"You can corrupt one man.
You can't bribe an army."

Raymond Postgate, founder of
The Good Food Guide, 1951

Please turn to the page number listed to find restaurant reviews for the corresponding region.

THE GOOD
FOOD GUIDE
2014

Distributed by Littlehampton Book Services Ltd
Faraday Close, Durrington, Worthing, West Sussex, BN13 3RB

Copyright © Which? Ltd, 2013
2 Marylebone Road, London NW1 4DF

Base mapping by Cosmographics Ltd
Data management and export by AMA DataSet Ltd, Preston
Printed and bound by Charterhouse, Hatfield

A catalogue record for this book is available from the British Library

ISBN: 978 1 84490 155 5

Maps designed and produced by Cosmographics Ltd, www.cosmographics.co.uk
Mapping contains Ordnance Survey data © Crown copyright and database right 2011
UK digital database © Cosmographics Ltd, 2013
Greater London map and North and South London maps © Cosmographics Ltd, 2013
West, Central and East London map data © Cosmographics Ltd, 2013 used with kind
permission of VisitBritain
Illustrations for features courtesy of Shutterstock
Mary-Ellen McTague courtesy of Jon Walsh
Restaurant of the Year winners courtesy of Jay Cain

Consultant Editor: Elizabeth Carter
Managing Editor: Rochelle Venables
Assistant Editor: Francesca Bashall

The Good Food Guide makes every effort to be as accurate and up to date as possible.
All inspections are anonymous, but every Main Entry has been contacted separately
for details. As we are an annual Guide, we have strict guidelines for fact-checking
information ahead of going to press, so some restaurants were dropped if they failed to
provide the information we required. Readers should still check details at the time of
booking, particularly if they have any special requirements.

www.thegoodfoodguide.co.uk

Contents

Introduction

For the past 63 years *The Good Food Guide* has consistently championed improved standards in food and restaurateuring. Recognising properly cooked food made from fresh ingredients has always been the Guide's main objective and this edition, my seventh as Consultant Editor, is no exception. Our resurgent pride in British produce and British cooking continues unabated – indeed, what this country now has to offer is barely recognisable from the first *Good Food Guide*s published in the 1950s.

With country pubs and neighbourhood restaurants becoming increasingly sophisticated, and value for money improving markedly in the mid-range, it makes the job of summing up a year of eating in restaurants across the UK tougher than ever.

On the cooking front it has been a fascinating year. London has consolidated its position as host to one of the world's most dynamic food scenes, this year given a fillip by some of our top-level chefs in expansionist mode. With the opening of Little Social and Social Eating House, Jason Atherton now has three (always packed) restaurants in the capital; Claude Bosi of Hibiscus has added a second pub to his portfolio (the very fine Malt House in Fulham); and Bruno Loubet and his partners at the Zetter Hotel have really hit the jackpot with Grain Store in King's Cross. And in the last year we've seen Nathan Outlaw open a branch of his superb Cornish seafood restaurant in the genteel environs of Knightsbridge's Capital Hotel – delivering some of the freshest fish in town to boot.

However, such is the strength and the individuality of the London restaurant scene that it's becoming a hard nut to crack for those not completely switched into its way of thinking. The Basque gastronomic legends Juan Mari and Elena Arzak failed to capture the London zeitgeist (or approval from Guide readers) with their Ametsa with Arzak Instruction at the Halkin, and neither did Hong Kong chef Alvin Leung with Bo London. And from New York, Keith McNally's long anticipated Balthazar, though briefly a hot ticket, failed to dent Chris Corbin and Jeremy King's dominance of the big French brasserie arena – their latest openings, Brasserie Zédel in Piccadilly and Colbert in Sloane Square, while not winning any points for originality, proved to be better-tested formulas.

And yet the most interesting new opening was not a London one. Simon Rogan's re-invigoration of the French at Manchester's Midland Hotel was a smash hit with Mancunians from the first week, ensuring that the 58-seater restaurant continually plays to a full house. The multi-course menus have Rogan's unique style stamped all over them; every dish is intriguing and extraordinary. After years of playing second-fiddle to Birmingham in the stellar foodie stakes, Manchester now hosts a real destination restaurant – even southerners are making the trip up north.

Improving the landscape of British food

So what are the latest trends? It's something that *The Good Food Guide* team is regularly asked. At long last we are seeing a welcome spread across the country of good-quality eateries in the middle and lower price bands. But if I had to pick one emerging trend this year, it would be the increasing popularity of part-time vegetarianism. The disconcerting horsemeat scandal touched on our daily lives, leaving people questioning the provenance of their meat. And with the growing awareness that eating more vegetables is both healthier and environmentally sound, observing a few meat-free days a week seems to be the way to go.

And chefs are stepping up to the plate. Many of Britain's premier chefs have been championing vegetables in recent years; their tasting menus now include two or three vegetable courses and their vegetarian menus are by no means an afterthought. In London, Bruno Loubet at Grain Store and Isaac McHale at the Clove Club have gone a step further – their menus reveal a more vegetable-based approach, with meat playing a bit part. In Belfast, Stephen Toman at OX also puts the emphasis on vegetables over animal protein, while at Bath's Menu Gordon Jones there's an 80 per cent vegetable slant on the day's surprise tasting menu (with a very good vegetarian alternative on request).

Vegetarian restaurants have always divided opinion among food lovers. Each year only a few are deemed good enough to be featured in *The Good Food Guide*, while token vegetarian dishes in many restaurants are frequently singled out by readers and inspectors for their sheer lack of imagination. But it is clear that a more balanced approach on the part of some very talented chefs, offering menus with a wider variety of vegetable dishes alongside meat, will lead the way to a significant (and welcome) change to the UK food landscape.

Redefining our ideas of 'good food' and 'good restaurants'

The yin to the vegetable's yang is the country's obsession with burger, steak and chicken restaurants – and I'm not referring to those mid-range, mid-market chain restaurants that swamp our high streets, but to urban pop-ups and one-hit wonders that celebrate the delights of top-quality burgers, steaks or roast chicken. Without a doubt, upmarket fast-food has had a great year, winning us over with its all-ages appeal and recession-defying affordability. Focusing on a few simple ingredients and doing them really well keeps prices down without sacrificing quality, while purposefully battered fixtures and fittings deliver the required utility feel – the result is affordable dining that suits modern lifestyles and modest budgets. Benson Blakes in Bury St Edmunds is one such new entry, its thoughtful local sourcing providing an example of how a small, owner-run burger joint can, and does, work in direct opposition to high street chains.

Tell us about it

We, the British public, are eating out in greater numbers than ever before. But where are we eating? We need you to tell us about your restaurant experiences, both good and bad. The Guide's perennial strength is that every single entry represents a range of meals taken in the last 12 months, eaten by genuine restaurant customers whether in celebration, on holiday, or in the normal course of business – people who claim no free meals, special service, recompense or reward. Indeed, our many years of success have depended on you, the reader, continuing to support us. Each year every entry is assessed afresh, based on feedback from you and backed up by anonymous, expert inspections. As a result, this edition lists some real gems and bargains. So please keep contributing by logging on to thegoodfoodguide.co.uk.

Although much has changed since Raymond Postgate founded *The Good Food Guide* in 1951, the ethos of the original book remains: we are completely impartial, we don't accept any sponsorship or free meals; and the essence of the Guide – its incisive writing and grading system – remains as important as ever. It is because of this, and because the Guide will always be the voice of the consumer, not the restaurant industry, that *The Good Food Guide* is still the UK's most trusted, best-loved restaurant bible.

Keep in touch.

Elizabeth Carter, Consultant Editor

P.S. New for this year you can view exclusive film interviews with top-rating chefs from *The Good Food Guide*, courtesy of www.coolcucumber.tv. Use the code GFG14 to view.

Editors' Awards

Every year *The Good Food Guide* team recognises excellence across
the restaurant industry with its Editors' Awards. For the 2014 edition,
the team is delighted to confer the following awards:

1. **Chef of the Year**
   David Everitt-Matthias, Le Champignon Sauvage, Gloucestershire

2. **Chef to Watch**
   George Blogg, Hotel TerraVina, Hampshire

3. **Best New Entry**
   The French, Manchester

4. **Best New Entry – Pub**
   The Richmond Arms, West Sussex

5. **Wine List of the Year**
   Cherwell Boathouse, Oxfordshire

6. **Pub of the Year**
   The Red Lion, East Chisenbury, Wiltshire

7. **Café of the Year**
   Eat Me Café, Yorkshire

8. **Best Value for Money**
   Bouchon Fourchette, East London

9. **Best Set Lunch**
   Outlaw's at the Capital, West London

Readers' Awards

The Good Food Guide Readers' Restaurant of the Year Awards are run annually in the spring, and champion great food and good service at local restaurants, pubs and cafés throughout the UK. This year an impressive 39,000 nominations poured into The Good Food Guide from across the country, as diners seized the chance to praise their favourite neighbourhood eateries. Consultant Editor Elizabeth Carter says, 'The dining-out public are at the heart of these awards. It's a fantastic opportunity to hear from them about where they really love to go when eating out, and to give those much loved regional restaurants the credit they deserve.' From a strong shortlist of regional winners, The Good Food Guide editors picked an overall Restaurant of the Year – Delifonseca, a restaurant, deli and food store on Liverpool's dockside. The Delifonseca team were presented with their award by Simon Rogan, chef-proprietor of L'Enclume in Cumbria.

The Readers' Restaurant of the Year 2014
Delifonseca, Liverpool

Regional Readers' Restaurant of the Year Winners

1. **Wales**
   Sosban, Llanelli

2. **East England**
   The Leaping Hare, Stanton

3. **London**
   Boqueria Tapas, Brixton

4. **North West**
   Delifonseca, Liverpool

5. **North East**
   Eric's, Huddersfield

6. **South East**
   Purefoy Arms, Preston Candover

7. **South West**
   The Seahorse, Dartmouth

8. **Midlands**
   Turners Restaurant, Birmingham

9. **Scotland**
   The Gardener's Cottage, Edinburgh

10. **Northern Ireland**
    Balloo House, Killinchy

Longest-serving restaurants

The Good Food Guide was founded in 1951. The following restaurants have appeared consistently since their first entry into the Guide.

The Connaught, London, 61 years

Gravetye Manor, West Sussex, 57 years

Porth Tocyn Hotel, Gwynedd, 57 years

Sharrow Bay, Cumbria, 53 years

Le Gavroche, London, 44 years

Ubiquitous Chip, Glasgow, 42 years

Plumber Manor, Dorset, 41 years

The Druidstone, Pembrokeshire, 41 years

The Waterside Inn, Berkshire, 41 years

Airds Hotel, Argyll & Bute, 38 years

Farlam Hall, Cumbria, 37 years

Corse Lawn House Hotel, Gloucestershire, 35 years

Hambleton Hall, Rutland, 35 years

The Pier at Harwich, Essex, 35 years

Magpie Café, Whitby, North Yorkshire, 34 years

RSJ, London, 33 years

The Seafood Restaurant, Padstow, Cornwall, 33 years

The Sir Charles Napier, Oxfordshire, 33 years

Le Caprice, London, 32 years

Little Barwick House, Somerset, 32 years

Inverlochy Castle, Fort William, 31 years

Ostlers Close, Fife, 31 years

Brilliant, London, 29 years

Clarke's, London, 29 years

Le Manoir aux Quat'Saisons, Oxfordshire, 29 years

Roade House, Northamptonshire, 29 years

Blostin's, Somerset, 28 years

Read's, Kent, 28 years

The Castle at Taunton, Somerset, 28 years

The Three Chimneys, Isle of Skye, 28 years

Wallett's Court, Kent, 28 years

Northcote, Lancashire, 27 years

ramsons, Greater Manchester, 27 years

The Old Vicarage, Ridgeway, Derbyshire 26 years

Cnapan, Pembrokeshire, 26 years

Kensington Place, London, 25 years

Le Champignon Sauvage, Gloucestershire, 25 years

Quince & Medlar, Cumbria, 25 years

Silver Darling, Aberdeen, 25 years

Plas Bodegroes, Gwynedd, 24 years

Bibendum, London, 24 years

The Great House, Suffolk, 24 years

Ynyshir Hall, Powys, 24 years

The Creel, Orkney, 24 years

Dylanwad Da, Gwynedd, 24 years

Eslington Villa, Tyne & Wear, 23 years

Top 50 restaurants 2014

A place on *The Good Food Guide*'s Top 50 list is greatly coveted by chefs and restaurateurs. This year has seen a reshuffle at the very top...

1. L'Enclume, Cumbria (10)
2. The Fat Duck, Berkshire (10)
3. Restaurant Nathan Outlaw, Cornwall (9)
4. Restaurant Sat Bains, Nottinghamshire (9)
5. Restaurant Gordon Ramsay, London (9)
6. Pollen Street Social, London (9)
7. Hibiscus, London (8)
8. The Square, London (8)
9. The Ledbury, London (8)
10. Le Manoir aux Quat'Saisons, Oxfordshire (8)
11. Le Champignon Sauvage, Gloucestershire (8)
12. The French, Manchester (8)
13. Marcus Wareing at the Berkeley, London (8)
14. Midsummer House, Cambridgeshire (8)
15. Le Gavroche, London (8)
16. Whatley Manor, The Dining Room, Wiltshire (8)
17. Alain Ducasse at the Dorchester, London (8)
18. The Waterside Inn, Berkshire (7)
19. Dinner by Heston Blumenthal, London (7)
20. Andrew Fairlie at Gleneagles, Tayside (7)
21. The Kitchin, Edinburgh (7)
22. Pied-à-Terre, London (7)
23. Fraiche, Merseyside (7)
24. Gidleigh Park, Devon (7)
25. Michael Wignall at the Latymer, Surrey (7)
26. Restaurant Martin Wishart, Edinburgh (7)
27. Murano, London (7)
28. The Peat Inn, Fife (7)
29. Fischer's Baslow Hall, Derbyshire (7)
30. Hambleton Hall, Rutland (7)
31. Artichoke, Buckinghamshire (7)
32. Paul Ainsworth at No. 6, Cornwall (7)
33. The Pass, West Sussex (7)
34. The Old Vicarage, Ridgeway, Derbyshire (7)
35. The Hand & Flowers, Buckinghamshire (6)
36. Mr Underhill's, Shropshire (6)
37. Hélène Darroze at the Connaught, London (6)
38. Purnell's, West Midlands (6)
39. The Sportsman, Kent (6)
40. Tyddyn Llan, Denbighshire (6)
41. The Yorke Arms, Ramsgill, North Yorkshire (6)
42. Freemasons at Wiswell, Lancashire (6)
43. OX, Belfast (6)
44. The Royal Oak, Paley Street, Berkshire (6)
45. The Red Lion, East Chisenbury, Wiltshire (6)
46. Castle Terrace, Edinburgh (6)
47. Simon Radley at the Chester Grosvenor, Cheshire (6)
48. The Clove Club, London (6)
49. The Box Tree, West Yorkshire (6)
50. Tuddenham Mill, Suffolk (6)

How to use the Guide

Each year *The Good Food Guide* is completely rewritten and compiled from scratch. Our research list is based on the huge volume of feedback we receive from readers; the list of many of our contributors at the back of the book is testimony to their dedication. This feedback, together with anonymous inspections, ensures that every entry is assessed afresh. To everyone who has sent us feedback over the last year, many thanks, and please keep the reports coming in via thegoodfoodguide.co.uk.

Symbols

Restaurants that may be given Main Entry or Also Recommended status are contacted ahead of publication and asked to provide key information about their opening hours and facilities. They are also invited to participate in the £5 voucher scheme. The symbols on these entries are based on this feedback from restaurants, and are intended for quick, at-a-glance identification. Our wine-bottle accolade recognises restaurants whose wine lists might be outstanding for one of a number of reasons, be it strong options by the glass, an in-depth focus on a particular region, or attractive margins on fine wines.

 Accommodation is available.

 It is possible to have three courses (excluding wine) at the restaurant for less than £30.

V The restaurant has a separate vegetarian menu.

 The restaurant is participating in our £5 voucher scheme. (Please see the vouchers at the end of the book for terms and conditions.)

 The restaurant has a wine list that our wine expert has deemed outstanding.

£XX The price indicated on each Main Entry review represents the average price of a three-course dinner, excluding wine.

Scoring

In our opinion the restaurants included in *The Good Food Guide* are the very best in the UK; this means that simply getting an entry is an accomplishment to be proud of, and a Score 1 or above is a significant achievement.

We reject many restaurants during the compilation of the Guide. There are always subjective aspects to rating systems, but our inspectors are equipped with extensive scoring guidelines to ensure that restaurant bench-marking around the UK is accurate. We also take into account the reader feedback that we receive for each restaurant, so that any given review is based on several meals.

Score 1   Capable cooking, with simple food combinations and clear flavours, but some inconsistencies.

Score 2   Decent cooking, displaying good basic technical skills and interesting combinations and flavours. Occasional inconsistencies.

Score 3   Good cooking, showing sound technical skills and using quality ingredients.

Score 4   Dedicated, focused approach to cooking; good classical skills and high-quality ingredients.

Score 5   Exact cooking techniques and a degree of ambition; showing balance and depth of flavour in dishes, while using quality ingredients.

Score 6   Exemplary cooking skills, innovative ideas, impeccable ingredients and an element of excitement.

Score 7   High level of ambition and individuality, attention to the smallest detail, accurate and vibrant dishes.

Score 8   A kitchen cooking close to or at the top of its game – highly individual, showing faultless technique and impressive artistry in dishes that are perfectly balanced for flavour, combination and texture. There is little room for disappointment here.

Score 9   This mark is for cooking that has reached a pinnacle of achievement, making it a hugely memorable experience for the diner.

Score 10   It is extremely rare that a restaurant can achieve perfect dishes on a consistent basis.

'New chef' in place of a score indicates that the restaurant has had a recent change of chef; we particularly welcome reports on these restaurants. Also Recommended reviews are not scored but our inspectors think they are worth considering if you are in the area. Readers Recommend reviews are supplied by readers. These entries are the local, up-and-coming places to watch and represent the voice of our thousands of loyal followers.

London Explained

London is split into six regions: Central, North, East, South, West and Greater. Restaurants within each region are listed alphabetically. Each Main Entry and Also Recommended entry has a map reference.

The lists below are a guide to the areas covered in each region.

London — Central
Belgravia, Bloomsbury, Covent Garden, Fitzrovia, Green Park, Holborn, Hyde Park, Lancaster Gate, Leicester Square, Marble Arch, Marylebone, Mayfair, Oxford Circus, Piccadilly, Soho, St James's, Westminster

London — North
Archway, Camden, Euston, Finsbury Park, Golders Green, Hampstead, Islington, Kentish Town, King's Cross, Neasden, Primrose Hill, Stoke Newington, Swiss Cottage, Willesden

London — East
Arnold Circus, Barbican, Bethnal Green, Blackfriars, Canary Wharf, City, Clerkenwell, Dalston, Farringdon, Hackney, Hackney Wick, Hoxton, Moorgate, St Paul's, Shoreditch, Spitalfields, Tower Hill, Wapping, Whitechapel

London — South
Balham, Battersea, Bermondsey, Blackheath, Borough, Brixton, Camberwell, Clapham, East Dulwich, Elephant and Castle, Forest Hill, Greenwich, Putney, South Bank, Southwark, Stockwell, Tooting, Victoria, Wandsworth, Wimbledon

London — West
Belgravia, Chelsea, Chiswick, Earl's Court, Ealing, Fulham, Hammersmith, Kensington, Knightsbridge, Ladbroke Grove, Notting Hill, Olympia, Pimlico, Shepherd's Bush, South Kensington

London — Greater
Barnes, Croydon, Crystal Palace, East Sheen, Harrow-on-the-Hill, Kew, Kingston-upon-Thames, Richmond, Southall, Surbiton, Sutton, Teddington, Twickenham, Walthamstow, Wood Green

LONDON

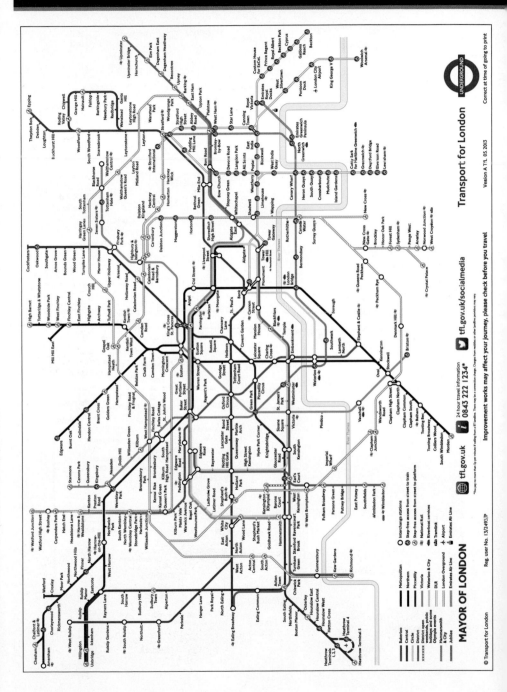

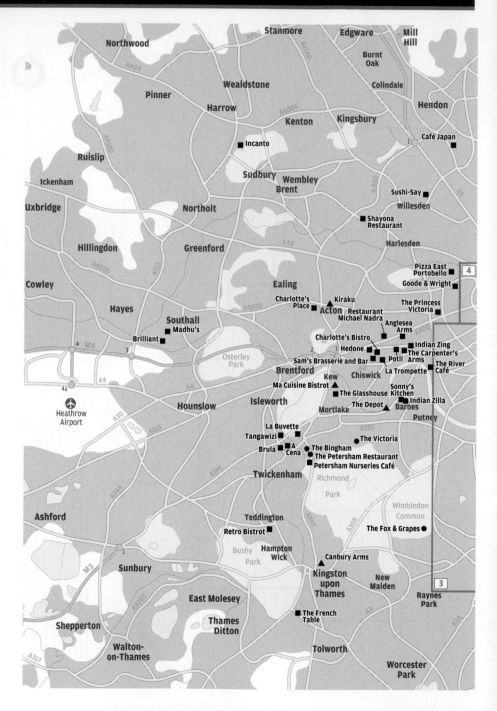

Northwood

Stanmore

Edgware

Mill Hill

Burnt Oak

Pinner

Wealdstone

Colindale

Harrow

Hendon

Kenton

Kingsbury

■ Incanto

1 Café Japan

Ruislip

Ickenham

Sudbury

Wembley

Sushi-Say ■

Uxbridge

Brent

Willesden

Northolt

■ Shayona Restaurant

Hillingdon

Greenford

Harlesden

Cowley

Ealing

Pizza East Portobello

4

Goode & Wright ■

Hayes

Charlotte's Place ■

▲ Kiraku

Acton

The Princess Victoria ■

Southall

Restaurant Michael Nadra

Anglesea Arms

■ Madhu's

Charlotte's Bistro ■

■ Brilliant

4 M4

3

1 Hedone

■ Indian Zing

The Carpenter's Arms

Osterley Park

2

Sam's Brasserie and Bar ■

■ Potli

■ The River Café

4

A4

Brentford

La Trompette

4a

Kew

Chiswick

Heathrow Airport

Ma Cuisine Bistrot ▲

Sonny's Kitchen

Hounslow

Isleworth

▲ The Glasshouse

■ Indian Zilla

The Depot ▲ Barnes

Mortlake

Putney

La Buvette ■

Tangawizi ■

■ The Victoria

Brula ■ ■ A Cena

■ The Bingham

The Petersham Restaurant

Petersham Nurseries Café

Twickenham

Richmond Park

Wimbledon Common

Ashford

Teddington

Retro Bistrot ■

The Fox & Grapes ●

Bushy Park

Hampton Wick

▲ Canbury Arms

Sunbury

Kingston upon Thames

New Malden

Raynes Park

East Molesey

Thames Ditton

■ The French Table

3

Shepperton

Tolworth

Walton-on-Thames

Worcester Park

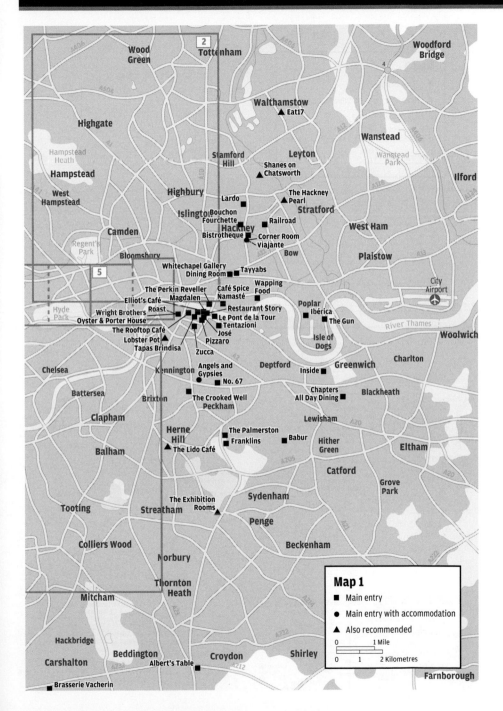

Map 1

- ■ Main entry
- ● Main entry with accommodation
- ▲ Also recommended

0   1 Mile

0   1   2 Kilometres

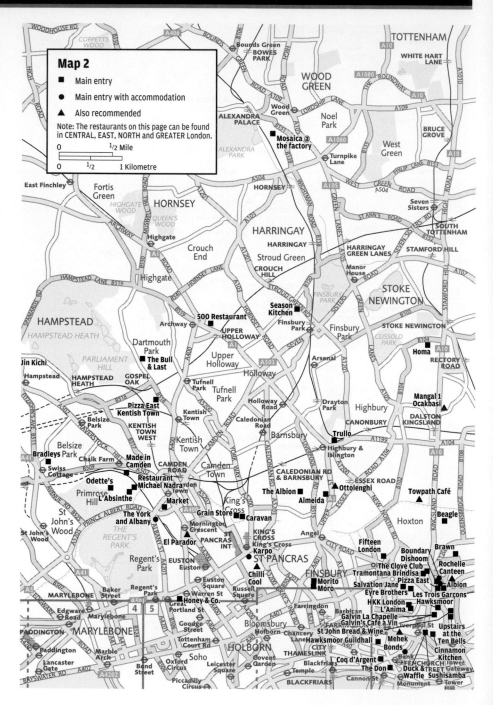

Map 2

- ■ Main entry
- ● Main entry with accommodation
- ▲ Also recommended

Note: The restaurants on this page can be found in CENTRAL, EAST, NORTH and GREATER London.

0 ¹/₂ Mile

0 ¹/₂ 1 Kilometre

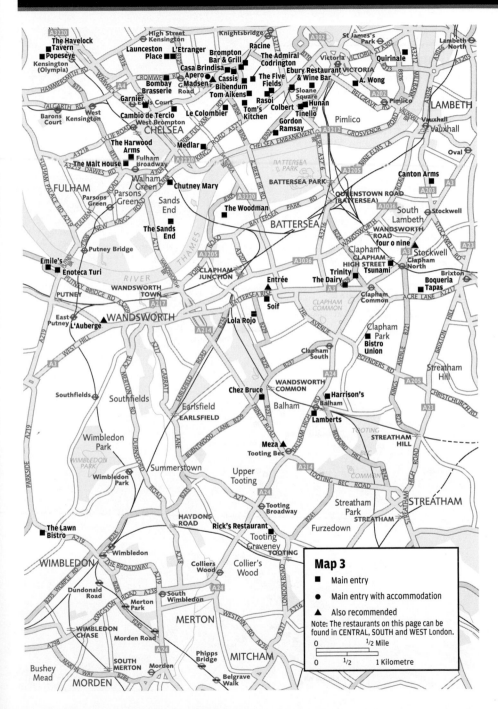

Map 3

- ■ Main entry
- ● Main entry with accommodation
- ▲ Also recommended

Note: The restaurants on this page can be found in CENTRAL, SOUTH and WEST London.

0 .... 1/2 Mile

0 ... 1/2 ... 1 Kilometre

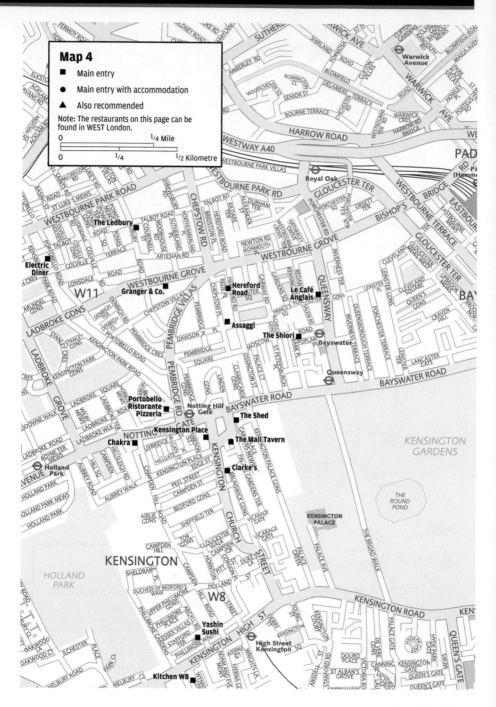

Map 4

■ Main entry

● Main entry with accommodation

▲ Also recommended

Note: The restaurants on this page can be found in WEST London.

0 — ¼ Mile

0 — ¼ — ½ Kilometre

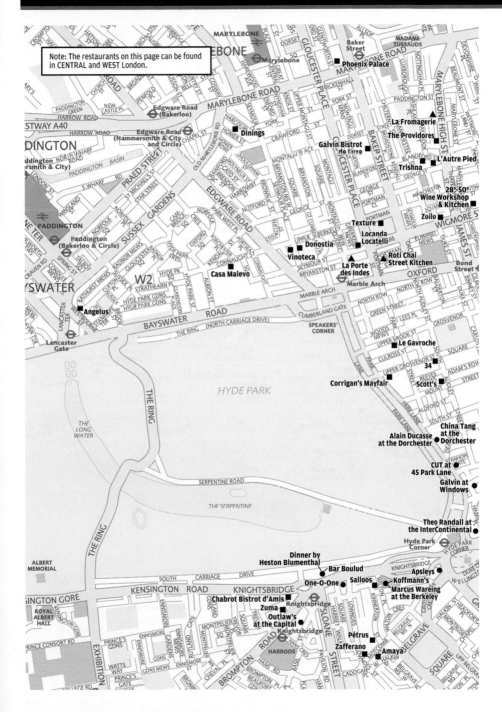

Note: The restaurants on this page can be found in CENTRAL and WEST London.

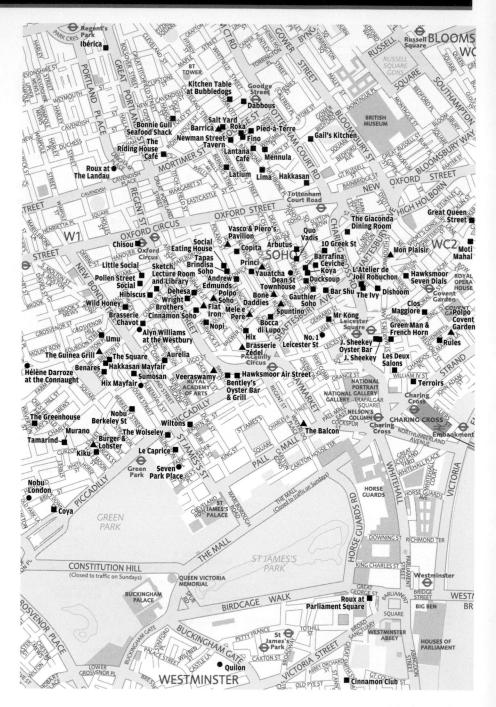

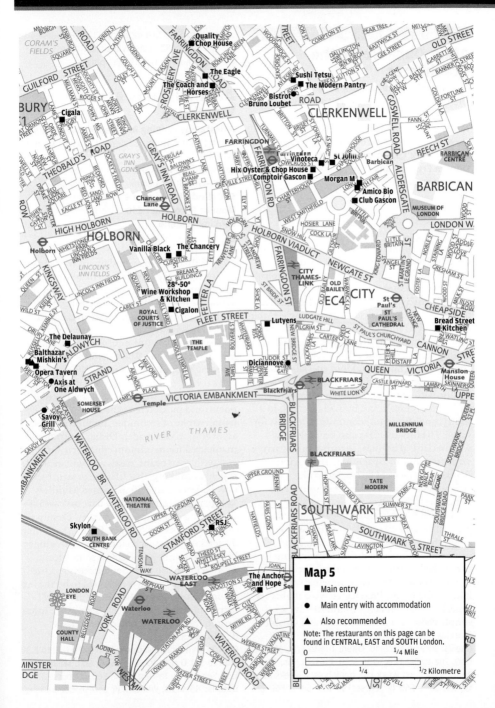

Map 5

■ Main entry

● Main entry with accommodation

▲ Also recommended

Note: The restaurants on this page can be found in CENTRAL, EAST and SOUTH London.

Alain Ducasse at the Dorchester

A corner of France on Park Lane
The Dorchester Hotel, 53 Park Lane, Hyde Park, W1K 1QA
Tel no: (020) 7629 8866
www.alainducasse-dorchester.com
⊖ Hyde Park Corner, map 4
Modern French | £85
Cooking score: 8

V

First-timers should prepare for the jolt in progressing from the long, ornate lobby – like a stage-set for the *Thousand and One Nights* – into the Ducasse dining room, with its determinedly deadpan demeanour of greenish panelling and buff upholstery. There are English grills and Chinese food elsewhere in the Dorchester's expanses, but this is where the falutin is at its highest. Ducasse is one of the senior generation of French maîtres, but among the least in hock to contemporary contrivance. The Lunch Hour specials (from which readers praise the duck and foie gras terrine with mango chutney, lobster in ink pasta with spinach, and braised ox cheek in a subtly amplifying jus) continue to impress for value. The full-on carte also keeps things within classical bounds, so turbot might arrive with crayfish and asparagus in sauce nantua, or Anjou pigeon could be teamed with artichokes and a little skewer of its innards. For dessert, chocolate and orange délice is made with finest Parisian ingredients, while a gracefully inflated soufflé of hazelnut is cut by razor-sharp pink grapefruit sorbet. The professional finish on dishes fully lives up to the exalted context, as does the impeccable service, not least from a sommelier who knows his onions. Preselected wine flights are superb, yet Lunch Hour might involve a simple choice between Sancerre and Chablis. Bottles start at £30.
Chef/s: Jocelyn Herland. **Open:** Tue to Fri L 12 to 1.30, Tue to Sat D 6.30 to 9.30. **Closed:** Sun, Mon, 26 to 30 Dec, 1st week Jan, bank hols, 2 weeks Aug.
Meals: Set L £60 (2 courses) to £55. Set D £60 (2

courses) to £85. Tasting menu £120 (8 courses) to £180. **Details:** 82 seats. Wheelchair access. Car parking. Children over 10 yrs only.

Alyn Williams at the Westbury

Painstaking cooking in preened surroundings
The Westbury Hotel, 37 Conduit Street, Mayfair, W1S 2YF
Tel no: (020) 7078 9579
www.alynwilliams.co.uk
⊖ Oxford Circus, map 5
Modern European | £50
Cooking score: 6

🛏 V

Alyn Williams' urbane restaurant within the glossy Westbury Hotel immediately catapults guests into the preened world of fine dining, yet never feels stuffy or intimidating. The dining room's rosewood panelling, cream velvet chairs and glass-walled private 'salon' may scream luxe, but measured service keeps the mood buoyant. Williams' stint as Marcus Wareing's deputy shows in his painstaking culinary approach: consider a plate of marinated quail with smoked egg, baked potato and pickled red cabbage – 'a masterstroke of technique, textures and tastes', according to one reader. Dishes are studiously manicured for maximum effect: translucent cod with coco beans, pastis and winter truffle is 'genius cooking' that lifts the prosaic fish to new heights, while 50-day-aged Middle White pork is a 'triumph of flavours' with its supporting cast of quince, chicory, parsnip and liquorice in perfect balance. Finally, 'tuck shop' desserts such as spiced cider jelly with ginger biscuit and milk pastilles toss some gleeful mischief into the mix. Set lunches are a steal and the tasting menu is reckoned to be 'the best value in London for cooking at this level'. Intriguing wine (and beer) pairings are spot-on and the heavy-duty list offers classy drinking from £19.50.
Chef/s: Alyn Williams. **Open:** Mon to Fri L 12 to 2.30, Mon to Sat D 6 to 10.30. **Closed:** Sun. **Meals:** Set L £25. Set D £50. Tasting menu £60 (7 courses).
Details: 45 seats. Wheelchair access. Car parking.

Andrew Edmunds

Wine-loving Soho stalwart
46 Lexington Street, Soho, W1F 0LW
Tel no: (020) 7437 5708
www.andrewedmunds.com
⊖ Oxford Circus, Piccadilly Circus, map 5
Modern European | £28
Cooking score: 2
🍷 £30

A Soho fixture since 1986, this old favourite still draws crowds. The early 18th-century town house – with crepuscular, candlelit interiors and cramped, white-clad tables – provides a backdrop for seasonally aware cooking with plenty of Eurozone and, occasionally Asian, influences. Well-sourced British products are to the fore. In early February that could mean roast pheasant breast wrapped in pancetta with braised red cabbage, and Herdwick lamb stew with pearl barley and roast root vegetables. May delivers goose rillettes with rhubarb confit, and twice-baked Stilton soufflé with English asparagus, artichokes and hazelnut salad. Dark chocolate and ginger tart makes a great finish, but a plate of Neal's Yard Dairy cheeses may be in order if you want to explore Andrew Edmunds' exemplary, wide-ranging wine collection that includes reasonably priced vintages and a detailed sweet wine and port list. Bottles from £17.50.
Chef/s: Roberto Piaggesi. **Open:** all week L 12 to 3.30 (12.30 Sat, 1 to 4 Sun), D 5.30 to 10.45 (6 to 10.30 Sun). **Closed:** 24 Dec to 2 Jan. **Meals:** alc (main courses £12 to £23). **Details:** 58 seats. 4 seats outside.

Angelus

A corner of France in London
4 Bathurst Street, Lancaster Gate, W2 2SD
Tel no: (020) 7402 0083
www.angelusrestaurant.co.uk
⊖ Lancaster Gate, map 4
Modern French | £49
Cooking score: 4

Tucked down a mews in a converted pub where Churchill once held meetings incognito, Thierry Tomasin's French restaurant looks a treat, the Art Nouveau fittings melding with the original dark panelling. Joe Howley became chef at the start of 2013 with a brief to maintain the broad range of inventive French brasserie food. Reporters are relieved to note the famous duck liver crème brûlée with caramelised almonds and toast still goes strong, or there might be home-cured salmon with salmon Scotch egg and garnishes of fennel, shallot rings and lemon. Fish impresses mightily, as in a perfectly timed main-course lemon sole with capers. Meat dishes can be pleasantly peasanty: perhaps braised beef shin with horseradish mash, bacon and mushrooms. Dark chocolate délice with praline and salted caramel ice cream is the star finale. Wines (from £25) take France as their starting point, with interesting bottles from the sud-ouest, Provence and Jura.
Chef/s: Joe Howley. **Open:** all week 10am to 11pm (10pm Sun). **Closed:** 24 Dec to 2 Jan. **Meals:** alc (main courses £20 to £29). Set L £20 (2 courses) to £25. **Details:** 40 seats. 12 seats outside.

Apsleys

Glamour, thrills and fabulous Italian flavours
The Lanesborough, Hyde Park Corner, Hyde Park, SW1X 7TA
Tel no: (020) 7333 7254
www.lanesborough.com
⊖ Hyde Park Corner, map 4
Italian | £70
Cooking score: 6

🛏 V

The principal dining room at the Lanesborough, a hulking slice of grand luxe on Hyde Park Corner, was reborn in 2009 under the aegis of Heinz Beck, proprietor of a much-garlanded restaurant in Rome. Adam Tihani's lavish interior has giant ring chandeliers dangling from an atrium roof, upholstery in taupe-hued plush and a neo-Romantic mural. The intention is to create a turbo-charged Venetian effect, backdrop for the dramatic modern-Italian stylings of Heros De Agostinis. Keeping to the quadripartite structure of Italian eating, but diverging from its simplicity, he offers starters of foie gras terrine with cherries, crispy quinoa and grappa jelly, or grilled scallops with puréed asparagus in basil vinaigrette. The house special pasta, mind-blowingly rich fagottelli carbonara, might follow, or a risotto of lime-marinated tuna. Mains journey to the wilder shores for pigeon with cassava and coffee crumble and sweetcorn purée, or play it safer with salt-baked sea bass and saffron potatoes. It all concludes with a svelte milk chocolate and coconut dessert, served with pineapple sorbet. The pneumatically priced wines take the Italian regions as their starting point, with bottles from £35, glasses £8.
Chef/s: Heros De Agostinis. **Open:** all week L 12.30 to 2.30, D 7 to 10.30. **Meals:** alc (main courses £29 to £38). Set L £25 (2 courses) to £35. D tasting menu £65 (5 courses) to £85 (7 courses). **Details:** 95 seats. Separate bar. Wheelchair access.

Arbutus

Groundbreaking Soho eatery
63-64 Frith Street, Soho, W1D 3JW
Tel no: (020) 7734 4545
www.arbutusrestaurant.co.uk
⊖ Tottenham Court Road, map 5
Modern European | £35
Cooking score: 5

There was a time when Arbutus, with its impressive sourcing and resolutely simple cooking, stood out as a beacon of innovation. That it is now part of the scenery is testament to how far-reaching the revolution it helped start has been. The unvarnished style of mostly European comfort food built around slow cooking and cheaper cuts of meat and less fashionable fish continues to strike a chord, and crowds still pack the dining room for the never-off-the menu squid and mackerel burger or, perhaps, a 'much enjoyed' warm pig's head terrine with potato purée and pickled turnip. The menu revels in strong natural tastes and contrasts: saddle of rabbit, for example, comes with a slow-cooked shoulder cottage pie in a separate dish, while a 'very good' Welsh Elwy Valley spring lamb is served 'navarin' style (a slow-cooked French classic) with young vegetables. To finish, a generous pear clafoutis with vanilla ice cream (for two to share) is outstanding. The lively, global wine list makes a harmonious match for the food, with everything available by the 250ml carafe and bottles from £19.50.
Chef/s: Tom Duffill. **Open:** all week L 12 to 2.30 (3 Sun), D 5 to 11 (10.30 Sun). **Closed:** 25 and 26 Dec, 1 Jan. **Meals:** alc (main courses £16 to £22). Set L £17.95 (2 courses) to £19.95. **Details:** 70 seats. Separate bar.

L'Atelier de Joël Robuchon

An indulgent line-up of innovative tasting-plates
13-15 West Street, Covent Garden, WC2H 9NE
Tel no: (020) 7010 8600
www.joel-robuchon.co.uk
⊖ Leicester Square, map 5
Modern French | £85
Cooking score: 6

V

Joël Robuchon's global empire is dedicated to entertaining jet-setters in the world's great cities, and his extravagant London outpost stays with the programme. Behind its discreet black frontage are layers of indulgent sensory pleasure. Thrill-seekers should stake their claim on the ground floor: a moody space furnished like a lacquered Japanese box in black and red, with a wall of greenery and stools at the counter. Top plaudits go to a line-up of innovative tasting plates; expect anything from artichoke and foie gras salad with truffles to confit aubergine with mushrooms, sesame and miso or crabmeat and avocado roll on blood-orange jelly. Other menus promise a more conventional spin on contemporary French cuisine: steak tartare, sea bass with Savoy cabbage, or a dramatic Manjari chocolate 'dome' with crunchy almonds and Cognac ice cream. Alternatively, La Cuisine on the first floor offers more sedate food in appropriately demure surroundings. A-list prices take no prisoners, although set deals mean you won't need to remortgage to sample the Robuchon brand. The wine list (from £29) scours France before whizzing off across the world – just like the man himself. **Chef/s:** Olivier Limousin. **Open:** all week L 12 to 3, D 5.30 to 11 (10.30 Sun). **Closed:** 25 Dec, 1 Jan, Aug bank hol. **Meals:** alc (main courses £19 to £42). Set L and D £28 (2 courses) to £33. Sun L £39. Tasting menu £125 (10 courses). **Details:** 43 seats. Separate bar. Wheelchair access.

Aurelia

Wildly delicious Mediterranean flavours in Mayfair
13-14 Cork Street, Mayfair, W1S 3NS
Tel no: (020) 7409 1370
www.aurelialondon.co.uk
⊖ Piccadilly Circus, Green Park, map 5
Mediterranean | £49
Cooking score: 4

£5
OFF

Step through the doors of this smart addition to the Roka/Zuma stable and you're in foodie heaven. Chef Alex Simone achieves a distinct blend of creativity and fashion in his Mediterranean-flavoured menus, ratcheting up the impeccably sourced components and tempting the assembled crowd with a salad of baby squid with Taggiasca olives, an oh-so-simple sea bass carpaccio with lemon and mustard dressing and a splendid rendition of a classic – linguine alle vongole veraci. From the rôtisserie and robata grill come examples of the kitchen's impressive capabilities, perhaps beef fillet with foie gras, Perigord truffle and croûtons or lamb cutlets with hot peppers and aubergine. Competitively priced set menus lure more than just Mayfair shoppers with plates of vitelo tonnato, and pappardelle with wild boar ragoût, while the all-day tapas menu offering the likes of charcuterie, calamaretti fritti and pizza is worth noting too. The Mediterranean wine list starts at £21. **Chef/s:** Alex Simone. **Open:** all week L 12 to 3 (11 to 5 Sun), Mon to Sat D 6 to 11.30. **Meals:** alc (main courses £14 to £37). Set L and D £24.50 (2 courses) to £28. Sunday brunch £40. **Details:** 120 seats. Wheelchair access.

L'Autre Pied

Genuinely exciting big-city cooking
5-7 Blandford Street, Marylebone, W1U 3DB
Tel no: (020) 7486 9696
www.lautrepied.co.uk
⊖ Bond Street, map 4
Modern European | £48
Cooking score: 6

The venue has been a fine-dining address for years, but has achieved its apotheosis as sibling of the acclaimed Pied-à-Terre (see entry), which acts partly as a feeder establishment for its chefs. Furnished in impeccable metropolitan understatement, with raspberry-hued banquettes, office-like chairs and unclothed tables, L'Autre Pied had one harrumphing reporter yearning for country-pub cheer, while nonetheless finding plenty to admire in Andy McFadden's creative repertoire. A tasting-menu dish of squid linguine with pine nuts and dried grapes (aka raisins) offered a great range of textures. Ideas spill forth, even on the good-value lunch menu where a winter main course was poached megrim in a delectable truffle crust, with blood orange, cauliflower and crab. Main ingredients are often surrounded by tiny (sometimes minute) supplementary flavours that offer interesting counterpoint – suckling pig is attended by grilled Nashi pear, Tokyo turnip and quince. Desserts don't scruple to indulge, as with caramelised banana cheesecake and passion fruit sorbet. Wines by the glass (from £5 for 125ml) head a list where bottles start at £25.
Chef/s: Andrew McFadden. **Open:** all week L 12 to 2.30 (3.30 Sun), Mon to Sat D 6 to 10.45. **Closed:** 24 to 27 Dec, 1 Jan. **Meals:** alc (main courses £28 to £32). Set L £22 (2 courses) to £25.50. Sun L £24.95. **Details:** 54 seats. 9 seats outside.

⫶⫶ Average Price

The average price listed in main-entry reviews denotes the price of a three-course meal, without wine.

Axis at One Aldwych

Thrilling interiors and satisfying food
1 Aldwych, Covent Garden, WC2B 4BZ
Tel no: (020) 7300 0300
www.onealdwych.com
⊖ Covent Garden, map 5
Modern British | £40
Cooking score: 2

£5 OFF 🚍 V

Axis is a 'beautifully appointed restaurant' in the handsome surrounds of One Aldwych Hotel, a landmark Edwardian building at the junction of Aldwych and the Strand. Reports suggest some inconsistency from this good-looking theatreland performer: one reader tells of 'beautifully cooked' halibut on the carte let down by 'salty and inedible' olive oil mash (docked from the bill 'without fuss') and a Kiwi Sauvignon that registered as merely 'OK'. There are plenty of positives, however: a good vegetarian menu, 'excellent' petits fours and some decidedly elegant dishes from Dominic Teague, including pot-roasted Yorkshire partridge, cauliflower and chicken jus, Cornish lamb with aubergine and lavender, and 'deconstructed' cherry Bakewell. Wines (from £23) cross the globe and please most pockets.
Chef/s: Dominic Teague. **Open:** Tue to Fri L 12 to 2.30, Tue to Sat D 5.30 to 10 (5 Sat). **Closed:** Sun, Mon, 19 Dec to 24 Jan, 2 weeks Aug, bank hols. **Meals:** alc (main courses £15 to £23). Set L and D £19.75 (2 courses) to £23.75. Tasting menu £45. **Details:** 120 seats. Wheelchair access.

ALSO RECOMMENDED

▲ The Balcon

Sofitel St James Hotel, 8 Pall Mall, St James's, SW1Y 5NG
Tel no: (020) 7968 2900
www.thebalconlondon.com
⊖ Piccadilly Circus, Charing Cross, map 5
Modern European

This dramatic double-height space plays the 'grand brasserie' role with commitment and dash. The menu is less French than at first appears (a consequence, perhaps, of the location within the Sofitel St James hotel), but Gallic influences meet British in dishes like Herefordshire snails with garlic jus, parsnip purée, French ham and croûtons (£10.50) or beef and foie gras cottage pie with chanterelles (£23). The charcuterie bar is an elegant setting in which to hit the wine list, which costs from £5.75 a glass, £16.50 a carafe. Open all week.

NEW ENTRY
Balthazar
Star-spangled brasserie
4-6 Russell Street, Covent Garden, WC2E 7BN
Tel no: (020) 3301 1155
www.balthazarlondon.com
⊖ Covent Garden, map 5
Modern European | £45
Cooking score: 2

In this year of grand London openings, there has been nothing like Balthazar, an enormous amber-hued dining room that's a legend in its own lifetime – although stories about the difficulties of getting a table are largely a product of the early months. The food, indeed the whole business, is part of an international love affair with the Paris brasserie, interpreted here (and across the pond) by that Englishman in New York, Keith McNally. Is this menu familiar? It's meant to be. You will not only be dining on 'smooth and velvety' onion soup, sardine tartine with salsa verde and 'exquisitely deep, rich' aubergine purée, and 'tender' grilled chicken paillard, but also a bar steak with béarnaise that's 'nothing different to what you would get in Cote'. 'Oily' gratin dauphinois and disappointing duck shepherd's pie need work, and one reporter has likened Balthazar to 'Café Rouge on speed'. Service, however, is 'very enthusiastic'. House wine £22.
Chef/s: Robert Reid. **Open:** Mon to Fri L 12 to 3.30, all week D 5.30 to 10. **Meals:** alc (main courses £13 to £38). **Details:** 150 seats.

❙❙◆ Also
❙❙ Recommended
Also recommended entries are not scored but we think they are worth a visit.

Bar Shu
Red-hot Szechuan lip-tingler
28 Frith Street, Soho, W1D 5LF
Tel no: (020) 7287 8822
www.bar-shu.co.uk
⊖ Leicester Square, map 5
Chinese | £45
Cooking score: 4

Be prepared for liberal doses of agony and ecstasy at this red-hot Szechuan eatery just a stroll from Soho's Chinatown. Chilli-heads will feel right at home here, surrounded by red walls, intricate carvings and ethnic paraphernalia, while the menu reaches parts that others dare not consider. Brace yourself for a sensory onslaught from the likes of 'numbing and hot' fish fillet, 'smacked cucumbers' with pungent mustard greens, fragrant chicken 'in a pile of red chillies' or boned pig's trotter (labelled 'as good as bear's paw'). But it's not all about lip-tingling spices and scary anatomical offcuts; there are complex undertones beneath the bravado, and some dishes are exceedingly gentle on the palate – try the beancurd skin with spring onion oil, Yunnanese chicken salad or dry-braised sea bass. Either way, prices are likely to burn a hole in your wallet. Soothing green-tea drinks are a better bet than the heavily marked-up wine list (from £21).
Chef/s: Xiao Zhong Zhang. **Open:** all week 12 to 11 (11.30pm Fri and Sat). **Closed:** 24 and 25 Dec.
Meals: alc (main courses £9 to £33). Set L £35 (2 courses) to £40. Set D £45 (2 courses) to £60.
Details: 100 seats. Wheelchair access.

Barrafina
Crammed with good things
54 Frith Street, Soho, W1D 4SL
Tel no: (020) 7813 8016
www.barrafina.co.uk
⊖ Tottenham Court Road, map 5
Spanish | £30
Cooking score: 4

Seven years on, there's still much to appeal at this open-hearted enthusiastic champion of Spanish tapas. The look is spare, with nothing but counter seating and space to queue at busy times, for the point is to ensure the food is accorded star status. Nothing is too complicated (a simple grilled quail with aïoli was a highlight for one visitor) which in part is the reason for Barrafina's success. From a carte that deals in classics – perhaps tortilla, razor clams, baby artichoke with aïoli, and morcilla Ibérica (spicy black pudding) with piquillo peppers and quails' eggs – raw materials, timing and production are impressive. To finish, there may be crèma catalana or turrón or a persuasively Spanish selection of cheeses. With behind-the-counter service hard to fault, and the likeable but short list of Spanish wines priced by the bottle (from £19) or glass (from £4), what's not to like?

Chef/s: Nieves Barragán Mohacho. **Open:** all week L 12 to 3 (1 to 3.30 Sun), D 5 to 11 (5.30 to 10 Sun). **Closed:** 25 and 26 Dec, 1 Jan, bank hols. **Meals:** alc (tapas £6 to £16). **Details:** 23 seats. 8 seats outside.

ALSO RECOMMENDED
▲ Barrica

62 Goodge Street, Fitzrovia, W1T 4NE
Tel no: (020) 7436 9448
www.barrica.co.uk
⊖ Goodge Street, map 5
Spanish

Tim Luther's mauve-fronted tapas bar just north of the West End makes a more assiduous effort than most to look and feel as authentically Spanish as possible, with bar seating and small tables down either side of a narrow sunny-yellow room. Padrón peppers (£4.95), ham croquetas (£2.75) and patatas bravas with allioli (£4.50) sound the right notes and might prime the appetite for something from the charcoal grill, perhaps hake with rhubarb and dill (£6.50) or beef topside with aubergine, chickpeas and turrón (£5.95). If the smoky mood has got to you, finish with smoked bourbon ice cream and caramelised hazelnuts (£3.95). Spanish wines from £16. Open Mon to Sat.

Benares

Supercharged Indian high-roller
12a Berkeley Square, Mayfair, W1J 6BS
Tel no: (020) 7629 8886
www.benaresrestaurant.com
⊖ Green Park, map 5
Indian | £60
Cooking score: 4

V

Appropriately pitched next door to a Bentley showroom, supercharged high-rolling Benares knows how to put on the style with its luxurious dark wood, leather and chocolate-toned trim. While staff ensure the first-floor dining room purrs contentedly, Atul Kochhar surprises his guests with sublime renditions of Indian regional cuisine overlaid with studious European culinary technique and oh-so-pretty presentation. It's all about confidence, light gestures and a commitment to sourcing – from line-caught Brixham cod served with vermicelli, coconut and curry leaf sauce to a contemporary take on rogan josh involving rack of Cornish lamb, polenta, pickled artichokes and spinach. The tandoor works its charred magic on everything from scallops and John Dory to Black Leg chicken, while vegetables and breads are taken to new Indian peaks. Desserts also break new ground: how about steamed yoghurt with raspberries and pistachio barfi (a fudge-like, bite-sized sweetmeat)? Spice-tolerant bottles pepper the well-considered wine list, although prices (from £28) will make your eyes water as surely as Kashmiri chilli.

Chef/s: Atul Kochhar. **Open:** Mon to Sat L 12 to 2.30, D 5.30 to 11. **Closed:** Sun, 24 to 26 Dec, 1 Jan. **Meals:** alc (main courses £24 to £45). Set L and D £29 (2 courses) to £35. Tasting menu £78 (6 courses). **Details:** 150 seats. Separate bar. Wheelchair access. No children after 7pm.

Bentley's Oyster Bar & Grill

'Consistently excellent' food and polished service

11-15 Swallow Street, Piccadilly, W1B 4DG
Tel no: (020) 7734 4756
www.bentleys.org
⊖ Piccadilly Circus, map 5
Seafood | £45
Cooking score: 4

Looking well set to celebrate its centenery in 2016, Bentley's has had renewed zest since being taken over by renowned chef Richard Corrigan in 2005. At street level is the more informal, slightly cheaper, wood and marble oyster bar, which offers 'some sort of perfection' when it comes to shellfish. Several varieties of oyster share the menu with impressive seafood platters, smoked salmon, fish pie, linguine vongole, even lamb cutlets, but the main action takes place in the upstairs grill. Despite its old-style William Morris wallpaper and white-clad tables, the décor is upbeat. Here, the menu contrives to comfort with familiarity yet excite with novelty, witness the shellfish bisque or pot of wild Cornish mussels alongside macaroni of lobster and basil, then mains of scallops with clementine, squid and broccoli. And meat? There's classic ribeye or garlic-roasted guinea fowl with bacon, sage and redcurrant. The globetrotting drinks list spills over with opulent, gorgeous wines. Some 20 by the glass or 500ml carafe (from £17) offer best value. Bottles from £25.
Chef/s: Michael Lynch. **Open:** all week L 12 to 3, Mon to Sat D 5 to 11 (Oyster Bar all week 12 to 12 (10pm Sun). **Closed:** 25 Dec, 1 Jan. **Meals:** alc (main courses £19 to £48). Set D £26 (2 courses) to £29. Sun L £45. **Details:** 100 seats. 24 seats outside. Separate bar.

🍴 Average Price

The average price listed in main-entry reviews denotes the price of a three-course meal, without wine.

Bocca di Lupo

Imaginative dishes bursting with Italian flavours

12 Archer Street, Piccadilly, W1D 7BB
Tel no: (020) 7734 2223
www.boccadilupo.com
⊖ Piccadilly Circus, map 5
Italian | £30
Cooking score: 3

Once Charlie Chester's casino, this nicely preserved brick-faced building had a contemporary Italian makeover when Bocca di Lupo opened in 2008. Imaginative, flavour-driven regional dishes, in varying portion sizes, have been offered ever since. A bilingual babble emanates from folk perched on the bar-stool seating and others at tables crammed in at the back. One reporter was fully appreciative of a repertoire that took in blood-orange and red-onion salad, fat griddled prawns with Merinda tomatoes and fennel, and a risotto of rabbit, pearl barley and wild garlic. Others have detected a slight loss of impetus since the early days. It seems quite a feat to turn roast partridge into 'nothing special', but then the tagliata (grilled bone-in sirloin, dressed in rosemary, balsamic, rocket and Parmesan) is exceptional. Finish with walnut and raisin crespelle dolloped with chocolate sauce. The Italian regional wines are good to magnificent, but aren't cheap: bottles from £20.50, half-litre carafes at £15.
Chef/s: Jacob Kenedy. **Open:** all week L 12.15 to 2.45 (12.30 to 3.30 Sun), D 5.15 to 10.45 (9.30 Sun). **Closed:** 24 Dec to 2 Jan. **Meals:** alc (main courses £10 to £28). **Details:** 75 seats. Wheelchair access.

ALSO RECOMMENDED

▲ Bone Daddies

31 Peter Street, Soho, W1F 0AR
Tel no: (020) 7287 8581
www.bonedaddiesramen.com
⊖ Leicester Square, Piccadilly Circus, map 5
Japanese

With its stripped-back interior, communal tapas-style tables and bar-stool seating, Bone Daddies is a happy-go-lucky amalgam of boisterous ramen-noodle bar and ever-so-casual dining room. It's at the hipster end of Peter Street and gets footfall from a young crowd who pop in for a quick ramen fix (from £9), perhaps tonkatsu ramen (spring onion, chashu pork in a rich 20-hour pork-bone broth), or to make more of a meal of it by adding sashimi or soft-shell crab (£8) as a starter and exploring the selection of saké and shochu. Wines from £16. Open all week.

NEW ENTRY
Bonnie Gull Seafood Shack
A handy local asset
21A Foley Street, Fitzrovia, W1W 6DS
Tel no: (020) 7436 0921
www.bonniegull.com
⊖ Oxford Circus, Goodge Street, map 5
Seafood | £32
Cooking score: 2
£5
OFF

A pop-up hit in Hackney, this single-minded restaurant has now found a permanent home in Fitzrovia where it has become a handy local asset. It's an unassuming little place done out with bare-boarded stark functionality. There are tightly packed tables, a shoehorned-in raw bar (majoring in oysters, but also clams, cockles, langoustines) and a short daily menu of sustainable seafood with a relatively painless price tag. Queenies (scallops) with chorizo, spinach and lemon purée or a small pot of mussels with diced bacon and Aspall cider give way to 'very well-presented' whole cracked crab with Shack mayonnaise or a straightforward lemon sole à la meunière. Chocolate brownie with Kirsch cherries and clotted cream is typical of desserts and you'll find gluggable, fish-friendly wines from £18.
Chef/s: Luke Robinson. **Open:** All week L 12 to 3 (4 Sat and Sun), D 6 to 10. **Meals:** alc (main courses £12 to £36). **Details:** 32 seats. 15 seats outside.

NEW ENTRY
Brasserie Chavot
A talented chef presents his Mayfair brasserie deluxe
41 Conduit Street, Mayfair, W1S 2YF
Tel no: (020) 7078 9577
www.brasseriechavot.com
⊖ Oxford Circus, map 5
French | £35
Cooking score: 5
£5
OFF

In Eric Chavot's haute cuisine days back at the Capital, his cooking always registered high on the 'delicious' scale. Even at its most refined, it seemed generous and soulful. So it's wonderful to see him in a buzzing brasserie – his own brasserie (attached to, though discrete from, Mayfair's Westbury Hotel) – where his spirit can really shine. The gorgeous mosaic floor, red banquettes and chandeliers look every inch the 'brasserie deluxe'. The service is pitched to suit: *madame*'s chair is pulled out, glasses are topped up. Chavot's technique is much in evidence: in the ethereal potato espuma atop a show-stopping (or should that be heart-stopping) snails bourguignon, in the petite dome of an île flottante, even in the near-perfect chips. Starters can be 'simple': oysters, charcuterie or thick sashimi-like slices of cured salmon with potato salad; the mains that follow are rich and generous, daube de boeuf, say, or grilled poussin with confit lemon. Prices are refreshing – perhaps less so on the Francophile wine list, though the sommelier recommended the house with pride (£13.50).
Chef/s: Eric Chavot. **Open:** all week L 12 to 2.30, D 6 to 10.30. **Meals:** alc (main courses £16 to £24). **Details:** 70 seats. Separate bar. Wheelchair access.

ALSO RECOMMENDED
▲ Brasserie Zédel

20 Sherwood Street, Soho, W1F 7ED
Tel no: (020) 7734 4888
www.brasseriezedel.com
⊖ Piccadilly Circus, map 5
French

'All in all a perfect, unaffected French brasserie,' enthuses a reader, who adds that Jeremy King and Christopher Corbin have not lost their touch. Descend a grand staircase to this enormous, 'fantastic-looking' space, all marble columns, velvet banquettes, close-packed tables and terrific buzz. OK, there are few surprises or 'frills and fusses' on the greatest-hits menu (céleri rémoulade, garlicky escargots, poulet au champagne) but you do get terrific value – soupe à l'oignon (£3.95), steak haché with frites (£7.95). Also 'superb' staff and wines from £16.95. Open all week.

READERS RECOMMEND
Briciole

Italian
20 Homer Street, Marylebone, W1H 4NA
Tel no: (020) 7723 0040
www.briciole.co.uk
'A proper trattoria serving on-the-money Italian classics. I always want to eat everything on the menu, and have never left disappointed.'

ALSO RECOMMENDED
▲ Burger & Lobster

29 Clarges Street, Mayfair, W1J 7EF
Tel no: (020) 7409 1699
www.burgerandlobster.com
⊖ Green Park, map 5
North American

When a novel idea flares up on the London food scene, it doesn't take long for the fire to spread: there are now branches of B&L in Soho (36 Dean Street, W1D 4PS), Farringdon (40 St John Street, EC1M 4AY) and City (1 Bread Street, EC4M 8SH), all with the same no-booking policy and inevitable queue as this still-hopping original. Tender, sweet and meaty whole lobsters or generously filled lobster rolls and 'gargantuan and very good' burgers – all with chips and salad for £20 – are the only things on the menu, backed up by well-managed, fast-paced service. Wine from £22. Open all day, all week.

Le Caprice

Famous Mayfair brasserie with loyal fans
Arlington House, Arlington Street, Mayfair, SW1A 1RJ
Tel no: (020) 7629 2239
www.le-caprice.co.uk
⊖ Green Park, map 5
Modern British | £45
Cooking score: 4

V

The Caprice is an island of stability amid the ever-changing West End restaurant scene: a supremely affable, welcoming place furnished in black-and-white with ranks of David Bailey photographs adorning the walls. Sit at the bar on comfortable stools or take a table on the main floor. Either way, it's an impressively smooth operation, with slick service and a menu of stolid, though occasionally dazzling, brasserie favourites. Caesar salad or steak tartare are obvious openers, or go nuts with a fragrant duck and pomelo salad scattered with spiced cashews. Mains keep things honest with a deep-pile salmon fishcake, served with buttered spinach and sorrel sauce, or slow-roast suckling pig in cider with smoked garlic mash. Just to show the tides of fashion haven't entirely washed past the door, sides include a warm salad of quinoa and sea veg. Finish with pistachio chocolate coupe. Wines cover all bases from Languedoc house blends at £27 to 1994 Château Latour at £1,200.
Chef/s: Andrew McLay. **Open:** Mon to Sun L 12 to 5.30 (11.30 to 4 Sat, 5 Sun), D 5.30 to 12 (11pm Sun). **Closed:** 25 Dec and 26 Dec. **Meals:** alc (main courses £16 to £35). Set D £19.75 (2 courses) to £24.25. **Details:** 76 seats. 10 seats outside. Separate bar. Car parking.

NEW ENTRY

Casa Malevo

Warm-hearted Argentinian dining
23 Connaught Street, Marylebone, W2 2AY
Tel no: (020) 7402 1988
www.casamalevo.com
Θ Marble Arch, map 4
Argentinian | £38
Cooking score: 2

This haven of Argentinian hospitality near Marble Arch, with charming staff and sleek décor, exudes South American warmth. An expertly made 'classic empanada' (with beef, potato and olive filling) or prettily presented 'mollejas al verdeo' (grilled sweetbreads with onions and lemon) gets things off to a strong start. Steaks are the stars of the show with prices to match: the 'Lomo' is a meltingly good pillow of pink, juicy beef fillet. Sides and sauces are extra but don't always deliver, such as a lacklustre potato and artichoke gratin. Silky crème brûlée with banana ice cream ends the meal on a high, and an all-Argentinian wine list (carafes from £10.95), makes it even easier to settle in and say *adiós* to your budget. **Chef/s:** Diego Jacquet. **Open:** all week L 12 to 2.30 (3.30 Sat and Sun), D 6 to 10.30 (10 Sun). **Meals:** alc (main courses £10 to £27). **Details:** 37 seats. 6 seats outside. Separate bar.

Ceviche

Peruvian flavour explosions
17 Frith Street, Soho, W1D 4RG
Tel no: (020) 7292 2040
www.cevicheuk.com
Θ Tottenham Court Road, map 5
Peruvian | £25
Cooking score: 2
£30

Since opening in 2012, Ceviche has proved to be an enjoyable, unpretentious and popular Frith Street venue. Though the post-work media crowds come primarily to down pisco sours, the kitchen is also a force to be reckoned with – but expect tasty Peruvian food rather than culinary fireworks. Everyone starts with a dish from the ceviche bar, say thinly sliced mackerel in gooseberry tiger's milk (the lime-based marinade used to make ceviche) served with pecan nuts and Panca chilli, then opts for lomo saltado (wok-cooked sliced beef fillet with red onions and tomato) or anticuchos (grilled skewers) of beef heart or octopus and chorizo. 'Great service' too. Wines start at £17.50.
Chef/s: Gregor Funcke. **Open:** Mon to Thur L 12 to 3, D 5 to 11.30. Fri to Sun 12 to 11.30. **Closed:** 24 to 26 Dec, 1 Jan. **Meals:** Ceviche from £5, alc (main courses £5 to £12). **Details:** 60 seats. 4 seats outside. Separate bar.

The Chancery

Fine-tuned cooking in lawyerland
9 Cursitor Street, Holborn, EC4A 1LL
Tel no: (020) 7831 4000
www.thechancery.co.uk
Θ Chancery Lane, map 5
Modern European | £35
Cooking score: 4

This bijou venue catapults guests (mostly the legal crowd) into a comfortable world of fine dining, yet never feels stuffy or intimidating. The dining room's fashionable pastel shades and leather seating are matched with white linen, contemporary art and mirrors. Measured service keeps the mood buoyant. Simon Christey-French's time spent with some stellar chefs (notably Philip Howard at the Square, and latterly as Jan Tanuka's head chef at the now-defunct Pearl) shows in his painstaking culinary approach: consider a plate of char-grilled Suffolk asparagus teamed with truffled egg, goats' curd, chicken crackling, summer truffle shavings and foraged barley grass. Spanking fresh John Dory epitomises mains, maybe served with 'superbly balanced' smoked courgette purée, aubergine caviar, pattypan (squash) and crisp bacon shards accompanying a razor clam in its shell. As for dessert, how about a wonderfully zesty grapefruit and lemongrass pannacotta with grapefruit sorbet, stem ginger and some amaretti crumb? Well-chosen wines fit the bill, starting at £17.50.

Chef/s: Simon Christey-French. **Open:** Mon to Fri L 12 to 2.30, Mon to Sat D 6 to 10.30. **Closed:** Sun, 23 Dec to 4 Jan, bank hols. **Meals:** Set L and D £28.50 (2 courses) to £35. Tasting menu £48.50 (six courses). **Details:** 70 seats. 14 seats outside. Separate bar.

China Tang at the Dorchester
Scintillating Shanghai glitz
The Dorchester Hotel, 53 Park Lane, Hyde Park, W1K 1QA
Tel no: (020) 7629 9988
www.chinatanglondon.co.uk
⊖ Hyde Park Corner, map 4
Chinese | £76
Cooking score: 3

🚗

Just to prove that if you wish hard enough in the world of five-star hotels, you can have anything you want, the Dorchester transports you to an Art Deco 1930s Shanghai in its basement Chinese restaurant. Classical, mainly Cantonese, cooking is Chong Choi Fong's stock-in-trade, and while many dishes may resemble those of Chinatown (apart from the prices), these are supremely elegant renditions. The simple won ton and hot-and-sour soups are 'the best I have eaten', said a reporter, the Peking duck first class (and not short on pancakes). Stir-fried king prawns with vegetables, and the ever-popular salt-and-pepper squid, are reliably superb, and scallops on tofu with black bean sauce is a peerless balance of flavours. Meats include barbecued pi pa duck and stir-fried minced pigeon wrapped in lettuce. Perfectly textured rice plates include a version with abalone. Wines encompass plenty of vibrant New World stunners, with prices that start at £26 and soon hit the roof.
Chef/s: Chong Choi Fong. **Open:** all week 11.30am to midnight. **Closed:** 25 Dec. **Meals:** alc (main courses £16 to £180). Set L £27.50. Set D from £75 (5 courses). **Details:** 120 seats. Separate bar. Wheelchair access.

Chisou
Authentic, unobtrusive Japanese favourite
4 Princes Street, Mayfair, W1B 2LE
Tel no: (020) 7629 3931
www.chisourestaurant.com
⊖ Oxford Circus, map 5
Japanese | £40
Cooking score: 4

£5 OFF V

Despite its location, just a minute's walk from Oxford Street, Chisou is surprisingly low on tourists and shoppers. Instead, Japanese businessmen, fashion-mag girls from nearby *Vogue* and aficionados of traditional cuisine come to savour the 'spirit of the feast' in modest, unobtrusive surroundings. An extensive menu covers all the staples, from zensai appetisers such as hijiki seaweed with soy or stir-fried pork belly with garlic and spicy Chinese cabbage, to grilled teriyaki, deep-fried tempura and udon noodles. Otherwise, sparklingly fresh sushi and sashimi are notable for their superlative raw materials and razor-sharp technique. Dish descriptions are clear, although courteous staff are always happy to explain the details. The saké selection is also a pleasure rather than a mystery, and the wine list offers sound drinking from £18.50. There's a dedicated sushi bar (Go Chisou) next door, and the restaurant has branches at 31 Beauchamp Place, Knightsbridge; tel: (020) 3155 0055 and 1-4 Barley Mow Passage, Chiswick; tel: (020) 8994 3636.
Chef/s: Dham Kodi. **Open:** Mon to Sat L 12 to 2.30 (12.30 to 3 Sat), D 6 to 10.30. Sun 1 to 9.30. **Closed:** 25 Dec to 1 Jan, bank hols. **Meals:** alc (main courses £5 to £32). **Details:** 70 seats. 6 seats outside.

Cigala

Old-school hispanic hangout
54 Lamb's Conduit Street, Bloomsbury, WC1N 3LW
Tel no: (020) 7405 1717
www.cigala.co.uk
⊖ Holborn, Russell Square, map 5
Spanish | £28
Cooking score: 1

£30

An institution keen to mark its territory among an abundance of trendy new Spanish joints, Bloomsbury's Cigala caters to a loyal roster of local patrons. The extensive tapas menu bypasses culinary innovation and pretence, instead offering a cornucopia of unfussy Iberian staples. Palate-pleasers include baked crab, pisto manchego and a cracking plate of mixed cheeses. Main dishes sometimes miss the mark, however, and reports that 'the whole experience is overpriced' imply the kitchen may occasionally rest on its laurels. The all-Spanish wine list offers carafes from £12.
Chef/s: Jake Hodges. **Open:** all week 12 to 10.45 (12.30 to 9.45 Sun). **Meals:** alc (main courses £14 to £20). Set L £17.50 (2 courses) to £19.50. Sun L £16. **Details:** 65 seats. 16 seats outside. Separate bar.

Cigalon

Platefuls of Provence
115 Chancery Lane, Holborn, WC2A 1PP
Tel no: (020) 7242 8373
www.cigalon.co.uk
⊖ Chancery Lane, map 5
French | £29
Cooking score: 3

£5 OFF   £30

There's a pleasing mix of the grandiose and the relaxed to Pascal Aussignac's homage to Provence in this former auction house. A glass ceiling floods the place with natural light – on a good day, it's as near to sun-splashed St Tropez as Chancery Lane gets. The list of classic south-eastern French dishes seems like a roll call of gastro-nostalgia: cassolette of snails and anchovies; salt cod in aïoli; pissaladière laden with black olives and caramelised onions; and, of course, proper niçoise salad. The set menus are good value, given the quality of the ingredients, and a two-course express lunch deal is perfect for those at the mercy of clock-watching office managers. The kitchen can also rustle up a grilled onglet. Finish with chocolate moelleux, its accompanying blackberry sorbet fragrant with lavender. Provençal and Corsican aperitifs augment a wine list where bottles cost from £19.50.
Chef/s: Julien Carlon. **Open:** Mon to Fri L 12 to 2.30, D 5.45 to 10. **Closed:** Sat, Sun, Christmas and New Year, bank hols. **Meals:** alc (main courses £10 to £19). Set L and D £19.50 (2 courses) to £24.50. **Details:** 68 seats. Separate bar.

Cinnamon Club

Exhilarating new-wave Indian cuisine
30-32 Great Smith Street, Westminster, SW1P 3BU
Tel no: (020) 7222 2555
www.cinnamonclub.com
⊖ Westminster, map 5
Indian | £47
Cooking score: 3

Enveloped by the baroque grandeur of the exquisite former Westminster Library, this decorous dining room certainly lives up to its gentlemanly name with shelves of leather-bound antiquarian books, dusky original features and seriously polished panelling all around. At first glance it can seem an odd backdrop for Vivek Singh's exhilarating take on his native cuisine, but there's no doubting that this trademark fusion of carefully sourced ingredients, silky European technique and pin-sharp Asian spicing is designed to thrill. Grilled scallops arrive with hot lentil chutney and smoked Devon crab purée; seared Ibérico pork turns up with a 'vindhalo' sauce and coriander mash; and char-grilled halibut is dressed with Kashmiri fennel and ginger sauce, curry leaf and quinoa. Not surprisingly, flamboyant desserts such as lassi pannacotta with wild rice crumble and melon carpaccio also add to the East/West crossover repertoire.

Breakfast is built for Westminster's politicos, likewise the aristocratic, big-money wine list; prices start at £22.
Chef/s: Vivek Singh. **Open:** Mon to Sat L 12 to 3, D 6 to 11. **Closed:** Sun, 1 Jan, bank hols. **Meals:** alc (main courses £16 to £40). Set L and D £22 (2 courses) to £24. Tasting menu £75. **Details:** 130 seats. Separate bar. Wheelchair access.

Cinnamon Soho

Streetwise Indian small plates
5 Kingly Street, Soho, W1B 5PF
Tel no: (020) 7437 1664
www.cinnamonsoho.com
Oxford Circus, map 5
Indian | £23
Cooking score: 3
£5 OFF £30

Mix the culinary creativity of the Cinnamon Club with the big-city pizazz of Cinnamon Kitchen (see entries), add some funky teasers for streetwise Soho and you have Indian maestro Vivek Singh's latest project: a slick, urban canteen that blends concrete and wood panelling with green banquettes and striking contemporary artworks. Sophisticated small plates are the thing here, typified by a range of colourful, vividly spiced 'balls' – crab cakes, potato bonda, Bangla Scotch eggs. Otherwise, make a meal from the likes of tandoori salmon with green pea relish, richly flavoured rogan josh 'shepherd's pie' or spiced mutton and lentil 'porridge' with a saffron bun. If you've room, indulge in sticky toffee pud spiced with garam masala for afters. Lunches 'al desko' are tailored to Soho's office slaves, while 'afternoon tiffin' suits those on the move. Asian-themed cocktails star on the drinks list, although you'll also find a decent choice of wines by the glass or carafe (from £11.70).
Chef/s: Vivek Singh. **Open:** all week 12 to 11 (4 Sun). **Closed:** 1 Jan, bank hols. **Meals:** alc (main courses £11 to £17). Set L and D £15 (2 courses) to £18. **Details:** 70 seats. 18 seats outside. Wheelchair access.

Clos Maggiore

Flexible French restaurant
33 King Street, Covent Garden, WC2E 8JD
Tel no: (020) 7379 9696
www.closmaggiore.com
Covent Garden, map 5
French | £35
Cooking score: 2
V

The competition's stiff in Covent Garden, but for 'intimate atmosphere' and old-school hospitality, Clos Maggiore is hard to trump. The flickering fire, candlelight and blossoms are nothing if not romantic. The French-Mediterranean cuisine (with vegetarian menu) is best described as modern classic: perhaps 'exquisite' crab, smoked anchovy mayonnaise and char-grilled cauliflower; Limousin veal belly with spätzle and Périgord truffle; then dark Valrhona chocolate fondant to finish. The useful theatre prix fixe (with wine included) comes recommended. 'Special mention' goes to friendly waiters who 'anticipate and rapidly attend to every need'. The wine list (from £18.50) 'resembles a bible' but comes with an interpreter, ie the excellent sommelier who knowledgeably guides guests through a roster of star producers from France and far beyond.
Chef/s: Marcellin Marc. **Open:** all week L 12 to 2.30, D 5 to 11 (10 Sun). **Closed:** 24 and 25 Dec. **Meals:** alc (main courses £18 to £28). Set L and D £15.50 (2 courses) to £19.50. Sun L £22.50. Tasting menu £59. **Details:** 67 seats. Children at L only.

Copita

Big flavours in small packages
27 d'Arblay Street, Soho, W1F 8EP
Tel no: (020) 7287 7797
www.copita.co.uk
Oxford Circus, Tottenham Court Road, map 5
Spanish | £17
Cooking score: 3
£30

Set up by the people behind Barrica (see entry), this effervescent tapas joint is pure Soho, sitting cheek-by-jowl with a specialist

waxing parlour and some rather dodgy venues. Inside, it's crammed and tight, with whirring ceiling fans, flickering candlelight, high stools at the bar and big wooden tables for sharing. The short, daily menu avoids worn-out clichés in favour of sharply executed plates of ajo blanco with beetroot, cured sardines on toast with apple, and pig's cheek with chocolate and hazelnuts – big flavours in small packages. Artisan charcuterie and cheeses are also worth ordering. Suckling pig is available for big groups, while a cleansing rhubarb and cava rosé sorbet should do the trick for dessert. More than a dozen prestigious sherries complement the thoughtfully compiled, drinker-friendly list of Spanish regional wines, with astute suggestions aplenty and a Verre de Vin system providing many by the glass. Bottles start at £16.50. Bookings at lunchtime only.
Chef/s: Nacho Pinilla. **Open:** Mon to Sat L 12 to 4 (1 Sat), D 5.30 to 10.30. **Closed:** Sun, 24 to 26 Dec, bank hols. **Meals:** alc (tapas dishes £3 to £7). **Details:** 50 seats. 8 seats outside.

Corrigan's Mayfair

Gilded Mayfair flagship
28 Upper Grosvenor Street, Mayfair, W1K 7EH
Tel no: (020) 7499 9943
www.corrigansmayfair.com
⊖ **Marble Arch, map 4**
Modern British | £50
Cooking score: 4

🍷 **V**

Regulars come to Corrigan's for a right royal cossetting, and they get it. The man himself might seem jovially down-to-earth, but his gilded Mayfair flagship is smart, smart, smart. In the dining room, joky references to the game season and portraits of musical greats tug the mood gently away from stifling clubbiness. Dishes like a starter of crubeens with truffle pommes purée – a little rough with a lot of smooth – characterise the approach. Readers have had 'disappointing' experiences for the price, and at inspection there was a shade of this in dull red wine-poached brill and clumsy, dry apple cake; a

fabulous chicken and morel pie, generously served with white asparagus and rivers of cream sauce, provided luxurious balance. The wine list isn't for the faint-hearted, and starts at £27.
Chef/s: Richard Corrigan and Chris McGowan. **Open:** Sun to Fri L 12 to 3 (4 Sun), all week D 6 to 10.30 (9.15 Sun). **Closed:** 25 and 26 Dec, 1 and 2 Jan. **Meals:** alc (main courses £22 to £42). Set L £31 (2 courses) to £37. **Details:** 70 seats. Separate bar. Wheelchair access.

NEW ENTRY

Coya

Slick, modern Peruvian cooking
118 Piccadilly, Mayfair, W1J 7NW
Tel no: (020) 7042 7118
www.coyarestaurant.com
⊖ **Hyde Park Corner, Green Park, map 5**
Peruvian | £50
Cooking score: 4

This new opening from Arjun Waney (of Roka and Zuma fame, see entries) is a slick operation offering evolved Peruvian cooking that promises exotic ingredients (not necessarily Peruvian) and current techniques. Ceviche (marinated and diced raw fish), for example, includes salmon, celery juice, ginger, daikon and wasabi tobiko alongside the more traditional sea bass with red onion, sweet potato and white corn. Ceviche, tiraditos (sashimi-style raw fish) and anticuchos (skewers of grilled meat and fish) are the small-plate mainstays of the menu, making bright, attractive lead-ins to deeply flavoured mains of Chilean sea bass with aji amarillo or Josper-grilled ribeye with chimichurri and aji rocoto salsa. The venue is located in a colourful, faux-industrial basement at the Park Lane end of Piccadilly. Staff are highly attentive and there's a thrum of activity thanks to an appealing bar – with room to sink a pisco sour or two. Otherwise, consult the global but steeply priced wine list (from £26). See opposite for details.

Chef/s: Sanjay Dwivedi. **Open:** all week L 12 to 3, D 6 to 10.45 (11.15 Thur to Sat). **Closed:** 25 Dec. **Meals:** alc (main courses £11 to £35). Set L £19.50 (2 courses) to £26.50. **Details:** 155 seats. Separate bar.

CUT at 45 Park Lane

Glitzy all-American steakhouse
45 Park Lane, Mayfair, W1K 1PN
Tel no: (020) 7493 4545
www.45parklane.com
⊖ Hyde Park Corner, map 4
North American | £55
Cooking score: 4

Fifth Avenue meets Park Lane at this ritzy outpost of Wolfgang Puck's US steakhouse chain. Dramatic draped curtains, mirrors, glitterball chandeliers and sumptuous furnishings create a mood of Liberace luxury in the narrow dining room. The kitchen takes its beef seriously, producing world-famous, cooked-to-perfection steaks. The char-grill/broiler double act is deployed for everything from Black Angus to gold-standard Australian Wagyu: prime cuts that arrive with 'four varieties of mustard' and terrific sides such as mushrooms with spicy green peppers. Fish fans needn't go hungry either – there's tuna tartare with wasabi aïoli or whole sea bass de-boned at the table – and the salads are stunning (butter lettuce, avocado and blue cheese with Champagne vinaigrette is a belter). The bread basket is unmissable, likewise tantalising transatlantic desserts such as the cheeky 'caramel chocolate bar'. CUT is also a red-hot ticket for breakfast (served 7 to 10.30; 8 to 10.30 Sat). The wildly extravagant wine list is notable for its cavalcade of Californian superstars (from £44).
Chef/s: David McIntyre. **Open:** all week L 12 to 2.30 (3.15 Sat and Sun), D 6 to 10.30. **Meals:** alc (main courses £14 to £82). Set L £29 (2 courses) to £35. Set D £55. Sun L £55 (2 courses). **Details:** 70 seats. Separate bar. Wheelchair access. Car parking.

Dabbous

A-list contender
39 Whitfield Street, Fitzrovia, W1T 2SF
Tel no: (020) 7323 1544
www.dabbous.co.uk
⊖ Goodge Street, map 5
Modern European | £45
Cooking score: 5

Ollie Dabbous is one of a new generation of personality chefs who have managed to rise above the clamour of central London and insist on their own distinctiveness. Thus, phone-bookers, be prepared to wait months (literally) for a table. On the other hand, rock up on a whim, and you never know. In a determinedly downbeat, post-industrial setting, a profoundly theorised form of cooking is offered: ingredient-led to the extent of often allowing virtually nothing else to offset the foregrounding of a principal component, and with the emphasis strongly on formal innovation. Strange substances arrive: vividly coloured rubble, conglomerates, pungent pastes. Open with a quarter of a tomato on dried Kalamata olive gravel in thin basilled-up juice, refreshing and bewitching. The white fish cooked in lemon verbena oil with celery and garlic remains a triumphant presentation, even if the ling itself might seem outsmarted by its assertive jus. Just-pink lamb seasoned with sweet-sour violet mustard, with cracked wheat and pickled vine leaves, is a joyous creation, its stringy char-grilled spring onions notwithstanding. The risk with such highly conceptualised food is that, if you don't get it, it teeters into the ridiculous: 'an endive salad was brutal and medicinal'; the wonderful meats turning up with accompaniments that seemed to 'bully them off the plate'. A reporter who ate here twice barely recognised the place from the first visit, suggesting consistency may be sacrificed to the desire to make statements. The now-famous coddled egg with smoked butter and morels, which, for one, is 'a fantastic take on comfort food, rich without being cloying', is for another vitiated by its 'overpowering whiff of smoke'. Desserts are thought to be where the effort most evidently flags: strawberries in super-sweet coulis with vanilla ice cream, a quarter of a peach in its own juice. Is he having a laugh, or what? The debate will doubtless continue. Wines start in Spain at £21 (£6 a glass), and cover much of the globe at prices that, in the context, are commendably restrained. An unequivocal bravo for that.

Chef/s: Ollie Dabbous. **Open:** Tue to Sat L 12 to 3, D 6.30 to 11.30 (5.30 Sat). **Closed:** Sun, Mon, 2 weeks Aug, 2 weeks Christmas. **Meals:** Set L £28 (4 courses). Set D £42 (4 courses). Tasting menu £59 (7 courses). **Details:** 40 seats. Separate bar.

Dean Street Townhouse

Glamorous Soho rendezvous
69-71 Dean Street, Soho, W1D 3SE
Tel no: (020) 7434 1775
www.deanstreettownhouse.com
⊖ Tottenham Court Road, map 5
Modern British | £40
Cooking score: 3

☐ V

Queen's song 'I want it all and I want it now' might be the signature tune for this glamorous Soho good-timer – a rendezvous for power breakfasts, working lunches, afternoon tea with buttered crumpets, pre-theatre suppers and more besides. A noisy gaggle of media folk, musos and fashionistas perpetually rams the zinc bar, and there's no let-up for those crammed elbow-to-elbow in the clubby dining areas. British sensibilities are writ large on a doughty menu that gathers together dishes old and new – from ham hock broth, grilled Dover sole and roast chicken to lamb's sweetbreads and mousseron mushrooms on toast or sea trout with fennel, cockles and samphire. Mince and potatoes is a rampant bestseller, while nostalgic puds such as custard tart or raspberry and sherry trifle tug at the heartstrings. The carefully curated, brasserie-style wine list has plenty by the glass or carafe; bottles start at £20.

Chef/s: Stephen Tonkin. **Open:** all week 12 to 12 (10.30pm Sun). **Meals:** alc (main courses £14 to £33). Set early D £16.50 (2 courses) to £19.50. Sun L £26.50 (2 courses) to £28.50. **Details:** 115 seats. 25 seats outside. Separate bar. Wheelchair access.

Dehesa

Agreeable tapas pit-stop
25 Ganton Street, Oxford Circus, W1F 9BP
Tel no: (020) 7494 4170
www.dehesa.co.uk
⊖ Oxford Circus, map 5
Tapas | £23
Cooking score: 2

£5 OFF £30

Competition is beginning to be fierce in this bustling little area south of Oxford Circus, but Simon Mullins' tightly packed neighbourhood tapas bar more than holds its own. It's an attractive place, run with the same conviction as its siblings Salt Yard and Opera Tavern (see entries), and the kitchen draws on the group's trademark Spanish and Italian influences to deliver some real treats. Expect plates of grilled chorizo with smoked aubergine and paprika oil; confit Old Spot pork belly with rosemary-scented cannellini beans; fantastic grilled Iberian ribs with celeriac purée, cavolo nero and pioppini agrodolce (sweet-and-sour mushrooms); and grilled sardine with cime di rapa, ajo blanci and blood orange. Desserts continue in a similar vein, say warm almond and clementine cake or affogato. Italian and Spanish wines open at £16.

Chef/s: Giancarlo Vatteroni. **Open:** Mon to Fri L 12 to 3, D 5 to 11. Sat and Sun 12 to 11 (10 Sun). **Closed:** 25 and 26 Dec, 31 Dec to 2 Jan. **Meals:** alc (tapas £4 to £10). **Details:** 40 seats. 40 seats outside. Separate bar.

The Delaunay
Strikingly handsome high-roller
55 Aldwych, Covent Garden, WC2B 4BB
Tel no: (020) 7499 8558
www.thedelaunay.com
⊖ Temple, map 5
Modern European | £35
Cooking score: 3

V

From the same mould as the all-conquering Wolseley on Piccadilly (see entry), this strikingly handsome, egalitarian high-roller is also modelled on Europe's grand cafés. Imagine a silky mélange of dark wood panelling, marble floors and polished brass fittings. Staff are snappy and metropolitan, ensuring no one feels out of place whatever the hour – from breakfasts of delectable patisserie, juices and coffee, through croques, paninis and pretzels mid-morning to slap-up afternoon teas and full-on dinners. The all-day menu is a *jeux sans frontières* trip back in time, summoning up generous prawn cocktails, chicken Kiev, omelette Arnold Bennett (a top version), frankfurters with sauerkraut and 'Cordon Bleu' schnitzels: not forgetting fruit crumbles, strudels and luscious ice-cream coupes (don't miss the gorgeously creamy Mont Blanc with chestnuts). The wine list offers an all-European selection with everything available by the glass or carafe (from £12.75). Otherwise, sip a Champagne cocktail and imagine you're swanning it on the Boulevard Saint-Germain.
Chef/s: Lee Ward. **Open:** all week 11.30am to midnight (11am Sun). **Closed:** 25 Dec. **Meals:** alc (main courses £10 to £28). **Details:** 160 seats. Wheelchair access.

> **¦|● Visit us**
> **||| Online**
> To find out more about
> *The Good Food Guide*, please visit
> www.thegoodfoodguide.co.uk

Les Deux Salons
Barnstorming French brasserie
40-42 William IV Street, Covent Garden, WC2N 4DD
Tel no: (020) 7420 2050
www.lesdeuxsalons.co.uk
⊖ Charing Cross, map 5
French | £40
Cooking score: 4

Success breeds success and this third restaurant in the Will Smith, Anthony Demetre stable (Wild Honey, Arbutus, see entries) got off to a cracking start when it opened in 2010. Ever since, Les Deux Salons' pitch-perfect interpretation of a Parisian brasserie has kept rolling on. The crowd-pleasing menu is a classic run through foie gras terrine, smoked and fresh salmon rillettes, steak tartare, specials of lapin à la moutarde and cassoulet, along with comforting fish pie and, from the Josper grill, steak frites, calf's liver with smoked bacon and sage, and veal chop. For dessert, the Paris Brest, especially, is well loved. The brasserie vibe has been nailed, too – big, bright and buzzy (even in the early evening) – and the look is spot-on (mosaic floors, wood panelling, plenty of brass). Service, however, occasionally lets the side down. Wines are served by the 250ml pot lyonnais or bottle (from £16.50).
Chef/s: Colin Layfield. **Open:** all week 12 to 11 (11 to 6 Sun). **Closed:** 25 and 26 Dec, 1 Jan. **Meals:** alc (main courses £15 to £32). Set L £18. Pre-theatre D £18 (2 courses) to £21. **Details:** 200 seats. Separate bar. Wheelchair access.

Dinings
Teeny-weeny Japanese thriller
22 Harcourt Street, Marylebone, W1H 4HH
Tel no: (020) 7723 0666
www.dinings.co.uk
⊖ Marylebone, map 4
Japanese | £40
Cooking score: 3

Squeezed into a teeny-weeny Marylebone town house, Dinings proves that size isn't everything – although creature comforts are thin on the ground, especially in the brutal basement bunker where most of the action takes place. Prices are high and the seats are hard, but the food offers a brilliant take on Japanese cuisine based around captivating, immaculately assembled small plates and more besides. 'Izakaya meets tapas bar' as the kitchen delivers everything from turbot sashimi and artichoke salad with yuzu and jalapeño dressing to sweetcorn and potato 'croquetas' with paprika relish. Clear, assertive flavours and striking contrasts also shine through in more substantial, luxury-laden showpieces such as Wagyu beef sukiyaki with sautéed foie gras, sweet port and soy. At the poky street-level counter, devotees watch the art of sushi and sashimi demystified. Obscure teas and shiso-leaf infusions suit the food; otherwise, three dozen wines start at £24.

Chef/s: Masaki Sugisaki. **Open:** Mon to Sat L 12 to 2.30 (3 Sat), D 6 to 10.30. **Closed:** Sun, 25 Dec to 3 Jan. **Meals:** alc (main courses £10 to £30). **Details:** 28 seats.

Dishoom

Funky all-day Indian café
12 Upper St Martin's Lane, Covent Garden, WC2H 9FB
Tel no: (020) 7420 9320
www.dishoom.com
⊖ Leicester Square, Covent Garden, map 5
Indian | £20
Cooking score: 2

£30

A convincing slice of the Subcontinent, styled after the faded, increasingly rare Persian-run old Bombay cafés, Dishoom serves up 'the most authentic Indian food in central London'. The day begins bright and early with everything from bun maska (bread roll and butter) to 'revelatory' bacon naan rolls, then segues into lunchtime salad plates (paneer and mango; prawn and pomelo) and filled naan parcels served by 'very quick, efficient and hospitable' staff. The main menu kicks off with small plates such as lamb samosas or 'the best chilli-cheese toasts outside Bombay' and sates larger appetites with the likes of sheekh kebab

or vegetable biryani. The house daal is 'seriously addictive'. Finish with basmati rice pudding or kulfi on a stick. Wines start at £18.90 a bottle.

Chef/s: Naved Nasir. **Open:** all week 8am to 11pm (12pm Thur and Fri, 9 to 12 Sat, 9 to 10 Sun). **Closed:** 25 Dec, 1 Jan. **Meals:** alc (main courses £7 to £12). Set L and D £27.50. **Details:** 140 seats. 20 seats outside. Separate bar. Wheelchair access.

NEW ENTRY
Donostia

Where to snack like the Basques
10 Seymour Place, Marylebone, W1H 7ND
Tel no: (020) 3620 1845
www.donostia.co.uk
⊖ Marble Arch, map 4
Spanish | £30
Cooking score: 3

Taking its name from that culinary hot spot, the Basque city of San Sebastian, this pintxo bar has a modern and bright outlook with white walls, blond bentwood chairs, shiny white table tops and a marble counter (where you can chat to the chefs). It's a 'recommended pit-stop when shopping on Oxford Street'. Two light prawn fritters with Bayonne ham and mango pieces, boquerones, Padrón peppers, and a 'beautiful' tortilla with cod and spinach hit all the right spots, but the kitchen excels at meat dishes. At inspection, pigeon breast with chestnut purée and morels proved to be rich and gamey. The good-natured service team here add to the appeal. Wines start from £17 and it's worth sampling the txakoli (a slightly sparkling dry white wine), which is poured from a height.

Chef/s: Damian Surowiec. **Open:** Tue to Sun L 12 to 3 (1 to 4 Sun), Mon to Sat D 6 to 11. **Closed:** 25 and 26 Dec. **Meals:** alc (tapas £5 to £20). **Details:** 40 seats. 12 seats outside. Separate bar.

¦¦¦• Visit us Online
To find out more about
The Good Food Guide, please visit
www.thegoodfoodguide.co.uk

Ducksoup

Rollickingly informal dining
41 Dean Street, Soho, W1D 4PR
Tel no: (020) 7287 4599
www.ducksoupsoho.co.uk
⊖ **Tottenham Court Road, map 5**
Modern European | £27
Cooking score: 2

£30

From the hard-working, tiny ground floor down to the basement dining room, it's all rollickingly informal at Ducksoup. The sparse, distressed décor works very well in Dean Street, lending itself perfectly to the simplicity of the whole operation. Seasonally inspired cooking forms the nerve centre, the short, scrawled daily menu offering dishes that range from shareable bar snacks (chopped hanger steak on toast, baby artichokes with pecorino and mint) to main-course plates. So take your pick from cuttlefish risotto, turmeric poussin with garlic, yoghurt, nettles and pappardelle, or oxtail with puntalette (pasta), skordalia and sourdough crumbs, and finish with baked ricotta and lemon cheesecake. Modest prices encourage evening queues – bookings are taken for lunch, but only for groups of three or more in the evening. Wines from £24.
Chef/s: Brett Barnes. **Open:** all week 12 to 10.30 (5 Sun). **Closed:** 25 and 26 Dec. **Meals:** alc (main courses £14 to £16). **Details:** 56 seats. 4 seats outside.

Fino

Big-hitting tapas restaurant
33 Charlotte Street (entrance in Rathbone Street), Fitzrovia, W1T 1RR
Tel no: (020) 7813 8010
www.finorestaurant.com
⊖ **Goodge Street, map 5**
Spanish | £35
Cooking score: 3

Part of the trendsetting Hart Brothers' stable, Fino 'gives a seriously good crack of the whip' to gutsy, authentic Spanish tapas, although there are some more newfangled ideas scattered about for good measure. It's a great bolt hole – a spacious, well-lit basement with a lively atmosphere – and everyone is here to tuck into platters of Spanish charcuterie, chipirones (baby squid), salt cod fritters or chicken wings in garlic, lemon and chillies. Recent highlights have included 'outstanding' marinated, grilled quail, crisp pork belly, and ribeye with Picos cheese and piquillo peppers. Desserts don't stray too far from Santiago tart and crema catalana, and the intelligent, all-Spanish wine list (from £19) has a classy selection of top sherries.
Chef/s: Nieves Barragán Mohacho. **Open:** Mon to Fri L 12 to 2.30, Mon to Sat D 6 to 10.30. **Closed:** Sun, 24 to 26 Dec, bank hols. **Meals:** alc (tapas £10 to £28). **Details:** 85 seats. Separate bar. Wheelchair access.

ALSO RECOMMENDED
▲ Flat Iron
17 Beak Street, Soho, W1F 9RW
www.flatironsteak.co.uk
⊖ **Leicester Square, map 5**
Steaks

From pop-up to permanent is a very 21st-century kind of restaurant trajectory, and it says something of the reorientation of British cooking that this eatery, now happily rooted in Soho, can make a name for itself by serving one thing – 'pink, juicy' high-quality steaks at just £10, with a choice of four sauces (£1 a small pot), and sides like 'delicious' creamed spinach or beef-dripping chips (£3). A no-booking policy can mean a wait in the bar and the no-frills surrounds extend to sharing tables if there are two of you, but everyone reports having a 'thoroughly good time'. Wines from £13.50. Open all week.

Also Recommended
Also recommended entries are not scored but we think they are worth a visit.

▲ La Fromagerie

2-6 Moxon Street, Marylebone, W1U 4EW
Tel no: (020) 7935 0341
www.lafromagerie.co.uk
⊖ Baker Street, Bond Street, map 4
Modern European

Patricia Michelson's affably run cheese shop-cum-deli in the heart of Marylebone village receives plaudits from readers for being an eye-catching oasis of good taste. Ogling the cheese and the shelves (and floors) laden with foodstuffs is a joy, not to mention a café menu that's astonishingly good value. Sit at communal tables and tuck into seasonal, perfectly ripe cheeseboards (from £8.75), a rare roast beef salad or duck rillettes with celeriac rémoulade (£10), or just pop in for coffee and an exceedingly good cake. Wines from £19.15. Open all week, closed D.

NEW ENTRY
Gail's Kitchen

A successful step from bakery to kitchen
11-13 Bayley Street, Bloomsbury, WC1B 3HD
Tel no: (020) 7323 9694
www.gailskitchen.co.uk
⊖ Tottenham Court Road, map 5
Modern British | £29
Cooking score: 2
£30

A confident foray into the restaurant business from this much-loved chain of bakeries sees their first venture pitched next to Gail's Bakery in Bedford Square – the entrance is via the lobby of the adjacent MyHotel. It's a small-plates set up: pick two or three dishes or 'supersize' one. At a test meal, thoughtful sourcing and punchy flavours impressed in a plate of buttery, wood-roasted English asparagus with a fried duck egg and Manchego, and in a 'plate-scrapingly moreish' helping of roasted beetroot, lentils, labneh and excellent flatbread. Smoked mackerel rillettes arrived in a tall jar, which presented practical difficulties, but the accompanying toasted rye was brandy-snap thin and pleasingly salty.

Simple desserts, such as fresh-from-the-oven 'cookies and milk', keep baking centre-stage. House wine from £19.
Chef/s: James Adams. Open: all week L 12 to 3 (4 Sun), Mon to Sat D 5.30 to 10.30 (11 Sat). Closed: 25 Dec. Meals: alc (main courses £7 to £14). Details: 54 seats.

Galvin at Windows

Precision-tuned food with a view
Hilton Hotel, 22 Park Lane, Mayfair, W1K 1BE
Tel no: (020) 7208 4021
www.galvinatwindows.com
⊖ Hyde Park Corner, Green Park, map 4
French | £65
new chef/no score
🛏

From its rarefied perch on the 28th floor of the Park Lane Hilton, Chris Galvin's glamorous window on the metropolis offers gasp-inducing wraparound views – including a peek into Her Majesty's backyard. Window seats are obviously at a premium in this slick eyrie, but the food also has much to dazzle the senses. As we went to press we learnt of the imminent departure of Galvin's dependable henchman André Garrett and that senior sous chef Joo Won is to take up the reins. With Chris Galvin overseeing the transition, we feel sure that the thoughtful, precision-tuned food and grand gestures for which Garrett was famed will continue. Witness fillet of Cumbrian beef paired with braised cheek bordelaise and a two-part dish of Landes chicken involving a poached breast and 'coq au vin' from the leg. Or a liking for oriental riffs in everything from scallop ceviche with soy, blood orange, cucumber and kohlrabi to potato-crusted brill fillet with enoki mushrooms, shellfish and dashi broth. To finish, marvel at the craftsmanship and invention involved in desserts such as buttermilk pannacotta with marinated pineapple, tapioca, coconut and lychee granita. The all-encompassing wine list courts big spenders, although you can drink affordably by the glass. Bottles start at £18. Reports please.

Chef/s: Joo Won. **Open:** Sun to Fri L 12 to 2.30 (11.45 to 3.30 Sun), Mon to Sat D 6 to 10.30 (11 Thur to Sat). **Closed:** bank hols. **Meals:** Set L £25 (2 courses) to £29. Set D £65. **Details:** 105 seats. Separate bar. Wheelchair access. Car parking.

Galvin Bistrot de Luxe
Big flavours and persuasive Gallic charm
66 Baker Street, Marylebone, W1U 7DJ
Tel no: (020) 7935 4007
www.galvinrestaurants.com
⊖ Baker Street, map 4
French | £36
Cooking score: 5

Unbridled Gallic generosity is alive and well in the Galvin brothers' Bistrot: a swaggering, confident venue that oozes persuasive charm and garrulous metropolitan bonhomie, without the pungent whiff of Gauloises cigarettes. Noise levels are invariably high as smartly garbed waiters work the close-packed tables and jolly crowds devour chunky bourgeois food beneath whirring ceiling fans. The masculine mahogany interior is matched by cooking that delivers punchy, immediate flavours and exemplary renditions of the classics: steak tartare with toasted sourdough; Roquefort, endive and walnut salad; daube of beef; braised pork 'osso buco' with choucroute and mustard cream. Don't be surprised to see plenty of sauces straight out of Larousse – 'maltaise' with pavé of halibut, 'diable' with a plate of crisp veal belly, celeriac purée and salsify, for example. Finish with rum baba, petit pot au chocolat or some creamy Brie de Meaux with excellent home-baked walnut and raisin bread. Prix-fixe deals win approval and the extensive wine list tips its beret to La Belle France, with plenty by the glass or pot lyonnais, and bottles from £20.25.
Chef/s: Luigi Vespero. **Open:** all week L 12 to 2.30 (3 Sun), D 6 to 10.30 (11 Thur to Sat, 9.30 Sun). **Closed:** 25 and 26 Dec, 1 Jan. **Meals:** alc (main courses £17 to £28). Set L £19.50. Set D £21.50. **Details:** 128 seats. 26 seats outside. Separate bar. Wheelchair access.

Gauthier Soho
Picture-pretty 'plats' at canny prices
21 Romilly Street, Soho, W1D 5AF
Tel no: (020) 7494 3111
www.gauthiersoho.co.uk
⊖ Leicester Square, map 5
Modern French | £40
Cooking score: 6
£5 OFF ♠ V

Alexis Gauthier has an idiosyncratic approach to modern French cuisine that leaves many reporters bowled over. His first- and second-floor rooms above Soho's hurly-burly have the feel of a private dining club, especially since a doorbell must be rung to gain admittance. Interiors are predominantly white: refreshing on a sunny lunchtime. 'The laid-back ambience, the wonderfully friendly service and the no-rush approach make this a real delight.' Choose from three to five courses, and prepare to be astonished. There are classic foundations, as in foie gras terrine with dandelion and chervil salad and port jelly, but some amazing innovations, too. Spelt and chlorophyll with cauliflower, broccoli and Parmesan crisps is one such conversation piece, while mains might deliver pink, flavourful onglet on strips of cardoon with onion and marrow gratin. To finish, Yorkshire's finest rhubarb could arrive poached with a Szechuan yuzu sorbet and white chocolate. A sommelier is on hand to present the fine wines, and the glass selections with the menus often spark engaged debate. Glasses start at £7, bottles £22. If you're on the wagon, try the volcanic Laotian wild tea.
Chef/s: Alexis Gauthier and Gerard Virolle. **Open:** Tue to Sat L 12 to 2.30, D 5.30 to 10.30. **Closed:** Sun, Mon, 25 and 26 Dec, bank hols. **Meals:** Set L £18 (2 courses) to £40. Set D £40 (3 courses) to £60. **Details:** 45 seats. Children over 5 yrs only.

Le Gavroche

Supreme gastronomic artistry
43 Upper Brook Street, Mayfair, W1K 7QR
Tel no: (020) 7408 0881
www.le-gavroche.com
⊖ Marble Arch, map 4
French | £100
Cooking score: 8

V

'There's nothing wrong with a bit of tradition . . . no smoke and mirrors here,' observed one reader who went on to eulogise about Le Gavroche in all its *classique* finery. 'Michel Roux was in attendance and spoke to every table,' he added with a note of comforting reassurance. Venturing into the exclusive confines of this green-hued subterranean dining room is like being willingly marooned in an outpost of indulgent extravagance. Eating here is all about being cherished: from your first mouthful of wickedly rich soufflé suissesse to the last spoonful of divine rum baba lovingly drizzled with dark spirit. The kitchen's repertoire is etched into the annals of restaurant history and it isn't about to surrender its laurels for the sake of newfangled shock tactics. Haute cuisine's legacy is safe here, judging by recent reports of supreme gastronomic artistry: marinated salmon with lemon and vodka jelly 'aigre-douce'; poached and roast calf's head and sweetbreads with sweet pepper, egg and caper dressing; turbot 'T-bone' with heritage carrots, radish and chive-butter sauce. When the shock of the new finally arrives, it's in the cunning guise of, say, an assiette of king crab with Asian dressing or fillet of stone bass perfumed with ras-el-hanout, fennel and red Camargue rice. After that, turn back time by revelling in the glorious fin de siècle luxury of an omelette Rothschild filled with apricots and Cointreau. The French service team never misses a beat, and 'truly wonderful' wines are handled with great insight – although prices zoom skywards from £24.

Chef/s: Rachel Humphrey. **Open:** Mon to Fri L 12 to 2, Mon to Sat D 6.30 to 11. **Closed:** Sun, 22 Dec to 7 Jan, bank hols. **Meals:** alc (main courses £27 to £61). Set L £52. Tasting menu £120. **Details:** 65 seats. Separate bar.

The Giaconda Dining Rooms

Expanded Tin Pan Alley eatery
9 Denmark Street, Soho, WC2H 8LS
Tel no: (020) 7240 3334
www.giacondadining.com
⊖ Tottenham Court Road, map 5
French | £40
Cooking score: 3

Expansion has added another dining room, and Paul Merrony can no longer boast that he cooks in London's smallest kitchen, but the increase in size has not changed the nature of his cooking. The Giaconda's menu continues to be a sincere exploration of the classic French repertoire and beyond, into pan-Med comfort food. The cooking is generally excellent in a homespun, straightforward way. Surprisingly, given the refit, it's the décor that's 'a bit dull', although lifted by 'first-class service'. 'Roast lamb smelt and tasted very good' is the sort of reaction the place seeks for dishes like leeks vinaigrette with egg mayonnaise, roast crottin on toast, lemon sole with cauliflower and cos lettuce, and veal T-bone with braised onions and saffron risotto. The mainly French wine list is sensibly priced with bottles starting at £19.

Chef/s: Paul Merrony. **Open:** Mon to Fri L 12 to 2.30, Mon to Sat D 5.30 to 10. **Closed:** Sun. **Meals:** alc (main courses £15 to £23). **Details:** 56 seats. No children under 4 yrs.

Symbols

🛏 Accommodation is available

£30 Three courses for less than £30

V Separate vegetarian menu

£5 OFF £5-off voucher scheme

🍾 Notable wine list

Great Queen Street

Fair prices and no frills
32 Great Queen Street, Covent Garden, WC2B 5AA
Tel no: (020) 7242 0622
⊖ Covent Garden, map 5
Modern British | £30
Cooking score: 3

This pub dining room off Covent Garden is run (like stablemates the Eagle and Anchor & Hope, see entries) with an understanding of one of life's simple pleasures: good food at reasonable prices. The sunny flavours of the Med combine well with great British ingredients: in cuttlefish braised in its ink, in early summer vegetable minestrone and wild garlic pesto, and in a crab, celeriac and leek pithiviers. Steak or chicken pies and rib of Hereford beef with chips and béarnaise (for two to share), and seven-hour lamb's shoulder (for four-ish) are typical of the kitchen's generous, convivial approach. Desserts are tarts or soft, creamy confections. The décor is plain – wood floor, bare tables – with a long, stool-lined bar, though laid-back, highly efficient staff and happy customers bring laughter and life. Wines from £15.
Chef/s: Tom Norrington-Davies and Sam Hutchins. **Open:** all week L 12 to 2.30 (1 to 3.30 Sun), Mon to Sat D 6 to 10.30. **Closed:** 23 Dec to 2 Jan, Easter, bank hols. **Meals:** alc (main courses £12 to £26). **Details:** 60 seats. 10 seats outside. Separate bar.

NEW ENTRY
Green Man & French Horn

The Loire Valley explored in food and wine
54 St Martins Lane, Covent Garden, WC2N 4EA
Tel no: (020) 7836 2645
www.greenmanfrenchhorn.co
⊖ Leicester Square, map 5
Modern French | £27
Cooking score: 3

🍸 £30 🍴

Part of Ed Wilson and Oliver Barker's mini foodie empire (see also Terroirs, Brawn, Soif), this tiny Covent Garden boozer turned French brasserie has been revamped with plenty of clattery urban pizazz – think bare brick, wood floors, cramped tables. The menu takes inspiration from the fertile Garden of France (aka the Loire Valley), so expect superb leeks vinaigrette with brown shrimps or rich pork belly rillons with endive and mustard, and for mains lovely surf clams with fennel and dill or venison with chard, celeriac, wild mushrooms and pickled walnuts, with pear, salted-butter caramel and a sable biscuit for dessert. It's all top-drawer stuff but even more compelling is the vast wine list, which explores the Loire in great depth: choice pickings especially from Saumur, Muscadet and Sancerre (from £18.50), plus the group's speciality – wines described as 'natural' or 'biodynamic'.
Chef/s: Ed Wilson. **Open:** Mon to Sat L 12 to 3, D 5.30 to 11. **Closed:** Sun, Christmas to New Year, bank hols. **Meals:** alc (main courses £11 to £28). **Details:** 54 seats.

The Greenhouse

Rarefied Mayfair oasis
27a Hay's Mews, Green Park, W1J 5NX
Tel no: (020) 7499 3331
www.greenhouserestaurant.co.uk
⊖ Green Park, map 5
Modern European | £75
Cooking score: 4

🍸 V

Reached via a serene, neatly landscaped garden decorated with stone sculptures from British artist Emily Young, the Greenhouse seems a world apart from surrounding Mayfair. The dining room, famed for its clubby, pinstriped masculinity, is now garbed in more feminine style with pale green and brown colours and miniature sculptures on each table. Chef Arnaud Bignon mines a modern vein that melds influences from all over – take a starter of Highland scallop with ponzu, mandarin, green mango and samphire or a more substantial serving of Yorkshire lamb with aubergine, sesame seeds, red spring onion and soy sauce. He adds gingerbread, pear and Tasmanian pepper to a dish of venison, and tantalises sweet-toothed palates with some unlikely pairings: pineapple with pine nut, lemon and lavender, for example. The wine list is old-school Mayfair to a T: a roll call of rare and expensive vintages with painful mark-ups, but some welcome financial relief by the glass. Bottles start at £19.

Chef/s: Arnaud Bignon. **Open:** Mon to Fri L 12 to 2.30, Mon to Sat D 6.45 to 11. **Closed:** Sun, bank hols. **Meals:** Set L £25 (2 courses) to £29. Set D £65 (2 courses) to £75. **Details:** 70 seats. Wheelchair access.

ALSO RECOMMENDED
▲ The Guinea Grill
30 Bruton Place, Mayfair, W1J 6NL
Tel no: (020) 7409 1728
www.theguinea.co.uk
⊖ Bond Street, map 5
British

A bastion of old England, this redoubtable hostelry still stands its ground. The décor pays no concession to modernity and the menu is a mixture of pub grub and gentleman's club dishes: think steak and kidney pie (£18) and grilled Dover sole (£33.50). The main draw are steaks from the Scotch Beef Club, considered among the best in town and cooked on a giant smoking grill. Needless to say, robust flavours are hallmarks and although it's not cheap, standards are consistently high. Wines from £21. Closed Sat L and Sun.

Hakkasan
Thrillingly seductive new-Cantonese food
8 Hanway Place, Fitzrovia, W1T 1HD
Tel no: (020) 7927 7000
www.hakkasan.com
⊖ Tottenham Court Road, map 5
Chinese | £65
Cooking score: 5
V

The crowds that continue to flock to the original Hakkasan, a Fitzrovia fixture since 2001, return for the highly glamorised Chinese cooking and the raunchy cocktails. The svelte basement room, with lighting levels conducive to calculated indiscretion, adds to the allure, as do the 'small eats' of the dim sum menu: golden-fried soft-shell crab

with red chilli, oat-coated aubergine, tea-smoked ribs. Among the main dishes, the famous grilled Chilean sea bass in honey is a sweetly delicious reference point, especially when offset with salty pak choi and moreish egg fried rice. Meat treatments may seem almost Westernised, as in the brilliantly tender stir-fried ribeye that comes in a potion of Merlot and black pepper, but there may also be venison with water chestnuts and Thai celery. Set menus are often the way to go, seeming to leave nothing essential out. Desserts are straight out of the French cookbook, as in orange and chocolate pot with orange sorbet, or pear and pistachio jalousie with ambrosially concentrated lemon curd. Wine prices are mostly eye-watering, but open at £28 for very good Spanish and Portuguese selections.

Chef/s: Tong Chee Hwee. **Open:** all week L 12 to 3.15 (4.15 Sat and Sun), D 6 to 11.15 (12.15 Thur to Sat). **Closed:** 25 Dec. **Meals:** alc (main courses £18 to £61). Set L and early D £28 (2 courses). Signature menus from £50. **Details:** 210 seats. Separate bar. Wheelchair access.

Hakkasan Mayfair
Slinky Chinese opulence
17 Bruton Street, Mayfair, W1J 6QB
Tel no: (020) 7907 1888
www.hakkasan.com
⊖ Green Park, Bond Street, map 5
Chinese | £80
Cooking score: 4

Its reach now extending across three continents from Mumbai via the United Arab Emirates to the US, Hakkasan is a globalised brand. The Mayfair branch is the second London incarnation (see entry above, Hanway Place), and the interior is quite as sleek, dark, streamlined and sexy as the original. The menu is short on neither classical Chinese skill nor bright ideas. You can be royally fed on salt-and-pepper squid, and stir-fried duck with Szechuan pepper and dried chilli, without scratching the surface of the repertoire. Whelk salad with iced apple; abalone and sugar-snaps in VSOP sauce; and Welsh black beef with pied bleu mushrooms and osmanthus flower wine extend the range extravagantly. Desserts wend their way westwards for chocolate marquise with poached kumquat and roast macadamia sorbet, or egg custard tart with roast banana. Wines by the glass include Alsace Sylvaner and German Pinot Noir, in the search for interesting flavours to suit the food. The illustrious main list shoots up from £28.

Chef/s: Tong Chee Hwee. **Open:** all week L 12 to 3.15, D 6 to 11 (11.45 Thur to Sat). **Closed:** 24 and 25 Dec. **Meals:** alc (main courses £16 to £61). Set L £50. Set D £65 to £130 (10 courses). **Details:** 212 seats. Separate bar. Wheelchair access.

NEW ENTRY

Hawksmoor Air Street
A temple to seafood and steak
5a Air Street, Soho, W1J 0AD
Tel no: (020) 7406 3980
www.thehawksmoor.com
⊖ **Piccadilly Circus, map 5**
British | £60
Cooking score: 4

Will Beckett and Huw Gott have done it again. This 'great addition to the Hawksmoor stable' is a first-floor bar and restaurant stretching along a length of Regent Street. The interior is a combination of period fidelity and contemporary gloss – buffed-up wood, stained glass, green leather – but then the duo always got the clubby, timeworn look right. Most come here for the expertly aged prime beef: weighty slabs of T-bone, fillet, bone-in sirloin, ribeye, plus a range of sauces. But in collaboration with Mitch Tonks of the Seahorse, Devon (see entry), very fresh fish is on the menu. Like the steaks, this goes in for minimum posturing: superb monkfish comes with a lovely char-grilled flavour and just a wedge of lemon; turbot is sold, like some of the beef, by the 100g; or there's Dover sole, royal bream and lobster. Add sides of, say, creamed spinach, start with shrimps on toast and finish with a generous scoop of Granny Smith sorbet. Wines from £19.

Chef/s: Richard Turner and Liam Kirwin. **Open:** Mon to Fri L 12 to 3, Sat and Sun 12 to 11 (10.30pm Sun), Mon to Fri D 5 to 10.30 (11 Fri). **Closed:** 24 to 27

Dec, 1 Jan. **Meals:** alc (main courses £20 to £35). Set L and D £23 (2 courses) to £26. Sun L £19.50. **Details:** 235 seats. Separate bar. Wheelchair access.

Hawksmoor Seven Dials
British beef at its best
11 Langley Street, Covent Garden, WC2H 9JG
Tel no: (020) 7420 9390
www.thehawksmoor.com
⊖ **Covent Garden, map 5**
British | £65
Cooking score: 4

Tucked away at the bottom of cobbled Langley Street, the street-level entrance at this branch of the upmarket meaty mini-chain may be dark and unprepossessing, but once downstairs you enter a fabulous twilight world. From a bar that's all leather chairs, dark wood, exposed brick and parquet flooring to a wide expanse of dining room held together with steel girders and piping – it's industrial-chic meets old-school gentleman's club, but with lashings of conviviality. Servers talk you through the menu: individual steaks or steaks to share, organised by cut and weight – a 'dinner-plate-sized' bone-in prime rib, perhaps, a magnificent porterhouse or a 'can't be beaten' ribeye. They also advise on sauces and side dishes, including béarnaise, triple-cooked chips and buttered greens. Alternatively, there's Brixham crab, lobster and free-range chicken. Reporters agree that the Hawksmoor crew has done a fantastic job here: 'the best steak restaurant in London'. Well-chosen wines start at £19.

Chef/s: Richard Turner and Mirek Dawid. **Open:** all week L 12 to 3 (4.30 Sun), Mon to Sat D 5 to 10.30 (11 Fri and Sat). **Closed:** 24 to 27 Dec, 1 Jan. **Meals:** alc (main courses £12 to £50). Set L and D £23 (2 courses) to £26. Sun L £19.50. **Details:** 140 seats. Separate bar. Wheelchair access.

Visit us Online
To find out more about *The Good Food Guide*, please visit www.thegoodfoodguide.co.uk

Hélène Darroze at the Connaught

Complex avant-garde thrills
16 Carlos Place, Mayfair, W1K 2AL
Tel no: (020) 3147 7200
www.the-connaught.co.uk
⊖ Bond Street, Green Park, map 5
Modern French | £85
Cooking score: 6

🚄 V

In Hélène Darroze, the august old Connaught has one of the capital's most interestingly creative chefs. Her culinary idiom starts from her native Landes and rolls out across the Pyrenees to Malaga, and ultimately to Vietnam, in one direction, to Hertfordshire and Northern Ireland in the other (for Lough Neagh river eel seared in beurre noisette, and tricked up with cauliflower mousse and Piedmontese hazelnuts in a garlic emulsion). Vietnam supplies the wild pepper that adds bang to the strong jus that comes with Challans duck: maple syrup-glazed breast and spring rolls of leg confit, along with citrus-spiked Tokyo turnip fondants. There's the odd bemused harrumph, as from the pair who relished foie gras terrine in mulled Madiran, with its rhubarb chutney and discs of lemon verbena jelly, but then found themselves bogged down in the potato ravioli, followed by a Texas-sized portion of John Dory with a smear of parsley jus. Faith is restored by desserts such as intense lime mousse in its chocolate and hazelnut case, or Cornice pear poached in sangria, with lemongrass pannacotta and blackcurrant sorbet. Wines from the 49-page list will raise the roof, or at least the bill, particularly if you accept a shot of Champagne from the trolley. Even 125ml glasses of wine start at £13 (bottles from £25).
Chef/s: Hélène Darroze. **Open:** Tue to Sat L 12 to 2.30 (brunch 11 to 2.30 Sat), D 6.30 to 10.45. **Closed:** Sun, Mon, 2 weeks Aug. **Meals:** Set L £35. Set D £85. Tasting menu £98 (6 courses) to £120 (9 courses). **Details:** 62 seats. Separate bar. Wheelchair access.

Hibiscus

Wildly creative, knockout dishes from a master
29 Maddox Street, Mayfair, W1S 2PA
Tel no: (020) 7629 2999
www.hibiscusrestaurant.co.uk
⊖ Oxford Circus, map 5
Modern French | £90
Cooking score: 8

V

The revamped dining room is a vast improvement. A solid oak floor replaces the carpet; the square room is lighter and looks bigger, more contemporary, the old corporate feel replaced by one of sophistication; and everyone – staff, customers – seems happier. As for the cooking, Claude Bosi has seized the occasion and is beginning to dazzle on a higher plane, presenting an experience unlike others around town. Menus allow you to chart paths of varying lengths, from three standard courses, to six or eight dishes, either chosen from a list of ingredients or as unspecified courses that Bosi selects for you. His food is French-grounded, but such classicism is woven deftly into the adventurousness of a new generation: sea bream stuffed with kaffir lime leaves and placed atop morels in a buttery tarragon and hazelnut purée, served at a March dinner, for example; or a fricassee of Herefordshire snails teamed with Scottish girolles, pig's cheek, and an egg-enriched vin jaune sauce from a June lunch. Some of Bosi's best work comes in small packages, like a springtime nettle and ricotta gnocchi served in a deliciously tart rhubarb and hibiscus jus; or an amalgamation of pea and mint arriving in a friable chocolate shell beside an intense coconut sorbet that brought a summer meal to an end. The fascinating wine list details scores of small producers, but it's hard to choose wine when you don't know what you're going to eat, so if your budget allows, go for the wine flights; if not, go for expert by-the-glass guidance – the sommelier can be trusted with such decisions. Bottles start at £26.

Chef/s: Claude Bosi. **Open:** Mon to Sat L 12 to 2.30, D 6.30 to 10 (6 Fri and Sat). **Closed:** Sun, Christmas to New Year, bank hols. **Meals:** Set L £29.50 (2 courses) to £34.95. Set D £65 (2 courses) to £87.50. Tasting menu £95 (6 courses), £105 (8 courses). **Details:** 48 seats.

Hix

über-cool Brit brasserie
66-70 Brewer Street, Soho, W1F 9UP
Tel no: (020) 7292 3518
www.hixsoho.co.uk
⊖ **Piccadilly Circus, map 5**
British | £40
Cooking score: 3

V

Mark Hix's all-day Soho flagship continues to delight. Style-wise the basement bar and ground-floor restaurant are cool and energetic, full of pulsating action and close-packed tables. A bevy of staff give 'very prompt service': necessary when there is a time limit on tables. The cooking, characterised by powerful British ingredients and an interest in foraging, delivers the very finest materials at their seasonal best. Menu choices in late winter, for example, produced purple sprouting broccoli with Berkswell (cheese) and pickled walnuts, Start Bay Dover sole with King's Lynn shrimps and sea purslane, a splendid hanger steak with baked bone marrow, and blood-orange blancmange. **Chef/s:** Damian Clisby. **Open:** all week 12 to 10.30. **Closed:** 25 Dec. **Meals:** alc (main courses £16 to £36). Set L and D £17.50 (2 courses) to £22.50. **Details:** 80 seats. Separate bar. Wheelchair access.

Hix Mayfair

Old-school charm and regional goodies
Brown's Hotel, 30 Albemarle Street, Mayfair, W1S 4BP
Tel no: (020) 7518 4004
www.thealbemarlerestaurant.com
⊖ **Green Park, map 5**
British | £46
Cooking score: 4

🛏 **V**

Lee Streeton remains at the kitchen helm as Mark Hix's representative in this august piece of Mayfair real estate. Rejigged British dishes are the declared intent, but there is more to the repertoire than watercress soup and fish and chips. A serving of white asparagus with Isle of Barra cockles in vinaigrette suggests the seasons aren't neglected, or there could be Dorset snails with bacon and black pudding. Mains run to Highland red deer with St George's mushrooms and varieties of allium (the onion family), and at lunchtime there's a daily changing roast trolley – Monday producing a hay-baked leg of Cornish lamb that was just a little too shocking-pink for one party. Finish with the newly ubiquitous Eton mess, ginger parkin or lemon posset. The wine list, according to its preface, is the product of 'some heated debate', at least some of which has been expended on finding wines at amenable prices for Mayfair, starting with Herefordshire Bacchus at £28. **Chef/s:** Lee Streeton. **Open:** all week L 12 to 3 (4 Sun), D 5.30 to 11 (7 to 10.30 Sun). **Meals:** alc (main courses £17 to £43). Set L and D £27.50 (2 courses) to £32.50. Sun L £36.50. **Details:** 70 seats. Separate bar. Wheelchair access.

NEW ENTRY
Honey & Co.
A truly special little gem
25a Warren Street, Euston, W1T 5LZ
Tel no: (020) 7388 6175
www.honeyandco.co.uk
⊖ Warren Street, map 2
Middle Eastern | £26
Cooking score: 2
£30

'The spartan, all-white space accessed from a barely marked frontage on a Fitzrovia back street brings new meaning to the word "cramped",' our inspector noted, happily tucking his elbows in amid an ambience of deeply endearing charm. Honey & Co. has personality in spades, typified by staff who do their best to fire you up with as much enthusiasm about its food as they have, all without an ounce of upselling cynicism. Tables are covered in paper pinned with clothes-pegs, and tap water is served in old milk-bottles. What more do you want? A concise menu of fresh, well-wrought Middle Eastern food perhaps. The kitchen knocks out one spanking-fresh zinger after another, with chickpea-dotted hummus, homemade labneh, cumin and chilli carrots, Yemeni falafels, butternut fritters and pickled cucumber starting things off in cornucopian style. For main, lamb shawarma is superb, the braised meat disintegrating obligingly into pittas with yoghurt, tomato and pomegranate. Finish with the house cheesecake, sweet-sour curd on kataifi pastry trickled with honey and roasted almond shards. Nine wines you may never have heard of start at £19.50 and are served in flat-bottomed tumblers.
Chef/s: Sarit Packer and Itamar Srulovich. **Open:** Mon to Fri 8am to 10.30pm (8 to 6 Mon, 9.30am to 10.30pm Sat). **Closed:** Sun. **Meals:** alc (main courses £11 to £14). **Details:** 26 seats. 6 seats outside.

Ibérica Marylebone
Classic and modern tapas with verve
195 Great Portland Street, Fitzrovia, W1W 5PS
Tel no: (020) 7636 8650
www.ibericalondon.com
⊖ Regent's Park, Great Portland Street, map 5
Spanish | £35
Cooking score: 2

'This does come over as a little corner of Spain, with many Spanish customers – greeting is always "hola".' Even after Ibérica opened a branch in Canary Wharf (see entry) it's good to see the original continuing to offer the real thing in a gregarious setting of dramatic Moorish lamps, intricately patterned tiles and large, central bar. For many it's still best for charcuterie, cheese and rice dishes – the 'impeccable quality' Sunday paella gets special mention. Nevertheless, the mix of modern and classic tapas is good, too: perhaps Galician seaweed salad with mussels, smoked cod fritters and lemon aïoli or Serrano ham croquettes. 'Intelligent, interactive and very helpful' staff are a bonus, and they're great at recommending just the right choice from the all-Spanish wine list. Prices from £19.
Chef/s: Miguel Garcia. **Open:** all week 11.30 to 10 (12 to 4 Sun). **Closed:** 25 and 26 Dec, bank hols. **Meals:** alc (main courses £7 to £24). Set L £10 (2 courses) to £15. Set D £28 (2 courses) to £35. **Details:** 100 seats. Separate bar. Wheelchair access.

The Ivy
A theatreland classic
1-5 West Street, Covent Garden, WC2H 9NQ
Tel no: (020) 7836 4751
www.the-ivy.co.uk
⊖ Leicester Square, map 5
Modern European | £39
Cooking score: 1

This theatreland classic is as glamorous yet comfortable as a pair of old sequinned slippers: from the long-standing favourites on its menu to the seasoned luvvies who gravitate here (the Ivy remains a good place for celebrity spotting if you favour national treasures over hip young things). The wood panelling, stained-glass windows and crisp napery could look old-fashioned, but add to the uncontrived retro vibe. Dishes like bang-bang chicken, salmon fishcake with spinach and a creamy sorrel sauce, and a well-made cottage pie are satisfying precursors to the nursery comforts of chocolate soufflé with mint ice cream. Wines start at £25.

Chef/s: Gary Lee. **Open:** all week 12 to 11.30 (10.30 Sun). **Closed:** 25 Dec. **Meals:** alc (main courses £15 to £35). **Details:** 105 seats. Separate bar.

J. Sheekey

Theatreland's seafood star
28-32 St Martin's Court, Covent Garden, WC2N 4AL
Tel no: (020) 7240 2565
www.j-sheekey.co.uk
⊖ Leicester Square, map 5
Seafood | £37
Cooking score: 4
V

The Sheekey lineage goes back to 1896, when one Josef of that ilk was first granted a franchise to serve fish and seafood here. Once just a humble oyster bar (see next entry), it metamorphosed after the war into an upmarket wood-panelled haven of fish cookery amid London's theatreland. Chef's specials come and go, but the formula doesn't change much – breathless innovation isn't needed in the preparation of sparklingly fresh seafood. Atlantic prawns by the quarter- and half-pint, whole Devon cock crab in the shell, oysters and caviar are all present, though a reporter notes a simple bowl of artichoke soup can be superb, too. The fish pie is legendary, but there are also fish stews, fish curries and grilled lobster, as well as more off-piste creations like sea trout with artichokes and fennel in blood-orange dressing. Finish with apple pie and clotted cream ice cream. A jumble of international wines, with more reds than you may expect, starts at £20.50.

Chef/s: James Cornwell. **Open:** all week L 12 to 3 (3.30 Sun), D 5.30 to 12 (6 to 11 Sun). **Closed:** 25 Dec. **Meals:** alc (main courses £16 to £28). **Details:** 93 seats. Separate bar. Wheelchair access.

J. Sheekey Oyster Bar

Sheekey offspring with speciality seafood
33-34 St Martin's Court, Covent Garden, WC2N 4AL
Tel no: (020) 7240 2565
www.jsheekeyoysterbar.co.uk
⊖ Leicester Square, map 5
Seafood | £26
Cooking score: 4
£30

Although the Sheekey operation began in the 19th century with a humble oyster bar, the venue so named today is actually the younger sibling, opening in 2008 next door to the original restaurant. A horseshoe-shaped seafood counter is its focal point, but more tables have been added to the main floor in the past year. The numerous staff are as perfectly proficient as they are next door. Celebrity photographer Alison Jackson provides starry wall decoration with portraits of Dame Eileen Atkins, John Hurt and others. The menu is a slimmed-down version of the original, retaining the oysters, naturally (try a mix of species with spicy boar sausages), the fruits de mer platters and the crab bisque, as well as the famous fish pie, the Cornish fish stew ('a delicious combination of seafood in a tasty broth') and populist desserts like banana sticky toffee pudding with crème fraîche. A condensed wine list opens at £19.75.

Chef/s: James Cornwell. **Open:** all week 12 to 12 (11pm Sun). **Closed:** 25 Dec. **Meals:** alc (main courses £9 to £14). **Details:** 51 seats. Separate bar. Wheelchair access.

Kiku

Bastion of cultured Japanese cuisine
17 Half Moon Street, Mayfair, W1J 7BE
Tel no: (020) 7499 4208
www.kikurestaurant.co.uk
⊖ Green Park, map 5
Japanese | £40
Cooking score: 4

Sibling establishment to the Mikuniya Onsen (Hot Spring) restaurant at Kinosaki, Kiku brought classical Japanese cuisine to Mayfair in

1978. In a spare and understated space, expansive tables in blond wood, delicate partitions and an elegant sushi counter contribute to the soothing ambience. Bilingual kaiseki menus offer the compendious experience, from clear soup in a dobin pot to sukiyaki and udon noodles, but the carte provides the best opportunity for newcomers to experiment. Grated yam on diced tuna, deep-fried aubergine slathered in sweet miso paste, grilled mackerel marinated in yuzu, and chicken and daikon casserole are totemic productions of the supremely skilled kitchen team, served alongside the more familiar sushi, sashimi and tempura. Set-lunch menus are built around favourite main dishes such as beef teriyaki and oroshi tonkatsu (breaded pork). Finish with a fruity sorbet or an ice cream made of adzuki beans or green tea. A full list of sakés and Japanese beers supplements a surprisingly gently priced wine list, from £15.50.

Chef/s: H Shiraishi, Y Hattori and M Anayama. **Open:** Mon to Sat L 12 to 2.30, all week D 6 to 10.15 (5.30 to 9.45 Sun). **Closed:** 25 to 27 Dec, 1 Jan. **Meals:** alc (main courses £12 to £39). Set L £15 (2 courses) to £20. Set D £20 (2 courses) to £50 (8 courses). **Details:** 100 seats.

NEW ENTRY
Kitchen Table at Bubbledogs
The ultimate chef's table
70 Charlotte Street, Fitzrovia, W1T 4QG
Tel no: (020) 7637 7770
www.bubbledogs.co.uk
⊖ Goodge Street, map 5
Modern British | £68
Cooking score: 5

Hot dogs and Champagne make the money in the fast-food eatery, while an evening-only 19-seater kitchen-restaurant ('the ultimate chef's table') satisfies James Knappett's creative urge. And he's firing on all cylinders with his 11–13-course, 'depending on the market' menu. Only key ingredients are listed – mackerel, kale, scallops – which translates as: mackerel diced raw, with apple purée, slivers of raw apple and a wine-infused snow; raw

young kale ('delicious') with an anchovy and Parmesan dressing; plump, sweet scallops with a dollop of diced cucumber in yoghurt, flavoured with dill, dill oil and bergamot. Dish after dish has subtle nuances or an inspired finishing touch, yet each succeeds primarily for simpler reasons: the happy marriage of crisp chicken skin, mascarpone and bacon jam; the simultaneously ethereal and earthy fresh egg pasta in a cloud of fresh truffle; smoked cod's roe topped with dried scallop powder and served with homemade rye bread (eclipsing any taramasalata you've ever had). Or there's the exquisite tenderness of venison, a delicate 'sweet-and-salty' Camembert and walnut tart, and among the lovely, finely wrought desserts, perhaps fresh mango with mango ice and jelly with yoghurt, coconut and fresh lime. If there is one complaint it is that 'the experience is over-long at three and a half hours when sitting at a counter on a high bar-stool in a stark kitchen'. Service is engaging and enthusiastic; wines start at a 'rapacious' £35.

Chef/s: James Knappett. **Open:** Tue to Sat D 6 and 7.30 (2 sittings). **Closed:** 23 to 27 Dec, first 2 weeks Jan, Easter bank hol, 2 weeks Aug. **Meals:** Tasting menu £68 (11 to 13 courses). **Details:** 19 seats.

Koya
Noodles with oodles of love and care
49 Frith Street, Soho, W1D 4SG
Tel no: (020) 7434 4463
www.koya.co.uk
⊖ Tottenham Court Road, map 5
Japanese | £15
Cooking score: 2
£30

'Udon noodles are wonderfully moreish with a fantastic toothsome bite' is one verdict on this premier-league Japanese fast-food outlet that lavishes love and care on them. Koya consists of a basic dining room (tiled floor, wooden chairs) and an open kitchen with a narrow four-stool counter at the back, so expect to queue and share tables. Hiya atsu (cold udon with hot broth) and yasai ten hiya atsu (with accompanying vegetable tempura) pleased one pair of reporters mightily, while another was taken by the salty, rich umami-filled flavours of atsu atsu buta miso (udon in a hot broth with pork and miso paste). Blackboard specials and donburi (rice bowls with miso soup) flesh out the repertoire. To drink, saké, shochu or beer may be preferable to wines (from £24). **Chef/s:** Junya Yamasaki and Shuko Oda. **Open:** all week L 12 to 3, D 5.30 to 10.30 (10 Sun). **Closed:** 24 to 26 Dec, 1 Jan. **Meals:** alc (main courses £7 to £15). **Details:** 46 seats.

Lantana Café
Lively Aussie brunch star
13 Charlotte Place, Fitzrovia, W1T 1SN
Tel no: (020) 7637 3347
www.lantanacafe.co.uk
⊖ Goodge Street, Tottenham Court Road, map 5
Australian | £12
Cooking score: 1
£30

This Aussie café off Goodge Street is run by people who understand life's simple pleasures: good coffee, good brekkie and an awesome brownie. A 'heaped, tottering plateful' of crisp-skinned chicken and bacon salad was, for one respondent, the 'tastiest tenner I've spent in a long time'. The sunny global flavours that Antipodeans do so well are everywhere: in squid, edamame and roast pepper salad, the ever-popular corn fritters with bacon, and toasted banana bread with raspberry labneh. Lantana has grown, too – into a take-away joint next door and a sister café, Salvation Jane, in Shoreditch (see entry). House wine £18. **Chef/s:** George Notley. **Open:** all week 8 to 3 (9 Sat and Sun). **Meals:** alc (main courses £7 to £12). **Details:** 30 seats. 12 seats outside.

╫╫ Average Price
The average price listed in main-entry reviews denotes the price of a three-course meal, without wine.

Latium
Smart Fitzrovia Italian with leanings towards Lazio
21 Berners Street, Fitzrovia, W1T 3LP
Tel no: (020) 7323 9123
www.latiumrestaurant.com
⊖ Goodge Street, Oxford Circus, map 5
Italian | £36
Cooking score: 3
£5 OFF

Bold artworks lend a splash of colour to the plain, Fitzrovia-smart restaurant of Claudio Pulze and chef/patron Maurizio Morelli. The Italian regions are well represented on the menu, with a little extra spotlight for dishes inspired by the culinary habits of Lazio – antipasti of Roman-style artichokes with smoked scamorza, seared mackerel and wild mint, perhaps. Pasta might be tagliatelle with guanciale, peas and red onions, and readers rate a 'classic' roast guinea fowl with grappa and dried plum, Savoy cabbage and baby carrots. To finish there's vanilla and goats' cream pannacotta with sour cherries and hazelnut biscotti, or a selection of sweet ravioli with fillings including apples with pine nuts and raisins. The all-Italian wine list shows no fear of big regional hitters, and starts at £16. **Chef/s:** Maurizio Morelli. **Open:** Mon to Fri L 12 to 3, Mon to Sat D 5.30 to 10.30 (11 Sat). **Closed:** Sun, 25 and 26 Dec, 31 Dec to 2 Jan, bank hols. **Meals:** alc (main courses £10 to £21). Set L £16.50 (2 courses) to 22.50. Set D £29.50 (2 courses) to £35.50. **Details:** 56 seats. Wheelchair access.

NEW ENTRY
Lima
Modest prices, vibrant, zingy food
31 Rathbone Place, Fitzrovia, W1T 1JH
Tel no: (020) 3002 2640
www.limalondon.com
⊖ Tottenham Court Road, map 5
£36
Cooking score: 2

For a new and exciting play on your senses head for Lima, a lovely contemporary space with whitewashed walls, banquette seating scattered with bright Peruvian cushions and a 'nice, chatty atmosphere'. 'Very fresh, very zingy' colourful plates are refined versions of peasant-style dishes where potatoes play a central role – perhaps jazzed up in starters such as tuna causa (composed mainly of mashed, lime-dressed potato with chopped tuna and ginger confit). Peru's unique eco-dried potato also features: accompanying a main course seco (superb slow-cooked lamb shoulder) to great effect, especially when combined with white grape and pisco mosto verde. Salmon tiradito, duck crudo and beef pachamanca have also been praised. Desserts (not a strong suit) generally consist of ice creams or mousses. Wines from a short, global list start at £18. **Chef/s:** Virgilio Martinez. **Open:** Mon to Sat L 12 to 2.30, D 5.30 to 10.30. **Closed:** Sun, 22 Dec to New Year. **Meals:** alc (main courses £16 to £26). Set L £17.50 (2 courses) to £20. **Details:** 65 seats. 8 seats outside. Separate bar.

NEW ENTRY
Little Social
A chip off the block
5 Pollen Street, Mayfair, W1S 1NE
Tel no: (020) 7870 3730
www.littlesocial.co.uk
⊖ Oxford Circus, map 5
Modern European | £35
Cooking score: 6

V

Right opposite Jason Atherton's Pollen Street Social (see entry), his new Little Social looks like many people's idea of a typical French bistro: a door-screening curtain, red banquettes, booth seating, French posters, faux nicotine staining and masses of dark wood. But the light, modern food with imaginative pairings and up-to-date treatments has more in common with the illustrious parent restaurant – although you can get a very good pork head and foie gras terrine and a choice of steaks (with chips). Canadian chef Cary Docherty may offer his own version of poutine, Canada's national dish – an awesome plate of chorizo, fries, curd

cheese and chilli – but he delivers real class in the shape of a sashimi-like slice of beetroot-cured sea trout with beetroot and a shallot dressing, or a deep, fulsome green pea and broad bean risotto with peppered ventrèche and mint ricotta. Spot-on cooking, too, in a beautifully creamy piece of roasted cod on butter beans, enlivened by 'the briny tang of the freshest cockles'. Bow out with a faultless tarte Tatin. Wonderfully dedicated, on-the-ball staff deserve much credit. A likeable wine list, strong of France, opens at £24. **Chef/s:** Cary Docherty. **Open:** Mon to Sat L 12 to 2.30, D 6 to 10.30. **Closed:** Sun, 25 and 26 Dec, 1 Jan, bank hols. **Meals:** alc (main courses £17 to £22). Set L £21 (2 courses) to £25. **Details:** 60 seats. Wheelchair access.

Locanda Locatelli
Classic Italian flagship
8 Seymour Street, Marble Arch, W1H 7JZ
Tel no: (020) 7935 9088
www.locandalocatelli.com
⊖ Marble Arch, map 4
Italian | £70
Cooking score: 4

🍾

Giorgio Locatelli's perennially glamorous hotel-restaurant on Portman Square is, at 12 years old, one of London's most famous Italians. The venue is a masterclass in design. Whether the curvy and capacious cream booths, gauzy drapes and fish-eye mirrors are to your taste or not, it's impressive how smoothly the operation segues from relaxed family lunches at weekends to chic see-and-be-seen eatery by night. The food eases the transition with impeccable homely options such as orecchiette with turnip tops or rabbit leg with polenta and radicchio cheek-by-jowl with luxurious pan-fried scallops with saffron vinaigrette, venison medallions with wild mushrooms, 'crema fritta' and radicchio and, of all things, banana and chocolate rice pudding with black truffle. The drinks list is an education in Italian wine (from £15) and includes Tuscan and Piedmont sections.

Chef/s: Giorgio Locatelli. **Open:** all week L 12 to 3 (3.30 Sat and Sun), D 6.45 to 11 (11.30 Fri and Sat, 10.15 Sun). **Closed:** 24 to 26 Dec. **Meals:** alc (main courses £14 to £33). **Details:** 82 seats. Wheelchair access.

ALSO RECOMMENDED
▲ Mele e Pere
46 Brewer Street, Soho, W1F 9TF
Tel no: (020) 7096 2096
www.meleepere.co.uk
⊖ **Piccadilly Circus, map 5**
Italian £5 OFF

'A delightful place to be' decided one reporter after a visit to this basement trattoria near Piccadilly Circus. A 'really relaxed atmosphere' and 'exceptionally friendly staff' add to the charm, as does a separate bar where sharing plates hold sway. In the dining room, tuck in to rustic Italian staples such as tagliatelle with beef ragù (£14.50) or turbot with broccoli, clams, anchovy and chilli (£16.50). Wines from £16.50. Open all week.

Mennula
Big-hearted Sicilian patriot
10 Charlotte Street, Fitzrovia, W1T 2LT
Tel no: (020) 7636 2833
www.mennula.com
⊖ **Goodge Street, map 5**
Italian | £35
Cooking score: 3
£5 OFF

Given that both chef and owner hail from the Sicilian province of Agrigento, it's no surprise that Mennula should take its name from the almond trees that are everywhere in the region. Mirrors, garish purple banquettes and stencilled motifs of nut-laden branches decorate the tidy little dining room, although rustic regional food is the real heartbeat of this proudly patriotic venue. The kitchen garners a larder full of British and imported ingredients for a menu peppered with good things from the volcanic island. Stuzzichini nibbles such as pan-fried Tuma goats' cheese with warm aubergine salad set the scene for rousing pastas

and big-hearted mains: squid ink ravioli with Devon crab and ricotta; pistachio-crusted Welsh lamb with 'sugo di carne'; wild Cornish sea bass steamed with clams and courgettes. To finish, try a plate of Sicilian sfinci (warm doughnuts with cinnamon sugar). Sicily also shines on the regional wine list, with prices from £19.80.

Chef/s: Santino Busciglio. **Open:** Mon to Fri L 12 to 3, Mon to Sat D 6 to 11. **Closed:** Sun, 2 to 8 Jan, bank hols. **Meals:** alc (main courses £18 to £35). Set L and D £16.95 (2 courses) to £18.95. **Details:** 30 seats. 10 seats outside.

ALSO RECOMMENDED
▲ Mishkin's
25 Catherine Street, Covent Garden, WC2B 5JS
Tel no: (020) 7240 2078
www.mishkins.co.uk
⊖ **Covent Garden, map 5**
American-Jewish

'A Jewish-style deli and cocktail bar that doesn't take itself too seriously' is how the management describes Mishkin's. Well, it's certainly not kosher. The faux-industrial look is everything you would expect from a Russell Norman joint, its style fits the multifarious nature of the clientele and service has a brisk charm. The whopping salt beef sandwich (£10) and the burger (from £6) are recommended, and there's praise for cod cheek popcorn, the lox bagel and dessert of banana Foster. The chicken matzo soup continues to draw complaints. Wines from £18. Open all week.

▲ Mon Plaisir
21 Monmouth Street, Covent Garden, WC2H 9DD
Tel no: (020) 7836 7243
www.monplaisir.co.uk
⊖ **Covent Garden, map 5**
French

With the Tricolore flapping proudly outside, posters on the walls and the sound of accordion music in the air, Mon Plaisir looks every inch the vintage French bistro. General de Gaulle was a famous visitor back in the early days, but the place is now a favourite with local thespians, tourists and theatre-goers. Generous helpings of 'entente cordiale' are the attraction, in the shape of ham and mushroom bouchées (£9.95), plaice meunière or roast guinea fowl with peas and morels (£19.95), followed by profiteroles or crémeux au chocolat. Patriotic wines from £18.50. Closed Sun.

Moti Mahal

Indian regional cook's tour
45 Great Queen Street, Covent Garden, WC2B 5AA
Tel no: (020) 7240 9329
www.motimahal-uk.com
⊖ Covent Garden, map 5
Indian | £35
Cooking score: 3

V

Spread over two snazzily decorated floors with a glassed-in kitchen for chef-watching in the basement, Moti Mahal takes Covent Garden's theatre-goers, tourists and business types on a fascinating culinary road trip along the Grand Trunk Road – an ancient 2,500km highway connecting Bengal to the North West Frontier. Pitch camp in Lahore for keema mirch (jumbo chillies stuffed with spiced mutton) or make a detour to Chennai for a crab and quail's egg roll with tomato and coriander chutney, before stopping off in the Punjab for a textbook tandoori with freshly made breads. Otherwise, stick a pin in Delhi (halibut with cumin, chilli and star-fruit salad), Benares (paneer simmered with walnuts in peppery tomato sauce) or Hyderabad (baby chicken cooked with spinach, garlic and ginger). Confident spicing and pretty new-wave presentation are the kitchen's trademarks, while the wine list is helpfully arranged for 'harmonious' food-matching. Prices start at £28.
Chef/s: Anirudh Arora. **Open:** Mon to Fri L 12 to 3.30, Mon to Sat D 5.30 to 11. **Closed:** Sun, 25 to 26 Dec, bank hols. **Meals:** alc (main courses £10 to £23). Set L £15 (2 courses) to £21. Set D £30 (2 courses) to £35. Tasting menu £45. **Details:** 80 seats. Wheelchair access.

Mr Kong

Cantonese old-stager
21 Lisle Street, Soho, WC2H 7BA
Tel no: (020) 7437 7341
www.mrkongrestaurant.com
⊖ Leicester Square, map 5
Chinese | £18
Cooking score: 1

V £30

Opened by Mr Kong and family in 1984, this old-stager has outlived many of its neighbours on ever-changing Lisle Street and still follows the old Chinatown ways as regards food and service. The Cantonese menu is as long as a New Year dragon, snaking its way through soups, hotpots, roast meats, rice plates and more, with seafood specials grabbing much of the limelight – think baked 'sandstone' lobster, steamed razor clams with glass noodles or pan-fried eel with stuffed chilli, prawn paste and black bean sauce. You may have to queue, even if you've booked: possibly a sign that redoubtable Mr Kong isn't immune to the neighbourhood's touristy vices. Wines from £11.50.
Chef/s: Kwai Kong and Y Wai Lo. **Open:** all week noon to 2.45am (1.45am Sun). **Closed:** 24 and 25 Dec. **Meals:** alc (main courses £8 to £32). Set L and D £10.80 (2 courses) to £25.80 (4 courses). **Details:** 120 seats.

★ TOP 50 ★

Murano

Paradigm of Mayfair exclusivity
20 Queen Street, Mayfair, W1J 5PP
Tel no: (020) 7495 1127
www.muranolondon.com
⊖ Green Park, map 5
Italian | £65
Cooking score: 7

🍾 **V**

There's a pleasing sense of light and fresh air to Angela Hartnett's Mayfair restaurant. The dining room may look studiedly mono-chrome, but plenty of natural daylight is let in on a space that's deepened with mirrors, where swirling scrolls etched on the walls suggest surging waves, and the one blot of colour comes from the foliage in the table decorations. It makes a thoroughly relaxing setting for some of central London's most inspirational contemporary cooking. The base camp may have been Italy when Hartnett arrived in 2008, but the kitchen now roams across a broader swathe of Europe. Dishes can seem dauntingly offbeat initially, but most make perfect sense on the plate, as was the case with a dinner that opened with beetroot, sweet potato and voluptuous, velvety goats' curd, followed by flawlessly executed pappardelle with succulent beef cheek. Fish is expertly timed, a piece of halibut arriving with steamed cockles, parsnip and trompettes. Pork belly with Scottish langoustines had a delicate balance underlined by garnishes of plum purée and smoked almonds. The fashion for texturally challenging desserts is celebrated in a grainy assemblage of toast parfait with burnt butter ice cream and granola. Murano's list of very fine wines is a detailed exploration of the French regions and Italy, but mark-ups give no quarter. Prices open at £29.50, or £6 for a small glass.

Chef/s: Angela Hartnett. **Open:** Mon to Sat L 12 to 3, D 6.30 to 11. **Closed:** Sun, 24 to 27 Dec. **Meals:** Set L £25 (2 courses) to £30. Set D £50 (2 courses) to £85 (5 courses). **Details:** 56 seats. Wheelchair access.

NEW ENTRY
Newman Street Tavern
A restaurant built on bulldog British produce
48 Newman Street, Fitzrovia, W1T 1QQ
Tel no: (020) 3667 1445
www.newmanstreettavern.co.uk
⊖ Goodge Street, map 5
British | £30
Cooking score: 3

Despite the name, the Newman Street Tavern is more a restaurant than a boozer – and a restaurant dedicated to meticulous sourcing. Cluttering the walls of the racing-green ground-floor 'raw bar' (there's also a quieter first-floor dining room) are portraits of scuttling crustaceans and content cows:

distant cousins of which figure on a menu evenly divided between land and sea. A capable hand in the kitchen was evident at an inspection meal: starting with a sublime splodge of brown crab on toast, moving on to delicately textured grilled cuttlefish sprawled over a bed of chilli and rocket. Meaty mains are just as spirited, and wisely don't over-complicate matters – try suckling kid with spring vegetables, or Middle White pork paired with beer onions although vegetarians might feel overlooked. One minor quibble was service, trundling along at glacial pace, albeit well intentioned. A thoughtfully arranged wine list opens at £3.50 a glass, £18 a bottle.

Chef/s: Peter Weeden. **Open:** Mon to Sat 12 to 11, Sun 10.30 to 5. **Closed:** 25 Dec, 1 Jan, bank hols. **Meals:** alc (main courses £12 to £22). **Details:** 90 seats. 6 seats outside.

Nobu Berkeley St
High-gloss celebrity hangout
15 Berkeley Street, Mayfair, W1J 8DY
Tel no: (020) 7290 9222
www.noburestaurants.com
⊖ Green Park, map 5
Japanese | £80
Cooking score: 4
V

The high-gloss Berkeley Street outpost of Nobu's glitzy global chain is party central for paparazzi hunting for eager celebs. Noise levels take no prisoners – especially among the braying throngs in the bar. Follow the money up the staircase to the sparkling futuristic dining room and you'll be rewarded with Nobu's trademark mix of tingling fresh sushi and sashimi, delicately astringent salads and top-end tempura, enriched with lashings of big-money luxury: think lobster with spicy lemon dressing, 'toro' tuna tartare with caviar or Wagyu rump teppanyaki with fresh truffles. Ceviches, tacos and grilled anticuchos skewers add Latin thrills, and this branch also has a wood oven (fired up from 6pm for the likes of roast poussin with cabbage or octopus with yuzu). Perching at the counter with a lunchtime bento box is a cheaper option. Rare imported sakés feature on a wine list stuffed with vintage treasures and super-sexy tipples at celebrity prices; bottles from £35.

Chef/s: Mark Edwards. **Open:** all week L 12 to 2.30, D 6 to 11 (12 Thur to Sat, 9.45 Sun). **Closed:** 25 and 26 Dec. **Meals:** alc (main courses £10 to £42). Set D £26 to £38. Tasting menus £75 to £105. **Details:** 180 seats. Separate bar.

Nobu London

Japanese fusion pioneer
Metropolitan Hotel, 19 Old Park Lane, Mayfair, W1K 1LB
Tel no: (020) 7447 4747
www.noburestaurants.com
⊖ Hyde Park Corner, map 5
Japanese | £75
Cooking score: 4

Nobu London's A-list glory days may be over, but this Park Lane icon remains a contender for those who like to show off with plates of black cod in miso or sea urchin tempura. As a Japanese fusion pioneer, it can still deliver clear flavours and supreme delicacy when it matters, as well as firing up proceedings with Peruvian anticuchos skewers, lobster ceviche and other Latino riffs. A fabulous assortment of sparkling nigiri and hand rolls suits the traditionalists, while others might venture into the crossover world of pan-fried Dover sole with red chilli and shiso salsa, tea-smoked lamb or squid 'pasta' with wild garlic sauce. Bento boxes and donburi rice bowls keep things casual at lunchtime, while zany East/West desserts such as 'I-pple'and 'banana split 3000' are tailor-made for fashionistas. High prices and strictly enforced table-turning come with the territory, and the celebrity wine list flaunts its wealth at every opportunity; bottles start at £27.

Chef/s: Mark Edwards and Hideki Maede. **Open:** all week L 12 to 2.15 (12.30 to 2.30 Sat and Sun), D 6 to 10.15 (11 Fri and Sat, 10 Sun). **Closed:** 25 and 26 Dec, 1 Jan. **Meals:** alc (main courses £10 to £42). **Details:** 150 seats. Separate bar. Wheelchair access.

Nopi

Inventive food to be fought over
21-22 Warwick Street, Soho, W1B 5NE
Tel no: (020) 7494 9584
www.nopi-restaurant.com
⊖ Piccadilly Circus, map 5
Middle Eastern-Mediterranean | £41
Cooking score: 3

V

Nearly three years on, Yotam Ottolenghi's striking, white-painted dining room still buzzes, surprising and delighting visitors with lively and intriguing Mediterranean and Middle Eastern-influenced dishes. The cooking is as joyous as it is seasonal, and vegetables are handled with as much vibrancy and imagination as meat and fish. The ever-innovative kitchen sends out a terrific array of sharing plates, combining burrata with blood orange, coriander seeds and lavender oil, wrapping spiced gurnard in banana leaf and teaming it with pineapple sambal, and serving lamb sweetbreads with black garlic, nettle, and parsley purée. Don't want to share? Then a short list of seductively flavoured main courses, say twice-cooked baby chicken with lemon myrtle salt and chilli sauce, should do the trick. There's 'sublime' rhubarb mess with lychee sorbet, stem ginger and chrysanthemum for dessert, black rice with coconut milk, banana and mango for breakfast and inventive cocktails to supplement the wine list, which opens at £25.

Chef/s: Yotam Ottolenghi and Ramael Scully. **Open:** Mon to Fri 8 to 2.45, D 5.30 to 10.15. Sat 10am to 10.15pm, Sun 10 to 4. **Closed:** 25 and 26 Dec, 1 Jan, 2 weeks Aug, bank hols. **Meals:** alc (main courses £17 to £30). Pre-theatre D £21.50 (2 courses). **Details:** 102 seats.

Average Price

The average price listed in main-entry reviews denotes the price of a three-course meal, without wine.

One Leicester Street

Spartan and spectacular British fare
1 Leicester Street, Leicester Square, WC2H 7BL
Tel no: (020) 3301 8020
www.oneleicesterstreet.com
⊖ Leicester Square, map 5
British | £30
Cooking score: 4

The epicurean pioneers of nose-to-tail dining at the St John group have bidden farewell to their West End hotel-restaurant venture, but one of the group's brightest stars, Tom Harris, continues to run the kitchen, albeit in softer environs. Now sporting Farrow & Ball hues, One Leicester Street has abandoned the austere setting, though the food remains resolutely spartan. The daily changing menu of sharing dishes sings an elegant hymn to Britain's seasonal produce. Humble grilled onion with goats' curd and wild fennel is revelatory: as vivid on the palate as the plate. From the best of beast and fowl – be it cheek, heart or robust smoked Dexter beef – to impeccably fresh seafood, each ingredient tastes of itself, masterfully cooked and heightened by judiciously chosen accompaniments, perhaps monk's beard, lovage or wild garlic. For an indulgent finale, brown-butter and honey tart won't disappoint. The eclectic European wine list opens at £5 a glass, £26 a bottle.
Chef/s: Tom Harris. **Open:** all week L 12 to 3 (1 to 3.30 Sat and Sun), D 5.30 to 11. **Meals:** alc (main courses £9 to £18). **Details:** 54 seats. Separate bar. Wheelchair access.

Symbols

🛏 Accommodation is available

💲30 Three courses for less than £30

V Separate vegetarian menu

£5 OFF £5-off voucher scheme

🍾 Notable wine list

Opera Tavern

Vibrant theatreland venue with lively tapas
23 Catherine Street, Covent Garden, WC2B 5JS
Tel no: (020) 7836 3680
www.operatavern.co.uk
⊖ Covent Garden, map 5
Tapas | £35
Cooking score: 3
£5 OFF

The Opera Tavern's trump card is its bustling atmosphere, the closely packed tables of the ground-floor bar and grill helping to crank up the volume. Even the more sedate restaurant upstairs (where tables are bookable) can become 'busy and lively'. What is offered is very much in tune with modern times, the menu turning its back on conventional courses, instead providing a choice of Spanish and Italian-inspired tapas as pioneered by older siblings Salt Yard and Dehesa (see entries). Simplicity and careful sourcing are seen in crisp-skinned confit of Old Spot pork belly with rosemary-scented cannellini beans, venison pinchos morunos (skewers) and char-grilled octopus with chickpea fritter, red pepper and mojo verde. The Ibérico pork and foie gras mini-burgers remain a highlight, and desserts feature an enticing cold chocolate fondant with salted-caramel and espresso ice cream. Wines start at £15.
Chef/s: James Thickett. **Open:** all week L 12 to 3 (5 Sat and Sun), Mon to Sat D 5 to 11.30. **Closed:** 25 and 26 Dec, 1 Jan. **Meals:** alc (tapas £4 to £10). **Details:** 76 seats. 6 seats outside. Separate bar. Children allowed in upstairs restaurant only.

Phoenix Palace

Hong Kong opulence and fresh dim sum
3-5 Glentworth Street, Marylebone, NW1 5PG
Tel no: (020) 7486 3515
www.phoenixpalace.co.uk
⊖ Baker Street, map 4
Chinese | £40
Cooking score: 2

Set beneath a vast apartment block not far from Baker Street, this sprawling, all-day restaurant decorated in the ubiquitous red, gold and dragon theme of many such Chinese food palaces, offers predominantly Cantonese cooking on its 200-dish menu. It's familiar territory, taking in chilli and garlic pork spare ribs, and shredded smoked chicken as appetisers, before crispy aromatic duck, fresh crab or lobster with ginger and spring onion, crispy shredded beef with chilli, and chicken with cashew nuts. But there's also eel fillet with belly pork and garlic casserole, wild boar fillet with lemongrass and beef brisket with noodles. Freshly made dim sum is the main daytime attraction. Wines are basic, starting at £19.

Chef/s: Marco Li. **Open:** all week 12 to 11 (11 to 10.30 Sun). **Closed:** 25 Dec. **Meals:** alc (main courses £8 to £36). Set L £15 (2 courses) to £25. Set D £28 (2 courses) to £40. **Details:** 300 seats. Separate bar. Wheelchair access.

★ TOP 50 ★

Pied-à-Terre
Bijou Fitzrovia aristocrat
34 Charlotte Street, Fitzrovia, W1T 2NH
Tel no: (020) 7636 1178
www.pied-a-terre.co.uk
⊖ Goodge Street, map 5
Modern French | £75
Cooking score: 7

🍷 V

Pedigree, precision and poise are the watchwords at this bijou aristocrat shoehorned into a Charlotte Street town house. Pied-à-Terre doesn't puff itself up or make grand overtures; instead it purrs contentedly, pleasing a knowledgeable dressed-up crowd with its serious food and equally serious wine. The narrow, dark-walled dining room is 'surprisingly compact' – a glass screen here, a floral arrangement there and two rows of tables either side of a walkway – but the mood is upbeat. Chef Marcus Eaves is really on song and everything about his cooking dazzles: from beautifully crafted canapés to a profusion of jewel-like petits fours with coffee. Just consider a three-part deconstruction of quail (roast breasts, crispy leg and a dinky little Kiev) accompanied by resinous Douglas Fir

purée and hazelnut dressing; or glazed shin of Aberdeenshire beef with baby leeks, pear and white wine purée, spelt and chervil roots; or even a colourful, virtuoso main course of roasted sea bass on aubergine purée with creamed polenta and vibrant red pepper essence – 'brilliant', intricate dishes fashioned with extraordinary care and attention to detail. Desserts are studiously assembled masterpieces, from a signature frozen rhubarb mousse with cardamom gel, rhubarb sorbet, yoghurt and vanilla foam to pear and cinnamon mille-feuille with verjus jelly. Service is discreet but 'always on hand when required', and the sommelier's wise counsel is priceless when it comes to navigating the stupendous, globetrotting list. Bespoke 'suggestions' (from £27) provide a mouth-watering snapshot of the complete cellar.

Chef/s: Marcus Eaves. **Open:** Mon to Fri L 12 to 2.30, Mon to Sat D 6 to 11. **Closed:** Sun, 23 Dec to 5 Jan. **Meals:** Set L £27.50 (2 courses) to £33.50. Set D £60 (2 courses) to £75. Tasting menu £99 (8 courses). **Details:** 44 seats. Separate bar.

★ TOP 10 ★

Pollen Street Social
Utterly brilliant uptown eatery
8-13 Pollen Street, Mayfair, W1S 1NQ
Tel no: (020) 7290 7600
www.pollenstreetsocial.com
⊖ Oxford Circus, map 5
Modern British | £60
Cooking score: 9

Jason Atherton's fingers are in so many pies, yet here at the mothership all remains well. Staff are friendly and attentive without being invasive and there's a happy, chatty buzz about the place that begins in the bar and extends to the restaurant where you could easily end up chatting with the folks on the next table; 'social' it most certainly is. The dining room lives very much in the moment and Atherton's menus are forever pushing forwards, finding an edible expression for his experiences around the world. Japan may inspire scallop sashimi, but it's not a dominant theme; the kitchen is equally happy taking a playful spin on British brunch or turning the classic combo of egg and asparagus into an extraordinary starter of barely poached egg on truffle purée with smoked eel, asparagus spears and an intense eel, pea and parsley soup. This is cooking to inspire gluttonous pleasure and there's no room for standing on ceremony. Opening nibbles focus on finger food, with brandade, beautiful fresh bread for dipping, fat Sicilian olives and airy pork scratchings with apple and mustard purée. Yet for all the lack of ceremony there's no missing the sophistication of Atherton's cooking. A main course of turbot with cauliflower and cheese purée, roasted carrot, broccoli, and cauliflower and cockle chowder is a case in point: everything is cooked with pinpoint accuracy, the flavours singing in close harmony with a sprinkling of seaweed salt adding a heavenly top note. Atherton handles flavour like a master, rustling up instant classics like camomile tea and cantaloupe melon sorbet with a sigh of yoghurt foam and a zing of fresh lime – a pre-dessert that threatens to overshadow anything that follows it. Fortunately the chef has more up his sleeve – maybe a dessert of 'PBJ': peanut parfait, peanut praline, a fruity blast of cherry yuzu sorbet and 'nitro peanut' (peanut mousse frozen with nitrogen to create a heavenly bubbly mass), and then, before coffee, two perfect, moist strawberry and almond financiers. Japan features on the wine list, but France gets the lion's share with all the major regions covered. There's also an impressive worldwide selection with plenty under £40; the starting price is £24.

Chef/s: Jason Atherton. **Open:** Mon to Sat L 12 to 2.30, D 6 to 10.30. **Closed:** Sun, bank hols. **Meals:** alc (main courses £27 to £36). Set L £24 (2 courses) to £27.50. Tasting menu £79 (8 courses). **Details:** 60 seats. Separate bar. Wheelchair access.

ALSO RECOMMENDED
▲ Polpo Covent Garden
6 Maiden Lane, Covent Garden, WC2E 7NA
Tel no: (020) 7836 8448
www.polpo.co.uk
⊖ Covent Garden, map 5
Italian

This Covent Garden spin-off from the original Polpo in Soho (there's also a branch in Smithfield) conforms neatly to Russell Norman's tried-and-tested formula of casual vibes and bàcaro-style food (aka Italian small plates). Cicchetti are there aplenty (from £3) as are pizzette – including a sweet Nutella version – plus a variety of meatballs (try the spicy pork and fennel), fritto misto (£9.50), duck and green peppercorn ragù with pappardelle, and affogato al caffè. Wines from £18. Open all week.

▲ Polpo Soho
41 Beak Street, Soho, W1F 9SB
Tel no: (020) 7734 4479
www.polpo.co.uk
⊖ Piccadilly Circus, Oxford Circus, map 5
Italian

As you head into deepest old Soho, the octopus (polpo) sign will be more eye-catching than the 'banged up' terracotta frontage. Along with the deliberately distressed interior, it is all part of Russell Norman's vision of a Venetian-inspired bàcaro – now with offshoots in Covent Garden (see entry above) and Smithfield. Polpo makes a serviceable street-food drop-in for inexpensive small plates, say anchovy and chickpea crostini (£3) or cured pork shoulder and pickled pepper (£6), plus larger helpings of cuttlefish and ink risotto (£8) and chicken involtini – though you may not love the evening no-booking policy. Wines from £18. Open all week.

▲ La Porte des Indes

32 Bryanston Street, Marble Arch, W1H 7EG
Tel no: (020) 7224 0055
www.laportedesindes.com
⊖ Marble Arch, map 4
Indian

'Not your run-of-the mill British Indian',
notes a fan of this flamboyant restaurant in a
high-ceilinged Edwardian ballroom. A
'jungle bar', tropical palms, palatial antiques
and a cascading water feature provide the
Bollywood backdrop for a menu inspired by
Les Indes Françaises. Garlicky grilled scallops
with saffron sauce (£12), a spicy seafood
cassoulet and Barbary duck breast with
tamarind sauce (£19) line up alongside
stalwarts such as tandoori chicken and pork
vindaloo. Sunday's jazz brunch is also worth
noting. Wines from £22. Open all week.

Princi

Good ingredients, good value, good buzz
135 Wardour Street, Soho, W1F 0UT
Tel no: (020) 7478 8888
www.princi.com
⊖ Tottenham Court Road, Piccadilly Circus,
map 5
Italian | £20
Cooking score: 2
£30

The London outpost of a Milanese bakery
chain, oh-so-cool Princi has been peddling
sandwiches, baked pastas, meaty stews, pizzas
and pastries in its (almost) self-service café for
some five years; now with the addition of a
pizzeria (complete with wood-fired oven) it is
still up for the gig. The café, with its
communal seating and laid-back vibe,
continues to do a roaring trade, but those
wanting waiter service and their own table
head for the pizzeria. Sunny flavours are in
abundance, found not only in the very good
pizzas, but also in heritage tomato salad with
buffala mozzarella, wild mushroom linguine
or Napoli sausage with polenta, roasted
peppers and onion gravy. It's also a handy

drop-in for breakfast and the coffee is superb.
The wine list is proudly Italian with prices
from £20.
Open: all week 8am to 11.30pm (8.30am to 10pm
Sun). **Meals:** alc (main courses £8 to £12).
Details: 46 seats. Wheelchair access.

The Providores

Fusion trailblazer
109 Marylebone High Street, Marylebone,
W1U 4RX
Tel no: (020) 7935 6175
www.theprovidores.co.uk
⊖ Baker Street, Bond Street, map 4
Fusion | £47
Cooking score: 2
🍸

The fashionable crowd may have moved on,
but Kiwi chef Peter Gordon's fusion trailblazer
still gets tongues wagging and taste-buds
jangling. Despite high prices, crowds are
happy to perch elbow-to-elbow in the street-
level Tapa Room: a jam-packed, no-bookings
grazing den serving popular fusion breakfasts
and kooky little dishes such as kohlrabi and
onion bhajias with plantain and date salsa,
sumac yoghurt and pomegranate mint sauce.
Upstairs in the more sedate Providores
restaurant, expect even more complicated
assemblages including crispy Cajun pork belly
with Puy lentils, pickled tomatoes, nashi pear,
apple, ginger and tamari 'slaw from a
challenging multi-course menu. The wine list
offers an incomparable tour of New Zealand's
10 major winemaking regions with rare
sampling opportunities by the glass or carafe.
Bottles start at £25.
Chef/s: Karl Calvert. **Open:** Mon to Fri L 12 to 2.45,
Sat and Sun 11 to 3, all week D 6 to 10 (9.45 Sun).
Meals: alc L (main courses £17 to £24), Set D £33 (2
courses) to £63 (5 courses). **Details:** 88 seats. 6
seats outside. Wheelchair access.

Quilon

Spot-on south Indian flavours
41 Buckingham Gate, Westminster, SW1E 6AF
Tel no: (020) 7821 1899
www.quilon.co.uk
⊖ St James's Park, Victoria, map 5
Indian | £48
Cooking score: 4
£5 OFF 🛏

Although there's no escaping the subdued surrounds and corporate anonymity of the Crowne Plaza Hotel, this revamped dining room now feels more approachable and glamorous with its moody lighting, amber tones, Indian artwork and bespoke Q Bar. Suave cosmopolitan styling is matched by refined south Indian cuisine full of innovative nuances, with considerable technique applied to a raft of smartly groomed, pinpoint dishes. Seafood is a strength: from oysters presented in an onion 'shell' with lemon, ginger and chilli or crispy fried squid matched with spice-pounded shrimps to lobster cooked with a rich amalgam of butter, pepper and garlic. Elsewhere, venison and coconut stir-fry, a ripe mango curry tempered with mustard and a rule-breaking dessert of lentil cappuccino with cardamom shortbread, fig and honey ice cream show Sriram Aylur's creativity across the board. Sakés and grappas are unexpected additions to the well-considered list of spice-friendly wines (from £23), but also check out the fascinating collection of globally sourced beers.
Chef/s: Sriram Aylur. **Open:** all week L 12 to 2.30 (12.30 to 3.30 Sat and Sun), D 6 to 11 (10.30 Sun). **Closed:** 25 Dec. **Meals:** alc (main courses £15 to £31). Set L £24. Set D £48. **Details:** 81 seats. Separate bar.

Quirinale

Intimate Westminster Italian
1 Great Peter Street, Westminster, SW1P 3LL
Tel no: (020) 7222 7080
www.quirinale.co.uk
⊖ Westminster, map 3
Italian | £45
Cooking score: 3

Well on its way to becoming a lovable old institution, Quirinale is a light-filled basement restaurant just off Millbank. It is also Parliament's local Italian, so earwigging on MPs' conversations is a distinct possibility. Kick off with one of the fabulous seafood-based starters, such as a well-constructed heap of cuttlefish, king prawns and tender squid, or scallops on vegetable purée with pine nuts and speck. The intermediate course might be a big plate of reimagined minestrone, bristling with spring veg and basil, or pastas such as orrechiette with ground boar, shallots and tomato. Main courses – monkfish with tapenade on chive mash, or a veal milanese the size of a frisbee – could seem pale by comparison. To finish, tiramisu was quite bland at inspection, but the Italian cheeses were superb. Wines, also Italian, are fair to middling, opening with a humdrum glass selection from £5. Bottles start at £21.
Chef/s: Stefano Savio. **Open:** Mon to Fri L 12 to 2.30, D 6 to 10.30. **Closed:** Sat, Sun, 1 week Christmas, Aug, bank hols. **Meals:** alc (main courses £18 to £29). Set L and D £19 (2 courses) to £23. **Details:** 50 seats.

Quo Vadis

Rejuvenated Soho legend
26-29 Dean Street, Soho, W1D 3LL
Tel no: (020) 7437 9585
www.quovadissoho.co.uk
⊖ Tottenham Court Road, map 5
British | £35
Cooking score: 4

'A terrific metro buzz, sharp uptown staff, bold seasonal flavours': no wonder rejuvenated legend Quo Vadis is set fair as a big player in Soho. The frisson of swinging through the revolving doors, past the bar and into the animated dining room never wanes; the vibe will pep you up as surely as a Campari aperitivo. Extravagant floral arrangements, distressed mirrors and discreet glass screens provide the backdrop, while the menu looks like an old broadsheet – complete with zany illustrations, news of special deals and even the weather forecast. The kitchen advertises its spiffing wares in bald, straight-talking lingo: celeriac and fennel soup; lamb's sweetbreads with capers and black butter; splendid ox liver with onions and sage; a fabulously fresh, spirit-lifting dish of brill with wild garlic and mussel broth. The day's 'pie and mash' goes down a treat, vegetables could include huge wedges of buttery spring cabbage, and there may be trifle to finish. Dependable Euro-accented wines start at £10 a carafe.

Chef/s: Jeremy Lee. **Open:** Mon to Sat L 12 to 2.30, D 5.30 to 10.30. **Closed:** Sun, 25 and 26 Dec, 1 Jan, bank hols. **Meals:** alc (main courses £16 to £20). Set L and theatre menu £17.50 (2 courses) to £20. **Details:** 60 seats. 20 seats outside. Separate bar.

The Riding House Café
All-day food everybody loves to eat
43 Great Titchfield Street, Fitzrovia, W1W 7PQ
Tel no: (020) 7927 0840
www.ridinghousecafe.co.uk
⊖ Oxford Circus, map 5
Modern British | £28
Cooking score: 2

£30

'A very lively outfit' begins one commentary on this all-day brasserie where food and drink are served from breakfast to last orders. Everyone seems to know the place – liking the vibrant bar, the casual vibes – and plenty return regularly. The cooking is Eurozone without fireworks: small sharing plates of clams, crayfish cocktail, soft-shelled crab or artichoke dip giving way to main courses of smoked haddock kedgeree with soft-boiled egg and pea shoots, roast rump of lamb with caponata and black olives, a burger with smoked Cheddar, gherkins and good chips,

and salt-baked sea bass for two to share. Cinnamon doughnuts with chocolate sauce are a good way to finish. Wines start at £18.

Chef/s: Paul Daniel. **Open:** all week 7.30am to 10pm (9am Sat, 9am to 9.30pm Sun). **Meals:** alc (main courses £11 to £25). **Details:** 150 seats. Separate bar.

Roka
Stylish urban Japanese eating
37 Charlotte Street, Fitzrovia, W1T 1RR
Tel no: (020) 7580 6464
www.rokarestaurant.com
⊖ Goodge Street, map 5
Japanese | £50
Cooking score: 4

'The place seems never less than rammed-full but service remains good,' noted a regular of this big-city eatery, which has a sheer-glass frontage opening on to the hustle and bustle of Charlotte Street. Cool, vibrant and resounding to a thumping soundtrack, the interior is a study in simplicity, drawing inspiration from the Japanese izakaya. Chefs work busily on the robata grill; you can take a ringside seat and watch the action or settle at one of the closely packed tables. The cooking gives a vigorous spin to Japanese classics, fusing new-wave Japanese with pan-Asian undertones. Standout dishes this year have included spicy Korean lamb chops, salmon teriyaki (wrapped in a houba leaf, with flesh that slipped apart into tiny creamy flakes), delicate tempura soft-shell crab, and sushi and sashimi that showed the excellent quality of the raw fish. The only misstep was French patisserie-style desserts. Wines (and saké), in tune with the food, start at £27.

Chef/s: Damon Griffin. **Open:** all week L 12 to 3.30 (12.30 to 4 Sat and Sun), D 5.30 to 11.30 (10.30 Sun). **Closed:** 25 Dec. **Meals:** alc (dishes from £5 to £15). **Details:** 88 seats. 24 seats outside.

ALSO RECOMMENDED

▲ Roti Chai Street Kitchen

3 Portman Mews South, Marylebone, W1H 6HS
Tel no: (020) 7408 0101
www.rotichai.com
⊖ Marble Arch, Bond Street, map 4
Indian

It's quite a treat to find a pleasant, amenably priced all-day eatery so close to Marble Arch. Tucked behind M&S, this brightly coloured, stylishly simple place offers a lively, shopper-friendly atmosphere and a kitchen dealing in Indian street food. There's a choice of appetisers such as bhel puri (puffed rice mixed with a tangy tamarind sauce), vegetable or meat-filled samosas (from £3.80) and Gujarati steamed chickpea cakes, as well as chicken (£7.90) or lamb curries. Open all week. (Note: the Dining Room is a more formal evening-only restaurant in the basement.)

Roux at Parliament Square

Luxe Anglo-French dining
12 Great George Street, Parliament Square, Westminster, SW1P 3AD
Tel no: (020) 7334 3737
www.rouxatparliamentsquare.co.uk
⊖ Westminster, St James's Park, map 5
Anglo-French | £65
Cooking score: 4

The nomenclature of fine dining is fully present throughout Roux at Parliament Square, from the muted plush interior within the prestigious home of the Royal Institute of Chartered Surveyors to the starched linen and eagerly solicitous staff. With Masterchef Professionals winner Steve Groves at the helm, and Michel Roux Jnr consulting, this Roux outpost shows no signs of flailing in the wake of expenses clampdowns. The modern-European menu offers distinctly British riffs on French haute cuisine, so while politicos conjugate and conspire you may opt for cheese and pickle, a voluminous foam of Lancashire bomb cheese punctured with immaculate pickled vegetables and oaty crumbs. Elegant mains run from Tamworth suckling pig three

ways with hazelnuts, cinnamon, apple and potato purée to lemon sole with crispy chicken wing and artichokes. To finish, linger perhaps over an English strawberry dessert with whipped yoghurt and a sprightly Douglas fir granita. Prix fixe is perfectly pleasant, but for a full technicolour experience, opt for a la carte. The French-dominated wine offers generous global reach by the glass (from £5). **Chef/s:** Steve Groves. **Open:** Mon to Fri L 12 to 2, D 6.30 to 10. **Closed:** Sat, Sun, 24 Dec to 2 Jan, bank hols. **Meals:** alc (main courses £17 to £27). Set L £35. **Details:** 51 seats. Separate bar. Wheelchair access.

Roux at the Landau

A paean to sumptuous luxury
The Langham, 1c Portland Place, Oxford Circus, W1B 1JA
Tel no: (020) 7965 0165
www.rouxatthelandau.com
⊖ Oxford Circus, map 5
Modern European | £50
Cooking score: 3
🚗 V

Formerly the Langham's Victorian ballroom, the Landau has been overhauled by David Collins as a paean to sumptuous luxury complete with spindly modern chandeliers, light-wood panelling and a superb curved banquette overlooking All Souls' Church. The Roux 'imprimatur' invites high expectations, and chef Chris King's team is capable of delivering concentrated, refined dishes in the modern idiom. Top-notch ingredients are the building blocks, from French white asparagus with butter-poached morels and soft herbs to spit-roast Orléans chicken with orzo pasta carbonara and Alsace bacon. To finish, the bitter chocolate mille-feuille with maple ice cream and salted pecans is a marvel to behold with its rigid, 'hair-thin' garnish of spun sugar. However, consistency is a bugbear and some reporters have bemoaned slapdash, 'one-dimensional' cooking and a miserly approach – although presentation is invariably picture-pretty. Service also has its ups and downs, from 'perfectly paced' and 'discreetly attentive',

to pushy and pretentious. The wine list is stuffed with aristocratic bottles at aristocratic prices (from £33).
Chef/s: Chris King. **Open:** Mon to Fri L 12.30 to 2.30, Mon to Sat D 5.30 to 10.30. **Closed:** Sun. **Meals:** alc (main courses £16 to £45). Set L £28 (2 courses) to £35. **Details:** 82 seats. Separate bar. Wheelchair access. Car parking.

Rules

Britannia rules in Covent Garden
35 Maiden Lane, Covent Garden, WC2E 7LB
Tel no: (020) 7836 5314
www.rules.co.uk
⊖ Covent Garden, Leicester Square, map 5
British | £47
Cooking score: 3

Born in 1798, this true patriot takes the blue riband as London's oldest restaurant – a landmark writ large in the capital's food heritage. More than two centuries on, few places can still deliver such an unreformed celebration of British victuals: it's enough to make you break into a rousing chorus of 'Rule, Britannia!'. In a deeply traditional, velvety setting of plush panelling and prints, staff serve up everything you might expect: bags of game (from 'famous grouse' to jugged hare), ribs of rare-breed beef from the trolley, gut-busting pies and memory-lane puds such as golden syrup sponge. The kitchen also flirts with foodie fashion by offering, say, sea bass fillet with endive, cauliflower purée and curry oil – although the wide-eyed crowds of camera-toting tourists, old-guard businessmen and celebrating families don't mind a jot. Rhône reds are top calls on the wine list (which starts at £24.50).
Chef/s: David Stafford. **Open:** all week 12 to 11.45 (10.45 Sun). **Closed:** 25 and 26 Dec. **Meals:** alc (main courses £18 to £36). **Details:** 95 seats. Separate bar.

Salt Yard

Versatile tapas hot spot
54 Goodge Street, Fitzrovia, W1T 4NA
Tel no: (020) 7637 0657
www.saltyard.co.uk
⊖ Goodge Street, map 5
Tapas | £30
Cooking score: 2
£5 OFF

Two minutes from the tube station, this Goodge Street tapas joint is one of a group of like-minded London enterprises (see also entries, Dehesa and Opera Tavern). Park yourself on bar-stool or banquette, or outside if it's fine, for a session of nibbles (olives, almonds, anchovies, quails' eggs), and perhaps move on to one or two modern tapas plates. The repertoire takes in salt-cod croquetas and char-grilled chorizo with cime di rapa, baby onions and thyme, as well as winter warmers such as a stew of char-grilled chicken, morcilla, pancetta and black beans. Spanish and Italian charcuterie is first rate, and sweet things include churros with chocolate sauce, and affogato with PX sherry-and-raisin ice cream. Spanish and Italian wines are arranged by weight, from £16 a bottle, £4 a glass.
Chef/s: Andrew Clarke and Ben Tish. **Open:** Mon to Fri L 12 to 3, D 5 to 11. Sat 12 to 11. **Closed:** Sun, 24 to 26 Dec, bank hols. **Meals:** alc (tapas £4 to £10). **Details:** 66 seats. 8 seats outside. Children allowed downstairs only.

Savoy Grill

An evocation of flavours past
The Savoy, Strand, Covent Garden, WC2R 0EU
Tel no: (020) 7592 1600
www.gordonramsay.com
⊖ Charing Cross, map 5
Anglo-French | £40
Cooking score: 2
🛏 V

Simple, expensive thrills – a shiny Art Deco dining room, trundling trolleys – create a sense of occasion when customers turn left through the lobby of one of London's grandest hotels. Like the setting, the Anglo-French

menu is knowingly old-school. Start with potted salmon, eggs en cocotte or omelette Arnold Bennett, to be followed by a hunky charcoal-fired pork chop or a meaty pie or pudding. It's busy, and the kitchen can't always cope. At inspection the richest pickings were from the lunch trolley, which conveys a different roast daily, and Welsh rarebit topped with a devilishly dark savoury paste. Service was polite yet inattentive, and ordering wine seems a more satisfying experience than ordering food; the list starts at £25 (£6.50 by the glass).
Chef/s: Andy Cook. **Open:** all week L 12 to 3 (4 Sun), D 5.30 to 11 (6 to 10 Sun). **Closed:** 25 Dec. **Meals:** alc (main courses £18 to £65). Set L £26. Pre-theatre D £22 (2 courses) to £26. **Details:** 126 seats. Wheelchair access.

Scott's

It's about luxury, comfort and indulgence
20 Mount Street, Mayfair, W1K 2HE
Tel no: (020) 7495 7309
www.scotts-restaurant.com
⊖ Green Park, map 4
Seafood | £45
Cooking score: 4

V

This vintage Mayfair hangout has been around for decades, but since 2005, when Caprice Holdings stepped on board, Scott's has taken on a breezy new lease of life with its ever-so-glamorous demeanour and nostalgic brasserie menu. Bivalves and crustacea are the kitchen's stock-in-trade, wolfed down by diners perched at the striking, central oyster bar or more comfortably ensconced at one of the white-clad tables. This is also the place to come if your fancy turns to shellfish bisque, lobster thermidor, Dover sole meunière, chicken, bacon and mushroom pie or Welsh rarebit. The cooking is not the most adventurous, but the quality-consciousness and precision is spot-on. The menu's scope is broad, taking in contemporary ideas (such as sautéed razor clams with wild boar sausage,

and roasted Gressingham duck with January King cabbage and blood orange) alongside the more traditional treatments. Wines from £25.
Chef/s: David McCarthy. **Open:** all week 12 to 10.30 (10 Sun). **Closed:** 25 Dec. **Meals:** alc (main courses £18 to £30). **Details:** 120 seats. 28 seats outside. Separate bar. Wheelchair access.

Seven Park Place by William Drabble

Wonderful, fastidiously detailed food
St James's Hotel and Club, 7 Park Place, Mayfair, SW1A 1LS
Tel no: (020) 7316 1600
www.sevenparkplace.co.uk
⊖ Green Park, map 5
Modern French | £58
Cooking score: 6

There's an element of plush-in-a-matchbox to this free-standing restaurant within the St James's Hotel, the 'sumptuous' pair of dining rooms seating just 26. It's this small scale and relative intimacy that attracts people, drawn too by 'good and helpful' service and by the understated finesse of William Drabble's cooking. Classic technique and flavour combinations rather than novelty are the keynotes here, but with a liberal sprinkling of high-end ingredients. Sliced morteau sausage, robustly paired with a grainy mustard potato salad, has enough oomph to assert itself; a cep butter sauce enhances rather than masks the delicate flavour of scallop mousse; a chunky fillet of cod – light, buttery crunch outside, almost translucent in the middle – is teamed with a silky white bean purée, seared squid adding texture and a foie gras vinaigrette giving an acid balance to the sweetness; a hot raspberry soufflé with bitter chocolate sauce is 'exemplary'. The set-menu format means bills are predictable, just as long as you don't get lost in the excellent global wine list – aimed at those prepared to pay for quality. The choice growers and vintages are hard to fault, however, and house selections start at £29.50.

Chef/s: William Drabble. **Open:** Tue to Sat L 12 to 2, D 6.30 to 10. **Closed:** Sun, Mon. **Meals:** Set L £24.50 (2 courses) to £29. Set D £52 (2 courses) to £58. Tasting menu £69 (6 courses). **Details:** 26 seats. Separate bar.

Sketch, Lecture Room & Library
An extravagant pleasure palace
9 Conduit Street, Mayfair, W1S 2XG
Tel no: (020) 7659 4500
www.sketch.uk.com
⊖ Oxford Circus, map 5
Modern European | £100
Cooking score: 6

V

An air of almost insane opulence permeates Sketch's arty pleasure palace, wafting upwards to the head-spinning excesses of the first-floor Lecture Room & Library: a nonconformist mix of gold walls, installations, oversized Ali Baba vases and creamy leather walls. It's audaciously ostentatious and you'll need a very deep wallet to appreciate Pierre Gagnaire's wickedly capricious food. To begin, wallow in the delights of 'perfume of the earth' (inspired by one of the chef's favourite *parfums*); costing £37, it brings a flavour-fest of jewel-like exhibits on separate plates – smoked cocotte of snails and vegetables, foie gras soup with white port, beef carpaccio, beetroot syrup with Colman's mustard, Sauternes jelly… and more. Next, brace yourself for even more grandiosity in the shape of, say, skate wings meunière with Oscietra caviar, steamed fennel, soft-boiled egg, mackerel bouillon and seaweed. Having come this far, give in to the 'grand dessert': a collation of sweets such as passion fruit with cream cheese mousse, candied chestnut and shortbread. 'Gourmet rapide' lunches offer some financial relief, but not so the 110-page wine list, which plunders France and beyond for big-hitting treasures. Prices zoom skywards from £25.
Chef/s: Pierre Gagnaire. **Open:** Tue to Fri L 12 to 2.30, Tue to Sat D 6.30 to 10.30. **Closed:** Sun, Mon, last 2 weeks Dec, last 2 weeks Aug, bank hols.

Meals: alc (main courses £43 to £55). Set L £35 (2 courses) to £40. Tasting menu £95 (6 courses). **Details:** 50 seats. Separate bar.

NEW ENTRY
Social Eating House
Smart-casual Soho hang-out
58 Poland Street, Soho, W1F 7NR
Tel no: (020) 7993 3251
socialeatinghouse.com
⊖ Oxford Street, map 5
Modern British | £30
Cooking score: 5

The third in Jason Atherton's trio of restaurants (see entries for Pollen Street Social and Little Social) has an altogether more swaggering, clubby interior – wood and gold and copper tones, a low mirrored ceiling, artfully distressed walls – that chimes well with the Soho media crowd, and there's the bonus of a standalone bar upstairs. Paul Hood has moved from Pollen Street Social to run the kitchen and his menu sports a mixed bag of smart-casual metropolitan dishes for big city palates: wild mushrooms served in a bag, with toast spread with cep purée; confit lamb neck with sheep's ricotta mashed potato, garlic, parsley and wild asparagus; flamed côte de porc with beetroot, white polenta, spring onion and summer savoury; and beautifully cooked Cumbrian native breed bavette served on a wooden board with duck-fat chips, green salad and béarnaise, have all been praised. Sharply executed desserts play the field, too, from London-honey almond sponge with goats' curd ice cream and orange to Szechuan and sea salt baked pineapple with lime and coconut. The wine list is no less delightful, well chosen and keenly priced, from £17.
Chef/s: Paul Hood. **Open:** Mon to Sat L 12 to 2.30, D 6 to 11. **Meals:** alc (main courses £16 to £24). Set L £18 (2 courses) to £21. **Details:** 70 seats. Separate bar. Wheelchair access.

ALSO RECOMMENDED

▲ Spuntino

61 Rupert Street, Soho, W1D 7PW
www.spuntino.co.uk
⊖ Piccadilly Circus, map 5
Italian-American

Russell Norman's machine-age Soho diner continues to score highly in the cool stakes and the lack of a phone or reservations book hasn't hampered its popularity. The transatlantic accent of the Italian 'tapas'-style menu means a cheeseburger with chipotle and jalapeño (£9) or pulled pork and pickled apple slider (£5) sits alongside braised octopus and borlotti beans (£9), with shoestring fries or 'slaw on the side. A short, sharp wine list starts at £18. Open all week.

★ TOP 10 ★

The Square

World-class gastronomy
6-10 Bruton Street, Mayfair, W1J 6PU
Tel no: (020) 7495 7100
www.squarerestaurant.com
⊖ Green Park, map 5
Modern French | £80
Cooking score: 8
🍷

Dealing in confidence without arrogance, Philip Howard and the Square rose to the top long ago, and have rightfully stayed there. The 'refined and clubby' Mayfair premises look the part thanks to wide open spaces and a subtle gleam from parquet and polished walls – no need for excess when the food has a colour and life all of its own. Keeping pace with the seasons, with signature dishes alongside, Howard's cooking is grounded in exceptional technique. It's the kind of craft that might sound like folly until the benefits are laid out on the plate. To start, a fat-bellied courgette flower is perfectly taut with coral-pink lobster mousse with lemon verbena, its tiny bubbles mimicked by a foaming shellfish sauce. On the tasting menu, there's the signature sauté of sweet langoustine tails with Parmesan gnocchi and potato and truffle emulsion. A main course of duck with cherries is complex rather than crowded: turnips and glazed endives contribute bitterness, there's depth and zest in a croustillant of leg meat spiked with orange, and a bold, bright cherry purée unifies the lot. To finish, Brillat-Savarin cheesecake is the rich classic (the extensive cheeseboard is another), and soufflés have impressive hats: chocolate with walnut ice cream is one winning combination. Professionalism and ease define the service, including the wine advice. There's much to fascinate on a fine and extensive French-led wine list populated by excellent producers; even single glasses are chosen thoughtfully. Bottles from £30.
Chef/s: Philip Howard. **Open:** Mon to Sat L 12 to 2.30, all week D 6.30 to 10 (10.30 Fri and Sat, 9.30 Sun). **Closed:** 25 and 26 Dec. **Meals:** Set L £30 (2 courses) to £35. Set D £80. Tasting menu £105 (9 courses). **Details:** 75 seats. Separate bar. Wheelchair access.

Sumosan

Glamorous modern Japanese
26b Albemarle Street, Mayfair, W1S 4HY
Tel no: (020) 7495 5999
www.sumosan.com
⊖ Green Park, map 5
Japanese | £50
Cooking score: 4
£5
OFF

Hailing from Moscow, now perfectly at home in London, this A-list Japanese venue feeds the blue blood and new blood of Mayfair. It is, at times, almost parodically extravagant; if you can serve something with truffles or lobster, Sumosan almost certainly will. Its 'T&T' (tuna and truffle) rolls are the most famous example, but toro stuffed with foie gras and spicy somen noodles with lobster make a similar point. You don't need a wealthy benefactor to dine here, however: set lunches allow diners to compose a bento of their own, choosing from the likes of seafood soup, lamb furikake and green-tea ice cream. Sushi and sashimi, also served at a small sushi bar, are prepared to an 'extremely high standard' and tempura, teppanyaki and creative salads deserve consideration, too. 'Discovery flights' of saké make a nice alternative to the usual Champagne and cocktails. House wine, £30. **Chef/s:** Bubker Belkhit. **Open:** Mon to Fri L 12 to 2.45, all week D 6 to 11.30 (10.30 Sun). **Closed:** 25 and 26 Dec, 31 Dec and 1 Jan, bank hols. **Meals:** alc (main courses £8 to £65). Set menus from £24.90. Tasting menu £75. **Details:** 100 seats. Separate bar. Wheelchair access.

Tamarind

A masterclass in Moghul cuisine
20 Queen Street, Mayfair, W1J 5PR
Tel no: (020) 7629 3561
www.tamarindrestaurant.com
⊖ **Green Park, map 5**
Indian | £50
Cooking score: 5
£5 OFF **V**

Tamarind fits its salubrious Mayfair location like a silky embroidered sari. It is posh, worldly and slightly ostentatious, with shimmering gold-hued columns, dusky tones, ambient Muzak and extravagant floral displays in the lustrous basement dining room. Alfred Prasad's sure-footed brigade takes its cue from the setting, conjuring up scintillating, tongue-tingling flavours and Euro-Asian crossovers for a suave international crowd. The sensory thrills come thick and fast, with vibrantly spiced starters leading the charge – try deep-fried gram-flour rolls filled with tilapia and mint chutney or three kinds of tandoori mushrooms with pickled onion in curry leaf dressing. Artfully marinated kebabs are a strong suit, and the kitchen also knows how to deliver consummate versions of curry-house evergreens: think rogan josh, murgh makhani or 'dum' biryanis cooked authentically under a pastry lid. Side dishes, vegetables and breads are exemplary, and it would be sinful to miss the warm, syrupy gulab jamun or the velvety pleasures of dark chocolate mousse with cinnamon and orange zest. Gold-star service helps justify the high prices, although the exhaustive wine list (from £28) is loaded with thoughtfully selected possibilities.

Chef/s: Alfred Prasad and Peter Joseph. **Open:** Sun to Fri L 12 to 3, all week D 5.30 to 11 (6 to 10 Sun). **Closed:** 25 and 26 Dec, 1 Jan. **Meals:** alc (main courses £12 to £36). Set L £19.50 (2 courses) to £22.50. Sun L £32. Tasting menu £56. **Details:** 84 seats. No children under 7 yrs after 7.

Tapas Brindisa Soho

Top-drawer Spanish provisions
46 Broadwick Street, Soho, W1F 7AF
Tel no: (020) 7534 1690
www.brindisa.com
⊖ **Oxford Circus, map 5**
Spanish | £25
Cooking score: 3
£30

This Soho link in the cheery Tapas Brindisa chain, with its authentic Spanish atmosphere, all-day opening and rather cramped dining room (the lighter, more attractive bar and open kitchen area is the preferred spot), can be counted on to produce convincing modern tapas. The Brindisa trademarks include plenty of Spanish specialities, ranging from assemblies of first-rate Iberian hams and cheeses, via quality tinned boquerones to Gordal olives stuffed with orange and oregano. Classic tortilla, pulpo a la gallega and patatas bravas appear alongside more evolved starter-sized plates of ox cheeks with purple potatoes and red wine or seasonal specials such as pheasant egg with morcilla and pancetta pan-fried mash. Desserts are missable, but not the concise, all-Spanish wine list (from £17.50), which includes a good selection of sherries.

Chef/s: Carles Ramon Aguilar. **Open:** all week 12 to 11. **Closed:** 25 and 26 Dec. **Meals:** alc (tapas £3 to £22). Set L for 2 £20 (mixed tapas plate). **Details:** 50 seats. 4 seats outside. Separate bar. Wheelchair access.

🍴 Also Recommended

Also recommended entries are not scored but we think they are worth a visit.

10 Greek Street

Nice vibes, sharp cooking, no reservations
10 Greek Street, Soho, W1D 4DH
Tel no: (020) 7734 4677
www.10greekstreet.com
⊖ **Tottenham Court Road, map 5**
Modern European | £31
Cooking score: 4
🍾

Soho's diners welcomed 10 Greek Street with open arms when it opened in 2012, and have kept it close to their chests ever since. They may not love the no-reservations at dinner policy (you're safe at lunch) but an international wine list of bottles from Burgenland to Barossa, all priced at less than a weekly travelcard, has softened the blow. Cameron Emirali's cooking is as joyous as it is seasonal. A February menu yielded potted pig with rhubarb jelly, red wine risotto with burrata and grilled Treviso, then Seville orange sorbet with gin – perfect cold-weather stuff. Substantial Welsh Black steaks or sharing dishes such as Gloucester Old Spot with Savoy and mustard mash are typical of the town-house restaurant's generous, convivial approach. It looks rather a plain Jane with simple wooden chairs and 'metro' tiles, but laid-back staff and happy customers fill it with joy. House wine is £16.
Chef/s: Cameron Emirali. **Open:** Mon to Sat L 12 to 2.30, D 5.30 to 10.45. **Closed:** Sun, 1 week Christmas, bank hols. **Meals:** alc (main courses £14 to £20). **Details:** 30 seats. 2 seats outside.

Terroirs

Crowd-pulling bistro with great wines
5 William IV Street, Covent Garden, WC2N 4DW
Tel no: (020) 7036 0660
www.terroirswinebar.com
⊖ **Charing Cross, map 5**
French | £32
Cooking score: 3
🍾

A Charing Cross hit, this single-minded wine bar/bistro is driven by a passion for all things French and artisan. The vibe works best in the packed-out ground floor with its exposed brickwork, Parisian posters, zinc bar and enticing 'pick and mix' menu. Here, breads, charcuterie, cheeses and small plates (garlicky snails with wild mushrooms, say) are bolstered by seasonal treats including red mullet with blood orange, capers and hazelnuts or boudin noir with heirloom beetroots and watercress. A slightly more formal menu is also available in the cosy basement hideaway. Ed Wilson and co now have three other eateries around town (Brawn, Soif and the Green Man & French Horn, see entries), and the increased pressure may explain recent gripes about a lack of service and inconsistent food. Mind you, Terroirs' trump card is ultimately its 'wild' list of organic and biodynamic wines, with insightful selections from France and Italy. Expect great drinking by the glass or 500ml 'pot', and bottles from £17.
Chef/s: Ed Wilson. **Open:** Mon to Sat L 12 to 3, D 5.30 to 11. **Closed:** Sun, 24 Dec to 1 Jan, bank hols. **Meals:** alc (main courses £16 to £20). **Details:** 130 seats. 6 seats outside. Separate bar.

Texture

High calibre Nordic-inspired cuisine
34 Portman Street, Marble Arch, W1H 7BY
Tel no: (020) 7224 0028
www.texture-restaurant.co.uk
⊖ **Marble Arch, map 4**
Modern French/Nordic | £51
Cooking score: 4
🍾 **V**

Six years on, in a grand Georgian setting with 'delightful ambience' that used to house a banking hall, the collaboration between chef Agnar Sverrisson and master sommelier Xavier Rousset continues to bear fruit. Technically astute fine dining is brightened and lightened by a touch of Nordic influence, care of Agnar's Icelandic heritage. Eschewing butter and cream in the main, he produces 'faultless' food from top-drawer ingredients. Delicate Anjou quail char-grilled with sweetcorn, shallot, bacon popcorn and red wine essence delights; and the signature Icelandic lightly salted cod with avocado, brandade, squid and chorizo yields to the fork effortlessly. Icelandic skyr (like strained yoghurt) with rye breadcrumbs and rhubarb marks a refreshing close to proceedings. Be prepared to dig deep for the fish tasting menu and à la carte choices, or alternatively plump for the wallet-friendly set menu. The prestigious and extensive wine list, with France to the fore, offers an enticing way in via glass and carafe. Bottles from £29.

Chef/s: Agnar Sverrisson. **Open:** Tue to Sat L 12 to 2.30, D 6.30 to 10.30. **Closed:** Sun, Mon, 23 Dec to 9 Jan, 2 weeks summer. **Meals:** alc (main courses £28 to £38). Set L £21.90 (2 courses) to £24.90. Tasting menu £79 (7 courses). **Details:** 52 seats. Separate bar. Wheelchair access.

Theo Randall at the InterContinental

Plate-lickingly good Italian food
InterContinental London Hotel, 1 Hamilton Place, Mayfair, W1J 7QY
Tel no: (020) 7318 8747
www.theorandall.com
⊖ Hyde Park Corner, map 4
Italian | £60
Cooking score: 6

🛏 V

Theo Randall's childhood trips to rustic Italy carried him to the River Café and eventually to the improbable environs of the InterContinental, a hunk of grande-luxe anonymity on Hyde Park Corner. A spare-looking dining room of caramel banquettes and concealed spotlighting creates a relaxed ambience for thoroughly researched modern Italian menus that keep things simple, while not stinting on prime ingredients. A dish of chicory shoots dressed in red wine vinegar, anchovy and capers bursts with savoury intensity, or you could up the ante for sea-fresh Devon crab with agretti (a marine succulent), datterini tomatoes and bottarga. Intermediates are hard to dodge, when they offer cappelletti stuffed with braised veal, pancetta and two types of mushroom. Main attractions might produce roast rack of Somerset lamb with wood-roasted vegetables,

golden beets and vivid salsa d'erbe. Sensational Amalfi lemon tart remains the crowd-puller at dessert, but then how to resist the little orange and honey cakes served with baked pear and crème fraîche? The Italian wine list, starting with Valdobbiadene Proseccos and motoring through all the regions, matches the mood, but prices are high. Glasses start at £8, bottles £34.

Chef/s: Theo Randall. **Open:** Mon to Fri L 12 to 3, Mon to Sat D 6 to 11. **Closed:** Sun, 25 and 26 Dec, 1 Jan, bank hols. **Meals:** alc (main courses £27 to £38). Set L and D £27 (2 courses) to £33. **Details:** 200 seats. Separate bar. Wheelchair access. Car parking.

34

Mayfair opulence and thrilling grilling
34 Grosvenor Square (Entrance on South Audley Street), Mayfair, W1K 2HD
Tel no: (020) 3350 3434
www.34-restaurant.co.uk
⊖ Bond Street, Green Park, map 4
Modern British | £37
Cooking score: 2

First and foremost, 34 is dedicated to the business of beef. Its entrance on South Audley Street, not far from the Connaught, gives on to a parquet-floored room in tones of burnt umber and lemon. Pedigree specimens from the grasslands of Argentina, Australia, the US and Scotland find their way on to the parrilla, a South American-style charcoal grill that's the kitchen's centrepiece. Yet as well as bavettes, ribeyes and T-bones, you'll find inspired seafood dishes such as grilled swordfish with squid, preserved lemon and rosemary salsa, and thoroughbred Spanish cured meats. Start with seared scallops, garlic mash, fennel and almonds, and end on jasmine rice pudding and mango – and the job's a good 'un. Wine prices open at £22.50, or £6.50 a glass.

Chef/s: Paul Brown. **Open:** all week 12 to 10.30. **Closed:** 25 Dec. **Meals:** alc (main courses £16 to £37). **Details:** 96 seats. Separate bar.

Trishna

Indian seafood star
15-17 Blandford Street, Marylebone, W1U 3DG
Tel no: (020) 7935 5624
www.trishnalondon.com
⊖ Marylebone, Bond Street, map 4
Seafood-Indian | £34
Cooking score: 3

🍷 V

Cool colours, expensive trappings and modernist light fittings set the tone in this sleek outpost of the famous Mumbai seafood specialist. Trishna courts the Marylebone vote with its delectable take on Indian fish cookery and more besides. Enthusiastic packed houses testify to the kitchen's prowess when it comes to 'expertly spiced' show-stealers such as crispy squid with poppy seeds, roasted rice, urd dhal and lime or the ever-popular hariyali bream with green chilli, coriander and tomato kachumber ('some of the best fish ever,' chimed one fan). There are hits in other departments, too, from 'original' duck seekh kebabs and quail pepper stir-fry to 'flavour-bursting' aubergine chaat with peanuts and tamarind. Trishna also caters for the business crowd with light 'lunch bites'. Five three-part wine flights provide a trailer for sommelier Sunaina Sethi's creative wine list, which offers top drinking by the glass or carafe and a classy choice of spice-tolerant recommendations from producers worldwide. Bottles start at £20.
Chef/s: Karam Sethi. **Open:** all week L 12 to 2.45 (12.30 to 3.15 Sun), D 6 to 10.45 (6.30 to 9.45 Sun). **Closed:** 25 to 28 Dec, 1 to 4 Jan. **Meals:** alc (main courses £10 to £23). Set L £17.50 (2 courses) to £22.50. Early D £20 (4 courses). Sun L £26 (4 courses). Tasting menu £32 (5 courses) to £55 (7 courses). **Details:** 75 seats. 8 seats outside.

NEW ENTRY

28°-50° Wine Workshop and Kitchen

Wine-centric bistro
15-17 Marylebone Lane, Marylebone, W1U 2NE
Tel no: (020) 7486 7922
www.2850.co.uk
⊖ Bond Street, map 4
French | £30
Cooking score: 3

🍷

Following on from the success of the Fetter Lane original (see entry), this Marylebone offshoot is housed more commodiously on two floors, incorporating a handsome V-shaped zinc bar (ground floor) and an open-to-view kitchen in the smaller basement dining room. But the same level of informality and sassy bistro dishes are standard, aided by on-the-ball service and cooking that hits 'just the right notes'. Marinated peppers and goats' curd in a grilled aubergine wrap could be followed by a juicy haunch of venison with wild garlic polenta. To finish, ginger pannacotta with blood oranges, rhubarb foam and caramelised oats makes a splendid dessert. Wines are taken seriously, with virtually everything on the 50-bin list available in quantities of 75ml (from £2.20), 125ml, 250ml sizes or by the bottle (from £19.50). Prestige labels are to be found on the Collectors List.
Chef/s: Paul Walsh. **Open:** all week L 12 to 2.30 (4 Sun), D 6 to 10 (10.30 Thur, Fri and Sat, 9.30 Sun). **Closed:** 25 Dec, 1 Jan, bank hols. **Meals:** alc (main courses £16 to £22). Set L £15.50 (2 courses) to £18.95. **Details:** 50 seats. Wheelchair access.

Umu

Gilt-edged Kyoto cuisine
14-16 Bruton Place, Mayfair, W1J 6LX
Tel no: (020) 7499 8881
www.umurestaurant.com
⊖ **Green Park, Bond Street, map 5**
Japanese | £90
Cooking score: 5

V

Apply your hand to the recess in the timber and bronze door, brush aside the curtains and enter Umu's slinky dining room – a calming sanctuary with rigorous floral displays, exclusive furnishings and bespoke Murano glassware dangling from the ceiling. There's studious Zen-like artistry in the open kitchen, as chefs demystify the intricacies of gilt-edged Kyoto cuisine with a series of ceremonial kaiseki menus. Clarity, balance and harmony are the unifying principles behind this relentlessly reverential approach, which showcases the full range of Japanese culinary styles. It may sound abstruse, but the results are stunning: consider 'nimonowan' (a 'chain' of simmered winter flavours involving burdock and kumquat with Jerusalem artichoke cake and blue tiger prawn) or hashiyasume (saké-steamed monkfish liver with ginger sauce and 'finger' lime). The kaiseki procession also features zensai appetisers, sashimi, meaty grills, tempura and more; the arrival of luxe nigiri or plates of wild mushroom rice with hot spring egg and pickles signal that meals are nearing their conclusion. Alternatively, pitch up at the sushi counter or try a lunchtime bento box if money and time are tight. Drinks-wise, the extravagant wine list (from £25) is outshone by an absolutely fabulous selection of premium sakés.

Chef/s: Yoshinori Ishii. **Open:** Mon to Fri L 12 to 2.30, Mon to Sat D 6 to 11. **Closed:** Sun, bank hols. **Meals:** alc (main courses £18 to £65). Set L from £25. Tasting menu £100. **Details:** 64 seats. Wheelchair access.

ALSO RECOMMENDED

▲ Vasco & Piero's Pavilion

15 Poland Street, Soho, W1F 8QE
Tel no: (020) 7437 8774
www.vascosfood.com
⊖ **Oxford Circus, map 5**
Italian

Vasco and Paul Matteucci's family-run restaurant is a popular old-stager among Soho's Italian restaurants, having clocked up more than 40 years as a consistently reliable destination. Expect full-bodied cooking with Umbrian roots, from handmade pasta – perhaps spinach and ricotta tortelloni with butter and sage (£9.50) – to loin of pork with fennel, polenta and cannellini beans (£19.50). The pleasant staff and cheery atmosphere score highly, too. Wines from £18.50. Closed Sat L and all Sun.

▲ Veeraswamy

Victory House, 99-101 Regent Street (entrance on Swallow Street), Piccadilly, W1B 4RS
Tel no: (020) 7439 8434
www.veeraswamy.com
⊖ **Piccadilly Circus, map 5**
Indian

First opened in 1926, Veeraswamy received a dynamic new lease of life when it came under the same ownership as Amaya and Chutney Mary (see entries). The modern menu now incorporates crispy chicken lollipops (£9.50) or venison and quail Scotch egg in tamarind glaze to start, with roast duck vindaloo (£25.50) and sea bass cooked with Keralan red spices in a banana leaf to follow. Finish with banana and date fritters (£9). House wine £30. Open all week.

Vinoteca

Welcoming, buzzy, bibulous brasserie
15 Seymour Place, Marylebone, W1H 5BD
Tel no: (020) 7724 7288
www.vinoteca.co.uk
⊖ Marble Arch, map 4
Modern European | £28
Cooking score: 2
🍷 £30

'This is a place I like a lot, no fuss, no pretension . . . really welcoming,' sums up one visitor, catching the tone of this bright, buzzy wine-bar-cum-restaurant. The offspring of Vinoteca in Farringdon (see entry), it's an enterprising addition to the Marylebone scene. The seasonally influenced menu changes often enough to keep regulars amused and there have been good reports of Norfolk asparagus with a bantam egg and truffle vinaigrette, Mersea Island sea bass with saffron courgettes and spring greens, and grilled, marinated bavette with watercress, horseradish and chips. The impressive wine list offers regular promotions, suggests a glass of wine to go with each dish (including cheeses from Neal's Yard Dairy) andm via detailed tasting notes, gives an overview of what is happening in current global viticulture. Bottles from £15.50.
Chef/s: Daniel Richards. **Open:** all week L 12 to 3 (4 Sun), Mon to Sat D 6 to 10. **Closed:** bank hols. **Meals:** alc (main courses £10 to £18). **Details:** 60 seats. 6 seats outside.

Wild Honey

A sense of comfort and indulgence
12 St George Street, Mayfair, W1S 2FB
Tel no: (020) 7758 9160
www.wildhoneyrestaurant.co.uk
⊖ Oxford Circus, Bond Street, map 5
Modern European | £45
Cooking score: 5

The Will Smith and Anthony Demetre stamp of relaxed Euro-modernity has been a Mayfair hit for some five years. Since the last edition of the Guide, the restaurant has been dealt the sleekest of 21st-century makeovers – leaving intact the dark oak panelling but removing 'the much-loved booths'. The menu, however, continues to offer a no-nonsense approach to food. Its sweep takes in an impressive range of calendar-correct materials and treatments, from seared foie gras with beetroot and buckwheat to a vibrant-sounding ravioli of wild Italian greens with hazelnut butter and sage, and wild sea bass with artichokes, girolles and pink grapefruit. Dishes don't try to be too clever, so the kitchen is not stretched beyond its capabilities, and a sense of comfort and indulgence pervades, exemplified by roast chicken with new-season morels and potato gnocchi. Desserts might include Alphonso mango (with yoghurt mousse, chilli and lime). For some, service is 'caring', others have been irritated by 'over-attentive water and wine pouring', and by 'very rapid attempts to get orders'. Just about everything on the modern, wide-ranging wine list is available by the carafe; bottles from £25.
Chef/s: Anthony Demetre and Patrick Leano. **Open:** all week L 12 to 2.30 (3 Sun), D 6 to 11 (10.30 Sun). **Closed:** 25 and 26 Dec, 1 Jan. **Meals:** alc (main courses £17 to £30). Set L £27. Sun L £33.50. **Details:** 50 seats.

Wiltons

Bastion of St James' tradition
55 Jermyn Street, Mayfair, SW1Y 6LX
Tel no: (020) 7629 9955
www.wiltons.co.uk
⊖ Green Park, map 5
British | £70
Cooking score: 4

Wiltons began selling shellfish from a stall to the London quality in 1742. It hasn't been in the Guide quite that long, but it remains a bulwark of British traditionalism. The furnishings are commodiously soft, the service discreet and £400 buys 50g of Beluga (financial crisis, what crisis?). For the rest of us, there's heartening comfort enough in dressed crab, potted shrimps and lobster bisque, as well as twice-baked Stilton soufflé, to start. Fish plainly grilled or poached, or perhaps lemon sole with brown shrimps and capers, is all impeccably timed, while meats encompass lamb cutlets with mint jelly, and whatever is on the carving trolley today. To finish, all the Mrs Beeton puddings turn up (crumbles, trifles, bread-and-butter), but there's also Amedei chocolate fondant with cherries and pistachio ice cream for diners hankering after the shock of the new. Wine pricing, untethered from its £30 moorings, majestically ascends like a hot-air balloon into the four-figure ether.

Chef/s: Daniel Kent. **Open:** Mon to Fri L 12 to 2.30, D 5.30 to 10.30. **Closed:** Sat, Sun, Christmas, bank hols. **Meals:** alc (main courses £19 to £60). Set L £38 (3 courses). Set D £26 (2 courses) to £30. **Details:** 100 seats. Separate bar. Wheelchair access.

The Wolseley

High-impact all-day brasserie
160 Piccadilly, Mayfair, W1J 9EB
Tel no: (020) 7499 6996
www.thewolseley.com
⊖ **Green Park, map 5**
Modern European | £35
Cooking score: 2

A heady cocktail of all-day dining and non-stop glamour (sit long enough and you'll see celebs) maintains the appeal of Corbin and King's original grand café. Book ahead for a run at an extensive menu big on European comforts such as chopped liver or onion soup, followed by the daily plat (salt beef, coq au vin, the house fish stew), steak frites or an endive, Roquefort and walnut salad. The pastry section exhibits skill and mettle at afternoon tea as well as providing desserts like custard tart or apple strudel. Service is well-drilled, though staff have a lot of silverware to juggle. Wine costs from £19.75.

Chef/s: Lawrence Keogh. **Open:** all week 7am to midnight (8am Sat, 11pm Sun). **Closed:** 25 and 26 Dec, Aug bank hol. **Meals:** alc (main courses £13 to £33). **Details:** 150 seats. Wheelchair access.

Wright Brothers

Good-value Soho seafood bar and restaurant
13 Kingly Street, Soho, W1B 5PW
Tel no: (020) 7434 3611
www.thewrightbrothers.co.uk
⊖ **Oxford Circus, map 5**
Seafood | £33
Cooking score: 2

With no frills or fripperies (bare wood underfoot, plain tables) and spread over several floors, this seafood bar and restaurant achieves a stylish informality that embraces the service as much as the food – a formula that attracts a full house. Simple treatments bring out the best of top-quality raw materials. Cornish crab, Atlantic prawns and Scottish langoustine are present for those wanting a pure seafood hit; otherwise the kitchen can run to, among starters, smoked cod's roe with pickled cucumber and a classic fish soup. For mains, you might encounter whole roast plaice with caper and brown shrimp butter, plus a few meaty alternatives like braised Dingley Dell pork belly with salsa verde. Finish with, perhaps, chocolate pot with hazelnut praline. The French-leaning wine list opens at £18.50. See also Wright Brothers entry in Southwark.

Chef/s: Jai Parkinson. **Open:** all week L 12 to 3 (3.30 Sat, 6 Sun), Mon to Sat D 5.30 to 10.45. **Closed:** 24 to 28 Dec, 1 and 2 Jan, bank hols. **Meals:** alc (main courses £12 to £18). Set L and D £14.50 (2 courses) to £16.50. Set D £16.50 (2 courses) to £18.50. **Details:** 96 seats. 24 seats outside.

Yauatcha

Drop-dead cool Chinese venue
15-17 Broadwick Street, Soho, W1F 0DL
Tel no: (020) 7494 8888
www.yauatcha.com
⊖ **Tottenham Court Road, map 5**
Chinese | £30
Cooking score: 3
V

As part of the Hakkasan Group, this Soho venue maintains the glamorous family resemblance (a drop-dead cool dim sum and

tea parlour on the ground floor and a moodily lit, low-slung basement) while aiming for a slightly simpler style in its approach to new-wave Chinese cooking. In addition to knocking out high-end renditions of Chinatown dim sum staples (char siu buns, sticky rice in lotus leaf, har-gau dumplings), served until last orders at night, the kitchen ups the ante with its signature venison puffs, steamed halibut with homemade chilli and salted radish, and braised Somerset lamb with black-pepper sauce. It's easy to order too much, but worth saving space for the exquisite patisserie, perhaps a yuzu-flavoured brûlée tart. The wine list offers a free-roaming global tour (from £28), but leans sensibly towards white for food-matching. Saké, smoothies, cocktails and a lengthy tea list are worth exploring, too.
Chef/s: Tong Chee Hwee. **Open:** all week 12 to 11.30 (10.30 Sun). **Closed:** 25 and 26 Dec. **Meals:** alc (dishes £9 to £29). **Details:** 191 seats. Separate bar. Wheelchair access.

Zafferano
Top Italian performer
15 Lowndes Street, Belgravia, SW1X 9EY
Tel no: (020) 7235 5800
www.atozrestaurants.com
⊖ **Knightsbridge, Hyde Park Corner, map 4**
Italian | £50
Cooking score: 5
♠

Zafferano fits polished Knightsbridge as neatly as a designer shoe. Pale tiled floors, extravagant sprays of flowers and 'gorgeous Italian staff' create a sunny Mediterranean feel, while smooth napery and sleek modern furnishings add a savvy metropolitan edge. There may be a new chef in the kitchen, but the thrust of the cooking remains the same: expect a sophisticated take on Italian classics, with no unnecessary fuss or adornments. Every element of each dish has earned its place, so the focus of your attention is often the sheer brilliance of the ingredients, as in a summer starter of beef carpaccio with baby spinach and generous shavings of black truffle, the wafer-

thin beef marbled and melt-in-the-mouth tender. The pasta here is legendary and the oxtail ravioli, silken and filled with fall-apart meat, deep and rich and perfectly seasoned, proves why. Only the tiramisu (a little dry in the middle) left one diner underwhelmed, but the whole experience was still deemed 'memorable in all the right ways.' The wine list delivers excellent regional coverage of Italy including a decent selection by the glass, all at Knightsbridge prices; bottles start at £34.
Chef/s: Miles Nixon. **Open:** all week L 12 to 3, D 6 to 11 (Sun 10.30). **Meals:** alc (main courses £10 to £30). Set L £21 (2 courses) to £30. **Details:** 140 seats. Separate bar. Wheelchair access.

NEW ENTRY
Zoilo
Drink to an Argentinian crowd-pleaser
9 Duke Street, Marylebone, W1U 3EG
Tel no: (020) 7486 9699
www.zoilo.co.uk
⊖ **Bond Street, map 4**
Argentinian | £30
Cooking score: 2
£5
OFF

A tiny bar-bistro behind Selfridges, Zoilo is an impressive newcomer to London's nascent Argentinian scene, so no surprise it has proved popular with its intriguing cooking, fantastic wines and attractive prices. The menu is neatly divided into bar snacks (try the braised pig's head with quince), empanadas (perhaps filled with spinach, raisins and pine nuts) and larger plates of 'very light and delicious' grilled black pudding on toasted bread or skirt steak with parsnips and parsley, with an 'exceptional' milk cake and passion fruit sorbet to finish. There's a great buzz to the long, narrow ground-floor bar with its small cramped tables. Downstairs, perch on counter stools and watch the chefs at work. The Argentinian wine list is startlingly good, with some reasonably priced easy drinking from £19.95.
Chef/s: Jacquet Diego. **Open:** all week L 12 to 2.30, D 6 to 10.30 (10 Sun). **Closed:** 23 to 27 Dec. **Meals:** alc (main courses £5 to £13). **Details:** 47 seats.

L'Absinthe

Cracking classics and stonking good value
40 Chalcot Road, Primrose Hill, NW1 8LS
Tel no: (020) 7483 4848
www.labsinthe.co.uk
⊖ Chalk Farm, map 2
French | £25
Cooking score: 3
£30

Serving Primrose Hill for some six years, this is the kind of smart bistro you would want in your neighbourhood. L'Absinthe is French through and through, from the closely packed tables (ground floor and basement), to the rustic, classical cooking. French onion soup and Chalk Farm smoked salmon with lentils vinaigrette and a poached egg are served without fuss or furbelows. Fillet of cod with ratatouille and pepper coulis yields satisfying results, too, while Toulouse sausage with lyonnaise potatoes and mustard sauce, and beef bourguignon represent the gutsier end of the spectrum. Desserts such as mousse au chocolat and Absinthe crème brûlée provide Gallic flavour to the end. The wine list, not surprisingly, is almost entirely French, with prices from £16.50. But L'Absinthe is also a wine shop – some of the classier wines are offered at shop prices plus £10 surcharge for drinking at table.
Chef/s: Christophe Fabre. **Open:** Tue to Sun L 12 to 2.30 (4 Sat and Sun), D 6 to 10.30 (9.30 Sun). **Closed:** Mon, 1 week Christmas, 2 weeks Aug. **Meals:** alc (main courses £10 to £20). Set L £10.95 (2 courses) to £13.95. Sun L £15.95 (2 courses). **Details:** 65 seats. 14 seats outside.

¡¡¡ Please send us your feedback

To register your opinion about any restaurant listed in the Guide, or a new restaurant that you wish to bring to our attention, please visit the web address at the bottom of the page. Your feedback informs the content of the book and will be used to compile next year's reviews.

The Albion

Lively Barnsbury local with no-frills Brit food
10 Thornhill Road, Islington, N1 1HW
Tel no: (020) 7607 7450
www.the-albion.co.uk
⊖ Angel, Highbury & Islington, map 2
British | £30
Cooking score: 2
V

This wisteria-covered Georgian hostelry found in the heart of the Barnsbury conservation area, achieves a stylish informality that embraces the service as much as the food. It's a formula that, together with a large sun-trap garden, real ales and winter fires, attracts full houses. Much is made of the sourcing of ingredients, with reassuring specifics such as Hansen & Lydersen's smoked salmon, potted Kentish mackerel and slow-roast Berkshire pork belly with wholegrain mustard mash and apple sauce. Readers highly recommend the triple-cooked chips, and warm vanilla rice pudding with strawberry jam makes a suitable retro finish. Cocktails fit the bill and the wine list is a global affair with prices from £16.
Chef/s: John Stanyer. **Open:** Mon to Sat L 12 to 3 (4 Sat), D 6 to 10. Sun 12 to 9. **Closed:** 25 Dec, 1 Jan. **Meals:** alc (main courses £10 to £21). **Details:** 126 seats. 129 seats outside. Separate bar. Wheelchair access.

Almeida

Long-running Islington performer
30 Almeida Street, Islington, N1 1AD
Tel no: (020) 7354 4777
www.almeida-restaurant.co.uk
⊖ Angel, Highbury & Islington, map 2
French | £40
Cooking score: 2

New talent in the kitchen has reinvigorated the long-established Almeida, attracting those heading for a show at the theatre opposite, and others in search of good food. The warehouse-style, glass and wood dining room may provide a slightly uninspiring setting, but the buzzing open kitchen confidently turns out

finely tuned starters like multicoloured salt-baked heritage carrots with hazelnut and date purée, goats' curd and orange, or pan-fried boudin blanc with choucroute, black pudding and apple. At inspection, main courses almost won standing ovations for the exacting technique displayed – so take a bow, poached breast and roast leg of chicken with truffle gnocchi, mushroom and tarragon; and crackling-crusted cod with white haricot beans, morteau sausage and sprouting broccoli. Local Italians also give a thumbs-up to the mushroom, truffle and Parmesan risotto. Afters might be lemon tart with basil ice cream or Keen's Cheddar with apple chutney and toasted walnut bread. House wine is £20.
Chef/s: Martin Nisbet. **Open:** Tue to Sun L 12 to 2.30 (3.30 Sun), Mon to Sat D 5.30 to 10.30. **Closed:** 26 Dec, 1 Jan. **Meals:** alc (£18 to £22). Set L and D £17 (2 courses) to £20. Sun L £20 (2 courses) to £25. **Details:** 110 seats. 10 seats outside. Separate bar. Wheelchair access.

Bradleys

Long-running French favourite
25 Winchester Road, Swiss Cottage, NW3 3NR
Tel no: (020) 7722 3457
www.bradleysnw3.co.uk
⊖ Swiss Cottage, map 2
French | £40
Cooking score: 3

£5
OFF

After 21 years, Simon Bradley's civilised establishment has built up a loyal following, not least because an early kick-off makes it convenient for a meal before a visit to the nearby Hampstead theatre. It's smart but informal: all pale-grey walls, wooden floor, undressed pale-wood tables and 'quietly excellent' service. A British slant to raw materials complements a fairly discreet French flavour. The food is a big hit, with a well-sourced menu providing plenty of sustenance for comfort-food lovers: a satisfying Mediterranean fish soup, perhaps, then venison haunch with celeriac fondant, beetroot confit and sauce poivrade or Orkney lamb with root vegetables and garlic purée. Finish with something like pear tarte Tatin or a rhubarb sablé with peppered yoghurt and rhubarb sorbet. House wines from £17.95.
Chef/s: Simon Bradley. **Open:** all week L 12 to 3, Mon to Sat D 6 to 11. **Meals:** alc (main courses £8 to £20). Set L £14.95 (2 courses) to £18.95. Set D £25.50. Sun L £24 (2 courses) to £28. **Details:** 60 seats.

The Bull & Last

Tried-and-true modern Brit dishes
168 Highgate Road, Hampstead, NW5 1QS
Tel no: (020) 7267 3641
www.thebullandlast.co.uk
⊖ Tufnell Park, Kentish Town, map 2
Modern British | £35
Cooking score: 3

Close to Hampstead Heath, this Victorian boozer has lots of charm and character, though it now trades as a serious eatery with strong patriotic inclinations. Pub classics (beer-battered haddock and chips) are outshone by an upbeat, daily changing menu that touts anything from char-grilled ox heart with beets, bone marrow and watercress to roast guinea fowl with a trotter-stuffed leg and parsley root. The homemade charcuterie board is a meat lover's bonanza, while fish fans might fancy roast Cornish cod with herb gnocchi, oxtail ragù, monk's beard and pan juices. Readers have also endorsed Dedham Vale onglet with chips, mixed leaves and béarnaise; Sunday roasts; and sticky prune pudding with butterscotch sauce. Wines from £16.
Chef/s: Oliver Pudney. **Open:** all week L 12 to 3 (12.30 to 4 Sat and Sun), D 6.30 to 10 (9 Sun). **Closed:** 24 and 25 Dec. **Meals:** alc (main courses £14 to £20). **Details:** 80 seats. 30 seats outside. Separate bar. Wheelchair access.

> ||♦ **Average Price**
> The average price listed in main-entry reviews denotes the price of a three-course meal, without wine.

Café Japan

Sparkling sushi at easy prices
626 Finchley Road, Golders Green, NW11 7RR
Tel no: (020) 8455 6854
⊖ Golders Green, map 1
Japanese | £25
Cooking score: 3
£30

Ignore the prosaic frontage, the cramped tables and the utilitarian blond-wood interior, because this evergreen Golders Green eatery has a rock-solid reputation when it comes to sparkling fresh sushi and other easily priced Japanese staples. Crowds come from all over to admire the seasoned chefs, whose knife skills, eye for detail and appreciation of quality are beyond reproach. The menu has a smattering of appetisers, tempura and grills such as butterfish teriyaki, but the real stars are bite-sized delicacies ranging from beautifully presented sashimi to nigiri, chirashi and some fascinating hand rolls. Try age-hamachi (crispy fried yellowtail, spring onion, sesame seeds and spicy mayo) or the giant futomaki loaded with omelette, pickled radish, cucumber, conger eel and prawn. Mixed platters are handy for ditherers who can't make up their mind. Drink green tea, beer, saké or wine (from around £14).
Chef/s: Shigeru Fukushima. **Open:** Tue to Sun L 12 to 2 (2.30 Sat and Sun), D 6 to 10 (9.30 Sun). **Closed:** Mon, 1 week Christmas, 1 week Aug. **Meals:** alc (main courses £11 to £28). Set L £8.50 (2 courses) to £13.50. Set D £14 (2 courses) to £28. Sun L £8.50. **Details:** 35 seats.

NEW ENTRY

Caravan

High-decibel King's Cross bolt-hole
Granary Building, 1 Granary Square (off Goods Way), King's Cross, N1C 4AA
Tel no: (020) 7101 7661
www.caravankingscross.co.uk
⊖ King's Cross, map 2
Global | £28
Cooking score: 2
£30

This high-decibel King's Cross bolt-hole with its stark, functional look and lively relaxed atmosphere occupies an extravagantly spacious warehouse. Its mission is to bring 'well-travelled food' to a part of the capital where, until now, good places to eat have been nonexistent. Popular with students from Central St Martins, the modestly priced menu is diverse enough for a knowledgeable palate and familiar enough for the novice. Breakfasts, good coffee, small sharing plates (chorizo and sweet potato croquettes; deep-fried duck egg with baba ganoush, chorizo oil and cumin) and pizzas (perhaps Serrano ham, tomato, jalapeño and Taleggio) are its stock in trade, but heartier appetites can tuck into lamb tagine or Wagyu ribeye. Then, if a plate of Swiss cheeses doesn't tempt, try coconut rice pudding with ginger mango sorbet. Wines from £17.
Chef/s: Sam Wilson. **Open:** Mon to Fri 12 to 10.30 (breakfast 8 to 11.30), Sat and Sun brunch 10 to 4, Sat D 5 to 10.30. **Closed:** Christmas, New Year. **Meals:** alc (main courses £14 to £16). Set L and D £20 (2 courses) to £28. **Details:** 120 seats. Wheelchair access.

ALSO RECOMMENDED
▲ Chilli Cool
15 Leigh Street, King's Cross, WC1H 9EW
Tel no: (020) 7383 3135
www.chillicool.com
⊖ Russell Square, King's Cross, map 2
Chinese

Students and locals are drawn to this modest Szechuan canteen between Bloomsbury and King's Cross by the authentic, unrefined heartiness of the cooking. Service is speedy, value great and the place wears its Szechuan colours on its sleeve – this is a cuisine that never compromises. Chilli heat meets beef and ox tripe (£5.80), a hotpot of sliced fish (enough for three to share) and crispy pork intestine (£8), and even accompanies beancurd, pork won tons and dumplings. Wines from £12.80, although tea and beer are better coolants. Open all week.

500 Restaurant
Genuine neighbourhood Italian
782 Holloway Road, Archway, N19 3JH
Tel no: (020) 7272 3406
www.500restaurant.co.uk
⊖ Archway, map 2
Italian | £30
Cooking score: 2
£5 OFF

'It is a shame that local restaurants like this are not in more neighbourhoods', observed one fan, and judging by reports, visitors can't get enough of this small, unpretentious Italian. Named after the dinky Fiat Cinquecento, it's as good for everyday dining as for celebrations, and offers an intelligent and gutsy take on modern Italian standards. From the well-priced menu a dish of fresh orecchiette pasta with spicy Italian sausage and broccoli soaks up most of the praise, although baked rabbit in balsamic vinegar sauce, and grilled lamb cutlets filled with mint and Parmesan, also get a share of the plaudits. To finish, quince and nougat ice cream has gone down a treat. Service is welcoming, and the all-Italian wine list opens at £14.50.

Chef/s: Mario Magli. Open: Fri and Sat L 12 to 3, Mon to Sat D 6 to 10.30. Sun 12 to 9.30. Closed: 10 days Christmas, 2 weeks summer. Meals: alc (main courses £12 to £17). Details: 40 seats.

NEW ENTRY
Grain Store
Raising the bar in King's Cross
1-3 Stable Street, King's Cross, N1C 4AB
Tel no: (020) 7324 4466
www.grainstore.com
⊖ King's Cross, map 2
Global | £26
Cooking score: 3
V £30

Grain Store is a massive, converted King's Cross warehouse bearing all the hallmarks of the nouveau brasserie – high ceilings, worn brick, metal piping, open-plan kitchen – its all-day opening blurring the line between restaurant and bar. Stellar chef Bruno Loubet oversees the menu (see entry Bistro Bruno Loubet) and much is made of careful sourcing, with his kitchen pulling off some neat tricks. Dishes are taken way beyond the meat-and-two-veg approach – indeed, vegetables have the starring role and there are interesting vegetarian-vegan choices. Flavour is everything in a starter of sprouting beans and seeds, miso aubergine, crispy chicken skin and potato wafer, and there's a kaleidoscope of world ingredients in dishes such as sticky rice with kim-chee cabbage and stuffed chicken wings steamed in a lotus leaf, or corn and quinoa tamale with salsa and sticky pork belly. It's hard to place this food into a neat category, especially when desserts include the likes of spiced candied tomatoes with goats' milk pannacotta. Wines from £20.
Chef/s: Bruno Loubet. Open: all week 11am to 11.30pm (12 Sat, 4.30 Sun). Meals: alc (main courses £10 to £23). Set L £30 ('surprise' menu, 5 courses). Set D £35 ('surprise' menu, 6 courses). Details: 120 seats. 80 seats outside.

The Holly Bush
British
22 Hollymount, Hampstead, NW3 6SG
Tel no: (020) 7435 2892
www.hollybushhampstead.co.uk

'A quintessential British pub with outrageously good comfort food: lamb rump with samphire; a huge steak and ale pie; bubbling, cheesy fish pie. I've tried them all – and will go back for more!'

Homa
Trendy brasserie with sunny food
71-73 Stoke Newington Church Street, Stoke Newington, N16 0AS
Tel no: (020) 7254 2072
www.homalondon.co.uk
⊖ Arsenal, map 2
Modern European | £30
Cooking score: 3
£5
OFF

'Really good place, just simple food cooked well,' is how one reader describes this lively Mediterranean eatery run by an Italian/Turkish couple. The cooking is fashionably straightforward, mostly seasonal and stands out through the sheer quality of ingredients. It certainly appeals to Stoke Newington residents who love the Georgian town house's stunning, contemporary interiors, easy-going service and flexible menus (opening with brunch at 10am each day). Typical of the style is a starter of poached salt cod with smoked aubergine, pancetta and sardine dressing, and mains of saddle and shoulder of Pyrenean lamb with onion purée and Savoy cabbage. A plate of pecorino, Gorgonzola and goats' curd, and sweet things such as yoghurt pannacotta with warm pistachio sponge and rhubarb sorbet, conclude things satisfyingly. Wines from £16.50.
Chef/s: Phil Jones. **Open:** all week 10 to 3 (4 Sat and Sun), D 6 to 10.30. **Closed:** 25 and 26 Dec. **Meals:** alc (main courses £12 to £22). **Details:** 85 seats. 35 seats outside. Separate bar.

Jin Kichi
Streetwise Japanese hangout
73 Heath Street, Hampstead, NW3 6UG
Tel no: (020) 7794 6158
www.jinkichi.com
⊖ Hampstead, map 2
Japanese | £30
Cooking score: 1

Blink and you can imagine you're in some backstreet Tokyo izakaya, slurping bowls of udon noodles in soup or grazing on chicken gizzard yakitori. Lanterns, prints, closely packed tables and a counter for perching are par for the Japanese course, but the food impresses with its pinpoint flavours. In addition to myriad signature skewers from the robata grill, also expect a fine selection of marinated vegetables, tempura and simmered dishes – plus nigiri, hand rolls and glistening sashimi for those who like their food raw. Wines (from £28) are limited and expensive, so stay with beer, saké or sexy shochu cocktails.
Chef/s: Rei Shimazu. **Open:** Tue to Sun L 12.30 to 2, D 6 to 11 (10 Sun). **Closed:** Mon, 25 and 26 Dec, 1 Jan, Tue after bank hols. **Meals:** alc (main courses £5 to £17). **Details:** 42 seats.

Karpo
A terrific addition to King's Cross
23 Euston Road, King's Cross, NW1 2SD
Tel no: (020) 7843 2221
www.karpo.co.uk
⊖ King's Cross, map 2
Global | £25
Cooking score: 2
£30

A decent feed, a good bottle of wine and an 'all-comers welcome' attitude is no longer a tall order in the environs of King's Cross station. Karpo, just a short trundle away with a suitcase, is a useful, zany-looking hotel-based all-dayer that nourishes its regulars (and 'irregulars') with good cheer and appealing, if variable, British/Mediterranean cooking. Even solo diners can relax here, over coffee and doughnuts, a full English or an on-trend assembly of burrata, blood orange and puntarelle, followed by wood-fired pork chop with cavolo nero and anchovy, with Androuet cheeses or apple crumble for afters. Wine from £16.

Chef/s: Joseph Sharratt. **Open:** all week L 12 to 3 (4 Sat and Sun), D 5.30 to 11. **Meals:** alc (main courses £12 to £16). Set L £15 (2 courses) to £18. Set D £20 (2 courses) to £25. Sun L £20. **Details:** 100 seats. Separate bar. Wheelchair access. No children after 6 in bar.

Made in Camden
A kaleidoscope of captivating sharing plates
Roundhouse, Chalk Farm Road, Camden,
NW1 8EH
Tel no: (020) 7424 8495
www.madeincamden.com
⊖ Chalk Farm, map 2
Modern British | £25
Cooking score: 3

V £30

Posters of shows past and present cover the walls, and the bare, unpretentious décor might be reminiscent of days in the student union, but the food at the Roundhouse's restaurant is serious business. An exquisite house meze of hummus, baba ganoush with pomegranate and parsley, beetroot purée, and green tahini with sumac almost merits the visit alone, similarly the seriously tasty jumble of grilled fennel salad with feta, pistachio and salted caramel. Vegetarians enjoy an above-average meat-free menu, but for others there might be grilled onglet with parsnip smash or a venison burger with basil mayo and pickled jalapeño. Readers rate dishes from 'full of flavour' to 'out of this world'. With set menus, the food is seriously good value, helping to make the venue 'a number one recommendation'. It's understandably busy, pre-show. Wine is £18 a bottle, although in-vogue drinks like Aperol spritz or Sipsmith G&T are worth trying.

Chef/s: Jean Baptiste Barbosa. **Open:** Tue to Sun L 12 to 2.30 (10.30 to 3 Sat and Sun), D 6 to 10.30. **Closed:** Mon, 25 and 26 Dec. **Meals:** alc (main courses £6 to £16). Set L £10 (2 courses). **Details:** 54 seats.

ALSO RECOMMENDED
▲ Mangal 1 Ocakbasi
10 Arcola Street, Stoke Newington, E8 2DJ
Tel no: (020) 7275 8981
www.mangal1.com
⊖ Dalston Kingsland, map 2
Turkish

It's raucous, cheap and full to bursting, but Mangal 1 is Stoke Newington's quintessential ocakbasi – fuelled by kebabs, chops and other meaty delights hot off the ocak grill. Steaming pide and sac breads accompany mezze starters (from £2), while the main events are served up with salads, yoghurt and various sauces. Top calls are the grilled quails (£10), lamb spare ribs and chicken wings, which can be followed by sticky baklava or sutlac (rice pudding). Drink Turkish beer or wine – although most people bring their own (no corkage). Open all week.

Market
Trendy eatery with plucky Brit food
43 Parkway, Camden, NW1 7PN
Tel no: (020) 7267 9700
www.marketrestaurant.co.uk
⊖ Camden Town, map 2
British | £28
Cooking score: 2

£30

When it opened in an unlikely part of London for good eating venues, Market was a place with a mission – elevating the humblest of eateries into somewhere that provided imaginative food at reasonable prices. Six years down the line and bare brick, bare boards and closely packed tables still keep things simple and relaxed, and the no-frills, fiercely seasonal modern British food continues to go down well. Indeed, there are some very good things to eat here, with a March menu producing squid, blood orange and fennel to start, then chicken and leek pie or cod, caponata and samphire, or even rose veal with wild mushrooms and sauté potatoes.

Vanilla cheesecake and forced rhubarb makes an ideal early-spring finale. Wines from £17.75.
Chef/s: Alan Turner. **Open:** all week L 12 to 2.30 (1 to 3.30 Sun), Mon to Sat D 6 to 10.30. **Closed:** 24 Dec to after New Year, bank hols. **Meals:** alc (main courses £13 to £18). Set L £10 (2 courses). Set D £17.50 (2 courses). **Details:** 50 seats. 4 seats outside.

Odette's

Letting quality ingredients do the talking
130 Regents Park Road, Primrose Hill, NW1 8XL
Tel no: (020) 7586 8569
www.odettesprimrosehill.com
⊖ Chalk Farm, map 2
Modern British | £36
Cooking score: 5

Odette's is a Primrose Hill institution that Welsh chef Bryn Williams has quietly made his own. A refurbishment of a few years ago has kept it current enough to stop passers-by in their tracks, but elegant enough to seduce its well-heeled regulars. Contemporary floral wallpaper, pleated shades, plush carpets and white tablecloths are suitably 'haute' yet defiantly stuffy. Williams' version of modern British is 'imaginative' and 'well executed', with a pronounced accent on seasonal ingredients. One reader's 'delightful' Cornish mackerel, rhubarb, apple and hazelnut starter is a case in point, and the ever-popular crayfish lasagne with salt-and-pepper squid never fails to impress. Whole lemon sole with brown shrimps, cucumber and sweet grapes, a steak tartare special ('as good as any in Paris') and the 'faultless' blackberry soufflé have also been name-checked by readers. Service is 'considerate and unhurried'. Friendly food-pricing goes down well, though there are grumbles about high mark-ups on the wine. On the plus side, there's plenty of choice by glass and carafe, and the 'house' is £19.50.
Chef/s: Bryn Williams. **Open:** all week L 12 to 2.30 (3 Sat and Sun), D 6 to 10 (10.30 Sat and Sun). **Closed:** 24 to 26 Dec, 1 Jan. **Meals:** alc (main

courses £16 to £22). Set L £17 (2 courses) to £20. Set D £22 (2 courses) to £25. Sun L £25. **Details:** 46 seats. 20 seats outside. Separate bar.

ALSO RECOMMENDED

▲ Ottolenghi

287 Upper Street, Islington, N1 2TZ
Tel no: (020) 7288 1454
www.ottolenghi.co.uk
⊖ Angel, Highbury & Islington, map 2
Mediterranean

The most restaurant-like of Yotam Ottolenghi's four-strong café chain, Ottolenghi plays to the crowds with its chic white interior, communal tables and cooking that draws on the flavours of the Mediterranean, Middle East and Asia. All the details are in place, whether you are in for breakfast, lunch or dinner. Consistency and quality are never in doubt, from a salad of roasted aubergine with Iranian lime yoghurt, pomegranate, spicy nuts and mixed herbs (£9) to seared lamb fillet with spiced peanut paste, anchovy and piquillo pepper salad (£12). Wines from £19. Closed Sun D.

▲ El Parador

245 Eversholt Street, Camden, NW1 1BA
Tel no: (020) 7387 2789
www.elparadorlondon.com
⊖ Mornington Crescent, map 2
Spanish £5 OFF

A Camden landmark since 1988, Carlos Horrillo and Patrick Morcas's small Spanish eatery has never lacked for enthusiastic, solid support, garnering praise for its lovely hidden garden and good-value, imaginative tapas menu. A long list of tapas (from £4.80 to £7.60) pushes well beyond the norms, with baked salt cod and coriander, ratte potatoes, harissa oil and wine, or rolled belly pork marinated in garlic, black pepper and dill and braised in Asturian cider. There are strong vegetarian choices, too. House Spanish is £15.20. Closed Sat and Sun L.

NEW ENTRY

Pizza East Kentish Town

On-trend pizzeria goes north
79 Highgate Road, Kentish Town, NW5 1TL
Tel no: (020) 3310 2000
www.pizzaeastkentishtown.com
⊖ Kentish Town, map 2
£24
Cooking score: 2

£30

The Soho House empire has gone all-out with
its third Pizza East outlet (see also Pizza East;
Pizza East Portobello), pitching up with a trio
of easy-eating joints – in the same building
are two new ventures: Chicken Shop and
Dirty Burger. More LA than Italy, Pizza East's
industrial-chic interior is thronged with cool
young things and families (children are
exceptionally well catered for). American-
style sourdough pizzas, puffed and charred
from the wood oven, are the main attraction.
The chewy 'cornicione' pleases purists, and
well-judged, gutsy flavours dominate. Try
perhaps the popular veal meatball, cream and
sage pizza, indulgent mac 'n' cheese or notable
antipasti. Wines from £18.
Chef/s: Theo Lewis. **Open:** all week 12 to 12 (9am
Sat and Sun), Fri and Sat 12 to 1am. **Meals:** alc
(main courses £8 to £17). **Details:** 160 seats.
Wheelchair access.

NEW ENTRY

Restaurant Michael Nadra

Affordable chic in Primrose Hill
42 Gloucester Avenue, Primrose Hill, NW1 8JD
Tel no: (020) 7722 2800
www.restaurant-michaelnadra.co.uk
⊖ Chalk Farm, map 2
Modern European | £35
Cooking score: 4

£5
OFF

Michael Nadra has created a chic venue in
boho Primrose Hill, boosted by caramel
leather, slate flooring and outside space. It is
larger and more ambitious than his restaurant
of the same name in Chiswick (see entry).
There are several dining options – bar,

conservatory, terrace, ground floor or
subterranean – and the menu travels the globe.
The kitchen takes this diversity in its stride,
delivering faultless renditions of tempura of
soft-shell crab with a julienne of daikon and
carrots ('a snappy match for a black sesame,
ginger and sweet chilli dressing') and a juicy
lamb rump ably accompanied by its
sweetbreads, swede fondant and a rosemary-
infused jus. Proper tarte Tatin is a good way to
conclude. Service is willing but at inspection
language skills lacked fluency. Nevertheless,
value for money is a big plus – especially for
set menus. The equally well-travelled wine
list, arranged by grape variety, starts from £17.
Chef/s: Michael Nadra. **Open:** all week L 12 to 2.30
(4 Sat and Sun), D 6 to 10.30. **Meals:** alc (main
courses £18 to £25). Set L £14 (2 courses) to £18.
Details: 86 seats. 34 seats outside. Separate bar.
Wheelchair access.

NEW ENTRY

Season Kitchen

Down-to-earth neighbourhood gem
53 Stroud Green Road, Finsbury Park, N4 3EF
Tel no: (020) 7263 5500
www.seasonkitchen.co.uk
⊖ Finsbury Park, map 2
Modern British | £25
Cooking score: 3

£5
OFF £30

A bijou dining room on an unpresuming
north London thoroughfare, Season Kitchen
has become a badly kept secret among local
food-lovers. It's a champion of seasonal
produce and the menu, a 'real gem', bristles
with infectious enthusiasm for down-to-earth
ingredients, from field to farm and sea to
shore. Expect focused cooking with an
experimental edge, as shown in the quirky
chicken starter: soup, mousse and skin (which
the 'cheerful front-of-house' will obligingly
describe). Alternatively, opt for full-blooded
maple-glazed beef short ribs paired with
Chantenay carrots. Breathtakingly fresh
poached wild Irish brown trout with almond
croquette and braised cucumber showcases
impressive sourcing and a deft touch. Desserts

are a knockout, and superb custard doughnuts with rhubarb sauce are a highlight. An attractive £15 dinner deal pulls in passers-by. The succinct list of natural wines is very well priced indeed, thanks to a gratifying 'pop without the rip' minimal mark-up policy (from £14.50).

Chef/s: Ben Wooles. **Open:** Tue to Sun D 5.30 to 10.30 (5 to 10 Sun). **Closed:** 25 and 26 Dec, 1 Jan. **Meals:** alc (main courses £13 to £18). Set D £20. **Details:** 35 seats.

Shayona Restaurant
Indian veggie with bargain buffet lunches
56-62 Meadow Garth, Neasden, NW10 8HD
Tel no: (020) 8965 3365
www.shayonarestaurants.com
⊖ Stonebridge Park, map 1
Indian Vegetarian | £13
Cooking score: 1
£5 OFF V £30

The splendour of the Swaminarayan Hindu temple rising up from a nondescript Neasden street is a sight to behold. With the belief that the body must be nourished as well as the soul, Shayona, a restaurant dedicated to Indian sattvic cooking (an easily digestible, light form of vegetarian cuisine), was established across the road. Chandeliers and colourful religious paintings form the backdrop to dishes that hail from across India: Punjabi samosa chaat, Mumbai bhel puri, south Indian dosas and rich curries. Service is friendly and helpful. A browse around the sweets bar (all sorts of Indian confectionery) and the adjacent (large) food shop is highly recommended. No alcohol.

Chef/s: Churaman Sharma. **Open:** Mon to Fri 11.30 to 10 (11 to 10 Sat and Sun). **Closed:** 25 Dec. **Meals:** alc (main courses £6 to £7). Buffet L (Mon to Fri) £7.99. **Details:** 150 seats. Wheelchair access. Car parking.

Sushi-Say
Japanese delicacies from a sushi master
33b Walm Lane, Willesden, NW2 5SH
Tel no: (020) 8459 7512
⊖ Willesden Green, map 1
Japanese | £28
Cooking score: 3
£30

'It's such a nice surprise to find good cooking and ingredients of this quality in Willesden Green,' says one regular of this friendly, family-run restaurant that's approaching two decades in business. Katsuharu and Yuko Shimizu's authentic Japanese restaurant offers sushi and sashimi the equal of the West End's big names as well as some less familiar, more homey, regional dishes including tempura, noodles and rice. To start, there's buta kakuni (braised pork belly), salted chicken gizzard skewers or, from the pristine sushi bar, ponzu-marinated salmon skin or tuna with natto (fermented soya beans). Larger dishes include menchi (minced beef) katsu with salad and grilled horse mackerel. No visit is complete without a selection of sashimi; take the chef's recommendations without hesitation. Dessert is homemade ice cream, perhaps shiso or ginger. Order wine (from £20) or stick to Japanese shochu, saké, beer or tea.

Chef/s: Katsuharu Shimizu. **Open:** Sat and Sun L 12 to 3, Wed to Sun D 6.30 to 10 (6 to 9.30 Sun). **Closed:** Mon, Tue, 25, 26 and 31 Dec to 2 Jan, 2 weeks Feb/Mar, 10 days Aug. **Meals:** alc (main courses £10 to £27). Set L £13.50 (2 courses) to £21. Set D £26.20 (6 courses) to £44.50 (8 courses). **Details:** 41 seats. Wheelchair access.

Trullo

Effortlessly likeable Italian eatery
300-302 St Paul's Road, Islington, N1 2LH
Tel no: (020) 7226 2733
www.trullorestaurant.com
⊖ Highbury and Islington, map 2
Italian | £31
Cooking score: 3

A handy local asset and cosy oasis on dreary, noise-ridden Highbury Corner, Trullo is the brainchild of two alumni from Jamie Oliver's Fifteen and the River Café (see entries). It's an unassuming little place done out in sparse contemporary style, with an extra dining room in the basement and a brigade of 'cheerful, confident' staff on hand to advise about the daily menu. Charcuterie boards loaded with artisan wonders, and well-wrought antipasti such as sweetbreads with wild garlic and Marsala on bruschetta, give way to sharply dressed salads, hand-rolled pasta (pappardelle with punchy beef shin ragù is a standout) and smoky specialities from the charcoal grill including mackerel with Castelluccio lentils and salsa rossa – 'bold flavours and interesting combinations' that come with a relatively painless price tag. The mood is buoyant, helped by plenty of Italian regional wines available by the glass or carafe; bottle prices start at £18.
Chef/s: Tim Siadatan. **Open:** all week L 12.30 to 2.30 (3 Sat and Sun), Mon to Sat D 6 to 10.15. **Meals:** alc (main courses £14 to £17). Set L £12 (2 courses). Sun L £30. **Details:** 74 seats.

The York & Albany

Metropolitan food for big-city palates
127-129 Parkway, Camden, NW1 7PS
Tel no: (020) 7388 3344
www.gordonramsay.com
⊖ Camden Town, map 2
Modern European | £30
Cooking score: 2

🛏 V

Grandness undiminished, this Regency-style town house by Regent's Park still attracts well-heeled or working locals, but the buzz has tempered somewhat since its 2008 opening. Modern artwork enlivens the otherwise neutral décor in the dining room. On inspection, a daily menu of silky cauliflower soup with smoked Applewood Cheddar, and a main course of char-grilled salmon with white beans and wild garlic was well-produced. The highlight was very fresh, herby gnocchi with poached egg and salsify, but in general dishes lacked the pizazz you might expect at such fine-dining prices. Keener value is evident with desserts; generous portions of dishes like crème brûlée with rhubarb ice cream are easily shared. More casual diners are tempted by homemade pizzas from a wood-fired oven in the stables next door. Wine from £18.75.
Chef/s: Simon Gregory. **Open:** Mon to Sat L 12 to 3 (12.15 Sat), D 6 to 11. Sun 12 to 8.30. **Meals:** alc (main courses £15 to £27). Set D £18 (2 courses) to £21. Sun L £17. **Details:** 120 seats.

Albion

Trendy all-day British caff
2-4 Boundary Street, Shoreditch, E2 7DD
Tel no: (020) 7729 1051
www.albioncaff.co.uk
⊖ Shoreditch, Liverpool Street, map 2
British | £25
Cooking score: 2

It's a versatile ground-floor space – café, bakery and food store – and a bright, lively venue that's part of Sir Terence Conran and Peter Prescott's Boundary project. Grab a quick breakfast (a bacon, sausage and egg sandwich, perhaps), stop by for a pot of tea and fruit cake or, better, savour more extensive all-day dining featuring such home-grown delights as British charcuterie and pickles, chicken and ham pie for two or three to share, and cauliflower cheese. Indeed, you can't go wrong with the menu, which lists the kind of comfort food everybody likes to eat: Welsh rarebit, shepherd's pie, fish and chips, and mussels in cider and cream. Friendly pricing and free Wi-Fi are a hit with locals. Wines from £18. **Chef/s:** Alex Umeh. **Open:** all week 8am to midnight. **Meals:** alc (main courses £10 to £14). **Details:** 70 seats. 30 seats outside. Wheelchair access.

Amico Bio

Green-thinking Italian veggie
44 Cloth Fair, Barbican, EC1A 7JQ
Tel no: (020) 7600 7778
www.amicobio.co.uk
⊖ Barbican, map 5
Vegetarian | £22
Cooking score: 1

V 🍴

'Green thinking . . . better living' is the worthy mantra behind Pasquale Amico's foray into Italian vegetarian cuisine, and he it backs up with ingredients from his organic farm near Naples. Expect a lively assortment of stuzzichini and antipasti ranging from kohlrabi carpaccio to Gorgonzola, apple and yellow-bean salad ahead of secondi such as pumpkin tofu with bulgur wheat and fennel or chickpea and carrot 'crocchetta' (croquettes). To finish, Italian artisan cheeses or rum baba with Amarena cherries might suffice. The informal interior blends wooden floors with photos of 1940s Italy, and the wine list (from £13.50) stays with the organic theme. There's a branch at 43 New Oxford Street, WC1A 1BH; tel: (020) 7836 7509. **Chef/s:** Pasquale Amico. **Open:** Mon to Fri 12 to 10.30. Sat D 5 to 10.30. **Closed:** Sun, 25 and 26 Dec, Easter, 1 week Aug, bank hols. **Meals:** alc (main courses £7 to £9). Set L £10. Set D £17.50. **Details:** 48 seats.

L'Anima

Gorgeous modern Italian food
1 Snowden Street, City, EC2A 2DQ
Tel no: (020) 7422 7000
www.lanima.co.uk
⊖ Liverpool Street, map 2
Italian | £48
Cooking score: 5

The chorus of praise for Calabrian chef Francesco Mazzei's stunning Liverpool Street Italian venue hasn't died down. Nor should it: this striking glass, stone and marble restaurant remains one of the City's hottest tickets. Mazzei is the consummate host. He and his kitchen colleagues can often be found 'circulating among the diners' making recommendations and checking all's well. Menus (complete with brief glossary – you'll need it) are as lively and intriguing as ever: octopus a la plancha with cannellini beans, ricotta mustia and paprika oil; black olive stracci with veal ragoût and pistachios; and beef tagliata with bone marrow, blu di capra cheese and Magliocco sauce are typical of his bold style. There are classics, too: the fritto misto and hand-carved ham to start are good examples of their kind, and fish stew with Sardinian fregola 'would warm up any chilly evening'. A Josper grill comes into its own for the likes of calf's liver and fresh tuna. Finish with sorbets or tiramisu. The wine list, from £22, celebrates modern Italian winemaking.

Chef/s: Francesco Mazzei. **Open:** Mon to Fri L 11.45 to 3, Mon to Sat D 5.30 to 11 (11.30 Sat). **Closed:** Sun, bank hols. **Meals:** alc (main courses £13 to £36). Set L and D £22.50 (2 courses) to £24.50. **Details:** 120 seats. Separate bar.

NEW ENTRY
Beagle
Great British cooking with seductive Med flavours
397-399 Geffrye Street, Hoxton, E2 8HZ
Tel no: (020) 7613 2967
www.beaglelondon.co.uk
⊖ Hoxton, map 2
British | £25
Cooking score: 3
£30

The extension of London's so-called 'Ginger Line' (East London line, as was) has opened up some exciting foodie enclaves. Underneath the arches at Hoxton station, just behind the Geffrye Museum, newcomer Beagle offers a coffee shop, bar and restaurant in one package. Chef James Ferguson comes from Rochelle Canteen, a local lunchtime institution (see entry), bringing with him a command of old-fashioned English cooking and a (not incompatible) love for seductive Mediterranean flavours. A late-spring inspection showed immense promise: octopus, tomatoes and coriander was a sprightly, colourful plateful, and the day's special delivered a gorgeous piece of wood-grilled turbot with Datterini tomatoes and softly roasted fennel. Onglet, duck-fat chips and anchovy sauce also hit the mark. Puddings weren't as precise: stracciatella ice cream was just too chocolatey (impossible, some might argue). Wine comes from an interesting Old World selection, with a dozen by the glass and bottles from £18.50.
Chef/s: James Ferguson. **Open:** Wed to Sun L 12 to 3 (6 Sun), Mon to Sat D 6 to 10.30. **Closed:** 25 and 26 Dec. **Meals:** alc (main courses £12 to £18). **Details:** 52 seats. 64 seats outside. Separate bar. Wheelchair access.

Bistrot Bruno Loubet
Clever cooking from a starry chef
The Zetter Hotel, 86-88 Clerkenwell Road, Clerkenwell, EC1M 5RJ
Tel no: (020) 7324 4455
www.bistrotbrunoloubet.com
⊖ Farringdon, Barbican, map 5
Modern French | £35
Cooking score: 3
≒

Packing a 'major punch' in Clerkenwell, Bruno Loubet's 'relaxed' bistro is just right for the Zetter Hotel. Full-height windows let plenty of light into a dining room where the décor has a touch of the Lewis Carrolls, and where Loubet's flights of fancy are brought to bear on French classics. His new King's Cross venture, the Grain Store (see entry), is all about vegetables; this is the place to enjoy what he can do with meat. To start, try Lyonnaise salad or venison carpaccio with pear and truffle dressing, then move on to one of the 'plates', such as a guinea fowl boudin blanc with broad beans ('bursting with flavour') that can be boosted into a main-course size. Braised beef indochine, with its lively herbed mango salad, reflects Loubet's time in Australia, while 'a glimmering example' of crêpes suzette brings it all home. Wines from £18.50.
Chef/s: Bruno Loubet. **Open:** all week L 12 to 2.30 (3 Sun), D 6 to 10.30 (10 Sun). **Closed:** 23 and 27 Dec. **Meals:** alc (main courses £17 to £19). **Details:** 80 seats. 40 seats outside. Wheelchair access.

Symbols
≒ Accommodation is available
£30 Three courses for less than £30
V Separate vegetarian menu
£5 OFF £5-off voucher scheme
🍾 Notable wine list

NEW ENTRY

Bistrotheque

Achingly cool east London pioneer – no sweat
23–27 Wadeson Street, Bethnal Green, E2 9DR
Tel no: (020) 8983 7900
www.bistrotheque.com
⊖ **Bethnal Green, map 1**
French | £35
Cooking score: 2

Credit to Bistrotheque, 10 years old this year, for keeping fashionable east London in good food well before anybody else dared open on these gritty, urban streets. The converted sweatshop is as achingly cool as ever: still with white walls, scuffed concrete floor and zero signage, but now with an attractive eating bar that brings laughter and life to the room. The occasional pianist performs a similar function. All-day brunch at weekends is wildly popular: tuck into pancakes, eggs Benedict, duck hash or excellent steak tartare. At dinner, go for pear and Stichelton cheese salad, then sea trout, samphire and hollandaise or an onglet steak, before making like a local and getting stuck into the 'pudding drinks' (espresso Martini, perhaps). European wines from £17.
Chef/s: Christopher Branscombe. **Open:** Sat and Sun L 11 to 4, all week D 5.30 to 12 (6 Sat and Sun). **Closed:** 24 to 26 Dec. **Meals:** alc (main courses £15 to £28). Set L and early/late D £17.50 (3 courses). Sun L £17.50. **Details:** 80 seats.

Bonds

Solid City pleaser
Threadneedle Hotel, 5 Threadneedle Street, City, EC2R 8AY
Tel no: (020) 7657 8088
www.bonds-restaurant.co.uk
⊖ **Bank, map 2**
Modern British | £42
Cooking score: 4

🍷 🛏

Dramatic classical columns, a high ceiling, subdued lighting and rust-red upholstery create a mood of pinstriped formality that befits the food in this sympathetically converted City banking hall. Stephen Smith's cooking is precise and risk-free, matching carefully sourced ingredients with smart, thoughtful technique. Dorset crab is served with wild cress salad, saffron, leek and clam vinaigrette, while steamed plaice fillets are dressed with a fricassee of spring vegetables and crispy squid. Pleasing meat and game dishes also stay firmly in the mainstream: from roast and confit chicken with Savoy cabbage, girolles, tomato and tarragon jus to grilled Black Angus ribeye with spinach and watercress purée, asparagus and thyme. To finish, cinnamon and apple crumble, orange crème brûlée and mixed berry Pavlova sound as safe as houses. There are wine suggestions for most dishes; the full list is an impressive compendium stuffed with big-ticket French names and serious stuff from the New World – plus a few bottles from England. Prices start at £22 (£6.50 a glass).
Chef/s: Stephen Smith. **Open:** Mon to Fri L 12 to 2.30, D 6 to 10. **Closed:** Sat, Sun, bank hols. **Meals:** alc (main courses £15 to £26). Set L and D £24 (2 courses) to £28. **Details:** 60 seats. Separate bar. Wheelchair access.

★ **BEST VALUE FOR MONEY** ★

NEW ENTRY

Bouchon Fourchette

A Gallic oasis in Hackney
171 Mare Street, Hackney, E8 3RH
Tel no: (020) 8986 2702
www.bouchonfourchette.co.uk
⊖ **Hackney Central, map 1**
French | £20
Cooking score: 2

£5 OFF £30

This Hackney newcomer is a little oasis of classic French cuisine on less-than-lovely Mare Street. Chef Jeremy Huguet has worked for *les grands noms* in France (Alain Ducasse and Pierre Gagnaire) and his experience shows in bistro cooking with a winningly purist streak. In the wrong hands, snails drenched in garlic, butter and parsley, coq au vin and crème caramel are clichés; in Huguet's, they're retro classics. Mackerel rillettes with cumin bread

and steak tartare and frites are similarly creditable. The food may be as French as the Marseillaise but the concrete floor and vintage chairs are pure east London. The wine list (from £17) is (almost) all French, and all bottles are available by the glass.
Chef/s: Jeremy Huguet. **Open:** Tue to Sun 9am to 10pm (11pm Fri and Sat). Mon D 5 to 10. **Closed:** 24 Dec to 2 Jan. **Meals:** alc (main course £8 to £12). Set L £7.99. **Details:** 40 seats. Separate bar.

NEW ENTRY
Boundary
Full-dress restaurant with a very posh wine list
2-4 Boundary Street (entrance in Redchurch Street), Shoreditch, E2 7DD
Tel no: (020) 7729 1051
www.theboundary.co.uk
⊖ Shoreditch, Old Street, map 2
Modern French | £50
Cooking score: 3

Sir Terence Conran's multi-purpose block of east London real estate, once a warehouse, is now a complex of three eating-spaces constructed around 17 guest-rooms, with a roof garden on top for good measure. Head down paint-daubed stairs and you could be forgiven for expecting the banging beat of a nightclub. But no, the basement is given over to the main restaurant where, under exposed vaulted brickwork a rather formal scene is set. The cooking is traditional French rather than modern: scallops are a trio, nicely rare, served with crumbed beignets of salt cod, assertively garnished with strips of fennel and segments of grapefruit, while red-rare Landais pigeon is robustly partnered with a lobe of duck foie gras, cubes of Alsace bacon and broad beans. To finish, there may be buttery sable sandwiching a gleaming chocolate ganache, alongside morello cherries doused in port and a puddle of melted cherry sorbet. The wine list is a very serious affair, full of elevated French gear at mark-ups that give no quarter.

Chef/s: Frederick Foster. **Open:** Mon to Sat D 6 to 10.30, Sun L 12 to 4. **Meals:** alc (main courses £18 to £36). Set D and Sun L £19.50 (2 courses) to £24.50

Brawn
Unbuttoned neighbourhood eatery
49 Columbia Road, Shoreditch, E2 7RG
Tel no: (020) 7729 5692
www.brawn.co
⊖ Shoreditch, map 2
French | £25
Cooking score: 4
£30

Ed Wilson and Oli Barker are dab hands at opening down-to-earth restaurants that only make a show of themselves where it matters: on the plate (see entries for Terroirs, Soif and Green Man & French Horn). Brawn's two rooms sport a simple palette – white walls and closely packed wooden tables, with natural light from large windows – that matches the straight-to-the-point cooking perfectly. The menu is a tribute to great British produce and plays off the seasons with mainly French-influenced dishes, say cauliflower and Westcombe Cheddar soufflé or Dorset clams with charred leeks and cidre beurre blanc. Dishes show minimum posturing, but are always comforting and big-flavoured, whether a main course of Tamworth pork and liver sausage with mash and pepper sauce, or a well-made treacle tart for dessert. Brawn also scores with its reasonable prices, a policy extending to the stash of modern wines that explores France with insightful selections, taking side trips mainly to Italy and Spain.
Chef/s: Owen Kenworthy. **Open:** Tue to Sun L 12 to 3 (4 Sun), Mon to Sat D 6 to 10.30 (11 Fri and Sat). **Closed:** 24 Dec to 2 Jan, bank hols. **Meals:** alc (main courses £5 to £16). Sun L £25. **Details:** 70 seats. Wheelchair access.

Bread Street Kitchen

Gordon's buzzy all-dayer
One New Change, 10 Bread Street, St Paul's,
EC4M 9AJ
Tel no: (020) 3030 4050
www.breadstreetkitchen.com
⊖ St Paul's, map 5
Modern British | £36
Cooking score: 2

Gordon Ramsay's City presence takes the form of a cavernous, somewhat zanily outfitted all-day brasserie over two floors in a sleek glass and steel mall. Usefully, its day begins at 7am with breakfast (ricotta hot cakes, sausage sandwiches and the like), after which the kitchen moves on to a vogueishly international repertoire that could take you from jalapeño-spiked salmon ceviche to short-rib beefburger with Monterey Jack, then griottine cherry Bakewell tart in the space of one meal. Steaks from the charcoal grill and pizzas round off the choice nicely. Some will relish the chance to sip an espresso Martini on a vintage vaulting horse in the bar; others may prefer the safety of the restaurant and its enticing, if expensive, wine list, from £22.
Chef/s: Erion Karaj. **Open:** Mon to Sat 7am to 11pm (11.30am Sat). Sun 11 to 8. **Closed:** 25 Dec. **Meals:** alc (main courses £12 to £43). **Details:** 312 seats. Separate bar. Wheelchair access.

Café Spice Namasté

High-rolling modern Indian
16 Prescot Street, Tower Hill, E1 8AZ
Tel no: (020) 7488 9242
www.cafespice.co.uk
⊖ Tower Hill, map 1
Indian | £30
Cooking score: 2
£5 OFF

Intriguing enough to pull in punters 'from 200 miles away', Cyrus Todiwala's high-rolling restaurant may be within reach of Brick Lane but it inhabits a very different world. Bold colours and rich swags add drama to the high-ceilinged dining room and the cooking melds Indian regional flavours with artisan British ingredients. The result is a 'damn good' menu with many surprises. Buccleuch beef appears as a tikka, rare-breed pork features in a genuine Goan vindaloo and home-reared lamb is the basis for a 'proper' dhansak – served with brown onion rice, a kebab and kachumber (onion salad). Also explore the outstanding 'in-season organic vegetables' (beetroot and coconut samosas for instance, or parsnip bhurta), and don't miss the gorgeous plate of mini kulfis to finish. Zippy, spice-friendly wines from £22.95.
Chef/s: Cyrus Todiwala. **Open:** Mon to Fri L 12 to 3, Mon to Sat D 6.15 to 10.30 (6.30 Sat). **Closed:** Sun, 25 Dec to 1 Jan, bank hols. **Meals:** alc (main courses £16 to £20). Set L and D £35. **Details:** 130 seats. Wheelchair access.

Cinnamon Kitchen

Sharp-suited City Indian
9 Devonshire Square, City, EC2M 4YL
Tel no: (020) 7626 5000
www.cinnamon-kitchen.com
⊖ Liverpool Street, map 2
Indian | £40
Cooking score: 4
£5 OFF

A far cry from the gentlemanly sobriety of the Cinnamon Club (see entry), this sharp-suited City offshoot struts its stuff in brash designer surroundings: cool grey colour schemes, elliptical lampshades and touches of warehouse chic. The kitchen delivers dazzling innovation and punchy flavours – no surprise given that executive chef Vivek Singh is behind the sprightly menu. A quick scan tells its own story: Goan-spiced duck breast with passion fruit raita; seared black bream with kokum berries, sprouting broccoli and quinoa salad; saddle of venison with chilli potato fondant – if it weren't for the tandoori chicken, lamb biryani, black dhal and Indian breads you might think you were in a trailblazing modern British eatery. Desserts indulge in East/West *jeux sans frontières*: think spiced pumpkin tart with clove ice cream or cumin profiteroles with cardamom

shortbread. Wacky Indian-themed cocktails are best enjoyed on the courtyard terrace, while spice-tolerant wines start at £26.
Chef/s: Abdul Yaseen. **Open:** Mon to Fri L 12 to 3, Mon to Sat D 6 to 11. **Closed:** Sun, bank hols. **Meals:** alc (main courses £13 to £40). Set L and D £19 (2 courses) to £21. Tasting menu £60 (6 courses). **Details:** 130 seats. 40 seats outside. Separate bar. Wheelchair access.

★ TOP 50 ★

NEW ENTRY

The Clove Club

Fashion-forward roots
Shoreditch Town Hall, 380 Old Street, Shoreditch, EC1V 9LT
Tel no: (020) 7729 6496
www.thecloveclub.com
⊖ Old Street, Shoreditch High Street, map 2
Modern European | £47
Cooking score: 6

V

Run by members of ostensibly curious culinary collectives, financed by a crowd-funding website and housed in Shoreditch Town Hall, it would be hard for the Clove Club to be any more in keeping with the zeitgeist. The good news is that, despite its fashion-forward roots in a Dalston pop-up of the same name, for the most part it's all about good, old-fashioned hospitality. The main dining-room – with its high ceilings, white-washed walls, stripped back ambience, teal-tiled kitchen and exposed pass – only opens in the evening to serve a five-course set menu that throws in various other little treats along the way. Lunch is served in the bar via a series of small plates and a more substantial dish of the day. Chef Isaac McHale, who also oversees 'The Young Turks' residence at the Ten Bells in Spitalfields (see entry), uses modern techniques in an unobtrusive fashion, and likes to focus on vegetables over animal protein in combinations such as poached leek, served complete with its roots and accompanied by mussels in a lemon-balm

sauce. The meat, when it appears, might be slices of ruby beef rib, simply but perfectly prepared. The wine list opens at £19.
Chef/s: Isaac McHale. **Open:** Tue to Sat L 12 to 2.30, Mon to Sat D 6 to 10. **Closed:** Sun, 24 Dec to 6 Jan. **Meals:** alc bar only (main courses £6 to £17). Tasting menu £47 (5 courses). **Details:** 42 seats. Separate bar.

Club Gascon

A lively sea of surrealist cooking
57 West Smithfield, City, EC1A 9DS
Tel no: (020) 7600 6144
www.clubgascon.com
⊖ Barbican, Farringdon, St Paul's, map 5
Modern French | £46
Cooking score: 6

♪ V

The former Lyons corner house next to Smithfield meat market has been home to Pascal Aussignac's dynamically creative French cuisine for a decade and a half now – and the chef remains restlessly inventive. In an atmosphere of studied, gently lit elegance, a conceptual approach is taken to the foodways of the Gascon south-west, with small dishes grouped thematically or a pre-selected market menu the possible routes. Some compositions sound almost straightforward, as in braised snails in diabolo sauce with wild fennel infusion, while others head for the wilder shores, as when a bowl of chestnut velouté is garnished with gnocchi, moss and Marmite clementine. Sceptics are often won over, as was the reporter who enjoyed pollack with black pudding reduction, de-boned partridge stuffed with chicken mousse and a 'glorious, clear mahogany-coloured sauce of wild mushrooms flecked with truffle'. A finale of almond sponge with blueberries, rosemary and fig crystals also garnered praise. The wine list concentrates on the south-western appellations – Irouléguy, Cahors and all – but also reaches out to the Midi, Provence and Corsica. Bottles start at £22, small glasses at £5. See overleaf for details.

Chef/s: Pascal Aussignac. **Open:** Mon to Fri L 12 to 2, Mon to Sat D 6.30 to 10 (10.30 Thur to Sat). **Closed:** Sun, bank hols. **Meals:** alc (main courses £19 to £23). Set L £25. Set D £28. Tasting menu £60. **Details:** 43 seats. Separate bar. Wheelchair access.

The Coach & Horses
British pub grub with a swagger
26-28 Ray Street, Clerkenwell, EC1R 3DJ
Tel no: (020) 7278 8990
www.thecoachandhorses.com
⊖ **Farringdon, map 5**
Modern British | £25
Cooking score: 2
£30

It's a Victorian backstreet pub you are unlikely to find by accident, and even if you did, you would probably pass by without a second glance – and miss a treat. This tremendous drinking and dining venue is noted for simple, rustic cooking that puts the emphasis on seasonality. Descriptions are straight to the point: a mound of 'melting' duck livers on toast with capers, sultanas and chicory epitomises content over style, while crab risotto or a fantastic rose veal chop with lemon, caper and parsley dressing, chips and a watercress and pear salad show that simplicity wins out. Sunday lunch with 'excellent' beef, crispy Yorkshire puddings and 'beautiful' goose-fat roast potatoes 'could hardly be bettered', and the succinct wine list (from £14.50) spreads itself geographically as well as economically.
Chef/s: Leigh Norton. **Open:** Sun to Fri L 12 to 3 (1 to 4 Sun), Mon to Fri D 6 to 10. **Closed:** Sat, 23 Dec to 3 Jan, bank hols. **Meals:** alc (main courses £11 to £17). Sun L £19.95. **Details:** 72 seats. 50 seats outside. Wheelchair access.

Comptoir Gascon
Earnest, brasserie-style Gallic cooking
61-63 Charterhouse Street, Clerkenwell, EC1M 6HJ
Tel no: (020) 7608 0851
www.comptoirgascon.com
⊖ **Farringdon, Barbican, map 5**
French | £27
Cooking score: 4
£5 OFF £30

Instantly appealing food is the deal at this unprepossessing bistro-deli with its good-time mix of buzz, bonhomie and fairly priced sustenance. Related to nearby Club Gascon (see entry), it, too, deals in the culinary essence of South West France but, unlike its smarter big brother, offers an unreformed style of Gallic cooking that's well matched by worn brick walls and too many tables. The kitchen shows its mettle with impeccable piggy treats (a charcuterie spread) or snails tartine with chickpeas, rocket and piquillo sauce, and makes the most of spiced veal kidney with sauté pine corn and persillade, duck confit and garbure béarnaise or French rabbit with mustard and olive oil crushed potatoes – although duck burger with fries has been underwhelming. To conclude, clementine cake with spiced yoghurt ice cream hits the spot. Growers from South West France make up the short, good-value wine list; prices from £17.
Chef/s: Pascal Aussignac. **Open:** Tue to Sat L 12 to 2.30 (11.30 Sat), D 6.30 to 10 (7 Sat). **Closed:** Sun, Mon, 22 Dec to 3 Jan, bank hols. **Meals:** alc (main courses £9 to £15). Set L £14.50. **Details:** 45 seats. 8 seats outside.

Coq d'Argent
Slick rooftop dining with spectacular views
1 Poultry, City, EC2R 8EJ
Tel no: (020) 7395 5000
www.coqdargent.co.uk
⊖ Bank, map 2
Modern French | £60
Cooking score: 2

The lift that whisks you off the street up to the top of 1 Poultry immediately makes you feel 'that little bit special', and there are tremendous views across the City skyline from the verdant garden bar/brasserie: the place to be in fine weather. Otherwise, the smart dining room is flooded with light from floor-to-ceiling windows. Simplicity is surely the key to success here – crab salad, plateau de fruits de mer, côte de boeuf – yet such dishes don't come cheap. Nevertheless, this popular establishment finds plenty willing to pay and you get decent French cooking for your money, including uncomplicated roast duck breast and confit leg with orange sauce, and roast cod with sauce américaine. For those feeling slightly less extravagant, the set-lunch menu doesn't skimp on quality. Wines from £22.50.
Chef/s: Mickael Weiss. **Open:** Sun to Fri L 11.30 to 3 (12 Sun), Mon to Sat D 6 to 10 (6.30 Sat). **Closed:** bank hol weekends. **Meals:** alc (main courses £17 to £35). Set L, D and Sun L £26 (2 courses) to £29. **Details:** 150 seats. 100 seats outside. Separate bar. Wheelchair access.

Corner Room
Trendy food and bang-for-buck
Town Hall Hotel, Patriot Square, Bethnal Green, E2 9NF
Tel no: (020) 7871 0461
www.cornerroom.co.uk
⊖ Bethnal Green, map 1
Modern European | £30
Cooking score: 4

This is the Town Hall Hotel's 'secret' restaurant, occupying a tiny, wood-panelled corner of the first floor. Its chef Nuno Mendes may be better known for his challenging modern cooking at the hotel's destination restaurant Viajante (see entry), but his hip bistro is arguably just as impressive within its category – and price grade. Don't expect steak frites: the Corner Room is rarely predictable and excels in fashionable international, often quite technical dishes. Good sourdough and sharing plates of ham and cheese are as conventional as it gets; after that, the menu could launch into squid with buttermilk and asparagus, then salmon confit, Japanese-style, with fried aubergine and agedashi, before finishing with frozen pannacotta with apple and hazelnuts. The wine list is brave to offer just a handful of each colour (all between £28 and £38) but they're smart choices and the gamble pays off. No bookings at dinner.
Chef/s: Nuno Mendes. **Open:** all week L 12 to 4, D 6 to 10.30. **Meals:** alc (main courses £12 to £14). Set L £17 (2 courses) to £21. **Details:** 30 seats. Separate bar. Wheelchair access.

Diciannove
Convivial City Italian
Crowne Plaza Hotel, 19 New Bridge Street, City, EC4V 6DB
Tel no: (020) 7438 8052
www.diciannove19.com
⊖ Blackfriars, map 5
Italian | £35
Cooking score: 2

The Italian refectory approach in the main eatery at the Crowne Plaza continues unabated, despite a change of name (from Refettorio to Diciannove). Big shared tables promote a convivial rather than monastic feel, and the pastas, risottos and classic main dishes continue to come up trumps. Lardo on toast as an appetiser is worth furring the arteries for, and there's tenderness and freshness in the octopus and potato salad with olives in lemon dressing. Reliable pastas take in paccheri with prawns and cherry tomatoes or spaghettini with crab, both cooked in white wine, garlic and chilli. After mains of char-grilled swordfish, perhaps, or beef fillet with stewed

onions and grilled asparagus, you can conclude proceedings traditionally with tiramisu or gelati. Wines from £19.50 (£5.50 a small glass).
Chef/s: Alessandro Bay. **Open:** Mon to Fri L 12 to 2.30, Mon to Sat D 6 to 10.30 (10 Fri and Sat). **Closed:** Sun. **Meals:** alc (main courses £18 to £26). Set D £25 (3 courses) to £65 (6 courses). **Details:** 100 seats. Separate bar. Wheelchair access.

NEW ENTRY

Dishoom
Buzzy all-day Bombay café
7 Boundary Street, Shoreditch, E2 7JE
Tel no: (020) 7420 9324
www.dishoom.com
⊖ **Old Street, Liverpool Street, map 2**
Indian | £25
Cooking score: 2
£5 OFF £30

Enter this homage to old Bombay's Irani cafés and wafts of incense assault the senses. Less refined than its precursor in Covent Garden (see entry), Shoreditch Dishoom rolls out the same all-day dining formula in a spacious subcontinental, faded Art Deco setting. Fragrant, spicy interpretations of Mumbai cookery include a vast array of sharing plates, snacks and grills. On inspection the skate-cheek morsels were pleasingly delicate deep-fried nuggets and the dhal rich and deeply flavoured. If you come as a crowd (recommended, as evening tables can only be booked by parties of six or more), try the signature lamb raan, a feast of braised, spiced meat, perhaps with 'awesome' fried okra, a cooling lassi and made-to-order naan from the in-house tandoor. Wines from £18.50.
Chef/s: Naved Nasir. **Open:** all week 8am to 11pm (9am Sat and Sun, midnight Thur to Sat). **Closed:** 25 and 26 Jan, 1 and 2 Jan. **Meals:** alc (main courses £6 to £22). Set L and D £20 (2 courses) to £35. **Details:** 190 seats. 40 seats outside. Separate bar.

The Don
Fine wines and enterprising cooking
The Courtyard, 20 St Swithin's Lane, City,
EC4N 8AD
Tel no: (020) 7626 2606
www.thedonrestaurant.co.uk
⊖ **Bank, Cannon Street, map 2**
Modern European | £38
Cooking score: 2
£5 OFF

'Overall a good place for lunch in the City,' remarks one who emerged from the wine-cellar-style bistro happy with the fair prices. A note of caution is added, though: 'if full it could be quite claustrophobic and the noise levels were high'. The Don occupies Sandeman's former offices – hence the name, the Madeira and port list, and the great character. In contrast, the ground-floor restaurant is strikingly modern, more discreet and offers a pleasingly varied menu. The food has a deep reassurance about it, thanks not least to steak tartare, dressed Cornish crab, potted salt beef, grilled calf's liver and steamed supreme of halibut topped with a shrimp mousse on a leek fondue. The highly individual wine list (one of the City's best) contains well-chosen Champagnes and top-name bottles from classic regions of France and around the globe. There's plenty of choice by the glass and bottles from £20.
Chef/s: Matthew Burns. **Open:** Mon to Fri L 12 to 2.30, D 6 to 10. **Closed:** Sat, Sun, 23 Dec to 2 Jan, bank hols. **Meals:** alc (main courses £17 to £29). Bistro menu (12 to 10) £18.95 (2 courses) to £22.95. **Details:** 100 seats. Separate bar. No children.

Average Price
The average price listed in main-entry reviews denotes the price of a three-course meal, without wine.

NEW ENTRY
Duck & Waffle
High-flyer with a bird's-eye view of the City
Heron Tower, 40th floor, 110 Bishopsgate, City,
EC2N 4AY
Tel no: (020) 3640 7310
www.duckandwaffle.com
⊖ Liverpool Street, map 2
Modern British | £46
Cooking score: 3

We could devote this entire entry to the glass lift that flies guests up to Duck & Waffle on the 40th floor of the Heron Tower, and to the views – oh, the views! Instead, to the food: the modern, madcap menu somehow meshes American junk, Mediterranean and British 'hipster' influences without discombobulating City diners. Things aren't always coherent in this energetic, 24-hour venue; even with the aid of the painstakingly helpful staff, it's tricky to get the right balance of starters, small plates and sharing plates for the table, and standards have been inconsistent. Sweet and savoury are often played off, most notably in the titular duck and waffle, a surprisingly successful combination of duck confit, fried egg and mustard maple syrup. Other hits have been ox cheek doughnut, bacon-wrapped dates and beetroot with goats' curd and honeycomb. Wine prices are steep, from £26. **Chef/s:** Daniel Doherty. **Open:** all week 24-hour opening. **Meals:** alc (main courses £7 to £13, small plates). **Details:** 116 seats. Separate bar. Wheelchair access.

The Eagle
Still a masterclass in running a modern pub
159 Farringdon Road, Clerkenwell, EC1R 3AL
Tel no: (020) 7837 1353
⊖ Farringdon, map 5
Modern European | £20
Cooking score: 2
£30

Those prepared to put up with the crowded single room and go *mano-a-mano* with drinkers for table space are rewarded with excellent food. The basic décor reflects Michael Belben's aim to provide great food and drink without breaking the bank, and the modern British-Mediterranean cooking is based on a zealous enthusiasm for entirely fresh ingredients. The Eagle was a mould-breaker when it opened in 1991, and over the years the consistent flow has not been interrupted – buy drinks, order and pay for the hearty food at the bar. The crowds keep returning for plates of cuttlefish stew with chickpeas, chilli, peppers, tomato, lemon and thyme; grilled Swaledale lamb marinated in rose-petal harissa; or the legendary never-off-the-menu marinated steak sandwich. You won't need a starter but pasteis de nata provide a sweet conclusion. The short wine list opens at £14.50. And reports please on a new opening, The Three Crowns, 8 East Road, London N5 2ET; tel: (020) 7842 8516.
Chef/s: Ed Mottershaw. **Open:** all week L 12 to 3.30 (4 Sun), Mon to Sat D 6.30 to 10.30. **Closed:** 24 Dec to 1 Jan, bank hol L. **Meals:** alc (main meals £6.50 to £15). **Details:** 60 seats. 24 seats outside. Separate bar.

Eyre Brothers
Broad-shouldered and beautiful Iberian cuisine
68-70 Leonard Street, Shoreditch, EC2A 4QX
Tel no: (020) 7613 5346
www.eyrebrothers.co.uk
⊖ Old Street, map 2
Spanish-Portuguese | £35
Cooking score: 4

A friendly buzz of contentment radiates from the sleek, light, wood-toned interior of the Eyre brothers' eatery not far from Old Street. Robust textures and upstanding flavours are the hallmarks of the kitchen's Spanish and Portuguese specialities. Squid is grilled with garlic and chilli, while chistorra (a thin chorizo variant from Burgos) comes with fried Padrón peppers and egg, among the starters. Main courses up the ante with Portugal's arroz de pato (a baked spicy rice dish with duck, chorizo and smoked bacon), or perhaps dourada (sea bream) with crushed ratte potatoes dressed in onion, black olives, capers, olive oil and coriander. Finish with crema catalana or tarta de Santiago with marmalade and cream. The viticultural map of the Iberian peninsula will help to orientate you in a list that's big on interest, voluble notes and value. Prices start at £19.50, or £5.50 a glass.

Chef/s: David Eyre and João Cleto. **Open:** Mon to Fri L 12 to 2.30, Mon to Sat D 6 to 11 (7 Sat). **Closed:** Sun, Christmas to New Year, bank hols. **Meals:** alc (main courses £10 to £30). **Details:** 70 seats.

Fifteen London

Modern British revamp from brand Jamie
15 Westland Place, Shoreditch, N1 7LP
Tel no: (020) 3375 1515
www.fifteen.net
⊖ Old Street, map 2
British | £35
Cooking score: 3

Jamie Oliver's flagship, not-for-profit enterprise, which has welcomed underprivileged young apprentices into its fine-food fold for over a decade, has celebrated its success with a welcome face-lift. The generous two-floor space (basement restaurant, ground-floor bar), given a typically Shoreditch industrial-chic restyle, has young urbanites flooding in to devour the all-new, pared-back British fare. Seasonal, unfussy offerings lay bare executive chef Jon Rotheram's credentials (he's an alumnus of St John, see entry) and are ideally suited to shared-plate dining. The menu changes daily, so spring might bring the delights of Dorset crab, rye cracker and dill, cured Middle White pork with pickled fennel, and punchy bocca di lupo (ravioli) with goats' cheese and nettles. Round off the tour of the best of British with signature rhubarb and custard eclair. The bar draws in walk-ins with its delectable snacks, craft beers, seasonal cocktails and relaxed vibes. Wines from £19.

Chef/s: Jon Rotheram. **Open:** all week L 12 to 3, D 6 to 10. **Closed:** 25 and 26 Dec, 1 Jan. **Meals:** alc (small/sharing plates £5 to £27). **Details:** 140 seats. Separate bar.

Galvin La Chapelle

Head-turning French class
35 Spital Square, Spitalfields, E1 6DY
Tel no: (020) 7299 0400
www.galvinrestaurants.com
⊖ Liverpool Street, map 2
Modern French | £48
Cooking score: 6

Housed in what was once the chapel of St Botolph's, a Victorian girls' school, is one of the Galvin brothers' more eye-catching venues. Soaring marble columns surround chocolate-brown banquettes, and the lighting is perfectly pitched to emphasise the drama of the setting. Zac Whittle has achieved a winning fluency in the Galvin group style, with menus that mingle French idioms with the contours of modern British cooking. The span of reference takes us from the wilder shores (smoked eel with caramelised pineapple and horseradish) to the beaten track (pressed ham hock and foie gras with onion marmalade), but always with a confident sense of orientation. The lasagne of Dorset crab with beurre nantais and pea shoots attracts high praise, while mains take in guinea fowl in Alsace bacon velouté and red mullet with artichokes and salsify in truffle butter. Classic French desserts like tarte Tatin and rum baba conclude matters. The wine list's highlight is a run of Jaboulet's glorious Hermitage La Chapelle, but there are many interesting wines from lesser-known corners of Europe. Prices start at £19.

Chef/s: Jeff Galvin and Zac Whittle. **Open:** all week L 12 to 2.30 (3 Sun), D 6 to 10.30 (9.30 Sun). **Closed:** 24 to 26 Dec, 1 Jan. **Meals:** alc (main courses £23 to £33). Set L £24.50. Early set D £29.50. Tasting menu £70 (7 courses). **Details:** 110 seats. 32 seats outside. Separate bar. Wheelchair access.

Galvin's Café à Vin

Good-value Galvin offshoot
35 Spital Square, Spitalfields, E1 6DY
Tel no: (020) 7299 0404
www.galvinrestaurants.com
⊖ **Liverpool Street, map 2**
Modern European | £30
Cooking score: 3

'I ventured deep into Spitalfields to enjoy an early dinner at this café next door to the grander and more ambitious Galvin La Chapelle,' noted one reporter, adding 'it has a pleasant vibe and cheerful and professional service'. A smart-casual kind of place, the Café à Vin is furnished in zinc and dark wood and has all the theatre of a 'see-through kitchen'. Tables outside provide a popular spot for lunch. The short repertoire majors in simple brasserie French food and flexible opening times. French onion soup, escargots and rump steak with Pont Neuf potatoes and sauce bordelaise represent the old guard, while wood-roast sole, cima di rapa and anchovy dressing strikes a more contemporary note. To finish, petit pot au chocolat is typical of the desserts offered. You can also enjoy all-day nibbles along with a good choice of wines by the glass or 'pot lyonnais'. Bottles from £18.
Chef/s: Jack Boast. **Open:** all week 11.30 to 10.30 (9.30 Sun). **Closed:** 24 to 26 Dec, 1 Jan. **Meals:** alc (main courses £12 to £19). Set L and early D £14.95 (2 courses) to £18.50. Sun L £14.95. **Details:** 45 seats. 110 seats outside.

The Gun

Docklands socialising and robust food
27 Coldharbour, Canary Wharf, E14 9NS
Tel no: (020) 7515 5222
www.thegundocklands.com
⊖ **Canary Wharf, map 1**
Modern British | £32
Cooking score: 1

Back in the 18th century, this old boozer was a haunt favoured by stevedores, smugglers and workers from the nearby gun-forging foundries. Fast-forward a few hundred years and it's now a cheery venue for Docklands socialising, with thrilling views of the Thames and O_2 thrown in. Tradition rules in the pubby bar and various interconnecting rooms, where visitors are treated to decent ales and a menu with strong British credentials. Nibble on Scotch eggs with HP sauce, steak sarnies and crispy brawn 'fingers' with fennel 'slaw, or plump for something larger: perhaps braised Yorkshire rabbit, slow-cooked Herdwick lamb neck or a well-rendered sea bass, queen scallop and sorrel risotto with crispy squid. Wines from £17.50. The AstroTurf terrace outside is now used for summertime gin parties, beer festivals and corporate jollies.
Chef/s: Quinton Bennett. **Open:** all week L 12 to 3 (4 Sat and Sun), D 6 to 10.30 (6.30 to 9.30 Sun). **Closed:** 25 and 26 Dec. **Meals:** alc (main courses £14 to £29). **Details:** 70 seats. 40 seats outside. Separate bar. Wheelchair access. No children in the bar after 8.

ALSO RECOMMENDED

▲ The Hackney Pearl

11 Prince Edward Road, Hackney Wick, E9 5LX
Tel no: (020) 8510 3605
www.thehackneypearl.com
⊖ **Hackney Wick, map 1**
Modern British

Unwavering local support is a given at this all-purpose bar-café-restaurant: a rollickingly informal spot with Formica-topped tables and school chairs. James Morgan's Antipodean-inspired cooking forms the nerve centre of the enterprise, so for weekend brunch expect sweetcorn fritters with chilli jam and yoghurt. Otherwise, split pea falafels with labneh and beetroot jam (£5.50) could give way to meatloaf with tomato sauce and swede mash (£13.50), then rhubarb jelly with roast rhubarb. Drink London-brewed real ales, classic cocktails or wine (from £14.20). Open all week.

Hawksmoor Guildhall

A sizzling advert for British beef
10-12 Basinghall Street, City, EC2V 5BQ
Tel no: (020) 7397 8120
www.thehawksmoor.com
⊖ Bank, map 2
British | £60
Cooking score: 4

'The best of London!' exclaimed a fan of Hawksmoor's Guildhall branch: the third London offering from Messrs Beckett and Gott's headlining steakhouse group. This sprawling basement may be deep in the Square Mile, but aficionados say it's like walking into a stateside 'speakeasy steak club' – imagine swathes of dark-wood panelling, mirrors and low ceilings. You can feast on veal chops, lobster and char-grilled monkfish, but this barnstormer is essentially a sizzling advert for slabs of well-aged, British-reared beef: strapping bone-in ribs, mature D-rumps and other sought-after cuts served with beef-dripping fries, macaroni cheese, fried eggs or unmissable grilled bone marrow. A starter of shrimps on toast or sticky Tamworth pork ribs should get the juices flowing, while puds such as sticky toffee sundae go for calorific overload. Power breakfasts (7 to 10am) are 'simply divine', too. Animated, on-the-ball staff are happy to impart their knowledge of Hawksmoor's fabulous cocktail selection and big, beefy wine list. Prices start at £19 (£5.75 a glass).
Chef/s: Richard Turner and Lewis Hannaford. **Open:** Mon to Fri L 12 to 3, D 5 to 10.30. **Closed:** Sat, Sun, 21 Dec to 2 Jan. **Meals:** alc (main courses £7 to £44). Early set D £23 (2 courses) to £26.
Details: 160 seats. Separate bar. Wheelchair access.

▮▮● Visit us
▮▮▮ Online
To find out more about
The Good Food Guide, please visit
www.thegoodfoodguide.co.uk

Hawksmoor

Prime British steakhouse
157a Commercial Street, City, E1 6BJ
Tel no: (020) 7247 7392
www.thehawksmoor.co.uk
⊖ Liverpool Street, Aldgate East, map 2
British | £60
Cooking score: 3

'Go ravenous' advises one reader, of the original steakhouse in a widely admired London mini-group (see entries). Yes, the trademark dry-aged Yorkshire Longhorn beef cuts, expertly cooked over charcoal, are big as well as 'awesome', but supporting dishes rightly take up their fair share of space. Add sides like triple-cooked chips, macaroni cheese or mash and gravy to the porterhouse or bone-in prime rib, plus anchovy hollandaise or bone marrow gravy, and you've got yourself a proper steak dinner. An express lunch, perhaps Doddington Caesar salad, gilthead bream and buttermilk pannacotta with raspberries, is a good way to tour the rest of the menu. Casual eats like a 'life-affirming' short-rib French dip are available in the basement bar, alongside the mixed drinks that receive special attention here. Wines are carefully chosen, from £19.
Chef/s: Richard Turner and Paul O'Dowd. **Open:** all week L 12 to 2.30 (4.30 Sun), Mon to Sat D 5 to 10.30 (6 Sat). **Closed:** 24 to 27 Dec, 1 Jan. **Meals:** alc (main courses £13 to £35). **Details:** 116 seats. Separate bar. Wheelchair access.

Hix Oyster & Chop House

A personal take on British ingredients
35-37 Greenhill Rents, Cowcross Street,
Clerkenwell, EC1M 6BN
Tel no: (020) 7017 1930
www.hixoysterandchophouse.co.uk
⊖ Farringdon, map 5
British | £45
Cooking score: 4

Mark Hix's restaurants are matched to their locales. His Smithfield chophouse, the first in a line-up that continues to grow, echoes the rawness and cacophony of the nearby meat

market with plain tiled walls, edgy artwork and cheek-by-jowl dining arrangements. 'X' marks the spot in many dishes, with 'snax' including pork crackling with apple sauce, Hix-cure smoked salmon with soda bread and a final course of a Hix Fix jelly shot (based on the house cocktail, with cherries in Somerset eau de vie). But the food is about great British flavours rather than ego, and dishes such as a starter of sand eels with ramson mayonnaise, followed by a poached turkey egg with heritage potato and green onion salad (from the dedicated veggie menu) bring some little-known ingredients into the light. Wine is from £18.75.
Chef/s: Jamie Guy. **Open:** all week 12 to 11 (9 Sun). **Closed:** 25 to 27 Dec, bank hols. **Meals:** alc (main courses £18 to £37). Set L and D £17.50 (2 courses) to £22.50. Sun L £17.50. **Details:** 70 seats.

NEW ENTRY
HKK London
Chinese cooking doesn't get any better
Broadgate West, Worship Street, City, EC2A 2BF
Tel no: (0203) 535 1888
www.hkklondon.com
⊖ Liverpool Street, map 2
Chinese | £45
Cooking score: 6

Secreted on an anonymous street not far from Liverpool Street Station, HKK eschews the high-spec glamour of its Hakkasan Group siblings for an understated, greyish-beige room — it is Tong Chee Hwee's exquisitely rendered modern Chinese and Cantonese cooking that stands out. It achieves striking results, thanks to sourcing, vibrant seasoning and ingenious grace notes. Highlights at inspection included three stunning dim sum (delicate, light silky dumplings of steamed prawn, and Szechuan chicken, with an amazing fried turnip roll 'the standout in a tight finish') and an 'all so delicious' version of Peking duck: shards of crisp skin and slivers of meat, with a sesame pancake roll of more duck meat, a smear of hoisin, a pinch of sugar (to dip the skin in) and a tangle of beautifully dressed leaves. In another knockout dish, jasmine tea-

smoked Wagyu beef made an impressive showing, braised to a state of almost criminal lusciousness, while a razor clam shell filled with chopped clams and chilli — a skilful balance of sweet and fiery notes — came with a wonderful sticky ball of glutinous rice. Then a delicate, wobbly postage-stamp-sized lychee tapioca with a passion fruit chiboust and passion fruit jam, followed by a pineapple fritter with salted lime jelly and a tiny dollop of vanilla ice cream. Prices are high, and that goes for wines, which start at £39.
Chef/s: Tong Chee Hwee. **Open:** Mon to Fri L 12 to 2.30, Mon to Sat D 6 to 9.45. **Closed:** Sun, 2 weeks Christmas, first week Jan. **Meals:** alc (main courses £16 to £38). Set L £28.50 (4 courses), £42 (5 courses) to £48 (8 courses). Tasting menu £95 (15 courses). **Details:** 58 seats. Separate bar. Wheelchair access.

Ibérica Canary Wharf
Top-tier tapas in Docklands
10 Cabot Square, Canary Wharf, E14 4QQ
Tel no: (020) 7636 8650
www.ibericalondon.co.uk
⊖ Canary Wharf, map 1
Spanish | £35
Cooking score: 2

In the heart of Canary Wharf, this striking restaurant pays homage to contemporary Spain: from its strident, bullish décor (a mix of leather, brick, iron and legs of ham) to the modern-Spanish approach of the cooking. Gazpacho of red berries, beetroot and anchovy, black rice with cuttlefish, prawns and allioli sauce, and oxtail ravioli with pumpkin purée achieve both balance and restraint in terms of their contrasting flavours. It's the same with desserts, which are generally as impeccable as the rest of the menu; tarta de Santiago with coffee, orujo (Galician brandy) and vanilla ice cream is one possible option. The exclusively Spanish wine list starts at £19.
Chef/s: Berto Romo. **Open:** all week 11.30 to 10 (12 to 4 Sun). **Closed:** 25 and 26 Dec, bank hols. **Meals:** alc (main courses £7 to £24). Set L £10 (2 courses) to £15. Set D £28 (2 courses) to £35. **Details:** 130 seats. Separate bar. Wheelchair access.

NEW ENTRY
Lardo
Hip-yet-homely pizzeria
205 Richmond Road, Hackney, E8 3NJ
Tel no: (020) 8985 2683
www.lardo.co.uk
⊖ Hackney Central, map 1
Italian | £25
Cooking score: 2
£30

Named after the cured fat that's here served over impeccable pizzas in melting sheets, Lardo is a love letter to Italy's humble food traditions. This hip-yet-homely pizzeria in a not-too-shady part of Hackney does what it can from scratch. We enjoyed a zesty straw-coloured homemade 'chinotto' soda, excellent pasta and Lardo's own speck (cured for it in Gloucestershire) in a delicious dandelion and celery salad. Don't leave without trying a pizza: crisp bases, sweet tomatoes and unusual toppings (such as cardoon, scamorza and olive) put them among London's best. It's hard not to fall instantly in love with Lardo but there are disappointments, including overly oily spaghettini spilling off tiny vintage plates and dry chocolate and walnut cake at inspection. Interesting European wine list, from £19.50.
Chef/s: Damian Currie. **Open:** Mon to Fri L 12 to 3, D 6 to 10.30. Sat and Sun 11 to 10.30 (9.30 Sun). **Meals:** alc (main courses £8 to £16). **Details:** 60 seats. 50 seats outside. Wheelchair access.

Lutyens
Smooth, seductive Conran classic
85 Fleet Street, City, EC4Y 1AE
Tel no: (020) 7583 8385
www.lutyens-restaurant.com
⊖ Chancery Lane, St Paul's, Temple, map 5
French | £45
Cooking score: 4

In a building designed by Sir Edwin Lutyens, which once housed the Reuters news agency, another branch of the new Conran empire has made its home. Inside is a bright, white, enlivening space furnished in pale shades, with a marble floor design that references the old ticker-tapes that used to deliver the news. Swedish chef Henrik Ritzen brings a subtle Nordic influence to bear, amid the expected pan-European brasserie dishes. The Raw Bar does what it says, offering oysters, sea bass ceviche and steak tartare. Otherwise, head for the house-smoked salmon with pickled cucumber. Specials might cast the net wider for saddle of rabbit with a pastilla of braised shoulder and cardamom yoghurt, while monkfish comes with celeriac and wild leeks. Finish with a blood-orange soufflé, or rum baba with roast pineapple and coconut. A very fine, classically based wine list (from £20) has all the serious French stuff, as well as a bushel of pedigree German Rieslings.
Chef/s: Henrik Ritzen. **Open:** Mon to Fri L 12 to 3, D 6 to 10. **Closed:** Sat, Sun, Christmas, New Year, bank hols. **Meals:** alc (main courses £14 to £36). Set L and D £22 (2 courses) to £26. **Details:** 120 seats. 20 seats outside. Separate bar. Wheelchair access.

ALSO RECOMMENDED
▲ Mehek
45 London Wall, Moorgate, EC2M 5TE
Tel no: (020) 7588 5043
www.mehek.co.uk
⊖ Moorgate, Liverpool Street, map 2
Indian £5 OFF

City suits hungry for a posh 'Ruby Murray' often convene at this swish Indian by London Wall, where swift, 'professional' service is much appreciated. Against a sexy backdrop created by a Bollywood set designer, they order spicy, 'fragrant' machi masala with king prawns (£14.90), Bengali-style guinea fowl with herbs, and chunks of punchy sukhi duck on banana leaves. Otherwise, kormas, vindaloos and jalfrezis (from £9.50) generally satisfy. Cocktails and fizz suit the bonus boys, while spice-friendly wines start at £16.95. Open Mon to Fri.

The Modern Pantry

Flexible fusion in Clerkenwell
47-48 St John's Square, Clerkenwell, EC1V 4JJ
Tel no: (020) 7553 9210
www.themodernpantry.co.uk
⊖ Farringdon, map 5
Fusion | £33
Cooking score: 3
£5 OFF 🍷

'Anna Hansen has a way of surprising your taste-buds' raves one fan of the New Zealand chef/owner at Clerkenwell's ever-innovative Modern Pantry. 'Fusion' food sometimes gets a bad rap, but Hansen could single-handedly repair its image. In her international box of tricks, she has green tea and kalamansi lime dressing and sumac sunflower seeds to go with scallop sashimi; miso to marinate onglet steak and pair with cassava chips; and a terrific array of desserts such as ginger pudding with bergamot cream cannoli and kumquats. Occasionally divisive, always interesting, Hansen's food is 'sheer joy for vegetarians'. Her restaurant is more than just a gastronomic experience; the gorgeously converted Georgian town house is a cool, 'vibey' place, with trendy locals filling both the street-level café and first-floor dining room. As modern and free-range as the food, the agreeably priced wine list (from £19.50) actively encourages guests to discover something new.
Chef/s: Anna Hansen and Robert McLeary. **Open:** Mon to Fri 8am to 10.30pm (10pm Mon). Sat 9 to 4, 6 to 10.30. Sun 10 to 4, 6 to 10. **Closed:** 24 to 26 Dec, 1 Jan, Aug bank hol. **Meals:** alc (main courses £16 to £22). Set weekday L and Sun L £22 (2 courses) to £27. **Details:** 100 seats. 30 seats outside. Wheelchair access.

Morgan M

French sophistication and precision
50 Long Lane, Barbican, EC1A 9EJ
Tel no: (020) 7609 3560
www.morganm.com
⊖ Barbican, map 5
Modern French | £44
Cooking score: 5
V

You'd have to look hard to find a restaurant as refreshingly uncool as Morgan Meunier's understated Smithfield venture (it made the move here from Islington in 2012). The place isn't dated – far from it – but this brand of reassuringly French cuisine and formal service is getting rather scarce. Morgan M is a 'slick operation': staff are 'highly attentive from the moment of arrival' and the split-level, ground-floor dining room is elegantly outfitted in leaf-green and cream, accessorised with white linen and sparkling ice buckets. Meunier's 'expertly prepared' dishes are quietly contemporary and imaginative, though firmly anchored in classic French technique. Poêlé of foie gras with orange sauce and toasted brioche makes a bright, attractive lead-in to a deeply flavoured main such as slow-cooked boar with celeriac purée, braised roots and sauce civet. Desserts continue to delight: pineapple soufflé with a pina colada sorbet 'could not be faulted'. Tasting, vegetarian and set menus are consistently good options, and French wines are the cellar's strong suit (from £19.50).
Chef/s: Morgan Meunier and Sylvain Soulard. **Open:** Mon to Fri L 12 to 2.30, Mon to Sat D 6 to 10.30. **Closed:** Sun, 24 to 31 Dec. **Meals:** alc (main courses £20 to £27). Set L and D £21.50 (2 courses) to £25.50. Tasting menu £52. **Details:** 65 seats.

Morito

Tiptop tapas
32 Exmouth Market, Clerkenwell, EC1R 4QE
Tel no: (020) 7278 7007
www.morito.co.uk
⊖ Farringdon, map 2
Tapas | £20
Cooking score: 4
£30

At this tiny, pared-down offshoot of Moro (next door), the simplicity of the tapas-only menu is entirely in keeping, and diners need to warm to the cramped bustle and general informality. Expect to queue (reservations at lunchtime only), but once you've secured a seat at the long bar or one of several small tables you'll realise it's worth the wait. Ingredients are given centre-stage prominence in dish after dish trumpeting spicy, fragrant Spanish and North African ideas. A must-order dish is fried chickpeas with pumpkin, coriander and tahini, but there's praise, too, for beetroot borani (purée) with feta and walnuts, and spiced lamb shredded on to aubergine, yoghurt and pine nuts. Palpable freshness means that traditional dishes such as a tortilla of potato, onion and peppers or jamón and chicken croquetas and patatas bravas are reliably superb. A good selection of sherries by the glass heads the short, Iberian wine list; prices from £16.
Chef/s: Samuel and Samantha Clark. **Open:** all week L 12 to 4, Mon to Sat D 5 to 11. **Closed:** 24 Dec to 2 Jan, bank hols. **Meals:** alc (tapas from £3 to £9). **Details:** 30 seats. 8 seats outside. Wheelchair access.

Moro

Good-time vibes and earthy Moorish food
34-36 Exmouth Market, Clerkenwell, EC1R 4QE
Tel no: (020) 7833 8336
www.moro.co.uk
⊖ Farringdon, map 2
Spanish-North African | £35
Cooking score: 4

It was a hit from the start and – 16 years later – Moro remains a rambunctious customer, packed with publishing types, the Sadler's Wells brigade and fans of fragrant, earthy Moorish food. The action-packed canteen resounds with chatter and clatter from the open kitchen, sultry aromas fill the air and a riotous time is had by all. Wood-roasting and char-grilling are the star turns: from 'beautifully tender' pork with crisp crackling, grilled onion salad, pomegranate and lentils to roast duck with figs and 'moros y cristianos' (rice and black beans) that was 'evocative of the Mediterranean'. Starters of quail in flatbread or pan-fried calf's liver with roast pumpkin and spiced labneh open proceedings with a bang; huge helpings of rich, oily patatas bravas are strictly for trencherman appetites; and few can resist yoghurt cake with pistachios to finish. The splendid Iberian wine list is stuffed with unusual delights from £19 (£4.50 a glass).
Chef/s: Samuel and Samantha Clark. **Open:** all week L 12 to 2.30 (12.30 to 2.45 Sun), Mon to Sat D 6 to 10.30. **Closed:** 24 Dec to 2 Jan, bank hols. **Meals:** alc (main courses £17 to £21). **Details:** 110 seats. 20 seats outside. Wheelchair access.

NEW ENTRY
Perkin Reveller

Tipples and tuck by the Tower
The Wharf at the Tower of London, Tower Hill,
EC3N 4AB
Tel no: (020) 3166 6949
www.perkinreveller.co.uk
⊖ Tower Hill, map 1
British | £30
Cooking score: 2

An airy haven amid the tourist throngs milling on the Wharf at the Tower of London, this modern bar and eatery is a study in understated style – simple furnishings deliberately playing second fiddle to the fabulous views of the Tower and Tower Bridge. It's a fine spot for a lazy drink (perhaps in the outdoor seating area), but the food deserves attention, too. British classics make a good showing, from Maldon rock oysters to Cornish fish stew, while elsewhere the menu looks to Europe: with chilled tomato and basil soup, say, or potato gnocchi with wild mushrooms and Jerusalem artichokes. Poached rhubarb with vanilla cream and shortbread is a smart way to finish. Take time with the wine list (from £17), which includes some fascinating organic finds.
Chef/s: Andrew Donovan. **Open:** all week L 11.30 to 3.30 (5 Sun), Mon to Sat D 5.30 to 10.30. **Closed:** 24 to 27 Dec, 1 Jan. **Meals:** alc (main courses £13 to £28). Set L £16 (2 courses) to £19. Set D £25 (2 courses) to £30. Sun L £16.50. **Details:** 110 seats. 100 seats outside. Separate bar. Wheelchair access.

Pizza East

Oh-so-cool Italian eatery
56 Shoreditch High Street, Shoreditch, E1 6JJ
Tel no: (020) 3310 2000
www.pizzaeast.com
⊖ Liverpool Street, Old Street, map 2
Italian-American | £25
Cooking score: 2
£30

'Very laid-back, very east London' noted one reporter after a visit to the Soho House Group's vast industrial-chic pizzeria in perennially trendy Shoreditch. On the ground floor of a former tea warehouse, the edgy, canteen-style room has a typically utilitarian look with plenty of exposed brick and concrete. The regulars may lean towards the fashion-conscious, but the food is far from frivolous and the authentic wood-fired pizzas are taken seriously, with a use of premium ingredients. Start, perhaps, with salt cod and fried polenta or octopus with celery hearts and capers, before pizzas topped with the likes of pork belly, tomato, mozzarella and mushrooms, or veal meatballs, prosciutto and cream. Pudding of peanut-butter parfait is worth leaving room for. Wines from £19.50.
Chef/s: Brian McGowan. **Open:** Mon to Fri 12 to 11 (midnight Thur, 1am Fri). Sat and Sun 9am to 1am (11pm Sun). **Closed:** 24 to 26 Dec. **Meals:** alc (main courses £7 to £16). **Details:** 170 seats. Separate bar. Wheelchair access.

NEW ENTRY
Quality Chop House

A Victorian gem reincarnated
94 Farringdon Road, Clerkenwell, EC1R 3EA
Tel no: (020) 7278 1452
www.thequalitychophouse.com
⊖ Farringdon, map 5
British | £27
Cooking score: 3
£30

Long ago, the working men of 19th-century Clerkenwell found their way to the Quality Chop House – a humble canteen serving simple sustenance to the masses. Ad execs may have long since replaced them on the church pew-style seating, but the original interiors have stubbornly survived: a glorious relic of Victoriana, with chessboard tiled floors and wainscotted walls. Reopened under new owners, the famous Chop House claims to have gone back to basics in the kitchen: evident in a simple but flawlessly executed starter of lamb ribs with mint sauce. Rich, rousing flavours characterised main courses at inspection – a meaty mountain of Longhorn mince atop dripping toast and a buttery thornback ray with capers and sea purslane. To finish, a silken crème brûlée raised the game again. Portion sizes are more suited to Mr Bumble than Oliver Twist, and service takes a similarly generous approach. The formidable wine list starts at £19.

Chef/s: Shaun Starley. **Open:** Mon to Sat L 12 to 3, D 6 to 10.30. **Closed:** 24 Dec to 2 Jan. **Meals:** alc (mains courses L only £12 to £22). Set D £35 (4 courses). **Details:** 80 seats. 6 seats outside. Separate bar.

ALSO RECOMMENDED
▲ Railroad

120-122 Morning Lane, Hackney, E9 6LH
Tel no: (020) 8985 2858
www.railroadhackney.co.uk
⊖ Bethnal Green, map 1
Global

'It's small and cramped but fun', aptly describes this admirable little café on a busy corner of Morning Lane. You'll sit at communal tables and marvel at how a tiny kitchen manages to produce excellent, freshly cooked food at such reasonably prices. Shakshuka ('a perfect balance of egg, tomato and herbs') has been praised, or try chicken livers cooked in wine, brandy and sage (£5) ahead of Catalan fish stew with potato, saffron and picada (£15.90). The bread is delicious and cakes such as coffee and chocolate are not to be missed. Wines from £16. Closed Mon and Tue.

▲ Rochelle Canteen

Rochelle School, Arnold Circus, E2 7ES
Tel no: (020) 7729 5677
www.arnoldandhenderson.com
⊖ Liverpool Street, map 2
Modern British

Breakfast, elevenses, lunch and tea are the main events at this offbeat, communal eatery housed in a converted school bike shed. Chef James Ferguson has moved on, but the kitchen still majors on broad-shouldered seasonal victuals with emphatic British overtones. Typical calls from the terse daily lunch menu might include rabbit terrine with pickled prunes, clams with potato, chorizo and parsley or lemon sole with borlotti beans and rocket (£14.50), followed by caramel ice cream or apricot and almond tart. Take a break outside when the sun shines. Unlicensed, but BYO wine (£5 corkage). Closed Sat and Sun.

St John

Provenance-driven nose-to-tail adventures
26 St John Street, Clerkenwell, EC1M 4AY
Tel no: (020) 3301 8069
www.stjohnrestaurant.com
⊖ Farringdon, map 5
British | £40
Cooking score: 5

Fergus Henderson and Trevor Gulliver have been responsible for one of the more important breakaway movements in London cuisine of the past 20 years. Here is where it more or less began: in a converted Smithfield smokehouse, between unadorned walls of operating-theatre white. Nose-to-tail eating means just that, at least where the noble pig is concerned. There are no unexpected garnishes or techno-faffing, no foams, no 'textures'. What you get is defiantly old-fashioned cooking. Long-staying dishes such as the roast bone marrow with parsley salad retain their supporters, but there are new things to try: venison as a starter with green beans and pickled walnuts; main courses of mutton and carrots in mint sauce, or gamey woodcock complete with a teaspoon for the brain. Fish is less the point, though you might open with a wing of skate on bread with green sauce or go for the uncomplicated freshness of lemon sole and tartare. Finish with bread pudding and butterscotch or rhubarb sorbet shocked up with vodka. A list of surprisingly refined French wines sets up an entertaining dialectic: Clos Vougeot with your pig's cheek and dandelion, perhaps? Prices start at £23.40, or £5.90 a glass.

Chef/s: Chris Gillard. **Open:** Sun to Fri L 12 to 3 (1 to 3 Sun), Mon to Sat D 6 to 11. **Closed:** 1 week Christmas, bank hols. **Meals:** alc (main courses £13 to £32). **Details:** 110 seats. Separate bar.

St John Bread & Wine
The laid-back second child
94-96 Commercial Street, Spitalfields, E1 6LZ
Tel no: (020) 3301 8069
www.stjohnbreadandwine.com
⊖ Liverpool Street, map 1
British | £28
Cooking score: 3
£30
⬇

'Although there was no sawdust on the floor', notes one reader, 'it would not have been out of place.' In comparison with its Clerkenwell big brother (see entry), Fergus Henderson's City-fringes outpost has an unselfconscious ease, which lubricates breakfast, lunch, afternoon tea and 'supper'. The well-known nose-to-tail approach (and horror at the prospect of irrelevant garnish) results in robust plain dishes and devastatingly good combinations. Beetroot salad with goats' cheese, or game offal with radishes and dandelion, might be followed by a 'very tasty' pheasant to share, with sprout tops and red wine gravy. The presence of the on-site bakery means excellent bread, and afters might be the signature Eccles cakes with Lancashire cheese or hot chocolate pudding. Wine is very French and from £23.40; bottles are also sold to take home. **Chef/s:** Lee Tiernan. **Open:** all week 9am to 11pm (9pm Sun). **Closed:** 25 Dec. **Meals:** alc (main courses £13 to £25). **Details:** 60 seats.

NEW ENTRY
Salvation Jane
Relaxed all-day Aussie café
Unit 2, 1 Oliver's Yard, 55 City Road, Shoreditch, EC1Y 1HQ
Tel no: (020) 7253 5273
www.salvationjanecafe.co.uk
⊖ Old Street, map 2
Australian | £20
Cooking score: 1
£5 OFF £30

Brunch has long held a special place in Australians' hearts, and Salvation Jane – the new, larger sibling to Fitzrovia's Lantana Café

(see entry) – garners high praise for its laid-back Antipodean fare. Locals linger over weekend brunch at the all-day café, which might feature a stack of corn fritters with bacon, spinach, avocado salsa and slow-roast tomatoes; salt beef hash-cakes with poached eggs; or coconut French toast. The dinner crowd is enticed, too, with larger dishes and inventive cocktails. Behind the relaxed attitude lies a serious dedication to coffee, so expect a superior brew. The concise wine list starts at £15 a carafe, £20 a bottle. **Chef/s:** Tim Dorman. **Open:** all week 8 to 3 (9 to 3.30 Sat and Sun), Tue to Fri D 6 to 9. **Closed:** 24 to 27 Dec, Easter Sun. **Meals:** alc (main courses 8 to £14). **Details:** 65 seats. 40 seats outside. Separate bar. Wheelchair access.

ALSO RECOMMENDED
▲ Shanes on Chatsworth
62 Chatsworth Road, Hackney, E5 0LS
Tel no: (020) 8985 3755
www.shanesonchatsworth.com
map 1
Modern British

The gastronomic energy that has recently infused east London has yet to reach the outer edges of Hackney and Homerton, but Shanes is leading the charge. On a street where launderettes and take-aways sit fairly comfortably (for now) alongside the first stirrings of gentrification, this little bistro with some eight tables is cramped but welcoming. It serves 'good, very British cooking' along the lines of pickled pear and Colston Bassett Stilton on chicory leaves (£5) and lamb chop with cauliflower purée and salsa verde (£11.95). Wine from £22. Closed Mon and L Tue to Fri.

Also Recommended
Also recommended entries are not scored but we think they are worth a visit.

NEW ENTRY
Sushi Tetsu

Best sushi quality in London
12 Jerusalem Passage, Clerkenwell, EC1V 4JP
Tel no: (020) 3217 0090
www.sushitetsu.co.uk
⊖ Farringdon, map 5
Japanese | £30
Cooking score: 4

An awkward booking policy combined with space for just seven diners means it's harder to get a reservation here than at the Fat Duck, but then this traditional Japanese counter-style restaurant does deliver 'the best sushi quality I have had in London'. Toru Takahashi's omakase is a good intro for those not familiar with sushi and sashimi, but if you are familiar, order from the carte and be guided by the excellent waitress. Startlingly fresh fish is well sourced and a test meal produced some real high points: scallop, seared on top, quickly marinated in lime underneath, 'a lovely contrast'; tuna that was 'absolutely fantastic'; wasabi imported from Japan and grated at table – an action that felt 'very Japanese'; and, always served last, tiny squares of superb sweet-steamed omelette. However, the 'easy listening music' was not appreciated and the tiny room ('bigger than a garden shed though not by much') lacks atmosphere. Drink green tea, Asahi or Sapporo beer or saké.
Chef/s: Toru Takahashi. **Open:** Tue to Fri L 12.30 to 1 (last sitting), Tue to Sat D 6 to 8.30 (last sitting). **Closed:** Sun, Mon. **Meals:** Sushi from £3.20 (1 piece), sashimi from £7 (3 pieces), minimum order L £20, dinner £30. **Details:** 7 seats.

❙❘❘ Please send us your feedback

To register your opinion about any restaurant listed in the Guide, or a new restaurant that you wish to bring to our attention, please visit the web address at the bottom of the page. Your feedback informs the content of the book and will be used to compile next year's reviews.

NEW ENTRY
Sushisamba

A lively mix of Japanese, Brazilian and Peruvian cuisines
Heron Tower, 110 Bishopsgate, City, EC2N 4AY
Tel no: (020) 3640 7330
www.sushisamba.com
⊖ Liverpool Street, map 2
Japanese-South American
Cooking score: 1

High in the Heron Tower, Duck & Waffle (see entry) snaffled the foodies, Sushisamba the drinkers – at 38 floors up its bar and outside terrace is spectacular, and fun. A desire to upgrade the food (no mean feat as the concept is a lively mix of Japanese, Brazilian and Peruvian), saw Cláudio Cardoso drafted in, and early results are promising. A cavalcade of small plates brings splendid wagyu gyoza, blistering chicharrón de calamar (baby squid) served with fried plantain, pico de gallo (tomato, onion, chilli), mint and tamarind, while the robata grill delivers excellent hamachi kama (yellow tail collar). Chocolate, red pepper and chilli is a 'truly astounding' finale. Wines from £24.
Chef/s: Cláudio Cardoso. **Open:** all week 11.30am to 12.30am (1.30am Sat and Sun). **Meals:** alc (small plates £8 to £17, large plates £15 to £35). Nigiri omakase £12 to £25, Sashimi omakase £22 to £58. **Details:** 120 seats. Separate bar.

Tayyabs

Rollicking Punjabi canteen with wicked spicing
83-89 Fieldgate Street, Whitechapel, E1 1JU
Tel no: (020) 7247 6400/9543
www.tayyabs.co.uk
⊖ Whitechapel, Aldgate East, map 1
Pakistani | £20
Cooking score: 2
V £30

'Queuing for food is part of the experience,' explains one reviewer gamely, putting a positive spin on what is, for many, the only downside of this fast-paced, crowded, 'slightly chaotic' Punjabi canteen. Tayyabs' many regulars all have their favourite dishes: for some, it's the 'tender, rich' dry meat, for others it's the mixed grill or vegetarian curries with pumpkin or lentils and baby aubergine. Most, however, seem united in their addiction to the 'hissing, sizzling' lamb chops, the wonderful breads ('you could order the naans alone and be happy') and the mango lassi, an effective salve for the fierce spicing. It's cheap and BYO (no corkage fee), which only 'adds to the allure'.

Chef/s: MS Tayyab. **Open:** all week L 12 to 3, D 4 to 11.30. **Meals:** alc (main courses £6 to £13). **Details:** 250 seats. Wheelchair access.

ALSO RECOMMENDED
▲ Towpath Café
42 De Beauvoir Crescent, Dalston, N1 5SB
www.towpathcafe.wordpress.com
⊖ Old Street, map 2
Modern European

Lori de Mori and Jason Lowe's idiosyncratic, joyous canal-side café is a spare operation, based around a few hatches, some rickety furniture (little of it under cover) and ditzy staff. Grab a quick breakfast (coffee and sourdough toast, perhaps) or – better – try the short seasonal lunch menu for perfect wild garlic revueltos (£6.50) or smoked mackerel fishcakes (£9.50) with a glass of biodynamic wine (from £21.50 a bottle). Open Tue to Sun, Mar to Oct only. No cards.

NEW ENTRY
Tramontana Brindisa
An homage to Catalonia and Mediterranean Spain
152 Curtain Road, Shoreditch, EC2A 3AT
Tel no: (020) 7749 9961
www.brindisa.com
⊖ Old Street, map 2
Spanish | £25
Cooking score: 3

£30

Named after the bracing north wind – the 'tramontana' – that whips Spain's Mediterranean coastline, Brindisa's fourth branch casts its considerable net of sourcing expertise over the eastern regions of Spain. Pull up a stool next to the open kitchen and watch head chef Alberto Torres and his team at work, or head for the welcoming dining room beyond. Impeccable ingredients are a given, and the imaginative menu ventures above and beyond standard tapas fare. Expect Padrón peppers, fluffy croquetas and outstanding charcuterie, certainly, but don't miss out on regional specialities: Catalonian rice dishes to share, white bean stew with clams and the standout dish on inspection: fideuà de sepia, a rich noodle seafood 'paella' with garlic allioli. The impressive regional wine list offers an extensive selection of cavas, and lesser-known Spanish bottles (from £18.50).

Chef/s: Alberto Torres and Nicolas Modat. **Open:** all week 12 to 11 (9 Sun). **Meals:** alc (tapas £5 to £12). Set L and D £25 to £30. **Details:** 130 seats. Separate bar. Wheelchair access.

Les Trois Garçons
High camp and vigorous French cooking
1 Club Row, Shoreditch, E1 6JX
Tel no: (020) 7613 1924
www.lestroisgarcons.com
⊖ Liverpool Street, map 2
French | £37
Cooking score: 2

'Glorious zany fun' in a high-camp setting of bejewelled taxidermy, dangling handbags, a cane-wielding crocodile and a bulldog with butterfly wings – this audaciously attired one-time boozer will stop you in your tracks. The kitchen tries hard to match the dining room's outrageous décor, although its take on modern French food can sometimes seem 'surprisingly orthodox', despite some rather mannered Asian inflections. Fillet of tea-smoked sea trout with a carrot spring roll, pickled shallots, blood orange and chilli sauce or spice-cured venison with won tons, Savoy cabbage, beetroot purée and Szechuan pepper jus show the kitchen's adventurous streak, while 'chaud-froid' of foie gras in Sauternes, chateaubriand and coconut nougat glacé are determinedly true to tradition. The French-accented wine list starts at £26 (£6.50 a glass).

Chef/s: Michael Chan. Open: Thur and Fri L 12 to 2, Mon to Sat D 6 to 9.30 (10.30 Fri and Sat). Closed: Sun, 23 Dec to 6 Jan, bank hols. Meals: alc (main courses £15 to £33). Set L £17.50 (2 courses) to £22. Details: 65 seats. Children at L and early D only.

28°-50° Wine Workshop and Kitchen

Dedicated to the fruit of the vine
140 Fetter Lane, City, EC4A 1BT
Tel no: (020) 7242 8877
www.2850.co.uk
⊖ Chancery Lane, map 5
French | £30
Cooking score: 3

With the looks and lively atmosphere of a modern Parisian wine bar, this Fetter Lane basement brasserie continues to pull in the crowds. The menu recreates French classics, perhaps a rich foie gras terrine or onglet with braised shallots, and confit duck with polenta, date and Seville orange. Alternatives include sharing plates of charcuterie or cheeses from La Fromagerie, plus an undeniably delicious grilled spatchcock chicken with béarnaise sauce. Dessert might be a cinnamon crème brûlée with apple compote or a rhubarb mousse with chocolate sorbet and crumble. The wine list is no less delightful: well chosen and keenly priced, starting with bottles of Chilean Carménère and Puglian Fiano for £19.50. One of the pleasing details is real choice by the glass – from a dinky 75ml, small 125ml to large 250ml measures. A branch of 28°-50° is in Marylebone Lane (see entry).
Chef/s: Paul Walsh and Ben Mellor. Open: Mon to Fri L 12 to 2.30, D 6 to 9.30. Closed: Sat, Sun, last Fri before Christmas to 2 Jan. Meals: alc (main courses £11 to £17). Set L £15.95 (2 courses). Details: 60 seats. Separate bar.

NEW ENTRY

Upstairs at the Ten Bells

Uber-cool Spitalfields hang out
84 Commercial Street, Spitalfields, E1 6LY
Tel no: (07530) 492986
www.tenbells.com
⊖ Liverpool Street, Aldgate East, map 2
Modern British | £30
Cooking score: 2

If it weren't already an ancient two years old, this pub dining room would be the last word in hipster dining. Fight your way through the rammed former 'Jack the Ripper' pub up to this one-time 'pop-up' created by Isaac McHale of the Clove Club (see entry). Traditional British ingredients and modern techniques combine on ex-Ledbury chef Giorgio Ravelli's carte. Begin with 'snacks' – buttermilk chicken and pine salt, say – before veal pastrami, tarragon, kohlrabi and flax seeds, then cod, monk's beard and grapefruit sauce vierge. Presentation can lack precision; desserts (Nutella and spelt waffle with unadvertised banana) were the weakest link in an interesting yet imperfect meal. Take note: music is loud, lighting low. An excellent choice of Italian and French wines starts at £19.
Chef/s: Giorgio Ravelli and Isaac McHale. Open: Tue to Sun L 12 to 2.30 (4 Sun), Tue to Sat D 6 to 10.30. Closed: Mon, 23 Dec to 6 Jan. Meals: alc (main courses £15 to £18). Set L £18 (2 courses) to £24. Set D £39. Details: 44 seats.

Vanilla Black

Proper cooking for neglected veggies
17-18 Tooks Court, Farringdon, EC4A 1LB
Tel no: (020) 7242 2622
www.vanillablack.co.uk
⊖ Chancery Lane, map 5
Vegetarian | £38
Cooking score: 2
V

Andrew Dargue's small restaurant in a cobbled street not far from Chancery Lane is a very personal enterprise. Run as a restaurant with a mission, it's a real one-off. The food is strictly

vegetarian, but leave any preconceptions behind. Space barely permits a comprehensive roll call of dishes that might take in Brie ice cream with pickled plum, mulled custard, sherry vinegar and cracked hazelnut ahead of seared seaweed and cabbage with pickled potatoes, soda bread sauce, pickled mustard seeds and foraged seaside vegetables. The kitchen shows real ambition – note liquid doughnut and espresso gel with milk parfait, yeast sugar and coffee crumbs – and results on the plate are more often than not a glorious mélange of flavours. Wines from £22.
Chef/s: Andrew Dargue. **Open:** Mon to Fri L 12 to 2.30, Mon to Sat D 6 to 10. **Closed:** Sun, 2 weeks from 25 Dec. **Meals:** Set L £18.50 (2 courses) to £23.50. Set D £28 (2 courses) to £38. **Details:** 45 seats. Wheelchair access.

Viajante
Truly original food that makes a splash
Town Hall Hotel, Patriot Square, Bethnal Green, E2 9NF
Tel no: (020) 7871 0461
www.viajante.co.uk
⊖ Bethnal Green, map 1
Modern European | £70
Cooking score: 5

Nuno Mendes' venue for the gastronomically curious inspires mixed reactions and wouldn't be doing its job if it didn't. This is one of London's most ambitious restaurants – and not simply because it dares to do (and charge) what it does in edgy Bethnal Green. Housed in the Victorian town hall-turned-boutique hotel, Viajante comprises a fashionably attired double dining room with open kitchen, from which Portuguese-born Mendes sends out his highly technical, 'east-west' menus of 3 (lunch only), 6, 9 or 12 courses. The tone is set immediately, with creative amuse-bouches such as potato with yeast and Gordal olive soup. What follows is a (sometimes rather slow) succession of perfectly plated, textural dishes: perhaps cod tripe with parsley, potatoes and onions; Dehesa lamb with black quinoa; or smoked bone marrow with morels

and beef broth. Dessert might be a 'riff' on milk. Some combinations 'take getting used to'; others suffer 'temperature issues' (blame sous-vide); still more are instant, roaring successes. 'It's an experience I am glad I had,' says one reader. Modern wines, from £32.
Chef/s: Nuno Mendes. **Open:** Fri to Sun L 12 to 2, all week D 6 to 9.30. **Closed:** bank hols. **Meals:** Set L £78 (6 courses) to £90. Set D 70 (6 courses) to £100. **Details:** 35 seats. Separate bar. Wheelchair access. No children under 11 yrs.

Vinoteca
Mediterranean flavours and interesting tipples
7 St John Street, Farringdon, EC1M 4AA
Tel no: (020) 7253 8786
www.vinoteca.co.uk
⊖ Farringdon, Barbican, map 5
Modern European | £28
Cooking score: 3

A big hit when it opened in 2005, this premier-league wine bar has gone from strength to strength, opening branches in Marylebone (see entry) and Beak Street, Soho. Vinoteca continues to draw praise for its now tried-and-tested formula of casual vibes, a worldwide wine list (with splendid tipples by the glass) and food that deals in bold Mediterranean flavours. Indeed, there are some very good things to eat here: crispy duck salad with blood orange and watercress; roast gurnard with spiced cauliflower, baba ganoush and golden beetroot; then pistachio and almond cake with cassata ice cream. The well-annotated wine list is a treasure trove, ticking all the boxes for serious intent, quality and value, and rewards experimentation. Prices start at £16.75.
Chef/s: John Cook. **Open:** Mon to Sat L 12 to 2.45 (4 Sat), D 5.45 to 10. **Closed:** Sun, 25 Dec to 1 Jan, bank hols. **Meals:** alc (main courses £12 to £18). **Details:** 37 seats. 6 seats outside. Separate bar.

Wapping Food

Skilful food in an industrial setting
Wapping Hydraulic Power Station, Wapping Walk,
Wapping, E1W 3SG
Tel no: (020) 7680 2080
www.thewappingproject.com
⊖ Wapping, map 1
Modern European | £36
Cooking score: 3
£5
OFF

Sure, tables in this vast space (a former hydraulic power station) are inserted in between chunks of machinery and dangling chains, and chairs are of the white plastic garden variety, but 'on a fine day when the sun is pouring through the part-glass roof and big windows, it's a great place to be'. Part art centre, part restaurant, Wapping Food is as endearingly unpretentious as its signature modern European cooking. Quality seasonal ingredients make up a cracking starter of cow's curd, bitter leaves, blood orange, salmon roe and bottarga, while mains could run to pork loin with artichoke, almond sauce, radicchio and anchovy dressing. Puddings are worth saving space for, especially the thick chocolate mousse with rye crumb, quince compote and yoghurt ice cream. Fans of Aussie wine will have a field day – everything on the short, fashionable list is from Down Under, with bottles from £19.
Chef/s: Matthew Young. **Open:** all week L 12 to 3 (1 to 3.30 Sat, 1.15 to 4 Sun), Mon to Sat D 6.30 to 11 (7 Sat). **Closed:** 23 Dec to 3 Jan, bank hols. **Meals:** alc (main courses £16 to £23). **Details:** 120 seats. 40 seats outside. Wheelchair access. Car parking.

Whitechapel Gallery Dining Room

Good value and flavours that sing
77-82 Whitechapel High Street, Whitechapel,
E1 7QX
Tel no: (020) 7522 7896
www.whitechapelgallery.org
⊖ Aldgate East, map 1
Modern European | £28
Cooking score: 3
£30

The restaurant at the Whitechapel Gallery, east London's artistic hub, is under the aegis of Angela Hartnett of Murano (see entry). A simple café-like ambience, and staff who reliably come in for applause for their warmth and proficiency, help make the place a success at what it offers. Emma Duggan's kitchen celebrates the pick of English regional produce, on show in starters such as asparagus with Bottisham smoked ham and a soft-boiled egg, or razor clams with peas, broad beans and gremolata, followed by the likes of Portland crab risotto with radicchio and basil, or a something-for-everyone dish of slow-roast pork belly with spiced greens and chorizo in cockle and cider cream. Finish with Eton mess, or buttermilk pannacotta and rhubarb compote. Wines start at £18.50, or £5 a glass, for a southern French Grenache-Syrah blend. The restaurant hasn't returned our questionnaire, so details below should be checked.
Chef/s: Emma Duggan. **Open:** Tue to Fri and Sun L 12 to 3 (4 Sun), Wed to Sat D 6 to 9.30. **Closed:** Mon, 25 Dec to 3 Jan. **Meals:** alc (main courses £12 to £17). Sun L £23 (3 courses). **Details:** 50 seats. Wheelchair access.

NEW ENTRY
A. Wong
A little Chinese gem in Victoria
70 Wilton Road, Victoria, SW1V 1DE
Tel no: (020) 7828 8931
www.awong.co.uk
⊖ Victoria, map 3
Chinese | £25
Cooking score: 4

£30

Victoria is an unlikely spot for an ambitious Chinese restaurant, but Andrew Wong's venture, set inside a modern and easy-going space, is a little gem. The menu is short, with dim sum at lunchtime, a tasting menu and cooking from an open-plan kitchen. A creative streak is shown from the off: witness an egg that has been tea-smoked at 63 degrees to maintain a runny yolk 'rather than the duller hard-boiled version you come across in China'. Next up, five-spiced smoked cod cheeks will jump-start any palate, while poached razor clam with sea cucumber and wind-dried sausage is a thrilling balance of textures. Applause, too, for the meringue snowball with lychee granita and mango purée. Food is slow coming out of the kitchen and portions are quite small, but the best dishes are big-league Chinese cooking without the price tag. Staff make every effort to be accommodating. Wines start at £14.
Chef/s: Andrew Wong. **Open:** Tue to Sat L 12 to 2.30, Mon to Sat D 5.30 to 10.30. **Closed:** Sun, 23 to 28 Dec. **Meals:** alc (main courses £7 to £12). Set L and D £12.95. Tasting menu £38.88 (8 courses). **Details:** 80 seats. 10 seats outside. Separate bar. Wheelchair access.

Symbols

🛏 Accommodation is available

£30 Three courses for less than £30

V Separate vegetarian menu

£5 OFF £5-off voucher scheme

🍶 Notable wine list

The Anchor & Hope
Hearty stuff from a foodie boozer
36 The Cut, South Bank, SE1 8LP
Tel no: (020) 7928 9898
⊖ Waterloo, Southwark, map 5
British | £25
Cooking score: 3

£30

An asset to the Waterloo area, the cooking at the Anchor & Hope celebrates British earthiness – the dishes are plain and unadulterated – and it does not go unnoticed that physically the dining area has the same attributes. The food struck an instant chord when the pub opened a decade ago, and the unbuttoned atmosphere suits it down to the ground. You can't book (except Sunday lunch) and you may have to share a table, but who cares when there's the prospect of huge helpings of cod brandade or duck hearts on toast to tuck into? Ingredients are all, given centre-stage prominence in the likes of slow-roast Middle White with smoked sausage, new potato and kale or seven-hour lamb shoulder. Desserts range from the traditional treacle tart to Muscat caramel custard. Wines from £15.
Chef/s: Jonathan Jones. **Open:** Tue to Sat L 12 to 2.30, Sun L 2 (1 sitting), Mon to Sat D 6 to 10.30. **Closed:** Christmas through New Year, bank hols. **Meals:** alc (main courses £11 to £24). Sun L £32. **Details:** 80 seats. 20 seats outside. Separate bar. Wheelchair access.

Angels and Gypsies
Take a pew for saintly tapas
33 Camberwell Church Street, Camberwell, SE5 8TR
Tel no: (020) 7703 5984
www.angelsandgypsies.com
map 1
Spanish | £30
Cooking score: 2

🛏

'Well-cooked, well-judged portion sizes, attentive service, definitely worth a return visit,' summed up a reporter after a visit to this modern Spanish tapas restaurant on the

ground floor of a boutique hotel. Brick walls, pews, old chapel chairs, atmospheric lighting and modern stained glass set the scene. The authentic food packs a punch and the bold décor matches the statements on the plate. A plate of Teruel ham, Galician chorizo in Basque hard cider or patatas pobres – sliced potatoes with sweet pepper and garlic – are among the more familiar items, whereas seared rabbit fillet with chickpeas, cumin and Moroccan chouk chouka (peppers, garlic and tomatoes) or Peterhead cod with celeriac, Manchego cheese and olive oil really catch the eye, as does macadamia nut cheesecake with nut brittle. A short list of mainly Iberian, South American and French wines opens at £17.95.
Chef/s: J Raido. **Open:** all week L 12 to 3 (3.30 Sat, 4 Sun), D 6 to 10.30 (11 Fri and Sat). **Closed:** 24 and 25 Dec, 1 Jan. **Meals:** alc (tapas £5 to £11). Set D £28 to £32 (3 tapas + dessert). **Details:** 50 seats.

ALSO RECOMMENDED
▲ L'Auberge
22 Upper Richmond Road, Putney, SW15 2RX
Tel no: (020) 8874 3593
www.ardillys.com
⊖ East Putney, map 3
French

Locals love this husband-and-wife-run bistro for its old-fashioned feel and proper French food. The solid wooden tables and chairs and motherly care of Madame Ardilly in the dining room are reassuring, and Monsieur Ardilly's renditions of foie gras torchon with sweet apple compote (£8.95) and a sweet/sour pavé of venison (£17.50) are perfect for nostalgic Francophiles. Puds are worth a look – chocolate moelleux (£6.95) is marvellously sweet and gooey. If you can, stretch beyond the house wine (£15.95), which is distinctly budget. Tue to Sat D only.

Babur
Classy surrounds, creative cooking
119 Brockley Rise, Forest Hill, SE23 1JP
Tel no: (020) 8291 2400
www.babur.info
map 1
Indian | £26
Cooking score: 2
£5 OFF   £30 ▼

Classy looking Babur goes where most suburban Indian restaurants fear to tread, the creative kitchen moving beyond the usual high-street clichés into adventurous modern Indian cuisine. As can be seen with a starter of clove-smoked lamb chops cooked in the tandoor and served with roasted garlic yoghurt, the cooking shows great respect for tradition but brings a measure of inventiveness. Creativity is given full rein in main courses such as seared Gressingham duck breast with sweet-and-sour plum sauce and carrot mash, but more conventional sounding alternatives might be lamb biryani served with boondi raita. Desserts include caramelised pineapple tarte Tatin with vanilla gelato. Wines are well chosen to go with the spicy food, with excellent recommendations by the glass for each dish. House wines from £19.25.
Chef/s: Jiwan Lal. **Open:** all week L 12 to 2.30 (4 Sun), D 6 to 11.30. **Closed:** 25 and 26 Dec. **Meals:** alc (main courses £12 to £17). Sun L £12.95 (buffet). **Details:** 72 seats.

READERS RECOMMEND
The Begging Bowl
Thai
168 Bellenden Road, Peckham, SE15 4BW
Tel no: (020) 7635 2627
www.thebeggingbowl.co.uk
'Such a boon for Peckham, serving really authentic Thai food; I had a coconut and galangal soup that was deliciously fragrant. Be prepared to queue; it's popular!'

Bistro Union
Straight-talking British bistro
40 Abbeville Road, Clapham, SW4 9NG
Tel no: (020) 7042 6400
www.bistrounion.co.uk
⊖ Clapham South, map 3
British | £23
Cooking score: 2
£30

A casually garbed, straight-talking kid brother to auspicious Trinity (see entry), Adam Byatt's mustard-fronted Bistro Union makes its case with reclaimed furniture, easy vibes, likeable prices and bags of British oomph in the kitchen. Perch at the all-day bar with a pint of Freedom organic lager and a black pudding and apple pasty fresh from the oven, or grab a table for something more filling. Salmon is smoked upstairs or you might begin with a bowl of potato, parsley and garlic soup; after that try fish pie, toad-in-the-hole with Guinness onions or cod with shrimps and capers. Still hungry? Why not order rhubarb trifle or a scoop of Eccles cake ice cream. A 500ml carafe of house wine is £12.50.
Chef/s: Karl Goward. **Open:** all week L 12 to 3 (11 to 3 Sun, 11 to 4 Sun), Mon to Sat D 6 to 10. **Closed:** 23 to 27 Dec. **Meals:** alc (main courses £10 to £24). Set L and D Mon to Fri £14 (2 courses) to £18. **Details:** 32 seats. 12 seats outside.

★ READERS' RESTAURANT OF THE YEAR ★
LONDON

Boqueria Tapas
Sparklingly fresh, authentic tapas
192 Acre Lane, Brixton, SW2 5UL
Tel no: (020) 7733 4408
www.boqueriatapas.com
⊖ Clapham North, Brixton, map 3
Spanish | £25
Cooking score: 3
£5 OFF £30

Both Clapham and Brixton foodies are claiming this trendy Acre Lane tapas bar as their own. Boqueria Tapas, named after Barcelona's renowned food market, wouldn't look out of place in the style-conscious Catalan capital. At the front is an appealing bar – with room to eat or sink a caña or two – and there's an attractive, contemporary dining room at the back. The extensive menu offers a pleasing mix of traditional tapas and more unusual items, with plenty more on the specials board. Of the classics, it's the ham croquetas, the arroz negro (black rice with squid and mussels) and the cured meats that are oft recommended, with special mention for the suckling pig, a creative dish with sweet potato crisps, apple sauce and lemon sorbet. Don't overlook dessert: the homemade crema catalana is excellent. Staff are 'charming' and bursting with enthusiasm for the all-Spanish wine list (from £16).
Chef/s: Jose Luis Gil. **Open:** Sat L 12.30 to 3.30, Sun L 12 to 5, all week D 5 to 11 (12 Fri and Sat). **Closed:** 25 and 26 Dec, 1 Jan. **Meals:** alc (tapas £4 to £11). **Details:** 80 seats. Separate bar. Wheelchair access.

Canton Arms
Revitalised local boozer
177 South Lambeth Road, Stockwell, SW8 1XP
Tel no: (020) 7582 8710
www.cantonarms.com
⊖ Stockwell, map 3
Modern British | £22
Cooking score: 1
£30

Recast and revitalised as a pub with sociable foodie aspirations, this new-age boozer now brightens up a scruffy stretch of South Lambeth Road with its rollicking bar and cosy dining room out back. Blood-red walls, shelves of books, polished panelling and jars full of chutney suggest the Canton Arms is courting the affluent local crowd, and the Med-influenced menu is spot-on for fashion-conscious appetites. Squid with tomatoes and garlic on toast; caponata with baked egg and watercress; braised rabbit legs with chorizo, red peppers and aïoli; Muscat crème caramel . . . say no more. Wines from £14. See overleaf for details.

Chef/s: Trish Hilforty. **Open:** Tue to Sun L 12 to 2.30 (4 Sun), Mon to Sat D 6 to 10. **Closed:** 25 and 26 Dec, 31 Dec and 1 Jan, bank hols. **Meals:** alc (main courses £10 to £16). **Details:** 60 seats. 40 seats outside. Separate bar.

Chapters All Day Dining
User-friendly neighbourhood brasserie
43-45 Montpelier Vale, Blackheath, SE3 0TJ
Tel no: (020) 8333 2666
www.chaptersrestaurants.com
map 1
Modern British | £25
Cooking score: 3
£30

From extended breakfasts and brunch to family suppers and late cocktails, all-day food and drink is, obviously, the name of the game at this user-friendly Blackheath brasserie. Start the morning with pancakes, kippers or croque monsieur, keep the hunger pangs at bay with a warm salad of salt beef and green beans or go the whole hog with three courses from the flexible, democratic menu. The Josper grill makes easy work of Herefordshire ribeyes, Angus fillets, burgers, Barnsley chops and spatchcock chicken, but the choice also extends to charcuterie boards, smoked haddock fishcakes and tagliatelle with wild mushrooms. After that, indulge in a helping of warm rice pudding with caramelised pineapple. Putting on the style is second nature here (think Art Deco mirrors, exposed brickwork and views of the heath from floor-to-ceiling windows) and service 'always goes that extra mile' – particularly for special occasions. Wines start at £16.50 (£4.60 a glass).
Chef/s: Alex Tyndall. **Open:** all week 8am to 11pm (9 to 9 Sun). **Closed:** 2 to 4 Jan. **Meals:** alc (main courses £9 to £25). Set L £12.95 (2 courses) to £14.95. Set D £14.95 (2 courses) to £17.95. **Details:** 100 seats. 20 seats outside. Separate bar. Wheelchair access.

Chez Bruce
Big-hitting neighbourhood star
2 Bellevue Road, Wandsworth, SW17 7EG
Tel no: (020) 8672 0114
www.chezbruce.co.uk
⊖ Balham, map 3
Modern British | £45
Cooking score: 6
🍾

Bruce Poole's big-hitting neighbourhood star is not only a local eatery of the best sort, it's also a model of understatement. Wandsworth's foodies certainly appreciate having such an even-tempered, accommodating treasure on their doorsteps. The surroundings are tailored to conversational, dressed-down get-togethers, and the cooking pleases, excites and soothes in equal measure – witness a beautifully composed starter of oxtail with herb tortellini and chanterelles or grilled baby squid with potent, punchy sidekicks including brandade fritters, chickpeas, chorizo and piquillo peppers. Earthy rustic tones and big-city flavours also meet in plucky mains such as roast cod with olive oil mash and gremolata or hefty pot-roast pork with soft polenta, grilled endive, crisp pancetta and wild mushrooms. Standards remain sky-high: whether you're sampling the gloriously ripe cheeses, indulging in a textbook crème brûlée or trying the caramel and hazelnut mille-feuille with caramelised apples. A premier-league sommelier provides verbal notes for the staggeringly good, all-encompassing wine list: a triumph of diversity, style and quality with representatives from big names and lesser known regions. A goodly clutch of house selections starts at £11.50 a carafe (£4.50 a glass).
Chef/s: Matt Christmas. **Open:** all week L 12 to 2.30 (3 Sat and Sun), D 6.30 to 10 (10.30 Fri and Sat, 9.30 Sun). **Closed:** 24 to 26 Dec, 1 Jan. **Meals:** Set £23.50 (2 courses) to £27.50. Set D £34.50 (2 courses) to £45. Sun L £35. **Details:** 90 seats. Wheelchair access. Children at L only.

The Crooked Well

A hunky-dory home from home
16 Grove Lane, Camberwell, SE5 8SY
Tel no: (020) 7252 7798
www.thecrookedwell.com
map 1
Modern British | £30
Cooking score: 3
£5
OFF

Brought back to life in 2011, this formerly threadbare Camberwell boozer now looks hunky-dory with vintage lighting, mirrors, scrubbed floorboards and elegant toile de jouy wallpaper giving the bar/dining room a decidedly Art Deco vibe. It feels like a local home from home, with occasional jazz nights and film screenings, Sunday roasts for the whole family and a very accommodating menu full of busy, fashionable flavours. Graze on a plate of sautéed scallops with pickled salsify, chicken wing and butternut squash purée, order a generous helping of roast venison with red cabbage, confit celeriac, white pudding and pomegranate sauce or share the spoils from a gut-busting fish pie. After that, keep it sociable by requesting extra spoons for the hot chocolate pudding with caramel ice cream or go solo with spiced orange cake and orange mascarpone. Draught beers are in good order and the well-chosen wine list offers decent drinking from £14.75.
Chef/s: Matt Green-Armytage. **Open:** Tue to Sun L 12.30 to 3 (4 Sun), all week D 6.30 to 10 (10.30 Fri and Sat, 7 to 9.30 Sun). **Closed:** 24 to 30 Dec. **Meals:** alc (main courses £10 to £19). Set L £10 (2 courses). **Details:** 60 seats. 40 seats outside. Separate bar. Wheelchair access.

NEW ENTRY

The Dairy

Flavour-driven small plates at a pulsating Clapham honeypot
15 The Pavement, Clapham, SW4 0HY
Tel no: (020) 7622 4165
www.the-dairy.co.uk
⊖ Clapham Common, map 3
Modern British | £30
Cooking score: 4

V

'It's kind of like a neighbourhood version of Roganic' is praise indeed for this hip, pulsating Clapham honeypot. The Dairy attracts buzzing hordes intent on socialising and grazing on some seriously inventive small plates. A tiny front bar gives way to a low-lit bistro area, its reclaimed furniture embracing the chilled-out vibe. Menus – printed on brown paper – list light, modern, colourful plates driven by flavour and seasonality (with some produce plucked from the restaurant's own urban garden). Think charred leek, sorrel and crisp toasted bread partnering intensely flavoured smoked cod brandade, or perhaps perfectly pink Somerset lamb served with aubergine and squeaky fresh broad beans, followed by a salted-caramel chocolate dessert with malted barley ice cream ('the best thing I've eaten this year'). Homemade sourdough comes with 'amazing' smoked bone-marrow butter, while wines (from £18) have a European leaning.
Chef/s: Robin Gill. **Open:** Wed to Sun 12 to 11 (midnight Fri, 10am to midnight Sat, 10am Sun). Tue D 6 to 11. **Closed:** Mon, 23 to 31 Dec. **Meals:** alc (small plates £5 to £10). Tasting menu £40 (7 courses). **Details:** 35 seats. 12 seats outside. Separate bar. Wheelchair access.

Elliot's Café

On-trend foodie canteen
12 Stoney Street, Borough, SE1 9AD
Tel no: (020) 7403 7436
www.elliotscafe.com
⊖ London Bridge, map 1
British | £30
Cooking score: 1
£5 OFF

Though Elliot's isn't a 'destination dinner spot', you'd certainly be happy if you lived or worked close to this rough-hewn, easy-going canteen carved out of the Borough arches. Charming staff squeeze you in wherever they can and the place buzzes with folk enjoying seasonal food sourced from Borough Market: say, crab on toast, Middle White pork terrine or gurnard and chickpea cassoulet. Ox cheek and onion pie (for two) and slow-cooked Herdwick lamb (for three or four) are deeply satisfying rustic dishes, and there are 40-day-aged Longhorn steaks cooked on the wood-fired grill. It's all realistically priced and broadly successful. Wines from £23.
Chef/s: Matt Tarantini. **Open:** Mon to Sat L 12 to 3 (4 Sat), D 6 to 10. **Closed:** Sun, 1 week Christmas, bank hols. **Meals:** alc (main courses £12 to £35). **Details:** 32 seats. 8 seats outside. Separate bar.

Emile's

Long-serving Putney favourite
96-98 Felsham Road, Putney, SW15 1DQ
Tel no: (020) 8789 3323
www.emilesrestaurant.co.uk
⊖ Putney Bridge, map 3
Anglo-French | £30
Cooking score: 1
£5 OFF

In a residential street not far from Putney High Street, and spread across two Victorian buildings and three dining areas, Emil Fahmy and Andrew Sherlock's long-standing restaurant continues to bring some culinary savoir-faire to chain-ridden Putney. An all-embracing European-influenced menu offers everything from grilled cod cheeks with marinated artichoke hearts, smoked tomato

passata and garlic butter to venison meatballs on homemade noodles. If you can resist the never-off-the-menu beef Wellington, try escalope of veal teamed with a fried duck egg, capers, anchovy fillets and Savoy cabbage with caraway and cream. Desserts such as apple and almond meringue with mango sauce hit all the right spots. Wines from £15.75.
Chef/s: Andrew Sherlock. **Open:** Mon to Sat D only 7.30 to 11. **Closed:** Sun, 24 to 30 Dec, 2 Jan, Easter Sat, bank hols. **Meals:** Set D £26 (2 courses) to £29.50. **Details:** 90 seats.

Enoteca Turi

Italian oenophile heaven with an inspired regional menu
28 Putney High Street, Putney, SW15 1SQ
Tel no: (020) 8785 4449
www.enotecaturi.com
⊖ Putney Bridge, map 3
Italian | £39
Cooking score: 3
🍷

Turn up early or pray your guest is late at long-standing Putney restaurant, Enoteca Turi: you will need – or, rather, want – plenty of time to pore over the 300-bin wine list (and perhaps knock back that sneaky first glass). This is Italian oenophile heaven, with a thoughtfully annotated list (from £19.50) drawn from top to toe of 'the boot', and with major producers well represented. 'By-the-glass' recommendations aren't foisted on guests; they're discreetly marked on the inspired regional Italian menu. Giuseppe Turi himself is involved in the kitchen so you will feel the spirit of his native Puglia in homemade orecchiette with turnip tops, alongside influences from elsewhere in the form of, say, baked Sardinian artichoke with deep-fried egg and Parmesan, and guinea fowl breast with Savoy cabbage and 'pearà' (Veronese bread sauce). Dessert could be ricotta cake with candied fruit and hot chocolate sauce.
Chef/s: Giuseppe Turi. **Open:** Mon to Sat L 12 to 2.30, D 7 to 10.30 (11 Fri and Sat). **Closed:** Sun, 25 and 26 Dec, 1 Jan. **Meals:** alc (main courses £13 to

£29). Set L £17.50 (2 courses) to £20.50. Set D £27.50 (2 courses) to £32.50. **Details:** 85 seats. Wheelchair access.

ALSO RECOMMENDED
▲ Entrée
2 Battersea Rise, Battersea, SW11 1ED
Tel no: (020) 7223 5147
www.entreebattersea.co.uk
⊖ Clapham South, map 3
Modern European

From the low-lit piano bar to the smart restaurant upstairs, Entrée is a rollickingly informal spot: an elegant yet simply run operation. Eurozone-inspired dishes form the nerve centre, so take your pick from pork rillettes with apple jelly (£7.50) or scallop and crab lasagne with chive beurre blanc, then confit lamb shoulder with aubergine caviar, slow-roasted onions, squash and chickpeas (£17) and lemon posset with pear and saffron compote to finish. Wines from £19. Restaurant open Sat and Sun L, all week D.

▲ four o nine
409 Clapham Road, Clapham, SW9 9BT
Tel no: (020) 7737 0722
www.fouronine.co.uk
⊖ Clapham North, map 3
Modern European

Enter this much-loved neighbourhood gem speakeasy-style: find the door next to the Clapham North pub, ring to be let in, climb stairs that lead to a terrace and head for the entrance. Inside there's a relaxed vibe and a kitchen that pumps out an inventive take on modern brasserie food: perhaps wild rabbit fricassee with spinach gnocchi, black olives and tomato fondue (£7.50), roast venison haunch (£19) or pork tenderloin stuffed with Clonakilty black pudding, then apple and pear crumble with salted-caramel ice cream. Wines from £22. Open Sat and Sun L, all week D.

The Fox & Grapes
Cut-above pub classics
9 Camp Road, Wimbledon, SW19 4UN
Tel no: (020) 8619 1300
www.foxandgrapeswimbledon.co.uk
⊖ Wimbledon, map 1
British | £35
Cooking score: 2

Like many of its cousins in the capital, this prettily located (just off the Common) neighbourhood pub takes a dressed-down, casual approach to things, with wood floors, polished tables and no standing on ceremony. The proprietor may be French chef Claude Bosi (Hibiscus, see entry) – with his brother Cedric managing day-to-day affairs – but earthy British pub food is what you get, perhaps with the odd brioche, sauce gribiche or cod brandade thrown in for good measure. Game terrine has been praised, as has a 'divine' bulgur wheat and goats' cheese cannelloni, and there's satisfaction to be had in a steak pie with a suet crust, roast hake and roasted cauliflower with capers and lemon-dressed baby gem, and good old treacle tart with clotted cream. Wines from £19.
Chef/s: Stephen Gadd. Open: Mon to Sat L 12 to 3, D 6 to 9.30. Sun 12 to 8. Closed: 25 Dec. Meals: alc (main courses £11 to £32). Details: 90 seats. Wheelchair access.

Franklins
Hugely likeable veteran bistro
157 Lordship Lane, East Dulwich, SE22 8HX
Tel no: (020) 8299 9598
www.franklinsrestaurant.com
map 1
British | £28
Cooking score: 2

Everybody has a good word to say about Franklins; indeed, some reckon there's no place like it. With a pared-back interior of wood and reclaimed furniture, and vigorously championed great British produce, this veteran bistro certainly puts on a convincing

show. Menus scream seasonal credentials: in March via the likes of Jerusalem artichokes, tomatoes, lamb's lettuce and goats' curd; in May through Synfield Farm asparagus and sauce gribiche. Simple presentations capture the essence of the main ingredient: ox tongue with chicory and bacon, or hake with mussels, fennel and saffron potatoes. Puddings carry on the theme of simplicity, with chocolate and Guinness cake. Wines from £14.50.
Chef/s: Ralf Wittig. **Open:** all week 12 to 11 (midnight Thur and Fri, 10am to midnight Sat, 10.30pm Sun). **Closed:** 25 and 26 Dec, 1 Jan. **Meals:** alc (main courses £13 to £21). Set L £13.95 (2 courses) to £16.95. **Details:** 72 seats. 30 seats outside. Separate bar. Wheelchair access.

Harrison's
Reinvigorated local brasserie
15-19 Bedford Hill, Balham, SW12 9EX
Tel no: (020) 8675 6900
www.harrisonsbalham.co.uk
⊖ Balham, map 3
Modern British | £28
Cooking score: 1
£5 OFF   £30

'Great atmosphere . . . nice to have somewhere so smart as a neighbourhood restaurant . . . new energy injected with a cocktail bar downstairs.' That's one verdict on Sam Harrison's reinvigorated local, a sibling of Sam's Brasserie in Chiswick (see entry). Harrison's continues to draw the Balham crowd with reasonable prices and a tried-and-trusted repertoire of breakfast staples (served 9am to 12) and brasserie classics. The kitchen belts out wild boar Scotch eggs, salt-and-pepper squid and fish soup, as well as robust versions of Goan fish curry, Welsh rarebit pork chop with braised red cabbage and caramelised apples, and a very good chocolate and pistachio fondant. Wines from £16.50.
Chef/s: Faycal Khiat. **Open:** all week L 12 to 4, D 6 to 10.30 (10 Sun). **Closed:** 24 to 26 Dec. **Meals:** alc (main courses £12 to £21). Set L and D £13.50 (2 courses) to £16.50. Sun L £21.50. **Details:** 90 seats. 12 seats outside. Separate bar. Wheelchair access.

The Hill
Mediterranean
89 Royal Hill, Greenwich, SE10 8SE
Tel no: (020) 8691 3626
www.thehillgreenwich.com
'I had scallops, followed by a delicious mushroom risotto; my son had ham croquettes, followed by rack of lamb, which was cooked just as he likes it and he was very satisfied.'

Inside
Stylish, buzzy neighbourhood bistro
19 Greenwich South Street, Greenwich, SE10 8NW
Tel no: (020) 8265 5060
www.insiderestaurant.co.uk
⊖ Greenwich, map 1
Modern European | £31
Cooking score: 2

Guy Awford's intimate neighbourhood restaurant has been a fixture on the Greenwich dining scene for 14 years. It's reliable, familiar and unchallenging in equal measure, and locals treat it as a place to sup or to celebrate – the hubbub of happy diners is all-pervading. First-class materials underpin the operation, from starters of beech-smoked salmon with butternut squash pancake, sour cream, dill and orange, or cod, lemon and parsley fishcakes, to successful mains of roast Barbary duck breast served with parsnips, spiced red cabbage and white bean, orange and chorizo casserole, or sea bass with chive mash, garlic spinach, fine beans and tomato coulis. Desserts stay on standard territory with treacle tart, chocolate and pecan brownie, and apple and rhubarb crumble. Wines from £16.50.
Chef/s: Guy Awford and Brian Sargeant. **Open:** Tue to Sun L 12 to 2.30 (3 Sat and Sun), Tue to Sat D 6.30 to 10.30 (11 Fri and Sat). **Closed:** Mon, 24 to 26 Dec. **Meals:** alc (main courses £14 to £20). Set L £12.95 (2 courses) to £17.95. Set D £19.95 (2 courses) to £24.95. Sun L £18.95 (2 courses) to £23.95. **Details:** 40 seats. Wheelchair access.

José

Stand up for triumphantly simple tapas
104 Bermondsey Street, Bermondsey, SE1 3UB
Tel no: (020) 7403 4902
www.josepizarro.com
⊖ **London Bridge, Borough, map 1**
Spanish | £25
Cooking score: 3
£30

José Pizarro was all set to become a dentist at the outset of his career when a life in gastronomy suddenly felt the more intuitive choice. London's Spanish scene would certainly have been the poorer if a life of root-canal work had won out, as this vibrant, bustling tapas-and-sherry joint near London Bridge volubly demonstrates. On ambience alone, you could be somewhere in the middle of Madrid, as little plates of boquerones in cava vinegar, hake in allioli, albondigas, croquetas and Marcona almonds mount up around you. The jamón and chorizo are sourced from a fine producer, and there is, of course, plenty of Jeréz's finest to go at in the drinking stakes. Lighter, drier sherries are very much drunk like white table-wine in Spain, and some of Lustau's most tempting bottlings are offered. Otherwise, choose from the short Spanish wine list, which opens with a Viura and a Cabernet-Bobal blend at £19.50.
Chef/s: José Pizarro. **Open:** all week 12 to 10.30 (5.30pm Sun). **Meals:** alc (tapas £4 to £10). **Details:** 17 seats. Wheelchair access.

Lamberts

Good-natured local asset
2 Station Parade, Balham High Road, Balham, SW12 9AZ
Tel no: (020) 8675 2233
www.lambertsrestaurant.com
⊖ **Balham, map 3**
Modern British | £32
Cooking score: 2
£5 OFF

'A great place to go for seasonal British food done well' thought one reader, who also enjoyed the 'casual, welcoming ambience' of this popular neighbourhood eatery. With a sure hand at the stove, the straightforward cooking relies on high-quality raw materials, and reporters have particularly liked the good-value set lunch, heaping praise on 'delicious' venison tartare, mackerel with radish and cucumber, and sea bream with spinach. Applause, too, for an April dinner that highlighted Herdwick lamb rump with Jerusalem artichokes, anchovy potato cake and wild garlic, and fillet of hake with parsnip purée, Shetland Black potatoes and mussel and cherry tomato vinaigrette. As for dessert, the simple unfussy approach extends to hot chocolate pudding with stout ice cream. The global wine list opens at £18.
Chef/s: Ryan Lowery. **Open:** Tue to Sun L 12.30 to 2.30 (12 to 5 Sun), Tue to Sat D 6 to 10. **Closed:** Mon, 25 and 26 Dec. **Meals:** alc (main courses £14 to £21). Set L £15 (2 courses) to £18. Midweek set D £17 (2 courses) to £20. Sun L £24. **Details:** 53 seats. 8 seats outside.

The Lawn Bistro

The perfect bistro
67 High Street, Wimbledon Village, Wimbledon, SW19 5EE
Tel no: (020) 8947 8278
www.thelawnbistro.co.uk
⊖ **Wimbledon, map 3**
Modern British | £38
Cooking score: 3
£5 OFF

With its wood floor, bare tables and neutral tones, Lawn Bistro achieves a stylish informality, projecting itself as a smart-casual sort of place. It has also become a foodie hot spot, for there's something reassuring about Ollie Couillaud's simple, well-prepared food with its penchant for strong French flavours and keen eye on the season. Starters range from a well-reported 'rustic slab of foie gras with hunks of toast' to beautifully presented crisp fillet of mackerel with crushed celeriac, spiced pear and smoked bacon salad. Main courses often appear with classic flavour combinations, as in a 'wonderfully flavoured' veal fillet with mushrooms and spätzle or rump of lamb and sweetbreads with shallot purée, croquette potatoes and rosemary jus, while dessert could be a Valrhona chocolate fondant with caramel ice cream and honeycomb. Wines from £19.50. Lawn Bakery, at 9 High Street, is a bakery/café offshoot for breakfast, lunch and afternoon tea.

Chef/s: Ollie Couillaud. **Open:** all week L 12 to 2.30 (3 Sun), Mon to Sat D 6.30 to 10.30. **Closed:** 25 and 26 Dec, 1 Jan. **Meals:** Set L £19.50 (2 courses) to £22.50. Set D £32.50 (2 courses) to £37.50. Sun L £29.50. **Details:** 69 seats. Separate bar.

ALSO RECOMMENDED
▲ The Lido Cafe

Brockwell Park, Dulwich Road, Herne Hill, SE24 0PA
Tel no: (020) 7737 8183
www.thelidocafe.co.uk
⊖ Brixton, map 1
Modern British

Found in the grounds of Brockwell Lido, this laid-back café is a 'really nice airy space', but can get 'a bit chock-a-block with mums and kids', according to one mum-with-kids reporter. Go for the candlelit dinner (Wed to Sat) if you prefer food without children on the side. Breakfast keeps the passing crowds replenished, but the café peaks at lunch when the menu deals in salads, charcuterie (from £6.95), char-grilled chicken and very good burgers (£10), as well as desserts like cardamom and pistachio tart. Wines from £18.50. Open all week.

▲ Lobster Pot

3 Kennington Lane, Elephant and Castle, SE11 4RG
Tel no: (020) 7582 5556
www.lobsterpotrestaurant.co.uk
⊖ Kennington, map 1
Seafood £5 OFF

Famed for its longevity as well as its eccentricity, Hervé Regent's Breton-themed surreal maritime old-timer is stuffed with nets, lifebelts, portholes and memorabilia. Menus are dictated by the markets and the

weather, but big platters of fruits de mer are the stars – closely followed by oysters gratinée with Champagne sauce (£11.50), bouillabaisse or skate with brown butter and capers (£19.50). Steaks and stews satisfy the carnivores. House French is £19.50. Closed Sun and Mon. Hervé's sons now run Toulouse Lautrec – a jazz bar/brasserie next door.

Lola Rojo

Creative contemporary tapas
78 Northcote Road, Battersea, SW11 6QL
Tel no: (020) 7350 2262
www.lolarojo.net
⊖ Clapham South, map 3
Spanish | £25
Cooking score: 2
£30

A passionate exponent of Spanish 'nueva cocina', Lola Rojo is on a mission to reinvent traditional tapas for today's inquisitive palates. Sit in the pretty dining room or the dinky wraparound terrace and pick from a menu that has no truck with tired westernised clichés. Instead, explore the delights of spicy chorizo lollipops with quince alioli, venison and Rioja stew with pumpkin purée or grilled sardines with Iberian bacon and smoked aubergine. Charcuterie, cheeses and paellas also feature, along with teasing desserts such as white chocolate soup with mango sorbet and red wine granita. A notable list of sherries and Spanish wines starts at £16 (£4 a glass). The owners also run Rosita – a jamón and sherry bar at 124 Northcote Road, tel (020) 7998 9093.

Chef/s: Antonio Belles. **Open:** Mon to Thur L 12 to 3, D 6 to 10.30. Fri to Sun 12 to 10.30. **Closed:** 25 and 26 Dec. **Meals:** alc (tapas £5 to £12). **Details:** 50 seats. 17 seats outside.

▮▮ Also Recommended
Also recommended entries are not scored but we think they are worth a visit.

Magdalen

Sophisticated, robust comfort food in a handsome bistro
152 Tooley Street, Southwark, SE1 2TU
Tel no: (020) 7403 1342
www.magdalenrestaurant.co.uk
⊖ London Bridge, map 1
Modern British | £34
Cooking score: 3

James Faulks's 'careful and intelligent' approach comes in for warm praise at this handsome London Bridge bistro. His is just the tack to take with the hearty and robust ingredients he often favours. It's not unusual to find a pie, offal and a handful of braises on the Magdalen menu, but Faulks's finesse keeps them at the sophisticated end of the comfort food spectrum. White tablecloths and blood-red walls present a dramatic backdrop. Modern British, Spanish and Italian dishes sit happily together on balanced, seasonal menus where Devon crab mayonnaise or cuttlefish and chickpeas might precede oxtail and polenta or fish stew with aïoli. Choose patriotically and have rhubarb trifle for pudding or take the French route with classic crème caramel. The carefully chosen, predominantly European wine list rises from a baseline of £21 in pleasingly small increments.
Chef/s: James Faulks. **Open:** Mon to Fri L 12 to 2.30, Mon to Sat D 6.30 to 10. **Closed:** Sun, 22 Dec to 3 Jan, bank hols. **Meals:** alc (main courses £14 to £23). Set L £15.50 (2 courses) to £18.50. **Details:** 80 seats. 4 seats outside. Wheelchair access.

ALSO RECOMMENDED

▲ Meza
34 Trinity Road, Tooting, SW17 7RE
Tel no: (07722) 111299
⊖ Tooting Bec, map 3
Lebanese

'What they do, they certainly do well,' comments a regular to this simple, honest and very tight-packed Lebanese pit-stop. Indeed, with just five tables, you need to book well in advance but there is always the take-away option. Open all day from noon, a hardworking kitchen sends out exemplary hummus (£3.25) and falafel, and everyone praises the minced lamb skewer with hot tomato sauce (£9) and the grilled baby chicken. Wine is Lebanese red, white or rose (£15). Closed Mon. Cash only.

READERS RECOMMEND

M1lk
Modern British
20 Bedford Hill, Balham, SW12 9RG
www.m1lk.co.uk
'Expect queues around the block, but it's worth it for the amazing breakfasts, including Kurdish baked eggs, and brilliant coffee.'

NEW ENTRY

No. 67

Laid-back gallery restaurant
South London Gallery, 67 Peckham Road, Peckham, SE5 8UH
Tel no: (020) 7252 7649
www.number67.co.uk
⊖ Peckham Rye, map 1
Modern European | £24
Cooking score: 1
£30

Appended to the South London Gallery, this ultra-relaxed spot is café by day and – later in the week – restaurant by night. Take a seat in the cosy main room or an airy space that leads into gardens at the back; out front, tables by the busy A202 are strictly for the determined. A short menu changes frequently and doesn't overreach itself. To start, the salt of cured tuna might be balanced by sweet grilled peppers. Follow it with cod with tomatoes and olives and lashings of shellfish sauce, and a 'dinner party' dessert like boozy chocolate mousse. The wine is from £16, but the boon for Peckhamites is priceless.
Chef/s: Nick Hardman. **Open:** Sun and Tue 8am to 6.30pm (10am Sun), Wed to Sat 8am to 11pm (10am Sat). **Closed:** Mon, 24 Dec to 2 Jan. **Meals:** alc (main courses £12 to £14). **Details:** 44 seats. 28 seats outside. Wheelchair access.

▌▌▌ JASON ATHERTON
Pollen Street Social

Why do you think food and cooking has become so fashionable?
Simple food is now very important to our way of life. We share meals together, we love to eat, and we use food to socialise.

The most underrated ingredient is...
Cabbage. I love it! Crazy, I know.

What's a common mistake that lets chefs down?
Not being humble.

Who do you think is the chef to watch in 2014?
Ollie Dabbous.

Which restaurant best sums up British cooking today?
There are many, but I love what Tom Kerridge is doing at the Hand & Flowers, Marlow. It's amazing, and so British.

Which out-of-the-way restaurant is worth the trip?
Sat Bains, Nottingham. You have to be crazy not to go there.

At the end of a long day, what do you like to cook?
Cornflakes.

NEW ENTRY

The Palmerston
A solid dining-pub that's on the up
91 Lordship Lane, East Dulwich, SE22 8EP
Tel no: (020) 8693 1629
www.thepalmerston.net
map 1
Modern British | £28
Cooking score: 1
£5 OFF £30 ▼

A solid corner pub, The Palmerston is a Lordship Lane stalwart, and reports suggest it keeps getting better. Regulars, however, urge it to 'go the whole hog' with softer lighting and food-centred service to complete the atmosphere in the appealing wood-panelled dining room. Here, Jamie Younger's European-inflected dishes include beer-battered courgette flowers oozing mozzarella, basil and anchovy, and roast pork tenderloin with 'just right' Gorgonzola polenta, gremolata and asparagus. Pudding might be fig and almond tart with 'superb' homemade buttermilk ice cream, or a chocolate marquise with oat and white chocolate cookies. House wine £16.
Chef/s: Jamie Younger. **Open:** all week L 12 to 2.30 (3 Sat, 3.30 Sun), D 7 to 10 (9.30 Sun). **Closed:** 25 to 27 Dec. **Meals:** alc (main courses £14 to £19.50) Set L £13 (2 courses) to £16.75. **Details:** 56 seats. 24 seats outside.

Pizarro
Thrilling fare from a Spanish food hero
194 Bermondsey Street, Southwark, SE1 3TQ
Tel no: (020) 7378 9455
www.josepizarro.com
⊖ London Bridge, Borough, map 1
Spanish | £30
Cooking score: 4

The tapas and sherry formula continues to be a hit with Londoners, and José Pizarro's laid-back venue in the trendy London Bridge catchment area is a-bubble with enthusiastic devotees. The chef himself is an evangelising author and regular TV presence, and offers an unswervingly authentic version of Spanish

cocina. Prawns with flat mushrooms, jamón and chilli, or sweetbreads in mustard mayonnaise, fire up the taste-buds, and might lead to cod with white beans, beef cheeks and celeriac or a fruity presentation of duck breast with pears and orange. Daily specials are chalked on the blackboard, and on weekdays, there's a top-value *menú del día*, offering the likes of cuttlefish and prawns with black rice, halibut with spinach and anchovies, and Santiago tart with yoghurt ice cream. A compact wine list does a whirlwind rip through the Spanish regions, not forgetting excellent cavas and sherries. Prices open at £19, or £6.50 for a 25cl carafe.
Chef/s: José Pizarro. **Open:** Mon to Fri L 12 to 3, D 6 to 11. Sat 10 to 11, Sun 10 to 10. **Closed:** 24 to 27 Dec. **Meals:** alc (main courses £12 to £16). Mon to Fri Set L £17 (2 courses) to £20. **Details:** 80 seats. Separate bar. Wheelchair access.

Le Pont de la Tour
Old-fashioned French favourite
36d Shad Thames, Bermondsey, SE1 2YE
Tel no: (020) 7403 8403
www.lepontdelatour.com
⊖ Tower Hill, London Bridge, map 1
Modern French | £45
Cooking score: 1

Beyond the (often packed) bar and grill is a more formal, white-clothed restaurant and a terrace whose stunning view of the Thames and Tower Bridge is Le Pont de la Tour's strongest card. The kitchen deals in conservative French food: plateau de fruits de mer, grilled Dover sole, roast beef fillet with pommes noisette, morel and Madeira sauce. The bar and grill wins more support for its good-value set deals than does the restaurant's à la carte, where prices invite sterner scrutiny, but the food is well executed and comfortably old-fashioned. Slick French staff give it all a certain polished charm. The wine list is a buff's delight, packed full of interesting bottles including Old World classics and New World stars. Prices start at £19.50 but rocket skyward too quickly.

Chef/s: Tom Cook. **Open:** all week L 12 to 3 (4 Sat and Sun), D 6 to 11 (10 Sun). **Closed:** 1 Jan. **Meals:** Set L and D £15 (2 courses) to £20. **Details:** 150 seats. 150 seats outside. Separate bar. Wheelchair access.

NEW ENTRY
Restaurant Story
Never-ending story
201 Tooley Street, Bermondsey, SE1 2UE
Tel no: (020) 7183 2117
www.restaurantstory.co.uk
⊖ London Bridge, map 1
Modern European | £45
Cooking score: 5

Tom Sellers' high-achieving, hard-edged Scandi-style Bermondsey restaurant tells its own story. Purpose built on the site of a demolished Victorian lavatory, its full-drop windows allow you to admire the view of the Shard – but also allows passers-by to admire you. Sellers has worked for Tom Aikens (London, see entry), Thomas Keller (Per Se, New York), René Redzepi (Noma, Copenhagen), and Adam Byatt (Trinity, London, see entry), and his thrill-inducing six- or ten-course tasting menus (delivered to table in an old book) are built around little platefuls of radical ideas, nostalgia and obscure ingredients. The story theme may seem pretentious, but the nursery rhyme-style bread and dripping candle and its four Mad Hatter-esque snacks (including an afternoon tea-style rabbit sandwich) have really captured readers' imagination, ditto the Goldilocks 'three bears' porridge and the Tunnock's dark chocolate teacake served with coffee. Other highlights have included: burnt onions and skins with apple, various foraged buds and leaves and a superb gin-and-thyme laced consommé; a light, buttery mash of heritage potatoes topped with asparagus heads, shavings, barley grass and a terrific coal oil dressing; and a wonderfully flavoured pigeon breast with pungent white summer truffle shavings enhancing the gamey flavour. Once you've acclimatised to the full on, rapid delivery service, this Story does 'live on in the memory'. Wines from £24.

Chef/s: Tom Sellers. **Open:** Tues to Sat L 12 to 2, D 6.30 to 9. **Closed:** Sun, Mon, 2 weeks Christmas. **Meals:** Set L and D £45 (6 courses) to £65. **Details:** 40 seats. Separate bar. Wheelchair access.

Rick's Restaurant

Tiny Tooting treasure
122 Mitcham Road, Tooting, SW17 9NH
Tel no: (020) 8767 5219
www.ricks-restaurant.co.uk
⊖ Tooting Broadway, map 3
Modern European | £30
Cooking score: 1

The hugely likeable Rick's is quite a local asset. With its reasonable prices, flexible menu, well-timed service and informal atmosphere, it feels just right. There are some very good things to eat here: small plates of stuffed piquillo peppers with sardines and egg or jamón croquettes with garlic mayo, platters of charcuterie and main courses of seared skirt of beef with peppercorn sauce or mussels with fries. Praise, too, for chocolate brownie with mascarpone as 'a good way to finish'. The set-lunch menu is fantastic value and the global wine list opens at £14.75.

Chef/s: Ricardo Gibbs. **Open:** Tue to Fri L 12 to 3, Mon to Fri D 6 to 11 (10 Mon). Sat and Sun 10am to 11pm (9pm Sun). **Closed:** 25 and 26 Dec, 1 Jan. **Meals:** alc (main courses £9 to £27). Set L £10. Sun L £12.50. **Details:** 38 seats.

Roast

Valiant British foodie patriot
Floral Hall, Stoney Street, Southwark, SE1 1TL
Tel no: (0845) 034 7300
www.roast-restaurant.com
⊖ London Bridge, map 1
British | £40
Cooking score: 2

V

Synonymous with new-Brit foodie patriotism, jam-packed Roast makes the most of a fabulous location above the gastronomic

melee of Borough Market. High decibels and equally lofty prices reflect the touristy allure of the old Floral Hall, but there's no disputing the valiant intent behind it all. The kitchen plucks the best from artisan producers across the land – so check the Roast 'roll of honour' to discover where it originated. The seasonal haul might bring Wye Valley asparagus soup with Herefordshire goats' curd ahead of Goosnargh guinea fowl pie with Bath Pig chorizo, Jersey Royal hash and white sprouting broccoli, with buttermilk pudding and poached Sussex strawberries to finish. Business breakfasts and family Sunday roasts are, unsurprisingly, a sell-out. Drinks also champion the British cause, with wines from £22.

Chef/s: Marcus Verberne. **Open:** Mon to Sat L 12 to 3.45, D 5.30 to 10.45 (6 Sat). Sun 11.30 to 6.30. **Closed:** 25 Dec and 26 Dec, 1 Jan. **Meals:** alc (main courses £16 to £35). Set L and D £30. Sun L £35. **Details:** 120 seats. Separate bar. Wheelchair access.

NEW ENTRY

The Rooftop Café

Quirky rooftop bolthole with gutsy cooking
The Exchange, 28 London Bridge Street, London Bridge, SE1 9SG
Tel no: (020) 3102 3770
www.theexchange.so
⊖ London Bridge, map 1
Modern Eclectic | £24
Cooking score: 4

£5 OFF £30

Quite literally in the shadow of the Shard, this quirky rooftop bolthole sits a comparatively modest six floors up, with Europe's tallest building bearing down on its decked terrace. The café operates as the canteen for the Exchange – which runs serviced workspaces in what, from the outside, looks like a rather nondescript office building – and definitely doesn't make itself easy to find. Tip: search out their name on the buzzer, head to the third floor via the lift and follow the low-key signage to discover an unexpectedly vibrant modern dining room overlooked by a simple galley-style kitchen. The compact daily-changing menu (five starters, five mains, three

desserts) from Australian chef Magnus Read combines gutsy St John-esque Britishness with European and Asian influences. That might mean bavette steak with kim-chee; Toulouse sausages with lentils; or a treacle tart with cream. House wine is £17.
Chef/s: Magnus Read. **Open:** Mon to Sat 8 to 3 (10 Sat), Thur to Sat D 6 to 10.30 (4 to 11 Sat). **Closed:** Sun, bank hols. **Meals:** alc (main courses £9 to £14). Set D £20 (3 courses). **Details:** 40 seats. 30 seats outside. Separate bar.

RSJ

Excellent-value food and astonishing wines
33 Coin Street, Southwark, SE1 9NR
Tel no: (020) 7928 4554
www.rsj.uk.com
⊖ Waterloo, Southwark, map 5
Modern European | £32
Cooking score: 3

£5 OFF ♦ V

Housed in a three-storey building that the Duchy of Cornwall once used for stabling, RSJ is now comfortably into its fourth decade in the Guide. The short journey from the South Bank has always been worth taking to sample the kitchen's modern-accented British and French food, and the determinedly singular wine list. Readers have been wowed by the precision timing of duck livers and spinach on rösti, with crispy bacon bits and a good sticky jus, and the freshness of potted mackerel tartare with lemon. Main courses show admirable balance, as in seared salmon with spinach mash in Noilly Prat pea cream or ample ox cheek with truffled pomme purée and tiny carrots. Round things off with excellent plum and almond tart and honey ice cream. The USP of the wine list has always been the Loire region. Beyond Sancerre and Pouilly-Fumé, you'll find Chinon, Bourgueil, Saumur-Champigny, Vouvray (in its array of styles) and full-on stickies from Bonnezeaux and the Coteaux du Layon. Surveying a run of vintages back to 1995, you might even wonder whether it's worth giving Muscadet another

whirl. (It is – the wine goes mellow and Burgundian in its maturity.) House Saumur is £18.95.
Chef/s: Ajo Plunkett. **Open:** Mon to Fri L 12 to 2.30, Mon to Sat D 5.30 to 11. **Closed:** Sun, 24 to 26 Dec, Easter bank hols. **Meals:** alc (main courses £13 to £23). Set L and D £16.95 (2 courses) to £19.95. **Details:** 90 seats. 12 seats outside.

READERS RECOMMEND

Saz
Turkish
23 Norwood Road, Herne Hill, SE24 9AA
Tel no: (020) 8671 3772
'If we fancy something a bit different from the usual night in the pub when we are in this area we head to Saz. The best Turkish food I've had outside of Turkey and the staff are great. The Turkish wine is worth a punt, too.'

Skylon
A riverside stunner in the Royal Festival Hall
Southbank Centre, Belvedere Road, South Bank, SE1 8XX
Tel no: (020) 7654 7800
www.skylon-restaurant.co.uk
⊖ Waterloo, map 5
Modern European | £48
Cooking score: 2

Spread over the third floor of the Royal Festival Hall with double-, even triple-height ceilings and floor-to-ceiling glass overlooking the Thames, 'there's no denying this is a stunner'. Skylon is part glamorous bar and casual grill, part elegant restaurant (the focus of our test meal) – it's all impressively sophisticated, yet understated. Service is seamlessly professional. Helena Puolakka has departed, her place taken by Adam Gray (a former Gary Rhodes lieutenant), whose cooking emphasises seasonality, exquisite presentation and imaginatively worked ingredients. Typical of the new style is a starter of 'pink and tender' squab pigeon breast, its sweetly marinated leg 'sticky and delicious', with apple and celeriac salad and hazelnut gravy. Characteristic too is a generous dish of perfectly cooked red mullet on a warm Jersey Royal and spinach salad (with 'beautifully tender' asparagus spears). Wines from £22.50. **Chef/s:** Adam Gray. **Open:** all week L 12 to 2.30 (4 Sun), Mon to Sat D 5.30 to 10.30. **Closed:** 25 Dec. **Meals:** Set L £25 (2 courses) to £29. Set D £42 (2 courses) to £47.50. Sun L £26. **Details:** 90 seats. Separate bar. Wheelchair access.

Soif

A chip off a fine block
27 Battersea Rise, Battersea, SW11 1HG
Tel no: (020) 7223 1112
soif.co
⊖ Clapham South, map 3
Modern European | £30
Cooking score: 2
🍷

A relaxed, noisy bar-cum-eatery, Soif, like its team mates (Terroirs, Brawn and the Green Man & French Horn, see entries), feeds the capital's appetite for fresh, seasonal ingredients delivered in rustic dishes such as duck rillettes and whole Dorset crab with mayonnaise. Everything on the concise, daily changing menu arrives in an unfussy style that perfectly matches the surroundings of bare boards and unclothed tables: perhaps roast bone marrow with pickled walnut relish and watercress, lemon sole meunière and braised shoulder of lamb with pearl barley and curly kale. To conclude, there's bitter chocolate pot or tarte aux pommes with crème fraîche. Wine fans will enjoy the great list, starting at £13 for 500ml, which is sourced with an eager eye for little-known gems and quality drinking all the way from France to the southern hemisphere. **Chef/s:** Pascal Wiedemann. **Open:** Tue to Sun L 12 to 3 (11 Sat, 11 to 4 Sun), Mon to Sat D 6 to 10.30. **Meals:** alc (main courses £17 to £18). Set L £10 (1 course). **Details:** 70 seats. 10 seats outside.

Tapas Brindisa

A tantalising taste of Spain
18-20 Southwark Street, Southwark, SE1 1TJ
Tel no: (020) 7357 8880
www.tapasbrindisa.com
⊖ London Bridge, map 1
Spanish | £20
Cooking score: 3
£30

Borough Market is a long way from Barcelona, but this founding member of the Brindisa group brings a tantalising taste of Spain to south London – thanks to imported provisions from the parent company. Artisan cheeses, breads and hand-carved charcuterie naturally hog most of the limelight, but the kitchen also knocks out a selection of tapas staples and seasonal specialities ranging from jamón croquetas, tortilla and garlicky gambas al ajillo to sautéed chicken livers with sherry, capers and red onion salad or ox cheeks braised in red wine with pumpkin. Drinks are equally patriotic, with a fine selection of sherries and beers alongside the well-tutored regional Spanish wine list; prices start at £18.95 (£4.25 a glass). Utilitarian décor, concrete floors, mirrored walls and closely packed tables are nothing to write home about, but no one seems to care, even if the melee gets too frantic. **Chef/s:** Roberto Castro. **Open:** Mon to Sat L 12 to 3 (4 Fri and Sat), D 5.30 to 11. Sun 12 to 10. **Closed:** 25 and 26 Dec, 1 Jan. **Meals:** alc (tapas £4 to £10). **Details:** 36 seats. 20 seats outside.

Tentazioni

Popular Italian cooking with a Sardinian tang
Lloyds Wharf, 2 Mill Street, Bermondsey, SE1 2BD
Tel no: (020) 7237 1100
www.tentazioni.co.uk
⊖ Bermondsey, London Bridge, map 1
Italian | £42
Cooking score: 3

Riccardo Giacomini's vibrantly buzzy Italian venue, not far from Tower Bridge, is a raspberry-red redoubt of traditional cooking, hung with works by showcased artists. The

food of Sardinia is the main draw. Giacomini and Alessandro Cattani head a busy kitchen, offering seasonal dishes such as pumpkin and porcini risotto and classic pasta variations like black olive tortelloni with puttanesca sauce, before the main attractions deliver beautifully marbled ribeye steaks, sea-bream simmered in seawater with cherry tomatoes, or a rather luxy rack of lamb stuffed with duck foie gras in cinnamon sauce. Finish with the signature deep-fried sheep's cheese raviolo served with abbamele (Sardinian honey reduced to the dark toffeeish consistency of molasses). Abruzzo house wines at £17.50 lead an Italian list that quickly gets into its price stride.
Chef/s: Riccardo Giacomini and Alessandro Cattani. **Open:** Mon to Fri L 12 to 2.45, Mon to Sat D 6 to 10.45. **Closed:** Sun, 24 to 26 Dec, bank hols. **Meals:** alc (main courses £10 to £29). Set D £25 (2 courses) to £29. Tasting menu £48.50 (7 courses). **Details:** 50 seats.

Trinity

Truly wonderful neighbourhood restaurant
4 The Polygon, Clapham, SW4 0JG
Tel no: (020) 7622 1199
www.trinityrestaurant.co.uk
⊖ Clapham Common, map 3
Modern British | £45
Cooking score: 5

Adam Byatt's Trinity proves that it isn't always necessary to head to the West End or City to find exciting contemporary cooking in London. The atmosphere is one of monochrome understatement, with sparkling-white linen and smart glassware. Byatt and his head chef Graham Squire have an evolutionary approach to the seasonal menus, adding new dishes at the rate of about one a week. The results of this prudent thought are shown in the food's sheer impact on the palate. A starter of pig's trotter and crackling, adorned with sauce gribiche and sourdough toast, achieves amazing depth. It might be succeeded by John Dory in an earthy mix of pumpkin and chanterelles, given weight by little dumpling bombs of oxtail, or

there may be Dexter sirloin with a persillade of snails, on-trend scorched onions and truffled mash. To finish, a new spin on Eton mess produces a bitter-chocolate and blood-orange reinvention. Trinity's wine list inspires confidence, with discerning selections from all over the world, including Austria's Burgenland and Lebanon's Bekaa Valley. Prices open at £13 for a half-litre carafe, £18 a bottle, or £4.50 a glass.
Chef/s: Adam Byatt. **Open:** Tue to Sun L 12.30 to 2.30 (3 Sun), Mon to Sat D 6.30 to 10. **Closed:** 23 to 27 Dec, 1 and 2 Jan. **Meals:** alc (main courses £18 to £28). Set L £20 (2 courses) to £25. Sun L £35. Tasting menu £50 (5 courses). **Details:** 60 seats. Wheelchair access.

Tsunami

Sleek Japanese fusion favourite
5-7 Voltaire Road, Clapham, SW4 6DQ
Tel no: (020) 7978 1610
www.tsunamirestaurant.co.uk
⊖ Clapham North, map 3
Japanese | £30
Cooking score: 3

Since setting up shop among Clapham's railway sidings some 12 years ago, Japanese fusion favourite Tsunami has proved the doubters wrong with its blend of sleek, sultry vibes and sophisticated food. Flamboyant floral displays add colour to the glass-ceilinged dining room, while the kitchen tempts its clientele with a savvy mix of fashionable and traditionally inspired dishes. Trendies might order an appetising salad of fresh crab with chicory leaves, pomegranate and peanuts; hamachi yellowtail with wasabi salsa; or black-cod tempura. Others might prefer agedashi tofu, chicken yakitori or grilled eel with rice and pickles. High-gloss sushi and sashimi also cover a lot of ground, from roast duck and foie gras nigiri to spicy lobster hand rolls with burdock root. To drink, serious sakés and flashy cocktails compete with global wines (from £20). There's a West End branch at 93 Charlotte Street W1; tel: (020) 7637 0050. See overleaf for Tsunami's details.

Chef/s: S W Cheung. **Open:** Sat and Sun L 12.30 to 4, all week D 5.30 to 10.30 (11 Fri and Sat, 10 Sun). **Closed:** 24 to 26 Dec. **Meals:** alc (main courses £8 to £28). Set L £15 (2 courses). **Details:** 80 seats. 20 seats outside. Separate bar. Wheelchair access.

NEW ENTRY

The Woodman

Unpretentious pub with civilised dining room
60 Battersea High Street, Battersea, SW11 3HW
Tel no: (020) 7228 2968
www.woodman-battersea.co.uk
⊖ Clapham Junction, map 3
British | £24
Cooking score: 2

£5 OFF £30

It may stand square on Battersea High Street but the Woodman is an archetypal country pub inside, complete with a fire-warmed bar and a civilised dining room. Service is smiley and warm and there's an air of relaxed unpretentiousness. Lunchtime sandwiches and bar snacks (wild boar Scotch egg gets the thumbs-up) please the locals, while the carte mixes standard pub food with more contemporary ideas. Thus home-cured gravlax with gin-and-tonic dressing, and fillet of sea bream with lemon-braised lentils, spinach and tossed salad, share the honours with, say, slow-braised venison, free-range pork belly and Dorset beefburger. Bringing up the rear is a cast list of desserts that might include sticky toffee pudding and rum-roasted pineapple with vanilla ice cream. Wines from £15.
Chef/s: James Rogers. **Open:** all week L 12 to 6, D 6 to 10 (9 Sat and Sun). **Meals:** alc (main meals £9 to £17). Sun L £13. **Details:** 70 seats. 25 seats outside. Separate bar.

⫙ INNOVATIVE COCKTAIL HOUR

Not content with serving some of the finest cocktails on the planet, London's bartenders are turning to some rather strange alternatives to attract curious drinkers. Head over to South African restaurant **Shaka Zulu** in Camden for a Meatequita cocktail containing tequila, chorizo and vegetable juice served with a biltong garnish, or grab a Bloody Bacon Mary made using bacon vodka.

If money is no object you can try the world's second most expensive cocktail at **Salvatore's Bar** at The Playboy Club in Mayfair. The drink, named Salvatore's Legacy, features some of the world's oldest Cognac and vermouth and will set you back a cool £5,500.

The latest trend in unusual cocktails is to age all or part of the drink in barrels at the bar to allow the flavours to develop. The **Rivoli Bar** at The Ritz serves a Manhattan made with one of three macerations aged in barrels for up to nine months: all spice, red fruits or orange and vanilla. Meanwhile **Worship Street Whistling Shop** in Shoreditch takes the idea one step further by ageing a rum and absinthe-based cocktail with radiation.

Wright Brothers Oyster & Porter House

Bivalves and 'black stuff'
11 Stoney Street, Southwark, SE1 9AD
Tel no: (020) 7403 9554
www.thewrightbrothers.co.uk
⊖ London Bridge, map 1
Seafood | £30
Cooking score: 2

'Fantastic food, great service and excellent, friendly staff,' is how a reader summed up the appeal of the Southwark arm of the Wright Brothers' seafood enterprise. Sit up at a wooden counter or roll yourself around a barrel amid the cheery hubbub. Then relish the sparklingly fresh simplicities of potted shrimps on toast, smoked mackerel pâté, fish soup and rouille, devilled whitebait, smoked salmon, moules marinière, dressed crab and what have you. Hot dishes include a traditional mash-topped fish pie stuffed with salmon and smoked haddock, and pastry-shelled beef and oyster pie with Guinness, but aficionados of British, Irish and French fresh oysters are the most indulged. Finish with a crème brûlée or a plate of chocolate truffles. House French is £20 a bottle, £4.90 a glass.
Chef/s: Phillip Coulter. **Open:** all week L 12 to 3 (4 Sat and Sun), D 6 to 10 (9 Sun). **Closed:** bank hols. **Meals:** alc (main courses £9 to £17). **Details:** 35 seats.

Zucca

Get-stuck-in, good-value Italian cooking
184 Bermondsey Street, Bermondsey, SE1 3TQ
Tel no: (020) 7378 6809
www.zuccalondon.com
⊖ London Bridge, Borough, map 1
Italian | £25
Cooking score: 3
🍾 £30

Another restaurant from a River Café alumnus, another reason to give praise to the gods of Italian food. Sam Harris's Zucca near London Bridge is the quintessential upbeat urban Italian. There's a thrum of constant activity thanks to the open kitchen, glass frontage and tightly packed dining room where appreciative diners of all ages tuck into Harris's deftly executed, ingredient-focused cooking. Reporters suggests there's some variance in portion size. One reader 'lucked out' with the 'utterly divine' signature 'Zucca' fritti, a generous mound of soft pumpkin in tempura batter followed by 'appealingly simple' whole mackerel, straight from the grill, with fennel salad ('I was thinking about it for days afterwards'). Others have found servings 'somewhat neat' but were nonetheless entranced by sea bass carpaccio, calf's liver with lentils and just-wobbly-enough pannacotta, all at ungreedy prices. The all-Italian wine list (from £28) is rich in new discoveries and fine producers.
Chef/s: Sam Harris. **Open:** Tue to Sun L 12 to 3 (3.30 Sat and Sun), Tue to Sat D 6 to 10. **Closed:** Mon. **Meals:** alc (main courses £5 to £17). **Details:** 60 seats. Separate bar. Wheelchair access.

The Admiral Codrington

A Chelsea favourite serving modern pub classics
17 Mossop Street, Chelsea, SW3 2LY
Tel no: (020) 7581 0005
www.theadmiralcodrington.co.uk
⊖ South Kensington, map 3
Modern British | £35
Cooking score: 2

The much-loved Cod is a well-designed west London hostelry, with a proper pub upfront and a pleasant, light-toned dining area at the back, split between tables for two and booth seating. The framed pictures of fish might get you in the maritime mood for feasting on perfectly crisp chilli squid with a fiery dipping sauce, followed by carefully timed sea bream with saffron potatoes and olives. Otherwise, contemplate a meatier route where steak tartare with grilled sourdough and salad could precede caramelised chicken breast in tarragon sauce. Chocolate mousse made with 72% Venezuelan gear should sort out the choc-heads, or there's pannacotta made with Greek yoghurt, served with rhubarb and pistachios. A short wine list, starting at £17, or £4.25 a glass, includes a slate of mature clarets.
Chef/s: Orrett Hoilett. **Open:** Mon to Sat L 12 to 2.30 (3.30 Sat), D 6.30 to 11 (7 Sat). Sun 12 to 9. **Closed:** 24 to 26 Dec. **Meals:** alc (main courses £14 to £28). **Details:** 55 seats. 20 seats outside. Separate bar.

Amaya

Sleek Indian with tapas-style tasting plates
15 Halkin Arcade, Motcomb Street, Knightsbridge, SW1X 8JT
Tel no: (020) 7823 1166
www.amaya.biz
⊖ Knightsbridge, map 4
Indian | £46
Cooking score: 3

From the group that also owns Chutney Mary and Veeraswamy (see entries), Amaya is the most chic of the lot: a Knightsbridge designer palace decked out in pink sandstone and rosewood panelling. Black-clad spotlit chefs at work in the open-to-view kitchen add to the sleek appeal. The format is tapas-style plates of contemporary Indian food, its greatest hits including flash-grilled rock oysters in coconut and ginger sauce, griddled king scallops in green sauce and show-stopping leg of lamb in cumin and garam masala. Gourmet menus provide an extensive introduction to the range, from mandarin and goats' cheese salad to griddled foie gras and masala lobster. Fragrant rose brûlée might conclude matters. The well-written wine list is intelligently compiled to suit the demands of the food, but mark-ups are stiff. A good selection by the glass opens at £6.25 for a fresh Cinsault rosé. Bottles start at £28.
Chef/s: Karunesh Khanna. **Open:** all week L 12.30 to 2.15 (2.45 Sun), D 6.30 to 11.30 (10.30 Sun). **Meals:** alc (main courses £10 to £36). Set L £29 (2 courses) to £35. Tasting menu £55. **Details:** 100 seats. Separate bar. Wheelchair access.

Anglesea Arms

Veteran neighbourhood pub
35 Wingate Road, Shepherd's Bush, W6 0UR
Tel no: (020) 8749 1291
www.anglesea-arms.com
⊖ Ravenscourt Park, map 1
Modern British | £30
Cooking score: 1

There's more competition in west London than when this four-square neighbourhood pub first appeared in the Guide in 1997, but although some reporters feel it is 'resting on its laurels', the Anglesea Arms is just about holding its own on the food front. A compact menu delivers hearty, uncomplicated cooking: perhaps 'rich' pappardelle pasta with a rabbit ragù or gurnard with cauliflower, Hispi cabbage and smoked red wine sauce. Start with beetroot, pickled radishes, walnuts, feta and black treacle dressing and finish with custard tart with white chocolate ice cream. Wines from £17.75.
Chef/s: Philip Harrison. **Open:** all week L 12.30 to 2.45 (3 Sat, 3.30 Sun), D 7 to 10.30 (10 Mon, 6.30 to 9 Sun). **Closed:** 23 to 27 Dec. **Meals:** alc (main courses £10 to £22). **Details:** 50 seats. 20 seats outside. Separate bar. Wheelchair access.

NEW ENTRY

Apero

Stylish Italian all-day dining
The Ampersand Hotel, 2 Harrington Road, South
Kensington, SW7 3ER
Tel no: (020) 7591 4410
www.aperorestaurantandbar.com
⊖ South Kensington, map 3
Mediterranean | £26
Cooking score: 3

🛏 £30

Sheltered from street-level clamour, Apero's
hip and plush interior is tucked in the vaults of
the boutique Ampersand Hotel. This relaxed,
Mediterranean-style outfit offers all-day
nourishment at the long marble bar or leather
snugs, and succeeds at combining refined,
modern ideas with the easy-going nature of an
all-day eatery with wallet-friendly prices. The
kitchen focuses squarely on light and bright
interpretations of Italian cookery. Expect
succinct small plates with a welcome spark of
ingenuity: delicate dishes such as grilled stone
bass marinated in sumac with burnt tomatoes
or gnocchi, white crabmeat and sprouting
broccoli. Show-off puddings and pastries are a
highlight – an almond parfait with chocolate
was 'a technical masterpiece'. Consider
eschewing the so-so selection of French and
Italian wines (starting at £17) for an Italian
aperitivo from the inventive cocktail list,
inspired by art at the nearby V&A.
Chef/s: Chris Golding. **Open:** all week L 12 to 2.30, D
6 to 10.30. **Meals:** alc (main courses £10 to £14). Set
L and D £26. **Details:** 40 seats. Separate bar.
Wheelchair access.

Assaggi

Fine-tuned rustic Italian food
39 Chepstow Place, Notting Hill, W2 4TS
Tel no: (020) 7792 5501
⊖ Notting Hill Gate, map 4
Italian | £45
Cooking score: 4

Exceptional quality and a lack of pretence are
the hallmarks of Nino Sassu's charming
neighbourhood restaurant above a former

pub. Notting Hill cool meets rustic Italian
brio in the vibrant, peach-toned dining room.
A cheery mood prevails as the kitchen dishes
up plates of finely tuned, boldly flavoured
food with a sunny disposition. Sassu's menu is
written in his native tongue and doesn't give
much away, but the food is guided by the
seasons, from polenta with sausage and leeks
or tagliolini with fresh herbs and walnuts to
venison with chestnut purée, fritto misto or
simply grilled veal chops – all served with
minimal fuss or adornment. Cheeses are
worth a sniff and desserts vary daily: although
there's usually something with fruit and
pastry, as well as classic tiramisu. The 36-bin
wine list packs plenty of Italian quality into a
small space, with prices from £23.95 (£5.50 a
glass).
Chef/s: Nino Sassu. **Open:** Mon to Sat L 12.30 to
2.30 (1 to 2.30 Sat), D 7.30 to 11. **Closed:** Sun, 2
weeks Christmas, bank hols. **Meals:** alc (main
courses £19 to £30). **Details:** 35 seats.

Bar Boulud

Glamour and finger-lickingly delicious food
Mandarin Oriental Hyde Park, 66 Knightsbridge,
Knightsbridge, SW1X 7LA
Tel no: (020) 7201 3899
www.barboulud.com
⊖ Knightsbridge, map 4
French | £38
Cooking score: 4

🛏

Housed beneath the Mandarin Oriental Hotel
in a swish mélange of banquettes, closely
packed tables, counter seating and soft
lighting, New York chef Daniel Boulud's
Knightsbridge spin-off is now in its fourth
year of bringing French-inspired brasserie
food to the capital. Bar Boulud does sociable
hubbub with aplomb – the main dining room
has lost none of its dynamic buzz – and the
kitchen knows how to deliver some truly
authentic food. The menu looks back with
affection when it comes to the likes of fromage
de tête (pig's head cheese terrine), jambon de
Paris, coq au vin and navarin d'agneau. But
you'll find some new tricks, too, from sea bass

fillet with crispy wild rice, sumac-glazed salsify, tastoi leaves and fig bordelaise, to the signature beefburgers and the outstanding coupe peppermint (flourless sponge with hot chocolate sauce and mint-chocolate ice cream). The wine list offers a winning selection of classy bottles, although prices, from £22.50, may deter experimentation. **Chef/s:** Dean Yasharian. **Open:** all week 12 to 11 (10 Sun). **Meals:** alc (main courses £12 to £30). Set L and pre-theatre D £23. **Details:** 169 seats. Separate bar. Wheelchair access.

Bibendum
Delightful design icon with seasonal classics
Michelin House, 81 Fulham Road, South Kensington, SW3 6RD
Tel no: (020) 7581 5817
www.bibendum.co.uk
⊖ South Kensington, map 3
French | £51
Cooking score: 4

Bathed in a glorious stained-glass glow, overpopulated by likenesses of a tubby man wrapped in bandages, Bibendum's dining room is one of the capital's most distinctive. At street level the Michelin building houses the oyster bar: a drop-in temple to crustacea and simple classics. On the first floor, Bibendum indulges in just enough pre-dinner folderol to evoke a sense of occasion, and the seasonally led, mainly French menu sees to the rest. To start, red-hot, deep-green, garlic-breathing escargots de Bourgogne are always on the menu alongside, perhaps, crab and octopus salad with avocado and saffron dressing. Main courses include confit of duck with Jerusalem artichokes, lentils and herb jus, or perhaps a special of nursery-soft sole paupiettes with a lobster and brown shrimp sauce. Elegance and comfort are key again in a raspberry and elderflower jelly with buttery madeleines. Further boons are the well-practised, assured service and the strong house selections (from £19.95) on the wine list. **Chef/s:** Matthew Harris. **Open:** all week L 12 to 2.30 (12.30 to 3 Sat and Sun), D 7 to 11 (10.30 Sun). **Closed:** 25 and 26 Dec, 1 Jan. **Meals:** alc (main

courses £18 to £33). Set L £26.50 (2 courses) to £30. Sun L and D £32.50. **Details:** 90 seats. Separate bar.

Bombay Brasserie
Born-again Indian veteran
Courtfield Road, South Kensington, SW7 4QH
Tel no: (020) 7370 4040
www.bombaybrasserielondon.com
⊖ Gloucester Road, map 3
Indian | £35
Cooking score: 3

It has been around for more than 30 years, but this maharaja among London's grand Indian restaurants seems to have found its second wind following a 2012 makeover. The dining room is still extravagantly decked out with plush colonial accoutrements, chandeliers and greenery, although some clean-lined fittings and a born-again conservatory (with a fiery open kitchen) have brought the whole place bang up to date. It's undeniably 'pricey' but the food is spot-on, with skilfully rendered regional specialities stealing the show. Mumbai roadside snacks such as ragda pattice (potato cakes with chickpeas and chutney) or Malabar soft-shell crabs give way to north Indian tandooris, prawns balchao spiked with Goan vinegar or Parsee-style lemon sole wrapped in a banana leaf. Knowledgeable staff are on hand to advise, although much of the repertoire is familiar enough. Drink by the carafe to get value from the wine list; bottles start at £22. **Chef/s:** Prahlad Hegde. **Open:** all week L 12 to 3, D 6.30 to 11.30 (10.30 Sun). **Meals:** alc (main courses £16 to £23). Set L £24. Sun L £26. **Details:** 185 seats. Separate bar. Wheelchair access.

Brompton Bar & Grill
Seductive neighbourhood bistro
243 Brompton Road, South Kensington, SW3 2EP
Tel no: (020) 7589 8005
www.bromptonbarandgrill.com
⊖ South Kensington, map 3
Anglo-French | £28
Cooking score: 2
£30

Just because you may live in Knightsbridge
doesn't mean you don't need a friendly
neighbourhood bistro, and in the grey-
fronted, jazz-tinged Brompton, the district
thankfully has one. Here you can tap a foot to
live swing on certain evenings, knock back a
cocktail at the zinc bar and begin a feast with
the likes of snails on toast, with bone marrow,
smoked bacon and garlic butter. The house
fish stew (a cavalcade of bream, gurnard,
salmon, mussels and clams) with aïoli might
follow, or grilled veal chop with polenta and
girolles, and there's a refreshing clementine
and pomegranate salad with almonds and
mint to round things off. You're likely to have
plenty of fun into the bargain. House wines
are £16 a bottle, £5 a glass.
Chef/s: Gary Durrant. Open: all week L 12 to 3 (3.30
Sat and Sun), D 6 to 10.30 (10 Sun). Closed: 25 Dec.
Meals: alc (main courses £13 to £30). Set L £18.50.
Sun L £22.50. Details: 50 seats. 4 seats outside.
Separate bar.

Le Café Anglais
Big-hearted brasserie pleasures
8 Porchester Gardens, Notting Hill, W2 4DB
Tel no: (020) 7221 1415
www.lecafeanglais.co.uk
⊖ Bayswater, map 4
Modern European | £30
Cooking score: 4

A Notting Hill landmark since it opened on
the second floor of Whiteley's shopping centre
in 2007 (with its own entrance in Porchester
Place), Le Café Anglais continues to deliver the
goods in its own inimitable style. The large
room with its massive windows and open-to-
view kitchen is a booming but bright space.

Rowley Leigh's menu continues to show the
eternal triangle of France, Italy and Britain as
the main influences, with the cooking
generally steering a course towards tried-and-
trusted flavours – the tone firmly set by the
famed Parmesan custard with anchovy toast,
roast Label Anglais chicken with bread
pudding and onion gravy and rump steak au
poivre. There's also turbot with salsa verde,
grilled pork chop with rosemary, polenta,
apple and lardo, and to finish, a very good
queen of puddings. An all-day oyster bar is an
added attraction, as is the Euro-accented wine
list with its useful, concise descriptions. Prices
from £19.50.
Chef/s: Rowley Leigh. Open: all week L 12 to 3.30, D
6.30 to 10.30 (10 Sun). Closed: 25 to 27 Dec, Aug
bank hol. Meals: alc (main courses £13 to £29). Set
L and D £20 (2 courses) to £25. Sun L £30.
Details: 120 seats. Separate bar. Wheelchair access.
Car parking.

Cambio de Tercio
Impressive, high-octane Spaniard
163 Old Brompton Road, Earl's Court, SW5 0LJ
Tel no: (020) 7244 8970
www.cambiodetercio.co.uk
⊖ Gloucester Road, map 3
Spanish | £40
Cooking score: 5
V

Flamboyant Cambio de Tercio, with tapas offshoots Capote y Toros all but next door and
Tendido Cero opposite, gives a real Spanish
flavour to this stretch of the Old Brompton
Road. Cambio has been playing to packed
houses since 1995, but has always moved with
the times; now twice its original size, latest
innovations include a fashionable gin-and-
tonic bar (serving some 50 different gins) and a
swanky new kitchen in the basement. Vibrant
coloured walls, bold oversized artworks, black
leather round-back chairs and slate flooring
provide the backdrop, while Alberto Criado's
thoroughly modern approach matches the
effervescent surroundings with creative, bold-
flavoured dishes. There may be traditional
tapas for conventional tastes (Iberica ham

croquetas), but Criado's signature tapas up the ante, perhaps a 'Neptune's supper' of plump oysters enhanced by the citrus zing of grapefruit 'air' and shallot vinaigrette or a stunning Andalusian gazpacho poured at the table on to wonderful olive oil lobster and a small quenelle of intense cherry ice cream. There's no three-course formula here, but large plates tempt with crisp-skinned, 'melt-in-the-mouth' suckling pig teamed simply with pumpkin, purple potatoes and roasting juices. Nor are desserts an afterthought – the high-octane Valrhona hot chocolate cake with roasted almonds and cooling coconut ice cream has fans aplenty, as does the corking 350-bottle all-Spanish wine list (from £23) with its astonishing list of 110 sherries.
Chef/s: Alberto Criado. **Open:** all week L 12 to 2.30 (3 Sat and Sun), D 7 to 11.30 (11 Sun). **Closed:** 22 Dec to 3 Jan. **Meals:** alc (main courses £18 to £23). Set L (Sat and Sun only) £26 (3 courses). **Details:** 55 seats. 8 seats outside. Separate bar.

The Carpenter's Arms
Jolly local with please-all food
89-91 Black Lion Lane, Hammersmith, W6 9BG
Tel no: (020) 8741 8386
www.carpentersarmsw6.co.uk
⊖ Stamford Brook, Ravenscourt Park, map 1
Modern European | £28
Cooking score: 2
£30

Bustling and noisy (blame the wooden floor, functional furniture and low ceiling), this energetic neighbourhood pub is a great hit with in-the-know locals. Things are equally upbeat in the kitchen, where big-hearted flavours are stuffed into a lively menu that might jump from charcuterie sharing platters to French onion soup or lobster salad with mango, chilli, coriander and toasted coconut. The rest of the repertoire is a zesty assortment of pub classics – braised lamb shank, fish and chips, burgers or grilled Dexter ribeye steak with peppercorn sauce and chips. The decent-sized beer garden is the place to be when the

sun comes out. Prices are keen and the short, worldwide wine list is equally affordable, with bottles from £17.20.
Chef/s: Nilton Campos. **Open:** all week L 12 to 3 (4 Sat, 6 Sun), D 6 to 10 (9 Sun). **Closed:** 26 to 28 Dec. **Meals:** alc (main courses £11 to £20). **Details:** 60 seats. 50 seats outside.

Casa Brindisa
Homage to Spanish provisions
7-9 Exhibition Road, South Kensington, SW7 2HE
Tel no: (020) 7590 0008
www.brindisa.com
⊖ South Kensington, map 3
Spanish | £20
Cooking score: 3
£30

Brindisa has become a byword for top-drawer Spanish provisions and its homage to the home country continues at this South Ken branch, which also sports a bar-cum-jamóneria and an amply stocked basement deli. As ever, it's all about the ingredients: tins of Ortiz tuna fill the window space, cutlery comes in pimentón tins and the menu is loaded with regional charcuterie, artisan breads, cheeses and other good things. 'Exquisitely flavoursome' chorizo tortilla, delicate wilted spinach with pine nuts and raisins, butifarra con mongetes (Catalan sausage with beans and allioli) and albondigas con sepia (meatballs with cuttlefish) have all been devoured with gusto, but also look for the special 'cider house' txuleta (Basque ribeye steak). It's honest, no-frills stuff, served with bags of energy by clued-up staff – although tables in the open-fronted, whitewashed dining room are jammed uncomfortably close together. To drink, explore the alluring sherries and Spanish regional wines (from £17.50).
Chef/s: Leonardo Rivera. **Open:** all week 11am to 11.30pm (10am Sat, 10.30pm Sun). **Closed:** 24 to 26 Dec, 1 and 2 Jan. **Meals:** alc (tapas £5 to £14). **Details:** 65 seats. 16 seats outside. Separate bar. Wheelchair access.

Cassis

Seductive, luxurious neighbourhood Italian
232-236 Brompton Road, South Kensington,
SW3 2BB
Tel no: (020) 7581 1101
www.cassisbistro.co.uk
⊖ South Kensington, map 3
Italian | £40
Cooking score: 4

Just off the mayhem of Brompton Road,
upmarket bistro Cassis is undergoing a
gradual metamorphosis. The plush, taupe
interior is earmarked for an overhaul, and a
changeover at the culinary helm has prompted
a continental shift, from elegant Provençal
cuisine to equally impressive Italian fare. Out
goes bouillabaisse, in comes a Tuscan cacciucco
(fish stew), bursting with flavour yet by no
means rustic – this is unashamedly seductive,
luxurious fare – along with elegant pasta
primi, perhaps seafood saffron scialatelli or
silky homemade fettuccine with mushrooms
and confit rabbit. Should you be coerced into
secondi there's plenty to please, perhaps veal
milanese with Sicilian orange and fennel salad
or roasted turbot. A dessert of Sicilian cannolo
with rice ice cream vexed on inspection, the
rice ice cream being an ill-judged addition to
the plate, but caramelised 'beignets' are a sure-
fire winner. Wine starts at £25, with plenty by
the glass.
Chef/s: Massimiliano Bladsone. **Open:** all week 12
to 11 (11am Sat and Sun). **Closed:** 25 and 26 Dec.
Meals: alc (main courses £17 to £28). Set L £18 (2
courses) to £22. **Details:** 90 seats. 10 seats outside.
Separate bar. Wheelchair access.

Chabrot Bistrot d'Amis

Diminutive bistrot with lots to like
9 Knightsbridge Green, Knightsbridge, SW1X 7QL
Tel no: (020) 7225 2238
www.chabrot.co.uk
⊖ Knightsbridge, map 4
French | £35
Cooking score: 5

It looked for a while as though London might
have to sail into the 21st century more or less
bereft of traditional French bistro cooking.
Ventures like this one have redressed the
balance. The environs of Knightsbridge
notwithstanding, there are no airs and graces
about the venue, which extends over two very
compact floors, or to Thierry Laborde's
cooking, which brings us the full panoply of
red mullet escabèche, foie gras terrine with
green beans, or smoked herring with potato
salad, to get the taste-buds motoring, ahead of
grilled Dover sole, bavette steaks, or sharing
mains such as shoulder of Pyrenean lamb in
spices, served with couscous full of dried fruits
and herbs. Dessert might be an impeccably
sticky tarte Tatin. Classic French wines come
in bottles (from £19.50), half-litre carafes
(£15) or glasses (£5.50). In March 2013, a
second venue, Chabrot Bistrot des Halles,
opened in Smithfield; 62-63 Long Lane,
EC1A 9EJ, tel: (020) 7796 4550. We were
unable to persuade Chabrot to return our
questionnaire this year, so please check the
website for details.
Chef/s: Thierry Laborde. **Open:** all week 12 to 11 (10
Sun). **Closed:** 25 and 26 Dec, bank hols. **Meals:** alc
(main courses £12 to £30). **Details:** 65 seats.

Chakra

Subcontinental sizzle and Notting Hill opulence
157-159 Notting Hill Gate, Notting Hill, W11 3LF
Tel no: (020) 7229 2115
www.chakralondon.com
⊖ Notting Hill Gate, map 4
Indian | £40
Cooking score: 3
£5
OFF

Plush and unashamedly opulent, Chakra invokes all sorts of Indian mystic notions in its quest for an identity – the name refers to the body's vital 'energy points' and inspiration apparently comes from the Vedic scriptures – although the venue is clearly dressed to impress big-spending Notting Hill hedge-funders and other well-to-do locals. One bijou room is done out in chocolate-brown tones, the other could have been lifted from a ritzy nightclub with its padded leather walls, squishy banquettes and weighty chandeliers. The menu name-checks legendary chefs from the Subcontinent's fabulous palace kitchens, so expect sizzling tawa grills and tandooris, salads, chaats and curries with distinctive regional flavours: from sizzling Lahori lamb kebabs and chickpea-crusted roast quail to Keralan prawn masala. Other ideas such as char-grilled asparagus spread with white miso paste or smoked duck breast with papaya seem far removed from the old ways, likewise the line-up of snazzy cocktails. Wines start at £29. **Chef/s:** Andy Varma. **Open:** all week L 12 to 3, D 6 to 11. **Closed:** 25 and 26 Dec, 1 Jan. **Meals:** alc (main courses £7 to £19). Set L £9.99 (2 courses) to £16.95. Set D £19.99 (2 courses). Sun L £16.95 (2 courses). **Details:** 70 seats. Wheelchair access.

> ## ⑪ Average Price
> The average price listed in main-entry reviews denotes the price of a three-course meal, without wine.

Charlotte's Bistro

Slick neighbourhood eatery
6 Turnham Green Terrace, Chiswick, W4 1QP
Tel no: (020) 8742 3590
www.charlottes.co.uk
⊖ Turnham Green, map 1
Modern European | £24
Cooking score: 2
£30

'What a great neighbourhood restaurant,' pronounced one reader, and such praise is echoed in many other reports. The key to success is simple: 'always friendly, always welcoming', with menus of sensible length focusing on showing off good raw materials. Sturdy comfort food could bring a 'very fresh' sea trout tart, followed by 'a wonderfully soothing, rich winter warmer' of slow-cooked rib of beef with bone marrow and roast sweet English onions, followed by a warm almond and blackberry Bakewell tart that's just 'too good to share'. The tiny front bar is a popular spot, too – for sipping cocktails and nibbling snacks such as patatas bravas or chunks of 'puffy pork crackling'. Wines from £18. Sister restaurant to Charlotte's Place in Ealing (see entry below). **Chef/s:** Alan Barrins. **Open:** Mon to Sat L 12 to 3, D 5.30 to 10. Sun 12 to 9. **Closed:** 26 Dec, 1 Jan. **Meals:** Mon to Fri set L £15.95 (2 courses) to £18.95. Sat and Sun L £19.95 (2 courses) to £23.95. Set D £24.95 (2 courses) to £29.95. **Details:** 60 seats. Separate bar. No prams allowed.

Charlotte's Place

Dependable, pleasing cooking and great value
16 St Matthew's Road, Ealing, W5 3JT
Tel no: (020) 8567 7541
www.charlottes.co.uk
⊖ Ealing Broadway, Ealing Common, map 1
Modern European | £29
Cooking score: 4
£30

Last year's reader-voted London restaurant of the year, Charlotte's Place by Ealing Common repays its guests' loyalty with good food and service they can rely on time and again. This

'treasure of a place' has an endearing 'quaintness' and the dining rooms (over two floors of an old house) are pretty cosy, but that doesn't mean the venue feels staid. The fixed modern European menus ('incredible value') are securely rooted in the classics, yet are never less than interesting. A porky trio of crisp pig's cheek, sausage roll and terrine kicks off proceedings in hearty fashion ahead of a 'surf and turf' combination of roast cod and braised oxtail with artichoke purée, followed by blood-orange sorbet with candied zest and Breton biscuit. Wine comes from a thoughtfully chosen classic selection (from £18) with plenty of sub-£50 bottles.
Chef/s: Greg Martin. **Open:** Mon to Sat L 12 to 2.30 (4 Sun) , D 6 to 9.30 (9 Sun). **Closed:** 26 Dec, 1 Jan. **Meals:** Set L £16.95 (2 courses) to £19.95. Set D £24.95 (2 courses) to £29.95. Sun L £20.95 (2 courses) to £24.95. **Details:** 54 seats. 16 seats outside. No prams allowed.

Chutney Mary

Indian culinary adventures in a lavish setting
535 King's Road, Fulham, SW10 0SZ
Tel no: (020) 7351 3113
www.chutneymary.com
⊖ Fulham Broadway, map 3
Indian | £40
Cooking score: 3

Some two decades down the line and Chutney Mary is holding up nicely. The lavish interior creates a big first impression, service remains well up to scratch, and you won't find many regular curry house dishes on the menu. Artichoke and spinach kebab, stuffed with chestnut, date and green chilli, shows the ambition among first courses. What follows is an intriguing blend of the modern and the classic. Lamb osso buco, which comes with caramelised beetroot, clove and vine-ripe tomatoes, and Gressingham duck breast, served pink and enlivened with Hunza apricot, chilli, jaggery and vinegar, for example, are served alongside very good renditions of lamb biryani or butter chicken masala. To finish, there might be dark chocolate and cinnamon fondant. A set-price

Saturday lunch and Sunday buffet are also available, and offer good value. The well-chosen, spice-friendly wine list opens at £25.
Chef/s: Manav Tulli. **Open:** Sat and Sun L 12.30 to 2.45, all week D 6.30 to 11.30 (10.30 Sun). **Meals:** alc (main courses £17 to £32). Set L Sat £24. Set D £45. Sun L £26. **Details:** 110 seats. Wheelchair access. Children over 3 yrs only; over 10 yrs after 8.

Clarke's

Landmark London eating address
124 Kensington Church Street, Notting Hill, W8 4BH
Tel no: (020) 7221 9225
www.sallyclarke.com
⊖ Notting Hill Gate, map 4
Modern British | £38
Cooking score: 4

In 2014, Sally Clarke will celebrate 30 years at the stoves here, and her commitment to quality produce prepared with sensitivity is undimmed. She can claim to be part of the late 1980s British renaissance in cooking, a champion of top-quality seasonal produce long before it became fashionable. Her cooking is at the gentler end of the modern British spectrum and depends on long-established connections with a trusted food network. Hence dishes might take in dill-marinated Scottish salmon with Colchester crab, beetroot, cucumber, castelfranco (radicchio), pea leaves and lemon, while breast of Goosnargh duck, roasted with orange, rosemary and red wine glaze, could be served with soft Parmesan polenta, baked trevisse and Jerusalem artichoke. It all comes with a wine list (from £19) that breathes class, with noble Burgundies and sexy Californians among its gems. Note that Clarke's café-bakery-deli has been moved to a new home across the road, allowing for expansion of the ground-floor restaurant (with a new kitchen and private dining room below).
Chef/s: Sally Clarke. **Open:** all week L 12.30 to 2 (12 Sat), Mon to Sat D 6.30 to 10. **Closed:** 10 days Christmas and New Year, 1 week Aug. **Meals:** alc (main courses £19 to £28). **Details:** 70 seats. Separate bar. Wheelchair access.

NEW ENTRY
Colbert
Feels like a lovely treat
50-52 Sloane Square, Chelsea, SW1W 8AX
Tel no: (020) 7730 2804
www.colbertchelsea.com
⊖ Sloane Square, map 3
French | £33
Cooking score: 2

The newest restaurant in the Corbin and King stable (Wolseley, Delaunay and Brasserie Zédel, see entries) can be found on a corner of Sloane Square, next door to the Royal Court Theatre. It's 'a beautiful place', every detail exquisitely rendered, from the black-and-white tiled floor and curved Art Deco woodwork to the red leather banquettes, 1930s posters and monochrome photographs – and it's so 'terribly Chelsea: we were sat next to Nigel Havers'. The Parisian tone is picked up on a menu that celebrates crustacea and bivalves, soupe de poisson, steak tartare, omelettes, endive salad with Roquefort and green beans, and a 'lovely and light' boudin blanc with Puy lentils. Service is 'slick and efficient' and the wine list is appropriately French with bottles from £19.75.
Chef/s: Andrew Woodford. **Open:** 8am to 11pm (11.30pm Fri and Sat, 10.30pm Sun). **Closed:** 25 Dec. **Meals:** alc (main courses from £10 to £30). **Details:** 115 seats. 22 seats outside. Separate bar. Wheelchair access.

Le Colombier
Pleasing French classics
145 Dovehouse Street, Chelsea, SW3 6LB
Tel no: (020) 7351 1155
www.le-colombier-restaurant.co.uk
⊖ South Kensington, map 3
French | £38
Cooking score: 2

There's a feeling of Gallic neighbourhood bonhomie about Didier Garnier's dyed-in-the-wool bourgeois bistro, and it chimes agreeably with the locals in this part of Chelsea. French to its fingertips, Le Colombier has a canopied terrace, bare floorboards and white-clad tables within, and

food that is unashamedly traditional. Come here for soupe de poisson, steak tartare and very good veal sweetbreads with wild mushrooms, or to share a côte de boeuf with sauce béarnaise. To finish, it has to be crème brûlée, unless you fancy tarte Tatin or a tranche of Brie de Meaux. The midday crowds certainly appreciate the set lunch, which 'represents excellent value in this expensive part of London'. French wines from £18.50.
Chef/s: Philippe Tamet. **Open:** all week L 12 to 3 (3.30 Sun), D 6.30 to 10.30 (10 Sun). **Meals:** alc (main courses £19 to £35). Set L £19.50 (2 courses). Sun L £23. **Details:** 45 seats. 25 seats outside.

★ TOP 50 ★

Dinner by Heston Blumenthal
A taste of history
Mandarin Oriental Hyde Park, 66 Knightsbridge, Knightsbridge, SW1X 7LA
Tel no: (020) 7201 3833
www.dinnerbyheston.com
⊖ Knightsbridge, map 4
British | £65
Cooking score: 7
🛏

Heston Blumenthal and chef Ashley Palmer-Watts spent months raiding the archives of British cookery to create this Knightsbridge epic: a high-profile campaigner for our native victuals. Jelly-mould light fittings, bare tables and leather panels set the scene in the rather masculine dining room – although most eyes are on the glass-walled kitchen. Efficient serving staff play it straight while their culinary ringmasters put on an explosive show. Expect gasps of delight as plates of spiced pigeon with ale and artichokes or roast halibut with leaf chicory and cockle ketchup reach the table. Heston's gastronomic joyride begins chronologically with 'rice and flesh' (inspired by *The Forme of Cury*, circa 1390) and ends with 'cod in cider' (a wartime rerun from 1940). Each item has a bibliographical reference. If that sounds dry and dusty, think again. This kitchen creates spectacular, historically charged flavours fit for inquisitive 21st-century palates. Watch out for battalia pie (a 17th-century heavyweight packed with sweetbreads, tongue, devilled kidneys and pigeon) or the superb buttered crab loaf (c. 1730): a veritable 'salmagundi' with assertive sweet-and-sour notes provided by cucumber, pickled lemon, herring roe and rock samphire. As for dessert, the chart-topping taffety tart and tipsy cake are now joined by yeasty brown-bread ice cream pointed up with pear and caramel. The wine list is stuffed with pedigree drinking, but prices (from £35) are daunting. **Chef/s:** Ashley Palmer-Watts. **Open:** all week L 12 to 2.30, D 6.30 to 10.30. **Meals:** alc (main courses £26 to £38). Set L £36. **Details:** 118 seats. Wheelchair access.

Ebury Restaurant & Wine Bar

Steadfast commitment to enjoyment
139 Ebury Street, Belgravia, SW1W 9QU
Tel no: (020) 7730 5447
www.eburyrestaurant.co.uk
⊖ **Victoria, map 3**
Modern European | £34
Cooking score: 2
£5 OFF

It's plain that this Belgravia old-timer understands what makes its regulars tick. The 'unique interior decoration' with hand-painted frescoes, 'immaculate' linen and 'appropriate' cutlery provides an atmosphere always conducive to imbibing. The glass of Champagne with the set lunch (three courses, £25) is one of many nice touches including food 'arriving hot', sauces served on the side and coffee with homemade whisky truffles. Service is 'attentive and unhurried'. Menus combine the old school (calf's liver and bacon, pork terrine, raspberry bavarois) with the more modish likes of beef tataki with edamame salad or chorizo-crusted cod with aubergine compote. Gluten- and dairy-free menus are available, too. Wines, from £17, include plenty of half-bottles, Champagnes and budget 'quaffers'.

Chef/s: Bernard Dumonteil. **Open:** all week L 12 to 3, D 6 to 10.15. **Closed:** 24 Dec to 2 Jan. **Meals:** alc (main courses £14 to £30). Set L and D £19 (2 courses) to £25. **Details:** 70 seats. Separate bar.

NEW ENTRY
Electric Diner

Fast food? You'll be hard-pressed to find better
191 Portobello Road, Notting Hill, W11 2ED
Tel no: (020) 7908 9696
www.electricdiner.com
⊖ **Ladbroke Grove, map 4**
French-American | £35
Cooking score: 2

'It's fun . . .a bit like eating in a tunnel, with a wood-clad arched ceiling, low-slung lighting and the ubiquitous red banquette seating lining up opposite a long New York-style bar.' So ran the notes of one reporter, smitten by this Ladbroke Grove fast-food diner, which seems to be doing everything properly with quality ingredients and care – 'I would go here over some of the new burger joints'. On offer could be honey-fried chicken (a huge heap of wings, leg and breast) with chilli and sesame seeds, perhaps an open-faced blue-cheese fondue sandwich (essentially a 'heavenly dish of melted cheese' with brioche on the side), moules frites (the skin-on fries are spot-on) and sea bass with capers and lemon. To finish, indulge in a Knickerbocker glory. Lovely service. Wines from £19.
Chef/s: Gilbert Holmes. **Open:** all week 8am to 11pm (Thur to Sat midnight, Sun 10pm). **Closed:** 25 Dec. **Meals:** alc (main courses £8 to £19). **Details:** 75 seats. 6 seats outside. Separate bar. Wheelchair access.

Symbols

🛏 Accommodation is available

£30 Three courses for less than £30

V Separate vegetarian menu

£5 OFF £5-off voucher scheme

🍾 Notable wine list

L'Etranger

Idiosyncratic Franco-Japanese creations
36 Gloucester Road, South Kensington, SW7 4QT
Tel no: (020) 7584 1118
www.etranger.co.uk
⊖ Gloucester Road, South Kensington, map 3
Modern French | £45
Cooking score: 4

Jérôme Tauvron is keen to stress that his Franco-Japanese approach is not about fusion, but an ecumenical exercise where maki and sashimi menus are offered alongside classic haute cuisine. Likewise, the décor features uncovered tables giving an oriental black lacquer effect, though neutral wood tones predominate. If nigiri octopus or sea bass tartare in yuzo miso aren't your thing, try instead the foie gras terrine with fig chutney and apple salad, before John Dory with clam risotto and baby leeks in Riesling, or truffled guinea fowl with red cabbage and chestnut purée. Finish with Earl Grey and dark chocolate crème brûlée, served with white chocolate ice cream. The wine list is one of London's finest: a weighty classical document full of grande marque Champagne, cru classé claret and grand cru Burgundy, supplemented by pedigree Californian enticements. Prices open at £22.50, with small glasses from £8. Set below the main restaurant, Meursault is the accompanying cool, sexy cocktail bar and dining lounge. Newly opened, it features a striking under-lit ceiling inspired by the Belle Epoque, and a menu that echoes the French-Japanese theme but with sharing platters, too. **Chef/s:** Jérôme Tauvron. **Open:** all week L 12 to 3, D 5.45 to 11 (5.30 Wed to Sat, 10 Sun). **Closed:** 26 Dec. **Meals:** alc (main courses £15 to £70). Set L £16.50 (2 courses) to £21.50. Early D £22 (2 courses) to £25. Sun L £25 (2 courses). Tasting menu £95. **Details:** 65 seats. Separate bar.

NEW ENTRY

The Five Fields

A new seed is planted
8-9 Blacklands Terrace, Chelsea, SW3 2SP
Tel no: (020) 7838 1082
www.fivefieldsrestaurant.com
⊖ Sloane Square, map 3
Modern British | £45
Cooking score: 4
V

Intimate and smart, this newcomer behind Sloane Square is fine dining through and through. American chef Taylor Bonnyman comes from New York's Corton, but ingredients are British, some from the restaurant's very own English garden. In a small dining room which feels almost padded, expect pretty, carefully-wrought dishes scattered with unusual herbs, and plenty of unbidden extras to add interest and gloss. A 'rock pool' of oyster tartare with Bloody Mary, crab, langoustine and red mullet plays with temperature and timing, while a main course of suckling pig gets the five-ways treatment with smoked potato and wild garlic. Pudding might be English goats' cheese with an olive-speckled madeleine and poached blackberries, or modish vegetable-based assemblies using Jerusalem artichoke or garden peas. Wines include special bottles from the private 'Sussex Collection' (which should be pre-ordered) and a French-skewed list from £29. **Chef/s:** Taylor Bonnyman. **Open:** Tue to Sat D only 6.30 to 10.30. **Closed:** 24 to 26 Dec, 2 weeks Jan, 2 weeks Aug. **Meals:** Set D £40 (2 courses) to £45. Tasting menu £65 (8 courses). **Details:** 40 seats. Separate bar.

NEW ENTRY

Garnier

As French as they come
314 Earl's Court Road, Earl's Court, SW5 9BQ
Tel no: (020) 370 4536
www.garnier-restaurant-london.co.uk
⊖ Earl's Court, map 3
French | £35
Cooking score: 2

'Earls Court . . . feels about 10 years behind the rest of London,' pronounced one reporter on discovering Didier and Eric Garnier's new gaff to be far less modern than the new breed of French brasserie (Colbert, Delaunay et al). However, as the area is hardly groaning under the weight of good restaurants, the consensus is that 'it will be here for years to come'. An unassuming place, Garnier is done up in cream and deep red, with two serried rows of linen-clad tables, red banquettes and large mirrors set with Art Deco light fittings. The menu is as French as they come: 'succulent and meaty' escargots; 'perfectly cooked' roast cod with a salty, crackly skin and a silky rich beurre blanc; and a delicious crêpe suzette. The wine list is all-French, too, opening at £18.50.
Chef/s: Andreas Engberg. **Open:** all week L 12 to 3 (3.30 Sun), D 6.30 to 10.30 (10 Sun). **Meals:** alc (main courses £18 to £32). Set L £18 (2 courses). Sun L £21. **Details:** 45 seats.

NEW ENTRY

Goode & Wright

Fabulous new unpretentious bistro
271 Portobello Road, Notting Hill, W11 1LR
Tel no: (020) 7727 5552
www.goodeandwright.co.uk
⊖ Ladbroke Grove, map 1
Anglo-French | £28
Cooking score: 3
£5 £30
OFF

This Notting Hill newcomer is an understated, completely unpretentious Anglo-French bistro knocking out superior food with the minimum of fuss and self-congratulation. There's an endearing quality to the narrow, dark-panelled dining room with its mirrors and blackboards and two rows of plain tables, down to the fantastic aromas wafting from the open kitchen. A May meal yielded buttermilk grilled oyster BLT – presented as a slider, with the breaded oyster, bacon and spinach in a brioche bun – and, from the specials board, fried black pudding with five fat wands of al dente asparagus and duck egg. A huge plaice heaped with sautéed fennel, and roast buttermilk marinated poussin (the skin 'sticky, sweet and caramelised'), with frites and salad, came next and the meal finished with the 'éclair du jour' filled with crème anglaise, topped with white chocolate and roughly chopped pistachios. The verdict? 'A fabulous experience'. Wines from £18.50.
Chef/s: Finlay Logan. **Open:** Tue D only 6 to 11. Wed to Sat 11 to 10 (10am Sat). Sun 10 to 4. **Closed:** Mon, 25 and 26 Dec, 1 and 2 Jan. **Meals:** alc (main courses £13 to £19). **Details:** 42 seats. 4 seats outside. Wheelchair access.

NEW ENTRY

Granger & Co.

A stunning line-up of wildly delicious flavours
175 Westbourne Grove, Notting Hill, W11 2SB
Tel no: (020) 7229 8944
www.grangerandco.com
⊖ Notting Hill Gate, map 4
Australian | £30
Cooking score: 3

Australian chef Bill Granger's all-day eatery is all about relaxation, enjoyment, spot-on service and quality ingredients. There's a no-bookings policy, so a jaunty apple-green canopy shelters the inevitable queue from the elements. Once you're inside, the light and airy dining room is 'swish but not ostentatious' with closely packed tables and a big marble bar with stool seating. On offer is a stunning line-up of wildly delicious flavours, seen in daytime sandwiches (miso-charred steak with pickled cucumber and red-eye mayo), salads, breakfast dishes, and even the great line-up of cakes. Mornings are especially popular, and fans come here in force for generous plates of the famed, pillowy

scrambled eggs or the ricotta hot cakes with banana and honeycomb butter. Dinner speaks of Granger's signature style, too, with shrimp tempura, sticky chilli belly pork or yellow fish curry with jasmine rice and cucumber relish ('a comforting but fresh plate of food'). Wines from £19.50.
Chef/s: Chris Clarke. **Open:** all week 7am to 11pm (10pm Sun). **Closed:** 25 and 26 Dec, Aug bank hol weekend. **Meals:** alc (main courses £13 to £23). **Details:** 70 seats. 6 seats outside. Wheelchair access.

The Harwood Arms
Gastronomic excellence and a fine wine-list
Walham Grove, Fulham, SW6 1QP
Tel no: (020) 7386 1847
www.harwoodarms.com
⊖ Fulham Broadway, map 3
British | £40
Cooking score: 5

At ease in residential Fulham, the Harwood Arms exudes an assured informality. It captures the style and atmosphere of a British pub perfectly, from weekly quiz nights and real ales, to the best in food and wine. There's an appealing bustle, with the opened-up space set around a large bar delivering a rustic elegance. A short, to-the-point menu reveals plenty of conscientious sourcing – provenance is everything, with dishes following the seasons beadily, whether it's West Country fish, seasonal game or Yorkshire rhubarb. This is rekindled British cooking of the best sort. Many start with the famed venison Scotch eggs, but how about a bowl of shellfish broth with cod cheeks and sea purslane to get your juices flowing? Then short rib of Ruby beef with purple sprouting broccoli and pickled walnuts or rump and shoulder of Herdwick lamb with artichokes, rosemary curd and garlic, with poached pear with walnuts and poached pear ice cream for a perfect finale. An intelligent and gently priced wine list (from £16) inspires you to try something new.

Chef/s: James Cochrane. **Open:** Tue to Sun L 12 to 3 (4 Sun), all week D 6.30 to 9.30 (7 to 9 Sun). **Closed:** 24 to 27 Dec, 1 Jan. **Meals:** alc (main courses £18 to £20). Set L £20 (2 courses) to £25. **Details:** 48 seats. Separate bar.

The Havelock Tavern
Bona fide local with eclectic food
57 Masbro Road, Shepherd's Bush, W14 0LS
Tel no: (020) 7603 5374
www.havelocktavern.com
⊖ Shepherd's Bush, Olympia, map 3
Modern British | £25
Cooking score: 2
£30

Although it's now under the wing of brewing giants Greene King, the Havelock Tavern still goes about its business as a bona fide neighbourhood local, complete with a Victorian blue-tiled frontage, regularly changing ales and a well-heeled, shabby-chic vibe. You can't book – so take pot luck at the bar, place your order and find a pew at one of the mismatched tables. The kitchen serves up well-crafted, eclectic dishes for robust appetites: think sea bass with spiced couscous, sticky braised pork belly on egg noodles or grilled lamb steak with Puy lentils, parsnips and ceps. If you still have room, round off with a helping of chocolate and caramel tart or toasted banana bread with ice cream and toffee sauce. Wines start at £17.50.
Chef/s: James Howarth. **Open:** all week L 12.30 to 2.30 (3 Sun), D 7 to 10 (9.30 Sun). **Closed:** 25 and 26 Dec. **Meals:** alc (£9 to £16). **Details:** 80 seats. 35 seats outside. Separate bar. Wheelchair access.

Hedone

Top-notch design and the best ingredients
301-303 Chiswick High Road, Chiswick, W4 4HH
Tel no: (020) 8747 0377
www.hedonerestaurant.com
⊖ Chiswick Park, map 1
Modern European | £50
Cooking score: 5

Mikael Jonsson is a force of nature, a strongly opinionated food blogger and apostle of contemporary cuisine who has crafted this Chiswick dining room in his own image. A row of stools flanks the kitchen pass, allowing views of the brigade at work, with Jonsson himself in charge of the final primping. In surroundings of bare brickwork, cave-art ceiling scrawls and heavy rustic furniture, the highly intellectualised food makes powerful statements. Ingredient buying has been honed to a fine-edged discrimination, dazzlingly exhibited on the Carte Blanche tasting menus (compulsory on Friday and Saturday evenings). A single oyster cooked for 20 minutes at 40°C sits on firm apple foam with vinegared shallots. Asparagus appears as whole spears and purée, with the yolk of a slow-poached egg and buttery morels, delivering astonishing clarity of flavour. The same can be said of the roasted and puréed carrots and foaming Jerusalem artichoke accompanying a thin tranche of suckling pig, and of gloriously fatty pink squab in foie gras sauce. When mistakes occur, they seem all the more jolting, as when brill, deliberately kept for four days, sits in a flavourless puddle of baked potato emulsion, or when ravioli in cloyingly sweet onion consommé burst open to exude an unexpectedly sour liquid Parmesan. Yet, in confidence-renewing contrast, a dessert study in lemon produces a pie of meringue strips and lemon curd, with sheets of lemon gel and a mouth-clenchingly pungent quenelle of lemon sorbet. The French-led wine list contains around 200 bins at relatively fair prices.

Chef/s: Mikael Jonsson. **Open:** Thur to Sat L 12 to 2.30, Tue to Sat D 6.30 to 9.30. **Closed:** Sun, Mon. **Meals:** Set L £35. Set D £55 (Tue and Wed only). Tasting menus £75 to £95. **Details:** 40 seats. Separate bar. Wheelchair access. No babies at D.

Hereford Road

Flag-waving Brit fare
3 Hereford Road, Notting Hill, W2 4AB
Tel no. (020) 7727 1144
www.herefordroad.org
⊖ Bayswater, map 4
British | £26
Cooking score: 2
£30

Blood-red banquettes and shiny white tiles hint at the butcher's shop it once was, but meat's not all that's on the menu at Hereford Road. Tom Pemberton is an ex-St John man (see entry), which suggests an enthusiasm for offal, game and braises (all present and correct) and a healthy respect for modest, oft-overlooked fish and vegetables. A set lunch of crispy pork, dandelion and mustard salad, followed by onglet and 'fantastic' chips hit the target, though mackerel with kohlrabi and sea dulse lacked balance. Nursery puds such as rice pudding and jam make a traditional finish. The lower dining room gets natural illumination from a skylight, but regulars prefer the curvy booths-for-two at street level. The list of all European wines starts at £19.50.

Chef/s: Tom Pemberton. **Open:** all week L 12 to 3 (4 Sun), D 6 to 10.30 (10 Sun). **Closed:** 24 Dec to 3 Jan, Aug bank hol. **Meals:** alc (main courses £10 to £16). Set L £13 (2 courses) to £15.50. **Details:** 55 seats. 6 seats outside. Wheelchair access.

Hunan

Chinese regional surprises
51 Pimlico Road, Chelsea, SW1W 8NE
Tel no: (020) 7730 5712
www.hunanlondon.com
⊖ Sloane Square, map 3
Chinese | £46
Cooking score: 3
V

It may look like another underwhelming provincial Chinese joint with its bare walls and crisp white linen, but pint-sized Hunan is a highly idiosyncratic one-off. There's no menu; instead, the deal is to go with the flow and put yourself in the hands of chef/proprietor Michael Peng. Simply discuss your preferences, pitch your budget and wait to be surprised. What follows is a bespoke feast of up to 18 beautifully fashioned 'tapas-style' dishes inspired by China's diverse regional cuisines. Steamed bamboo cup soup is a fixture, but other ideas are off-the-cuff – perhaps sticky radish cakes with Chinese leaves, curried beef flank, guinea fowl broth or ribeye with morning glory and fermented bean dressing. There's sweetness, too, in the shape of sticky toffee apples or red-bean pancakes. The well-considered wine and saké list has treasures in abundance to match the kitchen's cavalcade of complex flavours; prices start at £17.
Chef/s: Michael Peng. **Open:** Mon to Sat L 12.30 to 2, D 6.30 to 11. **Closed:** Sun, 24 Dec, 2 Jan, 1 week Easter, 2 weeks Aug, bank hols. **Meals:** Set L £29.80. Set D £45.80. **Details:** 48 seats.

Indian Zing

Cool vibes, thrilling food
236 King Street, Hammersmith, W6 0RF
Tel no: (020) 8748 5959
www.indianzing.co.uk
⊖ Ravenscourt Park, map 1
Indian | £27
Cooking score: 4
£5 OFF £30

Chef Manoj Vasaikar has established himself as one of the top performers on London's Indian restaurant scene, with several outlets in the capital (see entry, Indian Zilla in Barnes). His polished cooking is full of refreshingly light, up-to-the-minute flavours and thrilling contrasts, with free-range and organic ingredients given due respect. Zing's menu covers much ground – from baskets of crispy nibbles with piquant pickles and chutneys to tandoori figs with apple muesli crumble – but look for sophisticated dazzlers such as mussels simmered in tomato and tamarind broth, venison kofta spiked with methi leaves or chicken miravna with green herbs and 'virgin extract of coconut milk'. Colourful art and Indian antiques set the tone in the cool dining room, designed according to the harmonious mystical principles of Vastu Shastra; there's also a covered patio for alfresco meals. Wines (from £16) have been savvily chosen to match the spicy food.
Chef/s: Manoj Vasaikar. **Open:** all week L 12 to 3 (1 to 4 Sun), D 6 to 11 (10 Sun). **Meals:** alc (main courses £9 to £22). Set L £12 (2 courses) to £15. **Details:** 52 seats. 27 seats outside. Wheelchair access.

Kensington Place

Popular long-standing brasserie
201-209 Kensington Church Street, Notting Hill, W8 7LX
Tel no: (020) 7727 3184
www.kensingtonplace-restaurant.co.uk
⊖ Notting Hill Gate, map 4
Modern British | £30
Cooking score: 2

The floor-to-ceiling plate-glass windows, the black-and-white tiled floor, the bare wooden tables and the sheer size of the venue mean that a happy acceptance of noise, chatter, jollity and buzz is a prerequisite to a meal here – as is a matter-of-fact approach to the niceties of comfort. But this all makes Kensington Place what it is: a lively, informal brasserie that's great for dining with friends. Platters of shellfish, mackerel tartare, foie gras parfait, sea bass, mussels or ribeye steak with pommes frites are at the heart of the repertoire of modern British brasserie fare, while seasonal treats take in the likes of roast pheasant with

Savoy cabbage and bacon, and vanilla cheesecake with poached rhubarb and yoghurt sorbet. Wine starts at £19.50.
Chef/s: Daniel Loftin. **Open:** Tue to Sun L 12 to 3 (3.30 Sat, 4 Sun), Mon to Sat D 6.30 to 10.30 (11 Fri and Sat). **Closed:** Christmas, 1 Jan, bank hols. **Meals:** alc (main courses £12 to £26). Set L £17 (2 courses) to £20. **Details:** 100 seats. Separate bar. Wheelchair access.

ALSO RECOMMENDED
▲ Kiraku
8 Station Parade, Uxbridge Road, Ealing, W5 3LD
Tel no: (020) 8992 2848
www.kiraku.co.uk
⊖ Ealing Common, map 1
Japanese

Tucked into a parade of shops by the station, Kiraku delivers an authentic Japanese experience to Ealing's sushi-loving salarymen (and women). The menu deals in favourites from across Japan, with grilled salmon collar (£7.50), chilled soba noodles (£7.50) and squid and natto (£5.80) among the dishes you wouldn't encounter at a bland chain. Sushi and sashimi are serious classics, give or take the odd wacky maki roll. House wine is £15 but saké, shochu and beer are better. Closed Mon.

Kitchen W8
Big-city brio and neighbourhood glitz
11 Abingdon Road, Kensington, W8 6AH
Tel no: (020) 7937 0120
www.kitchenw8.com
⊖ High Street Kensington, map 4
Modern European | £42
Cooking score: 6

Within striking distance of Kensington High Street; affectionately supported by families living nearby; a place to take visiting business: Kitchen W8 serves many constituencies. Opened in 2009 by Philip Howard (of the Square, see entry) and restaurateur Rebecca Mascarenhas, it still achieves a freshness of welcome and attention that wins new friends. This is a neighbourhood restaurant par excellence. The food is at once familiar and

sufficiently aware of changes in taste to have popular appeal. Mark Kempson brings balance and a light touch to his remarkably consistent output, for example in a superb potted venison served with beetroot relish, walnut salad and black pudding Scotch egg, or in a well-timed whole lemon sole with sea beet, roasted cauliflower, kohlrabi, ras el hanout and pomegranate – the common thread running through all this is food that fully exploits contrasting flavours and textures. Equally, a beguiling combination of warm ginger financier with medjool date ice cream and whipped white chocolate rice pudding simply dazzles. The cosmopolitan wine list (starting at £20) offers impeccable choice and friendly mark-ups.
Chef/s: Mark Kempson. **Open:** all week L 12 to 2.30 (12.30 to 3 Sun), D 6 to 10.30 (6.30 to 9.30 Sun). **Closed:** 24 to 26 Dec, bank hols. **Meals:** alc (main courses £20 to £30). Set L £17.50 (2 courses) to £19.50. Early set D £21.50 (2 courses) to £24.50. Sun L £29.50. **Details:** 75 seats. Wheelchair access.

Koffmann's
The old master is back
The Berkeley, Wilton Place, Belgravia, SW1X 7RL
Tel no: (020) 7235 1010
www.the-berkeley.co.uk
⊖ Knightsbridge, Hyde Park Corner, map 4
French | £55
Cooking score: 5

🛏

After the closing of Tante Claire in Chelsea, it looked as though Pierre Koffmann was lost to London. His return in 2010 to these elegant premises in the Berkeley, a Knightsbridge hotel that has seen its fair share of fine dining, was welcomed with a tidal wave of affection from readers. Once again, the capital thrills to seared foie gras with pain d'épices and apple, grilled lobster with herb butter and, of course, the unforgettable pig's trotter stuffed with sweetbreads and morels, the epitome of earthy richness. There are excursions beyond the French fringes, productive ones too, such as squid tagliatelle or the main-course Ibérico pork with girolles. However, it's the *cuisine*

grande-mère dishes that still elicit raptures, such as the beef cheek daube, braised to gentle disintegration in red wine. A 15-minute dessert wait is rewarded by pillowy pistachio soufflé and coordinating ice cream, or there are old-school flamed crêpes suzette. South-west France is the compass point for the wine list, with good showings of Jurançon, Gaillac and Irouléguy. Prices open at £29.
Chef/s: Pierre Koffmann. **Open:** all week L 12 to 2.30, D 6 to 10.30. **Meals:** alc (main courses £22 to £60). Set L £21.50 (2 courses) to £25.50. **Details:** 115 seats.

Launceston Place
Fashionable without being frivolous
1a Launceston Place, South Kensington, W8 5RL
Tel no: (020) 7937 6912
www.launcestonplace-restaurant.co.uk
⊖ Gloucester Road, map 3
Modern British | £48
Cooking score: 5

Launceston Place is quite the ace to have up your sleeve when you're out to impress. It's most definitely a 'neighbourhood' restaurant (albeit a chi-chi South Kensington neighbourhood restaurant), and guests are made to feel not just welcome, but special. It is also a significant London destination with an ambitious gastronomic streak. Tim Allen has quickly found his stride here. His 'superb' cooking, 'exquisite to the finest detail', is fashionable without being frivolous. Lardo-wrapped veal sweetbread is enhanced by smoked sweetcorn purée, charred lettuce and sherry vinegar, and red mullet is given a subtle 'surf and turf' treatment with chicken oysters and brown-butter chicken jus. The excellent-value lunch menu might offer the delicious proposition of roasted Landes quail with bacon, organic brown chicken and truffle porcini potatoes, with English custard tart for pudding (all variations on themes from the carte). Nevertheless, the 'peaceful, relaxed' restaurant shines brightest come nightfall. A classy wine selection runs from £25 to four figures.

Chef/s: Tim Allen. **Open:** Tue to Sun L 12 to 2.30, all week D 6 to 10 (6.30 Sun). **Closed:** 24 and 25 Dec, 1 Jan, bank hols. **Meals:** Set L £19 (2 courses) to £25. Set D £48. Sun L £29.50. Tasting menu £65. **Details:** 60 seats. Separate bar. Wheelchair access.

★ TOP 10 ★

The Ledbury
Astonishing food from an Aussie star
127 Ledbury Road, Notting Hill, W11 2AQ
Tel no: (020) 7792 9090
www.theledbury.com
⊖ Notting Hill Gate, Westbourne Park, map 4
Modern European | £80
Cooking score: 8
♦ V

It may radiate old-school Notting Hill affluence, but the über-suave Ledbury is also a proper neighbourhood eatery – albeit one with arty chandeliers, leather chairs and mirrored walls. Foodies come to this cool, soigné cocoon for 'a good pampering' and a masterclass in sophisticated contemporary cuisine, courtesy of Brett Graham: a blazingly talented chef who cooks with vigour, authority and audacious brio. Tasting menus are the way to go: a procession of 'really tiny' but exquisite miniatures guaranteed to make you take notice. How about roast quail breasts with walnut milk, mousserons and pear, or a jokey textured 'risotto' fashioned from celeriac and new potato, sitting in a pool of parsley essence with a slice of almost translucent smoked eel laid on top? Glorious seasonal game always engenders rave reviews, from roast breast and confit leg of pigeon with foie gras, rhubarb and a profusion of pretty 'red' accompaniments, to saddle of roe deer 'at its finest': perhaps served with juniper-baked celeriac, wild garlic and hops pickled in beer. As the culinary barometer shifts towards sweetness, the kitchen responds by offering palate-jangling sorbets ahead of, say, a textbook passion fruit soufflé or a powerful pavé of full-on bitter chocolate with milk purée and lovage ice cream. Service is smart, professional and cosmopolitan. The opening salvos on the fabulous drinks list are provided by world beers, saké, sherry and brilliant wines by the glass. Big-name Bordeaux, sexy Italians, obscure German whites and bottles from Brett Graham's chums 'down under' are among the vinous treasures. Prices from £25. **Chef/s:** Brett Graham. **Open:** Tue to Sun L 12 to 2 (2.30 Sun), all week D 6.30 to 10.15 (7 to 10 Sun). **Closed:** 25 and 26 Dec, Aug bank hol. **Meals:** alc (main courses £30 to £32). Set L £30 (2 courses) to £35. Set D £80. Sun L £50. Tasting menu £105 (10 courses). **Details:** 55 seats. Wheelchair access.

ALSO RECOMMENDED

▲ Madsen

20 Old Brompton Road, South Kensington, SW7 3DL
Tel no: (020) 7225 2772
www.madsenrestaurant.com
⊖ South Kensington, map 3
Scandinavian

'Very Scandinavian – blond wood (floor, plain tables, chairs), white walls and lots of modern, white-shaded lights hanging from the ceiling,' noted a reporter of this informal Scandinavian eatery that's 'so handy for South Kensington tube'. Lunch simply on smushi (small versions of the Danish open sandwich) or dine on potato and onion pancake topped with lumpfish roe, sour cream and red onion (£6.95), then continue with Swedish 'wallenbergare': veal patty with peas, butter sauce and lingonberry jam (£13.95). Weekend brunch and Nordic Sunday roasts, too. Wines from £21. Closed Sun D.

The Mall Tavern

Comfort food with a dash of good humour
71-73 Palace Gardens Terrace, Notting Hill, W8 4RU
Tel no: (020) 7229 3374
www.themalltavern.com
⊖ Notting Hill Gate, High Street Kensington, map 4
Modern British | £29
Cooking score: 3

£30

Wittily presented comfort-food staples are the speciality at this Victorian pub a minute from Notting Hill Gate tube station. Dishes are served with a relaxing lack of ceremony (although the *salon privé* is a more sophisticated drawing room with swagged curtains). A jar of huge strips of pork crackling with a little mug of apple sauce is a good way to begin a Sunday lunch. 'Posh potted pâtés and pickles' is a tongue-twisting palate-pleaser and is typical of the good-humoured vein in evidence throughout the menu, where brand names from the heritage larder abound: Mother's Pride, Bird's Eye, Smash. Monkfish with cloud 'shrooms and scorched onions and finely sliced pink roast beef with crisp-fried cabbage, come in hugely satisfying portions. Sweet cravings are more than satiated by variations of Arctic roll in classic, yuzu, mango and Parma violet incarnations, among other desserts. Wines from £19, or £4.75 a glass.
Chef/s: Jesse Dunford Wood. **Open:** all week L 12 to 5, D 5 to 10. **Closed:** 1 week Christmas to New Year. **Meals:** alc (main courses £12 to £19). **Details:** 85 seats. 20 seats outside. Separate bar.

NEW ENTRY
The Malt House
A gem of a pub
17 Vanston Place, Fulham, SW6 1AY
Tel no: (0207) 385 3593
www.malthousefulham.co.uk
⊖ Fulham Broadway, map 3
British | £40
Cooking score: 4

'Such a pretty pub,' thought one reporter, taken by the light, airy look of this renovated Fulham hostelry (now with rooms). Claude Bosi's second pub (see also The Fox and Grapes, Wimbledon) is a chic foodie boozer combining pubby credentials with a kitchen that's capable of delivering some accomplished food – but then Marcus McGuinness was formerly Bosi's head chef at Hibiscus (see entry). A meaty piece of Cornish skate wing cooked in a rich, foamy brown butter, served with capers, lovely Kalamata olives and a little dish of buttery confit Jersey Royals, delighted one diner, as did the preceding sliced red and whole yellow beets, which came teamed with iced feta (aka feta sorbet) and balsamic vinegar, delivering a richly sweet-salty collation. Others have praised warm mussel and wild garlic broth with smoked bacon, wild rabbit and cider pie, and blood orange and thyme polenta cake. A concise international wine list opens at £19. Note: popular with supporters (well-mannered) when Chelsea are playing at home.
Chef/s: Marcus McGuinness. **Open:** Mon to Fri L 12 to 3, D 6 to 10 (10.30 Fri). Sat and Sun 12 to 10.30 (9.30 Sun). **Closed:** 25 Dec. **Meals:** alc (main courses £13 to £27). Set L £17.50 (2 courses) to £19.50. **Details:** 85 seats. 20 seats outside. Separate bar.

★ TOP 50 ★
Marcus Wareing at the Berkeley
Diverting menus from a stellar chef
The Berkeley, Wilton Place, Belgravia, SW1X 7RL
Tel no: (020) 7235 1200
www.marcus-wareing.com
⊖ Hyde Park Corner, Knightsbridge, map 4
Modern European | £80
Cooking score: 8

Much has been said about the hermetic nature of Marcus Wareing's dining room within the Berkeley Hotel. A womb-like place of dark panelling, oxblood chairs and soft lighting, it feels richly enveloping by night, though one may feel a trifle cut off from the daylight world of lunchtime. It is run with unexceptionable professionalism by staff who are invariably praised by reporters (the sommelier is a sympathetic paragon of the art), and makes a soothing and civilised setting for Wareing's intricately worked modern European dishes. The menu is written in sparse, shopping-list style. What you get is much more than what you see, as 'scallops, white asparagus and almond' add up to a carefully wrought medley of interactive textures, or 'foie gras, rhubarb and brioche' takes a classical approach to the counterpointing of sweet and tart. Materials are first-rate, as when Herdwick lamb turns up with broccoli and wild garlic, or Scottish halibut with fregola pasta, blood orange and sea kale. Sticky desserts may combine treacle, custard and dates, or banana, yuzu and popcorn. Sadly, the set lunch sits less comfortably with readers, with complaints of poor seasoning and 'not good enough' choice for a restaurant operating at this high level. The wine list is a plutocrat's paradise, however, with whole runs of Châteauneufs and Barolos to romp through. Wines by the glass, and the wine-pairing options, are probably the way to go. Bottles start at £35.

Chef/s: Marcus Wareing and Mark Froydenlund. **Open:** Mon to Sat L 12 to 2.30, D 6 to 10.45. **Closed:** Sun, 1 Jan. **Meals:** Set L £30 (2 courses) to £38. Set D £80. Chef's menu £120 (8 courses). **Details:** 70 seats.

NEW ENTRY

Medlar

A meal here is a real treat
438 King's Road, Chelsea, SW10 0LJ
Tel no: (020) 7349 1900
www.medlarrestaurant.co.uk
⊖ Sloane Square, Fulham Broadway, map 3
Modern French | £42
Cooking score: 4
🍷

The unprepossessing frontage may not stop you in your tracks, but persevere. For many, a meal here is a real treat, with one reporter singling out first courses for special mention, especially the crab raviolo with its rich bisque sauce. Contemporary crossover dishes such as sea bream carpaccio with sauce vierge, cucumber, seaweed purée and tempura prawns or a main course of wild turbot with ginger, mushroom and soy broth, white asparagus, pak choi and prawn dumplings reveal plenty of original ideas and novel presentations, but the focus is on sound culinary principles and traditional techniques. Note a rack of lamb with its confit shoulder and tongue, teamed with petits pois à la française and Jersey Royals. Portions are generous, cooked with total competence and flair, and served with grace by cheerful and patient staff. When it comes to wine, Medlar's first love is France but high standards are maintained for the rest of the world on a thoughtfully compiled list. Bottles from £25.

Chef/s: Joe Mercer Nairne. **Open:** all week L 12 to 3, D 6.30 to 10.30. **Closed:** 24 to 26 Dec. **Meals:** Set L Mon to Fri £21.50 (2 courses) to £26. Set L Sat and Sun £30. Set D £35 (2 courses) to £42. Sun D £30. **Details:** 80 seats. 8 seats outside.

🍴 A PRIZE MEAL AT THE BERKELEY

Last year we teamed up with Waitrose to search for budding restaurant inspectors, and after a day of foodie tests (and fun) at Waitrose cookery school, Laura LeBeau was named the overall winner. The prize: a meal for two at **Marcus Wareing at the Berkeley** and the chance to write up her meal for The Good Food Guide 2014. Here's her mouthwatering review.

Without pre-amble, the dinner I had at Marcus Wareing at the Berkeley was exceptional. The room is like a giant red-velvet jewellery box, meaning that you feel pleasingly cosseted and sparkly all evening.

The menu is £80 for three courses, with four choices at each stage. 'Foie gras, rhubarb, brioche' was warm and fried, rather than a cold terrine version. It came with brioche, brown butter (a revelation), rhubarb jelly and ginger yoghurt.

'Herdwick lamb, broccoli, wild garlic' was the apogee of a spring dish, whereas 'Venison, January king, almond' owed more to the winter months. Both had reached the levels of concentration in flavour that mark this kind of food apart. The attention to detail and technical skills involved in the sauces and garnishes are what make these plates astounding - nothing is superfluous.

The amuse-bouches that appeared in between - light gougère, agnolotti with pumpkin velouté, salt caramel truffles - were clever and well judged.

Wines were truly multicultural. We went by the glass, matched to each course, and explored new finds such as a Macvin du Jura and a Santa Monica Pinot Noir.

Marcus Wareing at the Berkeley is producing perfectly executed, thoughtful and interesting food, and must constitute one of the best evenings out in London this year.

One-O-One

Seafood with impeccable provenance
Sheraton Park Tower, 101 Knightsbridge,
Knightsbridge, SW1X 7RN
Tel no: (020) 7290 7101
www.oneoonerestaurant.com
⊖ Knightsbridge, map 4
Seafood | £62
Cooking score: 5

V

One-O-One is on the ground floor of the
Sheraton Park Tower Hotel and has its own
prominent entrance with no access to the main
building, but there's no escaping the fact that
this is a hotel dining room. Fish is the major
subject on a menu that has high aspirations and
prices (and it is certainly pricey). Breton chef
Pascal Proyart is a brand ambassador for the
Norwegian Seafood Council, so expect to see
wild Red King crab from the Barents Sea,
perhaps grilled with basil-tomato olive oil and
a citrus vierge, or slow-roasted wild Arctic cod
teamed with reserva chorizo, persillade
potato, piquillo, tomato and fennel and squid a
la plancha. Although some of the more
outlandish combinations do not always
balance – Proyart is a better judge of textures
than flavours – powerful French regional
dishes bear out the quality of his meat
cooking: Derbyshire beef fillet lyonnaise with
red Burgundy sauce, for example. There's little
financial relief to be found on the enticing
wine list, with prices starting at £34.
Chef/s: Pascal Proyart. **Open:** all week L 12 to 2.30
(12.30 Sat and Sun), D 6.30 to 10. **Closed:** 25 and 26
Dec, 1 Jan. **Meals:** alc (main courses £28 to £32). Set
L £17 (2 courses) to £22. Tasting menus £49 to £59
(6 courses). **Details:** 52 seats. 30 seats outside.
Separate bar. Wheelchair access. Car parking.

★ BEST SET LUNCH ★

NEW ENTRY

Outlaw's at the Capital

Flat-out excellent seafood
Capital Hotel, 22-24 Basil Street, Knightsbridge,
SW3 1AT
Tel no: (020) 7589 5171
www.capitalhotel.co.uk
⊖ Knightsbridge, map 4
Seafood | £50
Cooking score: 6

⇆ V

The restaurant at the Capital Hotel doesn't
make a big splash. A slip of a space, it has never
been considered an exciting room but, with
honey-coloured panelling and well-spaced
tables, it soothes. Since opening in the autumn
of 2012, Nathan Outlaw and head chef Peter
Biggs have tinkered with the format,
changing the focus from Outlaw's Grill in
Rock to that of his fine-dining restaurant (see
entries, Cornwall), but the emphasis has
always been on the fastidious sourcing of fish,
vibrant seasoning and ingenious grace notes.
By keeping the menu sufficiently succinct, by
making sure everything on it counts, it
certainly works. Meals are jump-started with
deep-fried fish balls and delicious bread.
Then, perhaps, 'gorgeously cooked' rosemary
cod, scampi and grilled leek, with orange
providing a subtle citrus zing. Monkfish, 'a
triumphant standout', comes wrapped in
smoked bacon, lightly dressed with carrots,
grapes and deep-flavoured mushroom
ketchup, a rape seed oil sauce, inflected with
the zip of an oaked Chardonnay reduction,
absorbing sweet, smoky notes as the dish is
eaten. As for dessert, char-grilled pineapple
with cream cheese ice cream and rum-
flavoured butterscotch sauce is clever and
innovative. The heavyweight wine list jets
skyward from £30.
Chef/s: Nathan Outlaw and Peter Biggs. **Open:** Mon
to Sat L 12 to 2.30, D 6.30 to 10.30. **Closed:** Sun.
Meals: alc (main courses £26 to £32). Set L £20 (2
courses) to £25. Tasting menu £70 (6 courses).
Details: 34 seats. Separate bar. Wheelchair access.

Pétrus

Fastidious, French-accented food
1 Kinnerton Street, Knightsbridge, SW1X 8EA
Tel no: (020) 7592 1609
www.gordonramsay.com
⊖ Knightsbridge, map 4
Modern French | £65
Cooking score: 5

V

Luxury with refreshing informality is the stated aim at Gordon Ramsay's reboot of the legendary Pétrus, and there's no denying it delivers the promise. The highly civilised, claret-toned dining room is soothing on the eye and easy on the ear – 'unlike some modern restaurants they have carpets', noted one couple, 'so we could hear without difficulty.' However, it's the food that really lifts the senses, and Ramsay's lieutenant Sean Burbidge knows how to impress without resorting to gimmicks or molecular wizardry. Skilled craftsmanship and intense flavours are a given in fastidious French-accented dishes ranging from crispy frogs' legs with broccoli purée, braised grelot onion, black garlic and Parmesan to sea bream with celery gnocchi, shimeji mushrooms and truffle emulsion. British ingredients such as Highland venison also have their say, and desserts set out to dazzle – who could resist the show-stopping chocolate sphere with milk ice cream and honeycomb? Service is beyond reproach, particularly when demystifying the vinous treasures lurking in the centrepiece glass-fronted wine store. Needless to say, ranks of ultra-rare Château Pétrus are beyond the reach of most mortals, but the list also features blue-blooded bottles for most occasions. Prices start at £33.
Chef/s: Sean Burbidge. **Open:** Mon to Sat L 12 to 2.30, D 6.30 to 10.30. **Closed:** Sun. **Meals:** Set L £30. Set D £55 (2 courses) to £65. Tasting menu £75 (5 courses). **Details:** 54 seats. Wheelchair access.

Pizza East Portobello

Crowd-pulling pizzas come west
310 Portobello Road, Ladbroke Grove, W10 5TA
Tel no: (020) 8969 4500
www.pizzaeastportobello.com
⊖ Ladbroke Grove, map 1
Italian-American | £25
Cooking score: 2
£30

The Pizza East concept (see also Pizza East, Pizza East Kentish Town) suits the way London wants to eat and drink these days, with an atmosphere of warm informality, all-day menus that allow for grazing and a decent choice of reasonably priced wines. It's not all about pizza, though with veal meatballs, prosciutto, cream and sage listed as one of the toppings, the selection is hard to bypass. Just about every dish begs to be ordered, whether bone marrow bruschetta or monkfish with Jersey royals and guanciale (smoked Italian bacon), a mac 'n' cheese or spring lamb shoulder from the wood oven. Salted chocolate caramel tart is still the star of dessert: one of those must-order puddings. Wine prices start at £19.50.
Chef/s: Kyle Boyce. **Open:** all week 8am to 11.30pm (12am Fri and Sat, 10.30pm Sun). **Closed:** 24 to 26 Dec. **Meals:** alc (main courses £8 to £17). Set L £25 (2 courses). Set D £30. **Details:** 127 seats. 42 seats outside. Separate bar. Wheelchair access.

Popeseye Steak House

A red-blooded steak-fest
108 Blythe Road, Olympia, W14 0HD
Tel no: (020) 7610 4578
www.popeseye.com
⊖ Olympia, map 3
Steaks | £20
Cooking score: 1
£5 OFF £30

Ian Hutchinson was peddling steak long before young pretenders such as Hawksmoor (see entries) turned it into the *viande du jour*. His unadulterated Olympia stalwart has been dishing up red-blooded meat-fests since 1995 and his approach couldn't be simpler. Just three cuts of properly aged, grass-fed Aberdeen Angus beef – sirloin, fillet and rump (aka 'popeseye') – are cooked on an open grill and served with chips plus an optional salad. All you need do is decide the weight and degree of cooking. That's it, apart from cheese, homemade puds and a short wine list dominated by beefy reds (from £13.50). Note: no credit cards. Also at 277 Upper Richmond Road, Putney; tel: (020) 8788 7733.

Chef/s: Ian Hutchinson. **Open:** Mon to Sat D only 6.45 to 10. **Closed:** Sun, Christmas, New Year, bank hols. **Meals:** alc (steaks £11 to £60). **Details:** 34 seats. Wheelchair access.

Portobello Ristorante Pizzeria

Eat-me pizza for sharing
7 Ladbroke Road, Notting Hill, W11 3PA
Tel no: (020) 7221 1373
www.portobellolondon.co.uk
⊖ Notting Hill Gate, map 4
Italian | £25
Cooking score: 1
£30

Regulars still regard this Notting Hill hot spot, which launched in 2008, as a 'real gem'. The busy, bustling interior is testament to the popularity of this little piece of Italy, and when the weather cooperates, the front terrace is a great place to enjoy a lazy lunch. If you can get past the imaginative selection of pizzas (which can come by the metre if you wish), just about every dish on the menu begs to be ordered: linguine with seafood, risotto al nero di sepia, char-grilled Italian sausage with roast potatoes and spicy diavolo sauce. House Sicilian is £17.95.

Chef/s: Andrea Ippolito. **Open:** all week 12 to 11.30. **Closed:** 25 and 26 Dec. **Meals:** alc (main courses £10 to £20). Set L £14.50 (2 courses). **Details:** 60 seats. 40 seats outside.

Potli

Authentic Indian street food
319-321 King Street, Hammersmith, W6 9NH
Tel no: (020) 8741 4328
www.potli.co.uk
⊖ Ravenscourt Park, Stamford Brook, map 1
Indian | £25
Cooking score: 3
£5 OFF £30

This laid-back turmeric-coloured 'Indian market kitchen' serves bazaar-inspired dishes to an appreciative and loyal west London clientele. Inside, nostalgia is stirred by Bollywood posters and tinplate ad boards. Chef Jay Ghosh is regarded as a 'total spice geek' by fans of his sure-handed blends, which enliven classic street snacks, curries, breads and preordered specials including a tandoor roasted leg of lamb for eight. Attention to detail – sustainable fish, homemade chutneys, British meat and vegetables – pays off. From the regular menu, a starter of chicken tikka three ways is singled out for praise. Mains of prawn narkel diye, cooked in a coconut sauce with mustard and coriander, and aloo udayagiri, with cumin, ginger, garlic and fresh herbs, are also admired, as is service that is 'unpretentious' but courteous. Prices are keen, with wine starting at £16.

Chef/s: Jay Ghosh. **Open:** Mon to Sat L 12 to 2.45, D 6 to 10.30 (11 Fri and Sat). Sun 12 to 10.30. **Meals:** alc (main courses £6 to £18). Set L £9.95. Sun L £10.99. **Details:** 67 seats. 24 seats outside. Separate bar. Wheelchair access.

The Princess Victoria

Superior pub food and glorious wines
217 Uxbridge Road, Shepherd's Bush, W12 9DH
Tel no: (020) 8749 5886
www.princessvictoria.co.uk
⊖ Shepherd's Bush Market, map 1
British | £27
Cooking score: 3
🍾 £30

Built on the site of the old Shepherd's Bush tram stop, at a time when the future Empress of India was still a princess, this William

Bruton pub with its graciously curved bar and interconnecting rooms dates from the gin-palace era. Its present-day business is in serving imaginative modern British food, including tempting bar snacks and world-class wines in a relaxed, friendly environment. Expect to find a bone marrow dumpling and chanterelles floating in your beef tea to start, before a meal rocks on with crisp-skinned bream on cep risotto, or Tamworth pork with braised celeriac, Swiss chard and smoked ham croquettes. Elegant pork boards and smoked fish plates supplement the individual dishes, and sublime stickiness turns up in the form of marmalade ice cream with kumquat compote. The wine list is a cracker, with bottles to suit the deepest of pockets and the tightest of card-margins: biodynamics, organics and naturals included. The house selection of nearly 20 bottles starts at £16.70, £11.40 a half-litre carafe, £4.20 the glass.

Chef/s: Matt Reuther. **Open:** all week L 12 to 3 (4.30 Sun), D 6.30 to 10.30 (9.30 Sun). **Closed:** 25 to 28 Dec. **Meals:** alc (main courses £10 to £24). **Details:** 120 seats. 40 seats outside. Separate bar. Car parking.

Racine

Classic and comforting French food
239 Brompton Road, Knightsbridge, SW3 2EP
Tel no: (020) 7584 4477
www.racine-restaurant.com
⊖ Knightsbridge, South Kensington, map 3
French | £35
Cooking score: 4

Henry Harris's *restaurant du quartier* just happens to be in a *quartier* that includes the Royal Albert Hall, and yet any tendency to grandeur is firmly resisted in the interest of creating a haven of honest-to-goodness French bourgeois cuisine. It's a simple enough room, not much resembling the bistro it is in spirit, but appealing nonetheless. Expect bone marrow persillade, mussels with a garlic and saffron mousse, or brains in black butter, to start, with follow-ons coming in the reassuring shapes of rabbit and bacon in mustard sauce or sea bass with wilted greens,

tomatoes and aïoli. The ratio of saucing to prime ingredient worried one reporter, and the seasoning – in a parsley job with otherwise perfect ox tongue, say, or the Roquefort butter paired with a great veal chop – can seem overpowering. Pear frangipane tart or raspberry and rose meringue close the deal. Lunch and pre-theatre menus are good value, and the wine list (from £22) includes some non-French interlopers.

Chef/s: Henry Harris. **Open:** all week L 12 to 3 (3.30 Sat and Sun), D 6 to 10.30 (10 Sun). **Closed:** 25 and 26 Dec, 2 weeks Aug, bank hols. **Meals:** alc (main courses £17 to £29). Set L and D Mon to Sat £15.50 (2 courses) to £17.75. Sun L £18 (2 courses) to £20. **Details:** 75 seats. 4 seats outside.

Rasoi

Luxurious Indian flagship
10 Lincoln Street, Chelsea, SW3 2TS
Tel no: (020) 7225 1881
www.rasoi-uk.com
⊖ Sloane Square, map 3
Indian | £60
Cooking score: 5
V

Vineet Bhatia's luxurious Chelsea town-house restaurant hasn't merely impressed this year – it has lifted guests 'into a state of euphoria'. Ironically, the joyous experience begins in slightly off-putting fashion with a ring on the doorbell to gain admittance, but once inside, the magic begins with a 'warm welcome', wafts of incense and shimmering colourful silks. This is 'evolved Indian' cooking, promising exotic ingredients (not necessarily from the Indian kitchen) and current techniques. The smoke-enclosed tandoori salmon starter with cooling cucumber dill salad has won raves, while a main course of prawns poached in kaffir lime and coconut sauce evokes 'holidays on the Indian coast'. Darjeeling tea chicken with goji berry pilau or lamb with walnut upma and blue cheese-seekh kebab are highly original combinations that demonstrate Bhatia's faculty with flavour. His chocolate samosa is now famous, but rose brûlée with rasgulla wheel is no less tempting.

Prices are high, yet this is 'brilliant cooking, terrific value'. Waiting staff 'enthuse knowledgeably' about the spice-appropriate if steeply priced wine list (from £20).
Chef/s: Vineet Bhatia. **Open:** Tue to Fri and Sun L 12 to 2.30, Tue to Sun D 6 to 10.30 (10 Sun). **Closed:** Mon, 25 and 26 Dec, 1 Jan. **Meals:** Set L £22 (2 courses) to £32. Set D £50 (2 courses) to £60. Tasting menu £89 (7 courses). **Details:** 54 seats.

★ TOP 10 ★

Restaurant Gordon Ramsay

A flagship evolves
68-69 Royal Hospital Road, Chelsea, SW3 4HP
Tel no: (020) 7352 4441
www.gordonramsay.com
⊖ Sloane Square, map 3
Modern French | £95
Cooking score: 9

⌀ V

Evolution, not revolution, is the order of things at the Chelsea flagship where Clare Smyth is now chef/patron. As well as taking a share of the business, she has overseen a refurbishment of the intimate dining room and added elegant, inventive dishes to the menu. It's all subtly done, since some still come for the Ramsay classics, but it's there if you look – and clearly a fillip for the 'veritable army' of staff, who can now revel both in the classy comfort of the old and the excitement of the new. Change can unbalance perfection, and the tiniest of wobbles is exposed here, where expectations are sky-high and 'special occasion' hovers constantly in the air. But readers feel it's 'as good as ever', and they might be thinking of puffy gougères, a little pea mousse with a mini garden of crisp baby vegetables and petals, or an iced pestle and mortar of crisp-frozen herbs to be crushed by the diner and mixed with a lime and cucumber sorbet as a sherbety pre-dessert. Seasonality and gorgeous colour are the key attributes of the best dishes; to start, a coeur de boeuf tomato stuffed with vivid caper-spiked tomato 'tartare' and surrounded by torn buffalo milk curds, black olive and Parmesan crisps, and to follow, Herdwick mutton with

the 'crunch and crackle' of puffed wild rice and a smoky aubergine purée. It is possible to play it too safe (suckling pig four ways, including a lovely chou farci, is immaculate but staid), but restraint works brilliantly in places. A quenelle of vanilla mousse in a garden of peach, strawberry and lemon verbena is the purest form of pudding art, though roast pineapple with buttery coriander financiers and coconut sorbet justifies the baker's intervention. The wine list puts a French foot forward, with plenty of quality and lots of stickies, but there is no obligation to go big or go home: bottles start at £28 for a white Bordeaux.
Chef/s: Clare Smyth. **Open:** Mon to Fri L 12 to 2.15, D 6.30 to 10.15. **Closed:** Sat, Sun, 25 and 26 Dec. **Meals:** Set L £55. Set D £95. Tasting menu £135 (7 courses) to £155. **Details:** 45 seats. Wheelchair access.

Restaurant Michael Nadra

Tasteful and satisfying Chiswick favourite
6-8 Elliott Road, Chiswick, W4 1PE
Tel no: (020) 8742 0766
www.restaurant-michaelnadra.co.uk
⊖ Turnham Green, map 1
Modern European | £35
Cooking score: 4

£5
OFF

Remarkably good value is a big selling point at Michael Nadra's popular Chiswick restaurant: a tasteful brasserie-style dining room kitted out with leather banquettes, tightly packed tables and slate floors. The kitchen knows how to mix and manage eclectic ingredients, as in a plate of olive-stuffed rabbit leg with stewed aubergines, garlic, piquillo peppers, Parmesan polenta and thyme jus. Confident seafood cookery harks back to the restaurant's former life as Fish Hook. Roast cod is served with a springtime assortment of ratte potatoes, samphire, fennel salad and chervil cream, while grilled lemon sole might be teamed with sautéed squid, flageolet beans, salsify and parsley purée – thoughtful, satisfying ideas with clear accents and contrasts. To conclude, invest in treacle tart or chestnut and caramel mille-feuille. The well-versed, 200-bin wine list has an excellent choice in the sub-£30 bracket, with house selections from £17 (£4.50 a glass). There's now a north London offshoot in Primrose Hill (see entry).

Chef/s: Michael Nadra. **Open:** all week L 12 to 2.30 (3.30 Sat and Sun), Mon to Sat D 6 to 10 (10.30 Fri and Sat). **Closed:** 25 to 27 Dec, 1 Jan. **Meals:** Set L £19.50 (2 courses) to £24, Set D £29 (2 courses) to £35. Tasting menu L £39 (6 courses). Tasting menu D £49 (6 courses). **Details:** 50 seats. Wheelchair access.

The River Café

Italian icon by the river
Thames Wharf, Rainville Road, Hammersmith, W6 9HA
Tel no: (020) 7386 4200
www.rivercafe.co.uk
⊖ Hammersmith, map 1
Italian | £80
Cooking score: 6

Down by the riverside, Ruth Rogers' world-renowned restaurant whirls like a merry-go-round, accommodating kids as easily as celebs. The setting is unbeatable for alfresco revelling, but there's also much to purr about in the cavernous, bright-white dining room with its high-arched ceilings, huge windows and photogenic clock. Ever-rising prices and strictly enforced time slots may grate, but there's no arguing when it comes to Rogers' now-legendary take on rustic Italian food. It's always been about ingredients, seasonality and bold flavours here, with salads and handmade pasta leading the pack – from a springtime plate of crab with sea kale, capers, red chicory leaves and Cedro lemon to fresh tagliatelle with new season's wet walnut sauce and panzotti stuffed with pumpkin and ricotta. The char-grill and showpiece wood-oven also have their say, turning out everything from sea bass fillet with salsa verde, potato, girolles and chanterelles to whole Anjou pigeon doused in Fontodi Chianti with sage, cavolo nero and polenta. To finish, peerless artisan cheeses await, along with the irresistible chocolate nemesis and lemon tart. The fabulous wine list wallows in the glories of Italian regional viticulture – from Abruzzo to Veneto and Sicily to Sardinia. Around £30 pays for an entry-level bottle.

Chef/s: Ruth Rogers. **Open:** all week L 12.30 to 2.15 (2.30 Sat, 12 to 3 Sun). Mon to Sat D 7 to 9 (9.15 Sat). **Closed:** 24 Dec to 3 Jan, bank hols. **Meals:** alc (main courses £32 to £45). **Details:** 115 seats. 75 seats outside. Separate bar. Wheelchair access. Car parking.

Salloos

Long-serving Pakistani stronghold
62-64 Kinnerton Street, Knightsbridge, SW1X 8ER
Tel no: (020) 7235 4444
www.salloos.co.uk
⊖ Knightsbridge, map 4
Pakistani | £40
Cooking score: 2

Ensconced on the first floor of a Belgravia mews house, this glamorous and rather exclusive dining room has established itself as a stronghold of authentic Pakistani cooking since owner Muhammed Salahuddin ('Salloo' to his friends) launched the place in 1976. Chef Abdul Aziz has been overseeing the pots and pans since day one, and he sees no need to modify or update a familiar, finely tuned menu that takes inspiration from family recipes and the old way of doing things. Salloos is noted for its exemplary tandooris – especially the ever-popular marinated lamb chops – but also look for signature dishes such as gurd masala (stir-fried kidneys with 'hot spices'), chicken with ginger or haleem akbari (shredded lamb with wheatgerm and lentils). Wines from £20.

Chef/s: Abdul Aziz. **Open:** Mon to Sat L 12 to 2, D 7 to 11. **Closed:** Sun, 25 and 26 Dec. **Meals:** alc (main courses £18 to £24). **Details:** 50 seats. Children over 5 yrs only.

Sam's Brasserie & Bar

Busy, buzzy neighbourhood brasserie
11 Barley Mow Passage, Chiswick, W4 4PH
Tel no: (020) 8987 0555
www.samsbrasserie.co.uk
⊖ Chiswick Park, Turnham Green, map 1
Modern European | £30
Cooking score: 2

Blurring the line between bar and restaurant, Sam's cool and casual vibe sets it apart from nearby rivals in Chiswick. The jazzed-up warehouse setting is unpretentious, informal and welcoming – all things that mark out neighbourhood success stories – with a flexible menu of modern classics from the kitchen. Starters range from a charcuterie board or a salad of celeriac and black radish dressed with pomegranate, pecorino and truffle dressing, to mains such as char-grilled leg of lamb teamed with aubergine and tomato stew with anchovy and pesto dressing: typical of the gutsy nature of much of the repertoire. Sticky toffee pudding is just one of the comfort-zone desserts. Breakfast and brunch (served all week 9am to 12) have their own fans. The global wine list opens at £16.50.
Chef/s: Mark Baines. **Open:** all week 9 to 3 (4 Sat and Sun), D 6.30 to 10.30 (9.30 Sun). **Closed:** 24 to 28 Dec. **Meals:** alc (main courses £12 to £22). Set L and early D Mon to Fri £13.50 (2 courses) to £16.50. Sun L £21.50 (2 courses) to £25.50. **Details:** 100 seats. Separate bar. Wheelchair access.

The Sands End

Nicely scrubbed-up pub with spirited food
135-137 Stephendale Road, Fulham, SW6 2PR
Tel no: (020) 7731 7823
www.thesandsend.co.uk
⊖ Fulham Broadway, map 3
British | £31
Cooking score: 3
£5
OFF

'Really good pub, smiley service and excellent cooking' is one visitor's verdict of this well-appointed hostelry in a Fulham residential street. The Sands End combines comfortably laid-back demeanour and mismatched pubby good looks with a kitchen that continues to keep customers satisfied with the straightforward cooking of high-class comfort food. Hand-cut steak tartare or country-style chicken liver and bacon terrine might be curtain raisers to Poole Bay cod with spinach and Puy lentils or Middle White pork belly with Hispi cabbage and wholegrain mustard sauce. Earthy flavours and astute cooking are the keys, and there's no messing around when it comes to desserts either: pecan pie with barley malt ice cream and maple syrup is par for the course. As with everything else, thought has been put into the decent selection of ales and the wine list (bottles from £17.50).
Chef/s: Kieren Steinborn. **Open:** Mon to Sat L 12 to 3 (4 Sat), D 6 to 10. Sun 12 to 9. **Closed:** 25 Dec. **Meals:** alc (main courses £12 to £23). Set L £14.50 (2 courses) to £17.50. **Details:** 65 seats. 16 seats outside.

NEW ENTRY
The Shed

All about big flavours and good provenance
122 Palace Gardens Terrace, Notting Hill, W8 4RT
Tel no: (020) 7229 4024
www.theshed-restaurant.com
⊖ Notting Hill Gate, map 4
Modern British | £23
Cooking score: 2
£30
▼

It's very jolly in the artfully ramshackle Shed (formerly The Ark). The interior is done out like a beach hut with an ad hoc mix of props (a row of spears, a ram's head). Tables are mix-and-match wood or converted steel drums in rainbow hues at which you perch (precariously) on uncomfortable stools. The small-plates menu is strong on provenance and divided into 'slow cooking' and 'fast cooking' with advice to order three dishes, perhaps fennel-cured, carpaccio-style pollack with mini-cubes of pickled cucumber and blobs of creamy lemon mayo; beautifully pink, Moroccan spice-crusted spring lamb with more cucumber, mint and a big slick of

wild garlic yoghurt; and monkfish cheeks with rainbow chard, samphire and lemon butter – the latter so over-generous it took away the appetite for dessert. Service 'needs work'. Wines from £20.
Chef/s: Oliver Gladwin. **Open:** Tue to Sat L 12 to 3 (5 Sat), D 6 to 11. **Closed:** Sun, Mon, 24 to 26 Dec. **Meals:** alc (small plates £6 to 9). **Details:** 55 seats. Separate bar.

NEW ENTRY
The Shiori
Small restaurant, faultless food
45 Moscow Road, Notting Hill, W2 4AH
Tel no: (020) 7221 9790
www.theshiori.com
⊖ Bayswater, map 4
Japanese | £65
Cooking score: 3

When Sushi of Shiori moved from Drummond Street in Euston to Moscow Road in Bayswater the name shortened, the seating capacity increased (from eight to 18) and it changed from a sushi-serving operation to one offering kaiseki (tasting menus). Takashi Takagi composes dishes in a quiet and meticulous manner behind a counter in the small and austere room. His tasting menus make ordering easier but Hitomi Takagi, who keeps a sweet and watchful eye on proceedings, gives guidance for some of the more exotic items. There has been praise for a superb appetizer of conger eel wrapped in tofu skin, high-gloss sashimi, an intense clear broth with abalone and mitsuba (Japanese parsley), outstanding red mullet, and nigiri sushi served with wasabi and soy sauce (a brush for applying the soy comes with the instruction 'to the fish only'). Lunch is limited to a couple of set deals and a pared down version of the evening kaiseki offering. Wines from £25.50.
Chef/s: Takashi Takagi. **Open:** Tue to Sat L 12 to 3, D 6 to 10.30. **Closed:** Sun and Mon, Christmas, Easter, 2 weeks Aug. **Meals:** Set L £28.50 (4 courses) to £50 (7 courses). Set D £65 (8 courses) to £105 (12 courses). **Details:** 18 seats. Wheelchair access.

Tinello
The Italians' Italian
87 Pimlico Road, Pimlico, SW1W 8PH
Tel no: (020) 7730 3663
www.tinello.co.uk
⊖ Sloane Square, map 3
Italian | £40
Cooking score: 4
🍾

Max and Federico Sali make every effort to bring the essence of Italian cooking to this smart corner of London via their low-key, faux industrial-style restaurant (brick walls, lots of hanging metal lamps). Chef Federico is a skilled interpreter of the cuisine and a passion for quality runs through every aspect, from antipasti of baby spinach salad with goats' cheese and walnuts to loin of venison served with stewed pumpkins, watercress and hazelnut salad in a red wine sauce – each dish owing everything to superb ingredients. Pasta remains a strength, with praise for homemade tagliatelle with Parma ham and Parmesan sauce. Seafood is also pitch-perfect, perhaps monkfish with baby artichokes, potato stew and grey mullet roe. Pear and almond tart with vanilla ice cream is a good way to finish. Italy continues to be the big player on the wine list, which also scours the world's major growing areas. Prices from £14.50.
Chef/s: Federico Sali. **Open:** all week L 12 to 2.30, D 6.15 to 10.30. **Meals:** alc (main courses £17 to £27). **Details:** 74 seats. 6 seats outside.

Tom Aikens
Fine art on a plate
43 Elystan Street, Chelsea, SW3 3NT
Tel no: (020) 7584 2003
www.tomaikens.co.uk
⊖ South Kensington, map 3
Modern European | £65
Cooking score: 6

Hard-edged Nordic minimalism has elbowed out suave French luxe at Tom Aikens' born-again flagship: swathes of bare wood, concrete, canvas and raw iron defining the interior; gastronomic quotes on the walls; and ever-so-cool staff in 'unsmart casual' mode flitting from table to table. Aikens' food is still about 'fine art on a plate', with bags of intensity and a new-found diversity of flavours. Baked scallop with yeasted potatoes, osso buco and toasted-bread soup tick all the fashionable boxes, and the menu is peppered with trendy details: homemade ricotta with green olive juice and honey jelly; crab with salt-baked celeriac; compressed pear with foie gras granules; thyme curd with Pyrenean lamb shoulder. Otherwise, braised and roasted piglet served with 'flavour-bomb' pineapple fondant has been well received, and desserts are a highlight, with nods to the vogue for savoury flavours (yoghurt parfait with sweetened beets or white chocolate parfait with black olive 'snow'). A clutch of esoteric bottled beers catches the eye, and the substantial, well-bred wine list has sound offerings across the range; prices from £23.

Chef/s: Tom Aikens. **Open:** Tue to Fri L 12 to 2.30, Tue to Sat D 6.30 to 10.30. **Closed:** Sun, Mon, 25 to 26 Dec, bank hols. **Meals:** alc (main courses £29 to £35). Set L £28 (2 courses). Set D £34 (2 courses). Tasting menu £90 (7 courses). **Details:** 55 seats. Wheelchair access.

Tom's Kitchen
Streetwise Brit-inspired brasserie
27 Cale Street, Chelsea, SW3 3QP
Tel no: (020) 7349 0202
www.tomskitchen.co.uk
⊖ Sloane Square, South Kensington, map 3
Modern British | £40
Cooking score: 2

It's only round the corner from Tom Aikens' pared-back flagship restaurant (see entry), but his streetwise brasserie inhabits a very different world indeed. Noisy fans of strapping, Brit-inspired food congregate here to scoff plates of shepherd's pie, venison casserole and calf's liver with fried egg and bacon alongside burgers, steak sarnies, fishcakes, macaroni cheese and Euro favourites such as confit duck cassoulet. Photos of 'food heroes' line the walls (should you wonder where your food comes from) and the clean-lined interior is a masculine mix of tightly packed tables and long benches. Breakfasts and weekend brunches also pull in the Chelsea crowds. Wines start at £18.50. Tom's Kitchen is now a burgeoning brand, with branches in Somerset House and Canary Wharf.

Chef/s: Tom Aikens. **Open:** all week 8 to 2.30 (10 to 3.30 Sat and Sun), D 6 to 10.30 (9.30 Sun). **Meals:** alc (main courses £14 to £30). **Details:** 80 seats. Separate bar. Wheelchair access.

La Trompette
A beacon of excellence
5-7 Devonshire Road, Chiswick, W4 2EU
Tel no: (020) 8747 1836
www.latrompette.co.uk
⊖ Turnham Green, map 1
Modern European | £43
Cooking score: 5

Chiswick is bursting with expensive places to spend money in, but news that ex-Square head chef Rob Weston has relocated here from Mayfair, combined with an expansive refurb, gives locals every reason to 'head down in droves'. The interior of dark-wood floors, rich gold banquettes and white linen is elegant, and yet La Trompette remains a relaxed local restaurant, the only soundtrack being lively conversation, spilling on to the small terrace and the boutiques of Devonshire Road. Readers report favourably on the quality of the food, and at inspection the delight in detail that pervades the menu translated directly on to the plate – whether the intricacies of nettle pesto with raviolo of smoked guinea fowl; or the smoked bone marrow that made for a glossy slow-cooked short rib of beef with pickled walnuts and scorched onions; or seaweed butter gently melting into Cornish mackerel teamed with homemade linguine, shrimps and fennel. Summer shone through in a dessert of Charentais melon with burnt vanilla cream, Lillet Blanc and verbena cream. Similarly detailed at 600-plus bins, the encyclopaedic wine list (from £21) may take some navigation.

Chef/s: Rob Weston. **Open:** all week L 12 to 2.30 (12.30 to 3 Sun), D 6.30 to 10.30 (7.30 to 9.30 Sun). **Closed:** 25 and 26 Dec. **Meals:** Set L £23.50 (2 courses) to £27.50. Set D £40 (2 courses) to £45. Sun L £27.50. **Details:** 86 seats. 14 seats outside. Wheelchair access.

Yashin Sushi

Sushi with a daring twist
1a Argyll Road, Kensington, W8 7DB
Tel no: (020) 7938 1536
www.yashinsushi.com
⊖ High Street Kensington, map 4
Japanese | £45
Cooking score: 3
V

'Without soy sauce – but if you want to' proclaims a neon sign on the wall of this innovative, hot-ticket Japanese joint done out with dangling lights, dark wood and green tiles. Set up by two chefs from Nobu (see entry), Yashin has a daring way of doing things, while maintaining the fundamentals of clean, expertly prepared sushi. Some items are seared with a blowtorch, others are dressed with anything from chilli ponzu jelly to Hawaiian salt and citrus yuzu. There are appetisers and salads too, plus a smattering of hot dishes: from a 'cappuccino' of miso soup topped with tofu espuma, to slow-cooked pork belly with mustard cream. Omakase tasting menus chosen by the chefs themselves are outstanding, although prices are steep; drinks are also expensive, with wines from £25. A second branch specialising in seafood is now open at 117-119 Old Brompton Road, SW7 3RN.
Chef/s: Yasuhiro Mineno and Shinya Ikeda. **Open:** all week L 12 to 3, D 6 to 10. **Closed:** 24, 25 and 31 Dec, 1 Jan, first Mon of every month. **Meals:** alc (dishes £14 to £60). Set L £20 (2 courses) to £30. Set D £40 (2 courses) to £60. **Details:** 37 seats.

Zuma

Slinky Knightsbridge high-roller
5 Raphael Street, Knightsbridge, SW7 1DL
Tel no: (020) 7584 1010
www.zumarestaurant.com
⊖ Knightsbridge, map 4
Japanese | £75
Cooking score: 5

The ultimate Knightsbridge trendsetter, relentlessly glamorous Zuma is a smouldering den of unyielding surfaces, rough-hewn wood, rock and steel: think post-industrial hardcore meets stripped-bare Zen. Normal socialising rules don't apply in this cocooned world where celebrity is king – from cocktail guzzlers to raw fish addicts getting their high-art fix at the sushi counter. Alternatively, sit in the main dining room and observe the chefs fashioning smart sharing plates inspired by the ever-evolving world of contemporary Japanese cuisine. Palate-sharpening thrills come thick and fast as the kitchen delivers waves of tantalising morsels ranging from fried tofu with mizuna, gobo and pickled carrots to seared Wagyu beef tataki with black truffle sauce. After that, graze your way through popcorn tempura with yuzu salt, roast lobster with green chilli and garlic butter, marinated black cod and miraculously good stuff from the robata grill: pork skewers with mustard miso, perhaps, or Dover sole with shiso, chilli and plum sauce. Such exquisite pleasures come at a mind-blowing cost, and drinkers take an additional hit if ordering rare seasonal sakés or prestigious globetrotting wines (from £22).
Chef/s: Perry Fuller. **Open:** all week L 12 to 2.30 (3.30 Fri, 12.30 to 3.30 Sat and Sun), D 6 to 11 (10.30 Sun). **Closed:** 25 Dec. **Meals:** alc (dishes £7 to £70). Tasting menu £96. **Details:** 175 seats. Separate bar. Wheelchair access.

A Cena

Attractive local Italian with reliable food
418 Richmond Road, Twickenham, TW1 2EB
Tel no: (020) 8288 0108
www.acena.co.uk
⊖ Richmond, map 1
Italian | £35
Cooking score: 2

Twickenham's snappily dressed A Cena is a 'really lovely' neighbourhood restaurant with 'charming staff, buzzing atmosphere'. Expect straightforward, authentic and comforting Italian cuisine – rather than culinary fireworks – which pays due attention to ingredients. The menu rolls out in traditional format, opening the show with, perhaps, antipasti of Tuscan-style bruschetta of braised beef in Chianti, and primi piatti of tomato and rosemary risotto with mascarpone. Secondi takes in sea bream fillet with white wine, thyme and celeriac parmigiano, and calf's liver in sage breadcrumbs with roast carrots, onions and sweet-sour tomato. Dolce delivers pannacotta with salted peanut brittle and coffee caramel. Wines on the (almost) all-Italian list open at £19.
Chef/s: Nicola Parsons. **Open:** Tue to Sun L 12 to 2, Mon to Sat D 6 to 10. **Closed:** 25 to 27 Dec, bank hols. **Meals:** alc (main courses £15 to £24). Sun L £21 (2 courses) to £25. **Details:** 60 seats. Separate bar. Wheelchair access.

Albert's Table

Confident and sophisticated local bistro
49b/c Southend, Croydon, CR0 1BF
Tel no: (020) 8680 2010
www.albertstable.co.uk
map 1
Modern British | £33
Cooking score: 3
£5
OFF

Joby Wells can congratulate himself on putting his experience at some of London's landmark restaurants (La Trompette, the Square, see entries) to good use in creating this well-supported and enterprising neighbourhood eatery near Croydon South station. In contrast to the bustling high street outside, the atmosphere at Albert's Table is calming and welcoming. The signature shortcrust tart of Dorset crab with rouille is a justly popular opener, while apple jelly lends class to a pork pie made with Old Spot and served warm with poached quails' eggs. Main courses extend from braised shoulder of salt marsh lamb with artichokes and chickpeas to whole baked plaice in shrimp and marjoram butter. Pudding could be a rather distinctive éclair or white chocolate and griottine cherries. An inspired collection of fairly priced wines accompanies the food, with bottles from £16.75, small glasses from £3.50.
Chef/s: Joby Wells. **Open:** Tue to Sun L 12 to 2.30 (3.30 Sun), Tue to Sat D 6.30 to 10.30. **Closed:** Mon. **Meals:** Set L £19.50 (2 courses) to £24. Set D £26 (2 courses) to £32.50. Tasting menu £45 (5 courses). **Details:** 60 seats. Wheelchair access. Car parking.

The Bingham

Supremely accomplished cooking near the Thames
61-63 Petersham Road, Richmond, TW10 6UT
Tel no: (020) 8940 0902
www.thebingham.co.uk
⊖ Richmond, map 1
Modern British | £45
Cooking score: 6
🍷 🛏 V

'An old favourite,' exclaim a couple who, like most customers, appreciate the gold and silver-hued glamour and excellent cooking at this 'quietly upmarket' hotel dining room overlooking the Thames. Much depends on Shay Cooper's supremely accomplished cooking, which is full of up-to-the-minute strokes. Reporters eat very well here, heaping praise on the ever-popular smoked haddock risotto (with cauliflower, curry spices, lime, dill and hollandaise) and salt marsh lamb (with glazed medjool date, spiced lamb faggot, braised onion, curry and apple). An enthusiastic nod is also given to the 'inspired' vegetarian menu where winter vegetable salad of candied walnuts, leaves and goats' curd with a walnut vinaigrette could be followed by

gnocchi with shaved truffles, truffle foam and morel mushrooms. Salted butter caramel, served with apple compote, cider cream, bitter chocolate and vanilla ice cream, makes a winning dessert. The whole experience is enhanced by 'extremely professional' staff who are 'free from any pretentiousness' and orchestrate meals at just the right pace. The wine list provides plenty to chew over, whether you prefer trendy New World names or a grand Bordeaux. Prices start at £19.
Chef/s: Shay Cooper. **Open:** all week L 12 to 2.30 (4 Sun), Mon to Sat D 7 to 10 (6.30 Thur to Sat). **Meals:** alc (main courses £25 to £29). Set L £22.50 (2 courses) to £25. Set D £45. Sun L £38. Tasting menu £65. **Details:** 38 seats. 14 seats outside. Separate bar. Wheelchair access. Car parking.

Brasserie Vacherin
Gallic flavours from start to finish
12 High Street, Sutton, SM1 1HN
Tel no: (020) 8722 0180
www.brasserievacherin.co.uk
map 1
French | £24
Cooking score: 2
£30

Malcolm John's restaurant is everyone's idea of a real, all-day French brasserie – right down to the red banquettes, polished floorboards and tiled walls. The menu is crammed with Gallic favourites and simple classics served without frills. The kitchen keeps things traditional for starters, from the twice-baked cheese soufflé, endives and walnuts to the escargots de Bourgogne. Mains take in duck and pork cassoulet; veal escalope, anchovy butter and sage; and smoked haddock, cavolo nero, poached egg and Dijon mustard. The dry-aged steaks cooked on the grill have also been applauded. End with bread-and-butter pudding with Agen prunes and Armagnac or a board of farmhouse cheeses. The French-heavy wine list starts at £13.50.

Chef/s: Ravi Geereedharry. **Open:** all week 12 to 11. **Closed:** 25 Dec. **Meals:** alc (main courses £11 to £21). Set L £14 (2 courses) to £15.95. Sun L £15.95. **Details:** 100 seats. 25 seats outside. Separate bar. Wheelchair access.

Brilliant
Chart-topping north Indian stalwart
72-76 Western Road, Southall, UB2 5DZ
Tel no: (020) 8574 1928
www.brilliantrestaurant.com
⊖ Hounslow West, map 1
Indian | £24
Cooking score: 3
£5 OFF £30

Opened as a 36-seater back in 1975, the Anand family's chart-topping Punjabi restaurant now boasts all mod cons from karaoke and plasma screens showing Bollywood films to a civil wedding licence, banqueting facilities and cookery classes. Celebs and royals drop by from time to time and the place packs 'em in with its down-home take on regional cooking. Fashion and fusion have no place here; instead the kitchen proves its worth with bold Punjabi flavours, fine-tuned spicing and a respect for family traditions. Butter chicken still reigns supreme as the signature starter, while curries such as palak lamb, keema peas and masala fish are served in 'regular' portions or mighty bowls for sharing. Veggies are well served and the menu also offers a range of 'healthy options'. Helpings are ginormous, but 'doggy bags' are happily provided for any leftovers. Wines start at £11, although most people prefer beer or lassi.
Chef/s: Jasvinderjit Singh. **Open:** Tue to Fri L 12 to 3, Tue to Sun D 6 to 11 (11.30 Fri and Sat). **Closed:** Mon, 25 Dec, bank hols. **Meals:** alc (main courses £5 to £14). Set L and D £20. **Details:** 225 seats. Car parking.

Brula
Hospitable local gem
43 Crown Road, St Margarets, Twickenham,
TW1 3EJ
Tel no: (020) 8892 0602
www.brula.co.uk
⊖ Richmond, map 1
French | £38
Cooking score: 3

V

'Simply the best'expresses a feeling shared by
many who have eaten at this gem of a
neighbourhood restaurant. Absolute, untiring
devotion, enthusiasm, skill and an innate sense
of hospitality make the place memorable. The
dining room with its pretty mirrors and
stained-glass windows is a charming setting: a
perfect backdrop for some modern French
cooking using top-drawer regional produce.
Openers might include the popular chicken
liver parfait with onion marmalade and warm
brioche, followed, perhaps, by slow-cooked
Gloucester Old Spot pork belly with 'some
really crisp crackling', creamed potatoes,
Savoy cabbage and cider jus, and a classic
crème brûlée to finish. The solid French wine
list offers 16 house selections by the glass,
250ml and 500ml carafes as well as by the
bottle (from £19.50).
Chef/s: Jamie Russell. **Open:** all week L 12 to 3, Mon
to Sat D 6 to 10.30. **Closed:** 26 Dec. **Meals:** alc
(main courses £17 to £25). Set L £18.50 (2 courses)
to £21.50. Set D £24.50 (2 courses) to £27.50.
Details: 48 seats.

La Buvette
Textbook French favourites
6 Church Walk, Richmond, TW9 1SN
Tel no: (020) 8940 6264
www.labuvette.co.uk
⊖ Richmond, map 1
French | £25
Cooking score: 3
£5 £30
OFF

A cosy, intimate bistro with a 'beautiful
courtyard' that reminds one smitten
correspondent of 'French holidays gone by'.

La Buvette isn't in sun-kissed Provence,
though, it's in the heart of Richmond, within
a pleasantly converted church annexe (once
used by the bridge club). Chef Buck Carter is a
stalwart presence behind the stove, where he
produces Gallic fare with the occasional twist,
but rarely anything so outré it would furrow
French brows. If you're in a traditional mood,
begin with classic fish soup with rouille and
Gruyère, then char-grilled onglet, herb butter
and chips, with crème brûlée to finish.
Otherwise, you could ring the changes with
roast monkfish, gremolata, tapenade and
spring onion tempura and a 'fabulous' caramel
and walnut tart. French wines, from £15.50,
come with almost comically brief but astute
annotations.
Chef/s: Buck Carter. **Open:** all week L 12 to 3, D 5.45
to 10. **Closed:** 25 and 26 Dec, Good Fri, Easter Sun.
Meals: alc (main courses £13 to £24). Set L £15.50 (2
courses) to £18. Set D £17.50 (2 courses) to £22.
Details: 46 seats. 36 seats outside.

ALSO RECOMMENDED
▲ The Canbury Arms
49 Canbury Park Road, Kingston Upon Thames,
KT2 6LQ
Tel no: (020) 8255 9129
www.thecanburyarms.com
map 1
Modern British £5
OFF

An agreeable Victorian pub 'only minutes'
walk from the shops and train station', the
Canbury Arms seems happy in its own skin.
The menu doesn't punch above its weight, nor
does the 'relaxed friendly' service. Reporters
praise the brunch, especially the eggs Benedict
and full English (Mon to Sat 9 to 4). Bar bites
of wild boar Scotch egg, and salt-and-pepper
squid (£4.90) are also admired, as are
generous mains such as the 'famous' Canbury
burger (£12) and chicken and mushroom pie.
Wines from £17.50. Open all week.

▲ The Depot

Tideway Yard, Mortlake High Street, Barnes,
SW14 8SN
Tel no: (020) 8878 9462
www.depotbrasserie.co.uk
map 1
Modern European

Irresistible river views and an atmospheric
Victorian stable-yard setting keep the Depot's
regulars coming back for more. The good-
looking brasserie deals in modern European
classics with va-va-voom: broccoli and rocket
salad with cashews (£6.50) and deep-fried
Brie de Meaux is hardly holier-than-thou,
and neither is John Dory with virtuous sea
kale but rich blood-orange hollandaise
(£15.50). Toffee apple and pecan tart with
English cream is a pretty representative pud.
House wine, £16.50. Open all week.

▲ Eat17

28-30 Orford Road, Walthamstow, E17 9NJ
Tel no: (020) 8521 5279
www.eat17.co.uk
⊖ Walthamstow Central, map 1
British

Known outside E17 for its bacon 'jam' (sold
nationally), Eat17 is rated in 'Walthamstow
Village' as a reliable choice for anything from
weekend brunch to cocktails. The menu is as
trendily eclectic as the designer interior.
Buttermilk fried chicken burger (£11) or
pulled pork and 'slaw (£10) are 'hipster'
favourites, though the kitchen will also do you
a '23-ingredient' lotus-root salad (£5.50) or
pineapple crumble with rum and salted-
caramel ice cream. Wines from £15. Closed
Sun D.

▲ The Exhibition Rooms

69-71 Westow Hill, Crystal Palace, SE19 1TX
Tel no: (020) 8761 1175
www.theexhibitionrooms.com
map 1
Modern British

Exposed brickwork, furniture in jaw-
dropping hues of violet and raspberry, and a
laid-back, stylish ambience characterise this
locally popular venue that recalls the great
days of the Crystal Palace exhibitions.
Contemporary brasserie dishes might include
fried sardines with beetroot and horseradish
jelly and pesto (£7.50), sea bream with caper,
vermouth and parsley butter (£17.50) and
apple and rhubarb crumble tart with clotted
cream. House Spanish is £16.50, or £5.50 a
large glass. Open Fri to Sun L, all week D.

The French Table

Fantastic neighbourhood restaurant
85 Maple Road, Surbiton, KT6 4AW
Tel no: (020) 8399 2365
www.thefrenchtable.co.uk
map 1
French | £37
Cooking score: 4
V

'Fantastic food – especially for the suburbs,'
declares a supporter of this chic Surbiton
neighbourhood restaurant. In fact, Eric
Guignard's accomplished modern French
cuisine needs no such qualifier. Such
effectively realised dishes as his scallop mille-
feuille starter with smoked salmon tartare,
Jerusalem artichokes and Parmesan froth or his
wild venison with pumpkin, chestnut,
pommes dauphines and sauce 'Grand Veneur'
could grace tables in a far glitzier postcode.
Guignard produces approachable,
internationally inflected fine dining with
regulars in mind: at times, comforting, at
others, luxurious. Exotic flavours are used
judiciously, particularly at the dessert stage
where crème brûlée is flavoured with rose, or
pineapple is roasted with Szechuan pepper.
White-clothed tables in a tastefully painted
bistro-style dining room set the food off well.
Prices aren't greedy: the five-course tasting
menu is £45; and the predominantly
European wine list begins at £16.95 for a
regional French red and white.
Chef/s: Eric and Sarah Guignard. Open: Tue to Sat L
12 to 2.30, D 7 to 10. Closed: Sun, Mon, 25 and 26
Dec. Meals: alc (main courses £19 to £27). Set L
£19.50 (2 courses) to £23.50. Tasting menu £45.
Details: 55 seats.

The Glasshouse
Low-key high-achiever
14 Station Parade, Kew, TW9 3PZ
Tel no: (020) 8940 6777
www.glasshouserestaurant.co.uk
⊖ Kew Gardens, map 1
Modern European | £43
Cooking score: 5
♦

Despite its low-key, suburban location in a parade of shops by Kew station, the Glasshouse doesn't need to flaunt its charms or puff itself up. One glance through the big glass frontage at the happy company of locals and foodies in the elegantly lit dining room is usually enough to do the trick. Sharp technique, intelligent ideas and a dedication to seasonal flavours set the culinary tone, and the daily menu is loaded with intriguing possibilities: crispy quails' eggs added to a salad of wood pigeon and white pear; a 'vermilion' goats' cheese raviolo with a dish of lamb rump, walnuts and beetroot; sweetly flavoursome slow-cooked pork belly with gutsy black pudding and potato gratin. After that, Valrhona chocolate mousse with iced coffee and milk ice cream provides a suitably 'decadent' finale. Service is 'faultlessly courteous', with top sommelier Sara Bachiorri receiving special praise for her consummate knowledge and helpful advice. The fascinating global list is full of oenophile distractions, from off-piste French varietals to Antipodean front runners; half-bottles and by-the-glass selections abound, with bottles starting at £20.
Chef/s: Daniel Mertl. **Open:** all week L 12 to 2.30 (3 Sun), D 6.30 to 10.30 (7 to 10 Sun). **Closed:** 24 to 26 Dec. **Meals:** Set L £23.50 (2 courses) to £27.50. Set D £37.50 (2 courses) to £42.50. Sun L £32.50. Tasting menu £60 (7 courses). **Details:** 65 seats.

Incanto
Local Italian with plenty to tempt
41 High Street, Harrow-on-the-Hill, HA1 3HT
Tel no: (020) 8426 6767
www.incanto.co.uk
⊖ Harrow-on-the-Hill, map 1
Italian | £35
Cooking score: 4
£5
OFF

The very fact of Incanto's existence – and the way it obviates the need for a trip into town – makes a lot of readers happy. This surprisingly airy space in Harrow's old post office has a deli attached, so it's no surprise that the antipasti selection has particular appeal. From an 'engaging' menu, readers also rate the delicate duck egg ravioli with red onion purée, wild mushrooms and black balsamic, and praise the 'attention to detail' evident in mains such as beef ribeye with smoked potato gratin, beef cannelloni, cavolo nero and wild mushrooms or fillet of cod with pearl barley risotto and lime and parsley gremolata. Mango soufflé with coconut sorbet is a popular finish, with salted-caramel pannacotta and peanut-butter ice cream also in the running. Wines come mainly from Italy, with a new dedication to organic, biodynamic and sustainable production methods; prices from £16.95.
Chef/s: Quentin Dorangeville. **Open:** Tue to Sun L 12 to 2.30 (12.30 to 4 Sun), Tue to Sat D 6.30 to 10.30. **Closed:** Mon, 25 and 26 Dec, 1 Jan. **Meals:** alc (main courses £15 to £20). Set L £17.95 (2 courses) to £19.95. Set D £19.95 (2 courses) to £23.95. **Details:** 62 seats. Wheelchair access.

Indian Zilla
Style, creativity and Indian pizazz
2-3 Rocks Lane, Barnes, SW13 0DB
Tel no: (020) 8878 3989
www.indianzilla.co.uk
map 1
Indian | £27
Cooking score: 4
£30

Zest, Zing and Zilla: Manoj Vasaikar's alliterative restaurant collection puts the pizazz into Indian cooking with a blend of classical training (he once worked for the luxe Oberoi hotel group on the Subcontinent) and modern ingenuity. Influences are drawn resourcefully from street food up to royal Mughal banqueting, with vivid seasonings and careful cooking in evidence all the way. A thali is the best way to experience the repertoire, but individual dishes shine, too. Griddled marinated scallops, or prawns and aubergine in caramelised onions, tomato and pickle, are vibrant openers to a meal that might continue with Mumbai chicken miravna, full of the greenness of herbs and the tang of coconut milk, or lobster tail in a hot sauce sweetened with jaggery. The signature finisher is tandoori figs with apple muesli crumble and vanilla ice cream. Rieslings, Sauvignons and Gewürztraminers are on hand to balance the finely tuned precision of the cooking with assertive aromatics. House French is £16.
Chef/s: Manoj Vasaikar. **Open:** Thur and Sun L 12 to 3, all week D 6 to 11. **Closed:** 25 Dec. **Meals:** alc (main courses £9 to £22). Set L £12 (2 courses) to £15. **Details:** 78 seats. 4 seats outside. Separate bar.

Symbols
🛏 Accommodation is available
£30 Three courses for less than £30
V Separate vegetarian menu
£5 OFF £5-off voucher scheme
🍷 Notable wine list

ALSO RECOMMENDED
▲ Ma Cuisine Bistrot
9 Station Approach, Kew, TW9 3QB
Tel no: (020) 8332 1923
www.macuisinebistrot.co.uk
⊖ Kew Gardens, map 1
French

Eggs Benedict, croque monsieur and crêpes suzette please the daytime crowd at John McClements' gingham-clothed 'bistrot' in Kew's old post office. Otherwise, drop by in the evening, when bourgeois cooking and rustic flavours hold sway: from baked Camembert with cured meats (£6.50) or ballotine of foie gras with Gewürztraminer jelly to coq au vin (£13.50), cassoulet, sea bass niçoise or slow-cooked pork belly with choucroute and morteau sausage. Just add lashings of make-believe Gallic frivolity. House vin de pays is £14.50. Open all week.

Madhu's
High-gloss Punjabi specialist
39 South Road, Southall, UB1 1SW
Tel no: (020) 8574 1897
www.madhus.co.uk
map 1
Indian | £23
Cooking score: 3
V £30

A fixture of the Southall scene for more than 30 years and now in the third generation of the Anand family, Madhu's is one of the big players in a neighbourhood rich in Indian eateries. The high-gloss interior, mirrors and shiny black surfaces might suggest some flashy Mayfair new-wave hangout, but the kitchen keeps its feet firmly on Punjabi soil for a menu of thoroughly traditional tandooris and curries. Loyal fans come here for big bowls of rogan josh, king prawn masala and other all-time favourites, but it pays to choose signature dishes marked with a red 'M' – perhaps pilli pilli boga (a deep-fried vegetable combo), jeera chicken with roasted cumin seeds or the deliciously named boozi bafu (lamb chops with a sumptuous onion and tomato sauce).

Top-notch ingredients, expert timing, gleefully rich flavours and deft spicing set this place apart from most of its rivals. Wines from £11.

Chef/s: Rakesh Verma. **Open:** Mon and Wed to Fri L 11.30 to 3, Wed to Mon D 6 to 11.30. **Closed:** Tue. **Meals:** alc (main courses £9 to £12). Set L and D £18 (2 courses) to £20. **Details:** 105 seats. Wheelchair access.

Mosaica @ the Factory
Funky flavour-fest
Chocolate Factory, 5 Clarendon Road, Wood Green, N22 6XJ
Tel no: (020) 8889 2400
www.mosaicarestaurants.com
⊖ Wood Green, map 2
Modern European | £30
Cooking score: 3

Twinkling fairy lights and flickering candles, black walls covered in wax, mismatched antique furniture, high industrial ceilings... welcome to Mosaica, a shabby-chic New York-style eatery in Wood Green's defunct chocolate factory (now a hub for local artists, musicians et al). Matching the food to this funky, gothic vibe is a tricky matter, but the guys in the open-plan kitchen do their best with a daily changing menu of vibrant modern dishes pulled from the European maelstrom. Char-grilled asparagus with 'gastrix and Parmy' sounds typically leftfield, while mains move into more orthodox territory for the likes of pan-fried sea bass with 'chorizo pots' and wilted baby spinach, braised oxtail, or corn-fed chicken with creamed Savoy cabbage, pancetta and black pudding. After that, consider dark chocolate and caramel torte with dulce de leche or 'Escoffier berries' with mango sorbet. The concise global wine list starts at £16 (£4 a glass).

Chef/s: Phil Ducker. **Open:** Tue to Fri L 12 to 2.30, Tue to Sat D 6.30 to 9.30 (7 to 10 Sat). Sun 1 to 4. **Closed:** 22 Dec to 31 Dec. **Meals:** alc (main courses £14 to £23). **Details:** 80 seats. 30 seats outside. Wheelchair access. Car parking.

Petersham Nurseries Café
Italian-inspired menus using home-grown produce
Church Lane, off Petersham Road, Richmond, TW10 7AG
Tel no: (020) 8940 5230
www.petershamnurseries.com
⊖ Richmond, map 1
Modern British | £45
Cooking score: 3

This one-of-a-kind restaurant 'at the back of a greenhouse, miles from anywhere and with precious little parking' is back in full bloom. The tables are no longer rickety and the staff don't wear wellies any more. Making best use of the home-grown produce from the beautiful nurseries and elsewhere, the kitchen produces a weekly changing Italian-inspired menu full of vibrant flavours and colours. Witness a monkfish stew with clams given brightness and sweetness with datterini tomatoes, peppery green nettle taglioni and a punchy lemon oil, soothed with a beautiful ricotta. Portions are delicate, which suits the coiffed lady lunchers perfectly (the occasional dinner services might be slightly more robust), but the bill is 'eye-wateringly expensive'. Budget-conscious diners can get a flavour of the place at half the price in the tea house next door. If you've time, browse the plants outside and the enticing objects in the shop. House wine starts at £9 for a 500ml carafe.

Chef/s: Lucy Boyd. **Open:** Tue to Sun L only 12 to 3. **Closed:** Mon, 25 and 26 Dec. **Meals:** alc (main courses £20 to £28). **Details:** 100 seats. 100 seats outside. Wheelchair access. Car parking.

The Petersham Restaurant
Sumptuous views and reinvented favourites
Nightingale Lane, Richmond, TW10 6UZ
Tel no: (020) 8939 1084
www.petershamhotel.co.uk
⊖ Richmond, map 1
Modern British | £36
Cooking score: 4
£5 OFF ➥ V

The heavy carpeting, acres of napery and hushed voices of both the staff and the customers give this hotel restaurant a distinctly grown-up, old-fashioned feel – and you'll find potted shrimps, fillet steak with béarnaise sauce and Dover sole to match. Dig a little deeper, however, and you'll also unearth beautifully made ham hock and prune terrine with lightly spiced pickled vegetables, or grilled skate with crispy squid, given richness from a long-cooked red wine sauce resonating with fennel and orange. Puddings such as rum baba and floating islands suit the traditionalists and are well executed and presented. The wine list (starting at £23.50) focuses on the Old World. Pleasant to visit on winter nights, the Petersham is even better in the summer when the 'one of the finest river views in England' – along the Thames and extensive surrounding greenery towards Hampton Court – can be enjoyed.
Chef/s: Alex Bentley. **Open:** all week L 12.15 to 2.15 (12.30 to 3.30 Sun), D 7 to 9.45 (8.45 Sun). **Closed:** 25 and 26 Dec, 1 Jan. **Meals:** alc (main courses £17 to £34). Set L and D £22.95 (2 courses) to £26.95. Sun L £34.50. **Details:** 90 seats. 12 seats outside. Separate bar. Wheelchair access. Car parking.

Retro Bistrot
Warm, buzzy French bistro
114-116 High Street, Teddington, TW11 8JB
Tel no: (020) 8977 2239
www.retrobistrot.co.uk
map 1
French | £35
Cooking score: 3
£5 OFF V

On Teddington's high street, flamboyant looks extend from the tongue-in-cheek luxe of Retro's decor to the characterful owner and host Vincent Gerbeau. Readers love the 'fun' ambience and the enthusiasm of the team – as well as the reassuringly classic French dishes with a few Italian touches. So a starter of ham hock tortellini comes with celeriac rémoulade, and mains might be a halibut fillet with black risotto, confit red peppers and samphire, or 'perfectly cooked' beef fillet with horseradish gnocchi. Chateaubriand with fondant potatoes and celeriac purée remains a favourite, and the kitchen rather kindly cooks it for one as well as for two. To finish, try a citrus terrine with madeleines and passion-fruit coulis, or a honey and fennel crème brûlée with a pistachio sablé. Wine is from £16.50 a bottle, with plenty by the glass.
Chef/s: Andrew West. **Open:** Tue to Sun L 12 to 3.30 (3 Sat), Tue to Sat D 6.30 to 11. **Closed:** Mon, 25 and 26 Dec, first 2 weeks Jan, first 2 weeks Aug. **Meals:** alc (main courses £12 to £27). Set L £10.95 (2 courses) to £14.50. Set D £17.50 (2 courses) to £19.95. **Details:** 110 seats.

Sonny's Kitchen
Revamped neighbourhood favourite
94 Church Road, Barnes, SW13 0DQ
Tel no: (020) 8748 0393
www.sonnyskitchen.co.uk
map 1
Modern European | £30
Cooking score: 2

'Terrific to have on your doorstep, but not a destination gaff' was one verdict on this revamp of Barnes's most recognisable eatery: a second bite of the cherry from Sonny's owner

Rebecca Mascarenhas in partnership with chef Phil Howard of the Square (see entry). The new incarnation has an immediately appealing vibe, with charming service, sympathetic lighting and lots of chat in the stylish dining room. The kitchen changes its menu each day, adding specials such as Jerusalem artichoke and chanterelle risotto to its regular line-up of generous warm salads, pastas, grills and European brasserie staples (calf's liver with creamed potatoes and balsamic onions, for example). Following a change of chef, the cooking seems to have lost some of its initial oomph, with dishes appearing 'overly rich' and 'short of the mark', but well-chosen wines (from £15.95), snappy aperitifs and takeaways from the adjoining 'foodstore' are reasons to be cheerful.

Chef/s: Tommy Boland. **Open:** all week L 12 to 2.30 (12.45 to 3.30 Sat and Sun), D 6 to 10.30 (11 Sat and Sun). **Closed:** 25 and 26 Dec, 1 Jan, bank hols. **Meals:** alc (main courses £13 to £21). Set L £16.50 (2 courses) to £18.50. Sun L £21 (2 courses) to £25. **Details:** 100 seats. Separate bar.

Tangawizi
Upmarket local Indian
406 Richmond Road, Richmond, TW1 2EB
Tel no: (020) 8891 3737
www.tangawizi.co.uk
⊖ Richmond, map 1
Indian | £27
Cooking score: 2
£30

'Smart, dark and modern to the point of glitziness', clever lighting and a chic purple interior set the bar reasonably high at this 'posh' local Indian restaurant. The charm of the welcome and the feel-good factor once you're inside take Tangawizi a notch further. Poppadoms served with at least six beautiful chutneys and relishes begin a meal well and could be followed by familiar staples such as chicken tikka or a biryani. However, the menu also has a page of 'new this month' dishes, and more adventurous diners will be enticed by the likes of jhinge coco (tandoor-grilled prawns marinated in coconut, ginger and

garlic). Sweets are old-school – carrot halwa and gulab jamun – and mango lassis are excellent, but there's also decent wine (starting at £14.50).

Chef/s: Surat Singh Rana. **Open:** all week D only 6 to 11 (10.30 Sun). **Closed:** 25 and 26 Dec, 1 Jan. **Meals:** alc (main courses £7 to £15). **Details:** 60 seats.

The Victoria
Appealing all-rounder
10 West Temple Sheen, East Sheen, SW14 7RT
Tel no: (020) 8876 4238
www.thevictoria.net
⊖ Richmond, map 1
Modern British | £30
Cooking score: 3
£5 OFF

As a good, old-fashioned park pub (albeit one with a restaurant and rooms), the Victoria near Richmond Park is practically duty-bound to offer shelter and a pint – or a latte – to dog owners, mums with strollers and walkers. It's 'the perfect combination of local pub and top-quality restaurant' in one regular's eyes and is 'never lacking in atmosphere'. The kitchen has strong credentials, with Paul Merrett at the helm. His lively menus roam the globe for inspiration but are, at heart, in the modern European style. Homemade goats' curd on toast with salt-baked beetroot makes an on-trend beginning, giving way to main course Dingley Dell pork chop 'au poivre' or an exotic rump of lamb 'massaman' with a peanut and chilli crust, and pistachio crème brûlée for dessert. The Victoria opens for breakfast, weekend brunch, bar meals and for summer barbecues in the leafy garden. Wines from £17.

Chef/s: Paul Merrett. **Open:** all week L 12 to 2.30 (3 Sat, 4 Sun), Mon to Sat D 6 to 10. **Meals:** alc (main courses £13 to £18). Set L and D £12.50 (2 courses). Sun L £24 (2 courses) to £28. **Details:** 100 seats. 50 seats outside. Separate bar. Car parking.

ENGLAND

Bedfordshire, Berkshire,
Buckinghamshire, Cambridgeshire,
Cheshire, Cornwall, Cumbria, Derbyshire,
Devon, Dorset, Durham, Essex,
Gloucestershire & Bristol,
Greater Manchester,
Hampshire (inc. Isle of Wight),
Herefordshire, Hertfordshire, Kent,
Lancashire, Leicestershire and Rutland,
Lincolnshire, Merseyside, Norfolk,
Northamptonshire, Northumberland,
Nottinghamshire, Oxfordshire, Shropshire,
Somerset, Staffordshire, Suffolk, Surrey,
Sussex – East, Sussex – West,
Tyne & Wear, Warwickshire,
West Midlands, Wiltshire, Worcestershire,
Yorkshire

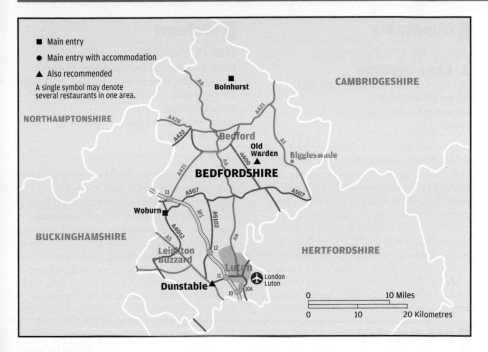

■ Main entry

● Main entry with accommodation

▲ Also recommended

A single symbol may denote several restaurants in one area.

▌Bolnhurst

The Plough

Big, true flavours and cracking wines
Kimbolton Road, Bolnhurst, MK44 2EX
Tel no: (01234) 376274
www.bolnhurst.com
Modern British | £35
Cooking score: 5

Savvy chef Martin Lee and his wife Jayne have worked miracles at the Plough, creating a fully rounded, top-end eatery in a good-natured Bedfordshire boozer without resorting to prissy amuse-bouches or highfalutin tasting menus. Beams, timbers, bare boards and floral walls set the tone, and the kitchen is pitched right behind the bar. Martin and his trusty brigade deliver food with real immediacy and impact, so expect big, true flavours: roast pigeon breast is invigorated with pickled onions, crisp celeriac and chilli flakes, while sticky beef cheeks are cooked overnight and served with horseradish mash, parsnips and

red wine sauce. Bolnhurst is a long way from the coast, but fish is always a good call: perhaps roast monkfish with a bright, sunny amalgam of cannellini bean purée, chorizo, confit red pepper, sun-dried tomato and parsley. Details such as the terrific home-baked breads, sharing nibbles and three cheese selections with appropriate accompaniments help make this 'a masterclass' and a joy. To cap it all, the wine list is a real cracker: 15 house recommendations precede a knowledgeable, worldwide compendium at drinker-friendly prices (from £16); also ask about BYO deals for special occasions.

Chef/s: Martin Lee and Graeme Ottewell. **Open:** Tue to Sun L 12 to 2, Tue to Sat D 6.30 to 9.30. **Closed:** Mon, first 2 weeks Jan. **Meals:** alc (main courses £16 to £27). Set L and D £16 (2 courses) to £20. Sun L £21 (2 courses) to £25. **Details:** 90 seats. 30 seats outside. Separate bar. Wheelchair access. Car parking.

Dunstable

ALSO RECOMMENDED
▲ Chez Jerome

26 Church Street, Dunstable, LU5 4RU
Tel no: (01582) 603310
www.chezjerome.co.uk
French £5 OFF

A sprightly antidote to Dunstable's junk-food joints, chains and takeaways, Jerome and Lina Dehoux's neighbourly oasis occupies a 15th-century timber-framed building just off the main drag. It's warm, sociable, cheery and enthusiastically run. The cooking is unreformed French bistro to the core – generous helpings of pigeon breast with walnut and orange sauce (£7.65), lamb fillet with rosemary jus or sea bass with lemon and garlic (£15.95), followed by crème brûlée, lemon cheesecake or crêpes suzette. House French is £14.25. Closed Sun D and Mon.

Old Warden

ALSO RECOMMENDED
▲ Hare & Hounds

High Street, Old Warden, SG18 9HQ
Tel no: (01767) 627225
www.hareandhoundsoldwarden.co.uk
Modern British

Jago and Jane Hurt have been presiding over this well-regarded village pub since 2000, and have kept the singular-looking building in fine fettle. Log fires and wood-burners warm on cold nights, there's a choice of dining areas, and sound seasonal ingredients find their way into unchallenging dishes – perhaps Norfolk pheasant braised in red wine (£16). In addition, expect Summerhill Farm Shop pork sausages, well-filled daily pies (perhaps steak and kidney) and 28-day aged steaks (from £18.90). Wines from £14.50. Closed Sun D and Mon.

Woburn

Paris House

Picture-perfect plates and pretty parkland
London Road, Woburn Park, Woburn, MK17 9QP
Tel no: (01525) 290692
www.parishouse.co.uk
Modern European | £67
Cooking score: 5
£5 OFF V

As is well known locally, this substantial half-timbered building was painstakingly transported from a spot by the Quai d'Orsay at the Paris Exposition of 1878 and rehomed amid acres of Bedfordshire parkland. It seems to have bedded in nicely. Well-spaced tables in the interconnecting dining rooms are provided with chairs that have fragments of magnified culinary text printed on their backs – giving some indication of Phil Fanning's inventive approach in the kitchen. Expect the unexpected, as a meal that might take you from prawn cocktail through steak and chips to banana split offers a parade of ingenious re-imaginings of British culinary populism. Otherwise, consider the likes of poached lobster with caviar, yuzu and oyster leaf, followed by venison from the Woburn estate, alongside a portion of the smoked heart, with turnips and ceps, the whole scented with truffle; or a curry of plaice, shellfish and artichoke. It all comes to a suitably innovative conclusion with poached rhubarb, served with duck-egg custard and coconut sorbet. The French-oriented wine list opens at £25, or £8 a glass.
Chef/s: Phil Fanning. **Open:** Wed to Sun L 12 to 2, Tue to Sat D 7 to 9. **Closed:** Mon, 24 Dec to 4 Jan. **Meals:** Tasting menu L £37. Tasting menu D from £67 (6 courses) to £95 (10 courses). **Details:** 47 seats. Car parking.

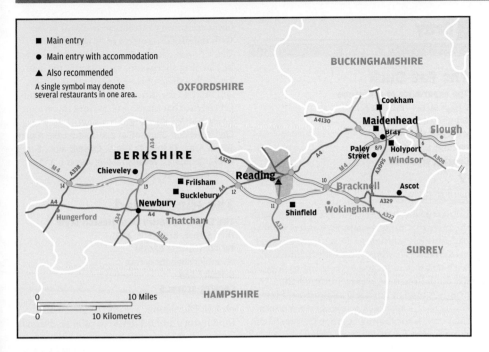

▮ Ascot

Restaurant Coworth Park

Intricate cooking in shiny, opulent surroundings
Coworth Park, London Road, Ascot, SL5 7SE
Tel no: (01344) 756784
www.coworthpark.com
Modern British | £65
Cooking score: 5

🛏 V

Heed the SatNav when you are trying to locate this idiosyncratically restored Georgian country house surrounded by 240 acres of lawns, meadows and woodland – although the Aston Martins and Bentleys parked outside will affirm that you've reached your destination. Huge panel-beaten mirrors, rich fabrics, leather chairs and a vast 'oak and acorn' copper corona shimmer in the autumnal-hued dining room, but there's 'real substance' beyond the opulent, big money look. Brian Hughson's kitchen is up to the task, matching the mood with confident displays of intricate contemporary cooking: soused Cornish mackerel is paired with smoked mussels, fennel and curried cream, while roast cutlet and slow-cooked neck of spring lamb are accompanied by wild garlic, potato purée and king oyster mushrooms. There's also plenty of interesting stuff on the tongue-in-cheek set lunch menu, from guinea fowl terrine with 'eggy bread' or a beautiful plate of pork belly, roast tenderloin, black pudding purée and apple 'dressed to look like tree', to a humorously deconstructed raspberry trifle ('a pud for people who don't like puds'). Service knows how to charm, but be prepared for shocks when it comes to the 'blindingly expensive' wine list – although 20 selections by the carafe (from £19.50) help to relieve the pain.
Chef/s: Brian Hughson. **Open:** Tue to Sun L 12 to 2.30, Tue to Sat D 6.30 to 9.30. **Closed:** Mon. **Meals:** Set L £29.95. Set D £40 to £65. Sun L £39.95. Tasting menu £85 (8 courses). **Details:** 66 seats. Separate bar. Wheelchair access. Car parking. No children after 7.30.

Bray

The Fat Duck

The experience of a lifetime
1 High Street, Bray, SL6 2AQ
Tel no: (01628) 580333
www.thefatduck.co.uk
Modern British | £195
Cooking score: 10

V

Even as the food landscape alters imperceptibly around it, the Fat Duck remains the prize that most restaurant-hunters want to bag. This has nothing to do with the physical surroundings (cottagey, pleasantly informal, with no dress code) and everything to do with the food. Inventive, clever, idiosyncratic, deeply rooted in nostalgia and history, Heston Blumenthal's approach is now better known than ever. If the familiarity that TV breeds can dim some of the magic, new dishes play a crucial role in the appeal at table. One such is lamb with cucumber, served with a crystal-clear jellied lamb consommé of incredible depth. The last thing you'd expect a meat dish to be is refreshing, but here it is, confounding expectations with good taste. Back at the beginning of a 14-course tasting menu, nitro-poached aperitifs are citrus-spiked iced puffs that zing about the palate like pinballs, performing cleansing work. Red cabbage gazpacho with grain-mustard ice cream is vivid and powerful; the famous snail porridge is silky, wild green and lifted by lemony fennel; and roast foie gras comes with leaves of crab biscuit and a nutty sesame crumb. Going off-piste here brings a world-beating scallop mirrored wittily with a daikon radish filled with scallop 'oil'. At its best, service is so well tuned that dietary requirements feel like a special privilege and left-handers' place settings are righted smoothly. Theatrics with dry ice and the swirling of a golden 'pocket watch' for Mad Hatter's tea are judged so as not to overwhelm, and some clever links between courses (single coriander seeds perched here and there, flavoured films of kombu or moss)

boost continuity. Attention to detail peaks with the 'BFG': a perfect re-imagining of Black Forest gâteau. A single cherry seems to be bleeding sharp-sour sauce down the side of a neat chocolate oblong full of good things, and there's a tiny knot tied jauntily in the stalk. Of course, that knot costs, as does the wine; house bottles start at £32.
Chef/s: Heston Blumenthal and Jonny Lake. **Open:** Tue to Sat L 12 to 2, D 7 to 9. **Closed:** Mon, Sun, 2 weeks Christmas. **Meals:** Tasting menu L and D £195. **Details:** 40 seats.

The Hinds Head

The English country pub, Heston-style
High Street, Bray, SL6 2AB
Tel no: (01628) 626151
www.hindsheadbray.com
British | £38
Cooking score: 5

Heston Blumenthal's research into British food history and his desire to offer traditional tavern cuisine suits this 'gorgeous' 15th-century pub a few steps from the Fat Duck. Ten years ago the intention was to maintain the Hinds Head as the village hostelry, but it has gradually become more 'special occasion', although drinkers still have their own beamed and timbered bar space and local ales, and the experience is never stuffy. (The village pub role has passed to the Crown down the road – acquired by Heston in 2010.) In the kitchen Kevin Love interprets the 'reinvented pub classic' style with considerable flair: from pea and ham soup, via the now-famous oxtail and kidney pudding and proper shepherd's pie, to more contemporary offerings such as cured duck salad with asparagus, artichoke and quail's egg, and roast fillet of stone bass with wild mushrooms, an intense beetroot purée and a roast chicken reduction. Posh bar snacks (Scotch eggs, devils on horseback) are available at the bar, the triple-cooked chips are a 'must have', and quaking pudding and rhubarb trifle are 'wonderful, if not perfect'. The well-chosen wine list opens at £19.95.

Chef/s: Kevin Love. **Open:** all week L 12 to 2.30 (4 Sun), Mon to Sat D 6.30 to 9.30. **Closed:** 25 Dec. **Meals:** alc (main courses £15 to £30). Set L £17.50 (2 courses) to £21.95. **Details:** 140 seats.

★ TOP 50 ★

The Waterside Inn
An irresistible package
Ferry Road, Bray, SL6 2AT
Tel no: (01628) 620691
www.waterside-inn.co.uk
French | £140
Cooking score: 7

Alain Roux's shrine to Gallic cuisine on the banks of the river Thames is as dependable now as when his father and uncle set it up over 40 years ago. Roux upholds its lovely traditions, from drinks on the riverside terrace to the continued presence of certain favourites on the menu – notably the pan-fried lobster medallions with a white port sauce and ginger-spiked vegetable julienne; and meltingly tender rabbit fillets on a celeriac fondant with candy-sweet chestnuts, an intense Armagnac sauce and ravioli of liver and kidney. These typify the scope of the menu, which upholds, but is never a slave to, the tenets of classical French cooking. The familiar is made remarkable here by being done very, very well: be it a light-as-air gougère or the sensible teaming of brandade with a pheasant's egg and silky red pepper sauce in an amuse-bouche. And then there is dessert: a crisp mille-feuille perhaps, with juicy strawberries in Melba sauce and mascarpone ice cream, almost overshadowed by the classic petits fours – all served with a winning blend of formality, warmth and efficiency. This brilliance comes with a gulp-inducing price tag, and you'll need to dig deep to get the most out of the impressive 1,000-bin exclusively French wine list, although prices start at a relatively accessible £29 a bottle.
Chef/s: Alain Roux. **Open:** Wed to Sun L 12 to 2 (2.30 Sun), D 7 to 10. **Closed:** Mon, Tue, 26 Dec to 23 Jan. **Meals:** alc (main courses £50 to £59). Set L £45.50 (2 courses) to £59.50 (weekdays). Sun L £79.50. Tasting menu £152.50. **Details:** 70 seats. Separate bar. Car parking. Children over 12 yrs only.

Bucklebury
The Bladebone Inn
Versatile village inn
Chapel Row, Bucklebury, RG7 6PD
Tel no: (0118) 9712326
www.thebladeboneinn.com
Modern British | £28
Cooking score: 1
£30

Kate and Wills Cambridge used to frequent this versatile, 17th-century country inn during their courting days, but you don't need to be a royal to enjoy its many pleasures. Drop by for coffee and cake, settle in the traditional bar with a hand-pulled pint and a jazzed-up Scotch egg or trade up to the bright conservatory dining room for food with bags of ambition. Salmon is cured over liquorice, pork belly comes with smoked apple mash, and sticky short-rib of beef appears with swede, a fricassee of snails, black kale and bone marrow. Wines from £15.
Chef/s: Kiren Puri. **Open:** all week L 12 to 2.30 (4 Sun), Mon to Sat D 6.30 to 9. **Meals:** alc (main courses £13 to £20). Set L £12.50 (2 courses) to £15. Tasting menu £45 (5 courses). **Details:** 42 seats. 24 seats outside. Separate bar. Car parking.

Chieveley
The Crab at Chieveley
Fresh seafood for landlubbers
Wantage Road, Chieveley, RG20 8UE
Tel no: (01635) 247550
www.crabatchieveley.com
Seafood | £35
Cooking score: 3
£5 OFF

The sight of a prosperous thatched pub/restaurant-with-rooms on a breezy hilltop in landlocked Berkshire might not conjure up thoughts of seafood, but the Crab is true to its maritime moniker. Nets, lobster pots, seafaring artefacts and other curios point up the theme in the fish bar, 'snug' and main restaurant, while the menu is dependent on deliveries from the West Country ports. Salcombe crab is a top shout, but the kitchen's global output spans everything from moules marinière and bowls of bouillabaisse to teriyaki sea bream with ginger and chilli pickle or poached lemon sole with maple-glazed pumpkin and sweet-potato risotto. Meat eaters can feed on game terrine or local venison with horseradish mash; sweets offer the likes of blackcurrant parfait with apple sponge and honeycomb. The informative wine list includes a commendable selection by the glass or carafe, with bottles from £16.50. **Chef/s:** David Horridge. **Open:** all week L 12 to 2.30, D 6 to 10 (9.30 Sun). **Meals:** alc (main courses £16 to £27). Set L and D £15.95 (2 courses) to £19.95. Sun L £22.50. **Details:** 80 seats. 40 seats outside. Separate bar. Wheelchair access. Car parking.

▌Cookham

Maliks

Dynamic Home Counties Indian
High Street, Cookham, SL6 9SF
Tel no: (01628) 520085
www.maliks.co.uk
Indian | £30
Cooking score: 2

£5 OFF

An ivy-clad frontage, rugged beams and open fires are reminders that this branch of Maliks was once a Home Counties boozer – although its swish interior, spotless layout, soothing ragas and enterprising menu are a long way from pies and pints. Die-hards can fill up on onion bhajias, bhunas and dhansaks, but it pays to explore some of the less-familiar ideas: marinated Sikandari lamb on the bone comes highly recommended, and it's also worth considering seafood specials including monkfish masala, Goan fish curry and fragrant steamed sea bass. To finish, don't miss the excellent firni (Bengali rice pudding). Wines start at £18. There are outlets at 14 Oak End Way, Gerrards Cross SL9 8BR; tel: (01753) 880888 and 101 High Street, Marlow; tel: (01628) 482180.
Chef/s: Malik Ahmed and Shapon Miah. **Open:** all week L 12 to 2.30, D 6 to 11 (10.30 Sun). **Closed:** 25 and 26 Dec. **Meals:** alc (main courses £8 to £16). Set L £12 (2 courses) to £15. Set D £24 (2 courses) to £30. Sun L buffet £12. **Details:** 66 seats. Wheelchair access. Car parking.

The White Oak

Desirable food in a desirable village
The Pound, Cookham, SL6 9QE
Tel no: (01628) 523043
www.thewhiteoak.co.uk
Modern European | £27
Cooking score: 3

£5 OFF   £30 ▼

Chef/patron Clive Dixon was at the Hinds Head in Bray (see entry) before taking over the reins at this popular red-brick pub in desirable Cookham. Drinkers can still sup in the bar, but most of the action takes place in the smart dining room with its coffee and taupe colour schemes, thick pine beams, mirrors and candelabra. Clive's cooking mixes forthright brasserie-style ideas with some clever technique and a nose for artisan ingredients – so expect to find plates of jamón Ibérico, home-cured Wagyu beef and 'hand-cut' pasta sharing the spotlight with more refined dishes such as monkfish sashimi or grilled Barnsley chop with quinoa salad, golden sultanas, marinated courgettes and piquillo peppers. It's all fairly priced and accessible, particularly when you factor-in fixed-price 'auberge' menus and special Sunday suppers. The Corney & Barrow wine list is peppered with bottles from reputable producers; prices start at £17.
Chef/s: Clive Dixon. **Open:** all week L 12 to 2.30 (3 Sat and Sun), D 6 to 9.30 (5.30 to 8.30 Sun). **Meals:** alc (main courses £14 to £22). Set L £12 (2 courses) to £15. Set D £15 (2 courses) to £19. **Details:** 100 seats. 40 seats outside. Separate bar. Wheelchair access. Car parking.

▋ Frilsham

The Pot Kiln

Lively cooking – if you can find it
Frilsham, RG18 0XX
Tel no: (01635) 201366
www.potkiln.org
British | £30
Cooking score: 2
£5
OFF

Mike Robinson's red-brick country inn sits amid fields and woodland, so well camouflaged that one couple, fuming along the country lanes, claimed 'It isn't possible to find it without SatNav or Tarot cards.' Persevere, and you'll be rewarded with Ben Fisher's lively modern British cooking, which takes in perfectly timed Cornish scallops seasoned with lemon thyme and garlic, and mains that might see John Dory paired with cockles in grape and Pernod sauce, or pork partnered by itself (rack and confit belly), alongside butternut squash, chestnuts and cabbage in mustard sauce. A Pangbourne specialist supplies the thoroughbred cheeses, as an alternative to the likes of buttermilk pannacotta with poached rhubarb and gingerbread croûtons. The distinguished wine list is full of helpful detail, and starts at £18.
Chef/s: Ben Fisher. **Open:** Wed to Mon L 12 to 2 (2.30 Sun), D 7 to 9 (6.30 to 8.30 Sun). **Closed:** Tue, 25 Dec. **Meals:** alc (main courses £15 to £20). Set L £13.95 (2 courses) to £17.50. **Details:** 48 seats. 100 seats outside. Separate bar. Car parking.

▋ Holyport

NEW ENTRY

The Belgian Arms

Good pub food at exactly the right price
Holyport, SL6 2JR
Tel no: (01628) 634468
www.thebelgianarms.com
British | £27
Cooking score: 3
£5
OFF £30

Dominic Chapman and Nick Parkinson of the Royal Oak, Paley Street (see entry), haven't put a foot wrong with their new venture. The village-green-with-pond setting and white walls of this 200-year-old pub might inspire 'olde-worlde' fantasies, but the lovingly revamped interior is modern, comfortable and relaxed, the menu pitched perfectly: good pub food at exactly the right price. The kitchen keeps chi-chi touches to a minimum, concentrating on first-class ingredients and reassuringly familiar dishes – roast sirloin and Yorkshire pudding for Sunday lunch, fried scampi with mayonnaise and an exemplary raspberry Knickerbocker glory – but there are a few modern-day surprises on the menu. Warm salad of Old Spot bacon with poached egg and frisée is a particularly modish starter, and a well-timed roast Cornish cod with baba ganoush and apricot and pine nut relish to follow continues in that vein. Brakspear supplies the ales and wines are from £14.95.
Chef/s: Ed Dutton. **Open:** all week L 12 to 2.30 (3.30 Sun), Mon to Sat D 6.30 to 9.30 (10 Fri and Sat). **Meals:** alc (main courses £12 to £19). **Details:** 46 seats. 30 seats outside. Separate bar. Wheelchair access. Car parking.

Maidenhead

Boulters Riverside Brasserie

A river runs past it

Boulters Lock Island, Maidenhead, SL6 8PE

Tel no: (01628) 621291

www.boultersrestaurant.co.uk

Modern British | £30

Cooking score: 2

£5
OFF

If you want river, Boulters has plenty of it. This old mill juts out over the Thames from its own island, with the first-floor bar and restaurant below both glazed to take in the views. In a neutral dining room, grills and salads appear alongside more inventive dishes; these are where the action is, though 'thrice-cooked' chips hold their own against Bray's best. At inspection, a pork belly starter with caramel apple sauce, apple salad and truffle was in need of extra freshness; duck with tomatoes, olives and a crisp-crusted potato cake flavoured with smoked bacon was a better testament to the kitchen's skills. To finish, try a passion fruit soufflé with dark and white chocolate. Wines from a free-thinking list start at £18.

Chef/s: Daniel Woodhouse. **Open:** Tue to Sun L 12 to 2.45, Tue to Sat D 6.30 to 9.30. **Closed:** Mon, 26 to 30 Dec. **Meals:** alc (main courses £14 to £28). Set L £15.95 (2 courses) to £19.95. Sun L £21.95 (2 courses). Tasting menu £35. **Details:** 70 seats. 20 seats outside. Separate bar. Wheelchair access. Car parking.

Newbury

The Vineyard at Stockcross

Formidable French cooking and epic wines

Newbury, RG20 8JU

Tel no: (01635) 528770

www.the-vineyard.co.uk

Modern French | £49

Cooking score: 6

£5 ♦ ⌐ V
OFF

Sir Peter Michael's Californian vineyard may be thousands of miles away, but at his ineffably stylish venue outside Newbury, a homage to world viticulture continues in full swing. Designed like a West Coast hacienda, with underfoot views into the cellar through a glass floor, the Vineyard is a treasure house for wine, but great vintages are only half the story. Chef Daniel Galmiche matches them with energetically creative cooking that leaves readers gasping. The format is a clever reappraisal of small-dish dining, with wines in various sizes to mix and match. Notes for each glass appear discreetly on its coaster. The deal at lunch is particularly good: consider exemplary duck foie gras with quince jelly; halibut with cucumber variations; John Dory with Jerusalem artichokes; Balmoral venison with butternut squash and pearl barley. Dishes rely on excellent materials rather than surreal combinations: free-range pork ribeye is teamed with spinach and onion seeds; the richness of Valrhona chocolate is counterpointed with top notes of ginger ice cream and tonka bean foam. The wine collection is among England's best, with superb choices from California as well as the pick of Burgundy, Italy, South Africa . . . Bottles start at £20, tasting samples at £7.

Chef/s: Daniel Galmiche. **Open:** all week L 12 to 2, D 7 to 9.30. **Meals:** Set L £29 (3 courses). Set D £49 (4 courses) to £89 (7 courses). Sun L £39. **Details:** 90 seats. 30 seats outside. Separate bar. Wheelchair access. Car parking.

Paley Street

★ TOP 50 ★

The Royal Oak

Classy inn with fine food

Littlefield Green, Paley Street, SL6 3JN

Tel no: (01628) 620541

www.theroyaloakpaleystreet.com

Modern British | £55

Cooking score: 6

♦ ⌐

The exterior may look unremarkable, but inside you'll discover an appealing bar area – sofas, a fireplace, space for a drink – leading to an interlinked pair of dining rooms, for the Royal Oak has been elegantly extended. The 'club-like' feel has been retained, though there's now the option of eating in a light airy dining room with glass doors giving on to a stylish paved terrace. And you can still expect some seriously classy food. Dominic Chapman's stellar cooking uses native British ingredients to telling effect; reports this year have listed rabbit lasagne, the Middle White pork and pigeon pithiviers, peppered haunch of venison, and 'fantastic' steaks cooked with marrow bone in a red wine jus as particular favourites. Praise, too, for linguine with a generous helping of lobster, perfect lemon sole with a delicate dill and lemon butter and dessert of egg custard tart. Indeed, 'from the little crusty loaves to the wonderful cheeseboard, it is difficult to find fault'. The wine list is a peach – a notable collection with plenty of big-hitters alongside more wallet-friendly bottles from £18.50.

Chef/s: Dominic Chapman. **Open:** all week L 12 to 2.30 (3.30 Sun), Mon to Sat D 6.30 to 9.30 (10 Fri and Sat). **Meals:** alc (main courses £17.40 to £32). Set L and D £25 (2 courses) to £30. **Details:** 80 seats. Separate bar. Car parking. Children over 3 yrs only.

∎ Reading

ALSO RECOMMENDED
▲ London Street Brasserie
2-4 London Street, Reading, RG1 4PN
Tel no: (01189) 505036
www.londonstbrasserie.co.uk
Modern European

'A lovely setting' was the verdict of one regular at this bustling riverside brasserie, another exclaiming that meals are 'always a delight'. This former tollhouse has become a popular fixture in Reading over the past 14 years. It's run by chef Paul Clerehugh, who offers a broad selection of European dishes, from seared diver scallops, chorizo and spiced yellow pepper sauce (£12) to rump of lamb, root vegetable gratin, winter greens and red wine jus (£18.90). Wines start at £19.50. Open all week.

∎ Shinfield

L'ortolan
Enticing menus full of impact
Church Lane, Shinfield, RG2 9BY
Tel no: (01189) 888500
www.lortolan.com
Modern French | £67
Cooking score: 6
£5 OFF ♦ V

Housed in a former vicarage amid beautifully manicured grounds on the leafy outskirts of Reading, L'ortolan has been a beacon of British haute cuisine for a generation. Its sparely decorated dining room is run with a consummate professionalism often praised by readers. Alan Murchison's focus is rather more French than modern British, although the boundaries are increasingly fluid. A short daily menu offers two starters and a trio of mains – perhaps seared mackerel with compressed melon, feta and fennel jam, followed by beef blade braised in red wine with violet potato purée and variously textured turnip – but it's the tasting menus that hold greatest excitement. Here, the range might extend from the dressing of crab in passion fruit and its partnering with ham hock, to the pairing of rabbit saddle and black pudding in sherry vinegar, finishing with toffee parfait, popcorn ice cream and banana bread. Natural wines made with minimal intervention are a highlight of the resourceful wine list, which also pulls in bottles from Mount Etna, Lebanon and Kent. Prices open at £19, or £7 a standard glass.

Chef/s: Alan Murchison. **Open:** Tue to Sat L 12 to 2, D 7 to 9 (9.30 Fri and Sat). **Closed:** Sun, Mon, 24 Dec to 3 Jan. **Meals:** Set L £28 (2 courses) to £31.50. Set D £39 (5 courses). Tasting menu £71 (7 courses) to £105. **Details:** 58 seats. Separate bar. Car parking.

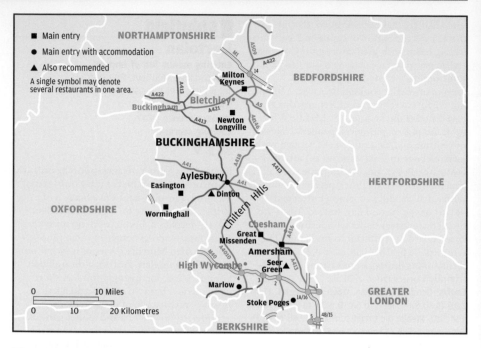

Amersham

★ TOP 50 ★

Artichoke

Confident Buckinghamshire barnstormer
9 Market Square, Amersham, HP7 0DF
Tel no: (01494) 726611
www.artichokerestaurant.co.uk
Modern British | £42
Cooking score: 7

🍷 V

'Fabulous food'; 'flawless service'; 'true inspired genius' – just some of the praise heaped on this Buckinghamshire barnstormer. Laurie Gear runs one of the 'calmest' open kitchens around. Quiet confidence is palpable the moment you enter the soft-toned, low-key dining room. Gear's cooking is on a roll, so expect razor-sharp, big-city techniques in a raft of increasingly impressive, highly detailed dishes. How about a tiny square of charred Cornish mackerel accompanied by cubes of salty Bute seaweed jelly, minuscule pickled mushrooms, sour pomelo and a brown-shrimp cracker? Or a daringly rich pairing of succulent smoked Severn eel with nuggets of orange curd and jelly on foie gras yoghurt? The local landscape has its say, as do ingredients from elsewhere: perhaps Chiltern pigeon breast in a gamey salad with smoked pheasant breast, 'mind-blowing' confit duck beignet and hazelnut powder; or rosy-pink, poached veal loin from Dorset with pungent wild garlic pesto, blobs of intense Parmesan custard and asparagus. Desserts also hit the high notes, from a slice of fruity mousse ('half white apple, half red blackberry') with hazelnut sponge and elemental blackberry sorbet to an extraordinary new-Nordic carrot cake: 'a piece of magical woodland' with little carrots popping out of a 'bed' of almond and chocolate crumb. Keen, personable staff do a 'brilliant' job, and the global wine list is packed with 'exceptional' bottles tailored to the food, from £24.50.

Chef/s: Laurie Gear. **Open:** Tue to Sat L 12 to 3, D 6.30 to 11 (6 Fri and Sat). **Closed:** Sun, Mon, 1 week Easter, 2 weeks Aug, 1 week Christmas, bank hols.

Meals: alc (main courses £19 to £23). Set L £21.50 (2 courses) to £25. Set D £38.50 (2 courses) to £45. Tasting menu L £35 (5 courses), D £65 (7 courses). **Details:** 48 seats. 2 seats outside.

ALSO RECOMMENDED
▲ Gilbey's
1 Market Square, Amersham, HP7 0DF
Tel no: (01494) 727242
www.gilbeygroup.com
Modern British

A dependable servant of Old Amersham, 'lovely' Gilbey's is run by delightful staff who are 'personable, but respectful too'. This honest, neighbourhood eatery occupies a converted grammar school with an inviting sun-trap courtyard. Its attractive, carefully crafted dishes range from seared pigeon breast with figs, almonds and parsnip purée (£9.75) to Anglesey sea bass with Jerusalem artichokes, chorizo and Puy lentils (£19.95). The Gilbey family are wine importers, so expect a sound list with good drinking from £16. Open all week.

▌Aylesbury
Hartwell House
Luxurious dining at a magnificent mansion
Oxford Road, Aylesbury, HP17 8NR
Tel no: (01296) 747444
www.hartwell-house.com
Modern European | £53
Cooking score: 3

🛏

Hartwell House is one of England's most spectacular stately homes. Over the centuries it has been the seat of the high and mighty (including the exiled court of Louis XVIII of France); today it operates as a country house hotel. Public rooms are grand, the grounds a joy and an old-fashioned charm permeates the place. But if there's a sense the kitchen hasn't quite moved with the times in culinary terms, the cooking is sound. Menus have their share of conservative dishes – from smoked salmon to twice-baked cheese soufflé – but there are

modern ideas, too: perhaps wood pigeon teamed with smoked Valrhona chocolate sauce; wild Atlantic cod with bacon and onion gnocchi, red wine-glazed salsify, baby onions and a white wine sauce; and pear tarte Tatin with Pedro Ximénez sherry ice cream. French-led wines fit the house style, but global choices share some of the glory; prices from £27.50.
Chef/s: Daniel Richardson. **Open:** all week L 12.30 to 1.45, D 7.30 to 9.45. **Meals:** alc (main courses £24 to £35). Set L £24.75. Set D £29.95. Sun L £34.95. **Details:** 60 seats. Separate bar. Wheelchair access. Car parking. Children over 5 yrs only.

▌Dinton
ALSO RECOMMENDED
▲ La Chouette
High Street, Dinton, HP17 8UW
Tel no: (01296) 747422
www.lachouette.co.uk
Belgian

'Classic cooking, plus the fun of discussing and disputing the world' lures fans to this unconventional time-warp auberge stuffed with chef/proprietor Frédéric Desmette's pictures of owls (chouettes). It's an acquired taste, but the prospect of Franco-Belgian cuisine ancienne generally entices, judging by reports of 'beautiful scallops' in saffron beurre blanc, wild pigeon breast salad (£9.80), pheasant brabançonne (£18.50) and leg of lamb with chicory. Terrific Belgian beers and a superlative Francophile wine list (from £16.80) are bonuses. Closed Sat L and Sun.

Symbols
🛏 Accommodation is available

💷³⁰ Three courses for less than £30

V Separate vegetarian menu

💷⁵ £5-off voucher scheme

🍾 Notable wine list

||| TOM KERRIDGE
The Hand & Flowers

What do you enjoy most about being a chef?
The alternative social life of being up later than everyone else, and also earlier. Having a strange enjoyment of hard work and spending time with people who are pirates and from the dark side...

Which of your dishes are you most proud of?
I love the simplicity of the smoked haddock omelette, but I'm probably most proud of the duck and duck-fat chips.

What food trends are you spotting at the moment?
A huge demand for top-quality, farmer- and producer-driven meat ingredients, prompted by the horse meat scandal.

What is your favourite time of year for food, and why?
I'm a big fan of autumn – I love root vegetables and cuts of meat that you have to slow cook.

Who are the chefs to watch in 2014?
For me, the future is in the safe hands of Paul Ainsworth (No. 6, Padstow) and Jonray and Peter Sanchez-Iglesias (Casamia, Bristol).

▌Easington
The Mole & Chicken
Attractive inn with sound cooking
Easington Terrace, nr Long Crendon, Easington, HP18 9EY
Tel no: (01844) 208387
www.themoleandchicken.co.uk
Modern British | £35
Cooking score: 1

This sensitively modernised country pub to the west of Aylesbury offers sofas for sinking into, a warren of little rooms and majestic views of the Buckinghamshire hills. Steve Bush cooks nicely judged modern pub food, with the dial set to 'eclectic'. Expect smoked eel with potato and horseradish salad, duck leg and merguez stew with garlic mash, and Norwegian skrei cod with herring roes, capers and parsley. Finish with dramatic blood-orange posset or Neal's Yard Dairy cheeses. Wines from a compact but serviceable list start at £18.50, or £3.95 a standard glass.
Chef/s: Steve Bush. **Open:** all week L 12 to 2.30 (4 Sun), D 6 to 9.30 (9 Sun). **Closed:** 25 Dec. **Meals:** alc (main courses £14 to £24). Set L and D £14.95 (2 courses) to £18.95. **Details:** 62 seats. 60 seats outside. Wheelchair access. Car parking.

▌Great Missenden
La Petite Auberge
Unswervingly French food
107 High Street, Great Missenden, HP16 0BB
Tel no: (01494) 865370
www.lapetiteauberge.co.uk
French | £37
Cooking score: 2

For over two decades the Martels' pristine and intimate French bistro has spread a blanket of joy across Great Missenden. The appeal of the menu (in French with English translations) is not difficult to spot. It delivers good renditions of dishes that soothe rather than challenge. The straightforwardness of the cooking is another confidence booster, the repertoire running from terrine of foie gras via coquilles St Jacques to carré d'agneau. The kitchen also presses the comfort button for classics as diverse as Scottish beef fillet with Madagascar green peppercorns and breast of duck with blackcurrant sauce. Desserts, such as caramelised lemon tart and chocolate mousse, confirm a commitment to simple, well-executed basics. The all-French wine list opens at £19.50.

Chef/s: Hubert Martel. **Open:** Mon to Sat D only 7 to 10. **Closed:** Sun (except Mothering Sun L), 2 weeks Christmas, 2 weeks Easter. **Meals:** alc (main courses £18 to £21). **Details:** 28 seats. Wheelchair access.

Marlow

★ TOP 50 ★

The Hand & Flowers
Big-hearted, resourceful cooking
126 West Street, Marlow, SL7 2BP
Tel no: (01628) 482277
www.thehandandflowers.co.uk
Modern British | £45
Cooking score: 6

'Immensely pleasurable and impossible not to like what's going on here', the most famous pub in Great Britain occupies a pretty roadside cottage on the edge of Marlow. It takes a lot to stand out from the competition in these parts, and while the interior still resembles a pub – flagged floor, low beams, scrubbed tables – Tom Kerridge's carte uncoils expansively into a repertoire of dishes with the crystal ring of modern British authenticity. How else to style a starter of blowtorched Scottish scallop with warm roast chicken bouillon, morels, nasturtium and apple? But on the whole the cooking says 'serious, but don't panic'. The high-end comfort food can produce a startling but moreish smoked mackerel and wild garlic Scotch egg with white onion soubise and charred English onion, and a 'flavoursome' tenderloin of Wiltshire pork with pickled mustard leaf, malt-glazed cheek, garlic sausage and potato dauphine. For pudding, a tonka bean pannacotta, with poached rhubarb, ginger wine jelly and rhubarb sorbet, has been described as the 'highlight of the meal'. Staff are 'chatty, bubbly, enthusiastic' in their black uniforms and black brasserie aprons. A thoroughly commendable job has been done on the global wine list, with assiduous notes, a selection of organic/biodynamic labels and house wines from £21.

Chef/s: Tom Kerridge. **Open:** all week L 12 to 2.45 (3.15 Sun), Mon to Sat D 6.30 to 9.45. **Closed:** 24 to 26 Dec. **Meals:** alc (main courses £24 to £32). **Set L** Mon to Sat £15 (2 courses) to £19.50. **Details:** 50 seats. 20 seats outside. Car parking.

The Vanilla Pod
Eminently civilised house of delights
31 West Street, Marlow, SL7 2LS
Tel no: (01628) 898101
www.thevanillapod.co.uk
Modern European | £45
Cooking score: 5

V

It's little wonder that readers endorse this small, tastefully laid out restaurant as being 'in a class of its own'. Here is a smart destination that puts comfort and hospitality above grand gestures, thanks to 'attentive service' and the inspired presence of chef-patron Michael Macdonald who is, notoriously, a one-man band, cooking alone in his 36-cover restaurant. He aims to impress with serious intentions, innovations and technical accomplishments, sourcing ingredients carefully and observing the calendar to produce food 'bursting with flavour'. One winter diner was pleased by a goats' cheese risotto given texture with hazelnuts and savoury crumbs, and saluted the excellent two-way serving of lamb – roast fillet and leg poached in olive oil – that followed. Others have commented on dishes 'packed with interest', perhaps loin of venison with pear and fondant potato, and crème brûlée ('up there with the best I have had'), beautifully arranged with a tiny jelly, condensed milk caramel, and popcorn ice cream. Recession-busting lunches make the prospect even more attractive, and the savvy, French-led wine list opens at £19.50. See overleaf for details.

Chef/s: Michael Macdonald. **Open:** Tue to Sat L 12 to 2, D 7 to 10. **Closed:** Sun, Mon, 2 weeks Christmas, bank hols. **Meals:** Set L £15.50 (2 courses) to £19.50. Set D £45. Tasting menu £55 (7 courses). **Details:** 36 seats. 15 seats outside. Separate bar.

Milton Keynes

Taipan

Best dim sum for miles
5 Savoy Crescent, Milton Keynes, MK9 3PU
Tel no: (01908) 331883
www.taipan-mk.co.uk
Chinese | £25
Cooking score: 3
£5 OFF V £30

Chinese diners make special trips to this vast restaurant in the pedestrianised theatre district of Milton Keynes. Spread across two open-plan floors with full-length windows adding to the bright, spacious interior, Taipan is renowned for its lunchtime dim sum, which draws a lively mix of suits, shoppers and Chinese families. Evenings are tailored slightly more to Western tastes via a range of set menus and an extensive carte offering the likes of spicy aubergine and minced pork hotpot, steamed eel with black bean sauce, and shredded chicken with jellyfish. Reporters have also applauded the steamed sea bass with ginger and spring onion and the stir-fried king prawn with cashew nuts. Drink tea, bottled Tsing Tao beer or choose from a wine list that opens at £14.50.
Chef/s: H Poon. **Open:** Mon to Sat L 12 to 3.30, D 5.30 to 11. Sun 12 to 10. **Closed:** 25 and 26 Dec. **Meals:** alc (main courses £7 to £34). Set D £15 (2 courses) to £22. **Details:** 140 seats. Wheelchair access.

🍴 **Average Price**

The average price listed in main-entry reviews denotes the price of a three-course meal, without wine.

Newton Longville

The Crooked Billet

Busy cooking in a pristine pub
2 Westbrook End, Newton Longville, MK17 0DF
Tel no: (01908) 373936
www.thebillet.co.uk
Modern British | £26
Cooking score: 2
🍴 V £30

The well-to-do village location, pristine thatched roof and sturdy antiquated frontage might suggest an affluent country boozer, but the Crooked Billet's interior tells a different story. Much of the space is taken up with properly laid tables and the menu makes fanciful reading – how about a busy plate of pan-fried mackerel fillet with griddled courgette, potato and chorizo terrine, red pepper and lemon yoghurt or a five-part discourse on duck (breast, sausage, confit leg, liver and egg) accompanied by spinach, quince and potatoes en cocotte? To finish, pistachio crème brûlée with cherry ice cream is one of the more straightforward offerings. Pride of place, however, goes to the remarkable 200-bin wine list: a treasure trove for curious imbibers, with bottles from £15 and almost everything available by the glass.
Chef/s: Emma Gilchrist. **Open:** Tue to Sun L 12 to 2 (3 Sun), Tue to Sat D 6.30 to 10. **Closed:** Mon, 25 and 26 Dec. **Meals:** alc (main courses £12 to £22). Set L and D £16.75 (2 courses) to £20.75. Sun L £21. Tasting menu £50 (5 courses). **Details:** 50 seats. 50 seats outside. Separate bar. Car parking.

Seer Green

ALSO RECOMMENDED
▲ **The Jolly Cricketers**
24 Chalfont Road, Seer Green, HP9 2YG
Tel no: (01494) 676308
www.thejollycricketers.co.uk
Modern British £5 OFF

'A spirited village boozer that really does cater for drinkers,' commented one visitor, noting at least four local ales. The impressively cluttered bar is adjoined by a cosy parlour-like dining room, though 'they've really overdone the cricketing theme'. Tasty food at fair pub prices sums up the repertoire of steak and kidney pie with cabbage and mash (£14) or ale-braised ham with colcannon and parsley sauce, and dessert of Bramley apple crumble with hazelnuts and vanilla ice cream (£6.50). Passable wines from £16.45. No food Sun D.

▌Stoke Poges

NEW ENTRY

The Garden Room

Drinks on the terrace at the manor
Stoke Place, Stoke Green, Stoke Poges, SL2 4HT
Tel no: (01753) 534790
www.stokeplace.co.uk
Modern European | £45
Cooking score: 4

Plenty of quirky, modern styling was blended into the original grandiosity of this brick-built manor house when it was restored. The Garden Room restaurant, with green herbaceous motifs and a terrace (for summertime drinks), enjoys views over sprawling lawns. Omitted from last year's Guide due to cooking that had become too clever to please customers, a test meal found chef Craig van der Meer back on course and cooking mostly with aplomb – though service still seems rather stiff. A first course of monkfish and lobster – an inspired pairing – was almost lost among its garnishes (tiny pickled mushrooms, tarragon mash, Parmesan shards) and three bubble-bath froths; more direct was a succulent, gamey wood-pigeon in asparagus velouté with powdered truffle. Mains extended from tender, flavourful pink veal loin with toasty sweetbreads, roasted artichoke and apricot variations, to a wonderfully expressive lemon sole with preserved orange, fennel and chive cream. Dessert brought a glossy biscuit-based chocolate and olive oil délice with dense pistachio ice cream. A resourceful wine list (from £19) contains many exciting choices, including much below £40. Half-bottle carafes broaden the options.

Chef/s: Craig van der Meer. **Open:** all week L 12 to 2.30, D 7 to 9.30. **Closed:** 24 Dec to 9 Jan. **Meals:** alc (main courses £21 to £25). Set L £15.50 (2 courses) to £19.50. Set D £35 (2 courses) to £45. Sun L £19.50. Tasting menu £55. **Details:** 36 seats. 25 seats outside. Children at lunch only.

▌Worminghall

NEW ENTRY

The Clifden Arms

A thoroughly satisfying country pub
75 Clifden Road, Worminghall, HP18 9JR
Tel no: (01844) 339273
www.theclifdenarms.com
British | £28
Cooking score: 2
£30

Matthew and Kate Butcher acquired the Clifden Arms in 2011 – a thatched pub with an endearing Toytown look from the outside (not least as there's a giant boot in the grounds for kids to play in). Low beams, tartan carpets, blackboard menus and notably hospitable staff compose the interior scene. Matthew Butcher has judged to a nicety what people want from a country-pub menu: coddled eggs with spinach purée, cumin dhal and parsnip crisps, perhaps, and mains of roast pork with a baton of crackling, on beetroot, spinach and puréed celeriac, or knots of poached lemon sole in mussel and lemongrass broth with chard from the garden. Finish with roasted figs, served with cinnamon ice cream and honeyed raisins. Good draught ales and a respectable wine list (from £14.50) complete a thoroughly satisfying picture.

Chef/s: Matthew Butcher. **Open:** Tue to Thur L 11 to 3, D 6 to 11. Fri to Sun 11am to 11.30pm (3 Sun). **Closed:** Mon. **Meals:** alc (main courses £10 to £20). **Details:** 36 seats. Separate bar. Car parking.

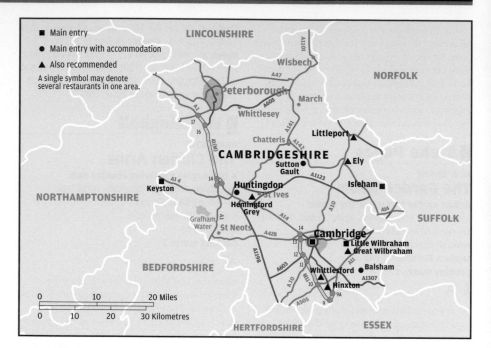

- ■ Main entry
- ● Main entry with accommodation
- ▲ Also recommended

A single symbol may denote several restaurants in one area.

LINCOLNSHIRE

Wisbech

NORFOLK

Peterborough

March

Whittlesey

Littleport

Chatteris

CAMBRIDGESHIRE

Sutton ●
Gault

Ely

Keyston

Huntingdon

Isleham

St Ives

NORTHAMPTONSHIRE

Hemingford
Grey

SUFFOLK

Grafham
Water

St Neots

Cambridge

Little Wilbraham
Great Wilbraham

BEDFORDSHIRE

Whittlesford

Balsham

Hinxton

0   10   20 Miles
0   10   20   30 Kilometres

HERTFORDSHIRE

ESSEX

■ Balsham

NEW ENTRY

The Black Bull Inn

Village hostelry with a fine line in pies
27 High Street, Balsham, CB21 4DJ
Tel no: (01223) 893844
www.blackbull-balsham.co.uk
British | £28
Cooking score: 1

🛏 £30

There are times when only a pie will do – and you're in luck if the urge hits you in Balsham. This fetching thatched freehouse produces a daily changing choice of densely filled delights. Beneath the crisp pastry lid, you might find venison and sage or village-bought Aberdeen Angus beef. From the à la carte, a potted rabbit starter at inspection lacked much rabbitiness (though wowed on the slate), and the pleasure of perfectly cooked scallops in a pan-fried sea bass main course was

only slightly diminished by an overly busy plate. Finish with a taster selection of puddings. House wine is £14.50.
Chef/s: Peter Friskey. **Open:** all week L 12 to 2 (2.30 Sun), D 6.30 to 9 (9.30 Fri and Sat). **Meals:** alc (main courses £12 to £22). Set L £13 (2 courses) to £17.50. **Details:** 90 seats. 60 seats outside. Separate bar. Wheelchair access. Car parking.

■ Cambridge

Cotto

Hard-to-fault sourcing and flavours
183 East Road, Cambridge, CB1 1BG
Tel no: (01223) 302010
www.cottocambridge.co.uk
Modern European | £50
Cooking score: 3

Shut the door on the noise of Cambridge's East Road and let Hans Schweitzer's culinary 'strokes of genius' and the gentle attention of his exemplary service team soothe and delight. Schweitzer's classical skills give weight to this tempting menu, but he's

cooking with a demanding modern diner in mind: someone more interested in provenance, sustainability and underused cuts of meat, than twiddly bits. So sourcing and flavours are hard to fault. A creamy organic barley seafood risotto with tiger prawn and roasted lobster juices is deftly seasoned, while a meltingly tender main of slow-braised pork cheeks, tenderloin and belly – all from those East Anglian champions of welfare-friendly pork, Dingley Dell – captures the mood precisely. Schweitzer is an expert chocolatier and an array of 'Hans-made chocolates' rounds things off nicely. Too full for them? A fiver gets you a box to take home. House wine from £17.50.
Chef/s: Hans Schweitzer. **Open:** Wed to Sat D only 6.30 to 10 (6 Sat). **Closed:** Sun, Mon, Tue, 1 week Easter. **Meals:** Set D £50 (£55 Sat). **Details:** 45 seats. Car parking. Children over 10 yrs only.

Fitzbillies
Delightfully donnish
51-52 Trumpington Street, Cambridge, CB2 1RG
Tel no: (01223) 352500
www.fitzbillies.com
British | £26
Cooking score: 1
£30

It can be difficult to avoid mediocrity if you're caught hungry in Cambridge. So escape to Fitzbillies, the bakery of Chelsea bun fame, where Rosie Sykes's food might make you 'weep with joy'. A beef patty with house relish, or egg and bacon pie, makes a satisfying lunch, while dinner – now three nights a week – offers more elaborate rose veal short ribs with horseradish dumplings and watercress, or pot-roast Norfolk quail, smoked pig's cheek and black cabbage. You won't go wrong with a chocolate and salt caramel pot for pudding. Wine from £16.
Chef/s: Rosie Sykes. **Open:** all week 10 to 6 (5 Thur to Sat), Thur to Sat D 6 to 9.30. **Closed:** 25 Dec to 3 Jan. **Meals:** alc (main courses £12 to £17). **Details:** 45 seats. Wheelchair access.

★ TOP 50 ★

Midsummer House
Cambridge's class act
Midsummer Common, Cambridge, CB4 1HA
Tel no: (01223) 369299
www.midsummerhouse.co.uk
Modern British | £75
Cooking score: 8
V

Reporters never fail to mention what a singular delight it is just to sit in Midsummer House. Even before you've picked up a menu, the daylight-filled dining room in a restored Victorian villa is a tonic for the senses. To linger on the upstairs terrace overlooking the Cam on a summer's day is idyllic. Daniel Clifford has worked conscientiously to make the venue not only a beacon of excellence in a once-underserved city, but also one of Britain's top destinations. The result is a finely judged balance of innovation and classicism, so that even the most speculative dishes speak of sound culinary logic. Copious praise continues to pour in from readers, whether singling out a straightforward gathering of Cashel Blue, broccoli and pear, a crisply sautéed scallop with celeriac and truffle or expressing delight at the ever-popular slow-roast pork, sauced with mead and accompanied by salt-baked carrots and sherry-pickled onions. Fabulous seasonal ingredients take centre stage, with a stunning velouté of English peas, chilled diced tomato and prawns, and a bravura fish dish of roast stone bass, briny surf calms, chargrilled cucumber, wasabi and sorrel sauce, forming part of one early summer meal, while lemon posset, blueberries and lemon espuma made a sharp, fresh finish; there are wonderful artisanal cheeses, too. Plentiful thoroughbred wines help to increase the bill substantially, beginning at £25 but soon soaring skywards.
Chef/s: Daniel Clifford. **Open:** Wed to Sat L 12 to 1.45, Tue to Sat D 7 to 9.30 (6.30 Fri and Sat). **Closed:** Sun, Mon, 2 weeks Christmas. **Meals:** Set L and D £40. Tasting menus £75 (6 courses) to £95 (10 courses). **Details:** 51 seats. Separate bar.

Restaurant Alimentum

Stimulating flavours in a modern urban eatery
152-154 Hills Road, Cambridge, CB2 8PB
Tel no: (01223) 413000
www.restaurantalimentum.co.uk
Modern European | £49
Cooking score: 6
£5
OFF

Alimentum is the image of a modern urban eatery. The inscrutable monochrome of dark undressed tables and a blond-wood floor is offset by wall panels of scarlet. A picture window allows views into the kitchen. Reports of staff on autopilot are happily in the past, and the place thrums with contentment and discovery. The menus favour the terse listing approach, to indicate that the range of technique and texture in a dish is too intricate for a concise summary. Flair resides in the innovative and stimulating juxtaposition of flavours. One reporter was thrilled by smoked eel with apple, horseradish and truffle, and a dessert comprising blackberry yoghurt, pistachio and tarragon. In between might be peanut-crusted cod with shrimp, mooli and grapefruit, or beef sirloin and oxtail with shallots and bone marrow. An efficient wine list productively combs the length and breadth of France before making fleeting calls elsewhere. Italian reds are good. Prices start at £19.50, or £15 for a half-litre carafe, £6.50 a glass.
Chef/s: Mark Poynton. **Open:** all week L 12 to 2.30 (3 Sun), Mon to Sat D 6 to 10. **Closed:** 23 to 30 Dec, bank hols. **Meals:** alc (£36 for 2 courses; £49 for 3 courses). Set L and early D £18.50 (2 courses) to £24.50. Tasting menu £72. **Details:** 62 seats. Separate bar. Wheelchair access.

▌Ely

ALSO RECOMMENDED
▲ The Boathouse
5-5a Annesdale, Ely, CB7 4BN
Tel no: (01353) 664388
www.theboathouseely.co.uk
Modern British

With Ely's cathedral nearby and dreamy views to admire, crowds descend on this restaurant by the Ouse. Like its sibling, the Cock at Hemingford Grey (see entry), the Boathouse excels in fish specials and homemade sausages, but the regular menu has plenty to tempt too: beetroot and goats' cheese salad (£5.75), perhaps, or pork tenderloin with bubble and squeak, wilted spinach and mustard sauce (£16). Languedoc wines are stars of the drinks list, with prices from £17.90. Open all week.

▌Great Wilbraham

ALSO RECOMMENDED
▲ The Carpenters Arms
10 High Street, Great Wilbraham, CB21 5JD
Tel no: (01223) 882093
www.carpentersarmsgastropub.co.uk
Modern European £5
OFF

A warming fire, real ales (Crafty Beers, the on-premises microbrewery), traditional décor: the Carpenters Arms looks and feels like a proper local. A big pull, however, are menus offering Gallic bistro classics as well as traditional British pub food. In the evening Heather Hurley reproduces the dishes she cooked at her restaurant in France – foie gras façon Tatin; chicken forestière (£14.50) – at lunchtime there are ploughman's, filled baguettes, the likes of venison pie, and gammon, egg and chips (both £9.95) and Sunday roasts. Wines from £14.95. Open all week except Sun D.

Hemingford Grey

ALSO RECOMMENDED
▲ The Cock

47 High Street, Hemingford Grey, PE28 9BJ
Tel no: (01480) 463609
www.thecockhemingford.co.uk
British

It may look like your average local on the main street of a strung-out village, but the Cock has two halves. Through the door marked 'pub' you'll find a rustic boozer with real ales; through the door marked 'restaurant' is a spacious dining room with blackboards offering ample choice. Homemade sausages with a choice of mash and sauce (£11.50) are favourites, but there are terrines, fish specials and the likes of lamb Barnsley chop with confit new potatoes (£15). Wines from £17. Open all week.

Hinxton

ALSO RECOMMENDED
▲ The Red Lion Inn

32 High Street, Hinxton, CB10 1QY
Tel no: (01799) 530601
www.redlionhinxton.co.uk
Modern British £5 OFF

An affluent village off the M11 south of Cambridge is the location for this striking, 16th-century timbered hostelry, now a thriving pub-with-rooms. Beams and bare boards in the bar add to the appeal, as do local ales and menus that combine popular pub food with more inventive dishes, perhaps turbot with gnocchi and saffron moules marinières (£22), trio of lamb with pea purée and fried sweetbread jus (£20) and chocolate tart with coffee anglaise and pistachio praline (£7.50). House wine is £14. Open all week.

Huntingdon

The Old Bridge Hotel

Oenophile oasis with vibrant seasonal food
1 High Street, Huntingdon, PE29 3TQ
Tel no: (01480) 424300
www.huntsbridge.com
Modern British | £30
Cooking score: 3

The ivy-clad Old Bridge Hotel has smart-casual hospitality down to a fine art, thanks to its upbeat, cosmopolitan vibes, enchanting riverside gardens and conservatory dining room emblazoned with classical trompe l'oeil friezes. The kitchen keeps an eye on the calendar, changes its menu each day and overlays a larder full of British produce with vibrant Mediterranean flourishes: lamb's sweetbreads partnered by cauliflower purée, crispy pancetta, capers and sage; line-caught sea bass pointed up with saffron dauphinois, braised fennel, cavolo nero and lobster sauce; poached and grilled saddle of rabbit enriched with borlotti beans, violetta artichokes, spring vegetables and tarragon sauce. Alternatively, go for something classic such as fish and chips followed by pannacotta with Champagne rhubarb. The Old Bridge is also a Mecca for oenophiles, with its own wine shop and a thrilling list of up-to-the-minute global varietals noted for their 'flat' mark-ups and brilliant by-the-glass possibilities. Bottles start at £16.95.
Chef/s: James Claydon. **Open:** all week L 12 to 2, D 6.30 to 10. **Meals:** alc (main courses £11 to £29). Set L and D £15.95 (2 courses) to £19.95. Sun L £29.50. **Details:** 80 seats. 40 seats outside. Separate bar. Car parking.

Isleham

NEW ENTRY
The Merry Monk
Generosity in a Fenland village
30 West Street, Isleham, CB7 5SB
Tel no: (01638) 780900
www.merry-monk.co.uk
British | £29
Cooking score: 3
£5 OFF £30 ▼

Fenland Cambridgeshire might not leap out as somewhere to eat well – but be prepared to change your mind for this gem of a village restaurant. Chef/owner Adrian Smith plunders the produce-rich surrounding area hungrily, so you might start with Norfolk mussels, chorizo, sea greens and parsley, or chicken liver parfait with pickled beetroot, Bramley apple chutney and brioche. A fillet of hake was memorably perfect, its gentle flavour enlivened by a fragrant drizzle of warm wild garlic butter and the salty, summery joy of early samphire. Portions are as generous as the service is friendly, so pace yourself because a pudding like bitter chocolate ganache, goats' milk ice cream, blueberries and praline is not to be missed. House wine, £17.95.
Chef/s: Adrian Smith. **Open:** Tue to Sun L 12 to 2, D 6.30 to 9. **Closed:** Mon, 25 and 26 Dec. **Meals:** alc (main courses £14 to 26). Set L £16 (2 courses) to £20. Sun L £25. **Details:** 60 seats. 24 seats outside. Car parking.

Keyston
The Pheasant at Keyston
Reborn thatched hostelry with big-city food
Loop Road, Keyston, PE28 0RE
Tel no: (01832) 710241
www.thepheasant-keyston.co.uk
Modern British | £28
Cooking score: 2
🍾 £30 ▼

John Hoskins MW, the oenophile brains behind the Old Bridge Hotel, Huntingdon (see entry), repurchased this dapper thatched hostelry in 2012 as part of his Huntsbridge

Group. It has been a turn for the better. Beams and open fires set the rustic tone, but the 'excellent cuisine' brings bright, big-city flavours and a sackful of British seasonal ingredients to the table. Home-cured bresaola with white bean purée, roast beetroot and truffle oil shares the billing with venison Scotch eggs, and the daily menu might also span everything from fish pie to superb poussin with sage gnocchi, leeks and artichokes. Hoskins' easily accessible, grown-up wine list is a 100-bin global stunner with thrilling modern names, plenty by the glass and admirable prices across the range. House selections start at £16.95 (£4.65 a glass).
Chef/s: Simon Cadge. **Open:** Tue to Sun L 12 to 2 (3 Sun), Tue to Sat D 6 to 9.30. **Closed:** Mon, 2 to 16 Jan. **Meals:** alc (main courses £13 to £24). Set L £14.95 (2 courses) to £19.95. Sun L £25. **Details:** 70 seats. 20 seats outside. Separate bar. Wheelchair access. Car parking.

Little Wilbraham
The Hole in the Wall
Refreshing cooking in a homely pub
Primrose Farm Road, Little Wilbraham, CB21 5JY
Tel no: (01223) 812282
www.holeinthewallcambridge.com
Modern British | £26
Cooking score: 1
£30 ▼

MasterChef finalists don't always make the best restaurateurs, but 2010 runner-up Alex Rushmer is doing Cambridgeshire proud with a little help from fellow chef/patron Ben Maud. Their 16th-century public house in a 'delightful fenland village' has the requisite real fires and bare beams and serves 'superb' food based around local ingredients. The 'short and flexible' menu flows with the seasons; a 'winter salad' of chicory, pear, walnut and blue cheese might precede poached chicken breast with potato and spring onion rösti, leek and mushrooms, and for dessert, fresh doughnuts with chocolate and griottine-cherry dipping sauce. Wines start at £18.

Chef/s: Alex Rushmer. Open: Wed to Sun L 12 to 3 (4 Sun), Tue to Sat D 6 to 10 (11 Fri and Sat). Closed: Mon, 23 Dec to 5 Jan. Meals: alc (main courses £12 to £20). Set L £14 (2 courses) to £16. Details: 80 seats. 25 seats outside. Separate bar. Wheelchair access. Car parking.

▌ Littleport

ALSO RECOMMENDED
▲ The Fen House
2 Lynn Road, Littleport, CB6 1QG
Tel no: (01353) 860645
Modern British

Talk about exclusive. David Warne's white-fronted cottage restaurant in the fenland near the Great Ouse, not far from Ely, opens for dinner on two nights a week only. The stock-in-trade is a fixed-price four-course menu at £40, comprising fragrantly seasoned modern British dishes, running from smoked salmon and dill mousse in lemon dressing to coriander-scented poached breast of guinea fowl with spiced lentil ragoût, and then cheeses, finishing up with lemongrass parfait on spicy pineapple salsa. Wines from £16.75. Open Fri and Sat D only.

▌ Sutton Gault

The Anchor Inn
Lovely old pub with lots of fans
Bury Lane, Sutton Gault, CB6 2BD
Tel no: (01353) 778537
www.anchor-inn-restaurant.co.uk
Modern British | £30
Cooking score: 2

£5 OFF ⊨

As a refuge from the chilly winds blowing across the fens, this slightly off-the-beaten track retreat is hard to beat, run with all the warmth and welcome you would hope to find in such an establishment. The Anchor is the real thing, over three centuries old, where amid head-cracking beams, crackling fires and scrubbed pine furniture you can sample real ales and generous cooking with a sharp seasonal sense. You might kick off with

scallops with tomato compote, chorizo crisps and a pepper-paprika sauce, go on to duck breast with sweet potato purée, purple sprouting broccoli and a blood orange and clementine sauce, and finish with lemon posset. Wines from £16.30.
Chef/s: Maciej Bilewski. Open: all week L 12 to 2 (3 Sun), D 7 to 9, (6.30 to 9 Sat and Sun). Meals: alc (main courses £12 to £24). Set L £13.95 (2 courses) to £17.95. Sun L £12.95. Details: 60 seats. 30 seats outside. Separate bar. Car parking.

▌ Whittlesford

ALSO RECOMMENDED
▲ The Tickell Arms
1 North Road, Whittlesford, CB22 4NZ
Tel no: (01223) 833025
www.cambscuisine.com
Modern European

This stylish addition to the Cambscuisine group (Cock, Hemingford Grey; Boathouse, Ely) is a pub/restaurant that carnivores will relish. A particular meat or fish is championed every couple of months, so you might follow beef carpaccio, shaved Parmesan and cep oil (£8.50) with star anise and liquorice-braised beef cheek, roast celeriac, oyster dumplings and chard (£18). Want something lighter? Try tempura squid with chilli and lime followed by pan-fried sea bream with ratatouille. Vanilla crème brûlée (£6.50) is a popular pud. A litre of house wine is £20.50. Open all week.

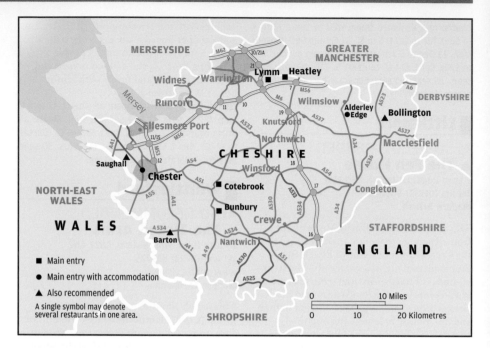

MERSEYSIDE

GREATER MANCHESTER

Lymm Heatley

Widnes Warrington

DERBYSHIRE

Runcorn Wilmslow

Alderley Edge Bollington

Ellesmere Port Knutsford

Macclesfield

Saughall C H E S H I R E

Winsford

Chester

NORTH-EAST WALES Cotebrook

Congleton

W A L E S Bunbury

Crewe

STAFFORDSHIRE

Barton Nantwich

E N G L A N D

■ Main entry
● Main entry with accommodation
▲ Also recommended
A single symbol may denote
several restaurants in one area.

SHROPSHIRE

0   10 Miles

0   10   20 Kilometres

▮ Alderley Edge

Alderley Edge Hotel

Modern cuisine in traditional surroundings
Macclesfield Road, Alderley Edge, SK9 7BJ
Tel no: (01625) 583033
www.alderleyedgehotel.com
Modern British | £46
Cooking score: 3

🍴 V

The JW Lees brewing concern owns this
delicious slice of Victorian Gothic, sited near
the renowned wooded ridge after which the
hotel is named. A dining room that extends
into a conservatory capitalises on the luxuriant
views, and Chris Holland cooks to a
regionally informed template, offering a
variety of menus. Signature creations include a
starter of slow-roast suckling pig with toffee
apple, pork popcorn and sage, and the duo of
Cheshire lamb for main (the loin aromatic
with garlic and parsley, the shoulder braised),
served with roast beetroot and champ. Fish-
lovers might head for roast monkfish and

brown shrimps, or 'delicate as a cloud' cod fillet
with creamed potato and nutmegged spinach.
Finish with sugar-crusted passion fruit soufflé
or lemon meringue cheesecake. An international selection of house wines starts
at £17.95.
Chef/s: Chris Holland. **Open:** all week L 12 to 2 (4
Sun), Mon to Sat D 7 to 10. **Meals:** alc (main courses
£24). Set L £23.95. Set D £34.50. Tasting menu
£58.50 (6 courses). **Details:** 80 seats. 26 seats
outside.

▮ Barton

ALSO RECOMMENDED
▲ The Cock O' Barton

Barton Road, Barton, SY14 7HU
Tel no: (01829) 782277
www.thecockobarton.co.uk
Modern European

A real Cheshire crowd-puller, the Cock O'
Barton is a fully switched-on country pub:
sprawling, stylish and thoroughly up to date,
serving food all day. And the menu does the

business: steak baguette (from £7.95) is great with a pint, and punters are well fed with generous helpings of game and mushroom terrine, fish and chips and slabs of pork belly with red cabbage (£13.50). In addition, the kitchen showcases locally produced Aberdeen Angus dry-aged steaks and an all-Cheshire cheeseboard. Wines from £14.95. Closed Mon.

◾ Bollington

ALSO RECOMMENDED
▲ The Lord Clyde
36 Clarke Lane, Kerridge, Bollington, SK10 5AH
Tel no: (01625) 562123
www.thelordclyde.co.uk
Modern British £5 OFF

'Still turning out stonkingly good food', is how one visitor summed up this 'find' of a hostelry. The kitchen plays it straight with the likes of twice-baked cauliflower cheese soufflé (£7.95) and sharing plates such as 'tastes of the North West' (£14.25) – black pudding fritters ('lovely and crisp'), Cheshire cheese croquettes ('oozing and with an apple chutney'), potted shrimps, Cumbrian air-dried ham and Cumberland sausage. Braised shin of beef with wild mushroom risotto makes a satisfying main course, and there's chocolate and salted pistachio caramel tart for dessert. Wines from £16. Closed Sun D, Mon.

◾ Bunbury
The Yew Tree Inn
Smart country local
Long Lane, Spurstow, Bunbury, CW6 9RD
Tel no: (01829) 260274
www.theyewtreebunbury.com
Modern British | £25
Cooking score: 2
£5 OFF £30

Eccentric design touches and an up-to-date menu confer a contemporary feel on a pub that has served Bunbury since the early 19th century. At the helm, Jon and Lindsay Cox give emphasis to beer lovers in the bar, but the food (and perhaps the possibility of eating it on the large terrace) is what draws many here. Readers report most success with pubby offerings such as a fish-finger barm with dripping chips, though more involved dishes include twice-baked Cheshire cheese soufflé with tomato relish; belly pork with black pudding mash, apple fritter, greens and a sage jus, and marmalade pudding with custard. Wines are from £14.95.
Chef/s: Mark Hughes. **Open:** Mon to Fri L 12 to 2.30, D 6 to 9.30 (10 Fri). Sat 12 to 10, Sun 11 to 8. **Closed:** 25 Dec. **Meals:** alc (main courses £10 to £20). **Details:** 65 seats. 60 seats outside. Separate bar. Wheelchair access. Car parking.

◾ Chester
Joseph Benjamin
Lively deli/eatery with foodie pleasures
134-140 Northgate Street, Chester, CH1 2HT
Tel no: (01244) 344295
www.josephbenjamin.co.uk
Modern European | £25
Cooking score: 2
£30

The Wright brothers haven't put a foot wrong with their easy-going deli-restaurant by Chester's city walls. They have the 'customer at the heart of everything they do'. Drop in for a latte and bacon sandwich breakfast, a deli platter or sandwich at lunch, or an 'interesting without being weird and wonderful' dinner with a well-chosen bottle of wine. Popular 'JB staples' include king prawns with chilli and garlic butter, and roast chicken, chips and aïoli. The classy combination of fruit cake, Stichelton blue cheese and a glass of Moscatel is a 'permanent fixture' for pudding. 'Eclectic' specials might be Shetland salmon with beetroot risotto or truffled macaroni cheese with caponata, to be enjoyed with charmingly annotated wines (from £15.95), bottled beers and old-school aperitifs.
Chef/s: Joe Wright. **Open:** Tue to Sun L 12 to 3 (4 Sun), Thur to Sat D 6 to 9.30. **Closed:** Mon. **Meals:** alc (main courses £11 to £17). Sun L £19.95 (3 courses). **Details:** 38 seats. 12 seats outside. Separate bar. Wheelchair access.

Michael Caines at ABode Chester

High-level dining in more ways than one

Grosvenor Road, Chester, CH1 2DJ
Tel no: (01244) 347000
www.michaelcaines.com
Modern British | £35
Cooking score: 5

🍽 V

The fifth-floor dining room has a magnificent view over Chester racecourse, and while the modernist interior decoration can feel rather anonymous, the front-of-house team put on a friendly face and the mood is far from stuffy. Reporters praise the 'absolutely delicious' food with its 'exquisite attention to detail', but then exact technique and an ability to bring both balance and masses of flavour to dishes are hallmarks of Michael Caines' ABode kitchens; here it is done consistently and, if you ever pop in for the race-day lunch, in volume too. Sound ingredients are the starting point, perhaps a terrine of local chicken with asparagus, quails' eggs and tarragon mayonnaise ahead of Welsh lamb loin teamed with onion purée, pressed potato, confit tomato and tapenade jus. Artisan British cheeses are a fine alternative to dessert, say mango and lime parfait with exotic fruit salad and confit-lime sorbet. The cannily chosen wine-list aims for value with bottles from £22.50.

Chef/s: Thomas Hine. **Open:** all week L 12 to 2.30 (12.30 Sun), Mon to Sat D 6 to 9.30 (9.45 Sun). **Closed:** bank hols. **Meals:** alc (main courses £17 to £25). Set L £14.50 to £19.50. Set D £16.50 to £22.50. Tasting menu £60. **Details:** 76 seats. 12 seats outside. Separate bar. Wheelchair access.

★ TOP 50 ★

Simon Radley at the Chester Grosvenor

Finely honed gastronomic delights

Eastgate, Chester, CH1 1LT
Tel no: (01244) 324024
www.chestergrosvenor.com
Modern European | £69
Cooking score: 6

🍷 🍽 V

Luxury comes as standard at the Chester Grosvenor – a prized asset that dominates the city with its extravagant half-timbered façade, lordly pedigree and reputation for fine food. At its heart is Simon Radley's restaurant, a gilded and pillared dining room manned by a battalion of punctilious waiters. It's worth shelling out top dollar for a chance to sample the chef's precise, assured creations – even if the dish names are pert and enigmatic. A starter called 'crown prince' brings saddle of French rabbit with hand-rolled bacon macaroni, pumpkin and poached langoustine, while a main course simply dubbed 'brace' involves wild mallard and Gressingham duck teamed with salt-baked beets, forced rhubarb and pain d'épices. Ingredients can't be faulted, whether rare-breed beef, Herdwick mutton, Ibérico pork or French Baeri caviar, and everything gels impressively on the plate. There's even room for some fun: how about a 'floating island' involving chilled blood-orange nectar, poached and crisp vacherins (meringue shells) and iced mandarin? Sommelier Garry Clark's 50-page wine list is an awesome tome that offers a palate-expanding tour of the winemaking planet, with lesser-known grapes and styles in abundance and with due attention paid to organic growers. Prices start at £22.

Chef/s: Simon Radley. **Open:** Tue to Sat D only 6.30 to 9. **Closed:** Sun, Mon, 25 Dec, 1 to 10 Jan. **Meals:** Set D £69. Tasting menu £90 (8 courses). **Details:** 42 seats. Separate bar. Wheelchair access. Car parking. Children over 12 yrs only.

NEW ENTRY
Sticky Walnut
Unstuffy food, sharply executed
11 Charles Street, Chester, CH2 3AZ
Tel no: (01244) 400400
www.stickywalnut.com
Modern European | £28
Cooking score: 4

£5 OFF   £30

With such a name, it's no surprise that Gary Usher's neighbourhood restaurant is resolutely unstuffy — yet Sticky Walnut still feels precision-tuned. It is set over two floors just off Hoole's main drag, with its innards neatly on display: wine and cookbooks on the shelves, a quiet open kitchen at the back and the makings of a bar. Prices are fastidiously controlled, giving a particular savour to the way each of the clever, seasonal dishes hits the spot. A starter of ox tongue comes licked with a glossy dressing of chicken jus and truffle mayonnaise, its texture echoed by the falling-apart insides of a couple of browned lamb croquettes. Mains might be arancini with a dab of Cashel Blue at the centre, served with walnuts, spinach and pears poached in red wine, or rolled, stuffed pork belly with lentils. For dessert, try a textbook apricot and almond tart, with biscuity pastry. Wines from £16.
Chef/s: Gary Usher. **Open:** Tue to Sat L 12 to 3 (2 Fri and Sat), D 6 to 10. **Closed:** Mon, Sun. **Meals:** alc (main courses £13 to £22). **Details:** 48 seats.

ALSO RECOMMENDED
▲ 1539 Restaurant & Bar
Watergate Square, Chester, CH1 2LY
Tel no: (01244) 304611
www.restaurant1539.co.uk
Modern British £5 OFF

The smart, chic interior at 1539 overlooks Chester Racecourse and has a bar and terrace above — it looks good in any weather. A large, bustling place ('lively on race days'), the restaurant is noted for an all-embracing menu and serious intent. Char-grilled Vale of Clwyd steaks and fish and chips (£13.50) are popular shouts, but there are also starters of fresh and smoked salmon lasagne with horseradish cream, mains of mackerel with confit fennel, lemon radicchio and Prosecco cream (£16), and chocolate and hazelnut cheesecake. Wines from £18. Closed Sun D.

▌Cotebrook
Fox & Barrel
Sunny flavours in a pubby setting
Foxbank, Cotebrook, CW6 9DZ
Tel no: (01829) 760529
www.foxandbarrel.co.uk
Modern British | £24
Cooking score: 2

£5 OFF   £30

This pub-restaurant in a village north of Tarporley has pubby attributes aplenty — beams, real fire, real ales — but its major draw is now the kitchen's vigorous cooking. Daily menus fuse regional ingredients with sunny Med flavours, promising anything from quail and pistachio terrine to pork and chorizo meatballs with pasta and a rich tomato sauce. Otherwise, expect please-all pub classics like fish and chips or venison and rabbit suet pudding. To finish, explore some excellent Cheshire cheeses and satisfy any sweet cravings with, say, bitter chocolate, cherry and almond cheesecake. Wines from £15.95.
Chef/s: Richard Cotterill and Aaron Totty. **Open:** all week 12 to 9.30 (9 Sun). **Meals:** alc (main courses £10 to £20). **Details:** 100 seats. 110 seats outside. Separate bar. Car parking.

▌Heatley
La Boheme
Fabulous value-for-money French food
3 Mill Lane, Heatley, WA13 9SD
Tel no: (01925) 753657
www.laboheme.co.uk
French | £27
Cooking score: 3

V   £30

'Good food that is consistently value for money' is the view of many who enjoy the classic French cooking of Olivier Troalen.

Smart, welcoming La Boheme is a well-oiled machine – the quality and consistency, especially at the prices charged, is impressive. Cognac-flavoured foie gras comes with aromatic pear chutney and toasted brioche. Alternatively, start with follie de porc: layers of French black pudding, shredded pork rillettes and gratinated Cheddar rarebit, served with a poached egg and a creamy white onion compote. Mains range from fillet of sea bass teamed with butternut squash, asparagus, baby carrot confit and a saffron sauce to veal rump with a vegetable parcel, white wine and morel sauce. Puddings feature the classics (crème brûlée; hazelnut parfait with poached pear and salted caramel) or perhaps a more showy chocolate assiette. The wine list majors in French wines and is as keenly priced as the food, with bottles starting at £16.50.
Chef/s: Olivier Troalen. **Open:** Tue to Fri L 12 to 2.30, Mon to Sat D 6 to 10 (10.30 Sat). Sun 12 to 9. **Meals:** Set L £15.95 (2 courses) to £20.95. Set D £21 (2 courses) to £26. Sun L £16.50 (2 courses). **Details:** 120 seats. Separate bar. Wheelchair access. Car parking.

Lymm
The Church Green
Smart British pub food
Higher Lane, Lymm, WA13 0AP
Tel no: (01925) 752068
www.aidenbyrne.co.uk
Modern British | £34
Cooking score: 2
V

This renovated hostelry in the heart of Lymm, slap-bang next to the church, has been transformed into a stylish and popular food-pub. Chunky wooden tables, high-backed leather chairs and a neutral colour scheme lend it a sophisticated look, and the kitchen makes impressive use of local ingredients. There's cottage pie, mussels, and honey-glazed gammon pork belly on the menu, but beef (cooked over coconut husk charcoals on an Inka grill) is the star; you are invited to mix-and-match your steak or burger with your choice of sauce, garnish and side dish. Saffron

risotto with king prawns and radicchio or pea mousse with Yellison goats' cheese and lemon emulsion make a good start, and desserts include the likes of lime cheesecake with roasted pineapple. Wine from £17.50.
Chef/s: Ian Matfin. **Open:** Mon to Fri 12 to 9, Sat and Sun 9am to 10pm (8pm Sun). **Closed:** 25 Dec. **Meals:** alc (main courses £9 to £39). Sun L £14. Tasting menu £60 (5 courses). **Details:** 80 seats. 120 seats outside. Separate bar. Wheelchair access. Car parking.

Saughall
ALSO RECOMMENDED
▲ The Greyhound Inn
Seahill Road, Saughall, CH1 6BJ
Tel no: (01244) 881122
www.thegreyhoundinnsaughall.co.uk
Modern British

'A little bit pub-in-a-box, with unadorned tables but a good size and with comfy chairs', this former coach house augments its menu of pub classics with diverting British tapas. You can mix and match for £3 per snack, ordering the likes of offal mixed grill (trotter, marrow, kidney), smoked salmon hotdog with beetroot ketchup or an excellent hot Scotch egg. Main courses range from conventional steaks or burgers to 'greedy pig, shrimp, crackle and pop': aka pork loin, belly, pig's cheek croquettes, with shrimp and cider sauce (£16). Wines from £11.50. Open all week.

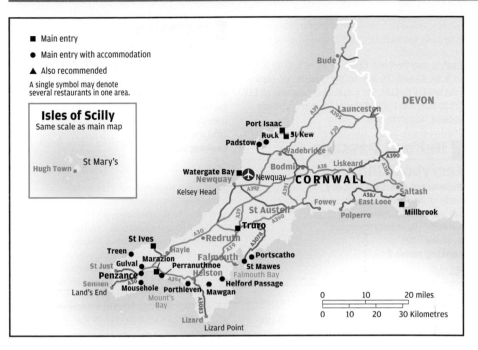

- ■ Main entry
- ● Main entry with accommodation
- ▲ Also recommended

A single symbol may denote several restaurants in one area.

Isles of Scilly
Same scale as main map

Hugh Town ● St Mary's

DEVON

Bude

Port Isaac
Rock ■ St Kew
Padstow ●
Wadebridge

Launceston

Bodmin
Watergate Bay ■ ✈
Newquay ● Newquay
Kelsey Head
CORNWALL
Liskeard
Saltash

St Austell
Fowey East Looe
Polperro
Millbrook

Truro
Redruth

St Ives ■
Treen ● Hayle
Marazion
St Just Gulval Perranuthnoe
Penzance
Helston
Semilen Porthleven
Land's End Mousehole Porthleven Mawgan
Mount's
Bay
Lizard
Lizard Point

Falmouth
Portscatho
St Mawes
Falmouth Bay
Helford Passage

0   10   20 miles
0 10 20 30 Kilometres

■ Falmouth

Rick Stein's Seafood Bar

Seafood
Events Square, Falmouth, TR11 3XA
Tel no: (01841) 532700
www.rickstein.com

'Most customers appeared to choose fish and chips. We had a starter of three battered scallops – unusual but very good – and mains of baked sea bass and hake fillet with cannellini beans and tomatoes in a superb lemon sauce.'

⌭⌭ Readers Recommend

A 'readers recommend' review is a genuine quote from a report sent in by one of our readers. We intend to follow up these suggestions throughout the year to come.

■ Gulval

The Coldstreamer Inn

Village local with fresh flavours
Gulval, TR18 3BB
Tel no: (01736) 362072
www.coldstreamer-penzance.co.uk
Modern British | £25
Cooking score: 2

£5 OFF 🛏 £30

'What a lovely find,' noted a visitor to this late-Victorian inn in the centre of the sprawling village of Gulval. The easy-going style here is much appreciated: eat from the same menu in the bar or adjoining dining room and expect cosmopolitan food with a feel for seasonality. The kitchen sensibly doesn't set itself over-ambitious targets, enabling it to draw applause for starters such as squid in red wine stew with aïoli or confit pork belly with celeriac purée and beetroot crisps; mains of whole lemon sole with parsley potatoes, prawns and wild mushrooms; and desserts of warm almond cake with poached pear and mascarpone. Fine

West Country cheeses are on hand, too, as are Cornish-brewed ales and a useful list of wines from £15.50.

Chef/s: Tom Penhaul. **Open:** all week L 12 to 3, D 6 to 9.30. **Closed:** 25 and 26 Dec. **Meals:** alc (main courses £11 to £18). Set L £14.50 (2 courses) to £17. Set D £21. Sun L £17. **Details:** 55 seats. 12 seats outside. Separate bar.

▌Helford Passage
Ferryboat Inn
Reinvented riverside hostelry
Helford Passage, TR11 5LB
Tel no: (01326) 250625
www.ferryboatinnhelford.com
Seafood | £25
Cooking score: 2
🛏 £30

From the well-kept St Austell Tribute ale to the please-all menu, there's plenty to entice at this 300-year-old pub – run by the Wright Brothers, who own a brace of London seafood restaurants. Its spectacular location overlooking the Helford estuary is a prime draw. The surge of visitors who negotiate the narrow lanes or (better still) arrive by ferry come for food that comforts rather than challenges. Expect uncluttered dishes such as fish soup, fish and chips, burgers and rump steak. Oysters arrive from the Duchy of Cornwall oyster farm along the river; the kitchen shows a light touch in cooking razor clams with white wine and garlic butter, as well as ling fillet with masala, red lentils and crab; and there's chocolate brownie with sour cherries and clotted cream for pud. Wines from £16.

Chef/s: Robert Bunny. **Open:** all week L 12 to 3, D 6 to 9. **Closed:** 25 Dec. **Meals:** alc (main courses £8 to £19). **Details:** 86 seats. 116 seats outside. Wheelchair access. Car parking.

▌Marazion
NEW ENTRY
Ben's Cornish Kitchen
Understated bistro making waves in Cornwall
West End, Marazion, TR17 0EL
Tel no: (01736) 719200
www.benscornishkitchen.com
Modern British | £33
Cooking score: 4
£5 OFF

Stylish yet understated, this bistro on Marazion's main street has rustic stone walls and modest furnishings; it's the inventiveness of the cooking that makes an impact. Chef/proprietor Ben Prior likes to keep things simple, using pinpoint accuracy of timing, careful balance and pretty much faultless composition. The supply lines are strong in these parts and the kitchen takes full advantage: wild garlic and potato soup with a poached egg and fennel seed roll, followed by 'pea-sotto' with preserved lemon, cheese crisp, Parmesan purée, mint and ricotta croquettes and pea shoots, then pineapple and lychee terrine with mango, ginger and coconut ice cream were the components of one successful lunch. Others have enjoyed 'delightful local mackerel, well cooked and presented lamb chops and an imaginative rhubarb (local) tasting plate'. The wine list (starting at £16) is a joy to behold.

Chef/s: Ben Prior. **Open:** Tue to Sat L 12 to 2, D 6.30 to 8.30. **Closed:** Sun, Mon, 25 and 26 Dec, 1 Jan. **Meals:** alc (main courses £14 to £24). Set L £15 (2 courses) to £18. Set D £25 (2 courses) to £32.50. **Details:** 30 seats. Wheelchair access.

Mawgan
New Yard Restaurant
A kitchen with its money on local produce
Trelowarren Estate, Mawgan, TR12 6AF
Tel no: (01326) 221595
www.trelowarren.com
Modern British | £30
Cooking score: 4

🛏

'Lovely place once you can find it,' noted one visitor, giving warning of the two-mile drive along a single-track private road to reach this converted coach house behind the Trelowarren estate office. It's an elegant, contemporary country restaurant cheered by a winter wood-burner, local art and fresh flowers. Max Wilson has taken up the reins following the departure of Olly Jackson, heading a kitchen that continues to put its money on local and regional produce. The result is intensely seasonal cooking that sings with flavour. Dinner could bring a terrine of local rabbit and grain mustard, enlivened by a pea, mustard leaf and broad bean salad, or a lovely piece of turbot with crab, fennel and orange dressing. Lunch is simpler: well-filled sandwiches, comforting dishes such as Cornish steaks or Helford mussels in a shallot and cream sauce, and Cornish artisan cheeses. Wines from £18.
Chef/s: Max Wilson. **Open:** all week L 12 to 2 (2.30 Sun), Mon to Sat D 7 to 9. **Closed:** Mon and Tue from Sept to Whitsun. **Meals:** alc (main courses £10 to £18). Sun L £20. **Details:** 50 seats. 20 seats outside. Wheelchair access. Car parking.

Symbols
🛏 Accommodation is available

£30 Three courses for less than £30

V Separate vegetarian menu

£5 OFF £5-off voucher scheme

🍷 Notable wine list

Millbrook
The View
Outstanding clifftop package
Treninnow Cliff Road, Millbrook, PL10 1JY
Tel no: (01752) 822345
www.theview-restaurant.co.uk
Modern British | £30
Cooking score: 2

Perched on the top of cliffs at Whitsand Bay with views as far as the Lizard Peninsula, Matt and Rachel Corner's simple restaurant certainly lives up to its name. The setting is stunning on a summer's day, yet the place is cosy in winter – 'you feel like you are in the teeth of the weather'. Visitors in their droves are attracted, for the food is just as big a lure. Very fresh seafood, mostly from Looe Harbour, is dealt with simply in the kitchen: roast scallops with chorizo and parsley cassoulet, say, followed by local haddock with herb crumb and red pepper coulis. Rump of lamb, portobello mushrooms and slow-roast onion is a not-so-token meat dish. To finish, try rhubarb fool with shortbread. Wines from £17.
Chef/s: Matt Corner. **Open:** Wed to Sun L 12 to 1.45, D 7 to 8.45. **Closed:** Mon, Tue, Feb. **Meals:** alc (main courses £15 to £24). Set L £10 (2 courses) to £12.95. **Details:** 42 seats. 26 seats outside. Car parking.

Mousehole
The Old Coastguard
Reborn hotel with confident local food
The Parade, Mousehole, TR19 6PR
Tel no: (01736) 731222
www.oldcoastguardhotel.co.uk
Modern British | £25
Cooking score: 3

£5 OFF 🛏 £30

Charles and Edmund Inkin have worked wonders at this old Cornish inn, upgrading, revamping and reinvigorating the place. An enclosed subtropical garden and lush terrace pull no punches when it comes to the majestic views across Mount's Bay, while the dining room with its cheerful colours, farmhouse tables and log fire matches the style of its stablemates (the Gurnard's Head nearby in Treen and Felin Fach Griffin in mid-Wales – see entries) with relaxed vibes and genuine hospitality. The kitchen looks to the locality for ingredients but also mixes up influences in a true modern British way: crab rarebit, and spiced belly pork with soy-marinated vegetables rub shoulders with plaice fillets and orange-cockle butter or lamb's shoulder shepherd's pie with minted peas, and desserts might produce brown sugar cheesecake, figs and Madeira. Wines from £19.

Chef/s: Tom Symons. **Open:** all week L 12.30 to 2.30, D 6.30 to 9. **Meals:** alc (main courses £10 to £13). Set L £14 (2 courses) to £17.50. **Details:** 60 seats. 30 seats outside. Car parking.

2 Fore Street

Unpretentious Cornish bistro
2 Fore Street, Mousehole, TR19 6PF
Tel no: (01736) 731164
www.2forestreet.co.uk
Modern British | £26
Cooking score: 2
£30

Joe Wardell's refreshingly unpretentious bistro is close to Mousehole harbour. Given the location, it's no surprise that fish is Fore Street's forte and the kitchen makes the most of seasonal hauls from the Cornish boats. A bowl of steamed Exe mussels should do the trick at lunchtime, while the evening menu touts everything from salt-and-pepper squid to lemon sole fillets with griddled baby leeks, clams and parsley butter. Alternatively, take the carnivorous route with confit duck, ribeye steak and chips or corn-fed chicken with Puy lentils, bacon and spinach before finishing off with lemon curd pannacotta. Wines from £15.50.

Chef/s: Joe Wardell. **Open:** all week L 12 to 3.30, D 6 to 9.30. **Closed:** Jan, Mon (Dec and Feb). **Meals:** alc (main courses £14 to £17). **Details:** 36 seats. 24 seats outside.

Padstow

★ TOP 50 ★

Paul Ainsworth at No. 6

Padstow's premier gastronomic address
6 Middle Street, Padstow, PL28 8AP
Tel no: (01841) 532093
www.number6inpadstow.co.uk
Modern British | £46
Cooking score: 7
£5 OFF V

With just two establishments in Padstow (see also Rojano's in the Square) Paul Ainsworth is hardly going *mano-a-mano* with the Stein empire, but there's no shortage of vocal support for this 'most impressive' chef whom 'we may well hear more about in the future'. A series of small rooms set over two floors, his intimate restaurant creates a subdued classy feel but without any stiff-collared formality. Regulars and newcomers are treated with equal courtesy, charm and genuine warmth. Ainsworth is a highly talented chef with classical technique in his blood and a nose for sharp seasonal partnerships – perhaps the crispy Porthilly oysters praised in several reports, their rich creaminess cut by shredded fennel and Granny Smith apple. Or Cornish cod, served with 'cod bubble' (two little balls of fried salt cod), thin slivers of crisp cauliflower, dabs of sweet raisin yoghurt and some restrained curry oil: the combination of sweet, salt and spicy working well. He can also play it straight and true, offering a flawless plate of 'wonderfully tasty' hogget (lamb) with sweetbreads, roasted beetroot and a rich lamb and red wine jus, as well as fashioning all manner of precision-tuned treats ranging from creamed smoked cod's roe with salty crumbled crackling to an 'unusual and very refreshing' dessert of chilled pineapple, 'almost confit in texture', flavoured with tarragon and served with set natural yoghurt and salt-and-pepper shortbread on the side. The kitchen knows how to impress and that extends to the wine list, which scours the world's vineyards

for fascinating flavours. There's no excess baggage, and mark-ups, from £20, are friendly.
Chef/s: Paul Ainsworth. **Open:** Tue to Sat L 12 to 3, D 6 to 10. **Closed:** Sun, Mon, 24 to 26 Dec, last 3 weeks Jan. **Meals:** alc (main courses £24 to £31). Set L £18 (2 courses) to £24. **Details:** 42 seats. 6 seats outside.

Rick Stein's Café
Feel-good crowd-pleaser
10 Middle Street, Padstow, PL28 8AP
Tel no: (01841) 532700
www.rickstein.com
Seafood | £25
Cooking score: 1
🛏 £30

Everyone seems to enjoy this immensely popular Padstein experience: an easy-going café, open from morning to night. Light wood, white walls and bright colours create a stylish, fresh look that complements a menu where fish obviously figures large. Typical of the bold, modern cookery are salt-and-pepper prawns and grilled hake with butter beans and aïoli, but Cornish ribeye features, too, or chicken supreme with a carrot, ginger and chilli sambal. At busy times you might prefer to join the swifter queue at Stein's Fish and Chips (takeaway and eat in) or settle for great takeaway pasties from Stein's Patisserie. Wines from £19.50.
Chef/s: David Sharland. **Open:** all week L 12 to 3, D 6.30 to 9.30. **Closed:** 25 and 26 Dec, 1 May. **Meals:** alc (main courses £11 to £17). Set L and D £22. **Details:** 36 seats. 10 seats outside. Wheelchair access.

¦¦¦ Visit us Online
To find out more about
The Good Food Guide, please visit
www.thegoodfoodguide.co.uk

Rojano's in the Square
Excellent pizzas pull the crowds
9 Mill Square, Padstow, PL28 8AE
Tel no: (01841) 532796
www.rojanos.co.uk
Italian | £26
Cooking score: 2
£30

When Paul Ainsworth (of nearby No. 6, see entry) bought this local institution right in the centre of Padstow's touristy hustle and bustle, all he did was update it – Rojano's remains a very welcoming Italian eatery. A dressed-down, casual approach is taken; from the hard-working ground-floor café and terrace to the upstairs grazing bar, it's all rollickingly informal. Take your pick from Italian charcuterie planks or smoked mackerel, then mains of linguine with Cornish white crabmeat or a burger made with local beef and Cornish blue cheese, although many diners are here just for the excellent thin-crust sourdough pizzas. Portions are generous, so perhaps share the Seville orange marmalade mascarpone cheesecake with Hobnob, praline and amaretti crumble. Wines from £18.45.
Chef/s: Rob Zabel. **Open:** all week L 12 to 3, D 5 to 10. **Closed:** 24 to 26 Dec, 5 Jan to 1 Feb. **Meals:** alc (main courses £8 to £25). **Details:** 70 seats. 22 seats outside.

St Petroc's Bistro
Stylish Padstein restaurant-with-rooms
New Street, Padstow, PL28 8EA
Tel no: (01841) 532700
www.rickstein.com
Modern European | £35
Cooking score: 2
🛏

A pair of reporters visiting the refurbished St Petroc's Bistro were delighted to find a new-found vibrancy to the spacious dining room, with service much improved. Although regarded as a younger sibling of the Seafood Restaurant (see entry), this venue is 'a considerable achievement in its own right' with menus far from being exclusively fish based. Grills are prominent, and dry-aged Scottish beef is a speciality. The food is generous and full-flavoured, whether lightly curried crab mayonnaise with rocket or baked scallops with paprika, Serrano ham, crisp garlic and olive oil. The kitchen can also do classic (grilled whole lemon sole teamed with brown shrimps and mushrooms, for instance) and desserts get a good press, too: perhaps pannacotta with vanilla-poached pears. Garden tables are at a premium in fine weather. Wines from £19.95.

Chef/s: Paul Harwood. **Open:** all week L 12 to 2, D 6.30 to 9.30. **Closed:** 25 and 26 Dec, 1 May. **Meals:** alc (main courses £15 to £30). Set L (winter only) £16.50 (2 courses) to £19.50. **Details:** 56 seats. 36 seats outside. Separate bar. Wheelchair access.

The Seafood Restaurant
Rick Stein's seafood original
Riverside, Padstow, PL28 8BY
Tel no: (01841) 532700
www.rickstein.com
Seafood | £60
Cooking score: 5
➿ V

With Nathan Outlaw top of the tree in this part of Cornwall and Paul Ainsworth snapping at his heels, the Seafood Restaurant has upped its game judging by the number of glowing reports received this year. The spacious, smart but unfussy dining room exudes an easy, informal ambience, while service strikes precisely the right balance: attentive and personal. Reporters not only applaud the breadth to the menu with its influences from the Med, Asia and the USA, but also highlight the classics of fish and shellfish soup, roast tronçon of turbot (rich, meaty and very fresh turbot roasted on the bone, served with a slick of hollandaise) and Padstow lobster, grilled or steamed, with mayonnaise. There has been praise, too, for 'lovely briny Palourde clams straight out of the estuary outside'; 'zingy, fresh-tasting' crisp smoked mackerel with green mango and papaya salad, Thai holy basil and bird's eye chilli and passion fruit pavlova with crème

chantilly. Prices are high, but the restaurant's seafood bar deals in good-value fish platters. A well-thought-out wine list opens with bottles at £22.

Chef/s: Stephane Delourme. **Open:** all week L 12 to 2, D 6.30 to 10. **Closed:** 25 and 26 Dec, 1 May. **Meals:** alc (main courses £18 to £49). Set L £29.95 (winter), £38 (summer). **Details:** 90 seats. Separate bar. Wheelchair access. Children over 3 yrs only.

▌Penzance

The Bakehouse
Funky eatery with good local food
Old Bakehouse Lane, Chapel Street, Penzance, TR18 4AE
Tel no: (01736) 331331
www.bakehouserestaurant.co.uk
Modern European | £25
Cooking score: 2
£30

'Great food, superb service', noted a reporter of this two-tiered eatery squirrelled away in a secluded palm-filled courtyard just off Chapel Street in Penzance's most historic quarter. Andy and Rachel Carr have been running the Bakehouse for some 10 years, never deviating from their dedication to the virtues of straightforward cooking. Menus offer something for everyone, be it Cornish Angus beef steaks with a choice of sauce, rub or flavoured butter; Cornish rare-breed pork loin with gremolata; marinated lamb; or scallops, 'lush and always cooked to perfection'; king prawns with sweet roasted vegetables; and hake fillet in Tuscan stew. Finish with a comforting fruit crumble or a meringue with berries and clotted cream. Wines from £14.

Chef/s: Andy Carr. **Open:** all week D only 6.15 to 9. **Closed:** Sun (Nov to Mar), 24 to 27 Dec, 1 to 14 Jan. **Meals:** alc (main courses £10 to £20). Set D £13 (2 courses before 7.15). **Details:** 56 seats. Separate bar.

The Bay

Art, views and Cornish flavours
Hotel Penzance, Britons Hill, Penzance, TR18 3AE
Tel no: (01736) 366890
www.thebaypenzance.co.uk
Modern British | £35
Cooking score: 3
£5 OFF 🛏 V

Adjacent to the Hotel Penzance, the restaurant offers views of Mount's Bay and plenty to divert the eye inside, too, as the owners are committed to showcasing the work of local artists in a series of exhibitions. The kitchen produces modern Cornish dishes with some Italian influence; fish and shellfish are a strong point. Begin with steamed mussels in an aromatic sauce of fennel, shallot, garlic and Pernod, or perhaps a rich, garlicky risotto topped with smoked local goats' cheese, before mains such as grilled red mullet with crabmeat, orzo pasta and orange and ginger salsa, or a duo of pigeon and partridge with a rosemary-scented polenta cake, sauced with dates in red wine. Chocolate and caramel are mainstays of the dessert repertoire, as in chocolate and honey tart with raisin purée and peanut-butter ice cream. A wide-ranging wine list includes Cornwall's finest, Camel Valley. Prices start at £17.75.
Chef/s: Steven Mesher. **Open:** Sun to Fri 12 to 10, Sat D 6 to 10. **Closed:** 2 to 16 Jan. **Meals:** Set L £12 (2 courses) to £15.50. Set D £24 (2 courses) to £32. Sun L £15.50. Tasting menu £49.50. **Details:** 40 seats. 10 seats outside. Separate bar. Wheelchair access. Car parking.

Harris's

Old favourite with satisfying food
46 New Street, Penzance, TR18 2LZ
Tel no: (01736) 364408
www.harrissrestaurant.co.uk
Modern European | £36
Cooking score: 2

'Our old faithful' is how a couple of regular visitors think of Harris's, which the Harris family has been running with commendable reliability for four decades. Although centrally located, the restaurant is tucked in a little alley, a small, genteel place with white tablecloths, warm service and a menu that reflects something of the region and the seasons. Roger Harris's cooking is underpinned by solid technical skills, positive flavours and workable combinations, as in crab florentine, and grilled smoked duck breast with endive and rocket salad and walnut oil dressing. Good supplies are evident at every turn – accurately timed noisettes of lamb, served with a fennel purée and rosemary sauce, for example – while desserts run to iced lemon soufflé and treacle tart. Wines from £17.50.
Chef/s: Roger Harris. **Open:** Tue to Sat L 12 to 2, Tue to Sat D 7 to 9.30. **Closed:** Sun, Mon, 4 weeks Jan to Feb. **Meals:** alc (main courses £15 to £35). **Details:** 32 seats. Separate bar. Children over 6 yrs only.

▮ Perranuthnoe

Victoria Inn

Historic inn with appealing cooking
Perranuthnoe, TR20 9NP
Tel no: (01736) 710309
www.victoriainn-penzance.co.uk
Modern British | £25
Cooking score: 2
£5 OFF 🛏 £30

Tucked away in the deep south-west of Cornwall, Stewart and Anna Eddy's place is a pink-tinged pub not far from St Michael's Mount, the South West Coast Path and Penzance. The location is beautiful and tranquil, and the Victoria Inn has an appealing, homely atmosphere. An extensive menu features much regional produce, and although descriptions look exhaustive, it all makes sense when the plates arrive. Start with wild mushrooms on garlic toast, garnished with a poached duck egg, crispy bacon and rosemary sauce, then move up to roast Cornish cod with seasonal greens and champ, in mussel and caper dressing. Rhubarb parfait with custard cream and almond crumble could provide the finale. A small but useful wine list opens with house French at £15.

Chef/s: Stewart Eddy and Paul Learney. **Open:** all week L 12 to 2 (3 Sun), Mon to Sat D 6 to 9. **Closed:** 25 and 26 Dec, 1 Jan, 1 week Jan. **Meals:** alc (main courses £11 to £19). **Details:** 60 seats. 20 seats outside. Separate bar. Wheelchair access. Car parking.

▌Port Isaac

NEW ENTRY

The Harbour

Intimate seafood bistro
1 Middle Street, Port Isaac, PL29 3RH
Tel no: (01208) 880237
www.theharbourportisaac.com
Seafood | £30
Cooking score: 2

Pitched at the top of Port Isaac's slipway, Emily Scott's good-natured 'gem of an unpretentious bistro' sits happily within the confines of two tiny, ancient, beamed fishermen's cottages with 'amazing views out across the pretty harbour'. Given the location, it's no surprise that locally caught fish feature strongly on the succinct, daily changing menu. Scallops are regularly endorsed (perhaps simply served with thyme and garlic), while monkfish might appear in company with chorizo, sun-blush tomatoes, rosemary, a creamy mash and rocket, or whole red mullet could arrive with focaccia crumbs, lemon, thyme and wilted spinach. Finish with flourless orange and almond pudding with vanilla-seeded ice cream or opt, perhaps, for British cheeses with fig chutney and crackers. Homemade bread is a delight, service 'exemplary' and wines start at £18.
Chef/s: Emily Scott. **Open:** Tue to Sat L 12 to 2, D 7 to 10. **Closed:** Sun, Mon, 23 to 28 Dec. **Meals:** alc (main courses £17 to £19). Set L £15 (2 courses) to £20. Set D £25.30 (2 courses) to £50. **Details:** 26 seats. Children over 4 yrs only at D.

▌Porthleven

Kota

Enticing gem with racy Pacific Rim flavours
Harbour Head, Porthleven, TR13 9JA
Tel no: (01326) 562407
www.kotarestaurant.co.uk
Fusion-Modern European | £30
Cooking score: 2

🛏

The Kereamas' harbour-head restaurant is appealing and spacious inside, with a tiled floor, raftered ceiling and unclothed tables making for a gently rustic look. Chef Jude has some Maori heritage, and the restaurant's name means 'shellfish' in that language, so Pacific Rim starters like scallop ceviche with fennel, apple, radish, wasabi roe and a dressing of pickled ginger and yuzu are entirely to be expected. Alternatively, there may be crab spring roll with tempura claws in wasabi mayo. Mains maintain the East Asian tone with fillet and short rib of local beef with Japanese mushrooms and celeriac in soy garlic jus, while roast turbot might appear with chanterelles, wakame seaweed and cauliflower in a tarragon-scented shellfish sauce. Finish with vanilla pannacotta, served with mango jelly, tamarind sorbet and palm-sugar caramel. Wine from £14.95.
Chef/s: Jude Kereama. **Open:** Mon to Sat D only 6 to 10 (check ahead for Mon openings). **Closed:** Sun, 25 and 26 Dec, 1 Jan to 28 Feb. **Meals:** alc (main courses £13 to £20). **Details:** 32 seats. Separate bar. Wheelchair access.

▌Portscatho

Driftwood

Elegant clifftop hotel with stylish food
Rosevine, Portscatho, TR2 5EW
Tel no: (01872) 580644
www.driftwoodhotel.co.uk
Modern European | £50
Cooking score: 5

'Although the weather was not good . . . this boutique hotel on the cliff above Gerrans Bay was stylish and warm, and the welcome and service first class. Chef Chris Eden is head and shoulders above most of his colleagues in Cornwall.' Thus concluded two Welsh travellers, won over by their first sampling of the sharp-toned cooking at Driftwood. The kitchen buys diligently from a network of local suppliers and transforms the haul into a bright, vibrant modern British menu with an acute seasonal edge. There's real flair and sensitivity when it comes to ingredients and a feel for their impact on the palate. Earthy flavours predominate – witness one visitor's account of a meal that progressed from lemon sole teamed with cauliflower, vanilla, lime and curry to loin of fallow venison, curly kale, beetroot, green peppercorns and pear, and finished with spiced pineapple with a toasted coconut meringue and lemongrass and lime sorbet. Everything, from the five types of homemade bread and inventive amuse-bouche to the pre-dessert, was pronounced 'impressive'. A short wine list opens at £19.
Chef/s: Chris Eden. **Open:** all week D only 7 to 9.30. **Closed:** early Dec to early Feb. **Meals:** Set D £50 (3 courses), tasting menu £80. **Details:** 34 seats. Separate bar. Wheelchair access. Car parking. No children under 5 yrs.

ALSO RECOMMENDED

▲ Rosevine

Rosevine, Portscatho, TR2 5EW
Tel no: (01872) 580206
www.rosevine.co.uk
Modern British £5 OFF

While this white-painted Georgian house with its beautiful location and lovely sea views is something of a canteen for a small holiday complex of apartments, it is well worth visiting for cooking that sets its sights absolutely in tandem with the available, very decent, skills in the kitchen. Newlyn crab salad with blood orange and spelt (£8) and whole grilled lemon sole (£18) are typical choices from the short carte, offered alongside a daily changing dinner menu (£23 for two courses), which could bring coq au vin or braised blade of beef. Wines from £17. Open all week.

▌Rock

Outlaw's

A breath of fresh air
St Enodoc Hotel, Rock Road, Rock, PL27 6LA
Tel no: (01208) 863394
www.nathan-outlaw.com
Seafood | £40
Cooking score: 4

An old hand reports that the more casual of Nathan Outlaw's two restaurants is 'better than usual . . . because the food is so good in its own right – excellent raw materials, and no unnecessary flourishes in the cooking.' The St Enodoc Hotel and its wide-screen views of the Camel Estuary provide the 'stunning' location, and although the emphasis is on fish from the Cornish coast or shellfish straight out of the estuary, one could choose duck ham, Puy lentils and butternut squash to start and rump of lamb, olives, aubergine and Cornish Earlies (potato) for a main course. There's no doubt that a very true judgement is at work, both in composing menus and fixing the level of complexity that should be permitted in the kitchen. 'The fish was in the peak of condition' was the admiring remark of one who started with the 'best hand-dived scallops this year', and a 'really simple, yet near-perfect' bream, served with nothing more than potted shellfish butter, potatoes and spinach. British cheeses follow or opt for the superb chocolate fondant tart with pistachio ice cream and cocoa syrup. Wines from £20.

Chef/s: Redas Katauskas. **Open:** all week L 12 to 2.30, D 6 to 9.30. **Closed:** 21 Dec to 30 Jan. **Meals:** alc (main courses £16 to £30). **Details:** 40 seats. 30 seats outside. Wheelchair access. Car parking. Children over 10 yrs only.

★ TOP 10 ★

Restaurant Nathan Outlaw
Spanking fresh seafood from a top talent
St Enodoc Hotel, Rock Road, Rock, PL27 6LA
Tel no: (01208) 862737
www.nathan-outlaw.com
Seafood | £99
Cooking score: 9
🍴 🛏 V

Nathan Outlaw presides over one of the most enjoyable places to eat in the country. It is also a serious restaurant, a real contender on the international food scene, using 'spanking fresh seafood of jaw-dropping quality' in an eight-course tasting menu of range and subtlety. The St Enodoc hotel, in which it is housed, overlooks the Camel Estuary and has all the trimmings of an upmarket seaside hotel – small spa, billiard room, garden, terrace, outdoor swimming pool – but despite its 20 bedrooms it could be viewed as a restaurant with rooms. There is a lounge but no bar, and the evening-only main restaurant closes on Sunday and Monday – though the more casual Outlaw's (see entry) is open every day. Nearly everyone who has eaten here in the last year has reported blisteringly successful evenings. Of the many dishes reported as outstanding, these score as being flawless: a single scampi in an intense red-pepper sauce; cured salmon, citrus and horseradish yoghurt; a carefully built mound of white crab set in a sweet crab sauce; cod with bacon, hazelnuts

and celeriac; fillets of red mullet served with delicious smoked tomato, the whole given a touch of green and contrast by an acidulated sauce of mint, caper, anchovy, gherkin and rocket. And then there is the turbot, cooked on the bone and served with a wonderful saffron and garlic aïoli. The magic of all these dishes is in their inherent simplicity and clever balance. Reporters agree that desserts have been a high point this year, especially local strawberries that were bursting with flavour and served with crumbled shortbread, and a brilliant gooseberry and peach tart served alongside a deeply flavoured peach sorbet, with hazelnuts adding some texture. Nothing jars here, staff know how to engage and respond warmly, and treasures abound on a wine list that finds space for some fascinating rarities. Everything is chosen with real authority and oenophile knowledge; it is well worth putting yourself in the hands of the 'incredibly knowledgeable' sommelier who proffers honest advice. Bottles from £20.

Chef/s: Nathan Outlaw. **Open:** Tue to Sat D only 6.45 to 9. **Closed:** Sun, Mon, 21 Dec to 30 Jan. **Meals:** Tasting menu £95 (8 courses). **Details:** 20 seats. No children.

■ St Ives

Alba
Ex-lifeboat house that lifts the spirits
Old Lifeboat House, Wharf Road, St Ives, TR26 1LF
Tel no: (01736) 797222
www.thealbarestaurant.com
Modern European | £28
Cooking score: 3
£5 OFF £30 🍷

Once the old lifeboat house of this gentrified coastal town, Alba has been a well-supported restaurant for the past 12 years. If you want unbeatable views over the harbour, ask for a window table on the upper floor – although the open kitchen downstairs provides ground-floor diners with theatre of a different kind. The clean, contemporary lines of the restaurant (and the striking modern art on the white walls) are complemented by bold flavour combinations and zingy globally influenced food. Local produce is taken seriously here, particularly locally landed fish and seafood. This plays a major role in the appealing menu, perhaps an 'outstanding, intensely flavoured' provençale fish soup, followed by fillets of plaice with curried mussels and leek and basmati rice. Rhubarb crumble sundae is one of the satisfying desserts. Wines cost from a reasonable £12.75. **Chef/s:** Grant Nethercott. **Open:** all week L 12 to 2, D 5 to 10. **Closed:** 25 and 26 Dec. **Meals:** alc (main courses £11 to £22). Set L and D £16.95 (2 courses) to £19.95. **Details:** 60 seats. Wheelchair access.

Alfresco
Vibrant harbour-front venue
The Wharf, St Ives, TR26 1LF
Tel no: (01736) 793737
www.alfrescocafebar.co.uk
Modern British | £32
Cooking score: 2

The far-reaching views across the harbour are hard to beat from open-fronted Alfresco, which is slap bang on St Ives promenade. Outdoor tables are the big draw when the sun appears, but the cheerful staff and bustling vibe of the contemporary dining room provide an ideal setting whatever the weather. Ozone-fresh local fish and seafood shines here in well-presented, imaginative dishes with punchy flavours to the fore. A starter of seared scallops, hog's pudding, squash, sage and amaretti might be followed by monkfish wrapped in chicken skin with pickled girolles, monkfish Kiev, leek fondue and thyme jus. If it's meat you're after, fillet of beef with Cornish Blue and walnut rarebit with fondant potato, confit tomato and watercress is one option. Wine from £14.95. **Chef/s:** Jamie Phillips. **Open:** Thur to Sat L 12 to 3, all week D 5 to 10. **Closed:** Jan. **Meals:** alc (main courses £14 to £22). Set L and D £15.95 (2 courses). **Details:** 26 seats. 12 seats outside. Wheelchair access.

The Black Rock
Friendly local eatery with imaginative menus
Market Place, St Ives, TR26 1RZ
Tel no: (01736) 791911
www.theblackrockstives.co.uk
Modern European | £26
Cooking score: 2
£5 OFF £30

A stone's throw from the harbour and surrounded by art galleries, this converted hardware shop has quickly made its mark in the crowded heart of St Ives. The Black Rock is just around the corner from the Barbara Hepworth museum. Works by local painters and potters line its walls and the laid-back mood of the contemporary dining room is complemented by an open kitchen that delivers well-defined flavours from premium ingredients. The intelligent cooking is well represented by dishes such as Fowey mussels steamed with coconut, curry, lime and herbs, which might precede a pan-roasted fillet of line-caught St Ives bass, cavolo nero, parsley gnocchi and lemon. Whisky and apple parfait with apple purée and salted caramel is a typical finale. Wine from £16.50. **Chef/s:** David Symons. **Open:** Mon to Sat D only 6 to 10. **Closed:** Sun, Nov, 23 to 26 Dec, Jan, Feb. **Meals:** alc (main courses £13 to £16). Set D £16.50 (2 courses) to £19.50. **Details:** 36 seats. Separate bar.

Blas Burgerworks
Feel-good eco-friendly burger bar
The Warren, St Ives, TR26 2EA
Tel no: (01736) 797272
www.blasburgerworks.co.uk
Burgers | £15
Cooking score: 1
V £30

Down a narrow street behind the harbour, this granite building was once a net loft, but it's now a boho, eco-friendly burger bar. Communal reclaimed-wood tables add to the utilitarian look of this marvellously laid-back operation where local produce is the kitchen's mantra. Burgers cooked on the char-grill come from impeccably sourced Cornish free-range beef and chicken. There's fresh fish from day boats and plenty of vegetarian options, too, but for many customers, it doesn't get any better than a beefburger topped with Cornish Blue and 'Primrose Herd' bacon, accompanied by a glass of local ale. House wine is £14.50. **Chef/s:** Sally Cuckson, Marie Dixon and Sarah Newark. **Open:** Mon to Sat D only 6 to 10, all week 12 to 10 during school hols. **Closed:** Sun, Nov to mid Feb. **Meals:** alc (main courses £8 to £11). **Details:** 30 seats.

Halsetown Inn
Passionate commitment to local sourcing
Halsetown, St Ives, TR26 3NA
Tel no: (01736) 795583
www.halsetowninn.co.uk
Modern British | £23
Cooking score: 2
£30

'Warm and welcoming as soon as you walk in' is the verdict of one visitor to this granite stone building in a village on the outskirts of St Ives. The pub is the second venture for the team behind Blas Burgerworks (see entry) and service is relaxed but professional. It's a traditional inn with a mix of flagstone floors and tiles, real fires and local art on the walls. The kitchen has a passionate commitment to local sourcing and sustainability. St Ives Bay crab with coriander, lime and chilli on toast is a typically vibrant starter and might be followed by Cornish hake with potato purée, pea, fennel and watercress salad and caper vinaigrette, or cottage pie with garlic and truffle mash. Wines from £14.75. **Chef/s:** Angela Baxter. **Open:** all week L 12 to 3 (4 Sun), Mon to Sat D 6 to 9. **Closed:** 6 to 13 Jan. **Meals:** alc (main courses £11 to £17). **Details:** 60 seats. 20 seats outside. Separate bar. Wheelchair access. Car parking.

NEW ENTRY
Porthgwidden Beach Cafe
An idyllic setting to sample local seafood
Porthgwidden Beach, The Island, St Ives, TR26 1PL
Tel no: (01736) 796791
www.porthgwiddencafe.co.uk
Modern British | £27
Cooking score: 1
£30

Lively little sibling to the more grown-up Porthminster Beach Café (see entry), this laid-back seaside café ('feels more Antipodean beach café in some ways') is in an idyllic position on a secluded beach overlooking St Ives Bay towards Godrevy Lighthouse. The no-frills, whitewashed room reflects the straightforward approach of the kitchen, which seeks to use only the best local seafood. A starter of chowder packed with smoked haddock and mussels might be followed by fish and chips or sea bass fillets with roast potatoes and salsa verde from the short specials board. Breakfasts and light lunches such as moules marinière are also served. Wines from £13.95. **Chef/s:** Matthew Foster. **Open:** all week L 12 to 3, D 6 to 9.30. **Closed:** 25 Dec. **Meals:** alc (main courses £10 to £14). **Details:** 34 seats. 40 seats outside.

Porthmeor Beach Café
Tapas and stunning St Ives sunsets
Porthmeor, St Ives, TR26 1JZ
Tel no: (01736) 793366
www.porthmeor-beach.co.uk
Tapas | £20
Cooking score: 1
£30

With windows on three sides, this conservatory-style café is a prime spot to watch stunning St Ives sunsets. It is owned by the team behind beach cafés at Porthminster and Porthgwidden, and there's a tangible Aussie air to the bright, bubbly interior with its white tables, lime-green chairs and pink plastic buckets of cutlery. From the tiny open kitchen, expect punchy, vibrant tapas such as harissa grilled mackerel or clams with chorizo, but also good-value grilled local hake with crunchy spring greens, dukkah new potatoes or mussels with smoked bacon, leek, white wine and cream. Wines from £13.95. **Chef/s:** Cam Jennings. **Open:** all week L 12 to 5, D 6 to 9.30. **Closed:** 1 week Oct, 1 week April. **Meals:** alc (tapas and main courses £3 to £16). **Details:** 28 seats. 80 seats outside.

Porthminster Beach Café

Beach hangout with enticing global dishes
Porthminster Beach, St Ives, TR26 2EB
Tel no: (01736) 795352
www.porthminstercafe.co.uk
Seafood | £35
Cooking score: 3
V

The position of this striking white Art Deco building by the sea is hard to beat. Porthminster beach is one of Cornwall's finest, with uninterrupted views over the waves. There's certainly a Mediterranean feel to a visit, whether you're dining on the terrace or in the bright, airy room with its driftwood mirrors and seahorse lampstands. Aussie chef Mick Smith makes good use of deliciously fresh local seafood, often adding Asian ingredients to give his own fusion-inspired twist. Although some reporters have noted prices rising and portion-sizes decreasing on certain dishes, the food still has the capacity to excite and service remains pin-sharp. A robust white fish chowder of local crab, mussels, clams and wild garlic has impressed, as has a precisely cooked pan-fried John Dory fillet with tempura scallops, white crabmeat, Asian salad and jasmine rice. Wines from £15.95. **Chef/s:** Mick Smith. **Open:** all week L 12 to 3.45, D 6 to 10. **Closed:** Jan. **Meals:** alc (main courses £10 to £24). **Details:** 60 seats. 70 seats outside.

¡¡¡ Average
Price
The average price listed in main-entry reviews denotes the price of a three-course meal, without wine.

St Andrew's Street Bistro

Vibrant eatery with Italian-inspired menus
16 St Andrew's Street, St Ives, TR26 1AH
Tel no: (01736) 797074
www.bistrostives.co.uk
Modern European | £27
Cooking score: 1
£5 OFF   £30 ▼

Tucked down a narrow street behind St Ives harbour, this buzzy evenings-only restaurant stands on the site of a former pilchard works. Inside, the Bistro is spread over two floors and sports eclectically bohemian décor. The seasonal European cooking style is straightforward and unfussy: a starter of pan-seared local scallops with black pudding, apple and whisky purée might be followed by confit duck leg with braised red cabbage and cherry jus. Chocolate fondant with clotted cream, raspberries and ice cream is a good way to finish. House wine is £14.95. **Chef/s:** Stephen Block. **Open:** Mon to Sat D 6.30 to 9 (6 Sat). **Closed:** Sun, Jan to Feb. **Meals:** alc (main courses £15 to £18). Set D £16.95 (2 courses) to £19.95. **Details:** 45 seats.

Seagrass Restaurant

Quality seafood in a stylish setting
Fish Street, St Ives, TR26 1LT
Tel no: (01736) 793763
www.seagrass-stives.com
Modern British | £35
Cooking score: 2
£5 OFF

'Where better to eat a seafood dish?' asks one reader of this contemporary but 'cosy' spot by the harbour beach at St Ives. Correspondents praise chef Lee Groves' creative take on local produce, with fish and seafood given due prominence. Start with fish soup or scallops with basil and apple and a lick of beef jus, followed by grilled pollack with a hearty garnish of mushrooms, leeks, cream and mussels. Game is strong, too, in dishes like Bodmin moor venison with poached pear, bramble jus and braised red cabbage. Puddings (lime posset with ginger sorbet, perhaps) are as

well liked as the carefully paced, friendly service. Wine starts at £16.95, with local beers and cider underlining hosts Scott and Julia Blair's strong sense of place.
Chef/s: Lee Groves. **Open:** all week L 12.30 to 2.30, D 5.30 to 10 (Oct to Apr D only, 5.30 to 10). **Meals:** alc (main courses £14 to £27). Set early D £15.95 (2 courses) to £19.95. **Details:** 32 seats. Separate bar.

READERS RECOMMEND

The Digey Street Tearoom
Modern European
6 The Digey, St Ives, TR26 1HR
Tel no: (01736) 799600
www.digeyfoodroom.co.uk
'A café and delicatessen in the heart of St Ives with stunning homemade food. Well worth a visit – if you can find a spare table!'

▌ St Kew

St Kew Inn
Ancient charm with locally rooted cooking
St Kew, PL30 3HB
Tel no: (01208) 841259
www.stkewinn.co.uk
Modern British | £25
Cooking score: 2
£30

Flagstone floors, beams, scrubbed tables, a wood-burning range, real ales from St Austell Brewery – little wonder that 'homely' and 'traditional' are two of the adjectives that visitors have used to describe this ancient village pub by the church. Out front there are friendly and helpful staff, while those in the kitchen produce no-nonsense, robust food. Classic pub grub like ham and eggs or fish and chips sit alongside locally rooted cooking such as Porthilly mussels with wine, garlic and cream, and homemade faggots with sage and onion gravy. Ale cake with golden syrup sauce has also been praised. Wines from £15.

Chef/s: David Trainer and Martin Perkins. **Open:** all week L 12 to 2, D 6.30 to 9. **Closed:** 25 Dec. **Meals:** alc (main courses £10 to £20). Sun L £19.50. **Details:** 70 seats. 50 seats outside. Separate bar. Car parking. Children not allowed in main bar.

▌ St Mawes

Hotel Tresanton
Stylish seaside bolt-hole
27 Lower Castle Road, St Mawes, TR2 5DR
Tel no: (01326) 270055
www.tresanton.com
Modern European | £45
Cooking score: 3
🛏

A Cornish yachtsmen's club in the 1940s, this nautical-looking cluster of buildings was taken over by Olga Polizzi in the late 1990s and it has been a fashionable seaside bolt-hole ever since. The location, overlooking the Fal estuary, is stunning and there's a distinctly Mediterranean feel to both the elegant dining room and the alluring sun-trap terrace. The kitchen has an Italian influence, producing refined dishes that make the most of high-quality local produce, whether it's fresh fish or Cornish meat and game. A starter of John Dory, globe artichoke, tomatoes, olives, saffron and aïoli might set things up for a main course of lamb cannon, rösti potato, green beans, olives and salsa verde, or a simple breadcrumbed fish of the day with chips, crushed peas and tartare sauce. Satisfying desserts keep things simple with, say, lemon tart and raspberry sorbet. Wines from £20.
Chef/s: Paul Wadham. **Open:** all week L 12.30 to 2.30, D 7 to 9.30. **Closed:** 2 weeks Jan. **Meals:** alc (main courses £20 to £24). Set L £22 (2 courses). Sun L £28. **Details:** 60 seats. 40 seats outside. Separate bar. Wheelchair access. Car parking. Children over 6 yrs only at D.

🍴 SWEET TOOTH

From the traditional to the innovative, these are our most memorable desserts from the past year.

Knickerbocker glory, The Belgian Arms
This good old-fashioned raspberry knickerbocker glory was properly made with lots of fresh raspberries, Chantilly cream, vanilla ice cream and raspberry sauce.

Milk cake, Zoilo
A square of pale, feathery sponge in a sweet condensed-milk puddle, matched brilliantly with heady passion-fruit ice.

Chocolate hazlenut-oil ganache, Dabbous
Beautifully executed, the rich ganache was accompanied by a fresh-flavoured basil foam and the lightest of sheep's milk ice cream.

Tarte Tatin, Little Social
This faultless apple tarte Tatin was everything it should be - loaded with rich, buttery, sweet apples.

Lemon tart with clove ice cream, Hibiscus
The pastry had a malty flavour with a savoury contrast to the sweetness of the lemon curd. The ice cream was light as a feather.

Black truffle ice cream, Whatley Manor
A revelatory sweet/savoury experience of truffle ice cream, truffle honey and creamed Roquefort with crisp tuiles and walnuts.

▌Treen

The Gurnard's Head
Clifftop pub with menus of 'sheer delight'
Treen, TR26 3DE
Tel no: (01736) 796928
www.gurnardshead.co.uk
British | £28
Cooking score: 3

£5 OFF 🚗 £30

'I will admit to being partial to the Gurnard's Head, just because I like its sister in the Brecon Beacons – the Felin Fach Griffin. Both are refreshingly laid-back, and both welcome children and dogs.' So enthused a visitor from Wales to this well-patronised clifftop bolt-hole, enchanted by the open fires, the pubby atmosphere and the 'sheer human interest' of the staff. 'Short, seasonal and simple' describes the menu, and you can rely on the food to be 'delicious'. The starting point is high-quality raw materials, so in spring this could translate as Jerusalem artichoke soup with oyster mushroom, followed by Noah's pork chop, macaroni cheese, Savoy cabbage and grain mustard, then brioche bread-and-butter pudding with marmalade ice cream as 'a more than adequate finish'. Wines start at £16.50, with many available by the carafe.
Chef/s: Bruce Rennie. **Open:** all week L 12.30 to 2.30 (2 Mon), D 6.30 to 9.30. **Closed:** 24 and 25 Dec, 4 days mid Dec. **Meals:** alc (main courses £15 to £17). Set L £15 (2 courses) to £18. **Details:** 50 seats. 40 seats outside. Separate bar. Car parking.

▌Truro

Tabb's
A beguiling favourite
85 Kenwyn Street, Truro, TR1 3BZ
Tel no: (01872) 262110
www.tabbs.co.uk
Modern British | £35
Cooking score: 5

£5 OFF

'True dedication' and 'my favourite restaurant', sum up the way most reporters feel about Nigel Tabb's intimate eatery. Once a pub, the

dining room is stylish 'in an understated way' with lilac walls, leather high-backed chairs and a slate floor. Tables are smartly dressed in crisp linen, and there are 'Riedel glasses and fine tableware in general'. Everything points to impressive cooking skills: from warm homemade bread to Nigel's chocolates served with the coffee. Excellent raw materials are cooked with precision timing, and the seasonal menus offer an intriguing array of dishes. An amuse-bouche – mushroom soup with truffle oil – ahead of ballotine of pork and duck with shredded iceberg, tomato sauce and homemade piccalilli got an inspection meal off to a good start. This was followed by 'commendable' slow-roast belly of pork with star anise gravy, chickpea hash and red pepper oil, and an outstanding medallion of monkfish with Cornish pancetta, artichoke purée and duck reduction. Desserts are equally well executed: baked lime and Earl Grey cheesecake, apple sorbet and orange sauce, for instance. A short wine list opens at £16.50.
Chef/s: Nigel Tabb. **Open:** Tue to Fri L 12 to 2, Tue to Sat D 5.30 to 9. **Closed:** Sun, Mon. **Meals:** alc (main courses £16 to £21). Set L £19.50 (2 courses) to £26.
Details: 30 seats. Separate bar.

▌Watergate Bay
Fifteen Cornwall
Zealously sourced ingredients with rustic punch
On the beach, Watergate Bay, TR8 4AA
Tel no: (01637) 861000
www.fifteencornwall.co.uk
Italian | £40
Cooking score: 4

'This is probably one of the most spectacular restaurants in Cornwall: its beach setting in Watergate Bay is stunning, even in rough weather, so grab a seat by the window if possible.' So advised one visitor who was completely bowled over by this enchanting venue. A refurbishment in early 2013 means there is now the theatre of an open kitchen to compete with that view. Fifteen is open for breakfast through to dinner, with a new pasta bar, sandwiches, light snacks and a kids' menu. There's no doubting the broad appeal (the

simple Italian cooking is based on some of Jamie Oliver's original ideas) or the fashionable spin in the tersely described dishes: 'risotto – Barolo – Taleggio', perhaps, followed by a main course of 'sea bass – lentils – aïoli', with 'lemon tart – rhubarb – clotted cream' for dessert. Service is knowledgeable and fast, and all profits go to the Cornwall Foundation of Promise's Apprenticeship Programme. Wines from £19.95.
Chef/s: Andy Appleton. **Open:** all week L 12 to 2.30, D 6.15 to 9.15. **Meals:** alc L (main courses £17 to £29). Set L £28. Set D £60 (5 courses) to £80.
Details: 120 seats. Separate bar. Wheelchair access. Children over 4 yrs only at D.

READERS RECOMMEND
The Beach Hut
Modern British
Watergate Bay Hotel, Watergate Bay, TR8 4AA
Tel no: (01637) 860877
www.watergatebay.co.uk
'No doubt about its attachment to the beach and the sea – and the food is completely delicious.'

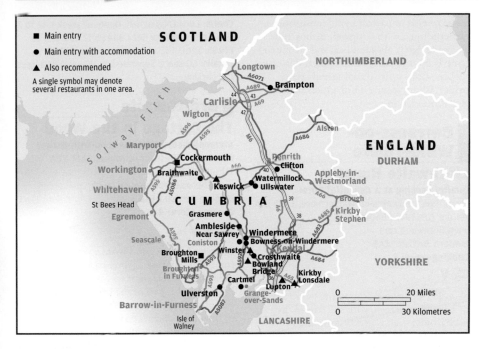

▌Ambleside

The Drunken Duck Inn

Handsome inn bursting with attributes
Barngates, Ambleside, LA22 0NG
Tel no: (015394) 36347
www.drunkenduckinn.co.uk
Modern British | £35
Cooking score: 2

🛏

Probably the best known of the South Lakes dining pubs, the Drunken Duck is one of those country hostelries that 'offer an escape from life itself: roaring log fires, their own brewery and some amazing comfort food'. There's a good-looking modern British menu for dinner, with serious intent shown when it comes to lamb's sweetbreads and tongue with goats' curd and courgettes, then roast cod with white bean purée, smoked ham and purple sprouting broccoli, and treacle tart with poached prunes and rice pudding ice cream. Lunchtime sandwiches are 'a good bet', much praised by reporters, especially the excellent

roast pork barmcake with 'really good apple sauce'; the salt beef, Emmental, sauerkraut and gherkins on toasted rye; and 'properly cooked chips'. Wines from £18.
Chef/s: Jonny Watson. **Open:** all week L 12 to 4, D 6 to 9. **Closed:** 25 Dec. **Meals:** alc (main courses £13 to £28). **Details:** 70 seats. 70 seats outside. Separate bar. Wheelchair access. Car parking.

▌Bowland Bridge

ALSO RECOMMENDED
▲ Hare & Hounds

Bowland Bridge, LA11 6NN
Tel no: (015395) 68333
www.hareandhoundsbowlandbridge.co.uk
British

The lovely location in the Winster Valley is as much a strong point as the carefully nurtured regional and local supply lines that keep the kitchen well endowed at this 17th-century coaching inn-with-rooms. Artisan cheeses, local game and free-range meats take their turn on a lively menu that might promise game terrine or leek and wild mushroom tartlet topped with Cropwell Bishop blue cheese (£5.50), ahead of beef and ale pie or lamb hotpot (£12.75) and familiar desserts such as sticky toffee pudding and crème brûlée. Wines from £13.75. Open all week. Accommodation.

Bowness-on-Windermere

Linthwaite House

Quality cooking at a delightful hotel
Crook Road, Bowness-on-Windermere, LA23 3JA
Tel no: (015394) 88600
www.linthwaite.com
Modern British | £45
Cooking score: 5

🚻 V

Wooded hills sweep around the broad expanse of Lake Windermere with the fells in the background – all is gently contoured tranquility in the view from the front terrace here. Within, this classic country house is furnished in vivid hues, and Chris O'Callaghan's locally based modern British food offers plenty of surprises, too. A pair of reporters dining in spring enjoyed an opening course of pink char-grilled pigeon breast with unusual accompaniments of sweetcorn granola and poached blueberries. To follow, a rather monochrome-looking main course of poached sole and a risotto of grapes and walnuts paled a little alongside more confident, well-timed loin of lamb with roasted turnips and swede purée. Desserts always seem to end things on a high, in this case a cylinder of dark chocolate ganache, purposefully contrasted with orange ice cream and a topping of almond brittle. Worries have been occasioned by the pace of service, which can be on the languorous side of relaxed. The wine list, arranged roughly by varietal, opens at £17.50 with glasses from £6.50.

Chef/s: Chris O'Callaghan. **Open:** all week L 12 to 2, D 6.30 to 9. **Meals:** Set L £14.95 (2 courses) to £19.95. Set D £52 (4 courses). Sun L £24.95. **Details:** 60 seats. Separate bar. Wheelchair access. Car parking.

Braithwaite

The Cottage in the Wood

Accomplished, ambitious food-with-a-view
Whinlatter Forest, Braithwaite, CA12 5TW
Tel no: (01768) 778409
www.thecottageinthewood.co.uk
Modern British | £40
Cooking score: 4

£5 OFF 🚻 V

Everybody has a good word to say about this rural, 17th-century former coaching inn; indeed, some reckon it serves 'the best food I've had in this part of the Lakes'. The views are sumptuous, and you won't lack for diversion in Ryan Blackburn's terrific menu, which includes plenty of seafood from the Cumbrian coast, local seasonal game and Herdwick hogget. Choice is commendably short and acutely seasonal. There's not too much flummery about Blackburn's style, but he's bursting with sharply executed ideas. Lobster ravioli, spelt and English girolle risotto, turbot with samphire – all have come in for praise, as has West Coast crab with pink grapefruit, avocado and relish, and 'tender' braised beef cheek with roasted carrots, chicory and monk's beard. Some consider puddings 'a weak spot' but local cheeses are up to the mark. The global wine list is a well-judged collection with prices from £19.
Chef/s: Ryan Blackburn. **Open:** Tue to Sat L 12.30 to 2, D 6 to 9. **Closed:** Sun, Mon, Jan. **Meals:** Set L £18.95 (2 courses) to £22.95. Set D £40. **Details:** 38 seats. Separate bar. Wheelchair access. Car parking. Children over 10 yrs only at D.

Brampton

Farlam Hall
Lovingly maintained Lakeland retreat
Brampton, CA8 2NG
Tel no: (016977) 46234
www.farlamhall.co.uk
Modern British | £48
Cooking score: 3

Lovingly maintained by the Quinion family since 1975, Farlam Hall is a civilised Victorian retreat on a personal scale. Tranquil gardens and an ornamental lake set the tone outside, while antique-filled lounges ooze chintzy charm and gracious hospitality within – a theme that extends to the elegant dining room with its starched napery and polished silverware. Barry Quinion's cooking is in the Lakeland country-house mould and his fixed-priced dinners are 'good enough to warrant a 70-mile round-trip over the fells at night'. Excellent sea bass fillet on a flavourful 'stew' of peppers, spicy slow-cooked pork with herbs and superb loin of Cumbrian lamb marinated in rosemary have been singled out, along with 'good seasonal' vegetables (except for baby corn in April – 'why?') and 'well-kept' cheeses. Carefully wrought desserts range from vanilla pannacotta with rhubarb compote to a 'proper custard tart' with 'unseasonal' strawberries. The extensive wine list starts at £25 (£5.50 a glass).
Chef/s: Barry Quinion. **Open:** all week D only 8 (1 sitting). **Closed:** 25 to 30 Dec, 6 to 23 Jan. **Meals:** Set D £47.50 (4 courses). **Details:** 40 seats. Car parking. Children over 5 yrs only.

Please send us your feedback
To register your opinion about any restaurant listed in the Guide, or a new restaurant that you wish to bring to our attention, please visit the web address at the bottom of the page. Your feedback informs the content of the book and will be used to compile next year's reviews.

Broughton Mills

Blacksmiths Arms
Quaint farmhouse inn with sturdy food
Broughton Mills, LA20 6AX
Tel no: (01229) 716824
www.theblacksmithsarms.co.uk
Modern British | £24
Cooking score: 2

With its crooked doorways, oak-lined passages, open fires and an original smoke-blackened range – not to mention a tiny one-table bar – this quaint farmhouse inn certainly justifies its listed status, but chef/landlord Michael Lane has a few contemporary tricks up his sleeve. A quick glance at his ever-changing menu reveals an adventurous spirit, as well as a liking for big, sturdy flavours: from fillet of salmon with a fricassee of peas, pancetta and broad beans to roast pork tenderloin with chorizo and chickpea casserole. Details such as potatoes roasted in duck fat are appreciated, while desserts keep it wholesome with the likes of sticky lemon sponge and custard. House wine is £13.50.
Chef/s: Michael Lane. **Open:** Tue to Sun L 12 to 2, D 6 to 9. **Closed:** Mon, 25 Dec. **Meals:** alc (main courses £11 to £17). Set L £12.95 (2 courses). **Details:** 45 seats. 24 seats outside. Separate bar. Car parking.

Cartmel

★ TOP 10 ★

L'Enclume
Miracles of nature
Cavendish Street, Cartmel, LA11 6PZ
Tel no: (015395) 36362
www.lenclume.co.uk
Modern British | £95
Cooking score: 10

Most chefs would claim to draw from nature's larder: few go to the lengths that Simon Rogan does. L'Enclume, where he 'makes local ingredients dance' to an inspired, thrillingly offbeat tune, is at the forefront of an enterprise which now includes north country farms and a new Manchester restaurant, The French, as well as Rogan & Company, also in Cartmel (see entries). In a period marked by change, including a kitchen extension and ancillary spruce-up, Rogan and his team have not missed a beat. L'Enclume's many-course dinner menu (don't panic, it's perfectly balanced) is simultaneously out-of-this-world and firmly rooted in it, through the clever use of top-notch Cumbrian ingredients and herbs from land and seashore. The exchange between nature and plate is reflected in everything from the slate-lined dining rooms and neat riverside garden to bare wooden tables dressed with pebbles and driftwood (and wine glasses, of course: they're not heathens). In the partly-open kitchen, the gadgets are there – for invention like this, they have to be – but they're deployed with care. A procession of canapés exhibits flair and humour: a little potato tartlet with shallot purée and onion ashes is a classy cheese and onion crisp; a tiny, rotund raw carrot with ham fat serves as a crudité; a Ragstone cheeseball is rolled in dark, malty powder. A crisp, juicy, smoky nugget of smoked eel and pork belly with lovage cream is one of the intense flavours that punctuate the menu at intervals. The courses get bigger. Cubed ox tongue comes with a borage emulsion and a dab of ricotta, draped with rich, thick meat jus. It's fresh and intense at the same time, with the first of many tiny vegetables – this one a courgette, complete with flower. Porcelain 'sacks' have a seasonal filling, perhaps crab with asparagus mousse and little rocks of sweet mushroom dust. Fish and seafood is a real strength, whether it's a cod brandade tucked inside a saffron 'yolk', with a foamy garlic 'white' and puffed rice in an addictive salt and vinegar powder, or a scallop dish in two parts, with a tartare of raw scallop on a linseed cracker and, hiding below it, a Japanese-style custard of the meat and roe freshened with the pop of raw peas. Dessert is where Rogan's approach really runs counter to convention, and it can be divisive. But without the deadening effect of too much

sugar, other flavours come through: the brown butter-soaked brioche in an ice cream served with sorrel and apple purées, and something sheepy – yoghurt, most likely – frozen in dry ice to serve with incredibly juicy cherries and a hazelnut crumb. With an extraordinary amount to communicate and a menu that, blessedly at this level, changes often, staff are friendly, relaxed and completely on top of their brief. Service extends to artful pouring of wine, so a single bottle can go the distance. The list starts at £28.50, with plenty to play with at the lower end as well as quality and breadth for those with deeper pockets.
Chef/s: Simon Rogan. **Open:** Wed to Sun L 12 to 1.30, all week D 6.30 to 9. **Meals:** Set L £32.50 (3 courses). Set D £95. **Details:** 60 seats. Wheelchair access. Car parking. No children under 10 yrs at D.

Rogan & Company
The Rogan diffusion line
The Square, Cartmel, LA11 6QD
Tel no: (015395) 35917
www.roganandcompany.co.uk
Modern British | £39
Cooking score: 4
£5
OFF

Simon Rogan's second Cartmel restaurant is, of course, a different proposition to the mothership. The food and the setting are simpler (and the service less smooth), but the parallels are there in dishes which recall L'Enclume as it started out – made, of course, with local ingredients and strewn with shoots and leaves. Attention to detail is here in a feather-light linseed cracker to dip in an amuse of Ragstone cheese with truffle and honey, and a starter of venison pastrami with vivid mustard emulsion and baby fennel, which is a clear relation of the tartare served across the way. Main courses might be a steak of Herdwick hogget shoulder with artichokes, broad beans and wild pea shoots, or Morecambe bay plaice cooked with a sure touch and served with shrimp, hunks of celeriac and sea greens. Pudding is a buttery deconstructed caramel peach pie, or British cheese with really good biscuits. Wine is from

£21. Note: in nearby Aynsome Road is Simon Rogan's recently acquired village hostelry, the Pig and Whistle, which serves simple pub food. Tel: (015395) 36482.
Chef/s: Simon Rogan and Danielle Barry. **Open:** Mon to Sat L 12 to 2, D 6.30 to 9. **Closed:** Sun. **Meals:** Set L and D £38.50. **Details:** 50 seats. Wheelchair access.

■ Clifton
George & Dragon
Country estate pub with strong local connections
Clifton, CA10 2ER
Tel no: (01768) 865381
www.georgeanddragonclifton.co.uk
Modern British | £24
Cooking score: 3
🛏 £30

This revitalised but genuinely unaffected 18th-century coaching inn, just five minutes from junction 40 of the M6, is making a name for itself with its big-hearted forays into the world of regional food. Produce from owner Charles Lowther's family estate leads by example: Askham garden vegetable and tomato tagliatelle, for instance, or Lowther Estate burger, and seasonal game. In the main it's generous, full-flavoured stuff, from a slow-cooked shin of beef with mashed potatoes served in the autumn to a pan-fried venison liver with wild-garlic mashed potato and crispy bacon that appeared in late spring. Home-cured gravlax, Brougham Hall smoked salmon, farmhouse cheeses (including a creamy Withnail Blue) and desserts such as sticky toffee pudding with fudge sauce keep the show firmly rooted. Fair prices are also a plus and this extends to the well-annotated global wine list; bottles from £15.50.
Chef/s: Ian Jackson. **Open:** all week L 12 to 2, D 6 to 9. **Closed:** 26 Dec. **Meals:** alc (main courses £12 to £23). **Details:** 80 seats. 40 seats outside. Separate bar. Wheelchair access. Car parking.

■ Cockermouth
Quince & Medlar
Long-serving Lakeland veggie
11-13 Castlegate, Cockermouth, CA13 9EU
Tel no: (01900) 823579
www.quinceandmedlar.co.uk
Vegetarian | £27
Cooking score: 2
V £30

When Quince & Medlar first opened in 1989 it felt like a breath of fresh green air in conservative Cockermouth. Now, the rather prim surrounds of a listed Georgian building by the castle seem out of touch with the prevailing vegetarian zeitgeist. The food has unmistakable echoes of eclectic meat-free dinner parties of the late 1980s, with tartlets, croustades, casseroles and colourful accompaniments dominating the menu. Celeriac, apple and blue cheese charlotte with red pepper sauce is a typical savoury idea, while pudding might be pear, apple and cinnamon crunch or chocolate mousse laced with crème de menthe on a biscuit base. Sadly, recent damning reports of frosty service and 'flavourless, overcooked food' suggest that this proverbial box of ripe fruit may be approaching its sell-by date. Two-dozen organic wines start at £16.50.
Chef/s: Colin Le Voi. **Open:** Tue to Sat D only 6.30 to 9.30. **Closed:** Sun, Mon, 24 to 26 Dec. **Meals:** alc (main courses £14). **Details:** 26 seats. Children over 5 yrs only.

■ Crosthwaite
The Punch Bowl
Keen prices and cosmopolitan ideas
Lyth Valley, Crosthwaite, LA8 8HR
Tel no: (015395) 68237
www.the-punchbowl.co.uk
Modern British | £33
Cooking score: 3
£5 OFF 🛏

An engaging and popular all-rounder, this reinvented country inn-with-rooms now markets itself as a luxury hotel, although it

sports a bona fide bar with real ales, exposed beams and log fire. Most come to eat and the kitchen obliges with 'quality, not quantity'. Twice-baked Lancashire cheese soufflé is a firm favourite with readers, as is roast partridge. Braised brisket of beef might also make an appearance, or rack of lamb with boulangère potatoes, roast artichokes and tarragon jus. Fish is good, perhaps roast loin of cod with vanilla potatoes, braised gem lettuce and cauliflower. 'Heavenly seasonal desserts' such as vanilla pannacotta with pomegranate glaze and clementine sorbet could conclude matters. This year, reports on service have found it 'second to none'. Wines from £21.95.
Chef/s: Scott Fairweather. **Open:** Mon to Fri 12 to 9, Sat and Sun L 12 to 4, D 5.30 to 9. **Meals:** alc (main courses £13 to £20). **Details:** 90 seats. 50 seats outside. Separate bar. Car parking.

Grasmere

The Jumble Room
Wacky Lakeland eatery
Langdale Road, Grasmere, LA22 9SU
Tel no: (015394) 35188
www.thejumbleroom.co.uk
Global | £35
new chef/no score

£5
OFF

Framed LP covers join paintings of cows and cockerels on the Jumble Room's ox-blood walls. Dinky lamps, teapots and other collectables also help this wacky Lakeland eatery live up to its name. The kitchen hitchhikes around the globe for ideas, picking up everything from colourfully topped crostini to roasted pumpkin and sweet potato with chickpea aloo. The regional larder is also plundered to produce a warm salad of oak-smoked eel, plates of Cumbrian sirloin steak or haddock and chips. Sticky toffee pudding, hot chocolate brownies and suchlike round things off nicely. Wines (from £15.99) follow the lively, eclectic theme. Just as we went to press The Jumble Room's former chefs, Trudy and David Clay, informed us of their departure; reports please.

Chef/s: Heath Calman. **Open:** Wed to Sun L 12 to 3, D 5.30 to 9. **Closed:** Mon, Tue, 12 to 27 Dec, Wed to Fri Jan. **Meals:** alc (main courses £15 to £27). **Details:** 50 seats. Wheelchair access.

Keswick

ALSO RECOMMENDED
▲ Swinside Lodge
Grange Road, Newlands, Keswick, CA12 5UE
Tel no: (017687) 72948
www.swinsidelodge-hotel.co.uk
Modern British £5
OFF

Built as a private dwelling in 1745, this family-run retreat is the epitome of low-key Lakeland serenity – complete with peaceful grounds and views towards Derwentwater. Four-course, country-house dinners (£45) tip their hat to the region's larder: think medallions of Thirlmere venison with candied pear and chestnuts followed by scallop-dusted roast salmon with courgettes, salmon fishcake and Pernod-laced prawn sauce. After that, perhaps warm ginger sponge pudding with spiced syrup and gooseberry compote or a 'slate' of North Country cheeses. Wines from £18.50. Open all week D only.

Kirkby Lonsdale

ALSO RECOMMENDED
▲ The Sun Inn
6 Market Street, Kirkby Lonsdale, LA6 2AU
Tel no: (015242) 71965
www.sun-inn.info
Modern British

Pleasing flexibility distinguishes this venerable inn-with-rooms, providing pints for drinkers, pub food for all-day grazers and something fancier in the intimate restaurant. Bar nibbles of grilled sardines on toasted sourdough or a generous portion of Cumberland sausage with mash, onion rings and onion gravy (£10.95) earn plaudits, while chicken livers and chestnut mushrooms on toasted brioche, then slow-roasted Saddleback pork belly with mustard mash and apple purée, from the three-course set menu

(£26.95), has gone down a treat in the restaurant. Wines from £16.25. Closed Mon L. Accommodation.

Lupton

ALSO RECOMMENDED
▲ The Plough

Cow Brow, Lupton, LA6 1PJ
Tel no: (015395) 67700
www.theploughatlupton.co.uk
British

On the A65, a few miles from junction 36 of the M6, this born-again hostelry has turned into an engaging place since the people who own the Punch Bowl at Crosthwaite (see entry) gave it a grand makeover. The menu is pubby in style and provides good local grub: a hearty ploughman's board of ham, cheese, pork pie and Scotch egg (£11.95); 'nice, crisp' rösti-topped chicken and mushroom bake (£12.95); and well-reported bread-and-butter pudding. Open all week. Accommodation.

Near Sawrey

Ees Wyke

Beatrix Potter bolt-hole
Near Sawrey, LA22 0JZ
Tel no: (015394) 36393
www.eeswyke.co.uk
Modern British | £35
Cooking score: 2

£5
OFF 🛏

A handsome Georgian house where Beatrix Potter and family once stayed on holiday, this Lakeland bolt-hole is tended with gracious care by Richard and Margaret Lee. The dining-room views over the water of Esthwaite to Coniston Old Man say it all. Richard cooks a daily changing five-course dinner menu, with a pair of choices at most stages, keeping things good and simple to let premier ingredients shine. Seared scallops dressed in balsamic might precede a leek tart with green peppercorn sauce, and then a Chinese-seasoned slow-roast duck leg:

pepped up by five-spice and star anise, sauced with honey and soy. Refreshing fruit sabayon with vanilla ice cream could then be followed by fine northern cheeses to round things off. House Chilean is £21 (£5.25 a glass).
Chef/s: Richard Lee. **Open:** all week D only 7.30 (1 sitting). **Meals:** Set D £35 (5 courses). **Details:** 16 seats. Car parking. Children over 12 yrs only.

▌ Ullswater

Sharrow Bay

Country-house comfort and fine food
Ullswater, CA10 2LZ
Tel no: (01768) 486301
www.sharrowbay.co.uk
Modern British | £45
Cooking score: 5

🍷 🛏 V

When Francis Coulson and Brian Sack founded the grande dame of all country house hotels in 1948, they dubbed it 'the gentle art of Sharrow'. More than 60 years later, this Lakeland retreat still glides along at a stately pace – oblivious to fashion, fads and anything remotely 'boutique'. The place virtually sells itself, with the waters of Ullswater lapping outside, acres of utterly English grounds and the peaks of Helvellyn looming in the distance. Inside, propriety reigns as guests take afternoon tea or assemble for meals in the chintzy dining room, where pampering and hushed tones are *de rigueur*, and the food seems to hark back to another era. Rich sauces and picture-book presentation are a given in finely executed dishes such as soufflé suissesse with spinach, Stilton and roasted onion, or noisettes of Matterdale venison with sherry lentils, braised red cabbage and a juniper-based reduction. After that, desserts merely pile on the creamy indulgence – from the iconic 'icky sticky toffee sponge' to cashew nut parfait with rum-roasted bananas. The magisterial wine list is awesome in scope, from the finest vintage Bordeaux to the most invigorating terroir-led organic tipples. Prices start at £25 (£6.50 a glass). See overleaf for details.

Chef/s: Colin Akrigg. Open: all week L 12 to 2, D 7 to 10. Meals: alc (main courses £15 to £25). Set L £27.50. Set D £45 to £75 (6 courses). Sun L £45. Details: 40 seats. Wheelchair access. Car parking. Children over 10 yrs only.

Ulverston

The Bay Horse
Romantic charm and breathtaking views
Canal Foot, Ulverston, LA12 9EL
Tel no: (01229) 583972
www.thebayhorsehotel.co.uk
Modern British | £36
Cooking score: 3

🛏 V

Once a pit-stop for stagecoaches crossing the sands of Morecambe Bay, this pedigree haunt by the water's edge still has the power to seduce visitors with its romantic charms and breathtaking views.'Dinner at eight' is the drill in the conservatory-style restaurant, where guests can partake of skilfully rendered dishes courtesy of long-serving chef/proprietor Robert Lyons. True-Brit classics and Aberdeen Angus steaks are the top sellers (try the homemade corned beef with white pudding mash, Cumberland sausages or crab and salmon fishcakes), but there are overseas riffs too – smoked duck breast with mango and passion fruit dressing or roast cod with a Dijon mustard and herb crust. Desserts might include dark chocolate and mascarpone cheesecake. Hot sandwiches and 'light bites' are served in the bar at lunchtime. The lively wine list is peppered with intriguing New World names; prices start at £13.50.
Chef/s: Robert Lyons. Open: all week L 12 to 2, D 7.30 for 8 (1 sitting). Meals: alc (main courses £14 to £27). Details: 50 seats. 20 seats outside. Separate bar. Car parking. Children over 9 yrs only at D.

The General Burgoyne
Reborn Lakes pub
Church Road, Great Urswick, Ulverston, LA12 0SZ
Tel no: (01229) 586394
www.generalburgoyne.com
British | £27
Cooking score: 3
£5 OFF £30

Old-fashioned Lakeland hospitality – they'll dry your boots by the fire – meets contemporary cuisine at this dog-, walker- and cyclist-friendly South Lakes pub. Fans enthuse about the beams, roaring fire, stone-flagged snug and beer garden of the 17th-century hostelry, while appreciating food that's a cut above the pub grub norm.'Deli boards', Sunday roasts, afternoon teas, steaks and 'pie and peas in the snug' are popular, but chef Craig Sherrington also has a creative streak best exemplified by the likes of a 'terrific' dish of smoked trout and brown shrimp served with tomato, spring onion and sweet cicely, a 'simple, perfectly cooked' black bream with baby leeks and potatoes in a light, buttery broth, and a delightful gooseberry mousse with squares of gin and tonic jelly ('properly tasting of gin!') with 'the most exquisite cucumber sorbet'. Helpful service 'lacks pomp and pretension'. Wines from £13.95.
Chef/s: Craig Sherrington. Open: Wed to Sat L 12 to 2, Tue to Sat D 6 to 9, Sun 12 to 8. Closed: Mon, first week Jan. Meals: alc (main courses £11 to £18), Sun L £17.95. Details: 33 seats. 12 seats outside. Separate bar. Car parking.

▌Watermillock

Rampsbeck Country House Hotel
Gracious comforts and fine contemporary food
Watermillock, CA11 0LP
Tel no: (017684) 86442
www.rampsbeck.co.uk
Anglo-French | £60
Cooking score: 4

🍷 🚒

Set in 18 acres of grounds and overlooking a fair stretch of Lake Ullswater, this 18th-century country house hotel is firmly of the old school – the Anglo-French cooking fits the place to a T. While the repertoire may hold few surprises, it certainly doesn't lack interest. At the five-course, fixed-price dinner (canapés in the lounge, a soup amuse-bouche ahead of the starter) main courses deliver fresh-tasting flavours in such dishes as spiced shoulder rack of lamb with sweet potato, aubergine, mint yoghurt mousse and feta or whole roast partridge with red cabbage, chestnuts and game chips. There's baked goats' cheese with fig chutney and rocket salad to start, Cumbrian cheeses and/or a well-reported soufflé to finish. The fairly priced, well-annotated wine list pays attention to the lower end as well as the top-class producers. France features most strongly but is complemented by intelligent selections from other regions, both European and New World; prices from £19.50.
Chef/s: Ian Jackson. **Open:** all week L 12 to 1.45, D 6 to 9. **Meals:** Set L £32. Set D £59.95 (5 courses). **Details:** 65 seats. 20 seats outside. Separate bar. Wheelchair access. Car parking.

▌Windermere

Gilpin Hotel & Lake House
Lakeside elegance and innovative cooking
Crook Road, Windermere, LA23 3NE
Tel no: (015394) 88818
www.gilpinlodge.co.uk
Modern British | £58
Cooking score: 5

£5 OFF 🍷 🚒

The Cunliffe family has carefully nurtured this pastoral resort on the shores of Lake Windermere for almost a century; it now comes complete with a lake house where you can contemplate the water from a jetty. The elegant, relaxing dining room – all flowers and candle-flicker – plays host to chef Daniel Grigg's innovative contemporary cooking. A reporter in May found the food 'a fine, fully appetising blend of flavours and textures'. First up, salt cod korma, an Indian-inspired dish, arrived with a crisp rice wafer, iced raita and curry powder 'that dissolved on the tongue like sherbet'. Another starter, seared foie gras, was garnished with crisped chicken skin and beetroot juice. Mains consist of meat in various cuts – Old Spot pork, Herdwick mutton or Cartmel venison (shank and loin) with choucroute, liquorice and blackberries – or sea bass with confit leeks, pistachios and variously textured heritage potato. Plum and cardamom soufflé with sugared almonds might conclude matters. The broad-minded, catholic wine list extends from the French heartlands across the world (including an enjoyable Georgian vintage), with good notes and fair prices all the way. Prices start at £20.
Chef/s: Daniel Grigg. **Open:** all week L 12 to 2, D 6.30 to 9.15. **Meals:** alc L (main courses £6 to £18). Set D £58 (5 courses). Sun L £35. **Details:** 65 seats. 30 seats outside. Separate bar. Car parking. Children over 7 yrs only.

Holbeck Ghyll
The finer things of life
Holbeck Lane, Windermere, LA23 1LU
Tel no: (015394) 32375
www.holbeckghyll.com
Modern British | £65
Cooking score: 5

£5 OFF 🍷 🛏

The tranquil grey-stone house – once Lord Lonsdale's hunting lodge – has become a linchpin of the Lakeland hospitality scene. Seductive views towards the Langdale Pikes help weave the Ghyll's magic, as does the friendly professionalism and David McLaughlin's cooking, which brings an invigorating dash of modern British style. The result is massively appreciated by reporters: 'every mouthful was a culinary delight, from the duck and foie gras terrine with homemade brioche, to venison infused with white truffle, and a chocoholic's playground for dessert.' To start, Scottish scallops are usually teamed with smoked bacon in sherry vinegar dressing, while sensitively handled fish main courses might include roasted brill with braised gem lettuce under cider foam. For dessert, those wanting a citric tang could sample a platter of lemon: mousse-filled mille-feuille, tart, sorbet, parfait and crème brûlée, with a little passion fruit sauce. Sommelier Stefan Lydka oversees a magisterial wine list that ranges from 'Fantastic Finds' from Margaret River, Oregon and the like, through an inspired exploration of the classics, incorporating plenty of halves. House selections from £27 a bottle, glasses £6.25.
Chef/s: David McLaughlin. **Open:** all week L 12.30 to 2, D 7 to 9.30. **Meals:** Set L £26 (2 courses) to £35. Set D £65. Sun L £26 (2 courses). Gourmet menu £85 (7 courses). **Details:** 52 seats. Separate bar. Wheelchair access. Car parking. Children over 8 yrs only at D.

ALSO RECOMMENDED
▲ Jerichos at the Waverley
College Road, Windermere, LA23 1BX
Tel no: (015394) 42522
www.jerichos.co.uk
Modern British

Chris and Jo Blaydes' handsome Victorian residence now runs primarily as an upmarket guesthouse, but the restaurant still does limited duty for those who enjoy vigorous modern cooking and thoughtfully chosen, food-friendly wines. The short menu might run from crispy confit duck with mustard mashed neeps, grilled black pudding and port reduction (£7.95) to raspberry and almond tart, via poached sea bass fillet on creamed 'hotpot' potatoes with dill-glazed roots, almonds, capers and Avruga caviar (£19.95). Wines start at £18. Open Sat D and bank hol weekends only.

▊ Winster
ALSO RECOMMENDED
▲ The Brown Horse Inn
Winster, LA23 3NR
Tel no: (015394) 43443
www.thebrownhorseinn.co.uk
Modern British £5 OFF

Locals show loyalty to the Brown Horse for good reason – it's worth knowing about if you're in the area. Overlooking the gently rolling countryside of the southern fringes of the Lake District National Park (best viewed from the terrace), it's a comfortable, sociable pub-with-rooms characterised by beams, open fires, polished tables and hand-pulled local and microbrewery ales. A straightforward menu deals in local, seasonal ingredients – Cumbrian black pudding teamed with scallops (£12.95) say, or slow-cooked shank of Kentmere lamb (£16.50). Wines from £15. Open all week. Accommodation.

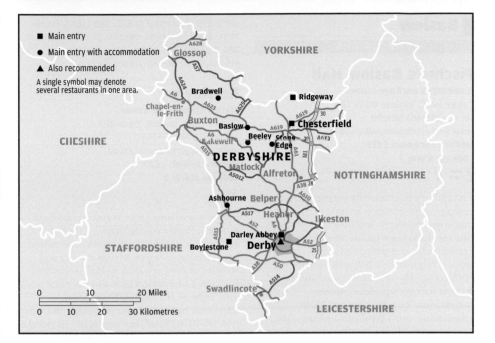

Map legend:

■ Main entry
● Main entry with accommodation
▲ Also recommended
A single symbol may denote several restaurants in one area.

YORKSHIRE
Glossop
A628
Bradwell
Chapel-en-le-Frith
Buxton
Baslow
Ridgeway
Chesterfield
CHESHIRE
Bakewell
Beeley
Edge
DERBYSHIRE
Matlock
Alfreton
NOTTINGHAMSHIRE
Ashbourne
Belper
Heanor
Ilkeston
STAFFORDSHIRE
Boylestone
Darley Abbey
Derby
Swadlincote
LEICESTERSHIRE

0   10   20 Miles
0   10   20   30 Kilometres

■ Ashbourne

The Dining Room

Finely honed, experimental tasting plates
33 St John Street, Ashbourne, DE6 1GP
Tel no: (01335) 300666
www.thediningroomashbourne.co.uk
Modern European | £40
Cooking score: 4

Open the gate and cross the cobbled courtyard to reach this endearingly wonky 17th-century building – home to Peter and Laura Dale's low-beamed, six-table Dining Room. Eating out doesn't get more intimate than this, and Peter runs the kitchen single-handedly: curing meat, smoking fish, baking bread and doing extraordinary things with produce from his local suppliers. Dinner consists of a preordained, no-choice succession of finely honed, experimental tasting plates. 'Finger food' nibbles and excellent sourdough with home-churned butter put down a serious marker, before the real action begins. One minute you're in the Far East for a dish of Goosnargh duck with salted 'umeboshi' plums, carrot kim-chee and red cabbage, the next you're sampling hand-dived scallops with morcilla, blood orange, fennel and homemade chorizo, or Jerusalem artichokes with sunflower seeds, sage and lemon. Cheeses get proper exposure, while desserts such as dark chocolate and peanut cake with salted caramel, popcorn and lime provide the final hurrah. Wines start at £24.

Chef/s: Peter Dale. **Open:** Tue and Wed D (by arrangement only), Thur to Sat D 7 (1 sitting). **Closed:** Sun, Mon, 1 week over Shrove Tue, 1 week Sept, last 2 weeks Dec. **Meals:** Set weekday D £40 (5 courses). Sat D £48 (8 courses). **Details:** 16 seats. Wheelchair access. Children over 12 yrs only.

¡¡● Average Price

The average price listed in main-entry reviews denotes the price of a three-course meal, without wine.

Baslow

★ TOP 50 ★

Fischer's Baslow Hall

A seductive package indeed
Calver Road, Baslow, DE45 1RR
Tel no: (01246) 583259
www.fischers-baslowhall.co.uk
Modern European | £72
Cooking score: 7

🍷 ⊨ V

The Hall is a meticulously detailed Edwardian homage to Restoration architecture, with mullioned windows and scalloped porch. Built for local bigwigs the Stockdales, this graceful edifice at the end of a tree-shaded drive now provides a home to both the Fischers' capably rendered hospitality and Rupert Rowley's protean culinary imagination. The dining room looks unassuming, with floral curtains amid the predominating beige, but the cookery fires the venue into another dimension. Dishes are carefully worked to achieve maximum impact without betraying the integrity of their materials, as when red mullet cooked over embers appears in Mediterranean livery with red pepper, aubergine and chorizo. The roast pumpkin mousse has left one or two baffled, but not so the local pork jowl, slow-cooked and caramelised in maltose, before being teamed with langoustines, honey-roast crackling, a raviolo of the cheek and a razor's edge of puréed grapefruit. An Indian approach suits a monkfish dish that comes with curried granola, roast cauliflower and razor clams, while the signature dessert of chocolate tree trunk, with its contrasting mousse and sorbet, proves reliably hard to resist. A lighter note is sounded by a serving of Yorkshire blackberries with camomile mousse and honey. The extensive wine list shows plenty of thought in its useful notes and fastidious choice of star growers. House wines are from £22, or £5.50 a glass.
Chef/s: Rupert Rowley. **Open:** all week L 12 to 1.30, D 7 to 8.30. **Closed:** 25, 26 Dec. **Meals:** alc (main courses £25 to £26). Set L £20 (2 courses) to £25.

Set D £55 (2 courses) to £72. Sun L £42. Tasting menu £50 (7 courses). **Details:** 55 seats. Separate bar. Car parking. Children over 7 yrs only at L, 10 yrs only at D. No restrictions for Sun L.

Rowley's

Stylish all-purpose venue
Church Lane, Baslow, DE45 1RY
Tel no: (01246) 583880
www.rowleysrestaurant.co.uk
Modern British | £29
Cooking score: 1

£30

Purple hues, lime-green furniture, modern artwork, floral extravaganzas . . . it's hard to believe this stylish all-purpose venue started life as a village boozer. Messrs Fischer and Rowley of Fischer's Baslow Hall (see entry) have worked wonders here and the place is now right on the money. Set lunches, afternoon 'light bites', fish and chips on Friday and drinks in the all-day bar satisfy the locals, while the full menu offers bright dishes without aftershocks. Retro prawn cocktail or Parmesan risotto might precede braised oxtail with mash, salmon with winter vegetable broth or confit duck and orange sauce. Espresso-spiked affogato provides an ideal finale. Wines from £16.95.
Chef/s: Jason Kendra, Ian Woodhead and Max Fischer. **Open:** Tue to Sun 12 to 9 (9.30 Sat, 4 Sun). **Closed:** Mon, 25 Dec. **Meals:** alc (main courses £12 to £20). Set L £16 (2 courses) to £20. Sun L £24. **Details:** 64 seats. Separate bar. Wheelchair access. Car parking.

READERS RECOMMEND

The Devonshire Arms

British
Nether End, Baslow, DE45 1SR
Tel no: (01246) 582551
www.devonshirearmsbaslow.co.uk
'Well-priced menus, lovely owners, great chef and stunning, unpretentious, lick-your-plate food.'

▌Beeley

The Devonshire Arms

Well-to-do country inn
Devonshire Square, Beeley, DE4 2NR
Tel no: (01629) 733259
www.devonshirebeeley.co.uk
Modern British | £32
Cooking score: 2

Set on the edge of the Chatsworth Estate, the Devonshire Arms is an 18th-century coaching inn with a 21st-century soul – all real fires, exposed stone and beams, offset by the striking contemporary pose of the adjoining brasserie. Fashionable menus are driven by local and seasonal produce, with simple pub classics worked into the mix: say honey-roasted Chatsworth ham 'n' eggs. The full menu shows a flair for invention, perhaps Chatsworth Estate wood pigeon carpaccio with crisp, slow-cooked leg, winter nuts and berries and mushroom duxelle to start, followed by baked cod with smoked cod brandade, cauliflower, English mustard and crispy cheese, then warm chocolate and olive pudding with chocolate custard to finish. Wines from £18.
Chef/s: Alan Hill. **Open:** all week L 12 to 3, D 6 to 9.30. **Meals:** alc (main courses £13 to £25). Set L £14.95 (2 courses) to £18.95. Sun L £14. **Details:** 78 seats. 20 seats outside. Car parking.

▌Boylestone

The Lighthouse Restaurant

A beacon for good local produce
New Road, Boylestone, DE6 5AA
Tel no: (01335) 330658
www.the-lighthouse-restaurant.co.uk
Modern British | £35
Cooking score: 2

'Well worth the effort to find,' enthused one reporter about this small village restaurant hidden behind the Rose and Crown pub. The modern, high-raftered dining room is rustically stylish (think exposed brick, wood and cream tones) with limited opening times,

but the kitchen proves its worth with some precise, assured cooking that celebrates good local produce. Chef/proprietor Jonathan Hardy's menus evolve with the seasons, his kitchen perhaps sending out Boylestone wild garlic and British asparagus risotto with Parmesan crisps, before red deer tenderloin with butternut squash purée, mulled red cabbage and a bitter chocolate demi-glace. Also finding favour have been scallops with pig's head beignet, apple, crackling and pancetta foam; 'a sea bass lattice with samphire'; Derbyshire beef steaks; and 'an amazing' deconstructed peanut butter and cherry cheesecake. Wines from £13.95.
Chef/s: Jonathan Hardy. **Open:** Thur to Sun D 7 to 12, Sun L 12 to 4. **Closed:** 24 to 26 Dec. **Meals:** alc (main courses £16 to £25). Set D £19.95 (2 courses) to £23.95. **Details:** 36 seats. Separate bar. Wheelchair access. Car parking.

▌Bradwell

The Samuel Fox Inn

Cut-above country pub
Stretfield Road, Bradwell, S33 9JT
Tel no: (01433) 621562
www.samuelfox.co.uk
British | £27
Cooking score: 3

Readers may remember James Duckett from the Old Custom House in Barnstaple, Devon, last in the Guide in 2012. He has now set up business in a revitalised village hostelry, developing it as a good place to eat. In the main his cooking is generous and full-flavoured, demonstrating sound talent and a commendable commitment to first-rate raw materials. Look out for pub classics such as fish and chips, cottage pie and the like, alongside sparkling versions of bang up-to-date modern dishes like game terrine, fillet of bream teamed with braised leeks, polenta and truffle sauce or haunch of venison with celeriac, red cabbage and red wine sauce, on a menu that concludes with a spot-on sticky toffee pudding with stout ice cream. Close attention to detail extends to excellent homemade bread and well-kept real ales – and it's all matched by cheerful service. Wines from £15.50.

Chef/s: James Duckett. **Open:** Wed to Sun L 12 to 2.30, Tue to Sat D 6.30 to 10.30. Sun 12 to 7.30. **Closed:** Mon, 2 to 16 Jan. **Meals:** alc (main courses £12 to £19). Sun L £19 (2 courses) to £24. **Details:** 36 seats. 12 seats outside. Separate bar. Wheelchair access. Car parking.

Chesterfield

Non Solo Vino

Trailblazing Italian wine shop-cum-restaurant
417 Chatsworth Road, Brampton, Chesterfield, S40 3AD
Tel no: (01246) 276760
www.nonsolovino.co.uk
Italian | £30
Cooking score: 3
£5
OFF

In the Brampton district of town, Non Solo Vino ('not just wine') is an Italian wine boutique that has branched out into feeding people. Locals firmly believe that Chesterfield has nothing to rival it, both for breezy informality and the quality of its fresh, seasonal dishes. A lot of Italian food settles for the simple and straightforward approach, but here you'll find a rich vein of creativity, manifested in goats' cheese mousse and spinach mille-feuille with Bloody Mary sorbet and powdered black olive. Mains follow suit, with the likes of salmon with kale and garlic mash in clam velouté, or duck breast with spiced red cabbage, puréed celeriac and orange and gin jelly. Dishes are accorded their Italian names throughout, at least until the menu gets to soufflé banoffi. Lincolnshire Poacher inveigles its way among the Italian cheeses. The enterprising wine list (opening at £14) roughly divvies up Italy.

Chef/s: Matt Bennison. **Open:** Tue to Sun L all day (3 Sun), Tue to Sat D 7 to 9. **Closed:** Mon, 25 and 26 Dec, 1 to 7 Jan. **Meals:** alc (main courses £14 to £24). Set D £32 to £39 (4 courses). Tasting menu £49 (7 courses) to £59 (9 courses). **Details:** 46 seats. Separate bar. Car parking.

Darley Abbey

Darleys

Tourist hot spot with capable food
Darley Abbey Mills, Haslams Lane, Darley Abbey, DE22 1DZ
Tel no: (01332) 364987
www.darleys.com
Modern British | £35
Cooking score: 3
V

Part of a vast World Heritage Site stretching across the Derwent Valley, this family-owned restaurant is housed in a converted cotton mill by a pretty weir. It's a sure-fire crowd-puller for tourists – especially when the sun shines on the decked waterside terrace. Bright contemporary surrounds, bold fabrics and clever design set the tone for a roster of ambitious modern dishes, with influences from home and abroad adding vibrancy and colour to proceedings. Confit salmon is served with cucumber Martini and tomato gel, cod loin turns up with a shrimp 'toasty' and green tapenade dressing, and a duo of pork comes with risotto-style potatoes and apple purée. To finish, mulled wine soufflé with candied ginger ice cream sounds promising. Service seems to have perked up lately, and the all-purpose, brasserie-style wine list promises sound drinking from £16.50.

Chef/s: Jonathan Hobson and Mark Hadfield. **Open:** all week L 12 to 2 (2.30 Sun), Mon to Sat D 7 to 9 (9.30 Fri and Sat). **Closed:** 25 Dec to 10 Jan. **Meals:** alc (main courses £19 to £22). Set L £18.95 (2 courses) to £20.95. Sun L £25. **Details:** 60 seats. Separate bar. Car parking.

Derby

ALSO RECOMMENDED
▲ Masa

The Old Wesleyan Chapel, Brook Street, Derby, DE1 3PF
Tel no: (01332) 203345
www.masarestaurantwinebar.com
Modern European £5 OFF

A one-time Wesleyan chapel just off the Derby inner ring road provides the setting for Paula and Didar Dalkic's highly idiosyncratic bar and restaurant. The light, many-tiered dining gallery (a popular wedding venue) has a well-deserved reputation for friendly hospitality and good food. Start with goats' cheese pannacotta with pickled carrot, pea and beetroot (£6.50), go on to braised blade of Derbyshire beef with boulangère potatoes (£18) and finish with dark chocolate parfait with caramel sauce and vanilla ice cream. Wines from £17. Closed Mon, Tue.

▲ Mumbai Chilli

28 Stenson Road, Cavendish, Derby, DE23 1JB
Tel no: (01332) 767090
www.mumbaichilli.com
Indian

Smart design touches and old curry-house favourites share the stage at this popular Indian restaurant. The repertoire spans everything from good tandooris, perhaps a mixed grill (£12.95), to lamb korma and chicken jalfrezi (£6.95), plus a few specials like chicken xacuti from Goa (the meat coconut-flavoured and cooked in a rich, mild curry sauce). Rice and breads are good, service pleasant. Drink beer or choose from the short wine list, which opens at £11.95. Open all week.

¶¶| Also Recommended

Also recommended entries are not scored but we think they are worth a visit.

Ridgeway

★ TOP 50 ★

The Old Vicarage

A beacon of natural-born cooking
Ridgeway Moor, Ridgeway, S12 3XW
Tel no: (0114) 2475814
www.theoldvicarage.co.uk
Modern British | £70
Cooking score: 7
£5 OFF 🍷

After more than 25 years at the Old Vicarage, Tessa Bramley's enthusiasm remains undimmed. 'It has never been easier to find good ingredients,' she reflects. The stone-built former clerical residence is less imposing than many of its era, but is furnished throughout in the unabashed comforts of yesteryear, with comfy cushions, ornately framed mirrors and spot-lit oils of pastoral scenes. Bramley's commitment to seasonality is more than skin-deep: it constitutes the lifeblood of her menus, garnishing a spring starter of roast quail and its deep-fried egg with leek purée, pea shoots and pine nuts, or adorning a winter main course of shorthorn beef fillet with crushed butternut squash, fresh morels and chestnut forcemeat. Dishes look complex in their descriptions, but make perfect sense, as when an Asian-influenced first course of John Dory and Manx queenies arrives with pak choi, candied chilli, mango salsa and lemongrass. A vegetarian main comprises spiced aubergine in coconut and tomato, saffron-braised fennel with ginger and cumin, and Indian-spiced sweet potato croquettes. Desserts mix old English favourites with the likes of bitter chocolate croquant of mocha mousse, with lemon curd ice cream and Limoncello jelly. An exceptional wine list, classified by style, reaches for the stars with the best Burgundy growers, the California elite and Italian stars. A page of recommendations neatly summarises the range. Prices start at £28.
Chef/s: Tessa Bramley and Nathan Smith. **Open:** Tue to Fri L 12.30 to 2, Tue to Sat D 6 to 9.30 (10 Sat). **Closed:** Sun, Mon, 26 Dec to 5 Jan, 2 weeks Aug,

bank hols. **Meals:** Set L £30 (2 courses) to £40. Set D £70 (4 courses) to £75. **Details:** 40 seats. 16 seats outside. Separate bar. Wheelchair access.

▌Stone Edge
Red Lion Bar & Bistro

Popular country-pub restaurant
Peak Edge Hotel, Darley Road, Stone Edge, S45 0LW
Tel no: (01246) 566142
www.redlionbarandbistro.com
Modern British | £28
Cooking score: 2

£5 OFF 🍽 £30

'Freezing outside, gorgeous cosy log fires, all candlelit, really nice atmosphere . . .' So writes someone who was happy to take pot luck on a wintry Sunday night and left impressed by the welcome, atmosphere and food. The Red Lion stands on the edge of the Peak District National Park, upbeat and modishly rustic in a 21st-century fashion (lots of dark beams, exposed stone walls, wood floors, leather chairs). The food straddles both traditional and contemporary – game terrine or smoked salmon with elderflower jelly, fresh radishes, fennel shoots, sour cucumber and lemon mayonnaise; slow-braised beef cheek with creamed mashed potato and bourguignon sauce or fillet of sea bream with brown shrimps, celeriac purée, wilted baby gem, horseradish sauce and pickled celery. Banana-and-date toffee pudding is a highlight among desserts and wine starts at £15.95.
Chef/s: Carl Riley and Daniel Laycock. **Open:** all week 12 to 9 (9.30 Fri and Sat). **Meals:** alc (main courses £11 to £22). Set L £12.95 (2 courses) to £14.95. Sun L £11.95. **Details:** 80 seats. 40 seats outside. Separate bar. Wheelchair access. Car parking.

▐▐ TESSA BRAMLEY
The Old Vicarage

What do you enjoy most about being a chef?
The freedom of expression through cooking and the ability to give pleasure. I love seeing plates scraped clean.

... And the least?
Washing up.

Which three ingredients couldn't you cook without?
Fresh herbs from the garden, the subtlety of sweet spices and unsalted English butter.

What do you think is a common mistake that lets chefs down?
Thinking that fashion is all and a pretty plate means you can cook. You need to know how to taste, how to season, and how to turn the good into the sublime.

Which chefs do you admire?
Raymond Blanc for his enthusiasm, skill and Gallic charm and Nathan Outlaw for his no-nonsense approach. There are so many great cooks around, but the modest ones do it for me.

At the end of a long day, what do you like to cook?
Nothing, I'm all cooked out!

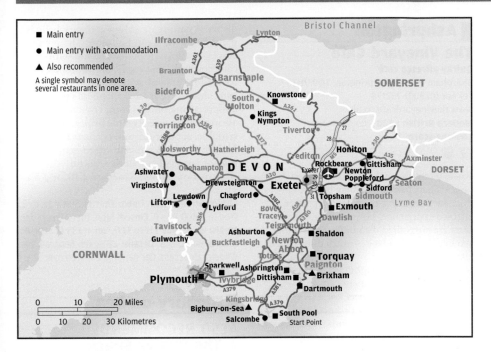

▮ Ashburton

Agaric
Heartfelt natural cooking
30 North Street, Ashburton, TQ13 7QD
Tel no: (01364) 654478
www.agaricrestaurant.co.uk
Modern British | £35
Cooking score: 4

£5 OFF 🚐

In a placid Devon stannary town near Newton Abbot, Agaric comprises a restaurant, accommodation (in a neighbouring handsomely restored Tudor house) and an adjoining shop in which chef/proprietor Nick Coiley gives cookery lessons. Many ingredients come from the Agaric smallholding, from lemongrass to edible flowers; stimulating modern dishes are the result. Smoked duck breast makes a robust opener, dressed in a salsa of pear, rhubarb and walnuts. Main courses are composed of layers of complementary flavours. A version of bourride is a sunny blend of tomato, orange

and saffron, as well as plenty of white fish, while best end of lamb might be crusted in herbs and tapenade and accompanied by celeriac mousse. Venison in a leg steak is a good cut, given the bourguignon treatment with smoked bacon, shallots and red wine, alongside horseradished potato gratin and parsnip purée. To finish, rhubarb and Pernod make a great double-act in a cleverly crumble-topped soufflé, served with custard. Wines start at £19.50.
Chef/s: Nick Coiley. **Open:** Wed to Fri L 12 to 2, Wed to Sat D 7 to 9. **Closed:** Sun to Tue, 2 weeks Dec. **Meals:** alc (main courses £16 to £23). Set L £15.95 (2 courses). **Details:** 28 seats. 15 seats outside. Separate bar. Wheelchair access.

🍴 Visit us Online
To find out more about
The Good Food Guide, please visit
www.thegoodfoodguide.co.uk

Ashprington

The Vineyard Café

Quirky alfresco café
Sharpham Estate, Ashprington, TQ9 7UT
Tel no: (01803) 732178
www.thevineyardcafe.co.uk
Modern British | £28
Cooking score: 1
£5 £30
OFF

Rosie Weston's quirky gem of a seasonal café on the Sharpham Estate may require effort to find, but its setting provides the perfect alfresco experience. The views over the river Dart are unrivalled. From the small trailer kitchen, local produce – much of it from the estate itself – appears on an ever-changing seasonal menu that might take in pork and prune terrine with runner bean chutney, followed by lamb and beef kofta served with broad bean and coriander couscous. Cardamom crème brûlée with roasted peach compote is a typical pudding. A range of Sharpham vineyard wines starts at £14.95. **Chef/s:** Charlie Goddard, Rosie Weston and Angela Howard-Chappell. **Open:** all week L only 12 to 2 (2.30 Sat and Sun). **Closed:** Oct to Easter. **Meals:** alc (main courses £10 to £15). Set L £13.50 (1 course) to £19.50. **Details:** 50 seats outside. Wheelchair access. Car parking.

Ashwater

Blagdon Manor

Hospitable West Country treasure
Ashwater, EX21 5DF
Tel no: (01409) 211224
www.blagdon.com
Modern British | £38
Cooking score: 2
🍽 V

The Moreys have fashioned their impressively professional, elegant country-house hotel out of a 17th-century west Devon farmhouse. Fine south-western produce flows into Steve's kitchen in abundance and emerges into the conservatory-style extension dining room in the form of carefully judged modern classic dishes. A pairing of scallop and pork belly is garnished with apple, pea shoots, honey and cloves, as a possible prelude to cod with cauliflower, raisins, capers and almonds, or roast rump of lamb with Cornish Gouda and leek, and a little crusted shepherd's pie. A dessert tasting offers a compendious assortment of cherry crème brûlée, peach crumble, apple fritter and coconut milk and Malibu sorbet. A separate vegetarian/vegan menu bears evidence of thoughtful construction. House wines are £16, or £5 a glass. **Chef/s:** Steve Morey. **Open:** Thur to Sun L 12 to 2, Wed to Sun D 7 to 9. **Closed:** Mon, Tue, 2 weeks Jan. **Meals:** alc (L only £11 to £17). Set D £35 (2 courses) to £40. Sun L £28. **Details:** 28 seats. Separate bar. Wheelchair access. Car parking. Children over 12 yrs only.

Bigbury-on-Sea

ALSO RECOMMENDED
▲ The Oyster Shack

Milburn Orchard Farm, Stakes Hill, Bigbury-on-Sea, TQ7 4BE
Tel no: (01548) 810876
www.oystershack.co.uk
Seafood

Chris Yandell and his crew have created something quite 'magical' here: from sunny chill-outs on the breezy sail-covered terrace to winter sojourns snuggled by the fire. The Shack deals in ozone-fresh Devon seafood plain and simple (oysters, mussels, cracked crabs, lobsters), but the kitchen also plays contemporary riffs with the day's catch. Expect anything from pan-fried scallops with pancetta and blue cheese salad (£9) to wild sea bass with chive and cockle velouté (£21), followed by local ice cream or lemon posset. Wines from £15.50. Open all week.

Also Recommended
Also recommended entries are not scored but we think they are worth a visit.

Brixham

ALSO RECOMMENDED
▲ The Brixham Deli
68a Fore Street, Brixham, TQ5 8EF
Tel no: (01803) 859585
www.thebrixhamdeli.co.uk
Modern British

The Deli is a double-fronted Victorian shop tucked just off the inner harbour of bustling Brixham. It's a useful place to stop for a quick bite, a hearty breakfast or sustaining lunch. Mounds of quality produce line the shelves. Reliable standards include sweet-cured herrings with chopped red onion and sour cream (£5.95), thick-sliced grilled ham with poached eggs and chips (£7.95), fritto misto based on the day's catch (£9.95) and fresh fruit tart with clotted cream. Wines from £10.99. Open daytime all week.

Chagford

★ TOP 50 ★

Gidleigh Park
Seductive Dartmoor setting
Chagford, TQ13 8HH
Tel no: (01647) 432367
www.gidleigh.com
Modern European | £110
Cooking score: 7

🍷 🚃 V

The narrow lane leading to Gidleigh Park seems to go on forever ('keep heart, you're almost there'), but eventually the seductive Dartmoor setting comes into view. From the moment you're greeted at the threshold, eating here is an impeccably paced experience. Take your ease in one of the lounges or sit on the terrace and await platters of exemplary nibbles. Meals are served in a couple of rather insular, detached dining rooms, which can sometimes make for a 'lonely start', but the food more than compensates. Despite his busy schedule, chef/proprietor Michael Caines still puts in the hours here, delivering subtly worked, delicately balanced dishes with clever

touches and a commitment to West Country produce. Almost every item is 'pinned' to the landscape: from Brixham scallops with truffle-infused celeriac purée, to Waddeton pheasant accompanied by cumin-spiked pumpkin purée, lentils, button onions and cumin-scented red wine sauce. To finish, utterly brilliant soufflés take some beating, although the exquisite hot chocolate fondant had one recipient swooning with delight; otherwise, an apple-themed plate of tarte Tatin mousse, ice cream and cider coulis chimes perfectly with the season. Service is top drawer and sensitive to customers' needs, although it can occasionally tail off towards the end of proceedings (a 'consistent failing with some top restaurants', noted one well-travelled reader). The authoritative wine list accommodates everything from breathtaking French classics to Californian superstars and South Africa's finest, alongside an enlightened choice of organic/biodynamic bottles. There's little below £35, but relief is provided by a profusion of half-bottles and by-the-glass selections.
Chef/s: Michael Caines. **Open:** all week L 12 to 2.30, D 7 to 9.30. **Closed:** 1 week Jan. **Meals:** Set L £42 (2 courses) to £55. Set D £110. Tasting menu £120 (5 courses) to £135 (8 courses). **Details:** 50 seats. Children over 8 yrs only.

Dartmouth

★ READERS' RESTAURANT OF THE YEAR ★
SOUTH WEST

The Seahorse
Approachable seafood eatery par excellence
5 South Embankment, Dartmouth, TQ6 9BH
Tel no: (01803) 835147
www.seahorserestaurant.co.uk
Seafood | £35
Cooking score: 5
🍷

Mitch Tonks is doing magical things with bracingly fresh fish and seafood at his restaurant overlooking the Dart estuary. The dining room's frisson of chatty contentment is helped along by the open kitchen, the

fabulous cooking aromas and Tonks's own willingness to nip out for a chat. Fish is given classic European treatment. 'We often share a monkfish tail', one couple reports, 'cooked on the char-grill and simply presented, best with tiny little courgette fritti.' Fried squid with artichoke hearts and lemon might precede the main event, or a bowl of sustaining fisherman's soup in the Italian style. Fire-roasting brings out the flavour of main-course fish, including sand-sole dressed only with olive oil and rosemary, while turbot on green lentils with spinach also benefits from a lack of complex saucing. Dessert almost seems an afterthought, but 'we are always excited if blood-orange and Campari jelly is on the menu'. The wine list has no truck with non-European vineyards, though the selections from the Iberian peninsula, French satellite regions and the house Portuguese blends are impressive. Bottles from £21.
Chef/s: Mitch Tonks and Mat Prowse. **Open:** Wed to Sun L 12 to 3 (12.30 to 2 Sun), Tue to Sat D 6 to 10. **Closed:** Mon, 24 to 26 Dec. **Meals:** alc (main courses £18 to £32). Set L and early D £20 (2 courses) to £25. Set D £20 (2 courses) to £25. Sun L £20. **Details:** 40 seats. 4 seats outside. Wheelchair access.

ALSO RECOMMENDED

▲ Rockfish Seafood and Chips

8 South Embankment, Dartmouth, TQ6 9BH
Tel no: (01803) 832800
www.rockfishdevon.co.uk
Seafood

A simpler proposition than seafood aficionado Mitch Tonks' other restaurants (see entries for the Seahorse, Dartmouth and Rockfish Grill, Bristol), Rockfish majors in beautifully fresh fish and chips (from £8.95) plus other piscine offerings including a bucket of prawns (from £7.45), freshly shucked oysters (£12 for six) and crispy soft-shell crab in a bun (£8.95). Welcoming staff, a superb quayside location overlooking the Dart Estuary and an 'inspired' interior complete this pretty picture. Wine from £16.95. Open all week.

▌ Dittisham

Anchorstone Café

Seafood lovers' paradise
Manor Street, Dittisham, TQ6 0EX
Tel no: (01803) 722365
www.anchorstonecafe.co.uk
Seafood | £23
Cooking score: 3
£30

The premises have housed a riverside café with views over the Dart since the 1950s, but have achieved their apotheosis under Clare Harvey's stewardship. Ethically caught and sustainable fish and seafood, much of it from the Dartmouth and Brixham day boats, is the prime attraction, winning the Anchorstone a strong local following. Prawns in Marie Rose sauce with brown bread or scallops in Caesar salad are simplicity itself, and the show continues with breaded whitebait or battered calamari, but it's to the daily specials board that most people look. Mussels from Elberry Cove just across the river, cooked with shallots and garlic in Devon cider; fantastic Start Bay crab; lobster; Looe haddock; and monkfish tail char-grilled with fresh herbs – all are worth snapping up when available. Or you might just be tempted by a ploughman's spread featuring locally made Poole Farm pork pie. Finish with plum crumble and clotted cream. House wine is £16.95.
Chef/s: Clare Harvey and Jasmine Harvey. **Open:** all week L 12 to 4, Thur to Sat D 6 to 8 (Jul and Aug only). **Closed:** Nov to Mar. **Meals:** alc (main courses £12 to £22). **Details:** 28 seats. 50 seats outside. Wheelchair access.

ᵢ║● Please send us your feedback

To register your opinion about any restaurant listed in the Guide, or a new restaurant that you wish to bring to our attention, please visit the web address at the bottom of the page. Your feedback informs the content of the book and will be used to compile next year's reviews.

■ Drewsteignton

The Old Inn

Exclusive little restaurant-with-rooms
Drewsteignton, EX6 6QR
Tel no: (01647) 281276
www.old-inn.co.uk
Modern European | £43
Cooking score: 3

'Very friendly service and excellent food' sums up the way most visitors feel about this village restaurant-with-rooms. The Old Inn appears to go from strength to strength – perhaps because the kitchen is more interested in cooking to please customers than to entertain itself. Duncan Walker is an experienced chef and over the years has gradually refined his version of modern European cooking. The result is a pared-back seasonal menu where crab raviolo with lobster sauce and monkfish with mussels have shone; likewise, the quality of herb-crusted rack of lamb as well as poached free-range chicken (served with gnocchi with thyme and chanterelle). Praise, too, for a simple almond tart with ice cream, but iced nougat with chocolate and glazed orange also entices. The short wine list opens at £21.
Chef/s: Duncan Walker. Open: Wed to Sat D only 7 to 10. Closed: Sun to Tue. Meals: Set L £29.50. Set D £37.50 (2 courses) to £42.50. Details: 16 seats. Children over 12 yrs only.

■ Exeter

NEW ENTRY
The Magdalen Chapter

Seasonally forceful food in a stunning setting
Magdalen Street, Exeter, EX2 4HY
Tel no: (01392) 281000
www.themagdalenchapter.com
British | £31
Cooking score: 3

One visitor found the Victorian red-brick façade of the former West of England Eye Hospital 'foreboding', but was delighted to discover an 'ultra-chic' hotel inside. Furnishings are classy and restrained, 'nothing jars', as traditional features blend seamlessly with the stunning modern interior. The dining room, with its open kitchen, brown leather banquettes, red leather chairs, high ceiling and striking, contemporary lighting is the setting for Ben Bulger's straightforward cooking that displays commendable seasonal force. The food is nearly always interesting, prices pretty fair and starters like grilled wood pigeon with leeks, smoked bacon and walnut dressing show quality from the off. A main course of whole roast wild sea bass with tomato, artichoke and olives has impressed, and there are steaks and burgers for those looking for something meaty. Finish with a 'comforting creamy' hot rice pudding with fresh new-season rhubarb. Wines from £17.50.
Chef/s: Ben Bulger. Open: all week L 12 to 2.30 (3 Sun), D 6 to 10 (9.30 Sun). Meals: alc (main courses £10 to £24). Set L and D £12.95 (2 courses) to £15.95. Sun L £15 (2 courses) to £17.95. Details: 74 seats. 22 seats outside. Separate bar. Wheelchair access.

Michael Caines at ABode Exeter

A polished set-up
Royal Clarence Hotel, Cathedral Yard, Exeter, EX1 1HD
Tel no: (01392) 223638
www.michaelcaines.com
Modern European | £50
Cooking score: 5

This bright fixture on the Exeter scene, delivering 'exemplary standards . . . memorable in its excellence', faces the Gothic frontage of Exeter Cathedral. It's a stylish outpost of Michael Caines' inventive gastronomy, with large mirrors, bold floral prints and the spotlighting of well-spaced tables. Professional yet engaging service, precise cooking techniques and the harmonious combination of ingredients amply justify readers' compliments.

Beautifully fresh regional ingredients are treated with respect, allowing the main component to shine. Brixham scallops, accurately timed to produce a caramelised crust and succulent flesh, come dressed with a celeriac purée of 'exemplary smoothness' and a light soy and truffle vinaigrette. Gentle spicing in main courses – five-spice jus with Creedy Carver duck, smoked paprika with Old Spot pork, cinnamon jus with Dartmoor lamb – is well judged, enhancing without overwhelming. Desserts are equally accomplished, notably a well-flavoured hot pistachio soufflé and a trio of chocolate mousse, parfait and ice cream. A good-value set-lunch menu supplements the carte. House wines, from a select list, start at £23.95 a bottle (£6.25 a glass).
Chef/s: Ian Webber. **Open:** Mon to Sat L 12 to 2.30, D 6 to 9.45. **Closed:** Sun. **Meals:** alc (main courses £23 to £27). Set L £14.50 (2 courses) to £19.50. Set early D £15 (2 courses) to £20. Tasting menu £60. **Details:** 75 seats.

Exmouth

NEW ENTRY
Les Saveurs at the Seafood Restaurant
A neighbourhood bistro from TV award-winners
9 Tower Street, Exmouth, EX8 1NT
Tel no: (01395) 269459
www.lessaveurs.co.uk
French | £31
Cooking score: 2

Olivier and Sheila Guyard-Mulkerrin came up in the world in 2013, when they won Channel 5's *Kitchen Wars*. Their neighbourhood bistro is a rough-and-ready amalgam of whitewashed and bare-brick walls, exposed floorboards and smart table linen, the setting for some neatly presented French cooking with the emphasis on seafood. A bowl of Mediterranean fish soup is deliciously intense, served with assertively hot rouille, or you might start with tiger prawns flamed in Pernod and garlic and finished in white wine and cream. Cream plays a big part, but the dishes have balance, as in main-course fish

options such as cod with a deeply coloured sauce of lentils and chorizo, which comes on pillows of (good) mash. There are meat dishes too, with dauphinois, and puddings take in sizeable dishes of Eton mess and darkly caramelised tarte Tatin. Wines from £17.50.
Chef/s: Olivier Guyard-Mulkerrin. **Open:** Tue to Sat D only 7 to 10. **Closed:** Sun, Mon, 3 weeks Jan, 1 week Oct. **Meals:** alc (main courses £17 to £18). **Details:** 30 seats. Wheelchair access. Children over 10 yrs only.

Gittisham
Combe House
Seductive hotel with seriously good dining
Gittisham, EX14 3AD
Tel no: (01404) 540400
www.combehousedevon.com
Modern British | £52
Cooking score: 5
£5 OFF 🍴 🚗 V

A well-maintained Elizabethan manor in rolling grounds, Combe House has a working Victorian kitchen garden at its disposal. One reporter enjoys 'the feeling of entering a proper country house', with 'wonderful views of the Devon countryside'. A mural of these vistas decorates one of the dining rooms. The glorious interiors make an elegant setting for Hadleigh Barrett's sustainably sourced cooking: a celebration of locally grown and reared produce. Dishes exhibit a fine-tuned precision, with three-dimensional flavours and juxtapositions that make sense. Taste the Asian notes of salmon confit with mooli and pickled cucumber dressed in wasabi mayonnaise and soy, before zipping over to North Africa for Moroccan-spiced loin and shoulder of pork with salted lemon couscous, butternut squash purée and almonds, or back home for mutton suet pudding with crushed roots and kale. Desserts take in Devon honey cake with caramel banana and peanut-butter ice cream, and the cheeseboard displays some notable regional specimens. The wine list skims the vinous world's surface, netting some fine growers; prices start at £24 (£6.50 a standard glass).

Chef/s: Hadleigh Barrett. **Open:** all week L 12 to 2, D 7 to 9.30. **Closed:** 2 weeks Jan. **Meals:** Set L £29 (2 courses) to £33. Set D £52. Sun L £37. **Details:** 75 seats. Separate bar. Wheelchair access. Car parking.

Gulworthy
The Horn of Plenty
Ravishing views and confident cooking
Gulworthy, PL19 8JD
Tel no: (01822) 832528
www.thehornofplenty.co.uk
Modern British | £50
Cooking score: 4

£5
OFF

The Horn of Plenty is a classic country house hotel found on the edge of Dartmoor National Park with glorious views over the Tamar Valley – it makes a popular wedding venue. Within, well-appointed public rooms have a comfortable feel and staff create a welcoming atmosphere that's anything but uptight. In the kitchen, a clear sense of purpose is evident. Scott Paton's cooking is ambitious, from homemade breads via a demi-tasse of celeriac soup to petits fours with coffee, and he deftly combines local produce and a few luxuries with contemporary ideas. Foie gras textures (parfait, terrine, pan-seared) for example, comes with apple, vanilla and truffle salad, while John Dory is teamed with lime pickle and curry spices, and roast loin of Exmoor venison comes with parsnip textures and chocolate jus. Desserts could include chocolate orange with chestnut ice cream and espresso. Lunch is 'a real bargain', and wines start at £19.50.
Chef/s: Scott Paton. **Open:** all week L 12 to 3, D 7 to 11. **Meals:** Set L £19.50 (2 courses) to £24.50. Set D £49.50. **Details:** 40 seats. 20 seats outside. Separate bar. Wheelchair access. Car parking.

Honiton
The Holt
Honest pub food
178 High Street, Honiton, EX14 1LA
Tel no: (01404) 47707
www.theholt-honiton.com
Modern British | £26
Cooking score: 1

£30

The narrow ground-floor bar of this rustic inn contrasts with the low-ceilinged but bright first-floor dining room. Here, Angus McCaig's capable British cooking has a strong sense of seasonal cohesion and attracts loyal locals. Hearty beef casserole with crispy dumplings is a deserved favourite, but deft contemporary touches can be seen in starters of crispy squid with tiger prawns or rare beef carpaccio with celeriac rémoulade. Traditional desserts such as bread-and-butter pudding are well executed, too. A recent popular addition is the good-value tapas selection. Fine ales from the Otter brewery make an enjoyable alternative to wines (which start at £20).
Chef/s: Angus McCaig. **Open:** Tue to Sat L 12 to 2, D 6.30 to 9.30 (10 Fri and Sat). **Meals:** alc (main courses £14 to £17). **Details:** 50 seats. Separate bar. Wheelchair access.

Kings Nympton
The Grove Inn
Proper country inn with local food
Kings Nympton, EX37 9ST
Tel no: (01769) 580406
www.thegroveinn.co.uk
British | £23
Cooking score: 2

£5
OFF V £30

Over the past decade or so Deborah and Robert Smallbone have done a grand job in maintaining this thatched village pub in pretty countryside a few miles from South Molton. The beamed interior oozes character and is still reminiscent of a traditional watering hole, but the real emphasis is on things culinary. The menu is perfectly pitched to suit locals and tourists with its all-day breakfasts, ham, egg and chips and mixed grills, but optimum use of local and regional produce remains at the heart of things, so expect to see creamy north Devon fish pie, Somerset pig's cheeks braised in cider, and an all-Devon cheeseboard, too. Wines from £15. **Chef/s:** Deborah Smallbone. **Open:** Tue to Sun L 12 to 2 (3 Sun), Mon to Sat D 6.30 to 9. **Closed:** Mon (Sept to Mar), 25 Dec. **Meals:** alc (main courses £8 to £18). Sun L £9.40. **Details:** 28 seats. 20 seats outside. Separate bar. Wheelchair access.

Knowstone

The Masons Arms
Fine dining in a village pub
Knowstone, EX36 4RY
Tel no: (01398) 341231
www.masonsarmsdevon.co.uk
Modern British | £42
Cooking score: 5

The name suggests a pub, but the Masons Arms is more a restaurant with bar: albeit a traditional village bar with open fire, thick walls and local ales. It's the more modern dining room and its wildly painted ceiling – far removed from the pub atmosphere skilfully retained in the bar – that gives the place its 'split personality'. But the Dodsons have put their all into the hospitality and fabric of this 13th-century thatched pub and the result is very personal. Mark's impeccable Roux-trained background dictates his concise menu, which offers classic technique allied to great generosity. He flits from seared, peppered tuna with oriental salad to wood pigeon with curried Brussels sprout purée and stuffing as easily as he does from potato-crusted brill with scallops, delicate salmon-mousse sausage and cider-cream sauce to roulade of pork belly, braised red cabbage and apple compote. Home-baked breads shine, Devon and Somerset supply good farmhouse cheeses and desserts have included a first-class trio of mixed berry desserts. All this plus glorious Exmoor views, and wines from £15.

Chef/s: Mark Dodson. **Open:** Tue to Sun L 12 to 2, Tue to Sat D 7 to 9. **Closed:** Mon, first 10 days Jan, 10 days following Aug bank hol. **Meals:** alc (main courses £19 to £25). Set L £20 (2 courses) to £25. Sun L £35.50. **Details:** 28 seats. 22 seats outside. Separate bar. Car parking. Children 5 yrs and over only at D.

Lewdown

The Harris Arms
Robust country cooking
Portgate, Lewdown, EX20 4PZ
Tel no: (01566) 783331
www.theharrisarms.co.uk
Modern British | £25
Cooking score: 2
£5 OFF   £30

Just a few miles from the Devon/Cornwall border, this 16th-century inn was once part of the Harris family estate (hence the name), although Andy and Rowena Whiteman have made it their own since arriving in 2003. The views and the decked garden are big selling points here, but Andy's take on robust country cooking also attracts the punters. Expect the best of both counties when it comes to sourcing regional produce for the no-frills menu: think slow-cooked local pork cheeks with sweet potato and mushroom hash, beer-battered Cornish fish, Devon ribeye steak or Creedy Carver duck with plum sauce. West Country cheeses are a star turn, while puds might include warm treacle sponge. To drink, Devon ales and local cider compete with 100 knowledgeably chosen wines (from £18).

Chef/s: Andy Whiteman. **Open:** Tue to Sun L 12 to 2, Tue to Sat D 6.30 to 9. **Closed:** Mon, 24 to 26 Dec, 1 and 2 Jan. **Meals:** alc (main courses £10 to £19). Sun L £15 (2 courses) to £18. **Details:** 60 seats. 30 seats outside. Separate bar. Car parking.

Lewtrenchard Manor

Personable charm and fine seasonal food
Lewdown, EX20 4PN
Tel no: (01566) 783222
www.lewtrenchard.co.uk
Modern British | £50
new chef/no score

🛏 **V**

Logged as a 'royal manor' in the Domesday Book, this dreamy grey-stone house peeps out invitingly from its wooded Dartmoor hollow. The place exudes a civilised, personable charm: from the beautifully preserved gardens, flamboyant architecture and ornate interiors to the quiet attentions of the staff. As we were preparing for publication we learned of the departure of John Hooker, too late to arrange an inspection. He has been replaced by Matthew Peryer, who arrives from the Atlantic Hotel in Jersey. We're confident that he will maintain Lewtrenchard Manor's reputation for assured cooking, with dinner bringing out the big guns. Lewtrenchard has its own kitchen gardens and much depends on Devon supply lines: from tastings of beetroot, whipped goats' cheese and candied walnuts, to assiette of Devon lamb, dauphinoise potato and lamb jus. Prices on the efficiently constructed wine list start at £25.
Chef/s: Matthew Peryer. **Open:** all week L 12 to 2, D 7 to 9. **Meals:** Set L £19.50 (2 courses) to £24. Set D £49.50. **Details:** 50 seats. 15 seats outside. Separate bar. Wheelchair access. Car parking. Children over 8 yrs only at D.

▌Lifton

The Arundell Arms

Civilised sporting retreat
Fore Street, Lifton, PL16 0AA
Tel no: (01566) 784666
www.arundellarms.com
Modern British | £43
Cooking score: 4

£5 OFF 🛏

Just a stone's throw from Dartmoor, and considered one of England's major hotels for country sports and fly fishing (it has 20 miles of fishing rights), this rambling former coaching inn is a combination of rustic pub, bar and chandeliered dining room – all owned by the same family since the early 1960s. Steven Pidgeon's cooking continues to be led by local produce, which he uses to create a simple yet sophisticated repertoire of dishes with a predominantly British flavour. Thus, starters might feature herb-crusted Falmouth Bay scallops with celeriac purée, smoked bacon and a simple butter sauce, while main courses include medallions of 'Week St Mary' wild venison with garlic mash, lovely spicy red cabbage and glazed salsify. For dessert, honey pannacotta could arrive with a red wine poached pear and malt ice cream. The wine list is a well-annotated, drinker-friendly collection with bottles starting at £20.
Chef/s: Steven Pidgeon. **Open:** all week L 12 to 2, D 6 to 9.30. **Closed:** 24 Dec to 26 Dec. **Meals:** Set L £19 (2 courses) to £22.50. Set D £37 (2 courses) to £42.50. Sun L £21.50 (2 courses) to £26.
Details: 100 seats. 30 seats outside. Separate bar. Wheelchair access. Car parking.

Lydford

The Dartmoor Inn

Proper comforts and West Country produce
Moorside, Lydford, EX20 4AY
Tel no: (01822) 820221
www.dartmoorinn.com
Modern British | £30
Cooking score: 3

£5 OFF 🛏 V

Since taking over this sturdy old inn on the fringes of Dartmoor in 1998, Karen and Philip Burgess have transformed it into a cultured country retreat abundant with proper comforts and West Country produce. Pitch up at the convivial bar or settle into the elegant dining room for plates of Falmouth Bay scallops, Devon Ruby steaks or more highly worked themes such as black bream fillet with shellfish risotto and crab bisque sauce. Meaty ideas work particularly well, judging by glowing reports of 'unbelievably good' slow-cooked beef short-rib with pickled walnut dressing and 'perfectly pink' roast rack of lamb. Desserts might include excellent vanilla pannacotta with rhubarb jelly. The whole show is personally driven by the owners, with help from a bevy of zippy staff who get top marks for their friendliness and professionalism. West Country ales vie with a thoughtfully assembled choice of wines from £16.50 (£4.50 a glass).
Chef/s: Andrew Honey and Philip Burgess. **Open:** Tue to Sun L 12 to 2.30 (3 Sat and Sun), Mon to Sat D 6 to 10. **Meals:** alc (main courses £13 to £25). Set L and D £15.75 (2 courses) to £19.50. Sun L £23.95. **Details:** 65 seats. 25 seats outside. Separate bar. Car parking.

Symbols

🛏 Accommodation is available

£30 Three courses for less than £30

V Separate vegetarian menu

£5 OFF £5-off voucher scheme

🍾 Notable wine list

Newton Poppleford

Moores'

Ticking all the right boxes
6 Greenbank, High Street, Newton Poppleford, EX10 0EB
Tel no: (01395) 568100
www.mooresrestaurant.co.uk
Modern British | £29
Cooking score: 1

£5 OFF 🛏 £30

The Moores' comfortingly homely restaurant-with-rooms commands great loyalty: 'very welcoming' notes one fan; 'everything was excellent' reports another. Jonathan Moore's cooking is rigorously seasonal, and impeccably sourced produce is a high priority – Brixham pollack, Devon-reared meats, seasonal game and West Country cheeses. Readers relish everything they are offered, from grilled local lemon sole fillets teamed with wild rocket and lemon vinaigrette, and confit leg of organic Creedy Carver duck enlivened by black pudding ravioli, braised red cabbage and celeriac purée, to apple frangipane tart with clotted cream and raspberry coulis. A wallet-friendly, well-annotated wine list starts at £13.95.
Chef/s: Jonathan Moore. **Open:** Tue to Sun L 12 to 1.30, Tue to Sat D 7 to 9.30. **Closed:** Mon, 2 weeks Jan. **Meals:** Set L £15.95 (2 courses) to £21.90. Set D £18.95 (2 courses) to £28.95. **Details:** 32 seats. 12 seats outside. Wheelchair access.

Plymouth

NEW ENTRY

Rock Salt

All things to all comers, run with good cheer
31 Stonehouse Street, Plymouth, PL1 3PE
Tel no: (01752) 225522
www.rocksaltcafe.co.uk
Modern British | £28
Cooking score: 2

£30

An all-things-to-all-comers operation on Plymouth's frankly unlovely western flank, Rock Salt efficiently caters for breakfasters, sandwich lunchers, Sunday-roasters and adventurous modern brasserie diners – all in a pint-sized corner site run with bustling good cheer. Dave Jenkins is a South-East Asian aficionado, so there are laksas, Thai and Vietnamese dishes among the steaks, fish and chips and burgers. The brasserie menu might begin with a light, refreshing assemblage of cured salmon, breadcrumbed mussels and wasabi sorbet, adorned with peanuts, lemon zest and crème fraîche. Mains could encompass stone bass in bouillabaisse nage with a deep-fried langoustine, or uncrackled pork belly with creamed cabbage and bacon and an intense, copper-coloured jus. Finish with chocolate fondant and popcorn ice cream or pistachio crème brûlée with fromage blanc sorbet and little doughnuts. Wines from £13.95.

Chef/s: David Jenkins. **Open:** Tue to Sat 8am to 9.30pm (10am Tue), Sun L 10 to 4. **Closed:** Mon, 1 week Jan. **Meals:** alc (main courses £10 to £20). **Details:** 45 seats.

Tanners
Contemporary cooking in an ancient setting
Prysten House, Finewell Street, Plymouth, PL1 2AE
Tel no: (01752) 252001
www.tannersrestaurant.co.uk
Modern British | £37
Cooking score: 3

The venerable stone walls of Plymouth's oldest domestic building (dating from the reign of Henry VII) make a grand setting for an informal modern eatery, with regal purple drapes adding a dashing note. The cooking is contemporary British in style, built on a foundation of high-quality south-western produce. Creedy Carver duck liver parfait with rhubarb and crunchy granola, or salmon tartare cured in whisky and brown sugar might get the show on the road. For mains, the boats at Looe provide such bounty as lemon sole with mussels, clams and sea greens, while Bodmin venison appears as the loin cut, with a potato galette, cavolo nero and tarka dhal. To finish, Valrhona chocolate comes in no fewer

than seven (count 'em) textures, or there could be lighter yoghurt pannacotta with pineapple. Regional cheeses are treated with respect, and an enterprising wine list has been carefully compiled, with prices from £17.95.

Chef/s: Martyn Compton, Chris and James Tanner. **Open:** Tue to Sat L 12 to 2.30, D 7 to 9.30. **Closed:** Sun, Mon, 24 to 31 Dec, first week Jan. **Meals:** alc (main courses £20 to £24). Set L £14 (2 courses) to £17. Set D £17 (2 courses) to £20. Tasting menu £55 (6 courses). **Details:** 60 seats. 50 seats outside. Wheelchair access.

ALSO RECOMMENDED
▲ Lemon Tree Café & Bistro
2 Haye Road South, Elburton, Plymouth, PL9 8HJ
Tel no: (01752) 481117
www.lemontreecafe.co.uk
Modern European

'A charming ambience and superb food' is one verdict on this small, family-run café close to Plymouth and the South Hams. Many friends have been won by the 'honest good-value dishes', from 'old favourites' croque monsieur/madame to the more substantial lamb and barley stew (£7.95) and pan-fried lemon sole fillets with new potatoes and courgette (£8.50). Finish with 'light as a feather' sticky toffee pudding. Wines from £13.95. Open Tue to Sat L, Mon to Sat D for private parties of 10 or more.

▌Rockbeare
The Jack in the Green
Roadside pub run with voluble warmth
London Road, Rockbeare, EX5 2EE
Tel no: (01404) 822240
www.jackinthegreen.uk.com
Modern British | £33
Cooking score: 1
£5 OFF V

About 15 minutes' drive from Exeter, the Jack has the trappings of a country pub – roughcast walls, pictures of pastoral scenes and several interlinked rooms – but one that's geared to accommodate the copious local business it attracts. Local suppliers are highlighted; choose dishes marked in bold on the menu and you'll be eating Devon all the way. Tender locally cured bresaola arrives with celeriac rémoulade and pickled walnuts, while *de rigueur* homemade Scotch egg is made with black pudding. Sensitively timed fish for main might be crisp-skinned sea bass with mushroom and leek fondue and chicken stock reduction. Wines start at £16.

Chef/s: Matthew Mason. **Open:** Mon to Sat L 12 to 2, D 6 to 9 (9.30 Fri and Sat). Sun 12 to 9. **Closed:** 25 Dec to 4 Jan. **Meals:** alc (main courses £19 to £26). Set D £25. Sun L £20 (2 courses) to £25. **Details:** 100 seats. 100 seats outside. Separate bar. Wheelchair access. Car parking.

◼ Salcombe
South Sands Beachside Restaurant
Seafood that's well worth seeking out
Bolt Head, Salcombe, TQ8 8LL
Tel no: (01548) 845900
www.southsands.com
Seafood | £35
Cooking score: 2
🛏

The hotel is a tantalisingly accurate homage to the New England style, its Beachside Restaurant overlooking a secluded inlet at Devon's southern tip. The dining room is airy and spacious, done in seashell colours and with fantastically cool staff. Stuart Downie's seafood-led menu plays it cool, too, with simple preparations of ringingly fresh marine life. A crayfish cocktail with pineapple salsa and wasabi mayo, or tempura soft-shell crab, might set things off, before mains of Fowey lobster in garlic butter with chunky chips, or turbot in béarnaise, turn up. There are meat dishes for the non-participants, and tempting puddings such as pistachio cake with cherry compote and goats' cheese cream. A sophisticated drinks list name-checks all the trending spirit brands, and wines start at £18, or £5 a glass.

Chef/s: Stuart Downie. **Open:** all week L 12 to 3, D 6 to 9.30. **Meals:** alc (main courses £15 to £30). Set L and D £17.95 (2 courses) to £22.95. Sun L £20 (2 courses) to £25. **Details:** 75 seats. 35 seats outside. Separate bar. Wheelchair access. Car parking.

◼ Shaldon
Ode Dining
Dazzling combinations from an organic champion
21 Fore Street, Shaldon, TQ14 0DE
Tel no: (01626) 873977
www.odetruefood.co.uk
Modern British | £40
Cooking score: 5
£5 OFF

Tim and Clare Bouget set up camp in a three-storey Georgian town house on the east Devon coast in 2006, and have won devotees for cooking that celebrates regional produce and maintains stringent ethical standards. Tim's resourceful repertoire draws on European and Asian techniques in the contemporary British manner. An evocatively North African-inspired fish starter might see cumin-crusted pollack teamed with smoked aubergine and cracked wheat in coriander oil, while a straightforwardly French approach produces pork liver terrine with red onion marmalade and homemade brioche. Steamed pak choi, egg noodles and soy-ginger sauce give an apt Chinese accent to seared sea bass, but local meats receive relatively mainstream treatments. Hence fabulous organic beef arrives with field mushrooms, roast garlic and shallots in red wine, while fallow deer is partnered by Jerusalem artichoke purée and kale. Desserts speak a whole new language, incorporating 'torched mallow', 'set pear' or perhaps a plum crumble tartlet with ginger-beer jelly and almond ice cream. Local cheeses come with honeycomb. A short, carefully chosen wine list of organics and biodynamics opens at £18 for a La Mancha Chardonnay.

Chef/s: Tim Bouget. **Open:** Wed to Sat D only 7 to 9.30. **Closed:** Sun to Tue, 2 weeks Oct, bank hols. **Meals:** Set D £35 (2 courses) to £40. **Details:** 24 seats. No children after 8 in restaurant.

Sidford

The Salty Monk

Industrious cooking and personal hospitality
Church Street, Sidford, EX10 9QP
Tel no: (01395) 513174
www.saltymonk.co.uk
Modern British | £43
Cooking score: 3

£5 OFF 🍽 V

On the main A-road through the village, the Witheridges' classy restaurant-with-rooms was once a storage depot for the salt traded by Exeter Cathedral. An attractive dining room looking over the gardens at the back is open evenings and Sunday lunches only, with a small bar fronting the operation at other times. Andy Witheridge's cooking has a hint of the old school about it, overlaid with a few modern touches. Layered fish mousses come with seared scallops in saffron foam, while main might be beef fillet on garlicky pasta with creamy mustard sauce. A summer lunch produced local asparagus thickly bandaged in smoked salmon with lemon cream, and then fillets of carefully timed silver mullet with a mini-turret of veg on a rösti base. Finish with chocolate brownie and mango compote. A decent little wine list opens at £16.
Chef/s: Andy Witheridge. **Open:** Thur to Sun L 12 to 1.30, all week D 6.30 to 9. **Closed:** Jan, 1 week Nov. **Meals:** Set L £25. Set D £42.50. Sun L £27.50. **Details:** 36 seats. 22 seats outside. Separate bar. Wheelchair access. Car parking.

South Pool

The Millbrook Inn

French food in a proper village pub
South Pool, TQ7 2RW
Tel no: (01548) 531581
www.millbrookinnsouthpool.co.uk
French | £35
Cooking score: 2

£5 OFF

With owners who are 'born to host', a divine setting by the Salcombe estuary, roaring fires, 'amazing gins' and Devon ales on tap, this cosy 17th-century village boozer seems to have it all. The Milbrook may be hailed as the 'best of English pubs', but the kitchen deals in French bourgeois food of the old school – think snails in garlicky Pernod butter, pan-fried duck foie gras, bowls of 'incredibly rich' bouillabaisse, petit salé, pot au feu and spectacular chocolate fondant. Game birds are also worth ordering, likewise the assiette of rabbit and the locally landed fish (perhaps seared brill with saffron mash). The short international wine list has house French from £15.50, but don't miss the brilliant Bloody Marys.
Chef/s: Jean-Philippe Bidart. **Open:** all week L 12 to 2 (3 Sun), D 7 to 9. **Meals:** alc (main courses £13 to £20). Set L £10 (2 courses) to £12. Sun L £16. **Details:** 40 seats. 40 seats outside. Wheelchair access.

Sparkwell

NEW ENTRY

The Treby Arms

Fine dining in a village pub from a MasterChef winner
Sparkwell, PL7 5DD
Tel no: (01752) 837363
www.thetrebyarms.co.uk
Modern British | £35
Cooking score: 4

This 'old-fashioned local boozer' is a work in progress for Anton Piotrowski, the 2012 winner of *MasterChef: The Professionals*. The Treby Arms was 'in the throes of transformation' at the time of inspection – the intention being to keep the feel of a village pub, retaining the original fireplace and wooden beams and continuing to welcome dogs in the small bar. Despite the upheaval, readers have been full of praise for the 'fantastic experience'. There's no doubting the quality or freshness of supplies (mostly from Devon). To start you'll usually find a soup based on 'what Dad got from the garden', or an assembly of hand-dived scallops, belly pork, pickled cockles and butternut squash purée. Next come mains of roast monkfish, brown shrimps and mussels, caper mash and malt vinegar crumble, or Cajun-spiced lamb rump with sweet potato purée. Invention is evident everywhere, and while presentation can be 'often quirky', this is certainly genuine cooking. Wines from £13.95.

Chef/s: Anton Piotrowski. **Open:** Tue to Sun L 12 to 2, D 6 to 9 (5.30 to 7.45 Sun). **Closed:** Mon. **Meals:** alc (main courses £13 to £26). Set L £16. Sun L £18. **Details:** 65 seats. 14 seats outside. Separate bar. Wheelchair access. Car parking.

Topsham
La Petite Maison
Engaging 'auberge' with assured cooking
35 Fore Street, Topsham, EX3 0HR
Tel no: (01392) 873660
www.lapetitemaison.co.uk
Modern European | £39
Cooking score: 4
£5
OFF

The Pestells' neighbourhood restaurant is on a bend in the hair-raising one-way street running through Topsham. A shop conversion has become two irregularly shaped rooms painted in bright white, hung with discreet pictures and furnished with smartly dressed tables. Elizabeth runs the front-of-house with warm, chatty aplomb, while Douglas cooks a menu of locally based ingredients in various European idioms. Starter might be a risotto of Lyme Bay crab topped with a fat king prawn and moated with creamy shellfish bisque, or a hearty, sustaining butternut squash and rosemary soup. Mains encompass breast and confit leg of Creedy Carver duck with caramelised kumquat and dauphinois, sauced with Cointreau; sea bass, monkfish and a scallop with vegetable 'spaghetti' in dill beurre blanc; or perhaps a fine tart of caramelised red onion, cherry tomato and Sweet Charlotte cheese. Puddings such as chocolate mousse cake with pecans will please the crowds. Decent wines start at £18, or £4.50 a glass.

Chef/s: Douglas Pestell and Sarah Bright. **Open:** Tue to Sat L 12.30 to 2, D 7 to 9.30. **Closed:** Sun, Mon. **Meals:** Set L and D £32.95 (2 courses) to £38.95. **Details:** 28 seats.

Torquay
The Elephant
Torquay's classiest destination
3-4 Beacon Terrace, Torquay, TQ1 2BH
Tel no: (01803) 200044
www.elephantrestaurant.co.uk
Modern British | £70
Cooking score: 5
£5
OFF

A gastronomic jumbo of two halves, the Elephant is situated by Torquay harbour front, with views over the sea and marina contributing to its status as the town's classiest destination. The ground floor is occupied by a brasserie serving snazzy dishes such as moules marinière, pulled pork burgers or slow-roasted onion tart, but chef/proprietor Simon Hulstone earns his rating in the upstairs Room, a smart space furnished with big mirrors, polished floorboards and antique lights. In the evening, this is the setting for an extended tasting menu full of sophisticated thrills. West Country produce, herbs and seaside flavours come together in a procession of little dishes that look as good as they sound: how about Devon scallops with sorrel, apple and Nepalese pepper, or skate with lovage, asparagus and sage buds? Away from the coast, quail might be paired with beetroot, verjus and radish shoots, while fallow deer sits well with garlic, capers and celeriac ash. For a fashionable sweet/savoury finish, try 'chocolate, malt, stout, coriander and nuts' or classic tarte Tatin upgraded with soy and apple brandy. The keenly priced wine list offers decent drinking from £17.50.

Chef/s: Simon Hulstone. **Open:** Tue to Sat L 12 to 2, D 6.30 to 9. **Closed:** Sun, Mon, first 2 weeks Jan. **Meals:** alc (main courses £17 to 24). Set L £16.95 (2 courses) to £19.95. Tasting menu £69.95 (10 courses). **Details:** 75 seats. Separate bar. Children in brasserie only.

ALSO RECOMMENDED
▲ The Orange Tree

14-16 Parkhill Road, Torquay, TQ1 2AL
Tel no: (01803) 213936
www.orangetreerestaurant.co.uk
Modern European

Tucked down a narrow backstreet near the harbour, the Orange Tree is a linen-clad, low-lit neighbourhood restaurant offering a broad repertoire of modern British cooking. Ambition shines in dishes such as gilthead bream and pancetta on leek fondue with grain-mustard vinaigrette (£7.50) and roast venison loin crusted in pumpkin seeds and peppercorns, with chestnut purée and wild cranberries (£19.50). Boozy sorbets feature as intermediate courses or desserts, the latter also including tiramisu with hazelnut praline and blood orange (£7). Wines from £16.50. Open Tue–Sat D.

■ Virginstow
Percy's

Excellent cooking in an alluring setting
Coombeshead Estate, Virginstow, EX21 5EA
Tel no: (01409) 211236
www.percys.co.uk
Modern British | £40
Cooking score: 4

Lauded as the 'place to get away from it all', the Bricknell-Webb's Devon retreat has been chugging along personably for almost two decades. Visitors love everything about it, from the extensive estate populated by horses, sheep, pigs and dogs to the old house where wood-burning stoves add warmth to the atmosphere. Local ingredients power Tina Bricknell-Webb's kitchen – many of them provided by the estate. These are worked into fixed-price, limited choice menus that change daily. Wild mushroom and pork liver parfait with sage toast, marrow, bean and onion chutney, and fillet of cod in tarragon and spring onion batter are typical of the plain-speaking style. Meat choice is often home-reared organic lamb, cooked pink and served with rosemary jus. Desserts are spot-on, and might feature white chocolate and cardamom pannacotta with mixed berries and blackcurrant coulis. Tony Bricknell-Webb can be relied upon to supply just the right bottle of wine (from £20).
Chef/s: Tina Bricknell-Webb. **Open:** all week D only 7 to 8.30. **Meals:** Set D £40. **Details:** 20 seats. Separate bar. Wheelchair access. Car parking. Children 12 yrs and over only.

■ Yelverton
READERS RECOMMEND
Prince Hall Hotel

British
Yelverton, PL20 6SA
Tel no: (01822) 890403
www.princehall.co.uk
'Situated in a glorious position on Dartmoor with stunning views. The food is exceptionally tasty as well as very reasonably priced.'

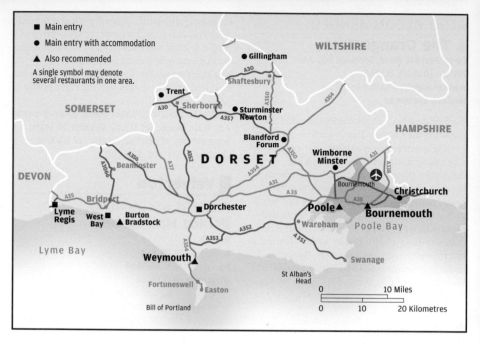

- ■ Main entry
- ● Main entry with accommodation
- ▲ Also recommended

A single symbol may denote several restaurants in one area.

▌Blandford Forum

Castleman Hotel

Hospitable dower-house hideaway
Chettle, Blandford Forum, DT11 8DB
Tel no: (01258) 830096
www.castlemanhotel.co.uk
Modern British | £26
Cooking score: 2

£5 OFF 🍴 £30

Occupying the former dower house in the Cranborne Chase village of Chettle, the Castleman is an idyllically located country restaurant-with-rooms with its own kitchen garden. Under an intricately moulded plasterwork ceiling, diners can set about a comforting menu of modern classics, starting perhaps with game terrine, celeriac rémoulade and pumpkin chutney, before main-course scallops with pancetta, dressed in garlic, basil and olive oil, or braised beef feather blade with parsnip mash and Puy lentils in red wine. The game season might bring on woodcock, served with bacon and potato rösti. Desserts take in lemon posset with rhubarb compote and shortbread, and there are classy regional cheeses. Half a dozen house wines are uniformly fairly priced at £14, or £3.50 a glass.
Chef/s: Barbara Garnsworthy and Richard Morris. **Open:** Sun L 12 to 2, all week D 7 to 9. **Closed:** 25, 26 and 31 Dec, Feb. **Meals:** alc (main courses £12 to £22). Sun L £24. **Details:** 45 seats. Separate bar. Wheelchair access.

▌Bournemouth

ALSO RECOMMENDED
▲ Koh Thai Tapas

Daimler House, 38-40 Poole Hil, Bournemouth, BH2 5PS
Tel no: (01202) 294723
www.koh-thai.co.uk
Thai

'It's a wonderfully relaxed atmosphere that somehow still manages to achieve a touch of glam,' noted a fan of this smart Thai restaurant, which continues to serve 'well-flavoured, unpretentious food'. Choose from a selection of tapas-sized plates, perhaps 24-hour pork ribs (£6.95), dim sum, chicken satay or Thai sliced crispy beef; other dishes come as main-course or tapas-sized, as in the popular massaman lamb curry (£5.95/£9.95). Look out, too, for fragrant soups, spicy salads and stir-fries. Wines from £14.95. Closed Mon L.

▲ The Print Room

Richmond Hill, Bournemouth, BH2 6HH
Tel no: (01202) 789669
www.theprintroom-bournemouth.co.uk
Modern European

The press room in the former *Daily Echo* building is the setting for this grand bar-cum-brasserie. Decorated in Art Deco style, with a lofty ceiling, vast arched windows and stunning crystal chandeliers, it offers a choice of banquette and intimate booth seating, plus a lengthy, please-all menu. Grills, sharing platters, salads and 'Print Room classics' sit alongside salt-and-pepper squid with chilli and rocket (£7.50), monkfish and king prawn red Thai fish curry (£14.95), and vanilla rice pudding (£5.50). House wine £16. Closed Sun.

▲ WestBeach

Pier Approach, Bournemouth, BH2 5AA
Tel no: (01202) 587785
www.west-beach.co.uk
Seafood

WestBeach is a relaxed and contemporary brasserie that buzzes from breakfast to dinner. The location is a 'priceless spot', so close to the sand and sea, with tables on the decked terrace the best place to enjoy the stunning views across Poole Bay. Interesting blackboard specials highlight local fish and seafood, perhaps brill fingers with gribiche (£7.50) and turbot with saffron potatoes, braised fennel, samphire, mussels and lobster bisque (£19), with ribeye steak, hand-cut chips and peppercorn sauce (£19.90) a perennial favourite. House wine £16.95. Open all week 9am to 10pm.

▌Burton Bradstock

ALSO RECOMMENDED
▲ Hive Beach Café

Beach Road, Burton Bradstock, DT6 4RF
Tel no: (01308) 897070
www.hivebeachcafe.co.uk
Seafood

The crowning glory of this beach-side fixture is a vast terrace well equipped to deal with the vagaries of the British weather. Casual – order at the bar, wait for your number to be called – the idea is that people can pop in for breakfast, for a West Country ham sandwich or a jacket potato filled with Weymouth crab (£10.95). Alternatively, settle down to a lunch of fresh local fish, say John Dory with new potatoes and salad (£16.95) or a hot shellfish platter. Wines from £12.80. Open all week, D in summer months only.

▌Christchurch

The Jetty

Slick new harbourside restaurant
Christchurch Harbour Hotel & Spa, 95 Mudeford, Christchurch, BH23 3NT
Tel no: (01202) 400950
www.thejetty.co.uk
Modern British | £35
Cooking score: 4
£5 OFF

'Beautiful even on a rainy day', the harbourside location of this contemporary 'gem' means views over rippling water to Mudeford Quay. Readers love the consistency of 'impeccable' service and chef Alex Aitken's 'exquisite' dishes. There's a strong seafood bent, though not to the exclusion of game in season. Readers have enjoyed the Weymouth scallops with cured pork and pea purée and a house signature trio of potted crab, shrimps and mackerel. To follow, duck breast is paired with squid stuffed with confit leg, and a duo of lamb comes with a mini shepherd's pie topped with buttery mash; there's a bit of offbeat cheek about a side dish of 'froggy' peas with bacon and lettuce. Pudding might be a passion fruit soufflé with matching sauce, or crunchy peanut-butter parfait with salted caramel and sesame thins. Wine costs from £17.95.

Chef/s: Alex Aitken. **Open:** Mon to Sat L 12 to 2.30, D 6.30 to 10 (6 Fri and Sat). Sun 12 to 8. **Closed:** 2 and 3 Jan. **Meals:** alc (main courses £16 to £29). Set L and D £17.95 (2 courses) to £21.95. Sun L £28.50. **Details:** 70 seats. 30 seats outside. Wheelchair access. Car parking.

▌Dorchester

Sienna

Tiny restaurant with big ideas
36 High West Street, Dorchester, DT1 1UP
Tel no: (01305) 250022
www.siennarestaurant.co.uk
Modern British | £45
Cooking score: 4

The Browns can feel proud at having transformed Dorchester's dining scene over the past decade. An unassuming converted shop on the high street, Sienna seats just 15, which certainly helps the kitchen keep its eye on the ball. West Country produce spills forth from the concise fixed-price menus, generously loading a spaghetti starter with lobster, courgette, tomato and crème fraîche. In contrast, mains occasionally look north for Goosnargh duck with leek and mushroom crumble and caramelised quince in thyme jus. Fish is handled dexterously, so roast cod might be teamed with creamed cabbage and bacon in a red wine reduction, while vegetarian butternut and sage risotto comes with an apposite salad of Taleggio, pumpkin seeds and watercress. Expect textural fireworks for dessert, when golden syrup and mascarpone mousse is offset by gingerbread crumb, lemon curd and lemon granita. Good breads and a modern miscellany of wines, from £20.25, provide accompaniment.

Chef/s: Russell Brown. **Open:** Wed to Sat L 12.30 to 2, Tue to Sat D 7 to 9. **Closed:** Sun, Mon, 2 weeks spring, 2 weeks autumn. **Meals:** Set L £26.50 (2 courses) to £29.50. Set D £38.50 (2 courses) to £45. Tasting menu £60 (7 courses). **Details:** 15 seats. Children over 12 yrs only.

▌Gillingham

Stock Hill House

Still flying the Austrian flag
Stock Hill, Gillingham, SP8 5NR
Tel no: (01747) 823626
www.stockhillhouse.co.uk
European | £40
Cooking score: 5

☞ V

Austrian-born Peter Hauser and his wife recently clocked up 27 years as caring custodians of this restful Victorian domicile reached via a meandering beech-lined drive. Chintz meets unshowy affluence in the grand dining room (think pink powder-puff colours, drapes and plush upholstery), while the cooking seems to evoke happier times past. 'Food is the only beautiful thing that nourishes', intones Peter on his menu, which flags up dishes from his homeland among a motley crew of 'high-quality', thoughtfully executed European staples. The Austrian cause is championed by the likes of flamed mackerel with cucumber salad, fennel and horseradish or seared loin of pork with paprika cream, while 'remarkably tender' poached Gressingham duck leg with green peppercorn sauce or red bream fillet dressed with a ragoût of Cornish squid, tomato and olive oil represent the other camp. Unsurprisingly, meals end strongly with Viennese patisserie in the shape of Linzer torte, apple flan topped with crème brûlée or dark chocolate and sour cherry gâteau. Big-name Austrians also stake a minor claim on the predominantly French wine list; house selections start at £24.95.

Chef/s: Peter Hauser and Lorna Connor. **Open:** all week L 12.15 to 1.45, D 7.15 to 8.45. **Meals:** Set L £19.50 (2 courses) to £26. Set D £40. Sun L £22.50 (2 courses) to £27.50. **Details:** 24 seats. 8 seats outside. Car parking.

Lyme Regis

Hix Oyster & Fish House

Marine cuisine and swoon-inducing views
Cobb Road, Lyme Regis, DT7 3JP
Tel no: (01297) 446910
www.hixoysterandfishhouse.co.uk
Seafood | £30
Cooking score: 2
V

Overlooking the harbour on one of the more breathtaking stretches of the Jurassic Coast, the Dorset arm of Mark Hix's network of seafood-based restaurants is the most scenically sited. Enjoy the views from an outdoor terrace while you set about native oysters on chervil mayo, cider-cured herrings in a sauce of Somerset's Kingston Black, prawn and butternut curry, or red gurnard with mussels and sea beet. Food is demonstrably fresh and mostly accurately cooked, although grumbles have surfaced with regard to the simpler dishes. Burned fish fingers with forgettable mushy peas are some way off their comfort-food mark. South-western cheeses should be a banker, if you're not in the market for apple fritters with gingerbread ice cream. Wines on the main list start at £20.50, with little glasses from £5.25. **Chef/s:** Lin Pidsley. **Open:** all week 12 to 10. **Closed:** Mon (Jan and Feb only), 25 and 26 Dec. **Meals:** alc (main courses £15 to £25). **Details:** 45 seats. 25 seats outside. Wheelchair access.

Poole

ALSO RECOMMENDED
▲ Guildhall Tavern

15 Market Street, Poole, BH15 1NB
Tel no: (01202) 671717
www.guildhalltavern.co.uk
French

'With a distinct French feel to the décor and French staff, you could think you were in France rather than Poole.' Thus noted one visitor to this former corner pub in Poole's Old Town, pleased he had nabbed the last table on a Tuesday lunchtime (booking advisable). The draw remains Frederic Seweryn's traditional 'and generous' French cooking of locally caught fish and seafood: typically, classic crab soup (£6.95) followed by sea bass flambéed with Pernod (£21.95). The set-lunch menu is good value at £14/£16.50 for two/three courses. Wines from £15.50. Open Tue to Sat.

Sturminster Newton

Plumber Manor

'What eating out in England should be'
Sturminster Newton, DT10 2AF
Tel no: (01258) 472507
www.plumbermanor.com
Anglo-French | £36
Cooking score: 2

The Prideaux-Brunes of Dorset built Plumber Manor in the early Stuart period and still run the place, though as a hotel these days. There's staying power for you. In an atmosphere of gracious country-house splendour, where swagged curtains frame the lovely garden views, Brian's thoughtfully conceived classic Anglo-French cooking brings on a shellfish trio (lobster, prawns and brown shrimps) to start, perhaps followed by guinea fowl on a bed of black-pudding bubble and squeak, or salmon in an eastern-influenced soy and ginger sauce. Finish with New York vanilla cheesecake. The French-based wine list opens at £17.50 and contains several half-bottles as well as one or two from Dorset. **Chef/s:** Brian Prideaux-Brune. **Open:** Sun L 12 to 2, all week D 7.30 to 9. **Closed:** Feb. **Meals:** Set D £29 (2 courses) to £36. Sun L £28. **Details:** 60 seats. Separate bar. Wheelchair access. Car parking.

Symbols

🛏 Accommodation is available

£30 Three courses for less than £30

V Separate vegetarian menu

£5 OFF £5-off voucher scheme

🍷 Notable wine list

Trent

The Rose & Crown
Rustic-thatched pub with adventurous food
Trent, DT9 4SL
Tel no: (01935) 850776
www.roseandcrowntrent.co.uk
Modern British | £26
Cooking score: 2

🍴 V £30

In a setting of rug-strewn stone floors, winter fires and old beams, Marcus Wilcox has been wowing locals and visitors with adventurous ingredients and flavour-combinations. Indeed, full-throated praise has come from a reader who, from the short dinner menu, enjoyed cod cheeks with shiitake mushroom, almonds, lemon jelly and tomato essence, ahead of duck breast with duck-leg hash, charred pineapple, roast cashews and orange jus, then an astounding Jaffa cake with hot chocolate fondant, orange curd and honeycomb. Elsewhere, this 'tucked away', rustic-thatched pub-with-rooms offers serene views across rolling countryside, best enjoyed from the terrace while tucking into lunchtime pub classics such as Scotch egg, fish stew, and ham, egg and chips. House wine from £14.95.
Chef/s: Marcus Wilcox. **Open:** all week L 12 to 3, D 6 to 9 (12 to 9 Sat). **Meals:** alc (main courses £10 to £22). **Details:** 65 seats. 45 seats outside. Separate bar. Wheelchair access. Car parking.

West Bay

Riverside Restaurant
Long-running favourite with heart-warming seafood
West Bay, DT6 4EZ
Tel no: (01308) 422011
www.thefishrestaurant-westbay.co.uk
Seafood | £39
Cooking score: 3

£5 OFF

'Customers are welcome to choose several starters if they so wish', states the menu at the Watsons' long-established restaurant, admirably demonstrating the flexibility of this waterside operation. Family-run and friendly, the approach has barely changed since the Riverside opened in 1960. Wide-ranging menus deal in locally landed fish and shellfish presented in an uncomplicated manner. Expect fishy classics, anything from a bowl of mussels or dressed crab, via salmon with hollandaise sauce, to dishes with a more lively global approach, say Szechuan-peppered sprats with saffron mayonnaise or baked brill fillet with Puy lentils, picante chorizo and char-grilled red peppers. Seafood platters are another option. To finish, there are tantalising desserts such as chocolate torte with beetroot syrup, candied baby beetroot and crème légère. A fish-friendly wine list starts at £13.75.
Chef/s: Tony Shaw. **Open:** Tue to Sun L 12 to 2.30, Tue to Sat D 6.30 to 9 (8.30 Tue and Wed). **Closed:** Mon, 2 Dec to 14 Feb. **Meals:** alc (main courses £13 to £30). Set L £19.55 (2 courses) to £26.50. **Details:** 80 seats. 25 seats outside. Separate bar. Wheelchair access.

Weymouth

ALSO RECOMMENDED
▲ Crab House Café
Ferryman's Way, Portland Road, Weymouth, DT4 9YU
Tel no: (01305) 788867
www.crabhousecafe.co.uk
Seafood

The wooden shack may be simple, but there are two great luxuries at this casual cafe: the sandy setting, overlooking Chesil beach, and an abundance of Dorset seafood including oysters from the owners' own beds. The catch dictates the menu, with fish piled high by the open kitchen. The crab's the thing (bash messily at a whole one for £19.25), book-ended perhaps by smoked mullet with Caesar salad (£6.50) and local cheese. House wine is from £14.50. Closed Tue and mid-Dec to Feb.

Wimborne

NEW ENTRY

Rock

Deep Dorset flavours
23 West Street, Wimborne, BH21 1JS
Tel no: (01202) 840700
www.rockrestaurants.co.uk
Modern British | £29
Cooking score: 3

🛏 £30

Rock is a sensitively renovated 17th-century building turned restaurant-with-rooms, with a distinct country-house feel to the bar and dining areas. In the kitchen, Victor Ferreira brings a lively sense of modernist ambition, taking his cue from the land and sea and exploiting ample local resources. Reporters speak of depths of flavour that linger in the memory – an intense wild mushroom soup for example, or a tender shank of spring lamb infused with the heady fragrance of rosemary. British classics such as handmade faggots, potato mash and red onion gravy are equally well executed. For dessert, sorbets, ice creams and hot chocolate fondant ('a model of its kind') hold most allure. Young, well-managed service is efficient and well informed, and the wine list starts at £16.50. A sister restaurant, Rock Westbourne, headed by former Chewton Glen chef Nick Atkins, is at Landseer Road, Westbourne, Dorset, BH4 9EH; tel (01202) 765696.

Chef/s: Victor Ferreira. **Open:** all week L 12 to 2, Mon to Sat D 6 to 10. **Closed:** 25 and 26 Dec.
Meals: alc (main courses £11 to £19). Sun L £25.
Details: 60 seats. 20 seats outside. Separate bar.

🍴 ONE-HIT WONDERS

Single-concept restaurants appear to be on every corner in Japan (ramen, sushi) and now eateries focusing on an individual dish or ingredient are popping up all over Britain (burgers, hotdogs, roast chicken). What they sell is usually made well, often in several different ways, with first-rate materials and maybe one or two side dishes. But menu options are limited, there's usually a no-booking policy and the unmistakable message is 'take it or leave it'. Many of us are taking it.

Niche restaurants are nothing new – the fish and chip shop is part of our DNA – but this latest trend demonstrates that the appetite for affordable comfort food shows no signs of abating. However, while single-concept restaurants are found countrywide (note the rash of burger joints), they tend to be more successful in cities where a dense, broad-based population guarantees a crowd for these one-hit wonders.

But are single-concept restaurants here to stay? Does such a narrow focus mean a better-executed dish? While not every comfort food has proved ready for such close scrutiny, the crowds tell a different story and single-concept restaurants continue to flourish.

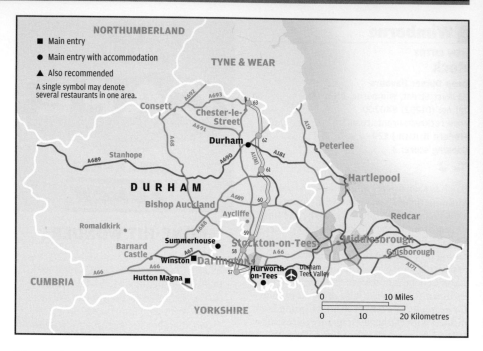

Durham

Bistro 21

Bucolic-style charmer delivering top comfort food

Aykley Heads House, Aykley Heads, Durham, DH1 5TS
Tel no: (0191) 3844354
www.bistrotwentyone.co.uk
Modern British | £27
Cooking score: 3

£30

North East food hero Terry Laybourne is held in high regard locally, thanks in no small part to this endearing rustic bistro in Durham. Trading for almost two decades, the striking yellow converted farmhouse restaurant (by Aykley Heads House registry office) is a charmer with its whitewashed walls, farmhouse chairs and flagstoned bar. The pretty central courtyard is particularly pleasant. On the menu, influences from France, Spain and Italy are caressed by modern British touches. Start with Ibérico ham

croquettes or home-smoked mackerel with beetroot and blood orange, then delve into appealing mains such as ribeye with tarragon and mustard butter or herb-crusted salmon with creamed leeks. The £15.50 express lunch is more overtly 'French bistro' in inspiration. Classics are given a twist for pudding: perhaps Bramley apple and cinder toffee parfait or rhubarb and ginger beer sorbet. A conservative wine list opens with a quaffable French number at £17.50.
Chef/s: Ruari MacKay. **Open:** all week L 12 to 2 (3.30 Sun), Mon to Sat D 5.30 to 10. **Meals:** alc (main courses £12 to £27). Set L £15.50 (2 courses) to £18. Set D £16.50 (2 courses) to £19.50.
Details: 70 seats. 22 seats outside. Separate bar. Wheelchair access. Car parking.

||♦ Visit us Online

To find out more about
The Good Food Guide, please visit
www.thegoodfoodguide.co.uk

Gourmet Spot
Small restaurant with big ideas
The Avenue, Durham, DH1 4DX
Tel no: (0191) 3846655
www.gourmet-spot.co.uk
Modern European | £40
Cooking score: 3
£5 OFF 🛏 V

A 'beautiful modern restaurant' decked out in red and black, the Gourmet Spot occupies the ground floor of the Farnley Tower Hotel – an imposing Victorian building in the upmarket Neville's Cross area of Durham. Simple menu descriptions belie the complexity and ambition of the cooking. 'Suckling pig belly with langoustines and English carrots' translates as a generous piece of belly with langoustines cooked in their own juices, carrot purée, baked carrots and raw slithers of marinated purple carrot, all finished with a sauce made from the langoustine shells. Pan-fried John Dory with 'shellfish and garlic variations' and shellfish bisque is a typical main, while a 'very simple but delicious' dessert teamed Yorkshire rhubarb mousse and pistachio ice cream with the 'wonderful spice' of set ginger custard. All this comes with a 'very modest' price tag and accompaniment from a decent selection of wines, grouped by style, starting at £18.50.
Chef/s: Stephen Hardy. **Open:** Tue to Sat D only 6.30 to 10. **Closed:** Sun, Mon, 25 and 26 Dec, first week Jan. **Meals:** Set D £32 (2 courses) to £40. Tasting menu £60 (8 courses). **Details:** 24 seats. Separate bar. Wheelchair access. Car parking.

▌Hurworth-on-Tees

The Bay Horse
Cut-above village pub
45 The Green, Hurworth-on-Tees, DL2 2AA
Tel no: (01325) 720663
www.thebayhorsehurworth.com
Modern British | £34
Cooking score: 4

Traditional features abound in this old village pub, but for all its beams, open fire and polished tables there is nothing cobwebby

about the operation. It provides an informal stage for Marcus Bennett's modern British cooking. He makes the most of local produce such as beef from Robin Hirst of Neasham Grange Farm in Darlington – 'one of the best steaks I have experienced' – and the cooking is exact and assured, coaxing maximum flavour from these top-quality ingredients. French black pudding is teamed with quail's breast and faggot, mushroom ketchup, bacon lardons, parsley oil and prune chutney, while for mains stone bass could share a plate with salt-and-pepper squid, sweet potatoes (roasted and puréed), shellfish cream and mussel beignet. A posh ploughman's lunch and a Grand Reserve fillet burger feature on the lunch menu, 'fantastic' bread is baked on the premises and desserts stay dependably in the comfort zone with sticky toffee pudding and lemon meringue pie. Wines from £16.95.
Chef/s: Marcus Bennett. **Open:** all week L 12 to 2.30 (4 Sun), D 6 to 9.30 (8.30 Sun). **Closed:** 25 and 26 Dec. **Meals:** alc (main courses £14 to £25). Set L £13.95 (2 courses) to £16.95. Sun L £23.95. **Details:** 40 seats. 40 seats outside. Separate bar. Wheelchair access. Car parking.

The Orangery
Gold-standard cooking with panoramic views
Rockliffe Hall, Hurworth-on-Tees, DL2 2DU
Tel no: (01325) 729999
www.rockliffehall.com
Modern British | £45
Cooking score: 5
🛏

With a golf course and spa, plus fishing and shooting, Rockliffe Hall isn't short of bells and whistles. It's an ambitious undertaking, coaxed back from near dereliction five years ago by owners Middlesbrough Football Club (whose training facilities are in Rockliffe Park). No expense has been spared on the luscious interior. The Orangery is the most extravagant of the three restaurants on site, with high glass ceiling, crisp napery and broad parkland views. Its new kitchen team, led by Dan Shotton (taking over from Kenny Atkinson), is keeping standards high. 'One of

the best dining experiences we've had,' says one recent visitor. Another praises a sweet/savoury starter of tender scallops with 'textures of cauliflower' and golden sultanas. Crisp-skinned sea bass with baby courgette, tapenade and puréed basil-infused potato is typical of the classically inspired mains, while a crisp-based apple and almond tart with toffee apple balls and apple sorbet makes a balanced, thoughtful end note. The exhaustive wine list is full of interest, tapping countries as diverse as Japan and Uruguay. Bottles start at £27, with plenty under £40.
Chef/s: Dan Shotton. **Open:** Mon to Fri L 12.30 to 2, Mon to Sat D 6.30 to 10. **Closed:** Sun. **Meals:** alc (main courses £20 to £35). Set L £19.50 (2 courses) to £25. L tasting menu £50. D tasting menu £65. **Details:** 60 seats. Separate bar. Wheelchair access. Car parking. No children.

■ Hutton Magna
The Oak Tree Inn
Village hostelry with high standards
Hutton Magna, DL11 7HH
Tel no: (01833) 627371
www.theoaktreehutton.co.uk
Modern British | £33
Cooking score: 3

Hutton Magna, to the west of Darlington, not far from Barnard Castle, floated out of the old North Riding of Yorkshire into Durham in the 1970s. It's a picturesque village set amid Pennine ruggedness, and is home to the Rosses' supremely appealing country inn. A nice contrast of roughcast walls and comfy sofas, bottle-green upholstery and undressed tables makes a cheering setting for Alastair's carefully worked modern British cooking. Main-course meats and fish are allowed to speak for themselves, the sea bass in a vegetable broth with brown shrimps and chunks of chorizo, or the saddle of lamb with provençale veg and rosemary-roast potatoes. Starters cast the net a little wider for influences, perhaps resulting in Shetland mussels in coconut, ginger and chilli, or tempura lemon sole on pea risotto. Desserts go the whole hog with a

semifreddo of orange, mascarpone and pistachio, served with orange sorbet and caramelised raspberries. Wines start at £15.
Chef/s: Alastair Ross. **Open:** Tue to Sun D only 6 to 9 (8 Sun). **Closed:** Mon, 24 to 27 and 31 Dec, 1 Jan. **Meals:** alc (main courses £20 to £24). **Details:** 20 seats. Separate bar. Car parking.

■ Summerhouse
The Raby Hunt
Clean-lined, unpretentious food
Summerhouse, DL2 3UD
Tel no: (01325) 374237
www.rabyhuntrestaurant.co.uk
Modern British | £42
Cooking score: 5
£5
OFF

The Raby Hunt is a sensitively renovated village hostelry turned restaurant-with-rooms, its interior décor all modern wood-toned understatement and white-clad well-spaced tables. James Close's sure-footed modern cooking is thus allowed to take centre stage: 'delicious, modern, eclectic and moreish' is one typically effusive verdict. He offers a style of clean-lined, unpretentious food, whether a perfect assembly of pan-fried lemon sole with caviar, radish and cockle jus, or excellent venison from the Raby estate – loin and ragù with an earthy slew of salt-baked beetroot and celeriac. Seasonality is king and the menu is tweaked as the months roll by: in winter a dish of 48-hour braised ox cheek appears in company with winter chanterelles, in late spring there could be razor clams with peas, morels, almond and brown shrimps before main courses explore the resonance to be teased from the likes of Goosnargh duck, poached and roasted, served with chicory jam and duck jus. For dessert, the Raby Hunt chocolate bar (served with vanilla ice cream) is a sublime signature dish. The well-considered wine list pulls together great stuff from reputable and forward-looking producers worldwide. Prices start at £18.50.
Chef/s: James Close. **Open:** Wed to Sat L 12 to 2, D 6.30 to 9. **Closed:** Sun, Mon, Tue, 25 and 26 Dec, 1 Jan, 2 weeks Aug. **Meals:** alc (main courses £20 to

£28). Set L £20.95 (2 courses) to £24.95. **Details:** 30 seats. 6 seats outside. Separate bar. Wheelchair access. Car parking.

▌Winston

The Bridgewater Arms

Character, warmth and local ingredients
Winston, DL2 3RN
Tel no: (01325) 730302
www.thebridgewaterarms.com
Modern European | £34
Cooking score: 1

The conversion of this former schoolhouse into an upbeat village pub that oozes unbuttoned charm and character hits all the right notes. A crowd-pleasing menu of straightforward British food is served in the fire-warmed bar or candlelit restaurant. Food has a high comfort factor, whether seafood pancake thermidor or mature Cheddar cheese and spinach soufflé. For mains expect rack of lamb with leek and potato cake or monkfish wrapped in pancetta on a curried prawn risotto, with Turkish delight ice cream and chocolate sauce to finish. House wine is from £15.
Chef/s: Paul Grundy. **Open:** Tue to Sat L 12 to 2, D 6 to 9 (9.30 Sat). **Closed:** Sun, Mon, 24 to 26 Dec. **Meals:** alc (main courses £14 to £30). **Details:** 50 seats. Wheelchair access. Car parking.

❙❙❙● TOM KITCHIN
The Kitchin

What do you enjoy most about being a chef?
I love the buzz of the kitchen, the adrenalin and the kick I get out of the pressures of each day.

Which of your dishes are you most proud of?
My shellfish rockpool: the shellfish and sea vegetables I use are inspired by nature and showcase the fantastic seafood Scotland has to offer.

What is your favourite time of year for food, and why?
Without a doubt the first grouse of the season. Gamekeepers, suppliers and chefs alike eagerly await the Glorious Twelfth (12th August), when the first birds arrive.

What food trends are you spotting at the moment?
In recent years a new genre of local pub has emerged in Britain, serving good, fresh food with quality, local ingredients.

At the end of a long day, what do you like to cook?
Langoustines, bread and butter with a crisp glass of white wine. Simple and uncomplicated food is sometimes the best.

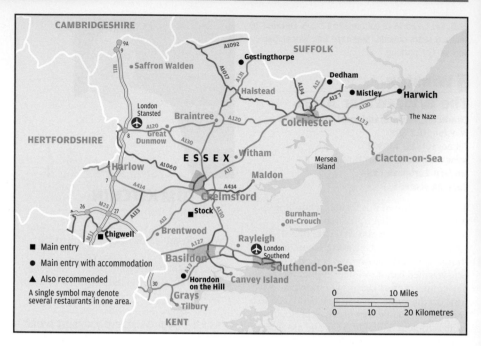

CAMBRIDGESHIRE

SUFFOLK

Gestingthorpe

Saffron Walden

Dedham

Halstead

Mistley

Harwich

London Stansted

Braintree

A120

Colchester

The Naze

HERTFORDSHIRE

Great Dunmow

A130

E S S E X • Witham

Clacton-on-Sea

Harlow

Mersea Island

Maldon

Chelmsford

Stock

Burnham-on-Crouch

Chigwell

Brentwood

Rayleigh

Main entry

London Southend

Main entry with accommodation

Basildon

Southend-on-Sea

Also recommended

A single symbol may denote several restaurants in one area.

Horndon on the Hill

Canvey Island

Grays

Tilbury

KENT

0   10 Miles

0   10   20 Kilometres

Chigwell

The Bluebell

Local asset with sound sourcing
117 High Road, Chigwell, IG7 6QQ
Tel no: (020) 8500 6282
www.thebluebellrestaurant.co.uk
Modern European | £37
Cooking score: 1

A world away from Essex bling and perma-tans, this sympathetically converted 500-year-old building looks as pretty as a picture with its bluebell colour schemes, pale woodwork and prints. Sound sourcing is at the culinary heart of things, from seared Devon scallops with honey-roast pork belly, Granny Smith apple, watercress and truffle dressing to a trio of Gressingham duck (roast breast, confit leg and pan-fried foie gras). Grass-fed Scottish beef is also a good call, while dessert might bring a trio of crème brûlée, semifreddo and tiramisu with cinnamon doughnuts. House wine is £16.95.

Chef/s: Gavin Maguire. **Open:** Tue to Sun L 12 to 2 (4 Sun), Tue to Sat D 6.30 to 9.30 (10.30 Sat). **Closed:** Mon, 26 and 27 Dec, 1 and 2 Jan. **Meals:** alc (main courses £17 to £29). Set L £16.95 (2 courses) to £19.95. Set D Tue to Thur £18.95 (2 courses) to £22.95. Sun L £18.95 (2 courses) to £23.95. **Details:** 90 seats. Separate bar. Wheelchair access.

Dedham

The Sun Inn

Classic inn with an Italian heart
High Street, Dedham, CO7 6DF
Tel no: (01206) 323351
www.thesuninndedham.com
Mediterranean | £25
Cooking score: 3
£5 OFF 🍷 🛏 £30

Everyone mentions the wonderfully warm welcome, engagingly friendly service and happy vibes pervading this 15th-century inn opposite the church in Dedham. The beams, wooden floors and oak panelling may speak of 'ye olde' England but expect a strong Italian accent in the food. Ingredients are impeccably sourced and generally the kitchen succeeds in its efforts to deliver confident, unpretentious food. Reporters have been delighted with a simple lunch of 'extremely well-cooked' salted cod, and a ploughman's-style platter of local cheeses, pickles and chutney with 'exquisite bread'. A dinner of braised clams and mussels with tomato, chilli, garlic and white wine, and beef shin with Parmesan polenta and black cabbage, also found favour. The wine list (starting at £15) is built on appeal and value, with a dedication to fine drinking from lesser-known sources. You'll find a decent choice by the glass and carafe, and eloquent food-matching notes.

Chef/s: Ugo Simonelli. **Open:** all week L 12 to 2.30 (3 Sat and Sun), D 6.30 to 9.30 (10 Fri and Sat). **Closed:** 25 and 26 Dec, 3 and 4 Jan. **Meals:** alc (main courses £9 to £20). Set L and D £12.50 (2 courses) to £15.50. Sun L £18.25. **Details:** 90 seats. 100 seats outside. Separate bar. Car parking.

■ Gestingthorpe
The Pheasant
Indulge in some comfort eating
Gestingthorpe, CO9 3AU
Tel no: (01787) 461196
www.thepheasant.net
Modern British | £25
Cooking score: 1
£5 OFF ⇔ £30

'What a delight', enthused one first-time visitor, smitten by the Donoghues' old-fashioned country inn with surprisingly up-to-date bedrooms looking out over the Stour Valley. It's a true local enterprise with own-grown fruit and vegetables, honey from the Pheasant's bees, local real ales and meats, and estate game. The result is a repertoire that ranges from chicken liver pâté with homemade piccalilli to pork belly with cider sauce, crackling and spring onion mash or confit Gressingham duck with apple and red onion tarte Tatin, then simple desserts like raspberries in jelly with stem ginger ice cream. Add a trio of homely rooms with beams, log-

burners and old polished tables and you have a 'proper pub serving proper pub grub'. Wines from £14.95.
Chef/s: James Donoghue. **Open:** all week L 12 to 2 (2.30 Sat and Sun), D 6.30 to 9. **Meals:** alc (main courses £11 to £19). Light L menu from £5.95. **Details:** 40 seats. 30 seats outside. Car parking.

■ Harwich
The Pier at Harwich, Harbourside Restaurant
Fine seafood and estuary views
The Quay, Harwich, CO12 3HH
Tel no: (01255) 241212
www.milsomhotels.com
Seafood | £38
Cooking score: 2
£5 OFF ⇔

Seafood is the main business in this cheery first-floor restaurant slap-bang on Harwich quayside and overlooking the Stour and Orwell estuaries. The kitchen takes the pick of the day's catch and the egalitarian menu pleases both traditionalists seeking seafood classics but also those in search of more contemporary dishes. Harwich crabs and lobsters are a speciality, though you might also be tempted by a starter of shell-baked scallops with chorizo and spinach before moving on to grilled fillet of hake with baked mussel Rockefeller. Those looking for something meatier should consider the char-grilled Dedham Vale steaks. Finish with quince crumble and cardamom custard. House wine is £18.95.
Chef/s: Tom Bushell. **Open:** Tue to Sun L 12 to 2 (3 Sun), D 6 to 9.30 (8.30 Sun). **Closed:** Mon. **Meals:** alc (main courses £16 to £39). Set L £20 (2 courses) to £25.50. Sun L £29. **Details:** 80 seats. Separate bar. Car parking.

▏▎● Average Price
The average price listed in main-entry reviews denotes the price of a three-course meal, without wine.

⫴ THE LUNCH CLUB

Take advantage of the 'all in' set lunches on offer in London to enjoy a fine-dining experience on a budget.

Murano
This restaurant may be a paradigm of Mayfair exclusivity, but the set lunch keeps it accessible with two courses for £25 or three for £30. A set lunch might include sea bream ceviche to start, followed by Cumbrian flank steak with romesco sauce.

Pétrus
Luxury with refreshing informality is the stated aim at Gordon Ramsay's legendary Pétrus, and there's no denying it delivers on the promise. For food that really lifts the senses, enjoy the set lunch at £35 for three courses.

Outlaw's at the Capital
Outlaw's at the Capital has a specific agenda: show what the sea can yield. A set lunch (excellent value at £25 for three courses) might open with a silky, intensely flavoured mushroom soup with pieces of salt cod, followed by ling served on a bed of shredded cabbage and bacon, finished with rich coffee cream topped by cinnamon and brandy doughnut balls.

▮ Horndon on the Hill
The Bell Inn
Medieval pub with comforting food
High Road, Horndon on the Hill, SS17 8LD
Tel no: (01375) 642463
www.bell-inn.co.uk
Modern European | £30
Cooking score: 2

In the same family for some 75 years, this 500-year-old inn is famed in the area for its rustic, pubby feel (rug-strewn wooden floors, oak settles, open fires, five ales on handpump) and for very good food. Stuart Fay's menu reflects a sound knowledge of modern ideas and imaginative pairings in dishes such as sea bass with confit pork belly and pea purée or veal chop with balsamic roast shallots, blackberries and blue cheese. Those with a sweet tooth get ample pleasure from the likes of dark chocolate fondant with caramelised banana and pistachio ice cream, but if you want to continue exploration of the Bell's impressive wine list, look to the selection of Neal's Yard Dairy cheeses. House wine £14.50.
Chef/s: Stuart Fay. **Open:** all week L 12 to 1.45 (2.15 Sun), D 6.30 to 9.45 (7 Sun). **Closed:** 25 and 26 Dec, bank hols. **Meals:** alc (main courses £9 to £23). **Details:** 80 seats. 36 seats outside. Separate bar. Wheelchair access. Car parking.

▮ Mistley
The Mistley Thorn
Upbeat eatery with painless prices
High Street, Mistley, CO11 1HE
Tel no: (01206) 392821
www.mistleythorn.co.uk
Modern European | £24
Cooking score: 2

British coastal cookery and sunny Californian touches (courtesy of American owner Sherri Singleton) make happy bedfellows at this former coaching inn-with-rooms. Throw in a few Italian influences and you have a likeable menu that transforms from kippers and porridge at breakfast to Mersea oysters, day-boat squid 'a la plancha', 'Cal-Ital' cioppino (seafood stew) and diver scallops with Puy lentils and spinach at lunch and dinner. 'Sherri's Mom's cheesecake' with toffee sauce is a hit for dessert. Refurbishment has upgraded the interiors, adding a cookery school and store. Guests praise the 'tiptop service' and 'homely atmosphere'. The wine list, from £14.95, holds a decent choice by glass, carafe and bottle. Wood-fired pizzas are the forte at sister venue Lucca Enoteca in Manningtree. **Chef/s:** Karl Burnside. **Open:** all week L 12 to 2.30 (4.30 Sat and Sun), D 6.30 to 9.30 (6 to 10 Sat and Sun). **Meals:** alc (main courses £10 to £18). Set L £12.50 (2 courses) to £15.00. Sun L £11.95 (2 courses) to £15.95. **Details:** 70 seats. 10 seats outside. Separate bar. Car parking.

█ Stock

NEW ENTRY
The Oak Room at the Hoop
Enthusiastically run local asset
21 High Street, Stock, CM4 9BD
Tel no: (01277) 841137
www.thehoop.co.uk
Modern British | £35
Cooking score: 1
£5 OFF

The Hoop has been feeding and watering the villagers of Stock for more than 450 years and still goes about its duties with real enthusiasm. Downstairs is a proper locals' drinking gaff, while the first floor is taken up with the Oak Room – a pretty, whitewashed restaurant serving well-crafted food with 'memorable attention to detail'. Starters of creamy Arbroath smokie pâté or goats' cheese, onion and thyme tart might give way to slabs of tender Dedham beef, native lobster ravioli or basil-crusted rack of Braxted lamb with ratatouille and olive mash. House wine is £13.50. **Chef/s:** Phil Utz. **Open:** Mon to Sat L 12 to 2.30, D 6 to 9 (9.30 Fri and Sat). Sun 12 to 5. **Meals:** alc (main courses £16 to £26). Sun L £25. **Details:** 40 seats. Separate bar. Wheelchair access.

█ Waltham Abbey

READERS RECOMMEND
Parsons Restaurant
Modern British
58 Sun Street, Waltham Abbey, EN9 1EJ
Tel no: (01992) 700616
www.parsonsrestaurant.com
'The service was extraordinarily good; the food, however, was the centrepiece of the evening. I started with an ox-cheek terrine with bread, followed by roast guinea fowl with truffle and potatoes. The quality of the flavours was amazing.'

█ West Bergholt

READERS RECOMMEND
The Treble Tile
Modern British
Colchester Road, West Bergholt, CO6 3JQ
Tel no: (01206) 241712
www.thetrebletile.co.uk
'A thoroughly welcoming place with great food and a sunny garden – a useful local find.'

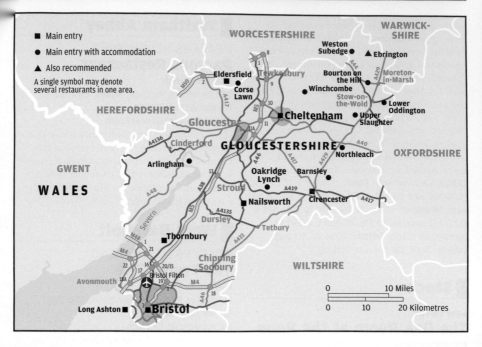

■ Main entry
● Main entry with accommodation
▲ Also recommended
A single symbol may denote several restaurants in one area.

Arlingham

The Old Passage

Pin-sharp seafood and fresh flavours
Passage Road, Arlingham, GL2 7JR
Tel no: (01452) 740547
www.theoldpassage.com
Seafood | £40
Cooking score: 3

It may be squirrelled away on a road that goes nowhere, but that doesn't stop visitors trekking out to Sally Pearce's charmingly run restaurant-with-rooms. A simply decorated, light-filled dining room with splendid views from the terrace over the river Severn sets the mood. Fish and seafood are the fortes. Plates of oysters, dressed crab and garlicky lobster are star turns, fish pie has plenty of takers and the choice might also stretch to whole-roasted lemon sole with nut-brown butter or roast cod with curried mussel fricassee. The menu also presses the comfort button, offering roast saddle of venison with braised red cabbage for those in the mood for meat. Some reporters baulk at the prices, but there's no arguing with the sheer quality of the food. Wines from £18.40.

Chef/s: Mark Redwood. **Open:** Tue to Sun L 12 to 2 (2.30 Sun), Tue to Sat D 7 to 9 (6.45 Fri and Sat). **Closed:** Mon. **Meals:** alc (main courses £19 to £49). Set L £15 (2 courses) to £20. **Details:** 40 seats. 22 seats outside. Wheelchair access. Car parking.

Barnsley

The Potager Restaurant

Rich pickings from Rosemary's garden
Barnsley House, Barnsley, GL7 5EE
Tel no: (01285) 740000
www.barnsleyhouse.com
Modern British | £40
Cooking score: 3

Named after garden legend Rosemary Verey's ornamental vegetable garden, which you can survey from the hotel dining room, the Potager celebrates the tradition of kitchen horticulture by continuing to produce much of its own provender. A long room furnished in uplifting light tones sets the mood for Graham Grafton's Italian-inflected English dishes. An opener of cod ceviche dressed in orange, lime and coriander could be followed by risotto verde or the famous vincisgrassi, a truffled baked pasta dish of Parma ham and porcini. Main courses run from a simple whole lemon sole in brown butter to the more complex proposition of Duchy venison with beetroot gratin, swede purée and peppercorn sauce. For pudding, early rhubarb is plucked from the soil to jolly up a traditional English burnt cream, or there's a different sort of tang from Sicilian citrus tart with apple sorbet. House wine is £24 or £12 for a half-bottle carafe.

Chef/s: Graham Grafton. **Open:** all week L 12 to 2 (2.30 Sat), D 7 to 9.30 (10 Fri and Sat). **Meals:** alc (main courses £19 to £27). Set L £22 (2 courses) to £24. **Details:** 60 seats. 20 seats outside. Separate bar. Car parking. Children over 14 yrs only at D.

ALSO RECOMMENDED

▲ The Village Pub

Barnsley, GL7 5EF
Tel no: (01285) 740421
www.thevillagepub.co.uk
Modern British £5 OFF

An ever-so-English village creates just the right impression for visitors to this well-groomed pub. Timbers and real fires reinforce the mood, and in keeping with the rustic-chic surrounds, the cooking is British executed in a modern style, tapping into a network of local producers. In the bar expect Welsh rarebit fritters or chorizo sausage, while options in the dining room could be an English charcuterie board (£9.25), smoked haddock fishcakes with poached egg, spinach and lemon butter sauce (£13.50) and Cox apple and treacle tart. Wines from £17. Open all week. Accommodation.

▮ Bourton on the Hill

Horse & Groom

Consistently satisfying hilltop inn
Bourton on the Hill, GL56 9AQ
Tel no: (01386) 700413
www.horseandgroom.info
Modern British | £25
Cooking score: 2
£5 OFF £30

Whether you're in for a quick pint, enjoying some capably rendered food, or staying over in one of the boutique rooms, this substantial Georgian inn knows how to deliver satisfaction – not surprising, given that owners Will and Tom Greenstock are old hands at the hospitality business. The hilltop setting provides great views of the Cotswolds, and the kitchen offers an inviting selection of contemporary pub dishes: from home-cured spiced beef with beetroot and horseradish relish to chocolate pannacotta with salted caramel. In between, expect vivid ideas inspired by well-chosen British ingredients: Dexter beef, Faroe Isles salmon, Middle White pork chops or local pigeon breasts with creamed celeriac purée, chorizo and thyme jus. Wines start at £14.25.

Chef/s: Will Greenstock. **Open:** all week L 12 to 2 (2.30 Sun), Mon to Sat D 7 to 9 (9.30 Fri and Sat). **Closed:** 25 Dec. **Meals:** alc (main courses £12 to £19). **Details:** 75 seats. 54 seats outside. Separate bar. Car parking.

▮ Bristol

Bell's Diner

Robust cooking from sunny climes
1-3 York Road, Montpelier, Bristol, BS6 5QB
Tel no: (0117) 9240357
www.bellsdiner.com
Mediterranean | £25
Cooking score: 4
£30

There has been a significant changing of the guard at this enduring neighbourhood restaurant located on a sunny corner in Bristol's bohemian quarter. After several years

at the helm, Chris Wicks hung up his apron in May 2013 and handed the baton to seasoned local restaurateur Connie Coombes. She immediately installed chef Sam Sohn-Rethel (ex-Flinty Red, see entry) to take this former grocer's shop back to its roots as an informal local bistro and bar. The food hails from the Mediterranean, the Middle East and North Africa, with exceptional ingredients treated with respect in robust, uncluttered dishes such as seared scallops with a Turkish-style chopped salad. Following on might be a light and fragrant main course of slow-cooked rabbit, morcilla, peas and mint. The selection of outstanding homemade ice creams for pudding could include orange ripple or Alphonso mango. A carefully constructed list of Eurocentric wines starts at £17.50.
Chef/s: Sam Sohn-Rethel. **Open:** Tue to Sun L 12 to 3 (11 to 5 Sun), Tue to Sat D 6 to 10. **Closed:** Mon, 25 Dec to 2 Jan. **Meals:** alc (main courses £11 to £17). **Details:** 40 seats.

NEW ENTRY
Bravas
Wonderfully atmospheric buzzy tapas bar
7 Cotham Hill, Bristol, BS6 6LD
Tel no: (0117) 3296887
www.bravas.co.uk
Spanish | £12
Cooking score: 2
£30

Bravas started life as a supper club run from Kieran and Imogen Waite's Bristol home, but once a permanent site was discovered, the couple set about creating the sort of small, buzzy tapas bar you find in Seville. With that on-trend look of exposed brick walls, copper piping and hessian coffee sacks covering old chairs, they have turned a former Greek restaurant into a wonderfully atmospheric place. Sit at the bar or grab a table at the back and order from a daily changing menu that may include octopus salad and white beans with leeks and fino. The plancha grill is the kitchen workhorse and comes into its own

when Ibérico pork or local lamb is available. A carefully sourced all-Spanish wine list starts at £15.
Chef/s: Imogen Waite. **Open:** Fri and Sat L 12 to 5, Tue to sat D 5 to 11. **Closed:** Sun, Mon, 24 to 26 Dec, 1 Jan. **Meals:** alc (tapas £2 to 7). **Details:** 30 seats. Separate bar.

Casamia
New tricks and experimental cuisine
38 High Street, Westbury on Trym, Bristol, BS9 3DZ
Tel no: (0117) 9592884
www.casamiarestaurant.co.uk
Modern British | £68
Cooking score: 5
£5 OFF V

Banish any thoughts of spag bol and *O Sole Mio* on arrival at Casamia. The name is a throwback to the old Sanchez-Iglesias family trattoria, but whizz-kid sons Jonray and Peter are creating something very different here. Their no-choice tasting menus (one per season) look as if they've been bashed out on a typewriter, yet there's nothing antiquated about the food – even if the kitchen is fond of taking trips down memory lane ('inspired' shepherd's pie or rhubarb fool anyone?). A winter opener of fruit-and-nut bread with 'cultured' butter closely followed by Keen's Cheddar and pickle might set you reminiscing about pub sandwiches, and there's a left-field contemporary British tone to other ideas: from rainbow trout with variations of cabbage or ham hock with swede to roe deer with parsnips and turnips. Nothing is quite what it seems in this 'new tricks' world of experimental cuisine. Dishes are deconstructed and reassembled in weird forms, presentation plays tricks on the senses and you might even find yourself picking at a Lilliputian salad with a pair of tweezers. The wide-ranging wine list (from £20.50) pays special attention to favoured growers such as Marchesi de Frescobaldi in Tuscany.

Chef/s: Jonray and Peter Sanchez-Iglesias. **Open:** Tue to Sat L 12 to 2, D 6 to 9.30. **Closed:** Sun, Mon. **Meals:** Tasting menu L £38 (3 courses) to £68 (11 courses). Tasting menu D £68 (Tue to Thur) to £88 (Fri and Sat). **Details:** 30 seats. Wheelchair access.

Flinty Red

Bright Mediterranean flavours and zesty wines
34 Cotham Hill, Bristol, BS6 6LA
Tel no: (0117) 9238755
www.flintyred.co.uk
Mediterranean | £25
Cooking score: 4
£30

Run in tandem with nearby wine merchant's Corks of Cotham, modestly appointed Flinty Red scores with its bright Mediterranean flavours and seasonal menu. This kitchen pays more than lip service to the calendar, although 'must-have' anchovy toasts and pasta dishes such as rabbit ragù with lardo and 'elbow-shaped' sourdough gomiti are regular attractions. Otherwise, daily treats might range from buffalo mozzarella with blood orange, fennel and black olives to char-grilled chorizo and kid's liver or pork collar cooked in milk with polenta and cavolo nero. Desserts move into the realms of buttermilk pudding with medjool dates and granola. Standards are 'consistently high' and 'experienced staff' know their way around the wine list, which offers around 20 zesty selections by the glass or carafe alongside bottles from £16. A spin-off entitled the Flinty Red Café Bar is now open at the Bristol Old Vic, King Street, BS1 4ED; tel: (0117) 9877877.
Chef/s: Matthew Williamson. **Open:** Tue to Sat L 12 to 3, Mon to Sat D 6.30 to 10. **Closed:** Sun, first week Jan, bank hols. **Meals:** alc (main courses from £12 to £16). Set L £9.95 (2 courses) to £14. Set D £15 (2 courses) to £20. **Details:** 36 seats.

NEW ENTRY

Gallimaufry

Relaxed by day, gastronomically rocking by night
26-28 The Promenade, Gloucester Road, Bristol, BS7 8AL
Tel no: (0117) 9427319
thegallimaufry.co.uk
Modern British | £22
Cooking score: 3
£30

A wall of nicotine-stained gig posters is the only real reminder of this venue's long history as one of Bristol's liveliest music venues. By day, the Gallimaufry is a relaxed bar where you can pop in for good coffee, hearty breakfasts, a cheap and satisfying lunch – but the food is ramped up considerably in the evening, when tables in the small dining area are highly prized by locals. Live music and DJs still appear, but it's ex-Casamia chef John Watson's British cooking that's making all the noise. His terse, well-priced menus are built around seasonal, impeccably sourced ingredients: scallops, chicken wings and silky butternut squash purée; pork ('perfect belly', slices of tender juicy tenderloin and a faggot with huge flavour') partnered by celeriac, turnip, apple and sage; a rich chocolate and rosewater fondant with almond ice cream, which 'worked brilliantly'. A concise wine list kicks off at £13, but local ales are also available.
Chef/s: John Watson. **Open:** all week 10 to 10 (Sun 5). **Meals:** alc (main courses £11 to £14). **Details:** 35 seats. 25 seats outside. Separate bar.

Greens

Welcoming bistro with wonderful food
25 Zetland Road, Bristol, BS6 7AH
Tel no: (0117) 9246437
www.greensbristol.co.uk
Modern European | £27
Cooking score: 3
£30

'The cooking still remains as competent as ever,' enthused one visitor to this much-loved neighbourhood restaurant, which changed hands at the end of 2012. Apart from a lick of paint and a shortening of the original name, little has changed – thankfully, for the quality of cooking and value for money. New chef/proprietor Martin Laurentowicz used to cook at Fishers Bistro in Edinburgh; here he ploughs a similar culinary furrow to his predecessors – simple, modern European dishes low on frills but big on flavour. Precisely cooked seared scallops with crispy chicken wing, Jerusalem artichoke and lettuce sauce makes a notable starter, followed, perhaps, by equally impressive sea bream fillets with crispy polenta, samphire and crab vinaigrette, and a warm chocolate and hazelnut tiffin served with caramel oranges and 'well-balanced' crème anglaise. The inherited £10 for two-course lunch menu remains a popular option, and the short, interesting wine list starts at £14.
Chef/s: Martin Laurentowicz. **Open:** Tue to Sat L 12 to 2.30, D 6 to 10. **Closed:** Sun, Mon, 25 and 26 Dec. **Meals:** alc (main courses £11 to £19). Set L £10 (2 courses) to £15. Set D £15 (2 courses) to £20. **Details:** 38 seats. 10 seats outside.

¡¡¡● Please send us your feedback

To register your opinion about any restaurant listed in the Guide, or a new restaurant that you wish to bring to our attention, please visit the web address at the bottom of the page. Your feedback informs the content of the book and will be used to compile next year's reviews.

Lido

Aromatic food in awesome surrounds
Oakfield Place, Clifton, Bristol, BS8 2BJ
Tel no: (0117) 9339530
www.lidobristol.com
Mediterranean | £31
Cooking score: 3
£5 OFF

It is six years since this Victorian lido was saved from demolition and restored to its former glory by Arne Ringner. With an open-air swimming pool, spa and stylish restaurant, it remains one of the city's singular dining experiences. Grab a window seat overlooking the heated infinity pool and enjoy chef Freddy Bird's robust seasonal cooking, which majors in local and wild ingredients but draws influences from the sunnier climes of the Mediterranean, the Middle East and North Africa. Many dishes are cooked in the searing heat of the wood-fired oven. A starter of wood-roast scallops, sweet herb and garlic butter might precede Ibérico pork cheeks cooked in Asturian cider with parsnip and vanilla purée and apple and watercress salad. A daily list of freshly churned ices could include banana, rum and pecan or passion fruit. The concise list of Europe-only wines opens at £17.50.
Chef/s: Freddy Bird. **Open:** all week L 12 to 3, Mon to Sat D 6 to 10. **Closed:** 25 and 26 Dec, 1 Jan. **Meals:** alc (main courses £16 to £26). Set L and D £16 (2 courses) to £20. **Details:** 90 seats. 45 seats outside. Separate bar.

NEW ENTRY

Manna

Tapas from around the Med
2B North View, Westbury Park, Bristol, BS6 7QB
Tel no: (0117) 9706276
www.mannabar.co.uk
Modern European | £25
Cooking score: 2
£30

Opened in 2012 as a more casual counterpoint to Prego (see entry) opposite, this small and buzzy room is a tapas bar in all but name –

although the geographical axis of the cooking owes as much to Italy and the Middle East as to Spain. Grab a stool in the window or settle down on soft leather banquettes and nibble on harissa and honey-roast nuts with a glass of manzanilla as you choose from the likes of gilt-head bream with tahini and tabbouleh; Somerset asparagus with quail egg and romesco; and bomba rice with slow-roast mutton and fresh new-season peas. A wine list dominated by bottles from Spain and Italy kicks off at £14.50 and there are plenty of local bottled beers.

Chef/s: Olly Gallery. **Open:** Mon to Sat D only 6 to 10 (9 Mon). **Closed:** Sun. **Meals:** alc (tapas £3 to £14). **Details:** Separate bar.

Prego
Tiptop local Italian
7 North View, Bristol, BS6 7PT
Tel no: (0117) 9730496
www.pregobar.co.uk
Italian | £25
Cooking score: 3
£30

Occupying a former shop in a leafy corner of Bristol, Prego opened three years ago in a well-heeled neighbourhood that was in desperate need of such a bustling local bistro. Chef/proprietors Julian Faiello and Olly Gallery have Italian roots and a regional rustic style drives their menu, which relies on top-drawer local produce and specialist Italian ingredients. The handmade pizzas are one popular option, although the carte and daily specials board are equally persuasive, listing starters like slow-cooked fennel bruschetta with buffalo mozzarella, capers and tarragon or pear and chicory salad with hazelnuts and Gorgonzola. These might be followed by Old Spot saltimbocca, truffle mash and spinach or linguine with river Exe mussels, Cornish clams, garlic, chilli and anchovy. Puddings include blood-orange pannacotta with rhubarb and pistachio praline. An all-Italian wine list starts at £13.50.

Chef/s: Olivier Gallery. **Open:** Tue to Sat L 12 to 2, Mon to Sat D 5.30 to 10 (9 Mon). **Closed:** 23 Dec to 3 Jan. **Meals:** alc (main courses £9 to £18). **Set L** £10. **Set D** £25. **Details:** 50 seats. 20 seats outside. Wheelchair access.

The Pump House
Waterfront venue with bold seasonal food
Merchants Road, Hotwells, Bristol, BS8 4PZ
Tel no: (0117) 9272229
www.the-pumphouse.com
Modern British | £30
Cooking score: 3
£5 OFF

Perched on the waterfront where Bristol's regenerated city docks meet the river Avon, this former Victorian pumping station is now a waterside pub with a separate upstairs restaurant. Toby Gritten is a keen forager and local food advocate and the menus in both bar and dining room reflect this unwavering commitment to seasonality. Grab one of the scrubbed pine tables in the bar and enjoy a bowl of river Exe mussels with cider, parsley and cream, local dry-aged steaks or the market fish of the day. Alternatively, order from the carte, which might kick off with new-season lamb sweetbreads, cauliflower, truffle and almond and then proceed with cod (both line-caught and salt cod) with oxtail, carrots and wild garlic. Desserts include 'mixed textures and temperatures' of bitter chocolate and blood orange. A range of regional ales in the bar is supplemented by an interesting wine list with bottles from £16.

Chef/s: Toby Gritten. **Open:** Tue to Sun L 12 to 3, all week D 6.30 to 9 (7 Thur to Sat). **Closed:** 25 Dec. **Meals:** alc (main courses £15 to £20). Set L and D £12.50 (2 courses) to £15. Tasting menu £45. **Details:** 80 seats. 80 seats outside. Separate bar. No children in restaurant.

riverstation

Consistently good waterfront veteran
The Grove, Bristol, BS1 4RB
Tel no: (0117) 9144434
www.riverstation.co.uk
Modern European | £28
Cooking score: 3
£5 OFF £30

Thoroughly glazed to take advantage of its waterfront location, this converted river police station provides arresting harbour views. Bristol's fluid food scene has as much going on underground as over, but riverstation's location, terraces and daily-changing menu makes the place a popular stalwart. In the lively water-level café-bar there's breakfast, brunch, cocktails and simpler plates, such as lentil salad with walnuts and goats' curd or Thai-spiced mussels. The restaurant menu tends towards smarter Med-influenced dishes, perhaps haricot and almond soup with mandarin oil and chervil root followed by venison haunch with chestnut spätzle, cavolo nero, chocolate and griottine cherries. Dessert could be a pistachio and rose-water torte with poached rhubarb. Parents will note that one child eats free with a paying adult during the day in the café-bar and at both services in the restaurant. Wine is from £15.95.
Chef/s: Toru Yanada and Peter Taylor. **Open:** all week L 12 to 2.30 (3 Sun), Mon to Thur D 6 to 10.30 (11 Fri and Sat). **Closed:** 24 to 26 Dec. **Meals:** alc (main courses £16 to £20). Set L £13 (2 courses) to £16. Set D £15 (2 courses) to £19. Sun L £20. **Details:** 120 seats. 30 seats outside.

Rockfish Grill

Quality seafood brasserie
128-130 Whiteladies Road, Bristol, BS8 2RS
Tel no: (0117) 9737384
www.rockfishgrill.co.uk
Seafood | £38
Cooking score: 4
£5 OFF

Sister restaurant to the Seahorse, Dartmouth (see entry), this stylish, unstuffy seafood brasserie feels much lighter since refurbishment resulted in the main entrance being moved. Although the small fishmonger's counter has now gone, there are plenty of pictures of Devon fishermen and owner Mitch Tonks on the walls to remind you that this is a restaurant that takes seafood very seriously. Fish is delivered daily from Brixham and the menu changes depending on the day's catch, perhaps a 'stunning, razor-thin' octopus carpaccio with fennel and tomato, and a 'generous piece' of red gurnard from the charcoal oven, served with a 'punchy' salsa verde. Meat seems to be gaining equal status here, with a section of the menu devoted to full-flavoured steaks and chops cooked in the Josper grill. End with vanilla pannacotta and rhubarb or seasonal cheeses from La Fromagerie. Wines from £18.
Chef/s: James Davidson. **Open:** Tue to Sat L 12 to 2.30, D 6 to 10 (10.30 Fri and Sat). **Closed:** Sun, Mon, 24 Dec to 4 Jan. **Meals:** alc (main courses £15 to £24). Set L and early D £12.50 (2 courses) to £15. **Details:** 48 seats.

NEW ENTRY

Wilks

A stylish new opening conjuring up full-flavoured food

1-3 Chandos Road, Bristol, BS6 6PG
Tel no: (0117) 9737 999
www.wilksrestaurant.co.uk
Modern European | £32
Cooking score: 4

£5
OFF

Before opening Wilks in late 2012, James Wilkins and Christine Vayssade did stints in many notable restaurants around the world, James working closely with the French chef Michel Bras. A gentle refurbishment of this compact restaurant – last seen in the Guide as Culinaria – has added a stylish edge. Slate-grey walls are offset by black enamel lamps and black seagrass-style coverings on the tables, which also boast cruet sets made by a local pottery. James demonstrates a solid grasp of classic techniques and uses the best available local produce to conjure up dishes high on flavour. A delicate tortellini of Hereford snails with pancetta, celeriac and a roast chicken jus might precede a precisely cooked rolled breast and leg of corn-fed Goosnargh guinea fowl with peas and morels. Poached rhubarb, orange jelly, strawberry jus, fromage frais sorbet and fresh mint is one light and fragrant dessert. A French-heavy wine list starts at £16.50.
Chef/s: James Wilkins. **Open:** Wed to Sun L 12 to 2 (4 Sun), D 6 to 10 (9 Sun). **Closed:** Mon, Tue, 2 weeks Jan, 2 weeks Aug. **Meals:** alc (main courses £14 to £20). Set L and D £16 (2 courses) to £19. Sun L £18 (2 courses) to £26. **Details:** 40 seats. 8 seats outside. Wheelchair access. Car parking. Children over 6 yrs only at D.

Visit us Online

To find out more about
The Good Food Guide, please visit
www.thegoodfoodguide.co.uk

▌Cheltenham

★ CHEF OF THE YEAR ★ TOP 50 ★

Le Champignon Sauvage

Prime ingredients and nice surprises

24-26 Suffolk Road, Cheltenham, GL50 2AQ
Tel no: (01242) 573449
www.lechampignonsauvage.co.uk
Modern French | £59
Cooking score: 8

Word has it that David and Helen Everitt-Matthias have never missed a service. After more than 25 years at this central Cheltenham restaurant that's astonishing. How David continues to turn out dish after dazzling dish, and Helen to look after guests with such warmth, is one of the mysteries of the cooking world. Nowadays it's rare for a chef of such calibre not to be seduced by TV or driven to sprout an empire. But thankfully diners can be confident they'll eat food cooked by the man himself. Expect surprises on a menu that remains rooted in classical France and the muscular flavours of 'terroir' cooking. An amuse-bouche of field mushroom soup with a bacon foam so light it evaporates as you sip, leaves your taste-buds dancing. The maple-glazed chicken wings that come with a starter of plump dived scallops are a 'contender for the most delicious thing I've ever put in my mouth' for one appreciative guest, while a ravioli of rabbit, with parsley cream and braised Hereford snails is a masterclass in combining the refined with the gutsy, the delicately translucent pasta bursting with subtle gaminess. Roast halibut with Jerusalem and globe artichokes is the hearty pick of the fish, while a silky-smooth parsnip cream and cockles give a lively sweet-salt dimension to an oh-so-tender slab of Cinderford lamb. The fragrant, herby flavours of fennel ice cream cut through the intensity of an oozing, bitter chocolate and green aniseed tart, though a lighter choice might be a frozen bergamot parfait, orange jelly and liquorice cream. The wine list takes you on an exhilarating tour of the classiest French wineries, with a nod

towards New World treasures. House wine at £18 is a steal, and there are plenty of half-bottles.
Chef/s: David Everitt-Matthias. **Open:** Tue to Sat L 12.30 to 1.15, D 7.30 to 8.30. **Closed:** Sun, Mon, 10 days Christmas, 3 weeks Jun. **Meals:** Set L and Tue to Fri D £26 (2 courses) to £32. Sat D £48 (2 courses) to £59. **Details:** 38 seats.

Lumière

A serious gastronomic contender
Clarence Parade, Cheltenham, GL50 3PA
Tel no: (01242) 222200
www.lumiere.cc
Modern British | £49
Cooking score: 5
£5 OFF **V**

Discreetly located in a small Regency house close to Cheltenham's main centre, Lumière is a serious gastronomic contender with an ever-growing reputation: 'we loved it and would go again, but we live near Leeds', commented one envious couple. Rich purple tones, mirrors, glass and an opalescent 'candle chimney' create an elegant mood in the dining room, as do classy details such as Riedel glassware and Bernardaud plates. There's plenty of class in the state-of-the-art kitchen, too, thanks to Jon Howe's confident approach to contemporary cuisine. Expect on-trend culinary complexity leavened with 'plenty of big flavours on the plate' – Looe skate with chicken wings, quinoa, salsify, red wine and squid, for instance, or Welsh hogget with pearl barley, chervil root, sprouting broccoli and a mini shepherd's pie. Superb breads demand second helpings, and meals are often interspersed with fashionable extras such as 'Tequila slammer' (salt tuile, with Tequila sorbet and a lime sphere). Desserts are also 'done to perfection': perhaps a 'big, fluffy' damson soufflé or dark chocolate délice with pecans, smoked salt, sesame and bourbon cheesecake. Service is professional but never snooty, and the wine list offers serious drinking from £16.
Chef/s: Jon Howe. **Open:** Wed to Sat L 12 to 1.45, Tue to Sat D 7 to 8.45. **Closed:** Sun, Mon, 2 weeks winter, 2 weeks summer. **Meals:** Set L £28. Set D

£49. Tasting menu L £55 (6 courses), D £70 (9 courses). **Details:** 34 seats. Children over 10 yrs only.

NEW ENTRY

Purslane

The perfect neighbourhood restaurant
16 Rodney Road, Cheltenham, GL50 1JJ
Tel no: (01242) 321639
www.purslane-restaurant.co.uk
Modern British | £30
Cooking score: 5

Off the main drag in Cheltenham's shopping area, in a quiet street populated by accountants and solicitors' offices, this pale yellow Georgian building certainly stands out. Inside, you'll find polished wooden parquet flooring and battleship-grey walls punctuated by colourful pictures of yellow rape fields under stormy grey skies – but the small dining room feels surprisingly light and the welcome from the staff is warm. Gareth Fulford arrived here after a stint at the Kingham Plough and he continues to use as much local and foraged produce as possible, but also majors in Cornish fish. Air-dried hogget ham with purple sprouting broccoli, local Sarsden sheep's cheese and a 'presse' of rare-breed hogget has made an impressive starter. A perfectly calibrated main of roast Cornish hake with whelk and wild mushroom fricassee, spinach and wild garlic sauce displays commendable lightness of touch. Harmonious flavour combinations continue for dessert, with rhubarb and goats' curd cheesecake served with stem-ginger ice cream. 'An exceptional meal' enthused one recent convert. The concise wine list starts at £18.
Chef/s: Gareth Fulford. **Open:** Tue to Sat L 12 to 2.30, D 6.30 to 9.30. **Closed:** Sun, Mon. **Meals:** alc (main courses £16). **Details:** 34 seats. 4 seats outside.

ALSO RECOMMENDED

▲ The Daffodil

18-20 Suffolk Parade, Cheltenham, GL50 2AE
Tel no: (01242) 700055
www.thedaffodil.com
British £5 OFF

Set in a restored Art Deco cinema, converted
to make a huge, lively but pleasant dining area
with first-floor bar, the Daffodil is 'an
enjoyable experience'. Regulars come here for
risk-free, old-wave dishes such as potted crab
(£7.50), twice-baked Double Gloucester
soufflé, and oxtail pudding with beef fillet
(£18.50). Other possibilities might be whole
char-grilled monkfish for two, excellent
steaks and very good bread-and-butter
pudding. Lunch and evening meal deals are
well reported, service is 'attentive and smiling',
and wines start at £16. Closed Sun.

▲ The Tavern

5 Royal Well Place, Cheltenham, GL50 3DN
Tel no: (01242) 221212
www.thetaverncheltenham.com
Modern British £5 OFF

A short walk from the spa town's central bus
station and Promenade, this former pub
morphed into an industrial Brooklyn-meets-
Soho diner and bar in 2012. On-trend enamel
lamps and exposed brickwork set the scene for
typewritten, brown parcel-paper menus
offering small plates, burgers, steaks and
salads. Blackened salmon with noodles (£9)
and braised feather blade, mash, pancetta and
button mushrooms (£16) are typical of the
style. Finish with a retro Cherry Coke float
(£3). Wines from £16. Open all week.

⅋ Also Recommended

Also recommended entries are not scored
but we think they are worth a visit.

▮ Cirencester

Jesse's Bistro

Folksy bistro with big ideas
The Stableyard, Black Jack Street, Cirencester,
GL7 2AA
Tel no: (01285) 641497
www.jessesbistro.co.uk
Modern British | £35
Cooking score: 1
£5 OFF

Secreted away among the low passages and
climbing plants of an old brick stableyard,
cute little Jesse's is a folksy number, cosily
decked out with grey-stone walls, oak beams
and polished tiled floors. By contrast, the
kitchen has big ideas and comes up with some
very busy combos – think wild sea bass with
salsify, little gem, panko-bread langoustine
and shellfish sauce, or duck breast with a ball
of juicy confit, carrot purée, baked endive and
a puff-pastry garnish. Simpler dishes from the
set menu tend to work best (salmon fillet with
braised lentils has been praised), and the
home-baked bread is unmissable. Wines
from £19.50.
Chef/s: Paul Driver Dickerson, David Witnall and
Andrew Parffrey. Open: Mon to Sat L 12 to 2.30 (3
Sat), Tue to Sat D 7 to 9.30. Closed: Sun, 27 and 28
Dec, 1 to 3 Jan. Meals: alc (main meals £13 to £24).
Details: 50 seats. 25 seats outside. Wheelchair
access.

Made by Bob

Deli-dining Mediterranean fun in the Cotswolds
The Corn Hall, Unit 6, 26 Market Place,
Cirencester, GL7 2NY
Tel no: (01285) 641818
www.foodmadebybob.com
Modern European | £28
Cooking score: 3
£5 OFF £30

When it opened six years ago, this chic café
and well-stocked deli was a godsend for
Cirencester and it has since established itself as
a gastronomic landmark in the heart of the
Cotswolds. Chef/proprietor James 'Bob'

Parkinson arrived here after working in notable London restaurants such as Bibendum (see entry). His simple, uncluttered modern European cooking can be observed first-hand by diners sitting at stools around the open kitchen in the centre of the café. The food is Mediterranean with occasional Asian influences: from the daily changing menu, lamb sweetbreads with French beans, watercress, lardons and mustard dressing may be followed by Asian braised octopus, grilled pork belly, pak choi, chilli, spring onions and coriander. Dessert could be milk chocolate bavarois with honeycomb. Many dishes are also available to take home from the deli. The concise, carefully considered wine list starts at £16.
Chef/s: Bob Parkinson. **Open:** Mon to Sat L 12 to 3, Thur and Fri D 7 to 9.30. **Closed:** Sun, 25 and 26 Dec, 1 Jan. **Meals:** alc (main courses £11 to £29). **Details:** 84 seats. Wheelchair access.

█ Corse Lawn

Corse Lawn House Hotel
Elegance and classic cooking
Corse Lawn, GL19 4LZ
Tel no: (01452) 780771
www.corselawn.com
Anglo-French | £35
Cooking score: 3
£5 OFF █ ⊨ V

Fronted by a photogenic ornamental pond, this immaculate Queen Anne house has been tended by members of the Hine family since 1978. True to the setting, it fosters a spirit of gracious English gentility – although the food mixes patriotic themes with a dollop of bourgeois French classicism. A starter of smoked eel, beetroot, horseradish and pancetta might sit alongside quails' egg salad niçoise, while mains might run from char-grilled calf's liver with bubble and squeak to grilled sea bream with cauliflower cream and caper dressing. To finish, a trolley of unpasteurised British cheeses competes with puddings such as 'the lemon collection' (posset, tart and ice cream). Simpler dishes are available in the adjoining Bistro. The vast wine list delves deep into the French regions, but also offers prestigious drinking from around the globe. More than 40 half-bottles are on show, while house selections start at £19 (£5 a glass).
Chef/s: Martin Kinahan. **Open:** all week L 12 to 2, D 7 to 9.30. **Closed:** 24 to 26 Dec. **Meals:** alc (main courses £15 to £23). Set L and D £15 (2 courses) to £20. **Details:** 70 seats. 40 seats outside. Wheelchair access. Car parking.

█ Ebrington

ALSO RECOMMENDED
▲ The Ebrington Arms
Ebrington, GL55 6NH
Tel no: (01386) 593223
www.theebringtonarms.co.uk
Modern British

Events such as the Sunday Social (music, comedy, quizzes) add novelty to this 17th-century inn overlooking the village green. The kitchen is noted for its home-baked breads as well as sprightly modern dishes ranging from beetroot soup with a crispy goats' cheese parcel (£5.50) to steamed pollack with vegetable tagliatelle, lemongrass and ginger sauce (£15). Blackboard specials and puds such as steamed pear sponge are also worth noting. Wines from £16.50 and tiptop local beers, too. Accommodation. Open all week.

█ Eldersfield

The Butchers Arms
Proper pub with confident, knowledgeable cooking
Lime Street, Eldersfield, GL19 4NX
Tel no: (01452) 840381
www.thebutchersarms.net
Modern British | £40
Cooking score: 4

Despite several accolades, chef/landlord James Winter insists the Butchers Arms is 'first and foremost a rural pub' serving Eldersfield and beyond, with an unreformed bar, local cask ales and wooden settles around a blazing fire.

The premises may be four centuries old, but there's nothing archaic about the 'magnificent' food offered in the pint-sized dining room. Zealous sourcing is key to the kitchen's efforts and fish is a strength: from sole fillets with crab ravioli, spinach and bisque sauce to 'precisely timed' monkfish with prawns and salsa verde. Succulent, crispy-skinned roast turbot is a winner, while others have devoured melting ribeye steak with oxtail dumpling, and there are vanilla doughnuts with strawberry sauce to finish. Prices can seem 'toppy' for a boozer, but this is 'confident and knowledgeable cooking' with bags of flair. Elizabeth Winter and her friendly staff are courteous, and wines start at £18.50 – should beer not appeal.

Chef/s: James Winter. **Open:** Fri to Sun L 12 to 1 (bookings only), Tue to Sun D 7 to 9. **Closed:** Mon, 24 to 27 Dec, 1 week Jan, last week Aug. **Meals:** alc (main courses £19 to £26). **Details:** 28 seats. Car parking. No children under 10 yrs.

▌Long Ashton
The Bird in Hand
Handsome village pub on the up
17 Weston Road, Long Ashton, BS41 9LA
Tel no: (01275) 395222
www.bird-in-hand.co.uk
British | £26
Cooking score: 2
£30

'Handsome food in a handsome pub', quipped a fan of this revitalised village boozer – a second venture from the guys behind the Pump House in Bristol (see entry). Old advertising signs, shelves of homemade preserves and walls plastered with pages from Mrs Beeton suggest serious intent, and the kitchen doesn't disappoint. Chunky wooden boards and steel slates are piled with honest, rustic dishes along the lines of baked duck egg and foraged mushrooms on brioche, fried Cornish hake with unmissable chips or a risotto of Dorset veal with bone marrow and saffron. But it's not all about the food: the

atmosphere is 'lovely' and the chummy bar is 'fab' if you fancy a coffee, a pint or a bottle of wine (from £16).

Chef/s: Jake Platt. **Open:** all week L 12 to 3 (4 Sun), Mon to Sat D 6 to 9. **Closed:** 25 Dec. **Meals:** alc (main courses £10 to £18). **Details:** 45 seats. 30 seats outside.

▌Lower Oddington
The Fox Inn
Olde-worlde warmth and charm
Lower Oddington, GL56 0UR
Tel no: (01451) 870555
www.foxinn.net
British | £27
Cooking score: 2
£30

Old Cotswold stone inns like the Fox are a fairly common fixture throughout 'the Chippings'. Visually, it's hard not to get excited – the rough-hewn stone, draped in climbing ivy, promises so much olde-worlde warmth and charm, which the ancient pub delivers in spades. The main feature is a polished flagstone floor that extends throughout the nooks, crannies, corridors and snugs that comprise what is in fact a very sizeable pub. Louise and Peter Robinson (of the Old Butchers, Stow-in-the-Wold) have taken over and their formula could scarcely be more winning. Peter Robinson's philosophy is all about straightforward seasonal flavours, with Bath chap, Scotch quail's egg, capers and radish, a richly flavourful Cornish fish soup and rump steak burger with Roquefort and bacon all praised by contented diners. Applause, too, for the warm bonhomie with which the place is suffused. Wines from £17.50.

Chef/s: Peter Robinson. **Open:** all week L 12 to 2 (3 Sun), D 6.30 to 9.30 (10 Fri and Sat, 7 to 9.30 Sun). **Closed:** 25 Dec. **Meals:** alc (main courses £10 to £20). **Details:** 85 seats. 100 seats outside.

Nailsworth

NEW ENTRY
Mark@street
Returning country boy makes his Mark
Market Street, Nailsworth, GL6 OBX
Tel no: (01453) 839251
www.marketstreetnailsworth.co.uk
Modern British | £32
Cooking score: 2

In the tranquil Cotswold mill town of Nailsworth, Mark Payne's debut restaurant is tucked down a narrow street lined with quirky crafts and interiors shops. With just a handful of tables, it is certainly intimate, but it's relaxed and unpretentious, too, and has quickly gained a local following. Prior to opening here, Payne worked at notable establishments in London and the Cotswolds, but he's a country boy at heart and much of the produce on the menu is either foraged or grown on his own allotment. Pressed chicken and parsley terrine is one way to start dinner, perhaps followed by loin of Gloucestershire rose veal with cottage pie and red cabbage. Finish with vanilla pannacotta and honey-roasted peaches. Wines from £16.
Chef/s: Mark Payne. **Open:** Tue to Sun L 12 to 2.30, Tue to Sat D 7 to 9.30. **Closed:** Mon, 26 Dec, 2 weeks Jan, 1 week Sept. **Meals:** alc (main courses £15 to £18.50). Set L £10 (2 courses) to £12.50. Sun L £16.50 (2 courses) to £19. Tasting menu £40 (5 courses). **Details:** 26 seats. Car parking.

READERS RECOMMEND
The Wild Garlic
Modern British
3 Cossacks Square, Nailsworth, GL6 0DB
Tel no: (01453) 832615
www.wild-garlic.co.uk
'We eat here regularly, especially for the Tasting Menu, and the flight of wines that accompany it.'

Northleach
The Wheatsheaf Inn
Captivating Cotswold coaching inn
West End, Northleach, GL54 3EZ
Tel no: (01451) 860244
www.cotswoldswheatsheaf.com
Modern British | £28
Cooking score: 3

Back in the 17th-century, the Wheatsheaf gained fame as a riotous hostelry dedicated to feeding and watering travellers on the coaching route to London. Fast-forward a few hundred years and it's now a captivating, wisteria-clad destination favoured by Cotswold tourists, families and locals – thanks to a telling blend of upmarket pubby virtues and more genteel, contemporary attributes. Log fires, good draught ales and mighty roast joints on Sundays tell one side of the story; boutique bedrooms and a menu of exemplary food with a strong seasonal accent complete an affable, cosmopolitan package. Generosity and big flavours are the kitchen's touchstones, from a twice-baked Cheddar cheese soufflé with spinach and mustard to rump of Cotswold lamb with braised peas, lettuce and wild garlic pesto. There are also steaks and calf's liver from the grill, while puds might feature rhubarb and custard with hazelnut granola. Carefully chosen wines start at £16. Sam and Georgina Pearman's latest venture is the Chequers, Churchill, Oxfordshire OX7 6NJ; tel: (01608) 659393.
Chef/s: Antony Ely. **Open:** all week L 12 to 3 (3.30 Sun), D 6 to 9 (10 Fri and Sat). **Meals:** alc (main courses £11 to £22). Set L £12.50 (2 courses) to £15. **Details:** 60 seats. 60 seats outside. Separate bar. Car parking.

◼ Oakridge Lynch

NEW ENTRY
The Butchers Arms
A tucked-away treat
Oakridge Lynch, GL6 7NZ
Tel no: (01285) 760371
www.butchersarmsoakridge.com
Modern British | £28
Cooking score: 2

Michael and Sarah Bedford have risen from
the ashes of their Chef's Table and taken the
French bistro food that made their Tetbury
restaurant popular to nearby Oakridge Lynch.
Make the effort to track down this unassuming
village pub to enjoy fish soup with properly
garlicky rouille, or smoked haddock and pea
risotto, 'a spot-on combination of saltiness,
creaminess and gorgeous yellowness'. Among
the mains, crisply coated chicken Kiev is
cooked to perfection, and ribeye steak with
fries and béarnaise sauce is a classic winner.
Homemade breads are irresistibly warm.
Indulge a sweet tooth with praline soufflé or
lemon polenta cake with raspberry sorbet.
House wine £16.60.
Chef/s: Michael Bedford. **Open:** Tue to Sun L 12 to
2.30, Tue to Sat D 7 to 9.30. **Closed:** Mon. **Meals:** alc
(main courses £10 to £19). **Details:** 48 seats. 30
seats outside. Separate bar. Car parking.

◼ Portishead

READERS RECOMMEND
The Lido Kitchen
Modern British
Portishead Lido, The Esplanade, Portishead,
BS20 7HD
www.thelidokitchen.com
'The jewel in the Lido's crown is its lengthy
tapas menu; the pink-hued cold roast lamb
rump positively melted in the mouth, its soft
sweetness perfectly accompanied by a vibrant
and zesty salsa verde.'

◼ Thornbury

Ronnie's of Thornbury
Low-key gem
11 St Mary Street, Thornbury, BS35 2AB
Tel no: (01454) 411137
www.ronnies-restaurant.co.uk
Modern European | £35
Cooking score: 3
£5 OFF

Regulars keep returning to this converted
school for the full 'Ronnies' treatment,
meaning 'first-rate' food − be that a bacon
butty at brunch or a five-course 'menu
surprise' − and a genuinely warm welcome.
Chef Ron Faulkner is back at the pass and
reports suggest the kitchen is well on song. His
classical style informs the range of menus
including a 'du jour' (two courses, £10) and a
dinner menu (two courses, from £25). On the
latter, wild mushroom risotto with
Champagne and truffle oil (a trusted favourite)
vies for attention with mullet and its vibrant
salad of fennel and orange with a salt cod
croquette, and a reassuringly old-fashioned
beef Wellington (for two). Comforting
classics are another strength, and the likes of
pressed ham hock with piccalilli, and apple
and blackberry crumble, in generous portions,
often work their way on to the menu. Global
wines start at £14.
Chef/s: Ronnie Faulkner. **Open:** Tue to Sun L 12 to
2.30 (3 Sun), Tue to Sat D 6.30 to 11. **Closed:** Mon,
25 and 26 Dec, 1 to 7 Jan. **Meals:** Set L £15 (2
courses) to £20. Set D £20 (2 courses) to £25. Sun L
£16 (2 courses) to £19. Menu surprise £45 (5
courses). **Details:** 66 seats. 36 seats outside.
Separate bar. Wheelchair access.

▌Upper Slaughter
Lords of the Manor
Cooking with a high degree of technical gloss
Upper Slaughter, GL54 2JD
Tel no: (01451) 820243
www.lordsofthemanor.com
Modern British | £69
Cooking score: 4

£5 OFF 🍷 🛏

One of the grandees of the English country house hotel scene, this secluded 17th-century rectory is a restful, atmospheric place. Richard Edwards now heads up the kitchen and he rises to the stately occasion with cooking that comes with a high degree of technical gloss. He serves salmon, for example, tucked into a cylinder of crisp potato strings and filled with finely diced beetroot, capers and horseradish, and teams foie gras with peaches (raw, dried and compressed) embellished with a little blob of sweet wine jelly and a purée of pain d'épices. Fillet of beef is subjected to similarly treatment – three small slices served with little chunks of cheek, a couple of Parmesan gnocchi, asparagus, girolles, Parmesan shavings and an onion purée. As for dessert, strawberry sorbet, vanilla ice cream and jellies of basil and strawberry are given texture by a little granola of freeze-dried strawberry, almonds and oats. The wine list gets rave reviews. As well as good representation for all the expected Burgundy and Bordeaux high rollers, they've put real effort into budget options (from £24), with quirky picks from less famous regions and each of their by-the-glass options matched to a dish.
Chef/s: Richard Edwards. **Open:** Sun L 12 to 2, all week D 7 to 9.30. **Meals:** Set D £69. Tasting menu £75. Sun L £40. **Details:** 52 seats. Separate bar. Car parking. No children.

▌Weston Subedge
The Seagrave Arms
A pub success story
Friday Street, Weston Subedge, GL55 6QH
Tel no: (01386) 840192
www.seagravearms.co.uk
Modern British | £28
Cooking score: 3

£5 OFF 🛏 £30

Here's an updated Georgian coaching inn of substance, though perhaps 'more a restaurant than a pub' these days with a small dining room that's 'wise to book at busy times'. It's also 'a nice place to stay' – no wonder the Seagrave Arms is a big hit. Local sourcing is at the heart of the commendably short, fiercely seasonal menu, whether it's breast of local wood pigeon with Puy lentils and blackberry dressing, confit of Madgett's Farm duck with white bean cassoulet or the 'beautifully cooked sole with crayfish sauce and samphire' that so impressed one reporter. A well-kept selection of Cotswold cheeses might follow, or desserts such as homemade vanilla ice-cream profiteroles with chocolate and Amaretto sauce. Service is simply 'delightful, unpushy, efficient'. The short wine list aims for value with bottles from £16.95.
Chef/s: Julien Atrous. **Open:** Tue to Sun L 12 to 2.30, D 6 to 9. **Closed:** Mon. **Meals:** alc (main courses £14 to £17). **Details:** 40 seats. 40 seats outside. Separate bar. Wheelchair access. Car parking.

▌Westonbirt
READERS RECOMMEND
Beaufort Restaurant
Modern European
Hare & Hounds Hotel, Westonbirt, GL8 8QL
Tel no: (01666) 881000
www.cotswold-inns-hotels.co.uk
'Over the last two years, the meals have evolved into excellence. As a bonus, the staff are welcoming, cheerful and enthusiastic.'

■ Winchcombe

5 North Street

Pint-sized eatery with stellar food
5 North Street, Winchcombe, GL54 5LH
Tel no: (01242) 604566
www.5northstreetrestaurant.co.uk
Modern European | £45
Cooking score: 6

V

The centre of Winchcombe is a pretty collection of mellow stone shops selling things you never knew you needed. The timbered frontage and quaint bow windows at 5 North Street slot in seamlessly, but inside there's a subtly modern edge, with contemporary art, cloth-free tables and lobster-red walls. It makes a cosy backdrop for Marcus Ashenford's artful, flavour-driven cooking. By turns earthy and ethereal, the food could take you from homely Welsh rarebit toasts to a dainty, truffle-scented leek and potato soup before the meal proper has even started. In Marcus's hands, diverse elements such as marinated scallop, sweetcorn, crab, horseradish, sunflower seeds and a Parmesan tuile pull together into one glorious whole. Juicy chump of lamb with sweetbread, pumpkin purée, shallot, bacon and lentil casserole and slow-cooked lamb shoulder with peas and mint typifies his flexible approach to British and classical themes. To finish, a dessert presentation of chocolate and raspberry (clafoutis, sorbet, pannacotta, mille-feuille) succeeds decadently at every step. The wine list lingers in France yet has good worldwide coverage, starting from £23.
Chef/s: Marcus Ashenford. **Open:** Wed to Sun L 12.30 to 1.30, Tue to Sat D 7 to 9. **Closed:** Mon, 2 weeks Jan, 2 weeks Aug. **Meals:** alc (main courses £20 to £23. Min spend D £40). Set L £24 (2 courses) to £28. Set D £40 to £50. Sun L £33. Gourmet menu £65 (7 courses). **Details:** 26 seats.

Wesley House

Refined home-style dishes
High Street, Winchcombe, GL54 5LJ
Tel no: (01242) 602366
www.wesleyhouse.co.uk
Modern European | £40
Cooking score: 2

£5 OFF 🛏

A 'quirky' proposition in a 15th-century merchant house, this long-standing restaurant with rooms has a 'cosy and smart' dining room – which comes as a surprise after the ramshackle half-timbered exterior and the cluttered lobby. Attentive service is a constant and the food, 'never less than enjoyable', puts a refined spin on home-style dishes such as a 'sterling' rack and belly of lamb with cauliflower purée and dauphinois potatoes. To start, try smoked and seared salmon with lemon and ginger crème fraîche and a fennel salad; finish with a dessert of vanilla-poached pear, walnut praline and brioche with home-pickled ginger. Wines are from £19.
Chef/s: Cedrik Rullier. **Open:** all week L 12 to 2, Mon to Sat D 6.30 to 9.30 (10 Sat). **Meals:** alc (main courses £16.50 to £32). Set L £14.50 (2 courses) to £18.50. Set D £20 (2 courses) to £25. **Details:** 60 seats. Separate bar.

ALSO RECOMMENDED

▲ The Lion Inn

North Street, Winchcombe, GL54 5PS
Tel no: (01242) 603300
www.thelionwinchcombe.co.uk
British £5 OFF

A worthy addition to the Winchcombe dining scene, this newly revamped inn was spruced up in 2012 without losing any if its 15th-century charm. The Lion is popular with locals, tourists and Cotswold Way walkers, who all flock here for reliable modern British food prepared from high-quality seasonal ingredients: whether a lunchtime seafood platter (£12) or dinner of scallops with saffron risotto (£9.50) followed by pork-shin osso buco with char-grilled polenta (£15). House wine is £18. Open all week.

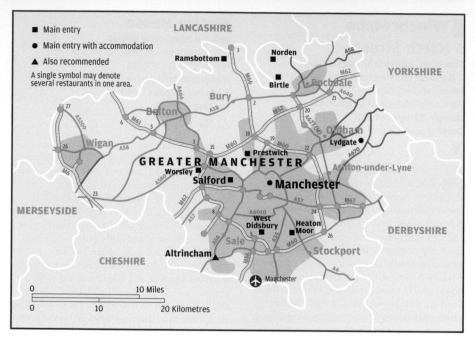

Legend:
- ■ Main entry
- ● Main entry with accommodation
- ▲ Also recommended

A single symbol may denote several restaurants in one area.

▐ Altrincham

ALSO RECOMMENDED
▲ Dilli

60 Stamford New Road, Altrincham, WA14 1EE
Tel no: (0161) 9297484
www.dilli.co.uk
Indian

One of the top Indian players in south Manchester's 'metro area', Dilli's intention is to recreate authentic regional dishes from all parts of the Subcontinent. Mumbai veggie street snacks (from £5), Punjabi tandooris and Keralan seafood specialities all get a look in, alongside marinated scallops with Goan 'peri-peri' masala, well-reported Hyderabadi bhuna gosht (£9.99) and crispy fried chicken from Andhra province. Sides of thick dhal makhani are top drawer, likewise rice and roti breads. The food generally passes muster, although service and housekeeping can become disorganised under pressure. Wines from £12.95. Open all week.

▐ Birtle

The Waggon at Birtle
Hearty modern British cooking

131 Bury and Rochdale Old Road, Birtle, BL9 6UE
Tel no: (01706) 622955
www.thewaggonatbirtle.co.uk
Modern British | £30
Cooking score: 2

£5 OFF

It is 11 years since this former pub on the road between Bury and Rochdale was knocked through to create a restaurant showcasing local ingredients. Its army of loyal customers continues to be rewarded with hearty dishes, whether they order from the carte or the terrific value fixed-price market menu. Tempura of Chadwick's Bury black pudding with apple, bacon, Lancashire cheese and mustard vinaigrette has become something of a signature dish and it might precede saddle of venison with spiced red cabbage, pommes purée, raspberry vinegar and bitter chocolate sauce. Hot chocolate and date pudding with chocolate sauce and marzipan ice cream is one of several desserts with a high comfort factor. Wines start at £14.95 (£3.95 a glass). **Chef/s:** David Watson. **Open:** Thur and Fri L 12 to 2, Wed to Sat D 6 to 9.30. Sun 12.30 to 7.30. **Closed:** Mon, Tue, first week Jan, 29 Jul to 11 Aug. **Meals:** alc (main courses £11 to £23). Set L and D £15.95 (2 courses) to £17.95. Sun L £11.95. **Details:** 45 seats. Separate bar. Wheelchair access. Car parking.

Heaton Moor

Damson

Colourful neighbourhood restaurant
113-115 Heaton Moor Road, Heaton Moor,
SK4 4HY
Tel no: (0161) 4324666
www.damsonrestaurant.co.uk
Modern British | £33
Cooking score: 2

🍾 V

Damson colour schemes and leaf-patterned chairs ram home the fruity point at this chic neighbourhood restaurant with a beautiful glass frontage. The setting comforts, and the kitchen brings bountiful North Country produce to the table – from a salad of Lancashire-grown beetroots with pickled shallots, candied walnuts and creamed goats' cheese to breast of Goosnargh duck with pak choi, spring onions and a port sauce tinged with bergamot and orange. Cheeses are supplied by local hero Peter Papprill, although desserts such as butterscotch pannacotta with caramel and hot cinnamon doughnuts also generate sighs of pleasure. The highly authoritative wine list (from £15.95) has a similar effect on oenophiles, with winners aplenty and fine selections by the glass. A second branch has opened in the Orange Building, Media City, Salford M50 2HF; tel: (0161) 7517020.
Chef/s: Simon Stanley. **Open:** Mon to Sat D only 5.30 to 9.30. Sun 12 to 7.30. **Meals:** alc (main courses £15 to £23). Set D and Sun L £15.95 (2 courses) to £18.95. **Details:** 70 seats. 8 seats outside. Separate bar. Wheelchair access.

Lydgate

The White Hart

Hilltop inn with some stellar food
51 Stockport Road, Lydgate, OL4 4JJ
Tel no: (01457) 872566
www.thewhitehart.co.uk
Modern British | £31
Cooking score: 4

£5 OFF 🛏 V

Perched on top of a Lancashire hill, the White Hart is a dignified old stone-built coaching inn. It displays all the expected period features inside (heavy oak beams, brick walls) and offers an abundance of eating environments: from the Brasserie to the Oak Room to the main Restaurant, a contemporary space that admirably suits Michael Shaw's trend-setting British food. Dishes challenge and satisfy in equal measure. Scottish scallops turn up in a parsnip cappuccino with apple and truffle, to be followed by venison loin with mulled pear, creamy cabbage and blackberries or the modishly Indian-influenced tandoori monkfish in red lentils and chickpeas, scented boldly with coriander. Tasting menus and vegetarian dishes give evidence of the earnest intent, as do ingeniously textured desserts such as lime curd meringue with coconut and sherbet marshmallow. A well-chosen wine list develops well from its French starting point, with bottles from £16.50.
Chef/s: Michael Shaw. **Open:** Mon to Sat L 12 to 2.30, D 6 to 9.30. Sun 1 to 8. **Closed:** 26 Dec, 1 Jan. **Meals:** alc (main courses £15 to £27). Set L £13.50 (2 courses) to £16.50. Sun L £22.50. **Details:** 48 seats. 10 seats outside. Separate bar. Car parking.

Manchester

NEW ENTRY

Albert Square Chop House
Boldly British chophouse
The Memorial Hall, Albert Square, Manchester,
M2 5PF
Tel no: (0161) 8341866
www.albertsquarechophouse.com
British | £32
Cooking score: 2

£5 OFF ▲

A confident remodelling has transformed a
neglected Victorian building into the newest
of Roger Ward's chophouses. This is the
foodiest of the four, with a bar at street level
and business-friendly restaurant below; clever
design allows the exchange of light and
atmosphere between them. Mancunian
heroes, shot in black and white, line the walls
and plush booths have 'long lunch' written all
over them. From the open kitchen, chefs
produce hefty British dishes with a boldly
offbeat spirit. There are grilled chops and
steaks aplenty, but also a vegetarian main
course of homity pie – gooey Lancashire
cheese, potato and onion in crisp pastry – and
starters like celery soup with blue cheese and
nettle dumplings, or Loch Duart salmon. The
French are admitted at dessert, with a punchy
raspberry soufflé alongside the trifle and
marmalade sponge. Sommelier George
Bergier's personal, spirited wine list starts
at £16.95.
Chef/s: Paul Faulkner. Open: Mon to Fri L 12 to 3, D
5 to 9.45. Sat and Sun 12 to 9.45 (8.30 Sun). Closed:
25 Dec. Meals: alc (main courses £12 to £28). Set L
£14 (2 courses) to £17. Details: 80 seats. Separate
bar. Wheelchair access.

🍴 **Visit us**
Online
To find out more about
The Good Food Guide, please visit
www.thegoodfoodguide.co.uk

Australasia
Funky big-city hangout
1 The Avenue, Spinningfields, Manchester, M3 3AP
Tel no: (0161) 8310288
www.australasia.uk.com
Pan-Asian | £50
Cooking score: 2

To find this funky big-city hangout, look for
the glass prism rising from the pavements of
Manchester's financial quarter. Once inside,
you'll discover a rocking subterranean venue
with sharp service, thumping music, lime-
washed walls and lots of beach-shack booths
dotted around. The food is backpacking pan-
Asian by inclination, with influences from
Japan to the Pacific Rim applied to a
hotchpotch of sharing plates, robata grills and
salads. Smoked duck 'dragon rolls' are a hit,
likewise bang-bang chicken, pan-fried
scallops on pork cakes and East-West
combinations such as pistachio-crusted
cannon of lamb with edamame ('a truly
amazing dish'). The high-octane bar deals in
glamorous cocktails and the Aussie-
dominated wine list (prices from £18) is
accessed via an iPad. Trendy or what?
Chef/s: Phil Whitehead. Open: Mon to Fri L 12 to 3,
D 5.30 to 11. Sat and Sun 12 to 11. Closed: 25 and 26
Dec, 1 Jan. Meals: alc (main courses £14 to £60).
Set L £11 (2 courses) to £15. Details: 150 seats.
Separate bar. Wheelchair access.

NEW ENTRY

Damson
Fine ingredients and a plum location
Media City, Manchester, M50 2HF
Tel no: (0161) 7517020
www.damsonrestaurant.co.uk
Modern European | £35
Cooking score: 2

£5 OFF

Damson has flourished in the suburbs but its
second site is a plum, overlooking the broad
sweep of Salford's revamped quays at
MediaCityUK. As befits the location, it's
bigger and sleeker than the original, but there's
continuity in the dark hotel-style fit-out and

in signature dishes such as Whitby crab and parsley risotto with salt-and-vinegar cockles. Classics and good northern ingredients make mains the highlight. Pork belly comes with a Lancashire cheese hash brown containing an oozing black pudding filling, while Cheshire beef is made into a filthy-rich bourguignon. A scattergun approach to pudding wastes the kitchen's skill: a fine pistachio financier doesn't need dry popcorn, and teaming pistachio crème brûlée with a chocolate and prune brownie makes less of both. Wine (from £15.95) is taken seriously.
Chef/s: Simon Stanley and Anshul Dhyani. **Open:** Mon to Sat L 12 to 3, D 5 to 10. Sun 12 to 7.30. **Meals:** alc (mains £13 to £20). Set L and D £15.95 (2 courses) to £18.95. **Details:** 140 seats. 30 seats outside. Separate bar. Wheelchair access. Car parking.

★ BEST NEW ENTRY ★ TOP 50 ★

The French
Manchester's hottest ticket
16 Peter Street, Manchester, M60 2DS
Tel no: (0161) 2363333
www.the-french.co.uk
Modern British | £67
Cooking score: 8
£5
OFF

The chorus of praise for Simon Rogan's stunning restaurant in the Midland Hotel has not died down. Nor should it: Rogan has re-invigorated the staid old French with a new sense of passion and enthusiasm, making it Manchester's hottest ticket. Opinion may be divided on the décor – opulent ceiling moldings are now painted white, there's sage green panelling, a carpet with the appearance of a hardwood floor, a magnificent pair of ethereal crystal chandeliers floating above canteen-style wooden tables – but it's the utterly brilliant food that's the primary source of pleasure. A pre-starter of a single mussel in an edible seaweed shell served in a bowl of pebbles – a variation on the oyster pebble served at l'Enclume (see entry, Cumbria) – is a sensational burst of flavour and a splendid indicator of what is to come. Dishes are shaped

by the cycle of the seasons – a May visit saw asparagus (spears and purée) accompanied by crevettes, crevette bisque, watercress and duck skin, served ahead of a vibrant, lively dish of late spring offerings – vegetables, herbs, flowers and lovage salt. But among a seemingly inexhaustible supply of brilliant ideas one dish almost steals the show – a diced rump of ox smoked in coal oil with pumpkin seeds, kohlrabi balls and sunflower shoots. When it comes to dessert a 'not too sweet, not too tart' camomile with Cheshire rhubarb, toasted oats and Douglas fir, and the incredible flavours, textures and contrasts of pear snow, meadowsweet purée and crisp rye alongside buttermilk and toasted linseeds are hard to trump. The wine list has plenty of well-considered drinking (from £25) though it pays to get direction from the sommelier.
Chef/s: Adam Reid. **Open:** Wed to Sat L 12 to 2, Tue to Sat D 6.30 to 9. **Closed:** Sun, Mon, 2 weeks Aug, 1 week Christmas. **Meals:** Set L £29. Tasting menus D £60 to £79. **Details:** 58 seats. Separate bar. Wheelchair access. Children over 8 yrs only.

Greens
Well-loved veggie with a thrill-factor
43 Lapwing Lane, West Didsbury, Manchester, M20 2NT
Tel no: (0161) 4344259
www.greensdidsbury.co.uk
Vegetarian | £25
Cooking score: 2
V £30

'Everybody seemed relaxed and happy,' says one reader of the restaurant that remains at the top of the Mancunian pile for vegetarian food in a contemporary setting. Out here in West Didsbury, trends roll on. Greens has moved with them, expanding to arrive at the wood-panelled dining rooms, hung with chandeliers, that appeal just as much as co-owner Simon Rimmer's TV profile. Much-loved dishes include deep-fried veggie black pudding with mustard mayo, or oyster mushrooms rolled into Chinese pancakes with plum sauce and cucumber. Readers also rate the Cheshire cheese and basil sausages with

celeriac, swede and potato mash and port gravy. Vegans will find plenty, including a weekly changing vegan dessert; for dairy fiends, pudding could be blueberry crème brûlée. Wine from £15.50.
Chef/s: Simon Rimmer. **Open:** Tue to Fri L 12 to 2 (2.30 Sat), Mon to Thur D 5.30 to 9.30 (10 Fri and Sat). Sun 12.30 to 9.30. **Closed:** 25 and 26 Dec, 1 Jan. **Meals:** alc (main courses £12 to £14). Set D £15 (2 courses). Sun L £12.95. **Details:** 80 seats. 8 seats outside.

The Lime Tree
Long-standing local favourite
8 Lapwing Lane, West Didsbury, Manchester, M20 2WS
Tel no: (0161) 4451217
www.thelimetreerestaurant.co.uk
Modern British | £30
Cooking score: 3

Legions of regulars have grown used to the luxury of having this consistent, relaxed bistro at hand in West Didsbury. A pleasant corner spot, the Lime Tree includes a sunny conservatory, and is staffed by an 'accommodating' team. The use of produce from Hardingland Farm, the restaurant's own smallholding near Macclesfield, adds allure, though international influences also help to keep the menu lively. Start with pan-fried scallops with sweet chilli and crème fraîche, followed by a plate of the Hardingland lamb, including slow-cooked shoulder, roast loin and shepherd's pie, or a tart of feta cheese, pine nuts and tomatoes with couscous. Finish with chocolate torte or iced tiramisu parfait with coffee crème anglaise. Wines of the month are highlighted on a long list that starts at £15.
Chef/s: Jason Parker. **Open:** Tue to Fri and Sun L 12 to 2.30, all week D 5.30 to 10 (9 Sun). **Closed:** 25 and 26 Dec, 1 Jan. **Meals:** alc (main courses £12 to £21). Set L £10 (2 courses) to £15.50. Set D £13.95 (2 courses) to £15.95. Sun L £19.95. **Details:** 75 seats. 15 seats outside.

Michael Caines at ABode Manchester
Classy city-centre dining
107 Piccadilly, Manchester, M1 2DB
Tel no: (0161) 2005678
www.michaelcaines.com
Modern European | £50
Cooking score: 5
🍴 V

The most urban of Michael Caines' hotel and restaurant ventures is, appropriately for Cottonopolis, set in a converted textile warehouse. Above ground, you're at the gritty end of town; below, in the basement restaurant flanked by its Champagne bar, all is settled and sleek. The menu combines Michael Caines' signature dishes, some in simplified form, with chef Robert Cox's own take on refined modern European cooking. The kitchen is well practised at small 'grazing' dishes, making the tasting menu (which changes weekly) a good bet. Otherwise, start with roasted scallops with Jerusalem artichoke, truffled egg yolk and crisp belly pork, then try welfare-friendly Cumbrian veal with a veal shin raviolo. Readers love the boudin of turbot and langoustine mousse with vanilla bisque. Puddings take classic combinations and tend towards the soft and bubbly; soufflés such as confit orange and Grand Marnier are consistently good. Wine, listed by grape, is from £26.
Chef/s: Robert Cox. **Open:** Mon to Sat L 12 to 2.30, D 6 to 10. **Closed:** Sun, 25 Dec to 1 Jan. **Meals:** alc (main courses £17 to £25). Set L £14.50 (2 courses) to £19.50. Set D £16.50 (2 courses) to £22.50. Tasting menu £60. **Details:** 65 seats. Separate bar. Wheelchair access.

The Northern Quarter
Well-established Mancunian brasserie
108 High Street, Manchester, M4 1HQ
Tel no: (0161) 8327115
www.tnq.co.uk
Modern European | £29
Cooking score: 2
£5 OFF £30

TNQ, as it's known, with its of-the-moment modern British brasserie menu and 'shabby chic' interior, is 'very much a child of its times'. Manchester's style-conscious diners have certainly taken to it, praising its seasonal approach, North West ingredients and all-round solid execution. Smoked Fleetwood haddock rarebit makes a cracking start, while slow-cooked pork belly ribs get the thumbs-up from several readers. Italian and French influences are keenly felt, though you're never far from a good local ingredient: Goosnargh duck leg confit with smoked garlic mash, say, or Garstang Blue brûlée with tomato and chervil scone. Pudding might be 'crumble' or 'something chocolatey'. Pricing is declared 'on the money for the city centre'; service 'friendly and attentive'. Global wines from £19.50. **Chef/s:** Anthony Fielden. **Open:** all week 12 to 10.30 (7 Sun). **Closed:** 24 to 26 Dec, 1 Jan. **Meals:** alc (main courses £10 to £22). Set L and D £13.95 (2 courses) to £16.95. **Details:** 58 seats. Wheelchair access.

NEW ENTRY
The Rose Garden
A worthy Burton Road newcomer
218 Burton Road, West Didsbury, Manchester, M20 2LW
Tel no: (0161) 4780747
www.therosegardendidsbury.com
Modern British | £32
Cooking score: 1

This 'very worthy addition' to the Burton Road enclave is set apart by its cool minimalist décor – white with slender lines of colour and 1960s-style chairs – and inventive approach. Dishes like the 'cracking' chip-shop prawns with mushy pea fritter, chips and tartare sauce are easier to eat than they are to contemplate. Diners risk brain freeze with every single element listed on the menu: as in roast Goosnargh duck breast, blackberry and lavender glaze, sweet potato mash, roast beetroot, sweet potato crisps, duck crackling and blackberry sauce. Puddings such as blood-orange posset need work, but service is sunny and obliging. Wines are from £15.95. **Chef/s:** William Mills. **Open:** Sun L 12 to 7.30, Mon to Sat D 6 to 9.30. **Closed:** 24 to 26 Dec, 1 Jan. **Meals:** alc (main courses £14 to £21). Set L and D £15.95 (2 courses) to £17.95. **Details:** 32 seats.

Second Floor
Fashionable food with views
Harvey Nichols, 21 New Cathedral Street, Manchester, M1 1AD
Tel no: (0161) 8288898
www.harveynichols.com
Modern European | £40
Cooking score: 4
V

The Manchester arm of Harvey Nicks has occupied pride of place in the Exchange Square development since 2003, with views of the bustle below from its second-floor complex of eating and drinking spaces. Apart from the lively bar and brasserie, the main restaurant adopts a more understated formal tone, with clothed tables in a monochrome setting. Sam Everett has an accurate grip on the group's culinary ethos, which is all about robust, traditional treatments offset by modish seasonings. First up might be pork terrine with black pudding, piccalilli and onion breadsticks, with follow-ups ranging from lemon sole on wild mushroom risotto to guinea fowl with braised red cabbage, celeriac and blackberries. Fun desserts include popcorn pannacotta with caramel mousse and maple-syrup jelly. Pedigree farmhouse cheeses, served with damson and fig chutney, roll round on a trolley. Match them with the reliable collection of HN own-label wines, starting at £19.50 for Bordeaux Sauvignon and a red blend from the Aude. See overleaf for details.

Chef/s: Sam Everett. Open: all week L 12 to 3, Tue to Sat D 6 to 10. Meals: Set L and D £32 (2 courses) to £40. Tasting menu £55. Details: 90 seats.

NEW ENTRY

Wing's

A city-centre Cantonese retreat

Heron House, 1 Lincoln Square, Manchester, M2 5LN
Tel no: (0161) 8349000
www.wingsrestaurant.co.uk
Chinese | £40
Cooking score: 3

Close to Manchester's business and financial districts, Wing's is a well-padded retreat for those fleeing the shops or the office. High-sided booths offer privacy in a dining room that is smart, if a little dated, and the uniformed staff are formal but friendly. The menu of mainly Cantonese dishes is pleasingly manageable and scores highly for quality. Start with a platter of steamed or crisp-fried dim sum or chilli duck in lettuce wraps. To follow, prawn-stuffed aubergine and tofu in black bean sauce is rich yet light; clay-pot beef brisket comes with chunks of unctuous tendon and an anise-scented sauce. Attention to detail here runs to superior prawn crackers and excellent boiled rice, as well as tender-crisp Chinese greens in potent garlic sauce. Wine costs from £17.90 a bottle.
Chef/s: Mr Chi Wing Lam. Open: Mon to Fri 12 to 12, Sat 4 to 12, Sun 1 to 11. Meals: alc (main meals £12 to £40). Set D £45 (4 courses). Details: 85 seats. Separate bar. Wheelchair access.

Symbols

🛏 Accommodation is available

💷³⁰ Three courses for less than £30

V Separate vegetarian menu

£5ₒғғ £5-off voucher scheme

🍶 Notable wine list

NEW ENTRY

Yuzu

Japanese food that hits the pleasure points

39 Faulkner Street, Manchester, M1 4EE
Tel no: (0161) 2364159
www.yuzumanchester.co.uk
Japanese | £20
Cooking score: 3
💷³⁰

Origami figures and multicoloured saké bottles add interest to a 'cosy' Japanese dining room on the fringes of Chinatown. Yuzu's simple menu goes straight to the pleasure points: chicken kara-age is blistered crisp on the outside and steamy-tender within, and generous prawn gyoza dumplings have a chunky filling and pleasing lick of sesame. There's no sushi, just sashimi, most of it served as donburi toppings – try the scallop, salmon, tuna and sweet prawn. Rice bowls can be topped with dark, grease-free and genuinely seasonal tempura, and lunch specials (with miso soup, rice and, perhaps, pork or chicken katsu) are exceedingly popular. Even when the wooden tables and communal countertops aren't fully occupied, service can be anything from excruciatingly slow to 'excellent'. Fair prices reward those who are willing to take the gamble. Saké from £28.
Chef/s: David Leong Nagami. Open: Tue to Sat L 12 to 2, D 5.30 to 10. Closed: Sun, Mon. Meals: alc (main courses £7.50 to £16.50). Details: 26 seats.

ALSO RECOMMENDED

▲ Teacup on Thomas Street

53-55 Thomas Street, Manchester, M4 1NA
Tel no: (0161) 8323233
www.teacupandcakes.com
Modern British

In the heart of Manchester's creative Northern Quarter, this bustling bohemian café is a contemporary take on the traditional English tea room. By day, be prepared to queue for a table to enjoy lunchtime dishes such as a pork and fig sandwich (£5) or the 'Northern Fettle' samosa (£9.50) filled with feta, flamed peppers and spinach. On Friday and Saturday, the 'supper and a cuppa' deal might include tiger prawn and fish curry (£9.50). Wines start at £16. Open all week.

READERS RECOMMEND

Glamorous
Chinese
Wing Yip Business Centre, 1st & 2nd Floor, Oldham Road, Ancoats, Manchester, M4 5HU
Tel no: (0161) 8393312
www.glamorous-restaurant.co.uk
'Greed got the better of us and we ordered skewers of thinly sliced chicken (slightly crisp, a bit overcooked), good satay sauce drizzled over); salt & pepper ribs (very meaty, good flavour of star anise coming through); and excellent sesame prawn toasts.'

Solita
Italian-American
Turner Street, Manchester, M4 1DW
Tel no: (0161) 8392200
www.solita.co.uk
'Brilliant flavour combinations, an Inka grill and marrow bone in the burgers make this place a meat-lover's dream.'

▮ Norden
Nutters
Wacky indulgence and serious purpose
Edenfield Road, Norden, OL12 7TT
Tel no: (01706) 650167
www.nuttersrestaurant.co.uk
Modern British | £34
Cooking score: 3
V

The Nutter family business has grown from its origins in a converted pub to a Georgian manor house, with six acres of parkland commanding imperious views over Ashworth Moors. That said, Andrew Nutter hasn't gone all snooty on us, but maintains his forte in good-humoured, lively modern British food. Fish starters consistently show up well, whether for turbot in lemon and Parmesan crumb with Champagne reduction, or skate

wing dressed in mango. The kitchen's common touch brings a main-course dish of pork variations with a sausage roll, or a duo of Limousin beef fillet with oxtail pudding, served with pea purée and shards of bacon. The sticky toffee pudding retains its fans, or there may be classic caramelised lemon tart, accompanied by gin-and-tonic sorbet. A wide-ranging selection of reliable wines starts at £15.25.
Chef/s: Andrew Nutter. **Open:** Tue to Sun L 12 to 2 (4 Sun), D 6.30 to 9.30 (8 Sun). **Closed:** Mon, 1 or 2 days after Christmas and New Year. **Meals:** alc (main courses £18 to £23). Set L £13.95 (2 courses) to £16.95. Gourmet D £40 (6 courses). Sun L £23.50.
Details: 146 seats. Separate bar. Wheelchair access. Car parking.

▮ Prestwich
Aumbry
Classy, complex food with an eye on the history books
2 Church Lane, Prestwich, M25 1AJ
Tel no: (0161) 7985841
www.aumbryrestaurant.co.uk
British | £40
Cooking score: 5
£5
OFF

Punching above its weight, this classy cottage restaurant continues to evolve. On the first floor, a refurbished lounge houses the old cookbooks from which head chef Mary-Ellen McTague takes inspiration. The small dining room, next to a semi open kitchen, is simple but not plain. A limited à la carte augments tasting menus of six, nine or twelve courses (or five for £25 on Tuesdays). You might as well be hanged for a sheep as a slow-cooked milk-fed goat with pearl barley, goats' curd and cauliflower. Readers regard the signature Bury black pudding Scotch egg as 'a belter', but game consommé with cured hare loin, turnip, barley grass and English truffle is a more complex dish. Local ingredients and old-fashioned preparations are carefully balanced. The rhythm of service occasionally misses a beat, but grapefruit posset with celery granita or beetroot and chocolate cake with

bee pollen, hazelnut, milk and honey restore the equilibrium. Attention is paid to drinks, from tea and coffee to saké and sherry, and wine costs from £20 a bottle.
Chef/s: Mary-Ellen McTague and Laurence Tottingham. **Open:** Fri to Sun L 12 to 2, Tue to Sat D 6 to 9.30. **Closed:** Mon, 25 and 26 Dec, 1 and 2 Jan. **Meals:** Set L £20 (2 courses) to £25. Tasting menus £55, £70, £90. **Details:** 32 seats. Separate bar. Wheelchair access.

▌Ramsbottom

NEW ENTRY
Hearth of the Ram
Classy food in relaxed surroundings
13 Peel Brow, Ramsbottom, BL0 0AA
Tel no: (01706) 828681
www.hearthoftheram.com
Modern British | £27
Cooking score: 3
£5 OFF £30

Euan and Dena Watkins' clever restoration of this 200-year-old pub has proved a hit with locals, especially as they have recruited Abdullah Naseem (ex ramsons, see entry) to head the kitchen. The interior has been stylishly transformed – red leather banquettes, stone floors, polished wood – while the cooking has modern British ideas as its bedrock, with additions from France, Italy and beyond. Traditional bar food includes raised pork pies, ploughman's and burgers, but a simple asparagus salad with quail Scotch eggs is a typically seasonal starter from the carte. Lining up alongside could be 'excellent quality' king prawns with a 'spicy hot' scotch bonnet sauce and 'lovely, light' coriander gnocchi. Mains might bring Bowland venison loin or fillet of bream with samphire and razor clam velouté – but save room for popcorn pannacotta with strawberry sorbet, a big hit at inspection. The good choice of wines (from £14.50) includes many by the glass.
Chef/s: Abdullah Naseem. **Open:** all week 10am to 10.30pm (Fri and Sat 11.30). **Meals:** alc (main courses £13 to £20). **Details:** 90 seats. 40 seats outside. Separate bar. Wheelchair access. Car parking.

♉ MARY-ELLEN McTAGUE
Aumbry

What do you enjoy most about being a chef?
The creative process, and making people happy via the medium of food.

... And the least?
Spending so much time away from my children. Although as we grow the team, I'm working on that!

How do you come up with new dishes?
A combination of looking through cookery books (particularly historical ones), seeing what's in season and sourcing new products. Dishes then get worked on for some time before going on the menu.

What would you be if you weren't a chef?
I would love to be a writer, as long as I could be a very successful one.

Which restaurant best sums up British cooking today?
L'Enclume, for its imaginative use of local produce.

Which three ingredients couldn't you cook without?
Salt, onions and fat.

ramsons

Winning friends with Italian-style fine dining
18 Market Place, Ramsbottom, BL0 9HT
Tel no: (01706) 825070
www.ramsons-restaurant.com
Italian | £38
Cooking score: 4
£5
OFF

There have been changes once more at ramsons with Louise Varley (formerly cooking downstairs in the Hideaway) taking over the kitchen. Her interpretation of the restaurant's trademark Italian style involves a straightforward approach to superb ingredients and a feel for balanced flavours – it's certainly winning friends. Witness a May meal that opened with a plate of gossamer-thin salami served with rocket and olives 'just to get the taste-buds going', then continued with 'perfectly cooked pink and plump' sautéed duck livers with a 'subtle' Marsala cream sauce, followed by a 'creamy, tasty' risotto with saffron, prawns, peas and beans, then a 'beautifully cooked' breast of duckling with mash and a bergamot and marmalade sauce ('duck à l'orange it was not!'), before finishing with a 'perfectly judged, wobbly, silky, almondy' pannacotta with fragolino purée. The wine list is 'a joy' and reflects owner Chris Johnson's continued passion with all things Italian. Prices start at £21.
Chef/s: Louise Varley. **Open:** Wed to Sat L 12 to 2.30 (1 to 3.30 Sun), Tue to Sat D 7 to 9.30. **Closed:** Mon, 26 Dec, 1 Jan. **Meals:** alc (main courses £11 to £24). Set L £15 (2 courses) to £20. Set D £16 (2 courses) to £21. Sun L £20 (2 courses) to £40. Tasting menu £56. **Details:** 34 seats.

Sanmini's

Terrific Indian with pitch-perfect flavours
7 Carrbank Lodge, Ramsbottom Lane,
Ramsbottom, BL0 9DJ
Tel no: (01706) 821831
www.sanminis.com
Indian | £25
Cooking score: 3
£5 V £30
OFF

Ramsbottom has seen its fair share of culinary fireworks over the years, but the Sankar family's south Indian restaurant, housed in a Victorian gate-lodge in the centre of town, stands out from the crowd. The atmosphere is homely and informal, with everybody pitching in, and the kitchen team produces reliable, vividly spiced and demonstratively fresh dishes from the repertoires of Chennai, Chettinad and Kerala, among others. A wide range of vegetarian food will allow even hardened carnivores a night off, but there are also fried king prawns in green chilli and ginger masala, mutton kuzhambu and chicken cooked in aromatic spice blends. Tiffin specialities and good-value thalis extend the range, and you can sweeten things up at the end with milk-cooked fragrant desserts such as beetroot with cashews and nutmeg, or carrots and cardamom. House Australian is £13.95, or else drink mango lassi.
Chef/s: Mr Sundaramoorthy and Mr Sathyanand. **Open:** Sat and Sun L 12 to 3, Tue to Sun D 6.30 to 9.30 (10.30 Fri to Sun). **Closed:** Mon, 25 and 26 Dec, 2 weeks Jan. **Meals:** alc (main courses £9 to £16). Sun L £17.50 (2 courses) to £29.95. **Details:** 40 seats. Separate bar. Wheelchair access.

Salford

The Mark Addy
The flavours of yesteryear
Stanley Street, Salford, M3 5EJ
Tel no: (0161) 8324080
www.markaddy.co.uk
British | £26
Cooking score: 2
£30

There's no going hungry in this pub by the river Irwell, where chef Robert Owen Brown deals in full measures of old-fashioned local dishes and personal tributes to the flavours of yesteryear. On the bar it's Spam fritters and Blacksticks Blue bhajias; classics include Lancashire hotpot; and the daily specials such as chicken and tarragon dumplings or cheese and onion pie are British (and northern) through and through. Wintry game is a strength, and summer takes guests on to the riverside terrace, away from the unreconstructed décor. To finish, try a sherry trifle or Eccles cake with Mrs Kirkham's Lancashire cheese – or, if you must, double cream. Wines are from £13.50.
Chef/s: Robert Owen Brown. **Open:** all week L 12 to 3 (5 Sat, 6 Sun), Mon to Sat D 5 to 9 (10 Sat). **Closed:** 25 to 27 Dec. **Meals:** alc (main courses £9 to £17). **Details:** 80 seats. 100 seats outside.

Worsley

Grenache
Popular local bistro
15 Bridgewater Road, Walkden, Worsley, M28 3JE
Tel no: (0161) 7998181
www.grenacherestaurant.co.uk
Modern British | £30
Cooking score: 2
£5 OFF

Readers say 'nothing is too much trouble' at Hussein Abbas's neighbourhood restaurant. The intimacy of the ground-floor dining room, which seats 34, allows the 'good fun' to spread, and the bar upstairs provides after-dinner breakout space. Chef Mike Jennings upholds standards with modern British dishes that use simple, effective combinations. To start, try pheasant terrine with pickled beetroot and an orange and watercress salad, followed by sea bass with a saffron and shellfish risotto and sweet curry oil. Puddings include deep-fried plums with damson sauce and clotted cream. Not surprisingly, house wines are dominated by Grenache blends, from £13.25.
Chef/s: Mike Jennings. **Open:** Sun L 1 to 5, Wed to Sat D 5.30 to 9 (9.30 Fri and Sat). **Closed:** Mon, Tue, first 10 days Jan, 1 week Aug. **Meals:** alc (main courses £10 to £23). Set D £14.95 (2 courses) to £17.95. Sun L £14.95. **Details:** 34 seats. No children after 7.30.

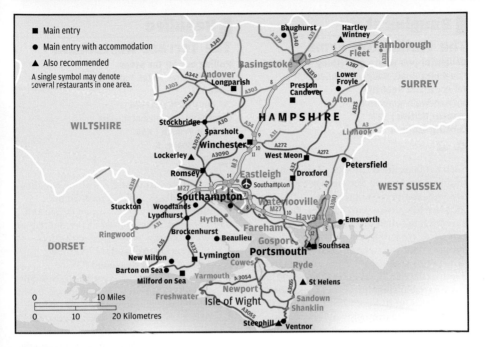

■ Main entry
● Main entry with accommodation
▲ Also recommended

A single symbol may denote
several restaurants in one area.

WILTSHIRE

DORSET

HAMPSHIRE

SURREY

WEST SUSSEX

Isle of Wight

0 10 Miles
0 10 20 Kilometres

▌ Barton on Sea

Pebble Beach

Glorious clifftop eatery with sparkling seafood
Marine Drive, Barton on Sea, BH25 7DZ
Tel no: (01425) 627777
www.pebblebeach-uk.com
French | £34
Cooking score: 3

'This place just keeps delivering wonderfully
consistent seafood,' enthused one reporter of
Pebble Beach, an enduring clifftop restaurant-
with-rooms. The venue boasts unbeatable
views of the Needles, with an open-air terrace
and open-plan kitchen adding to the theatre of
this relaxed eatery. Given the sea-facing
location, it's no surprise that the freshest fish
and seafood play a starring role, but there's
much more than scallops, crabs and lobsters
every which way. Kick off with twice-baked
smoked haddock soufflé, perhaps, before a
main of roasted monkfish with shrimp and
mussel risotto. Meat eaters and vegetarians
also do well with the likes of duck and pigeon
pie or wild mushroom ravioli with roasted
carrot and beetroot and cream sauce.
Caramelised apple pie with cinnamon cream
and blackberry ice cream makes a fine finish.
The lengthy, well-constructed wine list starts
at £17.75.
Chef/s: Pierre Chevillard. **Open:** all week L 11 to
2.30 (3 Sat, 12 to 3 Sun), D 6 to 11 (6.30 to 10.30
Sun). **Meals:** alc (main courses £14 to £46). Set L
and D £24.90 (2 courses) to £31.90. Sun L £14.95.
Details: 90 seats. 36 seats outside. Separate bar.
Wheelchair access. Car parking.

▮▯ Please send us your feedback

To register your opinion about any
restaurant listed in the Guide, or a new
restaurant that you wish to bring to our
attention, please visit the web address at
the bottom of the page. Your feedback
informs the content of the book and will
be used to compile next year's reviews.

Baughurst

The Wellington Arms

Delightful pub where everything's done well
Baughurst Road, Baughurst, RG26 5LP
Tel no: (0118) 9820110
www.thewellingtonarms.com
Modern British | £28
Cooking score: 4

🛏 £30

Such has been the Wellington Arms' success since Jason King and Simon Page took over this 18th-century country pub in 2005, that the place has grown with demand. Bedrooms have been installed and the restaurant extended, yet without losing that zest for doing everything so well. Jason King's food shines with seasonal goodness and remarkable depth of flavour. Food miles matter here, and farm-to-table cooking defines the kitchen, which feeds off its locality by fostering an army of hens, rearing pigs and sheep and growing vegetables. This self-reliant enterprise is backed up, wherever possible, by organic English produce. In summer expect gazpacho of home-grown tomatoes, cucumbers and red peppers with extra-virgin olive oil, home-reared roast rack of pork or Cornish skate with capers and brown butter. Autumn brings whole roast grouse or pot pie of local venison, with rhubarb and raspberry jelly and ice cream to finish. Wines start at £18.
Chef/s: Jason King. **Open:** all week L 12 to 1.30 (3 Sun), Mon to Sat D 6.30 to 9 (6 Fri and Sat). **Meals:** alc (main courses £11 to £21). Set L £15.75 (2 courses) to £18.75. **Details:** 36 seats. 20 seats outside. Wheelchair access. Car parking.

Beaulieu

The Terrace Restaurant

Pulling out all the stops
Montagu Arms Hotel, Palace Lane, Beaulieu, SO42 7ZL
Tel no: (01590) 612324
www.montaguarmshotel.co.uk
Modern French | £65
Cooking score: 5

🛏 V

The Montagu Arms, at the heart of Beaulieu's charming village, looks every inch the traditional hostelry. Its Georgian façade and 'days-of-yore' interior masks its credentials as a revered country-house hotel with a top-flight kitchen in the hands of Matthew Tomkinson. The aptly named Terrace overlooks lovely secluded gardens and, while the room has a 'lost in time' appearance (panelled walls, gilt-framed mirrors, white linen-clad tables and high-back chairs), the overall look is light – though uniformed staff heighten formality. 'Stiffly priced' menus take a surprisingly modern approach, inspired by the New Forest larder and vegetables and herbs from the hotel's potager, which the kitchen uses in a safe rather than ground-breaking manner. Witness a 'fresh and light' summer vegetable risotto (with globe artichokes, peas, lemon and Parmesan) or, from the Forest coast, a main course of wild Lymington sea bass fillet, teamed with watercress, Jerusalem artichoke purée, home-cured ham and red wine sauce. Desserts typify the kitchen's classical underpinning, maybe a praline soufflé or warm caramel fondant, while wines are a serious French-led bunch starting at £28.
Chef/s: Matthew Tomkinson. **Open:** Wed to Sun L 12 to 2.30, Tue to Sun D 7 to 9.30. **Closed:** Mon. **Meals:** Set L £22.50 (2 courses) to £27.50. Set D £50 (2 courses) to £65. Sun L £27 (2 courses) to £32.50. **Details:** 65 seats. Separate bar. Wheelchair access. Car parking. Children over 6 yrs only.

▌Brockenhurst

The Pig
Forward-thinking 'kitchen garden' enterprise
Beaulieu Road, Brockenhurst, SO42 7QL
Tel no: (01590) 622354
www.thepighotel.com
Modern British | £35
Cooking score: 4

🛏 V

Visitors to this forward-thinking boutique hotel can pull on their wellies, enjoy a meander through the impressively productive kitchen garden and even admire the pet porkers. Chef James Golding takes his cue from this self-sufficient bounty, and you can taste the results in a chill-out 'Victorian greenhouse' dining room – all terracotta flowerpots, boxes of seedlings, colourful floor tiles and a few too many tables. Home-grown produce and foraged pickings are supplemented by ingredients sourced from a 25-mile radius, and the results are 'just perfect'. Piggy plates (large and small) are always in demand: from baby BBQ ribs and crispy pork salad with homemade pickles to slow-roasted belly with crushed new potatoes and wild garlic. Otherwise, pan-fried scallops, game pie and juicy slabs of Pennington Farm sirloin go down well – likewise a 'heavenly' pavlova with forced rhubarb. Drink from a 'super choice of wines' from £16.50 (note the strong organic contingent).
Chef/s: James Golding. **Open:** all week L 12 to 2.15, D 6.30 to 9.30. **Meals:** alc (main courses £14 to £22). **Details:** 85 seats. Separate bar. Wheelchair access. Car parking.

Symbols
🛏 Accommodation is available
£30 Three courses for less than £30
V Separate vegetarian menu
£5 OFF £5-off voucher scheme
🍾 Notable wine list

▌Droxford

The Bakers Arms
Beguiling village pub
High Street, Droxford, SO32 3PA
Tel no: (01489) 877533
www.thebakersarmsdroxford.com
Modern British | £28
Cooking score: 3

£30

Modest, honest and generous, this cracking pub is located in the Meon Valley, within the South Downs National Park. Inside, beams and a mix of scrubbed and polished tables make a homely backdrop for some assured pub cooking. Dorset snails, juicy sausages and locally reared meats and cheeses are the building blocks for a line-up of dishes ranging from homespun English die-hards (faggots with mash and gravy) to more adventurous plates, say fillet of hake with sprouting broccoli and squid-ink sauce or slow-cooked pork belly with Puy lentils and red wine gravy. And when it comes to dessert, crème brûlée or sticky toffee pudding with caramel sauce and vanilla ice cream are a great way to finish. Wines from £14.95.
Chef/s: Richard Harrison. **Open:** Tue to Sun L 12 to 2 (3 Sun), Tue to Sat D 7 to 9. **Closed:** Mon. **Meals:** alc (main courses £11 to £19). Set L and D £13. Sun L £14.95. **Details:** 45 seats. 20 seats outside. Car parking.

▌Emsworth

Fat Olives
Imaginative championing of seasonal produce
30 South Street, Emsworth, PO10 7EH
Tel no: (01243) 377914
www.fatolives.co.uk
Modern British | £36
Cooking score: 3

Behind the smart frontage of a modernised 17th-century fisherman's cottage – easily spotted some 20 metres from the quay – is a charming dining room with a well-established husband-and-wife team at the helm. Lawrence Murphy does the cooking

while Julia runs front-of-house. The stylishly decorated room exudes a feeling of sincerity and goodwill, which counts for a lot. In the kitchen, the best seasonal produce is championed. The result is imaginative, confident dishes delivering well-balanced, emphatic flavours without overelaboration. Take brill served with roast chicory, brown shrimps, winter purslane and orange butter sauce or maybe roast and confit wild duck delivered with roast chervil roots, sherry vinegar and star anise jus. A starter of scallops with pancetta, pea velouté and shoots might catch the eye, while a selection of British cheeses makes an enjoyable alternative to desserts such as a 'well worth the 20-minute wait' lemon soufflé. Wines from £13.95.
Chef/s: Lawrence Murphy. **Open:** Tue to Sat L 12 to 2, D 7 to 9.30. **Closed:** Sun, Mon, 24 Dec to 1 Jan, 1 week Feb or Mar, 2 weeks Jun. **Meals:** alc (main courses £16 to £25). Set L £17.75 (2 courses) to £19.95. **Details:** 25 seats. 10 seats outside. Wheelchair access. Children over 8 yrs only (except Sat L where all ages welcome).

36 On The Quay
Destination restaurant-with-rooms
47 South Street, Emsworth, PO10 7EG
Tel no: (01243) 375592
www.36onthequay.co.uk
Modern European | £58
Cooking score: 6

Ramon and Karen Farthing's comfy retreat by Emsworth's cobbled quayside is a dream ticket for visitors – especially when you factor in the photogenic location, desirable letting rooms (named after spices) and a self-contained cottage in the village. The couple have been here since 1996, which shows in their thoughtful approach to hospitality and in Ramon's meticulous, multi-layered cooking. Given the waterside setting, it's no surprise that fish gets a starring role. A starter of seared scallops on creamed fresh crab with sugar snap peas and chestnut mushrooms is finished off with shellfish sabayon, while John Dory fillets are presented on white vegetables braised in

mussel and clam stock with tomato fondue and spiced courgette tempura. Meat also receives elaborate treatment, without too much jiggery-pokery: how about hay-roasted veal loin with compressed breast, nettles, charred Savoy cabbage heart and caramelised onion sauce? To finish, have fun with a combo of iced peanut parfait, butterscotch doughnuts and coffee foam or get citrus thrills from the five-part 'lemon presentation'. Zesty seasonal selections (from £19.50) kick off an idiosyncratic wine list that accommodates multifarious interesting grape varieties and styles geared for food-matching.
Chef/s: Ramon Farthing and Gary Pearce. **Open:** Tue to Sat L 12 to 1.45, D 7 to 9.30. **Closed:** Sun, Mon, 4 days Christmas, first 2 weeks Jan, last week May, last week Oct. **Meals:** Set L £23.95 (2 courses) to £28.95. Set D £57.95. **Details:** 50 seats. Separate bar. Wheelchair access.

▌Hartley Wintney

ALSO RECOMMENDED
▲ The Cricketers
The Green, Hartley Wintney, RG27 8QB
Tel no: (01252) 842166
www.thecricketers-hartleywintney.co.uk
Modern British £5 OFF

Trading on its village setting and views over the cricket green, this 'small yet beautifully formed pub' serves up real ales and honest local food ranging from honey-roasted Berkshire ham with eggs and triple-cooked chips right up to herb-crusted lamb. In between, expect twice-baked cheese soufflé (£6.95), sea bass with saffron potatoes, wilted spinach, red peppers and enoki broth (£13.95) and treacle and orange tart. Everyone praises the Sunday lunch, the warm welcome and 'very good' service. Wines from £16.50. Open all week.

▮▮● Also Recommended
Also recommended entries are not scored but we think they are worth a visit.

Isle of Wight

Appuldurcombe Restaurant
Refined dining and charm aplenty
The Royal Hotel, Belgrave Road, Ventnor, Isle of Wight, PO38 1JJ
Tel no: (01983) 852186
www.royalhoteliow.co.uk
Modern British | £40
Cooking score: 3
£5 OFF 🛏

Dating from the reign of William IV, the Royal is a stone-built hotel that has always prided itself on catering to the discerning traveller, tucked away as it is in the south-east corner of the Isle of Wight. The pale-hued dining room strikes a nice balance between traditional flounce and modern clean lines, with cooking to match courtesy of Steven Harris. A modish fish-and-flesh pairing might open proceedings, in the form of poached lemon sole and braised chicken wing, served with sweetcorn in chicken jus. Mains run from salmon with herb gnocchi and girolles in crab and ginger sauce, to venison loin and faggot, with the classic accoutrements of red cabbage, parsnip and mash, in bitter chocolate and port jus. The finale might be a proudly risen passion fruit soufflé with coconut sorbet. Eight wines by the glass from £4.75 lead a well-annotated list, with bottles from £18.
Chef/s: Steven Harris. Open: all week L 12 to 1.45, D 6.45 to 8.45. Closed: first 2 weeks Jan. Meals: Set L £15 (2 courses) to £19.50. Set D £31 (2 courses) to £40. Sun L £29. Tasting menu £50. Details: 110 seats. 50 seats outside. Separate bar. Wheelchair access. Car parking. Children over 3 yrs only at D.

Symbols
🛏 Accommodation is available
£30 Three courses for less than £30
V Separate vegetarian menu
£5 OFF £5-off voucher scheme
🍶 Notable wine list

NEW ENTRY
The Crab Shed
Alfresco café with super-fresh seafood
Tamarisk, Love Lane, Steephill Cove, Isle of Wight, PO38 1AF
Tel no: (01983) 855819
www.steephillcove-isleofwight.co.uk
Seafood | £15
Cooking score: 1
£30

You can practically dip your toes in the water at this no-frills alfresco café just yards from the sea at Steephill Cove, a picturesque sweep of coastline west of Ventnor. The Crab Shed's own fishing boat, *Endeavour*, delivers a daily haul of crab, lobster and mackerel, which goes into the simple salads and sandwiches on offer. Order at the counter then nab a bench table and tuck in to super-fresh seafood, including the famous crab pasties, with a glass of crisp Sauvignon Blanc. House wine £14.
Chef/s: Mandy Wheeler. Open: Wed to Mon L 12 to 3. Closed: Tue, Oct to Easter. Meals: alc (£4 to £18). Details: 30 seats outside.

The Hambrough
Boutique pizzazz and serious food
Hambrough Road, Ventnor, Isle of Wight, PO38 1SQ
Tel no: (01983) 856333
www.thehambrough.com
Modern British | £60
new chef/no score
🛏

High up on the cliffs overlooking Ventnor Bay, the Hambrough may still give the appearance of an imposing Victorian stone villa, but inside all is boutique pizzazz and style – complete with spectacular sea views from the windows of the understated dining room. Following the departure of chef/proprietor Robert Thompson, new owners have brought in Darren Beevers to head up the kitchen. His experience in big-name London venues such as Club Gascon and Chez Bruce (see entries) means that visitors can look forward to serious contemporary cooking in the modern vein – think roast quail with wild garlic, pickled beets and crunchy grains followed by pork loin and glazed cheek with apple gel, celery tops, balsamic onion 'petals' and smoked elderflower dressing. The food is matched by a concise but comprehensive wine list with prices from £25. Reports please.

Chef/s: Darren Beevers. **Open:** Wed to Sun L 12 to 1.30, Tue to Sat D 6.30 to 9.30. **Closed:** Mon. **Meals:** Set L £24 (2 courses) to £29. Set D £60. Tasting menu £85. **Details:** 35 seats. Separate bar.

ALSO RECOMMENDED
▲ Dan's Kitchen

Lower Green Road, St Helens, Isle of Wight, PO33 1TS
Tel no: (01983) 872303
www.danskitcheniow.com
Modern British £5 OFF

Locally sourced and seasonal are the buzz words at Dan and Carla Maskell's intimate neighbourhood restaurant located on the south side of St Helens' village green. It's a modern, bright eatery with wooden floors and simple, unadorned tables, noted for pleasant service and food that displays a little welcome ambition in dishes like a starter of local crab cakes with pickled vegetables and anchovies (£7.75) or mains of roasted loin of lamb with a mini shepherd's pie (£19.50). There's pear tarte Tatin with thyme ice cream to finish and wines from £13.95. Closed Sun, Mon, Tue L.

READERS RECOMMEND
Hillside Bistro

Modern British
30 Pier Street, Isle of Wight, PO38 1SX
Tel no: (01983) 853334
www.hillsideventnor.co.uk
'An open kitchen and a bustling, brilliant atmosphere; everyone enjoys themselves here. I highly recommend it.'

▌Lockerley

ALSO RECOMMENDED
▲ The Kings Arms

Romsey Road, Lockerley, SO51 0JF
Tel no: (01794) 340332
www.kingsarmsatlockerley.co.uk
British £5 OFF

Business has been brisk since this 18th-century pub close to Montisfont Abbey was spruced up a few years ago. It's a civilised place with polished tables, candles and winter fires, as well as an impressive landscaped garden for when the weather co-operates. The cooking is distinctly superior pub fare – from grilled Welsh rarebit with wild mushrooms (£6) via smoked haddock fishcakes with pea purée and poached egg or slow-braised ox cheek with garlic mash (£10), to cherry and almond tart. Wines from £15.95. Open all week.

▌Longparish
The Plough Inn

A proper foodie pub
Longparish, SP11 6PB
Tel no: (01264) 720358
www.theploughinn.info
Modern British | £30
Cooking score: 5
£5 OFF **V**

Chef James Durrant and manager Janet Cage earned their spurs at Gordon Ramsay's Maze before decamping to Hampshire. It's a big leap from Grosvenor Square to the Test Valley, but things have gone swimmingly since the couple took over this 18th-century village boozer. Ringwood ales, kids' menus and a full contingent of beams, timbers and old fireplaces are reminders that the Plough is still resolutely a pub rather than a restaurant manqué, and James has resisted any temptation to over-egg the 'excellent-value' gastronomic package. Evergreens such as delicate ale-battered haddock, mussels in cider or ribeye steaks on the bone are way above the norm, but there are bigger, more complex hits, too – from pork belly with a black pudding 'sausage roll' and cavolo nero to butter-roasted cod with an 'English breakfast' of smoked bacon, Toulouse sausage, poached egg and cep velouté. Be sure to order some chunky triple-cooked chips on the side, before pigging out over a bowl of creamy rice pudding with spiced plum jam. The wine list has decent drinking by the glass or carafe. Bottles from £14.

Chef/s: James Durrant. **Open:** all week L 12 to 2.30 (4.30 Sun), Mon to Sat D 6 to 9.30. **Meals:** alc (main courses £13 to £22). **Details:** 48 seats. 40 seats outside. Separate bar. Wheelchair access. Car parking.

▌Lower Froyle

The Anchor Inn

Cracking local with well-cooked classics
Lower Froyle, GU34 4NA
Tel no: (01420) 23261
www.anchorinnatlowerfroyle.co.uk
Modern British | £30
Cooking score: 2

This 16th-century inn in the heart of shooting country is an unabashed magnet for sportsmen. While it has been spruced up with some style, the Anchor has not lost its sagging beams, blazing winter fires and wooden floors – the atmosphere is one of a 'time-honoured' English inn. Just the sort of place to settle in with a newspaper and a pint of Ringwood ale or tuck into some proper British food: perhaps steak pie with triple-cooked chips and kale, whole lemon sole with caper and chive brown butter or local venison 'four ways' with parsnip purée and meat juices. Rice pudding with strawberry jam has received plaudits, likewise the plate of English cheeses with pickles. House wine £15.50.

Chef/s: Kevin Chandler. **Open:** all week L 12 to 2.30 (3 Sat, 4 Sun), D 6.30 to 9.30 (10 Fri and Sat, 7 to 9 Sun). **Closed:** 25 Dec. **Meals:** alc (main courses £13 to £24). Sun L £20.50 (2 courses) to £26.50. **Details:** 100 seats. 60 seats outside. Separate bar. Car parking.

▌Lymington

Egan's

Unpretentious neighbourhood eatery
24 Gosport Street, Lymington, SO41 9BE
Tel no: (01590) 676165
www.eganslymington.co.uk
Modern British | £30
Cooking score: 2
V

Housed in a late-Victorian building that once did duty as Lymington's police station, John and Debbie Egan's unpretentious neighbourhood eatery has become a fixture of the local scene over the years. Nothing disturbs the peace these days as the kitchen rolls out 'full-flavoured' food based on carefully sourced ingredients. The menu evolves at a steady pace, picking up a trend or two here and there. Clear tastes and pretty presentation are the hallmarks of dishes such as Dorset Blue Vinny pannacotta with crisp Bayonne ham and Waldorf salad or a duo of cod and hake with crab won tons and lemon butter sauce. To finish, white chocolate tart with blueberry compote is a typical call. House wine is £17.95.

Chef/s: John Egan. **Open:** Tue to Sat L 12 to 2, D 6.30 to 10. **Closed:** Sun, Mon, 2 weeks from 25 Dec. **Meals:** alc (main courses £16 to £24). Set L £15.95 (2 courses) to £17.95. **Details:** 50 seats. 20 seats outside. Separate bar. Wheelchair access.

▌Lyndhurst

NEW ENTRY

Hartnett Holder & Co.

Relaxed dining with an Italian accent
Beaulieu Road, Lyndhurst, SO43 7FZ
Tel no: (02380) 287167
www.limewoodhotel.co.uk
British-Italian | £38
Cooking score: 3

This New Forest country house hotel has been transformed (yet again). The rejigged restaurant now has bare-wood tables and country crockery, while a super-sized bar w

its red leather seating and walls covered in artwork has a modern clubby look – it's all billed as 'fun dining, not fine dining'. Head chef Luke Holder has joined forces with Angela Hartnett (of London's Murano, see entry), and the kitchen's approach is to combine seasonal British produce with Italian-accented cookery. Hartnett's influence is obvious. Signature pasta and risotto come as small or large plates (perhaps intensely flavoured veal cheek ravioli with tomato and green olive), or there are sharing plates of whole monkfish served with blackened red peppers, balsamic and basil alongside mains of halibut with diced scallop, peas and pea shoots. Reports in the main are positive, though side orders up-sold as necessities have not gone down well. An intelligent wine list starts at £17.50.
Chef/s: Luke Holder, Angela Hartnett. **Open:** all week 12 to 11. **Meals:** alc (main courses) £14 to £24. Set L £19.50 (2 courses) to £25. Sun L £37.50. Tasting menu £55. **Details:** 70 seats. 30 seats outside. Separate bar. Wheelchair access. Car parking.

▌ Milford on Sea

The Marine
Stylish Art Deco dining
Hurst Road, Milford on Sea, SO41 0PY
Tel no: (01590) 644369
www.themarinerestaurant.co.uk
Modern British | £30
Cooking score: 2
£5 OFF **V**

Right on the pebbled seafront, this spruced up Art Deco icon is perfectly positioned to capitalise on the view across the Solent to the Needles. Plenty of that luminous seaside glow finds its way into the smart first-floor restaurant (downstairs is an informal café bar-cum-bistro) via the floor-to-ceiling curved glass wall. The cooking ranges far and wide for culinary influences, turning out good gravlax and crab and potato cake with sweet chilli sauce among starters. For mains, the char-rilled ribeye steak, served with bacon and ive mash, mushroom fricassee and thyme

jus has been praised, as has supreme of chicken with sweet potato and chorizo croquettes. Rhubarb and apple crumble with custard makes a satisfying dessert. Wines from £14.95.
Chef/s: Mark Speller. **Open:** all week L 12 to 2.30 (3 Fri, Sat and Sun), Wed to Sat D 6 to 9.30. **Closed:** first 2 weeks Jan. **Meals:** alc (main courses £12 to £20). Set L and D £14.50 (2 courses) to £29.50. Sun L £11.50 to £17.50. **Details:** 40 seats. 74 seats outside. Separate bar. Wheelchair access. Car parking.

▌ New Milton

Vetiver
Aristocratic retreat with a contemporary outlook
Chewton Glen, New Milton, BH25 6QS
Tel no: (01425) 275341
www.vetiverchewtonglen.com
Modern British | £60
Cooking score: 5
♦ ⇌ **V**

Reporters find this ultra-smooth 'gem of a restaurant' difficult to fault for service and food, and while the 2012 remodelling continues to divide regulars, 'it manages to have a sense of occasion without being too formal or stuffy'. Spread over five rooms with 'a lovely outlook over the manicured gardens', Vetiver delivers a well-practised menu of modern British dishes, using many fine regional ingredients in a style that emphasises their pedigree. On a typical day, you might find Poole Bay mussels and clam linguine, although the kitchen could up the ante with foie gras and truffle terrine. Mains look to the enlightened brasserie repertoire for the likes of Jurassic Coast veal loin teamed with crisp sweetbreads and onion jam, a winning dish of Cornish sea bass with sea vegetables and salsa verde or, from the grill, excellent steaks and a 'superb' calf's liver with ventrèche bacon. To finish, dark chocolate terrine with Drambuie ice cream sent one reporter into raptures. The wine list is a grand tour of the Old and New World, with respected growers and fine vintages scattered liberally among its pages. Prices from £25.

Chef/s: Luke Matthews. **Open:** all week L 12 to 2.30, D 6 to 10. **Meals:** alc (main courses £22 to £44). Set L £20 (2 courses) to £25. Sun L £39.50. Tasting menu £75 (5 courses). **Details:** 173 seats. 46 seats outside. Separate bar. Wheelchair access. Car parking.

▮ Petersfield

Annie Jones

Amicable local restaurant and tapas joint
Lavant Street, Petersfield, GU32 3EW
Tel no: (01730) 262728
www.anniejones.co.uk
Modern European | £35
Cooking score: 2

£5
OFF

Chef/proprietor Steven Ranson's tapas sideline has proved so popular that he has extended the modest terrace/bar at the back of Annie Jones and taken over part of the shop next door – all in the attempt to satisfy Petersfield's appetite for chorizo croquetas, boquerones and pil-pil prawns. Otherwise, Ranson's intimate, boho-chic dining room provides an amicable setting for satisfying food with Anglo-European inflections: the likes of sticky char-grilled quail with carrot and ginger purée; fillet of turbot with lobster cannelloni, cauliflower and braised baby gem; or rump of lamb with confit shoulder and walnut pesto. Watch out for cheeky ideas such as a terrine of ham, egg and chips or lemon crunch with lime and mascarpone sorbet. House wine is £12.95.
Chef/s: Steven Ranson. **Open:** all week L 12 to 2, D 6 to 10. **Closed:** Sun, Mon (winter only), 25 to 27 Dec. **Meals:** Set L £14.95 (2 courses) to £17.95. Set D £27.50 (2 courses) to £35. Sun L £22.50. **Details:** 28 seats. 70 seats outside. Separate bar. No children after 9 Fri and Sat.

JSW

Less-is-more, fined-tuned artistry
20 Dragon Street, Petersfield, GU31 4JJ
Tel no: (01730) 262030
www.jswrestaurant.com
Modern British | £50
Cooking score: 6

🍾 🍽

Jake Saul Watkins (to fill out those initials) has achieved remarkable things at this converted 17th-century coaching inn since 2000. Inside, the look is contemporary with bright white décor, wicker chairs, slender wooden pillars and framed pictures. In such surroundings, Watkins offers a French-inflected version of modern Brit cuisine that delivers concentrated flavours teased from excellent raw materials. A starter of roast duck with a chicory tart and foie gras croûtons may sound like a main course, but is perfectly judged, or there may be a take on fish pie made from smoked haddock. When mains themselves come round, the techniques can be surprisingly old-fangled: tarragon-scented lamb navarin, for instance, or turbot with wild mushrooms. The five- or seven-course tasting menus hold most excitement, taking diners on a consummate tour of the repertoire, from scallops with celeriac purée and cep vinaigrette to a cheesecake loaded with tropical fruit. A conscientiously sourced wine list provides ample inspiring choice, including a generous slate of high-quality German Rieslings. Prices open at £19.
Chef/s: Jake Saul Watkins. **Open:** Tue to Sat L 12 to 1.30, D 7 to 9.30. **Closed:** Sun, Mon, 2 weeks Jan, May and Aug. **Meals:** Set L £17.50 (2 courses) to £22.50. Set D £27.50 (2 courses) to £32.50. Tasting menu £52.50 (5 courses) to £65 (7 courses). **Details:** 50 seats. 28 seats outside. Children over 8 yrs only at D.

Portsmouth

ALSO RECOMMENDED
▲ Abarbistro

58 White Hart Road, Portsmouth, PO1 2JA
Tel no: (023) 9281 1585
www.abarbistro.co.uk
Modern British

A couple of minutes from the cathedral and a short jog from the big-scale retail action at Gunwharf Quays, this whitewashed former pub was once used to house convicts awaiting transportation. These days it deals in modern brasserie food along the lines of seared pigeon breast with celeriac purée (£7), salmon Wellington with creamy dill sauce (£12) and black pepper and vanilla pannacotta with strawberries (£5.50). Wines from £14. Open all week.

Preston Candover

★ READERS' RESTAURANT OF THE YEAR ★
SOUTH EAST

Purefoy Arms

Welcoming hostelry with first-class Spanish-accented food
Alresford Road, Preston Candover, RG25 2EJ
Tel no: (01256) 389777
www.thepurefoyarms.co.uk
Modern European | £27
Cooking score: 3
£30

Spanish chef Andres Alemany and wife Marie-Lou swapped London for Hampshire's glorious Candover Valley back in 2009 and haven't looked back. Their unassuming brick pub, nicely spruced up and with a relaxed, contemporary feel, is drawing folk from afar for Andres' modern European-inspired menus. Handwritten daily, these bristle with homemade goodies (the delicious bread gets the thumbs-up) and quality ingredients: watercress from nearby Alresford, local seasonal game or the finest Serrano ham. Start with Spanish-inspired tapas – salt cod Scotch egg, perhaps, or Padrón peppers and grilled

chorizo Ibérico – or a perfectly timed risotto of goats' cheese, Muscat pears and chives. Main courses may take in cod fillet served with a rich stew of mussels, chorizo and tomatoes, and Dexter beefburger with dripping-cooked chips. Finish with crema catalana or Santiago tart with homemade ice cream. The sound European list of wines starts from £13.50.
Chef/s: Andres Alemany. **Open:** Tue to Sun L 12 to 3, Tue to Sat D 6 to 10. **Closed:** Mon, 26 Dec, 1 Jan. **Meals:** alc (main courses £11 to £28). **Details:** 55 seats. 65 seats outside. No children after 7.

Romsey

The Three Tuns

Local with updated pub classics
58 Middlebridge Street, Romsey, SO51 8HL
Tel no: (01794) 512639
www.the3tunsromsey.co.uk
Modern British | £25
Cooking score: 2
£30

Readers continue to endorse this picturesque, centuries-old listed pub, which is owned by the team behind Winchester's Chesil Rectory (see entry), taken by the flagstoned floors, old beams, bustling bar and relaxed pubby feel. Although drinkers are more than welcome, eager diners are drawn by the commitment to local and seasonal produce, perhaps in a dish of heritage beetroots with Rosary goats' cheese, walnuts and soft herbs or the Tuns pie (slow-cooked Hampshire ox cheek with mushrooms and horseradish) served with mash, seasonal greens, roasted carrots and beets. Lunchtime sandwiches, pub classics such as home-baked ham with egg and chips, British cheeses, real ales and wines from £15.50 complete the picture.
Chef/s: Andrew Yates. **Open:** all week L 12 to 2.30 (3 Fri, Sat and Sun), D 6 to 9 (9.30 Fri and Sat). **Closed:** 25 and 26 Dec. **Meals:** alc (main courses £10 to £17). **Details:** 50 seats. 30 seats outside. Separate bar. Wheelchair access. Car parking. No children under 7 at D.

▮ Southampton

The White Star Tavern

Lively urban bar and eatery
28 Oxford Street, Southampton, SO14 3DJ
Tel no: (023) 8082 1990
www.whitestartavern.co.uk
Modern British | £22
Cooking score: 1
£5 OFF   🛏   £30

A snappy, open-plan interior of wood floor and simple furnishings sets the tone for an unpretentious slice of high-street dining at this modern-day tavern (once a hotel for ocean-going passengers). The food aims to satisfy all requirements. The menu mixes contemporary European ideas with pub classics, offering the likes of garlic and thyme gnocchi with roasted carrot and truffled celeriac ahead of braised blade of beef with horseradish mash and bone-marrow gravy, alongside sausages with sage mash, apple sauce and cider gravy or fish and chips. Dessert could be a custard slice or apple and vanilla pie. Wines from £16.
Chef/s: Stewart Hellsten. **Open:** all week L 12 to 2 (3 Fri, 4 Sat), D 6 to 9.30 (10 Fri and Sat, 9 Sun). **Closed:** 25 to 27 Dec. **Meals:** alc (main courses £8 to £17). **Details:** 70 seats. 30 seats outside. Wheelchair access.

▮ Southsea

Montparnasse

Smart, inventive and much-loved bistro
103 Palmerston Road, Southsea, PO5 3PS
Tel no: (023) 9281 6754
www.bistromontparnasse.co.uk
Modern European | £38
Cooking score: 4

John Saunders' mission to bring relaxed, informal fine dining to Southsea has paid dividends. The Victorian town house near the common is a genteel but friendly venue for cooking that casts the net wide, to haul in a wealth of European reference points. Wayne Outram became head chef in 2012, and produces finely detailed dishes that celebrate pedigree Hampshire produce. A labour-intensive starter might see salmon fillet cured in salt and sugar, cooked sous-vide at 40°C, then chilled, diced and served with crispy salmon skin, sweetcorn purée and a lemon and soy vinaigrette. Next up could be fried fillet and braised shank of lamb, the latter shredded, mixed with olives and basil, crumbed and deep-fried, served with garlic tomatoes and basil jelly. The results feel deceptively effortless, deep studies in the essential flavours of their components – likewise, a dessert of macadamia praline parfait with poached pear and sesame tuile. A compact, stylish wine list opens at £18.50.
Chef/s: Wayne Outram. **Open:** Tue to Sat L 12 to 1.30, D 7 to 9.30. **Closed:** Sun, Mon, 25 and 26 Dec, 1 Jan. **Meals:** Set L and D £32.50 (2 courses) to £37.50. **Details:** 30 seats.

Restaurant 27

Clever, high-definition cooking
Burgoyne Road, Southsea, PO5 2JF
Tel no: (023) 9287 6272
www.restaurant27.com
Modern French | £40
Cooking score: 5
V

Despite sparse furnishings, barn-like dimensions and a slightly austere look (hangovers from its past as a chapel, gymnasium and grammar school), nothing eclipses Restaurant 27's 'boundary-pushing' food. Chef/proprietor Kevin Bingham describes his cooking as 'global French', and doubtless lists Ferran Adrià among his influences – judging by the gels, textures, powders and weird ideas characterising his clever, high-definition cuisine. Consider a chicken and carrot terrine paired with a 65°C egg yolk, salt-and-vinegar potato, hazelnut and apple; or a crazy-sounding 'fruit salad' involving liquid raspberry, lemon pannacotta, blueberry and coconut sorbet. In between, few can ignore the roast 'umami' duck with mango or the 'signature' pork belly, cooked for 30 hours, then served in all its rich glory with crab gnocchi, spring onion and a dusting of peanut: a combo eliciting gasps of amazement. Good-looking vegetarian dishes also create a stir: perhaps a risotto of Blacksticks Blue cheese and charred broccoli with burnt onion powder. Little extras 'make you feel valued', staff are attentive and the evolving 60-bin wine list starts with Pays d'Oc at £19.50.

Chef/s: Kevin Bingham. **Open:** Sun L 12 to 2.30, Wed to Sat D 7 to 9.30. **Closed:** Mon, Tue, 25 and 26 Dec, 1 Jan. **Meals:** Set D £40. Sun L £27. **Details:** 34 seats. Separate bar.

▌Sparsholt

NEW ENTRY

The Avenue

Technically assured cooking in handsome surroundings
Lainston House Hotel, Sparsholt, SO21 2LT
Tel no: (01962) 776088
www.lainstonhouse.com
Modern British | £55
Cooking score: 5

£5 OFF 🍴 V

'Exact cooking . . . ambition . . . balance and depth of flavour . . . quality ingredients – I think this is a real find.' So ran the notes of one visitor to Lainston House's handsome, polished mahogany and red-leather restaurant. As a leading member of Hampshire Food Fare and Farmers' Market (England's largest), chef Phil Yeomans is passionate about the sourcing of high-quality regional produce, the suppliers of which are credited on the menu. His cooking is a vigorous version of the modern British style, technically assured and showing a real understanding of taste and texture. You can eat very well here: unusual but well-thought out combinations such as scallops with smoked eel or veal rump with goats' curd and lemon, or meat dishes involving two cuts cooked differently: say roast loin of lamb with braised shoulder or pork fillet with braised pig's cheek. Equally, a beguiling combination of white chocolate, Hobnob biscuit, toffee popcorn and mandarin sorbet is a sweet hit. A

carefully chosen, cosmopolitan wine list is noted for friendly mark-ups, with prices starting at £20.

Chef/s: Phil Yeomans. **Open:** all week L 12 to 2, D 7 to 10. **Meals:** alc (main courses £35). Set L £22 (2 courses) to £32.50. Set D £45 (2 courses) to £55. Sun L £24.50. **Details:** 49 seats. 30 seats outside. Separate bar. Wheelchair access. Car parking. No children after 7.

▌Stockbridge

The Greyhound on the Test

A fresh new look
31 High Street, Stockbridge, SO20 6EY
Tel no: (01264) 810833
www.thegreyhoundonthetest.co.uk
Modern British | £35
Cooking score: 3

🍴

Since its revamp ('now more pubby than restaurant-with-rooms') this 15th-century inn has become extremely good at winning converts. The formula is an agreeable blend of rusticity (low beams, open fires, wooden floors), creature comforts and stylish informality. Locals, tourists and the fishing brigade – the Greyhound backs on to the river Test and has fishing rights – have all voiced their approval for the fresh new look, especially the new drinkers bar and the more relaxed feel. Alan Haughie remains at the stove and has risen to the occasion with panache, mixing an innovative streak with a flair for knowing his audience. Local and seasonal ingredients and an eye for detail are evident in dishes such as 'oysters on toast' (mushrooms and sage butter), braised cod cheeks with curried saffron sauce and linguine, bream with confit potato and tapenade, and rabbit cassoulet, followed by the likes of lemongrass pannacotta. House wine from £17.95.

Chef/s: Alan Haughie. **Open:** all week L 12 to 2 (2.30 Fri to Sun), Mon to Sat D 7 to 9 (9.30 Fri and Sat). **Meals:** alc (main courses £12 to £21). **Details:** 45 seats. 20 seats outside.

▌Stuckton

The Three Lions

Old-fashioned English auberge
Stuckton, SP6 2HF
Tel no: (01425) 652489
www.thethreelionsrestaurant.co.uk
Anglo-French | £40
Cooking score: 4

£5 OFF 🚃

Almost two decades down the line, the Womersleys' restaurant-with-rooms on a quiet lane on the western edge of the New Forest retains its comfortingly homely feel, matched by straightforward modern cooking. Mike Womersley doesn't go in for cutting-edge gastronomy – there is no attempt to scare the horses. Tersely worded menus look promising and compositions make sense, the finely honed repertoire delivering such dishes as pork loin with citrus stuffing and crackling or local venison accompanied by port and figs. To start, homemade salmon gravalax has 'very good flavour' according to one reporter, and the recipient of a fresh anchovy, bacon, confit pepper and oriental salad declared it 'a tasty little salad'. Desserts are good, especially a hot chocolate pudding with vanilla ice cream, and petits fours with coffee 'absolutely delicious'. An impressive, carefully annotated wine list draws together elite independent producers worldwide. House sections start at £14.75.
Chef/s: Mike Womersley. **Open:** Tue to Sun L 12 to 2, Tue to Sat D 7 to 9. **Closed:** Mon, last 2 weeks Feb. **Meals:** alc (main courses £19 to £27). Set L £22.50. Set D £28.50. **Details:** 60 seats. 10 seats outside. Separate bar. Wheelchair access. Car parking.

🍴 Average Price

The average price listed in main-entry reviews denotes the price of a three-course meal, without wine.

▌West Meon

The Thomas Lord

Country-pub charm and local fare
High Street, West Meon, GU32 1LN
Tel no: (01730) 829244
www.thethomaslord.co.uk
British | £25
Cooking score: 2

£30 🔻

True, the Thomas Lord has had a snazzy makeover, but the vibe is still that of a genuine country-village local. Named after the founder of Lord's, the pub has displays of cricketing paraphernalia (old bats and shoes) in its darkly beamed rustic bar, along with framed Player's cigarette cricket cards in the primped dining area. Twinkling candles, winter fires and period furniture add warmth. The kitchen 'tries to be a bit cheffy', but has more success when keeping things simple. Thus, Brit classics like a 'hearty' lamb hotpot are better bets than more fashionable pan-fried bream fillet teamed with herb-crushed new potatoes, (over) creamed leeks, mussels and spinach. The same goes for puds, where classic treacle tart trumps a smoked pineapple pannacotta. A trio of Upham ales and globetrotting wines (from £16.50) provide accompaniment.
Chef/s: Fran Joyce. **Open:** all week L 12 to 2.30 (3 Sat, 4 Sun), D 6 to 9.30 (10 Fri and Sat, 9 Sun). **Closed:** 25 Dec. **Meals:** alc (main courses £11 to £21). Sun L £15. **Details:** 65 seats. 70 seats outside. Separate bar. Car parking.

▌Winchester

The Black Rat

Lovely food awaits
88 Chesil Street, Winchester, SO23 0HX
Tel no: (01962) 844465
www.theblackrat.co.uk
Modern British | £35
Cooking score: 5

There's much to praise about this charmingly converted town boozer. Not only is it 'without question the best restaurant in our part of Hampshire', but it also 'guarantees top-class cooking every time'. Jamie Stapleton-Burns is an inspired chef and has gained in confidence since taking over the kitchen in April 2012. His cooking shows precision, imagination and flair, with great respect for the seasons. But it wouldn't work without sure-footed support from owner David Nicholson and his front-of-house team or, indeed, the loyal regulars who are voluble in their support, the detail of dishes lingering passionately in their memory. For one, it was exemplary smoked steelhead trout with 'super' heritage beetroot, a Japanese-style Aberdeen Angus tartare, 'succulent' New Forest venison and 'a clever, deconstructed' Black Forest gateau with a 'marvellous cherry sorbet'. For another, the highlight was new-season Yorkshire grouse, 'tender and full of the gamey, almost smoky flavour you expect' with the counterpoint of prime beetroot wedges and locally foraged girolles. Good bread, an excellent fixed-price lunch and wines from £18 complete the picture.

Chef/s: Jamie Stapleton-Burns. **Open:** Sat and Sun L 12 to 2.15, all week D 7 to 9.30. **Closed:** 2 weeks Christmas and New Year, 10 days Easter, 10 days Oct. **Meals:** alc (main courses £18 to £28). Set L £22.95 (2 courses) to £25.95. **Details:** 50 seats. 16 seats outside. Separate bar.

The Chesil Rectory

Half-timbered heritage and modern food
1 Chesil Street, Winchester, SO23 0HU
Tel no: (01962) 851555
www.chesilrectory.co.uk
Modern British | £32
Cooking score: 4

Blackened wooden timbers criss-crossing the crooked exterior remind everyone that this chunk of Winchester heritage is reckoned to be the oldest building in town. Once you're inside, creaking floorboards, ancient beams, tiny doorways and hunting-lodge taxidermy reinforce the mood – although the antiquity is tempered by stylish buttoned banquettes, vintage chandeliers and curios. The effect is 'classy but cosy': just right for cooking that

offers comfort, interest and satisfaction. Carpaccio of Blackmoor Estate venison is served with horseradish cream and tarragon pesto; a starter of warm black pudding and poached egg is enhanced by a piquant mustard sauce; and crisp pork belly appears in company with cipollini onions, smoked trout, apple and beetroot. Readers also recommend trying the fish: perhaps hake fillet with chorizo, chickpea and coriander broth. To finish, the raspberry soufflé is 'sensational'; otherwise, order the wicked espresso mousse with homemade doughnuts. Service is warm, friendly and courteous, and the carefully chosen wine list has plenty of reasonably priced drinking from £19.95.

Chef/s: Damian Brown. **Open:** all week L 12 to 2.20 (3 Sun), D 6 to 9.30 (9 Sun). **Closed:** 25 and 26 Dec, bank hols. **Meals:** alc (main courses £14 to £20). Set L and D £15.95 (2 courses) to £19.95. Sun L £21.95 (2 courses) to £26.95. **Details:** 75 seats. Separate bar. Children at L only.

▌Woodlands

★ CHEF TO WATCH ★

NEW ENTRY

The Dining Room at TerraVina

Ambitious, highly personal, modern dining experience
174 Woodlands Road, Woodlands, SO40 7GL
Tel no: (023) 8029 3784
www.hotelterravina.co.uk
Modern European | £78
Cooking score: 6

🍾 🍽

Although George Blogg is executive chef for the whole hotel, and thus oversees the main Hotel TerraVina dining room (see entry below), he concentrates specifically on this new venture – delivering a highly personal, dinner-only tasting menu (9 or 12 courses) to limited numbers on Saturday, Sunday and Monday evenings. The room may feel a little detached, more a homage to owner Gerard Basset's wine achievements (framed press cuttings cover the walls), though leather

seating and crisp white linen help 'pep things up', and the fine-tuned cooking more than compensates. George forages ingredients and sources produce exclusively from Hampshire and Dorset and delivers most dishes to the table himself – the cooking hitting the spot by combining formidable technical skill with flavours and textures. Menu descriptions are kept brief: thus turbot, tidal greens and cockles produces the freshest fish teamed with samphire and sea beet, cockles, toasted linseeds and 'exquisite' mini seaweed vinegar jelly balls. Earthier themes also surface in a complex dish of succulent local roe buck, served with spinach and spelt 'and much more besides', while dessert could bring acorn (brûlée), chocolate (dark chocolate sorbet) and sugars. The connoisseurs' wine list offers breadth with excellence of pedigree, with wine pairing available from 'a crack team'; prices from £17.50.
Chef/s: George Blogg. **Open:** Mon, Sat and Sun D 7 to 9. **Closed:** Tue to Fri. **Meals:** Tasting menu £72 (9 courses) to £85 (12 courses). **Details:** 18 seats. Separate bar. Wheelchair access. Car parking.

purée, cured ham, watercress and hazelnut crumb. But a classic bouillabaisse or roasted breast and confit leg of poussin, served with pomme Anna, wilted chard, baby carrots and broad beans are equally typical of his fresh, well balanced approach. Service keeps pace with the cooking, and it is all matched by a fittingly accomplished wine list. Gerard Basset is one of our leading wine gurus and his list, arranged by style, is suitably Bacchanalian: a deftly selective range of classics and new-wave wines, chosen for quality and value. Bottles from £17.50.
Chef/s: George Blogg. **Open:** all week L 12 to 2, D 7 to 9.30. **Meals:** alc (main courses £17 to £26). Set L £21 (2 courses) to £27. **Details:** 56 seats. 26 seats outside. Separate bar. Wheelchair access. Car parking.

Hotel TerraVina

A destination for food lovers
174 Woodlands Road, Woodlands, SO40 7GL
Tel no: (023) 8029 3784
www.hotelterravina.co.uk
Modern European | £35
Cooking score: 4

Nina and Gerard Basset's strikingly contemporary New Forest hotel has long been a destination for food lovers, but since the arrival of George Blogg, there is even more reason to beat a path to its door. Le Champignon Sauvage's former sous chef (see entry) has really stamped his mark on the place, overseeing all the cooking in this hotel of two parts – see entry above for the limited opening Dining Room. Blogg's enthusiasm and passion 'is so infectious', his flavouring partnerships well conceived with dishes deftly executed – as in a starter of slow-cooked marinated pigeon breast with black pudding

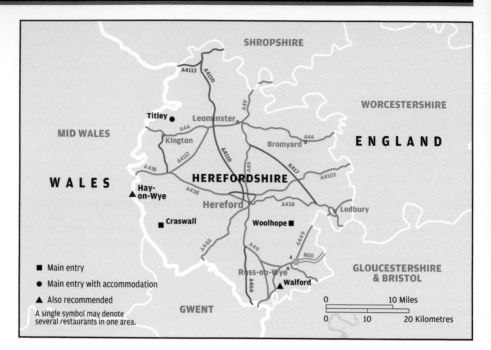

▌Craswall

The Bull's Head

Robust provender at a stone-walled hostelry
Craswall, HR2 0PN
Tel no: (01981) 510616
www.bullsheadcraswall.co.uk
Modern British | £29
Cooking score: 2

£5 £30
OFF

A recent recruit to the Bull's Head fan club starts with what this old Black Mountains 'dining pub' is not: 'it's not rundown, it's not twee, it's not olde-worlde'. . . The conclusion: 'It's just a great place.' Charles and Kathryn Mackintosh's lovingly kept stone-walled drovers' inn, just six miles from Hay-on-Wye, has quickly established a loyal local following, and the weekenders and festival-goers have cottoned on, too. Self-taught Charles's menus are French, Italian or British as the mood strikes. Rabbit rillettes and the Arbroath smokie pot make regular appearances, while robust mains might be Provence-style lamb shoulder with flageolet beans, or lamb tagine. Finish on a local note with Wimberry tart and cream or marinated Ledbury cherries. Drink European wines (from £16) or local cider and perry.
Chef/s: Charles Mackintosh. **Open:** Fri to Sun L 12 to 3, Fri and Sat D 7 to 11. **Closed:** Mon to Thur, 2 Jan to mid Feb. **Meals:** alc (main courses £12 to £23). **Details:** 36 seats. 12 seats outside.

▌Hay-on-Wye

ALSO RECOMMENDED
▲ Richard Booth's Bookshop Café

44 Lion Street, Hay-on-Wye, HR3 5AA
Tel no: (01497) 820322
www.boothbooks.co.uk
Modern British

More than just another bookstore, Richard Booth's Bookshop is a Hay cultural hub, complete with cinema, yoga classes and this picture-hung, stone-flagged café. The eatery is a 'pop in' sort of place where creative-but-comforting breakfasts, lunches and snacks are served. Try buttermilk pancakes with vanilla yoghurt and cinnamon syrup (£4.50), skirt steak sandwich with horseradish (£7.50) or rhubarb frangipane tart (£4). Drink coffee, wine (from £17) or a Bloody Mary as you see fit. Full menu Thur to Sun only. Closed Mon

Titley

The Stagg Inn
Foodie gem worth travelling to
Titley, HR5 3RL
Tel no: (01544) 230221
www.thestagg.co.uk
Modern British | £33
Cooking score: 5

£5 OFF 🍽 V

Built at the intersection of two drovers' roads, the white-fronted Stagg is an amalgam of medieval, Victorian and 1970s architecture, and yet every inch a cheering country pub. Three dining areas quickly fill at weekends, and the bar takes the overspill, but it's all run with impressive unflappability by Nicola Reynolds. Husband Steve is in the kitchen, drawing on trusted local suppliers to forge menus featuring familiar complementary flavours. Start with baked pressed brawn, served with shallot, pickled radish and parsley mayonnaise, or mackerel tartare with salsa verde and horseradish snow, before moving on, perhaps, to a fine seasonal game dish such as roast and confit partridge with figs, Savoy cabbage and lentils with bacon, or an accurately cooked sea bass with mushroom duxelles, charred leeks and dauphinois. The brilliant English and Welsh cheeses are hard to resist, if you haven't been snared by the tripartite brûlée set of vanilla, honey and ginger. A concise but impressive wine list keeps prices on a leash, and there are also thoroughbred West Country ciders and perries.

Chef/s: Steve Reynolds. **Open:** Tue to Sun L 12 to 2 (2.15 Sun), Tue to Sat D 6.30 to 9 (9.30 Sat). **Closed:** Mon, first 2 weeks Nov, 25 to 27 Dec, 1 to 3 Jan. **Meals:** alc (main courses £17 to £24). Sun L £20.90. **Details:** 70 seats. 20 seats outside.

Walford

ALSO RECOMMENDED
▲ The Mill Race
Walford, HR9 5QS
Tel no: (01989) 562891
www.millrace.info
Modern British £5 OFF

Boasting pretty views of Goodrich Castle, the Mill Race is an admirable pub-restaurant that makes the most of its Wye Valley location. Ingredients are plucked from the produce-rich local vicinity, so expect seasonal treats such as asparagus and duck egg or saddle and braised shoulder of lamb with shallot purée, artichoke and fondant potato (£20.25). Scotch eggs (£5.95), burgers and pies should satisfy the pub-grub fans, with a pizza menu thrown in to boot. House wines start at £15; open all week.

Woolhope

The Butchers Arms
Rustic pub with fresh flavours
Woolhope, HR1 4RF
Tel no: (01432) 860281
www.butchersarmswoolhope.com
Modern British | £24
Cooking score: 4

£30 ▾

Still a proper Herefordshire watering hole complete with beautifully kept cask beer, low beams and blazing fires, the Butchers Arms is simply a great place to be. Truly rural, it's a down-to-earth spot with a tremendous atmosphere and Fran Snell's sound cooking is based on shrewdly sourced local and regional produce. The approach is relatively simple, but there are some cleverly honed modern ideas (roast pheasant samosa, say) on the compact menu. 'Very fresh' fillet of gilthead bream on a bed of spinach with simply boiled potatoes, and 'a very generous portion' of roast pork tenderloin and black pudding with dauphinois potatoes and red cabbage, proved 'perfect for a bitterly cold day'. There's nothing like an old favourite at dessert stage, especially warm ginger cake with butterscotch sauce and treacle toffee ice cream. The wine list packs plenty of interest and serious drinking into a few pages. Prices from £16.

Chef/s: Fran Snell. **Open:** Tue to Sun L 12 to 2, Tue to Sat D 6 to 9. **Closed:** Mon, 25 Dec. **Meals:** alc (main courses £11 to £17). Sun L £18.50 (2 courses) to £24. **Details:** 60 seats. 30 seats outside.

DAVID EVERITT-MATTHIAS
Le Champignon Sauvage

What food trends are you spotting at the moment?
Deep fried artichoke skins, Nordic food and a return to good, local sourcing.

Name three chefs you admire.
Pierre Koffmann (Koffmann's), Eric Chavot (Brasserie Chavot) and Philip Howard (The Square).

Is there a restaurant you return to year after year?
Tom Aikens, Mayfair.

At the end of a long day, what do you like to cook?
We have a staff meal at 6.30, before service — something healthy, like Thai.

What would you be if you weren't a chef?
A money broker or a professional cricket player.

Which three ingredients couldn't you cook without?
Chocolate, duck fat and cheese.

Who are the chefs to watch in 2014?
George Blogg (Hotel TerraVina) and Rob Weston (La Trompette).

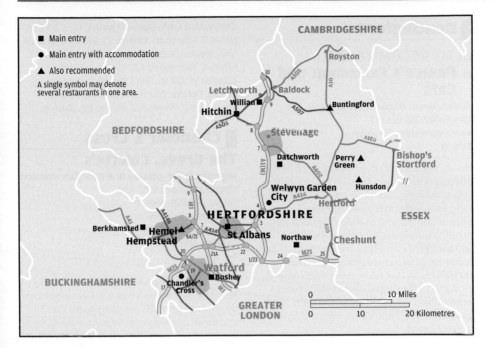

Map legend:
■ Main entry
● Main entry with accommodation
▲ Also recommended

A single symbol may denote several restaurants in one area.

▌Berkhamsted

The Gatsby
Deco decadence and artful food
Rex Cinema, 97 High Street, Berkhamsted, HP4 2DG
Tel no: (01442) 870403
www.thegatsby.net
Modern European | £35
Cooking score: 2

Housed within Berkhamsted's fabulously restored Rex Cinema, the Gatsby is a heady mix of Art Deco finery and up-to-the-minute accoutrements. The town's in-crowd rubs shoulders with movie-goers in the pulsating bar, while others sit under glittering chandeliers and sculpted ceilings in the pillared white dining room, dreaming of Garbo or Betty Grable. By contrast, Matthew Salt cooks in the modern idiom, fashioning artful plates from a battery of on-trend ingredients – perhaps tortellini of confit rabbit with carrot purée, bacon and tarragon foam or slow-cooked pork belly with crackling, mustard mash and buttered sprout tops. He also respects the old ways, presenting smoked salmon roulade with celeriac rémoulade, serving roast cannon of venison with pommes Anna and rounding things off with Bakewell tart. Wines start at £15.95.
Chef/s: Matthew Salt. **Open:** Mon to Sat L 12 to 2.30, D 5.30 to 10.30. Sun 12 to 9.30. **Closed:** 25 and 26 Dec. **Meals:** alc (main courses £16 to £27). Set L and D £14.95 (2 courses) to £20.90. Sun L £14.95. **Details:** 64 seats. 44 seats outside. Separate bar. Wheelchair access. No children after 6.

▕▏● Please send us your feedback

To register your opinion about any restaurant listed in the Guide, or a new restaurant that you wish to bring to our attention, please visit the web address at the bottom of the page. Your feedback informs the content of the book and will be used to compile next year's reviews.

Buntingford

ALSO RECOMMENDED
▲ **Pearce's Farmshop and Café**

Hamels Mead, Buntingford, SG9 9ND
Tel no: (01920) 821246
www.pearcesfarmshop.com
British

Beside the south carriageway of the A10 and offering wonderful views over the river Rib valley, this spacious, contemporary café-cum-farm shop welcomes punters with alluring piles of goodies and a modestly priced café menu. Sandwiches, salads, the likes of chicken and ham pie (£10.50) or toad in the hole and lovely cakes are served alongside a daily specials menu that takes its cue from what's available in the shop – perhaps tenderstem broccoli and sweet-potato gratin with roast guinea fowl (£11.50). Wines from £13.95. Open all week.

Bushey

St James
Doing Bushey proud
30 High Street, Bushey, WD23 3HL
Tel no: (020) 8950 2480
www.stjamesrestaurant.co.uk
Modern European | £29
Cooking score: 1
V £30

Much of St James's magic is down to host Alfonso La Cava, a 'garrulous, instantly welcoming chap full of gleeful bonhomie' who ensures you are 'always made to feel an important customer'. Nevertheless, the 'excellent well-cooked food' also makes its mark. Built on carefully sourced, super-fresh ingredients, it takes a broad view of British and French classics: maybe seared foie gras with oxtail casserole and then grilled medallions of beef with polenta chips, mushrooms, tomato ketchup and crispy shallots. Toblerone cheesecake is a regular dessert. Wines start at £15.95.

Chef/s: Matt Cook. **Open:** all week L 12 to 2.30, Mon to Sat D 6.30 to 10. **Closed:** 25 and 26 Dec, bank hols. **Meals:** alc (main courses £17 to £22). Set L £15.95 (2 courses) to £20.95. Set D £17.95 (2 courses) to £22.95. Sun L £20.95 (2 courses) to £25.50. **Details:** 100 seats. 25 seats outside. Separate bar. Wheelchair access. Car parking.

Chandler's Cross

The Grove, Colette's
Ingredients-led passion in a Georgian mansion
Chandler's Cross, WD3 4TG
Tel no: (01923) 296010
www.thegrove.co.uk
Modern British | £75
Cooking score: 6
⇋ V

A fetching Georgian mansion overlooking a bit of Hertfordshire known as Charlotte's Vale, the Grange provides the setting and the amenities (including an organic walled garden) for Russell Bateman's wide-ranging fixed-price menus of British cooking. Bateman's passion radiates out from both the masterclasses he gives and his culinary repertoire. It's the kind of food that's focused on the quality of its component parts, rather than cheffy fussiness, though there's no lack of innovation on display. Poached Fowey oysters, served with an oyster mushroom and foie gras in mushroom broth, has proved a hit with reporters, as has the relatively simple but sublime main course of Cotswold white chicken with cauliflower, Vacherin and truffle in poultry jus. Fish from the south west or Scotland is top-notch – perhaps brill with seaweed, sea kale, pickled clams and salsify – and desserts such as blood-orange tart with cardamom ice cream end things on a flourish. Intermediate courses, breads and cheeses all add lustre, as does the list of superb if expensive wines. Glasses start at £7.50, bottles £27.

Chef/s: Russell Bateman. **Open:** Tue to Sat D only 6.30 to 9.30. **Closed:** Sun and Mon. **Meals:** Set D £65. Tasting menu £85 (7 courses). **Details:** 42 seats. Separate bar. Wheelchair access. Car parking. No children.

▌Datchworth

The Tilbury
Generous, good-value British classics
Watton Road, Datchworth, SG3 6TB
Tel no: (01438) 815550
www.thetilbury.co.uk
Modern British | £28
Cooking score: 3
£5 OFF £30

You'll find bags of character at this roadside village inn, which incorporates a rustic bar, a slightly scuffed snug for light lunches and a smart dining room (comfortably attired in rich colours) for evening meals. The Tilbury also has a loyal band of regulars who praise the great food, atmosphere and service. Paul Bloxham's cooking is an expansive mix of big flavours and hearty portions, his passion for cooking and his dedication to unearthing first-class raw materials (some sourced locally) are without doubt. Indeed, ingredients are everything here, and Bloxham's menu makes choice hard – but there could be ham hock and salt beef terrine with mustard fruit pickle; roast sea trout with cauliflower couscous, ratatouille and salsa verde; and local honey pannacotta with red wine poached pear to finish. The short, global wine list opens at £18.95.
Chef/s: Paul Bloxham, Ben Crick and Martin Thurlow. Open: Tue to Sun L 12 to 3 (5 Sun), Tue to Sat D 6 to 11. Closed: Mon. Meals: alc (main courses £11 to £24). Set L and D £13.95 (2 courses) to £17.95. Sat D and Sun L £17.95 (2 courses) to £21.95. Details: 70 seats. 40 seats outside. Separate bar. Wheelchair access. Car parking.

▌▌Also Recommended
Also recommended entries are not scored but we think they are worth a visit.

▌Hemel Hempstead

ALSO RECOMMENDED
▲ Restaurant 65
65 High Street, Old Town, Hemel Hempstead, HP1 3AF
Tel no: (01442) 239010
www.restaurant65.com
Modern European £5 OFF

A valuable local asset, Grant and Gina Young's honest little restaurant offers a refreshing antidote to Hemel Hempstead's junk-food outlets. Despite pressure on the tiny kitchen, the food is well crafted in the Anglo-European vein – think sautéed chicken livers with black pudding, bacon and mustard sauce (£6.95); crispy slow-roast pork belly with tatties and neeps, apple purée and sage jus (£16.50); or warm pear and almond tart with cherry ice cream. House wine is £14.95. Closed Sun D and Mon.

▌Hitchin

Hermitage Rd
Sparky food and feel-good vibes
20-21 Hermitage Road, Hitchin, SG5 1BT
Tel no: (01462) 433603
www.hermitagerd.co.uk
Modern British | £25
Cooking score: 2
£30

Stylish to the hilt, the former first-floor dance hall is part of a group owned by the Nye family – see entries for the White Horse, Brancaster Staithe and Fox at Willan. The place is split into an all-day bar and a bold, high-decibel brasserie on a grand scale. Reporters are single-minded in their appraisal, giving the thumbs-up to the warm friendliness with which Hermitage Rd is imbued. At the centre of things is an open kitchen delivering a big-hearted line-up of generous dishes, from sharing boards and pots of Norfolk mussels, via steaks, burgers and ribs, to excellent fresh fish: fillet of pollack with mussel, leek and saffron chowder, perhaps. It's all 'very well done'. Wines from £16.50.

Chef/s: Kumour Uddin. **Open:** Tue to Sun L 12 to 2.30 (4 Sun), D 6.30 to 10 (5 to 8 Sun). **Closed:** Mon. **Meals:** alc (main courses £10 to £23). **Details:** 150 seats. Separate bar. Wheelchair access.

Hunsdon

ALSO RECOMMENDED
▲ Fox & Hounds

2 High Street, Hunsdon, SG12 8NH
Tel no: (01279) 843999
www.foxandhounds-hunsdon.co.uk
Modern British

There's no shortage of atmosphere at this village pub with its crackling fires, smart dining room and summer terrace. James Rix's bright, Mediterranean-infused menus major in hand-rolled pasta, local game and steak. Linguine with clams (£7.75), then venison loin, parsnip purée, Brussels tops and peppercorn sauce (£19.50), with apple tart fine and cinnamon ice cream (£6.25) for pudding would serve you very well. Drink local ale or (mostly) Old World wines (from £15.50). No food Sun D or Mon.

Northaw

The Sun at Northaw

Well-presented inn packed with robust delights
1 Judges Hill, Northaw, EN6 4NL
Tel no: (01707) 655507
www.thesunatnorthaw.co.uk
British | £29
Cooking score: 3
£5 OFF £30

This scrubbed-up village pub draws a well-heeled clientele with a credo of high-quality ingredients cooked simply and served generously. An unashamedly nostalgic menu name-checks local and regional suppliers and kicks off with snacks such as chips and curry sauce. Starters of razor clams with ramsons and smoked bacon or rolled pig's spleen with red onion, pickles and aïoli do their bit to

rekindle the embers of folksy British gastronomy, while the theme of posh, patriotic comfort food is reflected in main courses of hare and trotter suet-crust pie (with celeriac and thyme mash) and whole Aldeburgh lemon sole with spiced cockles and laverbread butter. Seville orange marmalade steamed sponge and custard, and buttermilk pudding with poached champagne rhubarb loom large among desserts. Wines from £17.

Chef/s: Oliver Smith. **Open:** Tue to Sun L 12 to 3 (4 Sun), Tue to Sat D 6 to 10. **Closed:** Mon. **Meals:** alc (main courses £12 to £24). Set L £12.95 (2 courses) to £14.95. Sun L £26.50 (2 courses) to £32.50. **Details:** 80 seats. 60 seats outside. Separate bar. Wheelchair access. Car parking.

Perry Green

ALSO RECOMMENDED
▲ The Hoops Inn

Perry Green, SG10 6EF
Tel no: (01279) 843568
www.hoops-inn.co.uk
British

This pretty, white-painted village hostelry has been given a smart, contemporary makeover by the Henry Moore Foundation. The pub makes a handy feeding and watering place for visitors to the artist's former estate. A big draw is the large terrace (which gets jammed on fine days) and the crowd-pleasing menu, which keeps things reassuringly pubby and simple. Expect good lunchtime soup, sandwiches (£4.50) and popular dishes such as moules marinière or braised lamb shank (£13.50). Wines from £13. Closed Mon, Tue and Sun D.

Symbols

🛏 Accommodation is available

£30 Three courses for less than £30

V Separate vegetarian menu

£5 OFF £5-off voucher scheme

🍷 Notable wine list

St Albans

Darcy's

A lot to like
2 Hatfield Road, St Albans, AL1 3RP
Tel no: (01727) 730777
www.darcysrestaurant.co.uk
Modern European | £30
Cooking score: 2
£5
OFF

'An amazing experience', 'great food', 'extremely accommodating' are plaudits tossed in the direction of Ruth Hurren's stylish St Albans favourite, which is spread over two floors with a courtyard for fine-weather eating. The kitchen casts its net wide, offering a lively, hubble-bubble mix of Mediterranean and Asian flavours. You might kick off with a sharing plate for two – sticky duck ginger gyoza, salt-and-pepper squid, miso wakeme soup – before herb-crusted cod with ratatouille and black olive tapenade or Gressingham duck breast with red cabbage, pancetta and hazelnuts. Dark chocolate and honeycomb bomb with milk chocolate sauce makes a great finish. In addition, the simpler lunch and early-bird menu is worth considering. Wines from £15.90.
Chef/s: David Christie. **Open:** all week L 12 to 2.30 (2.45 Sun), D 6 to 9.30 (9 Sun). **Closed:** 26 Dec, 1 Jan. **Meals:** alc (main courses £14 to £24). Set L and early D £12 (2 courses) to £15. Sun L £19.90. **Details:** 96 seats. 18 seats outside. Separate bar. Wheelchair access.

Lussmanns

Independently minded crusader
Waxhouse Gate, off High Street, St Albans, AL3 4EW
Tel no: (01727) 851941
www.lussmanns.com
Modern European | £27
Cooking score: 1
£5 £30
OFF

'Fish & Grill' is the full billing of this independent, family-owned crusader – a capacious eatery spread over three floors hard by St Albans Abbey and Cathedral. Lussmanns buys into the local/sustainable/free-range zeitgeist by sourcing carefully, cooking with the seasons and supporting regional enterprise. The result is user-friendly food with emphatic British and Mediterranean overtones. Come here for seared Cornish mackerel with soused vegetables, woodland-reared Sussex pork loin, chicken schnitzel with chilli linguine, steak frites and burgers, plus afters such as highly enjoyable orange bread-and-butter pud. Corney & Barrow house wine is £15.60. There's also a branch in Hertford.
Open: all week 12 to 10 (10.30 Fri and Sat, 9 Sun). **Closed:** 25 and 26 Dec. **Meals:** alc (main courses £12 to £19). Set L and early D £10.95 (2 courses) to £13.95. **Details:** 100 seats. Wheelchair access.

ALSO RECOMMENDED

▲ The Foragers

The Verulam Arms, 41 Lower Dagnall Street, St Albans, AL3 4QE
Tel no: (01727) 836004
www.the-foragers.com
Modern British £5
OFF

One regular highlighted the 'buzzing, friendly atmosphere' at this backstreet pub where diners are encouraged to take a walk on the wild side. The Forager is a foodie enterprise that organises regular foraging walks and wild-food banquets. Its rustic seasonal dishes take the form of smoked air-dried British mutton with three-corner leeks, hazelnuts and truffle and sherry dressing (£7.50), and wild duck with Jerusalem artichoke purée, creamed kale and nettles with game and elderberry jus (£15). Wines from £16. Open all week.

¶¶¶ Also Recommended
Also recommended entries are not scored but we think they are worth a visit.

▌ Welwyn Garden City
Auberge du Lac
Flamboyant food in polished surroundings
Brocket Hall, Brocket Road, Welwyn Garden City,
AL8 7XG
Tel no: (01707) 368888
www.brocket-hall.co.uk
Modern European | £60
Cooking score: 5

🍾 ⊨ V

The contrast between the velvety gloss of
Brocket Hall's corporate playground and the
intimacy of Auberge du Lac couldn't be more
striking: while the estate itself is all about big-
money hospitality and golfing breaks, the
restaurant feels like 'a much-loved family
home' – a photogenic *Country Life* hunting
lodge beside an ornamental lake, complete
with fabulous views and staff who get top
marks for polish and professionalism. Chef
Phil Thompson delivers flamboyant, highly
worked contemporary food designed to thrill
and satisfy in equal measure: in summer, for
example, that might mean John Dory with
salted lemon, young vegetables and oyster
velouté, roast shoulder of Ibérico pork with
petits pois and pork croquettes, or a dessert of
white peach with poached raspberries and
roasted pistachios. Lunch (with two glass of
superior wine included) is no poor relation
either, judging by glowing reports of smoked
eel with foie gras parfait and lightly pickled
radish, roast sea bass and a 'refined' take on
treacle tart involving cinnamon anglaise and
orange sorbet. The wine list is a 750-bin
blockbuster that celebrates the glories of
regional French winemaking, as well as lifting
beauties from Austria, Australia and beyond.
Prices from £28 (£6.50 a glass).
Chef/s: Phil Thompson. **Open:** Tue to Sat L 12 to
2.30, D 7 to 9. **Closed:** Sun, Mon, 27 Dec to 17 Jan.
Meals: Set L £39.50. Set D £60. Tasting menu £69 (6
courses) to £79.50 (9 courses). **Details:** 65 seats. 35
seats outside. Wheelchair access. Car parking.
Children over 12 yrs only.

▌ Willian
The Fox
Dining-pub gem
Willian, SG6 2AE
Tel no: (01462) 480233
www.foxatwillian.co.uk
Modern British | £29
Cooking score: 2

£30

The Nye family are no strangers to inn-
keeping (White Horse, Jolly Sailors in
Brancaster Staithe, Hermitage Rd in Hitchin)
and put their talents to good use in this
modernised 18th-century pub by the church
and village pond. Local and regional suppliers
play their part, alongside fresh fish and
shellfish delivered from the north Norfolk
coast. The produce is worked into 'an enjoyable
meal with some inventive dishes' according to
one reporter, who singled out starters of
truffled scrambled egg with mushroom, and
salt cod Scotch egg for particular praise.
Successes among mains have included hake
with chorizo and smoked paprika fricassee and
citrus aïoli, and venison fillet with a braised
oxtail and bone-marrow risotto, red wine and
mustard velouté. Wines from £16.50.
Chef/s: Sherwin Jacobs. **Open:** all week L 12 to 2 (3
Sun), Mon to Sat D 6.45 to 9 (9.15 Fri and Sat).
Meals: alc (main courses £10 to £20). **Details:** 70
seats. 80 seats outside. Separate bar. Wheelchair
access. Car parking.

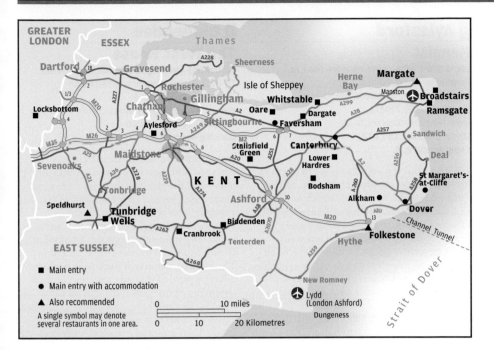

■ Alkham

The Marquis at Alkham
Chef with a foodie following
Alkham Valley Road, Alkham, CT15 7DF
Tel no: (01304) 873410
www.themarquisatalkham.co.uk
Modern British | £43
Cooking score: 4

🍽 V

Once you step inside, you wouldn't know that this former coaching inn is 200 years old. It has been spiffingly revitalised and stripped back, with muted colours and richly hued upholstery adding contemporary exclusivity. The Marquis now operates as a likeable restaurant-with-rooms, the kind of place that revels in regional produce. Indeed, with Godmersham hare, locally reared meats, fish from the South Coast, Kentish cheeses and foraged pickings, the seasonal menus reveal plenty of local interest, some unusual combinations and a feel for flavours and textures. Duck bresaola and rillettes with pickled damsons, Kent blue cheese and bitter chocolate is a typical starter, followed perhaps by a beautifully timed piece of cod with alexanders, celeriac, pork scratchings and cider. Soufflés with a scoop of ice cream are a must – pear with meadow sweet, for instance – or there may be new-season rhubarb with cherry kernel pannacotta and white chocolate crumble. Wines from £20.
Chef/s: Charles Lakin. **Open:** Tue to Sun L 12 to 2.30 (3 Sun), all week D 6 to 9.30 (7 to 8.30 Sun). **Meals:** alc (main courses £15 to £25). Tasting menus £30 (4 courses) and £55 (6 courses). **Details:** 55 seats. 30 seats outside. Wheelchair access. Car parking. Children over 8 yrs only at D.

🍴 Visit us Online
To find out more about
The Good Food Guide, please visit
www.thegoodfoodguide.co.uk

Aylesford

Hengist

Local asset with contemporary food in venerable surroundings
7-9 High Street, Aylesford, ME20 7AX
Tel no: (01622) 719273
www.hengistrestaurant.co.uk
Modern European | £42
Cooking score: 3

'Characterful', remarked a visitor to Richard Phillips' second restaurant (after Thackeray's, Tunbridge Wells, see entry), which occupies an ancient building in one of England's oldest villages. Almost five centuries of history – beams, standing timbers and stone walls, albeit cleverly reworked with some striking modern touches – create a fine atmosphere, matched by the kitchen's lively modern European style. A warm salad of Cornish red mullet with pickled shallots, carrots with saffron and a coriander and wild herb dressing is typical of the approach to starters. Kent lamb is given a decent outing, too (perhaps pressed breast and roast loin teamed with fondant potato, braised root vegetables, chervil root and vanilla purée). Desserts involve much time-consuming artifice in the form of spiced rum baba with passion fruit consommé, piña colada sorbet, pineapple gel and glass tuile. The French-dominated wine list is arranged by style and opens at £16.95.
Chef/s: Petrus Madutlela. **Open:** Fri to Sun L 12 to 2.30 (3 Sun), Tue to Sat D 6.30 to 10. **Closed:** Mon. **Meals:** alc (main courses £18 to £25). Set L £12.95 (2 courses) to £14.95. Set D £22.50 (2 courses) to £25.50. Sun L £18.95 (2 courses) to £22.95. **Details:** 70 seats. Separate bar. Car parking.

Biddenden

The West House

Innovative cooking in laid-back surrounds
28 High Street, Biddenden, TN27 8AH
Tel no: (01580) 291341
www.thewesthouserestaurant.co.uk
Modern European | £40
Cooking score: 5

Fashioned from late-medieval weavers' cottages, with heavily beamed ceilings and inglenook fireplace, Graham Garrett's gently modernised venue in a pretty Kent village has a fiercely loyal following, among both customers and suppliers. Garrett favours a vigorously innovative approach to modern British food, and has the skill to back it up. The familiar richness of duck liver parfait is offset by pickled rhubarb, a portion of duck confit, cured foie gras and a spin on pain d'épices. This might be a prelude to grilled sea bass with butternut squash risotto, wild mushrooms and crispy shallots, or Ibérico pig cheek, chorizo and scallop with a sauce of chickpeas. In between come cheesy crackers with dripping, an irresistible nibble if ever there was. Meals might conclude with the famous Crunchie tribute (a white chocolate honeycomb parfait with dark chocolate sorbet), or baked vanilla cheesecake with caviar jelly. An authoritatively written wine list includes a slate of natural wines, made with minimal intervention, as well as glasses from £5 and half-litre carafes from £12.
Chef/s: Graham Garrett. **Open:** Tue to Fri and Sun L 12 to 2 (3 Sun), Tue to Sat D 7 to 9 (9.30 Fri and Sat). **Closed:** Mon, 24 Dec to 6 Jan, 2 weeks Jul. **Meals:** Set L £25. Set D £35 (2 courses) to £40. Tasting menu £50. **Details:** 32 seats. Car parking.

Bodsham
The Timber Batts
Country pub, Anglo-French grub
School Lane, Bodsham, TN25 5JQ
Tel no: (01233) 750237
www.thetimberbatts.co.uk
Anglo-French | £32
Cooking score: 1

The Timber Batts is an ancient country pub in a glorious setting where beams, standing timbers and a pair of open fires keep the interior somewhere between hostelry and restaurant. Joël Gross remains firmly in charge. The dropping of the 'Froggies' moniker doesn't mean the Frenchman has lowered the tricolour, but signals that the food is now a stronger mix of pub classics (burgers, fish and chips, sharing platters of fish and meat) and French favourites, say crayfish tails with lobster bisque and Romney Marsh rack of lamb with dauphinois potatoes. Set lunches are good value, service is excellent and French wines cost from £18.50.
Chef/s: Joël Gross. Open: Wed to Sun L 12 to 2 (3 Sun), Tue to Sat D 7 to 9 (9.30 Sat). Closed: Mon, 29 Dec to 1 Jan, bank hols. Meals: alc (main courses £13 to £25). Set L £16 (2 courses) to £20. Sun L £20.50 (2 courses) to £25.65. Details: 50 seats. 50 seats outside. Separate bar. Car parking.

Broadstairs
Albariño
Spanish tapas making waves
29 Albion Street, Broadstairs, CT10 1LX
Tel no: (01843) 600991
www.albarinorestaurant.co.uk
Tapas | £18
Cooking score: 4
£30

'It's good to see Broadstairs finally attracting a decent chef/restaurant', sums up the way most visitors feel about Steven Dray's gutsy little Spanish tapas bar. Albariño is essentially about serving well-sourced ingredients in a perky space, the cramped tables and blackboards allowing no detraction from cooking that is distinguished by honesty, simplicity and full-on flavours. Trademarks, including chickpea and fennel chips with aïoli, sobrasada with garbanzo beans (chickpeas) and spinach, and slow-cooked ox cheek with liquorice, butternut squash and sage, share the billing with classics such as patatas bravas, cheese and charcuterie boards, and meatballs with aubergine and red peppers. Desserts are not to be missed, especially an indulgent honey and cardamom cream with glazed banana and crystalised orange. Wash it all down with first-rate sherries and Spanish regional wines from £14.
Chef/s: Steven Dray. Open: Mon to Sat L 12 to 3, D 6 to 11. Closed: Sun, 25 and 26 Dec, 1 Jan, first 2 weeks Nov. Meals: alc (tapas £6 to £8). Details: 20 seats. 2 seats outside.

Canterbury
The Goods Shed
Shedloads of good things
Station Road West, Canterbury, CT2 8AN
Tel no: (01227) 459153
www.thegoodsshed.co.uk
Modern British | £31
Cooking score: 2
£5 OFF

A happy din of chatter enlivens the farmers' market next to Canterbury West station six days a week, and weary shoppers appreciate the chance to eat in situ, at the platform restaurant overlooking the action. The huge blackboard menu changes through the day, perhaps offering pumpkin tart with Kentish cobnuts and peppery leaves, glistening sea trout with foraged samphire and sea-beet, and crisply rendered, pink cutlets of salt-marsh lamb with wilted greens. Recommended supper dishes have included squid and smoked egg salad with gremolata, and confit duck leg with prunes and bacon, while the signature pudding has to be shipwreck tart and clotted cream: a boozy, treacly hunk of gunge. Wines start at £15 (£4 a glass), and there are fine regional beers and ciders. See overleaf for details.

Chef/s: Rafael Lopez. **Open:** Tue to Sun L 12 to 2.30 (3 Sat and Sun), Tue to Sat D 6 to 9.30. **Closed:** Mon, 25 to 26 Dec, 1 and 2 Jan. **Meals:** alc (main courses £13 to £20). **Details:** 75 seats. Car parking.

Michael Caines at ABode Canterbury

Cooking with considerable panache
High Street, Canterbury, CT1 2RX
Tel no: (01227) 826684
www.michaelcaines.com
Modern European | £45
Cooking score: 5

The Canterbury branch of the ABode hotel group is in the heart of the pedestrianised city centre. Most of the ground floor of the former County Hotel is now dominated by a clean-lined contemporary restaurant showcasing the restrained cuisine of Michael Caines. Interpreting the MC menus, which present a considered tour of contemporary taste, is down to long-standing chef Jean-Marc Zanetti. His kitchen doesn't cut corners, so expect homemade everything (pretty much) and a wealth of the best regional ingredients. The excellent value three-course set menu is an inviting way to test the range, taking you from, perhaps, confit lamb served with braised potato, smoked yoghurt, peas, fennel and mint, via pan-fried pollack with beans, lettuce and pancetta, to a dessert of cherry and pistachio parfait with cherry coulis. For a higher outlay, you can choose from the main carte, where very good scallops with roasted cauliflower, apple and curry foam could precede 'a lovely combination' of Romney Marsh lamb (crusted loin 'all pink and tender', a 'superb' mini shepherd's pie) with crisp sweetbread and a fennel, pea and mint ragoût. The wine list opens at £24.50.
Chef/s: Jean-Marc Zanetti. **Open:** all week L 12 to 2.30, Mon to Sat D 6 to 10. **Meals:** alc (main courses £23 to £27). Set L £14.50 (2 courses) to £19.50. Set D £16.50 (2 courses) to £27.50. Tasting menu £60. **Details:** 72 seats. Separate bar. Wheelchair access.

▌Cranbrook

Apicius

Big-statement cooking in a tiny space
23 Stone Street, Cranbrook, TN17 3HF
Tel no: (01580) 714666
www.restaurant-apicius.co.uk
Modern European | £45
Cooking score: 6

A former weaver's cottage dating back some 600 years and named after the author of a celebrated Latin cookbook certainly has a due sense of history. It may look understated inside, but Apicius has garnered an enviable reputation over the past decade as a neighbourhood restaurant that looks beyond the tried and the tested. Tim Johnson's cooking is in the modern British vein, yet achieves great precision and depth from interesting treatments of reliable local supplies. A summer lunch party thoroughly enjoyed themselves by way of, among other things, satisfyingly textured deep-fried sweetbreads with puréed celeriac, baby artichokes and girolle velouté; properly crackled slow-roast pork shoulder with braised endive, prune purée and turnip galette; and a nicely judged fillet of John Dory with spinach, fennel and bitter strands of dried lemon. A sensitive approach to complexity was evident in a dish of roast brill and steamed mussels in mussel bouillon with spring onions, sweetcorn and confit potatoes. Hints of overseas flavours enliven desserts such as medjool date sponge with apricot salad, pistachio coulis and honey ice cream, and the compact wine list opens at £18 a bottle.
Chef/s: Timothy Johnson. **Open:** Wed to Fri and Sun L 12 to 2, Wed to Sat D 7 to 9. **Closed:** Mon, Tue, 2 weeks Jun/Jul, 2 weeks Christmas. **Meals:** Set L £27 (2 courses) to £32. Set D £34 (2 courses) to £40. **Details:** 30 seats. Children over 8 yrs only.

Dargate

The Dove Inn

Cosy pub with top-notch grub
Plum Pudding Lane, Dargate, ME13 9HB
Tel no: (01227) 751360
www.doveatdargate.co.uk
Modern British | £25
Cooking score: 2

£30

In a pretty corner of Kent, six miles from Canterbury, this 18th-century hostelry really looks the part. Amid scrubbed wooden tables and a roaring fire you can sample Shepherd Neame ales and a workmanlike version of honest pub food – simple stuff for weekdays (potted brown shrimps, locally smoked haddock macaroni, confit pork belly with black pudding, apple sauce and honey-glazed roots) and a touch more elaboration at weekends. Much of the repertoire has a cosmopolitan feel: say, cauliflower velouté with Stilton, toasted almonds and truffle oil; marsh lamb (roasted and confit) with Savoy cabbage and potato gratin; and classic crème brûlée. Reporters have found the Dove costly, but the food satisfies and service runs well. Wines from £15.
Chef/s: Phillip MacGregor. **Open:** Wed to Sun L 12 to 2 (2.30 Sat and Sun), Wed to Sat D 7 to 9. **Closed:** Mon, Tue, 1 week Jan, 1 week Feb. **Meals:** alc (main courses £13 to £19). **Details:** 25 seats. 40 seats outside. Separate bar. Car parking.

Dover

The Allotment

Interesting, good-value food
9 High Street, Dover, CT16 1DP
Tel no: (01304) 214467
www.theallotmentdover.com
Modern British | £23
Cooking score: 3

£5 OFF £30

'Don't just drive through Dover' advises one reader, who suggests a stop at Dave Flynn's 'convivial' restaurant on the high street. The former wine merchant's shop retains its stained-glass windows, with an open kitchen and courtyard garden adding further interest. Food is bright and fresh, with vegetables and fruit, some home-grown, given a strong billing. Readers have enjoyed spiced pumpkin soup, Spanish cured ham with celeriac rémoulade, and aged sirloin with blue cheese sauce. They also appreciate the little salad served between courses. Lesser-seen main courses such as Camargue-style beef and 'crying' shoulder of Canterbury lamb provoke conversations with the 'warm' staff. The house cheesecake (sometimes made with Allotment strawberries) has compelled one correspondent to make a return visit sooner than might be considered seemly. Wine from a short but considered list starts at £15.
Chef/s: David Flynn. **Open:** Tue to Sat 8.30am to 11pm. **Closed:** Sun, Mon, 24 Dec to 14 Jan. **Meals:** alc (main courses £9 to £16). **Details:** 26 seats. 24 seats outside. Wheelchair access.

Faversham

Read's

Elevated dining at a Georgian manor house
Macknade Manor, Canterbury Road, Faversham, ME13 8XE
Tel no: (01795) 535344
www.reads.com
Modern British | £60
Cooking score: 6

£5 OFF

This is Rona and David Pitchford's 28th season in the Guide and their long tenure tells of exemplary commitment. A meal at Read's has always felt like a very elevated occasion. The setting helps – a smartly appointed Georgian manor house surrounded by mature trees – but the rather regal tone is maintained within, with soft upholstery and swagged curtains in old gold. Nevertheless, the front-of-house welcome and the carefully considered, locally based food are achieved without recourse to grandiloquence. Naturally evolving with both the seasons and modern taste, the cooking remains pin-sharp and inspired. One way through the detailed menu would be to start with roast quail and

Kentish cobnuts on a celeriac tart with saladings in orange and tarragon; then poached cod with puréed cauliflower, pomegranate, capers and raisins; and caramel mille-feuille with roast pear and mascarpone sorbet. Many dishes reappear on the top-value set lunch. A condensed list of Best Buys is a user-friendly way into the extensive wine collection, where old-school classicism meets new-wave thinking from the Médoc to Margaret River. Prices start at £20.

Chef/s: David Pitchford. **Open:** Tue to Sat L 12 to 2, D 7 to 9. **Closed:** Sun, Mon, 25 to 27 Dec, first week Jan, first 2 weeks Sept. **Meals:** Set L £25. Set D £50 (2 courses) to £60. **Details:** 50 seats. 24 seats outside. Separate bar. Wheelchair access. Car parking.

Folkestone

ALSO RECOMMENDED
▲ Rocksalt

4-5 Fishmarket Road, Folkestone, CT19 6AA
Tel no: (01303) 212070
www.rocksaltfolkestone.co.uk
Seafood

Overlooking Folkestone harbour with views of boats bobbing in the water, this contemporary, glass-fronted restaurant with its wrap-round balcony is in an unbeatable location. Reporters have enthused about 'perfectly cooked' lemon sole with tomato and olive oil dressing, a 'beautifully sweet' whole grilled lobster for a 'well priced' £25 and a 'brilliant' cold chocolate and sea buckthorn fondant (£7.50), so it's a shame that complaints about inconsistent food and long waits between courses persist. Wines from £16. Closed Sun D. More reports please.

Locksbottom

Chapter One
Big-city cooking at local prices
Farnborough Common, Locksbottom, BR6 8NF
Tel no: (01689) 854848
www.chaptersrestaurants.com
Modern European | £38
Cooking score: 5
V

Andrew McLeish's Kent commuter-belt destination is a seasoned performer that knows what its clientele wants. This begins with an 'unstingy' way with bread and finishes over 'divine' salted caramels. In between, guests appreciate 'savvy and well-thought-out' cooking, matched by a touch of 'magic' from front of house. 'Savvy' is a good word for McLeish: he's up to speed on culinary trends; his food looks good 'without being too overdone'; and he knows when a classic is called for (witness ribeye, chips and béarnaise on the otherwise creative carte). Treacle-cured salmon with Asian flavours is a popular pick for starters, pitched against the likes of poached and roasted quail with parsnip consommé and sherry vinegar 'pearls'. For mains, braised and crispy suckling pig arrives with impeccable potato purée and black truffle butter. Desserts run the gamut from mainstream (chocolate fondant) to exotic (yuzu parfait, guava sorbet and basil cake). The broad lunch menu is excellent value, and there's bang for buck on the gently marked-up wine list, too, starting from £17.

Chef/s: Andrew McLeish. **Open:** all week L 12 to 2.30 (2.45 Sun), D 6.30 to 10.30 (9 Sun). **Closed:** first week Jan. **Meals:** alc (main courses £20 to £25). Set L £19.95. Sun L £22.95. **Details:** 120 seats. 20 seats outside. Separate bar. Wheelchair access. Car parking.

Lower Hardres
The Granville
Modern pub food in an expansive hostelry
Street End, Lower Hardres, CT4 7AL
Tel no: (01227) 700402
www.thegranvillecanterbury.com
Modern European | £28
Cooking score: 3
£30

A roadside pub not far from Canterbury, the Granville is leased from the Shepherd Neame brewery by the Harris family, who also run the Sportsman (see entry, Whitstable). The expansive space incorporates a leather-sofa'd lounge and an open-plan dining-room with glimpses of the kitchen, as well as a proper drinkers' bar. Jim Shave cooks a menu of modern pub food where there's plenty going on. Roast butternut squash soup with chestnuts makes a winter warmer and a half in December, and stalwarts include mussels simmered in white wine, garlic and thyme, as well as main-course fish such as grilled sea bass with pea sauce and bacon. Confit duck leg and crackled pork keep the regulars happy. Meals end with the likes of flourless chocolate cake, served with praline ice cream and raspberry sauce. Wines from a well-annotated list start at £15.50.
Chef/s: Jim Shave. **Open:** Tue to Sat L 12 to 2 (2.30 Sun), Tue to Sat D 7 to 9. **Closed:** Mon, 26 Dec, 1 Jan. **Meals:** alc (main courses £10 to £19). Set weekday L £12.95 (2 courses) to £15.95. Set D £19.50 (4 courses). **Details:** 55 seats. 35 seats outside. Separate bar. Wheelchair access. Car parking.

Margate
ALSO RECOMMENDED
▲ The Ambrette
44 King Street, Margate, CT9 1QE
Tel no: (01843) 231504
www.theambrette.co.uk
Indian £5 OFF

'A visit to the Turner Contemporary, then lunch at the Ambrette' would be one reporter's ideal day out in Margate. The 'relaxed and welcoming' contemporary Indian restaurant is overseen by Dev Biswal (as is sister operation, the Ambrette at Rye, see entry). He knows his local ingredients and his spices, combining them in 'unique dishes' such as Sussex beef feather blade with mango salad (£3.95), Kentish pork loin with aubergine mash and a garlic wine and malt-vinegar sauce (£12.95) and rose-scented crème brûlée (£4.95). House wine, £13.99. Closed Mon.

▲ GB Pizza Co
14a Marine Drive, Margate, CT9 1DH
Tel no: (01843) 297700
www.greatbritishpizzacompany.wordpress.com
Italian £5 OFF

The seafront space – a mix of vintage, industrial, gritty and modern with 'a cheeky twist' – is 'Margate in a nutshell', fuelled by the sheer enthusiasm for what the owners do. The menu, built around impeccable sourcing, is a simple list of six or seven wood-fired, thin-based pizzas: the 'Margate-arita' (£6), chilli and chorizo (£8.50) and daily specials like a 'seriously scrumptious' spiced Italian sausage with caramelised onions. Brilliant chocolate brownies and sea views are bonuses. Wine from £13. Open all week.

Oare
The Three Mariners
The full country-pub package
2 Church Road, Oare, ME13 0QA
Tel no: (01795) 533633
www.thethreemarinersoare.co.uk
Modern British | £25
Cooking score: 3
£30

A late 18th-century inn looking towards Oare Creek and close to the Oare Marshes Nature Reserve, the Three Mariners offers the full country-pub package, with terrace seating in summer, a roaring log fire in winter and real ales from Shepherd Neame. And it presses all the dining buttons, too, with a heavy reliance on local and seasonal produce, good pricing and eager young staff. What's not to like? Local skate cheeks with lemon, garlic and parsley, and pan-fried herring roes on toast are justly celebrated by readers, and there are fortifying cold-weather dishes such as venison pie with mashed potatoes, or paprika roast fillet of cod with butter-bean stew. To finish, you might indulge in pear and chocolate tart with espresso ice cream. Wines from £13.95 complete the picture.

Chef/s: John O'Riordan. **Open:** all week L 12 to 2.30 (3 Sat, 3.30 Sun), D 6.30 to 9 (9.30 Fri and Sat, 7 to 9 Sun). **Meals:** alc (main courses £11 to £19). Set L £11.95 (Mon to Sat). Set D £16.95 (Mon to Thur). Sun L £16.95. **Details:** 63 seats. 30 seats outside. Separate bar. Car parking.

▌Ramsgate

Age & Sons
Cut-above café and restaurant
Charlotte Court, Ramsgate, CT11 8HE
Tel no: (01843) 851515
www.ageandsons.co.uk
Modern British | £29
Cooking score: 1
£5 OFF V £30

The Victorian warehouse is tucked away in a small court not far from the harbour and is divided into a simple ground-floor café (with open-to-view kitchen) and a light-filled, raftered upstairs dining room. Service is pleasant, if casual, and the food is simple, seasonal and locally sourced where possible. The kitchen displays a little welcome ambition in dishes like a starter of pigeon pithiviers with a Waldorf salad. Attention to detail falters sometimes, but successes include bream with saffron risotto, brown shrimps, cockles and ginger sauce, and carrot cake with mascarpone icing and blood orange sorbet. Wines from £15.

Chef/s: Toby Leigh. **Open:** Tue to Sun L 12 to 3.30, Tue to Sat D 7 to 9.30. **Closed:** Mon, 2 to 17 January. **Meals:** alc (main courses £11 to £22). Set L and Sun L £9.95 (2 courses) to £12.95. Set D £12.95 (2 courses) to £15.95. **Details:** 58 seats. 30 seats outside. Separate bar.

READERS RECOMMEND

Royal Harbour Brasserie
Modern British
Royal Harbour Parade, East Pier, Ramsgate, CT11 8LS
Tel no: (01843) 599059
www.royalharbourbrasserie.co.uk
'The setting is amazing, and the menu features tons of Kentish produce: mussels, enormous cod goujons with the lightest batter, Puy lentils with goats' cheese, beautiful prawns in garlic and chilli oil.'

▌St Margaret's-at-Cliffe

Wallett's Court
Good food in a historical setting
Westcliffe, St Margaret's-at-Cliffe, CT15 6EW
Tel no: (01304) 852424
www.wallettscourt.com
British | £40
Cooking score: 1
🛏

Set in Kent's verdant pastures, just a stone's throw from Dover, this ancient manor house offers tranquil dining in a uniquely historical setting. When you're ensconced in the timber-beamed dining room, expect elegant plates striking a British pose: perhaps slow-roasted pork belly, black pudding, fondant potatoes and Savoy cabbage or grey mullet with ragoût of wild mushrooms and fennel and red onion marmalade. Starters and desserts can be lacklustre in comparison, bar the fulsome Kentish cheese plate, and the background music (Justin Timberlake, Kylie et al) might seem off-putting to some, and at odds with the setting. The extensive global wine list starts at £18.50.

Chef/s: David Hoseason. **Open:** all week L 12 to 2 (3 Sun), D 7 to 9. **Meals:** Set L £16.95 (2 courses) to £21.95. Set D £39.95. Sun L £16.95. **Details:** 70 seats. Separate bar. Car parking.

ALSO RECOMMENDED
▲ The Bay Restaurant
The White Cliffs Hotel, High Street, St Margaret's-at-Cliffe, CT15 6AT
Tel no: (01304) 852229
www.thewhitecliffs.com
Modern British £5 OFF

With the sea just a mile away, a cheery New England coastal vibe pervades this weatherboarded inn with stylish rooms. Fish and seafood landed from local day boats feature in the 'catch of the day' and a starter of Deal crab cakes with wasabi, Bramley apple and watercress salad (£6.95). Prices are keen, and the varied menu might augment pub staples with specials of roast rump of Romney Marsh lamb stuffed with anchovies, rosemary and wild garlic (£17.95). Wines from £14.95. Open all week.

∎ Speldhurst

ALSO RECOMMENDED
▲ George & Dragon
Speldhurst Hill, Speldhurst, TN3 0NN
Tel no: (01892) 863125
www.speldhurst.com
Modern British £5 OFF

It has been 10 years since Julian Leefe-Griffiths transformed this historic 13th-century hostelry (one of the region's oldest) into a thriving food pub. He's done a grand job, paying attention to local supply lines as well as the seasons. The menu reads well – a good balance of pub classics such as game terrine (£7.50) and Speldhurst pork sausage and mash (£10.50), showcase steaks ('quality meat and served on boards') and contemporary dishes like sea bass with saffron risotto and mussels (£15.50). Wines from £15, open all week.

∎ Stalisfield Green
The Plough
Big local flavours and Kentish ales
Stalisfield Green, ME13 0HY
Tel no: (01795) 890256
www.stalisfieldgreen.co.uk
British | £25
Cooking score: 2
£5 OFF £30

It may be in the middle of nowhere, but the atmosphere and service at this splendid medieval 'hall house' are guaranteed to put anyone 'in a good humour'. Everything from the weathered beams to the Kentish real ales and 'exceptionally good' home-baked bread is likely to please, and the kitchen is noted for its industrious streak. Big local flavours loom large, be it pressed pig's head with homemade piccalilli, lightly cured home-smoked partridge, fillet of gilthead bream with brown butter and shrimps or Farmer Palmer's 28-day aged Angus steak with chips and chophouse sauce. Sunday lunch brings cracking roast meats – perhaps full-flavoured free-range chicken or local beef cooked overnight – and the short wine list offers reasonably priced drinking from £16.
Chef/s: Alex Windebank. Open: Tue to Sun L 12 to 2 (3 Sat and Sun), Tue to Sat D 6 to 9. Closed: Mon. Meals: alc (main courses £12 to £20). Set L and D £13.95 (2 courses) to £16.95. Details: 65 seats. 40 seats outside. Separate bar. Car parking.

∎ Tunbridge Wells
Thackeray's
Classy French food with a touch of 'Vanity Fair'
85 London Road, Tunbridge Wells, TN1 1EA
Tel no: (01892) 511921
www.thackerays-restaurant.co.uk
Modern French | £60
Cooking score: 4
£5 OFF V

The Victorian novelist's elegant white clapboard house perched at one corner of Tunbridge Wells Common belies the suave vision of contemporary design within (and

the spacious Japanese Terrace at the back). In keeping with the sleek surroundings, the food is French done in a modern style, the meticulous, multi-layered cooking mixing classic ideas with less traditional pairings. A starter of chicken and foie gras 'coq au vin' ballotine, for example, takes in Parma ham, crisp chicken wings, chicken parfait, porcini mushrooms and a red wine reduction, while a main course of beautifully cooked wild sea bass might be served with fennel (braised and as a coleslaw), smoked eel, black truffle bonbon and fish cream velouté. Meat also receives elaborate treatment, with seasonal game always engendering good reports. Desserts might include apricot and tonka bean soufflé with apricot sorbet and hazelnut soup. Wines from £17.95.
Chef/s: Daniel Hatton. **Open:** Tue to Sun L 12 to 2.30 (3.30 Sun), Tue to Sat D 6.30 to 10.30. **Closed:** Mon. **Meals:** alc (main courses £22 to £27). Set L £16.95 (2 courses) to £18.95. Set D £24.50 (2 courses) to £28.50. Sun L £26.95. Tasting menu £69 (7 courses). **Details:** 60 seats. 25 seats outside. Separate bar.

▌Whitstable

JoJo's
Top-notch tapas by the sea
2 Herne Bay Road, Whitstable, CT5 2LQ
Tel no: (01227) 274591
www.jojosrestaurant.co.uk
Tapas | £25
Cooking score: 4
£30
♥

'Value for money and a happy ambience' are watchwords at this lively, popular restaurant looking out over the North Sea. It's the kind of place where loyal customers won't see favoured dishes disappear from the menu without speaking up, which lends a kind of community feeling. A wooden floor, kitchen tables, plain white walls and open-plan kitchen can ratchet up noise levels – but that's part of the appeal. Inspiration comes from across the Mediterranean: tapas such as patatas bravas, hummus, mutton and feta koftas, risotto balls, sharing plates of charcuterie, thinly sliced chargrilled venison loin and

calamari deep-fried in the lightest batter. Raw materials are conscientiously sourced, ensuring that quality imbues every dish, right through to desserts such as sticky toffee pudding. Happy staff help everyone feel at home, and if you have forgotten to BYO (corkage from £3), the good-value wine list (from £14) should keep all-comers smiling.
Chef/s: Nikki Billington, Jake Dellany and Sally Bambridge. **Open:** Thur to Sun L 12.30 to 2.30 (3.30 Sun), Wed to Sat D 6.30 to 9. **Closed:** Tue, Mon. **Meals:** alc (tapas £5 to £20). **Details:** 72 seats. Wheelchair access.

★ TOP 50 ★

The Sportsman
Astonishing food in the most congenial pub
Faversham Road, Seasalter, Whitstable, CT5 4BP
Tel no: (01227) 273370
www.thesportsmanseasalter.co.uk
Modern British | £38
Cooking score: 6

Superior simplicity – that's Steve Harris's approach to running his no-frills coastal pub. Sure, the Sportsman is in a rather bleak location 'but that makes it feel more homely inside', with the scrubbed, rustic interior designed to make people feel at ease. The quality of the food is outstanding, demonstrating a healthy obsession with local sourcing and a desire to show ingredients at their dazzling best. Oft-reported are the boards of homemade focaccia, soda bread and sourdough, the chilled beetroot soup, and a slab of seared thornback ray 'drenched in brown butter and scattered with cockles'. Everything is driven by simplicity and flavour. Take a coarse pork terrine wrapped in a neat ribbon of cabbage and served with pork crackling 'to make you sigh with delight', and your arteries panic' or lamb from nearby Monkshill Farm, pink and succulent with 'the fat seared to a lovely crispness' set on 'tender' emerald-green cabbage with a 'large wedge of potato cake' in a light gravy. There's praise, too, for gypsy tart, stewed apple and sour cream, 'good sensible service' and the astute wine list with bottles from £15.95.

Chef/s: Stephen Harris and Dan Flavell. **Open:** Tue to Sun L 12 to 2 (2.30 Sun), Tue to Sat D 7 to 9. **Closed:** Mon, 25 and 26 Dec. **Meals:** alc (main courses £18 to £23). **Details:** 50 seats. Car parking.

Wheelers Oyster Bar
British seaside through and through
8 High Street, Whitstable, CT5 1BQ
Tel no: (01227) 273311
www.wheelersoysterbar.com
Seafood | £35
Cooking score: 4

The candyfloss-pink and blue frontage of this quaint old oyster bar is British seaside through and through, as evocative on windswept afternoons as it is on sunny days when Londoners hit Whitstable. There's only space for 16 in the 'intimate and moody back parlour' and four at the seafood bar, though four sittings a day – remember to book – manage demand well. The modest surroundings 'juxtapose delightfully with the calibre of the food', an imaginative menu of six starters, mains and desserts, supplemented by a 'browsing menu' of global seafood classics from jellied eels to soft-shell crab tempura. Sample the Whitstable natives when in season before launching into hot favourites, such as 'delicate and satisfying' lobster lasagne with chanterelles or – 'the epitome of hearty comfort' – steamed steak and oyster pudding. Dessert might be pear tarte Tatin with blue cheese ice cream. BYO, corkage free of charge. **Chef/s:** Mark Stubbs. **Open:** Thur to Tue 1 to 7.30 (7 Sun). **Closed:** Wed, 2.5 weeks in Jan. **Meals:** alc (main courses £19 to £33). **Details:** Cash only. 16 seats. Wheelchair access.

Williams & Brown Tapas
Simple, flavour-packed tapas
48 Harbour Street, Whitstable, CT5 1AQ
Tel no: (01227) 273373
www.thetapas.co.uk
Tapas | £25
Cooking score: 2
£30

Ten years on, Christopher Williams's unpretentious little restaurant continues to enjoy faithful support. It's a strikingly light, utilitarian room where tightly packed tables sit perfectly with the straight-talking menu of Spanish tapas. Classics such as paella are given a modern workout when made with spinach, pine nuts, rosemary and roasted vine tomatoes, but the kitchen knows when to leave well alone when it comes to traditional recipes for chorizo in red wine, albondigas and tortilla. High-quality raw materials are apparent in straightforward dishes: say, local cod fillet with butter beans and aïoli or pork belly with a sage and red wine jus. Drink Spanish house wines from £15.50, and finish with tarta Santiago. **Chef/s:** Christopher Williams and Andrew Cozens. **Open:** all week L 12 to 2 (2.30 Fri, 3 Sat and Sun), D 6 to 9 (9.30 Fri, 9.45 Sat). **Closed:** 25 and 26 Dec, 2 and 3 Jan. **Meals:** alc (tapas £5 to £13). **Details:** 32 seats. 8 seats outside.

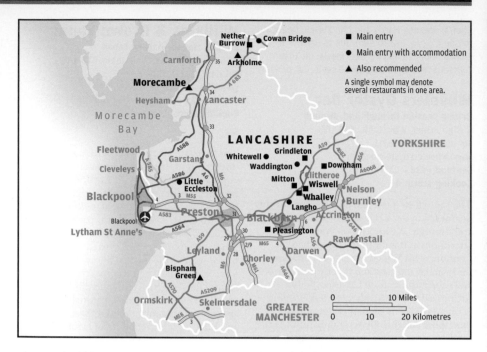

Map legend:
■ Main entry
● Main entry with accommodation
▲ Also recommended
A single symbol may denote several restaurants in one area.

Map labels: Nether Burrow, Cowan Bridge, Carnforth, Arkholme, Morecambe, Heysham, Lancaster, Morecambe Bay, LANCASHIRE, YORKSHIRE, Fleetwood, Grindleton, Whitewell, Garstang, Waddington, Downham, Cleveleys, Little Eccleston, Mitton, Clitheroe, Wiswell, Nelson, Blackpool, Whalley, Burnley, Langho, Preston, Blackburn, Accrington, Blackpool, Lytham St Anne's, Pleasington, Rawtenstall, Leyland, Darwen, Chorley, Bispham Green, Ormskirk, Skelmersdale, GREATER MANCHESTER, 0 10 Miles, 0 10 20 Kilometres

Arkholme

ALSO RECOMMENDED
▲ The Redwell Inn
Kirkby Lonsdale Road, Arkholme, LA6 1BQ
Tel no: (015242) 21240
www.redwellinn.net
Modern British £5 OFF

In essence, this enchanting 17th-century stone-built coaching inn set in the heart of the Lune Valley looks no different to any other Lancashire country pub. However, what sets it apart from your humble boozer is the on-site smokehouse and shop, along with cooking that delivers simple, modern and robustly flavoured dishes that rely on quality ingredients. The bar menu supplies own-smoked haddock fishcakes (£5.50), while the carte features pea and ham hock risotto and local veal steak and kidney pie with sweet pickled shallots (£12). Wines from £14.75. Food served Fri to Sun L, and Thur to Sat D.

Bispham Green

ALSO RECOMMENDED
▲ The Eagle & Child
Malt Kiln Lane, Bispham Green, L40 3SG
Tel no: (01257) 462297
www.eagleandchildbispham.co.uk
British £5 OFF

This big white ancient pub hides itself among the unclassified lanes of west Lancashire, but is worth tracking down for its convivial atmosphere and creative approach to food. Much of the produce hails from the surrounding farmland. The signature 'smokies' (£8) resemble brandade made from smoked haddock, 'a lovely dish'. Specials might include king prawn skewers with Thai dressing (£7.50), fine Cumbrian lamb rump with rösti (£14) and white chocolate and strawberry brûlée. Wines from £14. Open all week.

Burrow

The Highwayman
Local flavours and local enterprise
Main Road, Burrow, LA6 2RJ
Tel no: (01524) 273338
www.highwaymaninn.co.uk
British | £20
Cooking score: 2
£30

Once a haunt of Dick Turpin, the Highwayman now stands and delivers North Country 'food with roots' as one of Nigel Haworth's Ribble Valley Inns. It's a boisterous place with bags of atmosphere, bedded into the borderlands where Lancashire meets Yorkshire and Cumbria. A clean-cut foodie persona has been created here – complete with photos of gastro-heroes on the walls and a menu that celebrates local enterprise. Unmissable potted Morecambe Bay shrimps give way to a seasonal bonanza taking in everything from pheasant Kiev and fish pie to braised Herdwick mutton with black peas and salt-baked beetroot. Sunday roasts are the epitome of trencherman meatiness; puds might include Cumbrian rum nicky with lemon syllabub; and the regional cheeseboard is packed with artisan beauties. By contrast, the wine list offers serious global drinking from £15.50. **Chef/s:** Matt Thomson. **Open:** Tue to Sat L 12 to 2, D 5.30 to 8.30 (9 Fri and Sat). Sun 12 to 8. **Closed:** 25 Dec. **Meals:** alc (main courses £8 to £20). Set L and D £11.50 (2 courses) to £15. **Details:** 120 seats. 50 seats outside. Wheelchair access. Car parking.

Cowan Bridge

Hipping Hall
Up-to-date ideas in a historical setting
Cowan Bridge, LA6 2JJ
Tel no: (01524) 271187
www.hippinghall.com
Modern British | £55
Cooking score: 4
⇌ V

The main house may have been reconstructed in Queen Anne's reign, but the jewel of this richly historical country seat is its 15th-century dining hall, complete with minstrels' gallery and faded tapestries. Brent Hulena has brought the food up to date, so banish thoughts of roast pig's head, and instead consider starting with confit belly and braised tongue of pork adorned with chicory and orange, before proceeding to halibut, earthily accompanied by wild mushrooms, artichoke and leek. Herb-crumbed local hogget has a flavour of yore, to be sure, with its kidney and bashed-up swede, or there could be guinea fowl given three treatments: the breast poached, then roasted, the thigh as confit, garnished with chestnut and apricot in Albufera sauce. Dessert might be a comfortingly rich chocolate truffle, with hazelnut and coffee, or a lighter apple jelly and yoghurt sorbet. Every dish comes with an intelligent wine suggestion, culled from an enterprising, stylistically categorised list. Prices start at £20, or £5 a standard glass. **Chef/s:** Brent Hulena. **Open:** Sat and Sun L 12 to 2, all week D 7 to 9. **Meals:** Set L £32.50. Set D £55. Sun L £32.50. Tasting menu £65. **Details:** 30 seats. Separate bar. Wheelchair access. Car parking. Children over 12 yrs only at D.

Downham

NEW ENTRY

The Assheton Arms

Warm welcome, traditional surroundings,
modern food
Downham, BB7 4BJ
Tel no: (01200) 441227
www.asshetonarms.com
British | £28
Cooking score: 2
£30

At the foot of Pendle Hill, Downham is a
beautiful spot with a 'sublime village pub'. The
'gorgeous' Assheton Arms has each of its many
rooms tastefully decorated in muted colours
and rich fabrics. A log-burner adds to the
appeal, as does a menu that's an interesting mix
of local and regional produce, honest, down-
to-earth cooking and global influences.
Marine life is a forte: Muncaster dressed crab,
perhaps, or Caribbean salt-cod cakes with hot
pepper and mango salsa, and mains of a
'generously fishy' fish pie, char-grilled yellowfin tuna with spinach beurre blanc or a more
daring tikka-spiced monkfish. Barbecued
Goosnargh chicken might figure among the
meat choices, or poacher's pie with ham hock.
Finish with good old-fashioned steamed
syrup sponge with proper custard. Service is
'charming and genuine', and wine costs
from £14.95.
Chef/s: Antony Shirley. Open: Mon to Sat L 12 to 3,
D 6 to 9 (10 Fri and Sat). Sun 12 to 8. Meals: alc
(main courses £11 to £23). Details: 90 seats. 35
seats outside. Separate bar. Car parking.

Grindleton

The Duke of York Inn

Traditional pub with sharp seasonal food
Brow Top, Grindleton, BB7 4QR
Tel no: (01200) 441266
www.dukeofyorkgrindleton.com
Modern British | £31
Cooking score: 3
£5 OFF V

'Splendid old-fashioned service' and a chef/
landlord 'who talks to his customers' make a
visit to this thoroughly traditional, creeper-
clad pub in the Ribble Valley all the more
pleasurable. Main man Michael Heathcote is
also on first-name terms with many of the
growers and suppliers who provide him with
choice pickings throughout the year.
Faultlessly executed highlights from the menu
have spanned everything from seared Isle of
Man scallops with pork belly, black pudding
and spiced parsnip purée to a porcine
'hotchpotch' with mustard sauce, while the
steak and ale pud with triple-cooked chips is
reckoned to be 'a match for anywhere'.
Heathcote can also up the tempo with superb
bouillabaisse, venison with a wondrous
poached pear and chocolate sauce, and
textbook desserts such as passion fruit
pannacotta. Well-reported gastronomic
themed nights ring the changes. The wine list
kicks off with house bottles from £17.95, and
the beer's good too.
Chef/s: Michael Heathcote. Open: Tue to Sun L 12 to
2, D 6 to 9 (5 to 7.30 Sun). Closed: Mon, 25 Dec, Tue
following bank hols. Meals: alc (main courses £14
to £22). Set L £12.99 (2 courses) to £14.99. Set D
£13.99 (2 courses) to £15.99. Sun L £16.50 (2
courses) to £19. Tasting menu £42.50 (7 courses).
Details: 70 seats. 20 seats outside. Separate bar.
Wheelchair access. Car parking.

Langho

Northcote

A smart, timeless retreat
Northcote Road, Langho, BB6 8BE
Tel no: (01254) 240555
www.northcote.com
Modern British | £57
Cooking score: 6

♦ ⌐ V

A salubrious 19th-century manor in all but name, Northcote lives and breathes Lancashire when it comes to food and hospitality. Accrington-born Nigel Haworth is the cheerful culinary brains behind the set-up – although the kitchen is ably run by *Great British Menu* favourite Lisa Allen, who knows her onions when it comes to shrewd sourcing and muscular regional tastes. The result is precision-tuned cooking, from a 'rather fab' rabbit turnover served with turnip purée and diced pickled turnip to salt-baked beetroot with Bomber cheese fondue and warm onion bread. 'Flavour sensations' hit you from the start, but there's uncompromising Lancastrian gutsiness too – witness loin of lamb cooked rare with scorched leeks and hotpot potatoes. Flexible pricing means guests can flit between menus, although it would be sinful to miss desserts such as the 'lilting' Horlicks mousse topped with tiny pieces of Bramley apple. The kitchen's unbridled generosity is backed by 'absolutely charming' service – no wonder this smart, timeless retreat is a first choice for anniversaries and birthdays. Co-owner and passionate oenophile Craig Bancroft has curated a stupendous 50-page wine list. Growers are peerless, organic names show up well and half-bottles encourage exploration; house selections start at £24 (£6.50 a glass). **Chef/s:** Lisa Allen. **Open:** all week L 12 to 2, D 7 to 9.30 (6.30 to 10 Sat, 7 to 9 Sun). **Closed:** 25 Dec. **Meals:** alc (main courses £29 to £36). Set L £27.75. Set D £60 (5 courses). Tasting menu £85 (7 courses). Sun L £36 (4 courses). **Details:** 60 seats. Separate bar. Wheelchair access. Car parking.

Little Eccleston

The Cartford Inn

Handsome inn serving pub classics
Cartford Lane, Little Eccleston, PR3 0YP
Tel no: (01995) 670166
www.thecartfordinn.co.uk
Modern British | £25
Cooking score: 2

£5 OFF ⌐ £30

A 'lovely' setting on the river Wyre gives Patrick and Julie Beaume's boutique hotel and restaurant, in a 17th-century coaching inn, a peaceful appeal. Regulars like the 'courteous' service and attention to detail, which extends to Lancashire cheeses 'kept and served at a proper temperature'. Before you get to the Garstang Blue, try a platter of local antipasti or Fleetwood seafood, or loin of hare with tagliatelle in a mushroom cream sauce, followed by the signature oxtail suet pudding with beetroot salad. 'My partner wanted to order everything again,' says one reader, perhaps with an eye on the orange and spiced fig cheesecake. House wine is £14.75. **Chef/s:** Ian Manning. **Open:** Tue to Sat L 12 to 2, D 5.30 to 9 (10 Fri and Sat). Sun 12 to 8.30. **Closed:** Mon, 25 Dec. **Meals:** alc (main courses £10 to £23). **Details:** 80 seats. 30 seats outside. Separate bar. Wheelchair access. Car parking.

Mitton

The Three Fishes

Flying the flag for regional food
Mitton Road, Mitton, BB7 9PQ
Tel no: (01254) 826888
www.thethreefishes.com
British | £26
Cooking score: 2

£30

Following a complete refurbishment and a change of chef, the original member of Nigel Haworth's Ribble Valley Inns stable was about to relaunch with a bang as the Guide's deadline approached. Like its siblings in Burrow and Pleasington (see entries), this place pulls out all the stops in its quest for 'real food' and

staunch local producers. Stonkingly good fish pie and chunky Lancashire hotpot with red cabbage are all-time favourites, but the menu also celebrates the regional delights of potted Morecambe Bay shrimps, slow-braised rare-breed pig's cheeks with champ and black pudding, devilled chicken, and rhubarb crumble – not forgetting new-season's asparagus and the first strawberries, which are 'worth missing your main course for'. Drink fine North Country ales or impressive wines (from £15.50).
Chef/s: Darren Prideaux. **Open:** Mon to Sat L 12 to 2, D 5.30 to 8.30 (9 Fri and Sat). Sun 12 to 8.30. **Closed:** 25 Dec. **Meals:** alc (main courses £10 to £20). Sun L £16 (2 courses) to £19.50. **Details:** 120 seats. 40 seats outside. Separate bar. Wheelchair access. Car parking.

Morecambe

ALSO RECOMMENDED
▲ Sun Terrace Restaurant at The Midland
Marine Road West, Morecambe, LA4 4BU
Tel no: (01524) 424000
www.englishlakes.co.uk
Modern British

'Oh, I do like to be beside the seaside . . .' and you don't get much closer to the sea than the curved red-and-white restaurant of this renovated Art Deco hotel. Floor-to-ceiling windows give a grand view over Morecambe Bay, so ordering potted shrimps (£8.25) makes sense, perhaps following with monkfish, spinach and fennel with a 'scattering of juicy mussels and crisp samphire' (£16.50) or a blade of beef bourguignon with mash. Finish with crème brûlée and buttery shortbread. Wines from £17. Open all week. Accommodation.

⫢ Average Price
The average price listed in main-entry reviews denotes the price of a three-course meal, without wine.

Pleasington
The Clog & Billycock
Welcoming pub that champions local produce
Billinge End Road, Pleasington, BB2 6QB
Tel no: (01254) 201163
www.theclogandbillycock.com
British | £26
Cooking score: 2
£30

Readers in search of 'an afternoon well spent' find it at Nigel Haworth's food-focused pub, sister of the Highwayman and the Three Fishes (see entries). The trademarks are local produce, heritage details (black peas, oven-bottom muffins, cheese and onion pies) and lots of choice, served efficiently in a buzzy, busy setting. There's no going wrong with a shared platter of local seafood, including Morecambe Bay potted shrimps, followed by hotpot or devilled Goosnargh chicken. Traditional pancakes or a hefty local cheeseboard finish the job, and the children's menu eases parental consciences without being joyless. Wines are from £15.50, and readers report success with a tasting trio of real ales, served on 'beer bats'.
Chef/s: Steve Peel. **Open:** Mon to Sat L 12 to 2, D 5.30 to 8.30 (9 Fri and Sat). Sun 12 to 8.30. **Closed:** 25 Dec. **Meals:** alc (main courses £10 to £20). Sun L £12.50 (1 course) to £19.50. **Details:** 136 seats. 50 seats outside. Separate bar. Wheelchair access. Car parking.

Waddington
The Waddington Arms
Lovely, welcoming village local
Waddington, BB7 3HP
Tel no: (01200) 423262
www.waddingtonarms.co.uk
Modern British | £25
Cooking score: 1
£5 OFF £30

A local asset since 1994, the Waddington Arms creates a pleasing vibe with its pretty village location, open fires and cracking pub grub – 'the sort of place you'd drop into twice a week and be able to afford one course and a glass of

wine nicely'. The kitchen sends out a mixed bag of accessible dishes, ranging from Cajun-spiced salmon fishcakes with garlic mayonnaise to chocolate brownies, plus substantial mains such as pork loin with black pudding and Lancashire specialities like hotpot (with pickled red cabbage), and cheese, potato and onion pie. Staff are 'eager to please'. Local cheeses, hand-pulled beers and decent wines (from £14.25) complete the package.
Chef/s: Thomas Steele. **Open:** Mon to Fri L 12 to 2.30, D 6 to 9.30. Sat 12 to 9.30. Sun 12 to 9. **Closed:** 25 Dec. **Meals:** alc (main courses £12 to £19). Sun L £11.95. **Details:** 76 seats. 76 seats outside. Wheelchair access. Car parking.

▌ Whalley
Food by Breda Murphy
Café/deli with exciting, fresh cooking
Abbots Court, 41 Station Road, Whalley, BB7 9RH
Tel no: (01254) 823446
www.foodbybredamurphy.com
Modern British | £25
Cooking score: 2
V £30

Locals value the warmth of the service and relaxed atmosphere of this café and deli in one of Lancashire's prettiest spots. Breda Murphy's background is as a student and then teacher at Ballymaloe Cookery School, and it shows in her attention to detail and commitment to fine local ingredients – as well as in dishes such as chicken liver pâté made to the alma mater's buttery recipe. Salads and sandwiches, perhaps with Ribble Valley beef, make popular lunches, though there are also more substantial offerings such as slow-cooked shoulder of pork with black pudding, rhubarb compote and pommes amandine. Puddings and cakes, such as chocolate and gingerbread torte with pear and cardamom sorbet, are highlights. Wine starts at £13.95.
Chef/s: Gareth Bevan. **Open:** Tue to Sat L 11 to 5.30, occasional evenings 7 to 9. **Closed:** Sun, Mon, 24 Dec to 3 Jan. **Meals:** alc (main courses £11 to £17). Set D £42.50 (5 courses). **Details:** 50 seats. 20 seats outside.

▌ Whitewell
The Inn at Whitewell
Pleasing inn with bang-up-to-date cooking
Whitewell, BB7 3AT
Tel no: (01200) 448222
www.innatwhitewell.com
British | £35
Cooking score: 3
🛏

Carry on deep into the Trough of Bowland to locate this centuries-old inn set in glorious isolation beside the river Hodder. Run with seemingly effortless charm by Charles Bowman, it's a handsome, rambling place with a lived-in country-house feel and a relaxed atmosphere. Log fires, antique furnishings, even breathtaking views, are a given, but it's the competent modern British cooking that draws the crowds. There is nothing here to challenge, irritate or inflame the passions, but Jamie Cadman knows how to conjure up generous, satisfying dishes with all the right accents – whether it's a neatly contrived warm pigeon breast salad (with port and redcurrant dressing), or loin of Burholme Farm's lamb with mini shepherd's pie and rosemary jus. Finish with vanilla rice pudding with spiced plum compote, or a plate of Lancashire cheeses. The extensive global wine list, strong in France, opens at £13.
Chef/s: Jamie Cadman. **Open:** all week L 12 to 2, D 7.30 to 9.30. **Meals:** alc (main courses £27 to £42). **Details:** 150 seats. 35 seats outside. Separate bar. Car parking.

¡¦ Please send us your feedback
To register your opinion about any restaurant listed in the Guide, or a new restaurant that you wish to bring to our attention, please visit the web address at the bottom of the page. Your feedback informs the content of the book and will be used to compile next year's reviews.

Wiswell

★ TOP 50 ★

Freemasons at Wiswell
High-impact food that's getting noticed
8 Vicarage Fold, Wiswell, BB7 9DF
Tel no: (01254) 822218
www.freemasonswiswell.co.uk
Modern British | £35
Cooking score: 6

Currently the hottest ticket in this part of Lancashire, the Freemasons cuts quite a dash with its high-impact food, 'tasteful but informal surroundings' and urbane outlook. Chef Steven Smith has great talent for turning classic British flavour combinations and local ingredients into smart contemporary dishes full of vibrancy and bold strokes. Witness a conventional combination of char-grilled leek and smoked haddock, transformed into 'the silkiest, smoky velouté' topped with a soft pheasant's egg, or roast lamb's sweetbread teamed with won tons, goats' curd and hazelnuts. Mains showcase the quality of locally sourced produce, say Nidderdale lamb with cockles and capers and a mini shepherd's pie, or Anna's happy trotters – a startling combination of roast pork loin, black pudding purée, gammon, egg and pineapple and pork pie sauce. Desserts also dazzle, with Reg's duck egg (custard tart and rhubarb Arctic roll) and soufflés (perhaps pistachio and macaroon with hot chocolate sauce) getting special mention. The wine list has thoughtfully chosen examples from around the globe with sound advice on hand should you need it. Prices start at £16.95
Chef/s: Steven Smith. **Open:** Tue to Sun L 12 to 2.30, D 5.30 to 9 (6 to 10 Fri and Sat, 8.30 Sun). **Closed:** Mon, 1 to 15 Jan. **Meals:** alc (main courses £16 to £30). Set L and D £16.95 (2 courses) to £19.95. Tasting menu £60 (7 courses). **Details:** 70 seats. 16 seats outside.

AARON PATTERSON
Hambleton Hall

What do you enjoy most about being a chef?
The creativity, the ingredients, and the fact that I've been lucky enough to find a profession which I love and comes naturally.

… And the least?
Being mother, father and doctor to a brigade of chefs!

What food trends are you spotting at the moment?
Classic cooking with a modern twist – we've gone full circle.

Which restaurant best sums up British cooking today?
The Fat Duck.

How do you come up with new dishes?
I find seasonal foods and spend time at home in peace and quiet with my list of ingredients. I draw the dish and then start the cooking process.

What would you be if you weren't a chef?
A designer.

Who is the chef to watch in 2014?
Raymond Blanc.

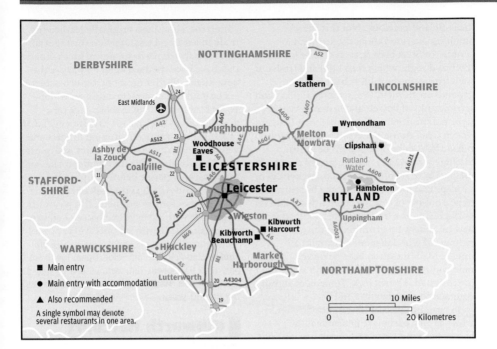

Clipsham

The Olive Branch

A well-honed country-pub operation
Main Street, Clipsham, LE15 7SH
Tel no: (01780) 410355
www.theolivebranchpub.com
British | £31
Cooking score: 3

Just a couple of miles away from the thundering A1 is the tranquil village of Clipsham and the mellow sandstone of this smart and successful dining pub. Pub classics proclaiming local provenance characterise the daily changing menu and specials board. Typically, expect smoked haddock bubble and squeak with soft poached egg, honey-roast belly pork and fish pie, with one or two more ambitious dishes at dinner. Eat at oak or rustic pine tables among beams and fires and horse brasses. On warm days the inviting garden is a draw for lunchtime tapas or evening cocktails. A thoughtful wine list that starts at £18 ranges through Old and New World specials and bin ends. Local craft ales, juices and cordials round off the pit-stop in a well-honed operation.
Chef/s: Sean Hope. **Open:** all week L 12 to 2 (3 Sun), D 7 to 9.30 (9 Sun). **Meals:** alc (main courses £15 to £24). Set L £16.95 (2 courses) to £19.95. Set D and Sun L £24.50. **Details:** 45 seats. 32 seats outside. Wheelchair access. Car parking.

Hambleton

★ TOP 50 ★

Hambleton Hall

Country-house grandeur and amazing food
Ketton Road, Hambleton, LE15 8TH
Tel no: (01572) 756991
www.hambletonhall.com
Modern British | £65
Cooking score: 7

The phrase 'quintessentially English' perfectly sums up this imposing Victorian mansion — as do other guidebook clichés like 'elegant',

'majestic' and 'gracious'. Not that there's anything overused about the setting. Co-proprietor Stefa Hart deserves credit for the interior design, which feels light and fresh but stays true to the building's history. The grounds are flawless, too; sculpted topiary and serried ranks of flowers and hedges give way to trees and the distant glassy expanse of Rutland Water. Chef Aaron Patterson has been a fixture here since 1992 and his beautiful, intelligent cooking is a large part of the hotel's magic. There are hints of techno-geekery, as in a canapé that looks like a raw egg but turns out to be a bubble of tomato essence that explodes with greenhouse freshness. He handles deeper flavours deftly, too, combining the melting richness of wood pigeon breast with an intense Madeira sauce, beer-flavoured macadamia nuts, salt-baked turnip and (intentionally) burnt leek. Tronçon of turbot comes with a verdant pea and bacon velouté, fresh peas, hogweed and chunks of bacon, while an airy passion fruit soufflé is the balancing point between a sweet passion fruit and banana sorbet and a tangy passion fruit and orange jelly. The international wine list favours small producers, with plenty of interesting finds at reasonable prices, kicking off at £22.
Chef/s: Aaron Patterson. **Open:** all week L 12 to 1.30, D 7 to 9.30. **Meals:** Set L £28.50 (2 courses) to £34.50. Set D £65. Sun L £45. Tasting menu £72. **Details:** 60 seats. Separate bar. Wheelchair access. Car parking. Children over 8 yrs only at D.

▌Kibworth Beauchamp
The Lighthouse
Much-loved Italian turns to fish
9 Station Street, Kibworth Beauchamp, LE8 OLN
Tel no: (0116) 2796260
www.lighthousekibworth.co.uk
Seafood | £26
Cooking score: 3
£5 £30
OFF

In a surprising change of tack, Lino and Sarah Poli's much-loved Firenze has re-branded as the Lighthouse and forsaken Italian regional food in favour of fish. It's also a personal dream

come true, since Lino originally learned his trade in a seafood restaurant on the Ligurian coast. Apart from a few nautical knick-knacks that have been dredged up to emphasise the new theme, the dining room is much as before – a tasteful and understated spin on white-walled trattoria cliché. Nibbles kick off a flexible 'bill of fare' that offers a choice of small or large plates (plus a smattering of meat and veggie options): a glass of crudités with garlic bread and bagna cauda for dipping makes an invigorating opener, before 'simple but effective' dishes such as pitch-perfect seared tuna niçoise, lobster spaghetti, fish pie or fillet of pollack with cabbage and bacon – all based on sustainable British supplies where possible. Thoughtfully chosen wines start at £15.50.
Chef/s: Lino Poli and Tom Wilde. **Open:** Tue to Sat D only 6 to 10. **Closed:** Sun, Mon, 25 and 26 Dec, 1 Jan, bank hols. **Meals:** alc (main courses £7 to £28). **Details:** 60 seats.

▌Kibworth Harcourt
Boboli
All-day Italian bristling with artisan treats
88 Main Street, Kibworth Harcourt, LE8 0NQ
Tel no: (0116) 2793303
www.bobolirestaurant.co.uk
Italian | £27
Cooking score: 1
£5 £30
OFF

This is what is meant by a neighbourhood restaurant: a sociable, welcoming place that has a good local following. Boboli looks after its customers well with generous portions of Italian food. Thinly sliced stuffed roast pork makes a diverting opener, teamed with celeriac rémoulade. You might then opt for an intermediate pasta course – perhaps pennette all'arrabbiata – or else steam into the main course, where saltimbocca alla romana or hearty fennel sausages with crushed potatoes and broccoli with chilli await. At other times drop in for stuzzichini (snacks) or pizza – smoked ham, Brie and onion marmalade has been a recent hit. The all-Italian wine list opens at £15.95. Related to the Lighthouse in Kibworth Beauchamp (see entry).

Chef/s: Lino Poli and Sergio Gisbert. **Open:** all week 10 to 9.30. **Closed:** 25 and 26 Dec, 1 Jan, bank hols. **Meals:** alc (main courses £8 to £21). Set L £13.50 (2 courses) to £18.50. Sun L £10.50 (1 course) to £22.50 (4 courses). **Details:** 90 seats. 28 seats outside. Separate bar. Car parking.

■ Leicester

Entropy
No-holds-barred seasonal cooking
42 Hinckley Road, Leicester, LE3 0RB
Tel no: (0116) 2259650
www.entropylife.com
Modern British | £32
Cooking score: 4

£5
OFF

A converted out-of-town butcher's shop just off the Narborough Road is the setting for Tom Cockerill's all-day eatery and bar. After 13 years, it's still doing the business. Don't be put off by the hip, laid-back vibe or the sight of 'hairy-legged waiters in shorts and waitresses with lip studs', because there's serious business at work in the open kitchen. Tom excels at no-holds-barred seasonal cooking, packing his menu with dishes that are straight and true: lamb's sweetbreads cooked in hay; mutton and caper suet pudding; whole Devon crab with roast garlic mayo and fries. Home-cured Dexter beef bresaola is a signature dish, and the family farm in Yorkshire also contributes Longhorn T-bone steaks and Southdown lamb (perhaps served with a sun-dried tomato crust, clay-baked root vegetables, rosemary and garlic jus). To finish, consider spotted dick or forced rhubarb crumble with gingerbread ice cream. Around 40 decent wines start at £15.50 (£5.25 a glass).
Chef/s: Tom Cockerill. **Open:** Tue to Sat 11 to 10 (10 to 10 Sat). Sun 10 to 5. **Closed:** 25 and 26 Dec, 1 Jan. **Meals:** alc (main courses £11 to £19). **Details:** 40 seats. Separate bar. Wheelchair access.

ALSO RECOMMENDED
▲ Maiyango
13-21 St Nicholas Place, Leicester, LE1 4LD
Tel no: (0116) 2518898
www.maiyango.com
Modern European £5
OFF

Dolled up like an exotic nightspot with tribal artefacts, beach shack cladding and swirling batik drapes, this boisterous venue attached to Hotel Maiyango rocks to a thumping soundtrack as punters swig cocktails and plunder the eclectic fixed-price menus (lunch £19.50, dinner £30). The kitchen thinks 'local', but absorbs flavours from all over – perhaps seared scallops with Thai-spiced mussels and cauliflower purée, lamb tagine with apricot and walnut jus or slow-roast blade of beef with wild mushrooms. Wines from £17.75. Open Wed to Sat L, all week D.

■ Stathern

Red Lion Inn
Satisfying, honest grub
2 Red Lion Street, Stathern, LE14 4HS
Tel no: (01949) 860868
www.theredlioninn.co.uk
British | £28
Cooking score: 2

V £30

With its low ceilings and beams, wood or stone floors, open fires and unclothed tables, the Red Lion is exactly what you might expect to find in a village hostelry. Local ales keep the drinkers happy, while gutsy, straight-talking food draws folk from further afield. Regional produce is sourced with a vengeance, just flip over the menu to see it all charted on a map. The result is a daily changing repertoire bursting with sharply executed ideas: Cropwell Bishop Stilton pannacotta with cider caramel, pickled walnuts and apple, or squid and oxtail with turnip rémoulade, then confit duck leg with carrot, fennel, orange and star anise. For afters, treat yourself to a dish of rhubarb, pannacotta and Champagne. Wines from £16.

Chef/s: Sam Britten. **Open:** Tue to Sun L 12 to 2 (3 Sun), Tue to Sat D 6.30 to 9.30 (7 to 9 Sat). **Closed:** Mon. **Meals:** alc (main courses £12 to £20). Set L £13.50 (2 courses) to £15. Set D £15. Sun L £15.50 (2 courses) to £19.50. **Details:** 60 seats. 30 seats outside. Separate bar. Wheelchair access. Car parking.

▌Woodhouse Eaves

The Woodhouse

Village restaurant with big ideas
43 Maplewell Road, Woodhouse Eaves, LE12 8RG
Tel no: (01509) 890318
www.thewoodhouse.co.uk
Modern British | £38
Cooking score: 3

V

The unassuming stone cottage on a street of stone cottages hasn't hindered the progress of Paul Leary's cutting-edge restaurant since he took over in 2005. The striking red interior forms a contrasting backdrop to the ambitious, often complex cooking. An ingenious starter of scallop teamed with Parmesan custard, butternut squash, pickled beech mushrooms, puffed rice and coriander 'excited and surprised' one reporter, while others have praised the perfectly cooked ras el hanout-spiced monkfish, and pheasant breasts served with trompette mousse, swede fondant, mushroom ketchup, cashew nuts, broccoli and truffle jus. A beautifully presented parsnip and Charnwood honey parfait with compressed apple, toasted brioche, caramelised walnut and honey tuile is typical of the noteworthy desserts. Wines, from £18, are listed by style.

Chef/s: Paul Leary. **Open:** Tue to Fri and Sun L 12 to 2 (4 Sun), Tue to Sat D 6.30 to 9.30. **Closed:** Mon, 26 Dec to 2 Jan. **Meals:** Set L £12.95 (2 courses) to £15.95. Set D £18.95 (2 courses) to £21.95. Sun L £24.95. Tasting menus £45 (7 courses) to £65 (10 courses). **Details:** 60 seats. Separate bar. Car parking.

▌Wymondham

The Berkeley Arms

Inviting country charmer
59 Main Street, Wymondham, LE14 2AG
Tel no: (01572) 787587
www.theberkeleyarms.co.uk
Modern British | £28
Cooking score: 3
£30

Neil and Louise Hitchen met while working at Hambleton Hall (see entry), but have been making waves in Wymondham since taking over this 16th-century village boozer in 2010. Readers adore its inviting atmosphere, with service getting full marks for cheery smiles and courtesy. Neil's cooking is right on the money, too, delivering big seasonal flavours from good ingredients – perhaps rabbit and prune pâté ('absolutely outstanding'), confit muntjac deer or roast partridge with red cabbage. Aside from bags of game, the kitchen knows how to please pub die-hards and adventurous foodies alike with everything from smoked haddock fishcakes to seared scallops with apple and vanilla purée or roast guinea fowl with wild mushroom and pearl barley risotto. British cheeses with home-baked biscuits make a 'brilliant' finish, or you could hit the sweet spot with hot chocolate fondant, cherry compote and pistachio ice cream. Tiptop beers, and decent wines from £15.50.

Chef/s: Neil Hitchen. **Open:** Tue to Sun L 12 to 2 (3 Sun), Tue to Sat D 6 to 9 (9.30 Fri and Sat). **Closed:** Mon, first 2 weeks Jan, 1 week Aug, Tue after bank hols. **Meals:** alc (main courses £10 to £23). Set L £14.95 (2 courses) to £18.95. Set D £18.95 (2 courses) to £22.95. Sun L £17.95. **Details:** 49 seats. 24 seats outside. Separate bar. Wheelchair access. Car parking.

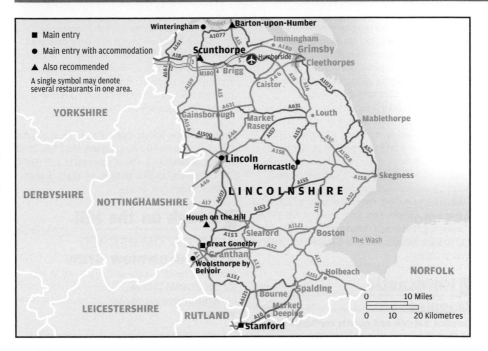

Map legend:
- ■ Main entry
- ● Main entry with accommodation
- ▲ Also recommended

A single symbol may denote several restaurants in one area.

■ Barton-upon-Humber

ALSO RECOMMENDED
▲ Elio's
11 Market Place, Barton-upon-Humber, DN18 5DA
Tel no: (01652) 635147
www.elios-restaurant.co.uk
Italian

Elio Grossi's redoubtable trattoria-with-rooms, established in 1983, is an enduringly popular fixture of the Humberside dining scene, noted for its conservatory/courtyard and daily board of fish specials. Pasta and pizzas are tried and tested favourites but it's worth going off-piste to try specials such as seared king scallops with truffle oil (£10.95); asparagus, mint and spinach risotto (£9.95); and osso buco alla milanese with saffron rice (£16.50). Many dishes are available as half-price tasters. The Italian-only wine list starts at £15.95. Open Mon to Sat D only.

■ Great Gonerby

Harry's Place
Keeping it personal
17 High Street, Great Gonerby, NG31 8JS
Tel no: (01476) 561780
Modern French | £60
Cooking score: 5

£5
OFF

A rare treasure or an 'exorbitantly priced let-down', this cocooned three-table dining room in Harry and Caroline Hallam's own home confounds expectations. Fresh flowers and family photos keep things personal (if rather 'joyless'), while the food evokes an era before bloggers started calling the shots. For more than 25 years, Harry has been scribbling his menus every day, offering just two choices at each stage and playing with recurring themes: the food can charm, but recent reports of 'anaemic' and erratic cooking suggest otherwise. To begin, the signature salad of Filey lobster, avocado and mango is probably a better bet than sautéed chicken livers, served chilled and 'enrobed in sherry aspic': a 'disgusting' throwback, according to one reader. After that, you might be offered lightly cooked brill with piccolo tomatoes or something from the old school of game cookery – roe deer with blueberries, mushroom duxelle and a boozy sauce laced with red wine, Madeira and Armagnac, perhaps. To finish, the cherry brandy jelly with yoghurt and black pepper continues to impress, although Harry can deliver textbook soufflés, too. Wines (from £20) are picked from a jumbled-up, single-page list.

Chef/s: Harry Hallam. **Open:** Tue to Sat L 12.30 to 2, D 7 to 8.30. **Closed:** Sun, Mon, 1 week from 25 Dec, 1 week Aug, bank hols. **Meals:** alc (main courses £37 to £40). **Details:** 10 seats. Car parking. Children over 5 yrs only.

Horncastle

Magpies

Genuine warmth and quietly confident cooking
73 East Street, Horncastle, LN9 6AA
Tel no: (01507) 527004
www.magpiesrestaurant.co.uk
Modern British | £45
Cooking score: 5

♦ ⇌ V

The very model of a personally run restaurant-with-rooms, Andrew and Caroline Gilbert's little beauty combines genuine warmth and honest intent with quietly confident cooking and fine wines. The dining room within this quaint Wolds cottage has been given a face-lift; duck-egg blue and cream tones now enhance the elegant, intimate vibe. Andrew's food shows a feel for what is right on the plate, and seasonal ingredients obviously play their part: from veal confit and spinach pithiviers with sautéed wild mushrooms to Lincolnshire Red beef fillet with oxtail ravioli, slow-cooked shin and horseradish rösti. The kitchen also calls on faraway themes – as in baked cod with lemongrass and ginger beurre blanc, butternut squash arancini and wilted Chinese greens. Caroline not only runs front-of-house, but also takes care of desserts. Her dark chocolate 'sweet shop' terrine with Turkish delight sorbet, banana gelato, pink-sugar tuile and Dolly Mixture syrup should whisk you right back to childhood. The food is reckoned to be 'jolly good value' and the well-balanced, manageable wine list is pure joy for both aficionados and everyday drinkers. Around 20 Corney & Barrow house selections start at £18.20.

Chef/s: Andrew Gilbert. **Open:** Wed to Fri and Sun L 12 to 2, Wed to Sun D 7 to 9. **Closed:** Mon, Tue, 26 to 30 Dec. **Meals:** Set L £20 (2 courses) to £25, Set £39 (2 courses) to £45. **Details:** 34 seats. 8 seats outside. Wheelchair access.

Hough on the Hill

ALSO RECOMMENDED
▲ The Brownlow Arms
Grantham Road, Hough on the Hill, NG32 2AZ
Tel no: (01400) 250234
www.thebrownlowarms.com
British

'Pretty well unchangeable' is one returning visitor's verdict on this 17th-century country pub-cum-restaurant-with-rooms, a stalwart of the Lincolnshire dining scene. The kitchen is not about to rock an exceedingly steady ship, and food remains true to the spirit of wholesome flavour and comfort. Warm seafood mousse with brown shrimp and beurre blanc (£7.50) and mains of classic beef bourguignon with butter mash (£14.50) or sea bream with fennel risotto, suit the tone of the place. Wines from £16.50. Open Tue to Sat D and Sun L.

||♦ Please send us your feedback

To register your opinion about any restaurant listed in the Guide, or a new restaurant that you wish to bring to our attention, please visit the web address at the bottom of the page. Your feedback informs the content of the book and will be used to compile next year's reviews.

▌Lincoln

The Old Bakery

Relaxed and idiosyncratic
26-28 Burton Road, Lincoln, LN1 3LB
Tel no: (01522) 576057
www.theold-bakery.co.uk
Modern European | £35
Cooking score: 2

Tracey and Ivano de Serio's welcoming restaurant-with-rooms inspires confidence in its regulars, who like the 'peaceful' conservatory and friendly service. Ivano's Puglian heritage shows in an eight-course Italian tasting menu, but on a personal, idiosyncratic à la carte, starters such as soft-shell crab with jambalaya rice and burnt-onion mayonnaise take their influences from further afield. Local pork is roasted in hay for a main course with pancetta potato gratin, apple and red cabbage with cinnamon and crispy pork popcorn. An extensive cheese selection, featuring some of the British Isles' greatest unpasteurised hits, is a big draw. Wine starts at £14.95.
Chef/s: Ivano de Serio. **Open:** Tue to Sun L 12 to 1.30, Tue to Sat D 6.30 to 9. **Closed:** Mon, 2 weeks Jan, 2 weeks Aug. **Meals:** alc (main courses £16 to £25). Set L £12.50 (2 courses) to £16.50. Sun L £17.95. Tasting menu £38. **Details:** 50 seats. Wheelchair access.

▌Scunthorpe

ALSO RECOMMENDED
▲ San Pietro
11 High Street East, Scunthorpe, DN15 6UH
Tel no: (01724) 277774
www.sanpietro.uk.com
Modern European

Over the past 10 years this Grade II-listed windmill with courtyard gardens has fared well under the stewardship of Piero and Michelle Catalano. The kitchen may have an Italian accent (risotto ai frutti di mare, lobster and truffle fettuccine) but it also soaks up influences from near and far. Expect to find pigeon stuffed with Lincolnshire sausage on a caramelised red onion galette (£8.95), duck breast with confit duck croquette, spiced red cabbage, potato fondant and orange and port jus (£25.95) and crème brûlée. Wines from £17.50. Closed Mon L and Sun.

▌Stamford

Jim's Yard

Terrific neighbourhood eatery
3 Ironmonger Street, Stamford, PE9 1PL
Tel no: (01780) 756080
www.jimsyard.biz
Modern European | £27
Cooking score: 2

£5 OFF   £30

Something about Jim's Yard hits exactly the right spot, perhaps because it's a refreshing and likeable antidote to most high-street eateries – smart and comfortable with great alfresco possibilities and a robust attitude to provenance and seasonality. Reporters certainly approve the welcoming atmosphere and applaud the kitchen's efforts. From the carte, a starter of crispy pancetta with roast black pudding, beetroot and Puy lentils has gone down well, but also look for slow-cooked belly pork with sage and onion mash, and fresh fish such as sea bream with roast sweet potato, wilted spinach and tomato butter sauce. Otherwise, investigate the British and French cheeses and desserts such as baked white chocolate cheesecake with mulled fruits. Wines from £14.95.
Chef/s: James Ramsay. **Open:** Tue to Sat L 12 to 2.30, D 6 to 9.30. **Closed:** Sun, Mon, 2 weeks from 26 Dec, last week Jul, first week Aug. **Meals:** alc (main courses £13 to £20). Set L 14.50 and pre-theatre D (2 courses) to £17.50. Set D 19.50.
Details: 70 seats. 20 seats outside. Separate bar. Wheelchair access.

¦¦¦ Also Recommended
Also recommended entries are not scored but we think they are worth a visit.

▌Winteringham

Winteringham Fields

A shining star
1 Silver Street, Winteringham, DN15 9ND
Tel no: (01724) 733096
www.winteringhamfields.co.uk
Modern European | £59
Cooking score: 5

£5 OFF 🍴 V

The McGurran family's former farmhouse on the Humber estuary has long been a compass point for English dining, but nothing prepares first-timers for Colin McGurran's artistry – unless they happened to see him on 2012's *Great British Menu*. The ambience remains chintzy, yet the painstakingly worked European techno-cooking is anything but. Reports relate all the details, starting with the tasty little crisps with wasabi mayo that titillate at the Menu Surprise's opening. Everybody loves the mock tomato: a bulging ball of gazpacho, accompanied by horseradish, frozen olives and smeared basil. 'Ham and peas' is full of astonishing little jokes: counter-intuitively coloured purées; pressed ham hock in powdered pea; pork scratchings in a minty salad. Fish could be super-fresh barbecued mackerel with a nori cracker and horseradish snow, or smoked haddock in a spicy chowder topped with a poached egg parcel done up in potato ribbon. The pièce de résistance is quail, sitting on a perch accompanied by its tempura-battered egg, amid blackberries, beetroot-stained pear and a cigarette of foie gras parfait. In comparison, the dessert of egg custard and nutmeg with Amaretto ice cream and boozed-up raisins, may seem almost prosaic. Many ingredients are supplied from Winteringham's own smallholding, making the show still more impressive. A compendious wine list (from £28) does its best to live up to the cooking.
Chef/s: Colin McGurran. **Open:** Tue to Sat L 12 to 2, D 7 to 10. **Closed:** Sun, Mon, Christmas, 3 days Apr, 3 weeks Aug. **Meals:** Set L £39.95. Set D £59 (3 courses) to £79 (10 courses). **Details:** 70 seats. Separate bar. Wheelchair access. Car parking.

▌Woolsthorpe by Belvoir

Chequers Inn

Honest country pub with no-nonsense victuals
Main Street, Woolsthorpe by Belvoir, NG32 1LU
Tel no: (01476) 870701
www.chequersinn.net
Modern British | £28
Cooking score: 1

£5 OFF 🍴 £30

This 17th-century inn close to Belvoir Castle has all the classic accoutrements: heavy beams, solid wooden furniture, log fire. Its easy-going approach is just the ticket, whether you fancy a pint, a snack or a full-blown meal. The Chequers earns its living from generous hospitality, real ales and satisfying food. Ribeye steak sandwich with frites is the best option at lunch, or look beyond pub grub to Belvoir pigeon with pickled plums, wild mushrooms and port jus, mains of hake with risotto of clams and pancetta, followed by chocolate tart with pistachio ice cream. House wine is £15.
Chef/s: Mark Nesbit. **Open:** all week L 12 to 2.30 (4 Sun), D 6 to 9.30 (8.30 Sun). **Meals:** alc (main courses £11 to £20). Set L £12.50 (2 courses) to £15. Set D £17.50. Sun L £13.95. **Details:** 90 seats. 50 seats outside. Separate bar. Wheelchair access. Car parking.

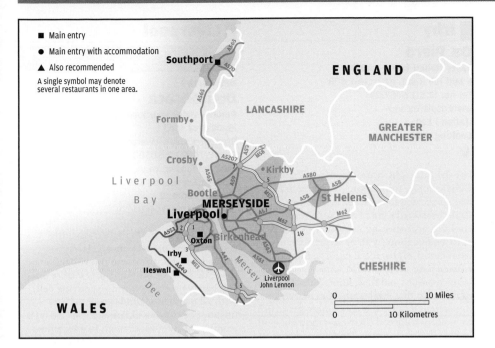

- ■ Main entry
- ● Main entry with accommodation
- ▲ Also recommended

A single symbol may denote
several restaurants in one area.

ENGLAND

Southport

LANCASHIRE

GREATER
MANCHESTER

Formby

Crosby

Kirkby

Liverpool
Bay

Bootle
MERSEYSIDE

St Helens

Liverpool

Oxton
Birkenhead

Irby

CHESHIRE

Heswall

Liverpool
John Lennon

WALES

Dee

Mersey

0   10 Miles

0   10 Kilometres

◼ Heswall

Nova

A hidden gem on the Wirral
68 Pensby Road, Heswall, CH60 7RE
Tel no: (0151) 3429959
www.novarestaurant.co.uk
Modern British | £30
Cooking score: 3

Jana and Moyo Benson are acquiring a loyal
following at this former shop turned smart
neighbourhood restaurant. 'Smart' also
describes the innovative cooking going on,
with 'imaginative ideas' seen in crab fishcake
with Thai-style salsa or a dish of grilled
mackerel teamed with apple tapioca,
Reblochon cheese and miso ('a lovely
combination of textures and flavours'). There's
plenty to applaud in main courses, too:
perhaps pork belly with the lightest, crispiest
pork skin, a beignet of black pudding and
asparagus or a 'great' dish of gigot of mutton
('in the style of pulled pork') teamed with an
'inspired' lightly curried potato. For dessert,
the kitchen contents itself with a gorgeously
tart rhubarb with sweet pannacotta-style set
cream and a pistachio biscotti, or roast
pineapple with its own sorbet atop a rum baba.
A short, well-chosen wine list starts at £14.
Chef/s: Moyo Benson. **Open:** Tue to Sat L 12 to 2.30,
D 6 to 9.30. Sun 12 to 8. **Closed:** Mon, 26 Dec, first 2
weeks Jan. **Meals:** alc (main courses £13 to 19). Set
L £12 (2 courses) to £15. Set D £15 (2 courses) to
£17.50. Sun L £15. **Details:** 42 seats. Wheelchair
access.

╫ Please send us your feedback

To register your opinion about any
restaurant listed in the Guide, or a new
restaurant that you wish to bring to our
attention, please visit the web address at
the bottom of the page. Your feedback
informs the content of the book and will
be used to compile next year's reviews.

Irby

Da Piero

Tasty Italian home cooking
5 Mill Hill Road, Irby, CH61 4UB
Tel no: (0151) 6487373
www.dapiero.co.uk
Italian | £30
Cooking score: 4

V

For the past eight years, Dawn and Piero di Bella's simple, front-room-style restaurant has been dedicated to the freshest and most straightforward kind of Sicilian home cooking, accentuating its rusticity. Consider curly endive soup (with pancetta, tomato and fresh herbs), tagliatelle al ragù, and duck legs roasted with herbs and red wine, served with sautéed onions and fresh mint. There's a roster of fresh fish that might run from marvellous tuna tartare prepared with sashimi-grade fish to Sicilian-style cod (in extra-virgin olive oil, garlic and vine tomato). Tender marinated and char-grilled beef is a popular choice, as are interesting side dishes of caponata (aubergines, celery, pine nuts, olive and capers) and crisp fennel salad. Finish with homemade ice cream. Some have found the food 'disappointing', but no such criticism can be levelled at the warm service or the small selection of Italian wines (from £19.20).
Chef/s: Piero Di Bella. **Open:** Tue to Sat D only 6 to 11. **Closed:** Sun, Mon, 25 and 26 Dec, 1 and 2 Jan. **Meals:** alc (main courses £11 to £25). **Details:** 32 seats.

Liverpool

★ READERS' RESTAURANT OF THE YEAR ★
NATIONAL WINNER

NEW ENTRY

Delifonseca

Popular neighbourhood restaurant with innovative food
Brunswick Quay, Liverpool, L3 4BN
Tel no: (0151) 2550808
www.delifonseca.co.uk
Modern European | £25
Cooking score: 2

£5 OFF £30

At first glance it looks like a classy little supermarket (and was once a Harry Ramsden's), but persevere and you'll find a nice café (cosy booths or comfy leather seats and bare wood tables) and an enticing deli with all manner of edible goodies. This offshoot of city-based Fonseca, (see entry) is gaining loyal followers with its welcoming service and range of tasting platters, sandwiches and salad staples. But it's the daily changing blackboard that demands attention – 'what I would call proper restaurant food' offering the likes of quail Scotch egg with celeriac remoulade ahead of fillet of salmon with caper and dill potato cake and a butternut squash purée, or a 'super' rainbow gratin of root vegetables with a cannellini and tomato ragù, and sheep's milk crème brûlée. A very short wine list starts at £14.95, but you can pick any wine from the deli and add £6.50 corkage or choose from a good list of speciality beers.
Chef/s: Martin Cooper. **Open:** all week 8am to 9pm (9.30 Sat, 10 to 5 Sun). **Closed:** 25 and 26 Dec, 1 Jan. **Meals:** alc (main courses £14 to £16). **Details:** 66 seats. Wheelchair access. Car parking.

Fonseca's
Wonderful deli with satisfying food
12 Stanley Street, Liverpool, L1 6AF
Tel no: (0151) 2550808
www.delifonseca.co.uk
Modern European | £25
Cooking score: 2
£5 OFF £30

Readers continue to sing the praises of Candice Fonseca's original deli-restaurant in the Stanley Street Quarter (see also Delifonseca Dockside). The restaurant, wedged above the magnificently stocked deli, is alive with chat, service is charm personified and the menu reads robustly. Expect salads and sandwiches or a 'very good' Welsh rarebit, along with enticing blackboard specials: perhaps breast of wild mallard 'bang-on at medium rare', served with chorizo, sun-dried tomatoes and sauté potatoes or a well-reported venison with beetroot, pickled mushrooms and a herby Stilton croquette. The deli supplies some cracking cheeses, or there could be raspberry and ginger jelly and mixed berry pannacotta served with a belting stem ginger ice cream. Wines from £13.95.
Chef/s: Andrew Hutchinson. **Open:** Mon to Thurs 12 to 9 (9.30 Fri and Sat). **Closed:** Sun, 25 Dec to 1 Jan, bank hols. **Meals:** alc (main courses £10 to £17). **Details:** 50 seats.

Hanover Street Social
Globetrotting all-day brasserie
Casartelli Building, 16-20 Hanover Street, Liverpool, L1 4AA
Tel no: (0151) 7098784
www.hanoverstreetsocial.co.uk
Modern European | £25
Cooking score: 1
£5 OFF £30

A funky playground for Liverpudlians, this brash all-day brasserie entertains with a lively bill of fare that stretches from breakfast to late-night cocktails. Bare brickwork, high ceilings, red leather banquettes and a black-and-white tiled floor set the scene for a globetrotting menu that peddles crustacea, char-grilled flatbreads, exotic salads (bang-bang chicken, for example) and an assortment of grills and roasts. Popular calls include the house burgers, tandoori salmon, duck breast with celeriac purée and good old fish and chips. Wines start at £14.50, with plenty offered by the glass or carafe. Related to the Salt House opposite (see entry).
Chef/s: Simon Wood. **Open:** all week 12 to 10.30 (12.30 to 10.30 Sun). **Closed:** 25 Dec. **Meals:** alc (main courses £9 to £17). Set L £9.95 (2 courses) to £12.50. Sun L £11.95 (2 courses) to £15.50. **Details:** 100 seats. Wheelchair access.

Host
Fast and friendly fusion
31 Hope Street, Liverpool, L1 9HX
Tel no: (0151) 7085831
www.ho-st.co.uk
Pan-Asian | £22
Cooking score: 1
V £30

Table sharing is encouraged at this funky pan-Asian canteen in Liverpool's trendy Georgian Quarter. The atmosphere fizzes as super-efficient staff whizz around, delivering myriad 'small' and 'big' plates to a diverse crowd in the retro, open-plan dining room. Big wholesome flavours and quick-fire chilli hits come thick and fast – from chicken satay or soy-cured salmon with Szechuan dressing to bowls of Vietnamese pho noodle soup, yellow seafood curry or chilli bean and smoked tofu stir-fry. For dessert, try peanut-butter brûlée with a jam crumble biscuit. House wine is £14.95, although bottles of Saigon beer suit the food. Related to 60 Hope Street (see entry).
Chef/s: David Fitzsimmons. **Open:** all week 11 to 11. **Closed:** 25 and 26 Dec. **Meals:** alc (main courses £10 to £15). **Details:** 140 seats. 25 seats outside. Separate bar. Wheelchair access.

LIVERPOOL

The London Carriage Works

Hot-ticket Merseyside brasserie
Hope Street Hotel, 40 Hope Street, Liverpool,
L1 9DA
Tel no: (0151) 7052222
www.thelondoncarriageworks.co.uk
Modern European | £39
Cooking score: 3
🛏

Looking at its open-plan interior, exposed brickwork and chunky oak floors, you might not guess that this hot-ticket, brasserie-style restaurant was housed in the 'Venetian palazzo' remains of a Victorian carriage maker's workshop – although the name gives a clue. It's resolutely understated in style, with a menu that aims to please: from sharing platters, deli sandwiches, classic salads and dry-aged steaks to daily fish specials from the market and dishes ranging from wild mushroom and pistachio pithiviers to an assiette of Wirral pork (tenderloin, cheek and belly) with celeriac purée, beetroot and green peppercorn jus. To finish, a dozen British regional cheeses line up alongside the likes of banana and toffee Eton mess or prune 'Bourdaloue' tart with crème anglaise and Earl Grey sorbet. Each dish is flagged with a suitable wine (or beer) from the extensive international list; prices start at £16.50 (£4.50 a glass).
Chef/s: Paul Askew. **Open:** Mon to Sat L 12 to 3, D 5 to 10. Sun 12 to 9. **Meals:** alc (main courses £8 to £30). Set L and D £15 (2 courses) to £20. **Details:** 60 seats. Separate bar. Wheelchair access.

Symbols

🛏 Accommodation is available
£30 Three courses for less than £30
V Separate vegetarian menu
£5 OFF £5-off voucher scheme
🍾 Notable wine list

Lunya

Vibrant Spanish eatery and deli
18-20 College Lane, Liverpool One, Liverpool,
L1 3DS
Tel no: (01517) 069770
www.lunya.co.uk
Spanish | £23
Cooking score: 2
£5 OFF £30

Peter Kinsella's vibrant and buzzy tapas restaurant and well-stocked deli continues to charm readers who travel from afar to order Catalan and Spanish specialities from the extensive menu. Lunya is situated deep in the heart of the bustling Liverpool One shopping development. Part of it occupies a centuries-old warehouse and the brick-lined dining room has a laid-back vibe. Many have been impressed by the 'sharp and attentive' service and 'varied and interesting' menu that enables you to mix and match the generously proportioned tapas. Try garlicky Catalan bread, 24-hour slow-roasted lamb with pomegranate and mint, or black rice and cuttlefish with calamari and squid ink. Finish with a classic crema catalana or a board of Spanish cheeses. House wine from £15.75.
Chef/s: Dave Upson. **Open:** all week 10 to 9.30 (10pm Wed, 10.30pm Thur, 11pm Fri and Sat). **Closed:** 25 Dec. **Meals:** alc (tapas £3 to £8). Set L £9.75. **Details:** 150 seats. 30 seats outside. Separate bar. Wheelchair access.

Salt House

Tapas with a buzz
Hanover Street, Liverpool, L1 3DW
Tel no: (0151) 7060092
www.salthousetapas.co.uk
Spanish | £14
Cooking score: 2
£30

In a prime location in 'new' Liverpool, this buzzy tapas spot confidently combines local essentials (people-watching opportunities, genuine hospitality and cocktails) with cool minimalism and good Spanish ingredients. The menu is by no means purist (witness

sweet-sour ribs and beer-battered fish sliders), but it's possible to steer an Iberian course with, perhaps, deep-fried Monte Enebro cheese with honey and red beetroot crisps, Ibérico ham croquettes, tortilla or hake with warm mussel escabeche. Turrón mousse with candied almonds, a long-standing house favourite, is the dessert to beat. House wine – Spanish, of course – is £14.50, but there's plenty of sherry and beer, including the results of Ferran Adrià's collaboration with Estrella, to explore.
Chef/s: Martin Renshaw. **Open:** all week 12 to 10.30 (11pm Fri and Sat). **Closed:** 25 Dec. **Meals:** alc (tapas £4 to £7). Set L £9.90. **Details:** 90 seats. 26 seats outside.

The Side Door
Welcoming, good-value bistro
29a Hope Street, Liverpool, L1 9BQ
Tel no: (0151) 7077888
www.thesidedoor.co.uk
Modern European | £30
Cooking score: 2
£5
OFF

A 'really lovely restaurant' with 'great atmosphere, great food', this characterful bistro has many loyal followers. Against an unfussy backdrop of stripped-back interior, natural light and utilitarian furnishings, the Side Door makes its mark with a raft of snappy European ideas. There's something to suit most preferences. You might open with smoked haddock and Jerusalem artichoke risotto, and follow with tandoori monkfish with spiced rice, green bean and coconut salad and a coconut curry sauce – though Goosnargh duck breast served with caramelised onion, Bury black pudding mash, Savoy cabbage and leeks is an enticing alternative. 'Finish in style' with a bitter chocolate tart with mango and passion fruit mousse. Service is 'very professional'. Wines from £13.95.
Chef/s: Michael Robinson. **Open:** Mon to Sat L 12 to 2, D 5.30 to 9.30 (10 Thur to Sat). **Closed:** Sun, 25 and 26 Dec, 1 Jan, bank hols. **Meals:** alc (main

courses £13 to £19). Set L £15.95 (2 courses). Set D £16.95 (2 courses) to £18.95. **Details:** 60 seats. 12 seats outside.

60 Hope Street
A smart eatery in the heart of town
60 Hope Street, Liverpool, L1 9BZ
Tel no: (0151) 7076060
www.60hopestreet.com
Modern British | £35
Cooking score: 1
V

This smart Georgian town house close to the Philharmonic Hall attracts early diners and business folk, thanks to good-value meal deals. Its 'nicely decked out' contemporary interior comes with polished floors that 'look great but provide an awful acoustic effect', though there's praise for the cooking. Dishes such as seared mackerel fillet with cucumber and coriander couscous, confit chicken terrine with pea and ham salad, and fillet of Cumbrian beef served with a mini-casserole of braised shin with herb dumplings are typical of the style. Puddings include staples such as crème brûlée or passion fruit cheesecake. A well-annotated wine list starts with house vin de pays at £19.95.
Chef/s: Damien Flynn. **Open:** Mon to Sat L 12 to 2.30, D 5 to 10.30. Sun 12 to 8. **Closed:** 26 Dec, 1 Jan. **Meals:** alc (main courses £15 to £39). Set L and D £20 (2 courses) to £25. **Details:** 150 seats. 15 seats outside. Separate bar.

Spire
Neighbourhood nirvana
1 Church Road, Liverpool, L15 9EA
Tel no: (0151) 7345040
www.spirerestaurant.co.uk
Modern European | £32
Cooking score: 4
£5
OFF

A neighbourhood bistro near Penny Lane, Spire is now a decade old and inspires great loyalty locally. It's an approachable place, run by the Locke brothers: Matt in the kitchen, Adam out front. The dining room is done up in blond wood and brick, with a splash of colour from paintings on the wall and flowers on the table. Matt cooks in a smart modern European style, producing dishes that offer innovative takes on new 'classics' and familiar pairings. Beetroot and goats' cheese are teamed with pear purée and caramelised onions, for instance; Cumbria beef comes with fondant potato and an unusual red cabbage purée; and chocolate fondant is paired with bitter orange ice cream. Set menus (both lunch and early evening) list old favourites such as steak and chunky chips, fish and chips, or a 'posh' prawn cocktail. Wines (from £14.95) are mainstream but kindly priced with plenty of choice sub-£20.

Chef/s: Matt Locke. **Open:** Tue to Fri L 12 to 2, Mon to Sat D 6 to 9 (9.30 Thur, Fri and Sat). **Closed:** Sun, first week Jan. **Meals:** alc (main courses £14 to £22). Set L £11.95 (2 courses) to £14.95. Set D £14.95 (2 courses) to £17.95. **Details:** 70 seats.

ALSO RECOMMENDED
▲ The Clove Hitch

23 Hope Street, Liverpool, L1 9BQ
Tel no: (0151) 7096574
www.theclovehitch.com
Modern British

The area close to the Philharmonic Hall is fast becoming a foodie hub. This all-day eatery offers relaxed surroundings, come rain or shine, in which to enjoy pancakes and maple syrup (£4.95), homemade burgers (£12.95) or fennel-roasted sea bass salad with roasted tomatoes, garlic wild mushrooms and toasted brioche. Heartier dishes can also be ordered: the likes of confit of duck with a leek rösti or rump of lamb, olive mash and Welsh rarebit. Choose from a global selection of wines (from £13.95) and beers. Open all week.

¶¶ Also Recommended
Also recommended entries are not scored but we think they are worth a visit.

Etsu
Japanese
25 The Strand (off Brunswick Street), Liverpool, L2 0XJ
Tel no: (0151) 2367530
www.etsu-restaurant.co.uk
'Food was fresh, tasty and worlds apart from the chain sushi restaurants that are springing up. It even bests some of the flashier high-end Japanese restaurants the city has to offer.'

▌Oxton

★ TOP 50 ★

Fraiche
Culinary wizardry on the Wirral
11 Rose Mount, Oxton, CH43 5SG
Tel no: (0151) 6522914
www.restaurantfraiche.com
Modern French | £65
Cooking score: 7
V

'Perfectionism', 'dedication' and 'innovation' – there's ample praise for Marc Wilkinson's highly popular one-man show. Every aspect of the experience is choreographed, from the dining room's uncluttered lines to the well-rehearsed, knowledgeable and attentive staff. The food, still influenced by cutting-edge culinary wizardry, has taken a turn for the orthodox (ingredients now speak for themselves more clearly) but those looking for food theatrics won't be disappointed. A 'signature' menu might open with 'refreshing' cucumber, apple and lime granita, made at table with liquid nitrogen, followed by mussels poached in ginger, samphire and garlic ('a delicious and intense mouthful'), a 'deconstructed' Spanish omelette (quail's egg, chorizo jelly, crispy shallots, potato cream) or the salt-sweet sensations of 'textures of carrot with feta' (roasted carrot with feta and carrot sorbet, wild garlic purée, truffle and a shard of toasted pain d'épices, finished with grated Perigord truffle). Scallop ceviche – slivers of scallop with apple, wild rice and oyster leaf

alongside a roasted scallop with smoked lime butter – shows a desire to ensure natural flavours remain true, as does aged barbecued beef (smoky beef fillet served with braised salsify and celeriac purée). No sleeping in the stalls for the last act either: cold, fizzing fresh grapes arrive as a refresher before the final course of 'salt' (a 'retro' cheese chariot) or 'sweet' (poached rhubarb with star anise cream and sesame crisp). The 300-strong, global wine list (from £21.50) is listed by style.
Chef/s: Marc Wilkinson. **Open:** Sun L 12 to 1, Wed to Sat D 7 to 8.30. **Closed:** Mon, Tue, 25 Dec, first week Jan. **Meals:** Set L £35. Tasting menu £65 (6 courses). **Details:** 14 seats. 6 seats outside. Separate bar. Wheelchair access. Children over 8 yrs only at D.

▌Southport

Bistrot Vérité
Homely eatery with Gallic classics
7 Liverpool Road, Birkdale, Southport, PR8 4AR
Tel no: (01704) 564199
www.bistrotverite.co.uk
French | £28
Cooking score: 3
£30

A few yards from the level crossing at Birkdale station, Marc Vérité's compact neighbourhood bistro continues to fly the Anglo-French flag for locally sourced, uncomplicated food. The place is run with consummate professionalism, which makes up for the muzak-augmented din created on busy evenings. Menus chalked on boards yield the likes of a fine terrine of smoked duck, foie gras and lentils, dressed with apricot purée; generous bowls of mushroom and tarragon soup; and mains of accurately cooked sea bass topped with a row of toasted scallops in spinach beurre blanc. A chorizo wrapping might out-shout some mildly flavoured collops of pork fillet, but the accompanying buttery leek fondue is a winner. Finish with a refreshingly straightforward crème brûlée with properly crisped top. The wine list is sloppily presented and rather piecemeal, though it starts with house French at a reasonable £16.75.

Chef/s: Marc Vérité. **Open:** Tue to Sat L 12 to 1.30, D 5.30 to 9.30. **Closed:** Sun, Mon, 25 and 26 Dec, 1 Jan, 1 week Feb, 1 week Aug. **Meals:** alc (main courses £13 to £20). **Details:** 45 seats. 14 seats outside.

READERS RECOMMEND

The Warehouse
Modern British
30 West Street, Southport, PR8 1QN
Tel no: (01704) 544662
www.warehousekitchenandbar.com
'The trio of Welsh lamb was just tenderness in its timbale, gold in its confit and melting perfection in its medallions.'

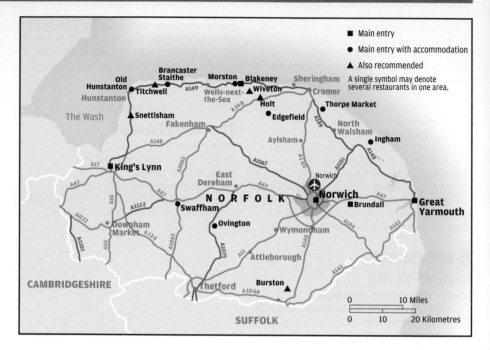

Blakeney

The Moorings

Endearing Norfolk bolt-hole
High Street, Blakeney, NR25 7NA
Tel no: (01263) 740054
www.blakeney-moorings.co.uk
Modern British | £30
Cooking score: 2

An endearing Norfolk bolt-hole with good intentions and a big heart, Richard and Angela Long's well-liked eatery occupies some converted (and extended) bait sheds just a hop from Blakeney quay. During the day, the Moorings runs along as a café, serving sandwiches, soups and salads to famished locals and out-of-towners, while candles and tablecloths signal that it's dressed for dinner. The kitchen makes good use of fish and other local pickings for a short evening menu that might yield spicy crab cakes, warm pigeon breast salad with figs and pancetta, lobster with hollandaise or rack of lamb with celeriac

purée and 'hedgerow' jus. To finish, Angela's puds have quite a reputation. The wine list is a little corker, with prices from £14.95.
Chef/s: Richard and Angela Long. **Open:** Tue to Sun L 10.30 to 4.30, Tue to Sat D 6.30 to 9.30. **Closed:** Mon, 16 to 26 Dec, 3 weeks Jan. **Meals:** alc (main courses £15 to £23). Sun L £17.50. **Details:** 50 seats.

Brancaster Staithe

The White Horse

Simple cooking lets the flavours shine
Brancaster Staithe, PE31 8BY
Tel no: (01485) 210262
www.whitehorsebrancaster.co.uk
Modern British | £30
Cooking score: 3

The conservatory dining area capitalises on stunning views across salt marshes, for one reporter a 'wonderful arena on a stormy Sunday'. Others have endorsed the contemporary 'seaside feel' and the comfort of the front bar, describing it as a 'valuable local resource and an agreeable stopover, too' – for this whitewashed inn is on the coast road linking King's Lynn to Cromer. The quality sourcing of local ingredients (from mussels, oysters and asparagus to game and meat) is a prime motivation for chef Avrum Frankel, and he fuses these great British ingredients with a light Mediterranean touch. Fish is a strength, but alternatives might be chicken ravioli with sprout leaves, pancetta, cider and Stilton velouté, or pan-roast lamb mini hotpot. Portions are generous, desserts hard to resist (try the lemon tart) and service is all it should be. Wines from £15.

Chef/s: Avrum Frankel. **Open:** all week L 12 to 2, D 6.30 to 9. **Meals:** alc (main courses £9 to £21). **Details:** 110 seats. 90 seats outside. Separate bar. Wheelchair access. Car parking.

ALSO RECOMMENDED
▲ The Jolly Sailors
Brancaster Staithe, PE31 8BJ
Tel no: (01485) 210314
www.jollysailorsbrancaster.co.uk
British

The bar dispenses own-brewed ale (Brancaster Brewery) and drinkers are welcomed, but good-value cooking is the thing at this rustic 18th-century roadside pub – which shares owners with the nearby White Horse (see entry). A please-all menu focuses on light bites (Scotch egg, crayfish salad), great pizzas, excellent Brancaster mussels and pub classics such as steak and chips (£14.50), curry or pie of the day, and ploughman's (£6.95). A sheltered courtyard and garden holds a summer ice cream hut. No bookings. House Georges Duboeuf is £15.50. Open all week.

▌ Brundall
The Lavender House
Delightfully unassuming foodie haven
39 The Street, Brundall, NR13 5AA
Tel no: (01603) 712215
www.thelavenderhouse.co.uk
Modern British | £43
Cooking score: 3
🍾

Chef/restaurateur Richard Hughes is big in Norfolk, with fingers in several pies, but this delightful 16th-century thatched cottage is mission control for his culinary crusade. Whether you are enrolled at his award-winning cookery school, sipping rare fizz in the Champagne bar or enjoying Sunday lunch in the Willi Opitz Room, there are beguiling pleasures aplenty to be enjoyed here. East Anglian flavours leap out from every skilfully rendered dish, be it roast cod with Brancaster mussels, saffron risotto and shaved fennel or fillet of Shropham beef with slow-cooked cheek, signature smoked mash, piccolo parsnips and black pepper. Smoked fish comes from Cley, pork is reared in Blythburgh and pungently ripe specimens from Norfolk's resurgent cheese-making scene round things off admirably. The auspicious wine list naturally includes tipples from the aforementioned Herr Opitz, vintages are peerless and personal selections abound. Prices start at £19.95 (£4.85 a glass).

Chef/s: Richard Hughes. **Open:** Sun L 12 to 3, Wed to Sat D 6 to 10. **Closed:** Mon, Tue, 26 to 31 Dec. **Meals:** Set D £42.50 (5 courses). Tasting menu £60 (9 courses). **Details:** 48 seats. Separate bar. Car parking.

Burston

ALSO RECOMMENDED
▲ The Crown

Mill Road, Burston, IP22 5TW
Tel no: (01379) 741257
www.burstoncrown.com
Modern European £5 OFF

Built in the late 16th century, this red-brick pub in a tranquil Norfolk village makes an inviting all-weather setting – either in the walled garden, or indoors where squishy sofas surround the wood-burner. Food is a mixture of pub classics and more enterprising specials, perhaps a shared Norfolk platter: Scotch egg, smoked pheasant, venison sausage, Norfolk Brie and pickle (£9.50). Thus fortified, proceed with wild boar steak in black radish, grape and white port butter sauce (£14.90), and finish with mixed berry semifreddo with warm chocolate sauce (£5.50). Wines from £16. Open Tue to Sat and Sun L.

Edgefield

The Pigs

Gutsy food in a bucolic boozer
Norwich Road, Edgefield, NR24 2RL
Tel no: (01263) 714810
www.thepigs.org.uk
British | £30
Cooking score: 1

🛏

Locally brewed ales, cribbage, dominoes and gutsy food are the calling cards at this bucolic boozer-with-rooms in a north Norfolk village. The kitchen procures produce from the county's food heroes for a stout-hearted menu with porcine overtones: crispy pig's ears, pork and apple burgers or slow-cooked belly with black pudding and baked beans. To start, order a selection of 'iffits' (small plates ranging from 'dirty' beef dripping on toast to cauliflower fritters); to finish, sample Norfolk artisan cheeses or old-fashioned banana custard with a caramel crust. Underage 'piglets' have plenty to enjoy, while grown-ups can sip wines from £16.95.

Chef/s: Tim Abbott. Open: all week L 12 to 2.30, D 6 to 9. Meals: alc (main courses £11 to £20). Set L and D £20. Sun L £14. Details: 134 seats. 30 seats outside. Separate bar. Wheelchair access. Car parking.

Great Yarmouth

Seafood Restaurant

Excellent seafood and homemade treats
85 North Quay, Great Yarmouth, NR30 1JF
Tel no: (01493) 856009
www.theseafood.co.uk
Seafood | £35
Cooking score: 2
£5 OFF

Originally a pub, the Seafood Restaurant has been in the safe hands of Christopher and Miriam Kikis for more than three decades. They are 'genuinely caring hosts' whose great relationship with their fishmonger guarantees a kaleidoscopic array of the freshest fish and seafood, from calamari in 'the most exquisite dark, yet light-textured batter' to a simple main course of turbot with herb butter. Christopher's cooking respects the freshness and delicacy of his ingredients, as in a seafood platter with a light garlic butter that 'did not overpower the subtle and sweet flavours of fresh prawns, scallops and fish'. The straight-talking, uncluttered approach extends to simple desserts such as American-style cheesecake. An international wine list opens at £14.50 a bottle.

Chef/s: Christopher Kikis. Open: Mon to Fri L 12 to 1.45, Mon to Sat D 6.30 to 10.30. Closed: Sun, 24 Dec to 7 Jan, last 2 weeks May, bank hols. Meals: alc (main courses £12 to £33). Details: 42 seats. Separate bar. Wheelchair access. Car parking. Children over 3 yrs only.

---

⑪• Visit us Online

To find out more about
The Good Food Guide, please visit
www.thegoodfoodguide.co.uk

Holt

ALSO RECOMMENDED
▲ Byfords
1 Shirehall Plain, Holt, NR25 6BG
Tel no: (01263) 711400
www.byfords.org.uk
Modern European

Reputedly the town's oldest building, this flint-fronted, listed property buzzes with life all the day, thanks to its location just off the Market Place and the quality of its food. Ingredients are sourced with an eye for freshness, with snacky options taking in 'posh pizzas' (from £7.50) and deli boards of seafood, antipasti and cured meats. Full meals have an international flavour, perhaps pork and fennel meatballs, followed by chicken curry or bouillabaisse (£14.95). Byfords is equally popular for breakfast (8 to noon) and coffee and scones. Wines from £17. Open all week. Accommodation.

Ingham

The Ingham Swan
Proper boozer with broad-minded food
Sea Palling Road, Ingham, NR12 9AB
Tel no: (01692) 581099
www.theinghamswan.co.uk
Modern European | £28
Cooking score: 2

🛏 £30

Moored not far from the Norfolk Broads and flanked by Ingham Priory, this fine-looking medieval thatched inn comes with bundles of boozy charm: from ancient beams and timbers to locally brewed Woodforde's ales. However, chef/landlord Daniel Smith jettisons the pub clichés when it comes to food – witness broad-minded dishes such as seared calf's liver with sweet carrot purée, Savoy cabbage, warm Serrano ham and shallot jus or baked smoked haddock with horseradish, crispy leeks, brown shrimps and caper beurre blanc. It may be a conventional spin of modern European cooking, but the results are reckoned to be 'top-notch'. Service hits the mark, too, and it's

also worth paying heed to Daniel's excellent wine suggestions on the menu. The full list is packed with interesting bottles from £20 (£5.25 a glass).
Chef/s: Daniel Smith. Open: all week L 12 to 2 (3 Sun), D 6 to 9. Meals: alc (main courses £15 to £26). Set L £13.95 (2 courses) to £17.50. Set D £18.95 (2 courses) to £23.95. Sun L £18.95. Details: 52 seats. 20 seats outside. Car parking.

King's Lynn
Market Bistro
Enterprising local asset
11 Saturday Market Place, King's Lynn, PE30 5DQ
Tel no: (01553) 771483
www.marketbistro.co.uk
Modern British | £22
Cooking score: 2

£5 OFF £30

Richard and Lucy Golding's happy-go-lucky eatery in a quaint, crooked house opposite King's Lynn's historic Saturday Market Place is an 'oasis' noted for its industrious home production, enthusiastic enterprise and dedication to Norfolk produce. Regulars rave about the 'orgasmic' burgers and 'heavenly' dark chocolate délice, although the kitchen can also deliver ham hock terrine with sourdough and homemade pickles, fish pie and Red Poll beef casserole with mustard mash. But it isn't all plain-speaking stuff – witness a vividly detailed plate of beetroot and goats' cheese with smoked beetroot purée, toasted hazelnuts and pretty nasturtium flowers. Portions are hearty enough to satisfy ravenous local farmers and fishermen, wines are 'sensibly priced' (from £11) and it's also worth sampling one of the quirky house cocktails.
Chef/s: Richard Golding. Open: Tue to Sat L 12 to 2, D 6 to 8.30 (9 Fri and Sat). Closed: Sun, Mon, 25 and 26 Dec. Meals: alc (main courses £9 to £19). Details: 40 seats. Wheelchair access.

Morston

Morston Hall

Accomplished country hotel
The Street, Morston, NR25 7AA
Tel no: (01263) 741041
www.morstonhall.com
Modern British | £62
Cooking score: 5

⇌ V

Many readers say there's 'never a disappointing meal' at Tracy and Galton Blackiston's small hotel near the north Norfolk coast. As part of the hosts' campaign of comfort, guests are spared the agony of decision making. Dinner is served in one sitting, and the menu (with an inventive and flavoursome vegetarian alternative) is set until pudding. Add well-drilled staff and plush, calm surroundings and the effect is somewhere between treat and retreat. Nevertheless, Galton doesn't coddle his guests with anything old-fashioned; his style has clarity and verve. Ingredients are mainly local, or home-smoked, cured or raised, so dinner might start with Jerusalem artichoke with Morston's own bacon and egg yolk, followed by sea bream with apple and curry sauce, and a rib of Blickling Hall beef, smoked with rosemary and juniper and served with tarragon purée, spätzle, ceps and raw chestnuts. A small dessert course leads on to a decision between British cheeses and, perhaps, fig clafoutis with honey ice cream (the honey from the Hall's own bees). A matching wine flight is well priced, or bottles start at £28.
Chef/s: Galton Blackiston and Richard Bainbridge.
Open: Sun L 12.30 for 1 (1 sitting), all week D 7.30 for 8 (1 sitting). **Closed:** 24 to 26 Dec. **Meals:** Set D £62. Sun L £33. **Details:** 50 seats. Separate bar. Wheelchair access. Car parking.

Norwich

Roger Hickman's

Clean, clear seasonal flavours
79 Upper St Giles Street, Norwich, NR2 1AB
Tel no: (01603) 633522
www.rogerhickmansrestaurant.com
Modern British | £40
Cooking score: 5

£5 OFF

Roger Hickman's civilised restaurant still beats the local competition hands down. There's something about its comforting surrounds that attracts both the Norwich old guard and new-breed foodies. 'Faultless' staff apply the personal touch in the cultured yet gregarious little dining room. Clean-cut, clearly defined flavours and 'incredible attention to detail' are the hallmarks of Hickman's spirited cooking – witness seasonally inspired dishes such as a zingy, multi-coloured combo of roast scallops with avocado purée, oyster, radish and lemongrass or pan-fried halibut with curly kale, roast parsnips and wild mushrooms. He can also conjure up rich, earthy plates of pot-braised pork with confit turnips, apple and ginger purée or loin of venison with celeriac, braised red cabbage and a dinky venison pie. High levels of painstaking skill are applied to desserts such as poached rhubarb with blood orange, vanilla pannacotta and cardamom ice cream. The 'superb', thoughtfully assembled wine list parades top names like Charles Melton's Rose of Virginia at manageable prices. Thirteen tiptop recommendations start at £20 (£5.25 a glass).
Chef/s: Roger Hickman. **Open:** Tue to Sat L 12 to 2.30, D 7 to 10. **Closed:** Sun, Mon, 1 week Jan, 1 week Aug. **Meals:** Set L £18 (2 courses) to £22. Set D £32 (2 courses) to £40. **Details:** 42 seats.

ALSO RECOMMENDED

▲ The Assembly House

Theatre Street, Norwich, NR2 1RQ
Tel no: (01603) 626402
www.assemblyhousenorwich.co.uk
Modern British

'Not quite the Ritz', quipped a reader, referring to the lofty, gold-tinged pillared hall and the chandeliers in the powder-pink dining room. But there's no doubt that the magnificent, listed Georgian Assembly House makes a stylish place to eat, whether you're in for lunch of fishcake with smoked paprika aïoli (£5.95) and slow-cooked beef cheek with bacon, horseradish dumplings and braised red cabbage (£10.95), or the 'must-book treat' of afternoon tea complete with finger sandwiches and tiered cake stands. Wines from £14. Closed Sun.

▲ Shiki

6 Tombland, Norwich, NR3 1HE
Tel no: (01603) 619262
www.shikirestaurant.co.uk
Japanese

On a leafy corner opposite Norwich Cathedral, rocking Shiki continues to deliver 'the best Japanese street food in town' backed by energetic service from T-shirted young staff. Honest nigiri, maki rolls and gunkan ('battleship' sushi) make the grade alongside gyoza dumplings (£2.80), yakitori skewers, seafood tempura (£10.50), beef teriyaki and other staples. Good-value bento boxes and nourishing donburi rice bowls are top calls for Japanese students, tourists and office workers at lunchtime, while teppanyaki grills steal the show come nightfall. Drink green tea, beer or shots of saké (from around £4). Closed Sun.

▌Old Hunstanton

The Neptune

Seriously good food
85 Old Hunstanton Road, Old Hunstanton, PE36 6HZ
Tel no: (01485) 532122
www.theneptune.co.uk
Modern British | £52
Cooking score: 5

Chef Kevin Mangeolles and his oenophile wife Jacki have done a grand job at this foliage-clad 17th-century inn, transforming it from a humdrum seaside watering hole into a sought-after restaurant-with-rooms favoured by the up-from-London crowd. Kevin can deliver some seriously good food inspired by local maritime pickings and seasonal produce from Norfolk's farmers and growers – think pan-fried mackerel with pickled carrot and spiced crab salad, monkfish with Brancaster mussels or loin of Houghton Hall venison with a celeriac tart, baby onions and Savoy cabbage. Clean-cut, balanced flavours and acutely sharp presentation also shine through in a complex starter involving a salad of pickled wild mushrooms and hazelnuts with truffled cheese on toast and mushroom consommé, while elaborately constructed desserts might feature a gilded take on sticky toffee pudding or chestnut parfait offset by blueberries and coconut sorbet. Prices may seem steep given the lack of full-dress protocol and haute cuisine finery in the unadorned, sea-grey dining room, but there's no eyebrow-raising when it comes to Jacki's thoughtfully constructed global wine list. Prices start at £19.50 (£5.95 a glass).
Chef/s: Kevin Mangeolles. **Open:** Sun L 12 to 1.30, Tue to Sun D 7 to 9. **Closed:** Mon, 2 weeks Nov, 26 Dec, 3 weeks Jan. **Meals:** Set D £52. Sun L £32.50. **Details:** 22 seats. Separate bar. Car parking. Children over 10 yrs only.

OVINGTON

Ovington

The Café at Brovey Lair
Thrilling gastro-theatre
Carbrooke Road, Ovington, IP25 6SD
Tel no: (01953) 882706
www.broveylair.com
Pan-Asian-Seafood | £53
Cooking score: 6

£5 OFF ⊑ V

Mike and Tina Pemberton's dining room in a village south of Norwich might seem straightforwardly domestic – this is, after all, their home – yet the place thrills readers with its originality. The menu is decided on after discussion with customers who've booked, then Tina cooks the food in a smartly designed kitchen-diner. The event becomes an absorbing tutorial, with guests getting up from their seats as they wish, to watch her at work. The result is vibrantly expressive seafood fusion cuisine (Tina has a teppan grill) that lingers in the memory. A summer reporter enjoyed five-spice-coated scallops on beanshoots dressed in spring onion, lime and ginger (something of a signature dish), then teppanyaki monkfish medallions on ink noodles with shiitakes stir-fried in tamari and saké. A simple but effective soup arrives before the main: perhaps spinach and sweet potato with cumin, lemon and toasted pumpkin seeds. Dessert produces something substantial such as pear and polenta cake, lightened with citrus-spiked pear sauce and crème fraîche. A short list of mostly white wines opens with an unoaked Spanish Viura at £17.50.
Chef/s: Tina Pemberton. **Open:** all week L by special arrangement, D 7.30 (1 sitting). **Closed:** 25 and 26 Dec. **Meals:** Set L and D £52.50 (4 courses). **Details:** 24 seats. 20 seats outside. Wheelchair access. Car parking. Over 16 yrs only.

⦿ Average Price
The average price listed in main-entry reviews denotes the price of a three-course meal, without wine.

Snettisham

ALSO RECOMMENDED
▲ The Rose & Crown
Old Church Road, Snettisham, PE31 7LX
Tel no: (01485) 541382
www.roseandcrownsnettisham.co.uk
Modern British £5 OFF

Thoughtfully constructed in the 14th century to cater for workers building the village church, the rose-covered inn opposite Snettisham's cricket pitch looks a picture, and the much sought-after beaches of north Norfolk aren't far away. Hearty modern pub cooking is the bill of fare, embracing the likes of Brancaster mussels marinière and crusty bread (£5.95), Norfolk venison casserole with thyme dumplings and honey-roast parsnip (£12.50) and chocolate tart with vanilla pannacotta and berry compote (£6.25). Wines from £14.50. Open all week.

Swaffham

Strattons
Eco champ with modish menus
4 Ash Close, Swaffham, PE37 7NH
Tel no: (01760) 723845
www.strattonshotel.com
Modern British | £36
Cooking score: 2

⊑

From the 'wonderful romantic setting' to the 'fires in the lounge and restaurant', readers continue to endorse the virtues of this 'beautiful characterful hotel', just off Swaffham's market place. Regulars appreciate the bonhomie and efficiency, and the fact that the Rustic restaurant has long been a champion of seasonal local ingredients. In turn, the kitchen knows its niche market: dishing up modish pastiches of pub food. Everyone praises the Scotch egg starter, the curried Ellingham goat burger – 'a true masterpiece' – and the Sunday roasts, but there's also rare-breed Norfolk Horn mutton broth and roasted T-bone turbot with braised oxtail, cockles and bacon fat-roasted chervil

root. Sticky toffee pudding and 'wicked' millionaires' shortbread are the pick of desserts. Wines from £19.
Chef/s: Sam Bryant. **Open:** Sun L 12 to 2.30, all week D 6.30 to 9.30. **Closed:** 1 week Christmas. **Meals:** alc (main courses £16 to £25). Set D £40. Set Sun L £19 (2 courses) to £25. **Details:** 40 seats. 12 seats outside. Separate bar. Car parking.

Thorpe Market
The Gunton Arms
Game-changer that fizzes with success
Cromer Road, Thorpe Market, NR11 8TZ
Tel no: (01263) 832010
www.theguntonarms.co.uk
British | £30
Cooking score: 5

Despite being four miles from the coast, the Gunton Arms has made waves since opening in 2011. Set in an idyllic 1,000-acre deer park, this baronial-style pub/hotel is certainly handsome, its interior kitted out with immense panache. Such flair also informs the cooking of Mark Hix protégé Stuart Tattersall, who employs high-quality, often local ingredients to create big, beefy flavours in the British idiom. Soups are a hit (cauliflower with cheese straws, say) and the first-course repertoire also extends to ham hock terrine with piccalilli, and a partnership of mixed beets, Binham Blue cheese and pickled walnuts. Hearty main courses might include farmhouse chicken, bacon and leek pie, or venison from the herd outside. The vast open fire in the Elk Room supplies roasted meats – perhaps rib of beef to share – while on-trend bar snacks encompass perfect venison sausage rolls and crab on toast. Finish with nostalgic desserts such as Yorkshire rhubarb and Bramley apple pie and custard. Value is fair throughout: for food, the superb service and the spot-on wine list (from £16). **Chef/s:** Stuart Tattersall. **Open:** all week L 12 to 3, D 6 to 10 (9 Sun). **Closed:** 25 Dec. **Meals:** alc (main courses £10 to £20). **Details:** 60 seats. 150 seats outside. Separate bar. Wheelchair access. Car parking.

Titchwell
ALSO RECOMMENDED
▲ Titchwell Manor
Titchwell, PE31 8BB
Tel no: (01485) 210221
www.titchwellmanor.com
Modern European £5 OFF

You could do worse than follow a bracing walk on the sandy expanses of the north Norfolk coast with dinner by Eric Snaith. His often daring eight-course tasting menu (£60) embraces all that's seasonal and local – look out for Brancaster mussels or venison from nearby Houghton estate. Going à la carte, start with 50°C smoked salmon, lemon miso curd, peanut, chicory (£10), followed by Dingley Dell smoked pork loin (£18), and finish with an Earl Grey burnt cream, blood orange and Eccles cake (£9). Wine from £18.

Wiveton
ALSO RECOMMENDED
▲ Wiveton Hall Café
Wiveton Hall, Wiveton, NR25 7TE
Tel no: (01263) 740525
www.wivetonhall.co.uk
Modern British

Part of an admirable local food enterprise built around Wiveton Hall, this quirky little café is set amid PYO strawberry and raspberry fields. 'A real find' was how one reporter described it: a Norfolk gem where a 'farm to table' approach to daily changing menus might offer game terrine, chutney and spelt toast (£7.50) and red onion and sorrel tart with new potatoes and salad (£10.50). House wine £14. Open all week Easter to end Nov (tapas Fri and Sat D).

Visit us Online
To find out more about *The Good Food Guide*, please visit www.thegoodfoodguide.co.uk

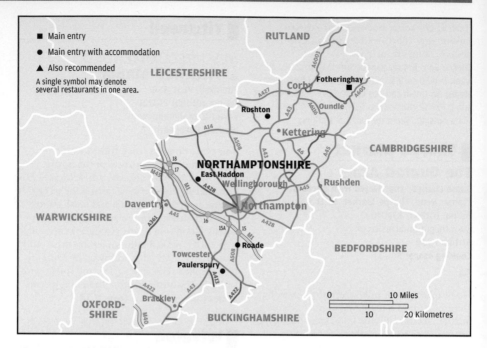

- ■ Main entry
- ● Main entry with accommodation
- ▲ Also recommended

A single symbol may denote several restaurants in one area.

RUTLAND
LEICESTERSHIRE
Fotheringhay
Corby
Oundle
Rushton
Kettering
CAMBRIDGESHIRE
NORTHAMPTONSHIRE
East Haddon
Wellingborough
Rushden
Daventry
Northampton
WARWICKSHIRE
Roade
BEDFORDSHIRE
Towcester
Paulerspury
OXFORD-SHIRE
Brackley
BUCKINGHAMSHIRE

0 __ 10 Miles
0 __ 10 __ 20 Kilometres

East Haddon

The Red Lion

A dining destination for the area
Main Street, East Haddon, NN6 8BU
Tel no: (01604) 770223
www.redlioneasthaddon.co.uk
Modern British | £27
Cooking score: 2

Could this be anywhere other than England?
A resounding 'no' is the answer, as you survey
the golden Northamptonshire sandstone and
thatch of this substantial, 17th-century
coaching inn. Inside is a vast, opened-out
interior with bare wooden tables dotted
around – the Red Lion is something of a
dining destination for the area (reasonable
proximity to the M1 is a plus). The
straightforward menu might start with the
likes of potted crab or the never-off-the-menu
pork Scotch egg with caper and parsley
mayonnaise. Beef slow-cooked in red wine
and served with smoked bacon cabbage and

creamy mashed potato is a popular main
course. Completing the flag-waving picture,
there's lemon posset and Cambridge burnt
cream for pud. Wines from £16.50.
Chef/s: Anthony Horn. **Open:** all week L 12 to 2.30
(4 Sun), Mon to Sat D 6 to 10. **Meals:** alc (main
courses £11 to £17). **Details:** 80 seats. 50 seats
outside. Separate bar. Wheelchair access. Car
parking.

Fotheringhay

The Falcon Inn

Well-heeled hostelry with robust food
Fotheringhay, PE8 5HZ
Tel no: (01832) 226254
www.thefalcon-inn.co.uk
Modern European | £28
Cooking score: 2

Synonymous with Mary, Queen of Scots,
who perished in its now-ruined castle, the
village of Fotheringhay is currently more
famous for its towering church and this well-

heeled stone hostelry. The Falcon has a robust foodie reputation hereabouts and the kitchen deals in mainstream European ideas, underpinned by sound sourcing from nearer home: perhaps rabbit rillettes with prune and Armagnac chutney, cod fillet with Parma ham and chorizo cassoulet or roast poussin with broad beans, peas and wild mushroom jus, followed by chocolate marquise with griottine cherry ice cream. Open sandwiches and simpler set menus are also available in the bar most sessions. Wines start at £16.75.

Chef/s: Danny Marshall. **Open:** all week L 12 to 2 (4 Sun), D 6 to 9 (8 Sun). **Meals:** alc (main courses £15 to £22). Set L and D £13.50 (2 courses) to £16.50. Sun L £15.95. **Details:** 70 seats. 60 seats outside. Separate bar. Wheelchair access. Car parking.

▌Paulerspury
The Vine House
Blissful restaurant-with-rooms
100 High Street, Paulerspury, NN12 7NA
Tel no: (01327) 811267
www.vinehousehotel.com
Modern British | £31
Cooking score: 4
£5 OFF ▆

Dubbed an 'oasis' in Northamptonshire's sparse foodie landscape, Marcus and Julie Springett's blissful 300-year-old farmhouse never fails to captivate visitors with its blend of personable courtesy, comfort and increasingly confident food. 'Marcus takes his cooking very seriously' and fans have had much to cheer of late: from a perfectly balanced starter of beetroot and goats' cheese salad with truffle dressing to Goosnargh duck with crushed peas or sea-fresh plaice with leeks, mustard mash and Parmesan crackling. Local venison and slow-roast Jacob's lamb are always worth ordering if available, and desserts are a strong suit: the 'exquisite' local honey pannacotta garners rave reviews, although readers also love on-trend savoury riffs such as dark chocolate terrine with hazelnuts, smoked bacon and sherry vinegar caramel. Everything is in its rightful place, the pace is restful and service is friendliness itself. If summer

romance is in the air, book the garden folly for an enchanting tête-à-tête. Well-chosen wines start at £17.95.

Chef/s: Marcus Springett, Kelly Kerley and Jordan Bateman. **Open:** all week L 12 to 1.30, D 6.30 to 9. **Meals:** Set L and D £27.50 (2 courses) to £30.95. **Details:** 33 seats. Separate bar. Car parking. Children over 8 yrs only.

▌Roade
Roade House
An oasis of calmness and respectability
16 High Street, Roade, NN7 2NW
Tel no: (01604) 863372
www.roadehousehotel.co.uk
Modern British | £35
Cooking score: 2
£5 OFF ▆

Roade is in farming country, a quiet village within easy reach of the M1 and handy for Althorp House and the racing at Towcester; it has been home to Chris and Sue Kewley's restaurant-cum-hotel since 1983. The nicely sized, beamed dining room may have a 'slightly old-fashioned feel', but the short-choice menu that mixes English modes with hints of warmer climes lifts the mood. A robustly native medallion of lamb, for example, teamed with a slow-roast shoulder shepherd's pie, might be followed by sticky toffee pudding with butterscotch sauce, but there could also be a starter of linguine with lime, chilli, coriander and prawns, and main courses like ribeye steak with rosemary roast potatoes and salsa verde. Wines from £16.

Chef/s: Chris Kewley. **Open:** Tue to Fri and Sun L 12 to 2, Mon to Sat D 7 to 9.30. **Closed:** 1 week from 24 Dec, bank hols. **Meals:** alc (main courses £16 to £22). Set L £20.50 (2 courses) to £23.50. Sun L £20.50. **Details:** 50 seats. Separate bar. Wheelchair access. Car parking.

∯ TOP DOG-FRIENDLY VENUES

Looking for an eaterie that welcomes furry friends? The following list of venues are all dog-friendly and they serve great food to boot.

Halsetown Inn, St Ives, Cornwall

Ferryboat Inn, Helford Passage, Cornwall

The Montague Inn, Shepton Montague, Somerset

The Bath Arms, Crockerton, Wiltshire

The Victoria, East Sheen, Greater London

Anglesea Arms, Shepherds Bush, London

GB Pizza Co., Margate, Kent

The Gunton Arms, Thorpe Market, Norfolk

The Falcon Inn, Fotheringhay, Northamptonshire

The Black Lion Inn, Llanfaethlu, North West Wales

Felin Fach Griffin, Powys, Wales

The General Burgoyne, Ullswater, Cumbria

▌Rushton

Rushton Hall, Tresham Restaurant

Satisfying food in venerable surroundings
Desborough Road, Rushton, NN14 1RR
Tel no: (01536) 713001
www.rushtonhall.com
Modern British | £46
Cooking score: 3

£5 OFF 🚬

Part 'princely residence', part heritage getaway, this magnificent medieval pile in the Northamptonshire countryside is a stately vision of heavy timber doors, elaborate carved stonework, tapestries, secluded cloisters and pristine grass quadrangles. The raftered, cathedral-like Great Hall now doubles as a bar/assembly point for the hotel's grand-looking, oak-panelled restaurant (named after Rushton's founding family, the Treshams). Service is full of measured gestures and politesse, although a refreshingly dressed-down vibe prevails as guests sample Adrian Coulthard's satisfying, seasonal food. The menu reads well (without scaring the horses), and there are some neatly considered ideas – from a two-part dish of quail with crisp egg, golden raisins and hazelnuts to cod poached in olive oil with chestnut mushrooms, samphire salad and artichoke velouté. To finish, complex fruity assemblages stand out: the clementine version involves marshmallow, sorbet, meringue and jelly. The huge, all-encompassing wine list opens with house selections from £18.50 (£5.50 a glass).
Chef/s: Adrian Coulthard. **Open:** Sun L 12 to 2, all week D 7 to 9. **Meals:** alc (main courses £20 to £29). Sun L £25. **Details:** 38 seats. Separate bar. Wheelchair access. Car parking. No children at D.

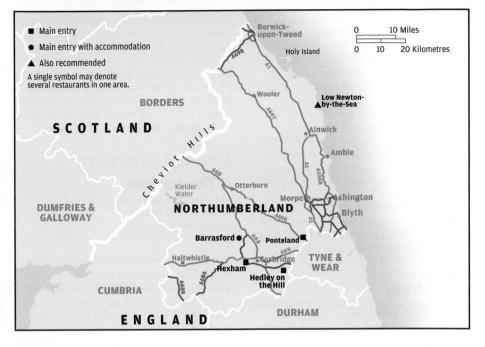

- ■ Main entry
- ● Main entry with accommodation
- ▲ Also recommended

A single symbol may denote
several restaurants in one area.

0   10 Miles
0 10   20 Kilometres

Berwick-upon-Tweed
Holy Island
Wooler
Low Newton-by-the-Sea
Alnwick
Amble
Otterburn
Kielder Water
Morpeth
Ashington
Barrasford
Ponteland
Blyth
Haltwhistle
Corbridge
Hexham
Hedley on the Hill

BORDERS
SCOTLAND
Cheviot Hills
DUMFRIES & GALLOWAY
NORTHUMBERLAND
TYNE & WEAR
CUMBRIA
DURHAM
ENGLAND

■ Barrasford

The Barrasford Arms
Well-run, no-frills village inn
Barrasford, NE48 4AA
Tel no: (01434) 681237
www.barrasfordarms.co.uk
Modern British | £25
Cooking score: 2

£5 OFF 🚗 £30 💷

With Hadrian's Wall and Haughton Castle just
a hike or a bike ride away, this sturdy village
pub-with-rooms isn't short on heritage appeal
or touristy clout. The regular influx of
outdoor types also need to be fed and watered,
and landlord/chef Tony Binks is a dab hand
when it comes to serving up proper sustenance
at keen prices. The kitchen knows its limits
and avoids anything too fancy, but there is
much to enjoy – from Yorkshire Blue cheese,
pear and walnut salad to roast rump of lamb
with cocotte potatoes, ratatouille and

rosemary. To finish, perhaps try raspberry and
Drambuie crème brûlée. Corney & Barrow
house wine is £13.95.
Chef/s: Tony Binks. **Open:** Tue to Sun L 12 to 2 (3
Sun), Mon to Sat D 6.30 to 9. **Closed:** 25 and 26 Dec,
bank hols. **Meals:** alc (main courses £10 to £17). Set
L £12 (2 courses) to £15. Sun L £15 (2 courses) to
£17.50. **Details:** 62 seats. Separate bar. Car parking.

■ Hedley on the Hill

The Feathers Inn
Cracking inn that's great value
Hedley on the Hill, NE43 7SW
Tel no: (01661) 843607
www.thefeathers.net
British | £25
Cooking score: 3

£5 OFF £30 💷

Exposed beams, open fires and traditional pub
games are a few of the reasons to search for this
difficult-to-find 200-year-old drovers' inn on
the old road between Hadrian's Wall and the
Derwent Valley – but then so is the no-frills,

locally sourced food. Homemade black pudding with poached free-range egg and devilled gravy, or a salad of endive, walnuts, red wine pears and 'perfectly ripe' Legram's organic blue cheese might start a meal here. Next could come mains of roast partridge, Toulouse sausage, rösti potatoes and choucroute cabbage, or grilled Dover sole with foraged alexanders, heritage new potatoes and buttered spinach. Finish with steamed marmalade pudding and vanilla custard. Check the handpumps for the current line-up of ales and the blackboards for wines, which start at £14.
Chef/s: Rhian Cradock. **Open:** Tue to Sun L 12 to 2 (2.30 Sun), Tue to Sat D 6 to 8.30. **Closed:** Mon, first 2 weeks Jan. **Meals:** alc (main courses £10 to £15). Sun L £13.50 (1 course) to £20 (3 courses). **Details:** 40 seats. 12 seats outside. Car parking.

Hexham
Bouchon Bistrot
Proper French cooking at gentle prices
4-6 Gilesgate, Hexham, NE46 3NJ
Tel no: (01434) 609943
www.bouchonbistrot.co.uk
French | £27
Cooking score: 4
£5 OFF   £30

Bouchon Bistrot in the heart of Hexham offers an 'object lesson' in French country cooking. It's all too rare a treat to encounter such comforting provincial classics as escargots with garlic and parsley butter ('à point in every way'), tartiflette savoyard, crisp duck confit with Lyonnaise potatoes, French beans and bacon, and Armagnac and prune clafoutis. There's room for creativity too: consider oxtail salad with pickled mushrooms and chervil roots or the monkfish with wild mushrooms and langoustine velouté that had one reader 'swooning'. Look to the early-bird and lunch menus for simpler classics at a fair price. Yes, the kitchen offers soothing cooking and, with its beams and real fire, the setting is comfortable, too, but regulars also use the place for special occasions. 'Get spoiled' here by smiling staff including the Loire-born

proprietor whose tricolore-waving drinks list (from £14.95) offers a wealth of regional French wines. Trust his choices: 'he knows what he's doing'.
Chef/s: Jérôme Cogné. **Open:** Mon to Sat L 12 to 2, D 6 to 9.30. **Closed:** Sun, 24 to 26 Dec, 1 Jan. **Meals:** alc (main courses £12 to £20). Set L £12.95 (2 courses) to £13.95. Set early D £14.50 (2 courses) to £15.95. **Details:** 150 seats. Wheelchair access.

ALSO RECOMMENDED
▲ The Rat Inn
Anick, Hexham, NE46 4LN
Tel no: (01434) 602814
www.theratinn.com
British

Overlooking the Tyne Valley, this homely, ivy-clad inn has been an alehouse for more than 200 years and retains its traditional feel with real fires, stone-flagged floors and a 'real-treat' of a bar. Daily changing menus, with much local produce in evidence, deal in hearty cooking and draw crowds for rib of beef (for two) or rack of lamb with olives, rosemary and oven-dried tomatoes (£13.95), then chocolate and Newcastle Brown ale cake with Jersey ice cream (£3.95). Wines from £14.95. No food Sun D and Mon.

Low Newton
ALSO RECOMMENDED
▲ The Ship Inn
Newton Square, Low Newton, NE66 3EL
Tel no: (01665) 576262
www.shipinnnewton.co.uk
British

Something about the Ship Inn hits the bulls-eye – this is one of the area's most popular pubs. Its location, in converted fishermen's cottages close to the beach, is a big draw, as is the on-site microbrewery. The simple lunch menu is prone to run out of hand-picked crab sandwiches (£6.75) and the like quite quickly, but there's always ploughman's with local unpasteurised cheese (£8.50) or Swallow's kipper with brown bread. Expect locally sourced lamb shanks or sirloin steak for dinner. Wines from £14.95. Open all week.

■ Ponteland

Café Lowrey

Setting the bar for neighbourhood eateries
33-35 The Broadway, Darras Hall, Ponteland, NE20 9PW
Tel no: (01661) 820357
www.cafelowrey.co.uk
Modern British | £30
Cooking score: 3

Ian Lowrey's well-supported neighbourhood restaurant is to be found in a parade of shops in a residential district, the perfect ambience for a what-the-heck midweek blowout. Expect modernised French bistro cooking of the kind that isn't necessarily always French (you might start with prawn spring rolls, served with pickled ginger and satay for an all-Asian preamble). That said, moules marinière and duck liver pâté with brioche, perhaps followed by confit duck with dauphinois in red wine jus, should orient things securely enough. Good steaks and comfort-food dishes such as fishcakes and chips in parsley sauce are the backbone of a bistro menu, and you can finish with sticky toffee pudding or poached pear in white wine sabayon. Special-event nights keep the place popular, and a short but fairly priced drinks list does the job, with house wines from Duboeuf at £16.50.
Chef/s: Ian Lowrey. **Open:** Fri to Sun L 12 to 2.30 (3 Sun), Tue to Sat D 5.30 to 10 (6 Sat). **Closed:** Mon, 26 Dec, bank hols. **Meals:** alc (main courses £14 to £25). Set L and early D £15.95 (2 courses) to £18.95. **Details:** 70 seats. Wheelchair access. Car parking.

❙❙◗ THE SWEET AND SAVOURY STUFF

The success of a tasting menu depends on balance and flow, and the yawning chasm between savoury and sweet courses can be the hole down which the rhythm of a multi-course meal disappears. A handful of high-end kitchens have bridged the gap (and identified the opportunity to show off some extra creativity) with small, neat savoury-sweet crossover dishes which lead naturally into dessert.

At **Sat Bains**, the crossover might be sharp beetroot custard lollies with raspberry vinegar, white chocolate and freeze-dried raspberries, or horseradish ice cream with elderflower granita and chickweed. At **L'Enclume**, Simon Rogan combines sea buckthorn with buttermilk, squash and sweet cicely, and at **Kitchen Table at Bubbledogs**, guests making their way towards the sweet end of a 14-course tasting menu encounter transition courses such as a tart of Calvados-soaked Camembert with walnut custard, braised Swiss chard and caramelised walnuts.

These are the dishes that are too sweet to be savoury, too savoury to be sweet, and too effective to be dismissed as mere menu-filler.

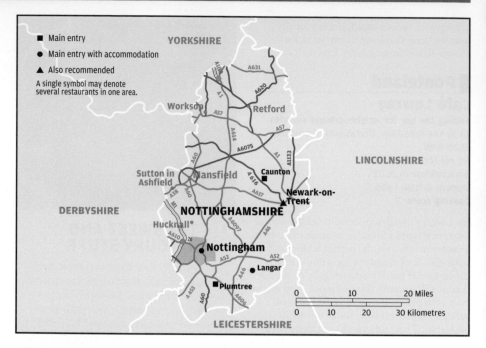

YORKSHIRE

A631

A620

Worksop   A57   Retford

A57

A614

A6075

A1   A1133

LINCOLNSHIRE

Sutton in Ashfield   Mansfield   A616   Caunton

A38   A60   A617   Newark-on-Trent

DERBYSHIRE   NOTTINGHAMSHIRE

Hucknall●   A6097   A46

A610   26   ● Nottingham

A52   A52

A446   A46   ● Langar

A453   ■ Plumtree   A60   A606

LEICESTERSHIRE

| 0 | | 10 | | 20 Miles |
| 0 | 10 | 20 | | 30 Kilometres |

▌Caunton

Caunton Beck

All-day treats in a rural retreat
Main Street, Caunton, NG23 6AB
Tel no: (01636) 636793
www.wigandmitre.com
Modern European | £27
Cooking score: 2

V £30

The setting is a little out of the way in rural Nottinghamshire, so the success of this extended 16th-century pub is a tribute to the dedication of Valerie Hope. The Beck still lives up to the title of free house, dispensing real ales, but is better known as an all-day venue for food, opening with breakfast at 8am. Throughout the day the carte is peppered with ideas that attempt to please all palates – a policy that seems to work well, as crowds of regulars keep the mood buoyant. The kitchen prides itself on good ingredients, delivering the likes of gammon steak, free-range duck egg and chips, locally sourced steaks (with

béarnaise and chips) or sesame-encrusted sea bass with Indian-spiced rice and katsu curry sauce. Wines from £14.50.
Chef/s: Valerie Hope. **Open:** all week 8am to 10pm. **Closed:** 25 and 26 Dec, 2 weeks Aug, bank hols. **Meals:** alc (main courses £11 to £24). Set L and D £13.95 (2 courses) to £16.50. **Details:** 100 seats. 60 seats outside. Separate bar. Wheelchair access. Car parking.

▌Langar

Langar Hall

A very English idyll
Church Lane, Langar, NG13 9HG
Tel no: (01949) 860559
www.langarhall.co.uk
Modern British | £40
Cooking score: 4

£5 OFF

A trip to this distinctive Victorian mansion begins with a leisurely drive past medieval ponds and croquet lawns. Guests then enter a civilised world where marble pillars, crystal

chandeliers and Grecian statues evoke a very English idyll. Imogen Skirving has imbued the place with her own personality since arriving in the 1980s, while her dedicated kitchen brigade delivers exact renditions of Anglo-European food based on ingredients from the Midlands and beyond. Twice-baked cheese soufflé is a fixture ('we can't take it off the menu'), likewise Belvoir game and lamb from the hotel's own pastures – perhaps served as an assiette with rosemary-tinged potato mille-feuille, baked white onion and Yorkshire rhubarb. The seasonal repertoire might run to Cornish turbot presented as a starter with roast chicken wings, cauliflower, white raisins and curry. Dessert could bring poached William pear with walnut granola and goats' cheese ice cream. Imogen's recommendations kick off the thoughtfully curated wine list; prices from £19.95.
Chef/s: Gary Booth and Ross Jeffery. **Open:** all week L 12 to 2, D 6 to 10. **Meals:** Set L £16.50 (2 courses) to £21.50. Set D £25 (2 courses) to £30. Sun L £35. **Details:** 60 seats. Separate bar. Car parking.

▌ Newark-on-Trent

ALSO RECOMMENDED
▲ Café Bleu
14 Castle Gate, Newark-on-Trent, NG24 1BG
Tel no: (01636) 610141
www.cafebleu.co.uk
Modern European

Down by the riverside and close to the castle, Café Bleu is Newark's favourite boho bistro – an eccentric mix of zany artwork, baroque fireplaces and occasional helpings of live jazz. Matching the mood is an eclectic menu of upbeat dishes ranging from tiger prawns with boudin noir, citrus fruit and orange reduction (£7.50) to osso bucco with saffron mash, sauce diable and crispy leeks (£16.45), backed by desserts such as lavender rice pud with plum compote. Wines from £13.95. Closed Sun D and Mon.

▌ Nottingham

Hart's
Putting on the style
Standard Hill, Park Row, Nottingham, NG1 6GN
Tel no: (0115) 9110666
www.hartsnottingham.co.uk
Modern British | £32
Cooking score: 5

With boutique rooms in the purpose-built hotel next door, Tim Hart's stylish venture in Nottingham's sedate Regency quarter is the complete package. The restaurant, occupying part of the old General Hospital building, has an elegant, soft-toned setting of polished wooden floors, discreet partitioned booths and abstract art. Likewise, the kitchen aims for urbane simplicity rather than florid gestures – what you see is what you get. Top-drawer ingredients form the backbone of a daily menu that might lead off with crispy squid, chorizo, chicory and avocado, before offering roast duck breast with butternut squash risotto or whole Cornish lemon sole with ratte potatoes, spinach and brown shrimp butter. Other dishes such as the signature seasonal salad, prawn cocktail and sirloin of beef Diane with Koffman cabbage are defiantly old-school, while desserts might bring apple crumble soufflé or the ever-popular sticky toffee pudding with date purée and cream-cheese ice cream. The even-handed, thoughtful wine list is testament to Tim Hart's enthusiasm for all things oenological, with mouthwatering selections helpfully laid out in drinker-friendly fashion for big spenders and everyday quaffers alike. Prices start at £18.50.
Chef/s: Dan Burridge. **Open:** all week L 12 to 2, D 7 to 10.30 (9 Sun). **Closed:** 1 Jan. **Meals:** alc (main courses £16 to £22). Set L £14.95 (2 courses) to £17.95. Set D £24. Sun L £23. **Details:** Cash only. 80 seats. Separate bar. Wheelchair access.

☰ OFFBEAT EATS

Predictability is a dirty word for the chefs enjoying the most attention-grabbing of recent trends. Deceptive dishes, favourites resembling something else, and throwaway ingredients elevated to star status are all part of the recent yen for offbeat eats.

Tom Sellers enlightens his diners to the charms of bread and dripping at **Restaurant Story**. The dripping is presented as an edible candle which melts at the table, with sourdough for dipping.

You've never had a breakfast like the duck muesli at **Restaurant Sat Bains**. This trompe l'oeil 'cereal' is made up of frozen granules of duck liver parfait, which gradually melt, to be offset with cranberries and crisp green beans.

If you've ever lifted the lid of a spent barbecue, inhaled deeply and enjoyed it, Simon Rogan at **The Midland** has a dish for you. His ox tartare with coal oil combines raw beef with an intense, smoky oil which works memorably with the ruby-red meat.

The dish known as 'chicken' at **Bubbledogs Kitchen Table** doesn't major on poultry protein. Instead, a wafer of chicken skin is spread with rosemary mascarpone and dotted with bacon jam.

The Larder on Goosegate
Vintage charm and gutsy food
16-22 Goosegate, Hockley, Nottingham, NG1 1FE
Tel no: (0115) 9500111
www.thelarderongoosegate.co.uk
Modern British | £28
Cooking score: 2

£5 OFF £30

Old medicine cabinets and salvaged apothecary bottles filled with flowers are reminders that these premises started life as a chemist's shop – the first retail venture from Nottingham lad Jesse Boot. Pork chops and pickled mushrooms have now replaced pills and poultices, as the Larder dispenses a different kind of therapy based largely on gutsy native ingredients. Duck hearts are popped into a stew with home-cured chorizo and rosemary, lamb's sweetbreads get a seasonal lift from wild-garlic buds and the aforementioned porcine cuts are served up with roasted carrots, salsify, quince and cumin-infused cider gravy. Elsewhere, braised Castelluccio lentils add depth to a dish of Cornish skate, fregola is matched with new season's asparagus and desserts might include sticky toffee carrot cake. Wines from £15.50.
Chef/s: Ewan McFarlane. **Open:** Thur to Sat L 12 to 4, Tue to Sat D 6 to 10. **Closed:** Sun, Mon. **Meals:** alc (main courses £13 to £20). Set L and D £13.95 (2 courses) to £15.95. **Details:** 65 seats.

★ TOP 10 ★

Restaurant Sat Bains
An extraordinary personal endeavour
Lenton Lane, Nottingham, NG7 2SA
Tel no: (0115) 9866566
www.restaurantsatbains.com
Modern British | £75
Cooking score: 9

🛏 V

'Who would have thought a sweet curry lollipop was a good idea?' wonders a correspondent bowled over by the brilliance of a 'crossover' course at one of the UK's most creative and forward-thinking restaurants.

The conclusion ('well, Sat Bains, obviously') says it all about a very personal endeavour, now impossible to imagine anywhere else but hunched in its famously unpromising location on the outskirts of Nottingham. In fact, even before one of the tasting menus (seven or ten courses) kicks off, there's a staunch culinary defence of the spot: a taster based on ingredients foraged from the restaurant's postcode, with a tiny horseradish ice cream sandwich providing a 'wonderful' play on texture and temperature. An 'original meal', with terrific combinations and execution' unfolds with carefully controlled creativity and skilful technique. Dishes are delicate and, on the whole, pretty, though the chunkier charms of hand-thrown bowls and proper bread and butter are also acknowledged. A first course might be scallop with vanilla mayonnaise, seeds, nuts and muscovado, followed by earthier, and perfectly balanced, pearl barley with Judas-ear mushrooms and a little truffle. Next, the 'sensational' duck liver muesli which is consistently mentioned in dispatches: a trompe l'oeil dish with the sweetness of apricot and the crunch of green beans and granola, and an introduction to the kitchen's fondness for little frozen crumbs. Slow-baked onion with thyme oil is a winning combination freshened with thyme granita, and lamb becomes a 'lovely plateful, deeply savoury' when the shoulder is braised and finished with seaweed. That 'crossover' lolly is a bridge between savoury and sweet, the latter perhaps a chocolate fondant topped with yoghurt sorbet with the 'unexpected, brilliant' addition of grated lime and a cumin caramel sauce. There's more spice in a cleverly nostalgic finish, which could be the end of an extraordinary, dazzling Sunday lunch: baked apples in caramel with star anise and cloves, cinnamon pastry and a frozen hailstorm of custard and apple juice crumbs. In a neutral dining space with a dark, slightly masculine feel, there are several options (chef's table, kitchen table and kitchen bench) besides the traditional table for two. 'Best ever' service contributes to a comfortably informal experience whether you're close to the action or not. Readers recommend wine pairings from an 'encyclopedically knowledgeable and extremely personable' sommelier. On a helpfully annotated list stuffed with quality at a price, bottles are from £32. **Chef/s:** Sat Bains. **Open:** Tue to Sat L 12 (1 sitting), Tue to Thur D 7 to 9, Fri 6.30 to 9.30, Sat 6 to 10. **Closed:** Sun, Mon, 2 weeks winter, 1 week Apr, 2 weeks Aug. **Meals:** Tasting menu £79 (7 courses) to £89 (10 courses). **Details:** 40 seats. Separate bar. Wheelchair access. Car parking. Children over 8 yrs only.

World Service

Ultra-cool, eclectic showpiece
Newdigate House, Castle Gate, Nottingham, NG1 6AF
Tel no: (0115) 8475587
www.worldservicerestaurant.com
Modern British | £35
Cooking score: 3

£5
OFF

It's nothing to do with the BBC, but the name of this ultra-cool venue says it all: outside is a Japanese pebble garden; inside, world music plays in the lounge bar, while the interior displays a cache of oriental statues, vases and masks. So far, so eclectic – but despite occasional appearances from crispy rice cakes, miso purée, morcilla crumbs and so on, the menu seems to have settled into a more orthodox groove. Dishes such as beetroot tarte Tatin with grilled goats' cheese and crispy viola flowers, line-caught bream with braised leeks, celeriac and brown shrimps or slow-cooked lamb rump with braised red cabbage and onion purée pass muster, yet they wouldn't be serious contenders in a global bunfight. Likewise, desserts play it pretty safe with the likes of salted-caramel and chocolate délice or coffee pannacotta with espresso granita. By contrast, the wine list is a fascinating 30-page compendium, with prices from £16 (£4.25 a glass). **Chef/s:** Jacque Ferreira. **Open:** all week L 12 to 2 (3.30 Sun), Mon to Sat D 7 to 10 (6.30 Mon and Sat). **Closed:** 25 and 26 Dec, 1 to 5 Jan. **Meals:** alc (main courses £15 to £26). Set L £14.50 (2 courses) to

£19.50. Set D Mon to Fri £19.50 (2 courses) to £24.50. **Details:** 80 seats. 30 seats outside. Separate bar. Children over 12 yrs only at D.

ALSO RECOMMENDED

▲ Delilah

12 Victoria Street, Nottingham, NG1 2EX
Tel no: (0115) 9484461
www.delilahfinefoods.co.uk
Modern European

A short move up the hill to a Victorian banking house has given this city-centre delicum-eatery more space – plus a proper café – and regulars are relieved to report that the 'quality remains the same'. A European charcuterie platter has particularly impressed, but with green eggs and ham (£7.95) for breakfast, bruschetta with chorizo and feta (£6.95), tapas, salads and blackboard specials, choice is wide. The selection of wines by the glass is 'even more appealing' than before; alternatively, choose any bottle from the deli and add £5 to the retail price. Open all week.

▲ Ibérico World Tapas

Shire Hall, High Pavement, Nottingham, NG1 1HN
Tel no: (0115) 9410410
www.ibericotapas.com
Spanish

'A regular lunch place for us' noted one fan of this laid-back cellar bar in a fantastically tiled and vaulted basement beneath Nottingham's old Courthouse. The menu is divided into 'Spanish' and 'World' tapas, which might mean tricky decisions between Iberian staples of chorizo in cider (£5.50) and Catalan fish stew (£5.50) and chicken wings with sweet yuzu chilli (£6.50). The 'fantastic value' express lunch (£11.95 for two tapas and dessert) has garnered particular praise. Wines from £16.50. Closed Sun.

▮ Plumtree

Perkins

Good-value family favourite
Station House, Station Road, Plumtree, NG12 5NA
Tel no: (0115) 9373695
www.perkinsrestaurant.co.uk
Modern European | £30
Cooking score: 2

'Well-balanced and well-presented menu; delicious flavours; reasonable prices; friendly and attentive service.' So ran one reader's notes on this long-standing family restaurant occupying a converted Victorian railway station. The cooking is never less than steady, with reports speaking favourably of 'beautifully presented' chicken liver parfait with onion jam, and chicken and sweetcorn soup, as well as mains of an 'utterly delicious' sea bass with sauté potatoes, green beans with shrimp and caper butter, and a 'very much enjoyed' combo of pork – fillet, cheek fritters, black pudding – with creamed potato, sautéed cabbage, smoked bacon and peas and Dijon hollandaise sauce. Crème brûlée is a popular dessert. House wine costs £16.75.
Chef/s: Sarah Newham. **Open:** all week L 12 to 2 (3.30 Sun), Mon to Sat D 6 to 10. **Meals:** alc (main courses £15 to £20). Set L £13.50 (2 courses) to £16.95. Set D £16.50 (2 courses) to £18.95. Sun L £15.50 (2 courses) to £18.95. **Details:** 73 seats. 22 seats outside. Separate bar. Wheelchair access. Car parking.

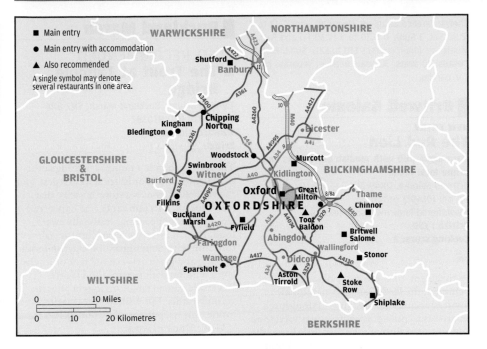

▮ Aston Tirrold

ALSO RECOMMENDED
▲ The Sweet Olive
Baker Street, Aston Tirrold, OX11 9DD
Tel no: (01235) 851272
www.sweet-olive.com
Modern British

It serves pints of ale in the bar, but the old wine boxes are the first clue that this wood-panelled village pub has a double identity as a French restaurant. The Alsatian proprietor conjures up Anglo-French classics for the blackboard menu that might kick off with Mediterranean fish soup (£7.95) followed by escalope of venison with creamed cabbage, port sauce and chips (£18.95). Alsatian wines dominate an interesting list starting at £18.95. Closed all day Wed and Sun D.

▮ Bledington
The King's Head Inn
Popular village hostelry
The Green, Bledington, OX7 6XQ
Tel no: (01608) 658365
www.thekingsheadinn.net
Modern British | £30
Cooking score: 1

Overlooking a glorious village green, this 16th-century hostelry is a popular operation, run as a proper village pub (a rustic bar, open fires, real ales). Nothing is posh or grand (book a table in the bar for the best atmosphere) and the menu is chock-full of hearty dishes. Devilled kidneys on toast is one way to start or there could be potted shrimps with beetroot salad, with mains of duck breast and braised pak choi, pilau rice and sweet-and-sour sauce or minute steak with skinny chips, green beans and garlic butter. Wines from £16.50.

Chef/s: Terence Gaughan. **Open:** all week L 12 to 2 (2.30 Sat, 3 Sun), D 6.30 to 9 (9.30 Fri and Sat). **Meals:** alc (main courses £10 to £21). Sun L £16.50. **Details:** 70 seats. 30 seats outside. Separate bar. Car parking.

█ Britwell Salome

NEW ENTRY

The Red Lion

Born-again pub with modish bar snacks and prime local meat

Britwell Salome, OX49 5LG
Tel no: (01491) 613140
www.theredlionbritwellsalome.co.uk
British | £29
Cooking score: 2
£30

Its turbulent, fine-dining spell as the Goose behind it, the Red Lion (new name, new owners) focuses on satisfying Oxfordshire's smart-casual pub-goers with hearty local food and ales. Step through the cosy little bar to the equally compact, burgundy-hued dining area. The kitchen's forte is in meat sourced from the neighbouring farm shop, and in excellent-value, modish bar snacks such as freshly cooked black pudding Scotch egg and mutton-breast rissoles with pungent wild-garlic mayo. At inspection, these out-performed a starter of scallop with smoked sausage. The concise main-course choice is boosted by specials such as rich slow-roast mutton in filo with cauliflower cheese purée and sublime gravy, before pudding of rhubarb and pistachio crumble with pannacotta. The appealingly priced global wine list (from £15.95) has ample choice by the glass.
Chef/s: Andrew Hill. **Open:** Wed to Sun L 12 to 2 (3 Sun), Tue to Sat D 6 to 9. **Closed:** Mon, 2 weeks Jan. **Meals:** alc (main courses £11 to £21). Sun L £19.50 (2 courses) to £23.50. **Details:** 40 seats. 30 seats outside. Separate bar. Car parking.

█ Buckland Marsh

ALSO RECOMMENDED
▲ The Trout at Tadpole Bridge

Tadpole Bridge, Buckland Marsh, SN7 8RF
Tel no: (01367) 870382
www.troutinn.co.uk
British £5 OFF

The setting, beside a humpback bridge over the Thames, is Oxfordshire at its prettiest, and the venerable Trout is a stone hostelry that hasn't forsaken its pub roots – so expect real ales alongside appealing, seasonally aware food. Recent hits have been Cornish crab tortellini with lemongrass and crayfish broth (£9.25) and rosemary-crusted rack of English lamb with fondant potatoes and faggot. Riverside garden tables are sought after in warm weather, but with log fires blazing inside, this is a pub for all seasons. Wines from £14.50. Open all week.

█ Chinnor

The Sir Charles Napier

Eccentric Chiltern charmer
Sprigg's Alley, Chinnor, OX39 4BX
Tel no: (01494) 483011
www.sircharlesnapier.co.uk
Modern British | £44
Cooking score: 4
♦ V

Red kites soar overhead; a sculpted black nude reclines on the lawn; crowds mingle under a vine-tangled pergola; crazy curios festoon the surreal dining room . . . welcome to the Napier, a lovably eccentric, Chiltern charmer high on Bledlow Ridge. Julie Griffiths has run the place since the 1970s, and it remains a sell-out for madcap Sunday lunches, boozy celebrations and romantic trysts over invigorating food. Menus follow the seasons, taking a full-blooded approach. Locally bagged game might yield grouse, partridge or mallard (perhaps with an earthy combo of endive tart, boudin and choucroute), while

Cornish fish could bring brill with pumpkin gnocchi, ceps and parsley root purée – emphatic flavours that chime with the calendar. Splendid desserts such as elderflower custard with gooseberry compote and mead jelly echo the theme, and the tray of ripe Anglo-French cheeses is a must. The wine list breathes class, with France, California and the Antipodes shining brightly; tantalising house selections start at £19.50.
Chef/s: Chris Godfrey. **Open:** Tue to Sun L 12 to 2.30 (3.30 Sun), Tue to Sat D 6.30 to 9.30. **Closed:** Mon, 25 to 28 Dec. **Meals:** alc (main courses £21 to £29). Set L and D Tue to Fri £17.50 (2 courses). **Details:** 70 seats. 70 seats outside. Separate bar. Car parking. Children over 5 yrs only at D.

▮ Chipping Norton
Wild Thyme

Sharply focused seasonal flavours
10 New Street, Chipping Norton, OX7 5LJ
Tel no: (01608) 645060
www.wildthymerestaurant.co.uk
Modern British | £35
Cooking score: 3

'A wonderful gem of a place: superb service, quality and atmosphere' enthused one regular of this smart little restaurant-with-rooms run by Nick and Sally Pullen. A serious approach to local sourcing and seasonality adds to the appeal of the finely tuned cooking, which certainly isn't shy of gastronomic innovation when it comes to bold and arresting flavour combinations. A light, fragrant salmon ravioli with a ragoût of Brixham mussels and lemongrass is a typical starter. It might line up alongside a robust main of roasted belly and tenderloin of local Tamworth pork with truffle mash, pig's cheek stew, shallots, prunes and baby carrots. Braised venison faggots with mash and root vegetables could make an appearance on the well-priced set menu, as might a dessert of apple, lemongrass and ginger crumble with honeycomb ice cream. Wines from £14.50, with ten offered by the glass.

Chef/s: Nicholas Pullen. **Open:** Tue to Sat L 12 to 2, D 7 to 9. **Closed:** Sun, Mon, first week Jan, 1 week May. **Meals:** alc (main courses £13 to £22). Set L £18 (2 courses) to £22.50. **Details:** 35 seats. 10 seats outside.

▮ Filkins

NEW ENTRY
The Five Alls

Confident, classy cooking in a Cotswolds inn
Filkins, GL7 3JQ
Tel no: (01367) 860875
info@thefiveallsfilkins.co.uk
Modern British | £30
Cooking score: 3

£5 OFF

The talk may be of Knightsbridge shopping rather than silaging at this concertedly casual Cotswolds pub, but social demographics – and the framed letter of thanks from local boy David Cameron – are soon forgotten when the kitchen's confident, classy output becomes apparent. The Five Alls was taken over in September 2012 by Sebastian and Lana Snow, who did great things at the Swan at Southrop nearby. Their new venture includes a woody bar lit by chandeliers, and two dining areas where prompt, practised staff serve a menu of British classics pepped up with Mediterranean flourishes. Thus meltingly tender tuna carpaccio could lead on to juicy roast new-season lamb (sourced from Devizes) boosted by punchy mint pesto. Likewise calf's liver might be enlivened by roast peaches and beetroot. Puddings are impressive constructions – whether a well-caramelised tarte Tatin or light, crunchy rhubarb crumble. Local real ales and a wine list (from £16.95) with ample choice by the glass enhance proceedings.
Chef/s: Sebastian Snow. **Open:** all week L 12 to 2.30 (3 Fri to Sun), Mon to Sat D 6 to 9.30 (10 Fri and Sat). **Closed:** 25 Dec. **Meals:** alc (main courses £12 to £23). Set L and D £15 (2 courses) to £19. Sun L £26. **Details:** 85 seats. 30 seats outside. Separate bar. Wheelchair access. Car parking.

Fyfield

The White Hart

Historic hostelry in good hands
Main Road, Fyfield, OX13 5LW
Tel no: (01865) 390585
www.whitehart-fyfield.com
Modern British | £32
Cooking score: 3

Built as a chantry house during the reign of
Henry VI and later owned by St John's College
in Oxford, this dreamy slice of ecclesiastical
heritage is currently in the capable hands of
Kay and Mark Chandler. The whole place
creaks with antiquity (don't miss the soaring
great hall and minstrels' gallery), but there are
green shoots aplenty in the increasingly
productive kitchen garden. Mark leavens his
harvest festival of native produce with sunny
Mediterranean touches – serving Fowey
mussels and cockles with char-grilled
bruschetta, matching roast rump of Cotswold
lamb with black olive and feta tart, and
assembling some splendid deli boards for
sharing. Elsewhere, regulars have lauded
everything from the 'melting' slow-roast
Kelmscott pork belly with crackling, celeriac
and cider jus to the instantly addictive sticky
toffee pudding. Kind staff 'really love what
they're doing' and there are some very decent
wines (from £16.50) on the 50-bin list.
Chef/s: Mark Chandler. **Open:** Tue to Sun L 12 to
2.30 (3 Sun), Tue to Sat D 7 to 9.30. **Closed:** Mon
(exc bank hols). **Meals:** alc (main courses £15 to
£21). Set L £17 (2 courses) to £20. Sun L £21 (2
courses) to £24. **Details:** 45 seats. 50 seats outside.
Separate bar. Car parking.

‖‖ Please send us your feedback

To register your opinion about any
restaurant listed in the Guide, or a new
restaurant that you wish to bring to our
attention, please visit the web address at
the bottom of the page. Your feedback
informs the content of the book and will
be used to compile next year's reviews.

Great Milton

★ TOP 10 ★

Le Manoir aux Quat'Saisons

Unashamed luxury and pure delight
Church Road, Great Milton, OX44 7PD
Tel no: (01844) 278881
www.manoir.com
Modern French | £120
Cooking score: 8
🛏 V

The honey-stone Oxfordshire house has been
Raymond Blanc's first love for nigh-on 30
years, its charm undiminished. Wandering the
grounds is a pleasure: especially the kitchen
garden and the water garden. Inside, a tone of
gracious civility prevails. The conservatory
dining room with its marquee-like ceiling is a
delight for a summer's lunch, yet equally
entrancing by night when candlelight flickers
among the table posies. Seasonality, as always,
remains the watchword of the monthly
menus. A couple dining in *août* opened with
pistou soup of stunning concentration, its riot
of summer veg topped with a floating
Parmesan croûton. That consummate balance
between English garden and French expertise
shines forth again in a pretty serving of salmon
marinated in lemon verbena with radishes,
yuzu cream and edible flowers. A trio of lamb
cuts is *de rigueur* nowadays, but this is the
benchmark: rare loin, braised shoulder and
half a kidney, amid a scattering of peas and
lettuce and a dab of garlic purée. *Octobre* for
another pair brought perfectly timed loin of
venison with braised chestnuts, to follow an
exquisite autumnal cep risotto with Alba
truffle fragrance. There's a hint of a simpler
style these days, which indicates the
confidence with which Blanc and Gary Jones
approach the task in hand. In due course, the
cheese chariot floats unmissably by, trailing
scents of pungently ripe Comté. Desserts, too,
endure in the memory, as in the summer
meringue that spilled forth a blackcurrant
purée, to add support to a sorbet and a
sprinkling of whole berries. English ales and
biodynamic ciders and perries supplement the

voluminous list of impeccably selected wines. Vinous advice has been oddly reticent on occasion, but if you know your onions, you won't know where to start. About £33 is the answer.

Chef/s: Raymond Blanc and Gary Jones. **Open:** all week L 11.45 to 2.15, D 6.45 to 9.30. **Meals:** alc (main courses £42 to £48). Set L £79 (5 courses) to £124 (7 courses). Set D £134 (6 courses) to £154 (9 courses). **Details:** 80 seats. Separate bar. Wheelchair access. Car parking.

Kingham
The Kingham Plough
A townie's rural dream
The Green, Kingham, OX7 6YD
Tel no: (01608) 658327
www.thekinghamplough.co.uk
Modern British | £32
Cooking score: 3

So sidetracked are readers by the superior bar snacks at the Kingham Plough, it's a wonder any get to sample the menu. In fact, beyond the hand-raised pork pie, 'Cotswold rarebit' and beer-battered cod cheeks of the bar, chef Emily Watkins produces a daily menu of quietly eccentric English cooking. Superb produce and Watkins' highly personal style shine through in such intriguing form as a mackerel burger starter with beetroot muffin and blood-orange chutney, or a clever 'Wellington' of pork and hotchpotch pudding with sage and onion purée. For afters, proper puddings (clementine meringue pie, for instance) are up against a truly local cheese selection; try the Jersey milk 'Kingham Green'. In such a 'lovely village pub' it would be remiss not to have an ale by the fire, but a classy European wine list, from £19, also beckons.

Chef/s: Emily Watkins and Ben Dulley. **Open:** all week L 12 to 2 (3 Sat and Sun), Mon to Sat D 6.30 to 9 (6 Sat). **Closed:** 25 Dec. **Meals:** alc (main courses £14 to £27). **Details:** 50 seats. Separate bar. Car parking.

Murcott
The Nut Tree Inn
Pubby vitality and cooking with conviction
Main Street, Murcott, OX5 2RE
Tel no: (01865) 331253
www.nuttreeinn.co.uk
Modern British | £38
Cooking score: 5
£5 OFF V

The sight of porkers rooting around in the garden of this beguiling 15th-century thatched pub might suggest folksy self-sufficiency, but this is no *Good Life* fantasy world. The Norths run their reinvented country boozer as a purposeful enterprise, with Mike and his sister taking care of business in the kitchen and wife Imogen handling things out front. Real ales, low beams and wood-burning stoves emphasise the Nut Tree's pubby vitality, yet the cooking shows real conviction and clout. Home-smoked Loch Duart salmon and home-baked breads put down a marker, and the menu has bags of seasonal cred: from pan-fried fillet of Cornish mackerel with bacon and clam chowder to olive oil-poached halibut on green herb risotto or roast cannon of Oxford Downs lamb with a torte of the braised shoulder, potato purée and meat juices. There's no diffidence about serving steak sandwiches, ploughman's or fish and chips at lunchtime, but things take a serious turn for pud: how about chocolate marquise with rum caramel and banana sorbet? Well-considered wines start at £16.

Chef/s: Michael and Mary North. **Open:** Tue to Sun L 12 to 2.30 (3 Sun), Tue to Sat D 7 to 9. **Closed:** Mon, 27 Dec to 3 Jan. **Meals:** alc (main courses £16 to £28). Set L and D £18 (2 courses). Tasting menu £55 (7 courses). **Details:** 60 seats. 30 seats outside. Separate bar. Car parking.

Oxford

Branca

Gregarious all-day Italian
111 Walton Street, Oxford, OX2 6AJ
Tel no: (01865) 556111
www.branca.co.uk
Italian | £25
Cooking score: 1
£5 OFF £30

'Fantastic value', all-day opening, weekend brunch and a vast garden terrace for alfresco grazing (rugs provided) are some of the reasons why this cheery old-stager is a hit with young families, students from nearby Jericho and couples out for some fun. Stone-baked pizzas, pastas, salads and risottos share the bill with a raft of trattoria staples ranging from char-grilled tuna with cannellini bean salad to calf's liver with pancetta, black cabbage and balsamic jus. Special menus for parties, kids and babies are also much appreciated by the talkative, gregarious crowds who congregate here. House wine is £15.95.
Chef/s: E Blandes. **Open:** all week 10am to 11pm.
Closed: 25 Dec. **Meals:** alc (main courses £11 to £19). Set L and early D £11.75 (2 courses). Sun L £11.95. **Details:** 110 seats. 60 seats outside. Separate bar. Wheelchair access.

★ WINE LIST OF THE YEAR ★

Cherwell Boathouse

Idyllic riverside favourite
50 Bardwell Road, Oxford, OX2 6ST
Tel no: (01865) 552746
www.cherwellboathouse.co.uk
Modern British | £32
Cooking score: 1
£5 OFF 🍾 V

It is not difficult to appreciate the appeal of this working boathouse (for the hire of punts) and adjoining restaurant on the banks of the river Cherwell; alfresco dining on the decked terrace is an added summer attraction. The kitchen specialises in vervy assemblies of English ingredients and Eurozone ideas such as rump of Torre Meadow lamb with parsnip

gnocchi, honey-roast root vegetables and red wine sauce, or confit duck leg with cassoulet and braised red cabbage, topped and tailed by butternut squash velouté and apple crumble. Winning our wine award this year, the list at the Cherwell Boathouse displays the oenological equivalent of perfect pitch. Classicists will love the selection of clarets and burgundies, many from great vintages, and there is a fine range of Riesling, particularly from JJ Prüm. But what will really make any wine lover purr with satisfaction is the extraordinary value for money it offers, especially at the top end, where prices are often below retail cost (and even the most parsimonious drinker will find much to enjoy, with prices starting at £14.75). As is entirely appropriate, this really is the best place in Britain to push the boat out.
Chef/s: Nick Welford. **Open:** all week L 12 to 2 (2.30 Sat and Sun), D 6 to 9.30. **Closed:** 24 to 30 Dec. **Meals:** alc (main courses £15 to £24). Set L £13.50 (2 courses) to £24.75. Set D £21.25 (2 courses) to £26.75. Sun L £24.75. **Details:** 65 seats. 45 seats outside. Separate bar. Wheelchair access. Car parking.

Gee's

Oxford landmark with easy-going food
61 Banbury Road, Oxford, OX2 6PE
Tel no: (01865) 553540
www.gees-restaurant.co.uk
Modern British | £27
Cooking score: 2
£30

A city institution for 30 years, Gee's is a good place for students to take visiting parents, as well as a destination dining venue for locals. The striking look (somewhere between a conservatory and a potting shed) is brimful of charm, the glass structure letting in plenty of daylight, with glass orbs providing illumination in the evenings. Jonas Lodge maintains the informal, unfussy style of pan-European cooking, perhaps lightly battered soft-shell crab with a blob of pungent aïoli or a main of sea-bream with butter-soft chunks of smoky fennel done in the wood-fired oven, as

well as black and green tapenade with a whack of anchovy to it. Things might conclude with a chocolate and hazelnut pot. Service sometimes seems barely up to coping with busy sessions, when cheerful chaos prevails. House French is £16.95.
Chef/s: Jonas Lodge. **Open:** Mon to Fri L 12 to 2.30, D 5.45 to 10, Sat 12 to 10.30, Sun L 10 to 4. **Closed:** 25 and 26 Dec. **Meals:** alc (main courses £7 to £27). **Details:** 80 seats. 25 seats outside. Separate bar. Wheelchair access.

My Sichuan

Lip-numbing Szechuan adventure
The Old School, Gloucester Green, Oxford, OX1 2DA
Tel no: (01865) 236899
www.mysichuan.co.uk
Chinese | £20
Cooking score: 3
£30

Housed in a converted Victorian schoolhouse close to Oxford coach station, this is a surprise package for fans of Szechuan cuisine in all its lip-numbing, chilli-spiked glory. High ceilings and a striking stained-glass dome add interest to a sprawling dining room that plays it safe with functional dark-wood furnishings, a curved bar and tacky paintings – although the food is what really attracts Chinese families, students and aficionados of the genre. The bilingual menu comes emblazoned with colour photographs of each dish in stark detail, but fortitude pays dividends: 'who dares wins' when it comes to glorious, rich broths and 'truly exceptional' plates of cold sliced pig's ears with sesame oil, steamed egg pudding with seafood, hot and spicy duck tongues or cumin-flavoured lamb ribs. At lunchtime, big noodle bowls and innovative Szechuan-style dim sum steal the show. Our questionnaire was not returned, so check the restaurant's website for details.
Chef/s: Jian Ju Zhou. **Open:** all week 12 to 11.
Meals: alc (main courses £7 to £19)

The Rickety Press

Reborn Jericho boozer
67 Cranham Street, Oxford, OX2 6DE
Tel no: (01865) 424581
www.thericketypress.com
Modern British | £28
Cooking score: 1
£5 OFF £30

A fixture of Oxford's Jericho district for many a year, the old Radcliffe Arms has been resurrected, renamed and rebranded as a thriving modern boozer. Students, affluent locals and staff from nearby Oxford University Press congregate in the real ale bar, while foodies veer towards the conservatory-style restaurant. The attraction is a monthly menu of smart pub food with on-trend flavours – think shredded confit duck salad with blood orange, radicchio and pecans; pork belly with apple purée and braised lentils; or black bream accompanied by creamed leeks, bacon and peas. Longhorn burgers and steaks with triple-cooked chips also have their say. Wines from £16.
Chef/s: Andrew Holland. **Open:** all week L 12 to 2.30 (3 Sun), D 6.30 to 9.30 (10 Fri and Sat). **Closed:** 25 and 26 Dec. **Meals:** alc (main courses £13 to £21).
Details: 70 seats. Separate bar. Wheelchair access.

Turl Street Kitchen

Vibrant charity venue
16-17 Turl Street, Oxford, OX1 3DH
Tel no: (01865) 264171
www.turlstreetkitchen.co.uk
Modern British | £20
Cooking score: 1
£5 OFF £30

There's a feeling of goodwill towards this town-centre bar-café-restaurant and not only because its profits support the Oxford Hub, a collection of charities based in the building. The 'casual but not-too-casual' all-day venue, now with guest rooms, does a nice line in freshly cooked, local eats. Vegetarians fare well with beetroot, spinach and Oxford Blue tart, then white bean stew with romanesco to follow, while beef shin pie or Sunday roast does the carnivores nicely. Chocolate brownie fool should please both. An extensive drinks list includes Turl Street Stout, wines from £14.50 and a choice of devilish hot chocolates. **Chef/s:** Carl Isham. **Open:** all week L 12 to 2.30 (3 Sun), D 6 to 10. **Closed:** 25 Dec to 2 Jan. **Meals:** alc (main courses £8 to £15). Set D £12.50 (2 courses) to £16. **Details:** 60 seats. Separate bar.

ALSO RECOMMENDED
▲ Edamamé
15 Holywell Street, Oxford, OX1 3SA
Tel no: (01865) 246916
www.edamame.co.uk
Japanese

A tiny, wallet-friendly Japanese canteen opposite New College, Edamamé serves unorthodox (but authentic) street food to enthusiastic crowds of students, tourists and locals who don't mind its limited opening hours and no-bookings policy. Lunch is a classic run through marinated chicken kara-age (£7.50), pork tonkatsu, salmon teriyaki (£9), curries and bowls of ramen noodles in soup – all with appropriate sides. Thursday evening brings a sparkling fresh sushi buffet, and there are extended, tapas-style suppers on Friday and Saturday nights. House wine £13. Open Wed to Sun L, Thur to Sat D.

▲ The Magdalen Arms
243 Iffley Road, Oxford, OX4 1SJ
Tel no: (01865) 243159
www.magdalenarms.com
British

Florence Fowler and Tony Abarno have injected new life into this suburban boozer and attract a loyal crowd. As graduates of London's Anchor and Hope (see entry), they don't indulge in posturing or frippery, just good, simple cooking that celebrates seasonal produce along the lines of warm English octopus with Little Gem and aïoli (£7.60), coq au vin (£12) or pot-roast pheasant with chestnuts, bacon and crème fraîche for two to

share. To conclude, a Muscat and caramel custard. The wine list opens at £13.80. No food Mon L.

▲ Sojo
6-9 Hythe Bridge Street, Oxford, OX1 2EW
Tel no: (01865) 202888
www.sojooxford.co.uk
Chinese

In a setting that is contemporary but functional, this small restaurant makes a bold attempt to serve proper regional Chinese food at reasonable prices – and it pays to be adventurous or give the helpful staff a budget and leave it to them. Here you will find braised Shanghai sweet-soy duck (£8), diced chicken with salted fish and aubergine pot, home-roast pork with crackling skin (£8.50), congees, rice bowls, soup noodles and much more besides. Dim sum is served until 5pm. Saké is an alternative to wine (from £16).

▮ Shiplake
Orwells
Menus sparkling with culinary fireworks
Shiplake Row, Shiplake, RG9 4DP
Tel no: (01189) 403673
www.orwellsatshiplake.co.uk
Modern British | £33
Cooking score: 5

It's hard to disagree with the diner who enthused over the 'insanely good' food emerging from this praiseworthy kitchen. Ryan Simpson and Liam Trotman's cooking is adventurous, but a relaxed, pubby feel to their restaurant ensures pomposity is avoided. A 'faultless' meal might start with smoked eel and foie gras, where tamarind, teeny marinated mushrooms and cubes of apple cut through the rich terrine. Fish is handled with flair, as evidenced by John Dory cooked to soft perfection and served with just-steamed asparagus and samphire, or a fillet of Brixham plaice with brightly green nettle and pearl barley and a salty sliver of Cornish fennel salami. The innovative 'box of delights' pudding menu involves a catalogue of unorthodox, playful flavours. Peppery ras-el-hanout ice cream makes an exotic foil to rich Chartreuse sabayon and light-as-air caramel cake. And don't miss the sorrel sorbet (oh, the perky tang!) and surprise hit of Poire Williams eau de vie in a translucent sliver of Bartlett pear on a walnut and goats' curd cheesecake. There's plenty to drink by the glass, knowledgeable guidance and house wine from £17.

Chef/s: Ryan Simpson and Liam Trotman. **Open:** Tue to Sun L 11.30 to 3 (3.30 Sun), Tue to Sat D 6.30 to 9 (10 Fri and Sat). **Closed:** Mon, first 2 weeks Jan, 1 week Apr, first 2 weeks Sept. **Meals:** alc (main courses £14 to £24). Set L £10 (2 courses) to £15.50. Sun L £24.95 (2 courses) to £29.95. **Details:** 55 seats. 40 seats outside. Separate bar. Wheelchair access. Car parking.

▌Shutford

NEW ENTRY

The George & Dragon
Rare finesse in a real pub
Church Lane, Shutford, OX15 6PG
Tel no: (01295) 780320
www.thegeorgeanddragon.com
British | £25
Cooking score: 3

£5 OFF   £30

Wedged into a hillock mere feet from Shutford's church, this venerable honey-stoned hostelry is the focus of village activities. Voluble locals discuss the relative merits of five cask ales in the bare-stone bar or perhaps eat a snack by the fire. A real pub, then, but in the compact back restaurant – a congenial spot open to the bar – the food transcends the setting. Simon Dyer has worked at Claridge's, and his hearty seasonal menus show rare finesse. Meat, sourced from a 20-mile radius, is a highlight. Modest pricing and few fripperies belie the quality of such dishes as pork belly on puréed white beans surrounded by plate-lickingly delectable truffle-spiked gravy. Herb-crusted rack of lamb, tender and pink, might follow, accompanied by miniature buttered leeks, carrots and champ. One reporter's slightly overcooked pecan tart was soon forgotten, given the solicitous service and great value – which extends to the appealing wine list (from £14).

Chef/s: Simon Dyer. **Open:** Fri to Sun L 12 to 2 (2.30 Sat, 3 Sun), Mon to Sat D 6 to 9. **Meals:** alc (main courses £10 to £18). Sun L £10. **Details:** 40 seats. 40 seats outside. Separate bar.

▌Sparsholt

NEW ENTRY

The Star Inn
Acute culinary talent in a scrubbed-up pub
Watery Lane, Sparsholt, OX12 9PL
Tel no: (01235) 751873
www.thestarsparsholt.co.uk
Modern British | £35
Cooking score: 4

🛏

With carefully preserved beams, a bucolic village setting and scrubbed pine furniture, the new-look Star may resemble a City banker's dream of rusticity, but there's acute talent in its kitchen. Chef/patron David Watts (ex-Cotswold House) spent eight years with Raymond Blanc at Le Manoir. Drinkers have two ales and a clutch of bar stools, though food dominates proceedings. Trendy bar snacks (Scotch eggs et al) are in place, as is a good-value set menu and a carte full of seasonal enticements. Jump into spring with milk curds, wild garlic, peas, pecan and rye, or succulent confit duck leg with orange segments and speckled endive, perhaps followed by a special of monkfish prettily presented on squid tentacles, fresh peas, broad beans and tiny St George's mushrooms – ask the well-spoken staff for details, as menu descriptions don't always tell the whole story. Puddings are spectacular – witness an intense chocolate tart counterbalanced by toasted oats and barley cream. Wines from £14.

Chef/s: Dave Watts. **Open:** Tue to Sun L 12 to 2.30 (3 Sat and Sun), Tue to Sat D 6.30 to 9.30. **Closed:** Mon, 6 to 20 Jan. **Meals:** alc (main courses £17 to £19). Sun L £23 (2 courses) to £28. **Details:** 60 seats. 20 seats outside. Separate bar. Wheelchair access. Car parking.

Stoke Row

ALSO RECOMMENDED
▲ The Crooked Billet
Newlands Lane, Stoke Row, RG9 5PU
Tel no: (01491) 681048
www.thecrookedbillet.co.uk
Modern European

Built in 1642, this beamed-and-flagged village pub is a favoured film location (credits include *Land Girls* and *Patriot Games*). Its rural setting doesn't deter crowds, here for the 'wonderful' atmosphere, food and live music. Local ingredients and eclectic ideas fill the quirky, handwritten menu, where the range is shown by crispy fried ham hock with caper salad and poached egg (£8); lime and coriander-crusted monkfish with a mussel, coconut and lime-leaf broth and ginger barley couscous (£20); and sticky toffee pudding. Wines from £20. Open all week.

Stonor

NEW ENTRY
The Quince Tree
A pristine rural venture packed with modish British delights
Stonor, RG9 6HE
Tel no: (01491) 639039
www.thequincetree.com
Modern British | £49
Cooking score: 4

To call the Quince Tree a pub tells a fraction of its story. This pristine complex dominates its rural locale, incorporating a well-stocked deli, all-day café (healthy breakfasts, brunches, cakes, light lunches) and a large bar opulently kitted-out with modern woody furnishings. Oxfordshire's moneyed thirtysomethings favour bar meals, where crayfish cakes might lead on to shin of beef cottage pie, but some plump for the full works in the adjoining Jazz Age-themed restaurant. Here, amid sunburst mirrors, early swing music and impressive flower displays, Peter Eaton's set-price menu comes packed with modish British delights. Delectable canapés and an intense basil and tomato foam pre-starter could precede a well-balanced assembly of pan-fried foie gras with duck crackling and quince and orange chutney. Juicy sea bass might follow, matched with battered anchovies, creamy white beans, samphire and chorizo. Excellent breads and a dessert of elaborately presented 'rhubarb and custard' (the lightly poached rhubarb enhanced by sorbet, jelly and gingerbread) confirm the kitchen's pedigree. Wine from £16.50.
Chef/s: Peter Eaton. Open: restaurant D only Fri and Sat 7 to 9. Pub all week L 12 to 2.30 (3 Sun), D Mon to Sat 6.30 to 9. Closed: 25 Dec. Meals: Set D £39.50 (2 courses) to £49.50. Details: 28 seats. Separate bar. Wheelchair access. Car parking.

Swinbrook

The Swan Inn
Idyllic village pub
Swinbrook, OX18 4DY
Tel no: (01993) 823339
www.theswanswinbrook.co.uk
Modern British | £30
Cooking score: 2

£5 OFF 🚗

A mid-16th-century village inn beside the river Windrush, the wisteria-clad Swan is every inch the Oxfordshire country pub. Winter fires, a beamed and timbered bar and a light conservatory-style dining room establish the mood. The cooking acknowledges current trends, as well as offering the occasional tried-and-true pub dish such as Tamworth pork sausages with mash and onion gravy and the popular Sunday roasts. A meal in January spoke of careful sourcing and ushered in some finely honed seasonal dishes: Jerusalem artichoke soup; roast local partridge with braised red cabbage, garlic potatoes and chestnut and juniper gravy; and mulled wine jelly with berry compote. When the sun shines tables are at a premium in the large garden (with wandering bantams). Local real ales are supported by a well-priced wine list (from £16.80).

Chef/s: Matthew Laughton. **Open:** all week L 12 to 2 (2.30 Sat, 3 Sun), D 7 to 9 (9.30 Fri and Sat, 8.30 Sun). **Closed:** 25 and 26 Dec. **Meals:** alc (main courses £14 to £20). **Details:** 70 seats. 100 seats outside. Separate bar. Wheelchair access. Car parking.

▌ Toot Baldon

ALSO RECOMMENDED
▲ The Mole Inn
Toot Baldon, OX44 9NG
Tel no: (01865) 340001
www.themoleinn.com
Modern British

Just a few miles from Oxford's dreaming spires, this refashioned 300-year-old inn is a tempting prospect with its traditional bar, extensive gardens and lively modern pub food. British and European themes meet on a menu that might run from ham hock and parsley terrine with a poached egg (£6.95) to roast cod with provençale dressing, chorizo, squid and celeriac mash (£17.50). Also try the offer of 28-day aged steak with a bottle of Mole Inn 'real underground ale'. Wines from £18.95. Open all week.

▌ Woodstock

The Feathers
Revamped coaching inn with modish menus
Market Street, Woodstock, OX20 1SX
Tel no: (01993) 812291
www.feathers.co.uk
Modern British | £50
new chef/no score

£5 OFF 🛏

A paragon of blue-blooded Oxfordshire life since the 17th century, the Feathers now puts on a thoroughly contemporary show, with boutique interiors, a dedicated gin bar and modish menus in the revamped restaurant. Jazzy carpets and vibrant artwork brighten the wood-panelled dining rooms, while in the past the kitchen has applied its skills to in-vogue ingredients: a tasting of beetroot might be embellished with watercress, aged

Parmesan and preserved lemon; Cotswold pheasant is teamed with smoked celeriac, pumpkin and trompette mushrooms; and there's Cornish turbot, too (perhaps with salsify, parsley soubise and sea kale). But, as we went to press, a new chef was in the process of being appointed. Cooking has occasionally seemed 'pretentious' and staff have sometimes been guilty of the same fault, but here's hoping the Feathers' new persona generally gets approval. The heavyweight wine list has plenty of recommendations from £19 (£5.50 a glass).
Open: all week L 12 to 2.30, D 7 to 9 (9.30 Fri and Sat). **Meals:** alc (main courses £19 to £26). Set D £55 (5 courses). Sun L £24.95. **Details:** 40 seats. 60 seats outside. Separate bar.

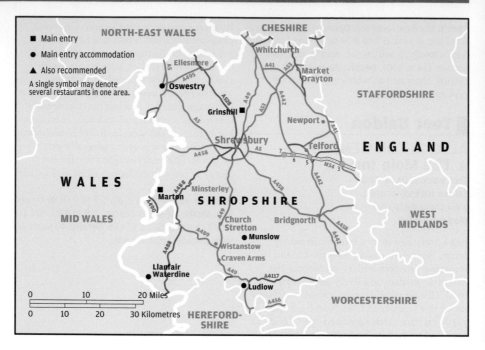

- ■ Main entry
- ● Main entry accommodation
- ▲ Also recommended

A single symbol may denote several restaurants in one area.

NORTH-EAST WALES
CHESHIRE
Whitchurch
Ellesmere
A41
A495
Market Drayton
Oswestry
STAFFORDSHIRE
Grinshill ■
Newport ●
A5
Shrewsbury
Telford
ENGLAND
A458
A5
M54
WALES
Marton ■
Minsterley
SHROPSHIRE
MID WALES
Church Stretton
Bridgnorth
WEST MIDLANDS
A489
● Munslow
Wistanstow
Craven Arms
Llanfair Waterdine
A49
A4117
● Ludlow
WORCESTERSHIRE
A456
HEREFORD-SHIRE

0   10   20 Miles
0   10   20   30 Kilometres

■ Grinshill

NEW ENTRY

The Inn at Grinshill

Gorgeous country inn with accomplished cooking
Grinshill, SY4 3BL
Tel no: (01939) 220410
www.theinnatgrinshill.co.uk
Modern British | £38
Cooking score: 3

The rather grand Grade II–listed inn with coach arches, tucked away in a pint-sized valley village, has been sensitively restored to achieve a clever balance of smart modernity with the requisite signs of structural age. As well as a commodious, hospitable bar, a glass-fronted, white-clothed dining room complete with ambitious chef is part of the package. Chris Conde is a confident exponent of the modern British genre, parcelling up quail breast en croute, its leg in crisp potato, alongside parsnip purée to start, before a fillet of turbot turns up, escorted by a brace of scallops, samphire and mushrooms in a deeply flavoured chicken stock sauce. Dessert could be a complex construction of chocolate mousse cake with cherry sorbet and crème fraîche ice cream. A decent little wine list opens with Spanish selections in three colours at £17.95, with glasses from £4.50.
Chef/s: Chris Conde and David Brazier. **Open:** Wed to Sun L 12 to 2.30 (3 Sun), Wed to Sat D 6.30 to 9.30. **Closed:** Mon, Tue, first week Jan. **Meals:** Set L and D £31.50 (2 courses) to £37.50. Sun L £20 (2 courses). Tasting menu £55.50 (7 courses).
Details: 60 seats. 8 seats outside. Separate bar. Car parking.

▌Llanfair Waterdine

The Waterdine

Foodie destination with unflashy cooking
Llanfair Waterdine, LD7 1TU
Tel no: (01547) 528214
www.waterdine.com
Modern British | £33
Cooking score: 4

The garden of this 16th-century thatched long house stands right on the border between Shropshire and Powys, with views of the Welsh Marches and rolling hills beyond. Once a refuelling point on the old drovers' route, the Waterdine is now a charmingly rustic foodie destination (with rooms) sporting leaded windows, sturdy wooden floors and thick stone walls. These days, chef/proprietor Ken Adams confines most of his culinary efforts to a modest dinner menu that allows room for local and organic ingredients. Grilled pork loin with garlic on mustard mash with braised Savoy cabbage is typical of his low-key approach. Supplies of Cornish fish mean the kitchen can also offer sea bass fillet on leek velouté with chive potatoes and samphire or roast monkfish with lemon and brown shrimp sauce. Desserts such as chocolate tart with ginger ice cream tread a safe path, Sunday lunch is thoroughly traditional and the wine list offers decent value from £18.50. Note: strictly 'bookings only'.
Chef/s: Ken Adams. **Open:** Sun L 12 to 3, Tue to Sat D 7 to 11. **Closed:** Mon, 24 to 26 Dec, 1 week spring, 1 week autumn. **Meals:** Set D £32.50. Sun L £22.50. **Details:** 20 seats. Separate bar. Car parking. Children over 8 yrs only at D.

▌Ludlow

La Bécasse

Classy Ludlow big-hitter
17 Corve Street, Ludlow, SY8 1DA
Tel no: (01584) 872325
www.labecasse.co.uk
Modern French | £60
new chef/no score

Occupying a 17th-century coaching inn, La Bécasse makes the most of the building's historic oak panelling and stone walls – although a swanky first-floor Champagne bar adds some modern-day glitz to proceedings. There's also a new dining room in the basement ('the vault'), where diners can get up close to the kitchen action. During a six-year stint as chef/patron, Will Holland gained a reputation for 'high-class consistency' with dishes such as fresh picked Devon crab with a lightly spiced fishcake and pickled papaya salsa or juniper-roasted haunch of Mortimer Forest venison with parsnips, blackberries and chestnuts. But following his departure the kitchen is now in new hands – although it's hoped that this big-hitting member of Alan Murchison's group of restaurants will continue to deliver top-class food backed by 'enthusiastic, correct service'. The wine list offers excellent drinking from reputable French sources and growers worldwide; current prices start at £27 (£7 a glass). Reports please.
Open: Wed to Sun L 12 to 2, Tue to Sat D 7 to 9 (9.30 Sat). **Closed:** Mon, 2 weeks Christmas and New Year. **Meals:** Set L £26 (2 courses) to £30. Set D £54 (2 courses) to £60. Gourmand menu £65 (7 courses). **Details:** 42 seats. Separate bar. Car parking.

The Green Café
Lovely watermill café with tasty lunches
Mill on the Green, Ludlow, SY8 1EG
Tel no: (01584) 879872
www.ludlowmillonthegreen.co.uk
Modern British | £19
Cooking score: 1
£30

'Sitting on the banks of the river Teme, you couldn't wish for a better location' is one verdict on this smashing converted watermill café. It 'fills a gap Ludlow has been missing for so long' by serving honest food at reasonable prices. Seasonal, often local ingredients appear on a short menu that might promise salt cod fritters with garlic mayonnaise ahead of braised beef short rib with parsley dumpling or homemade gnocchi with Italian-style pork and garlic sausage ragù. There are beautiful puddings, too, such as quince jelly with vanilla and rose-water custard. Drink local beers and ciders, or wines from £17.50.
Chef/s: Clive Davis. **Open:** Tue to Sun 10 to 4.30 (L 12 to 2.30). **Closed:** Mon, 24 Dec to 13 Feb. **Meals:** alc (main courses £7 to £11). **Details:** 30 seats. 25 seats outside. Wheelchair access.

★ TOP 50 ★

Mr Underhill's
Bewitching waterside hideaway
Dinham Weir, Ludlow, SY8 1EH
Tel no: (01584) 874431
www.mr-underhills.co.uk
Modern European | £65
Cooking score: 6

Chris and Judy Bradley's beloved restaurant-with-rooms by the river Teme 'moves along like a confident swan'. Its balmy hideaway charms never fail to bewitch, but there is also a genuine personal touch that's greatly appreciated. Fewer covers in the dining room (now garbed in French greys and greens) mean a sharper focus, while modifications to the kitchen have given Chris's team renewed impetus. 'No water baths: it's just proper

artisan cooking for us,' they say. The format remains unchanged – an eight-course market menu tailored to each guest – but new dishes are now appearing alongside fixtures such as the duck liver custard with sweetcorn cream. The result is a measured procession of precise, 'carefully crafted' flavours, say day-boat brill with pickled vegetables, vanilla and lime, ahead of slow-roasted Marches beef fillet with braised 'burgers', parsley and tarragon jus, creamed spinach and leek purée. After that, it's time for sweetness – perhaps Valrhona chocolate tart with blackcurrant ice cream and espresso caramel. Judy Bradley's wine list is a labour of love, accumulated over the years and properly attuned to quality, with regular 'guest' names, superb food-matching selections and plenty by the glass. Bottles start at £19.
Chef/s: Chris Bradley. **Open:** Wed to Sun D only 7.30 to 8.15 (1 sitting). **Closed:** Mon, Tue, 25, 26 and 31 Dec, 1 Jan, 1 week Jun, 2 weeks Oct. **Meals:** Set D £65 (8 courses). **Details:** 24 seats. 24 seats outside. Car parking.

Marton
The Sun Inn
Pubby hospitality, real ales, honest food
Marton, SY21 8JP
Tel no: (01938) 561211
www.suninn.org.uk
Modern British | £25
Cooking score: 1
£30

Hospitality is a strength of this 300-year-old pub-cum-restaurant on the Shropshire-Powys border, thanks to the warmth of the Gartell family, who create a refreshingly welcoming feel. Peter Gartell's cooking is honest and his menus aim to comfort rather than challenge. The repertoire ranges from goats' cheese, fig and honey tart, via roast rump of lamb marinated in Mediterranean herbs and served with butter beans, or beef bourguignon with mustard mash to traditional Sunday roasts. Puddings please,

too, including white chocolate and ginger cheesecake and lemon meringue pie. There are real ales in the bar and wines from £13.95.
Chef/s: Peter Gartell. **Open:** Wed to Sun L 12 to 2.30, Tue to Sat D 7 to 11. **Closed:** Mon. **Meals:** alc (main courses £10 to £17). Sun L £15.75 (2 courses) to £18.95. **Details:** 60 seats. 20 seats outside. Separate bar. Wheelchair access. Car parking.

▮ Munslow

The Crown Country Inn
Quirky old inn with fresh, simple food
Corvedale Road, Munslow, SY7 9ET
Tel no: (01584) 841205
www.crowncountryinn.co.uk
Modern British | £29
Cooking score: 2

On a winding country road leading to Ludlow, the Arnolds' hospitable country inn is eager to please. It's an imposing three-storey place with exposed stone walls and weighty beams inside, serving food that's high on comfort factor, but with a vein of ambition running through it, too. A breakfast-like starter of crisp-fried black pudding balls with bacon on Boston beans with a bit of fried bread is straightforward enough, but may be followed by hake with pancetta, sweet potato and sage purée and orange and ginger dressing, or beef brisket in chillified demi-glace with carrot and mango purée. Dishes are sometimes let down by acquiring one too many elements; as so often, simplicity would make a more direct appeal. Still, dessert might be caramel-coated pineapple with sprightly mango pannacotta and hazelnut ice cream, a thoroughly persuasive closer. Wines from £15.75.
Chef/s: Richard Arnold. **Open:** Tue to Sun L 12 to 2, Tue to Sat D 6.45 to 9. **Closed:** Mon, 25 and 26 Dec. **Meals:** alc (main courses £15 to £20). Set Sun L £22.95. **Details:** 60 seats. 24 seats outside. Car parking.

▮ Oswestry

Sebastians
A petit slice of France
45 Willow Street, Oswestry, SY11 1AQ
Tel no: (01691) 655444
www.sebastians-hotel.co.uk
French | £40
Cooking score: 3

'The small market town of Oswestry is very fortunate to have such a splendid establishment at its heart,' enthuses one visitor to Mark and Michelle Fisher's ancient, beamed coaching inn, now an immensely appealing restaurant-with-rooms. It's an opinion backed up by other warm and contented accounts of welcoming fires, friendly service and good food. The cooking has strong Gallic undertones and eating here is all about comfort, solace and familiarity, right down to the amuse-bouches and the mid-course sorbets. Expect sound renditions of foie gras and potato terrine, poached halibut with braised lettuce, peas and a horseradish cream sauce, and braised shin of beef with fondant potato, spinach purée and a red wine sauce. Finish with a trio of lemon desserts. French regional wines (from £17.95) open the well-chosen list.
Chef/s: Richard Jones. **Open:** Tue to Sat D only 6.30 to 9.30. **Closed:** Sun, Mon, 24 to 26 Dec, 1 Jan. **Meals:** Set D £19.95 and £39.50. **Details:** 35 seats. 20 seats outside. Car parking.

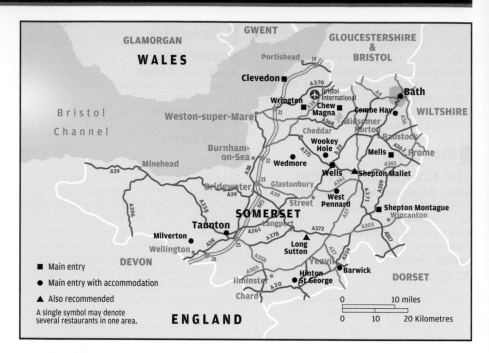

▌Barwick

Little Barwick House

A little English idyll
Rexes Hollow Lane, Barwick, BA22 9TD
Tel no: (01935) 423902
www.littlebarwickhouse.co.uk
Modern British | £44
Cooking score: 5

🍷 🛏

Tim and Emma Ford's listed Georgian dower house continues to charm visitors with its serene outlook and ever-so-comforting sense of decorum. Set in three acres of grounds close to the Dorset border, it's a little English idyll for those who crave personable R&R in meticulously polished surroundings. Much depends on the output of Tim's kitchen and his connections with the local food network. Rock-solid suppliers mean he can ring the changes while maintaining sky-high standards. Depending on the season, you might find pressed terrine of local game with plum chutney or Lyme Bay scallops with butternut squash purée and crispy bacon among a handful of starters, while mains might yield beef fillet, saddle of roe deer or Cornish sea bass with basil-crushed new potatoes and white wine sauce: classic stuff mercifully free of foams and whizz-bang trickery. Unwavering consistency is the kitchen's hallmark – witness impeccable desserts such as citrus posset with marmalade sponge, marinated orange and Grand Marnier ice cream. The distinguished global wine list is aimed at discerning connoisseurs and everyday quaffers alike, with plenty of half-bottles and 'stickies' to encourage off-piste excursions. Prices start at £19.95.
Chef/s: Tim Ford. **Open:** Wed to Sat L 12 to 2, Tue to Sat D 7 to 9. **Closed:** Sun, Mon, 3 weeks Jan. **Meals:** Set L £23.95 (2 courses) to £27.95. Set D £37.95 (2 courses) to £43.95. **Details:** 40 seats. 12 seats outside. Car parking. Children over 5 yrs only.

Bath

Allium Brasserie

Contemporary dining with big-city style
Abbey Hotel, North Parade, Bath, BA1 1LF
Tel no: (01225) 461603
www.abbeyhotelbath.co.uk
Modern British | £35
Cooking score: 4

🛏

'This place certainly stands out from the crowd', noted a visitor to the refurbished Abbey Hotel, much taken by its all-day brasserie 'with a touch of London pizazz' and 'trump-card' pavement terrace. Vibrant purple seating, oak flooring and striking modern art deliver cool good looks, while from the kitchen a variety of small-plate snacks are served all-day, or you can opt for the three-course carte at lunch and dinner. Chris Staines oversees it all, his cooking showing real panache. Top-notch ingredients and skilful execution, plus the occasional Asian influence, can be seen in dishes such as miso-cured Loch Duart salmon teamed with oyster fritter, pickled cucumber, grapefruit and a 'kick' of wasabi dressing. For mains, Cornish bream is served with sautéed potatoes, violet artichokes, octopus, salsa verde and an unusual ('if sweetish') savoury lemon curd. Lychee pannacotta topped with pineapple, mango and a 'lovely hit' of lemongrass granita makes a finish with a tropical flourish. Wines from £18.
Chef/s: Chris Staines. **Open:** all week 12 to 9.
Meals: alc (main courses £14.50 to £24.50). Set L £14.95 (2 courses) to £19. Set D £29 (2 courses) to £39. Sun L £20. **Details:** 70 seats. 50 seats outside. Separate bar. Wheelchair access.

The Bath Priory

Country-house elegance and accomplished food
Weston Road, Bath, BA1 2XT
Tel no: (01225) 331922
www.thebathpriory.co.uk
Modern European | £75
Cooking score: 5

🍷 🛏 V

It may be secreted in a residential area not far from the centre of Bath, but this many-winged Victorian pile is country-house elegance personified – complete with romantic gardens and generous, antique-filled interiors. The handsomely appointed restaurant provides a classy backdrop for Sam Moody's fine-tuned modern cuisine, which shows all the hallmarks of his mentor Michael Caines. West Country produce is given sympathetic treatment in accomplished dishes ranging from pan-fried Brixham sea bass with spring leeks, Avruga caviar and red wine jus to roast crown of local pigeon with chou farci, confit vegetables and Madeira consommé. One couple who navigated the tasting menu also found much to admire: from an 'unctuous' terrine of duck foie gras on a salad of green beans and truffles to perfectly cooked turbot embellished with crushed peas and bacon velouté. After that, Cassis-spiked soufflé with a glass of Canadian Icewine provided an 'amazing finale' to proceedings. Service is relaxed, expert, meticulous and accommodating – particularly when advising on the exhaustive 500-bin wine list. All-round pedigree, peerless growers and top vintages jump from every page, with 'sommelier highlights' starting at £25.
Chef/s: Sam Moody. **Open:** all week L 12.30 to 2.30, D 6.30 to 9.30. **Meals:** Set L £19.95 (2 courses) to £25. Set D £59 (2 courses) to £75. Sun L £42. Tasting menu £90 (7 courses). **Details:** 70 seats. 20 seats outside. Separate bar. Wheelchair access. Car parking. Children over 5 yrs only at L. Children over 12 yrs only at D.

Casanis

Charming bistro with Gallic classics
4 Saville Row, Bath, BA1 2QP
Tel no: (01225) 780055
www.casanis.co.uk
French | £28
Cooking score: 1
£30

Close to the Assembly Rooms in the heart of tourist Bath, compact two-tiered Casanis offers honest French cooking in a 'cosy, relaxing atmosphere' and is universally acclaimed by readers as good value. Fans are impressed by its simple, sympathetic décor, with white tablecloths setting the tone. The archetypal brasserie menu features the likes of soupe de poisson, excellent ravioles d'escargot and 'exceptional' stuffed quail with a lentil and pancetta ragoût, sautéed girolles, dauphinois potatoes and thyme jus. Finish with crème brûlée or tarte Tatin. Service is pleasant and the short, all-French wine list opens at £18.
Chef/s: Laurent Couvreur. **Open:** Tue to Sat L 12 to 2, D 6 to 10. **Closed:** Sun, Mon, 25 to 26 Dec, 2 weeks Jan, 1 week Jul/Aug. **Meals:** alc (main courses £14 to £22). Set L £16 (2 courses) to £20. Set D £18 (2 courses) to £22. **Details:** 40 seats. 16 seats outside.

The Circus Café & Restaurant

Refreshing two-pronged eatery
34 Brock Street, Bath, BA1 2LN
Tel no: (01225) 466020
www.thecircuscafeandrestaurant.co.uk
Modern British | £27
Cooking score: 3
£5 OFF   £30

'What a find!' trumpeted one reader after discovering Alison Golden's 'brilliant' eatery in a fine Georgian residence just off Bath's much-photographed Circus. During the day, visitors drop by for elevenses or light lunches of grilled mushrooms on Welsh rarebit, but come nightfall the place is transformed with candles on the tables and a menu that invokes the spirit of cookery writers old and new. In a soothing setting of muted green colours, original fireplaces and cornicing, guests can sample little pots of thyme-scented oxtail crumble or the fresh delights of confit Creedy Carver duck salad, followed by a schnitzel of Hampshire wild boar or some fish from the West Country day boats. To finish, it has to be 'whim-wham' (a decadently luxurious 18th-century trifle) or roast quinces in Muscatel. The 30-bin wine list is a hand-picked selection from small European growers, with prices from £14.90.
Chef/s: Alison Golden. **Open:** Mon to Sat L 12 to 3 (4 Sat), D 5.30 to 10 (10.30 Thur to Sat). **Closed:** Sun, 24 Dec to 17 Jan. **Meals:** alc (main courses £15 to £17). Set L £15 (2 courses) to £19.70. Set D £22 (2 courses) to £27. **Details:** 50 seats. 8 seats outside. Wheelchair access. Children over 7 yrs only.

NEW ENTRY

The Curfew

Show-stopping starters in a room over a pub
11 Cleveland Place, Bath, BA1 5DG
Tel no: (01225) 313747
www.curfewbath.co.uk
British | £29
Cooking score: 3
£30

Walk up the creaky stairs at the back of the small atmospheric bar (serving real ales) to find a light-filled, elegantly proportioned room with a huge picture window affording great views of the Georgian streets (and modern traffic). Chef/proprietor Rob Pearce not only knows how to cook, but also knows what people want to eat. Sunday lunch, for example, delivers generous roasts, enough to assuage the most ravenous appetite, if not the most enquiring palate. His creativity is channelled instead into show-stopping first courses – a plate of de-shelled razor clams with a spiky velvet butter-chilli sauce, given crunch with fennel and radish, or a vegetarian version with a peach and rhubarb dressing, which proved to be just as moreish. Pear clafoutis with homemade vanilla yoghurt seemed less exciting. Kind pricing, including house wine from £16, adds to the enjoyment.

Chef/s: Robert Pearce. **Open:** all week L 12 to 3.30 (5 Sun). Mon to Sat D 6 to 9.30. **Meals:** alc (main courses £10 to £21). Set L £12.95 (2 courses) to £14.50. **Details:** 35 seats. 15 seats outside. Separate bar. Children over 8 yrs only in restaurant.

King William
No-nonsense cooking in a boho pub
36 Thomas Street, Bath, BA1 5NN
Tel no: (01225) 428096
www.kingwilliampub.com
British | £28
Cooking score: 1
£5 OFF £30

Reports over the past couple of years suggested that Charlie Digney's unpretentious and diminutive city hostelry was suffering from inconsistency, but the King William appears to be back on track. It remains a shabby-chic slightly boho pub, but a renewed devotion to local ingredients and an understanding of our gastronomic heritage has led to a new menu of well-defined dishes such as curried beetroot soup and pan-fried plaice on the bone with shallot and caper potatoes and caper-butter sauce. Finish with pear, almond and fennel tart with ewes' cheese ice cream. Four excellent local ales are available alongside the French-heavy wine list (from £16).
Chef/s: Scott Galaway. **Open:** Mon to Sat L 12 to 2 (3 Sat), D 6 to 9 (10 Fri and Sat). Sun 12 to 9. **Closed:** 25 and 26 Dec. **Meals:** alc (main courses £12 to £18). **Details:** 62 seats. Separate bar.

The Marlborough Tavern
Stylish, popular food pub
35 Marlborough Buildings, Bath, BA1 2LY
Tel no: (01225) 423731
www.marlborough-tavern.com
British | £28
Cooking score: 2
£30

Just a few paces from Bath's famous Royal Crescent, this once run-down city-centre watering hole was given a sophisticated makeover in 2006 and is now a well-established local favourite. There has been a significant change in the kitchen since the last edition of the Guide, with Sam Coltman taking over the kitchen when his predecessor left after seven years at the helm. The style remains unfussy and seasonal, with plenty of local suppliers displayed on the menus. The daily changing line-up might start with salt-and-pepper squid with garlic aïoli. Next, a typical main could be a trio of Berkshire Boar pork, spring vegetables, mashed potato and rhubarb purée, followed by dessert of lemon and almond cake with lemon sorbet. House wine £15.90.
Chef/s: Sam Coltman. **Open:** all week L 12.30 to 2.30 (3 Sat, 4 Sun), D 6 to 9.30 (10 Fri and Sat, 9 Sun). **Closed:** 25 Dec. **Meals:** alc (main courses £11 to £27). Set L £12 (2 courses) to £15. **Details:** 80 seats. 90 seats outside. No children after 8.

Menu Gordon Jones
An exciting and refreshing new arrival
2 Wellsway, Bath, BA2 3AQ
Tel no: (01225) 480871
www.menugordonjones.co.uk
Modern British | £40
Cooking score: 4
🍷 V

An important new arrival on the crowded local scene, Menu Gordon Jones is 'a truly unique experience' according to one reporter. Another enthuses about 'fantastic food, beautifully and cleverly presented without pomp or ceremony'. With just seven tables, this modest little place occupies an unremarkable spot on a busy, dusty junction just outside Bath's city centre. The surprise, no-choice tasting menu concept may not be for those with more traditional tastes, but it is 'exciting and refreshing' and showcases Jones's 'flair and inventiveness'. A highly individual starter of 'sausage and eggs' (French sausage with smoked pheasant egg custard, baby turnips and purple potato crisps) might be followed by assiette of veal with roasted purple carrots and risotto-like minted oats with charred spring onion. Balsamic vinegar pannacotta with poached summer fruits and chocolate oil is one of the memorable desserts. A concise list of organic and biodynamic wines opens at £22.

Chef/s: Gordon Jones. **Open:** Tue to Sat L 12.30 to 2, D 7 to 9. **Closed:** Sun, Mon. **Meals:** Set L £35 (5 courses), Set D £45 (6 courses). **Details:** 16 seats. Children over 12 yrs only.

The Queensberry Hotel, Olive Tree Restaurant

Comfort, quirks and eclectic cooking
4-7 Russel Street, Bath, BA1 2QF
Tel no: (01225) 447928
www.olivetreebath.co.uk
Modern British | £45
Cooking score: 4
🍾 🛏

Since last year's Guide, there has been a change of chef at this elegant Georgian town-house hotel, a veteran of the Bath dining scene. Thankfully, quality and consistency remain high, indeed, 'many diners may not even notice the change'. The new man is Chris Cleghorn, who has an impressive CV of time spent with Michael Caines and Heston Blumenthal. Creative flair suffuses his modern European food, from a perfectly balanced smoked salmon mousse (the richness offset by an earthy, tart salad of beetroot, apple and lemon) to an excellent braised pork belly with nutty pearl barley and artichoke risotto. Passion fruit soufflé served with a refreshing coconut sorbet was 'as good as any soufflé I've eaten'. Warm lighting and colourful artwork brighten the basement dining room, as does confident, snappy service. An upbeat, winning choice of wines – with plenty to suit most palates and more than 30 by the glass – starts at £19.50.

Chef/s: Chris Cleghorn. **Open:** Tue to Sun L 12 to 2 (12.30 Sun), all week D 7 to 10. **Meals:** alc (main courses £17 to £27). Set L £18.50 (2 courses) to £22.50. Set D £32.50 (2 courses) to £38.50. Sun L £22.50. **Details:** 60 seats.

The White Hart Inn

Quirky pub with assertive cooking
Widcombe Hill, Widcombe, Bath, BA2 6AA
Tel no: (01225) 338053
www.whitehartbath.co.uk
Modern British | £25
Cooking score: 2
🛏 £30

A mere two-minute walk from Bath's railway station, the White Hart is reckoned to be one of the spa city's oldest watering holes. It has long enjoyed a loyal following for its consistently impressive and well-priced food. The backpackers' hostel above adds to the quirkiness, as does a pretty walled courtyard garden, which, in summer, wouldn't look out of place in Provence. Veteran Bath chef Rupert Pitt and his team cook with the seasons and the concise menu is packed with things you want to eat: slow-braised pork belly with salt-and-pepper squid might be followed by free-range chicken with baked squash, olives and green sauce. Vanilla pannacotta with rhubarb compote is one of the persuasive desserts. Wines from £15.50.

Chef/s: Rupert Pitt, Jason Horn and Steve Wesley. **Open:** all week L 12 to 2 (2.30 Sun), Mon to Sat D 6 to 10 (9 Mon and Tue). **Closed:** 25 Dec, 1 Jan, bank hols. **Meals:** alc (main courses £6 to £18). Set L £12.50. **Details:** 50 seats. 50 seats outside. Wheelchair access.

ALSO RECOMMENDED

▲ The Garrick's Head

7-8 St Johns Place, Bath, BA1 1ET
Tel no: (01225) 318368
www.garricksheadpub.com
Modern British £5

Occupying a historic site smack next to Bath's famous Theatre Royal, this 18th-century watering hole is a civilised spot for pre- or post-performance suppers in the bar or elegant dining room. It is related to the King William (see entry). Although the set-lunch/pre-theatre menu (£17.95 for three courses) has garnered particular praise for its good value, there have been reports of inconsistencies.

Nevertheless, a haunch of venison with venison cottage pie and redcurrant sauce (£16.95) impressed at inspection. Wines from £15. Open all week.

▲ Yak Yeti Yak

12 Pierrepont Street, Bath, BA1 1LA
Tel no: (01225) 442299
www.yakyetiyak.co.uk
Nepalese

On arrival at this characterful basement restaurant decorated with Nepalese memorabilia, you are given the choice of lounging on cushions Nepalese style or eating at tables. Wherever you choose, food will come out on big bronze trays – perhaps excellent polayko masu (grilled strips of spiced lamb with homemade chutney, £5.50) followed by chicken on the bone, stir-fried with ginger and garlic (£7.80) and teamed with well-reported orange lentil musurko dhal and basmati rice. Wines from £13.20. Open all week.

▌Chew Magna
The Pony & Trap

Versatile local food champion
Knowle Hill, Chew Magna, BS40 8TQ
Tel no: (01275) 332627
www.theponyandtrap.co.uk
Modern British | £30
Cooking score: 4

Bedded in lovely country between Bristol and Bath, this re-energised, 200-year-old cottage pub is immediately appealing. Josh Eggleton and family know how to keep customers satisfied, pleasing foodie types searching for 'proper cooking' as well as those after a lunchtime pint and plate of haddock and chips in the cutely restored bar. Josh is a champion of local food, gleaning ingredients from friends and small-scale Somerset producers for a switched-on daily menu that shows 'an intuitive feel for how flavours work': breast of lamb and lamb's sweetbreads offset by apple jelly and salsa verde; lemon sole embellished with brown shrimps, cucumber, lime and

caper butter; haunch of venison with ox tongue, red cabbage and potato cake. There are funkier ideas too (how about duck livers and hearts on toast or cod with 'chicken and mushroom pie' sauce). Desserts might bring chilled spiced rice pudding with rhubarb sorbet and wood sorrel. Wines start at £13.75. **Chef/s:** Josh Eggleton. **Open:** Tue to Sun L 12 to 2.30 (3.30 Sun), D 7 to 9.30 (9 Sun). **Closed:** Mon (exc Dec), 25 Dec. **Meals:** alc (main courses £12 to £22). Set L and D £22.95 (2 courses) to £27.95. Sun L £14.50. **Details:** 70 seats. 30 seats outside. Separate bar. Car parking.

▌Clevedon
Murrays of Clevedon

All-day Italian enterprise
87-93 Hill Road, Clevedon, BS21 7PN
Tel no: (01275) 341555
www.murraysofclevedon.co.uk
Italian | £22
Cooking score: 2

£30

Founded as a modest little tea shop back in 1984, the Murray family's admirable enterprise now consists of a deli, artisan bakery, wine shop and all-day Italian caffè under one roof. The venue has established itself as an eminently flexible set-up for locals, sightseers and shoppers after some provisions or a bite to eat. Drop by for breakfast, order a deli-style sandwich made with home-baked bread or relax with a plate of duck and quince terrine on crostini. Otherwise, go for something more substantial – perhaps brodetto of Cornish seafood, poached Kenn Moor ham hock in a light broth with salsa verde or home-salted cod in tomato sauce with pine nuts, capers and olives. Back-up comes from pasta and salads, while the minimal wine list offers decent Italian drinking from £13.50 (£3.95 a glass). **Chef/s:** Reuben Murray. **Open:** Tue to Sat 8.30 to 5. **Closed:** Sun, Mon, 25 to 27 Dec. **Meals:** alc (main courses £7 to £20). **Details:** 40 seats. 6 seats outside. Wheelchair access.

Combe Hay

The Wheatsheaf

Chic inn that oozes rustic sophistication
Combe Hay, BA2 7EG
Tel no: (01225) 833504
www.wheatsheafcombehay.com
Modern British | £32
Cooking score: 4

£5 OFF 🛏

A converted farmhouse dating back to the 16th century, the Wheatsheaf makes every effort to be an inn for all seasons, with log fires in winter and a delightful terraced garden for better weather. The kitchen is as much a hive of industry as the beehives that supply it. Ingredients also come from the vegetable garden and from Ian Barton's exertions during the game season. So far, so perfectly bucolic, but Eddy Rains cooks with an eye to polished city fashion, offering a risotto of leeks and Barkham Blue to start, or maybe lasagne of crab with samphire. Mains are all about pedigree prime materials, such as Somerset pork chop glazed in mustard and the inn's own honey, or poached breast of Wiltshire guinea fowl with wild mushroom fricassee and truffled mash. Warm treacle tart and malted milk ice cream makes a comforting conclusion. A commendably broad-minded wine list (from £15.95) offers plenty by the glass and half-bottle.
Chef/s: Eddy Rains. **Open:** Tue to Sun L 12 to 2 (2.30 Sun), Tue to Sat D 6.30 to 9. **Closed:** Mon, 25 and 26 Dec. **Meals:** alc (main courses £16 to £22). Set L £14 (2 courses) to £18. Sun L £19.50 (2 courses) to £24.50. **Details:** 55 seats. 80 seats outside. Car parking.

Symbols

🛏 Accommodation is available

£30 Three courses for less than £30

V Separate vegetarian menu

£5 OFF £5-off voucher scheme

🍾 Notable wine list

Hinton St George

The Lord Poulett Arms

Appealing village pub with seasonal food
High Street, Hinton St George, TA17 8SE
Tel no: (01460) 73149
www.lordpoulettarms.com
Modern British | £27
Cooking score: 2

🛏 £30

Ticking clocks, real fires, beams garlanded with hops – this 'super pub' delivers vintage charm by the bucketload. The casks behind the bar should keep ale lovers happy, and the menu includes pub classics such as fish and chips as well as chilli con carne with corn bread, sour cream and coriander. Other dishes, perhaps a warm salad of roasted quail with black pudding and a quail's egg, show more ambition. Spelt spätzle with wild garlic butter, local mushrooms, mozzarella and pine nuts makes an interesting and generous meat-free main, followed by a fun riff on tarte Tatin: tangy apple parfait on pastry with apple crisps and syrupy cooked apple. Wash it down with 'interesting, slightly pricey' wines from an international list starting at £18.50.
Chef/s: Philip Verden. **Open:** all week L 12 to 2.30, D 7 to 9.15. **Closed:** 25 and 26 Dec, 1 Jan. **Meals:** alc (main courses £13 to £23). Sun L £16 (2 courses) to £19. **Details:** 60 seats. 30 seats outside. Car parking.

Long Sutton

ALSO RECOMMENDED
▲ The Devonshire Arms

Cross Lane, Long Sutton, TA10 9LP
Tel no: (01458) 241271
www.thedevonshirearms.com
British

This grey-stone former hunting lodge faces the village green in the heart of the Somerset Levels. The Devonshire Arms has a clean-lined modern look inside, with pale wood tables and blackboard menus. Its appealing, modernised country-pub cooking ranges from leek tarte Tatin with goats' cheese and beetroot purée (£7.50) to lamb rump with black olive mash, red pepper and mint pesto (£16.50), followed by irresistible desserts such as chocolate and orange fondant with dark chocolate mousse and praline ice cream (£6.95). Wines from £16.50. Accommodation. Open all week.

▌Mells

NEW ENTRY

Talbot Inn

Historic coaching inn oozing civilised charm
Selwood Street, Mells, BA11 3PN
Tel no: (01373) 812254
www.talbotinn.com
British | £25
Cooking score: 3
£30

The 15th-century Talbot stands at the heart of a unique feudal village, overlooked by church and manor house. Push open the massive oak doors, enter the cobbled courtyard and step into a warren of passageways leading to beamed bars and dining rooms with open fires and candles on old dining tables. There's a relaxed and informal feel: the team behind the Beckford Arms (see entry Fonthill Gifford, Wiltshire) have worked their magic again and the place oozes civilised charm. Chef Pravin Nayar has moved across from the Beckford, but continues to deliver impeccable British food (with the occasional European accents) on his daily changing menus – veal carpaccio with capers, anchovies, Parmesan and rocket, perhaps, or leg of lamb with roasted garlic, mash and curly kale, or a pub classic like chicken, leek, tarragon and mushroom pie. Traditional desserts include buttermilk pudding with stewed rhubarb. House wine £17.
Chef/s: Pravin Nayar. **Open:** all week L 12 to 3, D 6 to 9.30. **Meals:** alc (main courses £8 to £19).
Details: 40 seats outside. Separate bar. Wheelchair access. Car parking.

▌Milverton

The Globe

Posh comfort food, served generously
Fore Street, Milverton, TA4 1JX
Tel no: (01823) 400534
www.theglobemilverton.co.uk
Modern British | £25
Cooking score: 2
£5 OFF 🛏 £30 🍽

A reader happily testifies that this pub-with-rooms some 15-minutes' drive from junction 25 of the M5 'is exactly the type of slightly remote country venue that the Guide must continue to promote'. Whether you are taking advantage of the terrace or warming yourself beside the wood burner (in an interior that's a lot more contemporary than indicated by this listed former coaching inn's façade), all is busy, convivial and unreservedly good-natured. The kitchen works in tandem with local and regional producers and imagination comes from near and far: chicken thighs stuffed with ricotta, spinach and semi-dried tomatoes; 'a good helping' of Creedy Carver duck breast with spiced plum sauce; and baked lemon cheese cake. Drink local ales or cider, or wines (from £13.95).
Chef/s: Mark Tarry and Kaan Atasoy. **Open:** Tue to Sun L 12 to 2, Mon to Sat D 7 to 9. **Meals:** alc (main courses £12 to £19). Sun L £12.95 (2 courses) to £15.95. **Details:** 50 seats. 20 seats outside. Wheelchair access. Car parking.

▌Shepton Mallet

ALSO RECOMMENDED
▲ Blostin's

29-33 Waterloo Road, Shepton Mallet, BA4 5HH
Tel no: (01749) 343648
www.blostins.co.uk
Modern British £5 OFF

Nick and Lynne Reed have done Shepton Mallet proud during their (almost) three decades in residence at this small bistro. As you might expect, Nick taps into the rich local and regional larder. His precise, uncluttered cooking is offered in the form of a short, set-price menu (£19 for two courses, £23 for three) or as seasonal specialities: perhaps Cornish crab tartlets with sauce grelette (£8.95) and rump of Exmoor venison with braised red cabbage and wild mushroom sauce (£19.95). Wines from £15.50. Open Tue to Sat D only.

■ Shepton Montague
The Montague Inn

A proper country pub with a pleasingly modern restaurant
Shepton Montague, BA9 8JW
Tel no: (01749) 813213
www.themontagueinn.co.uk
Modern European | £25
Cooking score: 1
£5 £30
OFF

Country pubs come in many guises, from gritty boozers to formal dining rooms – but some straddle the roles of pub and restaurant with ease. The Montague has a proper bar (complete with locals and dogs) as well as a bright, modern restaurant with lovely country views. Food ranges from a simple ploughman's to crispy egg with mushroom duxelles and bacon, followed by a tart of warm butternut squash, confit onion, vegetables and Taleggio. Finish with perfectly bittersweet chocolate brownie, peanut brittle and ice cream, or try the five-mile Cheddar board: five cheeses sourced within five miles of the pub. Wine from £14.50.
Chef/s: Matt Dean. **Open:** all week L 12 to 2 (2.30 Sun), Mon to Sat D 7 to 9. **Meals:** alc (main courses £12 to £19). **Details:** 70 seats. 50 seats outside. Separate bar. Wheelchair access. Car parking.

■ Taunton
Augustus Restaurant

Local hero goes solo
3 The Courtyard, St James Street, Taunton, TA1 1JR
Tel no: (01823) 324354
www.augustustaunton.co.uk
Modern British | £27
Cooking score: 5
£5 £30
OFF

The little nooks and crannies of Taunton are often hard to find if you're not in the local loop, but here's a venue definitely worth tracking down. Hiding in a little courtyard not far from the famous Castle Hotel, Augustus is a terraced restaurant fronted with French windows. It has a relaxed, informal ambience that contrasts favourably with the chef-patron's former residency at the Castle itself. Richard Guest is in full flow, cooking to a refined bistro template, with simple seasonal (sometimes gently inventive) dishes that are fully expressive of their ingredients. Deep-fried local goats' cheese is a universe away from the soggy pub norm, garnished with apple, pear, pomegranate and slivers of radish. Duck livers on toast with Calvados cream will waft you sensuously to Normandy, before mains follow on with an amply constituted fluffy-topped fish pie, or braised sika venison with ethereally light truffled gnocchi and cabbage. New spins on classic formulas produce fine pigeon Wellington or rabbit lasagne, and it all finishes with plum crumble or creamy rice pudding. A serviceable wine list opens at £17.
Chef/s: Richard Guest. **Open:** Tue to Sat L 12 to 3, D 6 to 9.30. **Closed:** Mon, Sun, 25 and 26 Dec, bank hols. **Meals:** alc (main courses £13 to £18). **Details:** 28 seats. 18 seats outside.

Castle Bow Bar and Grill
A suitably special setting for outstanding dishes
Castle Green, Taunton, TA1 1NF
Tel no: (01823) 328328
www.the-castle-hotel.com/brazz
British | £25
Cooking score: 5
🛏 £30

'Superb in every way,' says one reader of Liam Finnegan's clever, carefully considered cooking, which represents a return to form for a restaurant that has passed through the hands of some of the UK's leading chefs. A lusciously elegant, 1920s-style dining room, overseen by assured and friendly staff, makes a relaxed but suitably special setting for 'imaginative and creative' dishes informed by classic techniques and flavour combinations. An amuse of confit duck, red onion jam and pesto sets the bar high, the melting savoury notes of the duck brightened by sweet, acidic onions. Outstanding breads (try the honey and hop rolls) maintain that early promise, while scallops with pork belly, sorrel pesto and peas makes a generous, balanced starter. Finnegan's flair for flavour shines through in a main of gurnard with chive butter sauce, asparagus and succulent monk's beard, slivers of pickled beetroot striking a clever counterpoint to the mellow sauce. For dessert, try classic chocolate tart with white chocolate ice cream and Chantilly cream. A keenly priced list of international wines starts at £15.50.
Chef/s: Liam Finnegan. **Open:** all week L 12 to 3, D 6 to 9.30 (10 Fri and Sat). **Closed:** 25 Dec. **Meals:** alc (main course £10 to £18). **Details:** 55 seats. 8 seats outside. Separate bar. Wheelchair access.

The Willow Tree
Modish cooking in a low-beamed setting
3 Tower Lane, Taunton, TA1 4AR
Tel no: (01823) 352835
www.thewillowtreerestaurant.com
Modern British | £33
Cooking score: 5

A model of relaxed restraint in the heart of Taunton, this low-key neighbourhood restaurant works to a limited brief but still manages to generate fulsome praise from readers. 'Hard to fault' commented one satisfied customer, who also appreciated the 'efficient, friendly and unobtrusive service'. Chef Darren Sherlock and front-of-house partner Rita Rambellas go about their business in a low-beamed, 17th-century town house with cottagey interiors and logs in the inglenook, but there's nothing folksy about a menu that offers the likes of seared scallops with creamed leeks, tomato and chorizo dressing or lamb fillet on spinach accompanied by mini diced vegetables in a pastry box 'shaped like a miniature pie'. The kitchen also delivers satisfaction in the form of a three-part tasting of Loch Duart salmon and dresses up slow-cooked beef rib with red onion purée, a gateau of ox tongue and grilled aubergine. Dessert might bring the signature bread-and-butter pudding or something more modish such as star anise crème brûlée with toasted fennel and shortbread. Wines start at £18.95 (£5.75 a glass).
Chef/s: Darren Sherlock. **Open:** Tue, Wed, Fri and Sat D only 6.30 to 9. **Closed:** Mon, Thur, Sun, Jan, Aug. **Meals:** Set D Tue and Wed £27.95, Fri and Sat £32.95. **Details:** 25 seats. 10 seats outside. Separate bar.

Wedmore

The Swan

Simple, satisfying pub food
Cheddar Road, Wedmore, BS28 4EQ
Tel no: (01934) 710337
www.theswanwedmore.com
Modern British | £28
Cooking score: 2

🍽 £30

A sensitively refurbished Georgian coaching inn in a West Country village full of independent shops, the Swan is the embodiment of a country pub. It makes the most of the location (not far from Wells and the Levels) to draw on local farm supplies, which appear in a resourceful menu of modern European dishes. Ox heart bruschetta in apple balsamic isn't your pub staple, and nor is a main course of roast pollack with parsnip and chilli spelt risotto and salsa verde. That said, traditionalists are treated to the likes of Chew Valley rump steak with garlic butter and chips, char-grilled lamb burger or homemade ice creams such as raisin and cider brandy. House wines, Sauvignon and Sangiovese, cost £15.35, or £4.30 a glass. **Chef/s:** Tom Blake. **Open:** all week L 12 to 3, Mon to Sat D 6 to 9.45. **Closed:** 25 Dec. **Meals:** alc (main courses £11 to £22). **Details:** 115 seats. 70 seats outside. Separate bar. Wheelchair access. Car parking.

Wells

Goodfellows

Astute seafood cookery
5 Sadler Street, Wells, BA5 2RR
Tel no: (01749) 673866
www.goodfellowswells.co.uk
Modern British/Seafood | £42
Cooking score: 4

£5
OFF

'Surroundings are not luxurious but who wants luxury with food like this?' reports one happy regular of this 'excellent' seafood restaurant in the heart of Wells. What Goodfellows lacks in setting ('you're virtually

sitting in the kitchen') it more than makes up for in entertainment – it's a pleasure to watch the chefs at work. The results of their labours are perfectly timed, intelligent and deeply satisfying, from an opening pairing of soft brandade with crunchy red cabbage, sesame and the salty crunch of pancetta to a silky-fresh piece of sea bass with spring vegetables and umami-rich truffle sauce. For dessert you're shown a selection from the adjoining patisserie, perhaps a superb strawberry tart that teams sweet, juicy strawberries with white chocolate and perfect, crunchy pastry. Wash it down with decent international wines starting at £19.50. **Chef/s:** Adam Fellows. **Open:** Tue to Sat L 12 to 2, Wed to Sat D 6.30 to 9.30. **Closed:** Sun, Mon, 25 and 26 Dec, 5 to 20 Jan. **Meals:** alc (main courses £12 to £23). Set L £20 (2 courses) to £23.50. Set D £42. Tasting menu £58 (6 courses). **Details:** 40 seats. Wheelchair access.

The Old Spot

A supremely accomplished operation
12 Sadler Street, Wells, BA5 2SE
Tel no: (01749) 689099
www.theoldspot.co.uk
Modern British | £28
Cooking score: 4

£30

Diners come from far and wide to Ian and Clare Bates's city-centre restaurant, a converted Georgian town house with bow windows, backing on to the cathedral green. The winning formula is a combination of Clare's genuinely warm welcome, and Ian's finely tuned, confident cooking: a Franco-Italian celebration of West Country produce. Enthusiastic reporters have spoken of the warm salad of wood pigeon with bacon, pear and hazelnuts, or ham hock terrine with celeriac rémoulade, to start. Main-course successes have included roast halibut with fennel purée, peperonata and tapenade; crumbed pork loin with a fried egg, anchovy and capers; and perfectly timed onglet steak with horseradish cream, thick-cut chips and watercress. The fresh cream, sourced from

local Olive Farm, is 'out of this world', perhaps best enjoyed with a stickily impeccable rendition of tarte Tatin. An inspiring international miscellany of wines starts at £16.95 for Chilean Sauvignon or South African Pinotage.
Chef/s: Ian Bates. **Open:** Wed to Sun L 12.30 to 2.30, Tue to Sat D 7 to 10.30. **Closed:** Mon, 1 week Christmas. **Meals:** alc (main courses £13 to £22). Set L £15.50 (2 courses) to £18.50. Sun L £22.50. **Details:** 50 seats.

West Pennard
The Apple Tree Inn
Born-again village boozer
West Pennard, BA6 8ND
Tel no: (01749) 890060
www.appletreeglastonbury.co.uk
Modern British | £26
Cooking score: 3
£5 OFF 🍴 £30

Lee and Ally Evans have created 'the kind of place that everyone loves – not just foodies', claims an admirer of this born-again 16th-century hostelry. Flagstone floors, real fires, folksy handmade knick-knacks and five charming bedrooms are in tune with the rustic name, but Lee's kitchen is on the money when it comes to local sourcing and fresh, forthright seasonal flavours. British themes share the stage with ideas from faraway lands, so expect anything from mackerel fillet with green apple purée and celeriac, or braised blade of beef with parsley porridge and baby onions, to tea-smoked duck breast with confit gizzards and blood oranges or wild mushroom and spinach lasagne. There are fish specials from the day boats, too, as well as steaks with triple-cooked chips and mighty pork platters for sharing. The pub also has its own bakery, so bread is a must-have. Wines start at £14.50 (£3.90 a glass).
Chef/s: Lee Evans. **Open:** Tue to Sun L 12 to 2, D 6 to 8.30 (9.30 Sat). **Closed:** Mon, 25 and 26 Dec, 7 to 14 Jan. **Meals:** alc (main courses £12 to £19). Set L and early D £11.95 (2 courses) to £14.95. Sun L

£14.95 (2 courses) to £19.95. **Details:** 54 seats. 32 seats outside. Separate bar. Wheelchair access. Car parking.

Wookey Hole
The Wookey Hole Inn
Wacky, fun-loving village pub
High Street, Wookey Hole, BA5 1BP
Tel no: (01749) 676677
www.wookeyholeinn.com
Modern British | £30
Cooking score: 1
£5 OFF 🍴

Banging the drum for 'love, peace and great food', this singular village inn close to the famous caves is a live-wire hostelry with a good selection of real ale, including locally brewed Cheddar Ales. On the food front, too, due attention is paid to local produce – witness Wookey Hole cave-aged Cheddar sandwiches for lunch, and breadcrumbed Somerset Brie with plum chutney as a starter for dinner. There's also rump of West Country lamb with dauphinois potatoes and red onion tarte Tatin, and for dessert, caramelised poached pear with cinnamon sauce and vanilla ice cream. Wines from £15.50.
Chef/s: Adam Kennington. **Open:** all week L 12 to 2.30 (3 Sun), Mon to Sat D 6.30 to 9 (9.30 Fri and Sat). **Closed:** 25 and 26 Dec. **Meals:** alc (main courses £13 to £25). Sun L £16.95 (2 courses) to £19.95. **Details:** 66 seats. 75 seats outside. Car parking.

🍴 Please send us your feedback
To register your opinion about any restaurant listed in the Guide, or a new restaurant that you wish to bring to our attention, please visit the web address at the bottom of the page. Your feedback informs the content of the book and will be used to compile next year's reviews.

▌Wrington

NEW ENTRY

The Ethicurean

Garden-grown ingredients cooked with flair
Barley Wood Walled Garden, Long Lane,
Wrington, BS40 5SA
Tel no: (01934) 863713
www.theethicurean.com
British | £26
Cooking score: 2

£5 OFF £30

You can't get much closer to your ingredients than in a restored Victorian kitchen garden – and this one is a visitor attraction in its own right. The 'excellent' Ethicurean, located in a glasshouse, could easily have been a tagged-on tea room (tea and cakes are served) but the kitchen has real ambition, producing ethical and garden-grown ingredients with some originality and flair. Witness the spiky flavours of soused carrots, pickled rocket flowers and soused mackerel with cider brandy or the belly-warming comforts of 'melting' blade of beef with milk polenta ('as comforting as nursery food'), milk stout sauce and clove crumb. Chocolate brownie with salt-and-pepper caramel and toffee-apple sauce makes a rich, satisfying dessert. The wine list (from £21.50) includes some fascinating organic and English finds.
Chef/s: Matthew and Ian Pennington. **Open:** Tue to Sun L 10 to 4 (5.30 Sun), Fri and Sat D 7 to 10. **Closed:** Mon, 2 weeks mid Jan. **Meals:** alc (main courses £8 to £19). **Details:** 50 seats. 50 seats outside. Wheelchair access. Car parking.

🍴 JAMES KNAPPETT
Kitchen Table at Bubbledogs

Name three ingredients you couldn't cook without.
Liquorice, yoghurt and citrus fruits.

The most underrated ingredient is...
The potato.

What is your favourite time of year for food, and why?
Spring, because after a long winter of limited produce you start getting tons of ingredients to choose from.

Why do you think food and cooking has become so fashionable?
Because it's a great way to meet friends and family, and now there are so many choices and price points to please everybody.

What was your first professional dish?
Pear cake and liquorice ice-cream.

Which restaurant do you return to again and again?
Koya, Soho.

At the end of a long day, what do you like to cook?
Spicy Asian food.

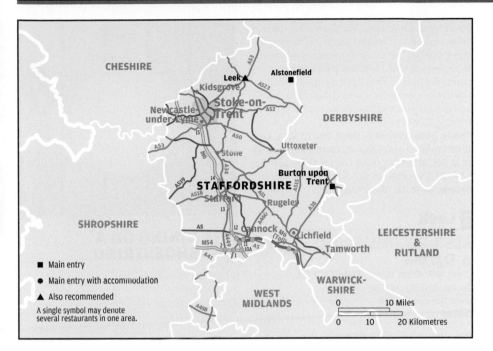

CHESHIRE

Leek▲

Alstonefield ■

Kidsgrove

Newcastle-under-Lyme

Stoke-on-Trent

A53
A523
A52
A50

DERBYSHIRE

Stone

Uttoxeter

STAFFORDSHIRE

Burton upon Trent ■

Stafford

Rugeley

A519
A518
A5

Cannock

Lichfield

Tamworth

M54
A449
A41
A458

LEICESTERSHIRE & RUTLAND

WARWICK-SHIRE

WEST MIDLANDS

■ Main entry
● Main entry with accommodation
▲ Also recommended
A single symbol may denote several restaurants in one area.

0   10 Miles
0   10   20 Kilometres

■ Alstonefield

The George
Village local with comfort food
Alstonefield, DE6 2FX
Tel no: (01335) 310205
www.thegeorgeatalstonefield.com
Modern British | £28
Cooking score: 2

£30

Emily Brighton's comforting village hostelry
commands great loyalty. 'We have been going
to the George for several years and while we
don't live in the immediate area we dine there
for special occasions and treats,' says one fan.
The pub with its snug and dining room and
simple country décor of open fire, bare
floorboards and tables with fresh flowers is run
with great warmth. To eat, reporters seem to
relish everything they are offered. Stilton
beignet with sautéed wild mushrooms and
spinach velouté makes a good start, followed
by roast rump and braised shoulder of lamb
with salsify, truffled dauphinois potatoes and

cabbage. Orange and chocolate tart with
crème fraîche ice cream concludes matters
sweetly. Wines from £15.
Chef/s: Chris Rooney. **Open:** all week L 12 to 2.30, D
6.30 to 9 (8 Sun). **Closed:** 25 Dec. **Meals:** alc (main
courses £11 to £28). **Details:** 46 seats. 60 seats
outside. Separate bar. Car parking.

■ Burton upon Trent

99 Station Street
Outstanding value from an old-town asset
99 Station Street, Burton upon Trent, DE14 1BT
Tel no: (01283) 516859
www.99stationstreet.com
Modern British | £35
Cooking score: 1

There is much to praise about this old-town
bistro a short walk from the train station. For a
start you'll find genuine hospitality here, and
Daniel Pilkington's simple bistro-style
cooking is underpinned by meticulously
sourced ingredients – as in a starter of confit
belly pork with locally produced black

pudding and red wine. Mains could include slow-braised and roasted shank of lamb with chive mashed potato or monkfish medallions with spinach and a tomato, prawn and coriander butter. Desserts keep up the standards, especially warm Bakewell tart with homemade jam and vanilla ice cream. Wines from £12.50.
Chef/s: Daniel Pilkington. **Open:** Wed to Sun L 12 to 2, Wed to Sat D 6.30 onwards. **Closed:** Mon, Tue, 24 to 31 Dec. **Meals:** alc (main courses £13 to £22). Set L £10.95 (2 courses) to £13. Sun L £16.95. **Details:** 44 seats. Wheelchair access.

Leek

ALSO RECOMMENDED
▲ Qarma
Cross Mill, Cross Street, Leek, ST13 6BL
Tel no: (01538) 387788
www.the-qarma.com
Indian

An innovative Indian restaurant in a former textile mill in a small-town location on the edge of the Peak District should have plenty going for it, and Qarma does. Its loyal band of regulars appreciates Abdul Malik's quality-led south Asian dishes, which reference the cuisines of Goa, Bangladesh and the Punjab, among others. Start with skewered king prawns in lime-spiked red masala (£4.95), and kick on with South Indian garlic chilli chicken from an organic corn-fed bird (£7.45), or aromatic minty lamb aloo (£8.75). There are old-time favourite dhansaks and pasandas as well, and a list of tandoori specials. Open all week D (lunch by reservation).

DINING ON A SHOESTRING

From a tiny coffee shop to a few tables at the back of a deli, from ethnic food to British pub classics, you really don't have to rely on swanky restaurants to celebrate the best of the country's food scene. Even better, you can enjoy these places without forking out too much. That revitalised Cambridge favourite, **Fitzbillies**, and Manchester's **Teacup on Thomas Street** are both well-known for their cakes, but simple savoury dishes do more than fill the gap between morning coffee and afternoon tea.

Superb local produce inspires the menu at **Pythouse Kitchen Garden Shop and Café**, Wiltshire, where soups, salads, savoury tarts and more are served in a bucolic setting. Alluringly stacked shelves, big wooden tables for sharing and a superior café menu are the attractions at **Brixham Deli**, Devon, while **Sojo**, Oxford, delivers proper Chinese food including congees, rice bowls and soup noodles.

Fantastic pizzas at the Dammone family's legendary **Salvo's**, Leeds, draw queues, but the budget prices of the broad-appeal menu help. If you're hankering for something more traditional, **The George**, Alstonefield, Staffordshire, is the place to go for fish and chips or local sausages.

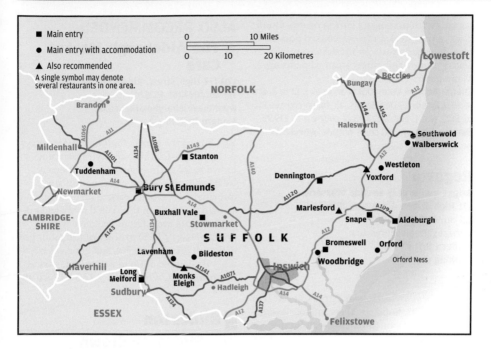

- ■ Main entry
- ● Main entry with accommodation
- ▲ Also recommended

A single symbol may denote several restaurants in one area.

0   10 Miles
0   10   20 Kilometres

NORFOLK

Lowestoft

Beccles

Bungay

Brandon

Halesworth

Southwold
Walberswick

Mildenhall

Stanton

Tuddenham

Westleton
Yoxford

Newmarket

Dennington

Bury St Edmunds

CAMBRIDGE-
SHIRE

Buxhall Vale

Stowmarket

Marlesford

Snape

Aldeburgh

S U F F O L K

Bromeswell

Orford

Lavenham

Bildeston

Woodbridge

Orford Ness

Haverhill

Long
Melford

Monks
Eleigh

Ipswich

Hadleigh

Sudbury

ESSEX

Felixstowe

■ Aldeburgh

The Lighthouse
Prime seafood and informal vibes
77 High Street, Aldeburgh, IP15 5AU
Tel no: (01728) 453377
www.lighthouserestaurant.co.uk
Modern British | £27
Cooking score: 1
£5 £30
OFF

Aldeburgh High Street is a competitive place to run a restaurant, but the informal Lighthouse meets the challenge, pulling in customers year round. They're tempted by fish – bought from boats selling the daily catch on the shingle beach and transformed by the duo of chefs, perhaps into a fish soup with rouille and croûton, or oven-baked cod on a mild tomato vegetable curry and rice. The meat menu is limited, though a slow-braised lamb shank on Savoy cabbage with new potatoes should satisfy. Any room? A chocolate truffle and marzipan cake is one way to end a meal here. House wine from £16.25.

Chef/s: Guy Welsh and Thierry Aubugeau. **Open:** all week L 12 to 2 (2.30 Sat and Sun), D 6.30 to 10. **Meals:** alc (main courses £11 to £22). Set L and D £10 (2 courses) to £15. **Details:** 90 seats. 16 seats outside. Wheelchair access.

One Five Two Aldeburgh
Unbuttoned neighbourhood eatery
152 High Street, Aldeburgh, IP15 5AX
Tel no: (01728) 454594
www.152aldeburgh.com
Modern European | £25
Cooking score: 1
£5 £30
OFF

Hidden down an alleyway between the High Street and the beach, One Five Two (or 152, if you prefer) occupies what was formerly Aldeburgh's music club. The tunesmiths have moved on, allowing the place to perform as an unbuttoned café-style eatery devoted to honest, unshowy cooking. Fish from the local boats is always a good shout on a menu that might run from rollmops with potato salad to

sea bass with prawn and saffron risotto. Confit duck, rump steak and slow-cooked pork belly please the carnivores, while desserts might feature honey and ginger steamed pudding. Wines from £14.95.
Chef/s: Andrew Lister. **Open:** all week L 12 to 3, D 6 to 10. **Closed:** 25 Dec. **Meals:** alc (main courses £10 to £19). Set L and D £13.95 (2 courses) to £19.95. **Details:** 53 seats. 20 seats outside. Wheelchair access.

Regatta
Bright and breezy seaside brasserie
171 High Street, Aldeburgh, IP15 5AN
Tel no: (01728) 452011
www.regattaaldeburgh.com
Modern British | £25
Cooking score: 1
£30

The Mabeys' stylish seaside restaurant caters to festival-goers, holidaymakers and locals with a menu of brasserie favourites, seafood specials and items smoked in-house over smouldering oak – the salmon with Thai cucumber salad is a banker. Otherwise, look to seared scallops with black pudding and bacon, and then piri-piri chicken on Caesar salad with jacket chips, or Gressingham duck breast on couscous in minted yoghurt dressing. Finish with the house summer pudding and cream in the season, or else a more fanciful Earl Grey pannacotta with fruit compote. Wines start at £15, or £4.50 a glass, for Chilean Merlot.
Chef/s: Robert Mabey. **Open:** all week L 12 to 2, D 6 to 10. **Closed:** 24 to 26 and 31 Dec, 1 Jan. **Meals:** alc (main courses £12 to £22). **Details:** 95 seats.

Symbols
🛏 Accommodation is available

£30 Three courses for less than £30

V Separate vegetarian menu

£5 £5-off voucher scheme

🍾 Notable wine list

ALSO RECOMMENDED
▲ The Aldeburgh Market Café
170-172 High Street, Aldeburgh, IP15 5AQ
Tel no: (01728) 452520
www.thealdeburghmarket.co.uk
Modern British £5 OFF

Sara Fox of the nearby Lighthouse (see entry) is responsible for this café-style restaurant linked to a fish shop and deli. It's a fiercely local foodie enterprise with an intimate, informal vibe, closely packed small tables and a menu majoring in fish. You'll find plenty of choice: from breakfast of kedgeree with poached egg (£6.75) to lunch of fish pie or pad thai with prawns (£8.50), and good cakes for tea – the lemon, almond and polenta cake is recommended. Wines from £12.50. Open all week.

▌Bildeston
The Bildeston Crown
Slick mix of old and new
High Street, Bildeston, IP7 7EB
Tel no: (01449) 740510
www.thebildestoncrown.co.uk
Modern British | £45
Cooking score: 4
£5 OFF 🛏

With a full contingent of beams, timbers and a roaring fire in the bar, plus bags of style throughout, this gentrified 15th-century inn-with-rooms certainly puts on a convincing show, good for both 'casual lunches and celebratory meals'. The kitchen's aim is to combine first-rate, well-sourced materials with uncomplicated modern cooking to produce a menu with broad appeal. From the complex to the straightforward, many dishes 'have been superb'. Simple classics have a please-all quality – for example, the well-reported 'speciality' burgers served with either Suffolk Gold cheese or foie gras and truffle – but the kitchen also turns out starters of sea trout with English snails, white beans and parsley, and mains of loin and braised shoulder of Suffolk venison with artichoke barigoule. There's applause, too, for the 'theatrical experience' of the tasting menu ('our best meal ever'), 'the attitude, knowledge and friendliness of the staff' and the 'well put together' wine list, which opens at £19. **Chef/s:** Chris Lee. **Open:** all week L 12 to 2.30, D 7 to 9.30. **Closed:** 24 to 26 Dec, 1 Jan. **Meals:** Set L and D £20.13. Sun L £25. Tasting menu £70 (8 courses). **Details:** 80 seats. 20 seats outside. Separate bar. Wheelchair access. Car parking.

▌Bromeswell

The British Larder

Enterprising regional food forays
Orford Road, Bromeswell, IP12 2PU
Tel no: (01394) 460310
www.britishlardersuffolk.co.uk
British | £30
Cooking score: 4
£5
OFF

With an online recipe hub spreading the word and a 'seasonal' cookbook under their belts, Ross Pike and Madalene Bonvini-Hamel are in bullish mood at their roadside pub. Not surprisingly, their forays into the world of regional food home in on Suffolk's larder: Butley oysters, Bramfield beef, Tunstall venison and Nacton beetroot all get a name-check on the daily menu. The food hits you with big, assertive flavours and the confidence is palpable: consider Cromer crab salad with avocado, watercress and crispy filo shards, or Bob Walden's rack of lamb with shoulder croquette, asparagus and wild garlic. The pair are also happy to give pub-grub throwbacks a shake-up, applying some canny on-trend touches here and there – witness a Dingley Dell pork tasting of hock Scotch egg, crispy bacon and frisée salad, raised pork pie and pork rillettes. To finish, 'divine desserts' have featured passion fruit pannacotta with coconut macaroon. Drinks run from local ciders, beers and juices to a short list of wines (from £16.50). **Chef/s:** Ross Pike and Madalene Bonvini-Hamel. **Open:** all week L 12 to 3 (3.30 Sun), D 6 to 9. **Closed:** Mon (7 Jan to 1 Apr). **Meals:** alc (main courses £13 to £22). Set L £15 (2 courses) to £18. **Details:** 73 seats. 100 seats outside. Separate bar. Wheelchair access. Car parking.

▌Bury St Edmunds

Maison Bleue

The freshest fish, worth seeking out
30-31 Churchgate Street, Bury St Edmunds, IP33 1RG
Tel no: (01284) 760623
www.maisonbleue.co.uk
Seafood | £34
Cooking score: 4

A few minutes' walk from St Edmundsbury Cathedral, in a light, comfortable setting that mixes ancient and modern trappings, this bastion of French seafood continues to impress. Traditional dishes such as fish soup with rouille and skate wing with capers make an appearance, but you can take a more adventurous journey if you like. Start, perhaps, with smoked eel with aged balsamic-glazed cauliflower, apple, green pepper, celery and prosciutto chips, then go on to red gurnard with glazed baby fennel, lemongrass and Chardonnay or monkfish with honeyed swede and a black peppercorn and veal reduction. With choice extending to saddle of venison with polenta, morel mushrooms and Cabernet Sauvignon sauce and pork with English chorizo sauce, meat is more than a sideline. Desserts can deliver a commendable honey and saffron crème brûlée. Expect excellent, efficient service, too, and a predominantly Gallic wine list with bottles from £16. **Chef/s:** Pascal Canevet. **Open:** Tue to Sat L 12 to 2, D 7 to 9.30. **Closed:** Sun, Mon, 3 weeks Jan, 2 weeks Aug. **Meals:** alc (main courses £17 to £30). Set L £18.50 (2 courses) to £22.50. Set D £32.50. **Details:** 65 seats.

▌♦ Visit us Online

To find out more about *The Good Food Guide*, please visit www.thegoodfoodguide.co.uk

Pea Porridge

Something quite special
28-29 Cannon Street, Bury St Edmunds, IP33 1JR
Tel no: (01284) 700200
www.peaporridge.co.uk
Modern British | £30
Cooking score: 3

Thank goodness for people like Justin and Jurga Sharp. The confident, original menu at the couple's adored neighbourhood restaurant makes welcome respite for diners fleeing chain-swamped Bury St Edmunds. Justin champions little-used cuts, so make him happy and choose a starter of grilled ox heart with dandelion, pickled walnuts and 'kohl' slaw, or subtly curried lamb sweetbreads. He's glad to buy locally, and braised Suffolk pig's cheek 'osso buco' style with saffron risotto, gremolata and crispy pig's ears is a popular main, but inspiration comes from further afield, too. A Lebanese-style lamb broth exudes Middle Eastern warmth, while cod with chickpeas, chorizo, piquillo peppers, mussels and aïoli whisks you straight to sunny Spain. End with an indulgent panettone bread-and-butter pudding. House wine starts at £14.95.
Chef/s: Justin Sharp. **Open:** Tue to Sat L 12 to 2, D 6 to 9.30 (10 Fri, Sat). **Closed:** Sun, Mon, 2 weeks Christmas and New Year, 2 weeks Sept. **Meals:** alc (main courses £13 to £20). Set L and D £12.50 (2 courses) to £16.50. **Details:** 46 seats. 8 seats outside. Children at lunch only.

ALSO RECOMMENDED
▲ Benson Blakes

88-89 St John's Street, Bury St Edmunds, IP33 1SQ
Tel no: (01284) 755188
www.bensonblakes.co.uk
Burgers

By day a great family-friendly, family-owned burger joint with 23 varieties and painless price tags; by night rammed with the youth of Bury, in for the fun bar atmosphere, fantastic craft beers and live music (Saturdays). This is an honest kitchen, a fine proponent of thoughtful local sourcing. Burgers are almost 100% Suffolk (local meat, daily baked buns) – wonderful when teamed with Suffolk black bacon, wholegrain mustard and red onion chutney (£6.95). Praise, too, for the pulled pork version with apple BBQ sauce (£9), the sweet potato chips and the excellent service.

▌ Buxhall Vale

NEW ENTRY
Buxhall Coach House
Bold Italian flavours in the depths of Suffolk
Buxhall Vale, IP14 3DH
Tel no: (01449) 736032
www.honortownsend.com
Italian | £31
Cooking score: 1
£5
OFF

Honor Townsend has finally brought years of cooking in Umbria back to Suffolk – and to judge by the full dining room, locals are glad. Expect bold, good food, generous portions and a welcome from Sarah, Honor's mother, as warm as the Italian sun. Apple and chilli jelly invigorates a sage-scented chicken liver parfait that's a meal in itself, while the robust flavours in sea bass with roast tomatoes, Umbrian lentils, peppers and basil pesto continue the hearty theme. Puddings delight: try a meringata semifreddo with raspberries and berry purée. With house wine at £22, this isn't a cheap night out, but it's worth it.
Chef/s: Honor Townsend. **Open:** Wed to Sun L 12 to 2.30, Wed to Sat D 7.30 to 9. **Closed:** Mon, Tue, 1 week Feb, 2 weeks Jul to Aug. **Meals:** alc (main courses £13 to £25). **Details:** 36 seats. 36 seats outside. Wheelchair access. Car parking.

▌▏● Readers Recommend

A 'readers recommend' review is a genuine quote from a report sent in by one of our readers. We intend to follow up these suggestions throughout the year to come.

Dennington

NEW ENTRY
The Dennington Queen
A welcoming pub in delightful village
The Square, Dennington, IP13 8AB
Tel no: (01728) 638421
www.thedenningtonqueen.co.uk
Modern British | £22
Cooking score: 1
£5 £30
OFF

Whether you're a fan of scrubbed floors, leather sofas and lots of taupe, or just want a break from the relentless bendiness of the Suffolk Tourist Route, it's worth paying homage to the Dennington Queen. The welcome is as friendly for passing trade as it is for the many loyal locals. Re-energise with softly sweet-braised new-season garlic with goats' cheese parfait, maybe followed by a lightly spiced Malaysian green beef curry, or hake fillet with a zesty cockle, caper and spring onion risotto. Chocolate soufflé is the gooey pick of the puds. House wine costs £14.50.
Chef/s: Martin Ryall. **Open:** all week L 12 to 2, D 6.30 to 9. **Meals:** alc (main courses £10 to £19). Set L £15 (2 courses) to £20. Set D £18.50 (2 courses) to £23.50. Sun L £11.50. **Details:** 55 seats. 30 seats outside. Car parking.

Easton

READERS RECOMMEND
White Horse
Modern British
The Street, Easton, IP13 0ED
Tel no: (01728) 746456
www.eastonwhitehorse.co.uk
'The menu, albeit quite small, was exactly what we were after. I had the salt-and-chilli squid, which was crispy and full of flavour. My main was pork belly, which had such a delicious crispy skin and the rest was melt in the mouth.'

Lavenham
The Great House
Impressive Gallic cooking
Market Place, Lavenham, CO10 9QZ
Tel no: (01787) 247431
www.greathouse.co.uk
Modern French | £40
Cooking score: 4

Is there any box the Great House doesn't tick? The (genteel) droves of returning diners are testament to the consistently exemplary cooking and faultless service that Régis Crépy and his team deliver. It's 'quite stunning' reported one regular, bowled over by another 'truly memorable' meal at this French restaurant in the photogenic heart of medieval Lavenham. The good-value set lunch gets applause, but popular à la carte options include roasted sardines filled with herbs, Parmesan and Swiss chard, tomato crostini and an anchovy, chilli and coriander dressing. Pan-fried calf's liver ('soft as butter') might follow, served with grilled bacon and raspberry sauce. The 'legendary' cheeseboard tempts many, but to finish on a sweet note, a rich dark chocolate and hazelnut tartelette accompanied by a clean blood-orange sorbet could fit the bill. By-the-glass options are plentiful on the drinks list, with house wine from just £15.95.
Chef/s: Régis Crépy. **Open:** Wed to Sun L 12 to 2.30, Tue to Sat D 7 to 9 (9.30 Fri and Sat). **Closed:** Mon, Jan, 2 weeks summer. **Meals:** alc (main courses £22 to £29). Set L £18.50 (2 courses) to £22.50. Set D and Sun L £33.50. **Details:** 50 seats. 20 seats outside. Car parking.

Long Melford

Scutchers

Quality ingredients and generous portions
Westgate Street, Long Melford, CO10 9DP
Tel no: (01787) 310200
www.scutchers.com
Modern British | £30
Cooking score: 2

A converted pub in the heart of Long Melford is home to Nick and Diane Barrett's personally run country restaurant. It's a model of tasteful domesticity and the food rings true. Opening only on Friday and Saturday is part of the appeal, and the menu treads a careful balance between modern ideas (salt-and-pepper tempura tiger prawn with a chilli dip) and the need to satisfy more conservative tastes (langoustine and avocado cocktail). Assertive European flavours are the hallmarks of dishes ranging from fillet of halibut with smoked haddock, prawn and leek chowder to roast loin of English lamb on crushed peas with wild garlic, rösti and a rosemary jus. Round off with apple pie ice cream with chocolate fudge sauce. Wines from £17.

Chef/s: Nick Barrett. **Open:** Fri and Sat L 12 to 2, D 7 to 9.30. **Closed:** Sun to Thur, 24 to 26 Dec. **Meals:** alc (main courses £16 to £28). **Details:** 60 seats. 40 seats outside. Separate bar. Wheelchair access. Car parking.

Marlesford

ALSO RECOMMENDED

▲ Farmcafé

Main Road (A12), Marlesford, IP13 0AG
Tel no: (01728) 747717
www.farmcafe.co.uk
British

For sheer unbranded oomph, this dedicated local food café and 'foodmarket' by the A12 knocks spots off most roadside pit-stops. Breakfast is the top deal, so pull in for a full Suffolk (£6.40), Orford kippers or organic mushrooms on toast. Come lunchtime, the emphasis shifts to colourful salads, ham-hock hash, bangers and mash, fish from the coast and double-crust pies with 'weird and wonderful' fillings (£9.90). Drinks range from yoghurt smoothies to Suffolk cider and wines from £3.40 (per quarter-bottle). Cakes, baguettes and take-aways, too. Open all week.

Monks Eleigh

ALSO RECOMMENDED

▲ The Swan Inn

The Street, Monks Eleigh, IP7 7AU
Tel no: (01449) 741391
www.monkseleigh.com
Modern British

Combining the virtues of a local pub and amenable village eating house, Carol and Nigel Ramsbottom's modernised thatched pub does the business with real ales on tap and an open fire in the bar, and a menu that deals in carefully sourced ingredients (local game, Brancaster mussels). The modern British brasserie cooking produces home-cured gravlax with lemon and mayonnaise (£6.75), individual beef Wellington with a mushroom duxelle and red wine sauce (£20.75), and iced brandy mousse. Wines from £14. Closed Mon.

Orford

The Trinity, Crown & Castle

Anglo-Italian flavours in a magical maritime setting
Orford, IP12 2LJ
Tel no: (01394) 450205
www.crownandcastle.co.uk
Modern British | £35
Cooking score: 4

V

Ruth and David Watson's career in the Guide has been an odyssey through some of East Anglia's premier destinations. Their present billet bears the hallmarks of simple elegance and lively informality, in a magical maritime setting by a 12th-century keep built for Henry II. To the untrained eye, the Trinity may look like a country pub, but in fact it's a showcase venue for Charlene Gavazzi's Anglo-Italian

cuisine. Start perhaps with a platter of salumi (finocchiona, coppa, wild boar and so forth), before sampling seared squid and pancetta with hummus. Modern Anglo dishes might encompass hake with saffroned cauliflower, raisins, pine nuts and aïoli, or pigeon breast and black pudding with confit garlic and mustard dressing. Crème caramel with prunes soaked in Earl Grey makes a fragrant finale. The colour-coded wine list looks as jolly as it drinks, with classification by grape and many creditable growers. Prices open at £17.95.
Chef/s: Charlene Gavazzi and Ruth Watson. **Open:** all week L 12.15 to 2.15, D 6.30 to 9.15. **Meals:** alc (main courses £15 to £25). **Details:** 50 seats. 50 seats outside. Separate bar. Wheelchair access.

Snape Maltings

NEW ENTRY
The Plough and Sail
Please-all pub with a maritime tang
Snape Maltings, IP17 1SR
Tel no: (01728) 688413
www.theploughandsailsnape.com
Modern British | £26
Cooking score: 1
£30

The twin brothers at the helm of this Snape Maltings pub are doing a grand job providing walkers, shoppers and concert-goers with a winning combination of 'courteous, charming, swift' service and a something-for-everyone menu. Fish gets star billing on a specials board where skate wing with anchovy, herb and caper butter, or locally caught slip Dover sole deliver well-cooked Suffolk flavours. A starter of homemade potted shrimps will get you in the coastal mood, and a lemon tart with poached rhubarb and crème fraîche makes a lively finish. House wine £14.50.
Chef/s: Oliver Burnside. **Open:** all week L 12 to 2.30, D 6 to late. **Closed:** 25 Dec. **Meals:** alc (main courses £11 to £18). **Details:** 75 seats. 30 seats outside. Wheelchair access. Car parking.

Southwold
The Crown Hotel
Buzzy pub with good food
90 High Street, Southwold, IP18 6DP
Tel no: (01502) 722275
www.adnams.co.uk
Modern British | £29
Cooking score: 2

'They now accept advance bookings,' yelped one regular visitor, referring to the characterful, often crowded bar of this 18th-century coaching inn. The Crown has been owned by Adnams, the Southwold-based wine merchant and brewer, for almost three decades. A penchant for local and regional supplies drives the menu, which might feature seafood (roulade of lemon sole with potato rösti, preserved lemon and brown shrimp butter, say) followed by whatever is currently available: maybe Simper Debden's mussels cooked with Broadside ale and bacon or braised lamb shoulder with kofte and sweetbread fritter. Finish with a cake of rhubarb and Norfolk-produced Binham Blue cheese. The Crown's jewel is undoubtedly its wine list. Defined by value and diversity, it offers around 20 varied house wines by the glass (from £5.50) and bottle (from £19.95) and moves on an illuminating tour through the world of serious modern drinking.
Chef/s: Tyler Torrance. **Open:** all week L 12 to 2 (2.30 Sat and Sun), D 6.30 to 9 (6 to 9.30 Sat). **Meals:** alc (main courses £14 to £20). Set L £14.95 (2 courses) to £16.95. Sun L £16.95 (2 courses). **Details:** 80 seats. 20 seats outside. Separate bar. Wheelchair access. Car parking.

Also Recommended
Also recommended entries are not scored but we think they are worth a visit.

Sutherland House

Oak-beamed heritage and low food miles
56 High Street, Southwold, IP18 6DN
Tel no: (01502) 724544
www.sutherlandhouse.co.uk
Modern British | £25
Cooking score: 2

£5 OFF 🍴 £30 🍷

Dating back partly to the mid–15th century, Sutherland House is named after a former ship's doctor turned Southwold mayor, so we're in venerable and exalted surroundings. Sustainable production and minimal food miles characterise the ethical approach of the kitchen, which turns out a sound seafood-based repertoire of modern dishes. Crab and avocado salad with tomato salsa, or steamed Asian-spiced red mullet on rice noodles blaze a trail for mains such as halibut with tiger prawns in bouillabaisse sauce, or perhaps braised belly and bacon-wrapped fillet of pork with apple fondant and mash, plus the award-winning house black pudding. Finish with brûlée-glazed bread-and-butter pudding and marmalade ice cream. House Chilean Sauvignon and Merlot are £17.
Chef/s: Jed Tedjada. **Open:** all week L 12 to 2, D 7 to 9. **Closed:** 2 weeks Jan, Mon (Oct to Mar). **Meals:** alc (main courses £18 to £26). Set L £12.50 (2 courses) to £16. **Details:** 48 seats. 30 seats outside. Wheelchair access.

▌Stanton

★ READERS' RESTAURANT OF THE YEAR ★
EAST ENGLAND

The Leaping Hare

Charming vineyard eatery
Wyken Vineyards, Stanton, IP31 2DW
Tel no: (01359) 250287
www.wykenvineyards.co.uk
Modern British | £27
Cooking score: 2

£5 OFF £30 🍷

'Warm, attractive, in a beautiful location' was one reporter's verdict on the Carlisles' 400-year-old barn conversion (now a well-bred, impressively timbered restaurant and café with a shop to one side). The Leaping Hare celebrated 20 years in 2013. It's a strongly rooted enterprise, noted for food that is estate grown or sourced, where possible, from the immediate locality. Lunch in the popular café – 'difficult to get a seat at weekends' – brings eggs Benedict, kedgeree, local sausages with mash and winter greens, and lovely cakes. Upgrade to the restaurant for the likes of Debden mussels cooked in Wyken white wine, cream and parsley, pheasant tagine with spiced giant couscous, and warm lemon meringue pie. Drink home-brewed Good Dog Ale or Chilean Sauvignon Blanc and Italian Barbera Amonte (£15). There's now little of the Wyken wine due to two years of appalling weather.
Chef/s: Jon Ellis. **Open:** all week L 12 to 2, Fri and Sat D 7 to 9. Café 10 to 6 (9am Sat, 10 to 5 Jan to Mar). **Closed:** 25 Dec to 5 Jan. **Meals:** alc (main courses £11 to £20). Set L £16.95 (2 courses) to £18.95. **Details:** 45 seats. 20 seats outside. Separate bar. Wheelchair access. Car parking.

▌Tuddenham

★ TOP 50 ★

Tuddenham Mill

Mesmerising skills in a seductive setting
High Street, Tuddenham, IP28 6SQ
Tel no: (01638) 713552
www.tuddenhammill.co.uk
Modern British | £40
Cooking score: 6

🍷 🍴

Rustic-chic, rural luxury, country-with-style – call it what you will, this is a place where sleek hospitality and classy, contemporary design collide joyfully with ancient beams, a dreamy millpond and acres of unspoilt Suffolk. Looks aren't everything, though, and Paul Foster cossets taste-buds with a 'natural modern British' menu that's as adventurous and on-trend as it is truly, deeply rooted in the location. He's a determined, nay, evangelical forager, but thankfully doesn't make a song and dance about it, preferring quietly, and ever so knowledgeably, to plunder the 12 acres around his kitchen. The edgy parsley/chervil flavour of alexander gives depth to a slow-cooked carrot, alexander soup and pine nut granola, while palate-cleansing mugwort, sheep's sorrel and wild garlic counter the richness of a salmon fillet. Lamb rump and shoulder, served simply with celeriac, salted pear and natural yoghurt is deemed 'excellent' by several enthusiastic diners, while Cornish plaice, salt-baked leek, aubergine and smoked roe is a natural bringing-together of four flavours that work. Ingredients here are celebrated and never unnecessarily over-worked. The purity of the cooking leads to blandness for the odd critic – an organic salmon 40°C fell into this trap for one diner, despite the thyme, oyster and sprout leaves. Of the puddings, chocolate, goats' milk and hazelnut with a scattering of mint is a deliciously bitter-sweet dream. House wine from £22.50.

Chef/s: Paul Foster. **Open:** all week L 12 to 2.15, D 6.30 to 9.15. **Meals:** alc (main courses £21 to £25). Set L and D £20 (2 courses) to £25. Sun L £25. **Details:** 54 seats. 40 seats outside. Separate bar. Car parking.

Walberswick
The Anchor
Eco-friendly seaside getaway
The Street, Walberswick, IP18 6UA
Tel no: (01502) 722112
www.anchoratwalberswick.com
Modern British | £25
Cooking score: 3

Sophie and Mark Dorber have created something special here, transforming this infectiously welcoming Arts and Crafts pub into a getaway du jour for Walberswick's weekenders and others who flit around self-styled 'Hampstead-on-Sea'. You can just glimpse dunes and sea from the dining room and terrace. As a disciple of the local/seasonal/free-range school of modern pub cooking, Sophie serves generous helpings of snappily presented food ranging from flavoursome

game terrine with home-baked bread or gin-cured gravlax with dill honey mustard to scallops with artichoke purée and fennel salad, and confit duck with chorizo and white bean stew. Drinks guru Mark provides illuminating suggestions for each dish: how about a glass of Endrizzi Brut Reserva fizz with beer-battered cod, or hot chocolate pudding accompanied by a bottle of Rochefort 10 Trappist ale? Breakfast and afternoon tapas complete an eco-friendly package, while wines (from £15.50) come courtesy of local boys Adnams.

Chef/s: Sophie Dorber. **Open:** all week L 12 to 3, D 6 to 9. **Closed:** 25 Dec. **Meals:** alc (main courses £14 to £23). Set L £14.50 (2 courses) to £17.50. **Details:** 60 seats. 100 seats outside. Separate bar. Wheelchair access. Car parking.

Westleton
NEW ENTRY
The Westleton Crown
Princely pickings at a tucked-away coastal treat
The Street, Westleton, IP17 3AD
Tel no: (01728) 648777
www.westletoncrown.co.uk
Modern British | £30
Cooking score: 1

No wonder William and Kate booked in here after a friend's wedding. This tucked-away coastal village is Suffolk at its pretty, pastel best, and the Westleton Crown will feed you well to boot. A rich, fragrant chicken liver and black truffle pâté makes a fine starter, and pan-fried tenderloin of Blythburgh pork with breaded crumb cheek boasts admirable local credentials. Leave room for pudding – and adequate time, as service can wobble. Crisp puff pastry, just-cooked fruit and a lively blackcurrant sauce make the pear tarte Tatin a choice fit for a king. House wine is a pricey £19.50.

Chef/s: Richard Bargewell. **Open:** all week L 12 to 2.30, D 6.30 to 9.30. **Meals:** alc (main courses £13 to £23). **Details:** 80 seats. 50 seats outside. Separate bar. Wheelchair access. Car parking.

▌Woodbridge

The Crown at Woodbridge
Stylish all-rounder
Thoroughfare, Woodbridge, IP12 1AD
Tel no: (01394) 384242
www.thecrownatwoodbridge.co.uk
Modern European | £25
Cooking score: 3

A lot of cash has obviously been lavished on this pristine-looking former coaching inn in the centre of Woodbridge. Inside, kooky novelties include a boat hull suspended over the granite-topped bar. The operation is unashamedly 21st century, with a lively and populist bar and plenty of opportunities for casual dining. Stephen David's intelligent and instinctively true contemporary cooking takes full account of East Anglian produce: in dishes such as roasted local mackerel (with heritage tomatoes, rocket, pesto and Suffolk trencher bread) or carpaccio of Suffolk beef, and in cider-braised local rabbit or roast Suffolk lamb rump (served with dauphinois potato, char-grilled globe artichoke, butternut squash purée and black olive jus). Crowd-pleasing finales have included dark chocolate fondant with chilli-spiced plums and lime-Tequila cream. Wines from £16.
Chef/s: Stephen David. **Open:** all week L 12 to 2.30, D 6 to 9.30. **Meals:** alc (main courses £13 to £25). Set L and D £18.50 (2 courses) to £23.50. Sun L £17.50. **Details:** 80 seats. 22 seats outside. Separate bar. Wheelchair access. Car parking.

The Riverside
Meals and movies by the river
Quay Street, Woodbridge, IP12 1BH
Tel no: (01394) 382587
www.theriverside.co.uk
Modern British | £26
Cooking score: 1
£30

An alfresco tapas lunch before the matinee is one reader's dream ticket at the Riverside – although special 'dinner and film' deals are the real money-spinners at this long-running restaurant embedded in Woodbridge's cinema/theatre complex. Either way, expect sound ingredients and confident cooking along the lines of ham-hock rillettes with pineapple and chilli salsa, sesame-crusted Blythburgh pork tenderloin or pan-fried hake with minted pea purée, langoustine tempura and straw potatoes. After that, roll the credits with Nanny Joy's sticky toffee pudding or an individual baked Alaska. House wine is £15.
Chef/s: Luke Parsons. **Open:** all week L 12 to 2.15 (2.30 Sun), Mon to Sat D 6 to 9.30 (10 Fri and Sat). **Closed:** 25 and 26 Dec. **Meals:** alc (main courses £13 to £25). Set D with film £30. **Details:** 40 seats. 34 seats outside. Separate bar. Wheelchair access.

▌Yoxford

ALSO RECOMMENDED
▲ Main's Restaurant
High Street, Yoxford, IP17 3EU
Tel no: (01728) 668882
www.mainsrestaurant.co.uk
Modern British

With a popular monthly bread-baking club and paupers' night (£14.40/£17 for two/three courses), a Saturday morning bakery (9am to 11am), and honest, seasonally aware dinners, Jason Vincent and Nancy Main's former draper's shop is quite a local asset. Come for dinner and white bean and roast garlic soup is a wholesome snip at £4, mains include slow-roast beef brisket with horseradish mash, and Dover sole with red pepper, oregano and sherry vinegar (£17), and irresistible desserts include îles flottante. Wines from £14. Open Thur to Sat D only.

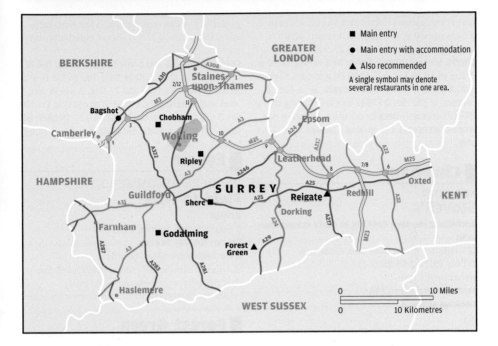

Bagshot

Michael Wignall at the Latymer

Breathless displays of contemporary cuisine
Pennyhill Park Hotel, London Road, Bagshot, GU19 5EU
Tel no: (01276) 486150
www.pennyhillpark.co.uk
Modern European | £78
Cooking score: 7

Sprawling Pennyhill Park could have been custom-built for photo-shoots. Château-style grounds envelop the greatly extended Victorian edifice, and the interior peddles luxury on a grand scale. Deep in the bowels of the hotel is Michael Wignall's Latymer Restaurant: a cocoon-like dining room fitted out with lime-green banquettes, latticed window panes and discreet glass screens. It's pure 'country house', with rather stiff, 'just so' service to match. In the kitchen, Wignall uses razor-sharp technique to 'bend and manipulate flavours': this is cooking as high-spec engineering, every detail precisely calibrated, refined and assembled in perfect symmetry. Although there is a carte, tasting menus provide the best opportunity to experience the results. The meat-free version offers a stunning play on vegetables in myriad forms – perhaps a 'booming savoury hit' involving roasted white asparagus and salsify on richly caramelised mushroom purée with a profusion of wild fungi, slivers of cleansing cured daikon and tarragon foam. Otherwise, expect breathless displays of contemporary cuisine: from an opener of cod poached in olive oil with confit organic egg yolk, harissa, Monmouthshire ham and shards of cabbage 'glass' to barbecued veal tongue and sweetbread in pork crackling with Hereford snail and pearl barley risotto. To conclude, desserts baffle, excite and seduce: try the sensational tiramisu 'made better' with rich coffee cream, a puff of almond espuma, milk ice cream, mocha butter and biscuit crumbs. The wine list is suitably plutocratic, with unforgiving prices (from £25.50).

Chef/s: Michael Wignall. **Open:** Wed to Fri L 12.30 to 2, Tue to Sat D 7 to 9.15 (9.30 Fri and Sat). **Closed:** Sun, Mon, first 2 weeks Jan. **Meals:** Set L £26 (2 courses) to £32. Set D £78 (3 courses). Tasting menu £92 (10 courses). **Details:** 50 seats. Separate bar. Wheelchair access. Car parking. Children over 12 yrs only.

Chobham

NEW ENTRY

Stovell's

Ambitious modern cooking in leafy commuter-land

125 Windsor Road, Chobham, GU24 8QS
Tel no: (01276) 858000
www.stovells.com
Modern European | £38
Cooking score: 5

£5
OFF

'All the food was absolutely fabulous, terrific tastes', is one enthusiastic verdict on the cooking at this impressively restored Tudor farmhouse on the outskirts of Chobham village. Inside, the old beams and timbers have been fashionably updated with a neutral colour scheme. It's unusual for a husband-and-wife team to both be in the kitchen, but Kristy and Fernando Stovell certainly know their stuff and the results are classy. A 'rich and full of flavour' leg of pata negra ham, displayed in the dining room, shows serious intent from the off (served as a special, hand-carved at table). Caramelised hand-dived Loch Leven scallops might appear with chorizo, ratte potatoes and a walnut dressing. Worth trying, too, is the trio of Hampshire rabbit (loin, leg and saddle), imaginatively teamed with pickled turnips, pistachio, yarrow and parsley purée. Alternatively, plump for the Cornish sea trout, partnered by grilled cucumber, ramsons (wild garlic), brown shrimps, yuzu and cashews, and don't miss the warm chocolate fondant to finish. Service is 'knowledgeable and

positively sunny-natured', and the first-rate wine list (from £17.50) shows equal attention to detail.

Chef/s: Fernando and Kristy Stovell. **Open:** Tue to Fri and Sun L 12 to 3.30 (4 Sun), Tue to Sat D 6 to 10.30. **Closed:** Mon, 26 and 27 Dec, 2 weeks Jan, 1 week Aug. **Meals:** Set L £15.50 (2 courses) to £19.50. Set D £30 (2 courses) to £38. Sun L £25. **Details:** 60 seats. 20 seats outside. Separate bar. Car parking.

Epsom

READERS RECOMMEND

Field to Fork

British
6 South Street, Epsom, KT18 7PF
Tel no: (01372) 744130
www.fieldtoforkrestaurant.com
'A relaxed atmosphere and a seasonal menu that celebrates the best of the English countryside and coast.'

Forest Green

ALSO RECOMMENDED
▲ The Parrot

Horsham Road, Forest Green, RH5 5RZ
Tel no: (01306) 621339
www.theparrot.co.uk
Modern British

With meat produced on the owners' 500-acre farm near Dorking, veg grown in the pub garden and even a shop selling appetising homemade comestibles, the enterprising Parrot certainly ticks all the boxes for provenance, food miles and sourcing. Visitors to this industrious village boozer can order from a tidy menu of robust dishes such as home-cured coppa with celeriac rémoulade (£6.85) or char-grilled hogget chops with rosemary-roasted potatoes and butternut squash (£16.95) as well as burgers, hotpots, pies and some fish from the South Coast. Wines from £17. No food Sun D.

Godalming

La Luna
Well-groomed Italian thoroughbred
10-14 Wharf Street, Godalming, GU7 1NN
Tel no: (01483) 414155
www.lalunarestaurant.co.uk
Italian | £28
Cooking score: 4

£5 OFF £30

Banish all memories of formula trattorias. Chic La Luna is all about Italian food in the modern era. A smart room in black and grey, with half-clothed tables in blond wood, it's a thoroughly relaxing space. Valentino Gentile is an enterprising chef, overlaying the age-old leave-it-alone philosophy of Italian eating with interesting combinations and techniques. A poached duck egg with crunchy walnut horseradish dressing, spinach and Parmesan is one way of embarking, and the ship sails on with a Gragnano pasta dish of monkfish, Gaeta olives and capers, or ink-black risotto with a seared scallop in gremolata. Main courses are slightly more traditional – witness chicken breast and leg cacciatora with cavolo nero and pancetta, or baked sea bream with herbed potatoes and smoked aubergine purée. Finish with vibrant Sicilian blood-orange tart with clotted cream – and watch out for special theme nights. The list of Italian regional wines is well-constructed, though mark-ups can be a touch heavy. Sicilian house wines are £15.50, small glasses £3.25.
Chef/s: Valentino Gentile. **Open:** Tue to Sat L 12 to 2, D 7 to 10. **Closed:** Sun, Mon, 2 weeks Aug. **Meals:** alc (main courses £12 to £20). Set L £13.50 (2 courses) to £16.50. **Details:** 58 seats.

Readers Recommend
A 'readers recommend' review is a genuine quote from a report sent in by one of our readers. We intend to follow up these suggestions throughout the year to come.

Reigate

ALSO RECOMMENDED
▲ The Dining Room
59a High Street, Reigate, RH2 9AE
Tel no: (01737) 226650
www.tonytobinrestaurants.co.uk
Modern British

A first-floor venue overlooking Reigate's High Street, Tony Tobin's smart restaurant remains abidingly popular with locals. It can run at a slightly brisk pace – too much so for one or two reporters – but the kitchen turns out commendable food. Chicken liver parfait ahead of turbot with creamed leeks, creamed potato and truffle dressing are typical of the carte (£31 for two courses); warm pea and pesto tart and slow-cooked lamb grace the set lunch and weekday dinner menu (£16.95 for two courses). Wines from £16.95. Closed Sat L and Sun D.

Ripley

Drake's Restaurant
Picture-perfect modern food
The Clock House, High Street, Ripley, GU23 6AQ
Tel no: (01483) 224777
www.drakesrestaurant.co.uk
Modern British | £60
Cooking score: 5

V

Steve and Serina Drake's landmark Georgian restaurant is recognisable by its old clock. The dining-room makes full use of towering windows, sturdy stripped beams and views over a beautifully maintained garden, a treat in the full bloom of summer. Fixed whole-table menus, labelled Journey and Discovery, are the heart of the operation, and represent a no-holds-barred tour of contemporary British technique. Tiny fragments of smoked mackerel with a seaweed dumpling might open proceedings, and be followed by a glazed scallop on celeriac purée with onion consommé poured over it. Ingredients stray beyond the mainstream for a course such as chicken hearts with raw broccoli and balls of liver parfait, where tough-textured astringency is a problem, and then there could be a sliver of grey mullet with samphire, oyster mayonnaise and miso foam. The principal item might be vigorously seasoned lamb loin on a mound of beans with charred aubergine purée, before an utterly bemusing presentation of frozen blue-cheese paste with a single raspberry and a pickled rose-petal arrives. If it all feels like too much of a stretch for the gastronomic sensibilities, relief is at hand in the form of a closer of 'chocolate breakfast', combining a mousse, milk ice cream, caramel and puffed rice. Steve Drake undoubtedly possesses the skill and intelligence to pull off avant-garde cooking with aplomb, but we wonder whether too many of these minuscule dishes represent a triumph of conception over properly joyous edibility. Neither do robotically chilly staff help, alas. On the resounding plus side, there is a very fine wine list, with much happy diversity, exciting quality and reasonable rates. Bottles start at £18, with an excellent range by the small glass from £5.50.

Chef/s: Steve Drake. **Open:** Wed to Sun L 12 to 2, Tue to Sun D 7 to 9.30. **Closed:** Mon, 25 and 26 Dec, 2 weeks Christmas, 2 weeks Aug. **Meals:** Set L £22 (2 courses) to £28. Set D £50 (2 courses) to £60. Journey menu £60. Discovery menu £84. **Details:** 40 seats. Separate bar.

▌Shere

Kinghams

Cottagey restaurant with creature-comfort niceties
Gomshall Lane, Shere, GU5 9HE
Tel no: (01483) 202168
www.kinghams-restaurant.co.uk
Modern British | £36
Cooking score: 2

£5
OFF

Paul Baker has clocked up two decades at this immensely likeable converted cottage on the edge of Shere. The sheltered garden with its heated gazebo is a huge draw. Inside feels very 'Sunday best' but without the stiff-collared formality: there are low beams, tables are

smartly laid and service runs along smoothly. Paul has built a reputation on a fail-safe formula of popular Anglo-French cooking that stays well within its comfort zone. Dishes are rich and sustaining, perhaps an open raviolo of smoked haddock with truffle-oil potato and a soft egg yolk to start, then loin of venison wrapped in a herb pancake with spinach, shallots and celeriac purée, with blackcurrant featuring in a baked cheesecake, compote and sorbet for dessert. Wines from £18.50.

Chef/s: Paul Baker. **Open:** Tue to Sun L 12 to 2 (5 Sun), Tue to Sat D 7 to 10. **Closed:** Mon, 25 Dec to 4 Jan. **Meals:** alc (main courses £15 to £21). Set L and D £16.95 (2 courses) to £23.90. Sun L £24.95. **Details:** 48 seats. 20 seats outside. Car parking.

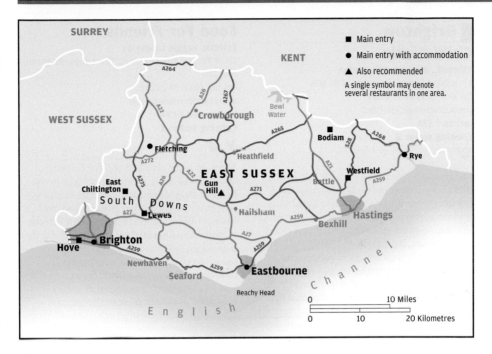

SURREY

KENT

- ■ Main entry
- ● Main entry with accommodation
- ▲ Also recommended

A single symbol may denote several restaurants in one area.

WEST SUSSEX

A264

Crowborough

Bewl Water

Bodiam

Rye

Fletching

Heathfield

EAST SUSSEX

Westfield

East Chiltington

Gun Hill

Battle

Hastings

South Downs

Lewes

Hailsham

Bexhill

Brighton

Hove

Newhaven

Eastbourne

Seaford

Beachy Head

English Channel

| 0 | 10 Miles |
| 0 | 10 | 20 Kilometres |

■ Bodiam

The Curlew

Seriously good stuff
Junction Road, Bodiam, TN32 5UY
Tel no: (01580) 861394
www.thecurlewrestaurant.co.uk
Modern British | £39
Cooking score: 4

£5 OFF **V**

The transformation of the Colleys' timber-framed 17th-century coaching inn into a sophisticated restaurant has removed all traces of rusticity. With its monotone grey walls, hung with prints depicting London landmarks, the place feels ready to head for the big city. On-view kitchen activities and a menu of modern British brasserie dishes seal the deal, and there's a commendable sense of fine-tuning to much of the cooking. A seared scallop, springy as marshmallow, is accompanied by crackled pork belly, apple cubes and blossom. The orchard-fruit theme might resurface in a main course of beautifully

judged pink venison with pickled Conference pear and creamy parsnip purée, while fish could be halibut with curried lentils in lemongrass sauce. A tart for two, topped with vanilla-infused pineapple and served with coconut and rum ice cream, is the splash-out way to finish. Biodynamic and natural wines are highlights of the stylistically arranged list. Try them by the glass from £7. Bottles of ordinary start at £18.50.

Chef/s: Andrew Scott. **Open:** all week L 12 to 2.30, D 6 to 9.30 (9 Sun). **Closed:** first week Jan. **Meals:** alc (main courses £18 to £23). Set L £20 (2 courses) to £25. **Details:** 64 seats. 32 seats outside.

Symbols

🛏 Accommodation is available

£30 Three courses for less than £30

V Separate vegetarian menu

£5 OFF £5-off voucher scheme

🍷 Notable wine list

▌Brighton

Chilli Pickle

Vibrant, idiosyncratic Indian
17 Jubilee Street, Brighton, BN1 1GE
Tel no: (01273) 900383
www.thechillipickle.com
Indian | £24
Cooking score: 3
£30

Originally a cult destination on The Lanes, this idiosyncratic Indian is now ensconced within the boutique confines of Brighton's myhotel. Mumbai market meets Bollywood in Chilli Pickle's glass-fronted, pastel-hued dining room, but it's the food that really fires up Brighton's spice lovers. Chef/proprietor Alun Sperring earned his stripes at London's Cinnamon Club (see entry), as shown in his fondness for vibrant contrasts, regional recipes and East-West crossovers. Lunch is a streetwise run through crisp nibbles, roti rolls and dosas, but the kitchen moves up a gear in the evening. The flavours come thick and fast, with accompaniments such as pungent homemade pickles making a big difference: steamed 'momo' dumplings are served with Tibetan vegetable broth, roasted tomato and timmur (Szechuan pepper) chutney; tandoori sea bream is coated in green peppercorn paste; and fragrant chicken biryani gets a kick from peanut and green-chilli relish. Cocktails, Belgian beers and punchy New World reds (from £19.95) match the food perfectly.
Chef/s: Alun Sperring. **Open:** all week L 12 to 3, D 6 to 10.30 (10 Sun). **Closed:** 25 and 26 Dec, 1 Jan. **Meals:** alc (main courses £10 to £19). Set D £23.50 (2 courses) to £26.50. Sun L £13 (2 courses). **Details:** 115 seats. 10 seats outside. Wheelchair access.

ᵾᵾ Visit us Online

To find out more about
The Good Food Guide, please visit
www.thegoodfoodguide.co.uk

Food For Friends

Eclectic veggie favourite
17-18 Prince Albert Street, The Lanes, Brighton, BN1 1HF
Tel no: (01273) 202310
www.foodforfriends.com
Vegetarian | £24
Cooking score: 1
V £30

Some 30 years on and Food for Friends continues to draw all manner of folk to the heart of Brighton's Lanes with its culinary circuit of the vegetarian globe. Head chef Michael Bremner has revitalised the eclectic menu with substantial yet sophisticated dishes, from open saffron ravioli with butternut squash to sweet Japanese tofu 'pockets'. Indulgent desserts take the form of coconut and sesame arancini and a rather gooey chocolate pudding. New to the menu is afternoon tea, featuring a selection of 15 brews and five homemade cakes and treats. House wine is £16.95.
Chef/s: Michael Bremner. **Open:** all week 12 to 10 (10.30 Fri and Sat). **Closed:** 25 Dec, 1 Jan. **Meals:** alc (main courses £12 to £14). Set L and D £20.95. Sun L £10.95. **Details:** 70 seats. 16 seats outside. Wheelchair access.

Gingerman

Jam-packed foodie hot spot
21a Norfolk Square, Brighton, BN1 2PD
Tel no: (01273) 326688
www.gingermanrestaurants.com
Modern European | £35
Cooking score: 3

Was it really as long ago as 1998 that Ben McKellar set about transforming the Brighton dining scene into the vibrant and enterprising attraction of today? His original venue was this small erstwhile tea room just up from the seafront, where brisk service and a menu of contemporary British food with an inventive edge continues to please. Among the latest offerings are a starter of white pudding made with pheasant, served with creamed cabbage and cherries cooked in port, and mains such as

slow-roast lamb shoulder with rosemary, anchovies and caper cream or cod with spätzle and baby fennel in red wine reduction. The fish of the day is always worth catching, and the soufflés (perhaps of mixed berries with frozen yoghurt and vanilla custard) also rise to the occasion. One guest left feeling 'relaxed and spoiled'. House Spanish is £15.50, or £3.90 a glass.
Chef/s: Ben McKellar and Simon Neville-Jones. **Open:** Tue to Sun L 12.30 to 2, D 7 to 10. **Closed:** Mon, 2 weeks Jan. **Meals:** Set L £15 (2 courses) to £18. Set D £30 (2 courses) to £35. Sun L £25. **Details:** 32 seats.

The Restaurant at Drakes
Fine dining at a classy boutique hotel
43-44 Marine Parade, Brighton, BN2 1PE
Tel no: (01273) 696934
www.therestaurantatdrakes.co.uk
Modern British | £40
Cooking score: 5

£5 OFF 🛏

The white-fronted boutique hotel on Brighton seafront, within virtual earshot of the screams of delight from the fairground rides on the pier, is a beacon of quality dining in Sussex's coolest and busiest coastal spot. Andrew MacKenzie's basement restaurant fits the place snugly, with a pleasantly laid-back but efficient ambience, and cooking that reaches into the European mainstream for dishes that do without the shock-tactic approach favoured elsewhere. A bowl of pea soup with Bellota ham and goats' curd raises the curtain on a summer tasting-menu that motors on with langoustine risotto garnished with coriander cress, before a satisfying main course of South Downs lamb with its sweetbreads, served with provençal veg and puréed dauphinoise. Anglo-European cheeses with fruit loaf and chutney pave the way for a perhaps too bracing lemon tart with matching sorbet. A relatively concise, serviceable wine list opens at £22 for Muscadet or Fleurie, with glasses from £6.50.

Chef/s: Andrew MacKenzie. **Open:** all week L 12.30 to 2, D 7 to 9.45. **Meals:** Set L £20 (2 courses) to £25. Set D £29.95 (2 courses) to £39.95. Sun L £25. **Details:** 38 seats. Separate bar. Car parking.

Terre à Terre
Quirky vegetarian favourite
71 East Street, Brighton, BN1 1HQ
Tel no: (01273) 729051
www.terreaterre.co.uk
Vegetarian | £30
Cooking score: 3
V

Fire caused by self-combusting tea towels forced this quirky veggie favourite to close for five months in early 2013, but Terre à Terre's colourful décor and forever-fervent demeanour is back with plenty of chutzpah – along with a smattering of eccentrically titled new dishes. Wild mushrooms and chestnuts abound in 'spruce shroom soufflé', while 'terre à tiffin' delights with a medley of zingy Indian treats. Regulars will be relieved to find the legendary 'rösti revisited' has returned, as has the amusingly named and lip-smackingly good pud 'nosey and nutty slack parkin'. Diners are spoilt for choice by a substantial list of extras and nibbles that includes cauliflower and ginger bhajis and deep-fried Grana Padano green olives. The sublime 'terre à tapas' – enough for two to share – epitomises the global melting pot of a menu. A good selection of wines is available by the glass, carafe or bottle from £17.80.
Chef/s: Phillip Taylor and Amanda Powley. **Open:** all week 12 to 10.30 (11 Sat, 10 Sun). **Closed:** 25 and 26 Dec. **Meals:** alc (main courses £15). Set D £30. **Details:** 110 seats. 15 seats outside. Wheelchair access.

ALSO RECOMMENDED

▲ Tookta's Cafe
30 Spring Street, Brighton, BN1 3EF
Tel no: (01273) 748071
Thai

Described as one of Brighton's best kept
secrets, this cosy Thai café on a quiet residential
street is overwhelmingly humble. Female
chef-owner Tookta dishes up a limited yet
freshly prepared and authentic menu of Thai
favourites. Mussels are delicately cooked in a
sweet chilli and basil sauce (£5.95), and the
spicy curries (from £9.95) are rich, decadent
and packed with crunchy vegetables and
succulent meats. The basic menu is surpassed
by Tookta's warm hospitality and an inviting
sense of dining in her eclectic living room.
Wine from £14. Open for D Tue to Sun.

East Chiltington

The Jolly Sportsman
Cheery hostelry that fits the bill
Chapel Lane, East Chiltington, BN7 3BA
Tel no: (01273) 890400
www.thejollysportsman.com
Modern British | £30
Cooking score: 2

With its weatherboarded exterior and an
interior that mixes rough stone walls with
warm colours and contemporary artworks,
Bruce Wass's lovely pub continues to draw the
crowds. The vibrant modern British bistro-
style dishes may be underpinned by classic
techniques but they are unfussy and driven by
prime local ingredients. Rye Bay scallops with
salt cod beignets, red pepper coulis and pea
velouté makes an enjoyable opener and might
precede a rump of local South Downs lamb
with peas, beans, artichoke and tarragon
served with dauphinois potatoes. The fixed-
price lunch and dinner menus are a bargain.
Finish with a no-frills pud such as rhubarb
fool and shortbread. The French-leaning wine
list opens at £16.50.

Chef/s: Anthony Masters and Bruce Wass. **Open:**
Tue to Sun L 12 to 2.30 (3.30 Sun), Tue to Sat D 6 to
9.30. **Closed:** Mon, 25 Dec. **Meals:** alc (main courses
£13 to £20). Set L £14.50 (2 courses) to £17.50. Set D
£19.50. Sun L £19.50. **Details:** 80 seats. 20 seats
outside. Separate bar. Wheelchair access. Car
parking.

Eastbourne

The Grand Hotel, Mirabelle
Gloriously traditional seafront hotel
King Edward's Parade, Eastbourne, BN21 4EQ
Tel no: (01323) 412345
www.grandeastbourne.com
Modern European | £50
Cooking score: 5
£5 OFF 🍴 🚗

A magnificent wedding cake of a building,
Eastbourne's Grand Hotel is the perfect setting
for this poised, elegant restaurant. Fine dining
is the name of the game: from the notice by
the door stipulating the dress code (jacket or
tie) to the extravagant drapery. Yet though
service is formal it isn't stiff, and the menu,
while broadly classic, is not as resolutely
backward-looking as the décor. An appetiser
of deconstructed goats' cheesecake with
beetroot marshmallow is a case in point. The à
la carte is exemplified by a 'perfectly risen' pike
mousseline soufflé with roast langoustine and
silky langoustine bisque. A main course of
roast sea bass with chorizo oil, aubergine
caviar, baby fennel and a black olive tapenade
cigar was equally sophisticated. This is
intelligent cooking, with keen attention to
flavour and texture, as shown in a 'crisp and
melting' dessert of rhubarb and apple filo pie
with brown-butter ice cream. A substantial
list of worldwide wines starts at £23.25 and
includes plenty by the glass or carafe.
Chef/s: Gerald Röser. **Open:** Tue to Sat L 12.30 to 2,
D 7 to 10. **Closed:** Sun, Mon, first 2 weeks Jan.
Meals: Set L £20 (2 courses) to £24. Set D £40.
Tasting menu £59.50. **Details:** 50 seats. Separate
bar. Wheelchair access. Car parking.

Fletching

The Griffin Inn
Recipe for a quality day out
Fletching, TN22 3SS
Tel no: (01825) 722890
www.thegriffininn.co.uk
Modern British | £30
Cooking score: 3

£5 OFF 🍷 🛏

Real fires, a glorious garden with stunning views, Sussex-brewed beers and pub food with big-city flavours reward visitors to this ancient village inn-with-rooms. It's a tribute to Nigel Pullen's 35 years of tenacity and dedication that he has managed to preserve the Griffin Inn as an honest-to-goodness country hostelry. It feels just right, so comfortable and easy is the atmosphere. The kitchen makes much of local produce but isn't immune to the charms of chorizo, couscous or an accurately made French sauce. Highlights include Rye Bay scallops with pumpkin purée, sage and capers, and roast rack of Romney Marsh lamb teamed with butternut squash, Puy lentils and salsa verde. Fancy a more homespun choice from the bar menu? Try chicken, leek and mushroom pie with parsley mash or char-grilled ribeye with chilli and garlic butter. Underpinning it all is a wine list offering tantalising drinking at ungreedy prices (from £14.90).
Chef/s: Matthew Sandells. Open: all week L 12 to 2.30 (3 Sat and Sun), Mon to Sat D 7 to 9.30. Closed: 25 Dec. Meals: alc (main courses £14 to £25). Sun L £25 (2 courses) to £30. Details: 60 seats. 25 seats outside. Separate bar. Wheelchair access. Car parking.

🍴 Average Price
The average price listed in main-entry reviews denotes the price of a three-course meal, without wine.

Gun Hill

ALSO RECOMMENDED
▲ The Gun
Gun Hill, TN21 0JU
Tel no: (01825) 872361
www.elitepubs.co.uk/the_gun
Modern British £5 OFF

Kid-friendly gardens overlooking the ancient Wealden Way are a highlight of this country inn reached up a long, winding road. The building has been extensively remodelled, giving the interior a deliberately rustic feel. Upmarket pub food is the order of the day: from open sandwiches and deli boards to wild mushroom and pheasant terrine (£5.80) or wild sea bass with spinach risotto, roasted fennel and crayfish sauce (£15.95). Home-baked breads, wholesome puds and real ales play their part, along with easy-drinking wines (from £17.60). Open all week.

Hove

The Foragers
Agreeable local with tasty flavours
3 Stirling Place, Hove, BN3 3YU
Tel no: (01273) 733134
www.theforagerspub.co.uk
Modern British | £23
Cooking score: 3

£5 OFF £30

With jumbled décor, real ales and simple wooden furnishings, the Foragers makes a good fist of being an ordinary street-corner boozer, but its kitchen, visible from the main bar, far exceeds expectations. True to the name, there are wild things on the menu, from ramsons to wood pigeon – maybe served as a starter with sautéed Portobello mushroom, parsnip purée and jus. A generous main course of roast duck breast with confit leg, potato fondant, red cabbage purée and orange jus is typical of the straight-talking style, which might also take in beef suet pie or beer-battered haloumi and chips. A slab of sticky toffee and walnut pudding with plenty of

sauce and homemade ice cream makes a wickedly moreish end note. The short selection of wines kicks off at £15.50.
Chef/s: Josh Kitson. **Open:** all week L 12 to 3 (4 Sat and Sun), Mon to Sat D 6 to 10. **Meals:** alc (main courses £9 to £15). Set L and D £12 (2 courses). **Details:** 80 seats. 80 seats outside. Separate bar.

The Ginger Pig
All-rounder with punchy flavours
3 Hove Street, Hove, BN3 2TR
Tel no: (01273) 736123
www.gingermanrestaurants.com
Modern British | £29
Cooking score: 4
£30

The original pub in Ben McKellar's Gingerman group would be a boon for any neighbourhood and is warmly appreciated by its followers. It works along comfortingly familiar lines, cleverly balancing all the virtues of a well-heeled hostelry thanks to genuine hospitality, real ales and good food. The kitchen is proud that it buys from local suppliers and while there's no standing on ceremony, the food can impress with a style that is unmistakably modern British brasserie. Recent highlights have been curried potted shrimps with fennel coleslaw and corn bread, confit pork belly with pineapple and chilli sorbet and peanut Asian salad, and a dish of chicken with pancetta, chorizo and crushed potatoes, which 'packed an enormous flavour punch'. Cheeses are always British and sweet treats to finish include lemon curd tart with star anise syrup and mascarpone ice cream. An international line-up of wines at fair prices (from £15.50) hits just the right note.
Chef/s: David Mothersill and Ben McKellar. **Open:** all week L 12 to 2 (3 Fri and Sat, 12.30 to 4 Sun), D 6.30 to 10 (9 Sun). **Closed:** 25 Dec. **Meals:** alc (main courses £13 to £19). Set L and early D £12.50 (2 courses). **Details:** 80 seats. 36 seats outside.

Graze
A romantic Regency-style showpiece
42 Western Road, Hove, BN3 1JD
Tel no: (01273) 823707
www.graze-restaurant.co.uk
Modern British | £34
Cooking score: 3
£5 OFF **V**

Luxury and low-key opulence sum up this lavishly appointed dining room: a romantic, Regency-style showpiece that fits well-to-do Hove like the proverbial kid glove. Red velvet upholstery, gilt-edged mirrors and flamboyant floral arrangements set the mood, while the kitchen puts great store by its extravagant seven-course tasting menus and thoughtful wine flights. Top seasonal produce and finely tuned technique are the hallmarks of muscular dishes including truffle-crusted halibut with cauliflower cheese and hand-rolled macaroni or shin of beef braised in Guinness with tongue, creamed parsnip, bone marrow and onions. The same ethos can be applied to lighter, more refreshing ideas ranging from tartare of Loch Duart salmon with apple, cucumber and poppy seeds to desserts such as blood-orange and vanilla pannacotta. Similar dishes are also available on the shorter (and cheaper) fixed-price menus. The wine list cherry-picks reputable names from around the globe, with prices from £18.
Chef/s: Adrian Hawkins. **Open:** all week L 12 to 2 (12.30 to 3.30 Sun), Mon to Sat D 6.30 to 9.30. **Closed:** 1 to 3 Jan. **Meals:** Set L £18. Set D £27 (2 courses) to £34. Sun L £18 (2 courses) to £22. Tasting menu £47 (7 courses). **Details:** 50 seats. 6 seats outside.

The Hove Kitchen
A buzzing hub for Hove
102-105 Western Road, Hove, BN3 1FA
Tel no: (01273) 725495
www.thehovekitchen.com
Modern European | £28
Cooking score: 2
£5 OFF £30

Big windows at the Hove Kitchen reveal an expansive space with tub chairs and bare-boarded floor, making the restaurant stand out from the plethora of eating options on this stretch of Western Road. Outdoor tables help, too. The kitchen knocks out energetic renditions of classic and modern Euro food, running from mussels in cider and cream or sticky deep-fried squid with fennel, chicory and pomegranate, through to satisfying main plates of cod and spinach with mash and olive sauce, or the cold-weather treat of breast and confit leg of locally shot pheasant with potato gratin, chestnuts, Brussels sprouts and quince. Alternatively, just order a cheeseburger with a big pile of fries, then a hunk of the famous River Café-inspired chocolate nemesis, dolloped with crème fraîche. Wines from £14.25.
Chef/s: Stephen Beadle. **Open:** all week 9am to 10pm (6 Sun and Mon). **Closed:** 26 Dec. **Meals:** alc (main courses £12 to £18). **Details:** 85 seats. 40 seats outside. Separate bar. Wheelchair access. No children after 9pm in restaurant.

NEW ENTRY
Little Fish Market
Neighbourhood newbie with maritime focus
10 Upper Market Street, Hove, BN3 1AS
Tel no: (01273) 722213
www.thelittlefishmarket.co.uk
Seafood | £31
Cooking score: 4

What better setting for a neighbourhood seafood restaurant than a former fishmonger's opposite an old fish market? The white-tiled premises were transformed into a bright yet modest space in early 2013 by chef/proprietor Duncan Ray (whose CV boasts the Fat Duck,

Bray and Pennyhill Park, Bagshot, see entries). Flying solo in the kitchen here, Ray seeks out the best of the local catch and serves it with a touch of unpretentious fine-dining swagger. Trout is delicately smoked with tea in an on-site smoker, 'meaty and rich' sea bass comes with crab ravioli. Finish with a decadent dark chocolate ganache with salted-caramel ice cream. Everything is made on the premises: bread, ice cream, even the butter is churned here. A fairly priced, concise wine list takes in California, New Zealand and Sussex varietals. Prices start at £18.
Chef/s: Duncan Ray. **Open:** Wed to Sun L 12 to 2 (3 Sun), Wed to Sat D 7 to 10. **Closed:** Mon, Tue, 24 Dec to 15 Jan. **Meals:** alc (main courses £17 to £19). **Details:** 22 seats.

▌Lewes
The Kings Head
Foodie pub for our times
9 Southover High Street, Lewes, BN7 1HS
Tel no: (01273) 474628
www.thekingsheadlewes.co.uk
Modern British | £22
Cooking score: 2
£30

Related to the Foragers in Hove (see entry), this born-again Victorian boozer occupies the site of a 16th-century alehouse not far from Southover Priory and Lewes Castle. As a foodie pub for our times, it sends out all the right signals − from organic bread and home-cured salmon to 'free-range' and 'local' tags across the menu. Ribeye steaks and Sussex cheeseburgers have a please-all appeal, but the kitchen also takes a broad-minded view of things: filling cannelloni with oxtail ragù; stuffing marinated Jerusalem artichokes with Comté cheese, hazelnuts and pickled chestnuts; serving dark chocolate and beetroot torte with malt caramel ice cream . . . and so on. Two dozen wines start at £15.50, or you might be tempted by a pint of locally brewed Harveys Sussex Bitter. See overleaf for details.

Chef/s: Jon Aldridge. Open: all week L 12 to 3 (4 Sun), Mon to Sat D 6 to 10. Meals: alc (main courses £10 to £19). Set L £12 (2 courses). Bar menu available. Details: 72 seats. 40 seats outside. Separate bar.

Rye

The Ambrette at Rye
Elegant Indian on top of its (local) game
White Vine House, 24 High Street, Rye, TN31 7JF
Tel no: (01797) 222043
www.theambrette.co.uk
Indian | £25
Cooking score: 1

£5 OFF V £30

Chef Dev Biswal moves between Rye and the original Ambrette in Margate (see entry), offering the same menu at both, though it's here at elegant White Vine House that his thoughtful cooking and the fine local ingredients come into their own. Biswal is strong on game, *viz* char-grilled clove-smoked partridge with pears to start or a main course of Kentish pheasant with a tomato, fenugreek and ginger sauce. That said, vegetarians fare well, too, with a dedicated menu of pan-Indian classics including cauliflower and carrot uppuma. Chocolate samosas with Darjeeling chai jelly make a choice finish. Wines from £14.95.
Chef/s: Dev Biswal and Deepak Suman. Open: Tue to Sun L 11.30 to 2.30, D 6 to 9.30 (5.30 to 10 Fri to Sun). Closed: Mon. Meals: alc (main courses £10 to £17). Set L £14.95 (2 courses) to £19.95. Tasting menu £40 (6 courses). Details: Wheelchair access.

Please send us your feedback
To register your opinion about any restaurant listed in the Guide, or a new restaurant that you wish to bring to our attention, please visit the web address at the bottom of the page. Your feedback informs the content of the book and will be used to compile next year's reviews.

The George Grill
Bolt-hole with quality crowd-pleasers
The George Inn, 98 High Street, Rye, TN31 7JT
Tel no: (01797) 222114
www.thegeorgeinrye.com
Modern European | £25
Cooking score: 2

You can see why the George in Rye is popular. A striking, centuries-old high street inn-cum-hotel with unusual flair, it can be thought of as a gentrified pub in two parts: where drinkers are welcome, and a smart grill-dining room delivering a menu of contemporary brasserie dishes. Basic materials are well sourced (many locally) and well handled, and simple classics have a please-all appeal, for example, 'the George' cheeseburger or ribeye with béarnaise. But the kitchen also turns out foie gras and chicken liver parfait; wood-grilled turbot with red chard, celeriac purée and sorrel; and Romney Marsh rump of lamb with pumpkin purée and rosemary jus. For dessert, there might be churros and hot chocolate sauce. Wines from £18.50.
Chef/s: Craig Wales. Open: all week 12 to 10. Meals: alc (main courses £8 to £32). Set L £16 (2 courses) to £19. Set D £33. Details: 75 seats. 20 seats outside. Separate bar.

Landgate Bistro
Landmark bistro that champions local food
5-6 Landgate, Rye, TN31 7LH
Tel no: (01797) 222829
www.landgatebistro.co.uk
Modern British | £29
Cooking score: 3

V £30

Martin Peacock continues to win over tourists and locals with his charming bistro in a pair of Georgian cottages next to the medieval Landgate. The kitchen is not trying to reinvent the wheel, but the carefully sourced local produce is precisely cooked and thoughtfully presented. One reporter has commended the homemade bread and 'helpful service', while another has praised the 'excellent food', which ranges from a starter of game terrine or fresh crab lasagne with white wine and lemon to a selection of cuts of Romney Marsh lamb, served with sugar snaps, baby carrots and gratin potatoes, and wild sea bass with a herb and cherry tomato risotto. A 'heavenly' chocolate brownie with cherries in Kirsch and homemade pistachio ice cream is among the impressive desserts. The modest wine list offers sound drinking from £15.

Chef/s: Martin Peacock. **Open:** Sat and Sun L 12 to 3, Wed to Sat D 7 to 10. Sun D 7 to 10 (bank hols only). **Closed:** Mon, Tue, 24 to 26 and 31 Dec, 1 Jan, 1 week Jun. **Meals:** alc (main courses £10 to £20). Set L £14.30 (2 courses) to £17.30. Set D £17.30 (2 courses) to £20.30. **Details:** 32 seats. Separate bar.

Webbe's at the Fish Café
Easy-going eatery with good local produce
17 Tower Street, Rye, TN31 7AT
Tel no: (01797) 222226
www.webbesrestaurants.co.uk
Seafood | £29
Cooking score: 2

£5 OFF   £30

The Webbes' restaurants and cafés are known locally for their emphasis on fresh, wild and seasonal food and this relaxed Rye brasserie is no exception. Seafood from local boats and ports is the focus, so you should certainly look out for Rye Bay scallops in carpaccio foam to start, and Loch Duart salmon and fennel salad or as a main with button onions, creamed potato, pancetta and vermouth sauce. Menus are lively and international. Bouillabaisse, tiger prawn noodle salad, fish and chips and wild sea bass with pesto tagliatelle coexist very happily here. Dessert might be local cheese or chocolate marquise mousse with griottine cherry. Crisp, dry French whites lead the wine list, from £15.95.

Chef/s: Matthew Drinkwater. **Open:** all week L 12 to 2.30, D 6 to 9.30. **Closed:** 24 to 26 Dec, 2 Jan for 2 weeks. **Meals:** alc (main courses £11 to £25). **Details:** 54 seats.

■ Westfield
The Wild Mushroom
Civilised country restaurant
Woodgate House, Westfield Lane, Westfield, TN35 4SB
Tel no: (01424) 751137
www.webbesrestaurants.co.uk
Modern British | £31
Cooking score: 2

A country sibling of Paul Webbe's Fish Café in Rye (see entry), this converted Victorian farmhouse is a likeable destination noted for its low-key sophistication, civilised charm, wallet-friendly prices and capable cooking. Clean, honest food with a nod to regional ingredients is the order of the day, as the kitchen works its way through a repertoire of unchallenging modern dishes ranging from dressed crab with Bramley apple jelly and cobnut toast or pan-fried Rye Bay scallops with creamed potato and chive velouté to breast and confit of Gressingham duck with damson sauce or slow-cooked ox cheek with garlicky herb mash and caramelised onion. To conclude, consider roast rhubarb with vanilla pannacotta and hazelnut macaroon. House wine is £16.95.

Chef/s: Chris Weddle. **Open:** Wed to Sun L 12 to 2 (2.30 Sun), Wed to Sat D 7 to 9.30 (10 Sat). **Closed:** Mon, Tue, 1 to 10 Jan. **Meals:** alc (main courses £13 to £20). Set L £16.95 (2 courses) to £19.95. Sun L £23. Tasting menu £34 (6 courses). **Details:** 40 seats. Separate bar. Wheelchair access. Car parking.

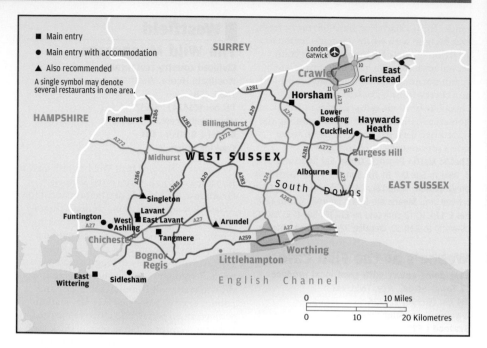

Map legend:
- ■ Main entry
- ● Main entry with accommodation
- ▲ Also recommended

A single symbol may denote several restaurants in one area.

SURREY
HAMPSHIRE
London Gatwick
Crawley
East Grinstead
Horsham
Fernhurst
Billingshurst
Lower Beeding
Haywards Heath
Cuckfield
Midhurst
WEST SUSSEX
Burgess Hill
Albourne
EAST SUSSEX
South Downs
Singleton
Lavant
Funtington
West Ashling
East Lavant
Arundel
Chichester
Tangmere
Bognor Regis
Littlehampton
Worthing
East Wittering
Sidlesham
English Channel

0 — 10 Miles
0 — 10 — 20 Kilometres

▌Albourne

The Ginger Fox

The complete package
Muddleswood Road, Albourne, BN6 9EA
Tel no: (01273) 857888
www.gingermanrestaurants.com
Modern British | £35
Cooking score: 4

Ben McKellar of Gingerman (see entry) owns a clutch of restaurants in Brighton and Hove, but he dipped a toe in the Sussex hinterland when he opened this thoroughly engaging country pub in 2008. Its thatched roof, trestle tables and vegetable beds look suitably rustic, and the bracing views over the South Downs help, too. James Dearden interprets the Ginger style well, innovative touches adding character to the oft-changing menu. An Indian-style mussel pakora accompanies mussel mouclade to start, while smoked ham hock with mustard gnocchi and cider cream makes a more hearty opener. Continue with sterling comfort food such as braised beef cheek with horseradish mash, or the more speculative likes of poached skate with clam and bacon chowder and sweetcorn ravioli. Rounding things off comes chocolate and bourbon tart with pecan praline ice cream. A short but serviceable wine list opens with house Spanish at £15.50.
Chef/s: James Dearden and Ben McKellar. **Open:** all week L 12 to 2 (3 Sat, 4 Sun), D 6 to 10 (6.30 Sat, 9 Sun). **Closed:** 25 Dec. **Meals:** alc (main courses £13 to £19). Set L £12.50 (2 courses). **Details:** 62 seats. 80 seats outside. Separate bar. Car parking.

▌Arundel

ALSO RECOMMENDED
▲ The Town House
65 High Street, Arundel, BN18 9AJ
Tel no: (01903) 883847
www.thetownhouse.co.uk
Modern British £5 OFF

Just steps from Arundel Castle, with an impressive Italian carved walnut ceiling dating from the 16th century and linen-swathed tables, Lee Williams' elegant restaurant (with-rooms) has many fans. His cooking is fashionably simple and mostly seasonal, standing out for the quality of ingredients and sheer good value. A dinner in February (£23.50 for two courses) produced beautifully presented warm chorizo, goats' cheese and cranberry salad, and whole-roasted partridge with spinach, wild mushrooms and game chips. Wines from £16.50. Closed Sun, Mon. Accommodation.

Chilgrove

READERS RECOMMEND
White Horse
Modern British
1 High Street, Chilgrove, PO18 9HX
Tel no: (01243) 519444
www.thewhitehorse.co.uk
'I see that the head chef is from the Ledbury. The food I sampled for lunch was really different − imaginative and good.'

Cuckfield
Ockenden Manor
Confident cooking with panache
Ockenden Lane, Cuckfield, RH17 5LD
Tel no: (01444) 416111
www.hshotels.co.uk
Modern French | £54
Cooking score: 5
£5 OFF 🛏

In the heart of Cuckfield, but hidden away in nine acres of pristine landscaped grounds, this thoughtfully extended 17th-century manor exudes an air of aristocratic gentility − even though it now sports all mod cons including a spa. Inside, it is grand in a low-key kind of way, whether you're relaxing in the public rooms or dining in the restaurant. Chef Stephen Crane has honed his confident approach to perfection over the past 12 years here, applying detailed composition and bags of panache to luxurious ingredients. Restraint and intricacy go hand in hand, witness an assiette of Longhorn beef involving bresaola,

bonbon, tongue and bone marrow fortified with horseradish, or a three-part dish of Balcombe venison. Fish also receives elaborate treatment, from hand-dived scallops with creamy cabbage, garlic crisps and red wine sauce to turbot partnered by artichokes, spring onions, purple sprouting broccoli and crispy shallots. Desserts such as milk chocolate délice with passion fruit sorbet and mango salad are marvels of the patissier's craft, and the wine list is a thoughtfully composed heavyweight, with house selections from £25 (£6.50 a glass).
Chef/s: Stephen Crane. Open: all week L 12 to 2, D 6.30 to 9. Meals: Set L £17.95 (2 courses) to £24.90. Set D £54. Sun L £34.50. Details: 80 seats. Separate bar. Wheelchair access. Car parking.

East Grinstead
Gravetye Manor
Enchanting Elizabethan charmer
Vowels Lane, East Grinstead, RH19 4LJ
Tel no: (01342) 810567
www.gravetyemanor.co.uk
Modern British | £58
Cooking score: 4
🍷 🛏

Built around 1598, this marvel of Elizabethan enchantment has always been a charmer, seducing guests with its grandiose architecture and lovingly arrayed gardens − reconfigured by Victorian horticultural godfather, William Robinson. A stroll around the grounds is a must, before sampling some finely executed contemporary cooking that combines a proper sense of ambition with an allegiance to native produce. Expect signature plates of butter-poached lobster, roast local partridge and Balcombe venison alongside complex pan-European assemblages such as seared pavé of Rougié foie gras with rich duck consommé, celeriac and apple, or fillet of red mullet with ratatouille, black olive tapenade and bouillabaisse sauce. To finish, soufflés such as passion fruit with coconut sorbet and passion fruit jelly are 'always impeccable'. Service is warm, sympathetic and knowledgeable, especially when navigating guests through the majestic 500-bin wine list: a paragon of good breeding, impeccable vintages and glorious drinking opportunities. Old World grandees dominate, but youth and vigour is here, too. Prices from £28.

Chef/s: Rupert Gleadow. **Open:** all week L 12 to 2, D 6.30 to 9.30. **Meals:** alc (main courses £27 to £32). Set L £25 (2 courses) to £29.50. Set D £40 (4 courses). Sun L £35. Tasting menu £75 (7 courses). **Details:** 40 seats. 20 seats outside. Separate bar. Wheelchair access. Car parking. Children over 7 yrs only.

East Lavant

NEW ENTRY
The Royal Oak Inn
Very much a dining destination
Pook Lane, East Lavant, PO18 0AX
Tel no: (01243) 527434
www.royaloakeastlavant.co.uk
Modern British | £33
Cooking score: 2
£5 OFF

With Chichester just two miles away, and the South Downs, Goodwood House and racecourse on the doorstep, this 200-year-old cottage-style pub thrives as a dining destination. Blazing winter fires and ales tapped from the cask contribute to the rustic mood, but wooden floors, leather sofas and fat candles on old dining tables create more of a restaurant feel. Bar snacks are served alongside a set-lunch menu of pub classics, with the more imaginative carte delivering reliable modern cooking in the shape of 'beautifully cooked and presented' panache of seafood (bream, hake, bass) with white wine cream, and duck, cooked pink, served on greens with dauphinois and red wine sauce. Round off with a 'zesty and delicious' lemon tart with homemade ice cream. Wines from £17.

Chef/s: Daniel Ward. **Open:** all week L 12 to 2.30, D 6 to 9 (9.30 Sat). **Meals:** alc (main courses £15 to £28). Set L £16.95 (2 courses) to £19.95. **Details:** 50 seats. 30 seats outside. Car parking.

East Wittering
Samphire
Laid-back by the beach
57 Shore Road, East Wittering, PO20 8DY
Tel no: (01243) 672754
www.samphireeastwittering.co.uk
Modern British | £35
Cooking score: 2
£5 OFF

It's billed as an English kitchen, but for one correspondent, Samphire's 'laid-back aesthetics and atmosphere' bring the Caribbean to mind. Wittering beach is just 50 metres from David Skinner's small, cosy restaurant. As you'd hope, the local catch makes appearances in dishes such as Selsey crab cake with crisp pork belly and a fennel, chilli and blood-orange salad, or a south coast fish stew packed with pollack, mussels and prawns. Service is 'warm', although there have been missteps with timing. To finish, there'll be something with seasonal fruit, such as a vivid forced rhubarb, apple and blood-orange crumble, or some Sussex cheese. Wine is from £15.

Chef/s: David Skinner. **Open:** all week L 12 to 2, D 6 to 9. **Closed:** Sun, 25 Dec to 25 Jan. **Meals:** alc (main courses £14 to £18). Set L £13 (2 courses) to £16. **Details:** 30 seats. 12 seats outside.

Fernhurst
The Duke of Cumberland Arms
Archetypal country pub with high aspirations
Henley, Fernhurst, GU27 3HQ
Tel no: (01428) 652280
www.dukeofcumberland.com
Modern British | £32
Cooking score: 4

On the one hand, this is an archetypal Sussex country pub, complete with ancient beamed bar, real ales tapped from the cask, tiered gardens, ponds and lovely terraces with bosky views over the Downs; on the other, it has high gastronomic aspirations. Ancient pubby virtues meet serious foodie intent here, and the kitchen proves its worth with a roster of dishes designed to show off its culinary skills and respect for Sussex produce. Head for the contemporary dining room if you hanker after pan-seared scallops with sweet potato purée, black pudding and truffle oil, followed by haunch of South Downs venison with braised red cabbage, roast beetroot, port and redcurrant jus. Alternatively, lap up the warm Mediterranean flavours of seafood linguine or pea, prawn and crayfish risotto. For afters, keep it seasonal with a three-part assiette of rhubarb or press the nostalgia button for brown-bread-and-butter pudding with vanilla custard. Wines start at £14 (£3.95 a glass).

Chef/s: Simon Goodman. **Open:** all week L 12 to 2, Tue to Sat D 7 to 9. **Closed:** 25 and 26 Dec. **Meals:** alc (main courses £15 to £32). **Details:** 60 seats. 130 seats outside. Wheelchair access. Car parking.

Funtington

Hallidays

Village restaurant with good-value food
Watery Lane, Funtington, PO18 9LF
Tel no: (01243) 575331
www.hallidays.info
Modern British | £35
Cooking score: 2
£5 OFF

For 17 years the Stephensons' charming thatched restaurant has been dispensing high-quality cooking with a resolute focus on value on the plate. Interiors are traditionally English with ceilings as beamed as you would expect in such a centuries-old building, but the kitchen is far from retro with Andy Stephenson using sound local and regional ingredients to create modern British dishes. Starters such as salt cod fritters with smoky paprika aïoli and mains of grilled monkfish with orange and onion confit or pot-roast rabbit with smoked aubergine purée and Serrano ham are typical choices. Desserts bring a rather fine Seville orange buttermilk

mousse with rhubarb and sugared almonds. Service is solicitous and the wine list opens at £18.75.

Chef/s: Andrew Stephenson. **Open:** Wed to Fri and Sun L 12 to 2. Wed to Sat D 7 to 10. **Closed:** Mon, Tue, 1 week Mar, 2 weeks Aug. **Meals:** alc (main courses £17 to £20). Set L £16 (2 courses) to £22.50. Set D £21 (2 courses) to £27.50. Sun L £23. **Details:** 26 seats. Separate bar. Car parking.

Haywards Heath

Jeremy's Restaurant

Special occasion dining at everyday prices
Borde Hill Garden, Balcombe Road, Haywards Heath, RH16 1XP
Tel no: (01444) 441102
www.jeremysrestaurant.co.uk
Modern British | £42
Cooking score: 4
£5 OFF

Within the pastoral purlieu of Borde Hill Gardens, Jeremy Ashpool's place is a treat at any time of year, but best in summer. Theme events include jazz lunches and barbecue evenings with expert wine tuition. The kitchen team specialises in a considered version of modern British food, full of interesting partnerships but without the techno-gimmicks. Crab arancini and squid in romesco, or a plate of local Balcombe Estate venison with puréed mushrooms and blood orange, make vibrant introductions to a menu that might go on to grilled hake with clams, sea purslane and gnocchi in cucumber sauce. Lamb is given the full treatment, with loin and confit belly, Swiss chard, saffron-scented sweetcorn purée and rosemary jus, before desserts with a savoury twist bring on poached pear with Slipcote cheese mousse, or pistachio olive cake with black olives and fennel sorbet in tarragon oil. Wines are grouped by style, opening at £16.50, or £5 a glass.

Chef/s: Jimmy Grey and Simon Denny. **Open:** Tue to Sun L 12.30 to 2.30, Tue to Sat D 7 to 9.30. **Closed:** Mon, first 2 weeks Jan. **Meals:** alc (main courses £15 to £25). Set L and D £16 (2 courses) to £19. Sun L

£24 (2 courses) to £29.50. **Details:** 55 seats. 40 seats outside. Separate bar. Wheelchair access. Car parking.

Horsham

Restaurant Tristan
Outstanding cooking at modest prices
3 Stans Way, Horsham, RH12 1HU
Tel no: (01403) 255688
www.restauranttristan.co.uk
Modern British | £42
Cooking score: 6

'Every visit we make provides a brilliant experience with food', is one regular's view of Tristan Mason's 'confident' restaurant secreted in a tranquil world of its own above the chef's all-day bar-café in a beamed, 16th-century house in old Horsham. His menu may be written in modern, understated fashion, but what turns up on the plate is always more expressive. A flawlessly prepared starter of plump, succulent scallops teamed with white chocolate risotto (served as arancini) and dill is an elegant surprise. Likewise, meaty monkfish – with beetroot textures, goats' curd and winter truffle – reinforces the impression of cooking that is at once sophisticated and accessible, reliant on fail-safe luxuries deployed in a modestly creative manner. Price-wise, it's a fair deal, considering the portions, the amuse-bouche, the pre-dessert and the very good and generously proffered bread – as well as the attentive, polite service. Indeed, one gloriously rich banana tarte Tatin, with dabs of intense lemon sauce, caramelised walnuts and an unusual parsley ice cream could easily satisfy two people. The wine list follows the menu's lead: urbane but approachable, with prices from £21.
Chef/s: Tristan Mason. **Open:** Tue to Sat L 12 to 2.30, D 6.30 to 9.30. **Closed:** Sun, Mon, first week Jan, last week Jul, first week Aug. **Meals:** Set L £18 (2 courses) to £24. Set D £34 (2 courses) to £42. **Details:** 34 seats. Separate bar.

Lavant

The Earl of March
Finely honed seasonal dishes
Lavant Road, Lavant, PO18 0BQ
Tel no: (01243) 533993
www.theearlofmarch.com
Modern British | £33
Cooking score: 4
£5 OFF V

The views out towards Goodwood and the South Downs haven't changed much since 1803, when William Blake was inspired to pen the words of 'Jerusalem' while admiring the prospect from this historic Sussex hostelry. These days, however, patriots are more likely to burst into song after sampling the fruits of Giles Thompson's culinary labours. Pub lunches are served in the bar, but it pays to trade up to the restaurant for an inviting checklist of finely honed seasonal dishes such as roast partridge with mulled plums, quail's egg, cep broth and pickled mushrooms. Thompson's forays into the Sussex larder and beyond might also yield anything from seared scallops with langoustines, pork belly, pea purée and Selsey bisque to Golden Cross goats' cheese, butternut squash and sage tart with purple kohlrabi salad, while dessert could bring warm lemon sponge with cherry compote. 'Mini gastronauts' have their own menu, Sussex real ales are on tap and the wine list offers decent pickings from £16.
Chef/s: Giles Thompson and Luke Gale. **Open:** all week L 12 to 2.30 (3 Sat and Sun), D 5.30 to 9.30 (6 to 9 Sun). **Meals:** alc (main courses £15 to £22). Set L and early D £18.50 (2 courses) to £21.50. **Details:** 70 seats. 60 seats outside. Separate bar. Wheelchair access. Car parking.

▌Lower Beeding

NEW ENTRY

The Crabtree

A genuine hostelry with sound culinary talent
Brighton Road, Lower Beeding, RH13 6PT
Tel no: (01403) 892666
www.crabtreesussex.co.uk
British | £30
Cooking score: 2

£5
OFF

'Family-run business that pays attention to detail' noted one reader, delighted to find this country pub given a new lease of life by Simon Hope (who ran Food For Friends in Brighton for many years). It's a genuine hostelry with a proper bar and a series of dining rooms offering the choice of 'olde-worlde' (inglenook and beams) or 'elegant rustic' (heritage colours, trendy wallpaper, wood-burners). The food demonstrates sound talent and a commendable commitment to seasonal and regional ingredients. Own-cured salmon and dill-cured mackerel arrive with potato and beetroot salad and pickled vegetables, rump of Sussex lamb comes with potato gratin and roasted shallot purée, while dessert could be a luscious dark chocolate brownie with berry compote and vanilla ice cream. Local ales and bar snacks emphasise the Crabtree's pub credentials, and the wine list opens at £16.
Chef/s: Mark Kinzel. **Open:** Mon to Sat L 12 to 3, D 6 to 9.30. Sun 12 to 7. **Closed:** 25 Dec. **Meals:** alc (main courses £13 to £20). Sun L £21. **Details:** 70 seats. 100 seats outside. Separate bar. Wheelchair access. Car parking.

░ Please send us your feedback

To register your opinion about any restaurant listed in the Guide, or a new restaurant that you wish to bring to our attention, please visit the web address at the bottom of the page. Your feedback informs the content of the book and will be used to compile next year's reviews.

★ TOP 50 ★

The Pass

Fireworks and fun in the kitchen
South Lodge Hotel, Brighton Road, Lower Beeding, RH13 6PS
Tel no: (01403) 891711
www.southlodgehotel.co.uk
Modern British | £60
Cooking score: 7

🍴 V

Chef's tables are virtually *de rigueur* these days, but the format has been refined at the South Lodge, a lovely Victorian country mansion near Horsham. A row of tables on an elevated platform overlooks Matt Gillan's brigade at work, while a bank of screens relays closed-circuit close-up footage. The chefs themselves bring the dishes to table, explaining their handiwork as they do – a personal touch keenly appreciated by one couple. The dishes remain as innovative as ever: thought-provoking geometrical compositions that explode with extraordinary flavours on the palate. Multi-course tasters are the backbone of the operation, but you can mix and match between menus. Ingredients are of the finest, and work well together: a starter of beetroot tartare and sorbet has its sweetness offset by blue cheese and Sardinian coppa. Rabbit ballotine with confit garlic, white beans and prune almost lulls diners into a sense of classical security, but then charred trout with watermelon, pickled apple and olives turns up. Another fine fish dish has been cod with baked salsify, grelot onions and yuzu curd, 'the last adding a delicious sweetness to the overall effect'. Meats such as breast, leg and neck of duck with pomegranate display peerless versatility. Dessert might be intensely concentrated pear parfait and terrine, scented with cinnamon and textured with smoked almonds. The vegetarian menus are equally imaginative. A strong wine list (from £24.50) is on hand, but finding much below £30 requires ferreting.
Chef/s: Matt Gillan. **Open:** Wed to Sun L 12 to 2, D 7 to 9. **Closed:** Mon, Tue, first 2 weeks Jan. **Meals:** Set L £25 (3 courses) to £55. Set D £60 (6 courses) to

£70. Sun L £35 (5 courses) to £55. **Details:** 26 seats. Separate bar. Wheelchair access. Car parking. Children over 12 years only.

Sidlesham

The Crab & Lobster

Contemporary seafood by a nature reserve
Mill Lane, Sidlesham, PO20 7NB
Tel no: (01243) 641233
www.crab-lobster.co.uk
Modern European | £32
Cooking score: 3
🛏

Facing the nature reserve of Pagham Harbour, not far from Chichester, the Crab & Lobster is a 350-year-old whitewashed country inn. The interior has been given a cool modern makeover, but retains its beams, low ceilings and flagged floors, and there are outdoor tables, too. Malcolm Goble oversees a menu of regionally sourced ingredients, including seafood from Selsey, dairy products from local farmers and honey from the village beekeepers. A traditional fish soup with rouille makes a hearty, generous start, as a prelude to herb-crusted veal with roasted roots and spinach in red wine jus, or fillet of stone bass with seaweed tagliatelle in a creamy sauce of mussels and bacon. Cherry Bakewell tart served warm with a matching ice cream is a good way to finish. A resourceful wine list covers plenty of ground, from £17.85, with loads by the glass in two sizes.
Chef/s: Malcolm Goble. **Open:** Mon to Fri L 12 to 2.30, D 6 to 9.30 (10 Fri). Sat and Sun 12 to 10 (9 Sun). **Meals:** alc (main courses £16 to £28). Set L £19.50 (2 courses) to £23. **Details:** 58 seats. 40 seats outside. Wheelchair access. Car parking.

🍴 **Average Price**
The average price listed in main-entry reviews denotes the price of a three-course meal, without wine.

Singleton

ALSO RECOMMENDED
▲ The Partridge Inn
Grove Road, Singleton, PO18 0EY
Tel no: (01243) 811251
www.thepartridgeinn.co.uk
British £5 OFF

Real ales and hearty pub classics set the tone at this centuries-old, 'spick and span' South Downs pub – a stable mate of the Earl of March in nearby Lavant (see entry). Rug-strewn wood-and-stone floors, crackling log fires, low ceilings and polished tables are matched by dishes such as house-potted brown shrimps with toasted soda bread (£7.25), steak, mushroom and ale pie (£11.95), macaroni cheese with garlic bread, and triple chocolate brownie. Wines from £15.95. Open all week.

Tangmere

Cassons
A love of all things French
Arundel Road, Tangmere, PO18 0DU
Tel no: (01243) 773294
www.cassonsrestaurant.co.uk
Anglo-French | £39
Cooking score: 3

Almost hidden by foliage along the busy A27, this unassuming low-ceilinged, narrow-roomed restaurant delights patrons with its friendly, accommodating service and assured, classically based Anglo-French cooking. Regulars agree on the 'exceptional value' of the à la carte and set menus in which luxuries such as scallops and foie gras appear without hefty supplements, and dishes are generously portioned and often understated. At Sunday lunch, 'roast pork' surprises guests as an assiette of succulent loin, belly and confit leg of suckling pig. Similarly, 'fish of the day' emerges as a trio of accurately timed sea bass, salmon and king scallops with a deeply flavoured prawn bisque. Desserts are a real strength, as seen in smooth, intensely flavoured ice creams and sorbets, delicate

mousses and fine pastry. The wine list offers equally good value with bottles starting from £20 (£6.25 a glass).
Chef/s: Vivian Casson. **Open:** Wed to Sun L 12 to 2, Tue to Sat D 7 to 10. **Closed:** Mon. **Meals:** Set L £15 (2 courses) to £20. Set D weekdays £24 (2 courses) to £31. Set D weekends £31 (2 courses) to £39. Sun L £22.50 (2 courses) to £28. **Details:** 36 seats. 16 seats outside. Car parking.

▌West Ashling

★ REST NEW ENTRY – PUB ★

NEW ENTRY

The Richmond Arms

Imaginative cooking at dining-pub gem
Mill Road, West Ashling, PO18 8EA
Tel no: (01243) 572046
www.therichmondarms.co.uk
Modern British | £35
Cooking score: 4

£5 OFF 🛏

'Magic on a bright sunny day', the Jacks' village pub-with-rooms close to the mill and pond is beginning to impress with its inventive modern cooking and good-natured service. It's only a small place with a 'dinky bar', but though dining predominates, drinkers are very welcome. Warming pastel tones, solid-wood tables and spindle-back chairs create 'a bit of style', while a renovated red Berkel meat slicer and a blackboard bulging with on-trend small-plate bar snacks (chorizo rolls to Thai-spiced fish tempura) show intent. William Jack is a local lad and his classy cooking is strong on local, seasonal produce, though wider influences reference his globe-trotting chef's career. From a 'wow-flavoured, hot-and-runny' venison Scotch egg with pickled fennel, to a 'succulent, melting' soy-lacquered pork belly 'imaginatively pepped up' by tangerine, mint, chilli, peanut and crisp iceberg lettuce, it's all about accessible food (and prices), with 'bags of innovation'. Traditional ales stay local, well-selected wines go global (from £14.75).

Chef/s: William Jack. **Open:** Wed to Sun L 12 to 2 (3 Sun), Wed to Sat D 6 to 9. **Closed:** Mon, Tue, 23 Dec to 11 Jan, 23 Jul to 1 Aug. **Meals:** alc (main courses £15 to £22). **Details:** 36 seats. 30 seats outside. Separate bar. Wheelchair access. Car parking.

▌West Hoathly

READERS RECOMMEND

The Cat Inn

Modern British
Queen's Square, West Hoathly, RH19 4PP
Tel no: (01342) 810369
www.catinn.co.uk
'Warm, cosy (log fires). Excellent service – very attentive but not intrusive.
Unquestionably one of the best restaurants around.'

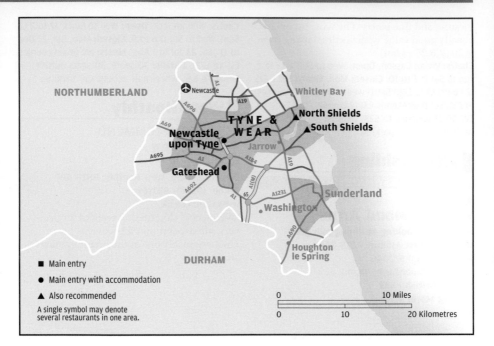

NORTHUMBERLAND

Newcastle

Whitley Bay

A19

TYNE & WEAR

North Shields

South Shields

Newcastle upon Tyne

Jarrow

A695 · A1

A184 · A19

Gateshead

A692 · A1(M)

65 · A1231

Sunderland

Washington

DURHAM

A690

Houghton le Spring

■ Main entry
● Main entry with accommodation
▲ Also recommended

A single symbol may denote several restaurants in one area.

0   10 Miles

0   10   20 Kilometres

Gateshead

Eslington Villa

Dependable cooking and a caring heart
8 Station Road, Low Fell, Gateshead, NE9 6DR
Tel no: (0191) 4876017
www.eslingtonvilla.co.uk
Modern British | £26
Cooking score: 2

£5 OFF 💤 £30

Although the view across the Team Valley from the Tulips' Victorian manor house may not enchant as it did in less developed days, the two acres of garden are well maintained and the food continues to please. Start with an assemblage of French black pudding, sauté potatoes, poached egg and mustard sauce or a more Francophile three-bird terrine with fine bean salad and sticky raisins. Then go on to, perhaps, black bream with new potatoes and tarragon crème fraîche. Lunch and early-bird meal deals offer the likes of smoked salmon or Caesar salad and braised beef with horseradish mash, and puddings (baked cheesecake, golden treacle tart, sticky toffee pud) will win friends. Wines from £17.50.

Chef/s: Jamie Walsh. **Open:** all week L 12 to 3 (4 Sun), D 5.30 to 10 (6.30 to 10 Sat, 9 Sun). **Closed:** 25 and 26 Dec, 1 Jan. **Meals:** Set L £13.95 (2 courses) to £16.95. Set D £21.95 (2 courses) to £25.95. Sun L £19.75. **Details:** 90 seats. 20 seats outside. Separate bar. Wheelchair access. Car parking.

Newcastle upon Tyne

Blackfriars Restaurant

Modern food where medieval monks dined
Friars Street, Newcastle upon Tyne, NE1 4XN
Tel no: (0191) 2615945
www.blackfriarsrestaurant.co.uk
British | £30
Cooking score: 3

£5 OFF

Readers love the dramatic historical location of this modern brasserie, sited in what was the refectory of a 13th-century Dominican friary in the heart of medieval Newcastle. You can

even book an old banqueting hall for a private party: a room where Edward III once received the Scottish royal claimant Edward Balliol. Gutsy regional cooking informs the menus, with Northumbrian oxtail in handmade pasta and sage butter, Wallington beef sirloin with butternut squash and Savoy cabbage, and Durham pork belly with black pudding, creamed sprouts and bacon all showing well in the meat department. Peppered mackerel provides a lighter starter, served with Yellison Yorkshire goats' cheese soufflé and horseradish cream, while Wylam 'Locomotion' doughnuts (made with local ale) feature among the puddings, accompanied by banana and stout jam and banana sorbet. Wines from a list grouped by style open at £17 (£4.40 a glass).
Chef/s: Troy Terrington. **Open:** all week L 12 to 2.30 (4 Sun), Mon to Sat D 5.30 to 10. **Closed:** bank hols. **Meals:** alc (main courses £12 to £21). Set L and D £15 (2 courses) to £18. Sun L £12. **Details:** 72 seats. 36 seats outside. Separate bar.

Café 21
Stylish quayside favourite
Trinity Gardens, Quayside, Newcastle upon Tyne, NE1 2HH
Tel no: (0191) 2220755
www.cafetwentyone.co.uk
Modern British | £45
Cooking score: 3
V

Newcastle's rampant food hero Terry Laybourne has been doing great things hereabouts for more than 20 years, and long-serving Café 21 is now firmly established as part of the Trinity Gardens quayside development. Polished woodwork, leather banquettes and linen-clad tables create a chic metropolitan vibe, while chef Chris Dobson pleases the city's smart foodie set with accomplished dishes inspired by big players from home and abroad: Basque charcuterie and Gallic 'salades gourmandes' line up alongside Craster kippers and Northumbrian venison (perhaps served with balsamic cherries, hazelnuts and spätzle) on a menu that gleefully ignores border controls. Steak tartare

arrives with hot toast or chips, while soufflés top and tail the repertoire: a classic Cheddar cheese and spinach version to start, a sweet pear variant with ginger ice cream to finish. The well-chosen wine list promises plenty of class by the glass or carafe, with bottles from £16.90; also note the list of world beers.
Chef/s: Chris Dobson. **Open:** all week L 12 to 2.30 (3 Sun), D 5.30 to 10.30 (9.30 Sun). **Closed:** 25 and 26 Dec, 1 Jan, Easter Mon. **Meals:** alc (main courses £16 to £30). Set L and early D £16.50 (2 courses) to £20. Sun L £18.50 (2 courses) to £21.50. **Details:** 85 seats. Separate bar. Wheelchair access.

David Kennedy's at The Biscuit Factory
Prime food to suit all pockets
Biscuit Factory, Stoddart Street, Newcastle upon Tyne, NE2 1AN
Tel no: (0191) 2605411
www.foodsocial.co.uk
Modern British | £28
Cooking score: 4
£5 OFF £30

David Kennedy's democratic and grown-up brasserie (formerly Food Social) looks right at home in Newcastle's renowned Biscuit Factory – the UK's largest art store and gallery. Leather sofas, soft lights, prints and sculptures create just the right cosmopolitan mood for an appetising menu that rings with seasonal flavours. North Sea fish gets a good outing (from roast hake with ratatouille to fillet of cod with creamed salsify and cod Kiev), while a gamey combo of venison with wild mushrooms and celeriac chimes perfectly with the calendar. For afters, keep it traditional with treacle tart and a dollop of lemon curd. Value for money means a lot here – not least the bargain set lunch, which has delivered fritto misto with 'gently warming' harissa mayo and a textbook twice-baked Gruyère soufflé with an autumnal salad of walnuts, apples and pear. Cocktails and wines (from £15) are in the same vein. David Kennedy also runs the River Café at 51 Bell Street, North Shields; tel: (0191) 2966168. See overleaf for details.

Chef/s: David Kennedy and Andrew Wilkinson. **Open:** all week L 12 to 2 (3 Sun), Mon to Sat D 5.30 to 9 (9.30 Sat). **Closed:** 25 and 26 Dec, 1 Jan. **Meals:** alc (main courses £12 to £20). Set L £10 (2 courses) to £12.95. Set D £12.95 (2 courses) to £15. Sun L £9.95. **Details:** 65 seats. Wheelchair access. Car parking.

Jesmond Dene House
Refined twirls and no-holds-barred flavours
Jesmond Dene Road, Newcastle upon Tyne, NE2 2EY
Tel no: (0191) 2123000
www.jesmonddenehouse.co.uk
Modern European | £52
Cooking score: 5
🛏

Just a few minutes' drive from Newcastle, Jesmond Dene is a peaceful wooded valley containing the suave late-Georgian mansion named after it. Within, the house is furnished in Arts and Crafts style, yet has been creatively remodelled to form a boutique hotel, complete with contrasting dining areas: a deep orange-hued brasserie with original moulded plaster ceiling, and a garden room opening on to a sun terrace with appetising views of the grounds. Michael Penaluna's kitchen uses the thoroughbred produce of respected suppliers, especially name-checked local farmers and fishermen, to produce contemporary dishes of generally unimpeachable quality: a starter of oak-smoked eel, perhaps, accompanied by the sharp, spicy notes of rhubarb and chorizo; or mains of sea bass with char-grilled leeks and mushrooms on wild rice, and seasonal pheasant with swede and onion galette, hazelnuts and kale. Taster menus (in both omnivorous and vegetarian versions) offer a six-course *tour d'horizon*, the whole routine finishing with a milk chocolate sphere containing praline ice cream. An enterprising wine list (from £18, £12 a half-litre carafe) provides good global coverage.
Chef/s: Michael Penaluna. **Open:** all week L 12 to 2 (12.30 to 2 Sat, 12.30 to 3.15 Sun), D 7 to 9.30 (6.30 to 10 Fri and Sat). **Meals:** alc (main courses £20 to £35). Set L £16.95 (2 courses) to £20.95. Set Sun L

£29. Tasting menu £65. Bar menu available. **Details:** 80 seats. 30 seats outside. Separate bar. Wheelchair access. Car parking.

Pan Haggerty
Suave city eatery with ambitious food
21 Queen Street, Newcastle upon Tyne, NE1 3UG
Tel no: (0191) 2210904
www.panhaggerty.com
Modern British | £35
Cooking score: 2

With its expanse of wooden flooring, bare tables and exposed brick, Pan Haggerty achieves a stylish informality, projecting itself as a smart-casual sort of place. There's no doubt that it's an appealing spot, and the menu offers sheer indulgence in the form of foie gras with apple and sage tarte Tatin, roast onion ice cream and white onion purée; and Galloway beef fillet with braised short rib and ox cheek tortellini. If both these dishes signal that prices can be high, look to the list of British classics, which includes the titular pan haggerty (a Northumberland potato dish) and fish and chips, or the good-value lunch and early evening meal deals. Wines from £16.95.
Chef/s: Kelvin Linstead. **Open:** all week L 12 to 2.30 (2 Sat, 3.30 Sun), Mon to Sat D 5.30 to 9.30 (5 Sat). **Closed:** 25 and 26 Dec, 1 and 2 Jan, bank hols. **Meals:** alc (main courses £13 to £23). Set L and D £14.95 (2 courses) to £17.95. **Details:** 65 seats.

ALSO RECOMMENDED
▲ Caffè Vivo
29 Broad Chare, Newcastle upon Tyne, NE1 3DQ
Tel no: (0191) 2321331
www.caffevivo.co.uk
Italian

Newcastle restaurant supremo Terry Laybourne says 'ciao' with this animated, all-purpose Italian that's tagged on to the Live Theatre. Occupying the shell of a 17th-century warehouse on trendy Quayside, Vivo serves soups, salads and sandwiches during the day before graduating to cicchetti, sharing 'planks', pasta and suchlike in the evening. Char-grilled squid with chilli and lemon

(£8.50) might precede saffron risotto with luganega sausage or roast pheasant with Umbrian lentils, spinach and vin santo (£16.50). The house aperitivo is 'out of this world', and wines start at £15.95. Closed Sun and Mon.

READERS RECOMMEND
Electric East
Pan-Asian
St James Boulevard, Waterloo Square, Newcastle upon Tyne, NE1 4DP
Tel no: (0191) 2211000
www.electric-east.co.uk
'The food is mainly Far Eastern with some fusion elements. We had strips of marinated beef on a Thai-style dressed salad, and tempura and tandoori fish with lime crushed peas and chunky Jenna potatoes – wonderful.'

■ North Shields
ALSO RECOMMENDED
▲ Irvins Brasserie
Union Road, The Fish Quay, North Shields, NE30 1HJ
Tel no: (0191) 2963238
www.irvinsbrasserie.co.uk
Modern British £5 OFF

From the generous bread board to the 'best in the world' complimentary madeleine at the end, readers happily endorse this bright, cheery all-day brasserie on North Shields' historic Fish Quay. It caters for most budgets and tastes, ranging from a £10 (two-course) set lunch to a 'far from bland' selection of vegetarian dishes. Otherwise expect excellent fish, say roast monkfish with curried cauliflower (£17.50), 'outstanding' venison, and duck confit with lentils, pak choi and five spice (£12.50). Friendly service, jazz evenings and wines from £16.95 complete the package. Closed Mon and Tue.

■ South Shields
ALSO RECOMMENDED
▲ Colmans
182-186 Ocean Road, South Shields, NE33 2JQ
Tel no: (0191) 4561202
www.colmansfishandchips.com
Seafood

'The finest fish and chips I have had in 65 years' was the verdict of one reporter after a meal at this evergreen family-run restaurant (established in 1926). Unpretentious, no-frills, high-quality fish cooked in 'secret recipe' batter, served alongside expertly fried chips are what keep Colmans ahead of the pack. Choose from the bestselling cod (£7.95), lemon sole (£13.95) or crab cake (£12.50). Wines from £12.95. Open all week.

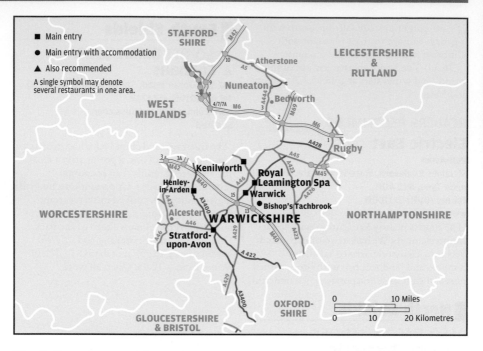

▉ Bishop's Tachbrook

Mallory Court, Main Dining Room

Pedigree package for country-house fans
Harbury Lane, Bishop's Tachbrook, CV33 9QB
Tel no: (01926) 330214
www.mallory.co.uk
Modern British | £60
Cooking score: 5

🍴 V

Sometimes only a creeper-covered old house set in ten acres of gardens, and equipped with an oak-panelled dining room, will do – and Mallory Court steps up to the mark. In sumptuous Warwickshire countryside near Leamington Spa, it's a professionally run, endearing place, the restaurant's low ceiling and swagged curtains contributing to the sense of benign enclosure. The modern British cooking maintains a balance between technological experimentalism and traditional technique. Start with a sandwich

perhaps, but a metaphorical one made of quail and foie gras, dressed with compressed apple and medjool dates, or perhaps a dual serving of mackerel (a glazed chunk and parfait) with mirin-marinated cucumber and mooli. Main course fish dishes can be daring – halibut with pak choi, citrus-dressed fregola pasta, pink grapefruit and black olives, for instance – while the more dignified red meats are left well alone, so beef fillet comes with red cabbage and beetroot in red wine jus. Vivid fruit flavours enliven desserts: kalamansi and lime soufflé with salt-baked pineapple, warm gingerbread with spiced pear, chocolate pannacotta with blood orange. The wine list offers all the sophistication expected at a Relais & Chateaux joint, with bottles from £20.
Chef/s: Simon Haigh and John Footman. **Open:** Sun to Fri L 12 to 1.30, all week D 6.30 to 9. **Meals:** Set L £27.50 (2 courses) to £32.50. Set D £45 (2 courses) to £59.50. Sun L £35. **Details:** 60 seats. 24 seats outside.

▌Henley-in-Arden

The Bluebell
Sharp food and cheery hospitality
93 High Street, Henley-in-Arden, B95 5AT
Tel no: (01564) 793049
www.bluebellhenley.co.uk
Modern European | £29
Cooking score: 3
£30

Slap-up afternoon teas (complete with pink fizz or Pimm's) are just one of the indulgent pleasures at this 500-year-old, half-timbered coaching inn. You'll also find parasols on the patio, an expansive dining area and a penchant for cheery hospitality. The 'attentive, well-trained staff' know their stuff, and the Bluebell's kitchen also comes up trumps thanks to a dependable menu of skilful pub grub and sharply executed restaurant-style dishes. Ale-battered fish and chips or venison and mushroom pie line up alongside the likes of crab spring rolls with spring onion vinaigrette, or pork fillet wrapped in Serrano ham with butternut squash purée, lentil and mustard cream. Likewise, for pud decide between a straightforward crème brûlée or a Bramley apple and Armagnac prune galette with cinnamon ice cream. Tapas-style nibbles and sharing boards fuel the drinkers – who also have the choice of two dozen competitively priced wines (from £15.50) as alternatives to pints of real ale.
Chef/s: Simon Malin. **Open:** Tue to Sun L 12 to 2.30 (3.30 Sun), Tue to Sat D 6 to 9.30. **Closed:** Mon. **Meals:** alc (main courses £13 to £23). Set L and D £15 (2 courses) to £18. Sun L £23. **Details:** 52 seats. 40 seats outside. Wheelchair access. Car parking.

▌Kenilworth

NEW ENTRY
Beef
On-the-money provincial steakhouse
11 Warwick Road, Kenilworth, CV8 1HD
Tel no: (01926) 863311
www.beef-restaurant.co.uk
Steaks | £40
Cooking score: 3

'A hot London trend hijacked for the provinces' is one way of describing this egalitarian steakhouse from Birmingham-based Andreas Antona (see entry for Simpsons). Regulation slate floors, cowhide banquettes and sauna-style woodwork set the tone for a menu built around 'satisfyingly beefy', skilfully butchered cuts ranging from British rump and USDA ribeye to luxurious Australian Wagyu – all stridently seasoned, seared to rich crustiness and served with beef-dripping chips and salad. The kitchen also takes proper care when it comes to starters, sides and puddings, from harmoniously blended crab hummus with tomato salad or gooey macaroni cheese to teasing mini-desserts (aka 'bonbons') served with coffee: ask for the maple waffle with pecan ice cream. Value for money and sharp service are plus points, while the one-page wine list keeps it short and simple; prices start at £19.
Chef/s: Marc Billings and Andreas Antona. **Open:** Mon to Sat L 12 to 3, D 6 to 10. Sun 12 to 6. **Closed:** 25 to 27 Dec, 31 Dec to 3 Jan, 2 weeks Aug. **Meals:** alc (main courses £11 to £38). Set L £16.95 (2 courses). Sun L £20.95. **Details:** 50 seats. Wheelchair access.

Leamington Spa

Restaurant 23

Cooking that fizzes with bright ideas
34 Hamilton Terrace, Leamington Spa, CV32 4LY
Tel no: (01926) 422422
www.restaurant23.co.uk
Modern European | £42
Cooking score: 4
£5 OFF

Regulars writing in to praise the well-oiled machine that is Peter Knibb's restaurant are unanimous in their enthusiasm for the consistency and attention to detail that distinguish a visit here. The cooking is a sure match for its stylish surroundings (in a listed Victorian building), offering precise (and for one fan 'never less than outstanding') dishes with an eye on the latest trends. A teaming of seared diver-caught scallops with carrot bhaji, curried yoghurt and coriander cress is right up there, likewise a voguish combo of rabbit loin stuffed with rabbit livers and served with pancetta, heritage carrots, quinoa, Savoy cabbage and semi-dried grapes. There's also room for well-tried partnerships in the shape of beef fillet with triple-cooked chips and béarnaise or a milk chocolate terrine with tangerine sorbet and candied orange. 'Attentive, efficient but unobtrusive' staff are a bonus, the sommelier's recommendations are always worth heeding and wines start at £14.50.
Chef/s: Peter Knibb. **Open:** all week L 12 to 2 (3 Sun), Mon to Sat D 6.15 to 9.30. **Closed:** 25 Dec. **Meals:** alc (main courses £20 to £27). Set L £14.95 (2 courses) to £18.45. Set D £25. Sun L £27. **Details:** 70 seats. 30 seats outside. Separate bar. Wheelchair access. No children after 7.

Also Recommended

Also recommended entries are not scored but we think they are worth a visit.

Stratford-upon-Avon

No 9 Church St

Capable cooking and keen prices
9 Church Street, Stratford-upon-Avon, CV37 6HB
Tel no: (01789) 415522
www.no9churchst.com
Modern British | £32
Cooking score: 1

Capable cooking, keen prices and 'service with a smile' are just some of the reasons why shoppers, tourists and Bard followers congregate at this quirky listed building in Stratford's old town. Ambitious dinners have their fans, but set lunches and pre-theatre menus draw the loudest applause – from warm duck liver salad with chorizo and Puy lentil dressing or melting pork shank glazed with honey and mustard syrup to niftily presented fish and chips. Puds can be more hit and miss, but if you're lucky there might be a 'totally delicious' deconstructed 'rocky road' or rhubarb and custard tart with stem-ginger sauce. Wines from £15.75.
Chef/s: Wayne Thomson. **Open:** all week L 12 to 2 (3 Sun), Mon to Sat D 5 to 9.30. **Closed:** bank hols. **Meals:** alc (main courses £14 to £22). Set L and pre-theatre D £13 (2 courses) to £17.50. Sun L £21.50. **Details:** 40 seats. Separate bar.

ALSO RECOMMENDED

▲ The Rooftop Restaurant

The Royal Shakespeare Theatre, Waterside, Stratford-upon-Avon, CV37 6BE
Tel no: (01789) 403449
www.rsc-rooftop-restaurant.co.uk
British

The striking wraparound restaurant atop Stratford's Royal Shakespeare Theatre hasn't been universally greeted with 'bravos', but it works hard to keep its offering relevant. A fixed-price menu is served all day (from £17.50), and Bard fans on a budget can enjoy the views over coffee and cake. Everything's geared towards smart theatre-goers. Mackerel tartare with rhubarb (£6.95), steak and ox cheek charlotte with polenta (£17) and gypsy tart (£6.95) are all fashionably British. House wine £20. Closed Sun D.

Warwick

NEW ENTRY

High Pavement
Quality-driven cooking with metropolitan sophistication
3 High Street, Warwick, CV34 4AP
Tel no: (01926) 494725
www.highpavementwarwick.com
Modern British | £25
Cooking score: 2

£5 OFF £30

A stylish new addition to Warwick's dining scene arrives in the form of this striking three-storey town-house conversion. The bar is the first arm of the operation, offering a cocktail list of metropolitan sophistication. In the restaurant, chairs upholstered in blue and yellow take their places at distressed-wood tables with painted metal rivets under warehouse-style light fittings. Modern brasserie food does the job, too, with crab ravioli and samphire in lemon butter, or spinach and ricotta gnocchi the kind of comfort to expect. Seasonal asparagus is jollied up with truffled brioche soldiers and a crisply cooked egg, while a main course might deliver a frankly stunning chicken pot-au-feu in tarragon-laced stock with carrots, turnips, leeks and spring onions. The little-plate approach is favoured for desserts, so an all-in price gets you a sublime quartet of, perhaps, dense chocolate mousse with honeycomb; praline parfait; Eton mess; and orange and cardamom crème brûlée. House wines are the expected Chilean varietals, Sauvignon and Merlot, at £14.95, or £4 a glass.
Chef/s: Martin Connolly. **Open:** all week 12 to 9.30 (7 Sun). **Closed:** 25 Dec. **Meals:** alc (main meals £11 to £15). **Details:** 80 seats. 20 seats outside. Separate bar. Wheelchair access.

Tailors
Dynamic duo's ritzy, glory-stealing food
22 Market Place, Warwick, CV34 4SL
Tel no: (01926) 410590
www.tailorsrestaurant.co.uk
Modern British | £35
Cooking score: 3

V

The setting in Warwick's market square is as traditional as can be, but chefs Dan Cavell and Mark Fry are distinguished by their inventive, slightly nostalgic approach. It's carefully done so that the joke is shared with customers, rather than played on them; readers are delighted by it. To start, try scallops with salt-and-pepper chicken, lime jelly and chestnut mushrooms or a reinvention of the all-day breakfast complete with fried slice. Mains might be duck with vanilla and lime doughnuts, red pepper purée, spinach and mojito jelly, or steak and chips for those who aren't in the mood. Well-reported puddings include a 'wow' take on Black Forest with sour cherries and Kirsch and buttermilk ice cream. Wines are from £17.95.
Chef/s: Dan Cavell. **Open:** Tue to Sat L 12 to 2, D 6.30 to 9.30. **Closed:** Sun, Mon, 25 to 31 Dec. **Meals:** Set L £12.95 (2 courses) to £16.90. Set D £29.50 (2 courses) to £34.50. **Details:** 28 seats.

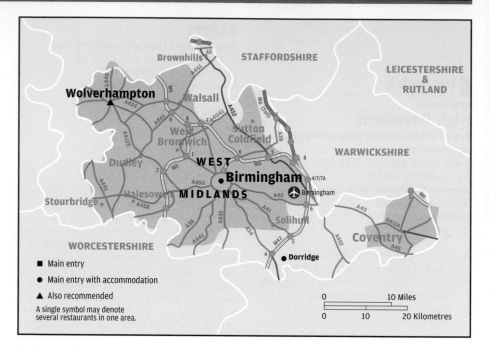

Brownhills
STAFFORDSHIRE
LEICESTERSHIRE & RUTLAND
Wolverhampton
Walsall
Sutton Coldfield
WEST
Bromwich
WARWICKSHIRE
Dudley
WEST
Birmingham
Birmingham
MIDLANDS
Stourbridge
Halesowen
Solihull
WORCESTERSHIRE
Coventry
Dorridge

- ■ Main entry
- ● Main entry with accommodation
- ▲ Also recommended

A single symbol may denote several restaurants in one area.

0		10 Miles
0	10	20 Kilometres

▌Birmingham

NEW ENTRY

Adam's

On-trend cooking underpinned by first-class produce
21a Bennetts Hill, Birmingham, B2 5QP
Tel no: (0121) 6433745
www.adamsrestaurant.co.uk
Modern British | £40
Cooking score: 5

£5 OFF **V**

Adam Stokes, previously lauded at Glennap Castle in Ayrshire (see entry, Scotland), hopes to break into the big league of new Brum gastronomy with this two-year 'pop-up'. The restaurant is on the edge of the central business district and makes the most of a tight space with trompe l'oeil, antique mirrors and faux marble décor, while on the food front all is on-trend with two tasting menus of five and nine-courses offered at dinner, plus a bargain three-course lunch. Everything is underpinned by first-class produce and the cooking shows real flair with Stokes' sound technique combining well with a witty streak that delivers trend-ticking extras such as an exploding 'roast chicken ball' canapé. Plenty of flavours are mobilised: a starter of deep-fried pig's trotter with smoked-eel and bacon 'jam' and a pre-dessert 'transition' course of rhubarb with grated foie gras exemplifies Stokes' repertoire of dishes that have the crystal ring of modern British authenticity. The wine list opens at £23.50.
Chef/s: Adam Stokes. **Open:** Tue to Sat L 12 to 2, D 7 to 9.30. **Closed:** 2 weeks Jul, 3 weeks Dec to Jan. **Meals:** Set L £21 (2 courses) to £25. Set D £40 (3 courses) to £45. Tasting menu £75. **Details:** 24 seats. Wheelchair access. Children over 5 yrs only at D.

❙❙❙ Visit us Online

To find out more about *The Good Food Guide*, please visit www.thegoodfoodguide.co.uk

Carters of Moseley
Food to capture the imagination
2c Wake Green Road, Moseley, Birmingham,
B13 9EZ
Tel no: (0121) 4498885
www.cartersofmoseley.co.uk
Modern British | £36
Cooking score: 3

£5 OFF

Set in a little row of shops a few minutes' walk
from Moseley's centre, this is the first solo
venture from chef Brad Carter and Holly
Jackson (front-of-house). Behind the tinted
plate-glass frontage there's an underwritten
mood of classy informality, but it's the food
that really captures the imagination.
Showcasing seasonal British produce is Ben's
business and he proves the point with a 'divine'
Scotch egg, and smoked wild pigeon with
cauliflower, black pudding and mustard leaf –
'a great piece of theatre'. Mains provide much
interest, too, particularly wild Cotswold
venison with spiced pumpkin, curly kale,
pickled pear and popped barley. Other
winning dishes come from the good-value
set-lunch menu: slow-cooked egg with
brandade bacon and wild garlic, and ox cheek
with parsley and beef barley and crispy potato
in beef fat. Clever desserts also earn top marks;
peanut-butter parfait with caramel sauce and
chocolate sorbet gets the nod this year. Wines
from £18.95.
Chef/s: Brad Carter. **Open:** Wed to Sun L 12 to 2, D
6.30 to 9.30 (7 Sun). **Closed:** Mon, Tue, 27 Dec, first
week Jan, 2 weeks Aug. **Meals:** alc (main course £14
to £25) Set L £18 (2 courses) to £20. Tasting menu
£65 (7 courses). **Details:** 30 seats. Wheelchair
access.

Symbols

🛏 Accommodation is available

£30 Three courses for less than £30

V Separate vegetarian menu

£5 OFF £5-off voucher scheme

🍷 Notable wine list

Lasan
Stylish Indian eatery
3-4 Dakota Buildings, James Street, St Paul's
Square, Birmingham, B3 1SD
Tel no: (0121) 2123664
www.lasan.co.uk
Indian | £47
Cooking score: 3

V

Tucked away in the historic Jewellery Quarter,
this smart but informal Indian restaurant
covers all bases. Chef Aktar Islam specialises in
modern takes on classic flavours, as in konkan
kekada, soft-shell crab in ajwain (lovage seed)
and Kashmiri chilli batter with a Devonshire
crab, pea and potato cake, served with raita and
sour raw mango chutney, or sarson ka jhinga
(tandoori prawns with baby radish and
grapefruit vinaigrette). But rustic dishes are
also done reassuringly well; goat biryani is
cooked in a sealed pot with cardamom, mace
and dum masala. First-rate produce such as
Cornish bass, wild venison or Wiltshire
Downs lamb (served as a marinated cutlet,
confit shoulder and shin patty, with tempered
lentils) elevates things further. Puddings cover
the traditional super-sweets such as gulab
jamun and pistachio kulfi, or introduce spice
via, perhaps, a lemon posset flavoured with
cardamom. Wines cost from £16.95 a bottle.
Chef/s: Aktar Islam. **Open:** Sun to Fri L 12 to 2, all
week D 6 to 11. **Closed:** 25 Dec. **Meals:** alc (main
courses £16 to £26). **Details:** 64 seats. Separate
bar. Wheelchair access. Car parking.

Loves
Intimate vibes and intricate food
Browning Street, Canal Square, Birmingham,
B16 8FL
Tel no: (0121) 4545151
www.loves-restaurant.co.uk
Modern British | £45
Cooking score: 4

🍷 V

First-timers, persevere. Loves may seem hard
to find, but the labour is worth it. It's a
converted woollen mill by the waterside, not

far from the Brindleyplace development. Claire Love presides impeccably out front, while Steve oversees a hard-working and principled kitchen, producing wonderful breads in-house, and balancing localism with quality-awareness for prime materials. Recommended dishes have included the sublimely intense Berkswell cheese gnocchi and chicken wings with braised lentils in garlic cream, and Hereford beef carpaccio with corned beef croquette, pickled veg, avocado and wasabi. The technical wizardry of contemporary cooking is evident in an array of slow-cooked pig's head with crispy ear, popcorn pork, tiger prawns, black pudding and smoked bacon relish, while fish might be more restrained, perhaps miso-glazed coley in tomato fondue with charred broccoli. Superlative regional cheeses are paired with their own chutneys, or there are texturally varied desserts such as apple cheesecake with caramelised apple, pear sorbet and pecan granola. A true enthusiast's wine collection has no notes, but includes benchmark producers from every region, including a good English spread. Prices start at £22, or £5.50 a standard glass, for an appetisingly scented Vouvray. **Chef/s:** Steve Love. **Open:** Fri and Sat L 12 to 1.45, Wed and Thur D 7 to 9, Fri and Sat D 6 to 9.30. **Closed:** Sun to Tue, 23 to 26 Dec, 1 to 9 Jan, 2 weeks Aug. **Meals:** Set L £25 (2 courses, Fri and Sat only) to £45. Set D £25 (2 courses, Wed and Thur only) to £45. Sun L £35 (3 courses). Tasting menus available. **Details:** 40 seats. Separate bar. Wheelchair access. Children over 8 yrs only at D.

Opus

Bullish Brummie brasserie
54 Cornwall Street, Birmingham, B3 2DE
Tel no: (0121) 2002323
www.opusrestaurant.co.uk
Modern British | £30
Cooking score: 2
£5
OFF

The epitome of a bullish Brummie brasserie, Opus parades its contemporary good looks with floor-to-ceiling windows, skylights and acres of wine racking. There's an unmistakable

metropolitan buzz about the place that suits its location in the city's financial district, but you'll find more than mere posturing here. The kitchen is serious about sourcing and hosts regular events celebrating regional food heroes – as well as producing 'consistently excellent', market-driven food. Fish always gets top reviews (scallops with pork belly and parsnip purée, lobster with fries, whole Brixham lemon sole with herb butter) and there's no arguing when it comes to plates of liver and bacon or slow-cooked ox cheek with Yukon gold potatoes and roasted beetroot. Welcoming, discreet service is applauded, and the wine list has ample tasty drinking from £14.95. **Chef/s:** David Colcombe. **Open:** Mon to Fri L 12 to 2, Mon to Sat D 6 to 9.30. **Closed:** Sun, 25 Dec to 3 Jan, bank hols. **Meals:** alc (main courses £14 to £28). Set L and D £15 (2 courses) to £17.50. **Details:** 80 seats. Separate bar. Wheelchair access.

Purnell's Bistro

Glynn Purnell's own brand of bistro
11 Newhall Street, Birmingham, B3 3NY
Tel no: (0121) 2001588
www.purnellsbistro-gingers.com
Modern French | £30
Cooking score: 2
V

In the autumn of 2012 Birmingham's favourite chef, Glynn Purnell (see entry, Purnell's), rebooted his second restaurant (formerly known as the Asquith), nailing his name firmly to the door. Some minor tweaking has opened up the large space – the snazzy cocktail bar remains at the front, but the bistro, now cloaked in warm shades of claret and browns, no longer feels cut off – and the menu has been pared back, too. At inspection a lightly cured salmon, served with a hen's egg filled with wasabi cream, made a lively start. Then a witty 'bourguignon' pie filled with venison and topped with mash was cleverly counterbalanced by a piece of roasted duck foie gras with spiced red cabbage. Pudding, an apple and pear crumble, ended matters comfortingly. Wines from £15.

Chef/s: Michael Dipple. **Open:** Sun to Fri L 12 to 1.45 (3.45 Sun), Mon to Fri D 6.30 to 9.30. Sat 12 to 9.30. **Closed:** 25 to 30 Dec, 1 Jan. **Meals:** alc (main courses £15 to £20). Set L and D £15 (2 courses) to £20. Sun L £22.95. **Details:** 90 seats. Separate bar.

★ TOP 50 ★

Purnell's

Dynamic cooking with a sense of fun
55 Cornwall Street, Birmingham, B3 2DH
Tel no: (0121) 2129799
www.purnellsrestaurant.com
Modern British | £50
Cooking score: 6

Brummie boy turned TV chef Glynn Purnell has made a real impact on his home turf and his flagship restaurant is 'still on excellent form'. The setting is a fashionably understated space in the city's financial district – a somewhat restrained backdrop for dynamic contemporary cooking with bags of personality and a sense of humour. Purnell shows his serious side with seasonal plates of, say, crunchy pork nuggets with parsnip purée, watercress, pear and black pudding or wild sea bass with mushroom purée, orange, pumpkin and coriander: but that's just the beginning. If you fancy some freewheeling gastronomic fun, book your seat for the eight-course 'tour': a roller-coaster ride through some of his more zany creations, all done in the best possible taste. Cue haddock and eggs with cornflakes and curry oil (breakfast kedgeree turned on its head), 'emotions of cheese and pineapple on sticks' (kitsch party nostalgia), Balmoral venison rolled in liquorice charcoal, and a quirky take on 'mint choccy chip'. 'It's quite an experience,' confessed one reader, 'and tremendous value for money'. France leads the way on the substantial wine list, with numerous house selections from £22.95 (£5.95 a glass). **Chef/s:** Glynn Purnell. **Open:** Tue to Fri L 12 to 1.30, Tue to Sat D 7 to 9. **Closed:** Sun, Mon, Christmas, New Year, Easter, first 2 weeks Aug. **Meals:** Set L £30. Set D £50. Tasting menu £80 (8 courses). **Details:** 45 seats. Separate bar. Wheelchair access. Children over 10 yrs only.

Saffron

Creative Indian cookery, with glitz
909 Wolverhampton Road, Oldbury, Birmingham, B69 4RR
Tel no: (0121) 5521752
www.saffron-online.co.uk
Indian | £20
Cooking score: 2
V £30

A stylish refurbishment has increased the space at this sophisticated Indian restaurant, which continues to curry favour with regulars by creating innovative, cleverly presented dishes. One reporter enthused about the 'wonderful flavours' of the delicately spiced food. The cooking is certainly a cut above the Brummie baltis of old, with starters such as salmon and crab cake, and saffron-scented sea bass roulade. Main courses show ambition and careful sourcing of top-drawer ingredients, with Scottish lobster peri-peri and achari venison among the choices – though tandooris, biryanis and kormas keep the old guard happy. Save some room for the rasmalai, a fragrant dessert of light sponge balls chilled in cold saffron milk topped with pistachios. Wines from £10.95. **Chef/s:** Sudha Shankar Saha and Avijit Mondal. **Open:** all week L 12 to 2.30, D 5.30 to 11. **Meals:** alc (main courses £8 to £20). **Details:** 92 seats.

Simpsons

Formidably accomplished suburban restaurant
20 Highfield Road, Edgbaston, Birmingham, B15 3DU
Tel no: (0121) 4543434
www.simpsonsrestaurant.co.uk
Modern French | £50
Cooking score: 6
🛏 V

Andreas Antona may justly claim to have spearheaded a culinary revival in Birmingham, with the supremely stylish Simpsons among the second city's box-office draws. In the placid purlieu of Edgbaston, in an ingeniously designed venue with alfresco tables and a glazed terrace, the kitchen sources from far and wide to allow itself the broadest canvas. The full panoply of taste categories, temperature ranges and textural contrasts is brought into play for compositions such as coriander- and lime-cured mackerel with salt-baked beetroot, herb oil and frozen horseradish. Spiced peanuts are on-trend as a garnish, seen here in a main course of sea bass, saffron potatoes and broccoli in crab sauce. There's no shyness about basing a dish on classic foundations, as when slow-cooked pork belly arrives with apple purée and cauliflower – albeit with the unexpected guest of a king prawn and a sauce of capers and raisins. Vibrant tropical flavours lift a presentation of rice pudding, made with deep-fried coconut, accompanied by pineapple, mango, and a passion fruit and lime-leaf sorbet. French aristocrats dominate the wine list, with much shorter shrift given elsewhere. Bottles start at £24, glasses £9.

Chef/s: Luke Tipping and Andreas Antona. **Open:** all week L 12 to 2 (2.30 Sun), Mon to Sat D 7 to 9 (9.30 Fri and Sat). **Closed:** 25 and 26 Dec, 31 Dec and 1 Jan, bank hols. **Meals:** alc (main courses £26 to £32). Set L £40. Tasting menu £90 (8 courses). **Details:** 70 seats. Wheelchair access. Car parking.

★ READERS' RESTAURANT OF THE YEAR ★
MIDLANDS

Turners Restaurant

A truly joyous surprise
69 High Street, Harborne, Birmingham, B17 9NS
Tel no: (0121) 4264440
www.turnersrestaurantbirmingham.co.uk
Modern British | £50
Cooking score: 5

You'd never know that behind this Harborne High Street shopfront lurks a glossy fine-dining restaurant where crystal sparkles, tasting menus seduce and Champagne cocktails are the drink of choice. Richard Turner's outward-looking modern British cookery suits the dramatic, contemporary backdrop of dark panels and mirrors. It's 'special occasion' without being stuffy. From bread and butter to the well-kept cheese, by way of amuse-bouches and pre-desserts,

Turner crosses the 'Ts' and dots the 'Is'. His tasting menus demonstrate classical nous with a modish touch in the form of slow-cooked duck egg with smoked winter minestrone and duck club sandwich, and fallow deer loin with salt-baked beetroot, chestnut, and chocolate sauce. Even the set lunch shows finesse; cod, lobster-claw 'bolognese' and hand-rolled linguine, and carrot cake with cream-cheese pannacotta are characteristically playful. Service has been frosty, but a report of waiting staff topping up a guest's parking meter suggests things have thawed. The wine list, from £26, is organised by varietal with a surprisingly good selection sub-£35.

Chef/s: Richard Turner. **Open:** Tue to Sat L 12 to 2, D 7 to 9.30. **Closed:** Sun, Mon, 1 week Christmas, 2 weeks Aug, bank hols. **Meals:** Set L £30 (2 courses) to £35. Set D £40 (2 courses) to £70. Tasting menu £60. **Details:** 20 seats. Wheelchair access.

ALSO RECOMMENDED

▲ Jyoti's Vegetarian

1045 Stratford Road, Hall Green, Birmingham, B28 8AS
Tel no: (0121) 7785501
www.jyotis.co.uk
Indian Vegetarian

Touristy, lager-swilling balti houses are now two a penny in this quarter of Birmingham, so it's refreshing to find a family-run veggie canteen that tries to buck the trend. Jyoti's kitchen is run by the ladies of the house and the menu taps into the Gujarati tradition, offering bargain-priced street snacks (from £1.65), big dosas, rich masalas and assorted curries ranging from aloo methi (£5.75) to makai patra (sweetcorn and colocasia leaves). Terrific thalis, too. Unlicensed, but you can BYO wine or sip lassi. Closed Mon.

🍴 **Also Recommended**
Also recommended entries are not scored but we think they are worth a visit.

∎ Dorridge

The Forest
On the right track
25 Station Approach, Dorridge, B93 8JA
Tel no: (01564) 772120
www.forest-hotel.com
Modern European | £28
Cooking score: 3

A 'routinely satisfying' destination, noted for its courteous staff, good manners and increasingly imaginative cooking, the Forest has come a long way since its days as a railway hotel – although it's still on the right track. There are touches of retro chintz about the informal dining room with its foliage-patterned décor, but the kitchen throws down some thoroughly modern challenges in the shape of, say, salt-baked celeriac with ceps, almonds and goats' cheese or barbecue-style monkfish with crispy squid and charred vegetable terrine. The attention to detail is 'impeccable', observes one reader. Chef Dean Grubb also knows his audience, offering steak and kidney pud, burgers and eggs Benedict for the traditionalists, along with generous Sunday roasts and some invitingly tweaked desserts: warm carrot cake with mascarpone and blond beer sorbet, for example. The food is complemented by some creditable wines from £13.95.
Chef/s: Dean Grubb. **Open:** all week L 12 to 2.30 (3 Sun), Mon to Sat D 6.30 to 10. **Meals:** alc (main courses £12 to £18). Set L and D £13.45 (2 courses) to £15.90. Sun L £16.50 (2 courses) to £19.75. **Details:** 55 seats. 50 seats outside. Separate bar. Wheelchair access. Car parking.

∎ Wolverhampton

ALSO RECOMMENDED
▲ Bilash
2 Cheapside, Wolverhampton, WV1 1TU
Tel no: (01902) 427762
www.thebilash.co.uk
Indian £5 OFF

Readers' expectations are exceeded by the Indian and Bangladeshi dishes at this Wolves veteran. Some classics, such as marinated, tandoor-charred Luknow lamb chops (£6.90) are left as they are; other dishes, including the 'beautifully presented' Bilash super (£13.90), a take on chicken tikka with a spiced tomato sauce, are unique and confidently presented – the restaurant claims you'll never want to try another chicken dish. Vegetarians have plenty to choose, including paneer in a moilee sauce. Wines start at £20. Closed Sun.

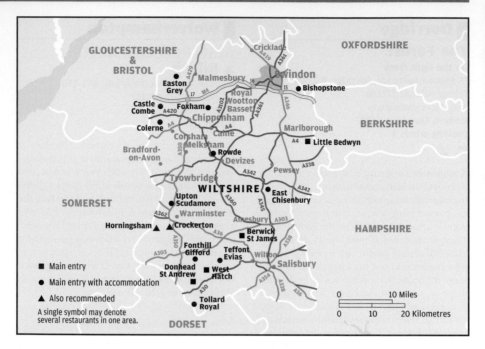

■ Berwick St James

The Boot Inn
Appealing pub with home cooking
High Street, Berwick St James, SP3 4TN
Tel no: (01722) 790243
www.bootatberwick.co.uk
British | £24
Cooking score: 1
£30

Tradition counts for much at this Till Valley flint-and-stone coaching inn, where drinkers get Wadworth beer, diners get brown Windsor soup, and both the sausage rolls and the brown sauce for dipping are made in-house. Readers rate hosts Cathy and Giles Dickinson for their professionalism, and the menu is written with a sharp understanding of appetite. Dishes such as home-smoked and cured meats and fish with relish and toast, mutton shepherd's pie with homemade baked beans or crumble and custard may be lionised in the urban jungle, but in walking country they make even more sense. Wines from £14.95.

Chef/s: Giles Dickinson. **Open:** Tue to Sun L 12 to 2.15 (2.30 Sun), Tue to Sat D 6.30 to 9.15 (9.30 Sat). **Closed:** Mon, 1 to 10 Feb. **Meals:** alc (main courses £10 to £16). Sun L £11 (1 course) to £18. **Details:** 35 seats. 25 seats outside.

■ Bishopstone

Helen Browning at the Royal Oak
Cheery organic pub-cum-B&B
Cues Lane, Bishopstone, SN6 8PP
Tel no: (01793) 790481
www.royaloakbishopstone.co.uk
British | £29
Cooking score: 3
£5 OFF 🍽 £30

Close to the Wilts-Oxon border, the Royal Oak is a country hostelry that's linked organically to its local community – in every sense. The pub is a stalwart of the contemporary food movement: rearing its own pork, beef and veal; sending raw milk for processing at a nearby dairy farm; and serving hand-pumped ales and ecologically produced wines. The kitchen doesn't disguise this bounty with freakish combinations and oddball technique; instead, it seeks to remind diners of the abundant merits of pork rillettes and cornichons, smoked mackerel pâté with pickled cucumber, ribeye steak with chips and garlic butter, and simply grilled fish such as grey mullet with warm broccoli salad. Occasionally, the menu wanders outside English shores, perhaps for ginger squid and kimchee, but its heart belongs to Blighty: right down to the treacle tart and cream, and English cheeses. The wines start at £19.50.

Chef/s: David Crabtree-Logan. **Open:** all week L 12 to 2.30 (3 Sat, 4 Sun), D 6 to 9.30 (6.30 to 8 Sun). **Meals:** alc (main courses £11 to £26). **Details:** 50 seats. 50 seats outside. Separate bar. Car parking.

▌Castle Combe

The Manor House Hotel, Bybrook Restaurant

Real verve and versatility
Castle Combe, SN14 7HR
Tel no: (01249) 782206
www.manorhouse.co.uk
Modern British | £60
Cooking score: 5

🛏 V

The 18th-century frieze in the Manor House's Shakespeare Room depicts Sir John Falstaff, the character reputed to have been based loosely on a former proprietor here. Set in a timeless Cotswold village, this building was a hospital during World War II, when its antique carved panelling and sumptuous views must have been thoroughly reviving to the spirits. The same could be said of the Bybrook dining room today, where candlelight sparkles off the silver and glass and Richard Davies formulates a menu of thoughtfully constructed modern British cooking. Basic techniques are traditional, as for truffled risotto with parsley purée, or ravioli of Salcombe crab, but often overlaid with novel touches, so the crab also comes with parsnip espuma, apple and vanilla.

Main-course meats often arrive in more than one cut – shoulder and loin of local lamb with potato terrine in rosemary jus – while fish and meat go harmoniously together, as in turbot with a fricassee of pancetta and celeriac. An artist's palette of ice creams and sorbets garnish desserts such as Valrhona fondant or ginger pannacotta. The wine list (from £24) leads with France, but with decent global support.
Chef/s: Richard Davies. **Open:** Tue to Sun L 12.30 to 2, all week D 7 to 9 (9.30 Fri and Sat). **Meals:** Set L £25 (2 courses) to £30. Set D £60. Sun L £35. Tasting menu £72. **Details:** 60 seats. Separate bar. Wheelchair access. Car parking. Children over 11 yrs only at D.

▌Colerne

Lucknam Park

Palatial grandeur and highly charged food
Colerne, SN14 8AZ
Tel no: (01225) 742777
www.lucknampark.co.uk
Modern British | £70
Cooking score: 6

🛏 V

The Lucknam Park country-house show begins as you process along the mile-long, tree-lined driveway that leads to this palatial Palladian mansion. Set in 500 acres of manicured grounds, it's a model of quiet aristocratic gentility – even though the hotel has all manner of latter-day accessories including a spa and an equestrian centre. The full-dress Park Restaurant occupies the original ballroom, resplendent with crystal chandeliers, gold silk drapes and a fabulous hand-painted ceiling. It makes a suitably sumptuous backdrop for highly charged, highly intricate modern cooking founded on solid principles. This kitchen can deliver anything from a torchon of duck foie gras with compressed pear, camomile and Sauternes jelly to grilled red mullet with glazed crayfish tails, broad beans and pak choi, while maintaining its sense of equilibrium. Game gets a gentlemanly airing (perhaps pot-roast grey-legged partridge with creamed Brussels sprouts, morteau sausage and salt-baked potato) and desserts marry classical prowess with flashes of whizz-bang eclecticism – say glazed passion fruit cream with lemongrass, lime leaf and mango. The food is matched by a grandiose wine list, with prices from around £25.

Chef/s: Hywel Jones. **Open:** Sun L 12 to 2, Tue to Sat D 6 to 10. **Closed:** Mon. **Meals:** Set D £70. Sun L £39. Tasting menu £90 (7 courses). **Details:** 80 seats. Wheelchair access. Car parking. No children.

Crockerton

ALSO RECOMMENDED
▲ The Bath Arms
Clay Street, Crockerton, BA12 8AJ
Tel no: (01985) 212262
www.batharmscrockerton.co.uk
Modern British

Pubby fare is the main thrust of this traditional village inn, where you can rub shoulders with the locals and their dogs, warm yourself by the log burner and enjoy a decent selection of real ales. Besides regular offerings like filled baguettes or meals with chips there are less predictable options such as a baked mushroom Welsh rarebit (£4.95) or sea bass with courgette and brown shrimps (£15.25). Mixed berry pavlova with vanilla cream (£5) is a typical dessert. Wines from £15.95. Open all week.

Donhead St Andrew
The Forester
Gently inventive cooking in a thatched hostelry
Lower Street, Donhead St Andrew, SP7 9EE
Tel no: (01747) 828038
www.theforesterdonheadstandrew.co.uk
Modern European | £29
Cooking score: 2

V £30

From its thatch to its oak beams, this is as traditional an English pub as you could hope to find – albeit one that's pitched towards dining. Well-worn stonework abounds inside, but there's nothing weary about the décor or the cooking. A starter of soft-boiled egg with

crispy pork soldiers pretty much sums up the menu, which manages to be comforting and gently inventive in equal measure. A 'beautifully balanced' plate of soft herring roes with pancetta, capers, lentils, parsley and toast impressed one reporter, while pan-fried fillet of Cornish brill with New Forest asparagus, ratte potatoes and hollandaise satisfied with 'top quality, fresh ingredients'. Desserts focus on British favourites – maybe Bakewell tart or sticky toffee pudding. A short but interesting selection of wines opens at £17.

Chef/s: Andrew Kilburn. **Open:** all week L 12 to 2, Mon to Sat D 6.30 to 9. **Closed:** 25 and 26 Dec. **Meals:** alc (main courses £12 to £20). Set L and D £16.50 (2 courses) to £19.50. **Details:** 60 seats. 40 seats outside. Separate bar. Car parking.

East Chisenbury

★ PUB OF THE YEAR ★ TOP 50 ★
The Red Lion
Much more than your average free house
East Chisenbury, SN9 6AQ
Tel no: (01980) 671124
www.redlionfreehouse.com
Modern British | £32
Cooking score: 6

£5 OFF

'A real joy' sums up reporters' unbridled enthusiasm for this acclaimed village pub (with guesthouse across the road), an unassuming little gem that's a vision of thatched roof, beams, crackling fires and lovely garden. Locals popping in for a drink add to the relaxed and informal atmosphere, but it is Guy Manning's compact, seasonal menus – built around excellent raw materials from trusted suppliers – that cause folk to 'regularly travel for almost an hour' to eat here. Deft handling and skilled cooking results in clear, well-defined flavours, as seen in a carefully judged roast rib of Wiltshire beef 'on the bone' with hand-cut chips and béarnaise or crisp fishcake and roast cod with purple sprouting broccoli, fondant potato, cep purée and hazelnuts. Start, perhaps, with a 'wonderful' crab tart or lemon sole goujons with homemade tartare sauce, and for dessert, Brittany Manning excels 'with one of the best crème brûlées in Christendom'. Own-baked bread, a compact yet imaginative wine list (from £17.50) and friendly, efficient service complete the pretty picture.

Chef/s: Guy Manning. **Open:** all week L 12 to 2.30 (3.30 Sun), D 6.30 to 9.30 (8.30 Sun). **Meals:** alc (main courses £15 to £25). Sun L £20 (2 courses). **Details:** 50 seats. 20 seats outside. Separate bar. Car parking.

Easton Grey

★ TOP 50 ★

Whatley Manor, The Dining Room

Some truly astounding food
Easton Grey, SN16 0RB
Tel no: (01666) 822888
www.whatleymanor.com
Modern French | £85
Cooking score: 8

As country house hotels go, this one's a thoroughbred, effortlessly outrunning other contenders with everything from 'supremely efficient' staff to 'sumptuous' surroundings. It dates from the 18th century, becoming a hotel in the 1980s and tactfully changing its original name (Twatley Manor) along the way. These days the place simply sparkles with class: the velveteen lawns, the pristine furnishings, the spa – and the thrilling show Martin Burge creates in the dining room. Fusing classical common sense with an adventurous spirit, he produces dishes that are consistently satisfying and often surprising. As an opening gambit, consider a shot glass of foie gras mousse with teriyaki jelly and a sesame croûton, one in a run of flavour-charged openers served against a backdrop of wood panelling and candlelight in the vast, rug-strewn lounge. In contrast, the dining room (housed in the former hunting lodge) is light and uncluttered, hung with modern art. Smoked haddock tartare with wasabi and cauliflower ice cream emphasises its contemporary leanings, and the flavour dial

stays at 11 for a starter of goats cheese ravioli with cauliflower foam, apple jelly, beetroot and hazelnut sherbert. Burge tends to divide dishes into several parts, as in a 'scintillating' main course of red mullet, cuttlefish and fennel with bouillabaisse purée and consommé and a separate plate of deep-fried cod cheeks with Parmesan rouille. Meals are never short of bells and whistles, so expect two pre-desserts ahead of your final course, when the 'revelatory' sweet/savoury combination of truffle ice cream, truffle honey and creamed Roquefort with crisp tuiles and walnuts comes highly recommended. Petits fours, too, are included in the 'good value for money' set meal. The extensive wine list (from £19.50) covers all the major areas, with helpful notes on each, and the sommelier can be relied on for intelligent recommendations.

Chef/s: Martin Burge. **Open:** Wed to Sun D only 7 to 10. **Closed:** Mon, Tue. **Meals:** Set D £85. Tasting menu £110 (7 courses). **Details:** 40 seats. Separate bar. Wheelchair access. Car parking. Children 12 yrs and over only.

Fonthill Gifford

Beckford Arms

Upper-crust rural inn
Fonthill Gifford, SP3 6PX
Tel no: (01747) 870385
www.beckfordarms.com
British | £25
Cooking score: 3

Dan Brod and Charlie Luxton's lovingly restored Beckford Arms wins advocates with its stunning rural location and agreeable blend of rusticity, creature comforts and affluent vibes. Very much a free house dispensing local real ales and genuine hospitality, it also successfully bridges the divide between country boozer and upper-crust inn-with-rooms. In the kitchen, dishes take their cue from the seasons and exploit local resources. Home-smoked salmon, locally shot game – in a terrine, for instance, or as a main-course venison loin with roasted shallots, bone marrow, parsnip purée and fried mushrooms

– and whole roast chickens for four to share for
Sunday lunch. Fish comes from Cornwall,
perhaps Newlyn pollack with mussels, white
wine, potatoes and cream, while dessert might
offer a rich chocolate fondant. The short,
modern wine list opens at £16.75.
Chef/s: Kevin Francis. **Open:** all week L 12 to 2.30 (3
Sat, 3.30 Sun), D 6 to 9.30. **Closed:** 25 Dec.
Meals: alc (main courses £9 to £24). **Details:** 60
seats. 30 seats outside. Separate bar. Wheelchair
access. Car parking.

Foxham

ALSO RECOMMENDED
▲ The Foxham Inn
Foxham, SN15 4NQ
Tel no: (01249) 740665
www.thefoxhaminn.co.uk
Modern British £5 OFF

Food at this 'welcoming' family-run country
inn-with-rooms is pitched above pub level,
though correspondents still rate Sunday lunch
as a high point. A menu peppered with the
names of local suppliers features dishes such as
lamb's sweetbreads in Marsala cream sauce
with rosemary (£6) and hake with creamed
potato, buttered spinach and a white wine
sauce (£16). Readers also praise the kitchen's
flexible, considered approach to cooking for
customers with allergies (given sufficient
notice). Wine from £13.90. Closed Mon.

Horningsham

ALSO RECOMMENDED
▲ The Bath Arms
Longleat Estate, Horningsham, BA12 7LY
Tel no: (01985) 844308
www.batharms.co.uk
Modern British

A handy refuelling point for visitors to
Longleat and its many attractions, this
rambling 300-year-old hostelry (once a coach
house) feeds and waters tourists, families and
locals. The kitchen supplies everything from
bar lunches (things on toast, salads, sarnies,
fishcakes) to more ambitious, restaurant-style

evening meals. For dinner you might find
beetroot risotto with goats' cheese cream
(£7.25) ahead of parsley-crusted roast cod
with samphire (£17.25) or roast organic pork
belly with Savoy cabbage ball, crackling and
pea shoots. House wine is £17. Open all week.
Accommodation.

Little Bedwyn

The Harrow at Little Bedwyn
Real food and extraordinary wines
High Street, Little Bedwyn, SN8 3JP
Tel no: (01672) 870871
www.theharrowatlittlebedwyn.com
Modern British | £55
Cooking score: 6

🍷 V

The name may conjure up visions of harvest
festivals and bucolic toil, but the Harrow's
solid brick-and-stone exterior conceals a top-
flight country restaurant dedicated to the
pursuit of 'real food' and extraordinary wines.
Muted modern colours and leather chairs set a
classy tone in the interconnecting dining
rooms, and chef/patron Roger Jones's
understanding of foodie supply lines shows in
every item on the precise menu. Wild
mushroom risotto with cep cream, Wiltshire
truffles and cep dust is a mycologist's dream,
while deep-fried Pembroke lobster gets a kick
from Halen Môn sea salt, chilli and ginger. As
for meat, expect anything from Highland
Shorthorn beef to organically reared Creedy
Carver duck. The result is 'outstanding haute
cuisine', with each dish allied to an appropriate
tipple. How about glazed bread-and-butter
pudding with prune and rum parfait, vanilla
pannacotta and a glass of plum-infused
Japanese umeshu. Also don't miss the
assortment of stonkingly fine cheeses from
Wiltshire and neighbouring counties. The
New World receives special attention in
Roger's lovingly curated wine list, but every
page is testament to oenology – from fabulous
Burgundies laid down over the years to rare
bottles of Spanish Viña Tondonia. Where to

begin? Two pages of irreproachable house selections (from £6 a glass) should set you on your merry way. **Chef/s:** Roger Jones and John Brown. **Open:** Wed to Sat L 12 to 3, D 7 to 11. **Closed:** Sun to Tue, 2 weeks from Christmas. **Meals:** alc (main courses £30). Set L £35. Set D £50. Tasting menu £50 (6 courses) to £75 (8 courses). **Details:** 30 seats. 20 seats outside.

■ Rowde

The George & Dragon
Proper period local with star seafood
High Street, Rowde, SN10 2PN
Tel no: (01380) 723053
www.thegeorgeanddragonrowde.co.uk
Modern British | £25
Cooking score: 3

It is everything you could want from an ancient village inn: oak floors, beamed ceilings and log fires, locals mingling in the bar drinking great real ales, while everyone in the dining room tucks into fish delivered daily from Cornwall. The formula is simple. The kitchen deals in seasonal produce, sending out well-wrought dishes that are fresh and flavourful – creamy baked potted crab (a repertoire favourite), a dish of fresh English asparagus or fresh figs stuffed with goats' cheese and prosciutto, perhaps, followed by lobster thermidor or char-grilled scallops with black pudding, or even roast rack of lamb with mint pea purée and red wine jus if you're not in the mood for fish. To finish, try the chocolate and orange bread-and-butter pudding. Wines from £14.50. **Chef/s:** Christopher Day. **Open:** all week L 12 to 3 (4 Sat and Sun), Mon to Sat D 6.30 to 10. **Meals:** alc (main courses £10 to £22). Set L and D £16.50 (2 courses) to £19.50. Sun L £19.50. **Details:** 48 seats. 20 seats outside. Car parking.

¶¶¶ Also Recommended
Also recommended entries are not scored but we think they are worth a visit.

■ Teffont Evias

Howard's House Hotel
Country comforts and quietly confident food
Teffont Evias, SP3 5RJ
Tel no: (01722) 716392
www.howardshousehotel.co.uk
Modern European | £45
Cooking score: 3
£5 OFF ➡ V

'Nothing is too much trouble' in this cocoon of country comforts: a carefree English pastoral idyll complete with a little stream, gardens and artistically trimmed topiary. Built as a dower house in 1623, the place now drifts along easily at its own pace – although long-serving chef Nick Wentworth keeps in touch with the trends. His quietly confident cooking finds room for Laverstoke Park black pudding, Dorset lamb and haloumi cheese from Somerset, as well as regular deliveries of Cornish seafood. The Brixham fish stew has gone down a treat, but the possibilities might extend to, say, wild sea bass fillet with parsnip and vanilla purée, crab beignet and basil. Readers have also praised the local Sika deer: 'cooked to perfection'. Desserts are 'melt-in-the-mouth gorgeous', and the well-spread wine list starts at £17. **Chef/s:** Nick Wentworth. **Open:** all week L 12 to 2, D 7 to 9. **Closed:** 24 to 27 Dec. **Meals:** Set L £25 (2 courses) to £29.50. Set D £36 (2 courses) to £45. Sun L £25 (2 courses) to £29.50. **Details:** 40 seats. 24 seats outside. Car parking.

■ Tollard Royal

The King John Inn
Popular village inn with unusual flair
Tollard Royal, SP5 5PS
Tel no: (01725) 516207
www.kingjohninn.co.uk
Modern British | £30
Cooking score: 3
➡

It's five years since Alex and Gretchen Boon rescued this Victorian inn set amid lovely surroundings on the Wiltshire/Dorset border.

Nowadays it successfully blends traditional country pub trappings (real ales, scrubbed wood tables, delightful garden) with swish boutique bedrooms and a tremendous wine list. On the food front, local and regional produce is at the heart of things, from wild duck consommé to a salad of pigeon with bacon and croûtons. Twice-baked Westcombe Cheddar cheese soufflé is one of chef Simon Trepess's standout dishes, served as a main course with salad, although he is equally confident tackling brill and smoked eel ravioli with a mussel and mushroom sauce, or Angus rump steak with chips and béarnaise. Desserts include 'amazing' apple doughnuts with toffee sauce and mulled cider. Wines from £16.95.
Chef/s: Simon Trepess. **Open:** Mon to Fri L 12 to 2.30 (3 Sat and Sun), Mon to Fri D 7 to 9.30 (10 Sat, 9 Sun). **Meals:** alc (main courses £13 to £23). **Details:** 60 seats. 60 seats outside. Separate bar. Wheelchair access. Car parking. Children over 8 yrs only at D.

Upton Scudamore

The Angel Inn
Welcoming and professional village hostelry
Upton Scudamore, BA12 0AG
Tel no: (01985) 213225
www.theangelinn.co.uk
Modern British | £30
Cooking score: 2

£5
OFF

Carol and Tony Coates have stamped their mark on this extended 17th-century inn (with rooms) on the edge of Salisbury Plain since moving in more than a decade ago. Reporters particularly like the spacious sheltered terrace and the fact that you can come just for a drink in the well-upholstered bar. Consistent, well-priced food served in the warm and welcoming dining room garners praise, too. Fish is a strong point – cured, just-seared mackerel with marinated beets, celeriac rémoulade, horseradish cream and pea shoots, or sea bass with organic buckwheat noodles, tiger prawn won tons and shiso broth – but there's also three-rib rack of lamb with sweetbreads, truffled pea purée, boulangère

potatoes and rosemary emulsion and jus. Finish with elderflower and lime cheesecake. Wines from £15.
Chef/s: James Maulgue. **Open:** all week L 12 to 2, D 6 to 10. **Meals:** alc (main courses £16 to £20). Set L £10 (2 courses) to £15. **Details:** 60 seats. 40 seats outside. Separate bar. Car parking.

West Hatch

Pythouse Kitchen Garden Shop and Café
Quaint kitchen garden eatery
West Hatch, SP3 6PA
Tel no: (01747) 870444
www.pythouse-farm.co.uk
British | £18
Cooking score: 2

£5
OFF £30

This charming Victorian walled garden produces fruit, vegetables and flowers for sale in a converted potting shed that serves as a small shop and rustic café – think winter wood-burner, summer views. Garden produce and local supplies appear on the short, daily changing menu: perhaps green bean, courgette and cavolo nero tart with mixed leaves or lamb from the Pythouse estate served with creamy leek ragoût and green bean and black onion-seed rice salad. There's praise for the lamb burger in a sourdough bun with beetroot, apple and thyme chutney, and for the dresser laden with 'yummy' cakes. Wines from £12.
Chef/s: Matthew Trendall. **Open:** Wed to Mon L 12 to 3, D Thur to Sat 6 to 10. **Closed:** Tue, 25 and 26 Dec, 1 Jan. **Meals:** alc (main courses £7 to £12). **Details:** 70 seats. 65 seats outside. Wheelchair access. Car parking.

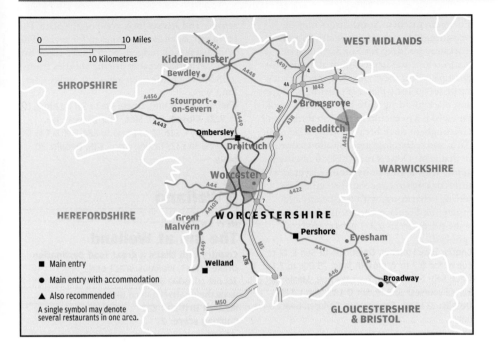

■ Broadway

Russell's

Inviting boutique brasserie
20 High Street, Broadway, WR12 7DT
Tel no: (01386) 853555
www.russellsofbroadway.co.uk
Modern British | £40
Cooking score: 4

£5 OFF 🚗

Occupying a remodelled furniture showroom in one of the prettiest Cotswold villages, Russell's is a sassy, eye-catching prospect with the promise of sound, regionally sourced food to boot. The place looks good in any weather, with its smartly chic interior and decked patio outside, and the all-embracing menu majors in gutsy bistro dishes and modern-day resolve. Start with broccoli pannacotta with saffron emulsion, go on to sea bass teamed with grilled fennel and vanilla and mussel broth or cannon of herb-crusted Lighthorne lamb accompanied by fondant potato, spinach and wild mushrooms, then finish with mandarin soufflé and bitter chocolate ice cream. One satisfied customer reported that a dinner of 'moules, a chicken dish with lovely tasting meat and sticky toffee pudding' was 'outstanding value', and singled out service for praise. Wines from £19.50.
Chef/s: Neil Clarke. **Open:** all week L 12 to 2.30, Mon to Sat D 6 to 9.30 (6.30 Sat). **Closed:** bank hols. **Meals:** alc (main courses £15 to £28). Set L and D £14.95 (2 courses) to £17.95. Sun L £21.95 (2 courses) to £24.95. **Details:** 60 seats. 25 seats outside. Separate bar. Wheelchair access.

■ Ombersley

The Venture In

Cracking food in a crooked inn
High Street, Ombersley, WR9 0EW
Tel no: (01905) 620552
Modern European | £37
Cooking score: 3

If the resident ghost at this quaint old timbered house (dating back to 1430) gets hungry, it can sate its appetite in the Venture In's modern

European kitchen. Some dishes may be reassuringly familiar – roast sirloin and Yorkshire pudding for Sunday lunch or venison loin and game faggot at dinner, for example – but there are a few modern-day surprises on Toby Fletcher's menu. Scallops and black pudding with beetroot and smoked rapeseed is a particularly modish starter, and Gressingham duck breast with pickled apple Tatin and seared foie gras to follow continues in that vein. Dessert might be caramelised apples with mascarpone mousse layered with tuiles or a warm chocolate brownie. The setting's charming, with oak beams and inglenook fireplace, service is friendly and wine prices (from £17) won't leave you spooked.

Chef/s: Toby Fletcher. **Open:** Tue to Sun L 12 to 2, Tue to Sat D 7 to 9. **Closed:** Mon, 25 Dec to 2 Jan, 1 week Feb, 1 week Jun, 2 weeks Aug. **Meals:** Set L £25 (2 courses) to £29. Set D £39. Sun L £29. **Details:** 32 seats. Car parking. Children over 10 yrs only.

Pershore
Belle House

Purveyor of upmarket meals
5 Bridge Street, Pershore, WR10 1AJ
Tel no: (01386) 555055
www.belle-house.co.uk
Modern British | £32
Cooking score: 3

Belle House enjoys a pleasant spot on the pretty market town of Pershore's traditional high street. Now entering its second decade, it boasts a deli-traiteur (doing a nice line in home-baked bread and upmarket 'takeaway' meals) and an approachable, 'always reliable' modern restaurant. Menus are Mediterranean-leaning, though can segue perfectly comfortably from an Asian-inspired king prawn and chilli risotto with soy honey syrup and sesame to a more typically Italian roast gurnard with Parmesan gnocchi and tomato fondue, followed by vanilla parfait with strawberry soup for dessert. Good technical skills in the kitchen ensure that deviations from the classical norm make sound culinary

sense – and always look good on the plate. The set lunch, once again, comes in for praise. The wine list is well judged, with lots to enjoy by the glass and agreeable pricing (bottles from £18.50) to ensure even a modest outlay goes a long way.

Chef/s: Steve Waites. **Open:** Tue to Sat L 12 to 2, D 7 to 9.30. **Closed:** Sun, Mon, first 2 weeks Jan. **Meals:** Set L £16 (2 courses) to £24. Set D £25 (2 courses) to £32. Tasting menu £45. **Details:** 80 seats.

Welland

NEW ENTRY
The Inn at Welland

Country pub that's a great food destination
Drake Street, Welland, WR13 6LN
Tel no: (01684) 592317
www.theinnatwelland.co.uk
Modern British | £27
Cooking score: 2

£5 OFF £30

A couple of years in, David and Gillian Pinchbeck's country hostelry in peaceful Welland has worn in and warmed up very nicely, and is now established as a great food destination. Sunday lunch here is an institution, but the rest of the week sees the whitewashed inn alive with customers enjoying the open fire, simple, modern décor, 'friendly, informative and efficient' service and very good food. The array of starters, sandwiches and main courses, such as slow-cooked shoulder of Cotswold lamb or roulade of free-range chicken, tells of a relationship with local suppliers, not the freezer. The menu is packed with goodies such as garden pea and Parmesan soufflé ('the best ever'), 'tender, almost sweet' pork belly with 'great crackling' and orange chocolate brownie with orange liqueur cream ('a triumph'). Wines from £13.95.

Chef/s: Chris Exley. **Open:** Tue to Sun L 12 to 2.30, Tue to Sat D 6 to 9.30. **Closed:** Mon. **Meals:** alc (main courses from £12 to £22). Set D and Sun L £19.50 (2 courses) to £25. **Details:** 50 seats. 30 seats outside. Wheelchair access. Car parking.

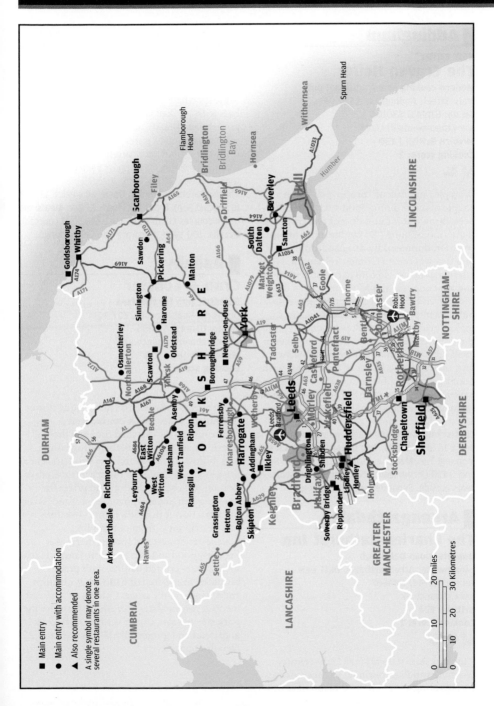

Addingham

NEW ENTRY
The Craven Heifer
Modern cooking in a traditional pub
Main Street, Addingham, LS29 0PL
Tel no: (01943) 830106
www.thecravenheifer.com
Modern British | £30
Cooking score: 2
£5 OFF 🛏

'It's a pleasing mix of "proper pub" with a couple of smart dining rooms; a lot of money's been thrown at it but it doesn't feel corporate, there's lots of quirk.' So ran the notes of one reporter, impressed by this handsome rural pub that was once a Chinese restaurant. Now, after scraping off old lino to reveal stone floors and papering walls in Mulberry tartan flock, the Craven Heifer's a comfortable place for a pint or a meal. Paul Jowett clearly wants to make a mark, his pared-down menu (typically three starters and mains) offering the likes of 'well judged and nicely presented' poached loin and confit leg fritter of local rabbit with boozy prunes, bubble and squeak beignets and Savoy velouté, but some feel he should 'bin the foams and the menu would be more accessible'. Wines from £14.
Chef/s: Paul Jowett and Mark Owens. **Open:** Wed to Sun L 12 to 2 (6 Sun), Wed to Sat D 6 to 9. **Closed:** Mon and Tue. **Meals:** alc (mains £14 to £23). Set L and D £20 (2 courses) to £23. **Details:** 60 seats. 20 seats outside. Separate bar. Car parking.

Arkengarthdale
The Charles Bathurst Inn
Unpretentious Dales pub
Langthwaite, Arkengarthdale, DL11 6EN
Tel no: (01748) 884567
www.cbinn.co.uk
British | £24
Cooking score: 1
£5 OFF 🛏 £30 🍸

This Yorkshire stalwart is an 18th-century coaching inn that continues to cheer visitors by providing a very civilised blend of real ales

and unfussy food, alongside beams, wood floors and open fires. The menu, scrawled on a mirror, cleverly mixes the familiar (Scotch egg, and braised pig's cheek with black pudding and honey mustard dressing) with some speculative efforts along the lines of sea bass with smoked salmon and Thai noodles, or guinea fowl breast and confit leg ballotine with sweet potato purée and Madeira jus. To round things off there might be old favourites like sticky toffee pudding or a selection of local cheeses. Wines from £15.95.
Chef/s: Gareth Bottomley. **Open:** all week L 12 to 2 (6 Sat and Sun), D 6 to 9. **Closed:** 25 Dec. **Meals:** alc (main courses £12 to £20). Sun L £10.50 (2 courses). **Details:** 100 seats. Separate bar. Car parking.

Asenby
Crab & Lobster
Eccentric pub for fish fans
Dishforth Road, Asenby, YO7 3QL
Tel no: (01845) 577286
www.crabandlobster.co.uk
Modern British | £38
Cooking score: 2
🛏

Lobster pots and old advertising signs clutter the outside walls, mock crustacea sit marooned on the thatched roof and the interior is stuffed with lifebelts, fog lamps, nets, billowing drapes and every nautical curio imaginable. Welcome to the eccentric Crab & Lobster. Of course, there are no prizes for guessing that 'superbly handled seafood' is the big attraction at this rather zany Yorkshire pub-restaurant – from outstanding Colchester oysters and lobster thermidor ('reliably good and rich') to more fanciful ideas such as crab-crusted halibut with prawn bisque or beer-battered haddock with chips and Chinese curry sauce. Otherwise, the vast menu accommodates everything from sticky pork ribs to roast loin of venison with pink grapefruit and ginger jelly. Wines start at £25. Details opposite.

Chef/s: Steve Dean. **Open:** all week L 12 to 2.30, D 7 to 9 (6.30 to 9.30 Sat). **Meals:** alc (main courses £17 to £22). Set L £16.50 (2 courses) to £19.50. **Details:** 110 seats. 45 seats outside. Separate bar. Car parking.

Beverley
Whites
Inventive food in unstuffy surroundings
12a North Bar Without, Beverley, HU17 7AB
Tel no: (01482) 866121
www.whitesrestaurant.co.uk
Modern British | £34
Cooking score: 2

Chef/proprietor John Robinson keeps it tight in his intimate and 'unstuffy' little restaurant-with-rooms, working from an open kitchen and eschewing the fripperies of fine dining in favour of bare tables and comforting, everyday touches. But there's nothing homespun about a tersely written, contemporary menu that might offer mackerel ceviche with fried wild rice, mango salsa and liquorice milk, 54-hour pork belly with apple textures or 'fabulous' venison cooked sous-vide with trompette mushrooms, cherry, leeks and 'light rosemary flavours'. Meals are fleshed out with top-drawer home-baked breads, amuse-bouches and palate-cleansing pre-desserts such as a raspberry jelly case with Campari filling and lemon verbena 'snow', while the fully loaded cheese trolley is accompanied by moreish savoury shortbread biscuits. Bright young staff provide charming, affable service, and the 'well-chosen' wine list promises dependable drinking from £18.50. **Chef/s:** John Robinson. **Open:** Sat L 12 to 2, Tue to Sat D 6.30 to 9. **Closed:** Sun, Mon, 1 week Christmas, 1 week Aug. **Meals:** alc (main courses £19 to £20). Set L £15.50 (2 courses) to £17.95. Set D £18.50 (2 courses) to £22.50. **Details:** 25 seats. Wheelchair access.

Bolton Abbey
The Devonshire Brasserie
Ducal eatery with a metropolitan edge
Bolton Abbey, BD23 6AJ
Tel no: (01756) 710710
www.devonshirebrasserie.co.uk
Modern British | £30
Cooking score: 2

The Devonshire Arms hotel achieves the often elusive trick of being an elegant country house with a fine-dining restaurant (the Burlington, absent from the Guide this year due to a late change of chef) that nonetheless retains the human touch. Much of this is down to its resolutely urban brasserie, a colourful juxtaposition of town and country with an informal approach. The food is all about brasserie favourites: meaty crowd-pleasers such as chicken liver parfait, ribeye steak with fat chips and peppercorn sauce, and duck breast with garlic-mashed potato. King scallop and salmon terrine with beetroot dressing is among the fish choices, as is sea bass fillet with scallops, tarragon risotto and braised fennel. Desserts include chocolate and orange marquise with praline ice cream. The wines are set out in style and the list offers good-value drinking (from £16.95) rather than impressing with unaffordable bottles – which you can find on the Burlington's 2,000-bin list encompassing the great, the good and the exceedingly rare. **Chef/s:** Daniel Field. **Open:** all week L 12 to 2.30 (4 Sun), D 6 to 9.30 (6.30 Fri and Sat, 9 Sun). **Meals:** alc (main courses £13 to £24). **Details:** 70 seats. 40 seats outside. Wheelchair access. Car parking.

Boroughbridge

The Dining Room

Welcoming family-run restaurant

20 St James Square, Boroughbridge, YO51 9AR
Tel no: (01423) 326426
www.thediningroomonline.co.uk
Modern British | £32
Cooking score: 3

£5
OFF

Dinner at this well-groomed little restaurant begins upstairs in the lounge, a room bursting with sofas, rococo chairs, vases, mirrors and ceiling fans. In contrast, the ground-floor dining room is more understated, making do with thick drapes, smart white tablecloths and maybe a vase holding a single pink tulip. The menu remains proficient if undemanding: prawn cocktail with brown bread and butter; venison terrine with Melba toast, followed by sea trout with samphire; duck confit with black pudding and apple compote or for a supplement, fillet steak with green pepper sauce and chips. Desserts follow a similar tried-and-tested route: sticky toffee pudding, crème brûlée with black cherry Kirsch ice cream or Yorkshire rhubarb fool with shortbread – all accurately prepared and served. Champagne and wines from a standard list start at £19.50.
Chef/s: Chris Astley. Open: Sun L 12 to 2, Tue to Sat D 6.30 to 9.15. Closed: Mon, 1 Jan, bank hols, 4 days Jan, 4 days Jun, 4 days Oct. Meals: alc (main courses £15 to £22). Set L £22 (2 courses) to £27.95. Set D £26 (2 courses) to £32. Sun L £26. Details: 32 seats. 20 seats outside. Separate bar.

⫷ Average Price

The average price listed in main-entry reviews denotes the price of a three-course meal, without wine.

Brough

READERS RECOMMEND

The Boar's Nest

Modern British

Rudstone Walk, South Cave, Brough, HU15 2AH
Tel no: (01482) 445577
www.theboarsnesthull.com

'Puddings shone. A toffee and almond île flottante was a classic done admirably and with imagination, while the special, a chocolate and poached stone-fruit mousse, almost floated away!'

Chapeltown

Greenhead House

Dinner-party vibes in a cottagey setting

84 Burncross Road, Chapeltown, S35 1SF
Tel no: (0114) 2469004
www.greenheadhouse.com
Modern European | £48
Cooking score: 2

A little way out of the city centre, Neil and Anne Allen's cottagey, suburban restaurant has been a fixture on the Sheffield dining scene for three decades. He cooks, she runs front-of-house, and there's a dinner-party feel to proceedings as you sip drinks in the lounge before making your way through to the dining room. The four-course evening menu changes frequently, allowing new ideas to filter through, but generally the cooking is grounded in classic techniques. Terrine of salmon with lemon might be followed by a fruit sorbet to ease you into a main course of roast Gressingham duck with bitter orange sauce. Finish with mixed berry, almond and marzipan pie. House wine is £21.
Chef/s: Neil Allen. Open: Fri L 12 to 1, Wed to Sat D 7 to 8.30. Closed: Sun to Tue, 1 week Christmas and New Year, 2 weeks Jun, 2 weeks Sept. Meals: Set L £22 (2 courses) to £29. Set D £48. Details: 30 seats. Separate bar. Wheelchair access. Car parking.

▌Drighlington

Prashad

Outstanding vegetarian cookery from Gujarat
and south India
137 Whitehall Road, Drighlington, BD11 1AT
Tel no: (01132) 852037
www.prashad.co.uk
Indian Vegetarian | £20
Cooking score: 3

V £30

Prashad has moved from an unglamorous,
windy corner location in Bradford to an old
stone pub on a windy corner in a gritty Leeds
suburb, but the flit seems to suit the Patels.
Mayur has been given free rein with design
and has done a great job, using vibrant colours
that nod to the family's Gujarati heritage. The
dining rooms are huge and ceilings high, but
the place feels cosy. Covers have doubled and
there's a handful of new dishes (including
paneer spheres, light as clouds, and 'wattana
and flower': a delicate, cumin-infused
cauliflower curry). Otherwise, the old menu
stands: a homage to the vegetarian cookery of
Gujarat and south India. The food is as
remarkable as ever, with sublime idli sambar,
masala dosa and tarka dhal ('overly spicy' for
one visitor). The restaurant is now licensed ('so
Tiger beers all round') and good advice has
been taken on wine (from £13.95), which
nicely complements the outstanding cuisine.
Chef/s: Minal Patel. **Open:** Tue to Thur D 5 to 11.30.
Fri to Sun 12 to midnight (9 Sun). **Closed:** Mon, 25
Dec. **Meals:** alc (main courses £7 to £10).
Details: 70 seats. Wheelchair access. Car parking.

▌East Witton

The Blue Lion

Gentrified Dales inn with generous food
East Witton, DL8 4SN
Tel no: (01969) 624273
www.thebluelion.co.uk
Modern British | £35
Cooking score: 3

🛏 V

Visitors to Paul Klein's gentrified Georgian
pub-with-rooms in a lovely corner of the
Dales can look forward to a 'friendly yet
respectful welcome', whether they are aiming
for the handsome, high-ceilinged dining
room or the thronged bar with its locally
brewed ales, flagstone floors and blazing fire.
A big blackboard spells out the day's food and
the cooking is right on the money ('high class
but not extravagant' noted one reader). Come
here for top-notch scallops with caramelised
cauliflower and hazelnut dressing, followed by
plates of pan-roasted wild duck with confit
hash, chanterelles and port jus, or tub-
thumping steak and kidney suet pud served
with North Country generosity. For dessert,
think liquorice Arctic roll or apple and
blackberry trifle with Calvados cream. The
well-spread, 100-bin wine list (from £18.65)
shows 'real quality and consideration'.
Chef/s: Michael McBride. **Open:** all week L 12 to 2, D
7 to 9. **Meals:** alc (main courses £17 to £23). Set L
£15.50 (2 courses) to £18.50. **Details:** 90 seats. 30
seats outside. Separate bar. Wheelchair access. Car
parking.

Ferrensby
The General Tarleton

High-profile foodie beacon
Boroughbridge Road, Ferrensby, HG5 0PZ
Tel no: (01423) 340284
www.generaltarleton.co.uk
Modern British | £30
Cooking score: 4

'It feels like coming home,' confessed a reader after visiting this high-profile foodie beacon in open country off the A1. Chef/proprietor John Topham made his name running the Angel at Hetton (see entry) before bringing its casual, open-minded concept to Ferrensby in 2003. Pick your spot in the formally laid-out dining room, grab a rattan chair in the courtyard or find a snug berth in the darkly traditional bar – the menu is the same throughout. 'Pub classics' such as burgers and smoked chicken Caesar salad share the billing with locally shot game and dishes inspired by North Country ingredients: think Northumbrian crab and scallop lasagne, twice-baked ewes' cheese soufflé or a tasting of Garstang suckling pig with black pudding and prunes wrapped in pancetta. To round things off, everyone loves the treacle sponge pud and the dark chocolate fondant with orange curd. 'Family simple suppers' show that the place understands its audience. The top-notch wine list offers sophisticated drinking from £18.95.
Chef/s: John Topham. Open: all week L 12 to 2, D 5.30 to 9 (9.15 Sat, 8.30 Sun). Meals: alc (main courses £11 to £23). Set L and D £15 (2 courses) to £18.50. Sun L £22.50. Details: 120 seats. 60 seats outside. Car parking.

Goldsborough
The Fox & Hounds

No fuss, just high-quality food
Goldsborough, YO21 3RX
Tel no: (01947) 893372
www.foxandhoundsgoldsborough.co.uk
Modern European | £34
Cooking score: 5

Jason and Sue Davies have been running this pint-sized country restaurant (seemingly in the middle of nowhere) for 10 years and have maintained a tenacious local following for well-crafted, seasonal dinner menus and amiable service. With just three choices per course (and one main always a steak), the brevity of the menu is the kitchen's strength. Local and regional raw materials, plus impeccably sourced produce from further afield, are the building blocks; bread is baked each day and the results are straight and true. Simplicity is evident in a dish of smoked haddock carpaccio with Savoy cabbage, capers and parsley, while mains could include a well-reported Saddleback pork shoulder braised in milk with smashed cannellini beans and curly kale. A sliver of dark chocolate truffle cake with espresso cream or rhubarb, blood orange and vanilla with crème fraîche could be offered alongside English cheeses, which are kept in their prime. The diverse wine list promises good drinking from £18.
Chef/s: Jason Davies. Open: Wed to Sat D only 6.30 to 8.30. Closed: Sun to Tue, Christmas, bank hols. Meals: alc (main courses £16 to £26). Details: 26 seats. Car parking.

▌Grassington

Grassington House Hotel
Impressive field-to-fork food
5 The Square, Grassington, BD23 5AQ
Tel no: (01756) 752406
www.grassingtonhousehotel.co.uk
Modern British | £33
Cooking score: 3

£5 OFF 🛏

With the majestic Yorkshire Dales all around, the Ruddens' capably refurbished hotel overlooking Grassington's cobbled square is perfectly situated for walkers and nature-lovers. Simple meals can be eaten in the bar, and an outdoor terrace comes into use on fine days, but the main business takes place in 5 The Square, the elegantly appointed dining room. Hand-reared rare-breed pork is a speciality, seen in a main course of loin and belly, fragrant with herbs, accompanied by pungent caper jus. The beef skirt rag pudding with filet mignon in red wine jus pleases reporters, too. Starters might encompass tempura tiger prawns with coriander marie-rose dressing and lime salt, while a meal could come to a triumphant conclusion with freshly baked tarte Tatin for sharing, served with thick vanilla cream. Wines from an international list start with Galician house selections at £15.25.
Chef/s: John Rudden. **Open:** Mon to Sun L 12 to 2.30 (4 Sat, 5 Sun), D 6 to 9.30 (8.30 Sun). **Closed:** 25 Dec. **Meals:** alc (main courses £12 to £24). Set L and D £13.50 (2 courses) to £16.50. Sun L £14.50. Bar menu also available. **Details:** 67 seats. 30 seats outside. Separate bar. Wheelchair access. Car parking.

▌Harome

The Pheasant Hotel
Impeccably modern food forged in a rustic setting
Mill Street, Harome, YO62 5JG
Tel no: (01439) 771241
www.thepheasanthotel.com
Modern British | £36
Cooking score: 4

🛏 V

In a village not short of culinary fireworks, the Pheasant's reputation is assured – Jacquie Pern from the nearby Star Inn (see entry) is a co-owner. The converted 17th-century forge, shop and barn with a wisteria-decked terrace overlooking the duck pond might make you expect something staid. Step inside, however, and the décor is sophisticated in contemporary browns, mushroom and creams, while Peter Neville's impeccably modern approach in the kitchen is light and seasonal. Pheasant ballotine and foie gras with sour pears, macadamia nuts and bread crisps is a typical starter, full of vivid contrasts and textures. Main-course halibut is cooked in brown butter and teamed with caramelised salsify, fresh chestnuts and pickled clams, and a trolley of fine farmhouse cheeses makes a tempting alternative to 'superb' lemon thyme pannacotta with Comice pear, Breton biscuit and brown-butter ice cream. Service is from a variously abled team. Wines from £19.
Chef/s: Peter Neville. **Open:** all week L 12 to 2, D 6.30 to 9.30. **Meals:** alc (main courses £21 to £24). Set L £23.50 (2 courses) to £28.50. Set D £36. Tasting menu £65 (7 courses). **Details:** 40 seats. 25 seats outside. Separate bar. Wheelchair access. Car parking.

The Star Inn
Highly popular hostelry with serious food
High Street, Harome, YO62 5JE
Tel no: (01439) 770397
www.thestaratharome.co.uk
Modern British | £40
Cooking score: 5

The reputation of Andrew Pern's gentrified thatched inn spreads far beyond its immediate locale, a tiny village on the edge of the North York Moors. So, you'll need to book a table in the comfortable, countrified restaurant, in the posher, welcome-to-the-21st-century dining room extension, or join the queues in the cosy old bar. Almost all the food is local, regional or home-grown – and the menu continues to flag up exciting treatments. In winter expect deep-fried Scarborough woof with brown crab mayonnaise, buttered marsh samphire and brown shrimps, ahead of locally shot hare with its own sausage roll, honeyed swede, celeriac purée, York ham and tarragon juices. Desserts, such as a melting baked dark chocolate and blood-orange pudding served with a sloe gin sorbet, don't let the side down, while the cheeseboard features half a dozen specimens (from Yorkshire, of course). The focus on quality sourcing continues on the drinks list, where a host of fine producers mingle under the banners of Europe and the New World. There's irresistible choice by the glass, and bottles from £18.95.
Chef/s: Andrew Pern. **Open:** Tue to Sun L 12 to 2 (12 to 6 Sun), Mon to Sat D 6.30 to 9.30. **Closed:** 1 Jan. **Meals:** alc (main courses £17 to £26). Set L and D £20 (2 courses) to £25. **Details:** 60 seats. 50 seats outside. Separate bar. Wheelchair access. Car parking.

‖‖ Visit us Online
To find out more about
The Good Food Guide, please visit
www.thegoodfoodguide.co.uk

▊ Harrogate

Orchid Restaurant
Well-crafted oriental cooking
Studley Hotel, 28 Swan Road, Harrogate, HG1 2SE
Tel no: (01423) 560425
www.orchidrestaurant.co.uk
Pan-Asian | £28
Cooking score: 2

In a setting that is contemporary but hardly 'designer', this comfortably appointed restaurant in the Studley Hotel continues to attract loyal followers, who come to enjoy satisfying pan-Asian food. Dishes are elegantly pared down and flavours restrained, but ingredients are fresh and carefully cooked – witness well-timed steamed sea bass fillets with spring onion and soy. The menu travels all over, providing a roll call of the most popular Chinese and Asian dishes: Cantonese sweet-and-sour prawns; Malaysian beef rendang; bang bang chicken from Szechuan; a Thai massaman curry; crispy duck from Hong Kong. Service is polite and pleasant. House wine is £17.80.
Chef/s: Kenneth Poon. **Open:** Mon to Fri and Sun L 12 to 2, all week D 6 to 10. **Closed:** 25 and 26 Dec. **Meals:** alc (main courses £9 to £20). **Details:** 85 seats. 24 seats outside. Separate bar. Car parking.

Sasso
Sound regional Italian cooking
8-10 Princes Square, Harrogate, HG1 1LX
Tel no: (01423) 508838
www.sassorestaurant.co.uk
Italian | £26
Cooking score: 3

The location may be the smart basement of a Georgian terraced house but the Italian heart of this restaurant shines through. Chef Stefano Lancellotti's trademark pasta has drawn praise once again this year (perhaps truffled pasta ribbons served with tiger prawn, scampi, lobster, crabmeat and asparagus sauce), while Yorkshire ribeye, hung for 40 days, local corn-

fed chicken and game, and venison cutlets wrapped in Tuscan pork and served with a berry sauce and chestnut mash all add merit. Antipasti include crab cakes with ginger, basil and sun-blushed tomatoes, served with a sweet caramelised lemon and garlic sauce, and dolci are true to form with tiramisu or homemade Italian ice creams, or there is a selection of Italian, French and English cheeses. The wine list is well put together (and not just from Italy), with bottles starting at £13.95.
Chef/s: Stefano Lancellotti. **Open:** Mon to Sat L 12 to 2 (2.30 Sat), D 5.45 to 10 (10.30 Fri and Sat). **Closed:** Sun, 25 and 26 Dec, 1 Jan. **Meals:** alc (main courses £13 to £22). Set L £8.95 (2 courses). **Details:** 90 seats. 20 seats outside.

Van Zeller
A chef firing on all cylinders
8 Montpellier Street, Harrogate, HG1 2TQ
Tel no: (01423) 508762
www.vanzellerrestaurants.co.uk
Modern British | £50
Cooking score: 4

£5 OFF **V**

In the heart of historic Harrogate, Tom Van Zeller's restaurant is small and narrow but also cordial, chatty and affably civilised. Many regulars return again and again to reclaim their favourite tables in the window. The menu is based on high-quality raw materials and, although there can be a lot happening on the plate, timing and technique have been praised. One reporter writes approvingly of a winter dinner that began with a 'very pretty dish' of East Coast crab served with mussel beignets, bisque, cauliflower, apple and Manzanilla olives, and then proceeded to tender Scottish red deer, with good smoked potato, chestnut purée, root vegetables and pepper, juniper and blackcurrant sauce. Desserts, too, show a kitchen that is innovative: chocolate orange ('rather like a posh jaffa cake') with 'lovely' popcorn ice cream. Service is pleasant and the wine list opens at £21.50.

Chef/s: Neil Bentinck. **Open:** Tue to Sun L 12 to 2, Tue to Sat D 6 to 10. **Closed:** Mon, 25 and 26 Dec, 1 to 9 Jan, 17 to 20 Feb, Easter, 29 to 5 Aug, 26 and 27 Aug. **Meals:** alc £49.50 (5 courses). Set L and early D £25 (5 courses). Seasonal menu £70 (7 courses). **Details:** 34 seats.

▌Hetton
The Angel Inn
Honest-to-goodness country pub for foodies
Hetton, BD23 6LT
Tel no: (01756) 730263
www.angelhetton.co.uk
Modern British | £30
Cooking score: 3

🛏 **V** £30

A fixture in this Guide for nearly 30 years, the Angel is a swish country inn covered in two shades of creeper. Within, you'll find ancient beams, guest rooms and an expertly constructed menu overflowing with pedigree meats from the Dales and Lancs, fish from both east and west coasts and produce from local farms. The appeal is easy to see, and dishes have a high success rate. To post notice of intent, the house black pudding comes with poached eggs and a balsamic-roasted pear in a mustard and red wine sauce. Game is a forte; 'fabulously tender' medallions and confit of partridge are served with cabbage and lardons, artichoke purée, beetroot fondant and pea shoots – a perfectly balanced dish. Dessert might be pumpkin and orange génoise with pumpkin-seed brittle and a pumpkin and lime sorbet. Service is 'wonderfully attentive', and house wines are £16.95, with glasses from £4.85.
Chef/s: Bruce Elsworth. **Open:** Mon to Sat L 12 to 2, D 6 to 9.45. Sun 12 to 8.30. **Closed:** 4 days Jan. **Meals:** alc (main courses £13 to £27). Set L and D £12.95 (2 courses) to £15.95. Sun L £27.50. **Details:** 120 seats. 20 seats outside. Separate bar. Wheelchair access. Car parking.

Honley

ALSO RECOMMENDED
▲ Mustard & Punch

6 Westgate, Honley, HD9 6AA
Tel no: (01484) 662066
www.mustardandpunch.co.uk
British

A 'great asset' to its home village near
Huddersfield, this 'welcoming' stone-built
British bistro is valued for its warm
atmosphere. Chef/owners Richard Dunn and
Wayne Roddis have a robust contemporary
outlook and a fondness for game, shown in
dishes such as pheasant rillettes with whipped
goats' cheese and pickled beetroot (£7.50) or
pan-fried saddle of hare with creamed peas,
bacon and cabbage (£16.50). 'Excellent'
house-made ice cream is available to take
home. The wine list opens at £16.50. Open
Tue to Sat D.

Huddersfield

Bradley's

Boisterous basement brasserie
84 Fitzwilliam Street, Huddersfield, HD1 5BB
Tel no: (01484) 516773
www.bradleysrestaurant.co.uk
Modern British | £27
Cooking score: 2

£5 £30
OFF

A loyal Huddersfield servant for many years,
Andrew Bradley aims to please all-comers in
the basement of this converted mill. Light
lunches provide easy-going, fairly priced
nourishment for shoppers and business types
who crowd the split-level dining room. By
contrast, lively evening menus go walkabout
in search of satisfaction and value. You might
follow smoked haddock and Cheddar rarebit
with the likes of roast pork fillet with black
pudding mash from the 'prime time' menu
deal, while home-cured monkfish gravlax
with beetroot blini and dill dressing, and
venison haunch with horseradish and thyme
rösti are highlights from the carte. For afters,
try the warm Bakewell tart with mango

coulis. Wines from £15.95. There's a branch at
46-50 Highgate, Heaton, Bradford; tel
(01274) 499890.
Chef/s: Jamie Rylance. **Open:** Tue to Fri L 12 to 2,
Tue to Sat D 6 to 10 (5.30 Fri and Sat). **Closed:** Sun,
Mon, 27 Dec for 1 week, bank hols. **Meals:** alc (main
courses £10 to £21). Set L £7.95 (2 courses) to £9.95.
Set D £14.45 (2 courses) to £21.45 (3 courses inc
wine). **Details:** 120 seats. Separate bar. Wheelchair
access.

ALSO RECOMMENDED
▲ T&Cake

91a Northgate, Almondbury, Huddersfield,
HD5 8RX
Tel no: (01484) 430005
www.t-and-cake.co.uk
British

Stephen and Tracy Jackson welcome everyone
to their pair of knocked-through terraced
houses, now a modern café. Casual flexibility
and commitment to local and home-grown
produce provide nourishment for shoppers
and business people alike, opening with
breakfast, delivering a superb range of
homemade cakes (lemon drizzle, £2.50), and
continuing with lunch of soup, Welsh rarebit
or club sandwich (both £7), perhaps roast
chicken Caesar salad. To drink you'll find
speciality teas, coffees and wines from £16.
Open Mon to Sat L.

Ilkley

★ TOP 50 ★

The Box Tree

One of Yorkshire's very finest destinations
35-37 Church Street, Ilkley, LS29 9DR
Tel no: (01943) 608484
www.theboxtree.co.uk
Anglo-French | £55
Cooking score: 6

🍷

'Expectation and delivery rarely match when
eating out, but the Box Tree never fails to
deliver, and nearly always exceeds
expectations.' So begins a regular's account of

the enduring appeal of Ilkley's finest. This elegant restaurant has an endearingly old-fashioned look, with striped wallpaper, paisley upholstery and charming prints. After a warm, efficient welcome, service is discreet and understated. Simon Gueller's food seems re-energised of late. There is real class in a Jerusalem artichoke velouté, with truffle providing the bass-note accompaniment. Mango, coconut and toasted almonds make modish enhancements to a lobster first course, and then there may be roast squab with seared foie gras, Puy lentils, bacon and shallots, or a fillet of John Dory adorned with truffled gnocchi, turnip and salsify purée. Our reporter's companion fell to awed silence during a pineapple Tatin with rum and raisin ice cream: sure sign of a fine final flourish. Patagonia is accorded nation status on a distinguished wine list that leaves no global stone unturned in its search for quality. Bottles are from £21.
Chef/s: Simon Gueller and Lawrence Yates. **Open:** Fri to Sun L 12 to 2, Tue to Sat D 7 to 9.30 (6.30 Sat). **Closed:** Mon, 26 to 30 Dec. **Meals:** Set L £28. Set D £60. Sun L £35. Gourmand menu £70. **Details:** 50 seats. Separate bar. Wheelchair access. No children under 10 yrs at D.

Farsyde
Long-running favourite with keenly priced specials
1-3 New Brook Street, Ilkley, LS29 8DQ
Tel no: (01943) 602030
www.thefarsyde.co.uk
Modern British | £28
Cooking score: 3
£5 £30
OFF

A 'wonderful' atmosphere and 'excellent' food continue to attract readers to this long-running Ilkley eatery. Chef/proprietor Gavin Beedham's contemporary take on classic brasserie cooking appeals to all-comers, whether it's traditional European dishes or flavours from further afield. To begin, smoked haddock and goats' cheese soufflé might sit alongside crispy duck, noodle, pepper, spring onion and watercress salad with plum

dressing. Typical mains could include fillet of salmon served with potted salmon and dill blini, crushed pea and mint and white wine and truffle sauce or a more classic fillet of beef with oxtail pudding, boudin noir, parsnip purée and red wine sauce. Warm parkin with praline ice cream, ginger sauce and damson compote provides a fitting finale. Good-value set lunches and early-bird dinners are a popular option, too. A reasonably priced wine list starts at £15.25.
Chef/s: Gavin Beedham. **Open:** Tue to Sat L 11.30 to 2, D 6 to 10. **Closed:** Sun, Mon, 25 and 26 Dec, 1 to 3 Jan. **Meals:** alc (main courses £15 to £22). Set L £15.85 (3 courses). Early D £15.95 (2 courses). **Details:** 82 seats. Separate bar. Wheelchair access.

Ilkley Moor Vaults
Pub with plenty to please
Stockeld Road, Ilkley, LS29 9HD
Tel no: (01943) 607012
www.ilkleymoorvaults.co.uk
Modern British | £23
Cooking score: 2
£5 £30
OFF

It's nigh-on eight years since Joe McDermott established his homely pub as one of the best in the area. It remains a local watering hole – stone floors, open fires and scrubbed pine tables help create a mood that is dressed down and relaxed – while the food taps into the current appetite for ingredient-led, straight-down-the-line dishes with clean-cut flavours. Lishman's rib of beef for two with béarnaise sauce is a meaty big hitter, but the menu covers a lot of ground, taking in everything from game terrine and Bleiker's smoked salmon to smoked haddock with mustard sauce, spinach and mash, and coq au vin. Desserts pitch chocolate and hazelnut truffle cake against homemade rice pudding with poached prunes. Wines start at £14.90.
Chef/s: Sabi Janak. **Open:** Tue to Sat L 12 to 2.30 (3 Sat), Tue to Sat D 5.30 to 9. Sun 12 to 7. **Closed:** Mon. **Meals:** alc (main courses £10 to £20). Early D £10 (2 courses) to £13.50. **Details:** 60 seats. 30 seats outside. Wheelchair access. Car parking.

Leeds

Brasserie Forty 4
A nice place to be
44 The Calls, Leeds, LS2 7EW
Tel no: (0113) 2343232
www.brasserie44.com
Modern European | £28
Cooking score: 2

£30

With a prime location on the banks of the river Aire, there is more to Brasserie Forty 4 than the mere novelty value of a city-centre riverside location in the Calls complex. Conversion has given the interior of this 18th-century corn mill a thoroughly modern urban look – though hard edges (painted brick walls, bare tables, wood floor) mean the place gets noisy when busy. The menu deals in an uncomplicated range of classic brasserie dishes: chicken liver parfait; venison haunch with roasted celeriac and juniper sauce; steak with peppercorn sauce. Oxtail risotto has been a hit this year, a daily fish special could be Cajun cod with spiced pilau rice and there's blueberry ripple cheesecake for afters. Wines from £16.25.
Chef/s: David Robson. **Open:** Mon to Sat L 12 to 2 (1 to 3 Sat), D 5.30 to 9.30 (5 Sat). **Closed:** Sun, 25 and 26 Dec, bank hols (exc Good Friday). **Meals:** alc (main courses £13 to £20). Set L and D £23.95 (3 courses, inc half-bottle of wine). **Details:** 120 seats. 18 seats outside. Separate bar. Wheelchair access. Children over 2 yrs only.

NEW ENTRY
Crafthouse
Grills in stylish surrounds
Level 5 Trinity Leeds, 70 Boar Lane, Leeds, LS1 6HW
Tel no: (0113) 8970444
www.crafthouse-restaurant.com
Modern British
Cooking score: 3

Trinity Leeds, the mega shopping centre that opened to much fanfare in 2013, features 20-plus chain restaurants and the flagship Crafthouse. Appropriately aloof on the fifth floor, the cool interior and wraparound glass looks on to a city roofscape, and from setting and service through to the food, it's a polished act. The menu majors on grills, produced on a Josper, with steaks sourced from Yorkshire farm Ginger Pig. Start with bacon chop and run pricily through sirloin, ribeye, rump and beef rib; lobster, sea bass and Dover sole also get a searing. Elsewhere are more homely dishes such as tarragon-flavoured chicken casserole and mash. Start with crab, potted shrimps or grilled oysters and finish with retro desserts such as sherry trifle or jelly and rhubarb. On the sixth floor, the more informal (and cheaper) Angelica has small plates to share, a raw bar, salads and mains of pasta, risotto, burgers and steaks. A well-drawn-up wine list starts at £17.
Chef/s: Lee Bennett. **Open:** all week L 12 to 3, D 5 to 11 (10 Sun). **Closed:** 25 Dec. **Meals:** alc (mains £15 to £38). Set L and early D £18.50 (2 courses) to £22.50. **Details:** 120 seats. Wheelchair access.

NEW ENTRY
The Reliance
An imaginative menu and spectacular beers
76-78 North Street, Leeds, LS2 7PN
Tel no: (0113) 2956060
www.the-reliance.co.uk
Modern British | £23
Cooking score: 3

£30

An informal bar-cum-restaurant on the edge of the city centre, the Reliance has ambition impressively beyond bar-food norms. Out of the open-plan kitchen in the big, unfussy dining room comes a tempting selection of provender, with pork products to the fore – including ham hock terrine and pork chops from the owners' own butchery. Pancetta, chorizo, lomo, coppa and aged ham are showcased on the charcuterie board and also sold as take-aways. There are appetising fish and vegetarian choices, too, while desserts give standard puds a shake-up, as in lemon Eton mess and grapefruit. Tall windows, Formica-topped tables and utility lamps characterise the congenial setting, with sharp service keeping everything switched on. The imaginative wine list opens at £14.25, and a spectacular, ever-changing beer menu spans the world: from Goole's Great Heck Brewing Company to Sierra Nevada's Torpedo. **Chef/s:** Simon Moxham. **Open:** Mon to Sun L 12 to 5 (11 to 4 Sun). Mon to Sun D 5.30 to 10 (6 to 9.30 Sun). **Closed:** 25 and 26 Dec, bank hols. **Meals:** alc (main courses £10 to £17). Pre-theatre D £13.95 (2 courses) to £17.95. **Details:** 128 seats. 6 seats outside. Separate bar.

Salvo's

Fantastic pizzas and budget prices
115 Otley Road, Headingley, Leeds, LS6 3PX
Tel no: (0113) 2755017
www.salvos.co.uk
Italian | £28
Cooking score: 2

£30

Firmly stamped with the individuality of its owners, this one-off Italian has a loyal band of regulars who praise its atmosphere, service and great food. Many ingredients come direct from Italy, the rest provided by a carefully nurtured network of local suppliers. Cooking is an expansive mix of big flavours and hearty dishes from across Italy. Try Puglian fishcake (sea bass layered with potatoes and pecorino), followed by agnello con faro (braised lamb shoulder with creamed potatoes and spelt). Pasta is also a sure-fire success and pizzas are among 'the best you will ever try' – worth queuing for if you can't get a reservation. Well-priced wines open at £16.50. Salumeria, the nearby sister café and Italian deli, is also 'outstanding'. **Chef/s:** Gip Dammone. **Open:** Mon to Sat L 12 to 2, D 6 to 10.30 (5.30 to 11 Fri and Sat). Sun 12 to 9. **Closed:** 25 and 26 Dec, 1 Jan. **Meals:** alc (main courses £10 to £22). Set L £11.50 (2 courses). Set D and Sun L £14.50 (2 courses) to £17.50. **Details:** 88 seats. 20 seats outside. Separate bar. Wheelchair access.

ALSO RECOMMENDED

▲ Fourth Floor

Harvey Nichols, 107-111 Briggate, Leeds, LS1 6AZ
Tel no: (0113) 2048000
www.harveynichols.com
Modern European

Harvey Nichols' Fourth Floor Café has always been a glam treat, especially with its new glitzy gold, teal and mirrored look. Classical, contemporary culinary skills are evident in a perfectly judged plate of pea and mint risotto with salt cod fritter and Parmesan crisp, while the beef flat-iron steak has been judged 'the best I've eaten this year': both dishes from a £20 three-course set lunch. Yes, there are inconsistencies – the confit salmon, the deconstructed peach Melba Eton mess – but the atmosphere is inclusive, fostered by carefully trained staff. House wine £19.50. Open all week except Sun and Mon D.

▲ Hansa's

72-74 North Street, Leeds, LS2 7PN
Tel no: (0113) 2444408
www.hansasrestaurant.com
Indian Vegetarian

'Gujarati vegetarian dishes, beautifully presented and delicious' is what Hansa Dabhi's homely restaurant on the edge of Leeds city centre is all about. Established in 1986, it gives a glimpse of real India via the spicy chilli paneer (£4.25) and stuffed paratha, the light, fresh and flavourful vegetable curries – say Indian baby pumpkin (£6.50) or delicious maag-ni-dhal (bean curry made with split mung beans and fenugreek leaves) – and the splendid mango kulfi for dessert. Service is polite and friendly. Closed Sun D and L Mon to Sat.

▲ Sukhothai

8 Regent Street, Chapel Allerton, Leeds, LS7 4PE
Tel no: (0113) 2370141
www.sukhothai.co.uk
Thai £5 OFF

The original of what is now a trio of restaurants, this much-loved Thai in Chapel Allerton remains the pick of the bunch. An epic menu requires some navigating, but there are savvy set deals for beginners (from £22), while the carte delivers some adventurous gems in the form of chicken and duck liver fried with garlic, black pepper, lime leaves, oyster sauce, onion and fresh chilli (£9.95), alongside the more familiar pad thai noodle dishes and massaman curry (from £9.50). Wine from £13.95. Closed Mon to Wed L.

▌Leyburn

The Sandpiper Inn

Highly polished Dales inn
Market Place, Leyburn, DL8 5AT
Tel no: (01969) 622206
www.sandpiperinn.co.uk
Modern British | £32
Cooking score: 3

It's nigh-on 15 years since the Harrisons took over this 17th-century inn at the heart of Leyburn, and it continues to go from strength to strength. An amenable place, the Sandpiper pleases with its country comforts – a wood-burning stove in the bar, oak floors and polished tables in the dining room – and Jonathan's seasonal menus yield interesting possibilities. He aims for a modern British approach, adding crab-apple jelly and pickled onions to a country terrine starter. Likewise, Swinton Park venison on a pearl barley and vegetable risotto with chestnut mushrooms, and slow-cooked Harrison-Topham lamb with smoked garlic, wilted greens and potato gnocchi are typical main courses. A few snacks and pubby dishes are offered in the bar at lunchtime. Desserts run the familiar gamut from crème brûlée to sticky toffee pudding. Wines from £14.95.

Chef/s: Jonathan Harrison. Open: Tue to Sun L 12 to 2.30, D 6.30 to 9 (9.30 Fri and Sat). Closed: Mon, Tue in winter. Meals: alc (main courses £14 to £20). Details: 40 seats. 20 seats outside. Separate bar. Car parking.

▌Lindley

★ READERS' RESTAURANT OF THE YEAR ★
NORTH EAST

Eric's

In tune with its customers
75 Lidget Street, Lindley, HD3 3JP
Tel no: (01484) 646416
www.ericsrestaurant.co.uk
Modern British | £30
Cooking score: 3

With readers keen on its 'seasonal changes, local produce and dedicated team', Eric Paxman's restaurant seems completely in tune with its customers. Set over two floors of a converted terrace, with local artwork on the walls, it's a 'warm, sociable' place to try dishes that please more often than they surprise. Even in the middle of the Pennines, fish is a strength. Start, perhaps, with crisp tandoori sea bass with spiced onion yoghurt, then Yorkshire spring lamb rack with a sunshine-evoking assembly of roast red peppers, feta, dill, lemon and harissa. Local pride is further stirred with Yorkshire versus Lancashire cheeses, or crème brûlée with ginger and Yorkshire rhubarb compote. House wine is £16.20, with plenty of bottles under £25.
Chef/s: Eric Paxman. Open: Tue to Fri L 12 to 2 (4 Sun), Tue to Sat D 6 to 10. Closed: Mon, 1 to 11 Jan. Meals: alc (main courses £13 to £26). Set L £14.95 (2 courses) to £16.95. Set D £18.95 (2 courses) to £21.95. Sun L £18.95 (2 courses) to £21.95. Details: 70 seats. Separate bar.

■ Malton

Talbot Hotel

Revamped hotel with a celeb chef
45 Yorkersgate, Malton, YO17 7AJ
Tel no: (01653) 639096
www.talbotmalton.co.uk
Modern British | £36
Cooking score: 3

🛏

TV chef James Martin was born in Malton and has returned to his home turf to head the kitchen at this expensively revamped, Grade II-listed hotel (part of the Fitzwilliam Estate). Horsey prints and other county paraphernalia point up the traditional dining room. Here, Yorkshire produce underpins the regularly changing menu – perhaps north-coast mackerel with beetroot dressing, blinis, herb crème fraîche and sorrel or a more exotic plate of pan-fried wreck fish with coconut-curried mussels, purple kale and lime-scented sauce. Meat eaters might plump for braised beef cheek in Riggwelter ale (from the Black Sheep brewery), while vegetarians could be swayed by an English truffle risotto with a slow-cooked egg. To conclude, desserts are a safe mix of homespun and fancy, from Bakewell tart to a crisp chocolate cylinder with blackberry mousse, Douglas Fir sorbet and pistachios. Wines start at £18.
Chef/s: James Martin. **Open:** all week L 12 to 2.30, D 6.30 to 9.30. **Meals:** Set D £30 (2 courses) to £36. Sun L £25. **Details:** 70 seats. Separate bar. Wheelchair access. Car parking.

■ Masham

Samuel's at Swinton Park

Exhilarating cooking and Gothic grandeur
Swinton Park, Masham, HG4 4JH
Tel no: (01765) 680900
www.swintonpark.com
Modern British | £52
Cooking score: 5

🛏 V

Nothing's done by halves at Swinton Park, where hotel residents can play at being aristocracy in the grand turreted house, vast estate and walled kitchen garden. The 'serene' dining room, with its ornate gold-leaf ceiling, is named after Samuel Cunliffe-Lister, who built it in 1890. His successors still run the place, combining heritage and heavy upholstery for a grand and cocooning experience. Chef Simon Crannage, reckoned by one correspondent to be 'at the top of his game', produces food with a matching sense of place and occasion. The Swinton larder is stuffed full of estate pheasant (perhaps pheasant rillettes with date purée, mulled turnips and game chips) and trout, Yorkshire meat and cheese, and the odd touch of spice – seen, perhaps, in fillet of stone bass with cumin-spiced mussels, toasted coconut and squash cream. Yorkshire rhubarb with granola, yoghurt mousse and rhubarb sorbet is among a slightly repetitive dessert selection, though readers praise the 'inventive' approach at work elsewhere. Wine starts at £21.50 from a manageable list divided by style.
Chef/s: Simon Crannage. **Open:** Tue to Sun L 12.30 to 2, all week D 7.30 to 9.30 (10 Fri and Sat). **Meals:** alc brasserie menu (£11 to £16). Set L £22 (2 courses) to £25.95. Set D £52. Sun L £28. Tasting menu £60 (7 courses) to £70 (10 courses). **Details:** 60 seats. Children over 8 yrs only at D.

Vennell's

Bringing metropolitan chic to Masham
7 Silver Street, Masham, HG4 4DX
Tel no: (01765) 689000
www.vennellsrestaurant.co.uk
Modern British | £28
Cooking score: 5

£5 OFF V £30

Now comfortable in its new skin following a 2012 makeover, this much-appreciated local restaurant brings metropolitan chic to provincial Masham with its striking interiors, cool first-floor bar, aubergine walls and sparkling gold mirrors. It feels serious, yet sociable – a mood reflected by good-humoured staff who manage just the right blend of dutiful intent and chatty informality. Jon Vennell's kitchen has turned out some marvellous food of late, including an amuse-bouche of delectable tomato consommé, venison carpaccio, roast partridge, and lamb presented three ways ('absolutely splendid in every respect', according to the happy recipient). Precisely handled fish is a regular star turn: anything from scallops with Jerusalem artichoke purée, micro cress and sweet-and-sour raisins to roast masala monkfish with braised lentils and pickled carrots or 'superb' sea trout with crab, buttered spinach and sauce gribiche. To finish, readers have praised the pear and frangipane pithiviers and the 'well-balanced', satisfying selection of Yorkshire cheeses (note the Barncliffe Brie). The wine list has been thoughtfully revamped with the menu in mind; 11 house selections start at £18.95 (£5.50 a glass).
Chef/s: Jon Vennell. **Open:** Sun L 12.30 to 4, Tue to Sat D 7.15 to 11.30. **Closed:** Mon, first 2 weeks Jan, 1 week Jun, 1 week Sept. **Meals:** Set D £24.50 (2 courses) to £27.99. Sun L £19.50. **Details:** 28 seats. Separate bar.

▌Newton-on-Ouse

The Dawnay Arms

Brit cooking with verve and gusto
Newton-on-Ouse, YO30 2BR
Tel no: (01347) 848345
www.thedawnayatnewton.co.uk
British | £30
Cooking score: 3

Bordering the Ouse, this 18th-century pub has its car park and garden running down to the river. Inside, rough chunky tables work well in the bar and the big, sunny dining room. A test meal in mid-spring began with an adequate potted Whitby crab and toast, and an exceptional crisp-coated, soft-boiled egg with asparagus, new potatoes and tarragon cream sauce. Salmon fillet excepted, meat dominated the mains. Roast chicken breast with risotto and asparagus was pleasing, as was wood pigeon 'Wellington' – although some greens alongside the black pudding, fondant potatoes and ultra-smooth celeriac purée would have relieved an otherwise monochrome plate. At dessert a pyramid of nougat ice cream, doused in passion fruit flesh and encased in caramel, stood out. The vegetarian choice is 'pedestrian', however, but service is charming 'despite being short-staffed and a large party in'. A standard wine list opens at £14.95.
Chef/s: Martel Smith. **Open:** Tue to Sun L 12 to 2.30 (6 Sun), Tue to Sat D 6 to 9.30. **Closed:** Mon, 1 week Jan. **Meals:** alc (main courses £17 to £20). Set L £12.95 (2 courses) to £15.95. Set D £13.95 (2 courses) to £16.95. Sun L £15.95 (2 courses) to £18.95. **Details:** 80 seats. 80 seats outside. Separate bar. Wheelchair access. Car parking.

▌Oldstead

The Black Swan
From family inn to garlanded restaurant
Oldstead, YO61 4BL
Tel no: (01347) 868387
www.blackswanoldstead.co.uk
Modern British | £45
Cooking score: 4
🛏 V

A veteran provider of hospitality in rural
North Yorkshire, the Black Swan started life as
a local pub – although it now flourishes as an
engaging country restaurant-with-rooms.
Inside it sports a stone-flagged bar with all the
appeal of an old-fashioned village hostelry and
an oak-floored dining room decorated in
traditional country-house style. Reporters
have emerged full of praise for the 'beautifully
presented food' with its strong seasonal accent.
Scallops with celeriac, pancetta, capers and sea
purslane might vie for attention with a
dynamic teaming of wood pigeon with
pickled vegetables, beetroot, watercress and
walnuts among starters. Main courses stretch
out expansively, encompassing the likes of
halibut with Jerusalem artichoke, squid, Pink
Fir potatoes and samphire, or ox cheek with
cauliflower cheese, macaroni, truffle and
salsify. To finish, there's praise for the rhubarb
soufflé with stem ginger ice cream and the
'well-balanced' selection of regional English
cheeses. Wines from £19.
Chef/s: Tommy Banks. **Open:** Thur to Sun L 12 to 2
(2.30 Sun), all week D 6 to 9. **Closed:** 2 weeks Jan.
Meals: alc (main courses £21 to £26). Set L and D
£25. Tasting menu L £35, D £70. **Details:** 50 seats.
20 seats outside. Separate bar. Car parking.

Symbols
🛏 Accommodation is available
£30 Three courses for less than £30
V Separate vegetarian menu
£5 OFF £5-off voucher scheme
🍷 Notable wine list

▌Osmotherley

Golden Lion
Warm-hearted Yorkshire watering hole
6 West End, Osmotherley, DL6 3AA
Tel no: (01609) 883526
www.goldenlionosmotherley.co.uk
Anglo-French | £26
Cooking score: 2
🛏 £30

No frills – that goes for the décor, menu and
food – just about sums up Christie Connelly's
village inn. The bar dispenses real ale and
drinkers are made very welcome, but good-
value cooking is the thing, and this is a
convivial place to eat. The endearingly
homespun menu might see the likes of king
prawns in garlic butter or barbecue pork ribs
to start, with mains of homemade chicken
Kiev, steak and kidney pie and fried fillet of
plaice with chips, peas and tartare sauce.
Desserts are pretty much in the 'like mother
used to make' vein – favourites such as ginger
sponge or bread-and-butter pudding – but
there's also a very good Middle Eastern orange
cake with marmalade cream. Wines
from £16.95.
Chef/s: Chris Wright. **Open:** Wed to Sun L 12 to 2.30,
all week D 6 to 9. **Closed:** 25 Dec. **Meals:** alc (main
courses £11 to £21). Sun L £12.95 (1 course).
Details: 63 seats. 16 seats outside. Wheelchair
access.

▌Pickering

The White Swan Inn
Big-hearted Yorkshire hospitality
Market Place, Pickering, YO18 7AA
Tel no: (01751) 472288
www.white-swan.co.uk
Modern British | £35
Cooking score: 3
🛏

Members of the Buchanan family have
presided over this 16th-century coaching inn
for more than three decades and still put their
faith in big-hearted Yorkshire hospitality.
Quaff a pint in the cosy bar or bag a seat in the

traditional dining room for carefully sourced food with North Country pedigree. Char-grilled rare-breed beef and pork from local heroes Ginger Pig play starring roles, but the menu spans everything from king scallops with sour apple purée and black pudding, or sautéed squid with rocket, chillies and crème fraîche to herb-crusted 'allotment pie' or free-range chicken breast with wild mushrooms and braised peas. For afters, try spiced apple crumble made with fruit from Ampleforth Abbey's renowned orchards. The Buchanans' prestigious wine list is notable for its personal collection of fabulous St Emilion vintages, although it's also peppered with serious bottles from lesser-known producers worldwide. Prices start at £16.45 (£4.25 a glass).
Chef/s: Darren Clemmit. **Open:** all week L 12 to 2, D 6.45 to 9. **Meals:** alc (main courses £13 to £28). **Details:** 55 seats. 20 seats outside. Separate bar. Wheelchair access. Car parking.

Ramsgill

★ TOP 50 ★

The Yorke Arms
A chef with stellar talents
Ramsgill, HG3 5RL
Tel no: (01423) 755243
www.yorke-arms.co.uk
Modern British | £65
Cooking score: 6

The expansive Georgian shooting lodge and coaching inn by the village green, smothered in Virginia creeper and set in the lush Nidderdale valley, has much going for it – not least gardens where some of the kitchen's produce is grown and dining rooms that have the air of a gracious private home. Frances Atkins has brought a forceful gastronomic presence to the Yorke since taking it over in the 1990s, cooking locally and seasonally in the modern way, but with real personality, too. A 'classics' menu features potted beef and ham hock terrine, as well as fillet steak with wild mushrooms in truffled jus, while the main carte takes wing with halibut in rolled oats

with anchovy, a smoked scallop and black pudding, then a partnership of venison saddle, veal kidney and oxtail to follow, accompanied by caramelised sour onion and juniper. Aromatic and intricate desserts include a délice of pistachio, olive and coconut with mint ice cream. The intelligently composed wine list (from £25 or £5.50 a small glass) is replete with quality growers and covers a broad geographical arc, with plenty below £30.
Chef/s: Frances Atkins. **Open:** all week L 12 to 1.30, Mon to Sat D 7 to 8.30 (Sun reservations only). **Meals:** alc (main courses £24 to £43). Set L £35. Sun L £40. Tasting menu £85. **Details:** 40 seats. 20 seats outside.

Richmond

The Punch Bowl Inn
Popular Dales refuelling point
Low Row, Richmond, DL11 6PF
Tel no: (01748) 886233
www.pbinn.co.uk
Modern British | £24
Cooking score: 1

The setting is a stone-built 17th-century pub-with-rooms looking out across Swaledale, and many original features have been retained. It's the sort of place for those who like minimal twee with their open fires. The menu seems designed for customers to eat and be pleased. Along with chicken liver parfait, fishcakes and steak with green peppercorn sauce, a few fancier dishes deliver bold flavours: perhaps roast chicken with linguine and blue cheese, or a tomato and smoked Wensleydale cheese tartlet with red onion jam and pesto dressing. Finish off with an espresso crème brûlée. Wines from £15.95.
Chef/s: Dani Grainger. **Open:** all week L 12 to 2 (2.30 Sun), D 6 to 9. **Closed:** 25 Dec. **Meals:** alc (main courses £11 to £20). Sun L £10.50. **Details:** 60 seats.

▮ Ripon

Lockwoods

Café-restaurant that aims to please
83 North Street, Ripon, HG4 1DP
Tel no: (01765) 607555
www.lockwoodsrestaurant.co.uk
Modern British | £27
Cooking score: 1
£30

'Our local taxi firm laugh each time we book them to take us to Lockwoods. They can't believe how often we visit,' confess fans of this popular café-restaurant, a short stroll from Ripon's Market Square. It's an opinion backed up by other warm and contented accounts of 'fantastic, friendly service' and good food. The kitchen is a champion of local produce – note the all-Yorkshire cheeseboard – though it looks across the Mediterranean for culinary inspiration, coming up with smoked haddock risotto, braised and rolled belly pork with homemade black pudding and sage and onion crushed potatoes, and pistachio and olive oil cake with rhubarb. Wines from £14.95.
Chef/s: John Malia. **Open:** Tue to Sat L 12 to 2.30, D 6 to 9.30 (10 Fri and Sat). **Closed:** Sun, Mon, 25 and 26 Dec, 1 Jan. **Meals:** alc (main courses £11 to £20). Set D £12.50 (2 courses) to £15.50. **Details:** 65 seats. Wheelchair access.

▮ Ripponden

El Gato Negro

No clichés, just sharp, honest tapas
1 Oldham Road, Ripponden, HX6 4DN
Tel no: (01422) 823070
www.elgatonegrotapas.com
Spanish | £25
Cooking score: 4
£5 OFF £30

Simon Shaw doesn't just know Spanish food; he knows what makes a good Spanish restaurant work. At his well-established Ripponden tapas bar, diners tick their selection of pan-Iberian modern classics on funky place-mat menus featuring sage words of advice: 'You can always order more – this is part of the fun of tapas.' There's no shortage of merriment and 'great ambience' in this cosy, rustic space. The convivial spirit is certainly encouraged by shared plates of high-quality jamón Ibérico, Manchego with bittersweet green figs, and Padrón peppers. More technical dishes such as pork belly, scallop, pig's cheek and morcilla or red wine-braised monkfish with oxtail and butter beans show a more gastronomic side. Wine forms a major part of tapas-bar fun, of course. El Gato Negro's list, drawn from Spain and Spanish-speaking countries, has a genuine personal touch and contains some interesting bottles. House is £15.95.
Chef/s: Simon Shaw. **Open:** Sat L 12 to 2, Tue to Sat D 6 to 9.30 (10 Fri and Sat). **Closed:** Sun, Mon, 2 weeks summer, 2 weeks winter. **Meals:** alc (tapas £4 to £16). Set D £35 for 2 (inc wine). **Details:** 54 seats. Wheelchair access.

▮ Sancton

The Star @ Sancton

Appealingly local menus and sound cooking
King Street, Sancton, YO43 4QP
Tel no: (01430) 827269
www.thestaratsancton.co.uk
British | £30
Cooking score: 4
V

Found in a farming village amid the gentle folds of the Yorkshire Wolds, Ben and Lindsey Cox's ancient pub is a cut above your average hiker-geared watering hole. A bar with its roaring wood-burner, local ales and reassuring pub-grub menu, may cater for locals and walkers fresh from the Wolds Trail, but it's in the dining room where Ben really shows his worth. Local produce starred in a well-reported meal that opened with smoked duck (raised by Mathison's of Leven, smoked at Staal Smokehouse) with confit rillettes, potted foie gras, and duck liver, served with beetroot and juniper chutney and celeriac crisps. For main course, East Coast cod loin with Shetland mussels, chorizo and Jerusalem artichokes was all 'smoothness and elegance', and a chocolate fondant ('the best any of us had

ever eaten') arrived with white-chocolate fudge cubes and damson ice cream. The set lunch is good value, and house wines start at £15.95.
Chef/s: Ben Cox. **Open:** Tue to Sun L 12 to 2 (3 Sun), D 6 to 9.30 (8 Sun). **Closed:** Mon, first week Jan. **Meals:** alc (main courses £11 to £25). Set L £15.95 (2 courses) to £17.95. **Details:** 80 seats. 40 seats outside. Separate bar. Wheelchair access. Car parking.

■ Sawdon

The Anvil Inn

Satisfying food in a former smithy
Main Street, Sawdon, YO13 9DY
Tel no: (01723) 859896
www.theanvilinnsawdon.co.uk
Modern European | £29
Cooking score: 2
🛏 £30

Two centuries ago this was Sawdon's village forge, although it now plies its trade as a 'comfortably smart', friendly and inviting little pub-with-rooms – complete with the original furnace and assorted blacksmith's tools on view. Chat and quaff a pint in the busy bar with a ploughman's or steak pie on the side, or enjoy the full gastronomic works in the cosy restaurant. Confit pork belly with king prawns, pak choi, orange and chilli glaze gets rave reviews, but readers also lap up the 'posh' burgers with onion marmalade and the special fish dishes: perhaps grilled lemon sole with a herb and Parmesan crust. Finish in North Country style with caramelised rice pudding and a dinky Eccles cake. Wines from £15.95.
Chef/s: Mark Wilson. **Open:** Wed to Sun L 12 to 2 (2.30 Sun), D 6.30 to 9 (8 Sun). **Closed:** Mon, Tue, 25 and 26 Dec, 1 Jan. **Meals:** alc (main courses £10 to £25). **Details:** 36 seats. 8 seats outside. Separate bar. Car parking.

■ Scarborough

NEW ENTRY

Eat Me Café

Cool, kitsch café on the Yorkshire coast
1 Hanover Road, Scarborough, YO11 1LS
Tel no: (01723) 373256
www.eatmecafe.com
Modern British | £20
Cooking score: 2
£30

Scarborough isn't short of cafés but expect queues outside Eat Me, tucked behind the Stephen Joseph Theatre. The kitsch interior has prints by Tretchikoff and condiments in Hovis bread tins, but the range of dishes is extraordinary. You could sit all day, from late breakfast through lunch to dinner (currently three nights a week), and work your way through the appealing menu. 'Tin plate lunches' include a deeply aromatic ramen noodle bowl, or there's the mighty Shetland pie or a hand-packed burger that's 'just how a homemade one should be, served in a wooden box with fab chips and a pile of brilliant house 'slaw'. The 'famous' grilled cheese sandwich with Parmesan crust is reason alone to visit. The café is unlicensed, but runs a BYO policy with corkage of £1 that goes to charity.
Chef/s: Martyn Hyde and Tali Escott. **Open:** Mon to Sat L 10 to 2.30, Thur to Sat D 5.30 to 10. **Closed:** Sun, bank hols, 3 weeks Dec/Jan. **Meals:** alc (main courses £10). **Details:** Cash only. 34 seats.

Lanterna

A proper Piedmontese ristorante
33 Queen Street, Scarborough, YO11 1HQ
Tel no: (01723) 363616
www.lanterna-ristorante.co.uk
Italian | £35
Cooking score: 3

Adopted tyke Georgio Alessio (his native Italian tongue tinged with pure Yorkshire, a beguiling mash-up) traipses down to the harbour most mornings to see what fish the boat has brought in. For more than 25 years he

has been buying the best the North Sea can offer. He then marries his Piedmont culinary heritage with this local bounty to feed and please folk in his unpretentious, cosy trattoria on a slightly dog-eared Scarborough backstreet. The style is simple but the outcome memorable: ling in a tempura batter that shatters on the fork; a silky, deeply rich dish of linguine with game ragoût. Sea bass and brill arrive unadorned and perfectly judged, with an old-school dish of al dente veg. 'It's always worth the 54-mile round trip,' says one frequent visitor; 'outstanding', agrees another. The redecoration is 'an improvement'. Wines from £14.95.
Chef/s: Giorgio Alessio. **Open:** Mon to Sat D only 7 to 9.30. **Closed:** Sun, 25 and 26 Dec, last 2 weeks Oct. **Meals:** alc (main courses £14.25 to £45). **Details:** 35 seats.

Scawton

NEW ENTRY
The Hare Inn
Contemporary cooking in a traditional country pub
Scawton, YO7 2HG
Tel no: (01845) 597769
www.thehare-inn.com
Modern British | £30
Cooking score: 2

£5
OFF

This is a curious place. A traditional 17th-century inn – all worn flagged floors and dark beams, scrubbed tables and cosy corners, dark red walls and fussy wallpaper – that's stuffed to the rafters with pubby ephemera (lots of copper). The bang-up-to-the-minute cooking is slightly at odds with this look, especially as chef/owner Paul Jackson's menu describes dishes in lists, as in 'wood pigeon: breast, foie gras, blackcurrant, pistachio' or 'duck: leg, breast, egg, beetroot, red cabbage, anise' (which arrives artfully arranged on a huge plate finished with dots, smears and tiny cubed vegetables). 'It's a bit fussy for the location but the lad can cook.' Jackson is

clearly out to impress; it remains to be seen whether the core customers approve. House wine costs £20.
Chef/s: Paul Jackson. **Open:** Tue to Sun L 12 to 2.30, Tue to Sat 6 to 9. **Closed:** Mon, last week Jan. **Meals:** alc (main courses £18.95 to £24.95). Set L and D £20.50 (2 courses) to £24.50. **Details:** 55 seats. Separate bar. Wheelchair access. Car parking.

Settle

READERS RECOMMEND
The Brasserie
Modern British
The Courtyard, Cleatop, A65, Settle, BD24 9JY
Tel no: (01729) 892900
www.brasserieinthecourtyard.co.uk
'Fresh and modern, serving stuff people like to eat.'

Sheffield

Artisan
Sharp neighbourhood eatery
34 Sandygate Road, Crosspool, Sheffield, S10 5RY
Tel no: (0114) 2666096
www.artisansheffield.co.uk
Modern British | £25
Cooking score: 3

£30

Richard Smith flies the seasonal and local flag at his eminently civilised neighbourhood eatery in Sheffield's leafy Crosspool suburb. Artisan – part of a growing local restaurant group – is modern and bright, with wooden flooring, plentiful white tablecloths and a first-floor private dining room. As a local boy approaching his second decade here, Smith knows his suppliers. The range of dishes is comforting: warm chorizo and beetroot salad to start, fishcake with spinach and hollandaise or belly pork with Normandy-style red cabbage, roast celeriac, casserole lentils, apple and sage with a cider sauce to follow, then Eccles cake with Lancashire cheese. One reader has nothing but praise for the accommodating staff, who have perfected the personable, unceremonious approach that delights visitors. A diverting beer list (with intriguing food matching) provides a fortifying accompaniment and the cosmopolitan wine list opens at £17. **Chef/s:** Ian Robley. **Open:** Tue to Thur D 5 to 10. Fri to Sun 11.30 to 10 (5 Sun). **Meals:** alc (main courses £12 to £22). Set L and early D £20. Sun L £22.50. **Details:** 80 seats. 6 seats outside. Separate bar. Wheelchair access.

The Milestone

Buzzy pub with kaleidoscope cooking
84 Green Lane, Sheffield, S3 8SE
Tel no: (0114) 2728327
www.the-milestone.co.uk
British | £25
Cooking score: 2
£5 OFF £30

The pre-Victorian building in the city's Kelham Island district was for many years a steelworkers' pub, but has been successfully converted into a vibrant modern venue dedicated to pedigree Yorkshire produce given the modern British treatment. Luke French finds inspired ways to combine big flavours, as in a starter of black pudding with cockles, chorizo and lemon mayonnaise, as well as conjuring memorable depth and impact from humble materials such as slow-roasted ox cheek, pot-roast chicken breast with carrot purée and bacon or freshly made fisherman's pie. The reference-point way to finish is with Yorkshire parkin, garnished eye-catchingly with apple, candied beetroot and thyme jelly. English and French cheeses look good, and wines begin with a solid house selection from £14.95 (£3.20 a small glass). **Chef/s:** Luke French. **Open:** Mon to Sun L 12 to 3 (11 to 4 Sat and Sun), all week D 5 to 10 (8.30 Sun). **Closed:** 25 and 26 Dec, 1 Jan. **Meals:** alc (main courses £13 to £17). Set L £12 (2 courses) to £14. Set D and Sun L £14 (2 courses) to £16.50. **Details:** 140 seats. Wheelchair access. No children after 8.30.

Moran's

Knockout food from a magpie chef
289b Abbeydale Road South, Sheffield, S17 3LB
Tel no: (0114) 2350101
www.moranssheffield.co.uk
Modern British | £32
Cooking score: 4
£5 OFF

A suburban cracker with knockout food, Bryan and Sarah Moran's neighbourhood restaurant occupies a converted showroom in Sheffield's leafy Dore district – and it knows how to put on the style. The interior is full of unprepossessing charm, with low lights, dark wood and exotic details that add to the effortlessly convivial vibe. Bryan Moran is a culinary magpie, stealing ideas from all over for his colourful menus: mackerel arrives with Spanish pepper and caper escabèche; salmon fillet is revved up with pickled ginger, crispy mussels and Thai salad; and twice-cooked duck breast appears on spicy pear compote with candied walnut and orange dressing. There are British riffs, too, from chicken and ham hock terrine to roast rump of lamb on pea and parsnip purée with sweetbreads, baby onions and redcurrant jus. To finish, stay on the eclectic track by ordering French-style white chocolate cheesecake embellished with mango sorbet, pineapple compote and coconut chilli brittle. Wines from £13.95. **Chef/s:** Bryan Moran. **Open:** Sat and Sun L 12 to 2.30 (3 Sun), Tue to Sat D 7 to 9. **Closed:** Mon, first 2 weeks Jan. **Meals:** alc (main courses £15 to £25). Sun L £22.95. **Details:** 60 seats. Separate bar. Wheelchair access. Car parking.

Wig & Pen by The Milestone
Good eating and good value
44 Campo Lane, Sheffield, S1 2EG
Tel no: (0114) 2722150
www.the-wigandpen.co.uk
British | £28
Cooking score: 2
£5 OFF   £30 ▼

This lively, modern, brasserie-style venue is an offshoot of the Milestone in Sheffield's Kelham Island district (see entry). Informal and flexible, it opens from breakfast through to late evening. Though reporters have found standards can be inconsistent, especially at busy times – and service, too, has disappointed – on the whole there is still plenty to recommend. The cooking takes as its mainstay good supplies and delivers robust, fairly priced English staples, along the lines of pub classics such as bangers and mash, fisherman's pie and steak and chunky chips. Poached egg with creamed leeks, spinach, Yorkshire mushrooms and Parmesan is a typical starter, and desserts run from English baked cream to a tasting of Yorkshire rhubarb. House wine is £14.95.
Chef/s: Matt Hodkin. **Open:** all week L 12 to 4, Mon to Sat D 5 to 10. **Closed:** 25 and 26 Dec, 1 Jan. **Meals:** alc (main courses £9 to £16). Set D £14 (2 courses) to £18. Sun L £16.50. **Details:** 82 seats. 30 seats outside. Separate bar. Wheelchair access.

ALSO RECOMMENDED

▲ Lokanta
478-480 Glossop Road, Sheffield, S10 2QA
Tel no: (0114) 2666444
www.lokanta.co.uk
Turkish £5 OFF

'Authentic Turkish food and wine and exceptional value for money' noted one visitor to the Günays' smart restaurant. The wide choice of meze (£4 to £6.80) can constitute an entire meal here, but don't restrict yourself when there are specials such as aubergine stuffed with minced lamb (£13.50) and monkfish sautéed with white wine, peppers, spring onion, mushrooms and tomatoes

(£16.50). Honey-soaked baklava (£5.50) provides a sweet conclusion. Turkish wines from £14. Open all week D and Sun L.

▲ Rafters
220 Oakbrook Road, Nether Green, Sheffield, S11 7ED
Tel no: (0114) 2304819
www.raftersrestaurant.co.uk
Modern British

'A great experience' was the verdict of one visitor to this neighbourhood eatery in a leafy Sheffield suburb. Look for the discreet entrance and head upstairs for chef/proprietor Marcus Lane's ambitious cooking. His fixed-price menus (£36.95 for three courses) have delivered white crabmeat with baby smoked haddock fishcake and rouille sauce, and pan-fried fillet of Angus beef with braised oxtail and shallot pie, crushed root vegetables and red wine sauce. House wine is £15.50. Open Mon to Sat D only.

▮ Shibden
Shibden Mill Inn
Captivating inn with solid cooking
Shibden Fold, Shibden, HX3 7UL
Tel no: (01422) 365840
www.shibdenmillinn.com
Modern British | £30
Cooking score: 3
⇆ V

Though not far from the centre of Halifax, Shibden Mill is definitely off the beaten track. It's sited at the bottom of a deep, lush valley beside a rushing mill stream – 'a fabulous location' for what is a quintessentially British inn tweaked for the 21st century. With open fires, low ceilings and beams, unclothed tables and a straight-talking menu, the 17th-century former spinning mill pleases a variety of customers. Fish and chips and steak sandwich are successful, but other dishes show serious intent and impeccable sourcing. Scallops teamed with crispy braised chicken wings and chorizo is one way to start, followed by lamb – tenderloin, confit breast, pressed shoulder, 12-

hour cooked leg – with aubergine purée, ratatouille and tapenade. An impressive selection of Yorkshire artisan cheeses is hard to resist, yet so is the winter berry soufflé admired by one reader. A global wine list opens at £15.70.

Chef/s: Darren Parkinson. **Open:** Mon to Sat L 12 to 2 (2.30 Fri and Sat), D 6 to 9.30. Sun 12 to 7.30. **Meals:** alc (main courses £11.95 to £19). Set L £12 (2 courses) to £15. Sun L £12.95. **Details:** 70 seats. 64 seats outside. Separate bar. Car parking.

▌Sinnington

ALSO RECOMMENDED
▲ Fox & Hounds

Main Street, Sinnington, YO62 6SQ
Tel no: (01751) 431577
www.thefoxandhoundsinn.co.uk
Modern British £5 OFF

Hop-garlanded oak beams and real ales define proceedings in the traditional bar of this 18th-century pub-with-rooms, but most people come for the food served in the more modern dining room. Thoughtful sourcing is at the heart of a menu that might kick off with game terrine or seared scallops with Calvados risotto (£7.95) before offering slow-braised shoulder of lamb, beef and oxtail Wellington (£14.25) or even battered haddock and chips. For afters, perhaps try blueberry pannacotta with poached apricots. Wines from £15.95. Open all week.

▌Skipton

Le Caveau

Retro bistro cooking in a secret cellar
86 High Street, Skipton, BD23 1JJ
Tel no: (01756) 794274
www.lecaveau.co.uk
Anglo-French | £30
Cooking score: 2
£5 OFF

It's not *that* old (opening in 1997) but there's something rather retro about Skipton cellar hideaway, Le Caveau. The melon fans, garlic mushrooms and lamb and redcurrant may

sound like they belong in the 1970s, yet behind the 'naive descriptions' can be 'imaginative food' and 'great flavours'. Goats' cheese roulade with walnuts and fig compote 'had a flavour dialogue that kept your interest all the way'; Gressingham duck breast came with 'glorious' port sauce and cherries. Puddings such as orange and Cointreau cheesecake with chocolate sorbet are 'part of what has made Le Caveau's reputation'. The vaulted ceilings and stone walls are charming, as is the 'hugely improved' service. A cheerful mix of international wines opens at £15, with plenty under £20.

Chef/s: Richard Barker. **Open:** Tue to Fri L 12 to 2, Tue to Sat D 7 to 9.30 (5 to 9.45 Sat). **Closed:** Sun, Mon, 25 Dec, first week Jan, first week Jun, first 2 weeks Sept. **Meals:** alc (main courses £14 to £20). Set L £9.95 (2 courses) to £12.95. Set D £16.95 (2 courses) to £20. **Details:** 26 seats. Separate bar.

▌South Dalton

The Pipe & Glass Inn

Pubby virtues and fine food
West End, South Dalton, HU17 7PN
Tel no: (01430) 810246
www.pipeandglass.co.uk
Modern British | £36
Cooking score: 5
£5 OFF ▐ ♚ V

James and Kate Mackenzie have worked minor miracles at this whitewashed Wolds hostelry, turning it into a marvel of honest pubby virtues, good-humoured hospitality and fine food. Log-burners crackle, music plays and a battalion of hand-pumped Yorkshire ales stands proud at the bar. Here, a blackboard promises sturdy plates of cider-braised Old Spot pork chops and the like. Alternatively, graduate to the thickly carpeted, conservatory-style dining room for some more auspicious, but equally robust cooking full of seasonal oomph. The poised kitchen can deliver hits of pure class (turbot fillet with richly sauced oxtail, cauliflower 'champ' and a monkfish-cheek fritter, for example), while giving the pub classics a thorough shake-up (ham hock, black pudding, leek and white bean crumble, anyone?). British regional cheeses get a vote of confidence and little savouries feature, too (Shepherd's Purse Blue with a port-poached fig and walnut bread, say); otherwise, keep it sweet with hot chocolate, juniper and sloe gin pudding. The knowledgeably chosen wine list shows its style and pedigree with fascinating food-matching suggestions, a terrific choice by the glass and very fair mark-ups. Bottles start at £15.50. **Chef/s:** James Mackenzie. **Open:** Tue to Sun L 12 to 2 (4 Sun), Tue to Sat D 6 to 9.30. **Closed:** Mon (exc bank hols), 25 Dec, 2 weeks Jan. **Meals:** alc (main courses £10 to £26). **Details:** 100 seats. 60 seats outside. Separate bar. Car parking.

Sowerby Bridge
Gimbals
Upbeat neighbourhood bistro
76 Wharf Street, Sowerby Bridge, HX6 2AF
Tel no: (01422) 839329
www.gimbals.co.uk
Modern European | £28
Cooking score: 4
£5 OFF £30

'I've never eaten at a better restaurant' notes one admirer of this neighbourhood bistro. Indeed, it's hard not to be impressed by the way the Bakers have not only maintained their enthusiasm after 15 years at the coal face, but also moved with the times. Janet's eye for design is keen and there's just the right amount of quirkiness. The result is a calm, happy dining experience: 'the atmosphere is unique, the welcome incredibly warm'. Husband Simon leads the team in the kitchen, where the emphasis still leans towards the rustic Mediterranean (but with nods to Yorkshire). So, expect the likes of cracked king crab with samphire, preserved lemon aïoli and soda bread crostini, or merguez with spiced couscous, smoked baby aubergines and pomegranate molasses – skilfully cooked, stunningly presented: summer on a plate. The wine list opens at £15.90. **Chef/s:** Ben Wood, Mark Ferrier, Simon Baker. **Open:** Tue to Sat D only 6 to 9 (9.15 Fri and Sat). **Closed:** Sun, Mon, 24 to 26 Dec, 1 and 2 Jan.

Meals: alc (main courses £13 to £22). Set D £16.90 (2 courses) to £19.90. **Details:** 50 seats. Wheelchair access.

West Tanfield
The Bruce Arms
Striking pub with splendidly rustic food
Main Street, West Tanfield, HG4 5JJ
Tel no: (01677) 470325
www.thebrucearms.com
Modern British | £29
Cooking score: 3
£5 OFF £30

Still a pub at first glance, the Bruce Arms is really all about food; the small bar area does dispense real ale and all, but people flock from miles around to eat here (York, Harrogate and the A1 are within easy reach). It's all well put together on a shoestring, with modern art, mismatched polished tables and cheerful log fires. In the kitchen Hugh Carruthers has settled in well after taking over in 2009, and the style continues to be straightforward modern British with the focus on clear, strong flavours and excellent raw materials. Chicken liver parfait with chutney and toast makes a 'tasty' start, while well-reported mains have included beef bourguignon, and pork belly with dauphinois potatoes and creamed spinach. While output is very consistent, occasionally service has been found wanting. Wines from £14.95. **Chef/s:** Hugh Carruthers. **Open:** Tue to Sun L 12 to 2.30 (3.30 Sun), Tue to Sat D 6 to 10. **Closed:** Mon, last 2 weeks Feb. **Meals:** alc (main courses £11 to £30). Set L £12.95 (2 courses). Set D £17.50. Sun L £16.95. **Details:** 43 seats. 25 seats outside. Car parking.

Also Recommended
Also recommended entries are not scored but we think they are worth a visit.

West Witton

The Wensleydale Heifer

Seafood and chic vibes in the country
Main Street, West Witton, DL8 4LS
Tel no: (01969) 622322
www.wensleydaleheifer.co.uk
Seafood | £35
Cooking score: 3

'The Heifer is a place which keeps pulling you back for return visits,' declares one fan of this updated 17th-century inn, now a chic boutique hotel – echoing the reams of praise for the 'superb', 'perfect' and 'fantastic' food offered. The main draw is spanking fresh fish, but the kitchen pleases just about everyone with its egalitarian menu. The renowned fish and chips 'does not come any better', but there's also chicken liver parfait or hand-picked Whitby crab teamed with gravlax, new potato, shallot and chive tian and warm-cured salmon to start, then fish and shellfish pie or a well-reported banana-leaf-baked sea bass with a subtle Thai curry. Traditional Sunday roasts are popular, desserts are 'just delicious', especially the Eton mess Knickerbocker glory, and service is 'relaxed but attentive'. House wine is £20.50.
Chef/s: David Moss. **Open:** all week L 12 to 2.30, D 6 to 9.30. **Meals:** alc (main courses £17 to £30). Set L and D £19.75 (2 courses) to £21.75. **Details:** 62 seats. 30 seats outside. Separate bar. Wheelchair access. Car parking.

Whitby

Magpie Café

Fish-and-chip champ
14 Pier Road, Whitby, YO21 3PU
Tel no: (01947) 602058
www.magpiecafe.co.uk
Seafood | £22
Cooking score: 2
£5 OFF £30

'Why try the rest?' asks one happy customer of Whitby's landmark fish and chip restaurant. The black-and-white building, with its views over the harbour and old town, has long formed part of seaside days out, and continues to earn its reputation with 'high standards' and 'good, freshly prepared food'. Whitby crab pâté or the house fishcakes will make a splendid start and it's a rare eater who walks away without trying the excellent haddock and chips with homemade tartare sauce, though the fish pie and haddock and salmon gratin are also rated. For afters, it's sticky toffee pudding and a lie down. Wine is from £14.95, but there's a strong argument for a pot of tea.
Chef/s: Ian Robson and Paul Gildroy. **Open:** all week 11.30 to 9. **Closed:** 25 Dec, 6 to 31 Jan. **Meals:** alc (main courses £7 to £23). **Details:** 120 seats. Wheelchair access.

The Woodlands Cafébar

Charming eatery by the sea
East Row, Sandsend, Whitby, YO21 3SU
Tel no: (01947) 893438
thewoodlands-sandsend.com
Modern British | £25
Cooking score: 1
£30

A chic cottage by the sea at Sandsend sounds idyllic: especially as this pretty whitewashed charmer is also a café and dining room for the nearby Woodlands B&B. Tartan walls and antlers might suggest a Lilliputian hunting lodge, although the food tells a different story. Emphatic seasonal flavours are the hallmarks of a tidy menu that might offer 'small' and 'large' plates ranging from Whitby crab vinaigrette with celeriac 'slaw to butternut squash risotto or braised pork belly with mustard mash, black pudding and Ampleforth cider. To finish don't miss the unbeatable rose-water meringues. Coffee, cakes and sandwiches fill the daytime gaps, and there's an inviting decked garden outside. Ten wines from £14.50.
Chef/s: Alexander Perkins. **Open:** Tue to Sun L 10 to 3, Fri and Sat D 6 to 9. **Closed:** Mon, 25 Dec. **Meals:** alc (main courses £10 to £19). **Details:** 34 seats. 30 seats outside. Separate bar. Car parking.

▌York

NEW ENTRY
The Blind Swine

Classic skills, clever pairings and youthful vigour
22-24 Swinegate, York, YO1 8AZ
Tel no: (01904) 634825
www.theblindswine.co.uk
Modern British | £45
Cooking score: 3
£5
OFF

Michael O'Hare swept into this city bar last year with a quirky, no-choice menu of nine small courses interspersed with cocktails and a feast of visual and oral puns. 'Edible stones' are clay-encrusted potatoes with yeast purée; a terracotta pot of horseradish emulsion and hazelnut 'soil' is planted with miniature radish and carrots. There is theatre – note the halibut with giant couscous topped with a fragile sheet of dehydrated milk skin – but the show is underpinned by classic skills and clever pairings. Take, for instance, the Whitby crab with crisp apple discs, sorrel juice, lobster oil and apple and elderflower jelly, or ice cream flavoured with Gammel Dansk bitters and served with violet meringue and salty raw milk crumbs. While the menu continues to evolve there's the odd miscue like the smoky bacon and Parmesan Margarita, but from the first gin sour with moss to the final Irish coffee, Blind Swine is bringing a whole new dimension to York dining.
Chef/s: Michael O'Hare. **Open:** Tue to Sat D 2 sittings 7.30 and 8.30. **Closed:** Mon, Sun, 1 to 12 Jan. **Meals:** Set D £45 (9 courses). **Details:** 18 seats. Separate bar. Wheelchair access. Car parking. No children.

¶¶● Visit us Online

To find out more about
The Good Food Guide, please visit
www.thegoodfoodguide.co.uk

Cabra Verde

Flexible café with its heart in Spain
1 Peter Lane, York, YO1 8SW
Tel no: (01904) 652920
www.cabraverde.co.uk
Spanish | £18
Cooking score: 2
£30

Portuguese chef Celia Marcos de Jesus Mendao arrived here last year strengthening the short but well-sourced menu of tapas, grills, meat and cheese plates at this cool, spare, tucked-away Spanish restaurant – formerly called de'Clare Café. Ibérico ham is hand sliced to order, and served with bread, olive oil and Pedro Ximénez vinegar. Menorcan Mahón cheese is teamed deliciously with honey and preserved green figs. Tortilla, sardines and skewers of chicken all tested well, but deep-fried squid rings on grilled apple and black pudding was a standout dish. Meringues and cakes are tempting, including a superior orange and almond Santiago tart. A short but pleasing drinks list contains Spanish wines from £16 and Pedro Ximénez sherries.
Chef/s: Celia Marcos de Jesus Mendao. **Open:** Mon to Fri 11 to 10.30, Sat 9.30 to 10.30, Sun 9.30 to 5. **Closed:** 25 and 26 Dec, Easter Sun. **Meals:** alc (main courses £10 to £16). Set L £9.95 (3 tapas plates). **Details:** 36 seats. Wheelchair access.

Le Langhe

Artisan foodie enterprise
The Old Coach House, Peasholme Green, York, YO1 7PW
Tel no: (01904) 622584
www.lelanghe.co.uk
Italian | £32
Cooking score: 4
£5
OFF

Ottavio Bocca's deli-restaurant, a recently spruced up homage to his Piedmontese upbringing, has taken root in the centre of York. Homemade pasta is the real deal here, freshly kneaded and hand-turned every day; you'll find it with game ragù, filled with pumpkin and goats' cheese, or scented with

shaved Alba truffle. First come appetisers, perhaps tender bresaola with rocket and Parmesan, while mains offer classic calf's liver with roasted onions, pancetta and sage or venison loin in bitter chocolate. Homemade ice creams and sorbets might be anointed with Prosecco or grappa; there's proper affogato and tempting tarts such as hazelnut, served with chocolate mousse. Italian wines are a major highlight. The list now approaches 700 bins, adding up to one fantastic cellar. Start, of course, in the Langhe hills of the north-west, and sweep down in a graceful arc through Franciacorta blends to ripe super-Tuscans and sinuous Sicilians. Prices remain reasonable throughout, with bottles starting at around £15, glasses at £4.95.
Chef/s: Ottavio Bocca. **Open:** Mon to Sat L 12 to 3, Fri and Sat D 6.45 to 10. **Closed:** Sun, 25 to 27 Dec, 1 to 14 Jan, 3 days Easter. **Meals:** alc (main courses £19 to £26). **Details:** 70 seats. 25 seats outside. Wheelchair access.

Melton's
Top-class cooking at fair prices
7 Scarcroft Road, York, YO23 1ND
Tel no: (01904) 634341
www.meltonsrestaurant.co.uk
Modern British | £35
Cooking score: 5
£5 OFF

'One word – sensational!' exclaims a devotee of Michael and Lucy Hjort's delightfully laid-back neighbourhood restaurant just a canter from York racecourse. Fans love its cute, idiosyncratic style, with close-packed tables, whimsical murals and well-worn furnishings adding to the charm. Lucy's 'honest' front-of-house team really know their way around the menu. 'Top-class, imaginative cooking' at very fair prices is the order of the day, and Michael's food is dependent on rigorous local sourcing: from Whitby crab and Holme Farm venison to artisan Yorkshire cheeses. Menus change regularly, but readers have singled out cured salmon enlivened with horseradish 'snow' and soused vegetables ('an interesting combination of textures and flavours'), home-salted coley

with fennel velouté, peas and saffron gnocchi, and a dazzling duo of Thirsk lamb – marinated like game and served 'osso bucco style' with soft polenta, swede purée and cavolo nero. To finish, warm Yorkshire parkin with toffee crunch ice cream vies with boozy seasonal soufflés such as apple and Calvados. Lucy Hjort's exemplary global wine list fits the restaurant's commendable credo to a T, with quality and value across the board, plus excellent food-matching suggestions. House recommendations are £16 (£3.90 a glass).
Chef/s: Michael Hjort. **Open:** Tue to Sat L 12 to 2, D 5.30 to 9.30. **Closed:** Sun, Mon, 2 weeks Dec. **Meals:** alc (main courses £15 to £20). Set L and early D £22 (2 courses) to £26. Tasting menu £38 (5 courses). **Details:** 42 seats.

Melton's Too
Flexible drop-in bistro with freewheeling food
25 Walmgate, York, YO1 9TX
Tel no: (01904) 629222
www.meltonstoo.co.uk
Modern European | £23
Cooking score: 2
£30

The merits of this bare-boarded all-day café-bistro, which occupies several floors of a 17th-century workshop, are its unpretentious atmosphere and flexible menus built around regional produce. Drop in for breakfast, an all-day lunch dish (perhaps smoked haddock and salmon fishcakes with a poached egg), to share tapas or just to enjoy a scone with a pot of tea. And there's more besides: simplicity of presentation appears to be the maxim behind dishes such as beef bresaola with horseradish cream and watercress; a rustic seafood, tomato and fennel stew (aka bouillabaisse); and a classic French cassoulet. Owned by Michael Hjort (see previous entry), Melton's Too has been a stalwart of the restaurant scene in York since 2001. Wine from £14.50.
Chef/s: Michael Hjort. **Open:** all week 10.30am to 10.30pm (10am Sat and Sun, 9.30pm Sun). **Closed:** 25 and 26 Dec, 1 Jan. **Meals:** alc (main courses £12 to £15). Set L and D £11.50 (2 courses) to £13. **Details:** 120 seats. Separate bar. Wheelchair access.

SCOTLAND

Borders, Dumfries & Galloway,
Lothians (inc. Edinburgh),
Strathclyde (inc. Glasgow), Central, Fife,
Tayside, Grampian, Highlands & Islands

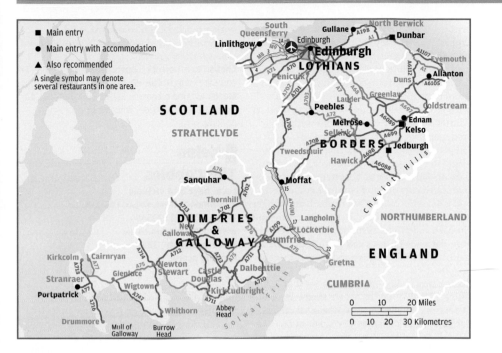

Allanton

The Allanton Inn

Hearty food and an eye for detail
Allanton, TD11 3JZ
Tel no: (01890) 818260
www.allantoninn.co.uk
Modern British | £28
Cooking score: 3

Reporters love the inviting atmosphere at this remodelled village inn, thanks to a telling blend of pubby virtues and more genteel, contemporary attributes. The cooking is right on the money, too, when it comes to local sourcing and fresh, forthright seasonal flavours – pleasing pub die-hards with steak, chips and peppercorn sauce, and adventurous foodies with everything from hot-buttered Eyemouth mackerel with warm potato salad and caramelised lime to lamb cutlets teamed with black pudding, truffle-scented mash, green beans and thyme jus. Blackboard specials, seasonal game and freshly baked bread are part of the package, Scottish cheeses make a brilliant finish, or you could hit the sweet spot with lemon and nutmeg brûlée. Tiptop beers and wines from £14.
Chef/s: Craig Rushton. **Open:** all week L 12 to 2.30, D 6 to 9. **Closed:** 25 and 26 Dec. **Meals:** alc (main courses £10 to £23). **Details:** 45 seats. 30 seats outside. Separate bar. Car parking.

Ednam

Edenwater House

Personally run borderland retreat
Ednam, TD5 7QL
Tel no: (01573) 224070
www.edenwaterhouse.co.uk
Modern British | £40
Cooking score: 4

'The formula we offer has not changed much over the past 15 years except that the menus and the wine list have kept up with food fashion and culinary style', write Jeff and Jacqui Kelly. Bravo! Their attractive 17th-century manse in the borderlands of the Upper Tweed Valley continues to delight a stream of visitors, despite the dining room having just four tables with residents taking precedence. The four-course, fixed-price dinners are built around Scottish produce, with Jacqui dreaming up some telling ideas. A demi-tasse of soup could be followed by spider crab salad with avocado cream, apple jelly and curried crème fraîche, with loin of Highland venison the centrepiece, served with parsnip and carrot mash, butternut squash, macerated currants and cumin, roasted beets and a red wine sauce, then rhubarb and ginger torte accompanied by pineapple ice cream and rhubarb and ginger syrup as a fitting finale. Regular wine tastings and themed dinners are held, and the well-structured wine list opens at £18.

Chef/s: Jacqui Kelly. **Open:** Mon to Sat D at 7, 1 sitting. **Closed:** 21 Dec to 28 Feb. **Meals:** Set D £40 (4 courses). **Details:** 16 seats. Wheelchair access. Car parking. Children over 12 yrs only at D.

▌Jedburgh

The Caddy Mann

Quirky local restaurant
Mounthooly, Jedburgh, TD8 6TJ
Tel no: (01835) 850787
www.caddymann.com
Modern British | £23
Cooking score: 2

£30

Stuffed with vintage knick-knacks, curios and pictures by local artists, this quirky little restaurant occupies a cluster of converted farm cottages just off the A68. Chef/co-proprietor Ross Horrocks is a dab hand in the kitchen – especially when it comes to cooking his beloved seasonal game. Reporters have endorsed richly flavoursome roast grouse with a pheasant boudin, but you might also find wild duck among the starters, venison in a steamed suet pudding or a boozy fricassee of grey squirrel with nut-crusted 'crispy squirrel balls' on the daily changing menu. Borders lamb receives special attention too, likewise fish from the coast (perhaps fillet of turbot

with air-dried Cumbrian ham, wild mushrooms and Madeira jus).'Sensibly priced' wines start at £13.75.

Chef/s: Ross Horrocks. **Open:** all week L 12 to 2, Fri and Sat D 7 to 9. **Closed:** 25 and 26 Dec, 1 to 3 Jan. **Meals:** alc (main courses £11 to £19). **Details:** 40 seats. 10 seats outside. Wheelchair access. Car parking.

▌Kelso

The Cobbles

Local beer and victuals
7 Bowmont Street, Kelso, TD5 7JH
Tel no: (01573) 223548
www.thecobblesinn.co.uk
Modern British | £25
Cooking score: 1

£30

This white-painted Victorian town-centre hostelry is noted for a relaxed vibe in its bar, the full range of Tempest ales (from its own microbrewery nearby) and some great modern pub food in the dining room. John Addy uses seasonal produce, much of it sourced locally, so starters might feature wood pigeon or home-cured gravlax. For mains, braised shoulder of pork with ginger and plums, sesame pak choi and coriander basmati rice might appear alongside sea bass with crab, lemon and garden-pea risotto and a mussel and pancetta white wine sauce. The bar menu brings lunchtime sandwiches as well as fish and chips and locally made sausages. Wines from £13.95.

Chef/s: John Addy. **Open:** Tue to Sun L 12 to 2 (2.30 Sat and Sun), D 6 to 9 (9.30 Fri and Sat, 8 Sun). **Closed:** Mon, 25 and 26 Dec. **Meals:** alc (main courses £9 to £21). Set D £20.95 (2 courses) to £24.95. Sun L £15.95 (2 courses) to £19.95. **Details:** 65 seats. 20 seats outside. Separate bar. Wheelchair access. Car parking.

Melrose

Burt's Hotel
Grand old inn with excellent ingredients
Market Square, Melrose, TD6 9PL
Tel no: (01896) 822285
www.burtshotel.co.uk
Modern British | £36
Cooking score: 2

At the heart of Melrose, which is, in turn, at the heart of the Scottish Borders, this smart town house is family-run and full of personal touches. The interior harks back to the building's origins as the home of a local dignitary, so expect elegance rather than slick styling. The restaurant is all crisp napery and sparkling glassware, with cooking that has more of a sense of occasion than in the bar. Pan-seared scallops, pancetta salad and cauliflower purée is a good way to begin, followed by a main-course roast rump of lamb with minted barley, confit tomatoes and cumin jus that puts an appealing spin on tradition. Finish with a trio of chocolate (Amaretto délice, fondant and chocolate ice cream). The wine list opens at £16.25.
Chef/s: Trevor Williams. **Open:** Sat and Sun L 12 to 2, all week D 7 to 9 (9.30 Fri and Sat). **Closed:** 25 and 26 Dec, 5 to 13 Jan. **Meals:** alc (main courses £13 to £24). **Details:** 50 seats. 24 seats outside. Separate bar. Car parking.

Peebles

Osso
Café by day, bistro by night
Innerleithen Road, Peebles, EH45 8BA
Tel no: (01721) 724477
www.ossorestaurant.com
Modern British | £28
Cooking score: 3
£30

These premises started off as a neighbourhood coffee shop, and buzzy Osso still does duty as an informal daytime drop-in for shoppers, buggy-pushing mums and passers-by. They come to enjoy reviving butties, deli salads, tapas nibbles and bigger lunchtime dishes such as smoked haddock and leek crumble. Come nightfall, the place puts on its glad rags and moves into serious gastronomic mode with a menu of 'interesting, innovative food': parsley soup surrounded by white crabmeat and a dish of coley accompanied by shards of fennel, samphire and a little pot of cheesy fish pie have gone down well; likewise, a clever dessert of Kirsch-infused cherries with tiny cubes of cherry jelly and goats' cheese sorbet. A pud teasingly entitled 'tea, milk and sugar' brings the venue back to its roots. House wine is £13.50.
Chef/s: Ally McGrath. **Open:** all week L 11 to 4.30, Tue to Sat D 6 to 9. **Closed:** 25 Dec, 1 Jan. **Meals:** alc (main courses £12 to £22). **Details:** 38 seats. 6 seats outside. Wheelchair access.

The Sutherland at Cringletie
Sumptuous country house hotel
Edinburgh Road, Peebles, EH45 8PL
Tel no: (01721) 725750
www.cringletie.com
Modern French | £45
Cooking score: 2

France meets Scotland in the restaurant of this small, luxurious hotel set in 28 acres. Chef Patrick Bardoulet puts produce from the walled garden and other local sources to work in dishes with contemporary kicks and twists. In the first-floor dining room, guests are met on all sides by lovely views: verdant Scottish countryside, a cherub-dotted hand-painted ceiling, and plenty more grandeur besides. To start, home-cured salmon might come with yoghurt marshmallow and sorbet, followed by Highland venison loin with game sausage, onion, mulled pear and a red wine sauce. A towering dessert of pear, chestnut, whisky and spiced bread ice cream pays tribute to the big ideas of the house's original architect. Wines from £19.
Chef/s: Patrick Bardoulet. **Open:** all week D 7 to 9. **Closed:** 3 weeks Jan. **Meals:** Set D £35 to £55. Sun L £22.50. **Details:** 30 seats. Separate bar. Wheelchair access. Car parking.

Moffat

NEW ENTRY

The Limetree Restaurant

Colourful cooking with emphatic flavours

Hartfell House, Hartfell Crescent, Moffat, DG10 9AL

Tel no: (01683) 220153

www.hartfellhouse.co.uk

Modern British | £28

Cooking score: 4

As a restaurant in a guesthouse, the Limetree could easily have been an afterthought, catering for a captive audience with a few wan offerings. It is anything but, and deserves a detour even if you're not staying in this handsome grey-stone building. The room is simple enough: small, wood-floored, with original artwork (for sale) on the walls and views of a particularly green corner of well-to-do Moffat. In contrast, the food has global reach: a starter of spiced chickpeas, char-grilled courgette, feta and mint delivered a 'lemony-fresh blast of the eastern Mediterranean', while a roast supreme of guinea fowl with chard, creamy mustard sauce and cabbage, bacon and melted onion potato cake delighted a visitor with its 'simplicity and emphatic flavours'. Finally, marmalade brioche pudding with passion fruit ice cream and poached rhubarb proved a 'classy but homely delight'. A modest list of reasonably priced wines starts at just £15.

Chef/s: Matt Seddon. **Open:** Sun L 12.30 to 2, Tue to Sat D 6.30 to 8.30. **Closed:** 24 to 30 Dec, 1 to 14 Jan, 10 days Oct. **Meals:** Set L £19.50 (2 courses) to £22.50. Set D £22.50 (2 courses) to £27.50. **Details:** 24 seats. Wheelchair access. Car parking.

Portpatrick

Knockinaam Lodge

Thrilling, windswept views and refined food

Portpatrick, DG9 9AD

Tel no: (01776) 810471

www.knockinaamlodge.com

Modern British | £58

Cooking score: 5

Surely this is heaven: an isolated cove framed by wind-sculpted trees; an immaculate lawn running to a sandy shoreline; waves changing from topaz to silver as the clouds come and go. Add thoughtfully composed dishes served by charming staff, and it's very hard to leave. The hotel – quietly luxurious, gracious yet homely – was originally a Victorian hunting lodge, and is impeccably run by David and Sian Ibbotson. Chef Tony Pierce coaxes the best from top-tier ingredients without resorting to fripperies – witness a firm and fresh fillet of turbot with a lemon-thyme and orange emulsion and little other adornment. Pierce knows when a dish is complete. Dine in late spring and you could progress via an intense asparagus and chervil soup to roast cannon of lamb with shallot purée, baked baby beetroot, confit garlic and a bell pepper and port reduction. A perfect rhubarb soufflé with clotted-cream ice cream is a good way to end. Be sure to explore David's lengthy wine list: the work of a true enthusiast, with everything from fine French vintages to New World discoveries, starting at £23.

Chef/s: Tony Pierce. **Open:** all week L 12 to 2, D 7 to 9. **Meals:** Set L £40 (4 courses). Set D £60 (5 courses). Sun L £30 (4 courses). **Details:** 24 seats. Separate bar. Wheelchair access. Car parking. No children at D.

▌Sanquhar

Blackaddie House Hotel

Foodie oasis in the borderlands
Blackaddie Road, Sanquhar, DG4 6JJ
Tel no: (01659) 50270
www.blackaddiehotel.co.uk
Modern British | £52
Cooking score: 4

£5 OFF 🚗

Crackling log fires, lots of original features, superbly crafted food and professional, charming staff with the gift of the gab – no wonder affectionate readers dub this converted 16th-century manse 'an oasis in the Scottish borderlands'. Ian McAndrew's culinary endeavours are based on fervent local sourcing and a feel for Scottish ingredients. 'Deeply flavoured' beef from a farm in Sanquhar is a regular attraction, while Borders lamb might be cunningly served four ways. Other intricately worked specialities have included ham hock terrine with pease pudding, mustard, apricots and lightly pickled shallots; seared scallops with parsnip and parsley purées, crumbled black pudding and lemon vinaigrette; and a 'heavenly' dessert of sweetcorn pannacotta with pine-nut ice cream and caramel. McAndrew has an 'obvious passion for his art', and his wine list is packed with food-friendly bottles from top producers. House recommendations start at £19.95 (£5.25 a glass).
Chef/s: Ian McAndrew. **Open:** all week L 12 to 2, D 6.30 to 9. **Meals:** Set L £24.50 (2 courses) to £30. Set D £24.50 (2 courses) to £52 (4 courses).
Details: 20 seats. Separate bar. Car parking.

🍴● CHRIS GALVIN
The Pompadour

What do you enjoy most about being a chef?
Cooking for customers, teaching, learning and knowing every day will be different.

What food trends are you spotting at the moment?
Increasing awareness of regional food, and suppliers sharing in the development of dishes.

At the end of a long day, what do you like to cook?
Normally fish – I never tire of cooking with a beautiful piece of fresh fish. I poach it and make a sauce from the cooking liquor.

How do you come up with new dishes?
I look at the ingredients available from the market, then think about flavour marriages and, finally, presentation.

Which of your dishes are you most proud of?
Daube of venison with quince and chestnuts.

What would you be if you weren't a chef?
An engineer, working with high-performance engines.

Dunbar

The Creel

Spanking-fresh food and keen prices
25 Lamer Street, Dunbar, EH42 1HJ
Tel no: (01368) 863279
www.creelrestaurant.co.uk
Modern British | £27
Cooking score: 3
£5 OFF £30

Shipshape and Dunbar-fashion, Logan Thorburn's small, nautical restaurant near the harbour feels 'very personal'. There's plenty of local fish on the menu, and readers are grateful for the kitchen's ability to deliver zingy flavours without overwhelming the central element of each dish. Steamed prawns with homemade mayonnaise is a constant alongside more complex starters such as confit ham rillettes with celery-scented quail's egg and pickled raisin vinaigrette. Pork loin might come with paprika rice, fennel and flageolet beans, but Thorburn is not above beer-battered Eyemouth haddock and chips. Dessert might be lemon posset with raspberries or a pecan and walnut brownie, and the cheese is local. Even with a few awkward supplements, a meal is 'great value' and served in friendly fashion. House wine starts at £15.95.
Chef/s: Logan Thorburn. **Open:** Wed to Sun L 12 to 2.30, D 6.30 to 9. **Closed:** Mon, Tue. **Meals:** Set L £14.50 (2 courses) to £17.95. Set D £23.50 (2 courses) to £26.50. **Details:** 36 seats. Wheelchair access. No children under 12 yrs after 7.30.

Edinburgh

Angels with Bagpipes

Uptown meets Old Town
343 High Street, Royal Mile, Edinburgh, EH1 1PW
Tel no: (0131) 2201111
www.angelswithbagpipes.co.uk
Modern European | £30
Cooking score: 3

It may be bang on the touristy Royal Mile, but this sharp cosmopolitan brasserie keeps tacky Rabbie Burns kitsch to a minimum – despite

the kitchen's fondness for haggis and whisky-laced cranachan. Cleverly rendered plates of Cairngorms venison (cooked perfectly rare with pearl barley and cabbage) have impressed: likewise, Orkney scallops with apple and black pudding, and a dish of beef tartare with truffle vinaigrette, green beans and quail's egg. Elsewhere, 'velvety' asparagus soup is poured from a teapot, spot-on fish and chips is served on a bed of 'incredible peas' and tiramisu is a far-from-ordinary mélange of parfait, Tia Maria, coffee, caramel, orange and espresso 'soil'. Dapper, on-the-ball staff work the contemporary-chic dining rooms with consummate aplomb. Suitably uptown drinks range from 'impressive' cocktails, 'fraoch' (heather) ale and rare malt whiskies to a cleverly assembled wine list with commendable names from across the globe. House selections start at £19 (£5 a glass).
Chef/s: Fraser Smith. **Open:** all week 12 to 10. **Closed:** 24 to 26 Dec. **Meals:** alc (main courses £13 to £22). Set L £12.95 (2 courses) to £15.95. **Details:** 70 seats. 16 seats outside. Wheelchair access.

Café St Honoré

Scottish produce in a Parisian setting
34 North West Thistle Street Lane, Edinburgh, EH2 1EA
Tel no: (0131) 2262211
www.cafesthonore.com
French | £35
Cooking score: 3
£5 OFF

A little time capsule from the days when every British city boasted Parisian bistros of this ilk, Café St Honoré is a short trot from Princes Street on a quiet back lane. The ambience could hardly be more French, fostered by tarnished mirrors, bentwood chairs and black-and-white floor, but chef Neil Forbes refuses to be constrained by Gallic clichés, and most of his daily changing menu acts as a showcase for top-quality Scottish produce. Expect to start with the likes of Mull scallops with Stornoway black pudding and Bramley purée, followed by hake with Shetland mussels and

razor clams, alongside stewed leek and fennel, or braised haunch of roe deer with red cabbage, dauphinois and thyme jus. Dark chocolate pithivier with coffee custard ends things on a caffeine high. Nor are wines exclusively French, although France provides the bedrock. Bottles start at £17.90, glasses at £5.10.
Chef/s: Neil Forbes. **Open:** all week L 12 to 2, D 5.15 to 10 (6 Sat and Sun). **Closed:** 25 to 27 Dec, 1 and 2 Jan. **Meals:** alc (main courses £14 to £23). Set L £15.50 (2 courses) to £19.50. Set D £18 (2 courses) to £22.50. **Details:** 48 seats.

★ TOP 50 ★

Castle Terrace

Superlative modern cooking
33-35 Castle Terrace, Edinburgh, EH1 2EL
Tel no: (0131) 2291222
www.castleterracerestaurant.com
Modern British | £60
Cooking score: 6

Å V

Spawned from Edinburgh high-flyer The Kitchin (see entry), Castle Terrace is a classy showcase for the superlative modern cooking of rising star Dominic Jack. Shades of purple and grey, opulent wallpaper and nifty designer detailing set the tone in the sumptuous dining room, and the kitchen is true to its strident credo. 'From nature to plate' is the message – and you'd better believe it. Brommie Bank hare is served 'à la royale' with 'forgotten vegetables' and wild watercress gnocchi, while stuffed saddle of Inverurie lamb comes with braised fennel, smoked aubergine, basil and olive jus. Dominic often plays Japanese japes with seafood, binding a mélange of brown crab, mango and red pepper with strips of avocado (like a sushi roll) and embellishing salmon tartare with white rice, black sesame seeds and wasabi ice cream. Tasting menus offer a procession of surprises 'from land and sea' and presentation is decidedly à la mode: all jokey constructions, arty squiggles, dots and cubes. Desserts such as pistachio soufflé with chocolate sorbet show the kitchen's mastery of the genre. The 300-bin global wine list is a serious tome noted for its reputable growers and vintages; prices start at £20 (£6 a glass).
Chef/s: Dominic Jack. **Open:** Tue to Sat L 12 to 2.45, D 6.30 to 10. **Closed:** Sun, Mon, 22 Dec to 21 Jan. **Meals:** alc (main courses £25 to £34). Set L £26.50. Tasting menu £70 (6 courses). **Details:** 65 seats. Separate bar. Wheelchair access. Children over 5 yrs only.

David Bann

Lustrous contemporary veggie
56-58 St Mary's Street, Edinburgh, EH1 1SX
Tel no: (0131) 5565888
www.davidbann.co.uk
Vegetarian | £22
Cooking score: 2

V £30

Smart as they come, David Bann's vegetarian eatery just off the Royal Mile adds lustre to Edinburgh's protean dining scene. A deep aubergine colour scheme and minimally dressed tables provide the setting for the kind of meat-free cooking that wins over even die-hard omnivores. Starters of aubergine, chickpea and cashew koftas, and smoked tofu with mango chutney compelled one pair of diners to make a return trip, while the outstanding main course has to be beetroot, apple and Dunsyre Blue pudding, a soufflé sauced with roasted red pepper and basil. Artfully constructed desserts include ginger and lime ice cream in a chocolate ganache bowl on orange drizzle cake. Good wines at manageable prices open at £14.75, £3.50 a glass; all, of course, are vegetarian or vegan.
Chef/s: David Bann. **Open:** all week 12 to 10 (10.30 Fri, 11 to 10.30 Sat, 11 to 10 Sun). **Closed:** 25 and 26 Dec, 1 Jan. **Meals:** alc (main courses £11 to £13). **Details:** 80 seats.

⁙ Average Price

The average price listed in main-entry reviews denotes the price of a three-course meal, without wine.

The Dogs

Hearty casual dining
110 Hanover Street, Edinburgh, EH2 1DR
Tel no: (0131) 2201208
www.thedogsonline.co.uk
Modern British | £22
Cooking score: 2
£30

Stamped with the individuality of its owner, this buzzy, popular first-floor eatery has a loyal band of regulars who praise the great food, atmosphere and service. The kitchen pilfers a few modern ideas (roasted squash, goats' cheese and spring onion barley risotto), but the rest is staunchly patriotic stuff – big on flavour dishes such as haggis, black pudding and bacon hash or devilled liver, onions, bacon and mushrooms on toast. Fish and chips with mushy peas or pork belly with sage and onion stuffing continue the theme. There are steaks, too, plus a raft of old-school desserts headed by lemon posset with an oat and ginger biscuit. A short list provides quaffable, inexpensive wines from £13.95.
Chef/s: Aitor Rodrigo. **Open:** all week L 12 to 4, D 5 to 10. **Closed:** 25 Dec, 1 Jan. **Meals:** alc (main courses £9 to £14). **Details:** 58 seats.

Fishers in Leith

Quirky nautical bistro with quality seafood
1 The Shore, Leith, Edinburgh, EH6 6QW
Tel no: (0131) 5545666
www.fishersrestaurantgroup.co.uk
Seafood | £28
Cooking score: 1
£30

The old watchtower overlooking the Leith shore makes an enticing venue for a repertoire of bistro seafood dishes. This is one of a trio of Fishers venues in Edinburgh. A mermaid figurehead floats serenely above the kitchen hatch, overseeing the consumption of inventive dishes such as queenie scallops with leek and black pudding butter, fillet of red mullet with fattoush and baba ganoush, or hake with roast beetroot and feta and rhubarb salad. Fill up with sticky toffee pudding and

vanilla ice cream. House Languedoc is £15.50, and there's an array of wines by the glass from £4.25.
Chef/s: Andrew Bird. **Open:** all week 12 to 10.30 (12.30 Sun). **Closed:** 25 and 26 Dec, 1 Jan. **Meals:** alc (main courses £14 to £23). Set L £13 (2 courses) to £16. **Details:** 38 seats. 18 seats outside. Separate bar.

Forth Floor Restaurant

Ambitious cooking, glorious views and shopping
Harvey Nichols, 30-34 St Andrew Square, Edinburgh, EH2 2AD
Tel no: (0131) 5248350
www.harveynichols.co.uk
Modern British | £37
Cooking score: 3

Perched atop Harvey Nichols, and slightly apart from the noisier bar-brasserie, the Forth Floor Restaurant's 'fat, red leather banquettes and chairs', polished mahogany floor, white linen and glass frontage ('stunning views over the city skyline') just about 'pulls off a convincingly chic sense of exclusivity'. Stuart Muir's dishes may sound complex in the billing, but they achieve well-judged culinary logic on the plate, and the quality of the Scottish regional produce is excellent. Poached oyster with squab lobster, crispy marrow bone, pickled shiitake mushroom, chicory, parsnip cream and bordelaise sauce starts things confidently, while a meatier choice at main course might be pork (braised cheek, fillet cordon bleu, crispy ear) teamed with caper and raisin purée, creamed cabbage and mustard seeds. Cappuccino soufflé with milk ice cream rounds thing off. Wines from £19.50.
Chef/s: Stuart Muir. **Open:** all week L 12 to 3, Tue to Sat D 6 to 10. **Closed:** 25 Dec, 1 Jan. **Meals:** alc (main courses £15 to £23). Sun L £30. **Details:** 45 seats. 31 seats outside. Separate bar. Wheelchair access. Car parking.

NEW ENTRY

Galvin Brasserie de Luxe

Big on flavour and quality
The Caledonian, Princes Street, Edinburgh,
EH1 2AB
Tel no: (0131) 222 8988
www.galvinrestaurants.com
French | £30
Cooking score: 3

The Galvin brothers have extended their
London empire with the opening of two
restaurants in the renovated slice of special-
occasion grandeur that is Edinburgh's
Caledonian Hotel. The Brasserie de Luxe is to
be found on the ground floor: three spacious
interconnecting rooms all modelled on a
Parisian brasserie and featuring a glamorous
circular bar. On the food front there's nothing
fussy or gratuitously showy. The assured
cooking has clear flavours, with crustacean
options and classic plats du jour (such as coq au
vin and poulet roti forestière) appearing
alongside 'suitably rich but light' crab lasagne
with beurre nantaise, and 'meltingly tender'
tagine of lamb shoulder re-formed into a large
tournedos with fragrant herb couscous and a
lively rose harissa. Reporters agree that
desserts are a high point – from the fine tarte
Tatin to the sublime passion fruit soufflé with
chocolate ice cream. Service is welcoming and
knowledgeable. House wines start at £19.
Chef/s: Craig Sandle. Open: Mon to Fri L 12 to 2.30
(12.30 to 3 Sat and Sun), D 6 to 10 (9.30 Sun).
Meals: alc (main meals £15 to £28). Set L and D
£15.50 (2 courses) to £18.50. Sun L £15. Details: 130
seats. Separate bar. Wheelchair access. Car parking.

Symbols

🛏 Accommodation is available

£30 Three courses for less than £30

V Separate vegetarian menu

£5 OFF £5-off voucher scheme

🍶 Notable wine list

★ READERS' RESTAURANT OF THE YEAR ★
SCOTLAND

NEW ENTRY

The Gardener's Cottage

Rural vibe in the heart of the city
1 Royal Terrace Gardens, London Road,
Edinburgh, EH7 5DX
Tel no: (0131) 558 1221
www.thegardenerscottage.co
British | £25
Cooking score: 2
£5 OFF £30

Praise pours in for Dale Mailley and Edward
Murray's Georgian cottage restaurant prettily
set in Royal Terrace Gardens. 'A truly
wonderful restaurant we are itching to get
back to,' reports one reader. Communal tables,
an open kitchen and a no-choice set menu,
posted each day on Facebook, is the deal. The
décor epitomises studied informality: paint-
splattered floorboards, scuffed paintwork,
Sunday school chairs, flowers and candles.
Produce from the cottage garden is used to
good effect in the kitchen. Garden salad, carrot
soup and hake with herb dumplings all tested
well, except for cold plates and lukewarm
dishes. A quiche of crowdie and Shimonita
onions was quiveringly perfect; so too was
rhubarb, oatcake, crowdie and soft meringue.
'Yum bloomin' scrum', reports another reader.
We concur. Excellent wines from £17.90.
Chef/s: Dale Mailley and Edward Murray. Open:
Thur to Mon L 12 to 2.30, D 5 to 10. Closed: Tue,
Wed, 25 Dec to 8 Jan. Meals: Tasting menu £25 (6
courses). Details: 30 seats. 10 seats outside.

La Garrigue

A taste of the Midi off the Royal Mile
31 Jeffrey Street, Edinburgh, EH1 1DH
Tel no: (0131) 5573032
www.lagarrigue.co.uk
French | £30
Cooking score: 3

Readers heap plaudits upon Jean-Michel
Gauffre's centrally located bistro, where the
flavours of le Midi are matched by staff who
are 'as genuine as the cuisine'. Not far from

Waverley station, La Garrigue is a convivial spot decorated in vivid Provençal hues, with bright paintings of sunnier climes hanging on the wood-panelled walls. It makes a heartwarming, friendly venue in which to sample food of the culinary *ancien régime*. Rabbit ravioli with spinach, chicken confit with potato and apple or generous seafood casserole might grace the regularly refreshed menu, but the gastronomic compass-point is usually set to the south, with fine renditions of cassoulet languedocien de rigueur. Finish with floating island pudding with fresh berries ('the perfect end to the meal') or a lavender-scented crème brûlée. Southern French wines populate a reasonably priced list that opens with glasses at £4.50 and half-litre pichets at £11.25.
Chef/s: Jean-Michel Gauffre. **Open:** all week L 12 to 2.30, D 6.30 to 9.30. **Closed:** 26 Dec, 1 and 2 Jan. **Meals:** Set L £12.50 (2 courses) to £15.50. Set D £25.50 (2 courses) to £30. **Details:** 45 seats. Car parking.

Guchhi Indian Seafood & Bar
Clubby vibes and trendy Indian food
9-10 Commercial Street, Leith, Edinburgh, EH6 6JA
Tel no: (0131) 5555604
www.guchhi.com
Seafood-Indian | £21
Cooking score: 2
V £30

A bright spark on Leith's trendy docklands scene, Guchhi hits the button with its fashionable blend of Indian tapas, clever seafood cookery and clubby vibes. Small plates are tailor-made for socialising: try artichoke pakoras with mango chutney; chicken, mushroom and chickpea puris; or mussels in coconut milk with a splash of white wine. Otherwise, fish fans should bypass the biryanis, kormas and rogan josh in favour of oven-baked scallops in the shell with 'Bombay duck' sauce or tandoori crab. You could even plump for westernised ideas such as lemon sole with shellfish sauce – and check out the Guchhi 'paella' for a sharing feast. Sip funky cocktails at the bar (Hindi punch, anyone?) or pick something from the fish-loving wine list; prices start at £14.95.
Chef/s: Vishant Das. **Open:** all week 12 to 11. **Meals:** alc (main courses £10 to £24). Set L £8.95 (2 courses) to £10.95. Set D £10.95 (2 courses) to £15.95. **Details:** 80 seats. 15 seats outside. Separate bar. Wheelchair access. Car parking.

★ TOP 50 ★

The Kitchin
Star player on the waterfront
78 Commercial Quay, Leith, Edinburgh, EH6 6LX
Tel no: (0131) 5551755
www.thekitchin.com
Modern European | £65
Cooking score: 7
Å V

Tom Kitchin's Commercial Street premises on the Leith waterfront may look unprepossessing from outside, but there's history in the stones. This was once a whisky warehouse, and its redesign makes a virtue of the old stone and wood structure: softening the interior with tones of smoky grey, enlivening it with daring turquoises and purples. Kitchin is devoted to his country's premium produce, and inspiration flows through his menus. Butchering and filleting of meats takes place in-house. Two diners conferring after a winter dinner voted respectively for the pig's head and ear salad, and the salmon and apple tartare as their favourites – but choosing is tough. Technical skills are astounding – witness a langoustine ravioli bound in virtually diaphanous cuttle-fish-ink pasta, floating on foamy shellfish bisque; or 'unbelievably tender' carpaccio of roe deer with pumpkin seeds, apple and herb cream. Neither does the repertoire lack for gutsiness: snipe from the game menu comes complete with brain; gloriously gamey hare arrives with chanterelles. Temper this robustness with a vivacious pud such as gorgeously ripe poached pear with sensuous toffee cake and terrific brown-butter ice cream. 'Each dish seemed to inspire its successor' commented one reader on a 'truly memorable' meal. Base

prices on the wine list are high (glasses from £9.50, bottles £29), but the intelligent, impeccably sourced selection offers a global distillation of modern vinous thinking.
Chef/s: Tom Kitchin. **Open:** Tue to Sat L 12.15 to 2.15 (2.30 Fri and Sat), D 6.30 to 10. **Closed:** Sun, Mon. **Meals:** alc (main courses £32 to £40). Set L £26.50. Tasting menu £70 (6 courses). **Details:** 55 seats. 32 seats outside. Separate bar. Wheelchair access. Children over 5 yrs only.

number one

Subtly inventive cooking that really surprises
The Balmoral, 1 Princes Street, Edinburgh, EH2 2EQ
Tel no: (0131) 5576727
www.restaurantnumberone.com
Modern European | £68
Cooking score: 6
🛏 V

The grand old Balmoral, which opened in 1902, was once very much the railway hotel, and had a separate entrance from what is now Waverley station. The clock in its august Edwardian tower runs three minutes fast, as a courtesy so you don't miss your train. Inside, everything speaks of imperial grandiloquence; there's a dedicated Bollinger Bar. The deceptively self-effacing number one (the principal dining room) features seating in golden velvet and walls in red Hong Kong lacquer. Messrs Bland and Boyter between them devise and enact a dynamic new Scottish cuisine, overlaid with modern French and east Asian influences. The results are seen in dishes such as poached scallop with Ibérico ham, pea purée, yuzu and kombu, followed perhaps by turbot with squid linguine and razor clam in shellfish sauce, or the glorious dry-aged Orkney beef, which comes with Barwheys cheese, asparagus, and onions simmered in dark ale. Look to the trolley for cheeses, or else contemplate a newfangled Caledonian dessert like raspberry crowdie and carrot sponge with chocolate sorbet. A compendious wine list, at mark-ups to suit the surroundings, opens at £28, or £9.50 a glass.

Chef/s: Billy Boyter and Jeff Bland. **Open:** all week D only 6.30 to 10. **Closed:** 26 Dec, first 2 weeks Jan. **Meals:** Set D £68. Tasting menu £75. **Details:** 55 seats. Separate bar. Wheelchair access.

Ondine

Sustainable seafood favourite
2 George IV Bridge, Edinburgh, EH1 1AD
Tel no: (0131) 2261888
www.ondinerestaurant.co.uk
Seafood | £45
Cooking score: 4

'Upstairs, well away from the pizza chain place below, we found this smart, modern dining room fashioned in a sweeping curve with views over one of the main arteries of Edinburgh.' The hard-to-find location doesn't stop Ondine filling up. Indeed, this dining room, which deals in seafood and sustainability, enjoys 'hidden gem' status. The menu steers an international course, taking in Cullen skink 'properly made with undyed smoked haddock and leek rather than onion'; tempura squid with Vietnamese dipping sauce; a 'very tasty' crab risotto with brown shrimps; 'delicious' haddock goujons with caper mayonnaise and 'a decent helping' of thin-cut chips in a paper cornet; and fish curry with raita and basmati rice. For dessert, a Trinity crème brûlée partnered by super local shortbread and honeycomb ice cream is considered a must-try. Service is 'relaxed, friendly and efficient'. Wines from £19.50.
Chef/s: Roy Brett. **Open:** Mon to Sat L 12 to 3, D 5.30 to 10. **Closed:** Sun, 24 to 28 Dec, 2 to 7 Jan. **Meals:** alc (main courses £15 to £50). Set L and D £17.95 (2 courses) to £21.95. **Details:** 80 seats. Wheelchair access.

🍴 Visit us Online

To find out more about *The Good Food Guide*, please visit www.thegoodfoodguide.co.uk

Plumed Horse

Harnessing powerful, sculpted flavours
50-54 Henderson Street, Edinburgh, EH6 6DE
Tel no: (0131) 5545556
www.plumedhorse.co.uk
Modern European | £55
Cooking score: 5

A small-scale restaurant with big ideas, Tony Borthwick's Plumed Horse is tethered in a red sandstone apartment block close to Leith's waterfront. Inside, light contemporary tones and shades of green soften the mood in the irregularly shaped, conjoined dining rooms. The kitchen continues to surprise. Tony's cooking is all about harnessing powerful, clear, sculpted flavours, with modern techniques given every opportunity to shine. Just consider chicken liver parfait with spiced foie gras butter, gingerbread foam, baked pear purée and watercress salad or ravioli of guinea fowl with guinea fowl consommé, oyster mushrooms and white spring truffles. Seasonal native ingredients are given due consideration, from blade of Scotch beef (served with spinach custard and basil gnocchi) to fish from the coast – perhaps crab and oyster quiche with curried foam or sautéed monkfish cheeks with langoustines, pancetta carbonara, quail's egg and Arënkha caviar. Desserts such as the signature coffee macaroon with citrus confit, honeycomb ice cream and hot toddy sauce also keep things interesting. France leads the way on the knowledgeable global wine list, with prices from £21.
Chef/s: Tony Borthwick. Open: Tue to Sat L 12.30 to 1.30, D 7 to 9 (6.30 Fri and Sat). Closed: Sun, Mon, Christmas. Meals: Set L £24. Set D £55. Details: 40 seats. Wheelchair access. No children under 5 yrs.

NEW ENTRY

The Pompadour by Galvin

Glamorous dining in the heart of the city
The Caledonian, Princes Street, Edinburgh, EH1 2AB
Tel no: (0131) 2228975
www.galvinrestaurants.com
French | £58
Cooking score: 5

The prettiest, priciest table in town when it opened in 1925, the Pompadour had faded from glory when the Hilton Group took over the Caledonian Hotel. The hotel's recent refurbishment cost £24 million and Hilton also brought in the Galvin brothers to relaunch the Pompadour and the Brasserie de Luxe (see entry). Pale grey walls, pink chandelier and restoration of the stucco cornices and hand-painted Chinese panels are part of the upgrade. This and views to the Castle complete one of the city's most glamorous dining rooms. The Galvins' French-inspired menu is overseen by Chris Sandle (ex-Balmoral Hotel) with considerable panache, and with service to match. A signature of poulet en vessie – chicken cooked in a pig's bladder broken open at the table and served with a foie gras sauce – features on the à la carte. An excellent-value seasonal menu celebrated spring with a roulade of guinea fowl and white asparagus. The showpiece seven-course menu gourmand with matching wines pleased one reader: 'Without exception every course was delicious.' Sommelier Peter Adshead impresses with his knowledge and quiet charm, advising on a list that starts at £27.
Chef/s: Craig Sandle. Open: Tue to Sat D 6.30 to 10. Closed: Mon, Sun, 26 Dec, first 2 weeks Jan. Meals: Set D £58 (3 courses) to £68 (7 courses). Details: 55 seats. Separate bar. Wheelchair access. Car parking.

NEW ENTRY
Purslane Restaurant
Intimate basement restaurant
33a St Stephen Street, Stockbridge, Edinburgh, EH3 5AH
Tel no: (0131) 2263500
www.purslanerestaurant.co.uk
Modern British | £26
Cooking score: 2
£5 OFF £30

A smart basement restaurant where chef/patron Paul Gunning's aspiring menu of precise dishes reflects his experience under the likes of Jeff Bland at Balmoral's number one (see entry). Belly, fillet and a rissole of pork looked a picture on its black plate with broccoli, turned potatoes, butternut squash purée and dashes of black pudding, but sadly looks won over flavour. By contrast, a crisp fried chicken and noodle salad and red mullet with crushed potatoes and green beans were all the more enjoyable for being simpler. Similarly crème brûlée with salted caramel triumphed over a fridge-hard coffee parfait, raspberry sorbet, fresh raspberry, and seed and nut brittle. More space between tables would also enhance this restaurant's high ambition. Wines start at £15.50.
Chef/s: Paul Gunning. **Open:** Tue to Sat L 12 to 2, D 6.30 to 10.30. **Closed:** Sun, Mon, 25 and 26 Dec, 1 to 4 Jan. **Meals:** Set L £12.95 to £16.95. Set D £22.95 to £26.95. **Details:** 24 seats. Children over 6 yrs only.

Restaurant Mark Greenaway
Harmonious cooking in new surroundings
69 North Castle Street, Edinburgh, EH2 3LJ
Tel no: (0131) 226 1155
www.restaurantmarkgreenaway.com
Modern British | £45
Cooking score: 4

In January 2013, Mark Greenaway moved his namesake restaurant uptown to 'elegant and darkly decorated premises immediately opposite Martin Wishart's bistro'. According to one reporter, 'most of the staff seem to have moved too, and the menu has moved more or less intact, with four choices at each stage.'

Tables may be tightly packed, and the chairs 'only moderately comfortable', but the new venue is proving popular. Attentive and professional, Greenaway produces food that is by turns inventive and orthodox, with a sharp focus on quality. Beautifully presented dishes might appear busy yet succeed with harmonious combinations: perhaps confit duck pavé with hot orange jelly or mosaic of rabbit terrine with carrot mayonnaise and carrot meringues. By contrast, main courses could receive more robustly traditional treatment – as in rump of lamb with 'shepherd's pie', thyme gnocchi and rosemary jus. Desserts tend to be subtle twists on familiar themes: rhubarb and custard 'fishbowl', say. The varied wine list (from £18) has reasonable mark-ups.
Chef/s: Mark Greenaway. **Open:** Tue to Sat L 12 to 2.30, D 5.30 to 10. **Closed:** Sun, Mon, 25 and 26 Dec, 1 and 2 Jan. **Meals:** alc (main courses £18 to £28). Set L and D £16.50 (2 courses) to £20. Tasting menu £65.50 (8 courses). **Details:** 60 seats.

★ TOP 50 ★

Restaurant Martin Wishart
Inspired cooking from a Caledonian star
54 The Shore, Leith, Edinburgh, EH6 6RA
Tel no: (0131) 5533557
www.martin-wishart.co.uk
Modern French | £75
Cooking score: 7

V

'Unforgettable', 'close to perfection', 'enough to make me move back to Edinburgh' . . . Readers confirm that Martin Wishart's restaurant is on blistering form, delivering brilliance at every turn – from anticipatory amuse-bouches (beetroot macarons, queenie scallops with crispy salsify, and more) to a cascade of petits fours and dainty homemade chocolates. The mood in the suave dining room is low-key and formal, but decidedly 'romantic', too, with gentle music playing and polite staff attending to every detail. Whether you eat from the carte or the tasting menu, this Caledonian star can deliver complex, intelligent and inspired creations, always with strong French accents but showing respect for the seasonal Scottish larder. Glowing recommendations tell their own story: sauté of duck foie gras with 'deliciously fruity' poached Mouneyrac pear, caramelised endive, bitter orange and a Szechuan-spiced meringue; a 'wow' combo of fregula sarda and veal sweetbreads roasted in buckwheat with winter chanterelles; onglet of beef pointed up with Swiss chard, Chinese artichokes, confit shallot and wasabi. Elsewhere, sea-fresh langoustines ('just out of the water') are teamed with melted smoked butter, sea lettuce and prawn crumbs – contrasting textures and flavours in perfect harmony. To finish, the exquisitely crafted caramel délice and peanut praline with poached pear, caramel and *fleur de sel* ice cream gets rave reviews. Matching wines are generally spot-on, and the superlative modern list admirably balances big hitters with bottles from lesser-known artisan producers. Prices start at £26 and half-bottles are numerous.

Chef/s: Martin Wishart. **Open:** Tue to Sat L 12 to 1.30, D 7 to 9 (6.30 to 9.30 Fri and Sat). **Closed:** Sun, Mon, 24 to 26 Dec, 2 weeks Jul. **Meals:** Set L £28.50. Set D £70. Tasting menu £75 (6 courses). **Details:** 48 seats. Wheelchair access.

Rhubarb at Prestonfield

Magnificent interiors and head-turning cooking
Prestonfield House, Priestfield Road, Edinburgh, EH16 5UT
Tel no: (0131) 2251333
www.prestonfield.com
Modern British | £50
Cooking score: 4

The white-faced William Bruce house with its curly gables was built in 1687 for the Lord Provost of Edinburgh. Maintained to a high standard throughout, its palatial interiors are stunning masterpieces of boudoir rococo that will reliably slacken the jaw. It seems a pity in the lavish circumstances that tables are so tightly packed in the dining-room, but staff compensate with the right balance of informality and polish. First up might be a rare-as-you-dare pigeon breast with malted spelt, mushrooms and cranberries in balsamic chocolate jus, followed perhaps by cod with preserved lemon, fennel and parsley roots. The kitchen's heart, though, seems to lie with red meats: chateaubriand in béarnaise for two, seasonal game like partridge with grelot onions in green olive oil, or surprisingly well-done Strathspey red deer with black pudding crumble, puréed red cabbage and a potato and Arran mustard mousse. The Valrhôna chocolate plate doesn't quite deliver the hoped-for hit, but more covetable might be a pear poached in Earl Grey with blackberries, sorrel sorbet, rice pudding and yoghurt ice-cream. The wine list is stunning in Europe, less so elsewhere, with prices from £24.

Chef/s: John McMahon. **Open:** all week L 12 to 2 (2.30 Sun), D 6.30 to 10 (11 Fri and Sat). **Meals:** alc (main courses £19 to £35). Set L £18 (2 courses). Set D £33 (3 courses). **Details:** 90 seats. 20 seats outside. Wheelchair access. Car parking.

Tanjore

Bargain-priced Tamil cooking
6-8 Clerk Street, Edinburgh, EH8 9HX
Tel no: (0131) 4786518
www.tanjore.co.uk
Indian | £15
Cooking score: 1
£5 OFF £30

Owned by Mrs Boon Ganeshram, who does some of the cooking, this informal, low-key restaurant in the Old Town focuses on south Indian Tamil cooking. Vegetarians (and vegans) do particularly well here – although the menu also contains meat and seafood dishes. Massive rolled-up dosas of every description are a speciality, but also look for uthappam (lacy savoury pancakes), steamed idli cakes, potato bonda and various veggie bhajis including 'raw' banana. Committed omnivores can enjoy the spicy delights of crab curry, Keralan-style fish, lamb pepper fry or chicken nilgiri with mint and coriander. At lunchtime, you can also build your own thalis for under a tenner. Unlicensed, but salt or sweet lassi are soothing sips.

Chef/s: Boon Ganeshram. **Open:** all week L 12 to 2.30 (3.30 Sat and Sun), D 5 to 10. **Meals:** alc (main courses £6 to £13). **Details:** 38 seats. 6 seats outside.

21212

Artful, offbeat food in sumptuous surrounds
3 Royal Terrace, Edinburgh, EH7 5AB
Tel no: (0131) 5231030
www.21212restaurant.co.uk
Modern French | £68
Cooking score: 5

Perhaps recalling Paul Kitching's madcap glory days in Altrincham, one Mancunian reader regularly makes the trip up north to the chef's latest venture – a 'truly undervalued' restaurant-with-rooms spread over four floors of a sumptuously decorated Edinburgh townhouse. With its beautifully quirky setting and artful, offbeat food, 21212 gets tongues wagging and devotees clearly love everything about the place. The meaning behind the venue's puzzling numeric moniker becomes apparent at lunchtime, when the menu offers two starters, one soup, two mains, one cheese and two desserts – although it perversely upgrades to 31313 in the evening. Either way, expect a truckload of ingredients deployed in predictably idiosyncratic style – from 'Waldorf-style' lamb with walnuts, celery and prunes, swede purée, seeds and chickpeas to a 'corned beef special' or pink trout with a hotchpotch of pineapple, kidneys and spicy prawns, soy, new potatoes, ginger and coriander cream. To finish, the 'classic speciality tart of 20 years standing' is always worth a punt – perhaps glazed lemon curd with honeydew melon milk. One fan also recommends dipping into the 'chef's dishes' – works in progress 'that haven't been named yet'. Friendly, helpful service guides things along nicely and the eclectic wine list offers daily selections by the glass, plus intriguing bottles from £25.

Chef/s: Paul Kitching. **Open:** Tue to Sat L 12 to 1.45, D 6.45 to 9.30. **Closed:** Sun and Mon, 10 days Jan, 10 days summer. **Meals:** Set L £20 (2 courses) to £52 (5 courses). Set D £48 (3 courses) to £68. **Details:** 38 seats. Children over 5 yrs only.

Valvona & Crolla Caffè Bar

Pioneering Neapolitan blockbuster
19 Elm Row, Edinburgh, EH7 4AA
Tel no: (0131) 5566066
www.valvonacrolla.co.uk
Italian | £25
Cooking score: 3

'A Mecca of Italian food and wine for any self-respecting foodie', the Contini family's deli-cum-caffè has gone 'from market stall to dom.com' since opening its doors in 1934. It's a brash, noisy and cosmopolitan Edinburgh star, equally popular with shoppers looking for imported provisions and peckish souls seeking robust, rustic food with a southern accent. The action starts with breakfast (don't miss the trademark 'panatella' sandwiches and bombolone doughnuts), although lunch is a real Neapolitan blockbuster. Top-drawer seasonal antipasti are closely followed by pizzas and handmade pastas (pappardelle with king prawns and artichokes, for example), as well as bigger plates of seasonal rusticity: say fritto misto or cotechino sausage with lentils and olive-oil mash. The Continis are also wine merchants, with the best Italian cellar in town, and you can sample affordably by dipping into their adventurous caffè list (check recommendations on the menu). Prices from £15.95 (£4.25 a glass). A branch called VinCaffè is housed in the Multrees Walk shopping complex; tel: (0131) 5570088.
Chef/s: Mary Contini. **Open:** Mon to Sat 8.30 to 5.30 (8 to 6 Fri and Sat, Sun 10.30 to 3.30). **Closed:** 25 and 26 Dec, 1 and 2 Jan. **Meals:** alc (main courses £10 to £16). **Details:** 60 seats.

The Witchery by the Castle

Some fancy trickery with Scottish produce
Castlehill, Royal Mile, Edinburgh, EH1 2NF
Tel no: (0131) 2255613
www.thewitchery.com
Modern British | £45
Cooking score: 2

On the last stretch of the climb towards the Castle, the Witchery is probably Edinburgh's most beautiful restaurant. You descend into a basement world of ornate wood panelling, hanging drapes and gargantuan floral displays sprouting from ornamental statuary. A menu of fairly modern Scottish dishes contains some fixtures (the preserved fish platter of smoked trout, smoked eel and mackerel ceviche with pickles), French delicacies such as foie gras terrine with Jerusalem artichoke purée, and mains like poached John Dory and mussels in curry-spiced sauce. Highland meats such as Cairngorm venison are royally treated, perhaps with roast squash and fig in chocolate oil, and puddings include passion fruit and mascarpone trifle with caraway biscotti. The huge wine list orders French classics in exhaustive detail, then branches out into the opulent best of Spain, Italy and the Americas, with a particularly fine US selection. Prices open at £21.50.

Chef/s: Douglas Roberts. Open: all week L 12 to 4 (5.30 Sat), D 5.30 to 11.30. Closed: 25 and 26 Dec. Meals: alc (main courses £23 to £39). Set L £15.95 (2 courses) to £33. Set D £33. Details: 95 seats. 20 seats outside. Children over 12 yrs only after 7.30.

ALSO RECOMMENDED

▲ Centotre

103 George Street, Edinburgh, EH2 3ES
Tel no: (0131) 2251550
www.centotre.com
Italian

Owned by the celebrated Contini family, who set up legendary Valvona & Crolla (see entry), this buzzy caffè in a converted bank feeds Edinburgh shoppers and tourists with everything from breakfast, mid-morning pastries and all-day aperitivi snacks to three-course suppers. Pizzas and classic pastas (from £8.95) are the mainstays of a menu that also runs to Tuscan-style grills and specials such as beetroot risotto (£12.95). Great handmade gelati too. The Continis are wine merchants par excellence, and their list is a treasure trove of classy regional Italian drinking from £15.95. Open all week.

▲ The Mulroy

11a-13a William Street, Edinburgh, EH3 7NG
Tel no: (0131) 2256061
www.themulroy.co.uk
French

This is the sort of charming French bistro where the basement location doesn't matter; intimate and elegant, it draws regulars 'from well beyond the city'. The set lunch (£16.50 for two courses) makes a good-value introduction: perhaps crab, saffron and leek risotto, then homemade venison sausage with vegetable, Puy lentil and cep ragoût. The set dinner (£39.50 for three courses) delivers more ambition and 'interesting combinations': for instance, lemon sole with sweet potato purée, squid-ink ravioli, North Sea shrimps and chive and mussel beurre blanc. Wines from £18.50. Closed Sun and Mon.

Gullane

Chez Roux

Graceful villa with Albert Roux menus
Greywalls Hotel, Muirfield, Gullane, EH31 2EG
Tel no: (01620) 842144
www.greywalls.co.uk
French | £35
Cooking score: 4

V

A country house designed by Lutyens in 1901, extended by Lorimer and with gardens laid out by Gertrude Jekyll makes a majestic setting for a meal. Thankfully, the food at Chez Roux bears all the hallmarks of the culinary royalty acknowledged in its name. Gavroche habitués of yore will recognise the soufflé suissesse that opens the entrées, and will

LOTHIANS

also remember the rather regal style of bilingual haute cuisine that informs the whole menu. A pot-au-feu of ox tongue and beef shin comes with sauce Albert, while the cheesy-coated lemon sole is filled with mushrooms and accompanied by brown shrimp gratin. Then there's a baked, spiced, flambéed banana for afters, served with rum and raisin ice cream. The cheese course is presented imaginatively, with a Roquefort mousse and pear compote. Staff are meticulous, and the wine list (from £22) provides ample luxurious bubbles, silky Chardonnay and velvety red blends from France and elsewhere.

Chef/s: Derek Johnstone. **Open:** all week L 12 to 2, D 6 to 10. **Meals:** alc (main courses £14 to £22). Set L £26.50 (3 courses). Set D £29.50 (3 courses). **Details:** 80 seats. Separate bar. Wheelchair access.

La Potinière

A cavalcade of immensely pleasurable food
34 Main Street, Gullane, EH31 2AA
Tel no: (01620) 843214
www.la-potiniere.co.uk
Modern British | £38
Cooking score: 6

A winter redecoration brought a fresh new look to La Potinière in 2013, but the ethos of the place remains sublimely unchanged. It's still like dining in somebody's front room – only with stellar culinary skills on display. Mary Runciman and Keith Marley are a formidable double-act and, with the aid of proudly listed local suppliers, have honed an impressive style of pin-sharp modern Scottish cooking. 'Absolutely first-class service – efficient, gracious and unobtrusive' helps too. A summer lunch that began with pea mousse in mint sauce, and proceeded to mains of lemon sole wrapped in salmon, and chicken breast with truffle jus, offered plenty to admire. Things get ritzier at dinner, when foie gras with duck, spiced plum, and sweetcorn custard might be the overture to a bowl of truffled celeriac soup, followed by poached and seared beef fillet with wild mushroom risotto in Madeira jus. Finish with crème

caramel and berries, or chocolate moelleux and lychee sorbet. An exhaustively noted wine list plays fair on price, opening at £16.75 or £3.25 a small glass.

Chef/s: Mary Runciman and Keith Marley. **Open:** Wed to Sun L 12.30 to 1.30, D 7 to 8.30. **Closed:** Mon, Tue, Jan. **Meals:** Set L £20.50 (2 courses) to £25. Set D £38 (3 courses) to £43. Sun L £25. **Details:** 24 seats. Wheelchair access. Car parking.

Linlithgow

Champany Inn
Pioneering steakhouse
Champany Corner, Linlithgow, EH49 7LU
Tel no: (01506) 834532
www.champany.com
British | £73
Cooking score: 3

An elegantly converted group of farmstead buildings, parts of which date back to the time of Mary Queen of Scots, has been consecrated to the unswerving celebration of fine Scottish beef. Hung for a minimum of three weeks and offered in a compendious variety of cuts, the meat comes with classic sauces such as Stilton and horseradish, peppercorn or wild mushroom and Pommery mustard. The steaks don't come cheap, but the quality is beyond question, and the accuracy in cooking – rare to medium timings work best – is a credit to the kitchen. If you're not up for a steak, try Dornoch lamb with apple and cinnamon jelly, or charcoal-grilled salmon with lemon butter, perhaps preceded by spanking-fresh langoustines and pasta in seafood bisque. Pudding might be a properly sticky pear tarte Tatin. Wines start at £20.50.

Chef/s: Clive Davidson and David Gibson. **Open:** Mon to Fri L 12.30 to 2, Mon to Sat D 7 to 10 (6.30 Sat). **Closed:** Sun, 25 and 26 Dec, 1 and 2 Jan. **Meals:** alc (main courses £29 to £49). Set L £22.50 (2 courses) to £30.50. Set D £42.50. **Details:** 50 seats. 20 seats outside. Separate bar. Wheelchair access. Car parking. Children over 8 yrs only.

Join us at www.thegoodfoodguide.co.uk

499

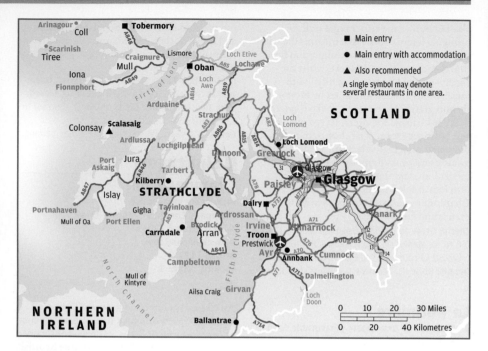

▌Annbank

Enterkine House

Splendour, charm and fine-tuned cooking
Enterkine Estate, Annbank, KA6 5AL
Tel no: (01292) 520580
www.enterkine.com
Modern European | £30
Cooking score: 4

£5 OFF ⇆

Set amid 350 acres of Ayrshire, Enterkine was built in the 1930s and still makes a wonderful getaway with its winding tree-lined drive. Browne's restaurant is kitted out with a less formal look than the country-house norm, with pine flooring and unclothed tables, all gently lit by standard lamps. It's a soothing setting for Paul Moffat's modern Scottish cooking, which draws inspiration from afar. Kicking things off might be smoked salmon tartare with mackerel, puréed pear, yuzu crème fraîche and Avruga caviar, or a hearty salad of French rabbit with black pudding, apple and a Sauternes dressing. Fillet of aged Buccleuch beef could follow, paired with the cheek, alongside horseradish mash in pink peppercorn sauce, or else John Dory with shaved fennel, kohlrabi and gnocchi in lemongrass velouté. The hot-ticket dessert is a parfait of Bramley apple crumble garnished with a sesame croquant and apple compote in fennel syrup. A brightly illustrated wine list opens at £19.50.
Chef/s: Paul Moffat. **Open:** all week L 12 to 2, D 7 to 9. **Meals:** alc (main courses £10 to £24). Set L £16.95 (2 courses) to £18.95. Set D £25 (2 courses) to £35. Sun L £25. **Details:** 45 seats. 12 seats outside. Car parking.

Symbols

⇆ Accommodation is available

£30 Three courses for less than £30

V Separate vegetarian menu

£5 OFF £5-off voucher scheme

♦ Notable wine list

▌ Ballantrae

Glenapp Castle

Formidable cooking at a top-notch hotel
Ballantrae, KA26 ONZ
Tel no: (01465) 831212
www.glenappcastle.com
Modern British | £65
Cooking score: 6

£5
OFF ⊟

A grand set of gates and a twisting woodland drive separate this other-worldly castle from the daily grind. Bear right at a Narnia-style lamppost and the building swings into view in all its fairytale splendour. The luscious interior – all antiques, oil paintings and chandeliers – is everything you could wish for. New chef Matt Worswick hails from Le Champignon Sauvage in Cheltenham (see entry), so he brings a knack for flavour-driven invention as well as a classical grounding befitting this location. A lunchtime dish of crisply seared gurnard with cauliflower purée makes the point well, bearing a fluffy powder of smoked almond to round up the flavours, while treacle braised brisket with watercress cream and rye flour macaroni is a devilishly rich, sure-footed main. Moist pistachio and orange cake with walnut crumble and dark chocolate sorbet is a good way to end, perhaps accompanied by something from the ample wine list, which has global coverage but a penchant for France, and opens at £28 a bottle.
Chef/s: Matt Worswick. **Open:** all week L 12.30 to 2, D 7 to 10. **Closed:** Christmas week, 3 Jan to late Mar. **Meals:** Set L £39.50. Set D £65 (6 courses). **Details:** 34 seats. Wheelchair access. Car parking. Children over 5 yrs only at D.

▮ Visit us Online

To find out more about
The Good Food Guide, please visit
www.thegoodfoodguide.co.uk

▌ Cameron House, Loch Lomond

Martin Wishart at Loch Lomond

Poised cooking in a baronial pile
Cameron House, Loch Lomond, G83 8QZ
Tel no: (01389) 722504
www.martinwishartlochlomond.co.uk
Modern French | £70
Cooking score: 6

⊟ V

While his multi-gonged Edinburgh restaurant (see entry) occupies one of the top branches of Scotland's gastronomic tree, Martin Wishart is developing a country outpost within the Cameron House Hotel: a grandiose baronial pile on the bonnie, bonnie banks of Loch Lomond, complete with ravishing views and lashings of designer gravitas. One of his protégés runs the kitchen, sending out food with real stature, poise and a sensitivity to Scottish produce – even if the predominant themes are from the Gallic half of the Auld Alliance. An invigorating combo of roasted Orkney scallop and bone marrow is overlaid with artichoke purée and smoked herring caviar, line-caught sea bass is baked in a salt meringue, and butter-poached John Dory fillets are speckled with ginger before being presented with cockles, purple sprouting broccoli and citrus beurre blanc. Meaty treasures could include roast saddle of Borders roe deer with oyster mushrooms, caramelised onion, baby turnips and grand-veneur sauce. Classic patisserie underpins such desserts as coffee parfait and crème mousseline with mango and kalamansi fruit sorbet. The wine list (from £28) is a global heavyweight tilted towards the Old World.
Chef/s: Graham Cheevers. **Open:** Sat and Sun L 12 to 2 (2.30 Sun), Wed to Sun D 6.30 to 9.30 (7 Sun). **Closed:** Mon, Tue, 25 and 26 Dec, first 2 weeks Jan, first week May. **Meals:** Set L £28.50. Set D £50 (2 courses) to £70. Tasting menu £75 (6 courses). **Details:** 48 seats. Separate bar. Wheelchair access. Car parking.

Carradale

Dunvalanree

Enchanting clifftop home-from-home
Port Righ, Carradale, PA28 6SE
Tel no: (01583) 431226
www.dunvalanree.com
Modern British | £28
Cooking score: 2

£5 OFF ⇌ V £30

Spectacular views across Port Righ Bay to the Isle of Arran come with the territory at this comfortable restaurant-with-rooms – in Alan and Alyson Milstead's capable hands since 1998. Alyson's enthusiasm for local and regional produce is as strong as ever, and her assured, quality-conscious style exudes and inspires confidence. The format never changes: drinks in the lounge, then a three-course dinner served at a single sitting, with daily changing dishes assiduously following the seasons. Reporters have praised fresh warmed figs with Strathdon Blue cheese and crispy prosciutto, and venison fillet steak with red onion, port and rowan jelly, as well as fresh mussels in a creamy white wine and dill broth, locally landed monkfish and crème brûlée with raspberries. Wines from £16. **Chef/s:** Alyson Milstead. **Open:** all week D only 7.30 for 8 (1 sitting). **Closed:** Christmas. **Meals:** Set D £24 (2 courses) to £28. **Details:** 20 seats. Car parking.

Dalry

Braidwoods

Precision-tuned cooking and incisive flavours
Drumastle Mill Cottage, Dalry, KA24 4LN
Tel no: (01294) 833544
www.braidwoods.co.uk
Modern British | £45
Cooking score: 6

Follow the twisting path that leads to a pair of whitewashed millers' cottages: only half an hour out of Glasgow, yet a giant leap into tranquil isolation. Here the Braidwoods pitched their camp two decades ago, establishing links to regional producers and following the seasons assiduously to craft a

classically based style of Scottish haute cuisine of persuasive intensity. Scallops from Wester Ross might kick off the game, bedded on leek purée in a buttery sauce of Arran mustard. After an intermediate such as Parmesan tart with red pepper coulis, mains might furnish forth best end and neck fillet of lamb in rosemary jus, or carefully carved red-legged partridge with puréed celeriac in thyme jus. Fish may be grilled turbot in a gentle sauce of chicken stock with braised fennel. The simplicity of it all, and the shining quality of the ingredients, make the place score highly. Artisanal British cheeses are one way of finishing, or there's vanilla rice pudding with rhubarb compote. A page of seasonal recommendations heads a resourceful wine list, with house selections from £23.95, or £5.95 a glass. **Chef/s:** Keith and Nicola Braidwood. **Open:** Wed to Sun L 12 to 1.45, Tue to Sat D 7 to 9. **Closed:** Mon, 25 Dec to 28 Jan, first 2 weeks Sept. **Meals:** Set L £25 (2 courses) to £28. Set D £43 (3 courses) to £49. Sun L £30. **Details:** 24 seats. Car parking. Children over 5 yrs only at L, over 12 yrs only at D.

Glasgow

Brian Maule at Chardon d'Or

Pleasing French food and exemplary wines
176 West Regent Street, Glasgow, G2 4RL
Tel no: (0141) 2483801
www.brianmaule.com
French | £45
Cooking score: 4

▲ V

Scottish-born Brian Maule quit the patrician world of Le Gavroche (see entry, London) to open Chardon d'Or in a porticoed Georgian town house not far from Glasgow city centre. That was in 2001, and the 'golden thistle' is still blooming – thanks to a combination of carefully judged French food and exemplary wines. There's 'no pressure' in the elegantly appointed, split-level dining room, which makes Brian's culinary efforts even more pleasing to the palate. Top billing goes to his showpiece 'duck trio' (foie gras, confit leg terrine and cured fillet with pistachios), but

visitors have also enthused about 'wonderfully tender' braised beef cheek with creamed celeriac and red wine sauce. Fish dishes such as pan-fried John Dory with baby leeks, salsify and macaroni stand out too, and there's much to enjoy for dessert: try coconut and lime yoghurt mousse with marinated pineapple, or keep it comforting with crème brûlée. The wine list is intelligently annotated, with many enterprising organic and biodynamic bottles alongside French grandees and seasonal recommendations. Prices start at £19 (£4.90 a glass).
Chef/s: Brian Maule. **Open:** Mon to Sat L 12 to 2.30 (3 Sat), D 5 to 10. **Closed:** Sun, 25 and 26 Dec, 1 and 2 Jan, bank hols. **Meals:** alc (main courses £23 to £28). Set L and D £18.95 (2 courses) to £21.95. Tasting menu £59.50 (6 courses). **Details:** 100 seats. Separate bar. No children after 7.

NEW ENTRY
Cail Bruich
Ambitious brasserie with excellent sourcing
725 Great Western Rd, Glasgow, G12 8QX
Tel no: (0141) 3346265
www.cailbruich.co.uk
British | £36
Cooking score: 3
£5 OFF V

Trendy, bohemian and slightly pampered, Glasgow's West End is well placed to support a restaurant of serious intent with a list of artisan suppliers as long as your arm. Cail Bruich ('Eat Well') rises effortlessly to the occasion. With dim lighting, red banquettes and worn floorboards it reads like a Parisian bistro, and there's a French inflection to the cooking – although you'll find Italian influences, too. Crab cannelloni with heirloom tomatoes translates as a crab-filled filo cigar, the tomatoes fruity and ripe enough to be stars of the show. An early-summer main of poached Scrabster cod with lobster tortellini, Jerusalem artichoke, samphire and shellfish emulsion exemplifies Chris Charalambous's commitment to seasonality, while a dessert of 'textures of Valrhona Manjari chocolate' (essentially ganache, brioche and homemade

Aero) with salted-caramel ice cream reflects his taste for top-drawer ingredients. A decent global wine list opens at £18 a bottle.
Chef/s: Chris Charalambous. **Open:** Tue to Sun L 12 to 2.30 (3 Sun), D 5.30 to 9.30 (8 Sun). **Closed:** Mon, 25 and 26 Dec, 1 and 2 Jan. **Meals:** alc (mains £15 to 25). Set L and D £14.95 (2 courses) to £17.95. Sun L £15.95. **Details:** 42 seats.

NEW ENTRY
Central Market
Breezy deli-restaurant
51 Bell Street, Glasgow, G1 1PA
Tel no: (0141) 5520902
www.centralmarketglasgow.com
Modern British | £25
Cooking score: 2
£30

Glasgow is a city of closely stacked opposites, so you never know whether there's a deli or a kebab shop around the next corner. Central Market ticks the first box but its main function is as a slick metropolitan restaurant. The interior (white tiled walls, slate floors, busy chefs on show) sports the kind of stripped-back, dining in-the-kitchen brand of cool that says the food is the star. And so it is. You can pick deli sandwiches, oysters, 'divine' mac 'n' cheese or smoky delights from the char-grill – maybe asparagus with goats' cheese, broad beans and sherry vinaigrette or Ibérico pluma steak with fennel, peppers and heritage potatoes. There's a good caramel tart, too, but the olive-oil-based caramel sauce won't suit all tastes. Wines start at £14.95.
Chef/s: Neil Palmer and Andrew Lambert. **Open:** all week 11 to 10. **Closed:** 25 and 26 Dec. **Meals:** alc (main courses £11 to £18). **Details:** 50 seats. 10 seats outside. Wheelchair access.

Average Price
The average price listed in main-entry reviews denotes the price of a three-course meal, without wine.

Gamba

First-class marine life with a hint of luxury
225a West George Street, Glasgow, G2 2ND
Tel no: (0141) 5720899
www.gamba.co.uk
Seafood | £35
Cooking score: 3

£5
OFF

You can't see the waves lapping up on the shore, but you can certainly imagine them at Derek Marshall's Glasgow seafood institution. It's a basement restaurant but a spacious and flatteringly lit one, with 'first class' service. First-class fish is the order of the day, too, and Marshall's menus run through variations on British, French and Asian seafood standards, often with a hint of luxury. Yellowfin tuna sashimi with wasabi, soy and ginger or hand-picked white crabmeat with horseradish and smoked caviar makes a fresh bright start before the kitchen powers up for lobster thermidor and chips, or seared king scallops, citrus dipping sauce and fragrant rice. Such cooking comes at a cost, so opt for lunch or pre-theatre if on a budget. Finish with rosemary crème brûlée or cherry and chocolate brownie with cinnamon ice cream. Wines are at the higher end with house at £18.95.
Chef/s: Derek Marshall. **Open:** Mon to Sat L 12 to 2.30, all week D 5 to 10 (9 Sun). **Closed:** 25 and 26 Dec, 1 to 8 Jan. **Meals:** alc (main courses £17 to £24). Set L and D £16.95 (2 courses) to £19.95. **Details:** 62 seats. Separate bar. No children after 10 in restaurant.

Stravaigin

Global food from prime Scottish ingredients
28 Gibson Street, Glasgow, G12 8NX
Tel no: (0141) 3342665
www.stravaigin.com
Modern European | £25
Cooking score: 2

£30

When the folks at Straivigin say they 'think global, eat local', they're not kidding. The 'adventurous' menu could almost give you jet lag. From fried sea bream with Louisiana-style

rice and pickled okra to Oaxacan beef and olive empanadas to start, and from 'battered fish supper' or haggis, neeps and tatties, to nasi goreng with Ramsay's of Carluke bacon and king prawns for mains – it's quite a ride. Vegetarians are 'spoiled': there's veggie haggis and more flamboyant creations such as parsnip and potato croquette with salsa verde and beetroot muhammara. Come dessert, the salted chocolate tart is 'amazing', the ice creams 'pure happiness'. The 'fabulous' atmosphere befits both 'posh nosh' and impromptu, casual meals. Global wines cost from £15.45; draught ales and cocktails add to the mix.
Chef/s: Kenny Mackay. **Open:** all week 9am to 11pm (11am Sat and Sun). **Closed:** 25 Dec, 1 Jan. **Meals:** alc (main courses £9 to £23). Set L £11.95 (2 courses) to £14.95. Set pre-theatre D £13.95 (2 courses) to £15.95. **Details:** 130 seats. 8 seats outside. Separate bar. Wheelchair access. No children after 10pm.

Ubiquitous Chip

Glasgow icon
12 Ashton Lane, Glasgow, G12 8SJ
Tel no: (0141) 3345007
www.ubiquitouschip.co.uk
Modern British | £40
Cooking score: 4

'I can see why it has been there since the 1970s,' says one reporter of this inimitable national treasure. The Ubiquitous Chip's success lies in its ability to move with the times without being enslaved by fashion; so while some dishes come and go, others (notably the kilt-swirling venison haggis) are in it for the long haul. Former stables set around a cobbled mews, the interior includes a dining area in a fabulous glass-roofed cobbled courtyard. Expect 'excellent service, a lively atmosphere' and cooking that while not always cutting edge, is 'perfectly honed'. The Jerusalem artichoke tarte fine with root vegetable caponata and rocket and hazelnut pesto comes well reported, as does a 'beautiful piece of halibut' served with crispy chicken wings, potato fondant and fennel purée. For a modern classic, finish with the Chip's 'famous' oatmeal ice cream. The monumental wine list is another delight, offering everything from mature clarets and Burgundies to rare gems from boutique wineries around the world, starting at £18.85.

Chef/s: Andrew Mitchell. **Open:** all week L 12 to 2.30 (12.30 to 3 Sun), D 5 to 11. **Closed:** 25 Dec, 1 Jan. **Meals:** Set L £15.95 (2 courses) to £19.95. **Details:** 100 seats. Separate bar. Wheelchair access. No children after 10.

La Vallée Blanche

Neighbourhood French bistro
360 Byres Road, Glasgow, G12 8AY
Tel no: (0141) 3343333
www.lavalleeblanche.com
French | £25
Cooking score: 3
£30 ▼

'Nowhere better in Glasgow – highest quality produce and perfect service' is one regular's view of this Francophile haven in the city's trendy West End. Inside it looks like an Alpine chalet, with rustic wood-panelled walls and simple wooden furnishings. The kitchen takes a broad view of the French theme, so options range from warm smoked haddock salad with onion bhajia, soft-boiled egg and light curry sauce to red wine and pearl barley cassoulet via veal osso buco with potato purée, truffle, French ceps, foie gras and port velouté. Desserts have a similar scope; try a simple apple soufflé with cumin caramel ice cream or chocolate tart with Catalan oranges, crème de cacao jellies and yoghurt ice cream. The Gallic wine list offers a broad range of styles, including lots of Champagnes and plenty by the glass. Bottles start at £17.95.

Chef/s: David Maxwell. **Open:** Tue to Sun L 12 to 2.15 (3.15 Sat and Sun), D 5.30 to 9.15 (10 Fri and Sat). **Closed:** Mon, 1 and 2 Jan. **Meals:** alc (main courses £15 to £25). Set L and D £12.95 (2 courses) to £14.95. Set L Sun £12.95 (2 courses) to £14.95. **Details:** 78 seats. No children after 9.

ALSO RECOMMENDED
▲ Number 16

16 Byres Road, Glasgow, G11 5JY
Tel no: (0141) 3392544
www.number16.co.uk
Modern British £5 OFF

'There's always something new and intriguing to try' noted one regular visitor to this intimate, two-floor neighbourhood bistro at the foot of the Byres Road. A laid-back dining area sets the scene for the unpretentious, confident cooking of the produce-driven kitchen. Typical dishes are roast Tuscan sausage with spiced Puy lentils and Parmesan mash (£6.50), which might precede pan-fried bavette with Hasselback potatoes, wild mushrooms and Café de Paris butter (£15.50). House wines are £14.95. Open all week.

■ Isle of Colonsay

ALSO RECOMMENDED
▲ The Colonsay

Scalasaig, Isle of Colonsay, PA61 7YT
Tel no: (01951) 200316
www.colonsayestate.co.uk
Modern British

People come to this far-flung outpost for pristine sandy beaches and the rich variety of wildlife. They stay for the log fires and unfussy comfort at this 18th-century inn, which seems to be run as a social service for the tourists and others who light upon the place. The menu is short, simple and steers clear of over elaboration: Colonsay oysters, linguine with wild garlic pesto (£9.50), baked haddock with herb butter and chips (£12.50) or chicken with lentils, roasted tomato and aïoli, finishing with warm apple and almond cake. Wines from £12.50. Closed Nov to March.

Isle of Iona

READERS RECOMMEND
Argyll Hotel
Modern British
Isle of Iona, PA76 6SJ
Tel no: (01681) 700334
www.argyllhoteliona.co.uk
'Stunning view across the strait to Mull, the better to enjoy dishes such as beautifully cooked langoustines in their shells with very garlicky aïoli; perfectly timed scallops with lemon, herbs and croûtons; and asparagus with cheese and polenta gnocchi.'

Isle of Mull
Café Fish
Fantastic no-frills seafood
The Pier, Main Street, Tobermory, Isle of Mull, PA75 6NU
Tel no: (01688) 301253
www.thecafefish.com
Seafood | £27
Cooking score: 3
£30

'Knock-'em dead stuff' enthuses one visitor to this family restaurant on the top floor of Tobermory's former ferry offices. It's not big, but it is clever, with a menu that makes the most of the owners' fishing connections, a sun terrace and views over the bay and beyond to the Sound of Mull. Landed by local boats including the café's own, the freshest fish and seafood is turned into no-fuss, hands-on dishes such as split creel-caught langoustine with garlic and herb butter, platters of shellfish either cold or roasted, a main course tom yam broth or a seafood stroganoff loaded with mussels, smoked haddock and salmon. For pudding, there's a chocolate pot with Tobermory whisky. It's all cooked with precision and served with 'affable professionalism'. Wine is from £15.
Chef/s: Liz McGougan. Open: all week L 12 to 3, D 5.30 to 10. Closed: Jan and Feb. Meals: alc (main courses £6 to £28). Details: 36 seats. 30 seats outside.

Kilberry
The Kilberry Inn
Dream destination with superlative seafood
Kilberry Road, Kilberry, PA29 6YD
Tel no: (01880) 770223
www.kilberryinn.com
Modern British | £32
Cooking score: 3

There's 'always a welcome at Kilberry', observed one couple who regularly make the tortuous trek along a single-track road to reach this windswept, rose-covered inn. It's miles from anywhere, but visitors can look forward to breathtaking views of the Hebrides and 'consistently excellent' food – as well as bags of warmth, care and attention in every department. 'Wee treats and nibbles' precede a menu that makes the best of regional produce, especially seafood. Readers have singled out the potted crab with fennel, citrus salad and a spelt-pastry 'crabstick', but the line-up could feature anything from hand-dived Jura scallops with Puy lentils and salsa verde to monkfish with pickled vegetable relish. There's fine Highland beef, lamb cooked pink and rose veal, too (perhaps served 'osso buco' style with buttery mash and gremolata), while desserts might range from 'sublime' sundaes to chocolate crème brûlée with banana ice cream. The 'surprisingly comprehensive' wine list offers admirable drinking from £18.
Open: Tue to Sun L 12 to 2, D 6 to 9. Closed: Mon, Jan, Feb, Sun to Thur (Nov and Dec). Meals: alc (main courses £14 to 22). Details: 30 seats. 12 seats outside. Wheelchair access. Car parking.

Oban

Waterfront Fishouse Restaurant

Minimal-frills, super-fresh seafood
1 Railway Pier, Oban, PA34 4LW
Tel no: (01631) 563110
www.waterfrontoban.co.uk
Seafood | £24
Cooking score: 1
£30

Majestic views over the Sound of Mull make an appetising backdrop for the seafood specialities at Alex Needham's alluring first-floor restaurant. The seasonally changing menus incorporate modern assemblies such as scallop salad with Serrano ham dressed in wholegrain mustard and honey, as well as various ways with oysters, and mains like whole char-grilled sea bass garnished with wild leaves or salmon in a coating of tomato and olives, with creamy pesto. When available, lobster thermidor and chips is hard to resist, while seafood refuseniks might choose roast duck breast in sesame and soy dressing. Finish with 'our famous sticky toffee pudding'. Wines from £13.95.
Chef/s: Roy Stalker. **Open:** all week L 12 to 2.15, D 5.30 to 9.30. **Closed:** 25 Dec. **Meals:** alc (main courses £9 to £20). Set L and D £9.95 (2 courses).
Details: 80 seats. 16 seats outside.

ALSO RECOMMENDED
▲ Ee-Usk

North Pier, Oban, PA34 5QD
Tel no: (01631) 565666
www.eeusk.com
Seafood £5 OFF

The modern glass building perched on the harbour's edge was purpose-built to maximise views over the water to the islands beyond (and terrific sunsets, too, if you're lucky); it gets so busy that booking ahead is recommended. Quality Scottish seafood is the name of the game, with visitors coming from afar for platters of oysters, mussels, crab claws, langoustines, scallops and smoked salmon

(£19.95), as well as smoked haddock chowder (£5.50), battered haddock and chips and scallops in mornay sauce. Wines from £15.95. Open all week.

Troon

MacCallums Oyster Bar

No fancy posturing, just prime seafood
The Harbour, Troon, KA10 6DH
Tel no: (01292) 319339
Seafood | £27
Cooking score: 2
£30

Devotees of this quirkily decorated seafooder are happy to clock up serious miles to experience its memorable charms. Housed in a former pumping station overlooking the boats unloading fresh fish in Troon's working harbour, the rustic interior is stuffed with America's Cup memorabilia. There's no posturing or gimmickry here, just top-class fish and shellfish cooked with natural acumen. Typically, you might begin with half a dozen oysters or grilled langoustines with garlic butter, move on to a generous shellfish linguine with garlic, chilli and lemon or a meaty piece of halibut with ratatouille, saffron potatoes and fish fumet. Recent standouts have included battered haddock with hand-cut chips, whole lemon sole and a very good sticky toffee pudding with homemade ice cream. Wines from £15.95.
Chef/s: Phillip Burgess. **Open:** Tue to Sun L 12 to 2.30 (3.30 Sun), Tue to Sat D 6.30 to 9.30. **Closed:** Mon, 3 weeks from 25 Dec. **Meals:** alc (main courses £13 to £28). Set L £13.95 (2 courses) to £17.95. **Details:** 43 seats. Car parking.

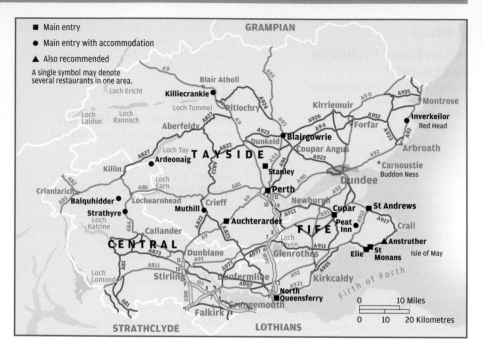

Legend:
- ■ Main entry
- ● Main entry with accommodation
- ▲ Also recommended

A single symbol may denote several restaurants in one area.

▌Ardeonaig

Ardeonaig Hotel

Deft loch-side cooking
South Loch Tay Side, Ardeonaig, FK21 8SU
Tel no: (01567) 820400
www.ardeonaighotel.co.uk
Modern British | £55
Cooking score: 4

🍽 V

The glorious loch views from the surprisingly grand dining room of this 17th-century drovers' inn (turned chic Tayside getaway) turn diners' thoughts to 'country' food: the wonderful game, fish, berries and mushrooms of Scotland's natural larder. These are, when in season, all present and correct – but in anything but rustic form. This impressive destination restaurant (bookings essential) set high standards within months of its 2011 opening and doesn't appear to have dropped the ball. The daily changing menu might include a precisely cooked dish of Glen Lyon wood-pigeon breast and confit leg with foie gras and consommé followed by very classical Boquhan Estate beef, braised shin, wild mushrooms, pommes purées and red wine jus. Dessert might be a complex study in chocolate, or local cheese and oatcakes. The wine list, from £15, is organised by varietal, with a sensible emphasis on enhancing the dining experience.
Chef/s: David Maskell. **Open:** Wed to Sun L 12.30 to 2, D 7 to 9. **Closed:** Mon, Tue, 7 Jan to 21 Jan.
Meals: alc (main courses £20 to £25). Set L £22.50 (2 courses) to £28.50. Set D £45 (2 courses) to £55. Sun L £28.50. Tasting menu £65. **Details:** 34 seats. 25 seats outside. Separate bar. Wheelchair access. Car parking. Children over 8 yrs only.

🍴 **Visit us Online**
To find out more about
The Good Food Guide, please visit
www.thegoodfoodguide.co.uk

▌Balquhidder

Monachyle Mhor
Family enterprise with a foodie heart
Balquhidder, FK19 8PQ
Tel no: (01877) 384622
www.mhor.net
Modern British | £50
Cooking score: 5

♦ ⇌ V

A Trossachs farmhouse furnished in a becoming shade of pale pink is home to the Lewis family's highly burnished hotel operation, reached along a single-track road by Loch Voil. The journey alone is a dream, but the stylish boutique décor and a restaurant offering a brisk version of modern Scots cooking seal the deal. The kitchen uses Highland materials to fine effect in dishes where the temptation to over-elaborate is resisted. A starter might be seared John Dory and crab with a salad of shaved fennel and sea kale, dressed in lemon and saffron. Local venison could follow, accompanied by spiced red cabbage, pearl onions, smoked pancetta and garlic mash. At dinner, appetisers and intermediate soup (celeriac and apple, perhaps) come into play, and a more than satisfactory conclusion is provided by dark chocolate and citrus ganache with chocolate fondant, blueberry compote and crème fraîche. The wine list, organised by grape variety, contains a section of 'Oddballs' ensuring that Albariño, Petite Sirah and England's rough diamonds aren't neglected. Prices open at £22, or £5.50 a glass.
Chef/s: Tom Lewis and Marysia Paszkowska. **Open:** all week L 12 to 2, D 7 to 9. **Closed:** 2 weeks Jan. **Meals:** alc (main courses £22 to £26). Set L £22 (2 courses) to £28. Set D £50. Sun L £32. **Details:** 40 seats. 16 seats outside. Separate bar. Wheelchair access. Car parking.

▌Strathyre

Creagan House
Delightful farmhouse with standout food
Strathyre, FK18 8ND
Tel no: (01877) 384638
www.creaganhouse.co.uk
French | £35
Cooking score: 4

£5
OFF ⇌

The Gunns' sublimely sited 17th-century former farmhouse enjoys direct access to Loch Lomond and the Trossachs National Park. It's a pretty lavish affair, the dining room well-nigh baronial, complete with monumental stone fireplace and vaulted ceiling. Gordon Gunn mixes old and new French styles in his cooking, adding what he calls 'strong Scottish overtones', evident in a starter called 'smokie in a pokie' (smoked haddock in a cone of smoked salmon). Otherwise, begin with a double-act of red gurnard and a scallop, with puréed courgette in star anise sauce, and continue with Gressingham duck breast in blackberry liqueur, or pheasant breast with a boudin of the leg meat, on celeriac and chestnut mash, sauced with Armagnac and thyme. At dessert comes a featherlight flory (puff pastry tart) of apple, prune and almond, served with clotted cream. Wines open with Argentinian Malbec at £18.70, the house-selection septet also available in half-litre carafes and small glasses.
Chef/s: Gordon Gunn. **Open:** Fri to Tue D only 7.15 for 8 (1 sitting). **Closed:** Wed, Thur, 24 to 26 Dec, 15 Jan to 13 Mar, 5 to 20 Nov. **Meals:** Set D £35. **Details:** 14 seats. Separate bar. Wheelchair access. Car parking. Children over 10 yrs only.

Anstruther

ALSO RECOMMENDED
▲ Anstruther Fish Bar
42-44 Shore Street, Anstruther, KY10 3AQ
Tel no: (01333) 310518
www.anstrutherfishbar.co.uk
Seafood

So close to the quay you could buy a take-away and watch the fishermen unloading their catch, this traditional chippy, a local institution, also does a great turn as an eat-in restaurant, with friendly if slightly erratic waitress service. Fresh, flaky haddock in a 'light as air' batter with 'excellent' chips (£8.25) is a favourite, and be sure to try the homemade ice cream, which comes in a kaleidoscope of flavours starting at £1.25 for a small cone. Wines are mostly French and priced from £9 a bottle. Open all week.

Cupar

Ostlers Close
Characterful cooking from a local hero
25 Bonnygate, Cupar, KY15 4BU
Tel no: (01334) 655574
www.ostlersclose.co.uk
Modern British | £41
Cooking score: 5

It may have entered its fourth decade but Jimmy and Amanda Graham's cosy little restaurant still has a spring in its step. Reached via an alleyway off Cupar's main street, it feels like a well-kept secret, yet its reputation extends to many happy regulars. There's a cottagey feel to the interior: terracotta walls, freshly picked flowers, country pine furniture smartened up with white linen — the whole thrust of the place is homely and personal. Get chatting to Amanda and she'll tell you where the ingredients came from: some home-grown, some gathered with chef Jimmy — for instance, the wild mushroom sauce that accompanies tender, rosy duck breast and spring greens. Before that might come pot-roast breast of wood pigeon with black pudding mash and a tangy beetroot sauce.

Like the décor, the presentation can err towards rusticity — as in a dessert of chunky meringues with salted-caramel ice cream — but the flavours always ring true. The handwritten, helpfully annotated wine list (from £18.50) has global reach and includes plenty of half-bottles.

Chef/s: Jimmy Graham. **Open:** Sat L 12 to 1.30, Tue to Sat D 7 to 9.30. **Closed:** Sun, Mon, 25 and 26 Dec, 1 and 2 Jan. **Meals:** alc (main courses £20 to £24). **Details:** 28 seats. Children over 6 yrs only.

Elie

Sangster's
Appealing Fife fixture
51 High Street, Elie, KY9 1BZ
Tel no: (01333) 331001
www.sangsters.co.uk
Modern British | £40
Cooking score: 4

With a serene air and timeless good looks, Sangster's slots neatly into the handsome thoroughfare that is Elie's High Street. Bruce and Jacqueline Sangster set up shop over a decade ago and have made fine dining their mission, throwing in lovely bells and whistles, from canapés to pre-desserts. Some dishes — like the Tobermory cheese soufflé — are perennials, but there's room for experimentation, too. A starter of braised pig's cheek croquette works well, with apple, vanilla and lemon compote striking a pleasing counterpoint to the dark intensity of the accompanying sauce. Occasionally, dishes go a flavour too far — as in a main course of Perthshire venison with red cabbage compote, butternut squash purée, gnocchi, port and red wine sauce and, less convincingly, feta — but the results are still enjoyable. Chocolate and salted-caramel tart is a thoughtfully composed dessert, and the wine list is carefully considered, too, offering good global reach and reasonable value, starting at £21.50.

Chef/s: Bruce Sangster. **Open:** Sun L 12.30 to 1.30, Tue to Sat D 7 to 8.30. **Closed:** Mon. **Meals:** Set D £33 (2 courses) to £45. Sun L £28. **Details:** 28 seats. Children over 12 yrs only.

North Queensferry

The Wee Restaurant

A diamond under the Forth Bridge
17 Main Street, North Queensferry, KY11 1JG
Tel no: (01383) 616263
www.theweerestaurant.co.uk
Modern European | £34
Cooking score: 3

Not quite so wee that it can't accommodate three dozen hungry customers, Craig Wood's appealing venue is housed in a century-old building that has served time as a prison, an ironmonger's and a post office. It is now a beacon of quality along the Firth of Forth: the model of a modern eatery, with unclothed tables, a neutral decorative tone and a menu of French-tinged modern Scottish brasserie cooking. Thoroughbred seafood goes into a boudin of salmon and crab, served with wilted spinach and samphire in lemon and caper dressing. Then there might be tender venison with lentils, girolles and herb gnocchi, or crisply grilled sea bass, given the Spanish treatment with chorizo and morcilla. Finish with apple frangipane galette and Calvados ice cream. House wines, South African Chenin and Cabernet, cost £16.75, or £5.50 a glass.
Chef/s: Craig Wood. Open: Tue to Sun L 12 to 2, D 6.30 to 9. Closed: Mon, 25 and 26 Dec. Meals: Set L £16.75 (2 courses) to £20. Set D £26 (2 courses) to £34. Details: 36 seats.

Peat Inn

★ TOP 50 ★

The Peat Inn

Oozing comfort and class
Peat Inn, KY15 5LH
Tel no: (01334) 840206
www.thepeatinn.co.uk
Modern European | £58
Cooking score: 7

During their few years in charge, Geoffrey and Katherine Smeddle have catapulted this quietly classy operation into Scotland's premier league. The Peat Inn is a simple-looking, whitewashed Georgian building. Its interiors are gentle on the eye, with neutral tones preferred in the three interlinked dining rooms. Geoffrey's French-accented modern Scottish cooking sets the place alight with excitement, never more so than on the six-course tasting menus that unfailingly astonish reporters. Dishes are models of ingenuity. A starter of oyster pannacotta with crisp basil langoustines, a little crabmeat, avocado crème fraîche and marinated cucumber makes a bravura opening statement: a bracing panoply of sea-fresh flavour. Main courses of maple-glazed duck breast with pickled peach in Madeira jus, or venison with its own boudin (along with glazed parsnips and salsify) in bay leaf jus are all about profundity through simplicity. Other seasonal game, such as pheasant with smoked pumpkin purée and black pudding, or exquisitely timed fish – perhaps seared hake with creamed Hispi and crosnes in shellfish dressing – maintain the standard. Nerveless technique for dessert produces a featherlight pear and gingerbread soufflé with vanilla ice cream. The classical wine list is replete with the stars of Bordeaux, Burgundy and the Rhône, but also finds space for newer-fangled thinking from Australia and South Africa. Prices open at £26.
Chef/s: Geoffrey Smeddle. Open: Tue to Sat L 12.30 to 1.30, D 7 to 9. Closed: Sun, Mon, Christmas, 2 weeks Jan, 1 week Nov. Meals: alc (main courses £23 to £27). Set L £19. Set D £45. Tasting menu £60. Details: 40 seats.

St Andrews

The Seafood Restaurant

Sustainable seafood in a spectacular setting
The Scores, Bruce Embankment, St Andrews, KY16 9AB
Tel no: (01334) 479475
www.theseafoodrestaurant.com
Seafood | £45
Cooking score: 3

'You are right on the shore line, in fact almost above the sea when the tide comes in,' enthused one visitor, referring to the striking glass cube that is the Seafood Restaurant. Inside, the activity in the completely open kitchen can draw the eye from the view. Sustainable fish is a strong suit, but chef Colin Fleming can also turn his hand to venison loin (with pommes dauphine, hazelnuts and Swiss chard) or pork belly. A seafood platter aside, back–to–the–roots familiarity is not the style here. To start, hot-smoked trout comes with apple, pear, horseradish and curry oil, while sea bass is fashionably partnered by beetroot, feta and squid. A hazelnut fondant served with carrot ice cream might end the meal. Service can be a tad too formal for the setting. Wines from £20.

Chef/s: Colin Fleming. **Open:** all week L 12 to 2.30 (12.30 to 3 Sun), D 6 to 10. **Closed:** 25 and 26 Dec, 1 Jan. **Meals:** Set L £22 (2 courses) to £26 + Mon to Fri £14.95 (2 courses). Set D £39 (2 courses) to £48.50. **Details:** 50 seats. 20 seats outside. Wheelchair access. Car parking.

ALSO RECOMMENDED
▲ The Doll's House

3 Church Square, St Andrews, KY16 9NN
Tel no: (01334) 477422
www.dollshouse-restaurant.co.uk
Modern European

Visitors, locals and students flock to this cheerful, casual Old Town stalwart, drawn by the sheer value for money of the straightforward cooking (note the two-course set lunch for £7.95) and relaxed service. Indeed, there's a comforting familiarity about a meal that begins with smoked trout and smoked mackerel with horseradish and chive cream (£5.95) and goes on to confit duck leg with apple, leek and Calvados cream (£13.75) or pheasant breast with a vegetable gratin. Wines from £14.95. Open all week.

▌St Monans
Craig Millar @ 16 West End

Dazzling seafood and spectacular harbour views
16 West End, St Monans, KY10 2BX
Tel no: (01333) 730327
www.16westend.com
Seafood | £50
Cooking score: 5
£5 OFF 🍾

If you are looking for an elegant restaurant by the sea you could do worse than head to St Monans and the smartly modernised fisherman's cottage where Craig Millar has nurtured his passion for dazzling Scottish produce for a dozen years or so. Unspoilt views look over the water to the Isle of May, but equally distracting is Millar's thoroughly modern cooking, which shows a degree of refinement. So, while beetroot-cured trout is served as a simple starter garnished with a quail's egg and potato salad, there might also be hand-dived scallops with salt-baked and pickled celeriac, truffle butter sauce and Jerusalem artichoke purée or halibut teamed with couscous, satay sauce, pickled vegetables and toasted cashew. Meat can be just as elaborate: perhaps loin of venison with Puy lentils, turnip fondant, choi sum and a duck confit bonbon. Desserts range from chocolate tart with banana ice cream and salted caramel to honey parfait with pickled plums and almond crumble. The wine list remains a high point, with France the focus, a good global choice by the glass and with notably fine bottles adding extra polish. Bottles from £22.

Chef/s: Craig Millar. **Open:** Wed to Sun L 12.30 to 2, D 6.30 to 9. **Closed:** Mon, Tue, 25 and 26 Dec, 2 weeks Jan. **Meals:** Set L £22 (2 courses) to £26. Set D £42. Tasting menu £60. **Details:** 35 seats. 32 seats outside. Separate bar. Wheelchair access. Car parking. Children over 12 yrs only at D.

Auchterarder

★ TOP 50 ★

Andrew Fairlie at Gleneagles

Awe-inspiring, luxurious French cuisine
Auchterarder, PH3 1NF
Tel no: (01764) 694267
www.andrewfairlie.co.uk
Modern French | £95
Cooking score: 7

V

The Gleneagles Hotel sits majestically amid an elegant 850-acre sprawl, much of which is devoted to golf. At the hermetically sealed heart of its ground floor is one of Scotland's premier dining destinations, conceived and executed by Andrew Fairlie, protégé of the great Gascon maître Michel Guérard. The large, black windowless space is sepulchrally lit, faintly resembling a well-appointed crypt, but it makes a suitably singular setting for the spectacular modern French food. The full panoply of artfully presented incidentals is on parade, from racks of canapés to ingenious petits fours, and the principal dishes are stunning. Marché and Dégustation menus may prove hard to resist for those with the resources, but there's plenty of diverting choice on the carte. Make an earthy start with truffled cep gratin, deepened further with puréed Jerusalem artichoke and jus gras, or in lighter mode, roast and tartared scallops garnished with a sublime squid cracker. Some ingredients are flown in from Paris's Rungis market, but there's also a strong commitment to Scots produce, as in Perthshire roe deer with glazed chestnuts and pommes dauphines, and superlative St Bride's Farm chicken served with foie gras parfait and fig toast. Cheeses are sourced from both sides of the Channel, and seductive desserts include perfectly executed pineapple soufflé with rum ice cream and coconut sauce, or chocolate and ginger tart with wonderfully fragrant vanilla ice cream. The wine list (from £30) takes no prisoners, but there's reasonable choice for £50.

Chef/s: Andrew Fairlie. Open: Mon to Sat D only 6.30 to 10. Closed: Sun, 25 and 26 Dec, 3 weeks Jan. Meals: Set D £95 (3 courses) to £125 (8 courses). Details: 50 seats. Wheelchair access. Car parking. Children over 12 yrs only.

Blairgowrie

Kinloch House Hotel

Grand Scottish hospitality
Dunkeld Road, Blairgowrie, PH10 6SG
Tel no: (01250) 884237
www.kinlochhouse.com
Modern British | £53
Cooking score: 5

A dignified showcase for grand Scottish hospitality, this ivy-clothed Victorian stone mansion comes with 25 acres of grounds overlooking Lunan Burn and the Perthshire Hills. Inside, the *Brigadoon* hunting lodge theme continues with blazing log fires in the richly panelled rooms, fabulous antique furniture, tartan fabrics and even a portrait gallery. Chef Steve MacCallum isn't about to frighten the horses but his kitchen knows how to please visitors, producing the likes of corn-fed chicken with onion confit, sweet potato, chanterelles and tarragon cream sauce. Scottish fish and local game are also treated with respect, from fillet of turbot with cockles, mussels, red wine risotto and roast fennel to an ultra-traditional plate of venison with spiced red cabbage, rösti, chestnuts and thyme sauce. Occasional flurries in the shape of piccalilli salad, deep-fried truffled eggs and candied beetroot keep the kitchen in touch with the times, but desserts revert to the norm: think baked lemon cheesecake or warm prune and almond tart. Unsurprisingly, the weighty wine list puts vintage Bordeaux and Burgundies in pole position. Prices start at £26.50.

Chef/s: Steve MacCallum. Open: all week L 12.30 to 2, D 7 to 8.30. Closed: 14 to 29 Dec. Meals: Set L £19.50 (2 courses) to £25.50. Set D £53. Sun L £30. Details: 30 seats. Separate bar. Wheelchair access. Car parking. Children over 5 yrs only at D.

READERS RECOMMEND

READERS RECOMMEND

Little's

Modern British
4 Wellmeadow, Blairgowrie, PH10 6ND
Tel no: (01250) 875358
www.littlesrestaurant.co.uk
'I have not met a better or fresher fish
selection.'

■ Inverkeilor

Gordon's

Cooking with vitality and dazzle
Main Street, Inverkeilor, DD11 5RN
Tel no: (01241) 830364
www.gordonsrestaurant.co.uk
Modern British | £50
Cooking score: 5

🚗

'At long last – an interior to match the food
and service; the khaki and maroon, with a
Scottish twist, makes the cooking taste even
better', notes a fan of the Watsons' high-
achieving restaurant-with-rooms. It's run
with great warmth out front by Maria, while
husband Gordon and son Garry are in charge
of the food. Their cooking is a vigorous
version of the modern British style,
technically assured and instinctively true, with
local, regional and seasonal raw materials the
mainstay of the short, set-price menus. One
reporter emerged full of praise for a meal that
opened with a double-baked soufflé of
Tobermory Cheddar, was followed by a 'rich
tasting' velouté of roast red pepper and plum
tomato, and went on to North Atlantic hake
with spiced couscous, pak choi, spring onion
beignets, coriander and 'a mild curry sauce,
which pulled everything together'. Elsewhere,
roast breast and leg of Gressingham duck,
served with glazed apple, celeriac and a sauce
of honey and cracked black pepper has been
praised, and desserts are bang on target:
perhaps an 'extremely tasty' pre-dessert
involving passion fruit and coconut, then a
'thin, crisp' apple tart with butterscotch sauce
and homemade vanilla ice cream. It's all
considered 'very good value for money'. Wines
from £17.95.
Chef/s: Gordon and Garry Watson. **Open:** Wed to Fri
and Sun L 12 to 1.45, Tue to Sun D 7 to 9. **Closed:**
Mon, 2 weeks Jan. **Meals:** Set L £28. Set D £50 (4
courses). **Details:** 24 seats. Car parking. Children
over 9 yrs only at D.

■ Killiecrankie

Killiecrankie House

Personally run Victorian retreat
Killiecrankie, PH16 5LG
Tel no: (01796) 473220
www.killiecrankiehotel.co.uk
Modern British | £42
Cooking score: 3

£5 OFF 🚗 V

Reports on this country house hotel set in a
beautiful part of Perthshire focus on the merits
of the kitchen. You can dine simply and
casually in the bar-conservatory, or more
formally in the 'intimate' dining room where
long-serving chef Mark Easton's menus have a
modern edge and take note of the seasons. In
spring, a warm salad of wild mushroom,
wood pigeon, black quinoa and roasted garlic
and rapeseed dressing could lead on to black
olive and herb-crusted best-end of local lamb
with fondant potato, creamed broccoli, carrot
spaghetti and a Madeira jus. In early summer,
hot-smoked salmon with asparagus and pesto
dressing might precede fillets of sea bream
served with a perfectly judged crab risotto.
Service has been described as 'friendly if
lacking polish'. Wines from £19.
Chef/s: Mark Easton. **Open:** all week L 12.30 to 2, D
6.30 to 8.30. **Closed:** 3 Jan to mid Mar. **Meals:** Set D
£42 (4 courses). Bar menu also available.
Details: 34 seats. Separate bar. Wheelchair access.
Car parking.

Muthill

Barley Bree

Scottish inn with French connections
6 Willoughby Street, Muthill, PH5 2AB
Tel no: (01764) 681451
www.barleybree.com
Anglo-French | £36
Cooking score: 3

£5 OFF 🛏

Since taking over this much-extended village inn, Fabrice and Alison Bouteloup have brought some Gallic *joie de vivre* and swagger to the place – much to the surprise and delight of locals and visitors. The name Barley Bree has a defiantly Scottish ring, but the kitchen quickly bypasses haggis and stovies in favour of local hare terrine with date purée, horseradish and pomegranate, or hake fillet with chorizo, squid, orzo pasta, samphire and crispy kelp seaweed. The underlying culinary accent is French, yet ingredients and ideas are snatched from all over: toasted cumin and pork puffs alongside a bowl of onion and real ale soup, cabbage tempura with seared mackerel, and so on. Desserts such as tarte Tatin or plum and griottine cherry clafoutis are true to *La Belle France*, and there's plenty of patriotic drinking on the wide-ranging wine list. Prices start at £16.95.
Chef/s: Fabrice Bouteloup. **Open:** Wed to Sat L 12 to 2, D 6.45 to 9. Sun 12 to 7.30. **Closed:** Mon, Tue, 25 to 27 Dec. **Meals:** alc (main courses £19 to £23). **Details:** 38 seats. 12 seats outside. Car parking.

Perth

Deans @ Let's Eat

Smart city-centre restaurant with eclectic flavours
77-79 Kinnoull Street, Perth, PH1 5EZ
Tel no: (01738) 643377
www.letseatperth.co.uk
Modern British | £30
Cooking score: 3

Look for the corner site with its bottle-green ground-floor frontage, a short trot from the city centre, the concert hall and theatre. Inside, the linen-clad tables and raspberry colour scheme play host to Willie Deans' locally sourced, modern cooking. This aims to offer a 'true taste of Scotland' with the odd divagation into Swiss cheese and Serrano ham for garnishing a chicken breast (served with steamed Rooster potatoes and courgettes provençale). Inspiration is plucked from far and wide, and dishes are often finely detailed, as in a starter of game pie, pink-cooked boar loin and rillettes in creamy truffle dressing, or a main course of sea bass in curry-leaf oil on mushroom velouté with a gratinated oyster and samphire. Dessert could be chocolate and cashew pudding with pineapple sorbet. Wines, starting at £16 a bottle, are arranged by style.
Chef/s: William Deans. **Open:** Tue to Sat L 12 to 2, D 6 to 10. **Closed:** Sun, Mon. **Meals:** alc (main courses £15 to £24). Set L £12.50 (2 courses) to £17.50. Set D £15.50 (2 courses) to £20.50. **Details:** 60 seats. Wheelchair access.

63 Tay Street

Championing the Scottish larder
63 Tay Street, Perth, PH2 8NN
Tel no: (01738) 441451
www.63taystreet.com
Modern British | £37
Cooking score: 3

V

Colourful wall hangings and pictures create a cosy, youthful vibe in this thriving neighbourhood restaurant by the river Tay. Chef/proprietor Graeme Pallister has stuck to his guns when it comes to 'local, honest and simple' (the restaurant's mantra) and is doing the Scottish larder proud in the process. Two returning regulars – up in Perth for the curling – rhapsodised about a classy risotto of Arbroath smokie with horseradish and Parmesan; whipped goats' cheese offset by spiced gingerbread and a crisp, fruity salad; and a stonkingly fine plate of home-smoked pork collar with salt-and-pepper pineapple, silky polenta and sauerkraut. There's roast Glenalmond venison too – cooked rare and served with some surprising accompaniments including monkey puzzle nuts. Char-grills are worth considering, while traditional puds might include treacle tart with maple custard. The wine list is a thoughtful selection of pedigree names from across the globe; prices start at £21 (£5.50 a glass).

Chef/s: Graeme Pallister. **Open:** Thur to Sat L 12 to 2, Tue to Sat D 6.30 to 9. **Closed:** Sun, Mon, 26 Dec to 9 Jan, 1 week Jul. **Meals:** alc (main courses £18 to £24). Set L £18 (2 courses) to £24. Set D £29 (2 courses) to £37. **Details:** 36 seats.

▌Stanley

The Apron Stage

Small is beautiful
5 King Street, Stanley, PH1 4ND
Tel no: (01738) 828888
www.apronstagerestaurant.co.uk
Modern British | £28
Cooking score: 3
£30

Shona Drysdale and Jane Nicoll set out to create the sort of endearing, pint-sized place you might discover down an alleyway in a southern French village. Seating just 18 covers, the Apron Stage is a sympathetically run venue that's big on charm. The operation is centred on a weekly changing blackboard menu, listing three or four starters (perhaps including spinach soup with egg butterballs, or caramelised salmon dressed in lime and soy) and then a straightforward choice of fish or meat for main. The former might be a seafood brochette on stir-fried veg with sticky coconut rice, the latter a roast rump of fine local lamb, teamed with a brioche-crusted noisette, sweet potato gratin and pea purée. Desserts aim to indulge with the likes of warm treacle tart or Moroccan-style rice pudding with rose-water plums. A short wine list opens with South African house blends at £15, £3.95 a glass.

Chef/s: Shona Drysdale. **Open:** Fri L 12 to 2, Wed to Sat D 6 to 10. **Closed:** Mon, Tue, Sun, 1 week May, 1 week Sept, 1 week Dec. **Meals:** alc (main courses £14 to £19). Set L £13.75 (2 courses) to £16.75. **Details:** 18 seats. No children.

▌▌● GEOFFREY SMEDDLE
The Peat Inn

What food trends are you spotting at the moment?
Specialised restaurants narrowing their focus to just one ingredient or a handful of ingredients, including wine and beer.

What do you think is a common mistake that lets chefs down?
Thinking that front of house staff are not as passionate or dedicated as the chefs behind the scenes.

Which of your dishes are you most proud of?
Not strictly a dish, but our cheese trolley, which showcases purely Scottish cheeses, and always at least 20, every night.

How do you come up with new dishes?
By always trying to look with totally fresh eyes at ingredients as they come back into season each year. It's like starting from scratch as a beginner, each season.

Who is a chef to watch in 2014?
Ian Scaramuzza, right hand man to Claude Bosi at Hibiscus, London.

At the end of a long day, what do you like to cook?
Welsh rarebit.

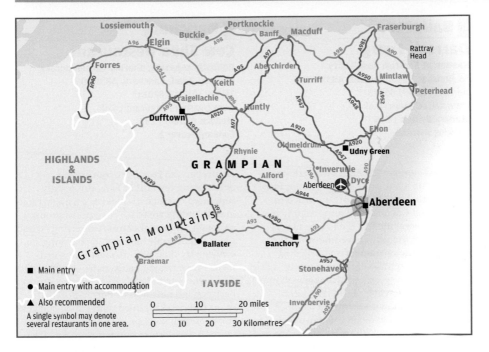

■ Aberdeen

Silver Darling

Fish-loving harbourside evergreen
Pocra Quay, North Pier, Aberdeen, AB11 5DQ
Tel no: (01224) 576229
www.thesilverdarling.co.uk
Seafood | £42
Cooking score: 3

A first-floor venue above the old customs
house, overlooking the harbour and the bay
beyond, Silver Darling is named after the term
of endearment by which the plentiful herring
was known to fishermen. You may not always
find this species on the menu, but you'll
certainly discover a copious haul of fresh
seafood: from tuna and sea bass tartare with
pickled veg, dressed in wasabi and coriander,
to main-course turbot, which comes with a
croquette of salt cod brandade, roast garlic and
a meaty thyme-scented jus. There's local
venison for those determined on meat, served
with a mushroom pithiviers and tartiflette in
peppery Madeira sauce. Dessert can be as

time-honoured as an array of crème brûlée
variations, or as off-the-wall as chocolate
mascarpone tart with mandarin and bee-
pollen sorbet in blood-orange and Grand
Marnier butter sauce. Wines start at £19.50, or
£5.50 a glass.
Chef/s: Didier Dejean. Open: Mon to Fri L 12 to 1.45,
Mon to Sat D 6.30 to 9.30. Closed: 2 weeks
Christmas and New Year. Meals: alc (main courses
£17 to £27). Set L £19.50 (2 courses) to £23.50.
Details: 50 seats. No children after 8.

READERS RECOMMEND

Moonfish Cafe

Modern British
9 Correction Wynd, Aberdeen, AB10 1HP
Tel no: (01224) 644166
www.moonfishcafe.co.uk
'A small rustic restaurant that produces five-
star food quality from fresh local produce. The
atmosphere is relaxed and the staff very
attentive.'

Ballater

Darroch Learg

Bastion of Scottish hospitality
56 Braemar Road, Ballater, AB35 5UX
Tel no: (013397) 55443
www.darrochlearg.co.uk
Modern British | £45
Cooking score: 5

Darroch Learg is a splendid Victorian residence on a human scale, a classic country house filled with good furniture allied to comfort and warmth. The personal touch is important here; indeed, the Franks family's 50 or so years at the helm have smoothed the front-of-house operation to a burnished gleam. John Jeremiah does the cooking: a fine compromise between Scottish materials and a style alert to the wider world. Ravioli of smoked haddock with a smoked haddock and Parmesan velouté and sauce vierge or some Loch Fyne scallops with sweetcorn purée, red pepper sauce and toasted sesame seeds could get the three-course dinners off to a fine start. Main course might be loin of Glen Muick venison with a braised haunch, red cabbage, parsnip purée and port wine sauce with, perhaps, grilled fillet of halibut with a saffron mussel broth as an alternative. High praise has gone to a lovely dark chocolate tart with mango ice cream. The wine list shows a preference for France, especially Burgundies, Bordeaux and Rhones, although enticing modern choices turn up elsewhere. Bottles start at £23.
Chef/s: John Jeremiah. Open: Sun L 12.30 to 2, all week D 7 to 9. Closed: 1 week Christmas, last 3 weeks Jan. Meals: Set D £45. Sun L £24. Details: 48 seats. Wheelchair access. Car parking.

¶¶¶ Average Price

The average price listed in main-entry reviews denotes the price of a three-course meal, without wine.

Banchory

Cow Shed Restaurant

Robustly seasonal, sharply contemporary
Raemoir Road, Banchory, AB31 5QB
Tel no: (01330) 820813
www.cowshedrestaurant.co.uk
Modern British | £37
Cooking score: 2

£5
OFF

Set deep in the Banchory countryside overlooking the Hill of Fare, this loyally supported restaurant is making a name with its grandstanding approach to regional produce, although a thoroughly modern setting (wood tones and neutral colours) and charming service play their part. Robustly seasonal menus are pitched exactly right, whether it's flavourful pigeon breast with celeriac, quince, beetroot and pine nuts or butter-poached monkfish cheeks teamed with a spelt and crab risotto, seared scallops, sorrel and shellfish sauce. A wonderful tasting of chocolate (aka 'my dream dessert') turned out to be a quenelle of dark chocolate grenache – bitter chocolate wafer filled with light chocolate mousse – chocolate ice cream with popping candy and drops of chocolate sauce around the plate. Wines from £20.
Chef/s: Graham Buchan. Open: Tue to Sat D 6.30 to 9.30, Sun L from 12.30. Closed: Mon, 25 and 26 Dec, 1 to 10 Jan. Meals: alc (£18 to £26). Set D £29 (2 courses) to £37. Sun L £22.50. Details: 56 seats. 15 seats outside. Wheelchair access. Car parking.

Dufftown

La Faisanderie

Confident French cooking
2 Balvenie Street, Dufftown, AB55 4AB
Tel no: (01340) 821273
www.lafaisanderie.co.uk
French | £35
Cooking score: 2

'French food with a Scottish flavour' is the promise at Eric Obry's rustic-style restaurant on the corner of Dufftown's main square. Yellow walls, antiques and pictures provide

the backdrop for some confident cooking – although service can sometimes seem preoccupied. Eric is a trained deer stalker as well as a chef, so his venison dishes are worth ordering. Other huntin' and fishin' fans also contribute to the kitchen, providing the raw materials for, say, 'melting' scallops in cream sauce or baked suprême of pheasant with Puy lentils, port and winter truffle jus. To finish, try the Speculoos biscuit crème brûlée or a 'chanson' of Russet apples with cinnamon ice cream and quince syrup. Burgundy grabs pole position on the regional French wine list, with prices from £15.45.
Chef/s: Eric Obry. **Open:** all week L 12 to 1.30, D 5.30 to 8.30. **Closed:** Tue and Wed (Nov to Mar), 16 Dec to 12 Feb. **Meals:** alc (main courses £18 to £23). Set L £14.50 (2 courses) to £18.50. Set D £25 (2 courses) to £35 (4 courses). **Details:** 28 seats. Wheelchair access.

▌Laurencekirk

READERS RECOMMEND
Balmakewan
British
Balmakewan House, Northwater Bridge, Laurencekirk, AB30 1QX
Tel no: (01674) 840888
www.balmakewan.co.uk
'I cannot praise highly enough the overall experience at Balmakewan. The beef was cooked to perfection. My wife had the duck dish which, in her own words, was the best she had ever tasted. I have to agree, succulent, tasty and beautifully presented.'

▌Udny Green
Eat on the Green
Delivering the Scottish larder to an old village post office
Udny Green, AB41 7RS
Tel no: (01651) 842337
www.eatonthegreen.co.uk
Modern European | £38
Cooking score: 2
V

Eat on the Green is unafraid of touting itself as a special-occasion restaurant and it knows when to pull out all the stops. 'It's not only the food . . . it's the whole package', rhapsodises one regular. Housed in the old stone post office in Udny Green, the venue provides an enticing and warm environment, with a candlelit lounge for aperitifs, a new chef's table and a handsome tartan-carpeted dining room Craig Wilson champions traditional Scottish produce without getting mired in old-fashioned cooking. There's Stornoway black pudding, in a warm duck confit salad with raspberry vodka and apple, or perhaps Perthshire venison with red cabbage, apricot dauphinois and dark chocolate and beetroot jus. Finish with a dessert 'taster' including lemon posset and berry pavlova. Global wines open at £18.95.
Chef/s: Craig Wilson. **Open:** Wed to Fri and Sun L 12 to 2, Wed to Sun D 6.30 to 8.30 (9.30 Fri, 5.30 to 9.30 Sat). **Closed:** Mon, Tue, 1 to 5 Jan. **Meals:** alc (main courses £20 to £27). Set L £21.95 (2 courses) to £24.95. Sat D £55. Sun L £24.95 (2 courses) to £29.95. **Details:** 80 seats. Wheelchair access. Car parking.

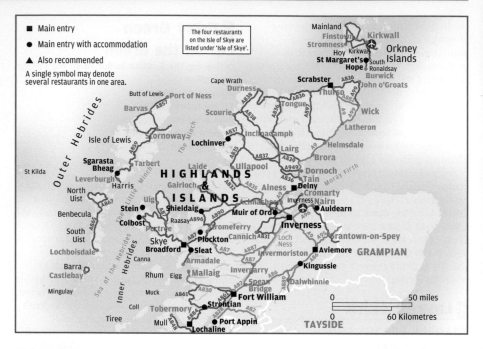

▊ Auldearn

Boath House

Country house with own-grown produce
Auldearn, IV12 5TE
Tel no: (01667) 454896
www.boath-house.com
Modern European | £70
Cooking score: 5

£5 OFF 🍴 V

From the charming gardens, complete with ornamental lake, to the gracious early 18th-century manor house, with its exquisitely furnished oval dining room, Boath House is the complete package. Charlie Lockley continues to devise daily changing menus that use the best Scotland and the manor's own garden have to offer. His dishes make a strong visual impact, but he is content to let ingredients speak naturally for themselves – six-course dinner menus, for example, are tersely described so that 'carrot, black olive' turns out to be a cup of intensely flavoured carrot soup topped with a black olive

emulsion. Food is delivered with unfailing prowess, sparkle and confidence, as seen in an inspired pairing of duck breast with pak choi and star anise, described as a perfect riff on oriental flavours. This year, however, one dish has stolen the show: foie gras with apple, quince and meringue that simply 'melted in the mouth'. A perfectly ripe Ardersier Clava Brie served with oatmeal wafers also receives praise. From a strong base in France, the wine list (starting at £24) turns up interesting bottles from across the world.
Chef/s: Charlie Lockley. **Open:** all week L 12.30 to 1.15, D 7 to 7.30. **Meals:** Set L £24 (2 courses) to £30. Set D £70 (6 courses). **Details:** 26 seats. Wheelchair access. Car parking. Children over 6 yrs only.

🍴 Visit us Online

To find out more about
The Good Food Guide, please visit
www.thegoodfoodguide.co.uk

▌Aviemore

Mountain Café
A jewel in the midst of Aviemore
111 Grampian Road, Aviemore, PH22 1RH
Tel no: (01479) 812473
www.mountaincafe-aviemore.co.uk
British | £20
Cooking score: 1
£5 OFF £30

Regulars vouch for the 'fantastic' service and 'beautifully presented, fresh food' at this 'affordable treat' of a café. Generous portions and wonderful views of the Cairngorm mountains are a bonus, and the fact that 'there is always a queue at the door' speaks for itself. The 'fabulous array' of home baking (especially the savoury cheese and cardamom scones) and the all-day breakfast feature in many reports this year, but there's praise, too, for chilli, pea and mint soup, cottage pie and homemade beef burgers. 'A jewel in the midst of Aviemore.' Wines from £13.
Chef/s: Kirsten Gilmour. **Open:** all week 8.30 to 5.30 (5 Tue to Thur). **Closed:** 25 and 26 Dec, 1 Jan. **Meals:** alc (main courses from £6 to £10). **Details:** 48 seats. 12 seats outside. Car parking.

▌Delny

Birch Tree
Much-loved country restaurant
Delny Riding Centre, Delny, IV18 ONP
Tel no: (01349) 853549
www.the-birchtree.com
Modern British | £28
Cooking score: 2
£5 OFF £30

There's a genuine feeling of affection from the many readers' reports we receive for this 'gem of a restaurant' located at the Delny Riding Centre. It's a real find in such a rural area and people appreciate the local sourcing and inventive touches with which Barry Hartshorne elevates his cooking above the standard bill of fare. Cheese soufflés, scallops (perhaps with a velvety smoked haddock velouté and caramelised fennel) and the good-value steak nights come in for consistent praise, as does the roast loin of venison and the feather blade of beef with tarragon mash. Desserts try out ingenious compositions such as Jerusalem artichoke and white chocolate cheesecake with peanut-butter ice cream. Wines from £15.95.
Chef/s: Barry Hartshorne. **Open:** Tue to Sat 6 to 9 (10 Fri and Sat). **Closed:** Sun, Mon. **Meals:** alc (main courses £14 to £23). Set D £20.95 (2 courses) to £24.99. **Details:** 32 seats. Wheelchair access. Car parking.

▌Fort William

Crannog
Fun fish restaurant on the pier
Town Pier, Fort William, PH33 6DB
Tel no: (01397) 705589
www.crannog.net
Seafood | £30
Cooking score: 1

An unmistakable lochside landmark, this converted bait shed is perched on the town pier right on Loch Linnhe in the heart of Fort William. It's an unpretentious spot, and unsurprisingly given that the owner runs his own fishing boat, West Highland seafood is showcased via a daily changing menu. A meal might kick off with a bowl of Cullen skink packed with smoked haddock, then move on to king scallops with leek mash, braised fennel and coral cream. Meat lovers may bag the venison with red cabbage, dauphinois potato and juniper jus. Finish with chocolate and orange torte. House wine is £16.60.
Chef/s: Stewart MacLachlan. **Open:** all week L 12 to 2.30, D 6 to 9. **Closed:** 25 and 26 Dec, 1 Jan. **Meals:** alc (main courses £15 to £20). Set L £12.95 (2 courses). **Details:** 60 seats. Separate bar. Wheelchair access. Car parking.

▮▮▮ Average Price
The average price listed in main-entry reviews denotes the price of a three-course meal, without wine.

Inverlochy Castle

Baronial pile with high-end contemporary food
Torlundy, Fort William, PH33 6SN
Tel no: (01397) 702177
www.inverlochycastlehotel.com
Modern British | £67
Cooking score: 6

🛏 V

As 'big hooses' go, this colossal study in Scottish baronial magnificence takes some beating – no wonder Queen Victoria wholeheartedly approved of the place, wrote about it in her diaries and even got out her paintbox to record the scene during an 1873 mini break. These days, visitors don their Barbours and deerstalkers to wander the estate, before dressing to dine in the hotel's extravagantly appointed restaurant (jacket and tie please, gentlemen). Scrupulous formality reigns amid the crystal chandeliers, oil paintings and rich antiques, service is a model of expertly drilled precision and the kitchen girds its loins for bravura displays of high-end contemporary cooking. Chef Philip Carnegie likes to give Scottish seasonal ingredients a luxurious spin – as in Loch Linnhe langoustines with crispy chicken, tomato croquette and Parmesan or Dingwall lamb with confit shoulder, tapenade, gnocchi and crottin beignets. He also assuages the die-hards with plates of Aberdeen Angus beef fillet and hollandaise sauce, before wowing everyone with dramatic desserts such as hot banana crumble soufflé or cold Valrhona chocolate fondant with lemon cream. The weighty, all-encompassing wine list is strictly for big spenders, with precious little below £40.
Chef/s: Philip Carnegie. **Open:** all week L 12.30 to 1.15, D 6 to 10. **Closed:** 24 to 26 Dec, 30 Dec to 1 Jan. **Meals:** Set L £28 (2 courses) to £38. Set D £67. Tasting menu £85 (5 courses). **Details:** 80 seats. Wheelchair access. Car parking. Children over 6 yrs only.

▌Inverness

Rocpool

Eye-catching riverside restaurant
1 Ness Walk, Inverness, IV3 5NE
Tel no: (01463) 717274
www.rocpoolrestaurant.com
Modern European | £33
Cooking score: 2

With its trendy glass frontage, 1930s-style lighting, bare surfaces and bold colours, this fizzy brasserie brings some suntanned metropolitan fizz to northerly Inverness. Eye-catching views of the river and ancient castle add to the thrill of eating here, while the kitchen adds plenty of global zing to well-sourced Scottish ingredients – including 'the best venison ever'. West Coast mussels are revved up with Thai curry and coconut cream, sea bream gets the tempura treatment and roast rump of lamb comes with a cassoulet of butter beans and chorizo, plus some crisp golden polenta. After that, keep it eclectic with warm pecan pie and panettone ice cream. Set deals get the thumbs-up and the wine list offers sound drinking from £16.50 (£4.95 a glass).
Chef/s: Steven Devlin. **Open:** Mon to Sat L 12 to 2.30, D 5.45 to 10. **Closed:** Sun, 25 and 26 Dec, 1 to 3 Jan. **Meals:** alc (main courses £13 to £24). Set L £14.95 (2 courses). Set D £16.95 (2 courses). **Details:** 55 seats.

▌Isle of Harris

Scarista House

Gorgeous getaway showcasing island bounty
Scarista, Isle of Harris, HS3 3HX
Tel no: (01859) 550238
www.scaristahouse.com
Modern British | £43
Cooking score: 2

🛏 V

The prospect of sandy beaches and heavenly sunsets combined with dramatic views of the billowing Atlantic are sufficient reasons to take the ferry to this gorgeous 200-year-old manse. But there's more to Scarista House than its miraculous topography: custodians Tim and Patricia Martin have a passion for all things local, organic and seasonal when it comes to feeding their guests. They grow what they can, bake bread, procure seafood from the boats and buy meat from their farming neighbours. The result is a menu that might feature Minches langoustine bisque, navarin of Harris lamb with aubergine purée or megrim sole with saffron risotto and saffron butter sauce. To finish, brilliant cheeses from the Scottish isles and beyond complement the likes of hazelnut meringue with raspberries and blueberry sorbet. House wine is £17. **Chef/s:** Tim and Patricia Martin. **Open:** all week D only 8 (1 sitting). **Closed:** 21 Dec to 31 Jan. **Meals:** Set D £43 to £49.50 (4 courses). **Details:** 20 seats. Car parking. Children over 8 yrs only.

■ Isle of Skye

Creelers of Skye

Delightful French-style seafood
Broadford, Isle of Skye, IV49 9AQ
Tel no: (01471) 822281
www.skye-seafood-restaurant.co.uk
French | £28
Cooking score: 2
£5 OFF £30

'The simplicity of the "shack" belies some accomplished cooking,' remarked one of Creelers' many followers. Seating just 26, it's a sympathetically run venue that's short on looks but big on charm. Tablecloths and napkins may be paper but the idiosyncratic David Wilson cooks with an instinctive use of the best ingredients. His French-tinged menu majors in thoroughbred seafood: note local shellfish (razor clams, surf clams, cockles and mussels) in an orange-scented liquor with shallots and kale; braised local monkfish tail in a light soy and Pernod cream reduction; or bouillabaisse for two or four to share. If you're determined on meat, pick 28-day-hung Angus sirloin with a sweet red wine reduction. Choose patriotically and have cloutie dumpling for dessert or take the French route with mousse au chocolat. Wines from £15.50.

Chef/s: David Wilson. **Open:** Mon to Sat L 12 to 4, D 4 to 9. **Closed:** Sun, 1 Nov to 1 Mar. **Meals:** alc (main courses £12 to £32). **Details:** 26 seats. Wheelchair access. Car parking.

Kinloch Lodge

Remote retreat with finely crafted food
Sleat, Isle of Skye, IV43 8QY
Tel no: (01471) 833214
www.kinloch-lodge.co.uk
Modern British | £70
Cooking score: 5
£5 OFF 🛏

Lord and Lady Macdonald's 17th-century hunting lodge on a hauntingly beautiful stretch of Skye shoreline sounds a rather grand address. In a way it is, complete with ancestors gazing out from oils on the dining room walls. But the operation is run with great warmth and bonhomie in this supremely relaxing location. Marcello Tully heads the kitchen, marshalling plentiful Highland and Island produce to fashion daily changing menus of classically inflected contemporary cooking. A serving of home-cured salmon with beetroot and dill crème fraîche might raise the curtain, to be followed by the house special seared scallop with Parma ham and peanut sauce. Mains could offer a choice of lamb fillet with pancetta, dauphinois and caramelised orchard fruits, or sea bass with pea purée in saffron cream, before dessert of vanilla pannacotta with raspberry sauce and caipirinha sorbet. Wines are a highfalutin bunch, with painstakingly detailed notes, at prices that might not shock. The starting point is £26 and there are plenty of half-bottles.

Chef/s: Marcello Tully. **Open:** all week L 12 to 2, D 6 to 9. **Meals:** Set L £29.99 (2 courses) to £34.99. Set D £65 (5 courses). Tasting menu £75. **Details:** 40 seats. Separate bar. Wheelchair access. Car parking.

Loch Bay

No flimflam, just spanking fresh fish
1-2 Macleod Terrace, Stein, Isle of Skye, IV55 8GA
Tel no: (01470) 592235
www.lochbay-seafood-restaurant.co.uk
Seafood | £30
Cooking score: 2

£5 OFF

'One room, a few wooden tables, local art on the walls, local pottery here and there, and a menu exclusively of fish,' is how Loch Bay was described by one reader. The report goes on to confirm the quality of the cooking at this small, ordinary looking restaurant in a 'remote and gorgeous setting' looking out to the Outer Isles. The value is remarkable, with simplicity the key when it comes to the spanking-fresh fish: steamed mussels, peat-smoked salmon, Loch Bay prawns grilled in garlic butter and seafood platters, served alongside blackboard specials such as red mullet fillet with beurre noisette and simply grilled Dover sole. Come pudding time, look for baked gooseberry and elderflower cheesecake or cloutie dumpling steamed for three hours. Wines from £17.70.
Chef/s: David Wilkinson. **Open:** Wed and Thur L 12 to 1.45, Tue to Sat D 6.30 to 9. **Closed:** Sun, Mon, mid Oct to week before Easter. **Meals:** alc (main courses £15 to £23). **Details:** 23 seats. 8 seats outside. Car parking. Children over 8 yrs only at D.

The Three Chimneys

Seductively isolated hotel
Colbost, Isle of Skye, IV55 8ZT
Tel no: (01470) 511258
www.threechimneys.co.uk
Modern British | £60
Cooking score: 6

They come from far and wide to Eddie and Shirley Spear's whitewashed croft conversion in the wilderness reaches of Skye, near Loch Dunvegan. It's spare and lovely country, the kind of location that provides abundant raw materials, and in which Michael Smith continues to forge a cutting-edge Scottish

cuisine with its own island identity. An individual haggis of Blackface lamb with neeps and greens in peaty gravy could hardly be a more regionally apposite way to start. To follow, the compendious seafood platters are sensational, though equally tempting is the Gigha halibut and squid with Anna potatoes in lobster coral butter. Meat comes with pedigree, too: Black Isle beef appears as charred blade, slow-cooked shin and tongue, in the company of tattie scones, celeriac rémoulade, watercress and pickled onion. Finish with chocolate and ginger ganache with caramelised pear – that's if you can resist the signature marmalade pudding with Drambuie custard. The wine list contains an agreeable mix of classic names and younger growers, with prices from £24 a bottle, or from £6 for the imaginative glass selection.
Chef/s: Michael Smith. **Open:** Mon to Sat L 12.15 to 1.45 (Sun L 12.15 to 1.45 May to Sept). All week D 6.15 to 9.45. **Closed:** 1 to 23 Jan. **Meals:** Set L £28.50 (2 courses) to £37. Set D £60. Tasting menu £90. **Details:** 40 seats. Wheelchair access. Car parking. Children over 5 yrs only at L, over 8 yrs only at D.

■ Kingussie

NEW ENTRY

The Cross

Assured cooking in a peaceful setting
Ardbroilach Road, Kingussie, PH21 1LB
Tel no: (01540) 661166
www.thecross.co.uk
Modern British | £50
Cooking score: 4

£5 OFF

'The whole experience was superb . . .nothing was rushed. The chef is obviously very passionate and staff were very knowledgeable.' Reporters have been quick to sing the praises of this converted tweed mill, which has survived its first year under new ownership (and chef) with honours all round – from the peaceful setting by the river Gynack to Ross Sutherland's contemporary cooking, which fizzes and pops with bright ideas. One visitor was full of admiration for a dinner 'of clean flavours, vibrant colours and exciting combinations', which took in 'crystal clear' chicken consommé with chicken wings and morels, an unusual but successful dish of scallops with squid ink purée and tapioca crackers, and turbot with chorizo, king prawn and a rich chicken sauce. A dessert of smoked chocolate crémeux with sea buckthorn and yoghurt impressed, too. And there's no questioning the commitment behind the high-quality wine list. It's arranged by style, deftly mixing Old World and New. Bottles from £22.

Chef/s: Ross Sutherland. **Open:** Tue to Sat D 7 to 8.30. **Closed:** Sun, Mon, 24 to 27 Dec, 2 Jan to mid Feb. **Meals:** Set D £50 (5 courses). **Details:** 30 seats. 10 seats outside. Car parking.

▌Lochaline
The Whitehouse Restaurant
The Highlands on a plate, with harbour views
Lochaline, PA80 5XT
Tel no: (01967) 421777
www.thewhitehouserestaurant.co.uk
Modern British | £40
Cooking score: 3

With food all around, the Morvern peninsula inspires hunger; Whitehouse co-owners Jane Stuart-Smith and Sarah Jones know how to feed the Highlands to their guests. Up the hill from the Mull ferry, their 'delightful' whitewashed restaurant is prettily plain, and the location has attracted a kitchen team with a strong pedigree. A fresh, appealing menu puts fish and seafood to the fore in dishes like partan bree or langoustine with rapeseed mayonnaise. Meat from the Ardtornish Estate is another feature, demonstrating the value of lasting local connections. Stag liver and kidneys, usually snaffled as a gun's treat, is served here with capers and whisky jus. Puddings are understandably boozy; try border tart with Tobermory malt whisky or a frozen Highland bellini with home-grown strawberries and Shetland gin. For those who can mix grape and grain, wine is from £15.95.

Chef/s: Mike Burgoyne. **Open:** Tue to Sat L 12 to 2.30 (12.30 Tue), D 5.30 to 10 (5 Tue). **Closed:** Sun, Mon, Nov to Easter. **Meals:** alc (main courses £17 to £29). Set L £16.95 (2 courses) to £19.95. **Details:** 24 seats. 8 seats outside. Wheelchair access.

▌Lochinver
Albannach
Solace, sustenance and fine hospitality
Baddidarroch, Lochinver, IV27 4LP
Tel no: (01571) 844407
www.thealbannach.co.uk
Modern British | £65
Cooking score: 6

Much of Sutherland looks like the surface of the moon: perfect walking country. Situated in a little harbour town in a deep sea-loch, Albannach takes full advantage of the tranquillity and views, with the twin peaks of Suilven and Canisp seen from the terrace and gardens. It's a big white 19th-century house, decorated old-school inside, the dining room a haven of candlelight and crisp linen – and of carefully worked modern Scottish cooking. The daily changing five-course fixed-price dinner menu offers the pick of regional produce. An autumn spread opened with seared wood-pigeon with chanterelle ravioli in a chocolatey game-stock sauce, followed by an intermediate Jerusalem artichoke tart with salads. Main was roast turbot with charred fennel and celeriac in red wine, before a cheese course (featuring Morangie goats'-milk Brie) ushered in dessert, a rhubarb and vanilla parfait with lemon caramel, and whole rhubarb poached in Muscat wine. In May, the starter was ham-wrapped monkfish with red pepper jus, the main wonderful slow-roasted Moray beef fillet with thyme mash, then pear tart and salted caramel to finish. The wine list (from £19) lingers in Bordeaux, Burgundy and the Rhône, before heading south.

Chef/s: Colin Craig and Lesley Crosfield. **Open:** Tue to Sun D only 8 (1 sitting). **Closed:** Mon, Mon to Wed in Nov and Dec, Jan to mid Mar. **Meals:** Set D £65 (5 courses). **Details:** 20 seats. Car parking. Children over 12 yrs only.

Muir of Ord

The Dower House

Inviting Highland hideaway
Highfield, Muir of Ord, IV6 7XN
Tel no: (01463) 870090
www.thedowerhouse.co.uk
Modern British | £38
Cooking score: 1

The Aitchisons' little white cottage in the Highlands is a heart-warming and homely spot, a refreshing change from the Scots baronial manner. Its comfortingly domestic feel inside extends to the food. Robyn Aitchison taught himself to cook, and cook well, offering straightforward three-course dinner menus that change every evening and feature fine regional produce. A bowl of crab bisque or pigeon breast in grain-mustard dressing might start things off, and be followed by halibut with mussels, bacon and mushrooms, or fillet of venison with a relish of fresh herbs. At the finishing stage comes peach soufflé or cherry tart. The wine list opens with house French in all three colours at £19.

Chef/s: Robyn Aitchison. **Open:** all week D only 6 to 10. **Closed:** 25 Dec, 31 Dec and 1 Jan. **Meals:** Set D £38. **Details:** 18 seats. 4 seats outside. Wheelchair access. Car parking. Children over 5 yrs only at D.

Orkney Islands

The Creel

Orcadian oasis dedicated to island produce
Front Road, St Margaret's Hope, Orkney Islands, KW17 2SL
Tel no: (01856) 831311
www.thecreel.co.uk
Modern British | £40
Cooking score: 6

The Craigies' enterprising spirit has carried them through nearly three decades at their Orcadian fastness. They live next door to the restaurant, which has rooms above. There's nothing grand about the dining room (a simple, white-walled space hung with colourful, quirky pictures) unless you count the views over the bay, which are priceless. Alan Craigie commits the kitchen wholeheartedly to the pick of island produce, with seafood leading the charge. Some streamlining of the operation in 2013, with fewer covers and a shorter menu offering a brace of choices at each stage, may help focus things even more sharply. First up might be a timbale of diamond-bright crab salad, with apple mayonnaise, avocado salsa and pickled cucumber, or a small fillet of seaweed-fed mutton in glazed pastry on tomato risotto. Mains bring on bracingly fresh steamed lemon sole, teamed with scallops and spiced cauliflower, or perhaps straightforward braised brisket with onion marmalade and glazed carrots. The lemon tart is legendary, and usually served with marmalade ice cream in a tuile cup, and the cheeses are peerless, too, paired with fruity membrillo. House wines from South Africa (Chenin and Shiraz) cost £15, or £4.50 a glass.

Chef/s: Alan Craigie. **Open:** Tue to Sat D only 6 to 10. **Closed:** Mon, Sun, Oct to Apr. **Meals:** Set D £35 (2 courses) to £40. **Details:** 16 seats. Wheelchair access. Car parking.

Plockton

Plockton Inn

Proving that simple can be best
Innes Street, Plockton, IV52 8TW
Tel no: (01599) 544222
www.plocktoninn.co.uk
Seafood | £23
Cooking score: 2

£30

There's no doubting readers' affection for this family-run pub-with-rooms where Mary Gollan has been feeding visitors for nigh on 17 years and 'fish is still a sure-fire bet on the menu' (meat dishes are offered, too). It's in a cracking location, some 100 metres away from the harbour – which means that ultra-fresh supplies are a given. Straightforward treatments include excellent spicy crab chowder as well as the oft-reported seafood

platter, which showcases the pub's own smoked fish and shellfish. A dozen locally caught langoustines, served hot with garlic butter, get plenty of votes, as does skate with black butter, and cranachan ice cream for afters. A warming fire, Plockton Brewery ale and quaffable wines (from £14.95) complete an admirable pub package.
Chef/s: Mary Gollan. **Open:** all week L 12 to 2.15, D 6 to 9. **Closed:** 25 and 26 Dec. **Meals:** alc (main courses £9 to £19). **Details:** 50 seats. 16 seats outside. Separate bar. Wheelchair access. Car parking.

▮ Port Appin

Airds Hotel

Former ferry inn full of delights
Port Appin, PA38 4DF
Tel no: (01631) 730236
www.airds-hotel.com
Modern British | £53
Cooking score: 5

🛒 V

As a top-notch country hotel, Airds looks the part and runs like clockwork. The views over Loch Linnhe still enchant, and visitors are treated to oodles of hospitality – without doubt this former 18th-century ferry inn is a destination for a wide region. 'We will rush back, driving hundreds of miles to eat dinner (not to mention the flawless breakfasts) here.' Since David Barnett's arrival in 2012, the kitchen has dazzled reporters with contemporary cooking full of imagination and polish. Ingredients have a strong Scottish allegiance, but there's a freewheeling spirit at work – witness scallops with tomato, Parma ham and yuzu dressing, or roast loin of venison served with braised Savoy cabbage, beetroot, celeriac and pickled apple. Dinner opens with an amuse-bouche, and dessert could be a masterly soufflé (the banana version comes with coconut ice cream and chocolate sauce), but the cheeseboard with 'real attention to the wonderful local cheeses' is also up to the mark. As is the wine list, which has an eclectic approach that mixes Old and New World names with thoughtfulness and enthusiasm. Bottles start at £23.50.
Chef/s: David Barnett. **Open:** all week L 12 to 1.45, D 7.30 to 9.30. **Closed:** 2 days each week Nov to Jan. **Meals:** Set L £18.95 (2 courses) to £21.95. Set D £53 (5 courses). Sun L £18.95. Tasting menu £72.50 (7 courses). **Details:** 32 seats. Car parking. Children over 8 yrs only at D.

▮ Scrabster

The Captain's Galley

Terrific harbourside eatery with sustainable seafood
The Harbour, Scrabster, KW14 7UJ
Tel no: (01847) 894999
www.captainsgalley.co.uk
Seafood | £49
Cooking score: 3

An ice house and salmon store built 200 years ago, the Cowies' harbourside Caithness seafood spot has bags of character. The aim is to offer at least 10 types of fresh fish and shellfish at each sitting, and not just the usual suspects. Starter could be mussels and razor clams in a Thai broth of coconut and lemongrass, or crispy squid fishcake with sweet chilli relish. A firm fondness for classic Asian treatments sees flame-grilled sea bass turn up in black bean sauce with noodles, or there might be a main-course serving of ling with razor clams, bacon, seaweed and samphire. Confirmed meat eaters will opt for duck breast with red cabbage in Madeira. Refresh with a blood-orange and Champagne granita, before a dessert such as summer berry lemon-meringue vacherin with strawberry sorbet. The white-dominated list opens with house French at £16.95.
Chef/s: Jim Cowie. **Open:** Tue to Sat L 12 to 2, D 7 to 9. **Closed:** Sun, Mon, 25, 26 and 31 Dec, 1 and 2 Jan. **Meals:** alc (main courses £25). Set L £12.50 (2 courses) to £15. Set D £49 (5 courses). Tasting menu £59 (7 courses). **Details:** 25 seats. 25 seats outside. Wheelchair access. Car parking.

Shieldaig

Tigh an Eilean Hotel

Enchanting, personally run getaway
Shieldaig, IV54 8XN
Tel no: (01520) 755251
www.tighaneilean.co.uk
Modern British | £45
Cooking score: 3

Located in a thriving fishing village on Scotland's rugged west coast, Tigh an Eilean (literally 'the house of the island') is a real beauty that fully lives up to its billing. This enchanting getaway also owes much to long-time custodians Chris and Cathryn Field: she is an ever-charming host, while he plunders the seasonal larder and holds sway in the kitchen. Chris's dinner menu changes each day, but typical choices might include locally smoked haddock tartare, medallions of Highland beef with cep, olive and Manchego butter or organic salmon escalope on seasoned Puy lentils with hot orange vinaigrette. After that, browse the artisan Scottish cheeseboard or try something sweet – perhaps chocolate roulade with macerated strawberries. House wines start at £17.50; also look for bottles from featured vineyards such as Guerrieri Rizzardi in Bardolino. Lunches and more casual meals are served in the adjoining Shieldaig Bar & Coastal Kitchen.
Chef/s: Christopher Field. **Open:** all week L 12 to 3 (bar only), D 6 to 9 (12 to 9 in high season). **Closed:** 25 Dec. **Meals:** alc bar L (main courses £6 to £17). Set D £45 (4 courses). **Details:** 54 seats. 50 seats outside. Separate bar. Car parking.

Strontian

Kilcamb Lodge

Welcoming retreat of the best Highland kind
Strontian, PH36 4HY
Tel no: (01967) 402257
www.kilcamblodge.co.uk
Modern British | £55
Cooking score: 4

The Lodge dates from Georgian times and is one of Scotland's oldest stone houses. Home to admirals, church ministers and teachers over the generations, as well as serving time as a hunting lodge, the building is now a country hotel – flourishing, for the past decade, in the hands of Sally and David Fox. Decorative improvements have resulted in a handsome lounge bar, and there is now a brasserie for less formal dining. The principal restaurant still trades in Gary Phillips' style of streamlined country-house cooking, with daily changing four-course dinner menus offering all the intermediate trimmings. A soufflé of Dunsyre Blue with caramelised walnuts might be the prelude to Angus fillet with haggis bonbon, wild mushroom gratin and roasted roots, or grilled lemon sole with a crab and sweetcorn pancake and braised baby gem: the whole rounded off with pear Tatin and marzipan ice cream. Wine prices start at £19.50.
Chef/s: Gary Phillips. **Open:** all week L 12 to 2 (3 Sun), D 5.30 to 9. **Closed:** Jan, Mon and Tue in Feb, Nov and Dec. **Meals:** alc L (main courses) £17 to £24. Set D £49.50 (5 courses). **Details:** 32 seats. 10 seats outside. Separate bar. Car parking.

WALES

Glamorgan, Gwent, Mid-Wales, North-East Wales, North-West Wales, West Wales

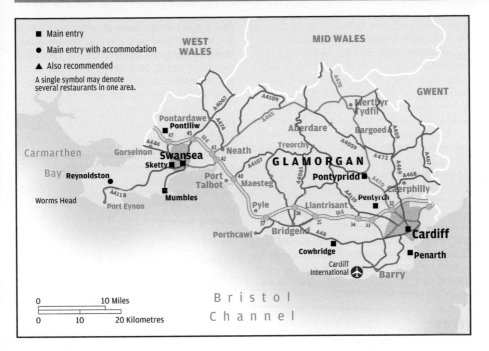

- ■ Main entry
- ● Main entry with accommodation
- ▲ Also recommended

A single symbol may denote several restaurants in one area.

■ Cardiff

Bully's

Long-running family-owned gem
5 Romilly Crescent, Cardiff, CF11 9NP
Tel no: (029) 2022 1905
www.bullysrestaurant.co.uk
Modern British | £34
Cooking score: 2
£5 OFF

A loyal local following has kept this neighbourhood gem going strong since 1996, but amazingly it still feels like a well-kept secret. Bully's is a specialist in all things Gallic (especially foie gras, which can be served on request with anything on the menu), and sports a shabby-chic interior that's slightly at odds with the precision of the cooking. Chicken liver parfait with pickled wild mushrooms and toasted croûtons is a classic opener, while char-grilled fillet of Welsh beef with purple kale, braised leeks, potato and Gruyère galette and a pink peppercorn sauce gives Welsh ingredients a French spin. Pear clafoutis with pear eau de vie caramel and sambuca sorbet is a good way to finish. International wines, including plenty of French classics, start at £21.
Chef/s: Gareth Farr. **Open:** Wed to Sun L 12 to 2 (3.30 Sun), Wed to Sat D 7 to 9 (10 Fri and Sat). **Closed:** Mon, Tue, check website for annual closures. **Meals:** alc (main courses £14 to £32). Set L £14 (2 courses) to £17.50. Sun L £16 (2 courses) to £19.50. **Details:** 40 seats. No children at D.

NEW ENTRY

Chapel 1877

Classic flavours in a unique setting
Churchill Way, Cardiff, CF10 2WF
Tel no: (029) 2022 2020
www.chapel1877.com
Modern British | £30
Cooking score: 2
£5 OFF

An extravagant refit of this former chapel has created a lively ground-floor bar and a mezzanine restaurant where you can choose to

have a view of the lower floor or to nestle in an intimate, velveteen booth. Original features include ornate patterned brickwork, but the overall feel is glossy and modern – especially given the brightly lit open kitchen. Well-sourced ingredients are employed to create a modern slant on classic pairings: fat scallops with a crunchy croquette of local chorizo and black pudding, perhaps, or a generous, tender helping of roast Breconshire venison loin with plump gnocchi and a Madeira cream sauce. An intense, pleasantly cakey chocolate fondant with ginger ice cream brings proceedings to a happy close. The satisfying selection of international wines kicks off at £15.
Chef/s: Kieran Harry. **Open:** Mon to Thur L 12 to 2.30, D 5.30 to 10.30, Fri to Sun 12 to 10 (5.30 Sun). **Closed:** 25 to 27 Dec. **Meals:** alc (main courses £12 to £29). Set L £12.95 (2 courses) to £15.95. **Details:** 80 seats. 25 seats outside. Separate bar. No children after 9 in restaurant.

ffresh
Flag-waving minimalist eatery
The Wales Millennium Centre, Bute Place, Cardiff, CF10 5AL
Tel no: (029) 2063 6465
www.ffresh.org.uk
Modern British | £26
Cooking score: 1
£5 OFF £30

Enveloped within the Millennium Centre waterfront development on Cardiff Bay, ffresh takes its chances amid a plethora of other eating options. Well-thought-out contemporary cooking is the attraction, presented on bilingual menus. Open with the citric tang of limoncello-cured salmon, served with beetroot relish, as a prelude to cider-braised pork belly with honey-glazed carrots and rösti, or skate and shrimps with sautéed potatoes and spinach, before concluding with benchmark Welsh cheeses and oatcakes, or pineapple carpaccio with coconut sorbet and mango foam. House French Sauvignon and Merlot are £14.95, or £3.95 a standard glass.

Chef/s: Kurt Fleming. **Open:** all week L 12 to 2.30 (5 Sun, 6 Mon), Tue to Sat D 5 to 9.30. **Closed:** 25 Dec. **Meals:** alc (main courses £12 to £19). Set L £16.50 (2 courses) to £19.50. Set D £19.50 (2 courses) to £23.50. **Details:** 120 seats. 60 seats outside. Separate bar. Wheelchair access.

NEW ENTRY
Fish at 85
Marine life fresh from the fishmonger's counter
85 Pontcanna Street, Cardiff, CF11 9HS
Tel no: (02920) 020212
www.fishat85.co.uk
Seafood | £40
Cooking score: 2
£5 OFF

Essentially a fishmonger's with a few seats for diners, this highly likeable little restaurant keeps everything simple. The menu offers classics such as moules-frites but the fun option is the 'catch of the day': you get to choose not just your fish (from the chiller counter that runs the length of the room), but also the cooking method, sauce and accompaniments. The chef is Padraig Jones – of late, great Cardiff restaurant Le Gallois – and although his cooking is pared down here, his technical skills shine through. Try a classic fish soup with rouille and croûton ahead of just-caught sea bass with romesco sauce, broccoli and silky smooth mash, then maybe a perfect crème brûlée for dessert. A modest international wine list kicks off at £14.95.
Chef/s: Padraig Jones. **Open:** Tue to Sat L 12 to 2.30, D 6 to 9. **Closed:** 25 to 27 Dec, 1 and 2 Jan. **Meals:** alc (main courses £14 to 24). Set L £12.95 (2 courses) to £15.95. **Details:** 24 seats.

｜♦｜ Average Price
The average price listed in main-entry reviews denotes the price of a three-course meal, without wine.

Mint & Mustard
Buzzy Indian with winning menus
134 Whitchurch Road, Cardiff, CF14 3LZ
Tel no: (029) 2062 0333
www.mintandmustard.com
Indian | £22
Cooking score: 2
V £30

Providing refined modern Indian cooking alongside familiar favourites is what this popular restaurant in suburban Cardiff is all about. The menu draws influences from across the Subcontinent. Starters of Scottish scallops simmered in lemon zest-flavoured coconut milk, Bombay chaat, or Keralan tiger prawns marinated in a paste of curry leaves, red chillies and garlic, might be followed by Goan 'porc vindalu' (from the Portuguese vin d'alho, meaning wine and garlic), a Malabar lamb biryani or chicken korma. For dessert, look out for tandoori pineapple with pistachio ice cream, but most people never get further than the chocolate and almond-filled samosas served with caramelised banana and vanilla ice cream. Wines from £15.
Chef/s: Santosh Nair. **Open:** all week L 12 to 2, D 5 to 11. **Closed:** 25 and 26 Dec, 1 Jan. **Meals:** alc (main courses £8 to £16). Set L £8.95. Tasting menu £37.50. **Details:** 100 seats. Separate bar. Wheelchair access.

The New Conway
Born-again suburban boozer
58 Conway Road, Pontcanna, Cardiff, CF11 9NW
Tel no: (029) 2022 4373
www.knifeandforkfood.co.uk/conway
Modern British | £23
Cooking score: 2
£30

This born-again Victorian boozer in a suburban terrace not far from Cardiff city centre strikes an admirable balance between local drinking den and good-looking foodie destination. The white-walled dining area has been kitted out like a chic living room with shelves of books and real fires. The blackboard menu offers upbeat food for all tastes – from rabbit and chervil ravioli with Hispi cabbage and chorizo, or an open lasagne of lemon sole with cockles and grilled cauliflower, to roast chicken or shepherd's pie to share. Drinks include a decent range of beers and wines (from £14), although cider is one reader's recommended tipple.
Chef/s: Stefan Nilsson and Lee Skeet. **Open:** all week 12 to 9.30 (10pm Fri and Sat, 9pm Sun). **Meals:** alc (main courses £9 to £19). **Details:** 70 seats. 40 seats outside. Separate bar.

Oscars of Cardiff
Homely comfort food with big flavours
6-10 Romilly Crescent, Cardiff, CF11 9NR
Tel no: (029) 2034 1264
www.oscarsofcardiff.com
Modern British | £25
Cooking score: 2
£30

A thoroughly infectious enthusiasm pervades Oscars: a family-friendly all-day venue with bubbly staff and a commitment to suiting all tastes. The menu changes seasonally, but is always supplemented by adventurous daily specials. Sharing boards and platters are right on the money, including meze and nachos versions. Asian and Mediterranean influences confer fire and sun on the main menu, which takes in crab cakes with chilli relish or green coconut chicken to start, and then lamb T-bone with vine tomatoes, feta and red onion, or Welsh ribeye given the bourguignon treatment for six hours and served with a grilled portobello mushroom. The house take on strawberry mess de-Etonises it with macaroons and candy floss, or there's bourbon vanilla, white chocolate and raspberry cheesecake. A brasserie-style wine list opens at £14.95.
Chef/s: John Cook. **Open:** Wed to Sun 12 to 11 (6 Sun). **Closed:** Mon, Tue, 25 and 26 Dec, 2 weeks Aug, bank hols. **Meals:** alc (main courses £10 to £22). Set L £10 (2 courses). **Details:** 60 seats. 12 seats outside. Wheelchair access. Car parking.

The Potted Pig

Snappy cooking and divine desserts
27 High Street, Cardiff, CF10 1PU
Tel no: (029) 2022 4817
www.thepottedpig.com
Modern British | £25
Cooking score: 2

£30

If you like a bit of utility chic (industrial lighting, exposed brickwork and piping), this converted bank vault is for you – especially if you're also keen on all things porcine. Potted pig with toast and pickles is a fixture on the straight-talking menu, perhaps washed down with a gin (from a long list), but there are pig-free options, too: whole bream with Jerusalem artichokes, for instance, with Savoy cabbage and béarnaise sauce. Classic puds include sticky toffee pudding and lemon and ginger posset. Besides gins (which feature as a partner for pork) there's a fair selection of wines, including plenty by the glass. Bottles start at £15. Consistency here can be a problem, and some diners say it's 'not what it was'. Reports please.
Chef/s: Gwyn Myring and Tom Furlong. **Open:** Tue to Sun L 12 to 2, D 7 to 9 (6.30 to 9.30 Fri and Sat). **Closed:** Mon. **Meals:** alc (main courses £9 to £27). Set L £12 (2 courses). Sun L £15 (2 courses). **Details:** 70 seats. Separate bar. Wheelchair access. No children at dinner.

NEW ENTRY

Purple Poppadom

Creative Indian cookery and a lively buzz
Upper Floor, 185a Cowbridge Road East, Cardiff, CF11 9AJ
Tel no: (029) 2022 0026
www.purplepoppadom.com
Indian | £28
Cooking score: 3

£30

Anand George made a name for himself at Mint & Mustard (see entry), but now he's giving his creativity free rein at the Purple Poppadom, a modest first-floor restaurant in Canton, serving a dazzling mix of inventive and traditional Indian dishes. Food is pitched significantly above your average curry house fare, and the funky pink and purple décor and lively buzz create a relaxed, informal mood. A starter of scallops poached in a moilee sauce set beside a spice-encrusted scallop with black grape and fresh ginger dressing is typical of George's ability to put a modern spin on traditional flavours. To follow, a main course of murgh chatpata Kolhapur (chicken with a thick tangy onion and tomato sauce flavoured with fenugreek leaves and lemon juice) has show-stopping freshness and complexity. For dessert, George's trademark chocomosa makes a fun and satisfying conclusion. A decent selection of wines kicks off at £15.95.
Chef/s: Anand George and Siddartha Singh. **Open:** Sun to Fri L 12 to 2.30, all week D 6 to 11 (Sun 5 to 9.30). **Meals:** alc (main courses £11 to £17). Tasting menu £39.95 (4 courses). **Details:** 74 seats. Separate bar.

Cowbridge

Bar 44

Unfettered enjoyment at a cheery tapas joint
44c High Street, Cowbridge, CF71 7AG
Tel no: (01446) 776488
www.bar44.co.uk
Tapas | £18
Cooking score: 2

£5 OFF £30

'There is always a warm and friendly welcome here,' says one reporter of this cheery first-floor tapas joint in the heart of Cowbridge. From the chalked cocktail list above the bar to the stools clustered around rustic tables, the emphasis is on earthy, unfettered enjoyment. 'Phenomenal' charcuterie with a chilled Estrella is one regular's idea of a good time; the 'simple but delicious' cider-poached chorizo made from the best Ibérico pork also gets the thumbs-up. Then there are the 'devilishly good' lamb, mint and chilli meatballs with red wine and tomato sauce; 'supremely crunchy' patatas bravas; and finally, moist flourless Catalan almond and lemon cake with citrus syrup and crème fraîche. An all-Spanish wine list opens at £14.95.

Chef/s: Tommy Heaney. **Open:** all week 9.30 to 9 (5 Mon). **Closed:** 25 Dec. **Meals:** Tapas (£3 to £8). Mon to Fri set L £10 (3 tapas) to £18 (6 tapas). **Details:** 60 seats.

Oscars of Cowbridge

Bright, breezy and imaginative cooking
65 High Street, Cowbridge, CF71 7AF
Tel no: (01446) 771984
www.oscarsofcowbridge.com
Modern British | £24
Cooking score: 1

£30

'Very friendly' staff give 'fantastic service' in this bright and breezy eatery that offers everything from coffee and cake to full evening meals. Imaginative menus pull in flavours from far and wide, with nibbles ranging from bacon and prunes on a stick with maple butter to roast butternut squash with pomegranate and feta. A starter of sea-salt chilli duck with smoked barbecue glaze and toasted sesame is 'amazing', while the 'delicious' six-hour beef brisket with mustard whipped potatoes and buttermilk onion rings also garners praise. Finish with chocolate macaroon mess with chocolate popping candy.

Chef/s: John Cook. **Open:** Mon to Sat midday to 9.30 (10 Fri and Sat). **Closed:** Sun, 25 and 26 Dec, 1 and 2 Jan. **Meals:** alc (main courses £10 to £17). Set L £10 (2 courses). **Details:** 40 seats. 20 seats outside. Wheelchair access. Car parking.

▌Mumbles

NEW ENTRY
Munch

Skilled cooking at a bargain price
650 Mumbles Road, Mumbles, SA3 4EA
Tel no: (01792) 362244
www.munchofmumbles.com
British | £25
Cooking score: 2

£5 OFF £30

Unadorned walls, the simplest furnishings, a set-price menu and a BYO policy might make Munch seem cheap and cheerful but the food has other ideas. Co-proprietor Ben Griffiths used to be chef at the now defunct Maes Yr Haf on the Gower and he's brought all his technical skill with him while abandoning some of the fuss. This is gutsy, clear-flavoured cooking that delivers excellent value. Springy, punchy garlic chilli bread got an inspection meal off to a good start, followed by a crisp salt-cod croquette with chorizo, squid ink aïoli and basil oil. Dry-aged Welsh beef rump with caramelised onion rösti, creamed cabbage and bacon and bordelaise jus made a full-flavoured, wintry main, while sticky treacle tart with spiced orange mascarpone was a comforting end note. Ben's wife Jacqui is an excellent hostess, and if you run out of BYO wine she'll sell you more, from £12 a bottle.

Chef/s: Ben Griffiths. **Open:** Wed to Sun L 12 to 2.30 (3 Sun), Wed to Sat D 6.30 to 9.30. **Closed:** Mon, Tue, 25 and 26 Dec, 1 Jan, 2 weeks Oct. **Meals:** Set L £15.95 (2 courses) to £18.95. Set D £25. Sun L £15.95 (2 courses) to £19.95. **Details:** 40 seats.

Penarth

The Fig Tree

Panoramic seaside views and sheer value
The Esplanade, Penarth, CF64 3AU
Tel no: (029) 2070 2512
www.thefigtreepenarth.co.uk
Modern British | £28
Cooking score: 3
£5 OFF £30

'Amazing food, great service and fantastic views' neatly sums up the reasons for visiting this beach-side restaurant. Even in rough weather, the converted Victorian beach shelter, just a few steps up from the main road, is magical. The two-level dining room has views across the Bristol Channel towards Somerset and the islands of Flat Holm and Steep Holm. It's in the open-plan kitchen that Mike Caplan-Hill and his team create straightforward dishes from raw materials sourced within a 30-mile radius (suppliers are credited). Start perhaps with Vale of Glamorgan rabbit terrine, served with grape chutney, followed by belly of Andrew Morgan's Welsh free-range pork (slow-roasted until crisp and served with wild garlic pesto, cherry tomatoes and spring greens). The homemade desserts make for a comforting finish, perhaps new-season rhubarb and chocolate bread-and-butter pudding with blood orange sorbet. Wines start at £14.
Chef/s: Mike Caplan-Hill and Tom Westerland. **Open:** Tue to Sun L 12 to 3 (4 Sat and Sun), Tue to Sat D 6.30 to 9.30. **Closed:** Mon. **Meals:** alc (main courses £11 to £19). Set L £11 (2 courses) to £13.50. Sun L £18.95. **Details:** 54 seats. 28 seats outside. Wheelchair access.

Symbols

🛏 Accommodation is available

£30 Three courses for less than £30

V Separate vegetarian menu

£5 OFF £5-off voucher scheme

🍶 Notable wine list

Pentyrch

Kings Arms

Worth a special journey
Church Road, Pentyrch, CF15 9QF
Tel no: (029) 2089 0202
www.kingsarmspentyrch.co.uk
Modern British | £25
Cooking score: 2
£5 OFF £30

Beckoning winsomely from the village of Pentyrch, just a short drive from Cardiff, the Kings Arms is a gently modernised version of a traditional village boozer, with flagstone floors, real ales and flickering fires. It's worth a visit for a pint in the snug, but is all the better for a relaxed meal in the restaurant. Rump or silverside of Breconshire beef is the obvious choice for Sunday visitors, though a starter of homemade Thai-style fishcakes with sautéed cockle butter, and a vegetarian dish of roasted swede stuffed with cannellini bean cassoulet better demonstrate the kitchen's international streak. Chestnut and whisky cheesecake finishes a meal on a rich note. The short wine list may not be the most inspired, but it starts at just £14.95.
Chef/s: Ken Bell. **Open:** all week L 12 to 3 (3.30 Sun), Mon to Sat D 6.30 to 9.30. **Meals:** alc (main courses £11 to £24.50). Sun L £12.50 (2 courses) to £15.50. **Details:** 70 seats. 60 seats outside. Separate bar. Car parking.

Pontlliw

NEW ENTRY
Rasoi

Lively Indian creations
Bryntirion Road, Pontlliw, SA4 9DY
Tel no: (01792) 882409
www.rasoiwales.co.uk
Indian | £20
Cooking score: 2
£5 OFF £30

Warm lighting and cosy booths give this out-of-town Indian restaurant an intimate feel despite its rambling size. Patterned panels and quirky carved wooden furniture lend plenty of character, and the open kitchen makes for a theatrical focal point. The menu combines familiar favourites, less well-known Indian classics and modern creations – all bursting with the flavours of freshly ground spices. Aloo tikki (pea and potato patties) gets a meal off to a punchy start, while lamb and courgette koftas with sweet potato and coriander purée and an intense mint sauce makes a comforting yet lively main. From an impressive selection of homemade desserts, a 'decadently sweet and syrupy' gulab jamun with vanilla ice cream gets the thumbs-up. The well-annotated, surprisingly substantial wine list starts at £12.95.

Chef/s: Mohammad Ashfaq Ansari. **Open:** all week L 12 to 2.30 (5 Fri to Sun), all week D 5.30 to 10. **Meals:** alc (mains £8 to £15). Set L £9 (2 courses) to £11. **Details:** 198 seats. 80 seats outside. Separate bar. Wheelchair access. Car parking.

▌Pontypridd
Bunch of Grapes
Hostelry that does the neighbourhood proud
Ynysangharad Road, Pontypridd, CF37 4DA
Tel no: (01443) 402934
www.bunchofgrapes.org.uk
Modern British | £30
Cooking score: 1
£5 OFF £30

'This is the kind of place you wish was your own local,' says one reporter who put her SatNav to good use to find this 'off-the-beaten-track' gem. A proper pub as well as a restaurant, it is equally at home dishing up hearty burgers and hand-cut chips as butternut squash risotto with pecan nuts, Perl Las cheese and Hafod-cheese crisps. Whichever end of the spectrum you settle on, you'll find a flair for flavours and attention to detail. Even the sandwiches, using homemade focaccia, are a cut above, and the chocolate fondant comes highly recommended. Wines, including some interesting Patagonian options, open at £15.90.

Chef/s: Sebastien Vanoni. **Open:** all week L 12 to 2.30 (3.30 Sun), Mon to Sat D 6.30 to 9.30. **Meals:** alc (main courses £13 to £25). **Details:** 60 seats. 24 seats outside. Separate bar. Wheelchair access. Car parking.

▌Reynoldston
Fairyhill
Smart hotel with uncluttered, clear-flavoured cooking
Reynoldston, SA3 1BS
Tel no: (01792) 390139
www.fairyhill.net
Modern British | £45
Cooking score: 4
♦ ⊨ V

As country house hotels go, this Georgian gem is at the boutique end of the market, both size-wise and in terms of personal service. Fairyhill lies at the heart of the Gower peninsula, surrounded by 24 acres of parkland, so is well placed to source produce from nearby farmers and fishermen. Steamed local mussels with leeks, garlic, white wine and herbs is a typical starter, while meat takes centre stage in a main course of loin and slow-cooked belly of Gower lamb with pea and mint, rosemary gravy and gratin dauphinois. The kitchen excels in uncluttered, clear-flavoured cooking: from canapés enjoyed in the elegant lounge through to gently inventive desserts such as green pistachio cake with rhubarb sorbet and roasted strawberries or rosemary pannacotta with blood-orange and rosemary jelly and biscotti. A weighty tome of a wine list (personally compiled by the owners) adds to the attraction, kicking off at £19.50.

Chef/s: David Whitecross. **Open:** all week L 12 to 2, D 7 to 9. **Closed:** 26 Dec, first 3 weeks Jan. **Meals:** Set L £20 (2 courses) to £25. Set D £35 (2 courses) to £45. Sun L £27.50. **Details:** 60 seats. 30 seats outside. Separate bar. Wheelchair access. Car parking. Children over 8 yrs only at D.

Swansea

Didier & Stephanie

Tasteful French cuisine
56 St Helen's Road, Swansea, SA1 4BE
Tel no: (01792) 655603
French | £30
Cooking score: 4

Since setting up their intimate little beacon of Gallic sophistication back in 2000, Didier Suvé and Stephanie Danvel have stayed true to their original intentions, matching highly personal service with their own brand of tasteful French cooking. Stephanie takes charge of proceedings in the smart, yellow-walled dining room, while partner Didier deals with business in the kitchen. Expect confident, generous and technically assured food with its heart in the world of bourgeois cuisine and an unwavering dedication to the classics – langoustine bisque, confit duck, chicken suprême stuffed with mushrooms, sea bass with saffron sauce. Regulars also come here for Didier's locally famous croustillant of boudin noir with mustard dressing, roast rack of Welsh lamb dressed with thyme jus, and deeply unfashionable desserts such as chocolate and mint mousse or poached pear in honey with ice cream. French regional names loom large on the wine list, from £14.90.
Chef/s: Didier Suvé. **Open:** Tue to Sat L 12 to 3, D from 7 onwards. **Closed:** Sun, Mon, Christmas to New Year, 2 weeks summer. **Meals:** alc (main courses £12 to £19). Set L £15.50 (2 courses) to £18.50. **Details:** 20 seats.

Hanson at the Chelsea

Convivial bistro amid Swansea's nightlife
17 St Mary Street, Swansea, SA1 3LH
Tel no: (01792) 464068
www.hansonatthechelsea.co.uk
Modern European | £30
Cooking score: 3
£5 OFF

In a cosy café with simple wooden chairs, yellow walls and a big cheering blackboard of daily fish specials, Andrew Hanson has created a thoroughly sympathetic city eatery in the midst of Swansea's vibrant nightlife. As befits the surroundings, the cooking has a bistro air to it, with classic European preparations creeping in among the modern British ideas. It could be something as simple as Parmesan-shaved wild mushroom risotto to start, followed by honey-glazed pork belly with sage and onion mash, apple compote and scrumpy sauce, or alternatively, flaked crab and prawn avocado with pink grapefruit, and then cod mornay, asparagus and tarragon butter. Desserts aim to please, with an array of cheesecakes, sticky toffee pudding and a version of bread-and-butter pudding ritzed up with honey and whisky. Wines are carefully annotated and fairly priced, opening with Chilean Sauvignon and Merlot at £13.95, or £3.75 a glass.
Chef/s: Andrew Hanson. **Open:** Mon to Sat L 12 to 2, D 7 to 9.30. **Closed:** Sun. **Meals:** alc (main courses £12 to £22). Set L £11.95 (2 courses) to £16.95. Set D £19.95. **Details:** 46 seats.

Pant-y-Gwydr Restaurant

French cooking that hits the spot
Oxford Street, Swansea, SA1 3JG
Tel no: (01792) 455498
www.pantygwydr.co.uk
French | £35
Cooking score: 3

Proudly Gallic at every turn, the Pant-y-Gwydr is Swansea's Cinderella story: a rundown street-corner boozer transformed into a stylish little restaurant that many rank as the best in town. Expect 'amazing classical French food' ranging from rustic fare to more inventive dishes – as in a starter of salmon rillettes with lemon confit and ginger wrapped in a parcel of smoked salmon and served with toasted sourdough. Pot au feu is a simple, homely main course, but alternatives include tournedos Rossini and goose three ways (rillettes, roasted magret and leg confit). The 'memorable' tarte au citron makes a satisfying finale, perhaps preceded by a cheeseboard featuring classics such as Brie de Meaux Dongé and organic Cropwell Bishop

Stilton. The all-French wine list covers the country's major regions, starting at just £14.95 a bottle. All round excellent value. **Chef/s:** Jacques Abdou. **Open:** Tue to Sat L 12 to 2, D 6 to 10.15. **Closed:** Sun (except 1 L a month), Mon, 2 weeks early Sept, 2 weeks mid Mar. **Meals:** alc (main courses £7 to £29). **Details:** 53 seats. Wheelchair access.

Slice

Personal service and menus that work
73-75 Eversley Road, Swansea, SA2 9DE
Tel no: (01792) 290929
www.sliceswansea.co.uk
Modern British | £35
Cooking score: 3

'This is one of the best restaurants in the area' is the view of a visitor to this cute 14-cover eatery in Sketty, a well-to-do corner of suburban Swansea. Named after the wedge shape of the building, Slice has been cunningly converted to house a ground-floor kitchen, where chef Phil Leach can be seen hard at work, and an upstairs dining room overseen by the 'excellent' Helen Farmer. The set-price menu is considered 'good value for the quality of cooking', which is classically rooted but not enslaved by tradition. Twice-baked goats' cheese soufflé with roasted cauliflower and hazelnut salad is a good way to start, while roast poussin with onion tarte Tatin and thyme velouté is typical of the polished, accessible mains. The bar stays high for desserts like chocolate mousse with soft almond meringue and rum and raisin ice cream. The international wine list opens at a reasonable £15. **Chef/s:** Philip Leach. **Open:** Thur to Sun D only 6.30 to 9. **Closed:** Mon to Wed, 24 Dec to 2 Jan. **Meals:** Set D £35. **Details:** 14 seats. Children over 10 yrs only.

STEPHEN TERRY
The Hardwick

Do you have a favourite new restaurant opening of the last year?
Wright's Independent Food Emporium, Nantgaredig.

Which three ingredients couldn't you cook without?
Halen Môn sea salt from the Isle of Anglesey, Ortiz anchovies and Blodyn Aur Welsh rapeseed oil.

How do you come up with new dishes?
By matching seasonal ingredients with core ingredients in a way that will be interesting to everyone, from the chef to the customer, whilst always remembering your marketplace.

Which of your dishes are you most proud of?
Crispy breadcrumbed middle-white pork belly and black pudding, with pickled fennel and apple and mustard sauce.

What do you think is a common mistake that lets chefs down?
Poor management skills.

What would you be if you weren't a chef?
A better father and husband!

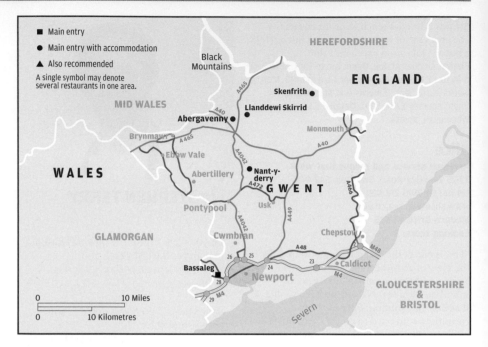

- ■ Main entry
- ● Main entry with accommodation
- ▲ Also recommended

A single symbol may denote
several restaurants in one area.

HEREFORDSHIRE

ENGLAND

MID WALES

Black
Mountains

Skenfrith ●

Llanddewi Skirrid

Abergavenny ●

Monmouth

WALES

Brynmawr

Ebbw Vale

Abertillery

Nant-y-
derry ●

GWENT

GLAMORGAN

Pontypool

Usk

Cwmbran

Chepstow

Bassaleg

Newport

Caldicot

GLOUCESTERSHIRE
&
BRISTOL

0   10 Miles

0   10 Kilometres

Severn

■ Abergavenny

The Hardwick

An all-round Welsh winner
Old Raglan Road, Abergavenny, NP7 9AA
Tel no: (01873) 854220
www.thehardwick.co.uk
Modern British | £40
Cooking score: 5

Since blasting on to the scene in 2005, Stephen
Terry's unflashy rural haven has pulled off
quite a coup. Few Welsh hostelries manage to
blend low-beamed rusticity with affluent
London ways, appealing both to pubby die-
hards and trend-hungry foodies. Even first-
timers are adopted as 'old friends' here. The
varnished wood and leather among the
bucolic trappings cajole the uptown crowd,
who are wooed by salt cod brandade with
fried chorizo tortilla, piquillo peppers and
olives, or confit duck pastilla with medjool
date purée, pomegranate, blood orange and
coriander. Others homesick for new Soho
might grab a native-breed hot dog. Bold,
brassy flavours, good sense and simple
comforts abound and everything is driven by
dedicated local sourcing – witness a bumper
tasting of Welsh beef (grilled fillet, oxtail suet
pudding, rib burger and braised shin) with
accompaniments including confit shallots,
greens, triple-cooked chips and bordelaise
sauce. A brilliant selection of Welsh cheeses
ends things on a grand-slam high, unless you'd
prefer sharing 'a plate of chocolate loveliness'.
The wine list is classy, modern and
democratic, with prices from £19.
Chef/s: Stephen Terry. **Open:** all week L 12 to 2.45,
D 6.30 to 9.15. **Closed:** 25 Dec. **Meals:** alc (main
courses £18 to £26). Set L £16.50 (2 courses) to £21.
Sun L £23 (2 courses) to £28. **Details:** 92 seats. 20
seats outside. Separate bar. Wheelchair access. Car
parking.

Restaurant 1861

Homely roadside restaurant
Cross Ash, Abergavenny, NP7 8PB
Tel no: (0845) 3881861
www.18-61.co.uk
Modern European | £37
Cooking score: 3
£5 OFF **V**

There's a genuine family feel to Simon and Kate King's homely roadside restaurant in a hamlet not far from Abergavenny. With its distinctive black-and-white frontage, the foursquare Victorian building looks a bit like an old 'railway station' house, although all is comfortable and tickety-boo within. Simon King has a strong culinary CV and is keen to promote the region's produce – local farmers provide various meats, while veg comes from his father in law's allotment. The result is a menu of astutely handled dishes with some neat contemporary accents: seared scallops are served with parsnip purée and chicken juices; ethically produced foie gras is offset by passion fruit sauce; and fillet of brill is poached in red wine. Other ideas show Simon's grounding in classically minded kitchens (braised stuffed pig's trotter, for example), and meals end on a high with desserts such as pear tarte Tatin. House wines from £17.
Chef/s: Simon King. **Open:** Tue to Sun L 12 to 2, Tue to Sat D 7 to 9. **Closed:** Mon, first 2 weeks Jan. **Meals:** alc (main courses £19 to £24). Set L £19 (2 courses) to £24.50. Set D £34. Sun L £22 (2 courses) to £25. Tasting menu £49.50 (7 courses). **Details:** 40 seats. Separate bar. Car parking.

Bassaleg

Junction 28

A lot to choo-choose from
Station Approach, Bassaleg, NP10 8LD
Tel no: (01633) 891891
www.junction28.com
Modern European | £30
Cooking score: 2

A stalwart of the Newport dining scene, this converted railway station restaurant (incorporating an original train carriage) continues to feed hordes of locals, families and tourists. A few readers have reported disappointing dinners, but others have found much to praise. The repertoire has a regional feel and the uncomplicated cooking has a slightly retro slant, so expect posh comfort food. Rich and creamy broccoli and Stilton soup is a well-reported starter, and those in the market for top-notch brisket of beef on mashed potato with wild mushroom sauce will not be sent away empty – especially if they conclude with sticky toffee sponge. The downside is the dated décor: 'straight out of the 1980s'. Wines from £15.95.
Chef/s: Simona Bordeianu. **Open:** all week L 12 to 2 (4 Sun), Mon to Sat D 5.30 to 9.30 (9.45 Fri and Sat). **Closed:** 26 Dec, 1 Jan, last week Jul, first week Aug. **Meals:** alc (main courses £13 to £24). Set L £14.45 (2 courses) to £16.45. Set D £18.45 to £21.95. Sun L £15.45 (2 courses) to £17.45. **Details:** 160 seats. Separate bar. Wheelchair access. Car parking.

Llanddewi Skirrid

The Walnut Tree

Homely inn harbouring a renowned chef
Llanddewi Skirrid, NP7 8AW
Tel no: (01873) 852797
www.thewalnuttreeinn.com
Modern British | £40
Cooking score: 6

After finding fame feeding the diners of Ludlow and Devon – where he put Gidleigh Park (see entry) on the gastronomic map – Shaun Hill reopened the Walnut Tree in 2008 and quickly restored its former glory: though 'glory' may be too pompous an epithet for this whitewashed country inn on the B4521 near Abergavenny. Inside is smart yet homely, with unclothed tables and bentwood chairs providing the backdrop for some engaging, and impressively precise, modern Welsh cooking. Game dishes are especially lauded: perhaps woodcock with braised lentils or 'the best, seasonally perfect hare dish I have ever eaten'. A first course of veal sweetbreads with a rich, full-flavoured pork cromesqui exhibits an assured flourish, while mains might feature delicately timed lemon sole with Jansson's temptation (the Swedish spin on dauphinois that's pungent with little fish). Desserts maintain the pace: baked marmalade pudding boosted with Penderyn (Welsh whiskey) custard, for instance, or apple and Calvados tart. An inspired slate of house wines, from £4.50 a glass, £18 a bottle, heads a carefully chosen global collection.

Chef/s: Shaun Hill and Roger Brook. **Open:** Tue to Sat L 12 to 2, D 7 to 9. **Closed:** Sun, Mon, 1 week Christmas. **Meals:** alc (main courses £15 to £25). Set L £20 (2 courses) to £26. **Details:** 50 seats. 16 seats outside. Separate bar. Wheelchair access. Car parking.

Nant-y-derry
The Foxhunter
Sheer indulgence and thoughtful food
Nant-y-derry, NP7 9DN
Tel no: (01873) 881101
www.thefoxhunter.com
Modern British | £35
Cooking score: 4

'I can't believe we've never eaten here before,' exclaims one new fan of Matt Tebbutt's popular country restaurant. A smartly converted former stationmaster's house in the tiny village of Nant-y-derry, the Foxhunter has been going strong for nearly 15 years. The draw is the 'professional, friendly and well-timed' service led by Matt's wife Lisa and the full-on flavours and unfussy presentation of Matt's cooking. 'There are no over-the-top embellishments, allowing the dishes to take centre-stage,' is a typical comment. Well-reported starters include octopus carpaccio and arancini with aubergine roulade. The European flavours extend to main courses such as Cornish mullet with smoked pancetta, courgettes, mussels and tarragon cream or rump of lamb with buttered spinach, rosemary, artichokes and tomatoes. Raspberry and whisky cranachan is typical of the 'gorgeous' desserts. A substantial, nicely annotated wine list includes plenty of half-bottles, with full bottles starting at £18.95.

Chef/s: Matt Tebbutt. **Open:** Tue to Sun L 12 to 2, Tue to Sat D 7 to 9.30. **Closed:** Mon, bank hols. **Meals:** alc (main courses £17 to £23). Set L £22.95 (2 courses) to £27.95. Sun L £23.95 (2 courses) to £28.95. **Details:** 40 seats. 8 seats outside. Separate bar. Wheelchair access. Car parking.

Skenfrith
The Bell at Skenfrith
Riverbank inn with a kitchen garden
Skenfrith, NP7 8UH
Tel no: (01600) 750235
www.skenfrith.co.uk
Modern British | £33
Cooking score: 4

The setting is as attractive as ever: a former 17th-century coaching inn on the outskirts of a pretty little village, overlooking the river Monnow and the ruins of Skenfrith Castle. The Bell combines its dual roles as local hostelry and upmarket eatery with agility – local real ales, flagstone floors, oak beams and antiques tick all the right boxes – and Alex Marston's food is based on industrious home production and keen sourcing, his larder boosted by produce from the inn's own kitchen garden. From a flavour-packed starter of beetroot (served three ways) with orange dressing and goats'cheese bonbon, and mains of fillet of cod with cod brandade, tarragon-crusted mussels, courgette ribbons, pea purée and citrus gel to a 'perfect' Sunday roast, many dishes have been superb. Desserts maintain the standard with a 'sublime' spiced apple trifle with local cider granita and fennel seed doughnuts. The food is matched by William Hutchings' enlightened wine list that favours elite independent growers from across the globe. Half-bottles are plentiful and bottle prices start at £16.

Chef/s: Kieran Goth. **Open:** all week L 12 to 2.30, D 7 to 9 (9.30 Fri and Sat). **Closed:** Tue (Nov to Mar). **Meals:** alc (main courses £15 to £23). Set L £18 (2 courses) to £22. Sun L £22 (2 courses) to £26. **Details:** 60 seats. 30 seats outside. Separate bar. Wheelchair access. Car parking.

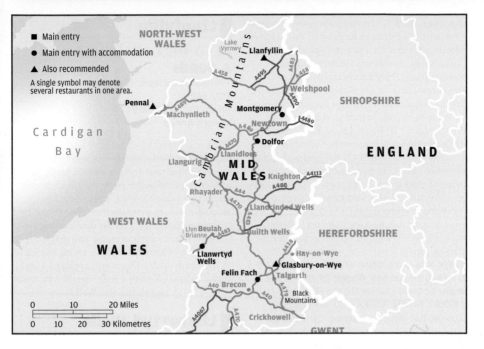

- ■ Main entry
- ● Main entry with accommodation
- ▲ Also recommended

A single symbol may denote several restaurants in one area.

NORTH-WEST WALES

Lake Vyrnwy   Llanfyllin

Welshpool

Pennal

Machynlleth

Montgomery

Newtown

Dolfor

Cardigan Bay

Llanidloes

Llangurig

MID WALES

Knighton

Rhayader

Llandrindod Wells

WEST WALES

Llyn Brianne   Beulah

Builth Wells

Llanwrtyd Wells

WALES

Felin Fach

Talgarth

Brecon

Crickhowell

SHROPSHIRE

ENGLAND

HEREFORDSHIRE

Hay-on-Wye

Glasbury-on-Wye

Black Mountains

GWENT

0   10   20 Miles
0   10   20   30 Kilometres

■ Dolfor

The Old Vicarage Dolfor

Charm, passion and kitchen-garden produce
Dolfor, SY16 4BN
Tel no: (01686) 629051
www.theoldvicaragedolfor.co.uk
Modern British | £30
Cooking score: 2

£5 OFF 🛏

Tim and Helen Withers run their red-brick Victorian B&B with immense enthusiasm – he in the kitchen, she a superb front-of-house. They are charming hosts, passionate about the environment and about food and wine. Visitors are full of praise for their personal approach and attention to detail. The emphasis is on the freshest seasonal produce, including ingredients from the Old Vicarage's own kitchen garden and polytunnels, as well as eggs from its free-range chickens. The result is a limited menu bursting with sharply executed ideas: from an 'exemplary' organic Hafod cheese soufflé, and a main-course Bryn

Derw free-range chicken with chorizo and peppers, saffron rice and sautéed courgettes, to a textbook rhubarb crumble. Wines from £15.
Chef/s: Tim Withers. Open: Sun L 1, all week D 7.30 (1 sitting). Closed: 25 and 26 Dec, 31 Dec and 1 Jan. Meals: Set D £25 (2 courses) to £30. Sun L £25. Details: 12 seats. Car parking.

■ Felin Fach

The Felin Fach Griffin

A beacon of Brecon hospitality
Felin Fach, LD3 0UB
Tel no: (01874) 620111
www.felinfachgriffin.co.uk
Modern British | £32
Cooking score: 4

🛏

A blazing beacon out in the Brecons, the Felin Fach Griffin pulls off an impeccable balancing act, giving equal weight to its duties as a gentrified Welsh boozer, away-from-it-all sleepover and serious country restaurant. Despite roaring fires and agricultural trappings, the kitchen takes a 'refined' modern view when it comes to feeding its flock: cured salmon arrives with a pea and broad bean Caesar salad, cod fillet is presented with pomme purée, Puy lentils and onions, while braised ox cheek is partnered by horseradish risotto. Sunday lunch brings huge tranches of roast meat, 'elegant brutes' in the shape of Welsh beef rib or leg of Llandefalle pork with all the desired accoutrements, followed by stamina-testing puds such as 'blindingly good' pistachio cake with poached pear and sour cream. Drinks include an ever-changing line-up of Welsh real ales, and there's also plenty to cheer about when it comes to the idiosyncratic, cliché-free wine list; bottles start at £16.50, with plentiful options by the glass or carafe.

Chef/s: Ross Bruce. **Open:** all week L 12 to 2.30, D 6 to 9 (9.30 Fri and Sat). **Closed:** 24 and 25 Dec. **Meals:** alc (main courses £16 to £19). Set L £21. Set D £28.50. **Details:** 45 seats. 30 seats outside. Separate bar. Wheelchair access. Car parking.

▌Glasbury-on-Wye

ALSO RECOMMENDED
▲ The River Café

Glasbury-on-Wye, HR3 5NP
Tel no: (01497) 847007
www.therivercafeglasbury.co.uk
Italian

The vast blackboard menu that's merrily wheeled from table to table makes the point well: everything here is fresh, with choices changing daily. The River Café is the good kind of idiosyncratic, with a light modern interior, bags of riverside alfresco seating and a penchant for things fishy, Italian, or both – try home-cured sewin (£7.50), fresh Cornish crab pappardelle (£13.50) and Italian chocolate and hazelnut cake (£5). A decent selection of mostly Italian wines opens at £13.95. Closed Sun D.

▌Llanfyllin

ALSO RECOMMENDED
▲ Seeds

5 Penybryn Cottages, High Street, Llanfyllin, SY22 5AP
Tel no: (01691) 648604
Modern British

Mark and Felicity Seager have been running this homely 16th-century cottage restaurant for more than two decades and are justly proud of their reputation for personable bonhomie and good-value cooking. Meals revolve around short set-price menus (£12.50 for two courses at lunch, £27.50 for three courses at dinner). On a typical evening you might open with grilled Cornish sardines, go on to rack of Welsh lamb with a Dijon and herb crust and round things off with treacle tart. Wines from £14. Closed Sun to Tue and Wed L.

▌Llanwrtyd Wells

Carlton Riverside

Smart yet homely riverside retreat
Irfon Crescent, Llanwrtyd Wells, LD5 4SP
Tel no: (01591) 610248
www.carltonriverside.com
Modern European | £30
Cooking score: 5
£5 OFF 🚃

For more than 20 years chef Mary Ann Gilchrist and her husband Alan have been plying their trade in Llanwrtyd Wells, first up the road in Carlton House and more recently in this attractive grey-stone property set snug to a tumbling river. Despite the dangers of trying to be all things to all people, they have mostly succeeded, giving locals a regular watering hole (the cellar bar, which serves all-day pizzas) and gastronomic tourists an impressive stopover in the form of a well-reported gourmet break (which comes with a specially created set menu). To experience Mary Ann at the top of her game, this is the best option, but there's also a regular carte offering simple brasserie fare: maybe tiger prawns with garlic and white wine ragoût and

orzo pasta, then fillet steak with mushroom and Parmesan gratin, dauphinois potatoes, carrots and green beans. The 'duo of chocolate' comprising fondant, trifle and milk ice cream gave one visitor 'a great finish to a memorable meal'. Ask Alan to guide you through his well-chosen international wine list, which opens at £16.
Chef/s: Mary Ann Gilchrist. **Open:** Mon to Sat D only 7 to 9. **Closed:** Sun. **Meals:** alc (main course £13 to £25). **Details:** 18 seats. Separate bar. Children over 8 yrs only.

Lasswade Country House
Thoroughbred local produce and Edwardian comforts
Station Road, Llanwrtyd Wells, LD5 4RW
Tel no: (01591) 610515
www.lasswadehotel.co.uk
Modern British | £35
Cooking score: 2
£5 OFF 🍴

A tall, trim country house looking out over the Brecon Beacons, Lasswade has been Roger and Emma Stevens' labour of love since 2001. The comforting Edwardian interiors include a well-stocked library; a log fire gets lit when the chill gets up; and Roger's cooking is solidly founded on thoroughbred local produce, much of which comes with the Royal imprimatur. Daily changing menus might proceed from locally smoked sewin with red cabbage chiffonade, apple and cucumber, topped with salmon caviar, to the superlative Cambrian hill lamb, regally presented as roast rump, breadcrumbed braised belly, and kidney sautéed in grain mustard and tomato, with root veg in a reduction of Madeira. Finish with rhubarb trifle made with zabaglione and amaretti, served warm. Wines from £13.65.
Chef/s: Roger Stevens. **Open:** all week D only 7.30 to 9. **Closed:** 25 and 26 Dec, Jan. **Meals:** Set D £35. **Details:** 20 seats. Wheelchair access. Car parking.

▌Montgomery

The Checkers
Faultless French food
Broad Street, Montgomery, SY15 6PN
Tel no: (01686) 669822
www.thecheckersmontgomery.co.uk
French | £50
Cooking score: 6
£5 OFF 🍴

Take one highly talented French chef, team him up with two Shropshire farmer's daughters and add stints in some of the UK's top kitchens before secreting them in one of Montgomery's old town boozers. The result: Checkers, a delightfully alluring restaurant-with-rooms. Drinks by the wood-burning stove in the cosy little lounge set the scene for meals in two gracefully appointed dining areas furnished with eau de nil panelling and antique French chairs. Despite the relaxed, country-style interiors, the food is as smartly turned out as can be – from home-baked breads and amuse-bouches to petits fours, and everything in between. Stéphane's cooking mixes classical haute cuisine with seasonal flavours and ingredients from his adopted region: perhaps 'meltingly tender' slow-cooked Shropshire pork belly with creamed potato, roasted pear and braising juices; or roast local partridge with confit leg, parsnip purée and thyme jus. To start, a perfectly risen soufflé suissesse is enhanced by the crunch and freshness of a Granny Smith apple and roasted almond salad, while fastidiously crafted desserts might feature a 'cigarette' of passion fruit and white chocolate. Around 100 reasonably priced wines start at £16.
Chef/s: Stéphane Borie. **Open:** Thur to Sat L 12 to 2, Tue to Sat D 6 to 9. **Closed:** Sun, Mon, 25 and 26 Dec, 2 weeks Jan. **Meals:** alc (main courses £19 to £28). **Details:** 45 seats. 15 seats outside. Separate bar. Wheelchair access. Children over 8 yrs only at D.

🍴 PRODUCED IN WALES

From rolling fields to rocky coast, Wales yields up some of the finest ingredients in the UK. To begin with a cliché, sheep are plentiful; look out for salt marsh lamb, which acquires a special sweetness from the rich herbage of the coastal marshes.

From the sea come mussels, lobsters and exceptional sea bass, while cockles are a national dish, served up with their classic partners – salty bacon and inky laverbread, made from cooked porphyra seaweed. Wild food is plentiful in Wales, with foraged mushrooms, ramsons and samphire making frequent appearances on menus.

The lowland areas support dairy farming and the production of a wide range of cheeses, from punchy Y Fenni to mellow Caerphilly. Try some cheese with that other great Welsh speciality – cawl, a hearty stew made with meat and native vegetables.

Sweet treats include Welsh cakes (flat scone-like cakes, delicious when warm) and bara brith – a rich raisin cake that sometimes pops up in bread and butter pudding. Above all, expect freshness and flavour when eating out in Wales – with a larder like this, there is no excuse for mediocrity.

▌Pennal

ALSO RECOMMENDED
▲ Glan Yr Afon
Pennal, SY20 9DW
Tel no: (01654) 791285
riversidehotel-pennal.co.uk
Modern British

'A must for anyone in the Pennal area', this 16th-century village inn has been transformed into a 'wonderful restaurant within a country pub'. Sound seasonal ingredients find their way into unchallenging dishes along the lines of fresh crab and fennel salad (£7.95) and Welsh Black sirloin steak with onion rings and peppercorn sauce (£18.95). Hits have included lamb's liver and bacon, fish stew with king prawns and chorizo, and a trio of Welsh cheeses that was 'enough for two people'. Wines from £14.50. Open all week.

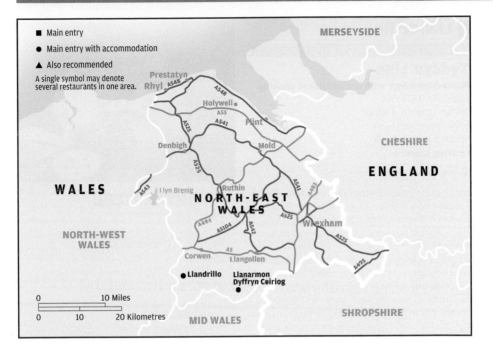

- ■ Main entry
- ● Main entry with accommodation
- ▲ Also recommended

A single symbol may denote several restaurants in one area.

Llanarmon Dyffryn Ceiriog

The West Arms Hotel

Characterful inn with fine local food
Llanarmon Dyffryn Ceiriog, LL20 7LD
Tel no: (01691) 600665
www.thewestarms.co.uk
Modern British | £25
Cooking score: 3

£5 OFF 🛏 £30

Conjure up an image of a picture-perfect, whitewashed Welsh country inn and you may see something like the West Arms near Wrexham. The 16th-century drovers' inn is as charming and well kept inside as it is out. The 'pleasing' lighting, 'adequately spaced' tables and comfortable seating that enhance the original features do not go unnoticed by readers. Polite, effective and 'appropriately paced' service is also commended. The inn's many regulars have come to expect 'considered flavours' and 'imaginative presentation' in the restaurant, more straightforward combinations in the bar (mussels with white wine, local gammon and hand-cut chips, perhaps) and strongly local ingredients in both. A representative dinner menu might include lobster and smoked salmon roulade with tarragon beurre blanc, Welsh lamb fillet with a Mediterranean soufflé and salsa verde, then honey and hazelnut parfait with raspberry and ginger tuile. The French-favouring wine list opens at £15.95.
Chef/s: Grant Williams. **Open:** all week 12 to 6.30, D 6.30 to 9. **Meals:** alc (main courses £10 to £19). Set D £27.95 (2 courses) to £32.95. **Details:** 72 seats. 40 seats outside. Separate bar. Wheelchair access. Car parking.

🍴 **Visit us Online**

To find out more about
The Good Food Guide, please visit
www.thegoodfoodguide.co.uk

Llandrillo

★ TOP 50 ★

Tyddyn Llan
Home-from-home with accomplished cooking
Llandrillo, LL21 0ST
Tel no: (01490) 440264
www.tyddynllan.co.uk
Modern British | £55
Cooking score: 6

🍷 ⇋ V

Set in three acres of grounds deep in the Welsh countryside, Tyddyn Llan was formerly the Duke of Westminster's shooting lodge, but since 2002 it has been home to Bryan and Susan Webb. Although some visitors think the old place is looking its age, few dispute there is much to appreciate when it comes to comfort, warmth and culinary accomplishment in the elegantly appointed (but 'dimly lit') dining room. Bryan has Welsh blood in his veins and tips his hat to the homeland, even if some of his seasonal ideas seem 'stuck in a 1980s time warp' – witness smoked salmon terrine with horseradish cream and cucumber salad or venison with goats' cheese gnocchi and port sauce. For the most part, however, the refreshing variations on familiar themes still have the power to surprise: from red mullet with aubergine purée, chilli and thyme oil to roast pigeon with chicory, rhubarb and fried polenta. Skilfully fashioned desserts also get good reviews – especially the Yorkshire rhubarb and Champagne trifle. The wine list is a labour of love, with kind mark-ups and real imagination when it comes to cherry-picking growers and grape varieties from around the globe. Prices start at £23.50.
Chef/s: Bryan Webb. **Open:** Fri to Sun L 12.30 to 2 (2.30 Sun), all week D 7 to 9 (9.30 Fri and Sat). **Closed:** last 2 weeks Jan. **Meals:** alc (main courses £21 to £29). Set L £19.50 (2 courses) to £26. Set D £45 (2 courses) to £55. Sun L £40. Tasting menu £85 (9 courses). **Details:** 40 seats. 10 seats outside. Separate bar. Wheelchair access. Car parking.

🍴🍽 BRYAN WEBB
Tyddyn Llan

What do you enjoy most about being a chef?
Being able to use the finest ingredients, and the buzz of a smooth service.

... And the least?
When suppliers send poor ingredients, and when service hits the rocks.

What food trends are you spotting at the moment?
Very little sauce on plates, which is not for me.

At the end of a long day, what do you like to cook?
Chicken, bacon and avocado salad, or a beefburger from my butcher in pitta bread with chilli sauce.

How do you come up with new dishes?
By eating in other restaurants, and testing ideas on my wife.

Name three chefs you admire.
Shaun Hill (The Walnut Tree), Philip Howard (The Square) and Pierre Koffmann (Koffmann's).

Who is the chef to watch in 2014?
Simon Rogan.

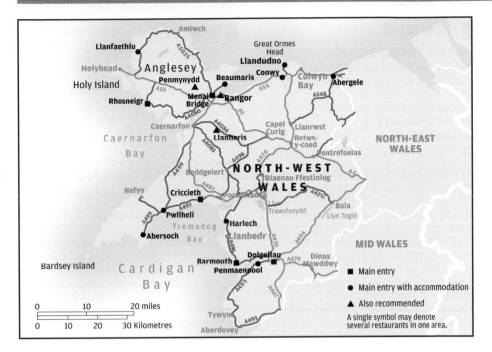

Abergele

The Kinmel Arms

Revitalised inn with fulfilling Welsh food
St George, Abergele, LL22 9BP
Tel no: (01745) 832207
www.thekinmelarms.co.uk
Modern British | £30
Cooking score: 4

'We were impressed with the way the place was run, the attention to detail, the décor, the open fire, the warm welcome and swift and attentive service,' fittingly sums up the appeal of this ancient but revitalised stone inn-with-rooms, which nestles (for once that is the apposite term) between the mountains and the sea. You can still sup real ales in the bar, but this place is all about sure-footed modern cooking starring excellent produce from local and regional suppliers. Reporters have emerged full of praise for a lunch that took in a medley of local seafood in a creamy Thai sauce, and bacon chop served with a poached egg, Pont Neuf potatoes, pineapple purée and béarnaise. Two recent hits from the dinner menu included breast of pigeon fashionably teamed with beetroot salad and quail's egg, and hake fillet with tomato confit, globe artichoke, celeriac and anchovy and caper butter. Wines from £16.50.

Chef/s: Wesley Oakley. **Open:** Tue to Sat L 12 to 2, D 6 to 9.30. **Closed:** Sun, Mon, 25 Dec, 1 Jan, bank hols. **Meals:** alc (main courses £15 to £23). **Details:** 88 seats. 24 seats outside. Separate bar. Wheelchair access. Car parking. No children after 9.

Please send us your feedback

To register your opinion about any restaurant listed in the Guide, or a new restaurant that you wish to bring to our attention, please visit the web address at the bottom of the page. Your feedback informs the content of the book and will be used to compile next year's reviews.

▋Abersoch

Porth Tocyn Hotel
Redoubtable family-run hotel
Bwlch Tocyn, Abersoch, LL53 7BU
Tel no: (01758) 713303
www.porthtocynhotel.co.uk
Modern European | £44
Cooking score: 3

🛏

A Guide stalwart for 57 years and counting, the Fletcher-Brewers' hotel overlooking Cardigan Bay is a smart choice for family holidays by the sea, but also cuts it as a destination for those who appreciate capably cooked Welsh ingredients. An unfettered 'dinner party' mood prevails in the restaurant as amicable staff serve up plates of unchallenging Anglo-European food – think seared local mackerel fillet with soused vegetables, shallot purée and lemon oil or braised oxtail and ox cheek with truffle mash, honey-roast parsnips and red cabbage. The kitchen also lets rip from time to time, conjuring up the likes of marinated duck breast with coconut 'rocks', coconut paste and deconstructed sushi, before easing back for warm chocolate brownie or chilled lemon posset. Light lunches, children's high teas, walking breaks and a list of thoughtfully chosen wines (from £16.95) complete a redoubtable package.
Chef/s: Louise Fletcher-Brewer and Martin Williams. **Open:** all week L 12.15 to 2.30, D 7.15 to 9 (9.30 in high season). **Closed:** Nov to week before Easter. **Meals:** Set D £37 (2 courses) to £44. Sun L £25. **Details:** 50 seats. 35 seats outside. Separate bar. Car parking. No children under 5 yrs at D.

Symbols
🛏 Accommodation is available

£30 Three courses for less than £30

V Separate vegetarian menu

£5 OFF £5-off voucher scheme

🍾 Notable wine list

▋Bangor

ALSO RECOMMENDED
▲ Blue Sky Café
Ambassador Hall, 236 High Street, Bangor, LL57 1PA
Tel no: (01248) 355444
www.blueskybangor.co.uk
British £5 OFF

An amiable daytime eatery housed in a former chapel, the Blue Sky Café begins the morning with lavish offerings ranging from a breakfast sundae to the hearty, bean-based 'cowboy breakfast'. After 11.30 other players enter the field: ever-changing soups, sandwiches (from £4.95), burgers and chef's specials such as fishcakes (£7.25) or meatballs with fusilli (£8.25). Finish with gluten-free Fairtrade organic chocolate brownies. Wines start at £11.75. Closed Sun and all evenings.

▋Barmouth

NEW ENTRY
Bistro Bermo
Pint-sized local bistro
6 Church Street, Barmouth, LL42 1EW
Tel no: (01341) 281284
www.bistrobarmouth.co.uk
Modern British | £25
Cooking score: 1
£5 OFF   £30

A shot in the arm for 'rundown' Barmouth, this pint-sized bistro is driven by an enthusiastic double act: Paul Ryder cooks on his own in the cellar kitchen; wife Emma deals efficiently with matters in the tastefully decorated dining room. Fresh fish from the nearby harbour crops up on the specials board, while the regular menu keeps it simple and honest with the likes of breaded field mushrooms with garlic mayo, twice-cooked 'aromatic' duck with plum and ginger sauce or 'totally boneless' shoulder of Welsh lamb with apple and mint gravy. To finish, check out the Snowdonia cheeseboard. Wines from £15.50.

The Good Food Guide 2014

Chef/s: Paul Ryder. **Open:** Wed to Sat L 12 to 2, all week D 6 to 9 (10 Fri and Sat). **Meals:** alc (main courses £13 to £25). **Details:** 18 seats. 2 seats outside.

■ Beaumaris

Cennin
Mecca for local meat
31 Castle Street, Beaumaris, LL58 8AP
Tel no: (01248) 811230
www.restaurantcennin.com
Modern British | £35
Cooking score: 4
V

The Leek (as the Welsh name translates) has taken root in a well-maintained Georgian house at the head of the Menai Strait. Modern décor with white walls under beamed ceilings makes an attractive atmosphere for Aled Williams' stirring Welsh dishes, which celebrate pedigree meats such as black beef, lamb and pork, all raised on Anglesey. There's fine seafood, too, seen at its most protean in a shellfish risotto stuffed with prawns, clams, scallops, brown shrimps and crab. Then gird your loins for a teaming of fine rump, sirloin, ribeye or fillet steak with a fritter of braised shin meat and horseradish, served with smoked mash. The pork appears as roast tenderloin, crispy belly and a bonbon of tongue in cheek, in a sauce of apple and local honey. After that, a lighter dessert may suffice, perhaps rhubarb and ginger parfait with apple jelly and mousse. The condensed drinks list contains a couple of Welsh wines. Bottles start at £15.95.
Chef/s: Aled Williams. **Open:** Sun L 12 to 4, Thur to Sat D 6 to 9. **Closed:** Mon to Wed. **Meals:** alc (main courses £18 to £27). Set Sun L £15.95 (2 courses) to £19.95. **Details:** 52 seats. Separate bar.

Ye Olde Bull's Head Inn, Loft Restaurant
Bull with pull
Castle Street, Beaumaris, LL58 8AP
Tel no: (01248) 810329
www.bullsheadinn.co.uk
Modern British | £43
Cooking score: 5

The venerable Bull has seen it all. Requisitioned by parliamentary forces during the Civil War, a Quaker meeting-house in the Georgian era, and favoured haunt of literary giants, from Dr Johnson to Dickens, it wears its history proudly on its sleeve in the ancient beams and brick fireplace of its bar. Up top, shoehorned into the old hayloft, is the Loft, the fine-dining venue under the aegis of Hefin Roberts. Light décor and partitions adorned with arabesques create a contemporary backdrop for his modern Welsh cooking, which doesn't fight shy of complexity in its determination to do creative things with sound regional produce. A duo of peppered beef and a curried oyster with watercress purée, or beetroot-cured salmon with a horseradish fritter and smoked yoghurt, might prepare the way for mains that encompass a versatile range of technique. A hearty vegetarian hot-pot of roots and red beans with spicy chickpeas and mushroom gravy is one possibility, or there may be monkfish and razor clams with leek, fennel and preserved lemon, or the old standby of Welsh beef fillet with an oxtail dumpling. Desserts ease things up a little, for the simplicities of tarte Tatin, or orange and cranberry sponge with marmalade ice-cream. A French-led wine list opens with house selections at £21, or £5.25 a glass. Simpler fare is on offer in the Brasserie.
Chef/s: Hefin Roberts. **Open:** Tue to Sat D only 7 to 9.30 (6.30 Fri and Sat). **Closed:** Sun, Mon, 25 and 26 Dec, 1 Jan. **Meals:** Set D £42.50 (3 courses). **Details:** 45 seats. Separate bar. Car parking. Children over 8 yrs only.

Colwyn Bay

READERS RECOMMEND

Hayloft

Modern British
Bodnant Welsh Food, Furnace Farm, Tal-y-Cafn,
Colwyn Bay, LL28 5RP
Tel no: (01492) 651100
www.bodnant-welshfood.co.uk
'Definitely the sort of place you would have on your regular dinner-venue list if you lived locally. I doubt you could get nearer to eating food at source.'

Conwy

Dawson's at the Castle Hotel

Rejuvenated dining room with local produce
High Street, Conwy, LL32 8DB
Tel no: (01492) 582800
www.castlewales.co.uk
Modern British | £30
Cooking score: 2
£5 OFF 🍴

Right in the centre of Conwy, this is a 'wonderful place to be', with diners tucking into meals from midday until late evening. Regulars are slowly adjusting to the bold look of the dining room, despite it clashing with the Shakespearean paintings by Victorian illustrator John Dawson-Watson. Food ranges from char-grilled steaks with a choice of sauces to pan-roasted fillet of cod on a crushed potato and basil cake with hot niçoise sauce, a soft-poached hen's egg and rich hollandaise sauce. Local ingredients get a big thumbs-up, particularly lamb, which might arrive in a hotpot with parsley mash. First, try Conwy mussels (food miles: just 100 yards). Desserts are classics like sticky toffee pudding. A 'well-chosen, fair value' wine list opens at £16.50. **Chef/s:** Andrew Nelson. **Open:** all week 12 to 9.30 (10 Sat, 9 Sun). **Meals:** alc (main courses £16 to £28). Sun L £11.95 to £13.95. **Details:** 80 seats. 30 seats outside. Separate bar. Car parking.

Criccieth

Tir a Môr

Corner bistro with comforting local food
1-3 Mona Terrace, Criccieth, LL52 0HG
Tel no: (01766) 523084
www.tiramor-criccieth.co.uk
European | £25
Cooking score: 1
£30

French chef Laurent Hebert makes good use of the bounty of land and sea at this corner bistro. Set on two floors, Tir a Môr is just a stone's throw from Tremadog Bay, but though fish is an avowed speciality, at inspection meat dishes predominated. A short list of blackboard specials adds to the choice. Aberdaron crab salad makes a pleasantly light starter, with spring onions, ginger, chilli, mayonnaise and seasonal leaves, followed perhaps by fillet of duck with star anise and orange sauce, or baked fillets of monkfish in a light curry sauce. Try the homemade pavlova for a gratifying finale. House wine is £17.50. **Chef/s:** Laurent Hebert. **Open:** Tue to Sat D only 6 to 9. **Closed:** Sun, Mon. **Meals:** alc (main courses £14 to £20). Set D £19.50 (2 courses) to £21.50. **Details:** 38 seats. Wheelchair access. Car parking. Children over 13 yrs only.

Dolgellau

Bwyty Mawddach

Mediterranean flavours on a Snowdonia family farm
Llanelltyd, Dolgellau, LL40 2TA
Tel no: (01341) 424020
www.mawddach.com
Modern British | £29
Cooking score: 2
£30

A 17th-century barn on the Dunn family farm has been strikingly converted to take full advantage of the 'stunning Snowdonia location'. The views from the clean-lined, slate-floored first-floor restaurant (the bar's on the ground floor) contextualise Ifan Dunn's intelligent British cooking; his menus don't have to shout about provenance – it's right there outside the window. For all that, Dunn's flavours are decidedly Mediterranean – for instance, a starter of thinly sliced slow-cooked pork shoulder with salsa verde and anchovy toast, or roast duck breast and risotto of offal with red wine. Orange and almond cake with orange custard pours on the summer sunshine, though the local cheese plate brings diners happily back to Wales. The 'excellent value' Sunday roast is recommended. Wine from £15.

Chef/s: Ifan Dunn. **Open:** Wed to Sun L 12 to 2.30, Wed to Sat D 6 to 9.30. **Closed:** Mon, Tue, 1 week Jan, 1 week Apr, 1 week Nov. **Meals:** alc (main courses £13 to £20). Sun L £20. **Details:** 50 seats. 50 seats outside. Separate bar. Wheelchair access. Car parking.

Dylanwad Da
Busy all-day asset
2 Ffôs-y-Felin, Dolgellau, LL40 1BS
Tel no: (01341) 422870
www.dylanwad.co.uk
Modern British | £28
Cooking score: 1

A veteran provider of hospitality in Dolgellau, Dylanwad Da flourishes as an engaging all-day café-bar-bistro providing soup and tapas during the day, more ambitious choices for dinner. Dylan Rowlands' food remains true to the spirit of generosity, wholesome flavour and comfort, with much reliance on good local produce and tried-and-trusted combinations. Minted Welsh lamb meatballs with red onion gravy could be followed by Bala sirloin steak with all the trimmings or local bass with a cream mango and mustard sauce, and desserts might feature homemade peach ice cream with raspberry sauce. Dylan is an independent wine merchant, too, and offers a cracking list of mainly European growers; prices (from £15.50) are exemplary.

Chef/s: Dylan Rowlands. **Open:** Tue to Sat L 10 to 3 (Tue and Wed high season only), D 7 to 9. **Closed:** Sun, Mon, Feb, early Mar. **Meals:** alc (main courses £15 to £20). Set D £21.50 (2 courses) to £26. **Details:** 28 seats. Separate bar.

Harlech
Castle Cottage
Accomplished restaurant-with-rooms
Y Llech, Harlech, LL46 2YL
Tel no: (01766) 780479
www.castlecottageharlech.co.uk
Modern British | £40
Cooking score: 2

A cosy restaurant-with-rooms close to Harlech's ruined castle, Castle Cottage may have been smartly modernised but still feels comfortably rustic, with exposed beams and a low ceiling in the dining room. Here crisp table linen and high-backed chairs set the scene for carefully considered cooking based around well-sourced ingredients. Starters such as moules marinière or roasted quail with truffle creamed potato, wild mushroom and Madeira jus are typical of the menu's European bent, but there are occasional forays further afield, as in a main course of Welsh cod marinated and grilled in miso and served with stir-fried noodles, sesame asparagus and miso and saké sauce. Desserts stick to familiar comfort – maybe apple crumble or Eton mess. A global selection of wines kicks off at £16.

Chef/s: Glyn Roberts. **Open:** all week D only 7 to 9. **Closed:** 3 weeks Nov. **Meals:** Set D £39.50 (3 courses). **Details:** 35 seats. Separate bar. Car parking.

Llanberis

ALSO RECOMMENDED
▲ The Peak
86 High Street, Llanberis, LL55 4SU
Tel no: (01286) 872777
www.peakrestaurant.co.uk
Modern British

'Always friendly and welcoming and the food is first class' was the verdict of one visitor to this unassuming village restaurant close to Snowdon mountain. High-quality Welsh ingredients inspire international dishes in the kitchen. Typical choices are Serrano-wrapped scallops with roasted tomatoes and balsamic syrup (£7.50), then maybe sautéed rump of Welsh lamb with cauliflower purée and redcurrant rosemary jus (£16.95). To finish, try chocolate pear and almond tart with crème fraîche (£5.50). Wines from £13.95. Open Tue to Sat D.

Llandudno
Bodysgallen Hall, The Dining Room
Full-dress heritage experience
The Royal Welsh Way, Llandudno, LL30 1RS
Tel no: (01492) 584466
www.bodysgallen.com
Modern British | £43
Cooking score: 4

Majestic gardens arrayed with follies, cascading water features, herb-scented hedges and other earthly delights are just part of the full-dress heritage experience at this ancient Welsh pile – a stately, centuries-old edifice looking out towards Snowdonia. Food-wise, the main focus is the smartly attired old-school Dining Room, where guests can sample Michael Cheetham's fancy-pants take on country-house cooking: think seared mackerel fillet with pickled carrots, Szechuan ice cream, coriander and cumin dressing or butter-poached chicken breast with red pepper croquettes, seared chorizo and paprika foam. Lunch dishes strike a lighter note (salmon fillet on lemon and chive risotto, say), although the kitchen lets rip again for desserts such as banana parfait with toffee ice cream, toffee popcorn and popping-candy brittle. The wine list is a well-travelled, classically schooled aristocrat with a liking for vintage Bordeaux, Burgundies, beefy Tuscans and other tasty offerings from around the vinous globe. House selections start at £19.50 (£5 a glass). Note: more casual food is available at the 1620 Bistro in Bodysgallen's converted coach house.
Chef/s: Michael Cheetham. Open: Tue to Sun L 12.30 to 1.45, Tue to Sat D 7 to 9. Closed: Mon. Meals: Set L £19.50 (2 courses) to £22.50. Set D £43. Sun L £27. Details: 50 seats. Separate bar. Wheelchair access. Car parking. Children over 6 yrs only.

St Tudno Hotel, Terrace Restaurant
Traditional hotel with well-judged dishes
Promenade, Llandudno, LL30 2LP
Tel no: (01492) 874411
www.st-tudno.co.uk
Modern British | £31
Cooking score: 2

Alice Liddell of *Alice in Wonderland* fame stayed at this seafront hotel the very year Lewis Carroll first met her. It feels as though little has changed since, the classically elegant interior harking back to a golden age of seafront promenades and afternoon teas. The pretty restaurant, sporting chandeliers, floral screens and a mural of Lake Como, belies the modern thrust of the cooking. Local ingredients star in baked mackerel with poached cod, tomatoes and cockles, while pan-roasted pork tenderloin with a pig's cheek parcel, fondant potato and cider sauce is typical of the 'very reasonably priced' mains. The attention to detail extends to desserts such as dark chocolate pavé with mandarin sorbet, milk chocolate truffle and orange. A lengthy international wine list opens at £17.50.

Chef/s: Andrew Foster. **Open:** all week L 12.30 to 2, D 6.30 to 9.30 (9 Sun). **Meals:** alc (main courses £19 to £22). Set L £22.50 (2 courses) to £27.50. Sun L £18.95 (2 courses) to £22.50. **Details:** 65 seats. 18 seats outside. Separate bar. Car parking. Children over 5 yrs only. Families can have full dinner in coffee lounge area.

▌Llanfaethlu

NEW ENTRY

The Black Lion Inn

Simple food in a lovely 18th-century pub
Llanfaethlu, LL65 4NL
Tel no: (01407) 730718
www.blacklionanglesey.com
Modern British | £25
Cooking score: 1

🍽 £30

This listed 18th-century country inn had been derelict for some years, but has now been sensitively restored. There's a spacious, dog-friendly bar – 'nicer to eat in than the dining room extension' – which retains the character of the original building (exposed stone wall, roughly plastered white walls), and chairs and tables are 'a pleasant mish-mash'. The place is run with panache, offering cooking that is simple and straightforward, based mainly on Anglesey produce. Salad champenois, with locally made black pudding, new potatoes, shallots and poached egg makes a good starter, followed by 'very tender' braised lamb Henry with carrots, butter beans and bacon, then cheesecake or crumble to finish. Wines from £14.70 a bottle.
Chef/s: François Letissier. **Open:** all week L and D 12 to 9. **Meals:** alc (main courses £10 to £19). Sun L £10.95. **Details:** 80 seats. 40 seats outside. Separate bar. Wheelchair access. Car parking.

▌Menai Bridge

NEW ENTRY

Sosban and the Old Butcher's

Civilised dining in a compact space
Trinity House, 1 High Street, Menai Bridge, LL59 5EE
Tel no: (01248) 208131
www.sosbanandtheoldbutchers.com
Modern British | £34
Cooking score: 4

Stephen and Bethan Stevens' converted butcher's shop has all the creature comforts of a smart, contemporary restaurant while incorporating the original slate slabs and ceramic tiles of its former incarnation. It's a simple set-up: he in the kitchen, she a genial front-of-house, and open for three evenings only. There are no printed menus, and no choice – 'for such a small operation, it makes sense', especially when the food taps into the current appetite for ingredients-led dishes with clean-cut flavours. An inspection meal started with an amuse-bouche (artichoke soup with wild mushrooms), went on to broccoli risotto topped with a slice of slow-cooked lamb strewn with almonds, then well-timed monkfish on a celeriac purée with a slice of oxtail. After rare beef topped with kipper butter and served on potatoes with capers, came 'lollipops' of elderberry and gin sorbet, and rice pudding with pistachios and grapes in Sauternes. Wines from £15.10.
Chef/s: Stephen Stevens. **Open:** Thur to Sat D only 7 to 11. **Closed:** Sun to Wed, 22 Dec to mid Feb. **Meals:** alc (main courses £16 to £22). Tasting menu £60. **Details:** 20 seats.

Penmaenpool
Penmaenuchaf Hall
Oak-panelled opulence and modern menus
Penmaenpool, LL40 1YB
Tel no: (01341) 422129
www.penhall.co.uk
Modern British | £43
Cooking score: 2

🍷 🛏

Pen Hall, as its website calls it (helping those with a shaky grip on Welsh pronunciation), is a long-standing Guide stalwart in the foothills of the Cader Idris range, on the edge of the Mawddach estuary. It is home to nearly 300 adorable horseshoe bats, but you wouldn't know that when in the crisply attired dining room that looks on to the gardens through conservatory windows. Justin Pilkington cooks in confident modern Welsh vein: partnering salmon fillet with foie gras and an apple and chilli chutney; bolstering seared brill with creamed leeks and star anise sauce; and giving fantastic black beef fillet the full Rossini. Dessert could be coffee pannacotta with Kahlúa syrup and chocolate brownies. A truly excellent wine list bears all the hallmarks of thoughtful selection and sheer passion. House wines alone lead from enterprising Spanish Monastrell and Pfalz Riesling to Viognier from Béziers and Mendoza Malbec – all at £20.95.
Chef/s: Justin Pilkington. Open: all week L 12 to 2 (Sun 2.30), D 7 to 9.30 (9 Sun). Closed: 3 to 17 Jan. Meals: alc (main courses £26 to £30). Set L £16.75 (2 courses) to £18.70. Set D £20 (2 courses) to £25. Sun L £18.95. Details: 36 seats. 16 seats outside. Separate bar. Wheelchair access. Car parking. Children over 6 yrs only.

🍴 **Visit us Online**
To find out more about
The Good Food Guide, please visit
www.thegoodfoodguide.co.uk

Penmynydd
ALSO RECOMMENDED
▲ **Neuadd Lwyd Country House**
Penmynydd, LL61 5BX
Tel no: (01248) 715005
www.neuaddlwyd.co.uk
Modern British

Built as a rectory in Victorian times, this fine-looking grey-stone retreat combines wonderful views of Snowdonia with pleasing accommodation and locally inspired food. Fixed-priced dinners (£42 for three courses, including extras) show a fondness for the seasons and the region – witness potted hot-smoked salmon with capers, local pheasant braised in Madeira or fillet of Welsh Black beef with garden vegetables and red wine sauce. To finish, don't miss the Anglesey farmhouse cheeses or the tarte Tatin with cinnamon cream. House wine is £14.95. Open Thur to Sat D only.

Pwllheli
Plas Bodegroes
Landmark hotel with impressive food
Nefyn Road, Pwllheli, LL53 5TH
Tel no: (01758) 612363
www.bodegroes.co.uk
Modern British | £45
Cooking score: 5

🍷 🛏

Readers find 'excellent cuisine, genuine friendliness and a complete absence of hype' at Chris and Gunna Chown's restaurant-with-rooms. Tranquillity comes from the secluded glory of its setting on the Llyn Peninsula and the lovely gardens with beech avenues. But this listed Georgian manor house, filled with well-chosen art, also has the calm 'ease and honesty' that's the result of years of good hospitality. Chris Chown's food is distinguished by the proud and intelligent use of excellent Welsh ingredients with outward-looking flair, so seared Cardigan Bay scallops come with asparagus, chorizo and preserved lemon, and a grilled fillet of cod is served with a smoked haddock spring roll and lemon butter sauce. Readers report 'the odd slip' in the extras but reserve 'adulation' for the main menu, including 'sophisticated' desserts such as Amaretto crème brûlée with poached plums. An extensive wine list features interesting expressions of grapes both widely used and lesser-known, plenty of them French. There are around 20 by the glass and lots of halves, with bottles from £19.50.

Chef/s: Chris Chown. **Open:** Sun L 12 to 2, Tue to Sat D 7 to 9. **Closed:** Mon, 1 Dec to 1 Mar. **Meals:** Set D £45. Sun L £22.50. **Details:** 40 seats. Wheelchair access. Car parking.

▮ Rhosneigr

NEW ENTRY
The Oyster Catcher
Please-all food with principles
Rhosneigr, LL64 5JP
Tel no: (01407) 812829
www.oystercatcheranglesey.co.uk
Modern British | £25
Cooking score: 1
£30

Housed in an environmentally friendly new building (designed and prefabricated in Germany) amid moving sand dunes on the western side of Anglesey, the Oyster Catcher is run on similar lines to Jamie Oliver's Fifteen social enterprise programme. It's an admirable local food initiative. The 'cadet' chefs cook perfectly acceptable dishes from a menu with a please-all appeal: not only oysters, baked mackerel, and fillets of trout, but also goats' cheese pannacotta with diced sweet potatoes and celery, homemade pastas, pizzas and burgers, and puddings such as warm chocolate sponge with a chocolate fudge sauce. Service can be somewhat erratic.

Chef/s: Mark Williams. **Open:** Mon to Fri L 12 to 2.30, D 6 to 9. Sat to Sun 12 to 9 (8.30 Sun). **Closed:** 25 to 26 Dec. **Meals:** alc (main courses £11 to £24). Sun L £13.50. **Details:** 135 seats. 90 seats outside. Wheelchair access. Car parking.

⫚ ALL THE FUN OF THE FARE

From single ingredient celebrations, to fairs showcasing London's best restaurants, there's a food festival to suit all palates.

Ludlow
This Marches town has hosted a festival since 1995. The food and drink fair, focused around the castle, features 160 independent producers as well as cookery demonstrations and competitions.

Abergavenny
Producers from Wales and the Marches are joined by experts from further afield at this charming, weekend-long festival. Highlights have included homegrown talent like Bryn Williams, Matt Tebbutt and Shaun Hill.

Great British Cheese Festival
With more than 600 varieties to try and buy, this annual festival, slap bang in the middle of Cardiff Castle, is a cheese lover's dream. Wet your whistle with some of the 200-odd ales and ciders on offer.

Taste of London
Enjoy a starter at **Le Gavroche**, main at **Benares** and pudding at **Pollen Street Social** at this four-day festival in Regent's Park, as 40 of the capital's best restaurants offer up samples of their signature dishes in the open air.

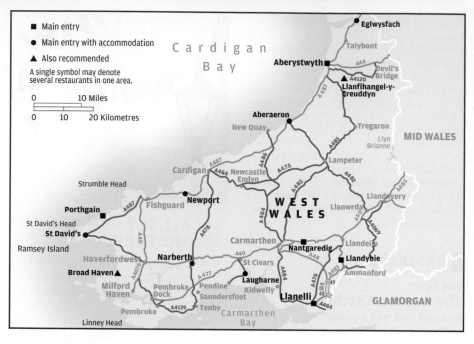

Main entry
Main entry with accommodation
Also recommended
A single symbol may denote several restaurants in one area.

0   10 Miles
0   10   20 Kilometres

Cardigan Bay

Eglwysfach
Talybont
Aberystwyth
Devil's Bridge
Llanfihangel-y-Creuddyn
Aberaeron
New Quay
Tregaron
Llyn Brianne
MID WALES
Lampeter
Cardigan   Newcastle Emlyn
Strumble Head
Porthgain   Fishguard   Newport
St David's Head
St David's
Ramsey Island
Haverfordwest   Narberth
Broad Haven
Milford Haven   Pembroke Dock   Pendine   Kidwelly
Saundersfoot
Pembroke   Tenby
Linney Head   Carmarthen Bay
WEST WALES
Llanwrda   Llandovery
Carmarthen   Nantgaredig   Llandeilo
St Clears   Llandybie
Laugharne   Ammanford
Llanelli
GLAMORGAN

Aberaeron

Harbourmaster

Sleek harbourside hotel
Pen Cei, Aberaeron, SA46 0BT
Tel no: (01545) 570755
www.harbour-master.com
Modern British | £30
Cooking score: 1

Pitched somewhere between a locals' hangout and a boutique retreat for weary Londoners, the Harbourmaster has allure: a buzzy bar, harbour views and a cool nautical dining room lit by retro bulbs. The menus flow with the seasons, trumpeting provenance at every course. Try Cardigan Bay crab spring rolls with tomato and chilli jam; pan-fried Montgomery chicken suprême with gnocchi, peas, broad beans and mustard cream; and maybe Bakewell tart and almond ice cream for dessert. Service can be sketchy, and one diner

balked at a jug of lumpy custard, but there's no doubt that intentions are good. A lengthy selection of wines starts at £15.
Chef/s: Kelly Thomas. **Open:** all week L 12 to 2.30, D 6.30 to 9. **Closed:** 25 Dec. **Meals:** alc (main courses £11 to £25). Set D £25 (2 courses) to £30. Sun L £17 (2 courses) to £23. **Details:** 95 seats. 15 seats outside. Separate bar. Wheelchair access. Car parking.

ALSO RECOMMENDED

▲ Ty Mawr Mansion

Cilcennin, Aberaeron, SA48 8DB
Tel no: (01570) 470033
www.tymawrmansion.co.uk
Modern British £5 OFF

Readers continue to endorse this hidden gem of a hotel in the Aeron Valley – taken by the Georgian house, the warmth of the service, good cooking and fair prices. Everything revolves around dinner and the set-price menus: three-courses for £29.95 (chicken liver parfait, local sirloin steak and sticky toffee pudding) or the more ambitious fine-dining menu (six courses for £39.95) which could take in ham hock, Cardigan Bay scallops, breast of duck and confit leg, and deconstructed tiramisu. Wines from £16.95. Open Mon to Sat D only.

Aberystwyth

Ultracomida

Well-endowed deli and tapas joint
31 Pier Street, Aberystwyth, SY23 2LN
Tel no: (01970) 630686
www.ultracomida.co.uk
Spanish | £20
Cooking score: 2
£30

Combining the virtues of a well-endowed deli with an all-day café/tapas joint, Ultracomida backs up its artisan Spanish provisions with produce from Wales, France and the Med. Nibbles and deli plates (boquerones, cheeses, charcuterie) supplement classics including albondigas, tortilla and hummus with minced lamb, while items such as slow-cooked beef cheeks in fino sherry with garlicky potato purée or baked hake on lentil, Serrano ham and chorizo stew can also be served in larger 'racione'-style portions. There are useful mixed selections for those who can't make up their minds, plus an assortment of 'barra gallega' sandwiches and assorted cakes for daytime fill-ups. House wine is £11.95.
Chef/s: Aled Jones. **Open:** Mon to Sat 10 to 9. Sun 12 to 3.30. **Closed:** 25 and 26 Dec, 1 Jan. **Meals:** alc (tapas from £3 to £9). **Details:** 32 seats. Wheelchair access.

ALSO RECOMMENDED
▲ Treehouse
14 Baker Street, Aberystwyth, SY23 2BJ
Tel no: (01970) 615791
www.treehousewales.co.uk
British £5 OFF

Vegetarian breakfasts (until 11.30am) open proceedings at this amenable, mainly meat-free bistro-cum-coffee house above an

excellent organic food shop. Lunchtime deals (£3.95 to £7) take over until 3.30pm, and the crowds flock in for Welsh ploughman's, quiches or filled baked potatoes, and a few more substantial offerings like aubergine and sesame falafel served in a wholewheat pitta with baba ganoush, harissa and tomato sauce (£7.70) or Welsh beef goulash with dumplings and cauliflower (£9.50). Wines from £9.95. Open all day Mon to Sat.

Broad Haven

ALSO RECOMMENDED
▲ The Druidstone
Broad Haven, SA62 3NE
Tel no: (01437) 781221
www.druidstone.co.uk
Global

In a wild garden, on a clifftop, the Bell family's Pembrokeshire hotel exudes a 'calm and rather bohemian' charm. 'The Dru' (established 1972) is as idiosyncratic as ever, with an events diary featuring 'pudding fests', Creole feasts and dancing. Its joyful global menus are unafraid to list rollmops (£7.50) alongside prawn toast (£7) to start, and salmon and cucumber pie alongside chicken korma (£11.50) for mains. Tremendous views over St Brides Bay. House wine is £13.90. Open all week.

Eglwysfach

Ynyshir Hall

Cooking that's moving into top gear
Eglwysfach, SY20 8TA
Tel no: (01654) 781209
www.ynyshirhall.co.uk
Modern British | £73
Cooking score: 5
£5 OFF

'Ynyshir is looking pristine and lovely,' write the Reens, rightly proud of the work they have put into this pretty 16th-century manor house since taking back ownership in late 2012. Magnificently shielded from the reality of 21st-century existence by mature trees, sweeping grounds and a remote location, it boasts a civilised and gracious interior. Here Joan Reen plays the host with enthusiasm and Paul Croasdale's cooking is moving into top gear. He sails confidently through the tricky waters of intricate modern cuisine, fashioning clever contemporary dishes from superlative raw materials, teaming roast scallops with earth-baked celeriac and muscatels, matching hake with a minestrone of globe artichoke, and venison with blackberry, parsnip and chocolate. From canapés via a 'really excellent selection' of breads to desserts such as bay leaf, sweet tomato and blood orange, attention to detail is impressive. The set lunch is reckoned to be good value – pot-roast chicken with confit garlic and wild mushrooms has been particularly praised – but Ynyshir really scores with its wine list. The global collection of cannily chosen, thought-provoking bottles and glasses offers fruitful, purposeful drinking throughout. Prices from £24.

Chef/s: Paul Croasdale. **Open:** all week L 12 to 2, D 7 to 9. **Closed:** 4 to 31 Jan. **Meals:** Set L £20 (2 courses) to £25. Set D £72.50. Tasting menu £90 (9 courses). Sun L £29.50. **Details:** 28 seats. Separate bar. Car parking.

Laugharne
The Cors
Romantic restaurant-with-rooms
Newbridge Road, Laugharne, SA33 4SH
Tel no: (01994) 427219
www.thecors.co.uk
Modern British | £35
Cooking score: 3
£5
OFF

Nick Priestland pitched his camp in this out of the way spot two decades ago and over time has reworked both the lovely Victorian house and the garden. There's a unique charm to the whole place and many visitors leave totally smitten by the highly individual setting, the exotic bog garden and the food. Nick's gutsy take on modern British cooking is distinguished by honesty, simplicity and full-on flavours. Sensible, unfussy dishes include beef carpaccio with Parmesan shavings, followed by turbot with samphire and a

lemon hollandaise or roast rack of Welsh salt marsh lamb served with a rosemary and garlic crust and caramelised onion gravy. Equally well-handled desserts have included a fine lemon tart. The short, modern wine list starts at £14.95.

Chef/s: Nick Priestland. **Open:** Thur to Sat D only 7 (1 sitting). **Closed:** Sun to Wed, first 2 weeks Nov. **Meals:** alc (main courses £16 to £26). **Details:** 24 seats. 10 seats outside. Separate bar. Wheelchair access. Car parking. Children over 12 yrs only.

Llandybie
Valans
Good-looking neighbourhood eatery
29 High Street, Llandybie, SA18 3HX
Tel no: (01269) 851288
www.valans.co.uk
Modern European | £28
Cooking score: 2
£30

At the heart of the local community, Valans hosts coffee mornings every Friday as well as offering special themed evenings. It's a simple but sleek bistro with an uncluttered red and black colour scheme – and the menu falls into step nicely, offering an unpretentious, modern take on Welsh and European classics. Perhaps start with cockles and laver bread, and then bouillabaisse with homemade bread and butter. Iced rhubarb parfait with warm orange and almond biscotti is a good way to finish, but then so is the chocolate crème brûlée with gooey chocolate cake, raspberry jelly and chocolate ganache. The wine list encompasses a broad range of prices, regions and styles, kicking off at £14.50.

Chef/s: Dave Vale. **Open:** Tue to Sat L 12 to 3, D 7 to 11. **Closed:** Sun, Mon, 24 Dec, 31 Dec, 4 to 12 Jun. **Meals:** alc (main courses £14 to £23). Set L £11.50 (2 courses) to £16. Set D (Sat only) £18.95 (2 courses) to £22.50. **Details:** 35 seats. Wheelchair access.

Llanelli

★ READERS' RESTAURANT OF THE YEAR ★
WALES

Sosban
Slick dockside contender
North Dock, Llanelli, SA15 2LF
Tel no: (01554) 270020
www.sosbanrestaurant.com
French | £30
Cooking score: 3

The Victorian engine pumphouse on Llanelli's North Dock has scrubbed up well, emerging as an 'elegant, even grand space' and seen by one visitor as 'a beacon in the darkness of the rest of the county'. Sian Rees has really stamped her mark on the kitchen, with reporters praising pithiviers of pigeon breast interlaid with spiced cabbage, the careful cooking of a Penclawdd shellfish gratin, superb lobster ravioli with shellfish sauce and a beautiful, gamey partridge with braised cabbage, celeriac and chestnuts. Homemade bread is 'very moreish'; the good-value set lunch and desserts such as lemon tart get the thumbs-up; and an all-Welsh cheeseboard might provide the finale. The 'excellent' ambience and 'friendly and helpful' staff also win hearts and minds. More than a dozen wines by the glass, carafe and bottle head a list ordered by style that opens at £15.
Chef/s: Sian Rees. **Open:** all week L 12 to 2.30, Mon to Sat D 6 to 9.30. **Closed:** 25 Dec, 1 Jan. **Meals:** alc (main courses £14 to £23). Set L and D £15 (2 courses) to £17. Sun L £15. **Details:** 90 seats. 80 seats outside. Wheelchair access. Car parking.

Llanfihangel-y-Creuddyn

ALSO RECOMMENDED
▲ Y Ffarmers
Llanfihangel-y-Creuddyn, SY23 4LA
Tel no: (01974) 261275
www.yffarmers.co.uk
Modern British £5 OFF

This charming village pub aims to please all-comers. Outside is glorious countryside; inside, oak floors, a wood-burner, real ales and

a totally relaxed vibe. Esther Prytherch is the amiable front-of-house; Rhodri Edwards runs the kitchen, putting local ingredients to good use in dishes such as game pâté with homemade chutney (£5.50), Penlan pork and apple pie (£9.50) and Ceredigion ribeye steak, with Welsh cheeses and bara brith bread-and-butter pudding bringing up the rear. Wines from £13.50. No food Sun D and Mon.

Nantgaredig

NEW ENTRY
Wright's Independent Food Emporium
Gloriously gutsy favourites at a cheerful deli/café
Nantgaredig, SA32 7NY
Tel no: (01267) 290678
www.wrightsfood.co.uk
Modern British | £12
Cooking score: 1
£30

Up a country lane, Wright's is the kind of spot you seek out rather than happening upon – a place where big flavours and bigger portions rule, and the roles of food store and café cheerfully overlap. Boxes of veg, delectable-looking loaves and a bench groaning with cakes lie right next to customers' mismatched tables and chairs. The rustic mood extends to the kitchen, which delivers a gloriously gutsy, rough-edged take on deli favourites, from a doorstep-sized Welsh rarebit, leek and spicy sausage sandwich (£7) to a stonking chunk of zesty lemon polenta cake (£2.50). Wines (sold from barrels at the back of the room) start at £12 a bottle.
Chef/s: Maryann Wright. **Open:** all week 9 to 7 (11am Sun to Tue, 5pm Sun). **Closed:** 25 and 26 Dec. **Meals:** alc (main courses £5 to £9). **Details:** 40 seats. 8 seats outside. Wheelchair access. Car parking.

Y Polyn

Broad-shouldered regional cooking
Capel Dewi, Nantgaredig, SA32 7LH
Tel no: (01267) 290000
www.ypolynrestaurant.co.uk
Modern British | £33
Cooking score: 3

Way out in the Carmarthenshire sticks, this striking half-timbered building began life as a tollhouse and lively drinking den. There's still plenty of life in the old place, but different times demand a different approach and Y Polyn now trades as an atmospheric *Country Living* pub-restaurant with a good line in broad-shouldered regional cooking. Air-dried Carmarthen ham with celeriac rémoulade is a fixture, but the menu roams freely, taking in smooth fish soup, a salad of skate with fine beans, ratte potatoes and anchovy dressing, thumpingly good free-range pork belly with Puy lentils, and wild sea bass with spinach and salsa verde. To finish, excellent Welsh cheeses vie with the likes of warm pear and frangipane tart. Boisterous Sunday lunches hark back to Y Polyn's former life, but service holds it all together with 'top manners, humour and friendliness'. Wines start at £14.

Chef/s: Susan Manson and Alix Alliston. **Open:** Tue to Sun L 12 to 2 (2.30 Sat and Sun), Tue to Sat D 7 to 9 (6.30 to 9.30 Fri and Sat). **Closed:** Mon. **Meals:** alc (main courses £12 to £17). Set L £12 (2 courses) to £14.50. Set D £26 (2 courses) to £32.50. Sun L £18.50. **Details:** 48 seats. 16 seats outside. Separate bar. Wheelchair access. Car parking.

▌Narberth

The Grove

Assured cooking in an idyllic setting
Molleston, Narberth, SA67 8BX
Tel no: (01834) 860915
www.thegrove-narberth.co.uk
Modern British | £49
Cooking score: 5
£5 OFF ⬛

'Go and eat there now,' urges one repeat customer of The Grove – before everybody else discovers this gastronomic getaway in the rolling Pembrokeshire countryside, being the inference. Chef Duncan Barham has ambition to spare and is building the reputation of this graceful and refined boutique hotel among food-loving weekenders, with his confident, stylish contemporary British cuisine. Barham takes his pick from the best local produce: St Brides Bay crab and Preseli Bluestone lamb for example, supplemented by fresh-as-a-daisy produce from the kitchen garden. From the seasonal carte, highlights have been Brecon red deer with a 'knockout' venison pudding and a 'pineapple textures' dessert that was positively 'crammed with ideas'. A summer tasting menu might reveal tried-and-true combinations such as goats' cheese with beetroot, blood orange and candied pecans or 'surf and turf' (Welsh Black featherblade with Caldey Island lobster) – but rendered with 'cheffy' touches that contribute something new to the conversation. Service is 'attentive and polished' and staff are fully conversant with the impressive globally minded wine list (from £22).

Chef/s: Duncan Barham. **Open:** all week L 12 to 2.30, D 6 to 9.30. **Meals:** Set L £18 (2 courses) to £22. Set D £39 (2 courses) to £49. Sun L £25. Tasting menu £65. **Details:** 60 seats. 30 seats outside. Separate bar. Wheelchair access. Car parking.

Ultracomida

Unpretentious tapas and great charcuterie
7 High Street, Narberth, SA67 7AR
Tel no: (01834) 861491
www.ultracomida.co.uk
Spanish | £20
Cooking score: 2

£30

This hybrid deli/restaurant is almost a foodie theme park. Visitors have to work their way through the well-endowed deli to reach the unpretentious tapas bar with its communal seating. The laid-back space has something of a canteen buzz and regularly plays to a full house − locals packing in for tapas such as grilled courgette with piquillo pepper and rocket leaf salad, chicken in almond sauce, and chorizo cooked in Welsh cider. Some tapas are also offered as a main course: albondigas (meatballs), for example, or prawns cooked in garlic, slow-cooked beef cheeks with a garlic potato purée, and deli plates of cheese and ham. Spanish wines from £11.95. There's another Ultracomida in Aberystwyth (see entry).

Chef/s: Padraig Nallen. **Open:** Mon to Sat 10 to 4.30. **Closed:** Sun, 25 and 26 Dec, 1 Jan. **Meals:** alc (tapas from £3 to £6). Ración options £9 to £10. **Details:** 30 seats.

▌Newport

Cnapan

Home-from-home with excellent ingredients
East Street, Newport, SA42 0SY
Tel no: (01239) 820575
www.cnapan.co.uk
Modern British | £32
Cooking score: 2

£5 OFF ⇔ V

'Always a wonderful welcome,' notes a fan of this 'lovely' restaurant-with-rooms, run by Michael and Judith Cooper for nearly 30 years. Old-fashioned chairs, a Welsh dresser and smart linen set the tone in the dining room, while in the kitchen ('always a quiet and calm area') Judith turns out an array of dishes defined by unfaltering consistency and the best local ingredients, including locally caught sewin (wild sea trout), local lobster and crab dishes. A starter of warm smoked duck breast is enriched by spicy sausage, poached plum and five-spice relish, while mains might offer Welsh lamb cutlets with minted pea purée and salsa verde. For dessert, try the banoffi pie with espresso coffee ice cream. Wines start at £15.
Chef/s: Judith Cooper. **Open:** Wed to Mon D only 6.30 to 9.30. **Closed:** Tue, Christmas through to mid Mar. **Meals:** Set D £26 (2 courses) to £32. **Details:** 35 seats. Separate bar. Wheelchair access. Car parking.

NEW ENTRY
Llys Meddyg

Doing the town proud, with clear flavours and artful presentation
East Street, Newport, SA42 0SY
Tel no: (01239) 820008
www.llysmeddyg.com
British | £33
Cooking score: 3

⇔ V

Snug beneath Carningli mountain (where Saint Brynach reputedly communed with the angels), other-worldly Newport has a dolmen and several bleakly beautiful beaches to its name. Llys Meddyg does the town proud. A proper boutique hotel from its Welsh wool blankets to its wood-burning stove, it breathes casual, modern-rustic style − perhaps with owner Ed wandering in, casually dressed, to exchange pleasantries. Laid-back it may be, but the kitchen doesn't sleep on the job. Expect clear flavours and artful presentation, from 'delectable' mussels in garlic soup with crunchy croûtons to mains such as meltingly good Welsh beef fillet with breaded slow-cooked ox cheek, truffle gnocchi, fennel, shallot and a dark, syrupy jus. Rich chocolate mousse with sticky toffee pudding, rum and pistachio ice cream is typical of the carefully considered desserts. Wines (from a mixed international selection) start at £16.59. See overleaf for details.

Chef/s: Patrick Szenasi. Open: all week D only 6.30 to 9.30. Closed: 2 weeks Jan. Meals: alc (main courses £15 to £24). Details: 40 seats. 40 seats outside. Separate bar. Car parking.

▌Porthgain

NEW ENTRY
The Shed

Homespun seafood cookery by the harbour
Porthgain, SA62 5BN
Tel no: (01348) 831518
www.theshedporthgain.co.uk
Seafood | £28
Cooking score: 1

£30

Lovely and infuriating in equal measure, The Shed occupies a rickety stone building right beside Porthgain harbour. The ingredients could virtually swim into the kitchen. Rustic and homespun, the restaurant collects seafood from its own boats and from local, ethically minded fishermen, and serves it with a genuine smile. Think tiger prawns with garlic butter, proper fish and chips and homemade tiramisu. Things do go wrong (orders not taken, a dish not as described), but somehow you end up loving the place anyway. Best first to mellow yourself with a glass or two of wine, from a sensible international selection starting at £15.50.
Chef/s: Carol Jones. Open: all week L 12 to 3, D 6 to 9. Closed: 1 to 26 Dec. Meals: alc (main courses £16 to £22). Details: 55 seats. 20 seats outside. Car parking.

▌St David's

Cwtch

Hearty, wholesome local food
22 High Street, St David's, SA62 6SD
Tel no: (01437) 720491
www.cwtchrestaurant.co.uk
Modern British | £30
Cooking score: 3

£5 OFF

'Fantastic and innovative local menu of classics and exciting dishes, all washed down with perfect recommended wines in a fabulous, contemporary setting with the kind of service that would make America blush,' is one reader's succinct summary of Cwtch's charms. A stripped-back interior full of exposed stone and beams sets the tone for an unpretentious style of cooking that plunders Pembrokeshire's bulging larder for the likes of Abercastle potted crab with lemon and dill crème fraîche, granary toast and a Brecon vodka shot; local 12-hour roasted pork belly with onion gravy, Trealy Farm black pudding, apple sauce and crackling; or Solva sea bass fillet with braised fennel and Penclawdd cockle and laver bread sauce. This is generous, big-hearted cooking with an eye for the crowd-pleasers – as in a dessert of chocolate pannacotta with salted caramel sauce, caramelised pears and toasted hazelnuts. International wines from boutique wineries start at £15.
Chef/s: Andy Holcroft. Open: all week D only 6 to 9.30. Closed: Sun and Mon (1 Nov to 31 Mar). Meals: Set D £24 (2 courses) to £30. Set early D £20 (3 courses). Details: 50 seats. Wheelchair access.

CHANNEL
ISLANDS

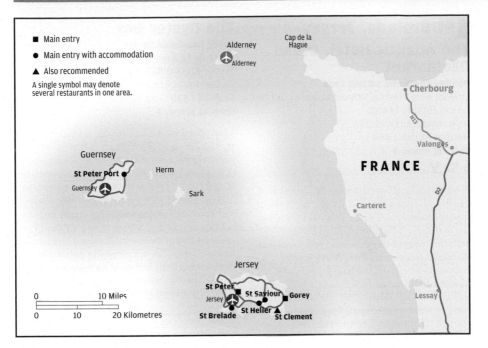

- ■ Main entry
- ● Main entry with accommodation
- ▲ Also recommended

A single symbol may denote
several restaurants in one area.

Alderney

Cap de la Hague

Cherbourg

Valognes

Guernsey

Herm

St Peter Port ●

Guernsey

FRANCE

Sark

Carteret

Jersey

St Peter

Jersey

St Saviour

Gorey

St Brelade

St Helier ▲

St Clement

Lessay

0   10 Miles

0   10   20 Kilometres

▌Gorey, Jersey

Sumas

No question, it's a beautiful spot
Gorey Hill, St Martin, Gorey, Jersey, JE3 6ET
Tel no: (01534) 853291
www.sumasrestaurant.com
Modern European | £34
Cooking score: 3

With terrace tables overlooking the flotilla of
boats bobbing off the east coast of Jersey,
Sumas enjoys a prime location. Neatly clothed
tables and smart glassware set the interior
scene, and in the kitchen Patrice Bouffaut's
mildly Mediterranean approach brings a
restrained sense of invention. The proceedings
might open with 'fabulous' poached oysters
with beurre blanc and cucumber or 'thick,
powerful' shellfish soup ahead of sea bass with
local vegetables and tomato broth – all a
showcase for Jersey produce. Not everything is
flawless: Gressingham duck breast with vanilla
mash, pak choi and blackberry and apples
seems contrived, even out of place, and from

the set-lunch menu fresh grilled plaice has
turned up on a cold salad of Jersey Royals,
green beans and semi-dried tomatoes – the
contrast of hot and cold 'failed to work'. In
contrast, rich lemon tart with honeyed Earl
Grey ice cream has been judged 'phenomenal'.
The thoughtfully compiled international
wine list is fairly priced, from £16.
Chef/s: Patrice Bouffaut. **Open:** all week L 12 to
2.30 (4.30 Sun), Mon to Sat D 6 to 9.30. **Closed:** 21
Dec to mid Jan. **Meals:** alc (main courses £15 to
£25). Set L and D £17.50 (2 courses) to £20. Sun L
£18.50 (2 courses) to £22.50. **Details:** 40 seats. 16
seats outside.

Symbols

🛏 Accommodation is available

£30 Three courses for less than £30

V Separate vegetarian menu

£5 OFF £5-off voucher scheme

🍷 Notable wine list

St Brelade, Jersey
The Atlantic Hotel, Ocean Restaurant
Holiday views and serious food
Le Mont de la Pulente, St Brelade, Jersey, JE3 8HE
Tel no: (01534) 744101
www.theatlantichotel.com
Modern British | £65
Cooking score: 4

🍷 ⇆ V

A boutique hotel overlooking St Ouen's Bay, the Atlantic has a tranquil setting that's also a conservation area. There's golf next door, but the real draw is the Ocean Restaurant, a beautiful room in marine blue and white with shuttered windows, where Mark Jordan elaborates a bells-and-whistles version of modern British cuisine. Dishes include 'sea shore', a tasting of bay-fresh seafood with foraged seaweed, anchovy 'sand' and tomato essence. That might lead to a fish-and-meat main course, such as pan-roast brill partnered by braised oxtail, salsify and wild mushrooms, or a full-on meat preparation like breast and leg of squab pigeon on pear and blue-cheese risotto, with raisin purée, in vanilla jus. Desserts sustain the pace with trending ingredients like tonka and kalamansi and Guanaja chocolate, or a pistachio and olive oil cake garnished with sour cherries and crème fraîche sorbet. The painstakingly crafted wine list (from £17) has runs of clarets and Chablis priced in the stratosphere.
Chef/s: Mark Jordan. **Open:** all week L 12.30 to 2.30, D 6.30 to 10. **Closed:** 2 Jan to 7 Feb.
Meals: Set L £20 (2 courses) to £25. Table d'hôte £55. Set D £65. Sun L £30. Tasting menu £80.
Details: 60 seats. Separate bar. Car parking.

🍴 **Visit us Online**
To find out more about
The Good Food Guide, please visit
www.thegoodfoodguide.co.uk

The Oyster Box
Perky beachside haven
Route de la Baie, St Brelade, Jersey, JE3 8EF
Tel no: (01534) 850888
www.oysterbox.co.uk
Seafood | £30
Cooking score: 3

Unrivalled views, a covetable alfresco terrace and stunning contemporary interiors chime perfectly with the fresh Jersey seafood on offer at this beachside haven. Rock oysters from the Royal Bay of Grouville get special treatment, but the global menu spans everything from sushi rolls to lobster risotto by way of squid a la plancha, cracked Chancre crab salad and grilled fillet of brill with buttered leeks and Jersey Royals. Meat fans might prefer confit duck spring rolls followed by roast loin of rose veal with wild mushroom fettuccine, but dietary preferences are ignored when it comes to desserts such as dark cherry soufflé with white chocolate sauce or coconut crème brûlée with mango, pineapple and red chilli compote. The wide-ranging, carefully chosen wine list kicks off with South African house recommendations from £17, but it's worth exploring the bottles from Jersey's La Mare Estate.
Chef/s: Patrick Tweedie. **Open:** Tue to Sun L 12 to 2.30, all week D 6 to 9.30 (5.45 Fri and Sat). **Closed:** 25 and 26 Dec. **Meals:** alc (main courses £9 to £28). **Details:** 90 seats. 60 seats outside. Separate bar. Wheelchair access.

St Clement, Jersey
ALSO RECOMMENDED
▲ **Green Island Restaurant**
Green Island, St Clement, Jersey, JE2 6LS
Tel no: (01534) 857787
www.greenisland.je
Seafood

Sitting at the top of the slipway, with ravishing views of the sparkling sea, Green Island majors in alfresco dining – though there are tables indoors for the unsunny seasons. The lively, often complex pan-European cooking ranges from apple- and beetroot-cured salmon with herb blinis, crème fraîche and caviar (£9.75), to beef fillet with wild mushrooms, horseradish rösti and cauliflower and blue cheese purée in red wine and veal stock jus (£26.95), with lemon tart to finish, served with clementine and hazelnut trifle and crumbled praline (£6.50). Wines from £15.50. Open Tue-Sat and Sun L.

▮ St Helier, Jersey

Bohemia
Fine-tuned contemporary cooking
The Club Hotel & Spa, Green Street, St Helier, Jersey, JE2 4UH
Tel no: (01534) 876500
www.bohemiajersey.com
Modern European | £59
Cooking score: 6

£5 OFF ╠ V

Tucked behind glass wine displays and sparkling metal railings, glitzy Bohemia might feel like a 'gauche' extension of the Club Hotel's bar, but it sails on regardless – despite changes in the kitchen during 2013. Following a nine-year residency, chef Shaun Rankin has moved on to open Ormer (see entry), but his successor is already dishing up top-drawer food with a real sense of generosity and value – especially when it comes to the little extras that can turn three courses into a veritable flavour-fest. Startling 'canapés' might feature a refreshing Middle Eastern riff built around curried aubergine purée, while pre-dessert could bring an eyebrow-raising combo of cherry sorbet, cherry gel, wheat-beer ice cream and meadowsweet cream. In between, expect 'class on the plate' in the shape of fine-tuned contemporary cooking – from a poached lobster claw dressed with peas, pistachios and deeply savoury pea purée to a trio of pink veal loin, gamey braised shank and 'toasty' sweetbread with onion purée, asparagus and broad beans. To finish, the aforementioned cherries also grace a complex, multi-part chocolate dessert packed with crystal-clear flavours – 'no frivolity, just

thrills' noted one reader. Service is 'just so' (if a little stiff), and the French-accented wine list offers food-friendly drinking from £18.
Chef/s: Steve Smith. **Open:** Mon to Sat L 12 to 2.30, D 6 to 10. **Closed:** Sun, 24 to 30 Dec. **Meals:** Set L £25 (2 courses) to £30. Set D £50 (2 courses) to £59. Tasting menus from £75 (8 courses). **Details:** 58 seats. Separate bar. Wheelchair access. Car parking.

NEW ENTRY

Ormer
Sophistication meets brasserie-style buzz
Don Street, St Helier, Jersey, JE2 4TQ
Tel no: (01534) 725100
www.ormerjersey.com
Modern French | £45
Cooking score: 5

Shaun Rankin's St Helier venture does nothing to hide its light under a bushel. An elongated, double-height frontage with blue shutters and rusted iron tubs of creative topiary shout for attention on the high street. Neither does the expansive dining-room have any truck with beige neutrality, but makes a vivid impression through mustard armchairs against bright blue buttoned banquettes, with lighting from wall-sconces and table-lamps. Rankin's kitchen, somewhere beyond the open illuminated pass, is a modern French enterprise, with many trusted flavour combinations nudged gently into modernity, viz a starter of scallops with curried granola, cauliflower salad, apple caramel and raisins. Roast foie gras with brioche and Sauternes gets a mint oil and pennywort shake-up, while a trio of oysters are delicately cooked and then submerged at table in garlic and parsley soup. The overall balance of a dish is sometimes questionable, as when a 'furiously savoury' accompaniment of barley, seaweed, aubergine and lamb (a kind of retooled moussaka) reduces a piece of poached turbot to the blandness of egg-white. Confidence is perhaps more inspired by a main of Goosnargh chicken with buckwheat, pine-nut muesli, pickled shimejis and salted popcorn. Desserts have been exemplary, from an unimprovable take on treacle tart with clotted-cream ice cream, to a triple-layered chocolate mousse with milk ice and salted caramel. A properly enterprising wine list suits the mood of excitement, with plenty of serious French product, but some imaginative buying outside Europe too. It starts at £18, with glasses from £5.

Chef/s: Shaun Rankin. **Open:** Mon to Sat L 12 to 2.30, D 6.30 to 10. **Closed:** Sun, 25 Dec. **Meals:** alc (main meals £22 to £29). Set L £19 (2 courses) to £24. Set D £30 (3 courses). **Details:** 50 seats. 20 seats outside. Separate bar. Wheelchair access. Car parking.

Tassili

Headline restaurant at a luxury spa hotel
Grand Jersey, The Esplanade, St Helier, Jersey, JE2 3QA
Tel no: (01534) 722301
www.grandjersey.com
Modern European | £49
Cooking score: 4

£5 OFF 🛏 V

A spa, a Champagne lounge and views of St Aubin's Bay are just some of the selling points at the luxe Grand Jersey hotel. The hotel's headlining Tassili restaurant – an intimate, peach-toned space – provides an understated setting for Richard Allen's creative contemporary cooking. If the dazzling marinated foie gras with smoked Creedy Carver duck doesn't appeal, try a luxurious Jersey lobster Caesar salad with shellfish jelly and Ebène caviar. Next, keep it local with lemon sole meunière, sea vegetables, poached langoustines, mussel and orzo broth or head inland for a two-part dish of rabbit embellished with crispy boudin noir, celeriac purée, gnocchi and more besides. Desserts give the kitchen free rein: witness an oriental kaleidoscope of caramelised banana, satay ice cream, green tea foam, lime jelly and sesame brittle. Also check out the 'latitude and longitude' menu, devoted to island produce. Wine flights are carefully managed and the serious list contains impeccable producers – particularly from France and Italy. Prices start at £16.95.

Chef/s: Richard Allen. **Open:** Fri and Sat L 12 to 2, Tue to Sat D 7 to 10. **Closed:** Sun, Mon, first 2 weeks Jan. **Meals:** Set L £18.95 (2 courses) to £24.95. Set D £40 (2 courses) to £49. Tasting menu £67 (6 courses) to £87 (9 courses). **Details:** 25 seats. Separate bar. Wheelchair access. Car parking.

ALSO RECOMMENDED

▲ The Green Olive

1 Anley Street, St Helier, Jersey, JE2 3QE
Tel no: (01534) 728198
www.greenoliverestaurant.co.uk
Mediterranean

'Passion on a plate' is the motto at this funky little first-floor restaurant overlooking St Helier's town centre, and chef/proprietor Paul Le Brocq proves the point with a menu of bright Mediterranean dishes based largely on Jersey produce. Dips, salads and risottos are mainstays, but the kitchen's eclectic output also runs from hand-dived scallops on cauliflower cheese, curry oil, pea shoots and pancetta dust (£8.95) to chicken burgers with beetroot slaw and green olives (£13.95). House wine is £16.95. Closed Sat L, Sun and Mon.

▮ St Peter Port, Guernsey

La Frégate

Stunning seascapes and complex cooking
Beauregard Lane, Les Cotils, St Peter Port, Guernsey, GY1 1UT
Tel no: (01481) 724624
www.lafregatehotel.com
Modern British | £38
Cooking score: 4

🛏

Sitting on its hill gazing loftily over the town and harbour, La Frégate presents a thoroughly modern vision of a luxury hotel, with stunning white interiors overlooking the marine views and a pretty terraced garden. The kitchen makes a valiant attempt to cover all bases, with an extensive carte, prix-fixe deals at lunch and dinner, a vegetarian menu and fish specials from the island catch, served with your choice of sauce – hollandaise, béarnaise, Champagne, lobster or chive butter. Otherwise, go Japanese with an opener of sea bass and salmon sashimi with marinated scallops, accompanied by wasabi and pickled ginger, before rack of lamb with smoked bacon rösti and braised shallots in port jus. To end with a flourish, crêpes suzette for two is set alight at the table, or there may be classic apple tarte fine with vanilla ice cream, or local and continental cheeses. House French is £20, or £6 a glass.

Chef/s: Neil Maginnis. **Open:** all week L 12 to 2, D 7 to 10. **Meals:** alc (main courses £20 to £25). Set L £17.50 (2 courses) to £22.50. Set D £33.50. Sun L £23.50. **Details:** 70 seats. 20 seats outside. Car parking.

ALSO RECOMMENDED
▲ Da Nello
46 Lower Pollet, St Peter Port, Guernsey, GY1 1WF
Tel no: (01481) 721552
www.danello.gg
Italian £5 OFF

The sea-blue frontage blends in well in the capital of Guernsey; the building, which dates from 1450, was once the principal defensive gateway to the port. These days, it hosts a vibrant Italian-oriented restaurant that's big on fresh seafood and classic dishes. Extensive menus take in avocado crab garnished with apple and grapes (£8.45), veal, spinach and mushroom cannelloni, beef medallions in Barolo cream sauce (£18.10), and chocolate-espresso brûlée with mandarin sorbet (£6.25). Wines from £15.95. Open all week.

||| Also Recommended
Also recommended entries are not scored but we think they are worth a visit.

■ St Peter, Jersey
Mark Jordan at the Beach
Down-to-earth venue, crowd-pleasing brasserie dishes
La Plage, La Route de la Haule, St Peter, Jersey, JE3 7YD
Tel no: (01534) 780180
www.markjordanatthebeach.com
Modern British | £35
Cooking score: 4

Mark Jordan's residency at the Atlantic Hotel (see entry, St Brelade) is supplemented by a more down-to-earth venue a little way along the seafront from St Helier. It's a vibrantly pinkish-red job on the outside, its windows filled with nautical trinkets. Inside, a pleasantly casual ambience reigns in the form of sturdy beechwood tables, wicker chairs and beach-themed artwork. Staff set a professional but relaxed tone that inspires confidence. Crowd-pleasing brasserie dishes with plenty of seafood are the bill of fare, from burgers and fishcakes to fried whitebait, grilled lobsters and Caesar salad. Good oysters come on a bed of mash, dressed in a thin beurre blanc, while main might deliver a wonderful plaice, cooked on the bone and dressed with fat cockles, prawns, capers, gherkins, croutons and a ton of butter. With a side of Royals on a summer's day, it's Jersey on a plate. Finish with enjoyable coconut crème brûlée and passion fruit sorbet, garnished with chunks of caramelised pineapple. The wine list in its plastic wallet could do with a bit more vim, the glass options especially boring. Prices start at £19.

Chef/s: Mark Jordan and Karl Tarjani. **Open:** all week L 12 to 2.30, D 6 to 9.30. **Closed:** Jan. **Meals:** alc (main courses £15 to £35). Set L £19.50 (2 courses) to £24.50. Set D £27.50 (3 courses). Sun L £29.50. **Details:** 50 seats. 30 seats outside. Separate bar. Car parking.

▌St Saviour, Jersey

Longueville Manor

A special place
St Saviour, Jersey, JE2 7WF
Tel no: (01534) 725501
www.longuevillemanor.com
Modern British | £58
Cooking score: 4

⟲ V

A lavishly decorated Norman manor house standing in 15 acres, Longueville has been surveying the Jersey scene since at least the 14th century. With its ornamental fountain, arched stone entrance and immaculately attired staff, it's a deeply impressive operation. Andrew Baird is now in his third decade heading the kitchen. As befits the Channel Island location, the cuisine is a harmonious amalgam of French and English cookery, using plenty of local materials (including vegetables and herbs from the kitchen garden). A typical route through the wide-ranging menus might be to start with langoustine tortellini in a truffle-perfumed spring array of baby leeks and peas, and then move on to roast best end and braised shoulder of Loch Erne lamb, served with potato gratin and artichokes in oregano jus. The gariguette strawberries are not to be missed when in season. Languedoc Chardonnay and Merlot at £25 open the bidding on an extensive wine list featuring plenty by the glass.

Chef/s: Andrew Baird. **Open:** all week L 12 to 2, D 6 to 10. **Meals:** Set L £22.50 (2 courses) to £27.50. Set D £50 (2 courses) to £57.50. Sun L £37.50. Tasting menu £75. **Details:** 90 seats. 35 seats outside. Separate bar. Car parking.

⊓⦶ HOME CHEESEMAKING

A fresh wave of home cooks are taking self sustainability to a new level by making their own cheese, and finding the process is not as complicated as it sounds.

The simplest cheese to make yourself is paneer, which can be made within an hour and requires only warmed whole milk and a few drops of lemon juice to form the curds. Once strained and pressed, the resulting firm-yet-crumbly blocks can be lightly fried and served in curries or salads. Add salt, plus a little chilli or fennel at the straining stage, for variation of flavour.

Other soft cheeses like ricotta or Boursin are equally simple, requiring few ingredients and little effort. Although these cheeses can take up to 24 hours to make, they are mightily satisfying when spread on crusty bread or stirred into pasta.

High street stores like Lakeland now sell starter kits, and there are many online retailers offering a variety of cultures, rennet, moulds and recipe books that are useful if you want to work your way up to harder cheeses like Camembert or mozzarella.

NORTHERN
IRELAND

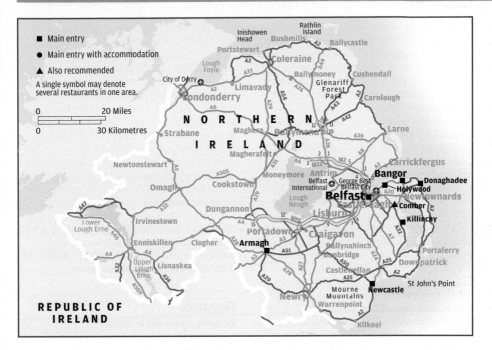

■ Armagh, Co Armagh
Uluru Bistro

An Aussie-in-Armagh experience
16 Market Street, Armagh, Co Armagh, BT61 7BX
Tel no: (028) 3751 8051
www.ulurubistro.com
Australian | £30
Cooking score: 2

V

'The quality of the food is consistently excellent, the atmosphere welcoming and lively' – that's the verdict of one regular who has been eating at this informal Antipodean-owned Armagh city bistro since it opened nine years ago. Despite the Australian connection, Northern Irish produce is the cornerstone of the kitchen here. Local seafood has star billing in dishes such as seared scallops with crispy pressed pork belly, buttered garden peas, cauliflower purée and beurre blanc sauce. Also well received has been an 'amazing' rolled shoulder of goat with spinach mash, wild mushrooms, red wine and thyme jus. Rose-water poached rhubarb and oranges, homemade honeycomb and vanilla ice cream is a typical dessert. House wine £15.
Chef/s: Dean Coppard. **Open:** Tue to Sat L 12 to 3, Tue to Sun D 5 to 9 (10 Fri and Sat, 8.30 Sun).
Closed: Mon, 25 and 26 Dec, 30 Dec to 2 Jan.
Meals: alc (main courses £17 to £24). Early D £16.95 (2 courses). **Details:** 32 seats. 8 seats outside. Separate bar. Wheelchair access.

■ Bangor, Co Down
The Boat House

Idiosyncratic harbourside gem
1a Seacliff Road, Bangor, Co Down, BT20 5HA
Tel no: (028) 9146 9253
www.theboathouseni.co.uk
Modern British | £35
Cooking score: 6

£5 OFF

An enchanting location by the Marina is only one of the assets of the Castel brothers' idiosyncratic enterprise. It's housed in the mid-Victorian harbourmaster's office, a tiny stone-

built edifice, blue-lit by night. Surprisingly, three dozen covers (and a few outside tables) are accommodated in the whitewashed, tiled and vaulted space, where a thrum of contentment prevails. Elder brother Joery is the chef, and cooks in the modern technological idiom that mixes local ingredients and international avant-garderie. You might open with a serving of glazed carrots, accompanied by Crozier Blue cream, pickled carrot, carrot meringue and a hemp-seed and carrot crisp, as well as cocoa-nibs, white chocolate and toasted hazelnuts. That could lead on to Glenarm salmon in potato sauce with frozen grapes and cardamom hollandaise, or breast of goose in liquorice and currant jus with puréed Jerusalem artichokes. A lemon tartlet comes with sweet yoghurt, thyme jelly, preserved blood-orange, raspberry and Champagne sorbet and poppy seeds. Such complex dishes deserve complex wines, and you can find them on a list that opens with Loire Chenin and California Zinfandel/Barbera at £17.50.
Chef/s: Joery Castel. **Open:** Wed to Sat L 12.30 to 2.30, D 5.30 to 9.30, Sun 1 to 8. **Closed:** Mon, Tue. **Meals:** alc (main courses £16 to £24). Set L £20 (2 courses) to £25. Set D £21 (2 courses) to £25. Tasting menu £50 (5 courses) to £70. **Details:** 36 seats. 8 seats outside. Car parking.

▌Belfast, Co Antrim

The Bar & Grill at James Street South
A casual offshoot with a Josper grill
21 James Street South, Belfast, Co Antrim, BT2 7GA
Tel no: (028) 9560 0700
www.belfastbargrill.co.uk
Modern British | £25
Cooking score: 3
£30

Housed in part of a previously derelict Victorian linen mill, the Bar & Grill opened in 2011 as a more informal offshoot of Niall McKenna's James Street South (see entry). It makes a casual setting, with its stylish first-

floor private dining room, top-floor cookery school and a ground-floor dining room complete with on-trend exposed brickwork, cool sea-blue panelling and sumptuous leather banquettes. Locally sourced steaks cooked with precision over charcoal are the focal point here, served with a choice of eight classic sauces. Otherwise, unashamedly retro starters of prawn cocktail or Caesar salad might be followed by crab and chilli linguine, confit pork belly with red cabbage or whole sea bass cooked on the Josper grill. Leave room for the chocolate brownie sundae. The intelligently designed, contemporary wine list starts at £15 a bottle (£4.25 a glass).
Chef/s: Carl Johannsen. **Open:** all week 12 to 10. **Closed:** 25 and 26 Dec, Easter Sun, 12 July. **Meals:** alc (main courses £10 to £23). **Details:** 55 seats. Separate bar. Wheelchair access.

Deanes
Versatile upmarket brasserie
36-40 Howard Street, Belfast, Co Antrim, BT1 6PF
Tel no: (028) 9033 1134
www.michaeldeane.co.uk
Modern European | £40
Cooking score: 5
V

Michael Deane's ubiquitous presence in Belfast gastronomy is thoroughly benign, and never more so than at this south Belfast brasserie, founded in 1997. The ambience is infectiously buzzy, with a bare-board floor and clothed tables making a nice contrast, and the walls sporting an appetising shade of russet. Staff are proficient and caring, and Simon Toye's brasserie menus offer resourceful pan-European ways with regional ingredients. A shellfish appetiser might set the ball rolling, perhaps a scallop or an oyster or two, before starters bring on roast squab with celeriac and spinach in Madeira, or salmon cured in beetroot and horseradish with sourdough bread. An eclectic approach to fish might see sea bass and clams turn up with Japanese mushrooms and crisped Parma ham in a soy dressing, while meats include local chicken cooked with morels and thyme, accompanied by a little onion tarte fine. Good counterpoints of flavour and texture are seen in a dessert of baked passion fruit custard with coconut sponge, passion fruit sorbet and coconut meringue. A page of seasonal wine suggestions heads an enterprising list, with bottles from £19.50, glasses £5.50.

Chef/s: Simon Toye. **Open:** Mon to Sat L 12 to 3, D 5.30 to 10. **Closed:** Sun, 25 to 26 Dec, 1 Jan, Easter Mon, 12 Jul. **Meals:** alc (main courses £14 to £28). **Details:** 100 seats. Wheelchair access. No children after 7pm in restaurant

Il Pirata

Casual 'small plates' Italian
279-281 Upper Newtownards Road,
Ballyhackamore, Belfast, Co Antrim, BT4 3JF
Tel no: (028) 9067 3421
Italian | £18
Cooking score: 3
£30

The style remains the same, but you can now book a table at Il Pirata – a casual city venue that prefers modish Italian small plates to trencherman trattoria helpings of spag bol or pizza margherita. Chunky wooden tables, dangling lamps and rather clinical white-tiled walls set the tone, while the menu kicks off with a fistful of cichetti snacks (perhaps confit squid with chilli, or roast onions with balsamic and mint), before trundling through assorted gnocchi, salads, risottos and bigger servings of fritto misto, pork saltimbocca or sea bass with roasted plum tomatoes and salad verde. Pasta also gets a look in, while desserts are standards such as tiramisu or Amaretto pannacotta. Drink Peroni beer, Maddens Irish cider or one of the Italian regional wines from £11 a carafe. The owners also run Coppi, another 'small plates' Italian on St Anne's Square, Talbot Street, Belfast BT1 2LD, tel: (028) 9031 1959.

Chef/s: Jonny Phillips. **Open:** all week 12 to 10 (11 Fri to Sun). **Closed:** 25 and 26 Dec. **Meals:** alc (main courses £9 to £15). **Details:** 80 seats. 10 seats outside. Wheelchair access. Car parking.

James Street South

Serious cooking at accessible prices
21 James Street South, Belfast, Co Antrim,
BT2 7GA
Tel no: (028) 9043 4310
www.jamesstreetsouth.co.uk
Modern European | £30
Cooking score: 6

If every great city needs a proper grown-up restaurant, James Street South is more important than ever to the fabric of Belfast. Gentle but constant evolution keeps Niall McKenna's assured, 'inviting' restaurant in the upper echelons. Following the successful addition of the Bar & Grill (see entry) in the other half of the old linen mill, there's now a cookery school, too. The contemporary dining room, with colourful modern art on white walls, makes a fine setting for serious French-inflected food. A sensible effort to remain accessible keeps prices reasonable given the amount of skill on display. Local ingredients get the classical treatment in dishes such as Lough Neagh smoked eel with horseradish cream, apple, raisin and truffle dressing, and readers love the pasta – perhaps herb and ricotta tortellini with butternut squash. Mains might be Tyrone venison with celeriac, beetroot, turnip, pear and red wine. Reports are particularly glowing when it comes to a dessert of chocolate and hazelnut crunch with Frangelico and Kirsch. Staff are 'attentive and knowledgeable', and wines start at £16.

Chef/s: Niall McKenna. **Open:** Mon to Sat L 12 to 2.45, D 5.45 to 10.45. **Closed:** Sun, 25 and 26 Dec, 1 Jan, 12 Jul, Easter Mon. **Meals:** alc (main courses £16 to £22). Set L £15.50 (2 courses) to £18.50. Set D £22.50 (2 courses) to £26.50. **Details:** 60 seats. Separate bar. Wheelchair access.

Molly's Yard

Unpretentious bijou bistro
1 College Green Mews, Botanic Avenue, Belfast, Co
Antrim, BT7 1LW
Tel no: (028) 9032 2600
www.mollysyard.co.uk
Modern British | £28
Cooking score: 2
£5 £30
OFF

Owned by pioneering Irish microbrewery
Hilden, who also run the Tap Room on the
Lisburn site where they make their beer,
Molly's Yard sits in a converted Victorian stable
in a courtyard off Botanic Avenue. Its beyond-
bijou dining room, built around a bar that
features those Hilden brews on tap, is an
exercise in rustic simplicity. The unpretentious
and reasonably priced bistro menu (the only
choice at lunch) sits alongside a marginally
more elaborate dinner menu that always
includes a simply prepared fish of the day.
Don't leave without trying the wheaten bread
made with chocolate stout, or having a look at
the dessert menu: the puddings and the Irish
cheese selection are a highlight here.
Chef/s: Ciarán Steele. **Open:** Mon to Sat 12 to 9
(9.30 Fri and Sat). **Closed:** Sun, 24 to 26 Dec, 1 Jan,
12 Jul. **Meals:** alc (main courses £15 to £23). Set D
£22.50 (2 courses) to £27.50. Pre and post theatre
Set D £15.50 (2 courses) to £18.50. **Details:** 55 seats.
20 seats outside. Wheelchair access.

Mourne Seafood Bar

Local seafood hero
34-36 Bank Street, Belfast, Co Antrim, BT1 1HL
Tel no: (028) 9024 8544
www.mourneseafood.com
Seafood | £25
Cooking score: 3
V £30

A big-city spin-off from the original in
Dundrum, Co Down, this branch of Mourne's
is easily found next to Belfast boozing legend
Kelly's Cellars. Inside, it's as traditional as can
be, with exposed brickwork and lots of dark
wood – plus an on-site fishmonger's and
cookery school to ram home the culinary

point. Eat in the street-level bar or the
swankier upstairs dining room from a menu
that majors in mussels, cockles and oysters
from the owners' beds in Carlingford Lough.
As well as bivalves every which way, you can
feast on daily consignments of seafood from
Annalong and Kilkeel. Well-tried classics (fish
fingers, for instance) sit alongside intriguing
daily specials such as prawn and chorizo
risotto with saffron butter or organic salmon
fillet with spicy aubergine relish and Tuscan
fries. 'The kitchen really knows its way
around,' noted one reader. Cocktails are a treat,
and fish-friendly wines start at £15.
Chef/s: Andy Rea. **Closed:** 24 to 26 Dec, Easter Sun
and Mon. **Meals:** alc (main courses £9 to £20).
Details: 80 seats. Separate bar. Wheelchair access.

★ TOP 50 ★

NEW ENTRY
OX

Creative cooking with vegetables taking centre
stage
1 Oxford Street, Belfast, Co Antrim, BT1 3LA
Tel no: (028) 9031 4121
www.oxbelfast.com
Modern European | £30
Cooking score: 6
£5
OFF

OX opened in April 2013 and immediately
softened the blow for Belfast restaurant-goers
of losing the long-running standard-bearer
that was Paul Rankin's Cayenne in the same
month. That the cooking, which takes a
modern approach to Ulster's fine larder of
produce, is of such a high standard will not
come as a surprise to anyone that came across
co-owner and head chef Stephen Toman when
he was in the kitchen at James Street South,
where he worked for Niall McKenna for a
decade (see entry). What's more surprising
about OX, located in what was an old tile shop
overlooking the river Lagan and the
Waterfront Centre, is that there's a freshness
and confidence to the whole proposition. The
stripped back, Scandinavian-style interior
benefits from high ceilings, lots of natural
light and handsome chairs reclaimed from a

church ('where the congregation must have sat comfortably'). The other co-owner is French front-of-house Alain Kerloc'h, an accomplished veteran of the Belfast restaurant scene, whose wine list is both adventurous and well-priced (offering tasters of wine in 7cl measures as well as by the glass and the carafe is a clever move). But it's Toman's creative cooking, with its emphasis on vegetables over animal protein in dishes such as Lough Neagh perch, basil gnocchi, mussel and tomato, and sweetbreads served with Comber carrots, wilted chicory, pearl barley and nettles, that is the star of the show.
Chef/s: Stephen Toman. **Open:** Tue to Sat L 12 to 2.30, D 6 to 9.30. **Closed:** Sun, Mon, 6 to 22 Jul. **Meals:** alc (main courses £16 to £22). Set L £13 (2 courses) to £16. Set D £24 (2 courses) to £30). Pre-theatre £20. **Details:** 40 seats. Wheelchair access. Car parking.

The Potted Hen
Lively contemporary bistro
11 Edward Street, Belfast, Co Antrim, BT1 2LR
Tel no: (028) 9023 4554
www.thepottedhen.co.uk
Modern European | £25
Cooking score: 3
 £5 OFF £30

Set under beautiful colonnades in St Anne's Square, this handsomely appointed bistro has established itself as a lively addition to Belfast's Cathedral Quarter. Inside, slate floors, iron struts and high ceilings create a laid-back, contemporary vibe, while the kitchen deals in up-to-the-minute flavours for city appetites. Homemade gnocchi and risottos provide some seasonal Mediterranean warmth, and the grill is also used to telling effect — try the Belfast ale-brined pork belly with roast shallots, creamy mash and spring cabbage. Otherwise, the menu spans everything from Ibérico ham salad with poached pear and salted walnuts to spiced monkfish fritters with skinny chips and curried celeriac rémoulade. There's also a colourful edge to desserts such as coconut and pineapple cheesecake with honeycomb, hazelnuts and pineapple purée.

Wines from £16.95. The Hen's owners also run Oregano at 29 Ballyrobert Road, Ballyrobert, Co Antrim; tel: (028) 9084 0099.
Chef/s: Dermot Regan. **Open:** Mon to Sat L 12 to 2.45, D 5 to 9.30 (10 Fri and Sat). Sun 12 to 9. **Closed:** 24 to 26 Dec, 1 and 3 Jan, 11 to 13 Jul. **Meals:** alc (main courses £14 to £18). Early D £15.95 (2 courses) to £17.95. Sun £18.95 (2 courses) to £21.95. **Details:** 120 seats. 40 seats outside. Wheelchair access. Car parking.

ALSO RECOMMENDED
▲ The Ginger Bistro
7-8 Hope Street, Belfast, Co Antrim, BT12 5EE
Tel no: (028) 9024 4421
www.gingerbistro.com
Modern European

A cheerful, cosy bistro where the kitchen has fun with Asian fusion flavours, but doesn't underestimate the value of good old comfort food. Simon McCance's cooking is imaginative yet unpretentious, described in plain English and cooked 'without fuss'. Fried squid with chilli sauce and garlic mayonnaise (£7.50) is a popular start, then sparklingly fresh cod fillet with crab risotto, garlic crab claws and asparagus (£17), finishing with sticky toffee pudding (£5.25). House wine £16. Closed Mon L and Sun.

▲ Little Wing
10 Ann Street, Belfast, Co Antrim, BT1 4EF
Tel no: (028) 9024 7000
www.littlewingpizzeria.com
Italian

This central Belfast outpost has arguably become the flagship for what is now a clever of quartet of pizza parlours, which includes two more branches in Belfast and another in the seaside suburb of Bangor. The formula is simple: Little Wing is open all-day, serving affordably priced, good quality, Naples-style pizzas (from £5.95) in a fun, timber-trimmed, diner-style setting with friendly service and, invariably, a quality soundtrack of classic rock on the stereo. The pizza averse can turn to simple pasta dishes such as lasagne

(£8.25), pesto fusilli (£7.25) or a chicken Caesar salad. The no-nonsense wine list starts at £14.95 a bottle.

Comber, Co Down

ALSO RECOMMENDED
▲ The Old Schoolhouse Inn
100 Ballydrain Road, Comber, Co Down, BT23 6EA
Tel no: (028) 9754 1182
www.theoldschoolhouseinn.com
Modern British £5 OFF

In a placid setting beside Strangford Lough, Will Brown's restaurant-with-rooms has been fashioned out of the former Ballydrain school. Its dining room, with burgundy walls and smart table settings, makes a sophisticated setting for some inventive modern dishes. Sea bass with mussels, cockles and samphire, alongside a scallop and crab mousse in beurre blanc (£8), is a busy starter, and might precede duck breast cooked in hay with a croustillant of the leg, braised red cabbage and cherries in jus gras (£19.50). Finish with chocolate délice with cocoa soil and mandarin foam (£5.50). Wines from £17.95. Open all week.

Donaghadee

NEW ENTRY
The Governor Rocks
Generous portions of fantastic fish and seafood
27 The Parade, Donaghadee, BT21 0HE
Tel no: (028) 9188 4817
www.thegovernorrocks.com
Seafood | £24
Cooking score: 3
£5 OFF £30

A recent arrival to the pretty seaside town of Donaghadee, on the north-east coast of the Ards Peninsula, the Governor Rocks is the second outpost of chef Jason More, who already runs the likeable central Belfast bistro CoCo. Its unpretentious dining-room does shabby-chic via mismatched furniture, antique mirrors of many shapes and sizes and nautical bric-a-brac brightening the walls. Although there's always a sirloin steak on the menu to appease the fish-a-phobic, given its setting overlooking the harbour the focus here is, understandably, on seafood. Expect generous portions of crab claws, fish pie, simply grilled hake or lobster served with garlic butter and fantastic chips – a triple-fried crunch on the outside and a perfect fluffy centre. Originally a BYO, the short serviceable wine list starts at £13.95.
Chef/s: Jason More and Conal Boyle. Open: Mon to Sat L 12 to 3, D 5 to 10, Sun 12 to 8. Meals: alc (main courses £10 to £20). Set L and D £15 (2 courses) to £20. Sun L £10. Details: 120 seats. Wheelchair access. Car parking.

Holywood, Co Down

The Bay Tree
Quirky quality café
118 High Street, Holywood, Co Down, BT18 9HW
Tel no: (028) 9042 1419
www.baytreeholywood.co.uk
Modern British | £20
Cooking score: 2
£30

The Bay Tree is, at heart, an all-day café, opening in time to feed work-bound punters on its famous cinnamon scones, and providing simple, sustaining lunch dishes in a down-to-earth ambience of plain white walls and tiled floor. On Friday nights only a full-scale dinner menu of Irish bistro cooking comes into play (book early!), offering the likes of Guinness-battered scampi with pea purée, pork medallions stuffed with pickled walnuts served with Savoy cabbage and baby onions in cider cream, and blackberry and ginger pudding with hot toffee sauce to finish. A single-page wine list starts from £13.50 (£3.75 a glass) for Chilean Sauvignon and Merlot.
Chef/s: Sue Farmer. Open: all week 8 to 3 (9 Sat, 10 Sun), Fri D 5.30 to 9.30. Closed: 25 and 26 Dec, 12 and 13 Jul. Meals: alc (main courses £10 to £17). Details: 60 seats. Car parking.

Killinchy, Co Down

★ READERS' RESTAURANT OF THE YEAR ★
NORTHERN IRELAND

Balloo House

Classy old coaching inn
1 Comber Road, Killinchy, Co Down, BT23 6PA
Tel no: (028) 9754 1210
www.ballooinns.com
Modern British | £22
Cooking score: 3
£30

Conviviality rules at this sturdy ex-farmhouse and old coaching inn, where the ground floor bar-bistro-pub has a kind of self perpetuating liveliness. Chef Danny Millar is in charge of food both here and in the more formal, intimate restaurant, Upstairs at Balloo. The two have local ingredients in common – crab and 'prawns' from nearby Strangford Lough, for example – and while Upstairs delivers winning dishes such as wild duck Wellington with braised red cabbage, roast apple, parsnips and potato gratin, it's the robust, rustic bistro food served downstairs that really shines. Try devilled kidneys with toasted brioche and bacon and mushroom cream, followed by simple Strangford crab linguini with parsley and lemon butter and the much-loved sticky toffee pudding with Bushmills butterscotch sauce. Wines from £14.95.
Chef/s: Danny Millar and Grainne Donnelly. **Open:** all week 12 to 9 (8.30 Mon and Tue, 9.30 Fri and Sat). **Closed:** 25 Dec. **Meals:** alc (main courses £7 to £19). Set L £12.95 (2 courses) to £16.95. Set D £13.95 (2 courses) to £17.95. Set Sun L £21.95. **Details:** 70 seats. 15 seats outside. Separate bar. Wheelchair access. Car parking.

Newcastle, Co Down

Vanilla

Local classics meet exotic fare
67 Main Street, Newcastle, Co Down, BT33 0AE
Tel no: (028) 4372 2268
www.vanillarestaurant.co.uk
Modern British | £29
Cooking score: 3
£30

Not far from the promenade where, as the old song goes, 'the Mountains of Mourne sweep down to the sea', Darren Ireland's 'cosy, friendly' bistro is a breath of fresh air. His kitchen pulls together international flavours in a colourful menu that runs from Thai quail Scotch egg with curry risotto to homely herb-crusted lamb rump with ratatouille, smoked aubergine purée and goats' cheese gnocchi. Ingredients are local where possible, and some are home-grown. 'Super value lunches' include 'excellent' sandwiches (maybe gammon and Cheddar with rocket and onion marmalade), while early evening diners could feast on falafel salad and local seafood pie for just £14.95. Desserts include favourites like the 'delicious and not too heavy' sticky toffee pudding, but Ireland also gives his creative streak free rein – as in an apple and vodka parfait with lime sorbet and whiskey fudge. A modest list of popular wines starts at £13.95.
Chef/s: Darren Ireland. **Open:** all week L 12 to 4 (3.30 Mon to Wed), D 5 to 9 (6 Fri and Sat, 8.30 Sun). **Closed:** 25 and 26 Dec. **Meals:** alc (main courses £14 to £22). Set L and D 14.95 (2 courses) to £18.95. **Details:** 40 seats. 6 seats outside. Separate bar. Wheelchair access.

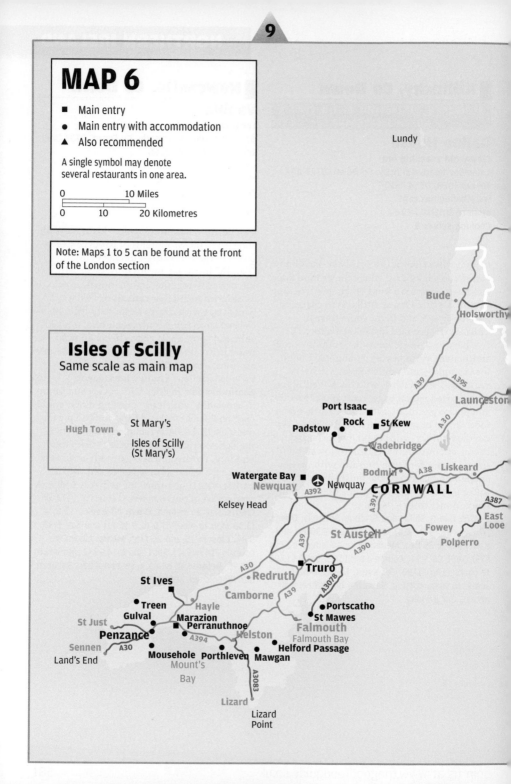

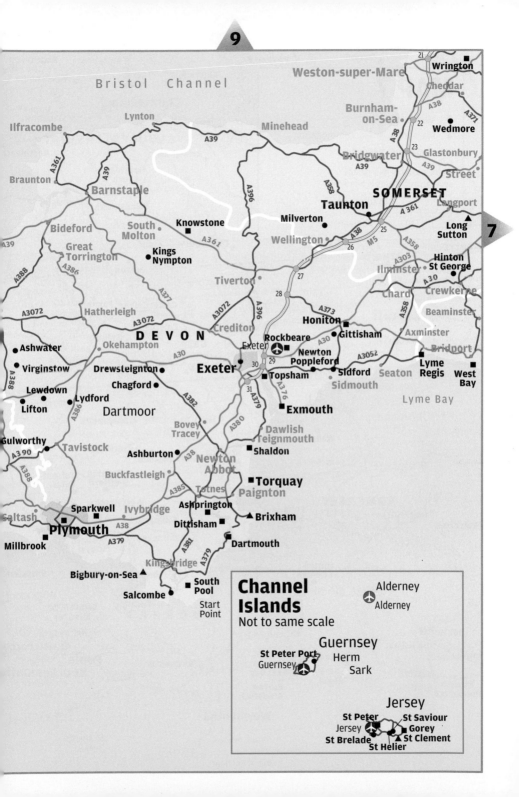

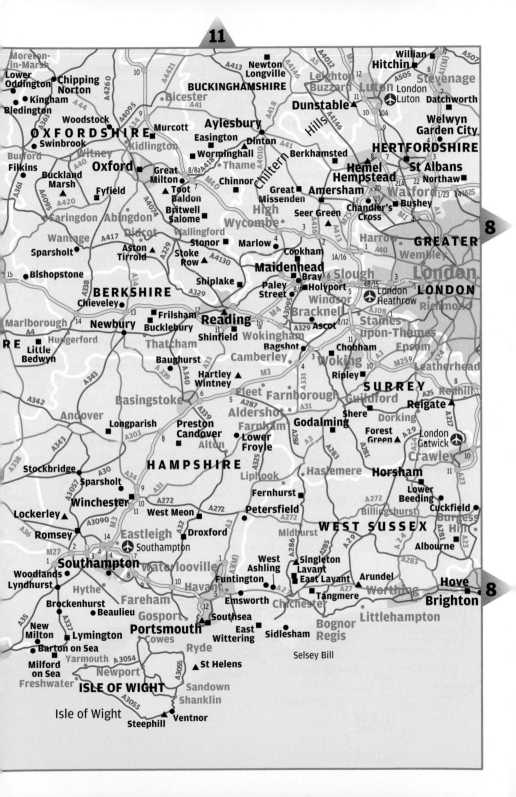

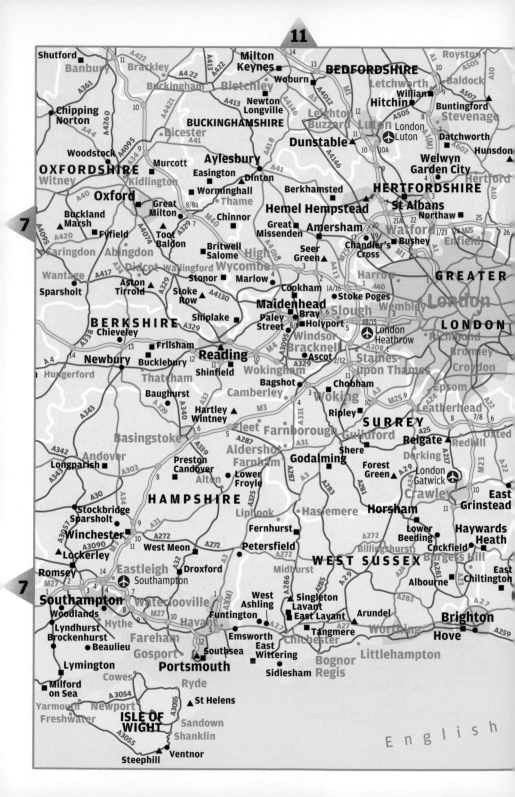

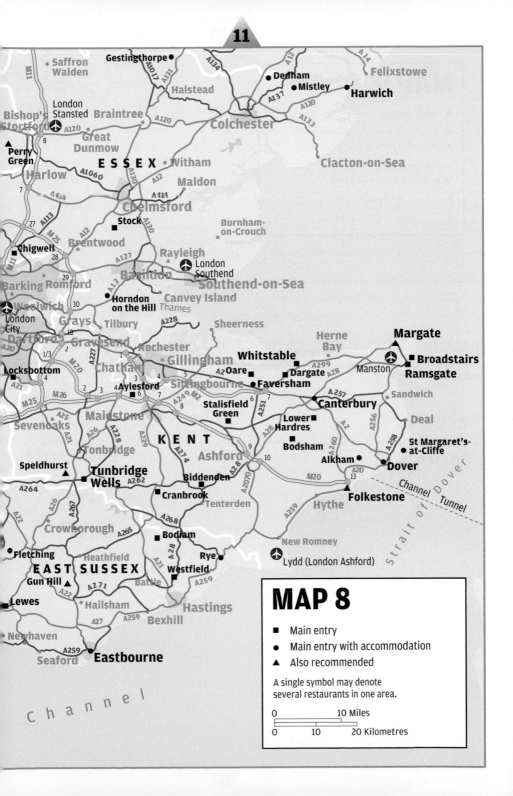

11

MAP 8

- ■ Main entry
- ● Main entry with accommodation
- ▲ Also recommended

A single symbol may denote several restaurants in one area.

0   10 Miles

0   10   20 Kilometres

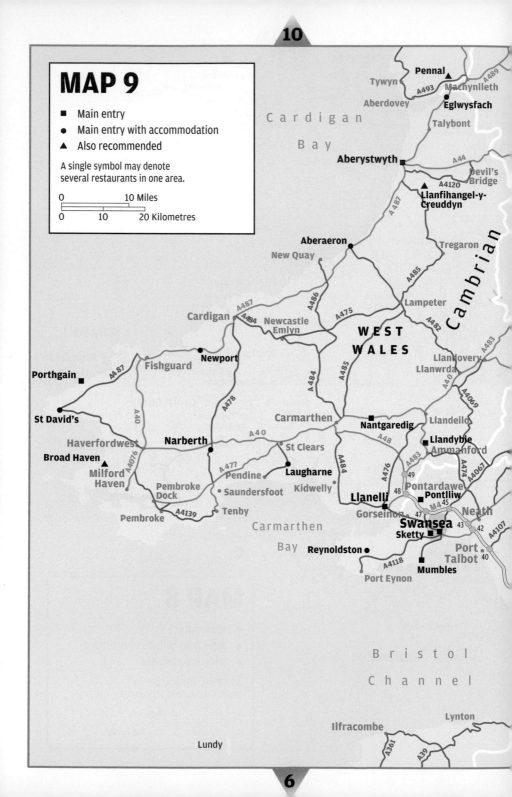

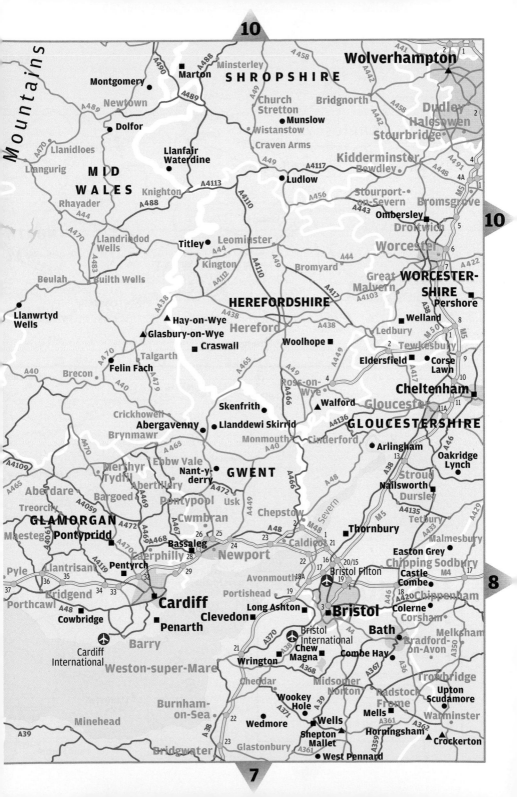

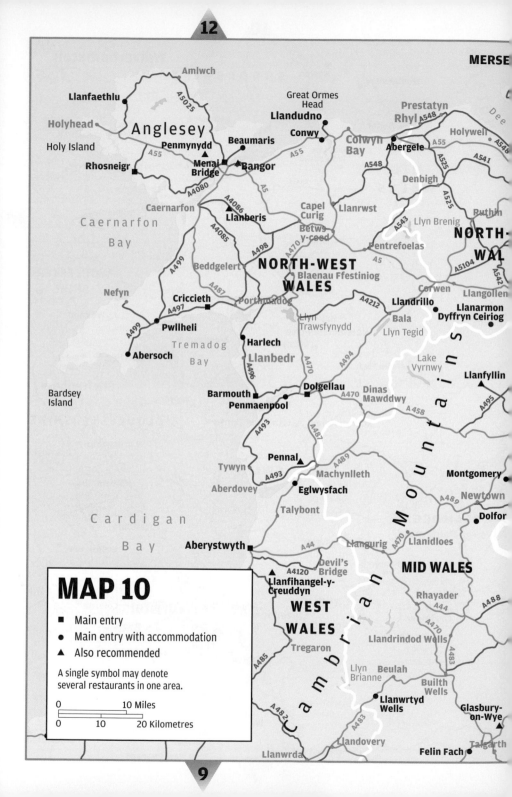

12

MERSE

MAP 10

- ■ Main entry
- ● Main entry with accommodation
- ▲ Also recommended

A single symbol may denote
several restaurants in one area.

0   10 Miles

0   10   20 Kilometres

Llanfaethlu
Holyhead
Holy Island
Rhosneigr
Amlwch
Anglesey
Penmynydd
Menai Bridge
Beaumaris
Bangor
Great Ormes Head
Llandudno
Conwy
Colwyn Bay
Abergele
Prestatyn
Rhyl
Holywell
Denbigh
Ruthin
NORTH-WAL
Caernarfon
Caernarfon Bay
Llanberis
Capel Curig
Betws-y-coed
Llanrwst
Llyn Brenig
Pentrefoelas
Beddgelert
NORTH-WEST WALES
Blaenau Ffestiniog
Corwen
Llangollen
Nefyn
Criccieth
Porthmadog
Llandrillo
Bala
Llyn Tegid
Llanarmon Dyffryn Ceiriog
Pwllheli
Llyn Trawsfynydd
Harlech
Llanbedr
Lake Vyrnwy
Llanfyllin
Abersoch
Tremadog Bay
Barmouth
Penmaenpool
Dolgellau
Dinas Mawddwy
Bardsey Island
Pennal
Tywyn
Aberdovey
Machynlleth
Eglwysfach
Talybont
Montgomery
Newtown
Dolfor
Cardigan Bay
Aberystwyth
Llangurig
Llanidloes
MID WALES
Devil's Bridge
Llanfihangel-y-Creuddyn
WEST WALES
Rhayader
Cambrian Mountains
Llandrindod Wells
Tregaron
Llyn Brianne
Beulah
Builth Wells
Llanwrtyd Wells
Glasbury-on-Wye
Llandovery
Felin Fach
Talgarth
Llanwrda
Dee

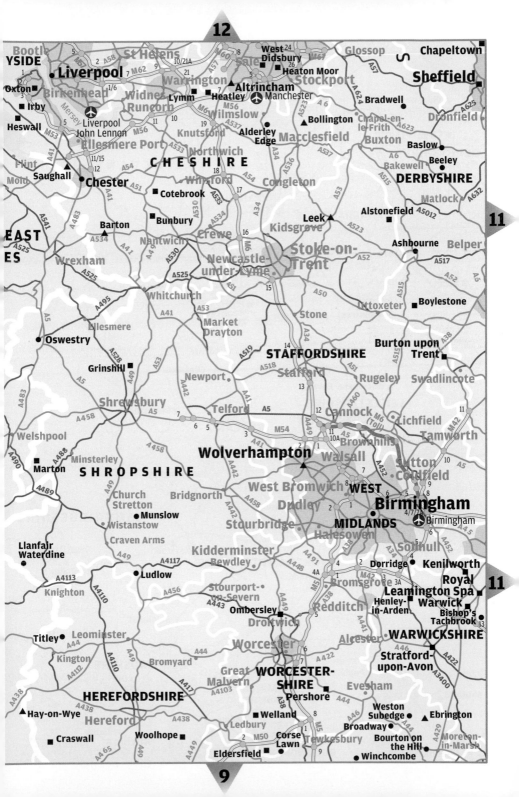

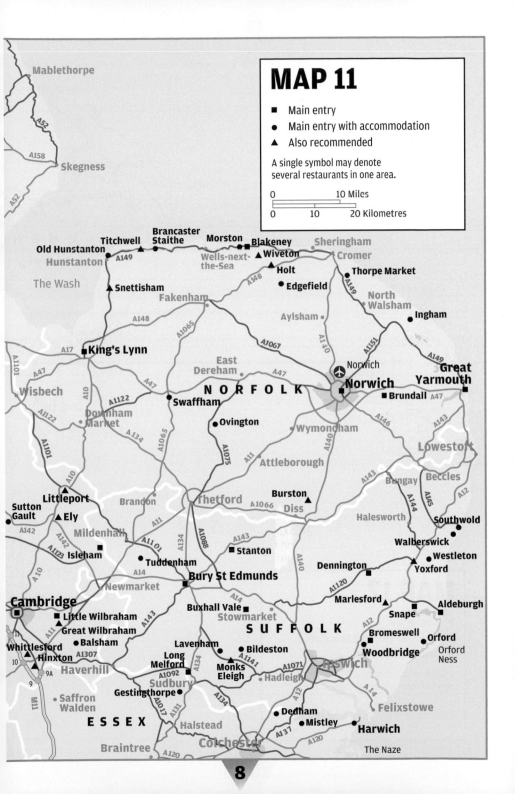

MAP 11

- Main entry
- Main entry with accommodation
- Also recommended

A single symbol may denote
several restaurants in one area.

0   10 Miles

0   10   20 Kilometres

Mablethorpe

A52

A158

Skegness

A52

The Wash

Old Hunstanton
Hunstanton
A149

Titchwell

Brancaster
Staithe

Morston
Wells-next-
the-Sea

Blakeney
Wiveton
Holt

Sheringham
Cromer

Thorpe Market

A149

Snettisham

Fakenham

A148

Edgefield

North
Walsham

Ingham

A148

A1065

Aylsham

A140

A151

A149

A17

King's Lynn

East
Dereham

A1067

Norwich

Great
Yarmouth

A1101

A47

A47

NORFOLK

Norwich

A47

Wisbech

A10

A1122

Swaffham

Brundall

A47

A143

A1122

Downham
Market

A134

A1065

Ovington

Wymondham

A146

Lowestoft

A1101

A10

A1075

A11

Attleborough

A140

Beccles

A143

Bungay

A145

A12

Littleport

Sutton
Gault

Ely

Brandon

Thetford

A1066

Burston

Diss

Halesworth

A144

Southwold

A142

A142

Mildenhall

A1101

A134

A1088

A143

Stanton

A140

Walberswick

Westleton

Yoxford

A1123

Isleham

Tuddenham

A14

Dennington

Newmarket

Bury St Edmunds

A1120

Marlesford

Aldeburgh

A10

Cambridge

Little Wilbraham
Great Wilbraham

Buxhall Vale
Stowmarket

A143

SUFFOLK

A14

Snape

Bromeswell

A12

Orford

Whittlesford
Hinxton

Balsham

A1307

Lavenham

Long
Melford

A134

Bildeston

A1141

Woodbridge

Orford
Ness

10

Haverhill

A1092

Monks
Eleigh

A1071

Ipswich

A14

9A

Sudbury

Gestingthorpe

A1017

A131

A134

Hadleigh

A12

Felixstowe

M11

Saffron
Walden

Dedham

Mistley

Harwich

ESSEX

Halstead

A137

A120

Braintree

A120

Colchester

The Naze

8

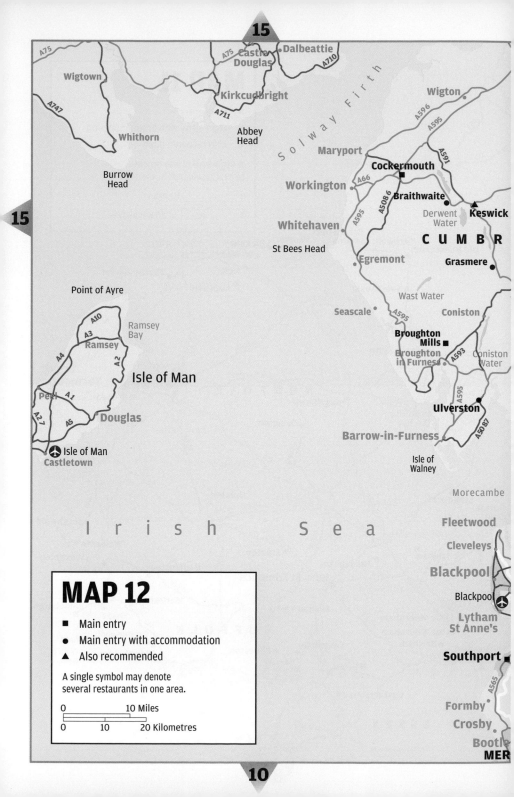

MAP 12

- ■ Main entry
- ● Main entry with accommodation
- ▲ Also recommended

A single symbol may denote
several restaurants in one area.

0   10 Miles
0   10   20 Kilometres

A75

Wigtown

A747

Whithorn

Burrow
Head

Point of Ayre

A10

A3

Ramsey
Bay

Ramsey

A4

A2

Isle of Man

Peel

A1

A27

A5

Douglas

Isle of Man
Castletown

Castle
Douglas

A75

Dalbeattie

A710

Kirkcudbright

A711

Abbey
Head

Solway Firth

Maryport

Cockermouth

Workington

A66

Braithwaite

A5086

Whitehaven

A595

A5086

Derwent
Water

Keswick

C U M B R

Grasmere

St Bees Head

Egremont

Wast Water

Seascale

A595

Coniston

Broughton
Mills

Broughton
in Furness

A593

Coniston
Water

A595

Ulverston

A5087

Barrow-in-Furness

Isle of
Walney

Irish   Sea

Morecambe

Fleetwood

Cleveleys

Blackpool

Blackpool

Lytham
St Anne's

Southport

A565

Formby

Crosby

Bootle

MER

Wigton

A596

A595

A591

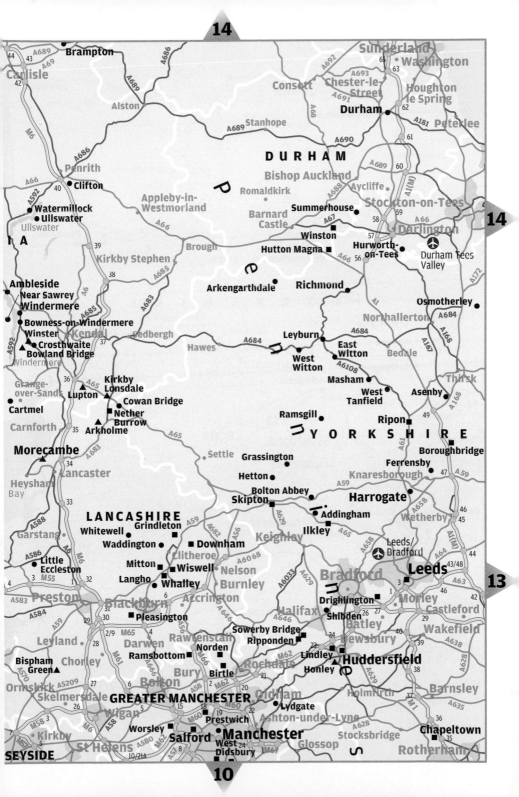

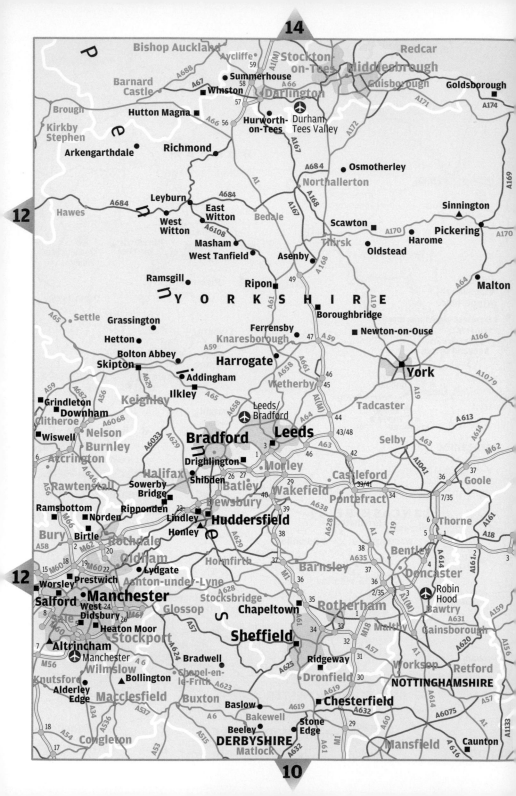

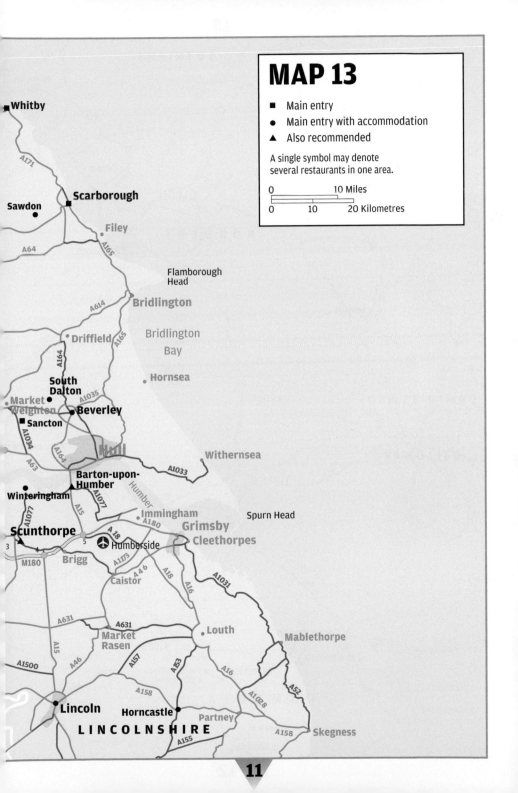

MAP 13

- ■ Main entry
- ● Main entry with accommodation
- ▲ Also recommended

A single symbol may denote
several restaurants in one area.

```
0                    10 Miles
0        10        20 Kilometres
```

■ Whitby

A171

Sawdon ●

■ Scarborough

● Filey

A64

A165

Flamborough
Head

A614

Bridlington

● Driffield

A165

Bridlington
Bay

A164

● Hornsea

South
Dalton

A1035

● Market
Weighton

● Beverley

■ Sancton

A1034

A164

Hull

A63

Withernsea

A1033

Barton-upon-
Humber

▲

Humber

● Winteringham

A1077

A1077

A15

Immingham

A180

Spurn Head

A1077

Scunthorpe

A18

Grimsby

3

▲

4

5

⊕ Humberside

Cleethorpes

M180

Brigg

A1173

A46

A18

Caistor

A16

A1031

A631

A631

Louth

Mablethorpe

Market
Rasen

A15

A46

A157

A153

A16

A52

A1500

A158

A1028

● Lincoln

Horncastle ●

Partney

A158

Skegness

LINCOLNSHIRE

A155

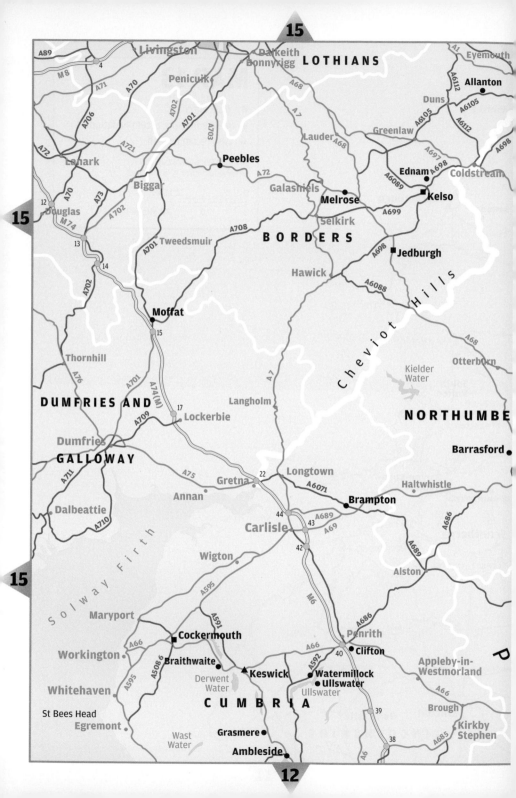

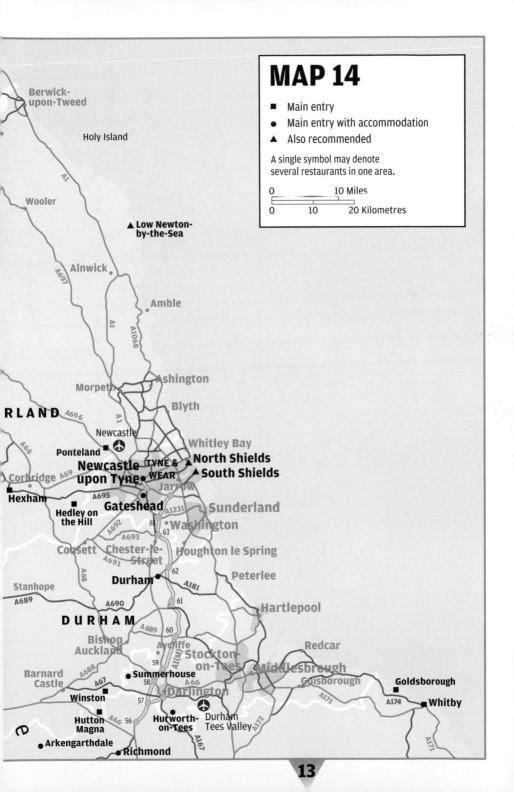

MAP 14

- ■ Main entry
- ● Main entry with accommodation
- ▲ Also recommended

A single symbol may denote
several restaurants in one area.

0   10 Miles

0 10 20 Kilometres

Berwick-upon-Tweed

Holy Island

Wooler

▲ Low Newton-by-the-Sea

Alnwick

Amble

Morpeth

Ashington

RLAND

Blyth

Newcastle

Ponteland

Whitley Bay

Newcastle upon Tyne

TYNE & WEAR

North Shields

▲ South Shields

Corbridge

Hexham

A695

Jarrow

Hedley on the Hill

Gateshead

Sunderland

Washington

Consett

Chester-le-Street

Houghton le Spring

Stanhope

Durham

Peterlee

A689

DURHAM

Hartlepool

Bishop Auckland

Aycliffe

Redcar

Barnard Castle

Summerhouse

Stockton-on-Tees

Middlesbrough

Guisborough

Goldsborough

Winston

Darlington

A174

Whitby

Hutton Magna

Hutworth-on-Tees

Durham Tees Valley

Arkengarthdale

Richmond

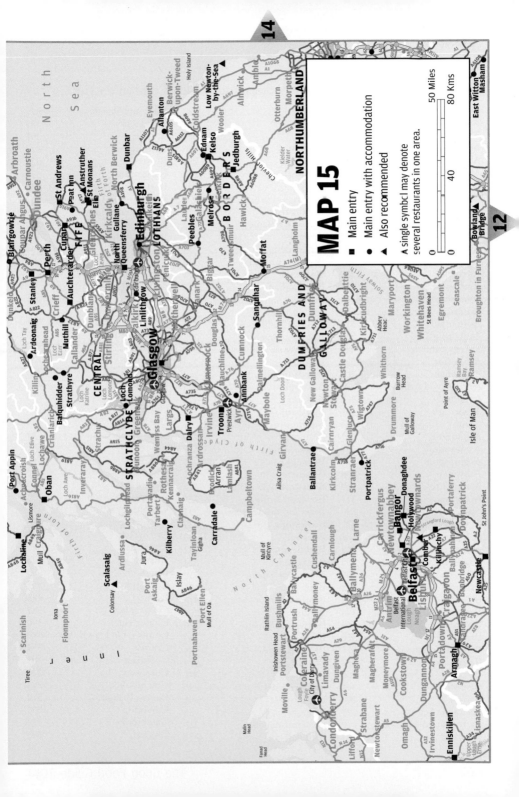

Note: The INDEX BY TOWN does not include London entries.

Features

Chef Interviews (alphabetically by surname)

The Good Food Guide 2014

Special Thanks

We would like to extend special thanks to the following people:

Kirstie Addis, Hilary Armstrong, Iain Barker, Ruth Coombs, Tom Fahey, Tessa Fox, Tim Goodson, Alan Grimwade, Phil Harriss, Ben Kay, Bill Knott, Jeffrey Ng, Laura Nickoll, Tom Roberts, John Rowlands, Emma Sturgess, Kerenza Swift, Mark Taylor, Stuart Walton, Jenny White, Gemma Wilkinson, Blanche Williams and Jane Wilson.

And an extra-special thanks to all of our hard-working inspectors.

This book couldn't have happened without a cast of thousands. Our thanks are due to the following contributors, among many others.

Dr Ian Aaronson
Mr Bimbi Abayomi-Cole
Mr John Abbey
Mr Neil Abbott
Mr Phil Abbott
Mr Gregory Abouna
Ms Alexandra Abrahams
Dr Ed Abrahamson
Mr John Abrook
Mrs Sally Ackerman
Mr Rob Adair
Miss Zoe Adamson
Miss Liz Addison
Miss Navneet Addy
Mr Nik Adhia
Mr Bill Adie
Miss Laura Agnew
Miss Catherine Ahern
Mrs Anke Ahmed
Mr Forhad Ahmed
Miss Asia Ahuja
Miss Mhairi Aikman
Mr John Aird
Mr John Aitken
Mrs Kay Akast
Mrs Janet Akers
Miss Taybah Akhtar
Mrs Catherine Aland
Mr Paul Albert
Miss Kirsty Alderson
Mr Tom Alderson
Mr David Alderton
Mr Neil Alderton
Ms Amy Aldred
Mr Mick Aldred
Mrs Jean Alen
Mr Douglas Alexander
Mr Gavin Alexander
Miss Caroline Allan
Mr John Allan
Miss Karan Allan
Mrs Ann Allen
Mr David Allen
Mr James Allen
Mr Jon Allen
Mr Michael Allen
Mrs Ruth Allen
Mr Simon Allen
Mr Tim Allen
Miss Hazel Allinson
Mr Seraphim Alvanides
Mrs Nicola Alvin-Smith
Mrs Angela Ambrose
Miss Ranna-Dey Amin
Miss Rupa-Dey Amin
Mr Lorraine Amos
Mrs Charlotte Anderson
Mr Joseph Anderson
Ms Susan Anderson
Mrs Kate Anderson-Glover
Mr Donald Andrews
Mr Michael Andrews
Ms Rachel Andrews
Mr Sebastian Anstey
Mr Mark Appalegate
Mr Emma Arakelova
Mrs Nicola Archer
Mrs Thelma Archer
Mr Graham Archibald
Mr Paul Argent
Mr Craig Armitage
Mr Peter Armour
Mrs Claire Armstrong
Mrs Debra Armstrong
Miss Gillian Armstrong
Mr Joe Armstrong
Miss Jemma Armytage
Miss Charlotte Arnold
Miss Jane Arnold
Mr Peter Arnold
Mrs Yvonne Arpino
Mr Michael Ashdown
Mr Michael Ashley

Miss Marie Ashpool
Mr Atom Asllani
Mr Gordon Astbury
Mr Mark Astbury
Dr Mark Aston
Mr John Asty
Ms Sarah Atcherley
Mr Chris Atherton
Mr Paul Atkins
Mr Brian Atkinson
Mr Christopher Atkinson
Mrs Jacqueline Atkinson
Mr Peter Atmore
Mrs Nikolina Attwood
Mr Christoph Auer
Mr Colin Avery
Dr Michael Awty
Mrs Michele Backer
Mrs Morag Bagley
Mr Christopher Baigent
Mr Bruce Bailey
Mrs Jenny Bailey
Mrs Debbie Baillie
Dr Nadia Bainbridge
Mr James Baird
Ms Linda Baird
Mr Michael Baird
Ms Robin Baird
Mrs Geraldine Bakelmun
Mr Alan Baker
Mr James Baker
Mrs Karen Baker
Mrs Mary-Louise Baker
Ms Niki Baker
Mr Stuart Baker
Ms Talya Baker
Mr Tony Bakinowski
Ms Urszula Balakier
Mr Phil Baldasera
Mrs Julia Balderstone
Mrs Heather Bamford
Mr Tim Bamford
Miss Jodie Bamforth
Mr Andrew Bamji
Ms Silvana Bandini
Mr Stephen Banks
Mr Michael Bannister
Mrs Jane Banton
Miss Bal Banwait
Miss Natalie Barber
Mrs J Bardsley
Mr Neil Barker
Mrs Nicholette Barker
Mrs Alison Barlow
Ms Anne Barlow
Mr Eric Barlow
Mr Ian Barnard
Mr David Barnes
Miss Debbie Barnes
Mrs Frankie Barnes
Mr Ian Barnes
Mrs Lita Barnes
Mr Andrew Barnett
Mr John Barnett
Mr Tim Barney
Mr Brian Barr
Mr Jon Barr
Miss Emma Barraclough
Mr Anthony Barrall
Mrs Jane Barranes
Miss Gemma Barratt
Mr Rod Barrett
Mrs Lesley Barrie
Dr Chris Barry
Mrs Jane Barry
Dr Buz Barstow
Dr Chloe Barter
Miss Catherine Bartlett
Mr Mike Bartlett
Miss Helena Bartley
Mr Andrew Barton
Mrs Dowana Barton
Mrs Karen Barton
Mr Martin Bashall

Mrs Nicola Bashall
Dr Tina Basi
Ms Sue Bastin
Ms Nayanika Basu
Mrs Catherine Bateman
Miss Natalie Batten
Mrs Jan Battrick
Mr Sydney Bayley
Mr Conrad Bayliss
Ms Lesley Beach
Mrs Daphne Beagrie
Mr Neil Beagrie
Mr Derek Beale
Mr Martin Bean
Mrs Penny Bean
Mrs Emma Beard
Mr Jo Beard
Miss Kate Beard
Mrs Louise Beardsworth
Mr Simon Bearryman
Mrs Wilma Beaton
Mr Donald Beattie
Mrs Liz Beauvoisin
Ms Allison Bechtloff
Mr Tim Beck
Mrs Ali Beckett
Mrs Heather Beckett
Mr Joe Beckett
Miss Amanda Beckwith
Miss Felicity Beddoes
Mr Martin Bedford
Mr Michael Bedford
Mrs Brenda Beech
Mrs Jane Beer-Jones
Miss Charlotte Beeson
Mr Shoki Begum
Mrs Janet Belcher
Mrs Joanna Belfield
Mrs Emma Bell
Dr Joanne Bell
Mr Michael Bell
Mr Wally Bell
Mr William Belton
Mrs Jane Benbow
Mr Ken Benbow
Ms Kate Bendix
Mr Darren Benedetto
Mr Darrell Benge
Mr Toby Benjamin
Mrs Anita-Dian Bennett
Mrs Camilla Bennett
Mrs Elizabeth Bennett
Mr Keith Bennett
Mrs Rhona Bennett
Mr Steve Bennett
Mrs Valerie Bennett
Mr Desmond Benning
Mrs Anne Benson
Mr Paul Benton
Mr Mike Benzimra
Miss Kate Bergel
Ms Erika Bernstedt
Mr Paul Bestall
Mr Michael Beswetherick
Mr Nicky Bevan
Mr Philip Bevan
Mr Alistair Beveridge
Mr Joe Beveridge
Mr Sean Beveridge
Ms Leah Bevington
Mrs Brita Bevis
Miss Kate Bex
Mrs Christine Beyga
Ms Karishma Bhalla
Ms Sonal Bhatt
Miss Alison Bicker
Miss Kat Bickmore
Miss Joanna Biddolph
Mr Gary Biggin
Mrs Laura Bignell
Mrs Josephine Bigwood
Mr Mark Billington
Mr Anthony Bingham
Miss Jo Bingham
Mrs Tracey Binns

Miss Emma Birch
Miss Lianne Birkett
Miss Kirsty Birse
Mr John Birtwell
Ms Annie Bishop
Mrs Marilyn Bishop
Miss Lyndsey Bittles
Mr Mark Bixter
Miss Kathy Black
Miss Natasha Black
Mrs Valerie Black
Mrs Sarah Blackwell
Mr Iain Blair
Mr Keith Blake
Mrs Pat Blake
Mr Peter Blake
Mr Enrique Blanco
Miss Katie Bland
Mrs Andy Bleasdale
Mr Stephen Block
Mr Dan Bluett
Miss Juliette Blum
Mr Andrew Blundell
Mrs Maria Blundi
Mr Matthew Blyth
Mr Peter Boardman
Miss Rebecca Boast
Miss Emma Boddington
Mrs Lyssa Bode
Mr Michal Bohanes
Mrs Julie Boland
Miss Johanna Bolhoven
Mrs Abi Bolter
Mr Matthew Bonnaud
Mrs Faith Bonner
Mr Neil Bontoft
Mrs Kathryn Boog
Mrs Denise Boom
Mr John Boon
Mr Tim Boon
Dr Ben Booth
Mrs Tracey Booth
Ms Cristina Borbilau
Ms Monika Borkowska
Dr Peter Borrows
Mr Tim Bostwick
Dr David Bosworth
Miss Anisa Bottrill
Mr Nicholas Bouckley
Mrs Sasha Boundy
Mrs Sally Bourn
Mr Mike Bourne
Ms Wendy Bourton
Mrs Gemma Bowcock
Miss Gillian Bowden
Miss Hattie Bowden
Mrs Isabelle Bowden
Mr Nick Bowden
Ms Lorraine Bowen
Mrs Wendy Bowen
Mrs Jennifer Bowers
Mrs Anna Bowes
Mrs Anita Bowman
Mrs Claire Bowman
Mrs Tatty Bowman
Miss Alice Bowyer
Miss Sophie Boyce
Mr Will Boyce
Mrs Diana Boyd
Mr Val Boyle
Mr Anthony Bradbury
Mrs Victoria Bradbury
Mrs Emma Bradder
Mr Harvey Braddock
Miss Gail Bradford
Mr Barry Brahams
Mr Bernard Brandon
Ms Jane Branley
Mr Craig Brannigan
Mr Ramon Bravo
Miss Jennifer Bray
Mrs Mary Bray
Mr Peter Breese
Ms Elizabeth Jane Bremner
Ms Annette Brennan

Mrs Helen Brennan
Mr Adam Brenner
Mr Ciaran Breslin
Mrs Maureen Brettell
Mr Ian Brewer
Mr Geoffrey Bridge
Mr Andrew Briers
Mr Alec Briggs
Miss Charlotte Briggs
Mr Peter Briggs
Mrs Sarah Briggs
Mr Robert Bright
Mr Clive Brightwell
Mrs Celia Brigstocke
Mr Tim Brigstocke
Miss Rachael Bristow
Mr Julian Britton
Mrs Susan Broadbent
Mr Michael Broadhurst
Mrs Leila Broadwater
Mrs Margaret Brobbin
Mr Francois Brocard
Mrs Rosemary Brocklehurst
Mr Andrew Brodie
Mrs Sasha Brompton
Mrs Jayne Brooke
Mr David Brookes
Mrs Kath Brookes
Dr Natalie Brookes
Mrs Polly Brookes
Ms Christina Brooks
Miss Deborah Brooks
Miss Sophie Brooks
Mr Paul Broome
Ms Theresa Brosnan
Mr Mark Broster
Mr Peter Broster
Mr Sarah Broughton
Mr Jasper Browell
Mr Alan Brown
Ms Ana Brown
Mr Andy Brown
Mr Christopher Brown
Mrs Deborah Brown
Mrs E Brown
Miss Emily Brown
Mrs Jayn Brown
Mr John Brown
Mr Keith Brown
Mr Kevin Brown
Mr Mally Brown
Miss Megan Brown
Mr Michael Brown
Mr Mitchell Brown
Miss Nikki Brown
Mr Paul Brown
Mrs Susan Brown
Mr Trevor Brown
Mrs Viven Brown
Mrs Barbara Brown
Mr Tim Browning
Dr Jacqueline Broxton
Mr Steven Bruce
Mr Stewart Bruce
Mrs Carolyn Bruce-Spencer
Miss Sophie Bruschan
Mr Derek Bryan
Miss Laura Bryans
Mrs Pauline Bryant
Mrs Ruth Bryant
Mrs Elizabeth Buchanan
Mrs Patricia Buckingham
Mr Alan Buckley
Mr Russell Buckley
Ms Lorna Bugeja
Miss L Bugsel
Mrs Carole Bullock
Mr Paul Bulteel
Mr David Bunce
Ms Emily Bunce
Mrs Abigail Bunney
Mr Jonathan Burden
Ms Nicki Burford

Mr Richard Burger
Mrs Alexandra Burgess
Mrs Katherine Burgess
Mr Simon Burke
Mr John Burley
Mrs Jane Burnett
Mrs Amanda Burnie
Mrs Claire Burnside
Mrs Kate Burr
Mr Richard Burridge
Mr Colin Burrows
Mrs Margaret Burrows
Mr William Burrows
Mrs Karen Burton
Ms Amy Buscombe
Ms Georgina Bush
Mr John Bustard
Mrs Barbara Butler
Mr Sean Butler
Miss Talwinder Buttar
Mr J M Butterfield
Mrs Hannah Butterworth
Mr Kenneth Buxton
Mrs Judith Byrne
Ms Simone Byrne
Ms Heather Cairncross
Mr Alan Cairns
Mrs Angie Callan
Mr Jonathan Calland
Mr Brian Cameron
Mrs Constance Cameron
Mr Donald Camilleri
Dr Tiziana Camilleri
Mrs Laura Campbell
Ms Linda Campbell
Mrs Lucy Campbell
Mr Rory Campbell
Mrs Wendy Campbell-Rice
Mr Anthony Campry
Mrs Sandra Cape
Mrs Rosalyn Caplan
Miss Zoe Caplan-Hill
Mr Phillip Cardwell
Mr Rob Carey
Mrs Stephanie Carey
Mrs Gilly Carliell
Mrs Felicity Carlton
Mrs Christine Carnegie-Brown
Mr Damian Carr
Ms Lesley Carr
Mrs Joanna Carreras
Mr James Carrier
Mr John Carroll
Mrs Rebecca Carroll
Dr David Carter
Mrs Sally Carter
Miss Susie Carter
Mr Tony Carter
Mrs Sarah Cartland
Mr Nigel Cartwright
Miss Vicky Cartwright
Mr Mike Carwithen
Mrs Judith Casey
Mr Peter Casey
Mr Alan Cassells
Mrs Sylvie Cassez
Ms Alexia Casson
Mrs Rachel Caswell
Mrs Harriet Cater
Mrs Amanda Cattrall
Miss Holly Cave
Mrs Judy Cave
Miss Anna Cavell
Miss Elizabeth Chadwick
Mrs Sue Chadwick
Miss Zoe Chadwick
Mr Will Chaloner
Mr Ajay Champaneri
Mrs Shikainah Champion-Samuel

Miss Candy Chan
Mr Stephen Chand
Miss Debbie Chapman
Ms Kim Chapman
Mrs Laurain Chapman
Mrs Lorraine Chapman
Mr Peter Chapman
Dr Robert Chapman
Mr Robin Chapman
Mr Simon Chapman
Ms Stephanie Chappell
Mrs Sarah Chapple
Mrs Charlotte Charlesworth
Mr Steve Charman
Mr Robert Charmer
Mrs Sue Charnley
Miss Kate Chartres
Mr Sarathi Chatterjee
Ms Roxanne Chavasse
Mrs Jean Cheesman
Mr David Chester
Mr David Chesters
Mrs Angelina Chik
Mr Timothy Childs
Mr Richard Chinnock
Ms Antonia Chitty
Mr David Chivers
Mr Jaspal Chowdhary
Mrs Chris Chubb
Miss Joanna Chubb
Miss Nina Claridge
Mr Jimmy Clark
Dr Jonathan Clark
Mr Martin Clark
Miss Melissa Clark
Mrs Penny Clark
Mrs Catherine Clarke
Mrs Jane Clarke
Mr Jeremy Clarke
Miss Rachael Clarke
Mr Richard Clarke
Mrs Sandra Clarke
Mrs Susan Clarke
Mrs Diana Clarkson
Mrs Sarah Clay
Mr Mark Clayson
Miss Emma Clayton
Mr George Clayton
Mrs Lesley Clayton
Mrs Mary Clayton
Mrs Kim Clayton-Jones
Mr Kevin Cleary
Mrs Barbara Clegg
Mrs Pauline Clegg
Mrs Liz Cleghorn
Miss Alexandra Clements
Miss Elizabeth Clements
Mrs Janet Clench
Miss Jane Clifford
Mrs Sarah Clifford
Mrs Sigrid Clou
Miss Ismena Clout
Mr Graham Clunan
Mrs Fiona Coad
Ms Clare Coard
Mrs Debbie Coates
Miss Laura Cobden
Mrs Beth Cockburn
Mr Richard Cockburn
Mrs Moir Cocker
Mr Paul Cocker
Ms Harriet Cockill
Mr Kevin Coen
Mrs Susan Coen
Mrs Rachel Coffey
Mr Ben Coffman
Ms Michelle Coggins
Miss Eilidh Coghill
Ms Dayna Cohen
Mr Patrice Cohen
Mr Henry Coldstream
Ms Alison Coldwell
Miss Rebekah Coldwell
Mr Jeff Cole
Mr John Cole
Mr Paul Cole
Mr David Coleman
Mr John Coleman
Mr Nick Coler
Mr Richard Colley
Mrs Lee Collier

Mr Michael Collier
Mrs Julie Collin
Mr Christopher Collins
Mr David Collins
Mr Gary Collins
Mrs Lindsey Collins
Ms Pippa Collins
Mr Richard Combe
Mr Christopher Comber
Miss Sam Complin
Mr Paul Concannon
Mr Eamon Condon
Mr Gary Condon
Ms Jane Coney
Mrs Gill Conneely
Mrs Sara Connor
Mr Si Conroy
Mrs Pauline Console
Miss Charlie Constant
Mr Phil Conway
Mrs Denise Cook
Dr Heidi Cook
Mrs Helen Cook
Mrs Jacqui Cook
Mrs Jeanette Cook
Mr Roger Cook
Miss Amy Cooke
Miss Selena Cooke
Mrs Sharon Cooke
Mr Derek Cooknell
Mr Adrian Cooling
Mr Ron Coomber
Mrs Samantha Coombs
Miss Julie Cooney
Mrs Geraldine Cooper
Mrs Gwyneth Cooper
Mr Ian Cooper
Mrs Janet Cooper
Mrs Katherine Cooper
Mr Peter Cooper
Miss Vanessa Cooper
Mr Bede Cope
Mr Richard Copley
Mrs Janet Copp
Mr Harcus Copper
Mr John Coran
Mr Ian Corburn
Dr R Corby
Mr Kevin Corcoran
Miss Hannah Cordingley
Mrs Roseanne Corlett
Ms Rebecca Cornelius
Mr Fred Cornell
Mr Richard Corney
Mrs Janice Cornish
Ms Gail Corrin
Mrs Annalisa Corsaro
Mr Stephen Cotsen
Mr Peter Cottam
Miss Sophie Cottam
Mr Peter Cottrell
Mr Jean-Pierre Couroulde
Mrs Geraldine Courtney
Mrs Lyndsey Courtney
Mr Richard Coward
Mr Katharine Cowherd
Mrs Vicki Cowin
Mr Richard Cowles
Mr Chris Cox
Miss Philippa Cox
Mr Steve Cox
Mrs Kelli Coxhead
Mr David Coxon
Mrs Jane Craddock
Miss Katie Cragg
Ms Kathlyn Craig
Mr Mark Crane
Mr Rob Crane
Mr David Craske
Mrs Sara Crawford
Mr Stephen Creed
Miss Kay Crewdson
Mr Andy Cripps
Mr Tim Croad
Miss Julie Crocombe
Mrs Dawn Croft
Mrs Jill Croft
Mr Roy Croft
Miss Lisa Crofts

Mrs Linda Crookes
Mr Jake Cross
Miss Sophie Crosse
Dr Alison Crossley
Mr Ian Michael Crossley
Mrs Pauline Crossley
Mr Peter Crown
Mrs Jane Crudace
Mr Adrian Crumpton
Mr Derek Crush
Mrs Alison Cruthers
Mr Andrew Culpin
Mrs Caroline Cummings
Mr Iain Cummings
Mr Edward Cummins
Ms Wendy Cunningham
Miss Denise Curi
Mr Rod Curtis
Miss Eleanor Curzon
Mr Michael Cuschieri
Mrs Tina Cussans
Mrs Angela Cutts
Miss Karolina Czaplak
Mrs Emma Daldorph
Mr Michael Dallas
Mr Daniele Dalle Mulle
Mrs Christine Dalton
Mr Howard Dalton
Mrs Irene Dalton
Mr Jon Dalton
Mrs Fiona Daly
Mr Manucher Daneshvar
Mr Arthur Daniels
Mrs Catherine D'Arcy
Mrs Jane D'Arcy
Mr Christopher Darlington
Mrs Sally Darnell
Miss Una Darrer
Mr Emile Darroch-Davies
Mrs Adeline Daurelio
Mrs Helen Davey
Mr Keith Davey
Mrs Chevonne Davidson
Mrs Sharon Davidson
Mr Alan Davies
Miss Angela Davies
Mr Ben Davies
Mrs Debra Davies
Miss Elizabeth Davies
Mr Guy Davies
Ms Judith Davies
Miss Julie Davies
Miss Katy Davies
Ms Lesley Davies
Mr Mike Davies
Mrs Patricia Davies
Mrs Sandra Davies
Mrs Stephanie Davies
Dr Thelma Davies
Mr Alan Davis
Miss Eleanor Davis
Ms Jane Davis
Mrs Jenni Davis
Miss Joanne Davis
Mr Andy Davison
Mrs Pollyanna Dawber
Mrs Patricia Dawkins
Mr Chris Dawson
Mr David Dawson
Mrs Rebecca Day
Mrs Andrea de Jesus
Ms Clara de Miguel
Mrs Alison de Salengre
Dr Hugo de Waal
Mr John Deacon
Ms Fiona Dealey
Mrs Sally-Anne Dean
Mrs Sue Dean
Mr Andrew Deas
Mrs M Debbage
Mr P Debbage
Mr Subhankar Debnath
Mr Richard Debney
Mr Richard Delval
Miss Alexandra Demper
Mr David Denness
Mr Ian Dent

Miss Amy Depledge
Mr Stephen Depoix
Mr Pierre Desmartin
Mr Adrian Desmond
Mrs Anne Devlin
Mr Andrew Dey
Mr Jorban Dhaliwal
Dr Anjan Dhar
Mrs Efrosini Diamond
Mr Jean Dickens
Mrs Sally Dickens
Dr Steve Dickinson
Mrs Mary Dickson
Miss Lauren Digby
Mr John Dilhorne
Mrs Rhiannon Dillon
Mr Les Diment
Miss Claire Dioszegi
Mrs Barbara Dittrich
Dr Colin Divall
Mrs Karen Dixey
Mr Ivan Dixon
Mrs Samantha Dixon
Mr Mark Dixon-Ives
Mrs Jane Doades
Mrs Amanda Dobinson
Mr Paul Dobson
Mrs Kate Docherty
Mrs Gillian Dodd
Mr Siegfried Dodd
Mrs Kate Dodson
Ms Ruth Dodson
Mr Aynsley Doherty
Mrs Joanne Dolan
Ms Aileen Donald
Miss Grace Donaldson
Mr Gerald Donnelly
Mrs Karen Donnelly
Mrs Daphne Donnison
Mr Mark Donohoe
Ms Mel Donohoe-Brown
Mr Chris Donovan
Mrs Linda Donovan
Mr Matthew Doonan
Mrs Annette Doran
Mrs Rachel Dorsett
Miss Patricia dos Santos
Mrs Margaret Double
Ms Diana Douglas
Dr Colin Dourish
Dr Rhid Dowdle
Ms Rebecca Dowling
Mr Brian Downs
Ms Rachel Downs
Mrs Sharon Drake
Mrs Allison Drakeley
Mr Marcus Draper
Mr Dudley Drayson
Mr James Drew
Mrs Siobhan Drew
Mr Adam Driscoll
Mrs Karen Drummond
Mr Adam D'Souza
Mr Ben Du Brow
Mr Chris P Duck
Mr John Ducker
Mr Neil Duckworth
Mr Philip Duffy
Mr Ali Dugdale
Ms Louise Dugmore
Mrs Sally Duhig
Miss Angela Duncan
Miss Karen Duncan
Mr John Dunsmure
Dr Claire Dunstan
Mrs Valerie Dunstan
Mr Francis Durham
Mrs Valerie Durli
Mr Paul Durrant
Miss Sandeep Dusanjh
Mrs Pamela Dutson
Miss Laura Dyer
Mrs Katherine Dyson
Mr Sam Dyson
Miss Caroline Eady
Mrs Amanda Earl
Mrs Michelle Earl
Dr Lindsay Easton
Mrs Sylvia Eastwood
Dr Mary Eaton
Mr Nathan Eaton-Baudains

Miss Jo Edge
Mrs Lisa Edmonds
Mr Neil Edmonds
Dr Pamela Edmonds
Mr Nigel Edmondson
Mrs Karen Edmunds
Mr Kenneth Edney
Mrs Pamela Edsall
Mr David Edward
Mr Colin Edwards
Mrs Gillian Edwards
Mrs Julie Edwards
Miss Kate Edwards
Mr Matthew Edwards
Mr Osian Edwards
Mr Paul Edwards
Mr Stephen Edwards
Mr Tim Edwards
Mrs Janet Egan
Mr Rod Eglin
Mrs Annie Eickhoff
Miss Danielle Eiseman
Mr Barry Eldon
Mrs Sandy Eldridge
Mrs Wendy Eley
Mr Michael Elia
Mr Korun Elliman
Mr Simon Ellingham
Miss Alice Elliott
Mrs Joanne Elliott
Mrs Lisa Elliott
Mrs Louise Elliott
Mrs Helen Elliott-Doyle
Miss Amy Ellis
Mrs Carole Ellis
Miss Charlotte Ellis
Mrs Lesley Ellis
Mr Terry Ellis
Mr Martin Ellison
Mrs Jane Ellison-Bates
Mr Charles Elvin
Miss Jane Elwine
Mrs Carole Embley
Mr David Emmott
Mrs Sally Engelbert
Mrs Natalie England
Mr Charlie Errock
Ms Nathalie Esparcieux
Mrs Linda Ettridge
Mr Barrie Evans
Miss Catherine Evans
Miss Claire Evans
Mr D Evans
Ms Daisy Evans
Ms Laura Evans
Miss Megan Evans
Dr Owain Evans
Mr Robert Evans
Mr Robin Evans
Miss Stacey Evans
Mrs Penelope Eveleigh
Mr Richard Everitt
Ms Petra Evison
Mrs Mary Eyers
Mrs Mel Eyers-Gibbs
Mrs Lynne Faccenda
Mr John Fairley
Mr Fraser Fairlie
Mrs Jacqueline Faller
Miss Catriona Faraday
Mr David Farber
Mr Benedict Faria
Mrs Heather Farmer
Dr Nicola Farmer
Mr John Farndell
Ms Dawn Farnworth
Miss Joanna Farr
Mrs Lorrie Farrall
Miss Frances Farrer
Mrs Willemijn Faulstich-Halsema
Mr Ian Featherstone
Ms Joy Fenton
Mr Peter Fenwick
Mr Gerry Fergus
Mr Alistair Ferguson
Mrs Sarah Ferguson
Mrs Lynda Fermor
Miss Sara Fernandez
Mrs Vikki Ferrie
Mrs Patricia Field
Mrs Susan Field

Mr Ashley Fieldhouse
Miss Diana Fieldwick
Mr Neville Filar
Miss Fiona Finch
Mr Robert Finch
Mr Norman Fincham
Mr Malcolm Fincken
Miss Heidi Finne
Mr Alan Finne
Mrs Nicola Finnigan
Mr Simon Finnigan
Dr Joan Firth
Mr Alan Fisher
Mr Brian Fisher
Mrs Kim Fishlock
Mrs Deirdre Fitzgerald
Miss Sarah-Anne Fitzsimmons
Dr Lisa Flanagan
Mr Trevor Flannery
Mrs Katarzyna Fletcher
Miss Eve Flett
Ms Carole Flint
Ms Anne-Marie Flood
Mr David Flynn
Miss Ella Flynn
Mr Sean Foley
Miss Vanessa Foley
Mr Wayne Foncette
Mrs Jane Ford
Ms Katie Ford
Mrs Linda Forde
Mr Carolyn Forman
Mr Kenneth Forrest
Mr Martin Forryan
Mr Sam Fortune
Mr Rob Foster
Mr Mike Fountain
Ms Alicia Fourie
Mr John Fowler
Miss Lucy Fowler
Mr Paul Fox
Mr Tom Foxwell
Mr Keith Fradgley
Ms A Francis
Mr Daniel Francis
Mrs Nicky Francis
Mrs Vera Francis
Mr Nick Frankgate
Mr John Fraser
Mrs Louise Freedman
Mr Michael Freedman
Mr Peter French
Mr Matthew Friel
Mrs Nancey Fromigia
Mrs Elaine Frost
Miss Janine Frost
Mrs Lauren Frost
Mrs Teresa Frost
Dr Carol Fry
Mr Daren Fulwell
Mrs Kate Fulwell
Mr Alexander Furber
Miss Helen Gadie
Dr Karl Gaffney
Mrs Sylvia Gagette
Mr Simon Gain
Mrs Helen Gale
Mr Craig Galvin-Scott
Mrs Carla Gardiner
Mrs Helen Gardner
Miss Edith Gargaud
Mr Clive Garlick
Mr Neil Garlick
Mr Gordon Garment
Mr Alan Garner
Mr Matthew Garner
Mr Lyn Garrihy
Mrs Massomeh Garshasebi
Mrs Nic Garvey
Mr Paul Garwood
Miss Natasha Gascoine
Mrs Shirley Gascoyne
Miss Rhiannon Gazeley
Mrs Claire Geach
Ms Keily Geary
Mrs Emily Gee
Mr Alastair Geldart
Mr Ashley Gent
Miss Jemma George
Mr Martin George
Mr Saul Gerald

Mrs Pauline Gerrish
Mrs Laura Gethen
Mrs Tavia Gethin
Mr Arthur Getz
Mrs Andrea Gibb
Mr Willie Gibbons
Mrs Marita Gibbons
Miss Charlotte Gibson
Mr Jonathan Gibson
Mrs Marilyn Gibson
Miss Natalie Gibson
Dr M Gifford
Mr Jonathan Gilbert
Mr Stuart Gilbert
Mrs Susan Gilbert
Mrs Guadalupe Gilbey
Mrs Susan Gilhespie
Mr Clive Gill
Mr Ian Gillett
Mrs Jackie Gillibrand
Mr Jon Gillmore
Mr Nick Gillott
Dr Jamie Gilmour
Mr John Ginman
Mr Alan Ginsberg
Mr Philip Girling
Mrs Vivien Gladen
Mr Bryan Glastonbury
Mrs Catherine Glazzard
Mr James Gleeson
Mrs Lucy Glenn
Miss Natalee Goas
Mr Dan Gobbitt
Mr Alan Godfrey
Ms Gail Godfrey
Mrs Margaret Godfrey
Mrs Joanna Godwin
Mr Ben Gold
Dr Penny Goldsbrough
Miss Barbara Goldsmith
Miss Janey Goodearl
Mr George Goodey
Mrs Pauline Goodson
Mr Andrew Goodwin
Mr Pam Goodwin
Mrs Janet Goodyer
Mr Alasdair Gordon
Mr Richard Gordon
Mr Nick Gore
Mrs Vicki Gorman
Miss Lauren Gornall
Mr Jindrich Gorner
Mrs Beryl Gorse
Mr Douglas Gosling
Miss Rachel Gough
Miss Abigail Gould
Mrs Lynne Gould
Mr Kieron Goulden
Mr Chris Gov
Mr Richard Gower
Mrs Jyoti Goyal
Ms Roshni Goyate
Mrs Claire Graham
Mrs Jane Graham
Mrs Lisa Graham
Mrs Wendy Graham
Mrs Judy Grainger
Mrs Sophie Granchi
Mr Alan Grant
Mr David Grant
Mr Luke Grant
Miss Sarah Grantham
Mrs Carol Graves
Mrs Christabel Gray
Mr Chris Green
Mrs Fiona Green
Mrs Jean Green
Mrs Jenny Green
Mrs Jessica Green
Mrs Jill Green
Mrs Jo Green
Dr Susanna Green
Mr Tony Green
Mrs Tracy Green
Mrs Della Greenaway
Mrs Helen Greene
Mrs Jill Greenfield
Mr Trevor Greenfield
Mrs Sheila Greenhalgh
Miss Emma Greenough
Dr Victoria Greensill
Mr Daniel Greenslade
Mr Richard Greenslade

Miss C Greenwood
Mr Dave Greenwood
Mr John Gregory
Miss Lorraine Gregory
Mr Stephen Gregory
Miss Amanda Griffith
Miss Ida Griffith
Mr Andrew Griffiths
Mr Brian Griffiths
Mrs Angela Grimes
Mr Mark Grimshaw
Miss Karolina Grochalska
Mrs Cheryl Grose
Mrs Paola Grossi
Mr Nick Grossman
Mrs Sarah Grout
Mrs Jane Grove
Mrs Julie Groves
Miss Jennifer Guest
Mrs Jenny Gunn
Mr Sandeep Gupta
Ms Annie Gurnett
Mr David Thomas Guthrie
Mr Shaun Guyver
Miss Georgina Haddon
Miss Fehmi Hafiz
Mr Dave Hagedorn
Mrs Jane Haka
Mr Geoff Halfhide
Mrs Jean Halfhide
Mrs Ann Hall
Mrs Carol Hall
Miss Charlotte Hall
Miss Deborah Hall
Mrs Julia Hall
Mrs Michele Hall
Ms Nicola Hall
Mrs Sharon Halle-Richards
Mr John Halliday
Mrs Clare Hallsworth
Mr Matthew Halsall
Miss Bryoni Halton
Mrs Joan Hambleton
Mr Kenneth Hamilton
Mrs Monika Hammel-Loho
Mr Chris Hammond
Miss Tracy Hammond
Mrs Zenobia Hammond
Mr Owen Hanbury
Mr Terry Hancock
Ms Karen Hands
Mr Wayne Hands
Mr Chris Hankinson
Mrs Julie Hanna
Mrs Deborah Hannah
Mr Iain Hannah
Mr Darryl Hanson
Mrs Heather Hanson
Mrs Sue Harbottle-Sear
Mrs Lisa Hardi
Mr Chris Hardie
Mrs Gail Hardwell
Miss Joy Hardy
Mrs Sara Hardy
Mr Cecily Harends
Mr David Hargreaves
Mr Bhavik Haria
Ms Laxmi Hariharan
Mrs Trina Harley
Miss Sera Harman
Mrs Helen Harold
Mrs Natalie Harper
Mr Peter Harper
Mr Stuart Harrell
Mr Matthew Harrington
Mrs Maxine Harrington
Mr Clive Harris
Mrs Gillian Harris
Mrs Kamila Harris
Mrs Karen Harris
Dr Malcolm Harris
Mr Steve Harris
Ms Theo Harris
Miss Annie Louise Harrison
Mr Anthony Harrison
Mrs Caroline Harrison

Dr Christopher Harrison
Mr David Harrison
Mr Dhani Harrison
Mrs Jane Harrison
Mrs June Harrison
Mr Lee Harrison
Miss Rebecca Harrison
Mrs Stephanie Harrison
Mr Stuart Harrison
Mrs Vanessa Harrison
Mrs Dilys Hart
Miss Justine Hart
Mr Martin Harte
Mr J D Hartley
Mr Peter Hartley
Ms Pippa Hartley
Mr Ben Harvey
Mrs Carol Harvey
Mrs Jane Harvey
Mr Lee Harvey
Mr Mark Harvey
Mr Tom Harvey-Brown
Mr Philip Harwin
Ms Carol Haskell
Mrs Debra Haslam
Mr David Hassall
Miss Elizabeth Haughey
Miss Shevaun Haughton
Miss Diana Havenhand
Mrs Rita Hawcock
Mr Paul Hawkes
Mrs Claire Hawkins
Mr David Hawkins
Ms Tracy Hawkins
Mrs Terry Hay
Mr Ric Hayden
Ms Ceri Hayes
Mrs Claire Hayes
Miss Rachael Hayes
Mrs Ann Hayne
Mrs Georgina Haynes
Mrs Jean Hayton
Miss Jill Hayward
Miss Sharon Hayward
Mr Chris Hazelden
Mrs Nicky Heather
Mrs Ann Hebden
Ms Julia Jane Heckles
Mrs Julie Heed
Mr Robert Heed
Mr Robert Hellen
Mrs Stephanie Helliwell
Ms Annie Hemmings
Ms Ann Henderson
Mr Gavin Henderson
Mr Jamie Henderson
Mr Jason Henderson
Mrs Stacey Henderson
Miss Clare Henley
Mrs Jacqueline Henness
Mrs Charli Henning
Ms Janice Henry
Mrs Judith Henshaw
Mrs Kathy Hepworth
Mr David Herbert
Miss Josephine Hercberg
Ms Fiona Hering
Mrs Tina Herlihy
Dr Michael Hession
Mr Paul Hetherington
Mr Gad Heuman
Mr Andrew Hewitt
Miss Jacqueline Hewitt
Mr Robert Hewitt
Mr Spencer Hewitt
Miss Tania Heyes
Mrs Jacqueline Heywood
Mrs Penelope Hickley
Miss Sharon Higginbotham
Mrs Ishbel Higgins
Mrs Julie Higgins
Mr Ken Higman
Mr Dan Hildreth
Mr Tim Hiles
Dr Allen Hill
Miss Charlotte Hill
Mr Colin Hill
Mrs Jo Hill

Mr Simon Hill
Miss Zoe Hill
Mr Simon Hillcox
Mrs Alison Hills
Mr Daniel Hills
Mrs Debby Hills
Mrs Emma Hillyard
Mr Ken Hilton
Mrs Nikki Hilton
Mrs Anne Hind
Miss Sarah Hindle
Mr Felix Hines
Mr Jawahar Hingorani
Mr David Hipple
Mr Chris Hirst
Mr LJ Hirst
Mr Timothy Hirst
Mr Alistair Hiscock
Mrs Antoinette Hiscock
Mrs Eleanor Hitchcox
Ms Claire Hitchen
Ms Barbara Hitchins
Mr Harry Hitman
Mrs Jean Hoare
Mr Brian Hoban
Mr Steven Hobbs
Mrs Jackie Hobbs-Mallyon
Mrs Helen Hobson
Mrs Gillian Hodge
Mr Jerry Hodgkinson
Ms Sharon Hogasian
Miss D Hogston
Mrs Linda Hohaia
Mr Craig Holden
Mrs Nicola Holden
Mr Grant Holder
Mr Peter Holdsworth
Mr Peter Hole
Mr Rob Holehouse
Mr Henry Holland
Mr Ros Hollingsworth
Mr Bernie Holloway
Mrs Jo Hollywood
Mr Clive Holmes
Mr David Holmes
Mrs Glynis Holmes
Mr Joy Holmes
Mr Nicholas Holmes
Ms Cheryl Holroyd
Mr Colin Honey
Miss Katie Honeyborne
Mr Adrian Hood
Mrs Alison Hood
Mr Josh Hoole
Mrs Susan Hoole
Mr George Hooper
Mr Mark Hooper
Ms Gemma Hope
Ms Lorna Hope
Mr Peter Hope
Mrs Helen Hopkins
Miss Sophie Hopkinson
Dr Barrie Hopson
Mrs Vicky Horn
Mr Richard Horner
Mrs Emma Horrocks
Mr Phillip Hoskins
Mrs Julie Hotham
Mr Esther Hothersall
Mrs Brigitte Houghton
Mrs Claire Houghton
Ms Diana Houghton
Mr Peter Houghton
Miss Zara Houghton
Mrs Gaynor Houghton-Jones
Mr Steven Hourston
Miss Alexandra Howard
Ms Kelly Howard-Garde
Mrs Zoe Howarth
Mr Lewis Howcroft
Mrs Donna Howden
Mr Abi Howel
Mrs Linda Howell
Dr Margaret Howells
Miss Andrea Howlett
Mrs Helen Hoyle
Mr Adrian Hudson
Mrs Chris Hudson
Mrs Cordelia Hudson
Mr Darren Hudson

Mrs Lynn Hudson
Mr Maxwell Hudson
Mr Tim Hudson-Brunt
Mr Colin Hughes
Mr Gwilym Hughes
Mr James Hughes
Mrs Sue Hughes
Mrs Yoshiko Hughes
Mr Richard Hugill
Mrs Pamela Humphreys
Mr Phil Humphreys
Mrs Becky Humphries
Mr Ian Hunneybell
Mrs Claire Hunt
Miss Lydia Hunt
Mr Martin Hunt
Miss Megan Hunt
Miss Rachael Hunt
Miss Gemma Hunter
Mr James Hunter
Mr Nigel Hunter
Mrs Sandra Hunter
Mr Ash Huntington
Ms Lesley Hurst
Mr Aaron Husain
Miss Jessica Husband
Mr Philip Husband
Mr Mohammed Hussain
Mrs Carol Hutchins
Mr Peter Hutchinson
Dr Sharon Hutchison
Mr Richard Hutley
Miss Jessica Huxtable
Mr David Hyett
Miss Rebecca Hyman
Mrs Pat Imrie
Mrs Rachael Ince
Mrs Patricia Inglis
Miss Carol Ingram
Miss Nikki Ingram
Miss Katrina Inkster
Miss Rebecca Inkster
Miss Simona Invernizzi
Miss Nadia Iqbal
Mrs Anne Ireland
Mr Deryck Irving
Mr Mel Irwin
Ms Michela Iseli
Ms Andrea Jackson
Mrs Antoinette Jackson
Miss Cheryl Jackson
Mr Garth Jackson
Mr Graham Jackson
Mrs Heather Jackson
Ms Jean Jackson
Mr Malcolm Jackson
Mr Peter Jackson
Mrs Sophy Jackson
Mr Wayne Jackson
Mr Paul Jacobson
Mr Simon Jacobson
Dr Christine Jagger
Mr Graham Jagger
Ms Kate Jales
Miss Christine James
Mr Ian James
Mr Kenni James
Mr Matt James
Mr Fraser Jamieson
Mr Janet Jamieson
Miss Vicki Jamieson
Mr James Jarvis
Mr Robert Jarvis
Mr Martin Jeeves
Mr Jody Jeffcoate
Mrs Mary Jefferies
Mrs Amanda Jefferson
Miss Katie Jefferson
Mrs Sinead Jefferson
Mr Andrew Jeffrey
Mrs Lesley Jeffrey
Mrs Jane Jeffreys
Mr John Jeffreys
Mr Stephane Jenaer
Mrs Kate Jenkins
Mr Richard Jenkins
Mr Stephen Jenkins
Miss Sue Jenkins
Mrs Susan Jenkins
Mr John Jennings
Miss Jo Jessop
Mr Oliver Jevons

Mr Martin Joce
Mr Paer Johansson
Mr Michael John
Mrs Lauren Johns
Mr Ben Johnson
Mrs Helen Johnson
Mr Jeffrey Johnson
Mr Kevin Johnson
Miss Lucy Johnson
Mr Nick Johnson
Mr Steve Johnson
Mrs Lorraine Johnson
Mrs Mary Jolly
Mr Andrew Jones
Mr Anthony Jones
Mr Brian Jones
Mrs Christine Jones
Mr Dilwyn Jones
Mrs Eileen Jones
Mrs Esther Jones
Mrs Fiona Jones
Mr Gareth Jones
Mr Jay Jones
Mrs Judith Jones
Mr Lee Jones
Mr Nigel Jones
Mrs Nikki Jones
Mr Roderic Jones
Mrs Sarah Jones
Miss Victoria Jones
Mrs Pauline Jorgensen
Mrs Joanne Joshua-Bevan
Mr Jonathan Michael Jowett
Ms Helen Judge
Mrs Sharon Kailou
Mr George Kallenos
Mr Rachit Kamath
Mr Chris Kangis
Mrs Emma Kangis
Mr Arun Kapil
Miss Nin Kaur
Mr Richard Kavanagh
Miss Sharon Kavanagh
Mrs Angelika Kawa
Mrs Naomi Kay
Mr Tom Kearney
Mrs Violet Keddie
Mr Jonathan Keegan
Mr John Keeley
Dr Kristina Keeley-Jones
Mr Alan Keen
Ms Clare Keenan
Mr Donald Keighly
Mrs Sheila Keighren
Mrs Joanne Kellett
Miss Danielle Kelly
Ms Judith Kelly
Mrs Becky Kemp
Ms Gill Kemp
Mr Ian Kemp
Ms Karen Kemp
Mrs Lisa Kempster
Mrs Hannah Kendall-Jones
Mrs Heather Kennard
Dr Camilla Kennedy
Mrs Jane Kennedy
Mrs Maureen Kennedy
Ms Clare Kenny
Mr Gary Kent
Mrs Susan Kent
Mr Tom Kentle
Mr Stuart Kenyon
Mr Lee Kevan
Mr Derek Key
Mrs Julie Keylock
Mrs Sheila Keynton
Mrs Asma Khan
Miss Elisha Khan
Mr Mohammad Khan
Ms Smriti Khanna
Mr Vimal Khosla
Mr Lindsay Kidd
Ms Hilary Kilburn
Mr John Kilby
Mr Keith Kilfoyle
Mr Stephen Kimberley
Mr Bill King
Mrs Elise King
Mrs Helen King

Mrs Jane King
Mr John King
Ms Lucy King
Mrs Rita King
Miss Sophia King
Mrs Vikki King
Mr Ross Kingsley
Miss Diana Kingsnorth
Ms Caroline Kinloch-Jones
Ms Susan Kinrade
Mrs Rachael Kinsella
Mrs Alison Kinsey
Mrs Danielle Kinsey
Mrs J M Kirker
Mr Alan Kirkham
Mrs Sue Kirkwood
Mrs Debbie Kirton
Mr Ian Kirvan
Mr Michael Kirwan
Mrs Julie Kitson
Mr Ian Kitts
Ms Colleen Klein
Mrs Helen Knibb
Mrs Christine Knight
Mr Daniel Knight
Mr Geoffrey Knight
Mr Wayne Knight
Ms Candace Knighton
Mrs Heather Knott
Mrs Lisa Koch
Mr Simon Kondal
Miss Monica Koo
Mrs Denise Kopyciok
Dr Paul Kuczora
Mrs Catherine Kurtz
Mr Martin Kutternik
Mr Paul Kyle
Mrs Victoria Kyte
Mr Ian Laidlaw-Dickson
Ms Sarah Laidler
Miss Rebecca Lain
Miss Barbara Lally
Ms Quynh Lam
Mr David Lamb
Mrs Kathryn Lamb
Mr Roger Lamb
Mrs Louise Lamberth
Mr Steve Lamond
Miss Kirsty Lamont
Miss Louise Lamont
Mr Paul Lane
Mr Robert Lane
Mrs Sue Lane
Mrs Patricia Lang
Mr Jonathon Langford
Ms Dawn Langton
Mrs Wendy Langwade
Mr Rob Larson
Mr Michael Laskey
Mrs Erica Lasparini
Mr Keith Latham
Mrs Stephanie Latham
Mrs Lilith Latham-Cruse
Ms Joanne Latta
Miss Sophie Laughlin
Miss Zoe Laurence
Mr Thibault Laurentjoye
Mrs Judith Lavender
Miss Alison Laverick
Mrs Vanessa Law
Miss Carole Lawford
Mrs Amy Lawrence
Mrs Anthea Lawrence
Ms Clare Lawrence
Mrs Maria Lawrence
Mr Peter Lawrence
Dr Thomas Lawrence
Mrs Vanessa Lawrence-French
Mr Barry Lawson
Mrs Catherine Lawson
Mr Matthew Lawson
Mr Stuart Lawson
Miss Tracey Lawson
Mrs Vivien Lawson
Mrs Caroline Lawther
Ms Karen Layton
Mr Chris Le Good
Miss Cheryl Leach
Ms Louise Leadbetter
Mr Alan Leading

Mr Hamish Leal
Miss Karla Leal
Mr Craig Lear
Mrs Jacqui Learoyd
Mrs Christina Lee
Mr Derek Lee
Mrs Jackie Lee
Mr Jason Lee
Miss Katie Lee
Mr Thomas Lee
Mr Tim Lee
Mrs Rebecca Leek
Mrs Sandra Leek
Mrs Sue Legat
Mr Allen Legate
Mrs Tessa Legg
Miss Nicole Leggett
Mrs Dianna Leighton
Mrs Ann Leitch
Mrs Barbara Leland
Ms Edina Lengyel
Mr Mike Lennard
Mr Mike Lennon
Mr James Lennox
Mr Daniel Leonard
Miss Eve Leonard
Miss Zlatica Leskova
Mr Gordon Lestrille
Miss Victoria Lethbridge
Ms Rebecca Leuw
Mr Jacob Leverton
Mr John Lew
Mr David Lewis
Mrs Dianne Lewis
Mrs Felicity Lewis
Ms Jill Lewis
Mr Paul Lewis
Mrs Rachael Lewis
Miss Shy Lewis
Ms Sian Lewis
Mr Jay Ley
Mrs Claire Lightley
Mrs Claudette Lilliefelth
Mrs Christine Lillington
Mr Brian Lindon
Mrs Katherine Lindop
Mr Roy Lindop
Mrs Margaret Lindsay
Mrs Sue Lindsay
Mrs Lorraine Line
Mr Andy Linfoot
Mrs Jan Ling
Mr David Linnell
Ms Karen Lipman
Miss Paula Lipscombe
Mrs Rosemary Lishman
Mr Roger Little
Mr Richard Littlejohns
Miss Alice Liverton
Miss Rosie Llewellyn
Mr Richard Llewellyn-Bell
Mrs Lisa Llewelyn
Miss Sian Llewelyn
Mr Brian Lloyd
Mr John Lloyd
Mrs Linda Locke
Mr Adrian Lockyer
Mr Adrian Lodge
Mrs Beth Lodwick
Miss Gillian Loney
Mr David Long
Mrs Elaine Longbottom
Miss Eleanore Longley
Mrs Marianne Looby
Miss Marion Look
Mr George Loudon
Mrs Janet Lougee
Mr Jon Lougee
Mr Graham Lovelady
Mr Robert Lovelady
Mr Geoffrey Lovelock
Ms Christine Lowe
Mrs Gill Lowe
Miss Elizabeth Lucas
Mrs Louise Lucas
Mrs Ruth Lucas
Mr Ian Ludlow
Mr Tino Luigi
Mrs Heidi Luke
Miss Roseanne Luther
Mr David Luxon
Mrs Tonia Luxton

Mrs Andrea Lynch
Mr Michael Lynch
Mr Stuart Lynch
Mr Andrew Lynn
Miss Deirdre Lyons
Mrs Catherine MacAllister
Mrs Susan MacArthur
Mrs Michaela MacAulay
Ms Hannah MacDiarmid
Mr Alasdair MacDonald
Mr David MacDonald
Dr Lesley MacDonald
Miss Lee-Anne MacDonnell
Miss Kirsty MacDougall
Miss Dede MacGillivray
Mrs Clair Machin
Mr Steve Machin
Mr Simon Machon
Mr John MacKay
Mr Raymond MacKay
Mrs Sara MacKay
Mr Gus MacKenzie
Mr Charles Mackintosh
Mr Daniel Mackley
Mrs Sharon MacLaren
Mrs Kate MacLean
Miss Kirsty MacLeod
Miss Rachel MacLeod
Mrs Meredith Macmillan-Scott
Mr Brian MacPhee
Mr Angus MacPherson
Mr Simon MacSorley
Miss Denise Madden
Mrs Anne Mader-Horne
Mr Per Mæland
Mrs Linda Magness
Mrs Liz Maher
Mrs Beryl Maidman
Mrs Jo Maidment
Miss Bev Mail
Mr Adam Major
Mr Ian Makin
Dr Priyanjali Malik
Miss Miranda Mallery
Ms Cecilia Malley
Mrs Sue Mallides
Mrs Jessica Mallinckrodt
Mr Alasdair Malloy
Mr Ian Malyk
Mrs Kate Malyon
Mr Stephen Mander
Mr Chris Mangle
Mr Brett Manley
Mrs Celina Mann
Mr Gerard Mann
Miss Katy Mannell
Mrs Mandi Manning
Mrs Alison Mansell
Mr Peter Manser
Mrs Sue Mansfield
Mrs Emily Manson
Mr Charles Mapleston
Mr Patrick Mapp-Smith
Mrs Madeline Marchand
Mr Adrian Markley
Ms Vicki Marks
Dr Charles Markus
Mrs Louise Markus
Mr Matt Markwick
Mr Paul Marland
Mrs Sue Marlow
Mr Justin Marriott
Mr Alan Marsh
Mr David Marsh
Mrs Jacqui Marsh
Mrs Kathryn Marsh
Mr Keith Marsh
Mrs Mary Marsh
Miss Diane Marshal
Mr David Marshall
Mrs Jennifer Marshall
Mrs Karen Marshall
Miss Philippa Marshall
Mr Robert Marshall
Mr St John Marston
Mr Alex Martin

Mr Andrew Martin
Miss Corrie Martin
Mr Dirk Martin
Mr George Martin
Mr Graham Martin
Miss Heidi Martin
Mrs Helen Martin
Ms Joan Martin
Ms Martina Martin
Miss Natalie Martin
Mr Paul Martin
Miss Samantha Martin
Mr Terry Martin
Mr Yannick Martin
Mr David Martindale
Mr Tony Martinez
Mrs Andrea Martin-Wright
Mr Andrew Marx
Mrs Adrienne Mason
Mrs Agnes Mason
Mr Darren Mason
Mrs Judy Mason
Mr Don Massey
Mrs Anna Mathias
Mr Euan Mathieson
Mr Paul Mathieu
Mr Peter Maton
Ms Sue Matthew
Mr Roger Matthews
Mr Barry Matthews-Keel
Mrs Trish Maunder
Mr Graham Maw
Mr John Mawer
Mr Jay Mawji
Mrs Sally Maxwell
Ms Julie May
Mrs Linda Mayer
Miss Rebecca Mayhew
Dr Stewart Mayne
Dr Gordon McAnsh
Ms Maria McArdle
Mr Hazel McAteer
Mrs Zoe McAvoy-Brown
Mrs Heather McCabe
Mrs Clare McCulloch
Mr Mark McCafferty
Mrs Angela McCall
Mrs Lynne McCall
Mrs Anne McCann
Ms Paulene McCaul
Ms Anne McClure
Ms Suzanne McClure
Mr Daniel McCoach
Mr Steve McCombe
Mr Alan McCormick
Mr Tim McCredie
Ms Fiona McCulloch
Mr Brendan McDonagh
Mr Douglas McDonald
Mrs Rachel McDonald
Mrs Alison McDonald-Brandes
Mrs Samantha McDonnell
Mrs Lisa McGeary
Dr Jenny McGeough
Mrs Margaret McGilloway
Mrs Sally McGraw-Brown
Mrs Amanda McGregor
Mrs Rebecca McIlgorm
Mrs Margaret McInerney
Dr Jeanie McIntee
Miss Christine McIntyre
Mr James McIntyre
Miss Andrea McKellar
Mrs Katie McKelvey
Mr Brooke McKenzie
Ms Mo McKnight
Dr James Gavin McLaggan
Mrs Jane McLaughlin
Ms Fiona McLean
Mr Ian McLean
Dr Ken McLean
Miss Jackie McLellen
Miss Janna McMahon

Mrs Trish McManus
Mrs Jo McNamara
Miss Lisa McNeice
Ms Martina McNeill
Miss Michelle McNulty
Mrs Catherine McWilliam
Mr David McWilliam
Miss Fiona McWilliam
Ms Di Meechan
Ms Mara Mehlman
Miss Rekha Mehr
Mr Bhavit Mehta
Mrs Jacq Mellor
Mrs Janice Mellor
Mrs Yin Mellor
Ms Sian Melvin
Mr Pierre Menard
Dr Malcolm Meneaud
Mr Simon Mercer
Mr Thom Meredith
Mr Alessandro Merlo
Mrs June Merrett
Ms Michele Mervin
Mr Steven Messer
Mr Jonathan Metcalfe
Miss Monika Michalak
Mr Gordon Michie
Mr Thomas Mill
Mr Ian Millar
Mrs Deborah Millard
Mrs Anistatia Miller
Mr Dan Miller
Mr Jonathan Miller
Mrs Karen Miller
Miss Louise Miller
Mrs Ruth Miller
Mrs Sally Miller
Mrs Sheila Miller
Mr Thomas Miller-Jones
Mrs Ann Millican
Miss Millie Milliken
Dr Michael Millington
Mr Chris Mills
Mr Paul Milne
Mrs Sylvia Milne
Mrs Georgina Milsom
Mr Christian Milton
Mr Ville-Aleksi Mineur
Mrs Alison Minns
Mrs Margaret Mirza
Mr Hitesh Mistry
Miss Rebecca Mitchell
Miss Sarah Mitchell
Mrs Tara Mitchell
Mrs Jenny Mitchell-Hilton
Mr G A Mitcheson
Mrs Melanie Mitchley
Mrs Yvonne Mobley
Mrs Kathryn Moffatt
Mrs Catherine Moger
Mr Arash Moghadam
Mr Richard Molineux
Miss Sara Monk
Mrs Susan Montgomery
Mrs Alexandra Moore
Mrs Carolyn Moore
Miss Clare Moore
Mrs Debbie Moore
Miss Emma Moore
Mrs Mary Moore
Mrs Sonia Moore
Mr Gary Moorshead
Miss Ciara Moran
Mr Craig Moran
Mrs Jennifer Moran
Mrs Louise Moran
Mr Loic Moreau
Mrs S Moreno-Henao
Mrs Louisa Moreton
Mr Sam Morey
Mrs Bev Morgan
Mrs Carole Morgan
Mrs Elisabeth Morgan
Mr Graham Morgan
Mr Jay-Asher Morgan
Mr Keanu Morgan
Mrs Louise Morgan
Mr Michael Morgan
Mr Steven Morgan-Cummins

Mrs Victoria Morgan-Cummins
Mr Carla Morgenstern
Mr Andrew Morley
Mr Michael Morley
Mr Katey Morrell
Mr David Morrill
Mrs Caroline Morris
Mrs Emma Morris
Mr Karl Morris
Mr Stuart Morris
Mrs Gaynor Morrison
Mrs Joan Mortimer
Miss Ceri Morton
Miss Alison Moss
Mr Craig Moss
Mrs R Moss
Mrs Susan Mottram
Miss Fiona Moucq
Mr Robin Moule
Mr Ian Mowat
Mrs Susan Moyler
Mrs Sally Muir
Miss Christine Mullaney
Mr Pat Mullaney
Mr Jane Mullee
Mr Alex Muller
Ms Ann Mulligan
Mrs B Munt
Mrs Allister Murdoch
Mrs Marie Murfitt
Miss Anna Murphy
Mrs Carol Murphy
Mr Mike Murphy
Mrs Angela Murray
Mrs Jill Murray
Mr Joshua Murray
Mr Keith Murray
Mrs Lyndsey Murray
Mr Paul Murray
Mrs Claire Musgrave-Brown
Mrs Heidi Mussett
Ms Havva Mustafa
Ms Sharina Mutreja
Mr Andrew Muzzelle
Mrs Alison Naeem
Mr Peter Napier
Mr Barry Nash
Mr David Nash
Mr Ryan Nash
Mr Naved Nasir
Mr Barry Natton
Mrs Jill Naylor
Mrs Christine Neale
Mr Mark Neil
Mrs Jean Neilan
Mrs Sylwia Nejman
Mrs Marilyn Nelson
Mr Peter Nelson
Ms Sally Neocosmos
Mr Arnold Nestler
Mrs Karen Nevshehir
Mr Austin Newberry
Mrs Caroline Newborn
Dr David Newby
Ms Julia Newcombe
Ms Janice Newlove
Mrs Carole Newman
Mr JJ Newman
Mrs Jackie Newport
Mrs Marjorie Newson
Mrs Susan Newsum
Mrs Christine Newton
Mrs Jill Newton
Miss Katie Ng
Miss K Niblo
Mrs Lori Nice
Mr Sarah Nicholson
Mr Steve Nicholson
Mrs Anica Nishio
Mrs Fiona Nixon
Ms KJ Noades
Ms Ann Noble
Mrs Caren Noble
Mrs Jane Noddings
Ms Sonja Noon
Mrs Louise Norfolk
Mrs Elizabeth Beryl Norgrove
Mrs Janet Norman
Mrs Lehni Norman
Mr Eddy North

Dr Aletta Norval
Mr Mike Nugent
Mr Scott Nugent
Mr Roger Nyeko
Miss Nikkita Oakes
Ms Zoe Oakley
Dr Kiri Oates
Miss Beth O'Brien
Ms Elizabeth O'Brien
Mr Niall O'Brien
Mrs Cheryl O'Carroll
Mrs Ann O'Connell
Miss Christine O'Connor
Mrs Diane O'Connor
Miss Stacey O'Connor
Mr Michael Odey
Dr Alice O'Grady
Dr Michael O'Grady
Mr Thomas O'Hara
Mr Shaun O'Keefe
Mr Jon O'Keeffe
Mrs Deborah Oldfield
Ms L Oldfield
Mrs Andrea Oliver
Mrs Christine Oliver
Mr Phillip Oliver
Mrs Joan Ollivier
Miss Laura Ollerton
Miss Jeanette O'Neill
Mr Joseph O'Neill
Miss Matilda O'Neill
Dr Pauline Ong
Mr Leon Opit
Ms Sue Oppenheimer
Miss Svetlana Orlova
Mr Simon Orphan
Mr Alex Ortiz
Mr Adria Osborne
Mrs Bobbie O'Shea
Mr Graham O'Sullivan
Mrs Susan Oswell
Ms Fiona Outram
Mr Conrad Owen
Ms Eirlys Owen
Mr Stuart Owen
Mrs Joanne Packwood
Dr Jonathan Page
Mr Richard Page
Miss Laura Painter
Ms Vivienne Palfreyman
Mrs Helen Palmer
Mrs Jacqueline Palmer
Mrs Karen Palmer
Mrs Lynn Palmer
Mrs Maria Palmer
Mrs Zoe Palmer
Mr James Pamphlion
Mrs Hilary Pankhurst
Mrs Eleni Papadopoulou
Mr Ketan Parikh
Mrs Mary Parish
Mrs Heather Park
Mrs Lou Park
Mrs Angela Parke
Dr Evan Parker
Mrs Joanna Parker
Mr Mike Parkin
Mr David Parkinson
Mrs Juliet Parkinson
Mr Robert Parkinson
Mrs Mary Parmenter
Miss Aimee Parnell
Mr Colin Parr
Mrs Susie Parrack
Mrs Barbara Parry
Mr Charles Parry
Mr Clive Parry
Dr Heather Parry
Miss Janine Parry
Mrs Alexandra Parsons
Mrs Francesca Parsons
Mr Ray Parsons
Mr William Parsons
Mr Paul Pashley
Miss Jessie Passmore
Mr Atul Patel
Miss Sona Patel
Miss Anjali Pathak
Mrs Lee Paton
Mrs Arlene Pattem
Miss Martina Patterson

Mr Raymond Pattison
Ms Victoria Patton
Mrs Lou Paul
Mr Steven Paul
Mrs Anna Payne
Mr Bernard Payne
Ms Helen Payne
Mrs Margaret Payne
Mrs Tania Payne
Mrs Susan Paynton
Mrs Karen Peach
Mr Chris Peacock
Mr David Peacock
Mr Nigel Peacock
Miss Sam Peacock
Mr David Pearce
Mr Wayne Pearman
Mrs Angela Pearse
Mrs Francesca Pearson
Mr James Pearson
Mr Shamsi Pearson
Mrs Maria Peavoy
Mr Alan Peebles
Miss Emma Peebles
Mrs Judith Peel
Mrs Andrea Pelling
Mrs Justine Pendlebury
Mr Iain Pennington
Mrs Karen Pennington
Dr Chris Pepper
Mrs Victoria Peppiatt
Mrs Mary Bindhu Pereira
Mr John Perkins
Mrs Zoe Perkins
Mr Christopher Perks
Mrs Sarah Perrott
Mr Stephen Perugi
Mrs Karen Peters
Mr Ralph Peters
Mrs Sam Petersen
Mr Ron Peterson
Miss Angela Petrocchi
Mr Peter Petts
Mrs B Phelps
Mr David Philip
Mrs Amy Philip-Price
Mr Adrian Phillips
Mrs Ann Phillips
Mr David Phillips
Mrs Janet Phillips
Mr John Phillips
Ms Julia Phillips
Mrs Nichole Phillips
Mr Norman Phillips
Mr Stanley Phillips
Mr Thomas Phillips
Mrs Wendy Phillips
Mr Dermot Philpot
Mr Darren Philpot
Mr Richard Philpott
Mrs C Phimister
Mrs Peta Phipps
Mr Josef Pichler
Mr Alan Pickering
Miss Louise Pickering
Miss Ria Pickles
Mr David Pickup
Miss Lorna Pickup
Mr Chris Pike
Mrs Margaret Pike
Ms Amanda Pilbeam
Miss Kira Pillai
Miss Sarah Pinder
Mrs Trudi Pinkerton
Miss Jeanette Piorkowska
Mr Harry Piper
Miss Joanne Piper
Mr Colin Pitcher
Mr Pat Pitcher
Miss Charlotte Pitt
Mr Ian Pitt
Mrs Lauren Pitts
Miss Lenna Pitts
Mrs Sophie Pizarro
Miss Jane Plackett
Mrs Anna Plant
Mr Andrew Ploutarchou
Dr Elliot Pocklington
Mr Dario Poddana
Mrs Ann Pointer
Mrs Heather Pollard

Mr Nigel Pollard
Mrs Tracey Pollock
Ms Jacqueline Polson
Mrs Magdalena Pomar-Lloyd
Mrs Georgette Pombreu
Mrs Sarah Poole
Mrs Michelle Pooley
Mr Nigel Pope
Mr Jeremy Porter
Mr Matthew Porter
Mr Raymond Postgate
Mrs Christine Pottage
Mr Nick Potter
Mr Tom Potter
Mr Chris Potts
Mrs Anne Poulson
Mrs Susana Poulson
Mr Ian Poultney
Mr Andrew Powell
Mr David Powell
Mr George Powell
Mrs Gillian Powell
Miss Hannah Powell
Mr Andrew Pownall
Mr Ian Pratt
Mrs Mary Pratt
Mr John Precious
Mr Barrie Preece
Miss Eleanor Prendergast
Mrs Aimee Preston
Mr Andrew Preston
Mrs Jane Preston
Mrs Claire Price
Mr Kenneth Price
Mr Peter Price
Mr Trevor Price
Miss Ella Prichard
Mr Charles Priday
Ms Amanda Pringle
Ms Jessica Proctor
Mrs Lesley Prothero-Smith
Mr Ewa Prygiel
Mr Debra Pugh
Mr David Purcell
Ms Sabrina Purchase
Mrs Shirley Purchese
Miss Joan Purdie
Mr John Pursall
Miss Georgina Pursey
Mrs Rachel Pybus
Mr Guy Pyle
Mrs Lowri Pytka
Mr Michael Quaife
Mr Jonathan Quilter
Miss Cheryl Quinn
Mr Chris Quinn
Miss Emma Quinn
Miss Sarah Quirie
Mrs Julie Quirk
Mrs Gillian Raab
Mr Frank Radcliffe
Mr Chris Radelaar
Ms Julie Radford
Mr Kush Kadia
Mr George Radice
Ms Jessica Radke
Mr Adam Raffa
Ms Sinead Rafferty
Mr Khalik Rahman
Ms Claire Raikes
Mr Stephen Raine
Mrs Alison Rainer
Miss Gemma Rainer
Mr Sahasranaman Ramachandran
Ms Jaya Raman
Mr Ben Ramsay
Mrs Emma Randall
Mr Thomas Randles
Mrs Chris Rankin
Mr William Rankin
Mr John Rannigan
Mr Andrew Rao
Mrs Charlotte Ratcliffe
Dr Deborah Rathbone
Mrs Elaine Rathbone
Mr Peter Ratzer
Mrs Faith Raven
Miss Kitty Raven
Mrs Kumud Rawal

Mrs K E Rawes
Miss Caroline Rawse
Ms Alison Rayner
Miss Michelle Re
Mrs Catherine Read
Mr Chris Read
Mr Christopher Reardon
Mr Erick Recalde
Mr Dieter Redden
Miss Lady Alexandra Redfearn
Mr Peter Redgrave
Mr Bill Redmond
Mrs Christine Redmond
Mrs Elizabeth Redshaw
Mr Jeff Redshaw
Mrs Carol Reece
Mrs Carmel Reed
Ms D Reeman
Mr Nick Rees
Mrs Anne Reeve
Mrs Rebecca Reeve
Mr Paul Regan
Miss Alyson Reid
Mr Mark Reid
Mr Paul Reid
Mr Norbert Reis
Mr Adam Rendle
Mrs Nicola Renshaw
Mrs Lesley Renteurs
Ms Claire Reuben
Mr Alistair Reynolds
Mr Geoff Reynolds
Mrs Georgina Reynolds
Ms Leigh Reynolds
Ms Patricia Reynolds
Mr Trevor Reynolds
Mr Josh Rhodes
Mrs Elle Ribbans
Mrs S Rice
Mrs Linda Rich
Mrs Zosia Rich
Ms Alice Richards
Mr Hywel Richards
Mr Keith Richards
Mr Michael Richards
Mr Yiannis Richards
Mr Andrew Richardson
Dr Donald Richardson
Mr Paul Richardson
Mr Will Richardson
Mr Alan Richell
Miss Sharon Riddell
Mr Ted Riddle
Mr Peter Ridley
Mr Malcolm Riedlinger
Miss Jodie Riley
Mr Joe Riley
Mr Jonathan Riley
Mrs Anne Rimer
Mrs Carol Rindone
Mr Karl Ringer
Mrs Jane Ripley
Mr Thomas Ripley
Ms Sonia Rishi
Mrs Jo Ritchie
Miss Tamsin Ritchie
Mr Paul Rivett
Mrs Beverley Roberts
Mr Derek Roberts
Miss Eleri Roberts
Miss Gwenan Roberts
Mrs Gwenda Roberts
Mr Julie Roberts
Ms Linda Roberts
Mrs Rachel Roberts
Mrs Victoria Roberts
Mrs Vikki Robertshaw
Mr John Robertson
Mrs Lisa Robertson
Mr Adrian Robins
Miss Catherine Robins
Miss Angela Robinson
Miss Beth Robinson
Ms Christine Robinson
Mrs Debbie Robinson
Miss Hen Robinson
Mrs Rachel Robinson
Mr Sean Robinson
Dr Charles Rodeck
Mr Kevin Roden

Ms Janet Rodgers
Mr Jose Rodriguez
Mrs Urvashi Roe
Mr Anthony Rogers
Mrs Nicki Rogers
Ms Helen Rogers
Mr Francisco Rojas
Mr Max Rollin
Mrs Tracy Rolling
Mrs Jan Rollinson
Mrs Molly Romanov
Miss Caroline Roney
Mr Kevin Rook
Miss Frances Rose
Mrs Pam Rose
Mrs Ruth Rose
Mrs Anna Ross
Mr Dave Ross
Mrs Mhairi Ross
Mrs Tracey Ross
Mrs Elaine Rothwell
Mr Morgan Rothwell
Mr Douglas Rounthwaite
Mrs Tracy Rowan
Miss Rachael Rowden
Mr Nigel Rowley
Mr St John Rowntree
Mr Sven Royall
Mrs Sandra Royston
Mr Clive Rozario
Miss Mel Rudder
Mr John Rudofsky
Ms Sonja Ruehl
Mr Ben Ruhle
Mrs Fran Rumbelow
Miss Hester Ruoff
Mr John Rush
Mrs Charmaine Rushton
Mr John Rushton
Mrs Margaret Russell
Miss Sarah Russell
Mr Terry Russell
Mrs Debi Rutter
Mrs Ann Ryan
Mr Gautam Sachdeva
Miss Syeda Sadiq
Mrs Kathryn Saegert
Mr Aroon Sahani
Dr Sanjay Sahi
Mr Sam Sahote
Mr Robin Sainty
Mr Ahmed Salahuddin
Mrs Elisabeth Salaman
Mr Vehid Salih
Mrs Karen Salisbury
Miss Abigail Salmon
Mrs Lisa Salter
Mr Keith Salway
Mr Raj Samuel
Miss Amy Sanderson
Mrs Penny Sanderson
Mr Robin Sanderson
Mrs Veronica Sanderson
Mrs Sandra Sandle
Mr Neeraj Sapra
Mr Carol Saunders
Mrs Lidia Saunders
Mrs Nancy Saunders
Mr Gary Savill
Mrs Sian Saxton
Mrs Kylie Sayers
Mrs Philippa Sayers
Miss Jodie Scales
Miss Georgina Scanes
Mrs Claire Scargill
Miss Joanna Scheidegger
Mr Simon Schiff
Mr Franck Schmidlin
Mrs Katharine Schofield
Mrs Annette Scott
Mrs Beverley Scott
Mrs Jill Scott
Ms Jo Scott
Miss Niamh Scott
Mr Nick Scott
Miss Nicky Scott
Mrs Penelope Scott
Miss Victoria Scrope
Mr Paul Scully

Mrs Miriam Seager
Miss Natalie Seager
Mr Barry Searle
Mr Anthony Seculer
Mrs Jillian Seddon
Mr Alan Sedgwick
Mr David Sefton
Mrs Toria Sefton
Mr Rod Seivewright
Mrs Dee Selby
Mr Angus Selstrom
Mr Richard Senior
Mrs Gillian Senkiw
Mrs Eileen R Senogles
Miss Leigh Setterington
Miss Hannah Seville
Miss Elisabeth Seymour
Mrs Joanna Seymour
Mr Ray Seymour
Mrs R M Shackleton
Mr Stef Shackley
Mrs Denise Shafeie
Mr Rohit Shah
Mrs Lynn Shakeshaft
Miss Anne-Marie Shanks
Mrs Margaret Shannon
Mr Vikrant Sharma
Mrs Amanda Sharman
Miss Penelope Sharp
Mrs Chris Sharpe
Mr Nick Sharpin
Mr Joseph Shaw
Mr Kevin Shaw
Mr Malcolm Shaw
Mr Martin Shaw
Mr Robert Shaw
Mr Chris Shearman
Mrs Michelle Shelton
Mr Dan Shepherd
Mr Philip Shepherd
Mrs Liz Sheridan
Mr Marek Sheridan
Miss Sara Sheridan
Mrs Susan Sheridan
Mr Robert Sherwood
Mrs Khushali Shingala
Mrs Magda Shonfeld
Dr Bernard Short
Mr Gilbert Short
Dr Paul Short
Dr John Shotton
Dr Jonathan Shribman
Ms Tracie Shroder
Mr Michael Shun
Miss Deborah Sibbald
Mr Vic Sibson
Mr Pavan Kumar Sikhakolli
Mrs Victoria Silcock
Mrs Bernadine Silver
Mr Mervyn Simmonds
Mr Michael Simmonds
Miss Christina Simmons
Ms Lesley Simmons
Miss Rebecca Simms
Mr Keith Simpson
Mr Michael Simpson
Mr Neil Simpson
Mrs Margaret Simpson
Mrs Colleen Sims
Mrs Gill Sims
Mr Cameron Sims-Stirling
Mr Alan Sinclair
Mr Kulwinder Singh
Mr Richard Singleton
Mrs Gaynor Sinton
Mr Brett Sirrell
Mrs Rachel Skells
Miss Elizabeth Skinner
Mrs Mary Skorupka
Mr Mark Slade
Dr Gary Slater
Mrs Lynette Slater
Mr Robin Slater
Mr Tom Smail
Mrs Sophie Smale
Ms Anais Smart
Miss Lucie Smidova
Mr Alastair Smith
Mrs Alex Smith
Mrs Alexandra Smith